W9-BGI-215

MANAGERIAL ECONOMICS
FIFTH EDITION

To Our Families

W. F. S
S. G. M

MANAGERIAL ECONOMICS
FIFTH EDITION

William F. Samuelson
Boston University

Stephen G. Marks
Boston University

WILEY

JOHN WILEY & SONS, INC.

ASSOCIATE PUBLISHER	Judith Joseph
SENIOR PRODUCTION EDITOR	Trish McFadden
DIRECTOR OF MARKETING	Frank Lyman
SENIOR DESIGNER	Madelyn Lesure
COVER PHOTO	Corbis Digital Stock
EDITORIAL ASSISTANT	Brigeth Rivera
SENIOR MEDIA EDITOR	Allison Morris

This book was set in 10/12 New Baskerville by Prepare, Inc. and printed and bound by Donnelley/Crawfordsville. The cover was printed by Lehigh Press, Inc.

This book is printed on acid-free paper.

To order books or for customer service please, call 1-800-CALL WILEY (225-5945).

ISBN-13 978-0-471-66362-1

ISBN-10 0-471-66362-X

Printed in the United States of America

10 9 8 7 6 5 4 3 2 1

PREFACE

The last decade has witnessed an unprecedented increase in competition in both national and world markets. In this competitive environment, managers must make increasingly complex business decisions that will determine whether the firm will prosper or even survive. Today, economic analysis is more important than ever as a tool for decision making.

OBJECTIVES OF THIS BOOK

The aims of this textbook are to illustrate the central decision problems managers face and to provide the economic analysis they need to guide these decisions. It was written with the conviction that an effective managerial economics textbook must go beyond the "nuts and bolts" of economic analysis; it should also show how these economic methods are used by practicing managers. Our experience teaching managerial economics to undergraduates, M.B.A.s, and executives alike shows that a focus on applications is essential.

KEY FEATURES

Managerial Decision Making

The main feature that distinguishes *Managerial Economics*, Fifth Edition, is its consistent emphasis on managerial decision making. In a quest to explain economics per se, many current texts defer analysis of such managerial decisions as optimal output and pricing policies until later chapters on market structure or special applications. In contrast, decision making is woven throughout every chapter in this book. Each chapter begins with a description of a real managerial problem that challenges students to ponder possible choices and is concluded by revisiting and analyzing the decision in light of the concepts introduced in the chapter. Without exception, the principles of managerial economics are introduced and analyzed by extended decision-making examples. Some of these examples include pricing airline seats (Chapter 3), producing auto parts (Chapter 6), choosing between risky research and development projects (Chapter 8), competing as a commercial day-care provider (Chapter 10), and negotiating to sell a warehouse (Chapter 16). In addition to reviewing important concepts, the summary at the end of each chapter lists essential decision-making principles.

The analysis of optimal decisions is presented early in the book. Chapter 2 introduces and analyzes the basic profit-maximization problem of the firm. Chapter 3 begins with a traditional treatment of demand and goes on to apply demand analysis to the firm's optimal pricing problem. Chapters 6 and 7 take a closer look at production and cost as guides to making optimal managerial decisions. The emphasis on decision making continues throughout the remainder of the book because, in our view, this is the best way to teach managerial economics. The decision-making approach also provides a direct answer to students' perennial question: How and why is this concept useful? A list of real-world applications used throughout the text appears on the inside of the front cover.

New Topics

At one time, managerial economics books most closely resembled intermediate microeconomics texts with topics reworked here and there. Due to the advance of modern management techniques, the days when this was sufficient are long past. This text goes far beyond current alternatives by integrating the most important of these advances with the principal topic areas of managerial economics. Perhaps the most significant advance is the use of game theory to illuminate the firm's strategic choices. Game-theoretic principles are essential to understanding strategic behavior. An entire chapter (Chapter 13) is devoted to this topic. Other chapters apply the game-theoretic approach to settings of oligopoly (Chapter 12), asymmetric information and organization design (Chapter 15), negotiation (Chapter 16), and competitive bidding (Chapter 17).

A second innovation of the text is its treatment of decision making under uncertainty. Managerial success—whether measured by a particular firm's profitability or by the international competitiveness of our nation's businesses as a whole—depends on making decisions that involve risk and uncertainty. Managers must strive to envision the future outcomes of today's decisions, measure and weigh competing risks, and determine which risks are acceptable. Other managerial economics textbooks typically devote a single, short chapter to decision making under uncertainty after devoting a dozen chapters to portraying demand and cost curves as if they were certain.

Decision making under uncertainty is a prominent part of *Managerial Economics*, Fifth Edition. Chapter 8 shows how decision trees can be used to structure decisions in high-risk environments. Chapter 9 examines the value of acquiring information about relevant risks, including optimal search strategies. Subsequent chapters apply the techniques of decision making under uncertainty to topics that are on the cutting edge of managerial economics: organization design, negotiation, and competitive bidding.

A third innovation is the expanded coverage of international topics and applications. In place of a stand-alone chapter on global economic issues, we have chosen to integrate international applications throughout the text. For instance, early applications in Chapters 2 and 3 include responding to exchange-rate changes and multinational pricing. Comparative advantage, tariffs and quotas, and the risks of doing international business are additional applications taken up in later chapters. In all, 17 of the 19 chapters contain international applications. In short, our aim is to leave the student with a first-hand appreciation of business decisions within the global economic environment.

A fourth innovation is the addition of end-of-chapter spreadsheet problems. In the last 20 years, spreadsheets have become the manager's single most important quantitative tool. It is our view that spreadsheets provide a natural means of modeling managerial decisions. In their own way, they are as valuable as the traditional modeling approaches using equations and graphs. (This admission comes from a long ago college math major who first saw spreadsheets as nothing more than "trivial" arithmetic and a far cry from "true" programming.) Optimization is one hallmark of quantitative decision making, and with the advent of optimizer tools, managers can use spreadsheets to model problems and to find and explore profit-maximizing solutions. A second hallmark is equilibrium analysis. Again, spreadsheet tools allow immediate solutions of what otherwise would be daunting sets of simultaneous equations.

Spreadsheets offer a powerful way of portraying economic decisions and finding optimal solutions without a large investment in calculus methods. We have worked hard to provide a rich array of spreadsheet problems in 17 of the 18 principal chapters. Some of these applications include optimal production and pricing, cost analysis with fixed and variable inputs, competitive market equilibrium in the short and long runs, monopoly practices, Nash equilibrium behavior, simulated evolutionary equilibrium, and the welfare effects of externalities. In each case, students are asked to build and analyze a simple spreadsheet based on an example provided for them. In addition, a special appendix in Chapter 2 provides a self-contained summary of spreadsheet optimization. In short, using spreadsheets provides new insights into managerial economics and teaches career-long modeling skills.

Organization, Coverage, and Level

This textbook can be used by a wide range of students, from undergraduate business majors in second-level courses to M.B.A. students and Executive Program participants. The presentation of all topics is self-contained. Although most students will have taken an economics principles course in their recent, or not so recent, past, no prior economic tools are presumed. The presentations begin simply and are progressively applied to more and more challenging applications. Each chapter contains a range of problems designed to test students' basic understanding. A number of problems explore advanced applications and are indicated by an asterisk. Answers to all odd-numbered problems are given at the end of the book. Suggested references at the end of each chapter direct students to extensions and advanced applications of the core topics presented in the chapter.

Although this text has many unique features, its organization and coverage are reasonably standard. All of the topics that usually find a home in managerial economics are covered and are in the usual sequence. As noted earlier, the analytics of profit maximization and optimal pricing are presented up front in Chapter 2 and the second part of Chapter 3. If the instructor wishes, he or she can defer these optimization topics until after the chapters on demand and cost. In addition, the book is organized so that specific chapters can be omitted without loss of continuity. In the first section of the book, Chapters 4, 5, and 6 fit into this category. In the second section of the book, Chapters 10, 11, and 12 are core chapters that can stand alone or be followed by any combination of the remaining chapters. The book concludes with applications chapters, including chapters on linear programming and capital budgeting that are suitable for many broad-based managerial economics courses.

Analyzing managerial decisions requires a modest amount of quantitative proficiency. In our view, understanding the *logic* of profit-maximizing behavior is more important than mathematical sophistication; therefore, *Managerial Economics*, Fifth Edition, uses only the most basic techniques of differential calculus. These concepts are explained and summarized in the appendix to Chapter 2. Numerical examples and applications abound throughout all of the chapters. In our view, the best way for students to master the material is to learn by example. Four to six "Check Stations"—mini-problems that force students to test themselves on their quantitative understanding—appear throughout each chapter. In short, the text takes a quantitative approach to managerial decision making without drowning students in mathematics.

THE FIFTH EDITION

While continuing to emphasize managerial decision making, the Fifth Edition of *Managerial Economics* contains several changes.

First, we have extensively revised and updated the many applications in the text. From analyzing the government's antitrust case against Microsoft, to using regression analysis to estimate box-office revenues for film releases in 2003, from considering the challenges of corporate governance in the aftermath of Enron, to formulating new auction mechanisms to sell the radio spectrum, these are all important and timely economic applications. Throughout the text, we have included a wider range of end-of-chapter problems from basic to advanced. Each chapter also contains a wide-ranging discussion question designed to frame broader economic questions. We have also revised each chapter's suggested bibliographic references including numerous Internet sites where students can access and retrieve troves of economic information and data on almost any topic.

The current edition examines the economics of information goods, e-commerce, and the Internet—topics first introduced in the fourth edition. While some commentators have claimed that the emergence of e-commerce has overturned the traditional rules of economics, the text takes a more balanced view. In fact, e-commerce provides a dramatic illustration of the power of economic analysis in analyzing new market forces. Any analysis of e-commerce must consider such issues as network and information externalities, reduced marginal costs and transaction costs, pricing and revenue sources, control of standards, e-commerce strategies, product versioning, and market segmentation, to name just a few topics. E-commerce applications appear throughout the text in Chapter 3 (demand), Chapter 7 (cost), Chapters 10 and 12 (competitive effects), and Chapter 15 (organization of the firm).

Finally, the fifth edition continues the emphasis on decision making under uncertainty by placing this important topic in the core of the text, Chapters 8 and 9. In this day and age, the process of confronting, analyzing, and making risky decisions is at the heart of management.

ANCILLARY MATERIALS

INSTRUCTOR'S MANUAL AND TEST BANK WITH TRANSPARENCY MASTERS
The instructor's manual includes suggestions for teaching managerial economics, additional examples to supplement in-text examples, suggested cases, references to current articles in the business press, anecdotes, follow-up on text applications, and answers to the even-numbered problems. The test bank contains over 500 multiple-choice questions, quantitative problems, discussion questions. The figures from the textbook are also included for instructors wishing to use black and white overheads.

STUDY GUIDE   The study guide is designed to teach the concepts and problem-solving skills needed to master the material in the text. Each chapter contains multiple-choice questions, quantitative problems, discussion questions, and mini-cases. All of the problems in the study guide were reviewed and checked for accuracy.

COMPUTERIZED TEST BANK   The test bank is available electronically in DOS and Windows versions. The ExaMaster system accompanying the computerized test banks makes it easy to create tests, print scrambled versions of the same test, modify questions, and reproduce any of the graphing questions.

WEB SITE   Professors using this textbook can find additional teaching materials such as PowerPoint versions of the text's figures and tables, spreadsheets, applications, and reference materials by accessing Wiley's Web site at www.wiley.com/college. The greatly expanded Web site is the place to look to access electronic versions of these materials.

ACKNOWLEDGMENTS

In preparing this important revision, we have benefited from suggestions from the following reviewers and survey respondents: Krishna Akkina, Kansas State University; Richard Beil, Auburn University; Gregory Brock, Georgia Southern University; Shawn Carter, Jacksonville State University; Richard Chisik, Florida International University; Michael Davis, Southern Methodist University; Mark Frescatore, Clarkson University; Ann Garnett, Murdoch University; Koushik Ghosh, Central Washington University; Theodore Groves, University of California–San Diego; Duncan Holthausen, North Carolina State University; John R. McNamara, Lehigh University; Kofi O. Nti, Pennsylvania State University; Nicola Persico, University of Pennsylvania; Franklin Robeson, College of William and Mary; Don Stengel, California State University–Fresno; Charles B. Wagoner, Delta State University; Craig Walker, Delta State University; Ron Wilder, University of South Carolina, and Chris Woodruff, University of California–San Diego.

We have also had valuable help from colleagues and students who have commented on parts of the manuscript. Among them are Alan J. Daskin; Cliff Dobitz, North Dakota State University; Howard Dye, University of South Florida; David Ely, San Diego State University; Steven Felgran, Northeastern University; William Gunther, University of Alabama; Robert Hansen, Dartmouth College; George Hoffer, Virginia Commonwealth University; Yannis Ioannides, Tufts University; Sarah Lane; Darwin Neher; Albert Okunade, Memphis State University; Mary Jean Rivers, Seattle University; Patricia Sanderson, Mississippi State University; Frank Slesnick, Bellarmine College; Leonard Tashman, University of Vermont; Rafael Tenorio, University of Notre Dame; Lawrence White, New York University; Mokhlis Zaki, Northern Michigan University; and Richard Zeckhauser, Harvard University. Other colleagues provided input on early teaching and research materials that later found prominent places in the text: Max Bazerman, Harvard University; John Riley, University of California–Los Angeles; James Sebenius, Harvard University; and Robert Weber, Northwestern University.

In addition, we have received many detailed comments and suggestions from our colleagues at Boston University, Shulamit Kahn and Michael Salinger. The feedback from students in Boston University's M.B.A. and Executive Programs has been invaluable. Special thanks to Diane Herbert and Robert Maurer for their comments and to Joseph Rosenfeld and Joseph Alexander for able research assistance.

Finally, we thank Susan and Mary Ellen.

William F. Samuelson
Stephen G. Marks

About the Authors

William F. Samuelson is professor of economics and finance at Boston University School of Management. He received his B.A. and Ph.D. from Harvard University. His research interests include game theory, decision theory, bidding, bargaining, and experimental economics. He has published a variety of articles in leading economics and management science journals including *The American Economic Review, The Quarterly Journal of Economics, Econometrica, The Journal of Finance, Management Science,* and *Operations Research.* His teaching and research have been sponsored by the National Science Foundation and the National Institute for Dispute Resolution, among others. He is currently on the editorial boards of the *Journal of Economic Behavior and Organization* and *Group Decision and Negotiation.*

Stephen G. Marks is associate professor of law at Boston University. He received his J.D., M.A., and Ph.D. from the University of California–Berkeley. He has taught in the areas of managerial economics, finance, corporate law, and securities regulation. His research interests include corporate governance, law and economics, finance, and information theory. He has published his research in various law reviews and in such journals as *The American Economic Review, The Journal of Legal Studies,* and *The Journal of Financial and Quantitative Analysis.*

Contents

CHAPTER 1

Introduction
to Economic
Decision Making

The crucial step in tackling almost all important business and government decisions begins with a single question: What is the alternative?

ANONYMOUS

Decision making lies at the heart of most important business and government problems. The range of business decisions is vast: Should a high-tech company undertake a promising but expensive research and development program? Should a petrochemical manufacturer cut the price of its best-selling industrial chemical in response to a new competitor's entry into the market? What bid should company management submit to win a government telecommunications contract? Should management of a food products company launch a new product after mixed test-marketing results? Likewise, government decisions range far and wide: Should the Department of Transportation impose stricter rollover standards for sport-utility vehicles? Should a city allocate funds for construction of a harbor tunnel to provide easy airport and commuter access? Should the federal government increase funding for the war on cancer? These are all interesting, important, and timely questions—with no easy answers. They are also all economic decisions. In each case, a sensible analysis of what decision to make requires a careful comparison of the advantages and disadvantages (often, but not always, measured in dollars) of alternative courses of action.

As the term suggests, **managerial economics** is the analysis of major management decisions using the tools of economics. Managerial economics applies many familiar concepts from economics—demand and cost, monopoly and competition, the allocation of resources, and economic trade-offs—to aid managers in making better decisions. This book provides the framework and the economic tools needed to fulfill this goal.

In this chapter, we begin our study of managerial economics by stressing decision-making applications. In the first section, we introduce eight decision examples, all of which we will analyze in detail later in the text. Although these examples cover only some applications of economic analysis, they represent the breadth of managerial economics and are intended to whet the reader's appetite. Next, we present a basic model of the decision-making process as a framework in which to apply economic analysis. This model proposes six steps to help structure complicated decisions so that they may be clearly analyzed.

After presenting the six steps, we outline a basic theory of the firm and of government decisions and objectives. In the concluding section, we present a brief overview of the topics covered in the chapters to come.

EIGHT EXAMPLES OF MANAGERIAL DECISIONS

The best way to become acquainted with managerial economics is to come face to face with real-world decision-making problems. The eight examples that follow represent the different kinds of decisions that private- and public-sector managers face. All of them are revisited and examined in detail in later chapters.

The examples follow a logical progression. In the first example, a global carmaker faces the most basic problem in managerial economics: determining prices and outputs to maximize profit. As we shall see in Chapters 2 through 7, making decisions requires a careful analysis of revenues and costs. In the second example, Disney's decision crucially depended on its ability to estimate demand and to forecast revenues, topics taken up in Chapters 4 and 5. The next two examples involve decision making under uncertainty. In the third example, a pharmaceutical company is poised between alternative risky research and development (R&D) programs. In the fourth example, a bank's loan department must assess the credit risk of a would-be borrower. Decision making under uncertainty is the topic of Chapters 8 and 9.

The next two examples highlight competition between firms, the subject of Chapters 10 through 13. In the first case, two large bookstore chains are battling for market share in a multitude of regional markets. Each is trying to secure a monopoly, but when both build superstores in the same city, they frequently become trapped in price wars. In turn, Texaco and Pennzoil are locked in a high-risk, high-stakes negotiation in the "shadow" of the courts. Competition in the contexts of negotiation and competitive bidding is taken up in Chapters 16 and 17.

The last two examples illustrate public-sector decisions: The first concerns funding a public project, the second is a regulatory decision. Here, a shift occurs both in the decision maker—from private to public manager—and in the objectives. As we argue in Chapter 14, government decisions are guided by the criterion of benefit–cost analysis rather than by profit considerations.

Multinational Production and Pricing

Almost all firms face the problem of pricing their product. Consider a U.S. multinational carmaker that produces and sells its output in two geographic regions. It can produce cars in its home plant or in its foreign subsidiary. It sells cars in the domestic market and in the foreign market. For the next year, it must determine the prices to set at home and abroad, estimate sales for each market, and establish production quantities in each facility to supply those sales. It recognizes that the markets for vehicles at home and abroad differ with respect to demand (that is, how many cars can be sold at different prices). Also, the production facilities have different costs and capacities. Finally, at a cost, it can ship vehicles from the home facility to help supply the foreign market, or vice versa. Based on the available information, how can the company determine a profit-maximizing pricing and production plan for the coming year?

Euro Disney

In 1987, Michael Eisner, the head of Walt Disney Co., signed the final contract with the French government to build and operate a $2 billion theme park outside of Paris. Euro Disney signaled the company's proposed entry into a soon-to-be-unified Europe.

In making its decision, Disney faced a monumental task of economic forecasting. Is a French location superior to a more temperate Spanish site? How much will the park cost to build? Can French workers deliver the high-quality customer service Disney expects? At what wage cost? Will Europeans flock to a fantasy theme park the way Americans have? How long will customers stay? Will they choose Disney's hotels? How much will they spend? How will these projections change if Europe encounters a prolonged recession?

Based on its long record of success, Disney's management team confidently embarked on a monumental investment: Besides creating the theme park, they intended to build over 5,000 hotel rooms, the necessary office space, hundreds of private homes, and a golf course. European banks lined up to provide loans to underwrite the Disney magic, and the French government offered tax concessions and low-interest loans. However, since opening in April 1992, Euro Disney's performance has been dismal, marked by lower-than-expected revenues and elevated costs. Though Euro Disney has achieved modest profits since 1998, its stock price remains at about one-tenth of its 1992 level. What factors are to blame for the park's poor operating results? Armed with more realistic forecasts, what might Disney have done differently?

An R&D Decision

A five-year-old pharmaceutical company faces a major research and development decision. It already has spent a year of preliminary research toward producing a protein that dissolves blood clots. Such a drug would be of tremendous value in the treatment of heart attacks, some 80 percent of which are caused by clots. The primary method the company has been pursuing relies on conventional, state-of-the-art biochemistry. Continuing this approach will require an estimated $10 million additional investment and should lead to a commercially successful product, although the exact profit is highly uncertain. Two of the company's most brilliant research scientists are aggressively advocating a second R&D approach. This new biogenetic method relies on gene splicing to create a version of the human body's own anticlotting agent and is considerably riskier than the biochemical alternative. It will require a $20 million investment and has only a 20 percent chance of commercial success. However, if the company accomplishes the necessary breakthroughs, the anticlotting agent will represent the first blockbuster, genetically engineered drug. If successful, the method will entail minimal production costs and generate annual profits two to five times greater than a biochemically based drug would. The question facing the firm: Which method should it choose for its R&D investment?

Predicting Credit Risks

For issuing banks large and small, the credit-card business is extraordinarily profitable—as much as three times more profitable than ordinary lending. However, this business is highly risky as well. Bank losses on accounts that are delinquent or in default can be considerable. Banks attempt to gauge a customer's risk from information provided on application forms: family income, employment history, home ownership, and other characteristics. In recent years, banks have increasingly turned to statistical measures, compiling computerized composite credit "scores" for customers as they use the cards. These scores incorporate factors such as past credit record, credit lines on other cards held, promptness and amount of payments, and credit-card spending patterns. A bank's aim is to distinguish high- and low-risk accounts, closing or reducing credit limits on the former and increasing limits on the latter.

Similar quantitative evaluation methods are also being adopted for ordinary business loans. Instead of bank loan officers relying on their long-time experience to make credit decisions, a software program (fed the appropriate information) would provide a quick and ready decision. The same quantitative method would track repayment behavior during the term of the loan.

How well can statistical computer scores predict and discern credit worthiness? Which perform more accurately, computer or human decision makers?

Market Entry

In recent years, the two giants of the book business—Barnes & Noble and Borders Group—have been engaged in a cutthroat retail battle. In major city after major city, the rivals have opened superstores, often within sight of each other. By the mid-1990s, more books were sold via chain stores than by independent stores, and both companies have continued to open new stores at dizzying rates.

The ongoing competition raises a number of questions: How does either chain assess the profitability of new markets? Where and when should each enter new markets? What if a region's book-buying demand is sufficient to support only one superstore? What measures might be taken by an incumbent to erect entry barriers to a would-be entrant? On what dimensions—number of titles, pricing, personal service—do the companies most vigorously compete? In view of emerging book sales on the Internet, what are the long-run growth prospects for retail book selling?

From 1984 to 1987, the dispute between these two oil companies set a gusher of records, including the largest court award in history, the largest bankruptcy filing, ultimately the greatest settlement, and collectively an unprecedented amount of legal expenses. The dispute arose from a takeover battle in which Texaco acquired Getty Oil, a move that allegedly wrecked a planned Pennzoil-Getty deal. Seeking damages, Pennzoil filed a lawsuit against Texaco, and thus began the first of many rounds of settlement negotiations. Following are some of the important company decisions (as well as key court outcomes) that took place during the protracted negotiations:

Texaco versus Pennzoil

- *January 1984.* Pennzoil offers to withdraw the lawsuit in exchange for the right to purchase 37 percent of Getty. Texaco refuses.
- *November 1985.* A Texas jury awards Pennzoil $10.5 billion from Texaco.
- *December 1985.* Texaco offers to sell 42 percent of Getty. Pennzoil refuses.
- *January 1986.* Texaco offers to take over Pennzoil, paying $83 per share. Pennzoil angrily refuses.
- *February 1987.* A Texas appeals court upholds all but $2 billion of the original judgment.
- *April 1987.* Texaco offers to pay $2 billion. Pennzoil refuses and demands $4.1 billion. Texaco refuses and files for bankruptcy, stopping Pennzoil from immediately securing its $10 billion judgment.
- *November 1987.* Pennzoil demands $1.5 billion and offers to cap its award at $5 billion even if the full award is upheld. Texaco refuses.
- *December 1987.* Pressured by a shareholders' committee, Texaco offers to pay $1.5 billion in exchange for a $3.5 billion cap. Pennzoil refuses.
- *December 19, 1987.* Texaco and Pennzoil agree on a $3 billion payment.

Put yourself in the companies' top leadership positions. Were the right decisions made? Which side, if either, "won" the negotiations?

As chief city planner of a rapidly growing Sun Belt city, you face the single biggest decision of your tenure: whether to recommend the construction of a new harbor bridge to connect downtown with the surrounding suburbs located

Building a New Bridge

on a northern peninsula. Currently, suburban residents commute to the city via a ferry or by driving a long-distance circular route. Preliminary studies have shown that there is considerable need and demand for the bridge. Indeed, the bridge is expected to spur economic activity in the region as a whole. The projected cost of the bridge is $75 million to $100 million. Part of the money would be financed with an issue of municipal bonds, and the remainder would be contributed by the state. Toll revenues on commuting automobiles and particularly on trucks would be instituted to recoup a portion of the bridge's costs. But, if bridge use falls short of projections, the city will be saddled with a very expensive white elephant. What would you recommend?

A Regulatory Problem

Environmental regulations have a significant effect on business decisions and consumer behavior. Charles Schultze, former chairperson of the President's Council of Economic Advisers, describes the myriad problems associated with regulations requiring electric utilities to convert from oil to coal.

> Petroleum imports can be conserved by switching [utilities] from oil-fired to coal-fired generation. But barring other measures, burning high-sulfur Eastern coal substantially increases pollution. Sulfur can be "scrubbed" from coal smoke in the stack, but at a heavy cost, with devices that turn out huge volumes of sulfur wastes that must be disposed of and about whose reliability there is some question. Intermittent control techniques (installing high smoke stacks and turning off burners when meteorological conditions are adverse) can, at a lower cost, reduce local concentrations of sulfur oxides in the air, but cannot cope with the growing problem of sulphates and widespread acid rainfall. Use of low-sulfur Western coal would avoid many of these problems, but this coal is obtained by strip mining. Strip-mine reclamation is possible but substantially hindered in large areas of the West by lack of rainfall. Moreover, in some coal-rich areas the coal beds form the underlying aquifer, and their removal could wreck adjacent farming or ranching economies. Large coal-burning plants might be located in remote areas far from highly populated urban centers in order to minimize the human effects of pollution. But such areas are among the few left that are unspoiled by pollution, and both environmentalists and the residents (relatively few in number compared to those in metropolitan localities but large among the voting populations in the particular states) strongly object to this policy. Fears, realistic or imaginary, about safety and accumulation of radioactive waste have increasingly hampered the nuclear option.[1]

[1] C. L. Schultz, *The Public Use of Private Interest* (Washington, D.C.: The Brookings Institution, 1977), 9–10.

Schultze's points apply directly to today's energy and environmental trade-offs. Actually, he penned this discussion in 1977! Important questions persist. How, when, and where should the government intervene to achieve and balance its energy and environmental objectives? How would one go about quantifying the benefits and costs of a particular program of intervention?

SIX STEPS TO DECISION MAKING

The examples just given represent the breadth of the decisions in managerial economics. Different as they may seem, each decision can be framed and analyzed using a common approach based on six steps, as Figure 1.1 indicates. With the examples as a backdrop, we will briefly outline each step. Later in the text, we will refer to these steps when analyzing managerial decisions.

Step 1: Define the Problem

What is the problem the manager faces? Who is the decision maker? What is the decision setting or context, and how does it influence managerial objectives or options?

FIGURE 1.1

The Basic Steps in Decision Making

The process of decision making can be broken down into six basic steps.

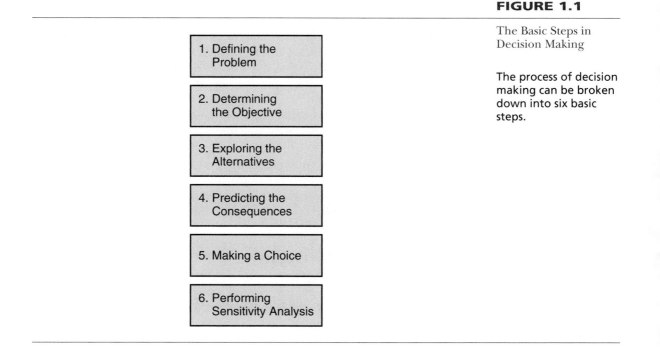

1. Defining the Problem

2. Determining the Objective

3. Exploring the Alternatives

4. Predicting the Consequences

5. Making a Choice

6. Performing Sensitivity Analysis

Decisions do not occur in a vacuum. Many come about as part of the firm's planning process. Others are prompted by new opportunities or new problems. It is natural to ask: What brought about the need for the decision? What is the decision all about? In each of the examples given earlier, the decision problem is stated and is reasonably well defined. In practice, however, managerial decisions do not come so neatly packaged; rather, they are messy and poorly defined. Thus, problem definition is a prerequisite for problem management. In fact, the decision in the last example—the conversion of utilities to coal—raises interesting issues concerning problem definition. How narrowly does one define the problem? Is the crux of the problem minimizing pollution from utilities? Presumably cost is also important. Thus, the problem involves determining how much pollution to clean up, by what means, and at what cost. Or is the problem much broader: reducing U.S. dependence on foreign energy sources? If so, which domestic energy initiatives (besides or instead of utility conversion to coal) should be undertaken? Is instituting an increase in the prices of oil and natural gas (to promote both conservation and domestic production) a better solution? Clearly, defining the problem is no easy matter.

A key part of problem definition involves identifying the setting or context. The majority of the decisions we study take place in the private sector. For instance, managers representing their respective firms are responsible for the decisions made in the first six examples. The final two examples occur in the public sector, where decisions are made at all levels of government: local, state, and national. For instance, the recommendation concerning construction of a new bridge is made by a city agency and must be approved by the state government. In the final example, the chain of decisions accompanying the conversion of utilities from oil to coal involves a surprising number of public-sector authorities, including the Department of Energy, the Environmental Protection Agency, state and local agencies, the Department of the Interior, and possibly the Nuclear Regulatory Commission. As one might imagine, the larger the number of bodies that share policy responsibility and the pursuit of different goals, the greater the likelihood that decision-making problems, conflicts, and impasses will occur.

Identifying the decision context and the decision maker represents a large step toward understanding the choice process. The particular setting has a direct bearing on both the decision maker's objectives and the available courses of action. The next two steps consider each of these aspects in turn.

Step 2: Determine the Objective

What is the decision maker's goal? What end is he or she pursuing? How should the decision maker value outcomes with respect to this goal? What if he or she is pursuing multiple, conflicting objectives?

When it comes to economic decisions, it is a truism that "you can't always get what you want."[2] But to make any progress at all in your choice, you have to know what you want. In most private-sector decisions, **profit** is the principal objective of the firm and the usual barometer of its performance. Thus, among alternative courses of action, the manager will select the one that will maximize the profit of the firm. Attainment of maximum profit worldwide is the natural objective of the multinational carmaker, the drug company, and the management and shareholders of Disney, Barnes & Noble, Borders Group, Texaco, and Pennzoil. Sometimes the manager focuses on the narrower goal of minimizing cost. For instance, the firm may seek to produce a given level of output at the least cost or to obtain a targeted increase in sales with minimal expenditure on advertising. In a host of settings, measures that reduce costs directly serve to increase profits.

The objective in a public-sector decision, whether it be building a bridge or regulating a utility, is broader than the private-sector profit standard. In making his or her choice, the government decision maker should weigh all benefits and costs, not solely those that accrue as revenue or are incurred as expenses. According to this benefit–cost criterion, the bridge in the seventh example may be worth building even if it fails to generate a profit for the government authority. And in the final example, the optimal means of regulating the production decisions of the utility depend on a careful comparison of benefits (mainly in the form of energy conservation) and costs (in dollar and environmental terms).

In practice, profit maximization and benefit–cost analysis are not always unambiguous guides to decision making. One difficulty is posed by the timing of benefits and costs. Should a firm (the drug company, for example) make an investment (sacrifice profits today) for greater profits 5 or 10 years from now? Are the future benefits to commuters worth the present capital expense of building the bridge? Both private and public investments involve trade-offs between present and future benefits and costs. Thus, in pursuing its profit goal, the firm must establish a comparable measure of value between present and future monetary returns.

Uncertainty poses a second difficulty. In many economic decisions, it is customary to treat the outcomes of various actions as certain. For instance, a fast-food chain may know that it can construct a new outlet in 45 days at a cost of $75 per square foot. The cost and timing of construction are not entirely certain, but the margin of error is small enough to have no bearing on the company's decisions and thus can be safely ignored. In contrast, the cost and date of completion of a nuclear power plant are highly uncertain (due to unanticipated design changes, cost overruns, schedule delays, and the like). At best,

---

[2] Many readers will recognize this quote as a lyric penned by Mick Jagger of the Rolling Stones. What many may not know is that Jagger briefly attended the London School of Economics before pursuing the path to rock stardom.

the utilities that share ownership of the plant may be able to estimate a range of cost outcomes and completion dates and assess probabilities for these possible outcomes. (With the benefit of hindsight, one now wishes that the utilities had recognized the risks and safety problems of nuclear plants 20 and 30 years ago, when construction on many plants was initiated.)

The presence of risk and uncertainty has a direct bearing on the way the decision maker thinks about his or her objective. The drug company seeks to maximize its profit, but there is no simple way to apply the profit criterion to determine its best R&D choice. The company cannot use the simple rule "choose the method that will yield the greater profit," because the ultimate profit from either method cannot be pinned down ahead of time. In each case, there are no profit guarantees; rather, the drug company faces a choice between two risky options. Similarly, public programs and regulatory policies generate future benefits and costs that cannot be predicted with certainty.

Step 3: Explore the Alternatives

What are the alternative courses of action? What are the variables under the decision maker's control? What constraints limit the choice of options?

After addressing the question "What do we want?" it is natural to ask, "What are our options?" The ideal decision maker, if such a person exists, would lay out all the available courses of action and then choose the one that best achieves his or her objective. Given human limitations, decision makers cannot hope to identify and evaluate all possible options. The cost of doing so simply would be too great. Still, one would hope that attractive options would not be overlooked or, if discovered, not mistakenly dismissed. No analysis can begin with all the available options in hand. However, a sound decision framework should be able to uncover options in the course of the analysis.

In our examples, the main work of problem definition has been carried out, making the identification of decision options relatively easy. In the first example, the carmaker is free to set prices at home and abroad. These prices are two of the firm's decision variables. In each market, the firm must choose a particular price to charge from a continuous range of prices. Obviously, these prices will largely determine the number of vehicles the firm can expect to sell in each market. It still remains for the firm to determine a production plan to supply its total projected sales; that is, the firm's other two decision variables are the quantities to produce in each facility. The firm's task is to find optimal values of these four decision variables, that is, values that will generate a maximum level of profit.

In most of the other examples, the decision maker faces a choice from a relatively small number of alternatives. But even when the choices are limited, there may be more alternatives than first meet the eye. Disney management had to decide whether to build the theme park and, if so, where and what size to build it. They also had to determine what prices to charge and how to advertise and promote the park. Similarly, the utilities example illustrates the way in which options can multiply. In this setting, the limitations and repercussions of the "obvious" alternatives lead to a wider consideration of other choices, which, unfortunately, have their own side effects.

The drug company might appear to have a simple either/or choice: pursue the biochemical R&D program or proceed with the biogenetic program. But there are other alternatives. The company could pursue neither program or both programs simultaneously. The latter strategy means investing resources and money in both, but it allows the firm to commercialize the superior program that emerges from the R&D competition. Alternatively, the company can institute sequential R&D development instead of simultaneous development. After observing the outcome of an initial R&D program, the company could choose to develop it or to reject it. In rejecting the initial program, the company could then invest in the second R&D approach. The question raised by the sequential option is: Which approach, the safer biochemical method or the riskier biogenetic alternative, should the company pursue first?

Most managerial decisions involve more than a once-and-for-all choice from among a set of options. Typically, the manager faces a sequence of decisions from among alternatives. For instance, before committing to computerized credit screening, bank management might prudently set up a small-scale test of the system. Thus, the bank might extend loans to a dozen clients based on the computer's recommendation and monitor their performance over the course of time. Alternatively, the bank could set 50 percent of its loan portfolio by computer and leave 50 percent in human hands, and compare performance. Or as economic and business conditions change, the bank might fine-tune the use of its computerized loan system. To sum up, in view of the myriad uncertainties facing managers, most ongoing decisions should best be viewed as *contingent* plans.

Sequential decision making also lies at the heart of the negotiation dilemma that Texaco and Pennzoil faced. Each side had to formulate its current negotiation stance (how aggressive or conciliatory an offer to make) in light of current court results and the offers (both its own and its opponent's) made to date. Thus, a commonly acknowledged fact about negotiation is that the main purpose of an opening offer is not to have the offer accepted (if it were, the offer probably was far too generous); rather, the offer should direct the course of the offers to follow.

Step 4: Predict the Consequences

What are the consequences of each alternative action? Should conditions change, how would this affect outcomes? If outcomes are uncertain, what is the likelihood of each? Can better information be acquired to predict outcomes?

Depending on the situation, the task of predicting the consequences may be straightforward or formidable. Sometimes elementary arithmetic suffices. For instance, the simplest profit calculation requires only subtracting costs from revenues. Or suppose the choice between two safety programs is made according to which saves the greater number of lives per dollar expended. Here the use of arithmetic division is the key to identifying the preferred alternative.

MODELS   In more complicated situations, however, the decision maker often must rely on a model to describe how options translate into outcomes. A **model** is a simplified description of a process, relationship, or other phenomenon. By deliberate intent, a model focuses on a few key features of a problem to examine carefully how they work while ignoring other complicating and less important factors. Of course, the main purposes of models are to explain and to predict—to account for past outcomes and to forecast future ones.

The kinds of predictive models are as varied as the decision problems to which they are applied. Many models rest on economic relationships. Suppose the multinational carmaker predicts that a 10 percent price cut will increase unit sales by 15 percent in the foreign market. The basis for this prediction is the most fundamental relationship in economics: the demand curve. The crux of Disney's decision problem was demand forecasting. Borders' decision of when and how to enter a new market depends on predictions of demand and cost and of how Barnes & Noble might be expected to respond in an effort to maintain its market share. These elements may be captured with a model of competitive behavior among oligopolists. Chapters 3 through 7 survey the key economic models of demand and cost used in making managerial decisions.

Other models rest on engineering, statistical, legal, and scientific relationships. The construction and configuration of the new bridge, its likely environmental impact, and the plan to convert utilities to coal depend in large part on engineering predictions. Evaluations of test-marketing results rely heavily on statistical models. Legal models, interpretations of statutes, precedents, and the like are pertinent to predictions of a firm's potential patent liability and to the outcome of the Pennzoil–Texaco lawsuit. Finally, the drug company's assessment of the relative merits of competing R&D methods rests on scientific and biological models.

So far as prediction is concerned, a key distinction can be drawn between deterministic and probabilistic models. A **deterministic model** is one in which the outcome is certain (or close enough to a sure thing that it can be taken as certain). For instance, a soft-drink manufacturer may wish to predict the numbers of individuals in the 10-to-25 age group over the next five years. There are ample demographic statistics with which to make this prediction. Obviously, the numbers in this age group five years from now will consist of those who today are between ages 5 and 20, minus a predictable small number of deaths. Thus, a simple deterministic model suffices for the prediction.

However, the forecast becomes much less certain when it comes to estimating the total consumption of soft drinks by this age group or the market share of a given product. Obviously, the market share of a particular drink—say, one with 10 percent or more real juice—will depend on many unpredictable factors, including the advertising, promotion, and price decisions of the firm and its competitors as well as consumer tastes. As the term suggests, a **probabilistic model** accounts for a range of possible future outcomes, each with a probability attached. For instance, the five-year market-share forecast for the natural-juice soft drink might take the following form: a 30 percent chance of less than a 3 percent share, a 25 percent chance of a 3 to 6 percent share, a 30 percent chance of a 6 to 8 percent share, and a 15 percent chance of an 8 to 12 percent share.

Step 5: Make a Choice

After all the analysis is done, what is the preferred course of action? For obvious reasons, this step (along with step 4) occupies the lion's share of the analysis and discussion in this book. Once the decision maker has put the problem in context, formalized key objectives, and identified available alternatives, how does he or she go about finding a preferred course of action?

In the vast majority of decisions we will encounter, the objectives and outcomes are directly quantifiable. Thus, the private firm (such as the carmaker) can compute the profit results of alternative price and output plans. Analogously, a government decision maker may know the computed net benefits (benefits minus costs) of different program options. Given enough time, the decision maker could determine a preferred course of action by **enumeration**, that is, by testing a number of alternatives and selecting the one that best meets the objective. This is fine for decisions involving a small number of choices, but it is impractical for more complex problems. For instance, what if the car company drew up a list of two dozen different pricing and production plans, computed the profits of each, and settled on the best of the lot? How could management be sure this choice is truly optimal, that is, the best of all possible plans? What if a more profitable plan, say, the 25th candidate, was overlooked? Expanding the enumerated list could reduce this risk, but at considerable cost.

Fortunately, the decision maker need not rely on the painstaking method of enumeration to solve such problems. A variety of methods can identify and cut directly to the best, or **optimal**, decision. These methods rely to varying extents on marginal analysis, decision trees, game theory, benefit–cost analysis, linear programming, and present discounted values, all of which we take up later in this book. These approaches are important not only for computing optimal decisions but also for checking why they are optimal.

Step 6: Perform Sensitivity Analysis

What features of the problem determine the optimal choice of action? How does the optimal decision change if conditions in the problem are altered? Is the choice sensitive to key economic variables about which the decision maker is uncertain?

In tackling and solving a decision problem, it is important to understand and be able to explain to others the "why" of your decision. The solution, after all, did not come out of thin air. It depended on your stated objectives, the way you structured the problem (including the set of options you considered), and your method of predicting outcomes. Thus, **sensitivity analysis** considers how an optimal decision would change if key economic facts or conditions were altered.

Here is a simple example of the use of sensitivity analysis. Senior management of a consumer products firm is conducting a third-year review of one of its new products. Two of the firm's business economists have prepared an extensive report that projects significant profits from the product over the next two years. These profit estimates suggest a clear course of action: continue marketing the product. As a member of senior management, would you accept this recommendation uncritically? Probably not. You naturally would want to determine what is behind the profit projection. After all, you may be well aware that the product has not yet earned a profit in its first two years. (Although it sold reasonably well, it also had high advertising and promotion costs and a low introductory price.) What is behind the new profit projection? Larger sales, a higher price, or both? A significant cost reduction? The process of tracking down the basic determinants of profit is one aspect of sensitivity analysis.

As one would expect, the product's future revenues and costs may be highly uncertain. As a consequence, management should recognize that the revenue and cost projections come with a significant margin of error attached. It is natural to investigate the profit effects if outcomes differ from the report's forecasts. What if sales are 12 percent lower than expected? What if projected cost reductions are not realized? What if the price of a competing product is slashed? By answering these what-if questions, management can determine the degree to which its profit projections, and therefore its marketing decision, are sensitive to the uncertain outcomes of key economic variables.

Sensitivity analysis is useful in (1) providing insight into the key features of the problem that affect the decision; (2) tracing the effects of changes in variables about which the manager may be uncertain; and (3) generating solutions in cases of recurring decisions under slightly modified conditions.[3]

---

[3] Sensitivity analysis might also include assessing the implementation of the chosen decision to see whether it achieved the desired solution. If so, management may be satisfied that it has made a sound choice. If not, why not? Has the decision setting been accurately described? Is the appropriate objective being pursued? Have all alternatives been considered? In light of an after-the-fact assessment, should the firm modify its original strategy?

PRIVATE AND PUBLIC DECISIONS: AN ECONOMIC VIEW

Our approach to managerial economics is based on a model of the firm: how firms behave and the objectives they pursue. The main tenet of this model, or **theory of the firm,** is that management strives to maximize the firm's profits, the difference between total revenues and total costs. This objective is unambiguous for decisions involving predictable revenues and costs occurring during the same period of time. However, a more precise profit criterion is needed when a firm's revenues and costs are uncertain and accrue at different times in the future. The most general theory of the firm states that:

| Management's primary goal is to maximize the value of the firm. |

Here, the firm's value is defined as the present value of its expected future profits. Thus, in making any decision, the manager must attempt to predict its impact on future profit flows and determine whether, indeed, it will add to the value of the firm.[4]

Value maximization is a compelling *prescription* concerning how managerial decisions *should* be made. Although this tenet is a useful norm in describing actual managerial behavior, it is not a perfect yardstick. After all, large-scale firms consist of many levels of authority and myriad decision makers. Even if value maximization is the ultimate corporate goal, actual decision making within this complex organization may look quite different. There are several reasons for this:

1. Managers may have individual incentives (such as job security, career advancement, increasing a division's budget, resources, power) that are at odds with value maximization of the total firm. For instance, it sometimes is claimed that company executives are apt to focus on short-term value maximization (increasing next year's earnings) at the expense of long-run firm value.

2. Managers may lack the information (or fail to carry out the analysis) necessary for value-maximizing decisions.

3. Managers may formulate but fail to implement optimal decisions.

Although value maximization is the standard assumption in managerial economics, three other decision models should be pointed out. The model of **satisficing** behavior posits that the typical firm strives for a satisfactory level of

[4] Students who previously have taken a course in finance will recall that, in reckoning the value of the firm, future profits are discounted relative to current profits. Thus, the value of the firm today is the sum of the flow of future profits (revenues minus costs), discounted at the appropriate interest rate. See Chapter 19 for a full explanation of the concept of present discounted value.

performance rather than attempting to maximize its objective. Thus, a firm might aspire to a level of annual profit, say $40 million, and be satisfied with policies that achieve this benchmark. This behavior is particularly prevalent if it is complicated and costly to identify and analyze other, potentially more profitable courses of action. More generally, the firm may seek to achieve acceptable levels of performance with respect to multiple objectives (profitability being only one such objective).

A second behavioral model posits that the firm attempts to **maximize total sales** subject to achieving an acceptable level of profit. Total dollar sales are a visible benchmark of managerial success. For instance, the business press puts particular emphasis on the firm's market share.[5] In addition, a variety of studies show a close link between executive compensation and company sales. Thus, top management's self-interest may lie as much in sales maximization as in value maximization.

A third issue centers on the **social responsibility of business**. In modern capitalist economies, business firms contribute significantly to economic welfare. Within free markets, firms compete to supply the goods and services that consumers demand. Pursuing the profit motive, they constantly strive to produce goods of higher quality at lower costs. By investing in research and development and pursuing technological innovation, they endeavor to create new and improved goods and services. In the process, firms bid for inputs and employ labor and capital. In the large majority of cases, the economic actions of firms (spurred by the profit motive) promote social welfare as well: Business production contributes to economic growth, provides widespread employment, and raises standards of living.

The objective of value maximization implies that management's primary responsibility is to the firm's shareholders. But the firm can be viewed as having other stakeholders as well: its customers, its workers, even the local community to which it might pay taxes. This observation raises an important question: To what extent might management decisions be influenced by the likely effects of its actions on these parties? For instance, suppose management believes that downsizing its workforce is necessary to increase profitability. Should it uncompromisingly pursue maximum profits even if this significantly increases unemployment? Alternatively, suppose that because of weakened international competition, the firm has the opportunity to profit by significantly raising prices. Should it do so? Finally, suppose that the firm could dramatically cut its production costs with the side effect of generating a modest amount of pollution. Should it ignore such adverse environmental side effects?

---

[5]It is fashionable to argue that raising the firm's current market share is the best prescription for increasing long-run profitability. In particular circumstances (for instance, when learning-curve effects are important), share increases may indeed promote profitability. But this does not mean that the firm's ultimate objective is gaining market share. Rather, gaining market share remains a means toward the firm's ultimate end: maximum value. (Moreover, in other circumstances, the goals of gaining market share and profitability will be in conflict.)

All of these examples suggest potential trade-offs between value maximization and other possible social values and objectives. Although the customary goal of management is value maximization, there are circumstances in which business leaders choose to pursue other objectives at the expense of some foregone profits. For, instance, management might decide that retaining 100 jobs at a regional factory is worth a modest reduction in profit. To assess trade-offs such as these, management should have a clear idea of the best strategies for pursuing value maximization.

To sum up, value maximization is not the only model of managerial behavior. Nonetheless, the available evidence suggests that it offers the best description of a private firm's ultimate objectives and actions.

Public Goals

In government decisions, the question of objectives is much broader than simply an assessment of profit. Most political scientists and economists would agree that the purpose of public decisions is to promote the welfare of society, where the term *society* is meant to include all the people whose interests are affected and supposedly considered when a particular decision is made. The difficulty in applying the social welfare criterion in such a general form is that public decisions inevitably carry different benefits and costs to the many groups of individuals they affect. Some groups will gain and some will lose from any public decision. In our earlier example of the bridge, businesses and commuters in the region can expect to gain, but nearby neighbors who will suffer extra traffic, noise, and exhaust emissions will lose. The program to convert utilities from oil to coal will benefit the nation by reducing our dependence on imported oil. However, it also will increase many utilities' costs of producing electricity, which will mean higher electric bills for many residents. The accompanying increase in air pollution will bring adverse health and aesthetic effects in urban areas. Strip mining has its own economic and environmental costs, as does nuclear power. In short, any significant government program will bring a variety of new costs and benefits to different affected groups.

The important question is: How do we weigh these benefits and costs to make a decision that will be best for society as a whole? One answer is supplied by benefit–cost analysis, the principal analytical framework used in guiding public decisions. **Benefit–cost analysis** begins with the systematic enumeration of all the potential benefits and costs of a particular public decision. It goes on to measure or estimate the dollar magnitudes of these benefits and costs. Finally, it follows this decision rule: Undertake the project or program if and only if its total benefits (to all affected groups) exceed its total costs. Benefit–cost analysis is similar in approach to the profit calculation of the private firm, with one key difference: Whereas the firm considers only the revenue it accrues and the cost it incurs, public decisions account for all benefits, whether or not recipients pay for them (that is, regardless of whether revenue is generated), and all costs (direct and indirect).

Lower Drug Prices in Africa

Since 2001, in response to growing international outcries, major American and European pharmaceutical companies have dramatically reduced the prices of AIDS drugs in Africa. Drug companies such as Abbott Laboratories, Bristol-Myers Squibb Co., GlaxoSmithKline PLC, and Merck & Co. have variously pledged to cut prices by 50% or more, sell the drugs at or below cost, or in some cases even supply the drugs for free.[6] Glaxo has offered its powerful cocktail of AIDS drugs at a price per patient of $1,300 per year in Africa (whereas the price was greater than $11,000 in the United States).

The problem of health and disease in the developing world presents a stark conflict between the private profit motive and social welfare. The outbreak of disease in sub-Saharan Africa is considered to be the world's No. 1 health problem. Some 30 million African inhabitants are infected with HIV, the virus that causes AIDS. Millions of others suffer from a host of tropical diseases including malaria, river blindness, and sleeping sickness. However, global pharmaceutical companies have little profit incentive to invest in drugs for tropical diseases because those afflicted are too poor to pay for the drugs. Given the enormous R&D costs (not to mention marketing costs) of commercializing new drugs, multinational companies maximize their profits by selling drugs at high prices to high-income nations. Over the past decade, such groups as the World Health Organization, Doctors Without Borders, and national governments of developing countries have argued for low drug prices and abundant drug supplies to deliver the greatest possible health benefits. Multinational drug companies made some price concessions but otherwise dragged their feet.

With the turn of the millennium, why the dramatic change in the drug companies' position? Pharmaceutical executives professed their willingness to cut prices and therefore sacrifice profit only after being convinced of the magnitude of Africa's health problem. In addition, the "voluntary" cuts in drug prices were spurred by two other factors. First was the competitive threat of two Indian companies that already were promoting and selling generic (copycat) versions of a host of AIDS drugs and other drugs in Africa. Second, several national governments, notably South Africa, threatened to revoke or ignore drug patents. (From the 1970s to the present, the Indian government has refused to acknowledge international drug patents.) In return for the companies' recent price concessions, the World Health Organization has reaffirmed the validity of the companies' patents. In addition, recognizing the severity of

---

[6]This account is based on many published reports including, "AIDS: The End of the Beginning?" *The Economist*, July 17, 2004, p.76; R. Thurow and S. Miller, "As U.S. Balks on Medicine Deal, African Patients Feel the Pain," *The Wall Street Journal*, June 2, 2003, p. A1; H. Cooper et al. "AIDS Epidemic Traps Drug Firms in Vice: Treatment vs. Profits," *The Wall Street Journal*, March 2, 2001, p. A1; and M. Schoofs and M. Waldholz, "AIDS-Drug Price War Breaks Out in Africa, Goaded by Generics," *The Wall Street Journal*, March 7, 2001, p. A1.

the AIDS epidemic, the World Trade Organization extended until 2016 the transition period during which developing countries could be exempt from patent requirements of certain pharmaceuticals. In short, the major multinational drug companies seem willing to make selective price cuts (they are unwilling to cut prices for the poor in industrial economies) in return for patent assurances. (For more on selective price cutting and the role of patents, see Chapters 3 and 14, respectively.)

Dramatic cuts in drug prices are but a first step. For instance, cutting the cost per patient per year from $1,000 to $200 for a combination dose of anti-AIDS medication is a strong achievement. But to be truly affordable in the poorest nations, the cost would need to be reduced to about $50 per person per year. In addition, the ultimate solution for the health crisis in developing nations will require additional initiatives such as (1) resources for more doctors and hospitals as well as for disease prevention and drug distribution; (2) improved economic conditions, education, and in many regions the end of civil war; and (3) monetary aid from world health organizations and foreign governments.

THINGS TO COME

Figure 1.2 presents a schematic diagram of the topics and decision settings to come. As the figure indicates, the central focus of managerial economics is the private firm and how it should go about maximizing its profit. Chapters 2 and 3 begin the analysis by presenting a basic model of the firm and considering the case of profit maximization *under certainty,* that is, under the assumption that revenues and costs can be predicted perfectly. Specifically, the chapters show how the firm can apply the logic of marginal analysis to determine optimal outputs and prices. Chapters 3, 4, and 5 present an in-depth study of demand analysis and forecasting. Chapters 6 and 7 present analogous treatments of production and cost. The firm's investment decisions and the use of linear programming are deferred to the final two chapters.

Chapters 10 through 13 focus on market structure and competitive analysis and comprise the second major section of the text. This discussion stresses a key point: The firm does not maximize profit in a vacuum; rather, the market environment it inhabits has a profound influence on its output, pricing, and profitability. Chapters 10 and 11 present overviews of perfect competition and pure monopoly. Chapter 12 examines the case of oligopoly and provides a rich treatment of competitive strategy. Chapter 13 applies the discipline of game theory to the analysis of strategic behavior.

Chapter 14 considers the regulation of private markets and government provision of goods and services. These topics are particularly important in light of the divergent views of government held by the "person on the street"—views often based on moral convictions, political beliefs, and ideology. Some see

FIGURE 1.2

Topics in Managerial
Economics

This flow chart shows
the relationship
among the main topics
in managerial econom-
ics: decisions of the
firm, market structure,
decisions under uncer-
tainty, and govern-
ment decisions.

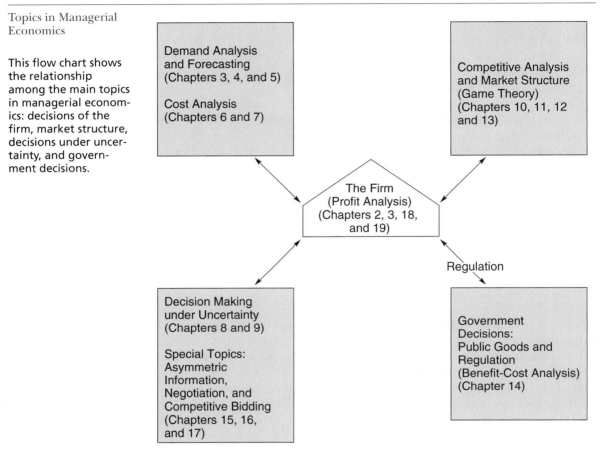

government as the essential engine to promote social welfare and to check private greed. Others call for "less" government, insisting that "for every action,
there is an equal and opposite government regulation." Our discussion does
not settle this dispute. But it does introduce the discipline of benefit–cost analysis to help evaluate how well government programs and regulations function.

Chapters 8 and 9 extend the core study of management decisions by incorporating risk and uncertainty. Managerial success, whether measured by a particular firm's long-run profitability or by the international competitiveness of
our nation's businesses as a whole, increasingly depends on making decisions
involving risk and uncertainty. Managers must strive to envision the future outcomes of today's decisions, measure and weigh competing risks, and determine
which risks are acceptable. Chapter 8 shows how decision trees can be used to

structure decisions in high-risk environments. Chapter 9 examines the value of acquiring information about relevant risks prior to making important decisions. Chapters 15, 16, and 17 present thorough analyses of four topics that are on the cutting edge of managerial economics and are of increasing importance to managers: asymmetric information, organizational design, negotiation, and competitive bidding.

The Aim of This Book

This book takes a *prescriptive* approach to managerial decisions; that is, it focuses on how managers can use economic analysis to arrive at optimal decisions. The aim of the prescriptive approach is to aid in solving important and difficult real-world decisions. One often hears the complaint, "That's fine in theory, but it wouldn't work in practice."[7] There is some validity to this objection; yet, in our view, the criticism misses the main point. To be useful, decision-making principles must be applicable to actual practice. In fact, most of the analytical methods we discuss were developed in response to important, recurring managerial decision problems. For instance, the value and flexibility of the six decision steps outlined in Figure 1.1 find strong support in the experience of practicing managers and decision analysts. Of course, one can expect that different decisions will call for varying degrees of analysis in each step. The degree to which a decision is analyzed (or the amount of information to be gathered) is itself a choice the manager must make. The key is to use the analytical approach flexibly.

In the course of our discussion, we will make frequent reference to the actual practice of managerial decision making—the customary methods by which business and government decisions are made. We need hardly point out that managerial practices frequently differ from our prescriptions. After all, if managers (and future managers like yourself) were always able to analyze perfectly the complex choices they faced, there would be little need for texts like this one. Actual managerial practice changes slowly. Many methods and practices accepted as essential by today's managers were unknown or untried by managers of earlier generations. These include many of the core decision methods of this book: optimal pricing and market segmentation, econometric forecasting, competitive analysis using game theory, benefit–cost analysis, resource allocation via linear programming, and the evaluation of investment projects based on net present value. The challenge of the prescriptive approach is to improve current and future practices.

---

[7] In many cases, the prescriptive approach turns the above criticism on its head by asking, "That's fine in practice, but does it make sense in theory?" In other words, is current practice the best way of making decisions, or could it be improved?

The value of a careful decision analysis is especially clear when one considers the alternatives. Individuals and managers have a host of informal ways of making decisions, relying on intuitive judgments, common sense, company policies, rules of thumb, or past experience, to name a few. In many cases these informal approaches lead to sound decisions, but in others they do not. For instance, one's intuitive judgments frequently are misleading or unfounded. A company's traditional rules of thumb may be inappropriate for many of the problems the firm currently faces. Often an optimal decision requires *uncommon* sense. For some managers (a small group, we hope), 10 years of experience may be equivalent to making first-year mistakes 10 times over. The point is that some kind of analysis, whether short or lengthy, is essential to keep the decision maker on firm ground. A choice inspired by company policy or past experience should be checked against the logic of a careful analysis. Has the manager kept clear sight of the essentials—the objectives and alternative courses of action? Has he or she evenhandedly considered all the economic factors, pro and con? What types of additional information does the manager need? How would the manager explain and justify his or her decision to others? A careful analysis that relies on the six steps defined earlier will provide the answers to just such questions.

A final advantage of the prescriptive approach is its emphasis on keeping things simple. A decision maker cannot consider everything. If he or she tried to, a choice probably would never be made. Rather, a sound decision-making approach should keep the manager focused on the several most important features of the decision he or she faces. The methods in this book do exactly that. Simplicity is essential not only for learning the methods but also for applying them successfully in future managerial decisions. An "optimal" decision procedure is of little value if it is too complicated to be employed. The decision settings and problems in this book are deliberately simplified. This is not to say that the decisions are "easy" (many are difficult and subtle); rather, they have been shorn of many real-world complications to direct maximum attention on the fundamental issues. To quote Albert Einstein, "The key is to make things as simple as possible, but not one bit simpler." Although they are illustrated in relatively uncomplicated settings, the principles and analytical tools presented in this book are equally applicable to complex decisions. In more complicated settings, of course, it is important to focus on the right problem. The danger lies in simplifying the problem beyond recognition, ultimately arriving at the "right" answer to the wrong problem. We are reminded of a chief executive who had commissioned a consultant to advise him on a vexing strategy problem of the firm. The consultant's highly technical report offered a score of impossible recommendations aimed at a company the chief could hardly recognize. As the executive used to say afterward, "Never have so many babies been thrown out with so little bath water."

SUMMARY

Decision-Making Principles

1. Decision making lies at the heart of most important problems managers face. Managerial economics applies the principles of economics to analyze business and government decisions.

2. The prescription for sound managerial decisions involves six steps: (1) define the problem; (2) determine the objective; (3) explore the alternatives; (4) predict the consequences; (5) make a choice; and (6) perform sensitivity analysis. This framework is flexible. The degree to which a decision is analyzed is itself a choice to be made by the manager. Different decisions will apply varying degrees of analysis to each step.

3. Experience, judgment, common sense, intuition, and rules of thumb all make potential contributions to the decision-making process. However, none of these can take the place of a sound analysis.

Nuts and Bolts

1. In the private sector, the principal objective is maximizing the value of the firm. The firm's value is the present value of its expected future profits. In the public sector, government programs and projects are evaluated on the basis of net social benefit, the difference between total benefits and costs of all kinds. Benefit–cost analysis is the main economic tool for determining the dollar magnitudes of benefits and costs.

2. Models offer simplified descriptions of a process or relationship. Models are essential for explaining past phenomena and for generating forecasts of the future. Deterministic models take the predicted outcome as certain. Probabilistic models identify a range of possible outcomes with probabilities attached.

3. The principal objective of management is to maximize the value of the firm by maximizing operating profits. Other management goals sometimes include maximizing sales or taking actions in the interests of stakeholders (its workers, customers, and neighbors). The principal objective of public managers and government regulators is to maximize social welfare. According to the criterion of benefit–cost analysis, a public program should be undertaken if and only if its total dollar benefits exceed its total dollar costs.

4. Sensitivity analysis considers how an optimal decision would change if key economic facts or conditions were altered.

Questions and Problems

1. What is managerial economics? What role does it play in shaping business decisions?

2. Management sometimes is described as the art and science of making decisions with too little information. What kinds of additional information would a manager want in the eight examples cited in the chapter?

3. Suppose a soft-drink firm is grappling with the decision about whether or not to introduce to the market a new carbonated beverage with 25 percent real fruit juice. How might it use the six decision steps to guide its course of action?

4. Listed here are several examples of bad, or at least questionable, decisions. Evaluate the decision maker's approach or logic. In which of the six decision steps might the decision maker have gone wrong? How would you respond in the final decision situation?

   a. Mr. and Mrs. A recently bought a house, the very first one they viewed.

   b. Firm B has invested five years and $6 million in developing a new product. Even now, it is not clear whether the product can compete profitably in the market. Nonetheless, top management decides to commercialize it so that the development cost will not be wasted.

   c. You are traveling on a highway with two traffic lanes in each direction. Usually traffic flows smoothly, but tonight traffic moving in your direction is backed up for half a mile. After crawling for 15 minutes, you reach the source of the tie-up: A mattress is lying on the road, blocking one lane. Like other motorists before you, you shrug and drive on.

   d. The sedative thalidomide was withdrawn from drug markets in 1962 only after it was found to be the cause of more than 8,000 birth defects worldwide. The United States chose to severely restrict the use of thalidomide.

   e. A couple, nervous about boarding their airline flight on time, patiently wait together in one of three baggage check-in lines.

   f. Each year, State F allocates $400,000 to provide special ambulance service for heart attack victims and $1,200,000 for improvements in highway safety (better lighting, grading, and the like). The former program saves an estimated 20 lives per year; the latter saves 40 lives. Recently the ambulance budget was cut by 40 percent and the highway safety budget increased by 10 percent.

   g. Mr. G is debating how to spend his summer vacation. Should he spend a quiet week at home, go to the beach, or go to the mountains, where his parents and several other relatives live? Unable to make up his mind, he decides to list the pros and cons of each option. The points he cares about are (1) relaxation and quiet, (2) some exercise, and

(3) seeing family and old friends. With respect to these points, he ranks the alternatives as shown in the table:

	Relaxation	Exercise	Family/Friends
Home	1st	3rd	2nd
Beach	2nd	1st	3rd
Mountains	3rd	2nd	1st

Now he is ready to compare the options. Which is his better choice: home or beach? Because home ranks higher than beach on two of the three points, he gives it two pros and one con and judges it the better choice. What about home versus mountains? Mountains versus beach?

h. Based on voter behavior, many political experts believe it is an advantage to be listed first on an election ballot. (What does this say about the decision processes of informed and not-so-informed voters?)

i. Ms. I is shopping for a new color TV set during a sale. The sale price is $300, and she is having trouble making up her mind. After deciding not to buy, she turns the sales tag over and sees that the standard price is $450. It is reduced by 33 percent, whereas most items are reduced by 10 percent. Therefore, she decides to buy.

j. "On the one hand, there is nuclear holocaust. On the other, there is abject surrender to the Soviet Union. The only sane alternative, then, is ratification of the proposed arms control treaty."

k. (1) You are given $1,000 to keep. You are then offered a choice between receiving an additional $500 for certain *or* taking a 50–50 gamble with outcomes of $1,000 and $0. Which would you choose?

   (2) You are given $2,000 to keep. You are then offered a choice between paying $500 for certain *or* taking a 50–50 gamble with outcomes of paying $1,000 and paying $0. Which would you choose?

5. Consider a firm that is in the business of treating hazardous waste. What kinds of economic constraints limit the scope of the firm's actions? What about technological constraints? Legal or regulatory constraints? Political constraints? Time constraints?

Discussion Question A town planning board must decide how to deal with the Kendall Elementary School building. Twenty years ago, the Kendall school (one of four in the town) was closed due to falling enrollment. For the past 20 years, the town has rented 60 percent of the building space to a nonprofit organization that offers classes in the creative and performing arts. The group's lease is up, and now the board is mulling other options:

a. Renew the current lease agreement. This will generate a small but steady cash flow and will free the town of building maintenance expenses (which under the lease are the tenant's responsibility).
b. Renegotiate the lease and solicit other tenants.
c. Use the building for needed additional town office space. (A minimal conversion would allow reconversion to a school in 5 to 10 years, when the elementary school population is expected to swell.)
d. Sell the building to a private developer, if one can be found.
e. Convert the building to condominiums to be sold by the town.
f. Raze the building and sell the site and all or part of the surrounding playing fields as building lots (from 6 to 12 lots, depending on how much land is sold).

Apply the six decision-making steps presented in the chapter to the town's decision. What objectives might the town pursue in making its decision? What additional information would the planning board need in carrying out the various steps? What kind of analysis might the board undertake?

Suggested References

A number of valuable references chart different approaches to analyzing and making decisions.

Bazerman, M. *Judgment in Managerial Decision Making,* Chapters 1 and 9. New York: John Wiley & Sons, 2005.

Bazerman, M. *Smart Money Decisions.* New York: John Wiley & Sons, 1999.

Hammond, J. S., R. L. Keeney, and H. Raiffa. *Smart Choices: A Practical Guide to Making Better Decisions.* Boston: Harvard Business School Press, 1999.

Kleindorfer, P. R., H. C. Kunreuther, and P. J. H. Shoemaker. *Decision Sciences: An Integrated Perspective,* Chapters 1 and 2. New York: Cambridge University Press, 1993.

Russo, J. E., M. Hittleman, and P. J. Schoemaker. *Winning Decisions.* New York: Bantam Dell Publishers, 2001.

Russo, J. E., and P. J. Schoemaker. *Decision Traps.* New York: Fireside, 1990.

For a comprehensive Web site about economics, firms, markets, government regulation, and much more (with links to many other sites), see: http://economics.about.com.

SECTION 1

Decisions within Firms

The main goal of a firm's managers is to maximize the enterprise's profit—either for its private owners or for its shareholders. The first section of this book, comprising Chapters 2 through 9, focuses squarely on this objective.

Chapter 2 begins the analysis by presenting a simple economic model of the firm and showing how managers identify optimal decisions. Chapters 3, 4, and 5 extend the discussion of optimal decisions by analyzing the market's demand for the firm's products. Chapter 3 considers optimal pricing, multiple markets, and price discrimination. Chapters 4 and 5 take a closer look at how managers can estimate market demand (based on past data) and how they can use forecasting techniques to predict future demand.

The business of firms is to produce goods and services that people want, efficiently and at low cost. Chapter 6 focuses on the firm's production decisions: how production managers determine the means to produce the firm's goods and services. Efficient production requires setting up appropriate facilities and estimating materials and input needs. Chapter 7 examines closely related issues concerning the firm's costs.

Managers are continually seeking less costly ways to produce and sell the firm's goods and services.

Decision making under uncertainty is the heart of Chapters 8 and 9. Managers must work hard at foreseeing changes in market demand, costs, competitors' actions, and government policies. Indeed, management is sometimes referred to as the "art of making decisions with too little information." Managers must measure and weigh competing risks and determine which risks are acceptable. Chapter 8 shows how managers can structure decisions in high-risk situations, whereas Chapter 9 examines the value of acquiring new information about relevant risks before making important decisions.

CHAPTER 2

Optimal Decisions Using Marginal Analysis

Government and business leaders should pursue the path to new programs and policies the way a climber ascends a formidable mountain or the way a soldier makes his way through a minefield: with small and very careful steps.

ANONYMOUS

Conflict in Fast-Food Franchising[1]

The rapid growth in franchising during the last three decades can be explained in large part by the mutual benefits the franchising partners receive. The franchiser (parent company) increases sales via an ever-expanding network of franchisees. The parent collects a fixed percentage of the revenue each franchise earns (as high as 15 to 20 percent, depending on the contract terms). The individual franchisee benefits from the acquired know-how of the parent, from the parent's advertising and promotional support, and from the ability to sell a well-established product or service. Nonetheless, economic conflicts frequently arise between the parent and an individual franchisee. Disputes even occur in the loftiest of franchising realms: the fast-food industry. In the 1990s, there were ongoing conflicts between franchise operators and parent management of McDonald's and Burger King.

These conflicts were centered on a number of recurring issues. First, the parent insisted on periodic remodeling of the premises; the franchisee resisted. Second, the franchisee favored raising prices on best-selling items; the parent opposed the change and wanted to expand promotional discounts. Third, the parent sought longer store hours and multiple express lines to cut down on lunchtime congestion; many franchisees resisted both moves.

---

[1] We begin this and the remaining chapters by presenting a managerial decision. Your first job is to familiarize yourself with the manager's problem. As you read the chapter, think about how the principles presented could be applied to this decision. At the chapter's conclusion, we revisit the problem and discuss possible solutions.

How does one explain these conflicts? What is their economic source? What can the parent and the franchisee do to promote cooperation? (At the conclusion of the chapter, we will revisit the franchising setting and offer explanations for these conflicts.)

This chapter introduces the analysis of managerial decision making that will occupy us for the remainder of the book. The chapter is devoted to two main topics. The first is a simple economic model (i.e., a description) of the private, profit-maximizing firm. The second is an introduction to marginal analysis, an important tool for arriving at optimal decisions. Indeed, it is fair to say that the subsequent chapters provide extensions or variations on these two themes. The present chapter employs marginal analysis as a guide to output and pricing decisions in the case of a single product line under the simplest demand and cost conditions. In Chapters 3 and 4, we extend marginal analysis to the cases of complex demand conditions, multiple markets, and price discrimination. In Chapters 6 and 7, we apply the same approach to settings that involve more complicated production technologies and cost conditions, multiple production facilities, and multiple products. In Chapters 10, 11, and 12, we analyze the key market environments—competition, oligopoly, and monopoly—in which the profit-maximizing firm operates. Together, these chapters demonstrate the great power of marginal analysis as a tool for solving complex decisions. Consequently, it is important to master the logic of marginal analysis at the outset. Toward this end, we start with a simple example before turning to the model of the firm.

Siting a Shopping Mall

A real-estate developer is planning the construction of a large shopping mall in a coastal county. The question is where to locate it. To help her in the decision, the developer has gathered a wealth of information, including the stylized "map" of the region in Figure 2.1. The county's population centers run from west to east along the coast (these are labeled A to H), with the ocean to the north. Since available land and permits are not a problem, the developer judges

FIGURE 2.1

Locating a Shopping Mall

At what site along the west–east coast, running from towns A to H, should a developer locate a shopping mall?

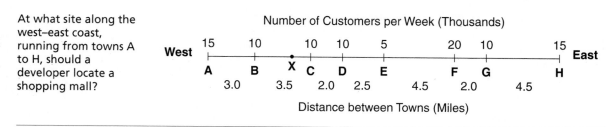

that she can locate the mall anywhere along the coast, that is, anywhere along line segment AH. In fact, the mall would be welcome in any of the towns due to its potential positive impact on the local economy.

According to an old adage, "The three most important factors in the real-estate business are location, location, and location." Accordingly, the developer seeks a site that is proximate to as many potential customers as possible. A natural measure of locational convenience is the total travel miles (TTM) between the mall and its customer population. Thus, Figure 2.1 notes the distances between towns in the county. It also shows the potential number of customers per week in each town. (Presumably these estimates have been derived via careful surveys.) Thus, the developer's key question is: Where along the coast should the mall be located to *minimize* the total travel miles?

To start suppose that the developer considers one site at a time, computes its TTM, and selects the site that has the lowest TTM. For example, the TTM at the possible site labeled X (a mile west of town C) is

$$(5.5)(15) + (2.5)(10) + (1.0)(10) + (3.0)(10) + (5.5)(5)$$
$$+ (10.0)(20) + (12.0)(10) + (16.5)(15) = 742.5.$$

The TTM is found by multiplying the distance to the mall by the number of trips for each town (beginning with A and ending with H) and summing.

We could try to solve the problem by enumeration. However, the method requires a good deal of computational "brute force"; it also offers no guarantee that an optimal location (i.e., one that has the lowest TTM of all possible candidates) will be found. The method only claims that its choice is the best of the limited number of candidates for which TTMs have been computed.

Fortunately, we can use a basic decision-making method, called marginal analysis, to identify the optimal site with much less computational effort and with certainty. **Marginal analysis** is the process of considering small changes in a decision and determining whether a given change will improve the ultimate objective. Because this definition is quite a mouthful, let's see how the method works in siting the mall.

Let's begin with an arbitrary location, say, point X. It is *not* necessary to compute its TTM. Instead, we consider a small move to a nearby site, such as town C. (The direction of the move, east or west, is unimportant.) Then we ask: What is the *change* in the TTM of such a move? The clear result is that the TTM must have declined. The eastward move means a one-mile reduction in travel distance for all customers at C or farther east (70,000 trip-miles in all). Therefore, the TTM is reduced by this amount. Of course, travel distances have increased for travelers at or to the west of X. For these customers, the TTM increase is 25,000 trip-miles. Therefore, the net overall change in TTM is $-70,000 + 25,000 = -45,000$ trip-miles. Total TTM has declined because the site moved toward a greater number of travelers than it moved away from. Town C, therefore, is a better location than site X.

Next, because the original move was beneficial, we try moving farther east, say, to town D. Again, the move reduces the TTM. (Check this.) What about a move east again to town E? This brings a further reduction. What about a move to town F? Now we find that the TTM has increased. (By how much?) Moreover, any further moves east would continue to increase the TTM. Thus, town E is the best site.

It is worth noting the simple but subtle way in which we found the optimal site. The simple maxim of marginal analysis is as follows:

> Make a "small" move to a nearby alternative if and only if the move will improve one's objective (in this case, reduce TTM). Keep moving, always in the direction of an improved objective, and stop when no further move will help.

The subtlety of the method lies in its focus on changes. One need never actually calculate a TTM (or even know the distances between towns) to prove that town E is the optimal location. (We can check that town E's TTM is 635.) One requires only some simple reasoning about the effects of changes.

Of course, on the tip of your tongue may be the declaration, "This problem is too simple; that is the only reason why the method works." This protest is both right and wrong. It is true that this particular location problem is special and, therefore, somewhat artificial. (Two-dimensional siting problems are both more realistic and more difficult.) But the simplicity of the setting was not the key to why marginal analysis worked. The method and its basic reasoning can be used in almost any optimization problem, that is, in any setting where a decision maker seeks to maximize (or minimize) a well-defined objective.

A SIMPLE MODEL OF THE FIRM

The decision setting we will investigate can be described as follows:

1. A firm produces a single good or service for a single market with the objective of maximizing profit.
2. Its task is to determine the quantity of the good to produce and sell and to set a sales price.
3. In this simple model, we begin by assuming the firm can predict the revenue and cost consequences of its price and output decisions with certainty. (We will deal with uncertainty in Chapters 8 and 9.)

Together these three statements fulfill the first four fundamental decision-making steps described in Chapter 1. Statement 1 specifies the setting and objective, statement 2 the firm's possible decision alternatives, and statement 3 (along with some specific quantitative information supplied shortly) the link between actions and the ultimate objective, namely, profit. It remains for the firm's manager to "solve" and explore this decision problem using marginal analysis (steps 5 and 6).

Before turning to this task, note the simplifying facts embodied in statement 1. Typically, a given firm produces a variety of goods or services. Nonetheless, even for the multiproduct firm, examining products one at a time has significant decision advantages. For one thing, it constitutes an efficient managerial division of labor. Thus, multiproduct firms, such as General Mills, assign product managers to specific consumer products. A product manager is responsible for charting the future of the brand (pricing, advertising, promotion, and production policies). Similarly, most large companies make profit-maximizing decisions along product lines. This product-by-product strategy is feasible and appropriate so long as the revenues and costs of the firm's products are independent of one another. (As we shall see in Chapters 3 and 7, things become more complicated if actions taken with respect to one product affect the revenues or costs, or both, of the firm's other products.) In short, the firm can maximize its total profit by separately maximizing the profit derived from each of its product lines. With this in mind, it is convenient to start with the single-product, single-market setting, important in its own right, before considering more complicated decisions.

A Microchip Manufacturer

As a motivating example, let's consider a firm that produces and sells a highly sophisticated microchip. A microchip, known more formally as an *integrated circuit*, is a small piece of semiconducting material that contains a large number of electronic circuits. Microchips are used for memory and data processing in computers and other electronic devices.

The firm's main problem is to determine the quantity of chips to produce and sell (now and in the immediate future) and the price. To tackle this problem, we begin by examining the manager's basic objective: profit. A simple accounting identity states that profit is the difference between revenue and cost. In algebraic terms, we have $\pi = R - C$, where the Greek letter pi (π) stands for profit. To see how profit depends on the firm's price and output decisions, let's examine the revenue and cost components in turn.

REVENUE   The analysis of revenue rests on the most basic empirical relationship in economics: the law of demand. This law states:

> All other factors held constant, the higher the unit price of a good, the fewer the number of units demanded by consumers and, consequently, sold by firms.

The law of demand operates at several levels. Consider the microchip industry as a whole, consisting of the manufacturer in question and a half-dozen major competitors. Suppose the leading firms raise their chip prices due to the increased cost of silicon. According to the law of demand, the industry's total sales of chips will fall. Of course, the law applies equally to a single-chip manufacturer. An individual firm competes directly or indirectly with the other leading suppliers selling similar chips. Let's suppose that currently there is a stable pattern of (different) prices and market shares for the leading firms in the industry. Consider what would happen if one of the firms unilaterally instituted a significant reduction in the price of its chips. The law of demand predicts that its microchip sales would increase. The sources of the increase are threefold: (1) increased sales to the firm's current customers, (2) sales gained from (and at the expense of) competing suppliers, and (3) sales to new buyers. Of course, each of these factors might be important to a greater or lesser degree.

Figure 2.2 graphically illustrates the law of demand by depicting the individual firm's downward-sloping **demand curve**. The horizontal axis lists the quantity of microchips demanded by customers and sold by the firm each week. For convenience, the quantity of chips is measured in lots consisting of 100 chips. The vertical axis lists the price per lot (measured in thousands of dollars)

FIGURE 2.2

The Demand Curve for Microchips

The demand curve shows the total number of microchips that will be demanded (i.e., purchased) by buyers at different prices.

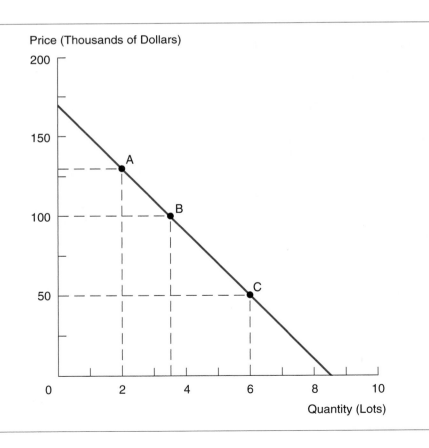

charged by the firm. Three particular points along the downward-sloping demand curve are noted. Point A corresponds to a quantity of 2 lots and a price of $130,000; this means that if the firm charges $130,000 per lot, its weekly sales will be 2 lots (or 200 chips). If the firm cut its price to $100,000, its sales would increase to 3.5 lots (point B). A dramatic reduction to a price of $50,000 would increase sales to 6 lots (point C). Thus, the demand curve shows the firm's predicted sales over a range of possible prices. The downward slope of the curve embodies the law of demand: A low price brings forth an increased quantity of sales.

Demand curves and demand equations have a wide variety of uses in economics. Predicting the profit consequences of selective fare discounts by airlines, the impact of higher oil prices on automobile travel, and the effect of government day-care subsidies for working mothers all require the use of demand curves. The properties of demand curves and the ways of estimating demand equations are important topics in Chapters 3 and 4. At present, we will focus on the firm's main use of the demand relationships:

> The firm uses the demand curve as the basis for predicting the revenue consequences of alternative output and pricing policies.

Quite simply, the demand curve allows the firm to predict its quantity of sales for any price it charges. In turn, revenue can be computed as the product of price and quantity. The most useful way to begin the revenue estimation task is to work with the mathematical representation of the demand curve. An algebraic representation of the demand curve in Figure 2.2 is

$$Q = 8.5 - .05P, \qquad [2.1]$$

where Q is the quantity of lots demanded per week and P denotes the price per lot (in thousands of dollars). In this form, the demand equation predicts the quantity of microchips sold at any given price. For instance, if P equals $50 thousand, then, according to Equation 2.1, Q equals 6 lots (point C in the figure); if P equals $130 thousand, Q equals 2 lots, and so on. *For any price the firm charges, the demand equation predicts the resulting quantity of the good that will be sold.* Setting different prices and computing the respective quantities traces out the demand curve in Figure 2.2.

With a bit of algebraic rearrangement, we can derive an equivalent version of Equation 2.1, namely,

$$P = 170 - 20Q \qquad [2.2]$$

This equation generates exactly the same price–quantity pairs as Equation 2.1; thus, the two equations are equivalent. The only difference is the variable chosen for placement on the left-hand side. Note the interpretation of Equation 2.2. For any quantity of microchips the firm plans to sell, Equation 2.2 indicates the price needed to sell exactly this quantity. For instance, setting Q = 3.5 lots in Equation 2.2, we find that P equals $100 thousand (point B in Figure 2.2). This price equation usually is referred to as the firm's *inverse demand equation.*[2]

Equation 2.1 (or the equivalent, Equation 2.2) contains all the information the firm needs to predict revenue. However, before launching into the revenue analysis, we should pause to make two points. First, the demand equation furnishes a quantitative "snapshot" of the *current* demand for the firm's product as it depends on price. Of course, many other factors, including competing firms' products and prices and the general strength of the computer industry, affect the firm's chip sales. The demand prediction of Equation 2.1 is based on the current state of these factors. If economic conditions changed, so too would the firm's sales at any given price; that is, Equation 2.1 would no longer be a valid representation of the new demand conditions. Keep in mind that our use of the demand equation takes other demand-relevant factors as *given*, that is, unchanged. (Chapters 3 and 12 take up the effects of changing market conditions and competitor behavior on a firm's demand.)

The second point is that we view the demand curve as **deterministic**; that is, at any given price, the quantity sold can be predicted with certainty. For a given price, Equation 2.1 furnishes a precise sales quantity. Conversely, for any targeted sales quantity, Equation 2.2 provides a precise market-clearing price. We acknowledge that such certainty is hardly the norm in the real world. To a greater or lesser extent, the quantity sold at any given price will vary. Nonetheless, the demand equation representation remains valid so long as the margin of error in the price–quantity relationship is relatively small. To become comfortable with the demand equations, think of a product with a long and stable history, allowing sales predictions to be made with very little error. (Clearly, a deterministic demand equation would be completely inappropriate in the case of a new-product launch. Other methods, which provide probability forecasts of possible sales, would be appropriate there. We consider these methods extensively in Chapters 8 and 9.)

Let's use Equation 2.2 to predict the revenues generated by alternative sales policies of the microchip manufacturer. Figure 2.3 contains the pertinent information and provides a graph of revenue. Column 1 of the tabular portion lists a spectrum of possible sales quantities ranging from 0 to 8.5 lots. It will be convenient to think of the sales quantity, Q, as the firm's decision variable, that is, the variable it explicitly chooses. For each alternative choice of Q, column 2 lists the corresponding sales price obtained from Equation 2.2. (Be sure you understand that the firm *cannot* set both Q and P independently. Once one is set, the other is determined by the forces of demand embodied in the demand

---

[2] An important special case occurs when the firm produces for a perfectly competitive market. (An extensive discussion appears in Chapter 10.) There the firm faces a horizontal demand curve instead of a downward-sloping curve. For example, suppose the inverse demand equation is P = 170. The firm can sell as much or as little output as it wishes at $170,000 per lot, the competitive price, and its actions will have no effect on this price.

equation.) Finally, column 3 lists the resulting revenue earned by the firm, where revenue is defined as $R = P \cdot Q$. From the table, we observe that revenue is zero when sales are zero (obviously). Then as Q increases, revenue initially rises, peaks, and eventually begins to fall, finally falling to zero at $Q = 8.5$ lots. (Note that to sell 8.5 lots, the requisite sales price from Equation 2.2 is zero; that is, the lots would have to be given away.) In short, the law of demand means that there is a fundamental trade-off between P and Q in generating revenue. An increase in Q requires a cut in P, the former effect raising revenue but the latter lowering it. Operating at either extreme—selling a small quantity at high prices or a large quantity at very low prices—will raise little revenue.

The revenue results in Figure 2.3 can be obtained more directly using basic algebra. We know that $R = P \cdot Q$ and that the market-clearing price satisfies $P = 170 - 20Q$ from Equation 2.2. Substituting the latter equation into the former yields the **revenue function**

$$R = P \cdot Q = (170 - 20Q)Q = 170Q - 20Q^2. \qquad [2.3]$$

Figure 2.3 also shows the graph of revenue as it depends on the quantity of chips sold. At the sales quantity of 2 lots, the market-clearing price is

FIGURE 2.3

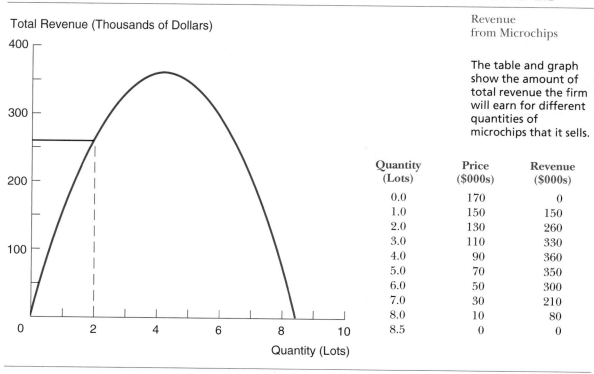

Revenue
from Microchips

The table and graph show the amount of total revenue the firm will earn for different quantities of microchips that it sells.

Quantity (Lots)	Price ($000s)	Revenue ($000s)
0.0	170	0
1.0	150	150
2.0	130	260
3.0	110	330
4.0	90	360
5.0	70	350
6.0	50	300
7.0	30	210
8.0	10	80
8.5	0	0

$130,000; therefore, revenue is $260,000. The graph clearly indicates that the firm's revenue rises, peaks, then falls as the sales quantity increases. (Some readers will recognize Equation 2.3 as a quadratic function. Therefore, the graph in Figure 2.3 is a simple parabola.)

CHECK STATION 1   Let the inverse demand function be P = 340 − .8Q. Find the revenue function.

COST   To produce chips, the firm requires a plant, equipment, and labor. The firm estimates that it costs $380 (in materials, labor, and so on) for each chip it produces; this is $38,000 per lot. In addition, it incurs fixed costs of $100,000 per week to run the plant whether or not chips are produced. These are the only costs. (Remember that we are constructing a highly simplified example.) The total cost of producing a given quantity of output is given by the equation

$$C = 100 + 38Q,$$ [2.4]

where C is the weekly cost of production (in thousands of dollars) and Q is the number of lots produced each week. This equation is called the **cost function** because it shows how total cost depends on quantity. By substituting in a given quantity, we can find the resulting total cost. Thus, the cost of producing Q = 2 lots is $176 thousand. Other quantities and costs are listed in Figure 2.4, which

FIGURE 2.4

The Cost of Microchips

The table and graph show the firm's total cost of producing different quantities of microchips.

Quantity (Lots)	Cost ($000s)
0.0	100
1.0	138
2.0	176
3.0	214
4.0	252
5.0	290
6.0	328
7.0	366

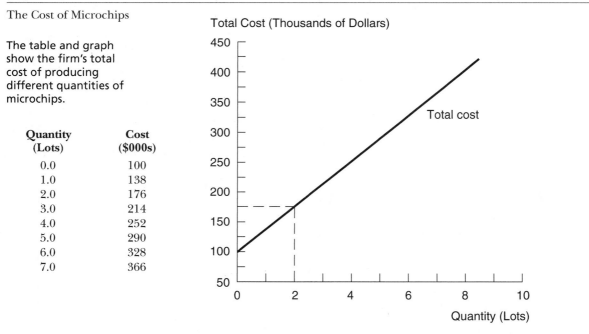

also shows the graph of cost versus output. As the graph shows, in this simple example the firm's total cost of production increases with output at a steady rate; that is, the slope of the cost function is constant.

PROFIT   From the preceding analysis of revenue and cost, we now have enough information to compute profit for any given output of microchips the firm might choose to produce and sell. These profit calculations are listed in Figure 2.5, where the profit column is computed as the difference between the revenue and cost columns reproduced from earlier figures. The graph in Figure 2.5 shows profit (on the vertical axis) as it varies with quantity (on the horizontal axis). For example, the level of profit associated with producing a weekly output of 2 lots is marked on the figure. Observe that the graph depicts the level of profit over a wide range of output choices, not just for the round-lot choices listed in the tabular portion of the figure. In effect, the graph allows us to determine visually the profit-maximizing, or optimal, output level from among all possible sales plans. In this case, the optimal output appears to be about 3.3 lots (or 330 microchips) per week.

FIGURE 2.5

Profit from Microchips

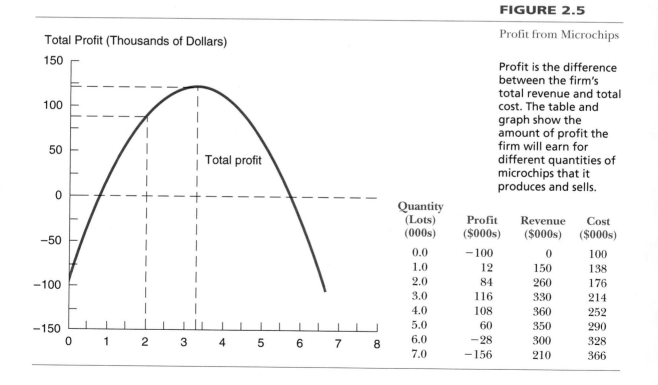

Profit is the difference between the firm's total revenue and total cost. The table and graph show the amount of profit the firm will earn for different quantities of microchips that it produces and sells.

Quantity (Lots) (000s)	Profit ($000s)	Revenue ($000s)	Cost ($000s)
0.0	−100	0	100
1.0	12	150	138
2.0	84	260	176
3.0	116	330	214
4.0	108	360	252
5.0	60	350	290
6.0	−28	300	328
7.0	−156	210	366

How were we able to graph the profit curve in Figure 2.5 so precisely? The graph was constructed from the following basic profit equation, often called the **profit function**:

$$\pi = R - C \hspace{3cm} [2.5]$$
$$= (170Q - 20Q^2) - (100 + 38Q)$$
$$= -100 + 132Q - 20Q^2.$$

In the second line, we have substituted the right-hand sides of the revenue and cost equations to express profit in terms of Q, the firm's decision variable. In the third line, we have collected terms. The important point about the profit equation is that it provides a numerical prediction of profit for any given quantity Q. To check that the equation is correct, simply substitute in a value for Q, say, 2 lots, and calculate profit: $\pi = -100 + (132)(2) - (20)(4) = \$84$ thousand, the same result as in Figure 2.5.

CHECK STATION 2 Suppose the inverse demand function is $P = 340 - .8Q$ and the cost function is $C = 120 + 100Q$. Write down the profit function.

MARGINAL ANALYSIS

Consider the problem of finding the output level that will maximize the firm's profit. One approach is to use the preceding profit formula and solve the problem by *enumeration*, that is, by calculating the profits associated with a range of outputs and identifying the one with the greatest profit. Enumeration is a viable approach if there are only a few output levels to test. Suppose that, for production reasons, the firm is constrained to produce in whole lots. Then Figure 2.5 effectively solves the decision by enumeration; it shows that the most profitable number of whole lots is 3. However, when the number of options is large, enumeration (and the numerous calculations it requires) is not practical. Instead, we will use the method of *marginal analysis* to find the "optimal" output level.

Marginal analysis looks at the change in profit that results from making a small change in a decision variable. To illustrate, suppose the firm first considers producing 3 lots, forecasting its resulting profit to be $116,000 as in Figure 2.5. Could it do better than this? To answer this question, the firm considers increasing production slightly, to, say, 3.1 lots. (One-tenth of a lot qualifies as a "small" change. The exact size of the change does not matter as long as it is small.) By substituting Q = 3.1 into Equation 2.5, we see that the new profit is $117,000. Thus, profit has increased by $1,000. The *rate* at which profit has changed is a $1,000 increase per 1/10 of a lot, or 1,000/.1 = $10,000 per lot.

Here is a useful definition: **Marginal profit** is the change in profit resulting from a small increase in any managerial decision variable. Thus, we say that the marginal profit from a small (.1 lot) increase in output starting from 3.0 lots is $10,000 per lot. The algebraic expression for marginal profit is

$$\text{Marginal profit} = (\text{Change in profit})/(\text{Change in output})$$
$$= \Delta\pi/\Delta Q = (\pi_1 - \pi_0)/(Q_1 - Q_0)$$

where the Greek letter delta (Δ) stands for "change in" and Q_0 denotes the original output level and π_0 the associated profit. The variables Q_1 and π_1 denote the new levels of output and profit. We abbreviate marginal profit by the notation $M\pi$.

Using the profit function you found in Check Station 2, find the marginal profit of increasing output from 99 to 100 units.

CHECK STATION 3

In Table 2.1, we have calculated marginal profits for various output levels. The marginal profit associated with a given change in output is calculated based on a .1-lot increase from the next lowest output. Thus, the $M\pi$ for an increase in output from 2.9 to 3.0 lots is ($116,000 - $114,600)/.1 = $14,000.

TABLE 2.1

Quantity	Profit	Marginal Profit (per Lot)
2.5	$105,000	
		$30,000
2.6	108,000	
		26,000
2.7	110,600	
		22,000
2.8	112,800	
		18,000
2.9	114,600	
		14,000
3.0	116,000	
		10,000
3.1	117,000	
		6,000
3.2	117,600	
		2,000
3.3	117,800	
		−2,000
3.4	117,600	
		−6,000
3.5	117,000	
		−10,000
3.6	116,000	
		−14,000
3.7	114,600	

Marginal Profit

Marginal profit is the extra profit the firm earns from producing and selling an additional unit of output.

How can the decision maker use profit changes as signposts pointing toward the optimal output level? The answer is found by applying the maxim of marginal analysis:

> Make a small change in the level of output if and only if this generates an increase in profit. Keep moving, always in the direction of increased profits, and stop when no further output change will help.

Starting from a production level of 2.5 lots, the microchip firm should increase output to 2.6 because marginal profit from the move ($30,000) is positive. Marginal profit continues to be positive up to 3.3 lots. Therefore, output should be increased up to and including a final step going from 3.2 to 3.3 lots. What about increasing output from 3.3 to 3.4 lots? Since the marginal profit associated with (a move to) 3.4 is negative ($-\$2,000$), this action would decrease profit. Having reached 3.3 lots, then, no further profit gains (positive marginal profits) are possible. Note that the final output, 3.3, could have been reached starting from a "high" output level such as 3.7 lots. As long as marginal profit is negative, one should reduce output (i.e., reverse field) to increase profit.

Marginal Analysis and Calculus

The key to pinpointing the firm's optimal quantity (i.e., the *exact* output level at which maximum profit is attained) is to compute marginal profit *at* any given level of output rather than *between* two nearby output levels. At a particular output Q, marginal profit is given by the slope of the *tangent* line to the profit graph *at* that output level. Figure 2.6 shows an enlarged profit graph with tangent lines drawn at outputs of 3.1 and 3.3 lots. From viewing the tangents, we draw the following simple conclusions. At 3.1 lots, the tangent is upward sloping. Obviously, marginal profit is positive; that is, raising output by a small amount increases total profit. Conversely, at 3.4 lots, the curve is downward sloping. Here marginal profit is negative, so a small reduction in output (not an increase) would increase total profit. Finally, at 3.3 lots, the tangent is horizontal; that is, the tangent's slope and marginal profit are zero. Maximum profit is attained at precisely this level of output. Indeed, the condition that marginal profit is zero marks this point as the optimal level of output. Remember: If $M\pi$ were positive or negative, total profit could be raised by appropriately increasing or decreasing output. Only when $M\pi$ is exactly zero have all profit-augmenting opportunities been exhausted. In short, when the profit function's slope just becomes zero, we know we are at the precise peak of the profit curve.[3] Thus, we have demonstrated a basic optimization rule:

---

[3] In some cases, the $M\pi = 0$ rule requires modification. For example, suppose demand and cost conditions are such that $M\pi > 0$ for all output quantities up to the firm's current production capacity. Clearly, the rule $M\pi = 0$ does not apply. However, the marginal profit message is clear: The firm should increase output up to capacity, raising profit all the while. (For further discussion, see the appendix to this chapter and Problem 5 at the end of the chapter.)

FIGURE 2.6

A Close-Up View
of Profit

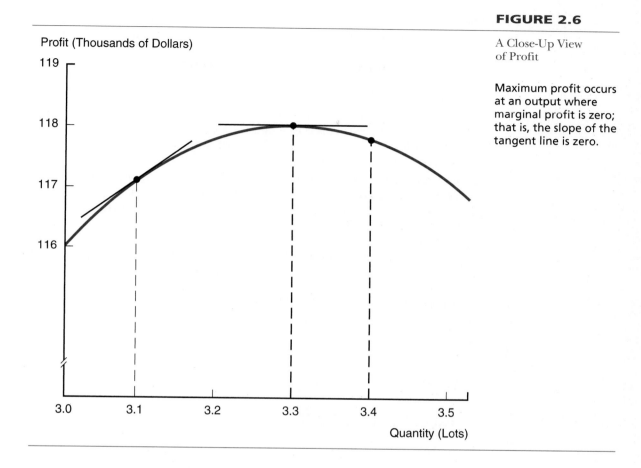

Profit (Thousands of Dollars)

Quantity (Lots)

Maximum profit occurs
at an output where
marginal profit is zero;
that is, the slope of the
tangent line is zero.

| Maximum profit is attained at the output level at which marginal profit is zero ($M\pi = 0$). |

A practical method for calculating marginal profit at any level of output is afforded by the simple rules of differential calculus. (For a thorough review, read the appendix to this chapter.) Consider once again the firm's profit equation:

$$\pi = -100 + 132Q - 20Q^2. \tag{2.6}$$

Marginal profit (the slope of the corresponding profit graph) is found by taking the derivative of this equation with respect to Q. The result is

$$M\pi = d\pi/dQ = 132 - 40Q. \tag{2.7}$$

With this formula in hand, we can find the marginal profit at any output level simply by substituting the specified quantity into the equation. For example, the marginal profit at Q = 3.0 is $12 thousand per lot.[4] In turn, we can immediately determine the firm's profit-maximizing level of output. Using Equation 2.7, we simply set $M\pi = 0$ and solve for Q:

$$M\pi = 132 - 40Q = 0.$$

Therefore, we find that Q = 132/40 = 3.3 lots. At 3.3 lots per week, the firm's marginal profit is zero. This is the output that maximizes profit.

Figure 2.7 graphs the firm's total profit (part a) as well as the firm's marginal profit (part b). Note that at the optimal output, Q = 3.3 lots, total profit reaches a peak in Figure 2.7a, whereas marginal profit is exactly zero (i.e., the marginal profit graph just cuts the horizontal axis) in part b.

A complete solution to the firm's decision problem requires two additional steps. We know the optimal quantity is Q = 3.3 lots. What price is required for the firm to sell this quantity? The answer is found by substituting Q = 3.3 into Equation 2.2: P = 170 − (20)(3.3) = $104 thousand. What is the firm's final profit from its optimal output and price decision? At this point, we can separately compute total revenue and total cost. Alternatively, we can compute profit directly from Equation 2.5 (with Q = 3.3). Either way, we arrive at π = $117,800. This completes the algebraic solution.

CHECK STATION 4   Once again consider the inverse demand curve P = 340 − .8Q and the cost function C = 120 + 100Q. Derive the formula for $M\pi$ as it depends on Q. Set $M\pi = 0$ to find the firm's optimal output.

MARGINAL REVENUE AND MARGINAL COST

The concept of marginal profit yields two key dividends. The general concept instructs the manager that optimal decisions are found by making small changes in decisions, observing the resulting effect on profit, and always moving in the direction of greater profit. A second virtue of the approach is that it provides an efficient tool for calculating the firm's optimal decision. The discussion in this section underscores a third virtue: Marginal analysis is a powerful way to identify the factors that determine profits and, more important, profit changes. We will look once again at the two components of profit, revenue and cost, and highlight the key features of *marginal revenue* and *marginal cost*.

---

[4] The difference between Equation 2.7 and Table 2.1 is that the latter lists marginal profit over small, discrete intervals of output, whereas the former lists marginal profit *at* particular output levels. When we use a very small interval, the discrete marginal profit between two output levels is a very close approximation to marginal profit at either output. For example, with an interval of .01, the discrete marginal profit at Q = 3 is the slope of the line connecting the points Q = 2.99 and Q = 3.00. This line is nearly identical to the tangent line (representing marginal profit) *at* Q = 3. Thus,

Using a .01 interval:	$M\pi = \$12,200$
Via calculus (Equation 2.7)	$M\pi = \$12,000$

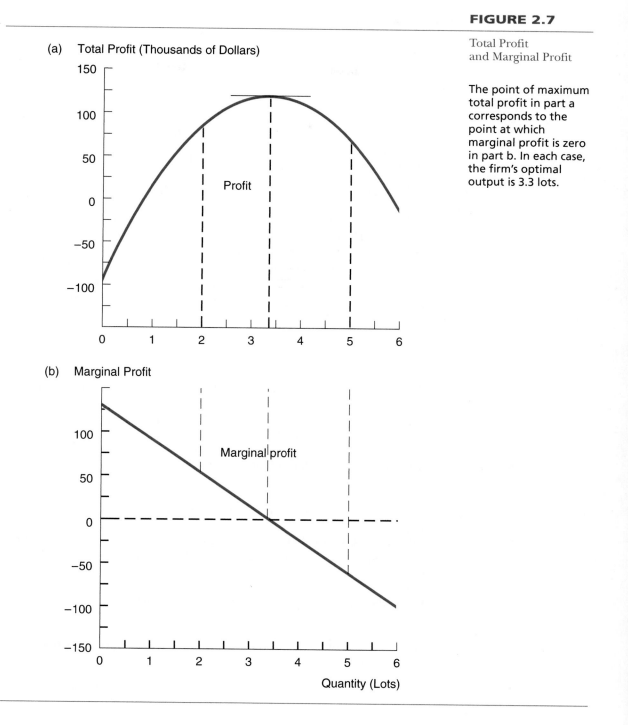

FIGURE 2.7

Total Profit
and Marginal Profit

The point of maximum
total profit in part a
corresponds to the
point at which
marginal profit is zero
in part b. In each case,
the firm's optimal
output is 3.3 lots.

(a)   Total Profit (Thousands of Dollars)

Profit

(b)   Marginal Profit

Marginal profit

Quantity (Lots)

Marginal Revenue

Marginal revenue is the amount of additional revenue that comes with a unit increase in output and sales. The marginal revenue (MR) of an increase in unit sales from Q_0 to Q_1 is

$$\text{Marginal revenue} = (\text{Change in revenue})/(\text{Change in output})$$
$$= \Delta R/\Delta Q = (R_1 - R_0)/(Q_1 - Q_0).$$

For instance, the MR earned by increasing sales from 2.0 to 2.1 lots is

$$(268.8 - 260.0)/(2.1 - 2.0) = \$88 \text{ thousand per lot.}$$

where 268.8 is the revenue from selling 2.1 lots and 260.0 is the revenue from selling 2.0 lots. The graphic depiction of the MR between two quantities is given by the slope of the line segment joining the two points on the revenue graph.

In turn, marginal revenue *at* a given sales quantity has as its graphic counterpart the slope of the tangent line touching the revenue graph. To calculate the marginal revenue at a given sales output, we start with the revenue expression (Equation 2.3), $R = 170Q - 20Q^2$, and take the derivative with respect to quantity:

$$MR = 170 - 40Q. \qquad [2.8]$$

We can use this formula to compute marginal revenue at any particular sales quantity. For example, marginal revenue at $Q = 3$ is $MR = 170 - (40)(3) = \$50$ thousand; that is, at this sales quantity, a small increase in sales increases revenue at the rate of $50,000 per additional lot sold.

A SIMPLIFYING FACT   Recall that the firm's market-clearing price is given by Equation 2.2:

$$P = 170 - 20Q.$$

Note the close similarity between the MR expression in Equation 2.8 and the firm's selling price in Equation 2.2. This similarity is no coincidence. The following result holds:

> For any linear (i.e., straight-line) demand curve with an inverse demand equation of the form $P = a - bQ$, the resulting marginal revenue is $MR = a - 2bQ$.

In short, the MR equation has the same intercept and twice the slope as the firm's price equation.[5]

---

[5] If $P = a - bQ$, it follows that $R = PQ = aQ - bQ^2$. Taking the derivative with respect to Q, we find that $MR = dR/dQ = a - 2bQ$. This confirms the preceding result.

Marginal Cost

Marginal cost is the additional cost of producing an extra unit of output. The algebraic definition is

$$\text{Marginal cost} = (\text{Change in cost})/(\text{Change in output})$$
$$= \Delta C/\Delta Q = (C_1 - C_0)/(Q_1 - Q_0)$$

The computation of MC is particularly easy for the microchip manufacturer's cost function in Equation 2.4. From the cost equation, $C = 100 + 38Q$, it is apparent that producing an extra lot (increasing Q by a unit) will increase cost by $38 thousand. Thus, marginal cost is simply $38 thousand per lot. Note that regardless of how large or small the level of output, marginal cost is always constant. The cost function in Equation 2.4 has a constant slope and, thus, also an unchanging marginal cost. (We can directly confirm the MC result by taking the derivative of the cost equation.)

Profit Maximization Revisited

In view of the fact that $\pi = R - C$, it should not be surprising that

$$M\pi = MR - MC. \qquad\qquad [2.9]$$

In other words, marginal profit is simply the difference between marginal revenue and marginal cost.

The logic of this relationship is simple enough. Suppose the firm produces and sells an extra unit. Then its change in profit is simply the extra revenue it earns from the extra unit net of its additional cost of production. But the extra revenue is MR and the extra cost is MC, so $M\pi = MR - MC$.

Thus far, we have emphasized the role of marginal profit in characterizing the firm's optimal decision. In particular, profits are maximized when marginal profit equals zero. Thus, using the fact that $M\pi = MR - MC$, an equivalent statement is $MR - MC = 0$. This leads to the following basic rule:[6]

| The firm's profit-maximizing level of output occurs when the additional revenue from selling an extra unit just equals the extra cost of producing it, that is, when MR = MC.

There are a number of ways to check the logic of the $MR = MC$ decision rule. Figure 2.8 provides a graphic confirmation. Part a reproduces the microchip manufacturer's revenue and cost functions (from Equations 2.3 and 2.4) in a

---

[6]According to Rule 4 in the appendix to this chapter, if $\pi(Q) = R(Q) - C(Q)$, then $d\pi/dQ = dR/dQ - dC/dQ$. In words, marginal profit is the difference between marginal revenue and marginal cost.

FIGURE 2.8

Marginal Revenue
and Marginal Cost

In part a, total profit is
shown as the
difference between
total revenue and total
cost. In part b, the
firm's optimal output
occurs where the
marginal revenue and
marginal cost curves
intersect.

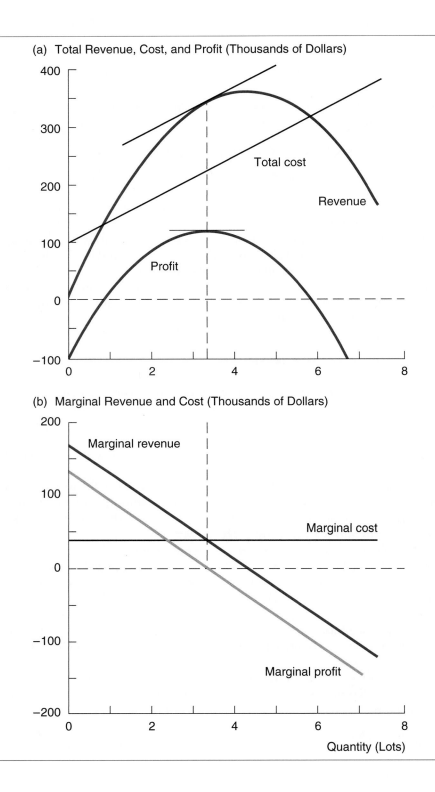

(a) Total Revenue, Cost, and Profit (Thousands of Dollars)

Total cost

Revenue

Profit

(b) Marginal Revenue and Cost (Thousands of Dollars)

Marginal revenue

Marginal cost

Marginal profit

Quantity (Lots)

single graph. The graph of profit also is shown in Figure 2.8a and, except for scale, is identical to Figure 2.5. (Note that, for any level of output, the firm's profit is measured as the vertical distance between the revenue and cost curves.) The firm's break-even outputs occur at the two crossings of the revenue and cost curves. At these outputs, revenue just matches cost, so profit is zero. Positive profits are earned for quantities between these two output levels. Of course, the firm incurs losses for very high or very low levels of production outside the break-even output levels. From the figure, we observe the profit peak at an output of Q = 3.3 lots.

Using the MR = MC rule, how can we confirm that the output level Q = 3.3 is profit maximizing? A simple answer is provided by appealing to the revenue and cost curves in Figure 2.8a. Suppose for the moment that the firm produces a lower quantity, say, Q = 2 lots. At this output, the revenue curve is steeper than the cost line; thus, MR > MC. Hence, the firm could increase its profit by producing extra units of output. On the graph, the move to a greater output widens the profit gap. The reverse argument holds for a proposed higher quantity, such as 4 lots. In this case, revenue rises less steeply than cost: MR < MC. Therefore, a reduction in output results in a greater cost saved than revenue sacrificed. Again profit increases. Combining these arguments, we conclude that profit always can be increased so long as a small change in output results in *different* changes in revenue and cost. Only at Q = 3.3 is it true that revenue and cost increase at exactly the same rate. At this quantity, the slopes of the revenue and cost functions are equal; the revenue tangent is parallel to the cost line. But this simply says that marginal revenue equals marginal cost. At this optimal output, the gap between revenue and cost is neither widening nor narrowing. Maximum profit is obtained.

It is important to remember that the Mπ = 0 and MR = MC rules are exactly equivalent. Both rules pinpoint the *same* profit-maximizing level of output. Figure 2.8b shows this clearly. At Q = 3.3 lots, where the profit function reaches a peak (and the profit tangent is horizontal) in part a, we note that the MR line exactly intersects the MC line in part b. This provides visual confirmation that profit is maximized at the output level at which marginal revenue just equals marginal cost.

In fact, the MR = MC rule often is the shortest path to finding the firm's optimal output. Instead of finding the marginal profit function and setting it equal to zero, we simply take the marginal revenue and marginal cost functions and set them equal to each other. In the microchip manufacturer's problem, we know that MR = 170 − 40Q and MC = 38. Setting MR = MC implies that 170 − 40Q = 38. Solving for Q, we find that Q = 3.3 lots. Of course, this is precisely the same result we obtained by setting marginal profit equal to zero.

Once again let us consider the price equation P = 340 − .8Q and the cost equation C = 120 + 100Q. Apply the MR = MC rule to find the firm's optimal output. From the inverse demand curve, find its optimal price.   **CHECK STATION 5**

SENSITIVITY ANALYSIS

As we saw in Chapter 1, sensitivity analysis addresses the basic question: How should the decision maker alter his or her course of action in light of changes in economic conditions? Marginal analysis offers a powerful answer to this question:

> For any change in economic conditions, we can trace the impact (if any) on the firm's marginal revenue or marginal cost. Once we have identified this impact, we can appeal to the MR = MC rule to determine the new optimal decision.

Figure 2.9 illustrates the application of this rule for the microchip firm's basic problem. Consider part a. As before, the firm's decision variable, its output quantity, is listed on the horizontal axis. In turn, levels of MR and MC are shown on the vertical axis, and the respective curves have been graphed. How do we explain the shapes of these curves? For MC, the answer is easy. The marginal cost of producing an extra lot of chips is $38,000 regardless of the starting output level. Thus, the MC line is horizontal, fixed at a level of $38,000. In turn, the graph of the MR curve from Equation 2.8 is

$$MR = 170 - 40Q.$$

We make the following observations about the MR equation and graph. Starting from a zero sales quantity, the firm gets a great deal of extra revenue from selling additional units (MR = 170 at Q = 0). As sales increase, the extra revenue from additional units falls (although MR is still positive). Indeed, at a quantity of 4.25 lots (see Figure 2.9) MR is zero, and for higher outputs MR is negative; that is, selling extra units causes total revenue to fall. (Don't be surprised by this. Turn back to Figure 2.3 and see that revenue peaks and then falls. When volume already is very large, selling extra units requires a price cut on so many units that total revenue drops.)

In part a of Figure 2.9, the intersection of the MR and MC curves establishes the firm's optimal production and sales quantity, Q = 3.3 lots. At an output less than 3.3 units, MR is greater than MC, so the firm could make additional profit producing extra units. (Why? Because its extra revenue exceeds its extra cost.) At an output above 3.3 units, MR is smaller than MC. Here the firm can increase its profit by cutting back its production. (Why? Because the firm's cost saving exceeds the revenue it gives up.) Thus, profit is maximized only at the quantity where MR = MC.

Asking What If

The following examples trace the possible effects of changes in economic conditions on the firm's marginal revenue and marginal cost.

FIGURE 2.9

(a) Marginal Revenue and Cost (Thousands of Dollars)

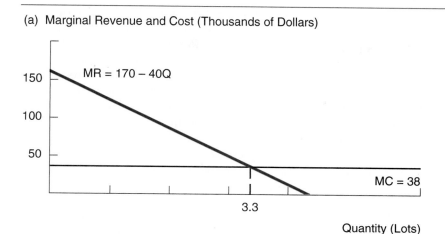

MR = 170 − 40Q

150

100

50

MC = 38

3.3

Quantity (Lots)

(b) Marginal Revenue and Cost (Thousands of Dollars)

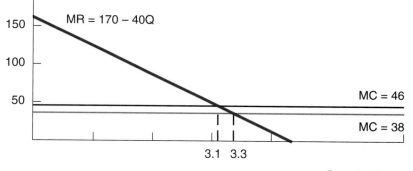

MR = 170 − 40Q

150

100

50

MC = 46

MC = 38

3.1   3.3

Quantity (Lots)

(c) Marginal Revenue and Cost (Thousands of Dollars)

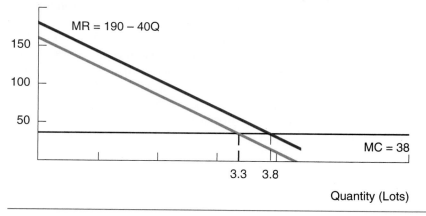

MR = 190 − 40Q

150

100

50

MC = 38

3.3   3.8

Quantity (Lots)

Shifts in Marginal Revenue and Marginal Cost

Part b depicts an increase in marginal cost as an upward shift in the marginal cost curve. As a result, the firm's optimal output level declines. Part c shows an upward (rightward) shift in marginal revenue resulting from an increase in demand. As a result, the firm's optimal output level increases.

INCREASED OVERHEAD   Suppose the microchip manufacturer's overhead costs (for the physical plant and administration) increase. Fixed costs were $100,000 per week; now they are $112,000. How will this affect the firm's operating decisions? The simple, albeit surprising, answer is that the increase in fixed costs will have no effect whatsoever. The firm should produce and sell the same output at the same price as before. There are several ways to see this.

First, note that the firm's profit is reduced by $12,000 (relative to its profit before the cost increase) *whatever its level of output.* Thus, whatever output was profit maximizing before the change must be profit maximizing after it.

Second, the revenue and cost graphs in Figure 2.8a provide a visual confirmation of the same reasoning. An increase in fixed cost causes the cost line to shift upward (parallel to the old one) by the amount of the increase. At any output, the revenue–cost gap is smaller than before. But note that the point of equal slopes—where $MR = MC$ and the profit gap is maximized—is unchanged. Profit is still maximized at the same output as before, $Q = 3.3$.

Finally, the MR and MC curves in Figure 2.9a make the same point. Has the increase in fixed cost changed the MR or MC curves? No! Thus, the firm's optimal output, where the MR and MC lines intersect, is unchanged.

INCREASED MATERIAL COSTS   Silicon is the main raw material from which microchips are made. Suppose an increase in the price of silicon causes the firm's estimated cost per lot to rise from $38,000 to $46,000. How should the firm respond? Once again the answer depends on an appeal to marginal analysis. In this case, the firm's MC per chip has changed. In Figure 2.9b, the new MC line lies above and parallel to the old MC line. The intersection of MR and MC occurs at a lower level of output. Because producing extra output has become more expensive, the firm's optimal response is to cut back the level of production. What is the new optimal output? Setting $MR = MC$, we obtain $170 - 40Q = 46$, so $Q = 3.1$ lots. In turn, the market-clearing price (using Equation 2.2) is found to be $108,000. The increase in cost has been partially passed on to buyers via a higher price.

INCREASED DEMAND   Suppose demand for the firm's chips increases dramatically. At the higher demand, the firm could raise its price by $20,000 per lot ($200 per chip) and still sell the same quantity of chips as before. The old price equation was $P = 170 - 20Q$. The new price equation is $P = 190 - 20Q$. What should be the firm's response? Here the increased demand affects the marginal revenue the firm obtains from selling extra chips. In fact, given the new price equation, the new MR equation must be $MR = 190 - 40Q$. Thus, the new MR curve in Figure 2.9c has a larger intercept than the old one, although the slope is the same. The upward parallel shift in the MR curve means the new intersection of MR and MC occurs at a higher output. What is the new optimal output? Setting $MR = MC$, we find that $190 - 40Q = 38$, so

$Q = 3.8$ lots. The corresponding market-clearing price (using the *new* price equation) is $114,000. The firm takes optimal advantage of the increase in demand by selling a larger output (380 chips per week) at a higher price per lot.

Domestic steel producers have long competed vigorously with foreign steel manufacturers for shares of the U.S. market. Given the intensity of price competition, global steel producers constantly strive to trim production costs to maintain profits. Over the last ten years, the competitive playing field has been buffeted by large swings in foreign exchange rates. For instance, between 1998 and 2000, the dollar's value fell (depreciated) from a high of about 130 Japanese yen per dollar to a level of about 100 yen per dollar. But, from 2000 to the winter of 2002, the dollar rose in value (appreciated) back to 132 yen per dollar before falling again to 109 yen by the end of 2003.

Responding to Exchange Rate Changes

What was the effect of the dollar's 2000–2002 appreciation on the competition for the domestic market between Japanese and U.S. steel producers?

The dollar appreciation (the fall in the value of the yen) conferred a relative cost advantage on Japanese producers to the detriment of domestic producers.

To see this, suppose that based on its current costs, a Japanese steel maker sets its 2000 price for a unit of specialty steel at 10,000 yen. When it sells to U.S. buyers, the company quotes a dollar price of $100 (based on the 100 yen per dollar exchange rate). Two years later, suppose that the Japanese supplier's costs and targeted price in yen are unchanged. However, with an exchange rate of 132 yen per dollar, the equivalent dollar price of its steel is now $10,000/132 = \$75.76$. Of course, the Japanese firm need not set its U.S. price this low. Perhaps, it will settle on $80 to $85, thereby increasing its yen-denominated price and profits while reaping a significant increase in demand from the 15 to 20 percent dollar price reduction.

Now let's turn our attention to U.S. steel producers. The effect of dramatically lower prices of imported steel is to shift the demand curve of a typical domestic firm inward, that is, downward and to the left. What is the domestic firm's profit-maximizing response to this adverse demand shift? Turning around the example of increased demand displayed in Figure 2.9c, we find that the domestic firm should plan to cut its output as well as to cut its price to meet the increase in foreign competition.

Suppose that with lower foreign prices, the domestic firm's demand curve experiences a parallel downward shift of $15. That is, in 2002 the firm would have to cut its price by $15 to maintain the same level of demand and sales as in 2000. Is such a price cut optimal?

CHECK STATION 6

Conflict in Fast-Food Franchising Revisited

The example that opened this chapter recounted the numerous kinds of conflicts between fast-food parents and individual franchise operators. Despite the best intentions, bitter disputes have erupted from time to time at such chains as McDonald's, Burger King, Wendy's, and Subway. A key source for many of these conflicts is the basic contract arrangement between parent and individual franchisee. Virtually all such contracts call for the franchisee to pay back to the parent a specified percentage of revenue earned. This total "royalty" comprises a base percentage plus additional percentages for marketing and advertising and rent (if the parent owns the outlet). Thus, the franchisee's profit begins only after this royalty (typically ranging anywhere from 5 to 20 percent depending on the type of franchise) and all other costs have been paid.

Thus, a key source of conflict emerges. Under the contract agreement, the parent's monetary return depends on (indeed, is a percentage of) the revenues the franchisee takes in. Thus, the parent wants the franchisee to operate so as to maximize revenue. What does the pursuit of maximum revenue imply about the franchisee's volume of sales? Suppose the revenue and cost curves for the franchisee are configured as in Figure 2.8a. (Ignore the numerical values and reinterpret the quantity scale as numbers of burgers sold rather than microchips.) We observe that the revenue-maximizing output is well past the franchisee's optimal (i.e., profit-maximizing) output. The range of economic conflict occurs between these two outputs—the franchisee unwilling to budge from the lower output and the parent pushing for the higher output.

The same point can be made by appealing to the forces of MR and MC. The parent always wants to increase revenue, even if doing so means extra costs to the franchisee. Thus, the parent wishes to push output to the point at which MR is zero. (Make sure you understand why.) But the franchisee prefers to limit output to the point at which extra costs match extra revenues, MR = MC. Past this point, the extra revenues are not worth the extra costs: MR < MC. In Figure 2.8b, the franchisee's preferred output occurs when MR = MC and the parent's occurs at the larger output when MR = 0.

The conflict in objectives explains each of the various disputes. In the parent company's view, all its preferred policies—longer operating hours, more order lines, remodeling, lower prices—are revenue increasing. In each case, however, the individual franchisee resists the move because the extra cost of the change would exceed the extra revenue. From its point of view (the bottom line), none of the changes would be profitable.

To this day, conflicts between parent and individual franchisees continue. Even McDonald's Corp., long considered the gold standard of the franchise business, is feeling the heat. McDonald's diverse efforts to increase market share have been fiercely resisted by a growing number of franchisees. What's good for the parent's market share and revenue need not be good for the individual franchisee's profit. Franchise owners have resisted the company's efforts to enforce value pricing (i.e., discounting). In 1997, widespread franchisee dissatisfaction led to the end of Campaign 55 (the 55-cent Big Mac). Finally, McDonald's strategy of accelerating the opening of new restaurants to claim market share means that new outlets inevitably cannibalize sales of existing stores. This is the latest conflict in the parent-franchisee relationship.

SUMMARY

Decision-Making Principles

1. The fundamental decision problem of the firm is to determine the profit-maximizing price and output for the good or service it sells.
2. The firm's profit from any decision is the difference between predicted revenues and costs. Output and sales should be raised provided this will increase profit, that is, so long as the extra revenue gained will exceed the extra cost incurred. Conversely, the firm will profit by cutting output if the cost saved exceeds the revenue given up.
3. If economic conditions change, the firm's optimal price and output will change according to the impact on its marginal revenues and marginal costs.

Nuts and Bolts

1. The basic building blocks of the firm's price and output problem are its demand curve and cost function. The demand curve can be used to predict (1) the quantity of sales for a given price or, conversely, (2) the price needed to generate a given level of sales. Multiplying prices and quantities along the demand curve produces the revenue function. The cost function estimates the cost of producing a given level of output. Combining the revenue and cost functions generates a profit prediction for any output Q.
2. The next step in finding the firm's optimal decision is to determine the firm's marginal profit, marginal revenue, and marginal cost.
   a. Marginal profit is the extra profit earned from producing and selling an additional unit of output.
   b. Marginal revenue is the extra revenue earned from selling an additional unit of output.
   c. Marginal cost is the extra cost of producing an additional unit of output.
   d. By definition, marginal profit is the difference between marginal revenue and marginal cost: $M\pi = MR - MC$. The $M\pi$, MR, and MC expressions can be found by taking the derivatives of the respective profit, revenue, and cost functions.
3. The firm's optimal output is characterized by the following conditions: (1) $M\pi = 0$ or, equivalently, (2) $MR = MC$. Once output has been determined, the firm's optimal price is found from the price equation, and profit can be estimated accordingly.

Questions and Problems

1. A manager makes the statement that output should be expanded so long as average revenue exceeds average cost. Does this strategy make sense? Explain.

2. The original revenue function for the microchip producer is $R = 170Q - 20Q^2$. Derive the expression for marginal revenue and use it to find the output level at which *revenue is maximized*. Confirm that this is greater than the firm's profit-maximizing output and explain why.

3. Because of changing demographics, a small, private liberal arts college predicts a fall in enrollments over the next five years. How would it apply marginal analysis to plan for the decreased enrollment? (The college is a nonprofit institution, so think broadly about its objectives.)

4. Suppose a firm's inverse demand curve is given by $P = 120 - .5Q$ and its cost equation is $C = 420 + 60Q + Q^2$.
   a. Find the firm's optimal quantity, price, and profit (1) by using the profit and marginal profit equations and (2) by setting MR equal to MC. Also provide a graph of MR and MC.
   b. Suppose instead that the firm can sell any and all of its output at the fixed market price $P = 120$. At any higher price, it will sell nothing. Find the firm's optimal output.

5. a. As in Problem 4, demand continues to be given by $P = 120$, but the firm's cost equation is linear: $C = 420 + 60Q$. Graph the firm's revenue and cost curves. At what quantity does the firm break even, that is, earn exactly a zero profit?
   b. In general, suppose the firm faces the fixed price P and has cost equation $C = F + cQ$, where F denotes the firm's fixed cost and c is its marginal cost per unit. Write down a formula for the firm's profit. Set this expression equal to zero and solve for the firm's break-even quantity (in terms of P, F, and c). Give an intuitive explanation for this break-even equation.
   c. In this case, what difficulty arises in trying to apply the MR = MC rule to maximize profit? By applying the logic of marginal analysis, state the modified rule applicable to this case.

6. A television station is considering the sale of promotional videos. It can have the videos produced by one of two suppliers. Supplier A will charge the station a setup fee of $1,200 plus $2 for each cassette; supplier B has no setup fee and will charge $4 per cassette. The station estimates its demand for the cassettes to be given by $Q = 1,600 - 200P$, where P is the price in dollars and Q is the number of cassettes. (The price equation is $P = 8 - Q/200$.)
   a. Suppose the station plans to give away the videos. How many cassettes should it order? From which supplier?

b. Suppose instead that the station seeks to maximize its profit from sales of the cassettes. What price should it charge? How many cassettes should it order from which supplier? (*Hint*: Solve two separate problems, one with supplier A and one with supplier B, and then compare profits. In each case, apply the MR = MC rule.)

7. The college and graduate-school textbook market is one of the most profitable segments for book publishers. A best-selling accounting text published by Old School Inc. (OS) has a demand curve $P = 150 - Q$, where Q denotes yearly sales (in thousands) of books. (In other words, $Q = 20$ means 20 thousand books.) The cost of producing, handling, and shipping each additional book is about $40, and the publisher pays a $10 per book royalty to the author. Finally, the publisher's overall marketing and promotion spending (set at the beginning of the year) typically has accounted for an average cost of about $10 per book.
   a. Determine OS's profit-maximizing output and price for the accounting text.
   b. A rival publisher has raised the price of its best-selling accounting text by $15. One option is to exactly match this price hike and so exactly preserve your level of sales. Do you endorse this price increase? (Explain briefly why or why not.)
   c. To save significantly on fixed costs, OS plans to contract out the actual printing of its textbooks to outside vendors. OS expects to pay a somewhat higher printing cost per book (than in part a) from the outside vendor (that marks up price above its cost to make a profit). How would outsourcing affect the output and pricing decisions in part a?

8. Modifying a product to increase its "value added" can benefit customers and enhance supplier profits. For example, suppose an improved version of a product increases customer value added by $25 per unit. (In effect, the demand curve undergoes a parallel upward shift of $25.)
   a. If the redesign is expected to increase the item's marginal cost by $30, should the company undertake it?
   b. Suppose instead that the redesign increases marginal cost by $15. Should the firm undertake it, and (if so) how should it vary its original output and price?

9. Firm Z is developing a new product. An early introduction (beating rivals to market) would greatly enhance the company's revenues. However, the intensive development effort needed to expedite the introduction can be very expensive. Suppose total revenues and costs associated with the new product's introduction are given by

$$R = 720 - 8t \quad \text{and} \quad C = 600 - 20t + .25t^2,$$

where t is the introduction date (in months from now). Some executives have argued for an expedited introduction date 12 months from now

($t = 12$). Do you agree? What introduction date is most profitable? Explain.

10. A producer of photocopiers derives profits from two sources: the immediate profit it makes on each copier sold and the additional profit it gains from servicing its copiers and selling toner and other supplies. The firm estimates that its additional profit from service and supplies is about $300 over the life of *each copier sold.*

There is disagreement in management about the implication of this tie-in profit. One group argues that this extra profit (though significant for the firm's bottom line) should have no effect on the firm's optimal output and price. A second group argues that the firm should maximize total profit by lowering price to sell additional units (even though this reduces its profit margin at the point of sale). Which view (if either) is correct?

11. Suppose the microchip producer discussed in this chapter faces demand and cost equations given by $Q = 8.5 - .05P$ and $C = 100 + 38Q$. Choosing to treat price as its main decision variable, the microchip producer writes profit as

$$\pi = R - C$$
$$= [P(8.5 - .05P)] - [100 + (38)(8.5 - .05P)]$$
$$= -423 + 10.4P - .05P^2.$$

Derive an expression for $M\pi = d\pi/dP$. Then set $M\pi = 0$ to find the firm's optimal price. Your result should confirm the optimal price found earlier in the chapter.

12. As the exclusive carrier on a local air route, a regional airline must determine the number of flights it will provide per week and the fare it will charge. Taking into account operating and fuel costs, airport charges, and so on, the estimated cost per flight is $2,000. It expects to fly full flights (100 passengers), so its marginal cost *on a per passenger basis* is $20. Finally, the airline's estimated demand curve is $P = 120 - .1Q$, where P is the fare in dollars and Q is the number of passengers per week.
   a. What is the airline's profit-maximizing fare? How many passengers does it carry per week, using how many flights? What is its weekly profit?
   b. Suppose the airline is offered $4,000 per week to haul freight along the route for a local firm. This will mean replacing one of the weekly passenger flights with a freight flight (at the same operating cost). Should the airline carry freight for the local firm? Explain.

13. Suppose a firm's inverse demand and cost equations are of the general forms $P = a - bQ$ and $C = F + cQ$, where the parameters a and b

denote the intercept and slope of the inverse demand function and the parameters F and c are the firm's fixed and marginal costs, respectively. Apply the MR = MC rule to confirm that the firm's optimal output and price are $Q = (a - c)/2b$ and $P = (a + c)/2$. Provide explanations for the ways P and Q depend on the underlying economic parameters.

* 14. Under the terms of the current contractual agreement, Burger Queen (BQ) is entitled to 20 percent of the revenue earned by each of its franchises. BQ's best-selling item is the Slopper (it slops out of the bun). BQ supplies the ingredients for the Slopper (bun, mystery meat, etc.) at cost to the franchise. The franchisee's average cost per Slopper (including ingredients, labor cost, and so on) is $.80. At a particular franchise restaurant, weekly demand for Sloppers is given by $P = 3.00 - Q/800$.

   a. If BQ sets the price and weekly sales quantity of Sloppers, what quantity and price would it set? How much does BQ receive? What is the franchisee's net profit?

   b. Suppose the franchise owner sets the price and sales quantity. What price and quantity will the owner set? (*Hint*: Remember that the owner keeps only $.80 of each extra dollar of revenue earned.) How does the total profit earned by the two parties compare to their total profit in part a?

   c. Now suppose BQ and an individual franchise owner enter into an agreement in which BQ is entitled to a share of the franchisee's profit. Will profit sharing remove the conflict between BQ and the franchise operator? Under profit sharing, what will be the price and quantity of Sloppers? (Does the exact split of the profit affect your answer? Explain briefly.) What is the resulting total profit?

   d. Profit sharing is not widely practiced in the franchise business. What are its disadvantages relative to revenue sharing?

15. Suppose a firm assesses its profit function as

$$\pi = -10 - 48Q + 15Q^2 - Q^3.$$

   a. Compute the firm's profit for the following levels of output: $Q = 2, 8$, and 14.

   b. Derive an expression for marginal profit. Compute marginal profit at $Q = 2, 8$, and 14. Confirm that profit is maximized at $Q = 8$. (Why is profit not maximized at $Q = 2$?)

Discussion Question   As vice president of sales for a rapidly growing company, you are grappling with the question of expanding the size of your direct sales force (from its current level of 60 national salespeople). You are considering hiring from 5 to 10 additional personnel.

* Starred problems are more challenging.

How would you estimate the additional dollar cost of each additional sales-person? Based on your company's past sales experience, how would you estimate the expected net revenue generated by an additional salesperson? (Be specific about the information you might use to derive this estimate.) How would you use these cost and revenue estimates to determine whether a sales force increase (or possibly a decrease) is warranted?

Spreadsheet Problems[7]

S1. A manufacturer of spare parts faces the demand curve,

$$P = 800 - 2Q,$$

and produces output according to the cost function,

$$C = 20,000 + 200Q + .5Q^2.$$

a. Create a spreadsheet modeled on the example shown. (The only numerical value you should enter is the quantity in cell B7. Enter appropriate formulas to compute all other numerical entries.)
b. What is the firm's profit-maximizing quantity and price? First, determine the solution by hand, that is, by changing the quantity value in cell B7. (*Hint:* Keep an eye on MR and MC in finding your way to the optimal output.)
c. Use your spreadsheet's optimizer to confirm your answer to part a.

	A	B	C	D	E	F	G
1							
2			THE OPTIMAL OUTPUT OF SPARE PARTS				
3							
4							
5		Quantity	Price	Revenue	Cost	Profit	
6							
7		20	760	15,200	24,200	−9,000	
8							
9							
10				MR	MC	Mprofit	
11							
12				720	220	500	
13							

---

[7] This chapter's special appendix reviews the basics of creating, using, and optimizing spreadsheets.

S2. Your firm competes with a close rival for shares of a $20 million per year market. Your main decision concerns how much to spend on advertising each year. Your rival is currently spending $8 million on advertising. The best estimate of your profit is given by the equation

$$\pi = 20[A/(A + 8)] - A,$$

where A is your firm's advertising expenditure (in millions of dollars). According to this equation, the firms' shares of the $20 million market are in proportion to their advertising spending. (If the firms spend equal amounts, A = 8, they have equal shares of the market, and so on.)

a. Create a spreadsheet modeled on the example shown. Determine the firm's optimal advertising expenditure. Refer to the appendix of this chapter if you are unsure about finding MR, that is, taking the derivative of the quotient, A/(A + 8).

b. Use your spreadsheet's optimizer to confirm your answer in part a. Is matching your rival's spending your best policy?

	A	B	C	D	E	F
1						
2		AN OPTIMAL ADVERTISING BUDGET				
3						
4						
5		Advertising	Revenue	Cost	Profit	
6						
7		8.00	10.00	8.00	2.00	
8						
9						
10			MR	MC	Mprofit	
11						
12			0.625	1.000	−0.375	
13						

S3. The accompanying spreadsheet lists the compass positions of the eight coastal cities of Figure 2.1 and the possible position of the shopping mall. By convention, the city positions are expressed in (x, y) coordinates. All cities are positioned "east–west" along the x-axis. Town A has coordinates (0, 0); Town B is located 3 miles due east, at coordinates (3, 0), and so on. The shopping mall is tentatively located at (5.5, 0), that is, a mile west of Town C (corresponding to position X in Figure 2.1).

In the spreadsheet, column M lists the population of shoppers in each of the towns, and column Q computes the distance between the mall and the various towns. For example, cell Q7 contains the distance formula

$$= ((I7 - D\$7)^2 + (J7 - E\$7)^2)^{.5},$$

that is, distance is the square root of the sum of squared differences of the x and y coordinates. Finally, cell E11 computes the total travel miles associated with the mall's location.

	A	B	C	D	E	F	G	H	I	J	K	L	M	N	O	P	Q	R	S	T	U	V
1																						
2		LOCATING A SHOPPING MALL																				
3																						
4				Location					Location				Population			Distance			Fraction That			
5				(x, y)			Towns		(x, y)				of Shoppers			from Mall			Visits Mall			
6																						
7		Mall		5.5	0		A		0.0	0			15			5.50			0.94			
8																						
9							B		3.0	0			10			2.50			0.99			
10																						
11		Total Travel Miles:		742.5			C		6.5	0			10			1.00			1.00			
12																						
13							D		8.5	0			10			3.00			0.98			
14		Total Visitors:		78.4																		
15							E		11.0	0			5			5.50			0.94			
16																						
17							F		15.5	0			20			10.0			0.80			
18																						
19							G		17.5	0			10			12.0			0.71			
20																						
21							H		22.0	0			15			16.5			0.46			
22																						

a. By trial and error, vary the mall's east–west location (cell D7) to minimize total travel miles. Use your spreadsheet's optimizer to confirm the optimal location.

b. More realistically, suppose the towns are scattered north–south as well as east–west. Set the y coordinates of Towns B, C, E, F, and H to 11, 7.5, 15, 12, and 8, respectively. Answer again the question in part a.

c. Column T provides estimates of the fraction of each town's shopping population that will actually frequent the mall. This fraction varies inversely with the square of the distance to the mall: $F = 1 - d^2/500$. Accordingly, the mall attracts 100 percent of the 10 thousand shoppers from nearby Town C but only 46 percent of the 15 thousand shoppers from Town H. Cell E14 lists the total number of mall visitors from all towns. (Be sure to check this formula.)

By trial and error and using your spreadsheet's optimizer, find the mall location that maximizes total visitors (and, thus, revenue) for the town locations of part a and part b.

Suggested References

The following references provide advanced treatments of marginal analysis using differential calculus.

Baldani, J., J. Bradford, and R. Turner. *Mathematical Economics.* Fort Worth, TX: Dryden Press, 1997.

Besanko, D., and W. R. Braeutigam. *Microeconomics: An Integrative Approach.* New York: John Wiley & Sons, 2002.

Valuable references on optimization methods include:

Fourer, R., and J.-P. Goux. "Optimization as an Internet Resource." *Interfaces* (March–April 2001): 130–150.

Fylstra, D. et al. "Design and Use of the Microsoft Excel Solver." *Interfaces* (September–October 1998): 29–55.

Can a disastrous decision result from mistaking a minimum for a maximum? For a dramatic example, see:

Biddle, W. "Skeleton Alleged in the Stealth Bomber's Closet." *Science*, May 12, 1989, 650–651.

A guide to optimization software and resources on the World Wide Web is provided by H. D. Mittelmann and P. Spellucci. "Decision Tree for Optimization Software." http://plato.la.asu.edu/guide.html.

**CHECK STATION
ANSWERS**

1. The revenue function is $R = 340Q - .8Q^2$.

2. The profit function is $\pi = R - C = -120 + 240Q - .8Q^2$.

3. At $Q = 100$, $\pi = -120 + (240)(100) - .8(100)^2 = 15,880$.
   At $Q = 99$, $\pi = -120 + (240)(99) - .8(99)^2 = 15,799.2$.
   Thus, $M\pi = (15,880 - 15,799.2)/(100 - 99) = 80.8$.

4. Marginal profit is $M\pi = d\pi/dQ = 240 - 1.6Q$. Setting this equal to zero implies that $240 - 1.6Q = 0$, or $Q = 150$.

5. Setting MR = MC implies that $340 - 1.6Q = 100$. Therefore, $Q = 150$. Substituting $Q = 150$ into the price equation implies that $P = 340 - .8(150) = 220$.

6. Cutting price the full amount to maintain sales at the same level is not optimal. A downward shift in the steel producer's demand curve implies a similar downward shift in the MR curve. Absent any other changes, the new intersection of the MR and MC curves is now at a lower output. Thus, the firm's profit-maximizing response in the face of lower prices from competing Japanese suppliers is to reduce its target level of output and to undertake a partial price cut.

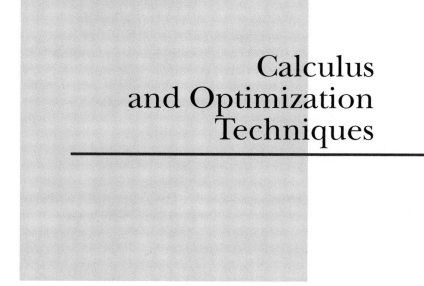

Calculus and Optimization Techniques

The study of managerial economics emphasizes that decisions are taken to maximize certain objectives. Although the precise objective may vary, the key point is that the manager should be able to quantify his or her ultimate goals. For instance, if the manager's objective is to maximize profit, he or she must be able to estimate and measure the profit consequences of alternative courses of action (such as charging different prices). This appendix introduces and reviews the use of calculus in optimization problems. These techniques will be applied throughout the book. Let's begin with an example.

MAXIMIZING PROFIT   A manager who is in charge of a single product line is trying to determine the quantity of output to produce and sell to maximize the product's profit. Based on marketing and production studies, she has estimated the product's profit function to be

$$\pi = 2Q - .1Q^2 - 3.6 \qquad \text{[2A.1]}$$

where π is profit (thousands of dollars) and Q is quantity of output (thousands of units). Here the level of output, Q, is identified as the manager's *decision variable*, the item the decision maker controls. The profit function shows the relationship between the manager's decision variable and her objective. (For this reason, it often is referred to as the *objective function*.)

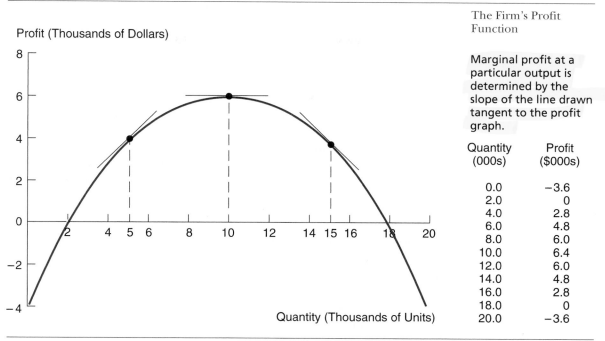

The Firm's Profit Function

Marginal profit at a particular output is determined by the slope of the line drawn tangent to the profit graph.

Quantity (000s)	Profit ($000s)
0.0	−3.6
2.0	0
4.0	2.8
6.0	4.8
8.0	6.0
10.0	6.4
12.0	6.0
14.0	4.8
16.0	2.8
18.0	0
20.0	−3.6

An equation is the most economical way to express the profit function, but it is not the only means. Figure 2A.1 presents a table listing the profit consequences of different output choices and graphs the profit function. (The graph plots profits across a continuum of possible output levels. Remember that output is measured in thousands of units. Thus, Q = 6.123 and Q = 6.124 are both legitimate output candidates.) According to convention, the graph plots the decision variable (also commonly referred to as the *independent* variable) on the horizontal axis and the objective (or *dependent* variable) on the vertical axis.

From either the table or the graph, we see that at very low output levels profit is negative. As the level of output increases, profit rises, becomes positive, and peaks. For still higher outputs, profit declines and eventually turns negative. The goal of management is to set production to generate positive profits—in particular, to attain maximum profit.

Marginal Analysis

The marginal value of any variable is the change in that variable per unit change in a given decision variable. In our example, marginal profit is the change in profit from an increase in output. A direct way to express marginal profit is to find the slope of the profit function at a given level of output. The graph in Figure 2A.1 shows how this is done. We start by specifying a particular level of output, say, Q = 5. Next, we draw a tangent line that just touches the profit graph at this output level. Finally, we find the slope of the tangent line. By careful measurement (taking the ratio of the "rise over the run" along the line), we find the slope to be exactly 1 (that is, the tangent happens to be a 45° line). Thus, the marginal profit at Q = 5 is measured as $1,000 per additional 1,000 units or, equivalently, $1 per unit.

The upward-sloping tangent shows that profit rises as output increases. Marginal profit measures the steepness of this slope, that is, how quickly profit rises with additional output. In the graph in Figure 2A.1, tangents also are drawn at output levels Q = 10 and Q = 15. At Q = 15, profit falls with increases in output; marginal profit (the slope of the tangent) is negative. At Q = 10, the tangent line is horizontal; marginal profit (again its slope) is exactly zero.

Why is marginal analysis important? The answer simply is that *marginal analysis allows the manager to identify an optimal decision*, that is, the course of action that will maximize his or her objective. To illustrate, consider once again the manager's profit-maximization problem. The table in Figure 2A.1 indicates that maximum profit is obtained at Q = 10,000 units. The profit here, $6,400, is greater than at any other round-number output level. Nonetheless, the table is hardly ironclad proof that this output is optimal. Perhaps Q = 10,500 will deliver greater profit. The profit graph in Figure 2A.1 provides stronger evidence that the output Q = 10,000 is optimal. But we still cannot be sure whether an output such as Q = 10,022 units would produce greater revenue.

Marginal analysis can identify the optimal output level directly, dispensing with tedious enumeration of candidates. The principle is this:

> The manager's objective is maximized when the marginal value with respect to that objective becomes zero (turning from positive to negative).

To maximize profit, the marginal principle instructs us to find the output for which marginal profit is zero. To see why this is so, suppose we are considering an output level at which marginal profit is positive. Clearly, this output cannot be optimal because a small increase would raise profit. Conversely, if marginal profit is negative at a given output, output should be decreased to raise profit. In Figure 2A.1, profit can be increased (we can move toward the revenue peak) if current output is in either the upward- or downward-sloping region. Consequently, the point of maximum profit occurs when marginal profit is neither positive nor negative; that is, it must be zero. As noted earlier, this occurs at output Q = 10,000, where the tangent's slope is flat, that is, exactly zero.

DIFFERENTIAL CALCULUS   To apply the marginal principle, we need a simple method to compute marginal values. (It would be tedious to have to compute rates of change by measuring tangent slopes by hand.) Fortunately, the rules of differential calculus can be applied directly to any functional equation to *derive* marginal values. The process of finding the tangent slope commonly is referred to as *taking the derivative of* (or *differentiating*) the functional equation.[1] To illustrate the basic calculus rules, let y denote the dependent variable and x the independent variable. We write $y = f(x)$, where $f(x)$ represents the (unspecified) functional relationship between the variables. The notation dy/dx represents the derivative of the function, that is, the rate of change or slope of the function at a particular value of x. (The d in this notation is derived from the Greek letter delta, which has come to mean "change in.") We list the following basic rules.

- *Rule 1.*   The derivative of a constant is zero. If $y = 7$, for example, $dy/dx = 0$. Note that $y = 7$ is graphed as a horizontal line (of height 7); naturally this has a zero slope for all values of x.

- *Rule 2.*   The derivative of a constant times a variable is simply the constant. If $y = bx$, then $dy/dx = b$. For example, if $y = 13x$, then $dy/dx = 13$. In words, the function $y = 13x$ is a straight line with a slope of 13.

- *Rule 3.*   A power function has the form $y = ax^n$, where a and n are constants. The derivative of a power function is

$$dy/dx = n \cdot ax^{n-1}.$$

For instance, if $y = 4x^3$, then $dy/dx = 12x^2$.

It is important to recognize that the power function includes many important special cases.[2] For instance, $y = 1/x^2$ is equivalently written as $y = x^{-2}$. Similarly, $y = \sqrt{x}$ becomes $y = x^{1/2}$. According to Rule 3, the respective derivatives are $dy/dx = -2x^{-3} = -2/x^3$ and $dy/dx = .5x^{-1/2} = .5/\sqrt{x}$.

- *Rule 4.*   The derivative of a sum of functions is equal to the sum of the derivatives; that is, if $y = f(x) + g(x)$, then $dy/dx = df/dx + dg/dx$. This simply means we can take the derivative of functions term by term. For example, given that $y = .1x^2 - 2x^3$, then $dy/dx = .2x - 6x^2$.

---

[1] The following are all equivalent statements:
1. The slope of the profit function at $Q = 5$ is $1 per unit of output.
2. The derivative of the profit function at $Q = 5$ is $1 per unit of output.
3. The marginal profit at $Q = 5$ is $1 per unit of output.
4. At $Q = 5$, profit is rising at a rate of $1 per unit of output.

[2] Notice that Rules 1 and 2 are actually special cases of Rule 3. Setting $n = 0$ implies that $y = a$, and, therefore, $dy/dx = 0$ (Rule 1). Setting $n = 1$ implies that $y = ax$ and, therefore, $dy/dx = a$ (Rule 2).

- *Rule 5.*   Suppose y is the product of two functions: $y = f(x)g(x)$. Then we have

$$dy/dx = (df/dx)g + (dg/dx)f.$$

For example, suppose we have $y = (4x)(3x^2)$. Then $dy/dx = (4)(3x^2) + 4x(6x) = 36x^2$. (Note that this example can also be written as $y = 12x^3$; we confirm that $dy/dx = 36x^2$ using Rule 3.)

- *Rule 6.*   Suppose y is a quotient: $y = f(x)/g(x)$. Then we have

$$dy/dx = [(df/dx)g - (dg/dx)f]/g^2.$$

For example, suppose we have $y = x/(8 + x)$. Then

$$dy/dx = [1 \cdot (8 + x) - 1 \cdot (x)]/(8 + x)^2 = 8/(8 + x)^2.$$

Let's derive an expression for marginal profit (denoted by Mπ) applying these calculus rules to our profit function:

$$\pi = 2Q - .1Q^2 - 3.6.$$

From Rule 4, we know we can proceed term by term. From Rule 2, the derivative of the first term is 2. According to Rule 3, the derivative of the second term is $-.2Q$. From Rule 1, the derivative of the third term is zero. Thus,

$$M\pi = d\pi/dx = 2 - .2Q.$$

Notice the elegance of this approach. By substituting specific values of Q, we can find marginal profit at any desired level of output. For instance, at $Q = 5$, we find that $M\pi = 2 - (.2)(5) = 1$; at $Q = 12$, $M\pi = -.4$; and so on.

To determine the firm's optimal output level, we set $M\pi = 0$. Thus,

$$2 - .2Q = 0.$$

Solving this equation for Q, we find $Q = 10$. This confirms that the profit-maximizing level of output is 10 thousand units.

THE SECOND DERIVATIVE   In general, one must be careful to check that a maximum, not a minimum, has been found. In the previous example, the graph makes it clear that we have found a maximum. But suppose the profit expression is more complicated, say,

$$\pi = 1.8Q^2 - .1Q^3 - 6Q - 10. \qquad [2A.2]$$

Figure 2A.2 shows the associated profit graph. Notice that there are two quantities at which the slope is zero; one is a maximum and the other is a minimum.

It would be disastrous if we confused the two. Taking the derivative of the profit function, we find

$$M\pi = d\pi/dx = 3.6Q - .3Q^2 - 6.$$

Substitution confirms that marginal profit is zero at the quantities Q = 2 and Q = 10. The graph shows that Q = 2 *minimizes* profit, whereas Q = 10 *maximizes* profit.

FIGURE 2A.2

A Second Profit Function

The manager must be careful to distinguish a maximum from a minimum.

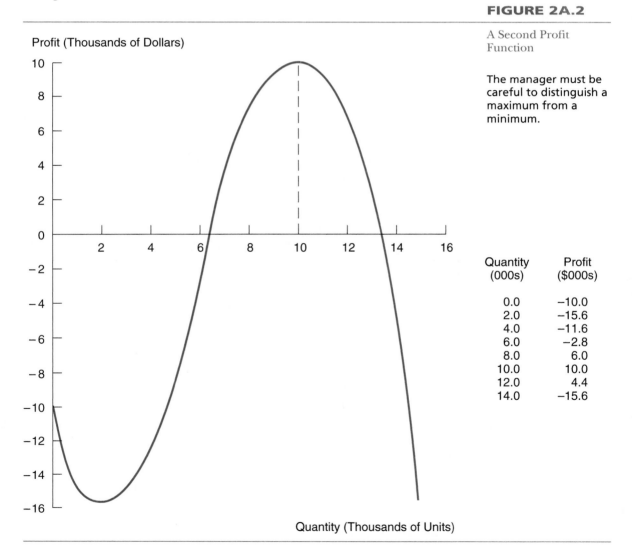

Profit (Thousands of Dollars)

Quantity (Thousands of Units)

Quantity (000s)	Profit ($000s)
0.0	−10.0
2.0	−15.6
4.0	−11.6
6.0	−2.8
8.0	6.0
10.0	10.0
12.0	4.4
14.0	−15.6

There is a direct way to distinguish between a maximum and a minimum. At a maximum, the slope of the profit function changes from positive to zero to negative as output increases; that is, the slope of the profit function decreases as output increases around the maximum. In contrast, at a minimum, the slope changes from negative to zero to positive; the slope is increasing. Because of this difference, the *second* derivative of the profit function can be used to distinguish between the two cases. The second derivative is found by taking the derivative of $d\pi/dQ$. If the second derivative is negative (i.e., the slope is decreasing), the point in question is a local maximum; if the second derivative is positive, the point is a local minimum. Taking the derivative of $d\pi/dQ$, we find the second derivative to be

$$
\begin{aligned}
d^2\pi/dQ^2 &= d(d\pi/dQ)/dQ \\
&= dM\pi/dQ = d(3.6Q - .3Q^2 - 6)/dQ \\
&= 3.6 - .6Q
\end{aligned}
$$

In finding the second derivative, we start from the original profit function and take the derivative *twice*. At $Q = 2$, we find that $d^2\pi/dQ^2 = 3.6 - .6(2) = 2.4$. Since this is positive, $Q = 2$ represents a local minimum. At $Q = 10$, we find that $d^2\pi/dQ^2 = 3.6 - .6(10) = -2.4$. Since this is negative, $Q = 10$ represents a local maximum.

MARGINAL REVENUE AND MARGINAL COST   We have seen that maximum profit is achieved at the point such that marginal profit equals zero, $d\pi/dQ = 0$. The same condition can be expressed in a different form by separating profit into its two components. Profit is defined as the difference between revenues and costs. Thus, the profit function can be written as

$$\pi(Q) = R(Q) - C(Q),$$

the difference between revenues and costs. In turn, the condition that marginal profit equal zero is

$$d\pi/dQ = dR/dQ - dC/dQ = MR - MC = 0.$$

In short, profit is maximized when marginal revenue equals marginal cost.

Maximizing Multivariable Functions

Frequently, the manager must determine optimal values for several decision variables at once, for instance, a product's price and its associated advertising budget. In this case, the product's profit would be expressed by the function $\pi = \pi(P, A)$, where P is the product's price and A is its advertising budget in dollars. Here the key to maximizing profit is to apply a double dose of marginal reasoning. Marginal profit with respect to each decision variable should be equated to zero. The optimal value of P is found where the "partial" derivative of profit with respect to P equals zero. This partial derivative is denoted by $\partial\pi/\partial P$ and is found by taking the derivative with respect to P, holding A (the other decision variable) constant. Similarly, the optimal value of A is found where $\partial\pi/\delta A = 0$.

PRICE AND ADVERTISING   Suppose the firm's profit function is

$$\pi = 20 + 2P - 2P^2 + 4A - A^2 + 2PA.$$

The partial derivative of profit with respect to P is

$$\partial\pi/\partial P = 2 - 4P + 2A$$

Notice that when we take the partial derivative with respect to P, we are treating A as a constant. Thus, 4A and A^2 disappear (Rule 1) and 2PA becomes 2A (Rule 2). The partial derivative of profit with respect to A is

$$\partial\pi/\partial A = 4 - 2A + 2P.$$

Setting each of these expressions equal to zero produces two equations in two unknowns. Solving these simultaneously, we find that P = 3 and A = 5. Thus, profit is maximized at these values of P and A.

Constrained Optimization

In the previous examples, the decision variables were unconstrained, that is, free to take on any values. Frequently, however, decision variables can be changed only within certain constraints. Consider the following example.

A SUPPLY COMMITMENT   A firm is trying to identify its profit-maximizing level of output. By contract, it already is committed to supplying at least seven units to its customer. Suppose that its predicted profit function is given by $\pi = 40Q - 4Q^2$. The firm seeks to maximize π subject to $Q \geq 7$. Setting marginal profit equal to zero, we have $d\pi/dQ = 40 - 8Q = 0$ so that Q = 5. But this value is *infeasible*; it violates the contract constraint. The constrained maximum occurs at Q = 7, where $d\pi/dQ = -6$. Note that, since marginal profit is negative, profit would decline if Q were increased. Thus, the firm would like to raise profit by decreasing Q, but this is impossible due to the binding contract constraint.

A different kind of constrained optimization problem occurs when there are multiple decision variables.

PROFITS FROM MULTIPLE MARKETS   A firm has a limited amount of output and must decide what quantities (Q_1 and Q_2) to sell to two different market segments. For example, suppose it seeks to maximize total profit given by

$$\pi = \left(20Q_1 - .5Q_1^2\right) + \left(40Q_2 - Q_2^2\right),$$

subject to $Q_1 + Q_2 \leq 25$. Setting marginal profit equal to zero for each quantity, we find that $Q_1 = 20$ and $Q_2 = 20$. But these desired quantities are infeasible; the total (40) exceeds the available supply (25). The manager must cut back one or both outputs. But how should she do this while maintaining as high a level of profit as possible? To answer this question, observe that if output is cut back in each market, the marginal profit in each market will be positive. What if the manager chose outputs such that marginal profit differed across the two markets, say, $M\pi_1 > M\pi_2 > 0$? If this were the case, the manager could increase her total profit by selling one more unit in market 1 and one less unit in market 2. She would continue to switch units so long as the marginal profits differed across the markets. At the optimal solution, marginal profits must be equal. Thus, $\partial \pi / \partial Q_1 = \partial \pi / \partial Q_2$ must hold as well as $Q_1 + Q_2 = 25$. Taking derivatives, we find the first condition to be $20 - Q_1 = 40 - 2Q_2$. Solving this equation and the quantity constraint simultaneously, we find that $Q_1 = 10$ and $Q_2 = 15$. This is the firm's optimal solution.

THE METHOD OF LAGRANGE MULTIPLIERS   The last two problems can be solved by an alternative means known as the *method of Lagrange multipliers.* To use the method, we create a new variable, the Lagrange multiplier, for each constraint. In the subsequent solution, we determine optimal values for the relevant decision variables and the Lagrange multipliers. For instance, in the supply commitment example, there is one constraint, $Q = 7$. (We know the constraint is binding from our discussion.) To apply the method, we rewrite this constraint as $7 - Q = 0$, create a new variable, call it z, and write

$$L = \pi + z(7 - Q)$$
$$= 40Q - 4Q^2 + z(7 - Q).$$

In short, we have formed L (denoted the Lagrangian) by taking the original objective function and adding to it the binding constraint (multiplied by z). We then find the partial derivatives with respect to the two variables, Q and z, and set them equal to zero:

$$\partial L / \partial Q = 40 - 8Q - z = 0$$
$$\partial L / \partial z = 7 - Q = 0.$$

Solving these equations simultaneously, we find that $Q = 7$ and $z = -16$. The value of Q is hardly surprising; we already know this is the best the manager can do. The interpretation of the Lagrange multiplier, z, is of some interest. The value of the multiplier measures the marginal profit ($M\pi = -16$) at the constrained optimum.

To apply the method in the multiple-market example, we write

$$L = \left(20Q_1 - .5Q_1^2\right) + \left(40Q_2 - Q_2^2\right) + z\left(25 - Q_1 - Q_2\right),$$

where the binding constraint is $Q_1 + Q_2 = 25$ and z again denotes the Lagrange multiplier. Setting the appropriate partial derivatives equal to zero, we find

$$\partial L/\partial Q_1 = 20 - 8Q_1 - z = 0$$
$$\partial L/\partial Q_2 = 40 - 2Q_2 - z = 0.$$
$$\partial L/\partial z = 25 - Q_1 - Q_1 = 0.$$

Notice that the third condition is simply the original constraint. We now find values that satisfy these three equations simultaneously: $Q_1 = 10$, $Q_2 = 15$, and $z = 10$. The values for Q_1 and Q_2 confirm our original solution. In addition, note that the first two equations can be written as $z = 20 - Q_1 = 40 - 2Q_2$, or $z = M\pi_1 = M\pi_2$. In other words, the multiplier z represents the common value of marginal profit (equalized across the two markets). The actual value of $M\pi$ in each market is $z = 10$. Thus, if the manager could increase total sales (above 25), she would increase profit by 10 per unit of additional capacity.

To sum up, the use of Lagrange multipliers is a powerful method. It effectively allows us to treat constrained problems as though they were unconstrained.[3]

Questions and Problems

1. In the late 1970s, the economist Arthur Laffer argued that *lower* tax rates, by stimulating employment and investment, could lead to *increased* tax revenue to the government. If this prediction is correct, a tax rate reduction would be a win-win policy, good for both taxpayers and the government. Laffer went on to sketch a tax revenue curve in the shape of an upside-down U.

   In general, the government's tax revenue can be expressed as $R = t \cdot B(t)$, where t denotes the tax rate ranging between 0 and 1 (i.e., between 0 and 100 percent) and B denotes the tax base. Explain why the

---

[3] It is important to note that the method of Lagrange multipliers is relevant only in the case of binding constraints. Typically, we begin by seeking an unconstrained optimum. If such an optimum satisfies all of the constraints, we are done. If one or more constraints are violated, however, we apply the method of Lagrange multipliers for the solution.

tax base is likely to shrink as tax rates become very high. How might this lead to a U-shaped tax revenue curve?

2. The economic staff of the U.S. Department of the Treasury has been asked to recommend a new tax policy concerning the treatment of the foreign earnings of U.S. firms. Currently the foreign earnings of U.S. multinational companies are taxed only when the income is returned to the United States. Taxes are deferred if the income is reinvested abroad. The department seeks a tax rate that will maximize total tax revenue from foreign earnings. Find the optimal tax rate if:
   a. $B(t) = 80 - 100t$
   b. $B(t) = 80 - 240t^2$
   c. $B(t) = 80 - 80\sqrt{t}$,
   where $B(t)$ is the foreign earnings of U.S. multinational companies returned to the United States and t is the tax rate.

3. A firm's total profit is given by $\pi = 20x - x^2 + 16y - 2y^2$.
   a. What values of x and y will maximize the firm's profit?
   b. Repeat part a assuming the firm faces the constraint $x + y \leq 8$.
   c. Repeat part a assuming the constraint is $x + .5y \leq 7.5$.

Optimization Using Spreadsheets

We have already encountered several quantitative approaches to optimizing a given objective: enumeration, graphic solutions, and (in the preceding appendix) calculus. To these we can add a fourth approach: spreadsheet-based optimization. Over the past 20 years, spreadsheets have become powerful management tools. Modeling a quantitative decision on a spreadsheet harnesses the power of computer calculation instead of laborious pencil-and-paper figuring. Besides helping to define and manage decision problems, spreadsheets also compute optimal solutions with no more than a click of a mouse. There are many leading spreadsheet programs—Excel, Lotus 123, Quattro Pro, to name three—and all work nearly the same way. To review the fundamentals of spreadsheet use, let's revisit the microchip example.

Table 2A.1 shows this example depicted in an Excel spreadsheet. The spreadsheet consists of a table of cells. Besides the title in row 2, we have typed labels (Quantity, Price, MR) in rows 5 and 10. We have also entered the number 2 in cell B7 (highlighted in colored type). This cell houses our basic decision variable, output. For the moment, we have set microchip output at 2.0 lots. Cells C7 to F7 show the price, revenue, cost, and profit results of producing 2.0 lots. These cells are linked via formulas to our output cell. For instance,

TABLE 2A.1

Optimizing a Spreadsheet

	A	B	C	D	E	F	G
1							
2		THE OPTIMAL OUTPUT OF MICROCHIPS					
3							
4							
5		Quantity	Price	Revenue	Cost	Profit	
6							
7		2.0	130	260	176	84	
8							
9							
10				MR	MC	Mprofit	
11							
12				90	38	52	
13							
14							

consider cell C7 showing a price of 130. When we created the spreadsheet, we typed the formula:

$$= 170 - 20*B7,$$

into cell C7 (and then pressed return). This formula embodies the price equation, $P = 170 - 20Q$. By entering the preceding spreadsheet formula, we are telling the computer to subtract 20 times the value of cell B7 from 170 and to enter the resulting numerical value in cell C7. (*Note:* We typed a formula, *not* the number 130, into this cell.)

The other numerical values are similarly determined by formulas. Thus, in cell D7, we entered the formula: $= B7*C7$, instructing the spreadsheet to compute revenue as the product of the price and quantity cells. In cell E7, we entered the cost formula: $= 100 + 38*B7$. In cell F7, we computed profit by entering: $= D7 - E7$, and in cell D12, we computed MR by entering: $= 170 - 40*B7$. Indeed, to gain experience with the ways of spreadsheets, we suggest that you start with a blank spreadsheet and re-create Table 2A.1 for yourself—that is, type in labels, numerical values, and formulas as indicated.

(*Note:* Typing in cell addresses is not the only way to enter formulas. The quickest way is to mouse click on the cell that is part of the formula.)

With the spreadsheet in hand, there are several ways to determine the microchip firm's profit-maximizing output. The most primitive way is to try various numerical values in cell B7, observe the resulting profit results in cell F7, and, thereby, identify the optimal output. This represents solution by enumeration. A second, more expeditious approach uses MR and MC as guides. Again, values in cell B7 are varied by hand but this time systematically. Output should be increased as long as MR exceeds MC; it should be cut if MC exceeds MR. When MR equals MC, the profit-maximizing level of output has been attained.

A third approach is to direct the computer to optimize the spreadsheet. The top menu in Table 2A.2 illustrates Excel's optimizer, called Solver, which is called by clicking on the Solver listing found under the Tools menu. By completing the menu in Table 2A.2, one instructs the computer to optimize the spreadsheet. In the menu, we have (1) entered target cell F7 (the profit cell), (2) to be maximized, (3) by varying cell B7. Then, after one clicks on the Solve box, the computer finds a new numerical value in cell B7 that maximizes cell F7. (The value you start with in cell B7 doesn't matter; the computer will replace it with the optimal value it finds.) Using an internal mathematical algorithm, Solver finds the optimal level of output, 3.3 lots, and places this value in cell B7, and the other cells (price, revenue, cost, and so on) change accordingly.

This simple example illustrates but does not do full justice to the power of spreadsheet optimization. In fact, optimizers are designed to solve complex problems involving many decision variables and multiple constraints. For instance, the firm's profit might well depend on several decision variables, such as output, advertising spending, and the size of its direct sales force. Here, in order to maximize profit, the manager would specify multiple variable cells in the Solver menu. In addition, the firm might face various constraints in its quest for maximum profit. For instance, suppose the microchip producer was quite sure that setting a price greater than $91,000 per lot would attract a cutthroat competitor whose sales of "cloned" chips would decimate the firm's own profit. In this case, management's *constrained* optimization problem would include the requirement that the value in price cell C7 should not exceed 91. The bottom menu in Table 2A.2 includes this new constraint. The spreadsheet's new optimal solution (not shown) becomes 3.95 lots, implying exactly a $91,000 price and a reduced profit of $109,350.

To sum up, the beauty of any spreadsheet-based optimization program is that, upon execution, it instantly computes all optimal values consistent with satisfying all constraints.

TABLE 2A.2

Optimizing a Spreadsheet

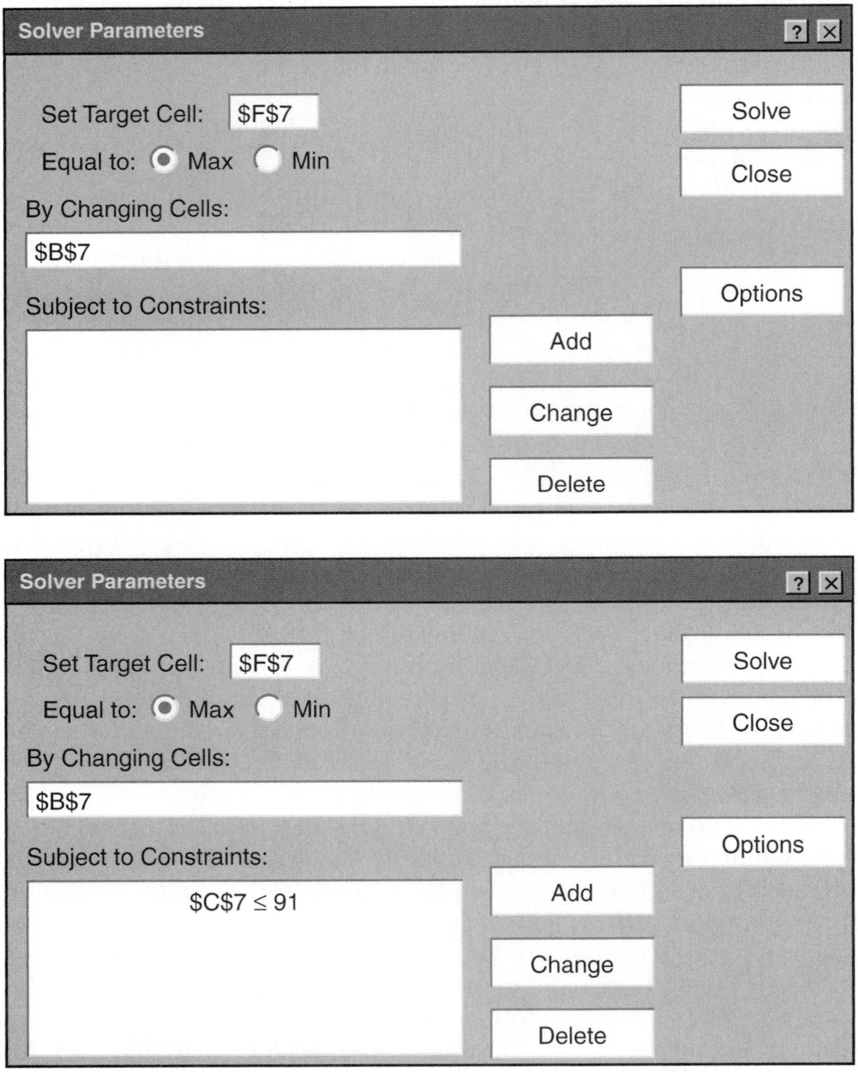

CHAPTER 3

Demand Analysis and Optimal Pricing

There's no brand loyalty so strong that the offer of "penny off" can't overcome it.

A MARKETING APHORISM

Anyone who has traveled via commercial airline, even on an infrequent basis, knows there is a bewildering plethora of fares for the same route. Besides the standard first-class and coach fares, there are discount fares for round-trip travel and for travelers who book two or more weeks in advance, leave during the week, stay over Saturday night, or fly standby. The fare structure is daunting not only for travelers but also for the airlines. For instance, in determining the standard coach fare on a particular route, the airline has to consider (1) the cost of the flight (including fuel, labor, and administrative costs), (2) the historical pattern of business and leisure use on the route, (3) overall economic conditions (which affect travel demand), and (4) the prices charged by competing airlines. Together the airlines mount some 14,000 domestic flights each day, and they repeatedly alter prices (often by computer) as conditions change.

Among airlines, the name of the game is *yield management*: how to price seat by seat to generate the greatest possible profit. For instance, airlines typically sell higher-priced tickets to business travelers who cannot take advantage of supersaver and other discount fares. At the same time, they sell other seats on the same flight at sharply lower prices to attract price-sensitive vacation travelers. A classic example of yield management is United Airlines Flight 815 (October 31, 1997) from Chicago to Los Angeles.[1]

Airline Ticket Pricing

[1] The following prices are reported in "So, How Much Did You Pay for Your Ticket?" *The New York Times*, (April 12, 1997), p. wk2.

79

Among the passengers holding tickets for the Chicago to Los Angeles segment only (i.e., excluding connecting passengers), there were some 27 different one-way fares, ranging from $1,248 for a first-class ticket bought on the day of departure to $87 for an advance-purchase coach ticket. Some travelers cashed in frequent flier miles. Some qualified for senior citizen discounts; others received lower fares for restricted tickets requiring Saturday stayovers. In general, early buyers paid less, but fares fluctuated day to day depending on demand.

The question here is: How can demand analysis help the airlines win the game of yield management?

In Chapter 2, we presented a simple model of profit maximization. There the manager began with demand and cost functions and used them to determine the profit-maximizing price and output level for a given product or service. In this chapter, we will take a closer look at demand and the role it plays in managerial decision making.

The notion of demand is much richer than the simple formulation given in Chapter 2. For instance, up until now we have studied the dependence of demand on a single factor: price. We begin this chapter by considering the *multiple* determinants of demand. Next, we look more closely at the responsiveness of demand to these factors, a concept captured in the basic definition of *elasticity*. In the remaining sections, we present a richer formulation of demand and show how it can be used to guide managers in their goal of maximizing profits. Toward this end, we will refine our optimization techniques to account for more complicated demand conditions—those that include the possibilities of market segmentation and price discrimination.

DETERMINANTS OF DEMAND

The Demand Function

To illustrate the basic quantitative aspects of demand, let's start with a concrete example: the demand for air travel.[2] Put yourself in the position of a manager for a leading regional airline. One of your specific responsibilities is to analyze the state of travel demand for a nonstop route between Houston, Texas, and a rapidly growing city in Florida. Your airline flies one daily departure from each city to the other (two flights in all) and faces a single competitor that offers two daily flights from each city. Your task is complicated by the fact that the number of travelers on your airline (and, therefore, the revenue your company earns) has fluctuated considerably in the past three years. Reviewing this past experience, you realize the main determinants of your airline's traffic are

---

[2] We are not ready yet to analyze the complicated problem of setting multiple fares described in the opening of this chapter. That must wait until the concluding section.

your own price and the price of your competitor. In addition, traffic between the two cities was brisk during years in which the Texas and Florida economies enjoyed rapid expansion. But, during the 1991 recession and the slowdown of 2001, air travel fell between the two cities.

Your immediate goal is to analyze demand for coach-class travel between the cities. (You also offer first-class accommodations, but these account for relatively little revenue despite the higher fare because fewer than a dozen such seats per flight are filled. Thus, we will ignore this category.) You begin by writing down the following demand function:

$$Q = f(P, P^\circ, Y). \tag{3.1}$$

This expression reads: "The number of your airline's coach seats sold per flight (Q) depends on (is a function of) your airline's coach fare (P), your competitor's fare (P°), and income in the region (Y)." In short, the **demand function** shows, in equation form, the relationship between the quantity sold of a good or service and one or more variables.

The demand function is useful shorthand, but by itself it does not indicate the exact quantitative relationship between Q and P, P°, and Y. For this we need to write the demand function in a particular form. Suppose the economic forecasting unit of your airline has supplied you with the following equation that best describes demand:

$$Q = 25 + 3Y + P^\circ - 2P. \tag{3.2}$$

Like the demand equations in Chapter 2, Equation 3.2 predicts sales quantity once one has specified values of the so-called explanatory variables appearing on the right-hand side.[3] What does the equation say about the present state of demand? Currently your airline and your competitor are charging the same one-way fare, $240. The current level of income in the region is 105.[4] Putting these values into Equation 3.2, we find that

$$Q = 25 + 3(105) + 1(240) - 2(240)$$
$$= 100 \text{ seats.}$$

A comparison of this prediction with your airline's recent experience shows this equation to be quite accurate. In the past three months, the average number of coach seats sold per flight (week by week) consistently fell in the 90- to

---

[3] Methods of estimating and forecasting demand are presented in Chapters 4 and 5.

[4] This value is an *index* of aggregate income—business profits and personal income—in Texas and Florida. The index is set such that *real* income (i.e., after accounting for inflation) in 2002 (the so-called base year) equals 100. Thus, a current value of 105 means that regional income has increased 5 percent in real terms since then. In the depth of the Texas recession, the index stood at 87, a 13 percent reduction in real income relative to the base year.

105-seat range. Since 180 coach seats are available on the flight, the airline's load factor is $100/180 = 55.5$ percent.

The demand equation can be used to test the effect of changes in any of the explanatory variables. From Equation 3.2, we see that

1. For each point increase in the income index, 3 additional seats will be sold.
2. For each $10 increase in the airline's fare, 20 fewer seats will be sold.
3. For each $10 increase in the competitor's fare, 10 additional seats will be sold.

Each of these results assumes the effect in question is the *only* change that occurs; that is, all other factors are held constant. In fact, the *total change* in demand caused by simultaneous changes in the explanatory variables can be expressed as

$$\Delta Q = 3\Delta Y + 1\Delta P^\circ - 2\Delta P, \qquad [3.3]$$

where Δ means "change in." Thus, if income increases by 5 percentage points while both airline prices are cut by $15, we find $\Delta Q = 3(5) + 1(-15) - 2(-15) = 30$ seats. Your airline would expect to sell 30 additional seats on each flight.

CHECK STATION 1   Use Equation 3.3 to compute the change in sales, ΔQ, that will result from $\Delta Y = -8$, $\Delta P^\circ = 12$, and $\Delta P = 20$.

The Demand Curve and Shifting Demand

Suppose that, in the immediate future, regional income is expected to remain at 105 and the competitor's fare will stay at $240. However, your airline's fare is not set in stone, and you naturally are interested in testing the effect of different possible coach prices. Substituting the values of Y and P° into Equation 3.2's demand function, we find that

$$Q = 25 + 3(105) + 1(240) - 2P, \qquad [3.4]$$
$$= 580 - 2P.$$

Like the basic demand equation facing the microchip producer in Chapter 2, Equation 3.4 relates the quantity of the good or service sold to its price. Here, however, it is important to remember that, in the background, all other factors affecting demand are held constant (at the values $Y = 105$ and $P^\circ = 240$). Of course, it is a simple matter to graph this demand equation as a demand curve. (Do this yourself as practice.) As usual, the demand curve is downward sloping.[5]

Starting from an initial price, by varying the coach fare up or down, we move *along* (respectively up and down) the demand curve. A higher price means lower sales. But what happens if there is a change in one of the other factors that affect demand? As we now will show, *such a change causes a shift in the demand curve.* To illustrate, suppose that a year from now P° is expected to be unchanged but Y is forecast to grow to 119. What will the demand curve look like a year hence? To answer this question, we substitute the new value, Y = 119 (along with P° = 240), into the demand function to obtain

$$Q = 622 - 2P. \qquad [3.5]$$

Now compare the new and old demand equations. Observe that they are of the same form with one key difference: The constant term of the new demand curve is larger than that of the old. Therefore, if your airline were to leave its own fare unchanged a year from now, you would enjoy a greater volume of coach traffic. Figure 3.1 underscores this point by graphing both the old and new demand curves. Note that the new demand curve constitutes a parallel shift to the right (toward greater sales quantities) of the old demand curve. At P = $240, current demand is 100 seats per flight. At the same fare, coach demand one year from now is forecast to be 142 seats (due to the increase in regional income), a gain of 42 seats. In fact, for *any* fare your airline might set (and leave unchanged), demand a year from now is predicted to grow by 42 seats. Thus, we confirm that there is a 42-unit rightward shift in the demand curve from old to new demand.

Another way to think about the effect of the increase in regional income is to write down the equations for the market-clearing price for the old and new demand curves. These are

$$P = 290 - Q/2 \text{ (old)} \qquad [3.6]$$
$$P = 311 - Q/2 \text{ (new)}$$

Thus, if your airline seeks to sell the same number of seats a year from now that it does today, it can do so while raising the coach ticket price by $21 (the difference between 311 and 290). To see this in Figure 3.1, fix the quantity and read the higher price off the new demand curve.

---

[5] We can graph the demand *curve* (by putting quantity and price on the respective axes), but we cannot graph the demand *function* (because this involves four variables and we do not have four axes). Thus, graphing a particular demand curve requires holding all other factors constant.

FIGURE 3.1

A Shift in Demand

Due to growth in regional income, the airline's demand curve in one year's time lies to the right of its current demand curve. At an unchanged price a year from now, it expects to sell 42 additional seats on each flight.

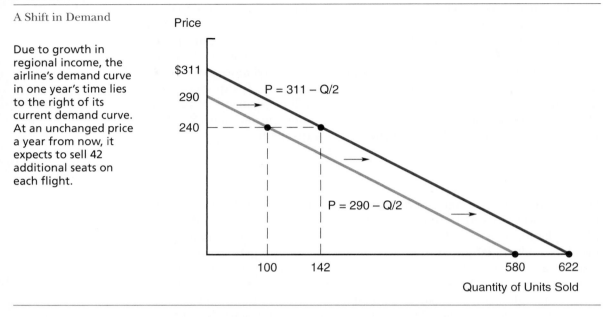

General Determinants of Demand

The example of demand for air travel is representative of the results found for most goods or services. Obviously, the *good's own price* is a key determinant of demand. (We will say much more about price later in the chapter.) Close behind in importance is the *level of income* of the potential purchasers of the good or service. A basic definition is useful in describing the effect of income on sales: A product is called a **normal good** if an increase in income raises its sales. In our example, air travel is a normal good. For any normal good, sales vary directly with income; that is, the coefficient on income in the demand equation is positive. As an empirical matter, most goods and services are normal. Any increase in consumer income is spread over a wide variety of goods and services. (Of course, the extra spending on a given good may be small or even nearly zero.) Likewise, when income is reduced in an economy that is experiencing a recession, demand falls across the spectrum of normal goods. For a small category of goods (such as certain food staples), an increase in income causes a reduction in spending. These are termed **inferior goods**. For instance, an individual of moderate means may regularly consume a large quantity of corned beef and beans. But, after experiencing an increase in income, the individual can better afford other foods and, therefore, can reduce his consumption of the old staples.

A third set of factors affecting demand are the prices of *substitute* and *complementary* goods. As the term suggests, a **substitute good** competes with and can substitute for the good in question. In the airline example, travel on one airline serving the same intercity route is a very close substitute for travel on the other. Accordingly, *an increase in the price of the substitute good or service causes an increase in demand for the good in question* (by making it relatively more attractive to purchase). Note that substitution in demand can occur at many levels. For instance, the airline's sales along the route are affected not only by changes in competing airline fares but also by train and bus fares and auto-operating costs. To a greater or lesser degree, these other modes of transportation are substitutes for air travel.

A pair of goods are **complementary** if an increase in demand for one causes an increase in demand for the other. For instance, an increase in the sales of new automobiles will have a positive effect on the sales of new tires. In particular, tire manufacturers are very interested in the prices car manufacturers announce for new models. They know that discount auto prices will spur not only the sales of cars but also the sales of tires. The price of a complementary good enters negatively into the demand function; that is, *an increase in the price of a complementary good reduces demand for the good in question.* For example, Florida resort packages and travel between Houston and Florida are to some extent complementary. Thus, the price of resort packages would enter negatively into the demand function for travel along the route.[6]

Finally, a wide variety of other factors may affect the demand for particular goods and services. Normal *population* growth of prime groups that consume the good or service will increase demand. As the populations of Houston and the Florida city grow, so will air travel between them. The main determinant of soft-drink sales is the number of individuals in the 10-to-25 age group; for beer sales, it is the number in the 18-to-45 age group. Changes in preferences and tastes are another important factor. Various trends over the past 15 years have supported growth in demand for new foods (diet, natural, fast), new electronic products (cell phones, digital cameras, CD and DVD players), new recreation services (exercise, travel, tanning salons, and so on). The list is endless.

Computers and Complementarity

In the computer industry, hardware (the computer itself) and software (programs that instruct the computer how to carry out its operations) are the ultimate complements. Customers do not value either for its own sake. Rather, they care about how well the combination performs necessary tasks: handling e-mail, managing databases, performing complex calculations, or word processing. Different firms dominate the hardware and software markets. Nonetheless, because of the close relationship between hardware and software, the fortunes of these firms are tied together.

---

[6]Although we say that autos and tires are complementary goods, the cross-price effects need not be of comparable magnitudes. Auto prices have a large impact on tire sales, but tire prices have a very minor impact on auto sales because they are a small fraction of the full cost of a new car.

Complementarity explains many of the basic features of the computer industry. For instance,

1. Over the last 30 years, the cost of building a computer's hardware has declined significantly, leading to lower prices, greater sales, and larger profits. However, software development costs rose sharply during the 1980s before moderating in the last decade. Packed with ever more numerous features, many of today's software programs suffer from "advancing bloat," hogging more and more memory while running slowly. It is an open question whether software advances will keep pace with hardware innovations in the future.

2. Compatibility is essential for both markets. To meet customer needs, a firm's computer must be able to run popular software programs. Conversely, regardless of its technical merits, a successful software program must be transferable across different types of computers. In short, without compatibility, the advantages of hardware-software complementarity are greatly diminished or even lost. The advantages of compatibility are evident in hindsight but were not so obvious at the time. IBM's "breakthrough" machines of the 1960s, its 360-computer line, offered full software compatibility—all machines in the line used the same system software—but at an enormous development cost to the company. The success of IBM's compatibility strategy (its existing customers moved up to more powerful IBM machines using familiar software) was not lost on the rest of the industry.

3. Companies quickly learned that price reductions in one market increased revenues not only directly but also in the complementary market. In particular, price cuts for popular software programs spurred purchases of personal computers. Selling computers bundled with low-priced software continues to be a common marketing strategy.

ELASTICITY OF DEMAND

Price Elasticity

Price elasticity measures the responsiveness of a good's sales to changes in its price. This concept is important for two reasons. First, knowledge of a good's price elasticity allows firms to predict the impact of price changes on unit sales. Second, price elasticity guides the firm's profit-maximizing pricing decisions.

Let's begin with a basic definition: The **price elasticity of demand** is the ratio of the percentage change in quantity and the percentage change in the good's price, all other factors held constant. In algebraic terms, we have

$$E_P = \frac{\% \text{ change in Q}}{\% \text{ change in P}} \qquad [3.7]$$

$$= \frac{\Delta Q/Q}{\Delta P/P} = \frac{(Q_1 - Q_0)/Q_0}{(P_1 - P_0)/P_0}$$

where P_0 and Q_0 are the initial price and quantity, respectively. For example, consider the airline's demand curve as described in Equation 3.4. At the current $240 fare, 100 coach seats are sold. If the airline cut its price to $235, 110 seats would be demanded. Therefore, we find

$$E_P = \frac{(110 - 100)/100}{(235 - 240)/240} = \frac{10.0\%}{-2.1\%} = -4.8.$$

In this example, price was cut by 2.1 percent (the denominator), with the result that quantity increased by 10 percent (the numerator). Therefore, the price elasticity (the ratio of these two effects) is -4.8. Notice that the change in quantity was due solely to the price change. The other factors that potentially could affect sales (income and the competitor's price) did not change. (The requirement "all other factors held constant" in the definition is essential for a meaningful notion of price elasticity.) In short, we observe that there is a large percentage quantity change for a relatively small price change. (The ratio is almost fivefold.) Demand is very responsive to price.

Price elasticity, as we shall see, is a key ingredient in applying marginal analysis to determine optimal prices. Because marginal analysis works by evaluating "small" changes taken with respect to an initial decision, it often is useful to measure elasticity with respect to an infinitesimally small change in price. In this instance, we write elasticity as

$$E_P = \frac{dQ/Q}{dP/P}. \qquad [3.8]$$

We can rearrange this expression to read

$$E_P = \left(\frac{dQ}{dP}\right)\left(\frac{P}{Q}\right). \qquad [3.8']$$

In words, the elasticity (measured at price P) depends directly on dQ/dP, the derivative of the demand function with respect to P (as well as on the ratio of P to Q).

The algebraic expressions in Equations 3.7 and 3.8 are referred to as *point elasticities* because they link percentage quantity and price changes *at a price–quantity point on the demand curve*. Although most widely used, point elasticity measures are not the only way to describe changes in price and quantity. A closely related measure is *arc* price elasticity, which is defined as

$$E_P = \frac{\Delta Q / \bar{Q}}{\Delta P / \bar{P}}$$

where $\bar{Q}$ is the average of the two quantities, $\bar{Q} = (Q_0 + Q_1)/2$, and $\bar{P}$ is the average of the two prices, $\bar{P} = (P_0 + P_1)/2$. In the airline example, the average quantity is 105 seats, the average price is \$237.50, and the arc price elasticity is $(10/105)/(-5/237.5) = -4.5$.

The main advantage of the arc elasticity measure is that it treats the prices and quantities symmetrically; that is, it does not distinguish between the "initial" and "final" prices and quantities. Regardless of the "starting" point, the elasticity is the same. In contrast, in computing the elasticity via Equation 3.7, one must be careful to specify P_0 and Q_0. To illustrate, suppose the initial airfare is \$235 and 110 seats are filled. The elasticity associated with a price hike to \$240 (and a drop to 100 seats) is $E_P = (-10/110)/(5/235) = -4.3$. Thus, we see that the elasticity associated with the change is -4.8 or -4.3, depending on the starting point.

The overriding advantage of point elasticities (Equation 3.8) is their application in conjunction with marginal analysis. For instance, a firm's optimal pricing policy depends directly on its estimate of the price elasticity, $E_P = (dQ/Q)/(dP/P)$. In this and later chapters (unless there is a statement to the contrary), we will focus exclusively on point elasticities in our analysis of optimal decisions.[7]

Elasticity measures the sensitivity of demand with respect to price. In describing elasticities, it is useful to start with a basic benchmark. First, demand is said to be **unitary elastic** if $E_P = -1$. In this case, the percentage change in price (the preceding denominator) is exactly matched by the resulting percentage change in quantity (the numerator) but in the opposite direction. In an important sense made explicit later, movements in price and quantity just cancel each other out. Second, demand is **inelastic** if $-1 < E_P < 0$. The term *inelastic* suggests that demand is relatively unresponsive to price: The percentage change in quantity is less (in absolute value) than the percentage change in price. Finally, demand is **elastic** if $E_P < -1$. In this case, an initial change in price causes a larger percentage change in quantity. In short, elastic demand is highly responsive, or sensitive, to changes in price.

The easiest way to understand the meaning of inelastic and elastic demand is to examine two extreme cases. Figure 3.2a depicts a vertical demand curve representing **perfectly inelastic** demand, $E_P = 0$. Here sales are constant

---

[7] So long as the price change is very small, the point elasticity calculated via Equation 3.7 will vary little whether the higher or lower price is taken as the starting point. Furthermore, this value will closely approximate the exact measure of elasticity given by Equation 3.8.

FIGURE 3.2

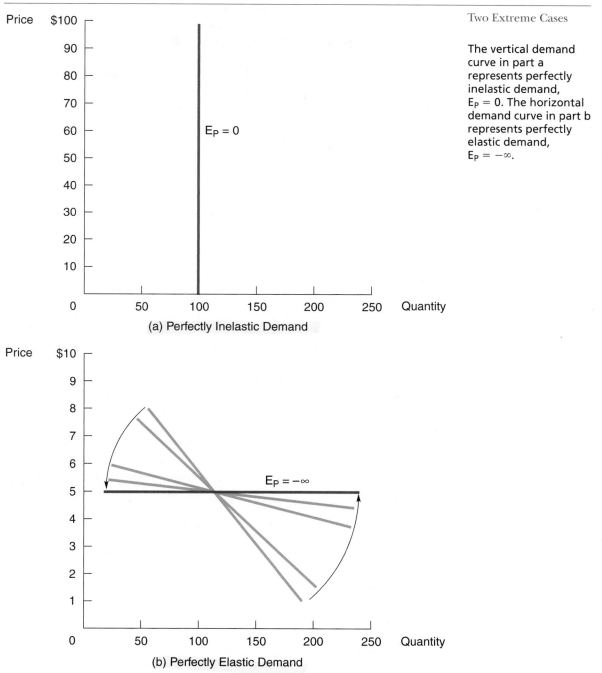

(a) Perfectly Inelastic Demand

(b) Perfectly Elastic Demand

Two Extreme Cases

The vertical demand curve in part a represents perfectly inelastic demand, $E_P = 0$. The horizontal demand curve in part b represents perfectly elastic demand, $E_P = -\infty$.

(at Q = 100) no matter how high the price charged. Thus, for any price change, the quantity change is zero and, therefore, so is the elasticity.[8] Figure 3.2b depicts the opposite extreme: a horizontal demand curve where demand is **perfectly elastic**, $E_P = -\infty$. The horizontal curve indicates that the firm can sell as much output as it likes at the given price; whether it sells a large or small output quantity will have no effect on its price. In this case, we say that the "market" determines the firm's price. (Note also that the firm can sell nothing at a higher-than-market price.) Demand is called perfectly elastic because sales are infinitely sensitive to price. To see this, consider the nearly horizontal demand curve in Figure 3.2 and observe that any small price change causes a very large quantity change in the opposite direction. For horizontal demand, the quantity change becomes infinite for any price change, even one approaching zero; thus, the elasticity ratio becomes infinite, $E_P = -\infty$.

CHECK STATION 2   "The demand for automobiles must be less elastic than the demand for CD players because a $50 reduction in the price of cars does not affect the number sold nearly as much as a $50 reduction in the price of CD players." Is this statement correct? Explain.

FACTORS AFFECTING PRICE ELASTICITY   What determines whether the demand for a good is price elastic or price inelastic? In general, we can identify four factors that affect elasticity. (The list is not exhaustive, but it does contain the most important factors.)

One important factor is the degree to which the good is a necessity. If a good or service is not considered essential, the purchaser can easily do without it—if and when the price becomes too high—even if there are no close substitutes. In that case, demand is elastic. If the good is a necessary component of consumption, it is more difficult to do without it in the face of a price increase. Thus, demand tends to be price inelastic.

A second important factor is the availability of substitutes. With many substitutes, consumers easily can shift to other alternatives if the price of one good becomes too high; demand is elastic. Without close substitutes, switching becomes more difficult; demand is less elastic. For this reason, *industry demand tends to be much less elastic than the demand facing a particular firm in the industry*. If one firm's price increases, consumers are able to go to other firms quite easily. Thus, the demand facing a single firm in an industry may be quite elastic because competitors produce goods that are close substitutes. But consider what happens if the *industry* price goes up; that is, all firms in the industry increase their prices in unison. In this case, price-sensitive consumers are limited in their course of action: One choice is to do

---

[8] Caution: The strictly vertical demand should be thought of as a hypothetical, limiting case, not something that could occur in practice. If it did occur, the firm could raise the good's price as high as it wished, maintaining an unchanged level of sales. By doing so, it would earn unlimited profit. We all know, however, that there is no such "free lunch" in the business world.

without the good, another is to find a good in another industry to replace it. If these options are infeasible, the third option is to pay the higher price. Thus, industry demand is less elastic. The same point applies to the case in which a single monopolist dominates an industry or product line. Other things being equal, the monopolist's demand is less elastic (since it is the sole producer) than the demand facing a particular firm in a multifirm industry.

A third determinant of price elasticity is the proportion of income a consumer spends on the good in question. The issue here is the cost of searching for suitable alternatives to the good. It takes time and money to compare substitute products. If an individual spends a significant portion of income on a good, he or she will find it worthwhile to search for and compare the prices of other goods. Thus, the consumer is price sensitive. If spending on the good represents only a small portion of total income, however, the search for substitutes will not be worth the time, effort, and expense. Thus, other things being equal, the demand for small-ticket items tends to be relatively inelastic.

Finally, time of adjustment is an important influence on elasticity. When the price of gasoline dramatically increased in the 1970s, consumers initially had little recourse but to pay higher prices at the pump. Most of the population continued to drive to work in large, relatively inefficient cars. As time passed, however, consumers made adjustments. Some commuters switched from automobiles to buses or other means of public transit. Gas guzzlers were replaced by smaller, more fuel-efficient cars. Some workers moved closer to their jobs, and when jobs turned over, workers found new jobs closer to their homes. Thus, in the short run, the demand for gasoline was relatively inelastic. But in the long run, demand appeared to be much more elastic as people were able to cut back consumption by a surprising amount. Thus, the time of adjustment was crucial. As the gasoline experience illustrates, it generally is true that demand is more elastic in the long run than in the short run.

Other Elasticities

The elasticity concept can be applied to any explanatory variable that affects sales. Many of these variables—income, the prices of substitutes and complements, and changes in population or preferences—have already been mentioned. (An additional important variable affecting sales is the firm's spending on advertising and promotion.) To illustrate, consider the elasticity of demand with respect to income (Y). This is defined as

$$E_Y = \frac{\% \text{ change in Q}}{\% \text{ change in Y}} = \frac{\Delta Q/Q}{\Delta Y/Y}$$

in a manner exactly analogous to the earlier price elasticity definition.[9] **Income elasticity** links percentage changes in sales to changes in income, *all other factors held constant.* For example, the income elasticity of demand for spending on groceries is about .25; that is, a 10 percent increase in income results in only about a 2.5 percent increase in spending in this category. In other words, a household's consumption of groceries is relatively insensitive to changes in income. In contrast, restaurant expenditures are highly sensitive to income changes. The income elasticity for this type of spending is about 3.0.

A main impact on the sales outlook for an industry, a firm, or a particular good or service is the overall strength of the economy. When the economy grows strongly, so do personal income, business profits, and government income. Gains in these income categories generate increased spending on a wide variety of goods and services. Conversely, when income falls during a recession, so do sales across the economy. Income elasticity, thus, provides an important measure of the sensitivity of sales for a given product to swings in the economy. For instance, if $E_Y = 1$, sales move exactly in step with changes in income. If $E_Y > 1$, sales are highly *cyclical,* that is, sensitive to income. For an inferior good, sales are *countercyclical,* that is, move in the opposite direction of income and $E_Y < 0$.

CROSS-PRICE ELASTICITIES A final, commonly used elasticity links changes in a good's sales to changes in the prices of related goods. **Cross-price elasticity** is defined as

$$E_{P^\circ} = \frac{\Delta Q/Q}{\Delta P^\circ/P^\circ}$$

where P° denotes the price of a related good or service. If the goods in question are substitutes, the cross-elasticity will be positive. For instance, if a 5 percent cut in a competitor's intercity fare is expected to reduce the airline's ticket sales by 2 percent, we find $E_{P^\circ} = (-2\%)/(-5\%) = .4$. The magnitude of E_{P° provides a useful measure of the substitutability of the two goods.[10] For example, if $E_{P^\circ} = .05$, sales of the two goods are almost unrelated. If E_{P° is very large, however, the two goods are nearly perfect substitutes. Finally, if a pair of goods

---

[9] If an infinitesimal change is considered, the corresponding elasticity expression is $E_Y = (dQ/Q)/(dY/Y)$. In addition, when multiple factors affect demand, the "partial derivative" notation emphasizes the separate effect of income changes on demand, all other factors held constant. In this case, we write $E_Y = (\partial Q/Q)/(\partial Y/Y)$.

[10] We could also examine the effect of a change in the airline's fare on the competitor's ticket sales. Note that the two cross-price elasticities may be very different in magnitude. For instance, in our example the airline flies only half as many flights as its competitor. Given its smaller market share and presence, one would predict that changes in the airline's price would have a much smaller impact on the sales of its larger rival than vice versa.

TABLE 3.1

Good or Service	Price Elasticity	Income Elasticity
Air travel:		
Business	−.18	1.1
Nonbusiness	−.38	1.8
Automobiles:		1.9
Subcompact	−.81	
Luxury	−2.1	
Beef	−.5	.51
Cigarettes:		
All smokers	−.7	
Ages 15–18	−1.4	
Gasoline (1-year)	−.32	.20
Housing		.34
Telephone calls:		
Long distance	−.5	1.0

Estimated Price and Income Elasticities for Selected Goods and Services

Source: Elasticities were compiled by the authors from articles in economic journals and other published sources.

are complements, the cross-elasticity is negative. An increase in the complementary good's price will adversely affect sales.

Table 3.1 provides estimated price and income elasticities for selected goods and services.

Price Elasticity and Prediction

Price elasticity is an essential tool for estimating the sales response to possible price changes. A simple rearrangement of the elasticity definition (Equation 3.7) gives the predictive equation:

$$\Delta Q/Q = E_P(\Delta P/P) \qquad [3.9]$$

For instance, in Table 3.1, the short-term (i.e., one-year) price elasticity of demand for gasoline is approximately −.3. This indicates that if the average price of gasoline were to increase from $1.50 to $1.80 per gallon (a 20 percent increase), then consumption of gasoline (in gallons) would fall by only 6 percent (−.3 × 20%). The table also shows that the price elasticity of demand for luxury cars is -2.1. A modest 5 percent increase in their average sticker price implies a 10.5 percent drop in sales. (Caution: Equation 3.9 is exact for very small changes but only an approximation for large percentage changes, over which elasticities may vary.)

How does one estimate the impact on sales from changes in two or more factors that affect demand? A simple example will illustrate the method. In Table 3.1, the price and income elasticities for nonbusiness air travel are estimated to be $E_P = -.38$ and $E_Y = 1.8$, respectively. In the coming year, average airline fares are expected to rise by 8 percent and income by 5 percent. What will be the impact on the number of tickets sold to nonbusiness travelers? The answer is found by adding the separate effects due to each change:

$$\Delta Q/Q = E_P(\Delta P/P) + E_Y(\Delta Y/Y) \qquad [3.10]$$

Therefore, $\Delta Q/Q = (-.38)(8\%) + (1.8)(5\%) = 6\%$. Sales are expected to increase by about 6 percent.

DEMAND ANALYSIS AND OPTIMAL PRICING

In this section, we put demand analysis to work by examining three important managerial decisions: (1) the special case of revenue maximization, (2) optimal markup pricing, and (3) price discrimination.

Price Elasticity, Revenue, and Marginal Revenue

What can we say about the elasticity along any downward-sloping, linear demand curve? First, we must be careful to specify the starting quantity and price (the point on the demand curve) from which percentage changes are measured. From Equation 3.8, we know that $E_P = (dQ/dP)(P/Q)$. The slope of the demand curve is dP/dQ (as it is conventionally drawn with price on the vertical axis). Thus, the first term in the elasticity expression, dQ/dP, is simply the inverse of this slope and is constant everywhere along the curve. The term P/Q decreases as one moves downward along the curve. Thus, along a linear demand curve, moving to lower prices and greater quantities reduces elasticity; that is, demand becomes more inelastic.

As a concrete illustration of this point, consider a software firm that is trying to determine the optimal price for one of its popular software programs. Management estimates this product's demand curve to be

$$Q = 1{,}600 - 4P,$$

where Q is copies sold per week and P is in dollars. We note for future reference that $dQ/dP = -4$. Figure 3.3a shows this demand curve as well as the

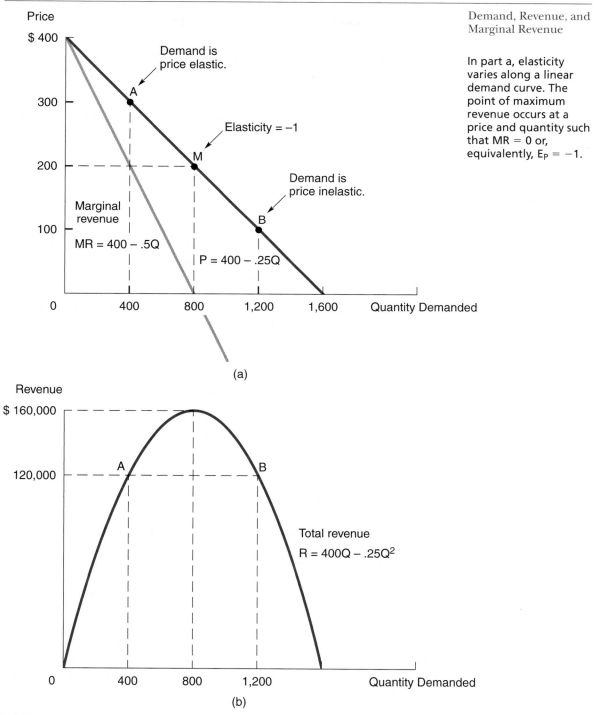

FIGURE 3.3

Demand, Revenue, and
Marginal Revenue

In part a, elasticity
varies along a linear
demand curve. The
point of maximum
revenue occurs at a
price and quantity such
that MR = 0 or,
equivalently, $E_P = -1$.

Price

$ 400

Demand is
price elastic.

300

A

Elasticity = −1

M

200

Demand is
price inelastic.

Marginal
revenue

B

100

MR = 400 − .5Q

P = 400 − .25Q

0   400   800   1,200   1,600   Quantity Demanded

(a)

Revenue

$ 160,000

120,000   A   B

Total revenue

R = 400Q − .25Q²

0   400   800   1,200   Quantity Demanded

(b)

associated marginal revenue curve. In the figure, the midpoint of the demand curve is marked by point M: Q = 800 and P = $200. Two other points, A and B, along the demand curve also are shown.

The figure depicts a useful result. The linear demand curve can be divided into two regions. *Exactly midway along the linear demand curve, price elasticity is unity.* To the northwest (at higher prices and lower quantities), demand is elastic. To the southeast (at lower prices and greater quantities), demand is inelastic. For example, consider a point on the inelastic part of the curve such as B: P = $100 and Q = 1,200. Here the point elasticity is $E_P = (dQ/dP)(P/Q) = (-4)(100/1,200) = -.33$. Conversely, at a point on the elastic portion of the demand curve such as A (P = $300 and Q = 400), the point elasticity is $E_P = (-4)(300/400) = -3.0$.

CHECK STATION 3   Compute the price elasticity at point M. Show that the elasticity is unity. This result holds for the midpoint of any linear demand curve.

Figure 3.3b depicts the firm's total revenue curve for different sales volumes. It displays the familiar shape of an upside-down U. Total revenue increases as quantity increases up to the revenue peak; at still higher quantities, revenue falls.

Let's carefully trace the relationship between changes in revenue and price elasticity. Suppose management of the software firm is operating at point A on the demand curve in Figure 3.3a. Its price is $300, it sells 400 copies of the software program, and it earns $120,000 in revenue per week. Could the firm increase its revenue by cutting its price to spur greater sales? If demand is elastic, the answer is yes. Under elastic demand, the percentage increase in quantity is greater than the percentage fall in price. Thus, revenue—the product of price and quantity—must increase. The positive change in quantity more than compensates for the fall in price. Figure 3.3b shows clearly that revenue increases from point A when the firm moves to greater quantities (and lower prices). Starting from any point of elastic demand, the firm can increase revenue by reducing its price.

Now suppose the software firm is operating originally at point B, where demand is inelastic. In this case, the firm can increase revenue by raising its price. Because demand is inelastic, the percentage drop in quantity of sales is smaller than the percentage increase in price. With price rising by more than quantity falls, revenue necessarily increases. Again, the revenue graph in Figure 3.3b tells the story. Starting from point B, the firm increases its revenue by reducing its quantity (and raising its price). So long as demand is inelastic, revenue moves in the same direction as price. By raising price and reducing quantity, the firm moves back toward the revenue peak.

Putting these two results together, we see that when demand is inelastic or elastic, revenue can be increased (by a price hike or cut, respectively). It follows that revenue is maximized when neither a price hike nor a cut will help; that is, when demand is unitary elastic, $E_P = -1$. In the software example, the revenue-maximizing quantity is Q = 800 (see part b of Figure 3.3b). This quantity (along with the price, P = \$200) is precisely the point of unitary elasticity (in part a).

Our discussion has suggested an interesting and important relationship between marginal revenue and price elasticity. The same point can be made mathematically. By definition, $MR = dR/dQ = d(PQ)/dQ$. The derivative of this product (see Rule 5 of the appendix to Chapter 2) is

$$MR = P(dQ/dQ) + (dP/dQ)Q \qquad [3.11]$$
$$= P + P(dP/dQ)(Q/P)$$
$$= P[1 + (dP/dQ)(Q/P)]$$
$$= P[1 + 1/E_P].$$

For instance, if demand is elastic (say, $E_P = -3$), MR is positive; that is, an increase in quantity (via a reduction in price) will increase total revenue. If demand is inelastic (say, $E_P = -.6$), MR is negative; an increase in quantity causes total revenue to decline. If elasticity is precisely -1, MR is zero. Figure 3.3a shows clearly the relationship between MR and E_P. More generally, the result in Equation 3.11 holds for *any* demand curve, not only for the case of linear demand.

Maximizing Revenue

As we saw in Chapter 2, there generally is a conflict between the goals of maximizing revenue and maximizing profit. Clearly, maximizing profit is the appropriate objective because it takes into account not only revenues but also relevant costs. In some important special cases, however, the two goals coincide or are equivalent. This occurs when the firm faces what is sometimes called a **pure selling problem**: a situation in which it supplies a good or service while incurring *no* variable cost (or a variable cost so small that it safely can be ignored). It should be clear that, without any variable costs, the firm maximizes its ultimate profit by setting price and output to gain as much revenue as possible (from which any *fixed* costs then are paid). The following pricing problems serve as examples.

- A software firm seeks to determine the optimal selling price for its software.
- A manufacturer must sell (or otherwise dispose of) an inventory of unsold merchandise.
- A professional sports franchise must set its ticket prices for its home games.
- An airline is attempting to fill its empty seats on a regularly scheduled flight.

In each of these examples, variable costs are absent (or very small). The cost of an additional software copy (documentation and floppy disk included) is trivial. In the case of airline or sports tickets, revenues crucially depend on how many tickets are sold. The cost of an additional passenger or spectator is negligible once the flight or event has been scheduled. As for inventory, production costs are sunk; selling costs probably are small. Thus, in each case the firm maximizes profits by setting price and output to maximize revenue.

How does the firm determine its revenue-maximizing price and output? There are two equivalent answers to this question. The first answer is to apply Chapter 2's fundamental rule: MR = MC. In the case of a pure selling problem, marginal cost is zero. Thus, the rule becomes MR = 0, exactly as one would expect. This rule instructs the manager to push sales to the point at which there is no more additional revenue to be had—MR = 0—and no further. If MR were positive, the firm should increase output to increase revenue. If MR were negative, the firm should cut back its quantity of sales. In short, the point of maximum revenue is attained at the sales quantity for which MR = 0.

From the preceding discussion, we have established a second equivalent answer: Revenue is maximized at the point of unitary elasticity. If demand were inelastic or elastic, revenue could be increased by raising or lowering price, respectively. The following proposition sums up these results.

| Revenue is maximized at the price and quantity for which marginal revenue is zero or, equivalently, the price elasticity of demand is unity (-1).

Note that this result confirms that the point of unitary elasticity occurs at the midpoint of a linear demand curve. For the sales quantity at the midpoint, marginal revenue is exactly zero (since the MR curve cuts the horizontal axis at the midpoint quantity). But when MR = 0, it is also true that $E_P = -1$.

CHECK STATION 4   The management of a professional sports team has a 36,000-seat stadium it wishes to fill. It recognizes, however, that the number of seats sold (Q) is very sensitive to average ticket prices (P). It estimates demand to be $Q = 60,000 - 3,000P$. Assuming the team's costs are known and do not vary with attendance, what is management's optimal pricing policy?

Pricing the Olympics Telecasts and Online Access

It is not easy to estimate the state of demand for a new product or one with a very short track record of sales. One famous example of overestimating demand involved Triplecast, NBC and Cablevision's pay-per-view cable coverage of the 1992 Summer Olympics in Barcelona. Based on extensive surveys of potential demand, the partners hoped to raise $250 million in revenue by attracting some 2 million subscribers for three channels of nonstop Olympics coverage over 15 days. Accordingly, NBC set the average package price at $125 for complete coverage and offered a separate price of $29.95 per day. However, as the games began, fewer than 300,000 homes had subscribed and even with aggressive price cutting no more than 500,000 sports fans tuned in.

America Online (AOL) experienced the opposite problem when it instituted a radical pricing shift in November 1996. In a bid to increase its customer base, it replaced its old monthly fee of $9.95 (good for five free hours) and $2.95 for each additional hour by a fixed monthly fee of $19.95 for unlimited access. The results should have been predictable. AOL's customer base did increase, but, more important, current customers more than doubled their daily time online. Constrained by a fixed capacity, AOL's system overloaded. Customers received busy signals and experienced interminable waits for access. One commentator likened the new pricing policy to offering a perpetual all-you-can-eat buffet to food lovers, who once seated would eat through breakfast, lunch, and dinner, fearing they would not get back in if they gave up their table. Customers were disaffected, and AOL was forced by regulators to give widespread refunds while it scrambled to increase its network capacity at a cost of $350 million.

What are the lessons from these examples? In the case of Triplecast, it appears that management faced a pure selling problem, the marginal cost of each additional subscriber being insignificant. Unfortunately, management dramatically misjudged its demand curve and also the point of maximum revenue along it. Once it recognized the depressed state of demand, management instituted a dramatic price cut—its best course of action to capture what revenue was available. Over time, the cable companies reduced their package price from $125 to $99 to $79 and the daily price from $29.95 to $19.95 to $11.95. However, these actions at best were able only to stem large losses.

For AOL, there appears to be a happier ending. Despite the high monetary and reputation cost of its one-price policy, the company achieved a key objective: raising its customer base over 18 months from 8 million to some 11 million subscribers. Fueled by revenues from retailers, advertisers, and publishers, who would pay for access to AOL's customers, the company earned its first quarterly profits in 1998. It has since raised its monthly fee to $21.95 while continuing to expand its network capacity.

THE CONSTANT ELASTICITY DEMAND FUNCTION   As we will see in Chapter 4, linear demand curves are commonly estimated in practice and have the advantage of being relatively easy to analyze. But they are not the only demand equations used in business forecasting and decision making. The **constant elasticity** demand equation also is used and estimated widely. This equation takes the form

$$Q = kP^{\beta}, \qquad\qquad [3.12]$$

where k and β are numerical coefficients. An example is the equation $Q = 100P^{-2} = 100/P^2$. (Here k and β take on the values 100 and -2, respectively.) Figure 3.4 shows the graph of this equation. As always, the demand curve is downward sloping, but here the graph is curved rather than linear. The

FIGURE 3.4

The Constant Elasticity Demand Function

Elasticity is constant along the demand curve shown.

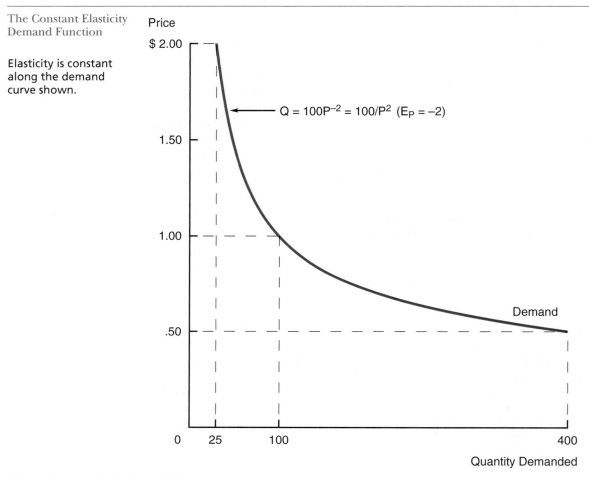

demand curve is convex; at low prices it is relatively flat, at high prices quite steep.

As the term suggests, this demand curve has a constant price elasticity at any point along its length. Let's check this for the equation $Q = 100P^{-2}$. Applying the appropriate derivative, we find $dQ/dP = (-2)(100)P^{-3}$. Thus, $E_P = (dQ/dP)(P/Q) = [-2(100)P^{-3}P]/[100P^{-2}] = -2$. For any P and Q pair along the demand curve, the elasticity is -2. What is true in this example holds generally: Price elasticity is exactly equal to the power β, $E_P = \beta$.

More generally, suppose the demand function includes multiple factors: say, price, income, and advertising. Then the general form of the power function is

$$Q = kP^{\beta}Y^{\varepsilon}A^{\alpha},$$ [3.13]

where the values ε and α measure the elasticities associated with income (Y) and advertising (A), respectively. For instance, if ε equals 2.1, then, other things being equal, a 3 percent increase in income will cause a 6.3 percent increase in sales.

Optimal Markup Pricing

There is a close link between demand for a firm's product and the firm's optimal pricing policy. In the remainder of this chapter, we will take a close and careful look at the trade-off between price and profit. Recall that in Chapter 2, the focus was squarely on the firm's quantity decision. Once the firm determined its optimal output by weighing marginal revenue and marginal cost, it was a simple matter to set price in order to sell exactly that much output. Now we shift our focus to price and consider a somewhat different trade-off.

To illustrate this trade-off, we can write the firm's contribution as

$$\text{Contribution} = (P - MC)Q,$$

where, for simplicity, MC is assumed to be constant. How should the firm set its price to maximize its contribution (and, therefore, its profit)? The answer depends on how responsive demand is to changes in price, that is, on price elasticity of demand. Raising price increases the firm's contribution per unit (or margin), $P - MC$. But to a greater or lesser degree, a price hike also reduces the total volume of sales Q. If sales are relatively unresponsive to price (i.e., demand is relatively inelastic), the firm can raise its price and increase its margin without significantly reducing quantity. In this instance, the underlying trade-off works in favor of high prices.

Alternatively, suppose demand is very elastic. In this instance, a price increase would bring a large drop in sales to the detriment of total contribution. Here the way to maximize contribution (and profit) is to play the other side of the trade-off. The firm should pursue a policy of discount pricing to maximize profitability. As we shall see, the correct pricing policy depends on a careful analysis of the price elasticity of demand. Indeed, when the firm has the ability to segment markets, it may benefit by trading on demand differences. As noted in this chapter's opening example, airlines set a variety of different ticket prices—charging high fares to less price-sensitive business travelers and discounting prices to economy-minded vacation travelers.

In Chapter 2, we focused on the application of the MR = MC rule as a way to determine the firm's optimal level of output. It is possible to write down and apply a modified (but exactly equivalent) version of the MR = MC rule to derive a simple rule for the firm's profit-maximizing *price*. The firm's optimal price is determined as follows:

$$\frac{P - MC}{P} = \frac{1}{-E_P}. \qquad\qquad [3.14]$$

This equation, called the **markup rule**, indicates that

> The size of the firm's markup (above marginal cost and expressed as a percentage of price) depends inversely on the price elasticity of demand for a good or service.

The markup is always positive. (Note that E_P is negative, so the right-hand side is positive.) What happens as demand becomes more and more price elastic (i.e., price sensitive)? The right-hand side of the markup rule becomes smaller, and so does the optimal markup on the left-hand side. In short, the more elastic demand is, the smaller the markup above marginal cost.[11]

The markup rule is intuitively appealing and is the most commonly noted form of the optimal pricing rule. Nonetheless, to make computations easier, it is useful to rearrange the rule to read

$$P = \left(\frac{E_P}{1 + E_P} \right) MC. \qquad [3.15]$$

Using this formula, Table 3.2 lists optimal prices by elasticity. Again, we see that greater elasticities imply lower prices.

A CAUTION   The markup rule, which characterizes the firm's optimal price, is applicable only in the case of *elastic* demand. Why not inelastic demand? The simple fact is that *the firm's price cannot be profit maximizing if demand is inelastic.* Under inelastic demand, the firm could raise its price and increase its revenue. Because it would sell less output at the higher price, it also would lower its production cost at the same time. Thus, profit would increase. In short, the firm should never operate on the inelastic portion of its demand curve. It should

TABLE 3.2

Elasticities and Optimal Prices	Elasticity	Markup Factor $E_P/(1 + E_P)$	MC	Price
The markup of price above marginal cost varies inversely with the elasticity of demand.	−1.5	3.0	100	300
	−2.0	2.0	100	200
	−3.0	1.5	100	150
	−5.0	1.25	100	125
	−11.0	1.1	100	110
	−∞	1.0	100	100

[11] Here is how the markup rule is derived. From Equation 3.11, we know that $MR = P[1 + 1/E_P]$. Setting $MR = MC$, we have $P + P/E_P = MC$. This can be written as $P − MC = −P/E_P$ and, finally, $[P − MC]/P = −1/E_P$, the markup rule. Thus, the markup rule is derived from and equivalent to the $MR = MC$ rule.

increase profit by raising price and moving to the elastic portion; the optimal markup rule tells it exactly how far it should move.

PRICING IN PRACTICE   The markup rule is a formal expression of the conventional wisdom that *price should depend on both demand and cost*. The rule prescribes how prices should be determined in principle. In practice, managers often adopt other pricing policies. The most common practice is to use *full-cost pricing*. With this method, price is

$$P = (1 + m)AC, \qquad [3.16]$$

where AC denotes total average cost and m denotes the markup of price above average cost.[12]

Our study of optimal managerial decisions suggests two points of criticism about full-cost pricing. First, full-cost pricing uses average cost—the incorrect measure of relevant cost—as its base. The logic of marginal analysis in general and the optimal markup rule (Equation 3.15) in particular show that optimal price and quantity depend on marginal cost. Fixed costs, which are counted in AC but not in MC, have no effect on the choice of optimal price and quantity.[13] Thus, to the extent that AC differs from MC, the full-cost method can lead to pricing errors.

Second, the percentage markup should depend on the elasticity of demand. There is considerable evidence that firms vary their markups in rough accord with price elasticity.[14] Gourmet frozen foods carry much higher markups than generic food items. Inexpensive digital watches ($15 and under) have lower markups than fine Swiss watches or jewelers' watches. Designer dresses and wedding dresses carry much higher markups than off-the-rack dresses. In short, producers' markups are linked to elasticities, at least in a qualitative sense. Nonetheless, it is unlikely that firms' full-cost markups exactly duplicate optimal markups. Obviously, a firm that sets a fixed markup *irrespective* of elasticity is needlessly sacrificing profit.

[12] Average total cost is defined as total cost divided by total output, or AC = C/Q.

[13] Fixed costs obviously are important for the decision about whether to produce the good. For production to be profitable in the long run, price must exceed average cost, $P \geq AC$. If not, the firm should cease production and shut down. Chapter 7 provides an extensive discussion of this so-called shut-down rule for firms producing single and multiple products.

[14] In evaluating the practice of full-cost pricing, the real issue is how close it comes to duplicating optimal markup pricing. Even if firms do not apply the optimal markup rule, they may price as though they did. For instance, a firm that experiments with different full-cost markups may soon discover the profit-maximizing price (without ever computing an elasticity). In contrast, a rival firm that retains a suboptimal price will earn a lower profit and ultimately may be driven from the highly competitive market. So-called natural economic selection (elimination of less profitable firms) means that the surviving firms are ones that have succeeded in earning maximum profits.
In some circumstances, full-cost pricing is a lower-cost alternative to the optimal markup rule. Estimating the price elasticities necessary for setting optimal markups is sometimes quite costly. Accordingly, the firm may choose to continue its current pricing policy (believing it to be approximately optimal) rather than generating new and costly elasticity estimates and setting a new markup.

The U.S. cigarette industry has negotiated with Congress and government agencies to set-tle liability claims against it. Under the proposed settlement, cigarette companies will make fixed annual payments to the government based on their historic market shares. Suppose a manufacturer estimates its marginal cost at $1.00 per pack, its own price elasticity at -2, and sets its price at $2.00. The company's settlement obligations are expected to raise its average total cost per pack by about $.60. What effect will this have on its optimal price?

Price Discrimination

Price discrimination occurs when a firm sells the same good or service to dif-ferent buyers at different prices.[15] As the following examples suggest, price dis-crimination is a common business practice.

- Airlines charge full fares to business travelers, while offering discount fares to vacationers.

- Firms sell the same products under different brand names or labels at different prices.

- Providers of professional services (doctors, consultants, lawyers, etc.) set different rates for different clients.

- Manufacturers introduce products at high prices before gradually dropping price over time.

- Publishers of academic journals charge much higher subscription rates to libraries and institutions than to individual subscribers.

- Businesses offer student and senior citizen discounts for many goods and services.

- Manufacturers sell the same products at higher prices in the retail market than in the wholesale market.

- Movies play in "first-run" theaters at higher ticket prices before being released to suburban theaters at lower prices.

When a firm practices price discrimination, it sets different prices for dif-ferent market segments even though its costs of serving each customer group are the same. Thus, price discrimination is purely demand based. Of course, firms may also charge different prices for the "same" good or service because

[15] Here we are discussing legal methods of price discrimination; that is, we are using the term *dis-crimination* in its neutral sense. Obviously, the civil rights laws prohibit economic discrimination (including unfair pricing practices) based on gender, race, or national origin. The antitrust statutes also limit specific cases of price discrimination that can be shown to significantly reduce competition.

of cost differences. (For instance, transportation cost may be one reason why the same make and model of automobile sells for significantly different prices on the West and East coasts.) But cost-based pricing does not fall under the heading of price discrimination.

Price discrimination is a departure from the pricing model we have examined up to this point. Thus far, the firm has been presumed to set a *single* market-clearing price. Obviously, charging different prices to different market segments, as in the examples just listed, allows the firm considerably more pricing flexibility. More to the point, the firm can increase its profit with a policy of optimal price discrimination (when the opportunity exists).

Two conditions must hold for a firm to practice price discrimination profitably. First, the firm must be able to identify market segments that differ with respect to price elasticity of demand. As we show shortly, the firm profits by charging a higher price to the more inelastic (i.e., less price-sensitive) market segment(s). Second, it must be possible to "enforce" the different prices paid by different segments. This means that market segments receiving higher prices must be unable to take advantage of lower prices. (In particular, a low-price buyer must be unable to resell the good or service profitably to a high-price buyer.) The conditions necessary to ensure different prices exist in the preceding examples. Sometimes the conditions are quite subtle. Business travelers rarely can purchase discount air tickets because they cannot meet advance-booking or minimum-stay requirements. First-run moviegoers pay a high ticket price because they are unwilling to wait until the film comes to a lower-price theater.

How can the firm maximize its profit via price discrimination? There are several (related) ways to answer this question. The markup rule provides a ready explanation of this practice. To illustrate, suppose a firm has identified two market segments, each with its own demand curve. (Chapter 4 discusses the means by which these different demand curves can be identified and estimated.) Then the firm can treat the different segments as separate markets for the good. The firm simply applies the markup rule twice to determine its optimal price and sales for each market segment. Thus, it sets price according to $P = [E_P/(1 + E_P)]MC$ (Equation 3.15) separately for each market segment. Presumably the marginal cost of producing for each market is the same. With the same MC inserted into the markup rule, the difference in the price charged to each segment is due solely to differences in elasticities of demand. For instance, suppose a firm identifies two market segments with price elasticities of -5 and -3, respectively. The firm's marginal cost of selling to either segment is $200. Then, according to the markup rule, the firm's optimal prices are $250 and $300, respectively. We see that the segment with the more inelastic demand pays the higher price. The firm charges the higher price to less price-sensitive buyers (with little danger of losing sales). At the same time, it attracts the more price-sensitive customers (who would buy relatively little of the good at the higher price) by offering them a discounted price. Thus, by means of optimal price discrimination, the firm maximizes its profit.[16]

Like the method just described, a second approach to price discrimination treats different segments as distinct markets and sets out to maximize profit separately in each. The difference is that the manager's focus is on optimal sales quantities rather than prices. The optimal sales quantity for each market is determined by setting the extra revenue from selling an extra unit in that market equal to the marginal cost of production. In short, the firm sets MR = MC in each market.

Multinational Production and Pricing Revisited

In the first example in Chapter 1, an automobile producer faced the problem of pricing its output at home and abroad. We are now ready to put demand analysis to work to determine the firm's optimal decisions. The facts are as follows: The producer faces relatively little competition at home; it is one of the most efficient domestic producers, and trade barriers limit the import of foreign cars. However, it competes in the foreign market with many local and foreign manufacturers. Under these circumstances, demand at home is likely to be much more inelastic than demand in the foreign country. Suppose that the price equations at home (H) and abroad (F) are, respectively.

$$P_H = 30{,}000 - 50Q_H \quad \text{and} \quad P_F = 25{,}000 - 70Q_F,$$

where price is in dollars per vehicle and quantities are annual sales of vehicles in thousands. Automobiles are produced in a single domestic facility at a marginal cost of $10,000 per vehicle. This is the MC relevant to vehicles sold in the domestic market. Shipping vehicles to the foreign market halfway around the world involves additional transport costs of $1,000 per vehicle. What are the firm's optimal sales quantities and prices?

Addressing this question is straightforward, but the answer may come as a surprise. The quantities of cars sold to the respective markets are determined by the conditions $MR_H = MC_H$ and $MR_F = MC_F$. Therefore, $30{,}000 - 100Q_H = 10{,}000$ and $25{,}000 - 140Q_F = 11{,}000$. The optimal quantities and prices (after substituting back into the demand curves) are $Q_H = 200$ thousand and $P_H = \$20{,}000$ in the domestic market and $Q_F = 100$ thousand and $P_F = \$18{,}000$ in the foreign market. The surprise comes when we compare domestic and foreign prices. Even though the marginal cost of vehicles sold in

---

[16] Here is another way to make the same point. Suppose the firm initially made the mistake of charging the same price to both market segments. The markup rule says it can increase its profit by raising one price and lowering the other. Let's check that this is the case. At the common price, let the first segment's demand be more elastic. Now suppose the firm lowers the price charged to the first segment and raises the price charged to the second in just the right amounts to maintain the same *total* sales. Given the differences in elasticities, it can do so while increasing the *average* price at which it sells units. With a higher average price and the same total number of units sold, the dual-pricing strategy has increased revenue. (The revenue gained from the first segment exceeds the revenue lost from the second.) With total output unchanged, profit has increased.

the foreign market is 10 percent higher than that of cars sold domestically, the foreign price is *lower*—by some 10 percent—than the domestic price. Why is it profitable for the company to sell on the foreign market at a much lower price than at home? It must be because demand is much more elastic abroad than it is domestically. Accordingly, the company's pricing policy is a textbook case of an optimal dual-pricing strategy.

DEMAND-BASED PRICING   As these examples indicate, the ways in which firms price discriminate are varied. Indeed, there are many forms of demand-based pricing that are closely related to price discrimination (although not always called by that name). For instance, resorts in Florida and the Caribbean set much higher nightly rates during the high season (December to March) than at off-peak times. The difference in rates is demand based. (The resorts' operating costs differ little by season.) Vacationers are willing to pay a much higher price for warm climes during the North American winter. Similarly, a convenience store, open 24 hours a day and located along a high-traffic route or intersection, will set premium prices for its merchandise. (Again, the high markups are predominantly demand based and only partly based on higher costs.) Likewise, golf courses charge much higher prices on weekends than on weekdays. Each of these examples illustrates demand-based pricing.

FORMS OF PRICE DISCRIMINATION   Finally, it is useful to distinguish three forms of price discrimination. The practice of charging different prices to different market segments (for which the firm's costs are identical) is often referred to as **third-degree price discrimination**. Airline and movie ticket pricing are examples. Prices differ across market segments, but customers within a market segment pay the same price.

Now suppose the firm could distinguish among different consumers within a market segment. What if the firm knew each customer's demand curve? Then it could practice perfect price discrimination. **First-degree**, or **perfect, price discrimination** occurs when a firm sets a different price for each customer and by doing so extracts the maximum possible sales revenue. As an example, consider an auto dealer who has a large stock of cars for sale and expects 10 serious potential buyers to enter her showroom each week. She posts different model prices, but she knows (and customers know) that the sticker price is a starting point in subsequent negotiations. Each customer knows the maximum price he or she is personally willing to pay for the car in question. If the dealer is a shrewd judge of character, she can guess the range of each buyer's maximum price and, via the negotiations, extract almost this full value. For instance, if four buyers' maximum prices are $6,100, $6,450, $5,950, and $6,200, the perfectly discriminating dealer will negotiate prices nearly equal to these values. In this way, the dealer will sell the four cars for the maximum possible revenue. As this example illustrates, perfect discrimination is fine in principle but much more difficult in practice. Clearly, such discrimination requires that the seller have an unrealistic amount of information. Thus, it serves mainly as a bench-mark—a limiting case at best.

Finally, **second-degree price discrimination** occurs when the firm offers different price schedules, and customers choose the terms that best fit their needs. The most common example is the offer of quantity discounts: For large volumes, the seller charges a lower price per unit, so the buyer purchases a larger quantity. With a little thought, one readily recognizes this as a form of profitable price discrimination. High-volume, price-sensitive buyers will choose to purchase larger quantities at a lower unit price, whereas low-volume users will purchase fewer units at a higher unit price. Perhaps the most common form of quantity discounts is the practice of *two-part pricing*. As the term suggests, the total price paid by a customer is

$$P = A + pQ,$$

where A is a fixed fee (paid irrespective of quantity) and p is the additional price per unit. Telephone service, electricity, and residential gas all carry two-part prices. Taxi service, photocopy rental agreements, and amusement park admissions are other examples. Notice that two-part pricing implies a quantity discount; the average price per unit, $P/Q = A/Q + p$, declines as Q increases. Two-part pricing allows the firm to charge customers for access to valuable services (via A) while promoting volume purchases (via low p).

Information Goods

In the last decade, we have witnessed explosive growth in the provision of **information goods and services**. The business press speaks of Internet industries and e-business markets. The "information" label is meant to be both more broadbased and more precise. An information good could be a database, a game cartridge, a news article (in electronic or paper form), a piece of music, or a piece of software. Information services range from e-mail and instant messaging, to electronic exchanges and auctions, to brokerage and other financial services, to job placements. Of course, information services also include all manner of Internet-based transactions, such as purchasing airline tickets, selling real estate, procuring industrial inputs, and gathering extensive data on potential customers.[17]

Although the information category is broad, all of the preceding examples share a common feature. *Information is costly to produce but cheap (often costless) to reproduce.* In short, any information good or service is characterized by high fixed costs but low or negligible marginal costs. With marginal costs at or near

[17] A superb discussion of the economics of information goods can be found in C. Shapiro and H. R. Varian, *Information Rules*, Chapters 1–3, 7 (Boston: Harvard Business School Press, 1999).

zero, the firm's total costs vary little with output volume, so that average cost per unit sharply declines as output increases. (Creating a $1 million database to serve 1,000 end-users implies an average cost of $1,000 per user. If, instead, it served 500,000 end-users, the average cost drops to $2 per user.) Moreover, with marginal costs negligible, a supplier of an information good once again faces a pure selling problem: how to market, promote, and price its product to maximize revenue (and thereby profit).

Not surprisingly, the early history of e-business activities has been characterized by high up-front costs and the pursuit of customers, revenues, and profits, in that order. In 1999 and 2000, Internet start-ups were the beneficiaries of enormous capital infusions by investors and spectacular market valuations, sometimes before a trace of revenue had been earned. These early Internet ventures are properly regarded as investments, and risky ones at that. Early losses are expected to be balanced by significant future revenues. For instance, strong revenue growth has been the pattern for such information goods as videotapes, CDs, and DVDs (once a critical mass of consumers had adopted the new technologies).

In many respects, however, information providers face special revenue issues. First, there are numerous ways in which revenues can be earned. The most familiar is simply setting a price per unit, as in the sale of a music CD, a movie videotape, a piece of software, or content to a Web site. Maximizing total revenue from sales means identifying the unit price such that $E_P = -1$. However, there are myriad other pricing options. When a movie producer sells a videotape to Blockbuster for rental, it receives a modest price of $8 per unit but shares roughly 40 percent of rental revenues with the video chain. Alternatively, software may be sold via site license, allowing group users to enjoy a kind of quantity discount. Internet services are sold by monthly subscription, by pay per use (or per download), or in some combination. Many information services, particularly search engines (such as Google) and high-traffic Web portals, earn the bulk of their cash flows from advertising revenues. Internet advertising includes banner ads, buttons, pop-up ads, e-mail advertisements, and even Web-page sponsorships to promote brand names. Finally, there are all kinds of indirect revenues. For instance, some information suppliers sell their customer lists to third parties. It is also important to recognize the numerous trade-offs between these different revenue sources. Outright video sales compete with video rentals. Raising subscription prices lowers traffic and, therefore, reduces the effectiveness of Web advertising. Obviously, these trade-offs complicate the task of maximizing total revenue. In effect, the information supplier faces multiple, interdependent, and imprecise demand curves.

Second, most information goods exhibit positive **network externalities**. This means that customers of a given information good obtain greater value with a larger network of other connected customers. For instance, wireless telephone customers benefit from the most fully developed nationwide (or worldwide) network, and air travelers benefit from airlines with integrated national and international routes offering multiple daily flights. Teenagers intensively utilize America Online's instant message service. The network need not be physical. For example, the global network of Microsoft's Windows-based operating system and Office applications allows easy file and software transfers among users. By contrast, the separate network of Apple Mac users is much more limited. The highly successful online auction company eBay, has attracted thousands of sellers and millions of buyers. This enormous network is valuable, not only for sellers who seek the greatest number of potential buyers (and vice versa), but also for eBay, which earns a percentage fee on all auction listings. In all these instances, positive network externalities imply that customer values and, therefore, underlying demand curves shift outward over time as the customer network expands.[18]

What are the strategic implications of network externalities for information providers? Clearly, there is a potential "first-mover" advantage in enlisting the greatest number of users of the information good in question. (We will say more about first-mover strategies in Chapter 13.) Users "in hand" are valuable to the firm not only for the revenue they directly generate but also because they enhance the value of other current and future users (from which the firm also gains revenue). Well aware of this dynamic, e-business firms have aggressively sought customers, not only via advertising and promotions but also by significant price cuts. The extreme cases of cutthroat competition have bred *free* information services of all kinds: electronic greeting cards, e-mail, Internet connections, and online newspapers and magazines. Interestingly, offering free services is a viable business strategy so long as the expanded customer base generates revenue via advertising or from any of the avenues mentioned earlier. In numerous instances, free downloadable versions of stripped-down software or Web content have enticed consumers to trade up to "professional" or "deluxe" versions, for which dollar fees are charged. In other cases, information providers have been locked in savage price wars or battles over free content that have decimated company revenues, thereby degenerating into "wars of attrition." To date, the identities of information suppliers with business plans capable of earning consistent and sustainable revenues are still being sorted out in the market.

CUSTOMIZED PRICING AND PRODUCTS   The emergence of electronic commerce and online transactions has greatly expanded the opportunities for market segmentation and price discrimination. From management's point of view, the beauty of information goods and services is that they can be sold over and over again (at negligible marginal cost). Moreover, unlike a traditional good

---

[18] Let there be n members of a network and suppose that each member's value is proportional to the number of other network members ($n - 1$). Then, according to Metcalf's "law," the total value of the network (summed over all members) is proportional to $(n)(n - 1) = n^2 - n$. In short, network value increases geometrically and rapidly as the square of the number of members. By this reckoning, a mega-network enjoys an enormous value advantage over a smaller network.

sold at a posted price from a store shelf, the price of an information good (transacted electronically) can be changed minute by minute, customer by customer. Sellers of sophisticated databases—from Reuters to Lexis-Nexis to Bloomberg financial information—set scores of different prices to different customers. As always, prices are set according to elasticities; the most price-sensitive (elastic) customers receive the steepest discounted prices. Consider the ways in which an airline Web site (such as www.delta.com) can price its airline seats. Each time a customer enters a possible itinerary with departure and return dates, the Web page responds with possible flights and prices. These electronic prices already reflect many features: the class of seat, 21-day, 14-day, or 7-day advance booking, whether a Saturday night stay is included, and so on. By booking in advance and staying a Saturday night, pleasure travelers can take advantage of discounted fares. Business travelers, whose itineraries are not able to meet these restrictions, pay much higher prices. Moreover, the airline can modify prices instantly to reflect changes in demand. If there is a surplus of unsold discount seats as the departure date approaches, the airline can further cut its price or sell them as part of a vacation package (hotel stay, rental car included) at even a steeper discount. (Airlines also release seats to discount sellers, such as Priceline.com, Hotwire.com, and Site59.com, which sell tickets at steep discounts to the most price-sensitive fliers.) Or some discount seats might be reassigned as full-fare seats if last-minute business demand for the flight is particularly brisk. Online the pricing possibilities are endless.

Closely akin to customized pricing is the practice of **versioning**—selling different versions of a given information good or service. Whether it be software, hardware, database access, or other Internet services, this typically means a "standard" version offered at a lower price and a "professional" or "deluxe" version at a premium price. The versions are designed and priced to ensure that different market segments self-select with respect to the product offerings. The inelastic demand segment eagerly elects to pay the premium price to obtain the more powerful version. The more elastic demand segment purchases the stripped-down version at the discounted price. Although customers may not know it, the firm's costs for the different versions are usually indistinguishable. In this respect, versioning is closely akin to third-degree price discrimination. In fact, some software firms begin by designing their premium products and then simply disable key features to create the standard version.

We are now ready to take a closer look at the pricing policy of the airline in the chapter-opening example and to suggest how it might succeed at yield management. Consider again Equation 3.4, which describes current demand:

Airline Ticket Pricing Revisited

$$Q = 580 - 2P.$$

At its present price, $240, the airline sells 100 coach seats (of the 180 such seats available per flight). Assuming the airline will continue its single daily departure from each city (we presume this is not an issue), what is its optimal fare?

The first step in answering this question is to recognize this as a pure selling problem. With the airline committed to the flight, all associated costs are fixed. The marginal cost of flying 180 passengers versus 100 passengers (a few extra lunches, a bit more fuel, and so on) is negligible. Thus, the airline seeks the pricing policy that will generate the most revenue.

The next step is to appeal to marginal revenue to determine the optimal fare. The price equation is $P = 290 - Q/2$. (Check this.) Consequently, $MR = 290 - Q$. Note: Even at a 100 percent load ($Q = 180$), marginal revenue is positive ($MR = \$110$). If more seats were available, the airline would like to ticket them and increase its revenue. Lacking these extra seats, however, the best the airline can do is set $Q = 180$. From the price equation, $200 is the price needed to sell this number of seats. The airline should institute a $40 price cut. By doing so, its revenue will increase from $24,000 to $36,000 per flight.[19]

Now let's extend (and complicate) the airline's pricing problem by introducing the possibility of profitable price discrimination. Two distinct market segments purchase coach tickets—business travelers (B) and pleasure travelers (T)—and these groups differ with respect to their demands. Suppose the equations that best represent these segments' demands are $Q_B = 330 - P_B$ and $Q_T = 250 - P_T$. Note that these demand equations are consistent with Equation 3.4; that is, if both groups are charged price P, total demand is $Q = Q_B + Q_T = (330 - P) + (250 - P) = 580 - 2P$, which is exactly Equation 3.4. The airline's task is to determine Q_B and Q_T to maximize total revenue from the 180 coach seats.

The key to solving this problem is to appeal to the logic of marginal analysis. With the number of seats limited, the airline attains maximum revenue by setting $MR_B = MR_T$. The marginal revenue from selling the last ticket to a business traveler must equal the marginal revenue from selling the last ticket to a pleasure traveler. Why must this be so? Suppose to the contrary that the marginal revenues differ: $MR_B > MR_T$. The airline can increase its revenue simply by selling one less seat to pleasure travelers and one more seat to business travelers. So long as marginal revenues differ across the segments, seats should be transferred from the low-MR segment to the high-MR segment, increasing revenue all the while. Revenue is maximized only when $MR_B = MR_T$.[20]

---

[19] The same point can be made by calculating the price elasticity of demand at $Q = 180$ and $P = 200$. Elasticity can be written as $E_P = (dQ/dP)(P/Q)$. From the foregoing demand equation, we know that $dQ/dP = -2$. Therefore, we find that $E_P = (-2)(200/180) = -2.2$. Since demand is elastic, the airline would like to increase revenue by cutting price and increasing the number of coach travelers. But because all its seats are full, the best it can do is set the full-capacity price, $200.

[20] The airline's decision is one example of constrained optimization problems (analyzed in the appendix to Chapter 2). The airline seeks to maximize total revenue: $TR = R(Q_B) + R(Q_T)$. The change in total revenue from small changes in the number of business and nonbusiness seats sold is $\Delta TR = MR_B \Delta Q_B + MR_T \Delta Q_T$. If the plane's capacity were not an issue, the airline would increase sales of each type of ticket until marginal revenue was zero: $MR_B = MR_T = 0$. On the other hand, if the plane is filled to capacity, $Q_B + Q_T = 180$, so $\Delta Q_T = -\Delta Q_B$. Selling one more business ticket means selling one less nonbusiness ticket. Therefore, $\Delta TR = (MR_B - MR_T)\Delta Q_B$ after substituting $\Delta Q_T = -\Delta Q_B$ into the preceding expression. Thus, no further increases in revenue are possible ($\Delta TR = 0$) if and only if $MR_B = MR_T$.

After writing down the price equations, deriving the associated marginal revenue expressions, and equating them, we have:

$$330 - 2Q_B = 250 - 2Q_T,$$

which can be simplified to $Q_B = 40 + Q_T$. The maximum-revenue plan always allocates 40 more seats to business travelers than to pleasure travelers. Since the plane capacity is 180, sales are constrained by $Q_B + Q_T = 180$. Therefore, the optimal quantities are $Q_B = 110$ and $Q_T = 70$. Optimal prices are $P_B = \$220$ and $P_T = \$180$. In turn, if we substitute $Q_B = 110$ into the expression $MR_B = 330 - 2Q_B$, we find that $MR_B = \$110$ per additional seat. (Of course, MR_T is also $\$110$ per seat.) Finally, total revenue is computed as $R = R_B + R_T = (\$220)(110) + (\$180)(70) = \$36,800$. Recall that maximum revenue under a single price system was $\$36,000$. Optimal yield management (price discrimination) has squeezed an additional $\$800$ out of passengers on the flight. As the chapter-opening example suggests, additional revenue can be gained by increasing the number of different fares, from two to as many as six or more.

CHECK STATION 6 Suppose the airline's management is considering adding an extra flight every second day. Therefore, average daily capacity would increase from 180 to 270 seats. The additional cost of offering this extra flight is estimated at $\$50$ per seat. Show that adding this "second-day" flight would be profitable but that an additional "everyday" flight would not. Determine the new ticket prices for the two classes.

SUMMARY

Decision-Making Principles

1. Optimal managerial decisions depend on an analysis of demand.
2. In particular, the firm's optimal uniform price is determined by the markup rule. This price depends on marginal cost and the price elasticity of demand.
3. When the opportunity exists, the firm can increase its profit by practicing price discrimination.

Nuts and Bolts

1. The demand function shows, in equation form, the relationship between the unit sales of a good or service and one or more economic variables.
   a. The demand curve depicts the relationship between quantity and price. A change in price is represented by a movement along the demand curve. A change in any other economic variable shifts the demand curve.

b. A pair of goods are substitutes if an increase in demand for one causes a fall in demand for the other. In particular, a price cut for one good reduces sales of the other.

c. A pair of goods are complements if an increase in demand for one causes an increase in demand for the other. In particular, a price cut for one good increases sales of the other.

d. A good is normal if its sales increase with increases in income.

2. The price elasticity of demand measures the percentage change in sales for a given percentage change in the good's price, all other factors held constant: $E_P = (\Delta Q/Q)/(\Delta P/P)$.

a. Demand is unitary elastic if $E_P = -1$. In turn, demand is elastic if $E_P < -1$. Finally, demand is inelastic if $-1 < E_P < 0$.

b. Revenue is maximized at the price and quantity for which marginal revenue is zero or, equivalently, the price elasticity of demand is unity.

3. The optimal markup rule is $(P - MC)/P = -1/E_P$. The firm's optimal markup (above marginal cost and expressed as a percentage of price) varies inversely with the price elasticity of demand for the good or service. (Remember that the firm's price cannot be profit maximizing if demand is inelastic.)

4. Price discrimination occurs when a firm sells the same good or service to different buyers at different prices (based on different price elasticities of demand). Prices in various market segments are determined according to the optimal markup rule.

Questions and Problems

1. During a five-year period, the ticket sales of a city's professional basketball team have increased 30 percent at the same time that average ticket prices have risen by 50 percent. Do these changes imply an upward-sloping demand curve? Explain.

2. A retail store faces a demand equation for Roller Blades given by:

$$Q = 180 - 1.5P,$$

where Q is the number of pairs sold per month and P is the price per pair in dollars.

a. The store currently charges P = $80 per pair. At this price, determine the number of pairs sold.

b. If management were to raise the price to $100, what would be the impact on pairs sold? On the store's revenue from Roller Blades?

c. Compute the point elasticity of demand first at P = $80, then at P = $100. At which price is demand more price sensitive?

3. Management of McPablo's Food Shops has completed a study of weekly demand for its "old-fashioned" tacos in 53 regional markets. The study revealed that

$$Q = 400 - 1,200P + .8A + 55Pop + 800P°,$$

where Q is the number of tacos sold per store per week, A is the level of local advertising expenditure (in dollars), Pop denotes the local population (in thousands), and P° is the average taco price of local competitors. For the typical McPablo's outlet, P = $1.50, A = $1,000, Pop = 40, and P° = $1.
   a. Estimate the weekly sales for the typical McPablo's outlet.
   b. What is the current price elasticity for tacos? What is the advertising elasticity?
   c. Should McPablo's raise its taco prices? Why or why not?

4. A minor league baseball team is trying to predict ticket sales for the upcoming season and is considering changing ticket prices.
   a. The elasticity of ticket sales with respect to the size of the local population is estimated to be about .7. Briefly explain what this number means. If the local population increases from 60,000 to 61,500, what is the predicted change in ticket sales?
   b. Currently, a typical fan pays an average ticket price of $10. The price elasticity of demand for tickets is −.6. Management is thinking of raising the average ticket price to $11. Compute the predicted percentage change in tickets sold. Would you expect ticket revenue to rise or fall?
   c. The typical fan also consumes $8 worth of refreshments at the game. Thus, at the original $10 average price, each admission generates $18 in *total* revenue for team management. Would raising ticket prices to $11 increase or reduce *total* revenue? Provide a careful explanation of your finding. (Hint: If you wish, you may assume a certain number of tickets sold per game, say 5,000. However, to answer the question the precise number of tickets need not be specified.)

5. a. General Motors (GM) produces light trucks in several Michigan factories, where its annual fixed costs are $180 million, and its marginal cost per truck is approximately $20,000. Regional demand for the trucks is given by P = 30,000 − 0.1Q, where P denotes price in dollars and Q denotes annual sales of trucks. Find GM's profit-maximizing output level and price. Find the annual profit generated by light trucks.
   b. GM is getting ready to export trucks to several markets in South America. Based on several marketing surveys, GM has found the elasticity of demand in these foreign markets to be $E_P = -9$ for a wide range of prices (between $20,000 and $30,000). The additional cost of

shipping (including paying some import fees) is about $800 per truck. One manager argues that the foreign price should be set at $800 above the domestic price (in part a) to cover the transportation cost. Do you agree that this is the optimal price for foreign sales? Justify your answer.

c. GM also produces an economy ("no frills") version of its light truck at a marginal cost of $12,000 per vehicle. However, at the price set by GM, $20,000 per truck, customer demand has been very disappointing. GM has recently discontinued production of this model but still finds itself with an inventory of 18,000 unsold trucks. The best estimate of demand for the remaining trucks is:

$$P = 30,000 - Q.$$

One manager recommends keeping the price at $20,000; another favors cutting the price to sell the entire inventory. What price (one of these or some other price) should GM set and how many trucks should it sell? Justify your answer.

6. Over the last decade, Apple Computer has seen its global share of the personal computer market fall from above 10 percent to less than 5 percent. Despite a keenly loyal customer base, Apple has found it more and more difficult to compete in a market dominated by the majority standard: PCs with Microsoft's Windows-based operating system and Intel's microchips. Indeed, software developers put a lower priority on writing Mac applications than on Windows applications.

a. In the 1980s, Apple vigorously protected its proprietary hardware and software and refused to license Mac clones. What effect did this decision have on long-run demand?

b. In the early 1990s, Apple enjoyed high markups on its units. In 1995 Apple's chief, John Sculley, insisted on keeping Mac's gross profit margin at 50 to 55 percent, even in the face of falling demand. (Gross profit margin is measured as total revenue minus total variable costs expressed as a percentage of total revenue.) At this time, the business of selling PCs was becoming more and more "commodity-like." Indeed, the price elasticity facing a particular company was estimated in the neighborhood of $E_P = -4$. Using the markup rule of Equation 3.14, carefully assess Sculley's strategy.

c. Recently, Apple has discontinued several of its lower-priced models and has expanded its efforts in the education and desktop publishing markets. In addition, recent software innovations allow Macs to read most documents, data, and spreadsheets generated on other PCs. Do these initiatives make sense? How will they affect demand?

7. As economic consultant to the dominant firm in a particular market, you have discovered that, at the current price and output, demand for your client's product is price inelastic. What advice regarding pricing would you give?

8. A New Hampshire resort offers year-round activities: in winter, skiing and other cold-weather activities and, in summer, golf, tennis, and hiking. The resort's operating costs are essentially the same in winter and summer. Management charges higher nightly rates in the winter, when its average occupancy rate is 75 percent, than in the summer, when its occupancy rate is 85 percent. Can this policy be consistent with profit maximization? Explain.

9. In 1996, the drug Prilosec became the best-selling anti-ulcer drug in the world. (The drug was the most effective available and its sales outdistanced those of its nearest competitor.) Though Prilosec's marginal cost (production and packaging) was only about $.60 per daily dose, the drug's manufacturer initially set the price at $3.00 per dose—a 400 percent markup relative to MC!

    Research on demand for leading prescription drugs gives estimates of price elasticities in the range −1.4 to −1.2. Does setting a price of $3.00 (or more) make economic sense? Explain.

10. Explain how a firm can increase its profit by price discrimination. How does it determine optimal prices? How does the existence of substitute products affect the firm's pricing policy?

11. Often firms charge a range of prices for essentially the same good or service because of cost differences. For instance, filling a customer's one-time small order for a product may be much more expensive than supplying "regular" orders. Services often are more expensive to deliver during peak-load periods. (Typically it is very expensive for a utility to provide electricity to meet peak demand during a hot August.) Insurance companies recognize that the expected cost of insuring different customers under the same policy may vary significantly. How should a profit-maximizing manager take different costs into account in setting prices?

12. In what respects are the following common practices subtle (or not-so-subtle) forms of price discrimination?
    a. Frequent-flier and frequent-stay programs
    b. Manufacturers' discount coupon programs
    c. A retailer's guarantee to match a lower competing price

*13. A private-garage owner has identified two distinct market segments: short-term parkers and all-day parkers with respective demand curves of $P_S = 3 - (Q_S/200)$ and $P_C = 2 - (Q_C/200)$. Here P is the average hourly rate and Q is the number of cars parked at this price. The garage owner is considering charging different prices (on a per-hour basis) for short-term parking and all-day parking. The capacity of the garage is 600 cars, and the cost associated with adding extra cars in the garage (up to this limit) is negligible.

*Starred problems are more challenging.

    a. Given these facts, what is the owner's appropriate objective? How can he ensure that members of each market segment effectively pay a different hourly price?

    b. What price should he charge for each type of parker? How many of each type of parker will use the garage at these prices? Will the garage be full?

    c. Answer the questions in part b assuming the garage capacity is 400 cars.

* 14. A golf-course operator must decide what greens fees (prices) to set on rounds of golf. Daily demand during the week is: $P_D = 36 - Q_D/10$ where Q_D is the number of 18-hole rounds and P_D is the price per round. Daily demand on the weekend is $P_W = 50 - Q_W/12$. As a practical matter, the capacity of the course is 240 rounds per day. Wear and tear on the golf course is negligible.

    a. Can the operator profit by charging different prices during the week and on the weekend? Explain briefly. What greens fees should the operator set on weekdays and how many rounds will be played? On the weekend?

    b. When weekend prices skyrocket, some weekend golfers choose to play during the week instead. The greater the difference between weekday and weekend prices, the greater are the number of these "defectors." How might this factor affect the operator's pricing policy? (A qualitative answer will suffice.)

Discussion Question The notion of elasticity is essential whenever the multiplicative product of two variables involves a trade-off. (Thus, we have already appealed to price elasticity to maximize revenue given the trade-off between price and output.) With this in mind, consider the following examples.

a. Why might a bumper crop (for instance, a 10 percent increase in a crop's output) be detrimental for overall farm revenue?

b. Court and legal reforms (to speed the process of litigation and lower its cost) will encourage more disputants to use the court system. Under what circumstances could this cause an *increase* in total litigation spending?

c. Despite technological advances in fishing methods and more numerous fishing boats, total catches of many fish species have declined over time. Explain.

d. Predict the impact on smoking behavior (and the incidence of lung disease) as more and more producers market low-tar and low-nicotine cigarettes.

Spreadsheet Problems

S1. Let's revisit the maker of spare parts in Problem S1 of Chapter 2 to determine its optimal price. The firm's demand curve is given by $Q = 400 - .5P$ and its cost function by $C = 20,000 + 200Q + .5Q^2$.

a. Treating price as the relevant decision variable, create a spreadsheet (based on the example shown) to model this setting. Compute the price elasticity in cell B12 according to $E_P = (dQ/dP)(P/Q)$.

b. Find the optimal price by hand. (*Hint:* Vary price while comparing cells E12 and F12. When $(P - MC)/P$ exactly equals $-1/E_P$, the markup rule is satisfied and the optimal price has been identified.)

c. Use your spreadsheet's optimizer to confirm the optimal price.

	A	B	C	D	E	F	G
1							
2		THE OPTIMAL PRICE FOR SPARE PARTS					
3							
4							
5		Price	Quantity	Revenue	Cost	Profit	
6							
7		780	10	7,800	22,050	−14,250	
8							
9							
10		Elasticity	MC		(P − MC)/P	−1/EP	
11							
12		−39.00	210		0.7308	0.0256	
13							

S2. On a popular air route, an airline offers two classes of service: business class (B) and economy class (E). The respective demands are given by:

$$P_B = 540 - .5Q_B \quad \text{and} \quad P_E = 380 - .25Q_E.$$

Because of ticketing restrictions, business travelers cannot take advantage of economy's low fares. The airline operates two flights daily. Each flight has a capacity of 200 passengers. The cost per flight is $20,000.

a. The airline seeks to maximize the total revenue it obtains from the two flights. To address this question, create a spreadsheet patterned on the example shown. (In your spreadsheet, only cells E2, E3, E4, C9, and D9 should contain numerical values. The numbers in all other cells are computed by using spreadsheet formulas. For instance, the total available seats in cell E5 is defined as the product of cells E2 and E3.)

b. What fares should the airline charge, and how many passengers will buy tickets of each type? Remember that maximum revenue is obtained by setting MR_B equal to MR_E. After you have explored the decision by hand, confirm your answer using your spreadsheet's optimizer. (*Hint:* Be sure to include the constraint that the total number of seats sold must be no greater than the total number of seats available—that is, cell E9 must be less than or equal to cell E5.)

c. Suppose the airline is considering promoting a single "value fare" to all passengers along the route. Find the optimal single fare using your spreadsheet's optimizer. (*Hint:* Simply modify the optimizer instructions from part b by adding the constraint that the prices in cells C11 and D11 must be equal.)

S3. Now suppose the airline in Problem S2 can vary the number of daily departures.

a. What is its profit-maximizing number of flights, and how many passengers of each type should it carry? (*Hint:* The optimal numbers of passengers, Q_B and Q_E, can be found by setting $MR_B = MR_E = MC$ per seat. Be sure to translate the $20,000 marginal cost per flight into the relevant MC per seat.)

b. Confirm your algebraic answer using the spreadsheet you created in Problem S2. (*Hint:* The easiest way to find a solution by hand is to vary the number of passengers of each type to equate MRs and MC; then adjust the number of planes to carry the necessary total number of passengers.)

c. Use your spreadsheet's optimizer to confirm the optimal solution. (*Hint:* Be sure to list cell E2 as an adjustable cell.)

	A	B	C	D	E	F
1						
2	DUAL AIRFARES			Planes	2	
3				Seats/Plane	200	
4				Cost/Plane	20,000	
5				Total Seats	400	
6						
7			Business	Non-Bus.	Total	
8						
9	Number of Seats		200	200	400	
10						
11	One-Way Fare		440	330	—	
12						
13	Revenue		88,000	66,000	154,000	
14	MR		340	280		
15						
16	MC		100	Total Cost	40,000	
17						
18				Total Profit	114,000	
19						

Suggested References

The following references illustrate the various uses of demand analysis, including the computation and application of elasticities.

Baye, M. R., D. W. Jansen, and J. W. Lee. "Advertising Effects in Complete Demand Systems." *Applied Economics* 24 (1992): 1087–1096.

Becker, G. S., M. Grossman, and K. M. Murphy. "An Empirical Analysis of Cigarette Addiction." *The American Economic Review* 84 (June 1994): 396–418.

Bordley, R. F. "Estimating Automotive Elasticities from Segment Elasticities and First Choice/Second Choice Data." *The Review of Economics and Statistics* 75 (August 1993): 455–462.

Gallet, C. A., and J. A. List. "Elasticities of Beer Demand Revisited." *Economics Letters* 61 (October 1998): 67–71.

Hagarty, J. C., and G. Russell. "Estimating Elasticities with PIMS Data: Methodological Issues and Substantive Implications." *Journal of Marketing Research* (1988): 1–9.

Hunt-McCool, J., B. F. Kiker, and Y. C. Ng. "Estimates of the Demand for Medical Care Under Different Functional Forms." *Journal of Applied Econometrics* 9 (1994): 201–218.

McCarthy, P. S. "Market Price and Income Elasticities of New Vehicles Demand." *Review of Economics and Statistics* 78 (August 1996): 543–547.

Pagoulatos, E., and R. Sorenson, "What Determines the Elasticity of Industry Demand?" *International Journal of Industrial Organization* 4 (1986): 237–250.

Schaller, B. "Elasticities for Taxicab Fares and Service Availability." *Transportation* 26 (August 1999): 283–297.

Silk, J. I., and F. L. Joutz. "Short- and Long-Run Elasticities in U.S. Residential Electricity Demand: A Cointegration Approach." *Energy Economics* 19 (October 1997): 493–513.

Subramanian, S., and A. Deaton. "The Demand for Food and Calories," *The Journal of Political Economy* 104 (February 1996): 133–162.

The following references contain discussions of optimal pricing, price discrimination, and advertising.

Dolan, R. J. "How Do You Know When the Price Is Right?" *Harvard Business Review* (September–October 1995): 174–183.

Grant, A. H., and L. A. Schlesinger. "Realize Your Customers' Full Profit Potential." *Harvard Business Review* (September–October 1995): 59–72.

Knetter, M. M. "International Comparisons of Pricing-to-Market Behavior." *The American Economic Review* 83 (June 1993): 473–486.

Tirole, J. *The Theory of Industrial Organization*, Chapters 2 and 3. Cambridge, MA: MIT Press, 1989.

Van Dalen, J., and R. Thurik. "A Model of Pricing Behavior: An Econometric Case Study." *Journal of Economic Behavior and Organization* 36 (August 1998): 177–195.

Demand characteristics and selling strategies for information goods and services are analyzed in:

Shapiro, C., and H. Varian. *Information Rules*, Chapters 1-3, 7. Boston: Harvard Business School Press, 1999, and at the associated Website, www.inforules.com.

CHECK STATION ANSWERS

1. $\Delta Q = -24 + 12 - 40 = -52$ seats.

2. The facts in the second part of the statement are correct, but this does not mean that auto demand is less elastic. Elasticity measures the effect of a percentage change in price, not an absolute change. The change in any good's sales is given by $\Delta Q/Q = E_P(\Delta P/P)$; that is, it depends both on the elasticity and the magnitude of the percentage price change. After all, a $50 auto price cut is trivial in percentage terms. Even if auto demand is very elastic, the change in sales will be small. By contrast, a $50 price cut

for a CD player is large in percentage terms. So there may be a large jump in sales even if player demand is quite inelastic.

3. $E_P = (dQ/Q)/(dP/P) = (dQ/dP)(P/Q)$. With $dQ/dP = -4$, the elasticity at $P = \$200$ and $Q = 800$ is $E_P = (-4)(200)/800 = -1$.

4. Since costs are assumed to be fixed, the team's management should set a price to maximize ticket revenue. We know that $Q = 60,000 - 3,000P$ or, equivalently, $P = 20 - Q/3,000$. Setting MR = 0, we have $20 - Q/1,500 = 0$, or $Q = 30,000$ seats. In turn, $P = \$10$ and revenue = \$300,000 per game. Note that management should *not* set a price to fill the stadium (36,000 seats). To fill the stadium, the necessary average price would be \$8 and would generate only \$288,000 in revenue.

5. Before the settlement, the cigarette company is setting an optimal price called for by the markup rule: $P = [-2/(-2 + 1)]1.00 = \$2.00$. The settlement payment takes the form of a fixed cost (based on past sales). It does not vary with respect to current or future production levels. Therefore, it does not affect the firm's marginal cost and should not affect the firm's markup. Note also that the individual firm faces *elastic* demand (because smokers can switch to other brands if the firm unilaterally raises prices), whereas industry demand (according to Table 3.1) is *inelastic*. If all firms raise prices by 10 percent, total demand will decline by only 7 percent.

6. The new seat allocations satisfy $MR_B = MR_T$ and $Q_B + Q_T = 270$. The solution is $Q_B = 155$ and $Q_T = 115$. In turn, $P_B = \$175$, $P_T = \$135$, and total revenue is \$42,650—approximately \$6,000 greater than current revenue (\$36,800). Since the extra cost of the "second day" is only \$4,500 ($90 \times \$50$), this expansion is profitable. Note, however, that the common value of marginal revenue has dropped to \$20. (To see this, compute $MR_B = 330 - 2(155) = \$20$.) Because the marginal revenue per seat has fallen below the marginal cost (\$50), any further expansion would be unprofitable.

Consumer Preferences and Demand

In this appendix, we provide a brief overview of the foundations of consumer demand—how consumers allocate their spending among desired goods and services. The analysis is important in its own right as a basis for downward-sloping demand curves. Perhaps its greater importance lies in the broader decision-making principle it illustrates. As we shall see, an optimal decision—made either by a consumer or a manager—depends on a careful analysis of preferences and trade-offs among available alternatives.

The Consumer's Problem

Consider an individual who must decide how to allocate her spending between desirable goods and services. To keep things simple, let's limit our attention to the case of two goods, X and Y. These goods could be anything from specific items (soft drinks versus bread) to general budget categories (groceries versus restaurant meals or food expenditures versus travel spending). The consumer faces a basic question: Given a limited amount of money to spend on the two goods, and given their prices, what quantities should she purchase?

INDIFFERENCE CURVES To answer this question, we will use a simple graphical device to describe the individual's preferences. Imagine that we have asked the consumer what her preferences are for alternative bundles of goods. Which do you prefer, 5 units of X and 10 units of Y, or 7 units of X and 6 units of Y? The answers to enough of such questions generate a preference ranking for a wide range of possible bundles of goods. Figure 3A.1 shows these possible bun-

FIGURE 3A.1

A Consumer's
Indifference Curves

Each indifference curve
shows combinations of
the goods that provide
the consumer with the
same level of utility.

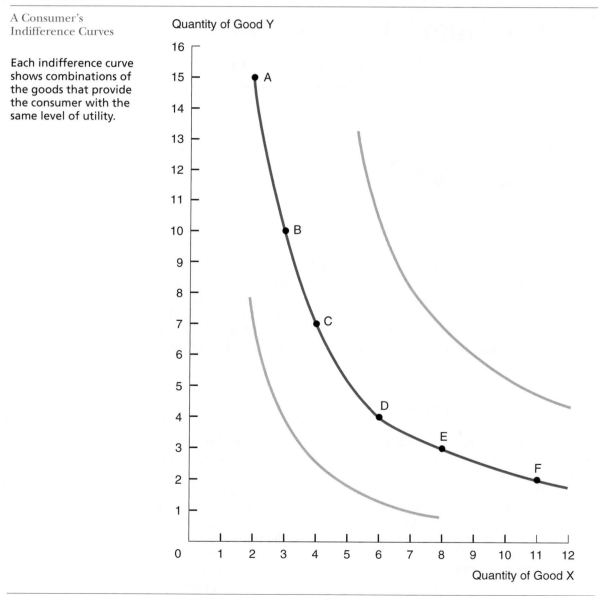

dles by listing the quantities of the goods on the respective axes. The figure also depicts a number of the consumer's indifference curves as a way of representing her preferences.

As its name suggests, an **indifference curve** shows all combinations of the goods among which the individual is indifferent. The consumer is indifferent between all bundles on the same curve. Using the middle indifference curve in the figure, we see that the consumer is indifferent between the bundle containing 15 units of Y and 2 units of X (point A), 10 units of Y and 3 units of X (point B), and 4 units of Y and 6 units of X (point D). The bundles corresponding to points C, E, and F lie on the same indifference curve and are equally preferred by the consumer.

We can make three observations about the consumer's indifference curves. First, as we move to greater quantities of *both* goods, we move to higher and higher indifference curves. The figure depicts three different indifference curves. The consumer's welfare increases as we move to curves farther to the northeast in the figure.[1] Second, we note that the indifference curve is downward sloping. Since both goods are valued by the consumer, a decrease in one good must be compensated by an increase in the other to maintain the same level of welfare (or utility) for the consumer.

Third, we note that the slope of each curve goes from steep to flat, moving southeast along its length. This means that the trade-off between the goods changes as their relative quantities change. For instance, consider a movement from A to B. At point A, the consumer has 15 units of Y (a relative abundance) and 2 units of X. By switching to point B, she is willing to give up 5 units of Y to gain a single additional unit of X. Thus, the trade-off is five to one. By moving from point B (where Y is still relatively abundant) to point C, the consumer is willing to give up another 3 units of Y to get an additional unit of X. Now the trade-off between the goods (while leaving the consumer indifferent) is three to one. The trade-offs between the goods continue to diminish by movements from C to D to E. Thus, the indifference curve is bowed. This shape represents a general result about consumer preferences:

> The greater the amount of a good a consumer has, the less an additional unit is worth to him or her.

This result usually is referred to as the *law of diminishing marginal utility.* In our example, moving southeast along the indifference curve means going from a relative abundance of Y and a scarcity of X to the opposite proportions. When X is scarce, the consumer is willing to trade many units of Y for an additional

---

[1] One way to think about the indifference curve is to view it as a contour elevation map. Such a map has contour lines that connect points of equal elevation. Theoretically, there is a line for every elevation. Practically, we cannot have an infinite number of lines, so we draw them for only a few elevations. Similarly, we draw a few representative indifference curves for the consumer. Bundles of goods lying on "higher" indifference curves generate greater welfare.

unit of X. As X becomes more abundant and Y more scarce, X's relative value diminishes and Y's relative value increases.

THE BUDGET CONSTRAINT   Having described her preferences, next we determine the consumer's alternatives. The amount of goods she can purchase depends on her available income and the goods' prices. Suppose the consumer sets aside $20 each week to spend on the two goods. The price of good X is $4 per unit, and the price of Y is $2 per unit. Then she is able to buy any quantities of the goods (call these quantities X and Y) so long as she does not exceed her income. If she spends the entire $20, her purchases must satisfy

$$4X + 2Y = 20. \qquad \text{[3A.1]}$$

This equation's left side expresses the total amount the consumer spends on the goods. The right side is her available income. According to the equation, her spending just exhausts her available income.[2] This equation is called the consumer's **budget constraint**. Figure 3A.2 depicts the graph of this constraint. For instance, the consumer could purchase 5 units of X and no units of Y (point A), 10 units of Y and no units of X (point C), 3 units of X and 4 units of Y (point B), or any other combination along the budget line shown. Note that bundles of goods to the northeast of the budget line are infeasible; they cost more than the $20 that the consumer has to spend.

OPTIMAL CONSUMPTION   We are now ready to combine the consumer's indifference curves with her budget constraint to determine her optimal purchase quantities of the goods. Figure 3A.3 shows that the consumer's optimal combination of goods lies at point B, 3 units of X and 4 units of Y. Bundle B is optimal precisely because it lies on the consumer's "highest" attainable indifference curve while satisfying the budget constraint. (Check that all other bundles along the budget line lie on lower indifference curves.)

Observe that, at point B, the indifference curve is tangent to the budget line. This means that at B the slope of the indifference curve is exactly equal to the slope of the budget line. Let's consider each slope in turn. The slope of the budget line (the "rise over the run") is -2. This slope can be obtained from the graph directly or found by rearranging the budget equation in the form $Y = 10 - 2X$. As a result, $\Delta Y/\Delta X = -2$. More generally, we can write the budget equation in the form:

$$P_X X + P_Y Y = I,$$

where P_X and P_Y denote the goods' prices and I is the consumer's income. Rearranging the budget equation, we find $Y = I/P_Y - (P_X/P_Y)X$. Therefore,

[2] Because both goods are valuable to the consumer, she will never spend *less* than her allotted income on the goods. To do so would unnecessarily reduce her level of welfare.

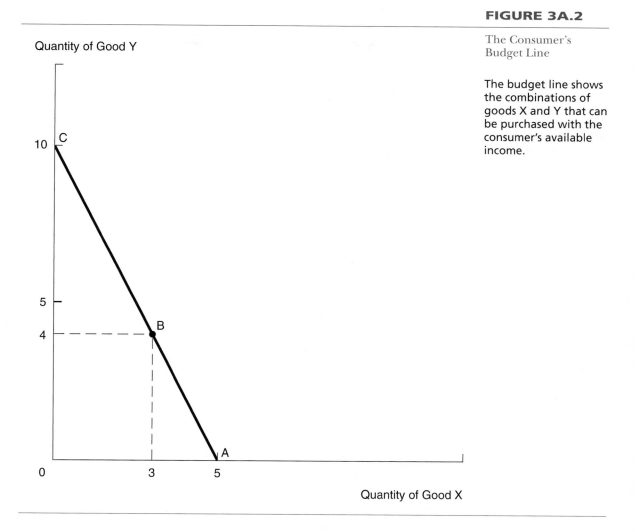

The budget line shows
the combinations of
goods X and Y that can
be purchased with the
consumer's available
income.

we have $\Delta Y / \Delta X = -P_X / P_Y$. The trade-off between the goods along the budget line is the *inverse* of the ratio of the goods' prices. Since the price of X is twice that of Y, by purchasing one less unit of X the consumer can purchase two additional units of Y. In short, $\Delta Y / \Delta X = -2$.

We already have commented on the slope of the consumer's indifference curve. Unlike the budget line, the indifference curve's slope is not constant. Rather, it flattens as one moves southeast along its length. The **marginal rate of substitution (MRS)** measures the amount of one good the consumer is willing to give up to obtain a unit of the other good. In other words, MRS measures the trade-off between the goods in terms of the consumer's preferences. To be

FIGURE 3A.3

The Consumer's
Optimal Consumption
Bundle

The consumer attains
her highest level of
welfare at point B,
where her indifference
curve is tangent to the
budget line.

specific, MRS measures the slope of the indifference curve at any bundle; that is, MRS $= -\Delta Y/\Delta X$ along the indifference curve. In the present example, the MRS at point B is 2.

Now we are ready to state a general result:

> The consumer's optimal consumption bundle is found where the marginal rate of substitution is exactly equal to the ratio of the product prices, MRS $= P_X/P_Y$.

Another way of saying this is that the consumer's preference trade-off between the goods should exactly equal the price trade-off she faces. The MRS represents the *value* of X in terms of Y, whereas P_X/P_Y is the *price* of X in terms of Y. If the relative value of X were greater than its relative price (such as is the case at point D), the consumer would shift to additional purchases of X and thereby move to higher indifference curves. At point E, the situation is reversed. The relative value of X falls short of its relative price, so the consumer would purchase less of X. The consumer's optimal purchase quantities (3 units of X and 4 units of Y) occur at point B. Here, MRS $= P_X/P_Y = 2$. No change in purchases could increase the consumer's welfare.

Demand Curves

The demand curve graphs the relationship between a good's price and the quantity demanded, holding all other factors constant. Consider the consumer's purchase of good X as its price is varied (holding income and the price of Y constant). What if the price falls from $4 per unit to $2 per unit to $1 per unit? Figure 3A.4 shows the effect of these price changes on the consumer's budget line. As the price falls from $4 to $2, the budget line flattens and pivots around its vertical intercept. (Note that, with the price of Y unchanged, the maximum amount of Y the consumer can purchase remains the same.) The figure shows the new budget lines and new points of optimal consumption at the lower prices.

As one would expect, reduction in price brings forth greater purchases of good X and increases the consumer's welfare (i.e., she moves to higher indifference curves). The figure also shows a **price–consumption curve** that passes through the optimal consumption points. This curve shows the consumer's optimal consumption as the price of X is varied continuously. Using this curve, we can record the consumption of X at each price. If we plot the quantity of X

FIGURE 3A.4

The Price–
Consumption Curve

The price–consumption curve shows that the consumer's demand for X increases as its price falls.

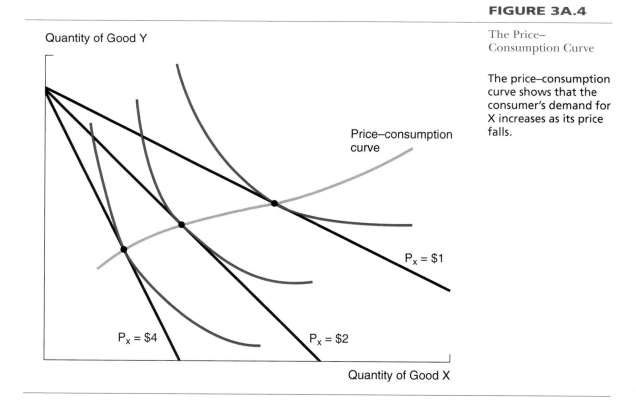

demanded versus its price, we arrive at the consumer's demand curve for X; it has the usual downward slope. The consumer increases her optimal consumption of X in response to lower prices.

Of course, different individuals will have varying preferences for goods and varying incomes. For these reasons, they obviously will have different demand curves. How do we arrive at the market demand curve (the total demand by all consumers as price varies)? The answer is found by summing the quantities demanded by all consumers at any given price. Graphically, this amounts to *horizontally* summing the individual demand curves. The result is the market demand curve.[3]

Questions and Problems

1. a. Consider a different consumer who has much steeper indifference curves than those depicted in Figure 3A.1. Draw a graph showing such curves. What do these curves imply about his relative valuation for good X versus good Y?
   b. Using the curves from part a and the budget line in Equation 3A.1, graph the consumer's optimal consumption bundle. How does his consumption bundle compare with that of the original consumer? Is it still true that MRS = P_X/P_Y = 2?

2. a. Suppose the income the consumer has available to spend on goods increases to $30. Graph the new budget line and sketch a new indifference curve to pinpoint the consumer's new optimal consumption bundle. According to your graph, does the consumer purchase more of each good?
   b. Sketch a graph (with an appropriate indifference curve) in which one of the goods is inferior. That is, the rise in income causes the consumer to purchase less of one of the goods.

3. Suppose that the price of good X rises and the price of good Y falls in such a way that the consumer's new optimal consumption bundle lies on the same indifference curve as his old bundle. Graph this situation. Compare the quantities demanded between the old and new bundles.

---

[3] Of course, market researchers do not investigate demand individual by individual. Rather, they survey random representative samples of potential consumers. The main point is that properties of individual demand curves—their downward slope stemming from optimal consumption behavior—carry over to the market demand curve itself.

Interdependent Demand

Almost all modern firms serve the marketplace by producing multiple (usually related) products that vary with respect to model, quality, and performance. Major automobile producers sell subcompacts, compacts, midsize cars, luxury cars, and sports cars. A large consumer-products firm (e.g., Procter & Gamble or General Foods) offers scores of brands. A giant computer firm (e.g., IBM) produces a range of computers for purchase or lease: personal computers, micro- and mini-computers, scientific workstations, and mainframe computers.

What effects do multiple products have on the firm's optimal pricing strategy? In the special case where demands for its products are *independent*, there is no real complication. The firm can analyze each product separately and determine a price and output to maximize that product's profit (by the means previously discussed). By maximizing profit product by product, the firm maximizes total profit. Complications arise when the demands for the firm's products are **interdependent**, that is, when there is competition or complementarity among the firm's products. In each of the examples just cited, the firm's own products (to a greater or lesser extent) compete with one another. Thus, in setting the price for a particular item, the firm must take into account the potential effects on its other products. For instance, a reduction in the price of compact cars increases sales in this category but partly at the expense of midsize and subcompact sales. A computer manufacturer faces similar interdependencies in demand.

The logic of marginal analysis can easily handle interdependent demand. Let's focus on a pair of products, A and B. We start by writing down the profit expression:

$$\pi = R_A(Q_A, Q_B) + R_B(Q_A, Q_B) - C_A(Q_A) - C_B(Q_B),$$

where the subscripts denote the product with which revenues and costs are associated. As indicated, a product's revenue depends not only on its own unit sales but also on the sales of the other product. Assuming products A and B are partial substitutes, an increase in sales of A (via a lower price) will *reduce* B's sales (and, therefore, revenue) and vice versa. How does the firm determine its optimal sales quantities? It produces up to the point where the increase in *total* revenue from selling an extra unit of A equals the extra cost of the unit of A and similarly for B. In algebraic terms,

and

$$MTR_A = \partial R_A/\partial Q_A + \partial R_B/\partial Q_A = MC_A$$

$$MTR_B = \partial R_A/\partial Q_B + \partial R_B/\partial Q_B = MC_B$$

where MTR denotes marginal total revenue.

Because the goods are substitutes, an increase in the sales of one reduces the revenue of the other; the so-called cross-marginal revenue terms, $\partial R_A/\partial Q_B$ and $\partial R_B/\partial Q_A$, are negative. (In contrast, if the demands were independent, these terms would be zero, and the problem would reduce to separate profit maximizations.) The negative cross-marginal revenue term in each equation lowers total MTR (in effect, it shifts the graph of MTR down and to the left). Consequently, the optimal sales quantity of each good is reduced and the good's price increased relative to the case of independent demands. (Check this by shifting the MR graph to the left and finding the new MR = MC crossing at a lower sales quantity.) This makes perfect sense. The firm neither lowers price nor expands sales as far when the goods are substitutes. It recognizes that the extra revenue it would get from selling slightly more of one good would come at the expense of some lost revenue on the other.

EXAMPLE   Suppose a firm produces goods A and B, which have constant marginal costs of 80 and 40, respectively. Demand for the goods is given by the price equations $P_A = 280 - 2Q_A$ and $P_B = 180 - Q_B - 2Q_A$. (Note that increased sales of A adversely affect demand for B but not vice versa.) Total revenue is

$$TR = R_A + R_B$$
$$= (280Q_A - 2Q_A^2) + (180Q_B - Q_B^2 - 2Q_AQ_B).$$

Therefore,

$$MTR_A = 280 - 4Q_A - 2Q_B$$

and

$$MTR_B = 180 - 2Q_B - 2Q_A.$$

Setting each product's marginal revenue equal to its marginal cost leaves two equations in two unknowns: $280 - 4Q_A - 2Q_B = 80$ and $180 - 2Q_B - 2Q_A = 40$. The solution is $Q_A = 30$ and $Q_B = 40$. Optimal prices (obtained by substituting Q_A and Q_B into the price equations) are $P_A = 220$ and $P_B = 80$. These quantities and prices comprise the firm's total profit-maximizing strategy.

In contrast, consider the outcome if product A's manager ignores the cross-effect of A and B and simply maximizes A's profit instead of total profit. Product A's revenue is $(280Q_A - 2Q_A^2)$, so marginal revenue is $280 - 4Q_A$. Setting this equal to MC (80), the manager sets $Q_A = 50$ and $P_A = 180$. Maximizing product A's profit alone results in too large a quantity. Taking into account the total revenue implications, the manager should lower A's output (from 50 to 30).

If the goods are complements (increased sales of one good enhance sales of the other), the effect is exactly the reverse. Then the cross-marginal revenue terms are positive. Relative to the case of independent demand, the firm increases the output of each good to take advantage of the positive cross-revenue effects. To illustrate, suppose that the price equation for product B is $P_B = 180 - Q_B + .35Q_A$ (i.e., demand for B depends positively on sales of A) with all other economic facts the same as before. It is easy to check that the marginal conditions are

$$MTR_A = 280 - 4Q_A + .35Q_B = 80$$

and

$$MTR_B = 180 - 2Q_B + .35Q_A = 40.$$

The resulting optimal outputs and prices are $Q_A = 57$, $Q_B = 80$, and $P_A = 166$ and $P_B = 120$. Relative to the case of independent demands, the firm cuts its price on product A, increasing unit sales (though sacrificing direct revenue) and in turn greatly spurring sales of product B.

CHAPTER 4

Estimating Demand

To count is a modern practice, the ancient method was to guess; and when numbers are guessed, they are always magnified.

SAMUEL JOHNSON

I know half the money I spend on advertising is wasted, but I can never find out which half.

LORD LEVERHULME OF UNILEVER

Estimating Movie Demand

Making movies is a risky business. Even if you find the most promising screenplay, assemble the best actors, finish the film on time and on budget, and mount a substantial marketing campaign, your film may still "bomb." Yet studios continue to produce movies and theaters continue to book them, and the profit of each depends directly on the demand that materializes in the first few weeks of play. (Studios also milk other sources of revenue: international receipts, DVD revenues, and TV sales, but the initial box-office response almost always predicts these other revenue flows. Rarely does a lackluster film turn a profit because of subsequent windfalls from TV runs and the like.)

Studios and theaters must forecast a film's potential box-office revenue. Studios need to discover what kinds of films to make and how much to invest in production and marketing. Theaters must decide which films to book, how much they should be willing to pay for the booking, and how much to charge customers. Indeed, forecasting the likely demand for new film releases has evolved from a subjective "art" to a hard-nosed, statistical "science." Decision makers use sophisticated mathematical forecasting techniques to derive better estimates of a film's likely box-office revenues. Up to a dozen variables—the film's genre, the quality of its cast and director, the timing of its release (time of year and number of competing films released at the same time), the breadth of its release (limited release in selected theaters or mass release nationwide), the magnitude of the advertising and promotional campaign, reviews and word of mouth—together influence the film's expected gross receipts earned per screen and per week.

Given this risky and complicated forecasting environment, how can film producers, distributors, and exhibitors derive sound quantitative predictions of a new film's likely box-office revenues?

In previous chapters, we used demand equations but we did not explain where they came from. The firm's forecasters collect a great deal of information about demand. They then must transform this information into demand equations that are crucial to management's decisions.

It is important to understand what one can expect to get out of business forecasts. The output of the forecasting effort comes in three forms: (1) the forecast itself, (2) the relationship between the forecast and the economic variables that influence it, and (3) an assessment of the accuracy of the forecast.

Consider once again the airline demand forecasts for the Houston–Florida route from Chapter 3. Recall that three main economic variables affect sales: the price charged by the airline, its competitor's price, and regional income. Suppose that we expect the airline and its competitor to maintain their current prices over the coming year and that income in the region will increase by 5 percent. Based on these assumptions, the firm's business economist predicts that in the coming year the airline will sell around 100 coach tickets per flight.

This numerical forecast—the first result of the forecasting effort—is of obvious importance to the manager. But, as we saw in Chapter 3, the forecast by itself does not capture all the information about demand that management needs. A more complete description of demand is given by the airline's demand equation,

$$Q = 25 + 3Y + P^° - 2P, \qquad [4.1]$$

where Q denotes number of seats sold, Y is regional income, $P^°$ is the competitor's price, and P is the airline's own price. This equation summarizes the relationship between the level of sales and the factors that influence it. From this, we can generate specific forecasts under different assumptions. (For example, inserting Y = 105 and the current prices, P = $P^°$ = \$240, into Equation 4.1 produces the forecast Q = 100.) In addition, the manager can use the equation to test the effect on sales of alternative forecasts of income and prices.

The demand equation tells us a lot more than a single forecast but, to make good decisions, we need more. Just as important is the *accuracy* of our predictions. In previous chapters, it has been assumed that the volume of sales, revenue, and costs could be predicted with certainty. Obviously, under this assumption, forecast accuracy is not an issue. But we know that in the real world uncertainty clouds the future, and forecasts suffer from significant errors that can destroy whole businesses and bring down careers. Thus, the manager should consider three basic kinds of questions:

1. What is the "best" forecasting equation that can be obtained (estimated) from the available data? How well does this equation explain changes in the economic variable of interest?

2. What does the equation *not* explain? What can be said about the likelihood and magnitude of forecast errors?

3. What are the profit consequences of such errors?

In this chapter and Chapter 5 (dealing with forecasting), we focus on the first two questions; in Chapters 8 and 9, we address the third.

This chapter is organized as follows. In the next section, we examine sources of information that provide data for forecasts. These include consumer interviews and surveys, controlled market studies, and uncontrolled market data. In the following sections, we explore regression analysis, a statistical method widely used in demand estimation.

SOURCES OF INFORMATION

Consumer Interviews and Surveys

A direct way to gather information about demand is to ask people. Face-to-face, by telephone, online, or via direct mail, companies use interviews and marketing surveys to ask current and prospective customers a host of questions: How much of the product do you plan to buy this year? What if the price increased by 10 percent? Do price rebates influence your purchase decisions and, if so, by how much? What features do you value most? Do you know about the current advertising campaign for the product? Do you purchase competing products? If so, what do you like about them? To those subjected to the questioning, the list of questions may seem endless.

Consumer-products companies use surveys and interviews extensively to glean valuable information. In a given year, Campbell Soup Company questions over 100,000 consumers about foods and uses the responses to modify and improve its product offerings. A well-designed survey administered to a large and representative number of consumers provides estimates of planned product purchases under different price and quality conditions. From this information, the firm constructs appropriate demand equations. For instance, the southern airline described in the previous section could ask a sample of Houston residents, business travelers, and nonbusiness travelers about their travel plans to Florida. Specific questions would concern the prices, services, convenience, and visibility of the airline and of competing airlines. Other questions would seek to determine how personal income and business conditions affect travel frequency. From these ingredients, the firm's management could construct a demand equation, such as Equation 4.1, for use in forecasting and in making managerial decisions.

A classic example of the consumer survey method is illustrated by the design of the hotel chain, Courtyard by Marriott.[1] Marriott Corporation undertook extensive market research before establishing (and subsequently introducing nationwide) its new hotel design: a small, quiet, informal, high-value hotel attractive to price-sensitive business and vacation travelers. The company surveyed over 600 consumers in four cities, paying people to come to a central location and complete a survey concerning some 50 hotel attributes related to room design, food, services, leisure activities, security, hotel location, price, and so on. Table 4.1, reproduced from the study, summarizes the alternatives participants faced. Marriott market researchers designed the survey to check and cross-check participants' responses. For instance, after asking participants to evaluate individual hotel features at given prices, they then asked participants to reevaluate the *total* hotel package they had selected, indicating whether they found it attractive at the implied price or whether it could be improved further.

According to the survey results, respondents clearly preferred a type of hotel not then offered in the marketplace. Using information from the survey, Marriott estimated price and cross-price elasticities of demand with respect to major competitors, as well as expected market shares under different (what-if) assumptions. It turned out that the "optimal" hotel design differed significantly from what management had originally envisioned (a "smaller" Marriott offering features similar to the trademark hotel). The new hotel attracted so many customers that by the end of 1989, Marriott had opened 150 new Courtyard by Marriott hotels. By 2005, the number had grown to over 600 nationwide allowing the company to continue a strategy of expansion and profitability. Predictably, at least five "clone" chains have been opened by other hotel groups.

SURVEY PITFALLS   The Marriott example demonstrates the advantages of consumer surveys. Yet managers must also consider the pitfalls. For example, market researchers may ask the right questions but of the wrong people. Economists call this **sample bias**. In some contexts, random sampling protects against sample bias. In other cases, marketers design surveys to select a representative sample of the relevant market segment under examination.

A second problem is **response bias**. There is always the danger that respondents might report what they believe the questioner wants to hear. ("Your product is terrific, and I intend to buy it this year if at all possible.") Alternatively, the customer may attempt to influence decision making. ("If you raise the price, I definitely will stop buying.") Neither response will likely reflect the potential customer's true preferences.

A third problem is **response accuracy**. Even if unbiased and forthright, a potential customer may have difficulty in answering a question accurately. ("I think I might buy it at that price, but when push comes to shove, who knows?").

Courtyard by Marriott

---

[1] A discussion and analysis of this marketing study appear in J. Wind et al., "Courtyard by Marriott: Designing a Hotel Facility with Consumer-Based Marketing Models," *Interfaces* 19 (1989): 25-47.

TABLE 4.1

Results of
Marriott Survey

Marriott used a survey
that sought
information about 50
features and services
of its Courtyard hotels.
The 50 factors that
describe hotel features
and services and the
associated (167) levels
are categorized under
seven headings. The
italicized items were
included in the final
design of the hotel.

External Factors
Building shape
  L-shaped w/landscape
  Outdoor courtyard
Landscaping
  Minimal
  Moderate
  Elaborate
Pool type
  No pool
  Rectangular shape
  Free-form shape
  Indoor/outdoor
Pool location
  In courtyard
  Not in courtyard
Corridor/view
  Outside access/restricted
    view
  Enclosed access/unrestricted
    view/balcony or window
Hotel size
  Small (125 rooms,
    2 stories)
  Large (600 rooms, 12
    stories)
Rooms
Entertainment
  Color TV
  Color TV w/movies at $5
  Color TV w/30-channel
    cable
  Color TV w/HBO, movies,
    etc.
  Color TV w/free movies
Entertainment/rental
  None
  Rental cassettes/in room
    Atari
  Rental cassettes/stereo
    cassette playing in
    room
  Rental movies in-room
    BetaMax
Size
  Small (standard)
  Slightly larger (1 foot)
  Much larger ($2\frac{1}{2}$ feet)
  Small suite (2 rooms)
  Large suite (2 rooms)

Quality of decor (in
  standard room)
  Budget motel decor
  Old Holiday Inn decor
  New Holiday Inn decor
  New Hilton decor
  New Hyatt decor
Heating and cooling
  Wall unit full control
  Wall unit soundproof full
    control
  Central H or C (seasonal)
  Central H or C (full
    control)
Size of bath
  Standard bath
  Slightly larger, sink separate
  Much larger bath w/
    larger tub
  Very large tub for 2
Sink location
  In bath only
  In separate area
  In bath and separate
Bathroom features
  None
  Shower massage
  Whirlpool (Jacuzzi)
  Steam bath
Amenities
  Small bar soap
  Large soap/shampoo/
    shoeshine
  Large soap/bath gel/
    shower cap/sewing kit
  Above items +
    toothpaste, deodorant,
    mouthwash
Food
Restaurant in hotel
  None (coffee shop next
    door)
  Restaurant/Lounge combo,
    limited menu
  Coffee shop, full menu
  Full-service restaurant,
    full menu
  Coffee shop/full menu
    and good restaurant
  None

Restaurant nearby
  None
  Coffee shop
  Fast food
  Fast food or coffee shop
    and moderate
    restaurant
  Fast food or coffee shop and
    good restaurant
Free continental
  None
  Continental included in
    room rate
Room service
  None
  Phone-in order/guest to
    pick up
  Room service, limited
    menu
  Room service, full menu
Store
  No food in store
  Snack items
  Snacks, refrigerated
    items, wine, beer,
    liquor
  Above items and
    gourmet food items
Vending service
  None
  Soft-drink machine only
  Soft-drink and snack
    machines
  Soft-drink, snack, and
    sandwich machines
  Above and microwave
    available
In-room kitchen facilities
  None
  Coffee maker only
  Coffee maker and
    refrigerator
  Kitchen in room
Lounge
Atmosphere
  Quiet bar/lounge
  Lively, popular bar/lounge
Type of people
  Hotel guests and friends
    only

TABLE 4.1

(continued)

Open to public—general appeal
Open to public—many singles
Lounge nearby
None
Lounge/bar nearby
Lounge/bar w/ entertainment nearby
Services
Reservations
    Call hotel directly
    800 reservation number
Check-in
    Standard
    Pre-credit clearance
    Machine in lobby
Check-out
    At front desk
    Bill under door/leave key
    Key to front desk/bill by mail
    Machine in lobby
Limo to airport
    None
    Yes
Bellman
    None
    Yes
Message service
    Note at front desk
    Light on phone
    Light on phone and message under door
    Recorded message
Cleanliness/upkeep/ management skill
    Budget motor level
    Holiday Inn level
    Nonconvention Hyatt level
    Convention Hyatt level
    Fine hotel level
Laundry/Valet
    None
    Client pick up and drop off
    Self-service

Valet pick up and drop off
Special services (concierge)
    None
    Information on restaurants, theaters, etc.
    Arrangements and reservations
    Travel-problem resolution
Secretarial services
    None
    Xerox machine
    Xerox machine and typist
Car maintenance
    None
    Take car to service
    Gas on premises/bill to room
Car rental/airline reservations
    None
    Car rental facility
    Airline reservations
    Car rental and airline reservations
Leisure
Sauna
    None
    Yes
Whirlpool/Jacuzzi
    None
    Outdoor
    Indoor
Exercise room
    None
    Basic facility w/ weights
    Facility w/Nautilus equipment
Racquetball courts
    None
    Yes
Tennis courts
    None
    Yes

Game room/entertainment
    None
    Electric games/pinball
    Electric games/pinball/ ping pong
    Above + movie theater, bowling
Children's playroom/ playground
    None
    Playground only
    Playroom only
    Playground and playroom
Pool extras
    None
    Pool w/slides
    Pool w/slides and equipment
    Pool w/slides, waterfall, equipment
Security
Security guard
    None
    11 A.M. to 7 P.M.
    7 P.M. to 7 A.M.
    24 hours
Smoke detector
    None
    In rooms and throughout hotel
Sprinkler system
    None
    Lobby and hallways only
    Lobby/hallways/rooms
24-hour video camera
    None
    Parking/hallway/public areas
Alarm button
    None
    Button in room, rings desk

Potential customers often have little idea of how they will react to a price increase or to an increase in advertising. In other words, response accuracy may be low.

A final difficulty is **cost**. Despite the falling cost of computer analysis and the emergence of firms specializing in the provision of consumer-survey information, conducting extensive consumer surveys is extremely costly. As in any economic decision, the costs of acquiring additional information must be weighed against the benefits. For instance, there is no point in conducting extensive consumer surveys that merely confirm what the company already knows about its customers' needs and preferences.[2]

An alternative to consumer surveys is the use of controlled consumer experiments. For example, consumers are given money (real or script) and must make purchasing decisions. Researchers then vary key demand variables (and hold others constant) to determine how the variables affect consumer purchases. Because consumers make actual decisions (instead of simply being asked about their preferences and behavior), their results are likely to be more accurate than those of consumer surveys. Nonetheless, this approach shares some of the same difficulties as surveys. Consumers know they are participating in an experiment and this may affect their responses. For example, they may react to price much more in an experiment than they do in real life. In addition, controlled experiments are expensive. Consequently, they generally are small (few participants) and short, thus limiting their accuracy. As the following example shows, consumer surveys and experiments do not always accurately foretell actual demand.

New Coke

In April 1985, Coca-Cola Company announced it would change the formulation of the world's best-selling soft drink to an improved formula: New Coke. This move followed nearly five years of market research and planning—perhaps the most intensive and costly program in history. In some 190,000 taste tests conducted by the company, consumers favored New Coke consistently over the old (by 55 to 45 percent in blind tests) and, perhaps more important, over Pepsi. In the 1980s, the company's market share had fallen due to competition from Pepsi. Moreover, Pepsi had beaten the old Coke convincingly in highly publicized taste tests.

With the advantage of 20-20 hindsight, we all know that the taste tests were wrong. (It just goes to show that you can succeed in doing the wrong thing, even with 190,000 people backing you up.) New Coke did not replace the old Coke in the hearts and mouths of soft-drink consumers. Why? The tests failed to measure the psychological attachment of Coke drinkers to their product. In response to the protests of die-hard old-Coke drinkers and evidence that the old Coke was outselling New Coke by four to one, Coca-Cola Company revived the old Coke (three months after announcing its discontinuance) and apologized to its customers. With its quick about-face, Coca-Cola minimized the damage to its flagship product, now called Coke Classic. In the last 20 years, Coca-Cola has greatly

---

[2] The same point applies to setting the design and size of a given consumer survey. In principle, the number of respondents should be set such that the marginal benefit from adding an additional respondent in the sample matches its marginal cost.

expanded its cola offerings: Diet Coke, Cherry Coke, and Caffeine-free Coke, among other offerings. On the advertising, image, taste, and new-product fronts, the cola wars between PepsiCo and Coca-Cola continue.

Controlled Market Studies

Firms can also generate data on product demand by selling their product in several smaller markets while varying key demand determinants, such as price, across the markets. The firm might set a high price with high advertising spending in one market, a high price and low advertising in another, a low price and high advertising in yet another, and so on. By observing sales responses in the different markets, the firm can learn how various pricing and advertising policies (and possible interactions among them) affect demand.

To draw valid conclusions from such market studies, all other factors affecting demand should vary as little as possible across the markets. The most common—and important—of these "other" demand factors include population size, consumer incomes and tastes, competitors' prices, and even differences in climate. Unfortunately, regional and cultural differences, built-up brand loyalties, and other subtle but potentially important differences may thwart the search for uniform markets. In practice, researchers seek to identify and control as many of these extraneous factors as possible. Moreover, as we shall see later in the chapter, there are statistical techniques to account for and measure the impact of these uncontrolled factors. Partial control is far better than no control.

Market studies generate **cross-sectional data**—observations of economic entities (consumers or firms) in different regions or markets during the same time period. Another type of market study relies on **time-series data**. Here the firm chooses a single geographic area and varies its key decision variables over time to gauge market response. The firm might begin by setting a high price and a low advertising expenditure and observing the market response. Some time later, it may increase advertising; later still, it may lower price; and so on. Time-series experiments have the advantage that they test a single (and, one would hope, representative) population, thus avoiding some of the problems of uncontrolled factors encountered in cross-sectional studies. However, over a lengthy period, other factors may change. (Even the change in the seasons may significantly affect demand.) The time-series approach also suffers from the problem that consumers respond not only to today's factors but to yesterday's as well. For example, high advertising will affect demand not only in the current period but also in subsequent periods. Thus, neither cross-sectional market experiments nor time-series market experiments produce data that are completely "clean." Again, statistical techniques can help resolve some of the problems of interpreting the data.

Market experimentation is expensive—often extremely so. A very rough rule of thumb holds that it costs $1 million to conduct a market test in 1 percent of the United States. Part of the cost comes from the effort of locating suitable markets and of customizing the experiment for each market. A substantial part comes from the experiment itself. In the preceding example, two of the markets featured a low price and two of the markets had high advertising expenditures. As a result, researchers generally run such experiments for short periods of time and for very limited markets. Consequently, the data generated may tell something about short-term demand but very little about long-term demand. Because of the limited amount of data, estimates of demand have large margins of error. Thus, one must not read too much into the data. Despite these qualifications, however, firms use market experiments frequently and such experiments do generate useful information.

Shopping in the Virtual Store

Goodyear Tire & Rubber had always sold its tires through its own stores. When the company decided to make its tires available to tire retailers, it faced a number of questions. How would the Goodyear tire fare when placed side by side with competitors? How much was the Goodyear name worth? Did the name justify charging a premium? Should Goodyear try to compete on price or warranty? To answer these questions, Goodyear turned to a new methodology made possible by the rapid advance of computer technology: the virtual store.[3]

A virtual store simulates the shopping experience. Using either a computer screen or, for greater realism, a head-mounted display, a computer creates images that simulate the experience of a consumer walking down a store's aisles. As the consumer progresses, products become visible on shelves. By touching the image on the computer screen, the consumer picks up the product, turns it around, examines it, and ultimately, if the consumer so desires, puts it in the shopping basket. The computer records the consumer's shopping behavior, including the order in which the consumer perused the items, the amount of time spent examining various facets of the item, and the quantity that the consumer purchased.

By creating the virtual store, researchers simulate realistic environments. Consumers see the product on the shelves surrounded by competitive products and competing distractions. In addition, researchers can easily change the look of the packaging, the attributes of the product, its location, and its price. This test-marketing methodology fits nicely with computer-aided design. Designers create product images that they can put into the virtual store for test marketing. Once the virtual store is up and running, researchers recruit representative consumers, telling them that they are involved in a test of a new way to shop by computer and asking them to shop in their normal way.

A number of studies have indicated that such simulations produce sound predictive results. In the case of Goodyear, researchers created a virtual retail store that featured Goodyear tires side by side with competitors' tires. Almost 1,000 consumers participated in the study, each taking a trip through the virtual store. The computer varied the price and warranty coverage of the Goodyear and competitors' tires.

The possibilities of the virtual store are almost limitless. One candy manufacturer employed this technique by creating a virtual vending machine. The

---

[3] The information in this section is based on R. Burke, "Virtual Shopping," *OR/MS Today* (August 1995).

computer varied the price and availability of the manufacturer's products and those of competitors. Retailers have also employed the virtual store to help determine store layout and display.

An airline is considering expanding its business-class seating (offering more room and amenities to business travelers at a slightly higher fare than coach). Which method, survey or market study, would you recommend to gather information for this decision?

CHECK STATION 1

Uncontrolled Market Data

In its everyday operation, the market itself produces a large amount of data. Many firms operate in multiple markets. Population, income, product features, product quality, prices, and advertising vary across markets and over time. All of this change creates both opportunity and difficulty for the market researcher. Change gives researchers the opportunity to view how changing factors affect demand. With uncontrolled markets, however, many factors relevant to demand change simultaneously across markets and over time. How, then, is a firm to judge the effect of any single factor on demand? Fortunately, statisticians have developed methods to handle this very problem. We examine these techniques in detail in the next section.

During the last decade firms have increasingly used sophisticated, computer-based methods of gathering market data. Today more than three-quarters of all supermarkets employ check-out scanners. These not only improve inventory control but also provide enormous quantities of data about consumer purchases. In addition, more and more people shop via the Internet. As customers make electronic purchases, computer programs automatically enter their data into databases. Retailers use the information and also sell it to product manufacturers. Thus, a cereal producer can observe how its pricing and promotional policies affect sales. Gathering this (relatively uncontrolled) data is quick and cheap—as little as one-tenth the cost of controlled market tests.[4] Indeed, this data mining has reached new and ever more sophisticated heights. Using new computers featuring massively parallel processors and neural networks, companies can search through and organize millions of pieces of data about customers and their buying habits. With these data, companies can divide the market into segments based on customer characteristics and can market products to customers based on their propensity to buy and their price elasticity of demand. (See the discussion of price discrimination in the previous chapter.) Financial services companies (such as American Express) and travel services companies (primarily airlines), among

---

[4] This kind of market research can track even the behavior of consumers from the TV set to the checkout counter. A household's television viewing is tracked by microcomputer and its supermarket purchases recorded using a special identification card. Market researchers attempt to discern the effects of television advertising on consumption behavior. (Some companies even test specially designed advertisements this way.)

others, pioneered these advances. Consumer-products companies, such as Kraft and Unilever, also use such database marketing.

Firms also purchase data and access publicly available data. For example, the University of Michigan publishes surveys of consumer buying plans for durable items and also an index of consumer optimism or pessimism. The U.S. Bureau of the Census disseminates *Consumer Buying Intention* and the Consumers Union publishes *Consumer Reports*. Often the firm spends less using published or purchased forecasts than by gathering and processing the data itself. Firms frequently need off-the-shelf forecasts as inputs to its own firm-generated model. For example, a firm may have determined, via its own studies, that gross domestic product (GDP) greatly affects the demand for its product. The firm may purchase forecasts of GDP that are more accurate than those it could produce itself at a similar cost.

Tracking Movie Revenues

In 1975, when the movie *Jaws* opened in theaters, there existed no systematic reporting of nationwide gross revenues.[5] *Variety* magazine reported on film openings and estimated box-office results in major markets such as New York and Chicago. Tracking nationwide gross revenues began with Art Murphy, a reporter for *Variety* and a former Navy systems analyst. In 1985, he published "Art Murphy's Box Office Register," which listed films, their grosses, per-screen averages, and other information. Murphy wrote, "Box office grosses represent the responses of PEOPLE to films. To ignore those numbers—and those people—is to risk business failure and worse to inhabit the catatonic world of the aesthete." Still, it was not until 1996 that *Variety* began publishing Monday-morning estimates of weekend grosses.

Meanwhile, in the late seventies, Joe Farrell, a former political pollster backed by director Francis Ford Coppola, brought modern survey techniques to the task of predicting audience reaction. Farrell's firm developed extensive databases listing each film's revenues along with its key characteristics. Today research firms collect data at the point of sale. Movie grosses become available instantaneously permitting studios and movie theater chains to estimate grosses based on a wide variety of characteristics. Nonetheless, movie studios and theaters still experience unexpected successes and failures.

REGRESSION ANALYSIS

As already noted, statistical methods can be used to help resolve some of the problems in analyzing uncontrolled market data. **Regression analysis** is a set of statistical techniques that quantify the dependence of a given economic variable on one or more other variables. The method uses past observations to find (or estimate) the equation that "best" summarizes the relationships among the variables. Because regression analysis is a powerful and widely employed tool, it is important to understand how it works, its main assumptions, and potential problems encountered with its use. The method requires that analysts (1) col-

[5] This account is based on D. Hayes and J. Bing, "The Hollywood Horse Race," *The Boston Globe*, September 19, 2004.

lect data on the variables in question, (2) specify the form of the equation relating the variables, (3) estimate the equation coefficients, and (4) evaluate the accuracy of the equation. Let's begin with a concrete example.

Ordinary Least-Squares Regression

In the central example in Chapter 3, an airline's management used a demand equation to predict ticket sales and to make operating decisions along a Texas–Florida air route. Now let's examine how the airline can use regression analysis to estimate such an equation. The airline begins by collecting data on ticket sales from the recent past. The second column of Table 4.2 shows the average number of coach seats sold per flight for each quarter (i.e., 90 days) over the last four years. We observe that sales vary quarter by quarter. In the best quarter, customers bought over 137 seats on each flight; in the worst, only a year earlier, customers bought just under 34 seats. Over the four-year period, the airline sold 87.2 seats on average.

The **mean** (i.e., the average) gives us some idea of the level of sales we can expect. We would also like some idea of how much the sales can deviate from the average. The usual measure of variability is called the **sample variance** defined as:

$$s^2 = \frac{\sum_{i=1}^{n} (Q_i - \overline{Q})^2}{n - 1}$$

TABLE 4.2

Year and Quarter		Average Number of Coach Seats	Average Price	Ticket Prices and Ticket Sales along an Air Route
Y1	Q1	64.8	250	
	Q2	33.6	265	
	Q3	37.8	265	
	Q4	83.3	240	
Y2	Q1	111.7	230	
	Q2	137.5	225	
	Q3	109.6	225	
	Q4	96.8	220	
Y3	Q1	59.5	230	
	Q2	83.2	235	
	Q3	90.5	245	
	Q4	105.5	240	
Y4	Q1	75.7	250	
	Q2	91.6	240	
	Q3	112.7	240	
	Q4	102.2	235	
Mean		87.2	239.7	
Standard deviation		27.0	12.7	

Here Q_i denotes each of the quarterly sales figures, $\overline{Q}$ is the overall mean, and n is the number of observations. In short, we look at the difference between each observation and the mean, square these differences, and then average them. (We use n − 1 instead of n for technical reasons.) As the dispersion of the observations increases, so does the variance.

In turn, the sample **standard deviation** s is simply the square root of the variance. By taking the square root (after squaring the differences), we ensure that the standard deviation is measured in the same units as the sample observations. In the present example, we can compute the sample variance to be $s^2 = 11{,}706/16 = 731.6$. In turn, the standard deviation of the airline's sales is given by s = $\sqrt{731.6}$ = 27.0 seats

Now consider a basic question: Knowing only the past 16 quarters of sales (nothing else), how can we best predict next quarter's sales and how good will this prediction be? We might use 87.2 seats, namely, the sample mean. After all, the mean is intended to capture the central tendency of the (admittedly dispersed) sample. This is the right answer, and there is a precise sense in which it is right.

When we computed sample variance, squared differences were measured from the mean, 87.2. But what if we had chosen some other value, say, 83 or 92, as our estimate of the sample's central tendency? Computing the sum of squares around either of these values, we find that it is much larger than around the mean. Employing calculus techniques, we can show that using the sample mean always *minimizes* the sum of squared errors. In this sense, the sample mean is the most accurate estimate of the central tendency of past observations. Of course, we should recognize the considerable chance of error in using 87.2 as next quarter's forecast. Given the variability in past sales, next quarter's sales are very likely to fluctuate above or below 87.2. But how accurate is this best guess? As a rough rule of thumb we can expect sales to be within two standard deviations of the mean 95 percent of the time. In our example, this means we can expect sales to be 87.2 plus or minus 54 seats (with a 5 percent chance that sales might fall outside this range).

Naturally, with more information, we hope to do better in explaining past ticket sales and predicting future sales. Invoking the basics of demand analysis, we begin with the past record of the airline's prices. These prices (quarterly averages) are listed in the third column of Table 4.2. Again there is considerable variability. It is apparent that the airline began with relatively high prices in the first year, lowered prices substantially in the second year, and settled on prices in the neighborhood of $240 in the most recent years. These data suggest a downward-sloping demand relationship. At high prices, the airline sold relatively few seats; when the airline cut prices, sales increased. Figure 4.1 provides a visual picture of the relationship. Each of the 16 points represents a price–quantity pair for a particular quarter. As Yogi Berra once said, "You can observe a lot by looking." The scatter of observations slopes downward: High prices generally imply low ticket sales, and vice versa. In short, based on the data collected and the scatter plot, there is strong qualitative evidence of downward-sloping demand.

The next step is to translate this scatter plot of points into a demand equation. A linear demand equation has the form

$$Q = a + bP.$$

The equation predicts ticket sales Q at a given price P. The left-hand variable (the one being predicted or explained) is called the *dependent* variable. The right-hand variable (the one doing the explaining) is called the *independent* (or explanatory) variable. As yet, the coefficients a and b have been left unspecified (i.e., not given numerical values). The coefficient a is called the constant term. The coefficient b (which we expect to have a negative sign) represents the slope of the demand equation. Up to this point, we have selected the *form* of the equation (a linear one) without writing down a particular equation. We

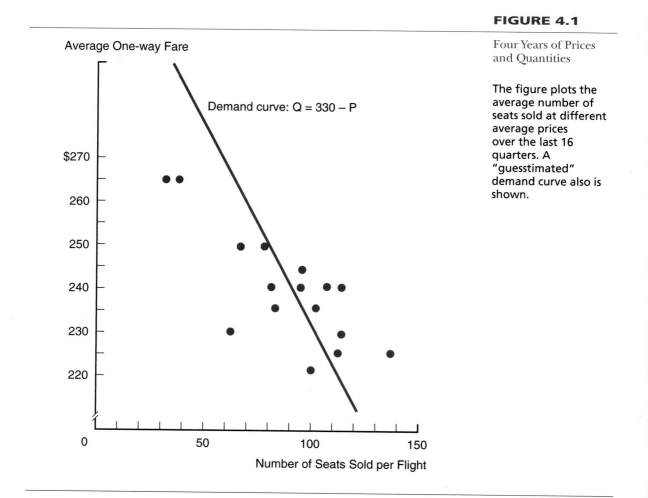

FIGURE 4.1

Four Years of Prices and Quantities

The figure plots the average number of seats sold at different average prices over the last 16 quarters. A "guesstimated" demand curve also is shown.

now can use regression analysis to compute values of a and b—values that will produce a specific equation that best fits the data.

The most common method of computing coefficients is called **ordinary least-squares (OLS) regression**. To illustrate the method, let's start by arbitrarily selecting particular values of a and b. Suppose a = 330 and b = −1. With these values, the demand equation becomes

$$Q = 330 - 1P. \qquad [4.2]$$

We plot this demand equation in Figure 4.1. Notice that the demand curve lies roughly along the scatter of observations. In this sense, the equation seems to provide a "good fit" with past observations. However, the fit is far from perfect. Many of the actual observations lie far from the equation line. This does not surprise us because sales can vary due to random factors or to other factors that have yet to be included in the equation (competing prices, income, and so on).

Table 4.3 lists Equation 4.2's sales predictions quarter by quarter. For instance, in the second column, the first quarter's sales prediction (at a price

TABLE 4.3

Predicted versus Actual Ticket Sales Using Q = 330 − P

Year and Quarter		Predicted Sales (Q*)	Actual Sales (Q)	Q* − Q	(Q* − Q)²
Y1	Q1	80	64.8	15.2	231.0
	Q2	65	33.6	31.4	986.0
	Q3	65	37.8	27.2	739.8
	Q4	90	83.3	6.7	44.9
Y2	Q1	100	111.7	−11.7	136.9
	Q2	105	137.5	−32.5	1,056.3
	Q3	105	109.5	−4.5	20.3
	Q4	110	96.8	13.2	174.2
Y3	Q1	100	59.5	40.5	1,640.3
	Q2	95	83.2	11.8	139.2
	Q3	85	90.5	−5.5	20.3
	Q4	90	105.5	−15.5	240.3
Y4	Q1	80	75.7	4.3	18.5
	Q2	90	91.6	−1.6	2.6
	Q3	90	112.7	−22.7	513.3
	Q4	95	102.2	−7.2	51.8
Mean		90.3	87.2	+3.1	376.7
				Sum of squared errors	6,027.7

of \$250) is computed as $330 - 250 = 80$. The third column lists actual sales. The fourth column lists the differences between predicted sales (column 2) and actual sales (column 3). In some quarters, the error is small; in others it is quite large. This difference (positive or negative) is referred to as the *estimation error*. To measure the overall accuracy of the equation, the ordinary least-squares regression method first squares the error for each separate estimate, then adds up the errors. The final column of Table 4.3 lists the squared errors. The total sum of squared errors comes to 6,027.7. The average squared error is $6{,}027.7/16 = 376.7$.

The sum of squared errors (denoted simply as SSE) measures the equation's predictive accuracy. The smaller the SSE, the more accurate the regression equation. (In fact, if all the price–quantity observations lay exactly on the equation line, the equation would predict each quarter without error, and SSE would be zero.) The reason for squaring the errors is twofold. First, by squaring, one treats negative errors in the same way as positive errors. Either error is equally bad. (If one simply added the errors over the observations, positive and negative errors would cancel out, giving a very misleading indication of overall accuracy.) Second, large errors usually are considered much worse than small errors. Squaring the errors makes large errors "count" much more than small errors in SSE. (We might mention, without elaborating, that there are also important statistical reasons for using the sum of squares.)

As the term suggests, **least-squares regression** computes coefficient values that give the smallest sum of squared errors. Using calculus techniques, statisticians have derived standard formulas for these least-squares estimates of the coefficients.[6] Based on the airline's 16 quarters of price and sales data, we have computed the least-squares estimators: $a = 478.6$ and $b = -1.63$. Thus, the estimated OLS equation is

$$Q = 478.6 - 1.63P. \qquad [4.3]$$

Table 4.4 lists Equation 4.3's sales forecasts and prediction errors quarter by quarter. The total sum of squared errors is 4,847.2—significantly smaller than the SSE (6,027.7) associated with Equation 4.2. Of all possible linear equations, Equation 4.3 produces the smallest sum of squared errors.

---

[6] Finding the least-squares estimators is itself an interesting optimization problem that can be solved using marginal analysis. In the foregoing problem, the coefficients a and b are chosen to minimize SSE. As always, the optimal coefficient values are found when no further change in either value can improve SSE; that is, marginal SSE with respect to each coefficient is zero. Indeed, the least-squares problem is roughly analogous to the mall-siting problem in Chapter 2. Think of the equation line in Figure 4.1 as a new highway to be located as near as possible to population centers, that is, the price–quantity points.

We provide the general formulas for the least-squares estimators for the interested reader. Suppose the estimated equation is of the form $y = a + bx$ and that the data to be fitted consist of n pairs of x-y observations (x_i, y_i), $i = 1, 2, \ldots, n$. Then the least-squares estimators are $b = [\Sigma(y_i - \bar{y})(x_i - \bar{x})]/[\Sigma(x_i - \bar{x})^2]$ and $a = \bar{y} - b\bar{x}$. (Here, $\bar{y}$ and $\bar{x}$ are the mean values of the variables, and the summation is over the n observations.)

TABLE 4.4

Predicted versus Actual Ticket Sales Using $Q = 478.6 - 1.63P$	Year and Quarter		Predicted Sales (Q*)	Actual Sales (Q)	Q* − Q	(Q* − Q)²
	Y1	Q1	71.1	64.8	6.3	39.7
		Q2	46.6	33.6	13.0	170.3
		Q3	46.6	37.8	8.9	78.3
		Q4	87.4	83.3	4.1	16.8
	Y2	Q1	103.7	111.7	−8.0	64.0
		Q2	111.8	137.5	−25.7	657.9
		Q3	111.8	109.5	2.3	5.5
		Q4	120	96.8	23.2	538.2
	Y3	Q1	103.7	59.5	44.2	1,953.6
		Q2	95.5	83.2	12.3	152.5
		Q3	79.3	90.5	−11.2	126.6
		Q4	87.4	105.5	−18.1	327.6
	Y4	Q1	71.1	75.7	−4.6	21.2
		Q2	87.4	91.6	−4.2	17.6
		Q3	87.4	112.7	−25.3	640.1
		Q4	95.5	102.2	−6.7	44.2
					Sum of squared errors	4,847.2

MULTIPLE REGRESSION   Because price is not the only factor that affects sales, it is natural to add other explanatory variables to the right-hand side of the regression equation. Suppose the airline has gathered data on its competitor's average price and regional income over the same four-year period. In management's view, these factors may strongly affect demand. Table 4.5 lists the complete data set. Management would like to use these data to estimate a **multiple regression** equation of the form

$$Q = a + bP + cP° + dY.$$

In this equation, quantity depends on own price (P), competitor's price (P°), and income (Y). Now the OLS regression method computes four coefficients: the constant term and a coefficient for each of the three explanatory variables. As before, the objective is to find coefficients that will minimize SSE. The OLS equation is

$$Q = 28.84 - 2.12P + 1.03P° + 3.09Y. \qquad [4.4]$$

TABLE 4.5

Airline Sales, Prices,
and Income

Year and Quarter		Average Number of Coach Seats	Average Price	Average Competitor Price	Average Income
Y1	Q1	64.8	250	250	104.0
	Q2	33.6	265	250	101.5
	Q3	37.8	265	240	103.0
	Q4	83.3	240	240	105.0
Y2	Q1	111.7	230	240	100.0
	Q2	137.5	225	260	96.5
	Q3	109.5	225	250	93.3
	Q4	96.8	220	240	95.0
Y3	Q1	59.5	230	240	97.0
	Q2	83.2	235	250	99.0
	Q3	90.5	245	250	102.5
	Q4	105.5	240	240	105.0
Y4	Q1	75.7	250	220	108.5
	Q2	91.6	240	230	108.5
	Q3	112.7	240	250	108.0
	Q4	102.2	235	240	109.0

Table 4.6 lists the predictions, prediction errors, and squared errors for this regression equation. The equation's sum of squared errors is 2,616.4, much smaller than the SSE of any of the previously estimated equations. The additional variables have significantly increased the accuracy of the equation. A quick scrutiny of Table 4.6 shows that, by and large, the equation's predictions correspond closely to actual ticket sales.

This example suggests the elegance and power of the regression approach. The decision maker starts with uncontrolled market data. The airline's own price, the competitor's price, and regional income all varied simultaneously from quarter to quarter over the period. Nonetheless, the regression approach has produced an equation (a surprisingly accurate one) that allows us to measure the separate influences of each factor. For instance, according to Equation 4.4, a $10 cut in the competitor's price would draw about 10 passengers per flight from the airline. In turn, a drop of about $5 in the airline's own price would be needed to regain those passengers.

The regression approach both can complement and act as a substitute for controlled market studies. Of course, many managers would like to see with their own eyes the separate effects of various pricing, promotion, and

TABLE 4.6

Predicted versus Actual
Ticket Sales Using
$Q = 28.84 - 2.12P$
$+ 1.03P° + 3.09Y$

Year and Quarter		Predicted Sales (Q*)	Actual Sales (Q)	Q* − Q	(Q* − Q)²
Y1	Q1	77.7	64.8	12.9	166.4
	Q2	38.2	33.6	4.6	20.9
	Q3	32.5	37.8	−5.3	28.0
	Q4	91.7	83.3	8.4	70.4
Y2	Q1	97.4	111.7	−14.3	203.3
	Q2	117.8	137.5	−19.7	387.1
	Q3	97.6	109.5	−11.9	140.7
	Q4	103.2	96.8	6.4	40.8
Y3	Q1	88.2	59.5	28.7	822.0
	Q2	94.0	83.2	10.8	117.7
	Q3	83.7	90.5	−6.8	46.7
	Q4	91.7	105.5	−13.8	190.7
Y4	Q1	60.7	75.7	−15.0	224.9
	Q2	92.2	91.6	.6	.4
	Q3	111.3	112.7	−1.4	2.1
	Q4	114.7	102.2	12.5	155.0
			Sum of squared errors		2,616.4

advertising policies—hence, the appeal of controlled market tests. But even without conducting (and paying for) controlled market tests, the firm can obtain the same kind of results. Regression analysis sees through the tangle of compounding and conflicting factors that affect demand and, thus, isolates *separate* demand effects.

CHECK STATION 2   Management believes price changes will have an immediate effect on ticket sales, but the effects of income changes will take longer (as much as three months) to play out. How would one test this effect using regression analysis?

INTERPRETING REGRESSION STATISTICS

A great number of computer programs are available to carry out regression analysis. (In fact, almost all of the best-selling spreadsheet programs include regression features.) These programs call for the user to specify the form of the regression equation and to input the data necessary to estimate it: the values of the dependent variable and explanatory variables. Besides computing the ordinary least-squares regression coefficients, the program produces a set of statistics indicating how well the OLS equation performs. Table 4.7 lists the standard computer output for the airline's multiple regression. The regression coefficients and constant terms are listed in the third-to-last line. Using these, we obtained the regression equation:

$$Q = 28.84 - 2.12P + 1.03P° + 3.09Y.$$

To evaluate how well this equation fits the data, we must learn how to interpret the other statistics in the table.

R-SQUARED   The **R-squared statistic** (also known as the *coefficient of determination*) measures the proportion of the variation in the dependent variable (Q in our example) that is explained by the multiple regression equation. Sometimes we say that it is a measure of *goodness of fit*, that is, how well the equation fits the data. The total variation in the dependent variable is computed as $\Sigma(Q - \overline{Q})^2$, that is, as the sum across the data set of squared differences between the values of Q and the mean of Q. In our example, this total sum of squares (labeled TSS) happens to be 11,706. The R-squared statistic is computed as

$$R^2 = \frac{TSS - SSE}{TSS}. \qquad [4.5]$$

TABLE 4.7

Regression Output

Airline Demand
Regression Output

Dependent variable: Q

Sum of squared errors	2616.40			
Standard error of the regression	14.77			
R-squared	0.78			
Adjusted R-squared	0.72			
F-statistic	13.9			
Number of observations	16			
Degrees of freedom	12			

	Constant	P	P°	Y
Coefficients	28.84	−2.12	1.03	3.09
Standard error of coefficients		0.34	.47	1.00
t-statistic		−6.24	2.20	3.09

The sum of squared errors, SSE, embodies the variation in Q *not* accounted for by the regression equation. Thus, the numerator is the amount of explained variation and R-squared is simply the ratio of explained to total variation. In our example, we can calculate that $R^2 = (11{,}706 - 2{,}616)/11{,}706 = .78$. This confirms the entry in Table 4.7. We can rewrite Equation 4.5 as

$$R^2 = 1 - (SSE/TSS). \qquad [4.6]$$

Clearly, R-squared always lies between zero and one. If the regression equation predicted the data perfectly (i.e., the predicted and actual values coincided), then SSE = 0, implying that $R^2 = 1$. Conversely, if the equation explains nothing (i.e., the individual explanatory variables did not affect the dependent variable), SSE would equal TSS, implying that $R^2 = 0$. In our case, the regression equation explains 78 percent of the total variation.

Although R^2 is a simple and convenient measure of goodness of fit, it suffers from certain limitations. The value of R^2 is sensitive to the number of explanatory variables in the regression equation. Adding more variables results in a lower (or, at least, no higher) SSE, with the result that R-squared increases. Thus, it is a mistake to regard the main goal of regression analysis as finding the equation with the highest R-squared. We can always jack up the R-squared by throwing more variables into the right-hand side of the regression equation—hardly a procedure to be recommended.

ADJUSTED R-SQUARED   A partial remedy for this problem is to adjust R-squared according to the number of degrees of freedom in the regression. The number of *degrees of freedom* is the number of observations (N) minus the number of estimated coefficients (k). In the airline regression, the number of observations is 16, and the number of coefficients (including the constant term) is 4. Thus, the degrees of freedom are $N - k = 16 - 4 = 12$. The adjusted R-squared is given by

$$\hat{R}^2 = 1 - \frac{SSE/(N - k)}{TSS/(N - 1)}. \qquad [4.7]$$

The difference between R^2 and $\hat{R}^2$ is the adjustment for the *degrees of freedom* in the latter. One can show that $\hat{R}^2$ always is smaller than R^2. In our example, $\hat{R}^2 = .72$. Furthermore, the smaller the number of degrees of freedom $(N - k)$, the greater the downward adjustment. In this way, the adjusted R-squared accounts for the fact that adding explanatory variables inevitably produces better predictions (reduces SSE) but at the "cost" of lost degrees of freedom.

Suppose the airline's management had only eight quarters of data. For dramatic effect, suppose it estimated Equation 4.4 using data from only odd-numbered quarters: Q1, Q3, . . . , Q15. How would this affect the quality of the regression? Would it adversely affect R-squared? The adjusted R-squared?

CHECK STATION 3

THE F-STATISTIC   The *F-statistic* is similar to the adjusted R-squared statistic. It is computed as

$$F = \frac{R^2/(k - 1)}{(1 - R^2)/(N - k)}.$$ [4.8]

Here we divide the explained variation (R^2) by the unexplained variation $(1 - R^2)$ after correcting each for degrees of freedom. The more accurate the predictions of the regression equation, the larger the value of F.

The F-statistic has the significant advantage that it allows us to test the overall statistical significance of the regression equation. Consider the hypothesis that all the coefficients of the explanatory variables in the airline regression are zero: $b = c = d = 0$. If this were true, then the regression equation would explain nothing. The simple mean would do just as well. Note, however, that even under this assumption both R-squared and F will almost certainly be above zero due to small accidental correlations among the variables. In general, very low (but nonzero) values of F indicate the great likelihood that the equation has no explanatory power; that is, we are unable to reject the hypothesis of zero coefficients.

Under the assumption of zero coefficients, the F-statistic has a known distribution (see Table 4B.1 in the chapter appendix for an abbreviated table of the F distribution). To test whether the regression equation is statistically significant, we look up the critical value of the F-statistic with $k - 1$ and $N - k$ degrees of freedom. Critical values are listed for different levels of confidence, with the 95 and 99 percent confidence levels being the most common. If the equation's F-value is greater than the critical value, we reject the hypothesis of zero coefficients (at the specified level of confidence) and say that the equation has explanatory power. In our example, the F-statistic is $F = (.776/3)/(.224/12) = 13.86$ and has 3 and 12 degrees of freedom. From the F-table in the chapter appendix, we find the 95 and 99 percent critical values of F to be 3.49 and 5.95, respectively. Since F is larger than 5.95, we can reject the hypothesis of zero coefficients with 99 percent confidence. The equation, thus, has significant explanatory power.[7]

STANDARD ERRORS OF THE COEFFICIENTS   Computerized regression programs calculate estimates for the coefficients. In addition to the values of the coefficients themselves, we would like to have a measure of their accuracy. After

---

[7] If our computed F had been 5.0, we could reject the hypothesis of zero coefficients with 95 percent confidence but not with 99 percent confidence. F must surpass a higher threshold to justify a higher confidence level.

all, the coefficients' computed values depended directly on the set of observations with which we started. If we continued to collect more quarters of data, we could recalculate the coefficients and get different estimates. Because the data themselves are subject to random errors (there is always some amount of SSE left unexplained), so, too, are the estimated coefficients. (The estimated values would equal the true, but unknown, coefficient values only if we had an infinite number of observations available.) On average, the OLS estimate for each coefficient is equal to the true value; that is, the OLS coefficient estimates are unbiased. Nonetheless, there is a considerable dispersion of the estimate around the true value.

The **standard error of a coefficient** is the standard deviation of the estimated coefficient. The lower the standard error, the more accurate is the estimate. Roughly speaking, there is a 95 percent chance that the true coefficient lies within two standard errors of the estimated coefficient.[8] For example, the estimate for the price coefficient is -2.12 and its standard error is .34. Two times the standard error is .68. Thus, there is roughly a 95 percent chance that the true coefficient lies in the range of -2.12 plus or minus .68, that is, between -2.80 and -1.44. True, we would prefer greater accuracy, but remember that our estimate is computed based on only 16 observations. Increasing the number of observations would significantly improve the accuracy of the estimates.

THE T-STATISTIC   The *t-statistic* is the value of the coefficient estimate divided by its standard error. The t-statistic tells us how many standard errors the coefficient estimate is above or below zero. For example, if the statistic is 3, then the coefficient estimate is three standard errors greater than zero. If the t-statistic is -1.5, then the coefficient estimate is one and one-half standard errors below zero. We use the t-statistic to determine whether an individual right-hand variable has any explanatory power. Consider the so-called *null hypothesis* that a particular variable—say, the competitor's price—has no explanatory power; that is, the true value of this coefficient is zero ($c = 0$). Of course, the regression results show this estimated coefficient to be 1.03, a value seemingly different from zero. But is it really? The value of the coefficient's standard error is .47. If the "true" value of c really were zero, there would be a roughly 95 percent chance that the coefficient estimate would fall within two standard errors of zero, that is, between $-.94$ and $+.94$. The actual coefficient, 1.03, is outside this range and, therefore, appears to be significantly different from zero.

The t-statistic tells the precise story. Its value is $t = 1.034/.47 = 2.20$. Again, this ratio says that the estimated coefficient is more than two standard errors

---

[8] The statement is strictly true only for a very large N (i.e., for an unlimited number of observations), in which case the coefficients estimated by OLS are normally distributed. For a fixed set of observations, the coefficient estimates follow a t-distribution. As N increases, the t-distribution comes closer and closer to being normal.

greater than zero. We appeal to the exact distribution of the t-statistic to pin-point the degree of confidence with which we can reject the hypothesis $c = 0$. To do this, we note that the computed t-statistic has $N - k = 16 - 4 = 12$ degrees of freedom. Using the table of the t-distribution (Table 4B.2) in the appendix to this chapter, we note that, under the null hypothesis, there is a 95 percent chance that the t-statistic would be between -2.18 and 2.18. That is, there would be a 5 percent chance that the estimate would lie in one of the tails beyond 2.18 or -2.18. Because the actual value of t is 2.20 and lies outside this range, we can reject the null hypothesis $c = 0$ with 95 percent confidence.[9]

From Table 4.7, we observe that all of the coefficients have t-values that are much greater than 2 in absolute value. Thus, all are significantly different than zero. Each variable has explanatory power. If additional explanatory variables were to be included, they would have to meet the same test. If we found that a given coefficient was not significantly different than zero, we would drop that explanatory variable from the equation (without a compelling reason to the contrary).

Finally, we can use this same method to test other hypotheses about the coefficients.[10] For instance, suppose the airline's managers have strong reasons to predict the coefficient of the competitor's price to be $c^\circ = 1$. The appropriate t-statistic for testing this hypothesis is

$$t = \frac{c - c^\circ}{\text{standard error of } c}$$

$$= \frac{1.04 - 1}{.47} = .085.$$

Since this is near zero, that is, smaller than 2, we cannot reject this hypothesis. Applying similar tests to the other coefficients, it is clear that there is little to choose between Equation 4.4 and the "rounded" regression equation, $Q = 29 - 2P + P^\circ + 3Y$, used in Chapter 3.

---

[9] We reject the hypothesis of a zero coefficient for positive *or negative* values of the t-statistic sufficiently far from zero. For this reason, it usually is referred to as a *two-tailed test*. Thus, we select the 97.5 percent fractile of the t-distribution to construct the 95 percent confidence interval. If the t-value lies outside this interval (either above or below), we can reject the hypothesis of a zero coefficient with 95 percent confidence.

From Table 4B.2 in the chapter appendix, we note that as the number of observations increases, the 97.5 percent fractile approaches 1.96. This justifies the benchmark of 2 as the rough boundary of the 95 percent confidence interval.

[10] We can use the F- and t-statistics to perform complex coefficient tests. For a good reference, see R. S. Pindyck and D. L. Rubinfeld, *Econometric Models and Economic Forecasts* (New York: McGraw-Hill, 1997).

CHECK STATION 4 Again, suppose the demand equation is estimated using only odd-numbered quarters in the regression. How do you think this will affect the equation's F-statistic? The standard errors of the coefficients?

STANDARD ERROR OF THE REGRESSION   Finally, the **standard error of the regression** provides an estimate of the unexplained variation in the dependent variable. Thus far, we have focused on the sum of squared errors as a measure of unexplained variation. The standard error of the regression is computed as

$$s = \sqrt{SSE/(N - k)}. \tag{4.9}$$

For statistical reasons, we divide the sum of squared errors (SSE) by the degrees of freedom (instead of by N) before taking the square root. The standard error is useful in constructing confidence intervals for forecasts. For instance, for regressions based on large samples, the 95 percent confidence interval for predicting the dependent variable (Q in our example) is given by the predicted value from the regression equation (Q*) plus or minus two standard errors.

Potential Problems in Regression

Regression analysis can identify successfully the separate influences of key factors on the dependent variable. Besides the estimated equation itself, the regression method provides statistics describing the explanatory power and margin of error of the equation. Nonetheless, it is important to be aware of the limitations and potential problems of the regression approach. We now take these up in turn.

EQUATION SPECIFICATION   Rarely is the decision maker certain of the correct form of the regression equation. In our example, we assumed a linear form, and the resulting equation tracked the past data quite well. However, the real world is not always linear; relations do not always follow straight lines. Thus, in choosing a linear form, we may be making an error in specification. A poorly specified equation means that prediction errors will be inevitable.

When theory does not suggest an appropriate equation form, the data themselves might do so. Thus, a wise decision maker will be flexible in his or her choice of equation, testing a number of different specifications. As we noted in Chapter 3, besides the linear form, a common specification for demand equations is the power, or constant elasticity, form. For the airline example, we would have

$$Q = aP^b(P^\circ)^c Y^d, \tag{4.10}$$

where, again, a, b, c, and d are to be estimated. Here, b, c, and d represent the (constant) elasticity of demand with respect to each explanatory variable. We can rewrite Equation 4.10 as

$$\log(Q) = \log(a) + b\log(P) + c\log(P°) + d\log(Y) \qquad [4.11]$$

after taking logarithms of each side. This log-linear form is estimated easily using the ordinary least-squares method.[11]

A related problem is that of **omitted variables**. Recall that we began the analysis of airline demand with price as the only explanatory variable. The resulting OLS equation produced predictions that did a reasonably good job of tracking actual values. However, a more comprehensive equation, accounting for competitor's price and income, did far better. In short, leaving out key variables necessarily worsens prediction performance. Omitting key variables is tantamount to acting as though they had zero coefficients, that is, no influence on demand. The multiple regression results clearly show that this is not the case. In fact, omission of these other variables also affects the coefficients of the included variables. For instance, the price coefficient is -1.63 when it is the sole explanatory variable. This is quite different from the estimated multiple regression coefficient -2.12. Thus, the single-variable regression underestimates the magnitude of the true price effect.

MULTICOLLINEARITY When two or more explanatory variables move together, **multicollinearity** occurs. In this case, it is difficult to tell which one is affecting the dependent variable. Suppose demand for a firm's product is believed to depend on only two factors, price and advertising. However, the firm is not sure how important each factor is. The data show that whenever the firm initiated an aggressive advertising campaign, it invariably lowered the good's price. Sales increased significantly as a result. When the firm decreased advertising spending, it also increased price and sales dropped. The question is: Should the changes in sales be attributed to changes in advertising or to changes in price? Unfortunately, it is impossible to tell, even with regression. If two right-hand variables move together, regression cannot separate the effects. Regression does *not* require that we hold one of the factors constant as we vary the other, but it does require that the two factors vary in different ways.

What happens when the forecaster runs a regression based on these data? If the right-hand variables are perfectly correlated, the computerized regression program will send back an error message. If the right-hand variables are not perfectly correlated but move very closely together (either directly or inversely), the program will provide very imprecise estimates. In this case, the standard errors of the estimates will be very large and the t-statistics very small.

Can the firm still use the equation to forecast? Yes and no. It can if it plans to continue the pattern of lowering price whenever it increases advertising. In that case, it need not care about the separate effects. However, if it plans to lower price without an advertising campaign or to advertise more

---

[11] Another common specification is the quadratic form $Q = a + bP + cP^2$ because this allows for a curvilinear relationship among the variables.

without lowering price, the forecast will be very unreliable. (Nevertheless, the firm may want to do exactly that to generate some new data that are less collinear.)

SIMULTANEITY AND IDENTIFICATION   This brings us to a subtle but interesting and important issue. In the preceding discussion, we assumed that the firm had explicit control over its price. In many settings, however, price is determined by overall demand and supply conditions, not by the individual firm. Here the firm must take the price the market dictates or else sell nothing. Such settings are called *perfectly competitive markets*, which we will discuss in detail in Chapter 10. For now, note that price and quantity in competitive markets are determined *simultaneously* by supply and demand. Let's consider the implications of this with a simple example.

Suppose both the quantity supplied and the quantity demanded depend only on price, except for some random terms:

$$Q_D = a + bP + \varepsilon$$
$$Q_S = c + dP + \nu$$

where ε and ν are random variables. The random terms indicate that both the supply and demand curves jump around a bit. The equilibrium will be determined by the intersection of the supply and demand curves. Figure 4.2a shows these curves with random shifts, as well as the price–quantity outcomes that these curves might generate.

Now, look only at the points in part a of Figure 4.2 and imagine trying to use these data to estimate either supply or demand. For this particular example, the "best line" appears in part b of the figure. Is this an estimate of the supply curve, the demand curve, or what? The problem is that, because price and quantity are determined simultaneously, we cannot tell whether two points differ because of randomness in supply, in demand, or in both; that is, we cannot *identify* which curve is responsible. **Simultaneity** (in the determination of price and quantity) means that the regression approach may fail to identify the separate (and simultaneous) influences of supply and demand.

When is identification possible? The easiest case occurs when supply fluctuates randomly but demand does not. This leads to a situation like the one portrayed in Figure 4.2c. In this case, all of the points will be along a stationary demand curve. Consequently, there is no problem estimating demand, although estimating supply remains impossible. We say that demand is identified but supply is not. In the converse case, where demand fluctuates but supply does not, only the supply curve is identified. What if both demand and supply fluctuate? If the supply or demand functions depend on other variables, we can use specific statistical techniques to identify one or both functions. These techniques are beyond the scope of this book. For our purposes,

FIGURE 4.2

Shifts in Supply and
Demand

The scatter of points in
parts a and b is caused
by shifts in both supply
and demand. To
estimate a demand
curve (as in part c),
shifts in supply are
crucial.

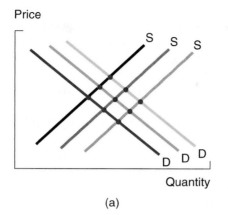

Price

Quantity

(a)

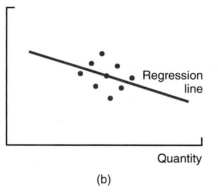

Price

Regression
line

Quantity

(b)

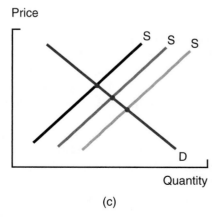

Price

Quantity

(c)

the lesson is that we must look carefully at the relationships being estimated and be on the lookout for simultaneously determined variables.

OTHER PROBLEMS　Finally, it is important to recognize that the regression approach depends on certain assumptions about randomness. To be explicit, let us rewrite Equation 4.1 as

$$Q = a + bP + cP° + dY + \varepsilon. \qquad [4.12]$$

Here we have added the term ε. This random term indicates that sales depend on various variables plus some randomness. The statistical properties of regression come from the assumptions one makes about the random term ε. The key assumption is that this term is normally distributed with a mean of zero and a constant variance and that it is completely independent of everything else. If this assumption is violated, regression equations estimated by ordinary least squares will fail to possess some important statistical properties. In such a case, modifications to the OLS method must be made to estimate a correct equation having desirable statistical and forecasting properties.

Two main problems concerning random errors can be identified. First, **heteroscedasticity** occurs when the variance of the random error changes over the sample. A simple way to track down this problem is to look at the errors that come out of the regression: the differences between actual and predicted values. We can, for example, divide the errors into two groups, one associated with high prices and one with low prices, and find the sum of squared errors for each subgroup. If these are significantly different, this is evidence of heteroscedasticity.

Serial correlation occurs when the errors run in patterns; that is, the distribution of the random error in one period depends on its value in the previous period. For instance, the presence of positive correlation means that prediction errors tend to persist: Overestimates are followed by overestimates and underestimates by underestimates. There are standard statistical tests to detect serial correlation (either positive or negative). The best-known test uses the **Durbin–Watson statistic** (which most regression programs compute). A value of approximately 2 for this statistic indicates the absence of serial correlation. Large deviations from 2 (either positive or negative) indicate that prediction errors are serially correlated. The regressions reported for air travel demand in our example are free of serial correlation and heteroscedasticity.

Predicting Presidential Elections

Every four years, U.S. citizens face the question: Which candidate and party will win the presidential election? Of course, political pundits and authoritative election predictions abound. Nonetheless, presidential elections are notoriously hard to predict. Reporters, commentators, and business leaders have turned increasingly to models created by political scientists and economists to explain and predict the patterns of election results. There are two customary ways of devising such forecasts. One approach relies on polling. A common poll question might be: "If the presidential election were held today, who would you vote for?" Such polls provide valuable information but are subject to the same response errors and biases as other surveys. Moreover, because likely candidates are known only six to eight months before the election, these predictions are necessarily very short term. A second approach is to make forecasts based on voting patterns from past elections. The most sophisticated models examine the past voting records state by state and combine this with an assessment of current party strength based on polls and incumbency considerations. (Historically, Utah and Idaho have had the strongest tendency to vote Republican, Arkansas and Rhode Island to vote Democratic.)

In striking contrast to these traditional methods, analysts have applied economic models to election forecasting, incorporating key economic indicators as determinants of voter demand. The forecasting formula of Professor Ray Fair of Yale University has received much attention in the business press because it invokes a basic political tenet: Americans vote their pocketbooks.[12] The Fair equation predicts the percentage of the popular vote (of the total two-party vote) for the incumbent party based on the average rate of economic growth (both during the election year and during previous quarters), the average rate of inflation, the duration that the incumbent party has held office, whether the president is running for reelection, whether the party in power is Democrat or Republican, and whether the country is at war. Fair's equation looks very much like an "incumbency demand curve." According to the equation, high rates of inflation (higher prices) and reduced rates of economic growth (meaning lower income and higher unemployment for voters) lead to a lower popular vote for the incumbent party.

To estimate his regression equation, Professor Fair considered elections from 1916 to 2000, using data on the percentage of the popular vote, the rate of economic growth, and the rate of inflation. The equation fits the past data quite well with an R-squared of .947 and a standard error of the regression (for the incumbent party's percentage of the popular vote) of 2.2 percent. Indeed, there are now numerous rivals to the Fair model. The most successful combine both economic and political variables. For instance, a popular equation includes the economy's recent rate of growth and a measure of presidential job approval the May before the election.

These models and equations show that the state of the economy has an important impact on presidential elections. But other factors matter as well. Historical state voting patterns matter. Opinion polls, volatile as they are, matter. Personalities of the candidates matter. Unexpected events, such as the appearance of third-party candidates (Ross Perot, Ralph Nader) matter. Traumatic national events, such as the terrorist attacks of 9/11, matter. All of these factors are hard to gauge.

---

[12] See Ray C. Fair, *Predicting Presidential Elections and Other Things* (Stanford: Stanford Business Books, 2002) and Fair's website http://fairmodel.econ.yale.edu. For a clear discussion of the competing models see J. E. Campbell and T. E. Mann, "Forecasting the Presidential Election, 1996," *The Brookings Review* (Fall 1996): 26–31.

In the 1992 election, most of the leading models underestimated the strength of the Clinton challenge to President Bush. Relying only on economic factors, the Fair model mispredicted that the senior Bush would be reelected. Other models held that the election was too close to call (Bush leading 51 to 49 percent but with a 3 percent margin of error). The Fair model rebounded to make accurate predictions of the popular vote in the 1996 and 2000 races. Interestingly, foreseeing the popular vote does not always mean correctly predicting the presidential winner. For instance, on October 27, 2000, Fair predicted that Al Gore would receive 50.8 percent of the two-party vote. Gore actually received 50.3 percent of the vote. Though he won the popular vote, Gore lost in the electoral college. (Of course, no expert or model could have foreseen the chaotic counts and recounts for Florida's electoral votes.) For the 2004 election, Fair predicted on July 31, 2004, that George Bush would receive 57.48 percent of the two-party vote. Though Fair correctly predicted the presidential winner, his popular vote forecast turned out to be a significant overestimate. Bush ultimately received 51.3 percent of the two-party vote and was narrowly reelected.

Choosing a Regression Equation

Demand estimation is as much an art as a science. This chapter has presented many of the most important statistical techniques currently available. But the analyst (and the manager) must never let these techniques themselves be the final arbiter of the quality of demand equations and forecasts. Judgment plays as important a role as statistics in evaluating demand equations. Thus, the evaluation of an estimated demand equation depends on the answers to a number of important questions.

1. Does the equation (or equations) make economic sense? What is the underlying economic relationship? Are the "right" explanatory variables included in the equation? Might other relevant variables be included? What form of the equation is suggested by economic principles?

2. Are the signs and magnitudes of the estimated coefficients reasonable? Do they make economic sense?

3. Based on an intelligent interpretation of the regression statistics, does the equation have explanatory power? How well did it track the past data? What factors are most important in determining quantity demanded?

If the equation successfully answers the foregoing questions, the manager can be confident that it embodies an accurate depiction of demand.

A top executive of a major chain of movie theaters is preparing to negotiate with a major film studio over the price the chain will pay for an upcoming release. The executive seeks to use demand analysis to produce the best possible prediction of the film's weekly gross revenue per screen. The chain's profit directly depends on this prediction. For instance, a contract having the chain pay the studio $4,500 per screen per week (for a four-week guaranteed run) would be a bargain if the film turns out to be a megahit and earns gross revenue of $8,000 per screen per week. The same contract is a losing proposition if the film bombs and brings in only $1,500 per screen per week.

Estimating Movie Demand Revisited

The theater chain's staff economists have used data from 204 major film releases during the preceding calendar year to estimate a demand equation to predict average revenues for a typical film. The estimated demand function posits that demand depends on the number of screens, the release date, the quality of the cast, and the type of film. More specifically, the best regression equation fitting the data is found to be

$$AR = 12{,}697 N^{-.197}(1.31)^S(1.27)^H(1.22)^C(1.15)^A \qquad [4.13]$$

The dependent variable is the average revenue per screen per week (during the first four weeks of the film's release). In turn, N denotes the number of nationwide screens on which the film is playing. The other explanatory variables are dummy variables: $S = 1$ for a summer release, $H = 1$ for a holiday release, $C = 1$ if the cast contains one or more proven blockbuster stars, and $A = 1$ if the film is a large-budget action film. (If a film does not fall into a given category, the dummy variable is assigned the value of 0.)

Let's explore the implications of this revenue equation. According to Equation 4.13, a nondescript film ($S = H = C = A = 0$) released in 2,000 theaters nationwide would generate revenue per screen per week of $AR = 12{,}697(2{,}000)^{-.197} = \$2{,}841$. Consider the effect of varying the number of screens. The negative exponent $-.197$ means that average revenue *per screen* falls with the number of screens playing the film. A film in narrow release (e.g., in an exclusive engagement on single screens in major cities) earns much more revenue per screen than a film in the widest release (3,500 screens nationwide), which inevitably leaves many seats empty. Thus, the same nondescript film released on only 100 screens nationwide would earn $AR = 12{,}697(100)^{-.197} = \$5{,}125$ per screen per week. Next, note the effect of each dummy variable. The multiplicative factor associated with S (1.31) means that, other things equal, a summer release ($S = 1$) will increase AR by a factor of $(1.31)^1$, or 31 percent. Similarly, a starry cast will increase predicted AR by 22 percent and an action film will raise AR by 15 percent. It is easy to check that releasing a summer action film with a starry cast increases revenue by a factor of $(1.31)(1.22)(1.15) = 1.84$, or 84 percent.

Now consider exactly how the equation was estimated. The data on all variables needed to estimate Equation 4.13 (average revenues, numbers of screens, and so on) is readily available from the weekly entertainment maga-zine *Variety* for all major U.S. film releases. The theater chain has collected these data for 204 films. As noted earlier in the chapter, Equation 4.13's multiplicative form must be estimated (via ordinary least squares) in the equivalent log-linear form. Thus, the actual regression equation (from which Equation 4.13 is derived) is

$$\log(AR) = 9.45 - .197\log(N) + .27S + .23H + .20C + .14A. \qquad [4.14]$$

In short, OLS regression of log(AR) for 204 films against log(N) and the respective dummy variables generates the coefficient estimates in Equation 4.14. To go from Equation 4.14 to Equation 4.13, we take the antilog of Equation 4.14's coefficients. (The antilog or exponential function is part of any financial calculator, spreadsheet, or standard set of mathematical tables.) Thus, antilog(9.45) = 12,697, antilog(.27) = 1.31, antilog(.23) = 1.27, and so on. The regression output associated with estimated Equation 4.14 shows that the explanatory variables are all statistically significant (according to their t-values) at a 99 percent degree of confidence. The variables N, S, and C exhibit a moderate degree of multicollinearity (summer films tend to have starry casts and very wide releases), but, given the large sample (204 observations), this does not unduly affect the validity of the individual coefficients.

However, the R-squared of the regression equation is only .31—that is, the equation explains only 31 percent of the variation in revenues for the films released that year. This should not be very surprising. As noted, film revenues are inherently unpredictable. To explain 31 percent of these variations is a solid achievement. Of course, a better demand equation could be built if more information were available. Clearly, a theater executive could make a better forecast if he or she knew the magnitude of the studio's advertising and promotion budget, the kind of reviews the film will receive, and the strengths of competing films for release during the same time period.[13] (Including these variables might raise R-squared well above .5.) However, at the time he must contract for films, this information is unavailable. Given the large standard error of the regression, the margin of error surrounding AR is in the neighborhood of plus or minus 33 percent. Predicting movie revenues will always be a risky proposition.

SUMMARY

Decision-Making Principles

1. Decision making is only as good as the information on which it is based. Accurate demand forecasts are crucial for sound managerial decision making.

2. The margin of error surrounding a forecast is as important as the forecast itself. Estimates of the margin of error are needed for good sensitivity analysis.

3. Important questions to ask when evaluating a demand equation are the following: Does the estimated equation make economic sense? How well does the equation track past data? To what extent is the recent past a predictable guide to the future?

---

[13] Conspicuously missing as explanatory variables in Equation 4.14 are price and income. These variables have no demand effects because both are essentially fixed over the one-year time period (and theaters do not vary ticket prices across films).

Nuts and Bolts

1. Forecasting can provide the manager with valuable information to aid in planning and pricing. Ideally, the forecasting process should provide (1) the forecast, (2) an estimate of its accuracy, and (3) an explicit description (an equation) of the dependency relationships.

2. Estimating demand can be divided into two categories: data collection and data analysis. Data can be collected from consumer interviews and survey techniques, controlled market studies and experimentation, uncontrolled market data, and purchased or published forecasts.

3. Regression analysis is a set of statistical techniques that quantify the dependence of a given economic variable on one or more other variables. The first step in regression is to formulate a model of this relationship in terms of an equation to be estimated. The second step is to estimate an equation that best fits the data. The usual criterion is based on minimizing squared errors (so-called ordinary least squares).

4. Regression analysis provides not only coefficient estimates but also statistics that reflect the accuracy of the equation. Important statistics include the equation's R-squared, F-statistic, and standard error, and the standard errors and t-statistics for individual coefficients. These statistics indicate the explanatory power of individual variables and of the equation as a whole.

Questions and Problems

1. Discuss and compare the advantages and disadvantages of survey methods and test marketing.

2. Coca-Cola Company introduced New Coke largely because of Pepsi's success in taste tests head-to-head with Coke Classic.
   a. Consider the following hypothetical information: (1) In blind taste tests, 58 percent of subjects preferred Pepsi to Coke Classic; (2) in similar tests, 58 percent of subjects preferred the taste of New Coke to Pepsi. From these findings, what can Coca-Cola's management conclude about consumers' preferences between Coke Classic and New Coke?
   b. Consider the following preference rankings of three different types of consumers A, B, and C:

	A (42%)	B (42%)	C (16%)
Most preferred	Pepsi	Coke Classic	New Coke
Second choice	Coke Classic	New Coke	Pepsi
Least preferred	New Coke	Pepsi	Coke Classic

As the table shows, 42 percent of consumers are "type A," whose top preference is Pepsi, followed by Coke Classic and New Coke. Are these preferences consistent with the information in part a? What do you predict would be the result of a blind taste test between Coke Classic and New Coke?

   c. From the information in part b, what brand strategy would you recommend to Coca-Cola's management? What additional information about consumer preferences might be useful?

3. A financial analyst seeks to determine the relationship between the return on PepsiCo's common stock and the return on the stock market as a whole. She has collected data on the monthly returns of PepsiCo's stock and the monthly returns of the Standard & Poor's (S & P) stock index for the last five years. Using these data, she has estimated the following regression equation

$$R_{Pep} = .06 + .92R_{S\&P}.$$

Here returns are expressed in percentage terms. The t-values for the coefficients are 2.78 and 3.4, respectively, and the equation's R-squared is .28.
   a. Do the respective coefficients differ significantly from zero?
   b. The value of R-squared seems quite low. Does this mean the equation is invalid? Given the setting, why might one expect a low R-squared?
   c. Suppose the S&P index is expected to fall by 1 percent over the next month. What is the expected return on PepsiCo's stock?

4. To what extent do you agree with the following statements?
   a. The best test of the performance of two different regression equations is their respective values of R-squared.
   b. Time-series regressions should be run using as many years of data as possible; more data means more reliable coefficient estimates.
   c. Including additional variables (even if they lack individual significance) does no harm and might raise R-squared.
   d. Equations that perform well in explaining past data are likely to generate accurate forecasts.

5. A 1984 study of cigarette demand resulted in the following logarithmic regression equation:

$$\log(Q) = -2.55 - .29 \log(P) - .09 \log(Y) + .08 \log(A) - .1W.$$
$$(-2.07) \quad (-1.05) \quad (4.48) \quad (-5.2)$$

Here Q denotes annual cigarette consumption, P is the average price of cigarettes, Y is per capita income, A is total spending on cigarette advertising, and W is a dummy variable whose value is 1 for years after 1953 (when the American Cancer Society linked smoking to lung cancer) and 0 for earlier years. The t-statistic for each coefficient is shown in parentheses. The R-squared of the equation is .94.

a. Which of the explanatory variables have real effects on cigarette consumption? Explain.

b. What does the coefficient of log(P) represent? If cigarette prices increase by 20 percent, how will this affect consumption?

c. Are cigarette purchases sensitive to income? Explain.

6. The following regression was estimated for 23 quarters between 2000 and 2004 to test the hypothesis that tire sales (T) depend on new-automobile sales (A) and total miles driven (M). Standard errors are listed in parentheses.

$$\% \Delta T = .45 + 1.41(\%\Delta M) + 1.12(\%\Delta A)$$
$$(.32) \qquad (.19) \qquad\qquad (.41)$$

Here N = 23, corrected R-squared = .83, F = 408, standard error of the regression = 1.2, and Durbin–Watson statistic = 1.92.

a. Does the regression equation (and its estimated coefficients) make economic sense? Explain.

b. Based on the regression output, discuss the statistical validity of the equation.

c. Do the coefficients on "miles driven" and "new-auto sales" significantly differ from 1.0? Explain why we might use unity as a benchmark for these coefficients.

d. Suppose that we expect "miles driven" to fall by 2 percent and "new-auto sales" by 13 percent (due to a forecasted recession). What is the predicted change in the sales quantity of tires? If actual tire sales dropped by 18 percent, would this be surprising?

7. A water expert was asked whether increased water consumption in a California community was lowering its water table. To answer this question, he estimated a linear regression equation of the form

$$W = a + bt,$$

where W = height of the water table and t = time measured from the start of the study period. (He used 10 years of water-table measurements.) The estimate for b was b = −.4 with a t-value of −1.4.

a. From this evidence, would you conclude that the water table was falling?

b. A second expert suggests yearly rainfall also may affect the water table. The first expert agrees but argues that total rainfall fluctuates randomly from year to year. Rainy years would cancel out dry years and would not affect the results of the regression. Do you agree?

8. A food-products company has recently introduced a new line of fruit pies in six U.S. cities: Atlanta, Baltimore, Chicago, Denver, St. Louis, and Fort Lauderdale. Based on the pie's apparent success, the company is considering a nationwide launch. Before doing so, it has decided to use

data collected during a two-year market test to guide it in setting prices and forecasting future demand.

For each of the six markets, the firm has collected eight quarters of data for a total of 48 observations. Each observation consists of data on quantity demanded (number of pies purchased per week), price per pie, competitors' average price per pie, income, and population. The company has also included a time-trend variable for each observation. A value of 1 denotes the first quarter observation, 2 the second quarter, and so on, up to 8 for the eighth and last quarter.

A company forecaster has run a regression on the data, obtaining the results displayed in the table.

	Coefficient	Standard Error of Coefficient	Mean Value of Variable
Intercept	−4,516.3	4,988.2	—
Price (dollars)	−3,590.6	702.8	7.50
Competitors' Price (dollars)	4,226.5	851.0	6.50
Income ($000)	777.1	66.4	40
Population (000)	.40	.31	2,300
Time (1 to 8)	356.1	92.3	—
N = 48.	R^2 = .93.	Standard error of regression = 1,442.	

a. Which of the explanatory variables in the regression are statistically significant? Explain. How much of the total variation in pie sales does the regression model explain?
b. Compute the price elasticity of demand for pies at the firm's mean price ($7.50) and mean weekly sales quantity (20,000 pies). In turn, compute the cross-price elasticity of demand. Comment on these estimates.
c. Other things equal, how much do we expect sales to grow (or fall) over the next year?
d. How accurate is the regression equation in predicting sales next quarter? Two years from now? Why might these answers differ?
e. How confident are you about applying these test-market results to decisions concerning *national* pricing strategies for pies?

Discussion Question There is an ongoing debate about the roles of quantitative and qualitative inputs in demand estimation and forecasting. Those in the qualitative camp argue that statistical analysis can only go so far. Demand estimates can be further improved by incorporating purely qualitative factors. Quantitative advocates insist that qualitative, intuitive, holistic approaches only serve to introduce errors, biases, and extraneous factors into the estimation task.

Suppose the executive for the theater chain is convinced that any number of bits of qualitative information (the identity of the director, the film's terrific script and rock-music sound track, the Hollywood "buzz" about the film during production, the easing of his ulcer) influence the film's ultimate box-office revenue.

How might one test which approach—purely qualitative or statistical—provides better demand or revenue estimates? Are there ways to combine the two approaches? Provide concrete suggestions.

Spreadsheet Problems

S1. Studies of automobile demand suggest that unit sales of midsize cars depend principally on their average price and consumers' real personal income. Consider the historical record of sales shown in the table.

Year	Sales (Millions of Cars)	Average Price (Thousands of Dollars)	Personal Income (2000 = 100)
2001	2.00	20.0	100
2002	1.86	20.8	95
2003	1.94	20.0	97
2004	1.90	22.0	100
2005	1.90	24.0	105

a. Estimate the point elasticity of demand with respect to price. (Be sure to choose two years in which all other factors are constant.)
b. Estimate the income elasticity of demand.
c. Given the elasticities in parts a and b, what change in sales do you expect between 2004 and 2005? How closely does your prediction match the historical record?
d. Estimate a linear demand equation that best fits the data using a regression program. Comment on the accuracy of your equation. Is this degree of accuracy realistic?

S2. To help settle the scientific debate in Problem 7, an expert has provided annual data on the water table and rainfall over the last decade.

					Year					
	1	2	3	4	5	6	7	8	9	10
Water Table	17.6	19.2	14.8	18.1	13.2	15.1	20	14.6	13.9	13.5
Rainfall	36	52	34	44	26	48	56	45	39	42

a. Using the 10 years of data, estimate the equation $W = a + bt$, where W is the water table and t is time in years. Comment on the statistical validity of your equation. Can you conclude that the water table level is dropping over time?

b. Did the region have greater yearly rainfall in the first five years or the last five years of the decade? Should rainfall be added as an explanatory variable in your regression equation? If it were, what would be the effect on the estimate of b? Explain.

c. Now estimate the equation $W = a + bt + cR$ where R denotes annual rainfall. Answer the questions posed in part a above. Is this equation scientifically superior to the equation in part a?

S3. A soft-drink bottler collected the following monthly data on its sales of 12-ounce cans at different prices.

	Month											
	1	2	3	4	5	6	7	8	9	10	11	12
Price	.45	.50	.45	.40	.35	.35	.50	.55	.45	.50	.40	.40
Quantity	98	80	95	123	163	168	82	68	96	77	130	125

a. Use a regression program to estimate a linear demand equation. If price is cut by $.10, by how much will the volume of sales increase?

b. Plot the 12 data points and the estimated regression line on a quantity–price graph. Does the scatter of points look linear?

c. Use a log-linear regression to estimate a demand curve of the form $Q = kP^{\beta}$. What is the price elasticity of demand? Does this equation fit the data better than the linear equation in part b? Explain.

Suggested References

Recommended articles on data collection and market experimentation include:

DeJong, D. V., and R. Forsythe. "A Perspective on the Use of Laboratory Market Experimentation in Auditing Research." *Accounting Review* 67 (January 1992): 157–170.

Norwood, J. "Data Quality and Public Policy." *Journal of Economic Perspectives* 4 (Spring 1990): 3–12.

The following are valuable references on demand estimation and forecasting.

Berk, K. N., and P. Carey. *Data Analysis with Microsoft Excel.* Duxbury, MA: Duxbury Press, 1995.

Pindyck, R. S., and D. L. Rubinfeld. *Econometric Models and Economic Forecasts,* Chapters 1–6. New York: McGraw-Hill, 1997.

Here is a wonderful article on the application (and misapplication) of regression techniques.

Barnett, A., and H. Tress. "Rain Men." *Interfaces* (March–April 1990): 42–47.

For interesting applications in communications and advertising, see:

Acton, J. P., and I. Vogelsang. "Telephone Demand over the Atlantic: Evidence from Country-Pair Data." *Journal of Industrial Economics* 40 (1992): 305–323.

Mazis, M. B., D. J. Ringold, E. S. Perry, and D. W. Denman. "Perceived Age and Attractiveness of Models in Cigarette Advertisements." *Journal of Marketing* 56 (January 1992): 22–37.

Web sites that discuss forecasting presidential elections include: http://fairmodel.econ.yale.edu/vote/vot1198.htm and http://www.brook.edu/press/review/man2fa96.htm.

CHECK STATION ANSWERS

1. Both surveys and test marketing would appear to be feasible methods for acquiring the requisite information. Since the target population (business travelers) is specific and easy to identify, surveying should be relatively accurate and inexpensive. For instance, we could distribute a questionnaire to passengers on flights known to be dominated by business travelers or send it to the airline's frequent fliers. In addition, business travelers probably would have more incentive than the typical respondent to express their true preferences about air travel. The airline also could test different types of business-class seating (at different fares) on various flights. Obviously, the company must extend the test long enough and publicize it adequately so that business travelers will have time to make up their minds about the new options. Although information from the actual test may be more accurate than that gleaned from surveys, it is also likely to be much more expensive.

2. The most direct way is to estimate the equation

$$Q = a + bP + cP° + dY_{-1},$$

where Y_{-1} denotes last quarter's income. For instance, the relevant data for the second quarter of year 1 is $Q = 33.6$, $P = 265$, $P° = 250$, and $Y_{-1} = 104$ (i.e., first quarter's income).

3. Reducing the number of data points typically worsens the quality of the estimated regression equation. R-squared may decrease or increase. (By luck, the remaining points may or may not lie more nearly along a straight line.) The reduction in observations tends to produce a reduction in the adjusted R-squared. Using only the odd-numbered quarters, R-squared falls to .72 and adjusted R-squared is .65.

4. With fewer data points for estimation, one would expect the F-statistic to fall (because of fewer degrees of freedom), the coefficient estimates to change, and their standard errors to increase. The regression output based on odd-numbered quarters confirms this: $F = 3.43$. Since the critical F-value (3 and 4 degrees of freedom) is 6.59, the equation lacks overall explanatory power at the 95 percent confidence level. The estimated equation is

$$Q = 71.7 - 2.81P + .74P° + 3.5Y.$$

The respective standard errors are 19.4, .72, .76, and 1.9. Applying a t-test shows that $P°$ and Y are not significantly different than zero. With so few data, it is impossible to detect the real effects of these two variables. Finally, the standard error of the regression increases to 19.4.

Regression Using Spreadsheets

Today most spreadsheet programs give you the power to run multiple regression programs. In this appendix we review the steps of running a regression using Microsoft's Excel spreadsheet program using the airline example in the text.

Simple Regression

Step One: Enter the data. Recall that in Table 4.2, the average number of coach seats is the *dependent variable*, and the average price is the *independent variable*. The data for both of these variables must be entered into the spreadsheet as columns, as Table 4A.1 shows.

Step Two: Call up the regression program. The method for calling up a regression program may vary a bit depending on the version of the program. In Excel, calling up the regression program involves these steps: Under the Tools menu select Data Analysis, then select Regression, and click OK. A regression dialog box will appear, such as the one in Figure 4A.1. The following steps show how to complete this box.

Step Three: Designate the columns of data to be used in the regression. The regression program has to be told where to find the data. This is done by entering the cells in the boxes labeled "Y Input Range" and "X Input Range." The

	A	B	C	D	E
1					
2	**Seats**	**Price**	**C Price**	**Income**	
3	64.8	250	250	104.0	
4	33.6	265	250	101.5	
5	37.8	265	240	103.0	
6	83.3	240	240	105.0	
7	111.7	230	240	100.0	
8	137.5	225	260	96.5	
9	109.5	225	250	93.3	
10	96.8	220	240	95.0	
11	59.5	230	240	97.0	
12	83.2	235	250	99.0	
13	90.5	245	250	102.5	
14	105.5	240	240	105.0	
15	75.7	250	220	108.5	
16	91.6	240	230	108.5	
17	112.7	240	250	108.0	
18	102.2	235	240	109.0	
19					

FIGURE 4A.1

The Regression Menu

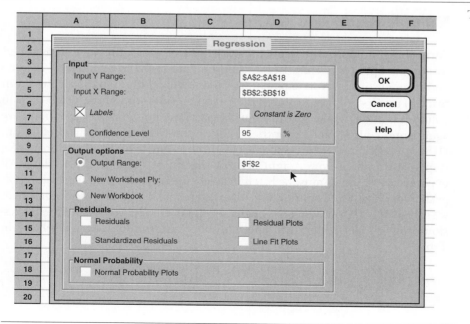

Y Input Range refers to the dependent variable. In our case, the Y data range from cell A3 to cell A18. Thus, we could simply type A3:A18 into the box.

Alternatively, we could select the range, pointing the mouse at A3, clicking, holding, and then dragging to cell A18. There will appear in the Input Range box the entry $A$3:$A$18. (Do not worry about the dollar signs.) If you wish to include the column label in cell A2, simply select the range $A$2:$A$18. Then click on the label box. (In our example, we chose to include the label.) The advantage of using the label is it will appear in the output statistics, making these statistics easier to read.

The X Input Range refers to the independent variable. In our case, the X Input Range is from cell B3 to cell B18. To input the cells for this range, repeat the procedure described previously.

Step Four: Inform the program where you want the output. The regression program needs to be told where to put the output. This is known as the Output Range. Simply type in a cell name (or point and click). The program will start with that cell and work to the right and down. It really does not matter where you put the output except that you do not want to put it over the data, thereby destroying the data. Thus, you should put the output either below or to the right of the data. We specified F2 as the output range. Some programs, such as Excel, will allow you to put the output in a separate spreadsheet.

Step Five: Run the regression. Simply click OK. For the airline example, the program produces the output shown in Table 4A.2.

Multiple Regression

Performing multiple regression analysis involves virtually the same steps as performing simple regression. Recall that the data in Table 4.5 include income and competitor's price as explanatory variables in addition to the airline's own price. The first step is to enter the income and competitive price data in columns C and D of the spreadsheet. After calling up the regression menu, we again enter cells A2 to A18 for the Y range. However, next we enter cells B2 to D18 for the X range. (We designate the three columns of data by selecting the upper left and the lower right cells of the range containing the data. All explanatory variables must be listed in adjacent columns.) The regression program recognizes each column of data as a separate explanatory variable. Next, we specify the Output Range to begin in cell F2. Finally, we execute the regression program by clicking OK. The multiple regression output is displayed in Table 4A.3.

TABLE 4A.2

Simple Regression
Results

	E	F	G	H	I	J	K	L	M
1									
2		SUMMARY OUTPUT							
3									
4									
5		*Regression Statistics*							
6		**Multiple R**	0.765						
7		**R Square**	0.586						
8		**Adjust R Square**	0.556						
9		**Standard Error**	18.607						
10		**Observations**	16						
11									
12		**ANOVA**							
13			*df*	*SS*	*MS*	*F*	*Signif F*		
14		**Regression**	1	6,858.8	6,858.8	19.81	0.00055		
15		**Residual**	14	4,847.2	346.2				
16		**Total**	15	11,706.0					
17									
18			*Coefficients*	*Stand Error*	*t Stat*	*P-value*	*Lower 95%*	*Upper 95%*	
19		**Intercept**	478.55	88.039	5.436	0.00009			
20		**Price**	−1.633	0.367	−4.451	0.00055	−2.419	−0.846	
21									

TABLE 4A.3

Multiple Regression
Results

	E	F	G	H	I	J	K	L	M
1									
2		SUMMARY OUTPUT							
3									
4									
5		Regression Statistics							
6		**Multiple R**	0.881						
7		**R Square**	0.776						
8		**Adjust R Square**	0.721						
9		**Standard Error**	14.766						
10		**Observations**	16						
11									
12		**ANOVA**							
13			*df*	*SS*	*MS*	*F*	*Signif F*		
14		**Regression**	3	9,089.6	3,029.9	13.90	0.0003		
15		**Residual**	12	2,616.4	218.0				
16		**Total**	15	11,706.0					
17									
18			*Coefficients*	*Stand Error*	*t Stat*	*P-value*	*Lower 95%*	*Upper 95%*	
19		**Intercept**	28.84	174.67	0.165	0.872			
20		**Price**	−2.124	0.340	−6.238	0.00004	−2.865	−1.382	
21		**Competitor's P**	1.035	0.467	2.218	0.04664	0.018	2.051	
22		**Income**	3.089	0.999	3.093	0.00931	0.913	5.266	
23									

Statistical Tables

TABLE 4B.1

Fractiles of the
F-Distribution

.95 Fractiles

$k - 1 =$	1	2	3	4	5	6	7
$N - k = 1$	161.40	199.50	215.70	224.60	230.20	234.00	236.80
2	18.51	19.00	19.16	19.25	19.30	19.33	19.35
3	10.13	9.55	9.28	9.12	9.01	8.94	8.89
4	7.71	6.94	6.59	6.39	6.26	6.16	6.09
5	6.61	5.79	5.41	5.19	5.05	4.95	4.88
6	5.99	5.14	4.76	4.53	4.39	4.28	4.21
7	5.59	4.74	4.35	4.12	3.97	3.87	3.79
8	5.32	4.46	4.07	3.84	3.69	3.58	3.50
9	5.12	4.26	3.86	3.63	3.48	3.37	3.29
10	4.96	4.10	3.71	3.48	3.33	3.22	3.14
11	4.84	3.98	3.59	3.36	3.20	3.09	3.01
12	4.75	3.89	3.49	3.26	3.11	3.00	2.91
13	4.67	3.81	3.41	3.18	3.03	2.92	2.83
14	4.60	3.74	3.34	3.11	2.96	2.85	2.76
15	4.54	3.68	3.29	3.06	2.90	2.79	2.71
16	4.49	3.63	3.24	3.01	2.85	2.74	2.66
17	4.45	3.59	3.20	2.96	2.81	2.70	2.61
18	4.41	3.55	3.16	2.93	2.77	2.66	2.58
19	4.38	3.52	3.13	2.90	2.74	2.63	2.54
20	4.35	3.49	3.10	2.87	2.71	2.60	2.51
21	4.32	3.47	3.07	2.84	2.68	2.57	2.49
22	4.30	3.44	3.05	2.82	2.66	2.55	2.46
23	4.28	3.42	3.03	2.80	2.64	2.53	2.44
24	4.26	3.40	3.01	2.78	2.62	2.51	2.42
25	4.24	3.39	2.99	2.76	2.60	2.49	2.40
30	4.17	3.32	2.92	2.69	2.53	2.42	2.33
40	4.08	3.23	2.84	2.61	2.45	2.34	2.25
60	4.00	3.15	2.76	2.53	2.37	2.25	2.17
120	3.92	3.07	2.68	2.45	2.29	2.17	2.09
∞	3.84	3.00	2.60	2.37	2.21	2.10	2.01

TABLE 4B.1

(continued)

				.99 Fractiles			
k − 1 =	1	2	3	4	5	6	7
N − k = 1	4052	4999.5	5403	5625	5764	5859	5928
2	98.50	99.00	99.17	99.25	99.30	99.33	99.36
3	34.12	30.82	29.46	28.71	28.24	27.91	27.67
4	21.20	18.00	16.69	15.98	15.52	15.21	14.98
5	16.26	13.27	12.06	11.39	10.97	10.67	10.46
6	13.75	10.92	9.78	9.15	8.75	8.47	8.26
7	12.25	9.55	8.45	7.85	7.46	7.19	6.99
8	11.26	8.65	7.59	7.01	6.63	6.37	6.18
9	10.56	8.02	6.99	6.42	6.06	5.80	5.61
10	10.04	7.56	6.55	5.99	5.64	5.39	5.20
11	9.65	7.21	6.22	5.67	5.32	5.07	4.89
12	9.33	6.93	5.95	5.41	5.06	4.82	4.64
13	9.07	6.70	5.74	5.21	4.86	4.62	4.44
14	8.86	6.51	5.56	5.04	4.69	4.46	4.28
15	8.68	6.36	5.42	4.89	4.56	4.32	4.14
16	8.53	6.23	5.29	4.77	4.44	4.20	4.03
17	8.40	6.11	5.18	4.67	4.34	4.10	3.93
18	8.29	6.01	5.09	4.58	4.25	4.01	3.84
19	8.18	5.93	5.01	4.50	4.17	3.94	3.77
20	8.10	5.85	4.94	4.43	4.10	3.87	3.70
21	8.02	5.78	4.87	4.37	4.04	3.81	3.64
22	7.95	5.72	4.82	4.31	3.99	3.76	3.59
23	7.88	5.66	4.76	4.26	3.94	3.71	3.54
24	7.82	5.61	4.72	4.22	3.90	3.67	3.50
25	7.77	5.57	4.68	4.18	3.85	3.63	3.46
26	7.72	5.53	4.64	4.14	3.82	3.59	3.42
27	7.68	5.49	4.60	4.11	3.78	3.56	3.39
28	7.64	5.45	4.57	4.07	3.75	3.53	3.36
29	7.60	5.42	4.54	4.04	3.73	3.50	3.33
30	7.56	5.39	4.51	4.02	3.70	3.47	3.30
40	7.31	5.18	4.31	3.83	3.51	3.29	3.12
60	7.08	4.98	4.13	3.65	3.34	3.12	2.95
120	6.85	4.79	3.95	3.48	3.17	2.96	2.79
∞	6.63	4.61	3.78	3.32	3.02	2.80	2.64

Source: This table is abridged from Table 18 of the *Biometrika Tables for Statisticians*, Vol. 1, with the kind permission of E. S. Pearson and the trustees of Biometrika.

TABLE 4B.2

Degrees of Freedom	Fractile .95	Fractile .975	Fractiles of the t-Distribution
1	6.31	12.71	
2	2.92	4.30	
3	2.35	3.18	
4	2.13	2.78	
5	2.01	2.57	
6	1.94	2.45	
7	1.90	2.36	
8	1.86	2.31	
9	1.83	2.26	
10	1.81	2.23	
11	1.80	2.20	
12	1.78	2.18	
13	1.77	2.16	
14	1.76	2.14	
15	1.75	2.13	
16	1.75	2.12	
17	1.74	2.11	
18	1.73	2.10	
19	1.73	2.09	
20	1.72	2.09	
40	1.68	2.02	
60	1.67	2.00	
∞	1.64	1.96	

CHAPTER 5

Forecasting

If today were half as good as tomorrow is supposed to be, it would probably be twice as good as yesterday was.

NORMAN AUGUSTINE, AUGUSTINE'S LAWS

Forecasting the Nickel Market

Put yourself in the position of senior management of one of the world's largest nickel mining companies in 1990. Currently your company has about a 30 percent share of world nickel sales, and your largest mine, in Canada, produces nickel more cheaply than anyone else. The company correctly predicted the high growth in demand for nickel in the 1980s and profited handsomely from it. Management has just completed a long-range forecast (for the next decade) of the nickel market. The forecast predicts that:

1. World nickel sales (in tons) will increase at an average rate of 6 percent per year during the coming five years and 4 percent for the remainder of the decade.

2. Nickel prices will remain strong, growing at an average of 7 percent per year, considerably faster than the overall rate of inflation.

3. Continuing the trend of the past five years, new competitors will expand into the industry. The likely effect is an erosion of the firm's market share from 30 to 25 percent.

4. Together, input prices (labor, plant and equipment, energy), extraction costs, and transport charges will raise nickel's cost per ton by an average of 4.5 percent per year over the decade.

In light of these forecasts, the company has decided to undertake a $1 billion investment to expand production facilities in Guatemala and Indonesia. With this expansion in capacity, the company should profit from growth in the nickel market and minimize the potential loss of market share. From its past record of forecasting accuracy, management is confident in its long-range plan. But a final evaluation of its strategy can be made only seven to ten years from now.

In the previous chapter, we began the discussion of forecasting by considering demand estimation. As we saw, demand estimation consists of a number of steps: (1) identifying key explanatory variables (based on the economic theory of demand), (2) collecting past data on these variables, and (3) using statistical techniques to estimate demand equations that best fit the past data. This chapter builds on Chapter 4 by considering a wide variety of forecasting methods.

Forecasting models often are divided into two main categories: structural and nonstructural models. *Structural models identify how a particular variable of interest depends on other economic variables.* Chapter 4's airline demand equation (4.1) is a single-equation structural model. Sophisticated large-scale structural models of the economy often contain hundreds of equations and more than a thousand variables and usually are referred to as econometric models.

Nonstructural models focus on identifying patterns in the movements of economic variables over time. One of the best-known methods, *time-series analysis*, attempts to describe these patterns explicitly. A second method, *barometric analysis*, seeks to identify leading indicators—economic variables that signal future economic developments. (The stock market is one of the best-known leading indicators of the course of the economy.)

This chapter is divided into four main parts. The first two sections consider nonstructural models: time-series analysis and barometric forecasting. The third section discusses econometric models. The final section discusses the accuracy of economic forecasts.

TIME-SERIES MODELS

Time-series models attempt to identify patterns in a single variable over time. By paying strict attention to past patterns, this method seeks to predict outcomes simply by extrapolating past behavior into the future.

Decomposing Time Series

Time-series patterns can be broken down into the following four categories.

1. Trends
2. Business cycles
3. Seasonal variations
4. Random fluctuations

A **trend** (sometimes called a secular trend) is a steady movement in an economic variable over time. The total production of goods and services in the United States (and most other countries) has moved steadily upward over the years. Demand for many categories of goods, from automobiles to computers, also has risen. Obviously, variables do not always trend upward. For instance, the number of farmers in the United States has steadily declined.

Superimposed on such trends are periodic **business cycles**. Economies experience periods of expansion marked by rapid growth in gross domestic product (GDP), investment, and employment. Typically, however, economic growth may slow and cease for a variety of reasons including high interest rates, inflation fears, jumps in energy prices, or reductions in government spending. A sustained fall in (real) GDP and employment is called a recession. For the U.S. economy, recessions have become less frequent and less severe since 1945. Nonetheless, the business cycle—with periods of growth followed by recessions, followed in turn by expansions—remains an economic (and political) fact of life.

Seasonal variations are shorter demand cycles that depend on the time of year, the season, or other conditions. Seasonal factors affect a great many retail products and services, such as tourism and air travel, tax preparation services, and clothing. Analysts compute seasonal indexes to gauge the magnitude of seasonal fluctuations around the general trend.

Finally, one should not ignore the role of **random fluctuations**. In any short period of time, an economic variable may show irregular movements due to essentially random (or unpredictable) factors. For instance, a car dealership may see 50 more customers walk into its showroom one week than the previous week and, therefore, may sell eight more automobiles. Management is grateful for the extra sales even though it can identify absolutely no difference in economic circumstances between the two weeks. Indeed, our discussion of regression analysis in Chapter 4 should remind us that random fluctuations will inevitably occur. No model, no matter how sophisticated, can perfectly explain the data. The sum of squared errors reminds us of the presence of random fluctuations. These fluctuations and unexpected occurrences are inherent in almost all past time series, and we must acknowledge such randomness when it comes to making predictions.

Figure 5.1 provides a graphical illustration how a time series (a company's sales, let's say) can be decomposed into its component parts. Part a depicts a smooth upward trend. Part b adds the effect of business cycles to the trend. Part c shows the regular seasonal fluctuations in sales over the course of the year added to the trend and business cycles. Although we do not show the random fluctuations, we can describe their effect easily. If we took an even "finer" look at the data (plotted it week by week, let's say), the time series would look even more rough and jagged.

The relative importance of the components—trend, cycles, seasonal variations, and random fluctuations—will vary according to the time series in question. Sales of men's plain black socks creep smoothly upward (due to population

FIGURE 5.1

The Component Parts
of a Time Series

A typical time series
contains a trend,
cycles, seasonal
variations, and random
fluctuations.

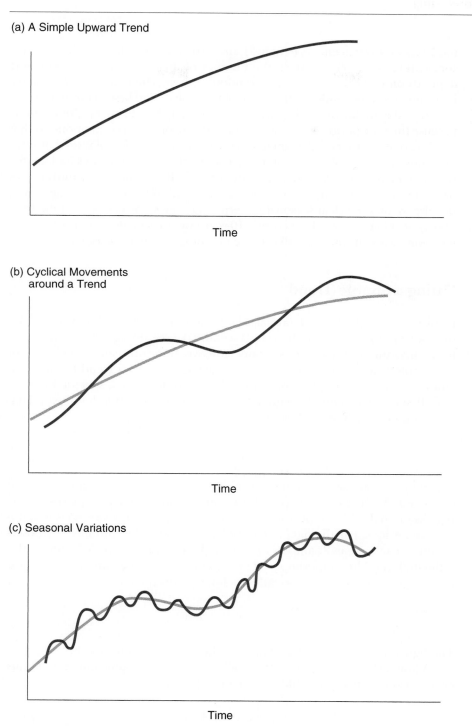

(a) A Simple Upward Trend

Time

(b) Cyclical Movements
around a Trend

Time

(c) Seasonal Variations

Time

increases and replacement demand) and probably show little cyclical or seasonal fluctuations. By contrast, the number of lift tickets sold at a ski resort depends on cyclical, seasonal, and random factors. The components' relative importance also depends on the length of the time period being considered. For instance, day-to-day or week-to-week changes may be purely random, simply because the time period is too short to identify the other three components that we observe. For instance, data on day-to-day sales over a period of several months may show a great deal of randomness. The short period precludes looking for seasonal, cyclical, or trend patterns. By contrast, if one looks at monthly sales over a three-year period, not only will day-to-day randomness get averaged out, but also we may see clear seasonal patterns and even some evidence of the business cycle. Finally, annual data over a 10-year horizon will let us observe cyclical movements and trends but will average out and, thus, mask seasonal variation.

Fitting a Simple Trend

Figure 5.2 plots the level of annual sales for a product over a dozen years. The time series displays a smooth upward trend. (We see no sign of a cyclical pattern, and random fluctuations around the overall trend seem small.) One of the simplest methods of time-series forecasting is fitting a trend to past data and then extrapolating the trend into the future to make a specific forecast. Let's first estimate a linear trend, that is, a straight line through the past data. We represent this linear relationship by

$$Q_t = a + bt, \tag{5.1}$$

where Q_t denotes sales at time t. As always, the coefficients a and b must be estimated. As we saw in Chapter 4, we can use ordinary least-squares (OLS) regression to do this. To perform the regression, all that is required is to number the periods. For the data in Figure 5.2, it is natural to number the observations: year 1, year 2, and so on, through year 12. Figure 5.2a shows the estimated trend line superimposed next to the actual observations. According to the figure, the following linear equation best fits the data:

$$Q_t = 98.2 + 8.6t$$

The figure shows that this trend line fits the past data quite closely.

A linear time trend assumes that sales increase by the same number of units each period. Instead we could use the quadratic form

$$Q_t = a + bt + ct^2. \tag{5.2}$$

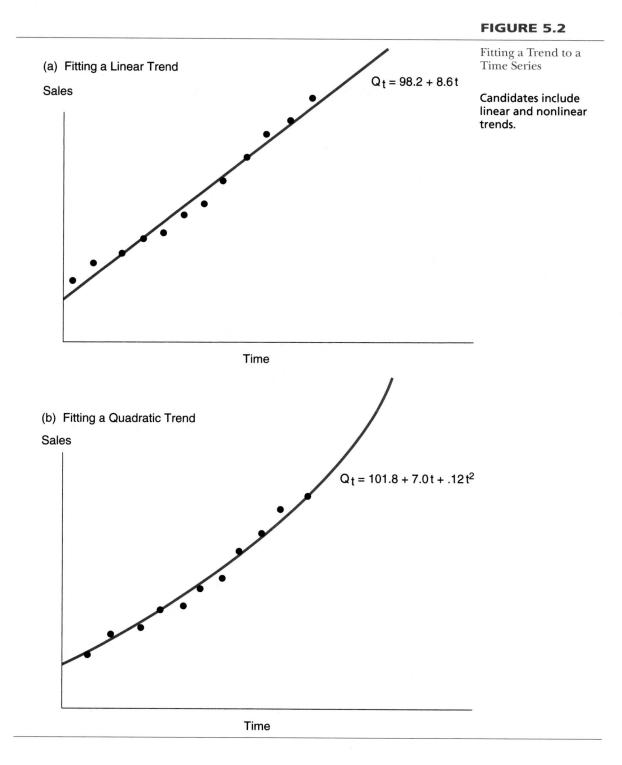

FIGURE 5.2

Fitting a Trend to a
Time Series

**Candidates include
linear and nonlinear
trends.**

(a) Fitting a Linear Trend

Sales

$Q_t = 98.2 + 8.6\,t$

Time

(b) Fitting a Quadratic Trend

Sales

$Q_t = 101.8 + 7.0\,t + .12\,t^2$

Time

A positive value of the coefficient c implies an increasing rate of growth in sales over time; that is, sales tend to trend more steeply upward over time. Conversely, if c is negative, sales grow more slowly over time. The quadratic form includes the linear equation as a special case (when c equals zero). Thus, suppose the manager runs a regression of sales versus the pair of explanatory variables, t and t^2, and arrives at the equation

$$Q_t = 101.8 + 7.0t + .12t^2$$

where, according to t-tests, the constant term and both coefficients are statistically significant. In such a case, the quadratic specification fits the past time-series data better than the linear specification and has a higher adjusted R^2. The bottom portion of Figure 5.2 shows the time series and the fitted quadratic equation.

Besides the quadratic equation, forecasters often use the exponential form,

$$Q_t = br^t, \tag{5.3}$$

where the coefficients b and r are to be estimated. Here the coefficient r is raised to the power t. Thus, if r is greater than 1, then sales Q_t grow proportionally as time advances. For instance, if r equals 1.04, then sales grow by 4 percent each year. Alternatively, if the estimated r falls short of 1, then sales decrease proportionally. If r equals .94, then sales fall by 6 percent per period. In general, the proportional change in sales per period is $r - 1$.

As it stands, the exponential equation is not in a form that allows direct estimation of b and r. One additional step is needed. The trick is to take logarithms of both sides of Equation 5.3 to arrive at

$$log(Q_t) = log(b) + log(r)t, \tag{5.4}$$

where log denotes the natural logarithm. Note that Equation 5.4 is linear. Thus, we can run an OLS regression with $log(Q_t)$ as the dependent variable and time t as the explanatory variable to produce estimates of the constant term $log(b)$ and time's coefficient $log(r)$.

To illustrate, suppose that the manager decides to fit an exponential equation to the time series in Figure 5.2. The resulting least-squares equation is

$$log(Q_t) = 4.652 + .0545t,$$

with both coefficients statistically significant. Here 4.652 represents our best estimate of $log(b)$ and .0545 is our best estimate of $log(r)$. To find the corresponding estimates of b and r, we take the antilog of each coefficient: b = antilog(4.652) = 104.8 and r = antilog(.0545) = 1.056. (All standard regression programs, even most handheld calculators, have an antilog or exponential function.) Thus, the fitted exponential equation becomes

$$Q_t = 104.8(1.056)^t.$$

In other words, the exponential trend estimates annual growth of 5.6 percent per year. Given only 12 observations in the time series, the quadratic and exponential equations give closely similar results. Both curves have about the same shape and fit the data equally well. (Thus, we have not provided a separate graph of the exponential curve.)

When it comes to forecasting, the significant difference is between the linear and nonlinear specifications. For example, using the linear equation, we forecast sales for the next year (year 13) to be

$$Q_{13} = 98.2 + (8.6)(13)) = 210.0.$$

The forecasts for quadratic and exponential equations are slightly higher, 213.1 and 212.4, respectively. The gap between the predictions widens as we forecast further and further into the future. The linear equation predicts constant additions to sales year after year; the nonlinear equations predict steeper and steeper sales increases over time. Therefore, the respective forecasts for year 16 are 235.8, 244.5, and 250.1; for year 20, they are 270.2, 289.8, and 311.0. Note that, as the time horizon lengthens, the exponential predictions exceed the quadratic predictions by a greater and greater margin. As time goes by, one can compare these predictions to actual sales experience to judge which equation produces the more accurate forecasts on average.

In 1970, Company A's common stock sold for $50 per share, the same price as a share of Company B's stock. Over the next 35 years, the value of A's stock increased at an average rate of 5 percent per year; the value of B's stock increased by 6 percent per year on average. Find the 2005 price for each company's stock. Comment on your findings.

CHECK STATION 1

The Effect of Today on Tomorrow

In many economic settings, the value of a variable today influences the value of the same variable tomorrow. Increased sales in one month frequently mean increased sales in the following month. An elevated rate of inflation in the current quarter is likely to spell higher rates in succeeding quarters. To consider the simplest case, suppose that a firm's sales in the current period depend on its sales in the previous period according to

$$Q_t = a + bQ_{t-1},$$

where a and b are coefficients. We can estimate this equation by OLS regression using last period's sales (or sales "lagged" one period) as the explanatory variable. For instance, if the constant term a is positive and b is greater than 1, then sales grow (more than proportionally) over time. Many other patterns are also possible.

FORECASTING CABLE TELEVISION CUSTOMERS   Suppose that a cable television company has watched its number of subscribers steadily increase over the past 10 quarters. With 500,000 subscribers in hand, the company naturally wants to predict how many additional subscribers it can expect one, two, or five years into the future. Figure 5.3 shows the time-series trend over the past 10 quarters. The figure also shows a smooth curve fitted to the past data and extrapolated into the future. The shape of the curve suggests that cable subscriptions have increased steadily in the last two and one-half years, although at a decreasing rate. It appears that some sort of "diminishing returns" have begun to set in. Will subscriber growth continue to flatten in the future?

Answering this question requires us to extrapolate the past into the future. But what equation should we estimate and what regression should we run? Suppose the company has the following information: (1) About 98 percent of current customers retain their subscriptions each quarter. (2) The market contains about 1 million potential customers of which 500,000 potential customers have not yet enlisted. (3) New subscribers each quarter comprise about 8 percent of the current pool of unsigned potential customers. These facts suggest the following equation for the number of subscribers each quarter:

FIGURE 5.3

Approaching Saturation
in the Cable TV Market

The number of cable
customers is best
described by a lagged
equation.

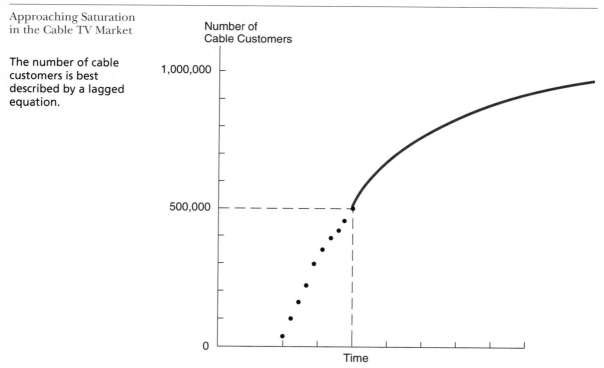

$$Q_t = .98Q_{t-1} + .08(1,000,000 - Q_{t-1}).$$

The first term on the right side of the equation represents the number of customers retained from last quarter; the second term represents the number of new subscribers.

Now, suppose the company does not have precise information on the retention rate, the new subscriber sign-up rate, and the size of the total market. Treating these as parameters to be estimated, we can write down the equation:

$$Q_t = rQ_{t-1} + s(N - Q_{t-1}),$$

where r denotes the retention rate, s the new subscriber rate, and N the total market. Combining the terms involving Q_{t-1}, we can rewrite the equation as

$$Q_t = sN + (r - s)Q_{t-1},$$

or

$$Q_t = a + bQ_{t-1},$$

where the constant term a stands for sN, and the coefficient b stands for r − s. This is exactly the lagged equation presented at the opening of this subsection.

To complete our discussion, suppose that the cable company's management runs a regression on the past 10 quarters of data and arrives at the estimated equation

$$Q_t = 113,400 + .88Q_{t-1}.$$

The predictions generated by this equation are graphed as a smooth curve in Figure 5.3. This curve fits the past data quite well. Of equal interest are the equation's predictions of future subscriber growth. Starting from 500,000 current customers, the estimated forecast for the coming quarter is $Q_{11} = 113,400 + (.88)(500,000) = 553,400$. In turn, the forecast for the following quarter is $Q_{12} = 113,400 + (.88)(553,400) = 600,392$.

Forecasts for succeeding quarters can be computed recursively. The one-year forecast (quarter 14) is 678,136. The two-year, three-year, four-year, and five-year forecasts are 784,963, 849,826, 887,445, and 910,485, respectively. The pattern of these forecasts should be readily apparent. As the market becomes saturated (as the subscribers make up 70 percent, then 80 percent, then 90 percent of the market), the rate of increase in the subscriber base becomes smaller and smaller. There are simply fewer and fewer possible new recruits.[1]

---

[1] The maximum number of subscribers can be found by setting $Q_t = Q_{t-1}$ in the estimated regression equation. (This implies no increase in Q). The solution is $Q_t = 113,400 + .88Q_t$, or $Q_t = 945,000$, a figure slightly lower than the company's subjective estimate of 1,000,000.

CHECK STATION 2   Consider a firm whose current average cost of production is $2.00 per unit. The firm has estimated the regression equation $AC_t = .3 + .6AC_{t-1}$, after collecting data on average-cost levels over the past 19 quarters of operation. Using this equation, provide forecasts of the firm's average costs for the next three quarters. What kind of average-cost behavior is being predicted? Where are average costs ultimately heading?

THE DEMAND FOR TOYS   To illustrate some of the issues involved in time-series modeling, consider the market for children's toys. We have collected sales data for 40 quarters over the period from 1995 to 2004. The tabular portion of Figure 5.4 shows these hypothetical data. The figure also displays a graph of toy sales over time. The data show an unmistakable upward trend. They also indicate some obvious seasonal behavior. The pattern does not seem completely regular, however, which indicates the presence of a random element.

Let's begin by estimating the long-term trend in toy sales. Assuming a linear trend, we can use any standard computer program to estimate the OLS regression equation

$$Q_t = 141.16 + 1.998t.$$

We have labeled the first quarter (winter 1995) as period 1, the second quarter (spring 1995) as period 2, and so on. We list the complete regression statistics in Table 5.1. The high F-statistic indicates that the equation has

TABLE 5.1

Time Trend of
Toy Sales

Regression Output

Dependent variable: Q

Sum of squared errors	11,968.8	
Standard error of the regression	17.75	
R-squared	0.64	
Adjusted R-squared	0.63	
F-statistic	67.59	
Number of observations	40	
Degrees of freedom	38	

	Constant	**t**
Coefficient(s)	141.16	1.998
Standard error of coefficients	5.72	.24
t-statistic	24.68	8.22

FIGURE 5.4

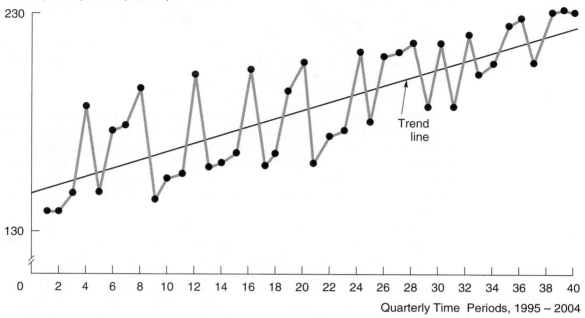

Quantity of Toys Sold (Millions)

Quarterly Time Periods, 1995 – 2004

Seasonal Toy Sales over Ten Years

1	Winter 1995	133	21	Winter 2000	158
2	Spring 1995	135	22	Spring 2000	169
3	Summer 1995	140	23	Summer 2000	171
4	Fall 1995	181	24	Fall 2000	209
5	Winter 1996	141	25	Winter 2001	172
6	Spring 1996	170	26	Spring 2001	207
7	Summer 1996	172	27	Summer 2001	209
8	Fall 1996	186	28	Fall 2001	214
9	Winter 1997	143	29	Winter 2002	183
10	Spring 1997	148	30	Spring 2002	212
11	Summer 1997	150	31	Summer 2002	184
12	Fall 1997	194	32	Fall 2002	219
13	Winter 1998	154	33	Winter 2003	185
14	Spring 1998	156	34	Spring 2003	190
15	Summer 1998	158	35	Summer 2003	222
16	Fall 1998	196	36	Fall 2003	227
17	Winter 1999	153	37	Winter 2004	199
18	Spring 1999	161	38	Spring 2004	228
19	Summer 1999	193	39	Summer 2004	230
20	Fall 1999	204	40	Fall 2004	229

considerable explanatory power. The time coefficient estimate has a low standard error (relative to the coefficient), which indicates that we can explain at least some of the variation in sales by a time trend. Roughly, sales have gone up an average of 2 million per quarter.

We can use this equation to forecast future sales. For instance, winter 2005 corresponds to $t = 41$. Inserting this value into the equation implies the forecast $Q_{41} = 223.08$.

SEASONAL VARIATION   Now we must account for seasonality. One would expect most sales to occur in the fall quarter (October to December) prior to Christmas and the fewest sales in the winter quarter (following the holidays). Indeed, this is exactly what one observes in the quarterly data. A simple timeline prediction does not account for this seasonal variation. Table 5.2 shows that the trend model consistently underpredicts fall sales and overpredicts winter sales.

A simple way to adjust for seasonality is to find the average prediction error for each season. Carrying out these computations, we find that actual fall sales exceed the predicted time trend by 20.78 on average, and that winter sales are 17.03 below the trend, spring sales are 3.53 below the trend, and summer sales are .22 below the trend. Thus, we can improve our forecast by taking these data into account. For example, a better forecast for winter 2005 is found by adjusting the time trend prediction, 223.08, downward by 17.03; the new forecast is 206.05.

Another way to correct for seasonality is through the use of dummy variables. The equation is set up as follows:

$$Q_t = bt + cW + dS + eU + fF.$$

The last four variables, W, S, U and F, represent the seasons of the year. They are called dummy variables. They take on only the values 0 and 1. For instance, the winter dummy (W) takes on the value 1 if the particular sales observation occurs in the winter quarter and 0 otherwise. Similarly, the dummy variable S is assigned the value 1 during the spring and 0 otherwise. We assign values for the dummy variables for summer (U) and fall (F) in the same manner. Once we have assigned dummy values, we perform an OLS regression to estimate the coefficients b, c, d, e, and f. We obtain:

$$Q_t = 1.89t + 126.24W + 139.85S + 143.26U + 164.38F.$$

As we expect, the coefficient for fall is greatest and the coefficient for winter is lowest. To generate a forecast for winter 2005, we simply set $t = 41$, $W = 1$, and $S = U = F = 0$. The computed value for next quarter's sales is $Q_{41} = 203.73$. Accounting for seasonality via dummy variables gives better predictions than the simple average adjustment made earlier. Nonetheless, it should not be surprising that the methods lead to similar, though not identical, forecasts.

TABLE 5.2

Predicted versus Actual
Toy Sales

This forecast consis-
tently underpredicts
fall sales and overpre-
dicts winter sales.

Time	Date	Q	Estimated Q	Error
1	Winter 1995	133.00	143.16	10.16
2	Spring 1995	135.00	145.16	10.16
3	Summer 1995	140.00	147.16	7.16
4	Fall 1995	181.00	149.16	−31.84*
5	Winter 1996	141.00	151.16	10.16
6	Spring 1996	170.00	153.15	−16.85
7	Summer 1996	172.00	155.15	−16.85
8	Fall 1996	186.00	157.15	−28.85*
9	Winter 1997	143.00	159.15	16.15
10	Spring 1997	148.00	161.15	13.15
11	Summer 1997	150.00	163.14	13.14
12	Fall 1997	194.00	165.14	−28.86*
13	Winter 1998	154.00	167.14	13.14
14	Spring 1998	156.00	169.14	13.14
15	Summer 1998	158.00	171.14	13.14
16	Fall 1998	196.00	173.13	−22.87*
17	Winter 1999	153.00	175.13	22.13
18	Spring 1999	161.00	177.13	16.13
19	Summer 1999	193.00	179.13	−13.87
20	Fall 1999	204.00	181.13	−22.87*
21	Winter 2000	158.00	183.12	25.12
22	Spring 2000	169.00	185.12	16.12
23	Summer 2000	171.00	187.12	16.12
24	Fall 2000	209.00	189.12	−19.88*
25	Winter 2001	172.00	191.12	19.12
26	Spring 2001	207.00	193.11	−13.89
27	Summer 2001	209.00	195.11	−13.89
28	Fall 2001	214.00	197.11	−16.89*
29	Winter 2002	183.00	199.11	16.11
30	Spring 2002	212.00	201.11	−10.89
31	Summer 2002	184.00	203.10	19.10
32	Fall 2002	219.00	205.10	−13.90*
33	Winter 2003	185.00	207.10	22.10
34	Spring 2003	190.00	209.10	19.10
35	Summer 2003	222.00	211.10	−10.90
36	Fall 2003	227.00	213.09	−13.91*
37	Winter 2004	199.00	215.09	16.09
38	Spring 2004	228.00	217.09	−10.91
39	Summer 2004	230.00	219.09	−10.91
40	Fall 2004	229.00	221.09	−7.91*

A utility that supplies electricity in Wisconsin is attempting to track differences in the demand for electricity in the winter (October through March) and the summer (April through September). Using quarterly data from the last five years, it estimates the regression equation $Q = 80.5 + 2.6t + 12.4W$, where W is a dummy variable (equal to 1 in the winter quarters, 0 otherwise). Has the utility made a mistake by not including a summer dummy variable? Now, suppose the utility believes that the rate of increase in demand differs in the winter and the summer. Think of an equation (using an additional dummy variable) that incorporates this difference.

BAROMETRIC MODELS

Barometric models search for patterns among different variables over time. Consider a firm that produces oil drilling equipment. Management naturally would like to forecast demand for its product. It turns out that the seismic crew count, an index of the number of teams surveying possible drilling sites, gives a good indication as to changes in future demand for drilling equipment. For this reason, we call the seismic crew a **leading indicator** of the demand for drilling equipment.

　　Economists have identified many well-known leading indicators. The number of building permits indicates the number of housing starts. Stock market indices (such as the Dow Jones Industrial Average) indicate future increases and decreases in economic activity (expansions or recessions). Such indicators, however, are not without certain problems.

1. Leading indicators are not always accurate. According to one humorous economic saying, declines in the stock market have predicted fourteen of the last eight recessions.
2. The amount of time between the change in the leading indicator and the change in the forecasted series varies. Leading indicators may say a change is coming, but they often cannot say when.
3. The change in the leading indicator rarely gives much information about the size of the change in the forecasted series.

　　Frequently, leading indicators are averaged to form a *composite* leading indicator. This helps eliminate some of the randomness and makes the indicator more accurate. The U.S. Bureau of Economic Analysis has developed (and publishes) the **Index of Leading Indicators**. This index signals future changes in the course of the economy. The revised index is a weighted average of 11 economic series.

1. Weekly hours of manufacturing workers
2. Manufacturers' new orders
3. Changes in manufacturers' unfilled orders
4. Plant and equipment orders

5. The number of housing building permits
6. Changes in sensitive materials prices
7. Percentage of companies receiving slower deliveries
8. The money supply
9. The index of consumer confidence
10. The index of 500 companies' common-stock prices
11. Average weekly claims for unemployment insurance

Positive changes in the first 10 indicators (and a decline in the last) indicate future economic growth, whereas persistent declines in the index presage a weak economy and possible recession. On average, the composite index tends to turn down nine months before the onset of recession. The index increases about four to five months before the economy bottoms out and begins to grow.

ECONOMETRIC MODELS

Econometric models provide forecasts for important aspects of the economy. A particular model might portray *microeconomic* relationships: estimates of economies of scale within a firm, demand and supply for a particular market, or the effect of a regulatory measure on a given industry. Alternatively, a model might describe the *macroeconomy* and forecast key economic measures such as gross domestic product (GDP), inflation, unemployment, interest rates, and international trade. Of course, senior managers in a particular company have more particular concerns—forecasting demand for goods and services, estimating input prices and related costs, and anticipating changes in borrowing rates. However, most macroeconomic trends have clear and direct effects on particular industries, product lines, and firms. Thus, business economists within companies—besides generating their own forecasts—use the output of macromodels to link movements in the wider economy to their own business lines.

An **econometric model** is a set of estimated equations describing relationships between key economic variables. A "very small" macromodel might contain as few as a dozen equations and 20 to 30 major variables. Today's largest macromodels contain over 1,000 equations and variables. The size of a macromodel depends on its degree of disaggregation. For instance, a small-scale model (part of which will be described later) might forecast total consumption spending (on all goods and services) via a single equation. A medium-scale model would estimate separate equations for various consumption categories: services, retail goods, consumer durables, and so on. A large-scale model might employ dozens of equations to predict consumption sales industry by industry: for automobile sales, truck sales, computer sales, and so on.

Econometric models have a number of key advantages relative to other forecasting methods. First, the model's equation structure makes explicit the links between economic variables. (This is in contrast to time-series methods that look at past trends to predict future values and barometric methods that track qualitative patterns among variables.) Second, econometric models attempt to provide a *complete* and *consistent* description of the economy. Such models use multiple equations to predict most (if not all) of the key macrovariables driving the economy (and affecting firms' profits).

Third, econometric models capture the *interdependence* of economic variables. The volume of goods and services produced by firms depends on expected consumption demand. But this demand depends on consumer income, which, in turn, depends on wage rates and the level of employment, which, in turn, depend on overall production levels. In short, there are all varieties of feedback effects among macrovariables. (Macroeconomics sometimes has been described as, "Everything depends on everything else, in more than one uncertain way.") By explicitly modeling these interdependencies, econometric models provide the potential for a better understanding of markets, industries, and the macroeconomy and for more accurate forecasts.

A Simple Macromodel

The best way to understand how macromodels work is to consider a small-scale example. (Actually, you should think of this as a partial skeleton—the backbone, perhaps—of a macromodel.) Consider the following six equations involving nine variables:

$$Y_t = C_t + I_t + G_t + X_t - M_t \qquad [5.5]$$

$$C_t = a + b[Y_t - T_t] + dP_{t-1} \qquad [5.6]$$

$$T_t = e + fY_t \qquad [5.7]$$

$$I_t = h + jY_{t-1} + kR_t \qquad [5.8]$$

$$M_t = n + qY_t \qquad [5.9]$$

$$P_t = s + uY_t + vP_{t-1}. \qquad [5.10]$$

Here Y denotes the economy's total production (equivalently, GDP or income). The first equation breaks Y down into its component parts, consumption spending, investment spending (including factories, plant and equipment, housing, and inventories), government spending, exports, and imports. We call Equation 5.5 an **identity**, that is, a relationship that is true by definition. Increased spending in any of these categories will augment total domestic output.

The remaining equations are to be estimated using regression methods. Each is a **behavioral equation**; that is, each describes the way the spending category has behaved in the past as a function of the explanatory variables on the right side. For instance, Equation 5.6 states that planned consumption spending principally depends on after-tax income, $Y - T$, where T denotes total taxes. The equation also indicates that consumption may be influenced by last period's price level (P_{t-1}). For instance, a sudden surge in recent prices may cause individuals to reign in their spending.

The other behavioral equations are suggested by basic economic theory. For instance, the tax equation (Equation 5.7) reflects the notion that tax revenues rise with income. (Note that the modeling approach dispenses with the intricacies of the tax code; Equation 5.7 is simply an average aggregate relationship.) Equation 5.8 states that planned investment depends on income and the average level of interest rates (R). (We would expect that higher sales would prompt increased investment, and higher interest rates would deter it.) According to Equation 5.9, some portion of total income is spent on imported goods. Finally, Equation 5.10 states that today's average price level depends on yesterday's price level and on the level of output. (Price increases begin to accelerate when the economy is booming.) Note the central role that Y plays in this small-scale model; it appears as an explanatory variable in each of the behavioral equations. In turn, each of the behavioral equations affects Y.

Thus far, we have formulated a bare-bones model of the macroeconomy. The next step is to estimate the model using regression techniques. This requires estimation methods that go beyond ordinary least-squares regression and beyond the scope of this book.[2] However, the general method resembles that used in single-equation estimation. Using time-series data on the included economic variables, the manager employs regression methods to estimate equations that best fit the past observations. The output of such a regression consists of coefficient estimates (in Equations 5.5 through 5.10, numerical values for the lowercase coefficients a to v) and the usual statistics (F values and t values, and R^2 for the individual equations). Using these statistics, the manager can assess the validity of the component equations. (According to their t-values, which explanatory variables are statistically significant?) One can also try alternative variables and equation forms that might better describe the past behavior of the economy. (We chose the linear forms in the foregoing equation system for reasons of analytical simplicity; we could also estimate nonlinear forms.)

Moving one step forward, let us suppose that the manager has estimated Equations 5.6 through 5.10. After carefully scrutinizing each equation's predicted values and comparing them to actual values, the manager is satisfied that the model accurately describes the past data and that it makes economic sense. The next step is to put the model in a form that is suitable for forecasting. To do this, we solve the system of simultaneous equations—a process called putting the equations in **reduced form**. We can illustrate the process using the 5.5–5.10 equation system. The main step is to solve for output Y (on which all

[2] For a very readable treatment of these methods, see R. Pindyck and D. Rubinfield, *Econometric Models and Economic Forecasts* (New York: McGraw-Hill, 1997).

the other variables depend). To find Y, we substitute each of the behavioral equations into the income identity (Equation 5.5) and arrive at

$$Y = [a + b(Y - e - fY) + dP_{-1}] + [h + jY_{-1} + kR] + G + X - [n + qY].$$

To economize on notation, we have dropped the t subscript. By moving all "Y terms" to the left side of the equation, we can solve for output:

$$Y = \frac{a - be + h - n + dP_{-1} + jY_{-1} + kR + G + X}{1 - b(1 - f) + q} \qquad [5.11]$$

How can the manager use this equation? Suppose that the objective is to forecast the level of output next period. The manager knows the current values of all economic variables and, of course, the manager knows the values of all the estimated coefficients (a to q). Thus, to forecast output next period, the manager inserts the coefficient values and the known values of P_{-1} and Y_{-1} (current output and price level) into Equation 5.11. To complete the forecast, the manager also must supply values for R, G, and X. These are called **exogenous variables** because their values come from outside the model. We might know the value of an exogenous variable (the government might have announced its spending plans); otherwise, we must forecast it independently outside the model.

The output variable Y is an **endogenous variable**; its predicted values are determined inside the model (specifically, by reduced-form Equation 5.11). The other endogenous variables are C, T, I, M, and P. We can solve for the reduced-form equation of each of these other variables by substituting the right side of Equation 5.11 for Y in the particular behavioral equation. Thus, in all, the model contains six endogenous variables and three exogenous variables.

Suppose the manager wishes to make forecasts for all six endogenous variables for five periods into the future. For instance, starting in year 2004, the manager first seeks a forecast of next year's output (2005 GDP) using Equation 5.11 (and supplying 2005 values for the exogenous variables G, R, and X). With this forecast in hand, the manager then could compute 2005 tax revenues, consumption spending, investment (also dependent on 2005 interest rates), imports, and the price level using the respective behavioral equations. To extend forecasts two years into the future, the manager repeats the process. To make 2006 forecasts, the manager uses the same equations after supplying 2006 values for the exogenous variables. However, there is one point of difference. According to Equation 5.11, the forecast of Y for year 2006 depends on the values of Y and P for 2005 (the preceding year's output and price). Of course, when the manager formulates forecasts in year 2004, he or she does not know the actual values of these variables for 2005. Thus, the manager simply uses the 2005 forecasts for these variables. In short, the manager can make forecasts one period at a time, producing future forecasts by "bootstrapping" on previous ones. (Of course, the manager may want to reestimate the forecasts for 2006 once he or she gets to 2005. At this point the manager can rerun the regression with 2005 data and use these new coefficients and new data to improve the forecast for 2006.)

FINAL REMARKS   As formulated, our simple macromodel has focused on planned spending; in this respect, the model is relatively complete. Before concluding the discussion, however, it is important to note the numerous ingredients that the model has omitted. These include the following.

1. **The Labor Market.** There is no mention of wages, employment, or composition of the labor force. Labor-market conditions clearly affect production and prices.

2. **The Financial Sector.** Obvious variables include the wealth and liquidity of individuals and firms, the demand and supply of loans, and interest rates. By treating the level of interest rates as an exogenous variable, the simple macromodel omits the financial sector altogether.

3. **Government Policies.** The government influences the macroeconomy through fiscal policies and monetary policies. Our model allows a role for government spending and taxation. A fully developed model would include the financial sector and incorporate the effect of Federal Reserve Board policies on the money supply, interest rates, and bank reserve requirements.

4. **The International Economy.** Although exports comprise only about 12 percent of the total GDP of the United States, international trade and international financial markets have important impacts on the economy. A more complete model would incorporate exchange rates, trade and capital flows, and trade barriers.

Forecasting the Fate of Euro Disney Revisited

As noted in Chapter 1, Walt Disney Company embarked in 1987 on an ambitious project to open a $2 billion theme park outside of Paris. Besides the park, Disney's investment encompassed over 5,000 hotel rooms, office space, hundreds of private homes, and a golf course. However, since opening in April 1992, Euro Disney has floundered with lower-than-expected revenues and elevated costs. In the low season (November through March) Disney's luxury hotels averaged only 10 percent occupancy rates. Indeed, there were no buyers for the additional hotels that the company planned to build and sell. The average European visitor spent far less on food, lodging, and merchandise than the average visitor to the company's American parks.

In making its decision to build the park, Disney faced a monumental task of economic forecasting: the company's planning relied on both microeconomic and macroeconomic predictions. Based on the evidence to date, the company made a host of crucial mistakes in its forecasting. One mistake the company readily admits: It did not anticipate the length and depth of the recession in Europe. (However, the European slowdown was foreseen and predicted by most international forecasters.) The recession meant fewer visitors, less spending, and a disastrous fall in real-estate prices.

Failed *microeconomic* forecasts also contributed to Euro Disney's operating problems. In envisioning the opening of Euro Disney, the company confidently cited its previous experience in opening its Tokyo theme park. But the reasons for the success of the Japanese park did not carry over to France. Work rules, effective in Japan, did not suit the French labor environment. The Japanese visitor, with a higher income than its European counterpart, was happy to spend two to five days at the park. Europeans, accustomed to month-long, extended vacations in Mediterranean climes, did not. Nor were Euro Disney's visitors as willing to wait in long lines. Also, French visitors insisted on sit-down, high-quality meals. When it first opened, Euro Disney delivered snack food and did not serve beer or wine. Not surprisingly, European visitors preferred Parisian hotels 30 minutes away to Disney's high-priced "fantasy" accommodations.

In short, most of Disney's problems stemmed from the company's inability to forecast fundamental demand for its services and products. Based on its experience, the company has instituted many changes in Euro Disney's operations. It has lowered ticket prices for the park and hotel rates, revamped its restaurant service, loosened stringent employee work rules, and changed its marketing campaign. In spite of these changes Euro Disney continues to struggle. As of summer 2004, Euro Disney was reporting record losses and was negotiating with creditors to avoid bankruptcy. Its shares were trading at around .26 euros, only about 25 percent of its equivalent share price in 1992.[3]

Forecasting Accuracy

The forecast accuracy of a given equation or model typically is measured by how closely its predictions match the actual realizations of the variable in question. Usually, such an evaluation is based on a comparison of many forecasts and realizations. For instance, a frequently quoted performance measure is the average absolute error (AAE):

$$\text{AAE} = \frac{\Sigma |Q - Q^*|}{m}$$

where Q^* denotes the forecast, m is the number of forecasts, and Q is the realized future value. An equation's root mean squared error (RMSE) is similarly defined:

[3] This account is based on F. Norris, "Euro Disney Secures Plan to Ward Off Bankruptcy," *The New York Times* (September 29, 2004), C4; P. Prada, "Euro Disney Does Nicely. So Why Are Investors Grumpy?" *The Wall Street Journal* (September 6, 2000), A20; J. Solomon, "Mickey's Trip to Trouble," *Newsweek*, (February 14, 1994), 34–38; and on other published reports.

$$RMSE = \sqrt{\frac{\Sigma(Q - Q^*)^2}{m - k}}.$$

Like the goodness of fit measures discussed in Chapter 4, the RMSE depends on the sum of squared errors. Here, however, the issue is the error in forecasting future values rather than how well the equation fits the past data. Note that the "average" is based on degrees of freedom, that is, on the number of forecasts minus the number of estimated coefficients (k).

Forecasts suffer from the same sources of error as the estimation discussed in Chapter 4. These include errors due to (1) random fluctuations, (2) standard errors of the coefficients, (3) equation misspecification, and (4) omitted variables. In addition, forecasting introduces at least two new potential sources of error. First, the true economic relationship may change over the forecast period. An equation that was highly accurate in the past may not continue to be accurate in the future. Second, to compute a forecast, one must specify values of all explanatory variables. For instance, to predict occupancy rates for its hotels in future years, Disney's forecasters certainly would need to know average room prices and expected changes in income of would-be visitors. In this sense, its forecasts are *conditional*—that is, they depend on specific values of the explanatory variables, prices of competitors, and so on. Uncertainty about any of these variables (such as future regional income) necessarily contributes to errors in demand forecasts. Indeed, an astute management team may put considerable effort into accurately forecasting key explanatory variables. Finally, even if we correctly specified the equation, even if we could perfectly know all of the coefficients, and even if we could predict perfectly the values of the explanatory variables, the forecast will still differ from what actually happens due to random, unpredictable fluctuations.

In light of the difficulties in making economic predictions, it is important to examine how well professional forecasters perform. Stephen McNees, an economist at the Federal Reserve Bank of Boston, has analyzed the track records of major forecasters and forecasting organizations. The methods examined include sophisticated econometric models, barometric methods, time-series analysis, and informal judgmental forecasts. Thus, his analysis strives for an even-handed comparison of a wide variety of forecasting methods. He has come to several interesting conclusions.[4]

Forecasting Performance

First, forecast accuracy has improved over time due to better data and better models. Forecasters did better in the 1980s than in the 1970s. Forecasters have made reasonably accurate forecasts of annual real GDP (though they have been less accurate in predicting economic "turns") and of inflation, except in instances of large inflation shocks (as in the 1974 oil shock or the 1982 recession). Energy forecasts have improved dramatically. But in the 1990s, further incremental gains in accuracy have been small.

[4] See S. K. McNees, "An Assessment of the 'Official' Economic Forecasts," *New England Economic Review* (July–August 1995): 13–23, and S. K. McNees, "How Large Are Economic Forecast Errors?" *New England Economic Review* (July–August 1992): 25–42.

Second, many economic variables still elude accurate forecasting. To be useful, any prediction also should report a margin of error or confidence interval around its estimate. One way to appreciate this uncertainty is to survey a great many forecasters and observe the range of forecasts for the same economic variable. (But even this range understates the uncertainty. A significant portion of actual outcomes falls outside the surveyed range—that is, the outcomes are higher than the highest forecast or lower than the lowest.)

Third, the time period for making forecasts matters. On average, accuracy falls as the forecasters try to predict farther into the future. The time interval forecasted also matters. (Forecasts of annual changes tend to be more accurate than forecasts of quarterly changes.) Fourth, no forecaster consistently outperforms any other. Rather, forecast accuracy depends on the economic variable being predicted, how it is measured, and the time horizon. But the differences in accuracy across the major forecasters are quite small. Overall, macromodels performed better than purely extrapolative models, but, for many economic variables, the advantage (if any) is small.

Forecasting the Nickel Market Revisited

Recall that the large mining company was "bullish" on the prospects of world nickel sales during the 1990s after seeing its own shipments steadily increase during the 1980s. In fact, based on a linear time trend fitted to the past data, it estimated its own growth in nickel shipments roughly at an additional 12,000 thousand tons per year (see Figure 5.5a). At this rate, demand would outstrip capacity in fewer than five years. Accordingly, the firm began expansion of its Indonesian and Guatemalan facilities. So long as actual nickel sales tracked the company's projections, it would earn healthy (perhaps even "obscene") profits and remain the world's leading producer of nickel.

With 20-20 hindsight (Figure 5.5b), one observes that the demand for the company's nickel did not quite unfold as forecasted. Shipments in 1990 were 242,000 tons and only 259,000 tons per year a decade later. Shipments declined steeply in the early 1990s, recovered in the middle of the decade, then took a smaller dip before the decade closed. Used in many metal products (especially stainless steel), electronic products, and industrial processes, nickel demand closely tracked the business cycle falling during the 1990–1991 recession in the United States and collapsing further with the prolonged 1991–1994 European recession. With the worldwide recovery, nickel demand rebounded, only to fall again during the East Asian financial crisis and recession.

Not only did the company's nickel shipments stagnate, but the price of nickel during the decade dropped as well. Nickel prices dropped from $9,000 per ton in 1990 to as low as $6,000 a ton in 1993. Although prices recovered, they dipped again during 1998 and finally regained the $9,000 level by 2000. The price drops were due not only to cyclical declines in nickel demand but also to overcapacity in the industry. The large nickel company was not alone in expanding capacity in the early 1990s. The third and fourth largest companies also expanded their production facilities, driving down prices. All three firms failed to make any profits in the early 1990s. The number-one firm returned to profitability in the

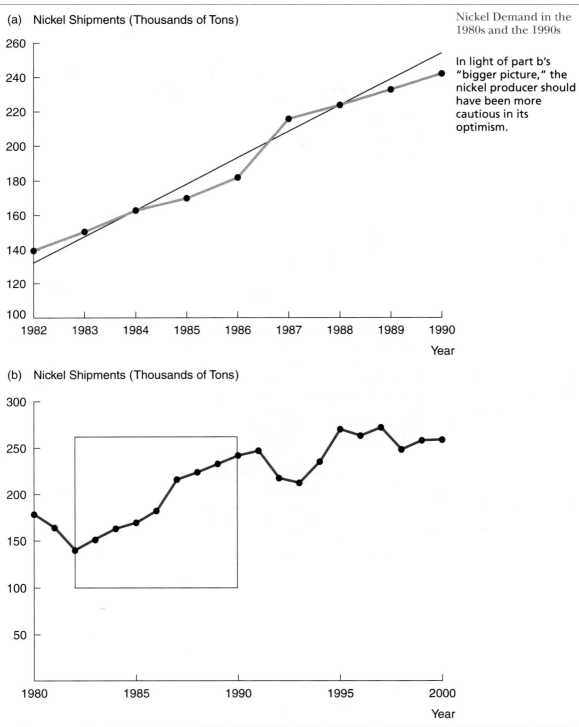

FIGURE 5.5

(a) Nickel Shipments (Thousands of Tons)

Nickel Demand in the
1980s and the 1990s

In light of part b's
"bigger picture," the
nickel producer should
have been more
cautious in its
optimism.

Year

(b) Nickel Shipments (Thousands of Tons)

Year

middle years of the decade, beginning to pay back its investment in expanded capacity. However, higher energy prices at present threaten profits. (Processing the kind of ore found in the tropics takes 1.5 times as much energy as Canadian ores require.)[5]

The large company's myriad problems resulted from a combination of bad forecasting and bad luck. Could the company have planned better for the coming turbulence in world markets? The "bigger" picture of the nickel market depicted in Figure 5.5b suggests that the answer is yes. The company's 1980s time series of shipments (magnified in part a) appears in the small box in part b. The bigger picture suggests the following conclusions:

1. The company's shipment history during the 1982–1990 period was unusually steady. However, during 1981 and 1982 (a time of worldwide recession), its shipments had fallen significantly. In fact, part of the company's high growth probably represented recovery from previous depressed levels. Moreover, a look at the *nickel industry as a whole* would have revealed much greater volatility in demand year to year during the decade. Though the firm's nickel sales grew steadily in the 1982–1990 period, how long could the company remain shielded from the reality of global fluctuations?

2. A linear time trend probably overstates the company's long-term growth prospects. (A quadratic specification, allowing for slackening growth, probably would have fit the data better.) Whatever the specification, the company should be aware of the standard error surrounding its forecast. Had anyone asked, the standard error for the linear time trend was large—plus or minus 8 thousand tons around the annual forecast. Moreover, this error will increase as forecasts become increasingly long range.

3. The time series did not take into account a key determinant of total nickel demand: the worldwide level of economic activity (especially steel production). Nor did it include an important factor influencing the company's share of demand: the supply and prices of its leading competitors. These omissions increase dramatically the margin of error in the company's forecast.

4. Japan's decade-long recession, the East Asian financial crisis, and recent oil price shocks were all nearly impossible to predict. The company's exposure to these adverse developments could well be attributed to bad luck.

The moral of this story? Often the worst mistake a company can make is to ignore uncertainty. Even if its forecasts had been correct on average, the company faced the risk that nickel demand could fall well below its expected projection. Given the uncertainty surrounding nickel demand, such a scenario was a significant possibility. Accordingly, the firm's production planning should have taken uncertainty into account.[5]

---

[5] Another moral is taken up in Chapter 10: Never ignore the principles of supply and demand. A naive manager might take the view, "Nickel is essential. The economy will always demand nickel. Therefore, we should march ahead as the world's leading supplier." Of course, this caricatures the real point: Do projected demand and supply conditions warrant the company's expansion?

SUMMARY

Decision-Making Principles

1. Managers depend on economic forecasts in making decisions.
2. An appreciation of the margin of error surrounding the forecast is as important as the forecast itself. Disasters in planning occur when management is overly confident of its ability to predict the future.

Nuts and Bolts

1. Forecasters use two main categories of forecasting methods. Structural forecasts rely on estimated equations describing relationships between economic variables. Nonstructural forecasts look at observed patterns among economic variables over time.
2. Time-series analysis relies on the identification of trends, cyclical fluctuations, and seasonal variations to predict the course of economic variables.
3. Barometric methods (leading indicators) are used to forecast the general course of the economy and changes in particular sectors.
4. Econometric models consist of systems of equations (behavioral equations and identities) that attempt to describe the economy's interdependent relationships and dynamics. The reduced form of the model provides forecasts of all endogenous variables after supplying values for all exogenous variables.
5. Forecasting accuracy has improved over time, but incremental gains have been small.

Questions and Problems

1. A chemical company uses large amounts of shredded steel scrap metal in its production processes. Most of this scrap comes from 12-ounce beverage cans (soft-drink and beer cans). On behalf of the company, you are responsible for forecasting the availability (and price) of this type of scrap over the next decade.
   a. What kinds of information would you need to make such a forecast?
   b. What factors—demographic, economic, technological, or political—might be important in your projection? Which could you most easily predict? Which would be highly uncertain?

2. The following table lists the Neebok Company's sales (in millions of dollars) in each of its five department stores. Management expects total sales to increase 10 percent in the coming year.

	Store A	Store B	Store C	Store D	Store E	Total
2004	8	9	10	11	12	50
2005	?	?	?	?	?	55

   a. Provide forecasts of each store's sales in the coming year. What assumptions underlie your forecasts?
   b. A fellow manager points out that last year's sales pattern is typical; sales vary considerably across stores for unpredictable reasons. Sales at a particular store may vary up or down by 10 to 20 percent from year to year. A store may be a leader one year and a laggard the next. What effect might this have on your 2005 forecasts? Explain.

3. a. Discuss and compare the relative merits of time-series and structural economic forecasts.
   b. Suppose a firm recently introduced cable television service into a rapidly growing city and surrounding suburbs in the Southwest. Which forecasting method might be most useful in predicting the total number of cable customers over the next five years?
   c. A producer of cable programming (such as Home Box Office) seeks to forecast its number of subscribers over the same time period. Which method would you recommend?

4. The following table lists your company's sales during the last four years.

	Year 1	Year 2	Year 3	Year 4
Sales	100	110	105	120

   a. A fellow manager points to the 15-unit increase between year 3 and year 4. Extrapolating this trend, he predicts 135 units will be sold in the coming year (year 5). Do you agree? Explain.
   b. A second manager notes that annual sales increases have averaged $(120 - 100)/3 = 6.67$ units per year. Accordingly, his forecast for the coming year is 126.67 units sold. Do you agree with this prediction? Explain.

5. Consider again the data in Problem 4.
   a. Using a computer program, estimate the linear increasing trend equation, S = a + bt, using ordinary least-squares regression.
   b. According to your regression statistics, how well does your estimated equation explain past variations in sales?
   c. Use your equation to forecast sales in the coming year. What margin of error would you attach to your forecast?

6. As the name suggests, a lagging indicator is an economic variable whose movements occur after movements in the overall economy.
   a. A number of employment measures are lagging indicators. Consider the following variables: (1) increased use of temporary workers, (2) increases in new hires, (3) a decline in the number of workers laid off, and (4) increase in overtime hours. In an economic recovery from a recession, which of these variables would have the shortest and longest lags?
   b. Top management of a company that produces luxury yachts has been waiting anxiously for the end of the recession and a resurgence in orders. Why might the company pay more attention to lagging indicators than to leading indicators? Explain.

7. A publisher of an industry newsletter wants to forecast the number of firms that are likely to subscribe in future years. Total subscriptions in a given year consist of renewals by current subscribers (O_t) and new subscriptions (N_t):

$$Q_t = O_t + N_t.$$

The publisher's best estimate of the number of new subscribers is

$$N_t = 1.25(Q_{t-1} - Q_{t-2}).$$

In words, the larger the recent increase in subscriptions, the more attractive is the newsletter to new subscribers. Finally, 95 percent of current customers renew their subscriptions.
   a. Use the given information to write down a reduced-form equation for Q_t as it depends on Q_{t-1} and Q_{t-2}.
   b. The number of subscribers increased from 100 last year to 120 this year. Provide subscription forecasts for the next seven years. Explain the predicted pattern of sales.

8. Over a span of 170 years, the men's world record for the mile run was reduced from 4 minutes and 56 seconds in 1804 to Roger Bannister's 3:59.4 in 1954 to John Walker's 3:49.4 in 1975. The graph records times by years and suggests that a straight line provides a good fit. A time-series regression produces the equation t = 16.473 − .0064Y, where t is the time in minutes (i.e., t = 4.1 means 4 minutes and 6 seconds) and Y is the year.

    a. According to the equation, the passing of each decade should reduce the record by how many seconds?

    b. Steve Cram's 1985 world record was 3:46.32. Hichman El Guerouj holds the current world record of 3:43.13 set in 1999. How accurate is the equation's forecast for each of these times?

    c. What is the predicted world record time for 2010? Would it be reasonable to use the equation for 2050?

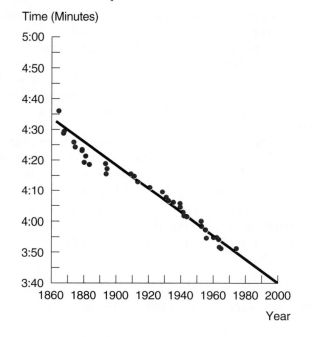

Discussion Question Companies such as Toyota, Dell, and Benetton have pioneered just-in-time production (JIT). Firms that practice JIT production carry low or no inventories of finished products. Rather, they build only those products that customers order. JIT production processes can adjust quickly to consumer demand both in terms of quantity and in terms of product characteristics. Does JIT production eliminate, reduce, or change the need to forecast demand? Discuss the role of forecasting, if any, in a JIT production environment.

Spreadsheet Problems

S1. There is considerable debate within your firm concerning the effect of advertising on sales. The marketing department believes advertising has a large positive effect; others are not so sure. For instance, the production and technical staffs believe the quality of the product itself largely determines sales. To clarify the debate, you have gathered the following data for the last 24 quarters.

Quarter	Unit Sales	Advertising
1	120	39
2	115	36
3	97	38
4	118	39
5	88	23
6	63	22
7	82	40
8	80	42
9	95	36
10	106	49
11	105	66
12	136	65
13	122	51
14	112	56
15	116	60
16	104	51
17	137	55
18	114	47
19	104	50
20	122	47
21	108	32
22	94	41
23	98	45
24	104	34

a. Does advertising affect unit sales? Base your answer on a regression analysis.

b. Others in the company argue that the last quarter's sales best predict the current quarter's sales. Test this hypothesis via regression analysis. Compare the performances of the regressions in parts a and b.

c. Some believe the impact of advertising takes time (as long as three months) to affect sales. Perform a regression to test this hypothesis.

S2. Your company's sales have been growing steadily over the last 17 quarters, as shown in the following table:

Quarter	Quantity Sales	Quarter	Quantity Sales
1	103.2	9	137.1
2	105.7	10	140.9
3	111.3	11	142.7
4	113.8	12	149.3
5	116.9	13	154.4
6	121.8	14	158.1
7	125.0	15	164.8
8	132.4	16	172.0
		17	181.3

You wish to predict the next four quarters' sales. (You are aware that your product's sales have no seasonal component.)

a. Using regression techniques, find the linear time trend that best fits the sales data. How well does this equation fit the past data?

b. Now estimate the constant-growth equation $Q = br^t$. Find the coefficients for b and r. Does this equation perform better than the linear form in part a? Explain.

c. Predict sales for the next four quarters using both equations.

Suggested References

The following are fine references on forecasting.

Armstrong, J. S. (Eds.). *Principles of Forecasting.* Boston: Kluwer Academic Publishers, 2001.

Granger, C. W. J. *Forecasting in Business and Economics.* New York: Academic Press, 1989.

Pindyck, R. S., and D. L. Rubinfeld. *Econometric Models and Economic Forecasts,* Chapters 1–6. New York: McGraw-Hill, 1997.

The following references discuss macroeconomic forecasting, the business cycle, and forecast accuracy.

McNees, S. K. "An Assessment of the 'Official' Economic Forecasts." *New England Economic Review* (July–August 1995): 13–23.

Stock, J. H., and M. Watson (Eds.). *Business Cycles, Indicators, and Forecasting,* Chicago: University of Chicago Press, 1993.

Zarnowitz, V., "Theory and History Behind Business Cycles: Are the 1990s the Onset of a Golden Age?" *Journal of Economic Perspectives,* Spring 1999, 13, 69–90.

Forecasting Web sites include The Conference Board www.conference-board.org and www.tcb-indicators.org (which lists various series of leading indicators), Professor Ray Fair of Yale University http://fairmodel.econ.yale.edu, and Data Resources, Inc. www.dri.mcgraw-hill.com.

1. The value of Company A's stock after 35 years will be $P_A = 50(1.05)^{35} = \$275.80$. (We can find this value by direct calculation or by using a future-value table found in most finance textbooks.) In turn, the value of Company B's stock will be $P_B = 50(1.06)^{35} = \$384.30$. The lesson is that small differences in average growth rates (when compounded over long periods of time) can lead to very large differences in value.

2. With $AC_1 = \$2.00$, it follows that $AC_2 = .3 + (.6)(2) = \$1.50$, $AC_3 = .3 + (.6)(1.5) = \$1.20$, and $AC_4 = .3 + (.6)(1.2) = \$1.02$. Obviously, the prediction is for falling average costs, presumably due to learning-curve effects. To discover how far AC could eventually fall, suppose that after many periods AC converges to some level denoted by c, $AC_t = AC_{t-1} = c$. Substituting c into the regression equation, we have $c = .3 + .6c$, implying $c = \$.75$. Over time, the firm's average cost per unit approaches a lower bound of \$.75.

3. The utility has not erred in using only a single dummy. By setting $W = 0$, the utility obtains the summer equation, $Q_t = 80.5 + 2.6t$. By setting $W = 1$, it has the winter equation, $Q_t = (80.5 + 12.4) + 2.6t = 92.9 + 2.6t$. Thus, the coefficient 12.4 represents the difference in the constant terms between summer and winter. To allow different rates of increase, the company could estimate the equation $Q_t = a + cW + bt + d(Wt)$. The last term includes an additional explanatory variable, the product of the winter dummy and the time variable. To illustrate, suppose the estimated equation is found to be $Q_t = 78.4 + 2.9t + 13.2W - .7(Wt)$. Then the summer equation (setting $W = 0$) is $Q_t = 78.4 + 2.9t$, and the winter equation (setting $W = 1$) is $Q_t = 91.6 + 2.2t$. Here the winter and summer seasons display different constant terms and different time coefficients.

CHAPTER 6

Production

One-tenth of the participants produce over one-third of the output. Increasing the number of participants merely reduces the average output.

NORMAN AUGUSTINE, AUGUSTINE'S LAWS

Allocating a Sales Force

To a greater or lesser extent, almost all firms face the task of finding and retaining customers for the goods and services they produce. For many service-intensive companies, the sales force is as important as—and, indeed, may outnumber—the production workforce. How to best utilize these sales personnel is a crucial question.

Consider an office equipment company that leases copiers, word processors, computers, and various types of office furniture to large and small firms. Because of the nature of the business, equipment leases rarely last more than one year in duration. Thus, the firm's extensive sales force is continually occupied with finding new customers, reenlisting current customers, and attempting to capture competitor's customers. A key question faces the company's sales and marketing director: Of the firm's current sales force (18 strong), how many "reps" should specialize in the larger accounts, which currently lease equipment (either the firm's own or a competitors'), and how many should devote themselves to new, smaller accounts, which have no current lease commitents? Could a reallocation of effort between these customer segments increase the firm's total sales?

To the person on the street, the nuts and bolts of management is deciding how to produce the firm's goods and services. This is the task of the firm's production managers. In Chapter 2 we introduced a bare-bones description of the firm's cost of production. In this chapter we examine production in more detail and in Chapter 7 we study issues of cost.

Production and cost are closely linked. The main task of the production manager is to determine how to produce a given level of output at minimal total cost. Thus, efficient production requires setting up appropriate facilities and estimating materials and input needs. It also means paying close attention to the costs of inputs and continually seeking to find less costly ways to produce the firm's goods and services.

We open this chapter by examining the production function, a quantitative summary of the firm's production possibilities. Next, we look closely at production in the short run and examine the impact on output of changing a single input. Then we consider production in the long run, when the firm has the flexibility to vary the amounts of all inputs. Next, we turn to the various types of production functions and discuss the means by which they are estimated. Finally, we consider a number of constrained production decisions involving the allocation of inputs (in fixed supply) to multiple plants or products, or both.

BASIC PRODUCTION CONCEPTS

Production Technology

Production is the process of transforming inputs into outputs. For instance, the production of automobiles requires a wide variety of inputs (also called factors of production): raw materials (steel, plastic, rubber, and so on), factories, machines, land, and many different categories of workers. For the purpose of analysis, it is convenient to refer to three main categories of inputs—materials, labor, and capital—with each category broadly defined. Materials include raw materials, intermediate goods (such as parts), water, electricity, and other energy sources. Labor encompasses all categories of workers employed by the firm: production workers, marketers, and managers at all levels. Capital includes buildings, equipment, and inventories.

The firm's **production function** indicates the maximum level of output the firm can produce for any combination of inputs. As we shall see, the production function can be expressed equivalently as an equation, a table, or a graph. A shorthand general description of a production function often is written as

$$Q = F(M, L, K). \qquad [6.1]$$

This states that the firm's quantity of output depends on the respective quantities of materials (M), labor (L), and capital (K) used in production. For instance, a major domestic automobile manufacturer might plan to produce 3 million passenger cars per year, using materials (of all kinds) that cost $24 billion, a total nationwide labor force of 80,000 workers, and a total capital stock valued at $100 billion. In its planning, management would be well aware that it could achieve the 3-million-unit target using alternative combinations of inputs. For instance, by making additional capital expenditures (in automatic, robotic assembly lines), the firm could reduce its labor force. It also knows that raising its production target to 3.2 million cars would require additional materials, labor, capital, and energy inputs in various proportions.[1]

We should emphasize one aspect of the preceding definition: The firm's production function specifies the *maximum* output for a given combination of inputs. Profit maximization by managers assumes that production is technically efficient; that is, neither inputs nor outputs are wasted or misused. Clearly, management should not continue to use an inefficient method of production if a superior method could increase its output using the same quantities of inputs. Obviously, production technologies improve over time, and efficient firms vigorously pursue these improvements. Thus, the production function is not "etched in stone." When we speak of a production function at any moment in time, we assume the firm is currently using the best available production technology. (Of course, the manager should never assume efficient production but rather should monitor continually that this is the case.)

A PRODUCTION FUNCTION FOR AUTO PARTS   Consider a multiproduct firm that supplies parts to two of the three major U.S. automobile manufacturers. Table 6.1 tabulates the firm's production function for one such specialty part. The table lists the quantities of output that can be produced using different combinations of two inputs, labor and capital.[2] Each entry lists the output generated by using a given amount of labor (listed by row) and a given plant size (listed by column). For instance, the first entry indicates that an output of 93 specialty parts per day can be produced employing 10 workers in a 10,000-square-foot plant. Alternatively, employing 60 workers in a 40,000-square-foot plant would increase the rate of output to 510 parts per day.

---

[1] Obviously, this example of a production function occurs at a very high level of aggregation: the company level. One just as well could speak of a production function for a specific car model at a particular plant. At this level, a detailed production function might disaggregate materials into scores of categories, separate labor into numerous job descriptions, and disaggregate capital expenditures.

[2] Production also requires a third input: materials. The assumption is that the firm has little or no flexibility with respect to this input. Each part requires a fixed amount of raw materials; producing twice as many parts requires twice as much raw materials and so on. Accordingly, the production function focuses on labor and capital and does *not* list the implicit amount of raw materials associated with each level of output.

TABLE 6.1

A Production Function
for a Specialty Part

This production func-
tion shows the quan-
tity of output that can
be obtained from vari-
ous combinations of
plant size and labor.

| Number of | Plant Size (Thousands of Square Feet) | | | |
Workers	10	20	30	40
10	93	120	145	165
20	135	190	235	264
30	180	255	300	337
40	230	315	365	410
50	263	360	425	460
60	293	395	478	510
70	321	430	520	555
80	346	460	552	600
90	368	485	580	645
100	388	508	605	680

PRODUCTION WITH ONE VARIABLE INPUT

Short-Run and Long-Run Production

Our analysis of production and cost makes an important distinction between
the short run and the long run.

The **short run** is a period of time in which the amount of one or more of the
firm's inputs is fixed, that is, cannot be varied. Inputs that cannot be changed in
the short run are called **fixed inputs**. Typically, a firm's capital stock requires time
to change; for example, expanding an existing plant or building a new one may
take years. Reducing the firm's capital stock also may be difficult or impossible
in the short run. If an oil producer finds it has a large excess of refining capacity in place (relative to demand), it may be impossible to sell or convert this capacity in the foreseeable future. If a firm operates under restrictive, long-term labor
contracts, its ability to vary its labor force may be limited over the contract duration, up to three years. In this case, labor could be a fixed input in the short run.

The **long run** is a period of time sufficiently long to allow the firm to vary
all of its inputs. In the long run, the firm could vary the size and scale of its
plant (as well as the amounts of all other inputs). In the short run, in contrast,
the size of this plant would be fixed at existing levels. To produce more output
in the short run, the firm would have to use the existing plant more intensively,
that is, by employing more labor and scheduling additional production runs.
There is no universal rule for distinguishing between the short and long runs;

rather, the dividing line must be drawn on a case-by-case basis. For a petro-chemical refinery, the short run might be any period less than five years (the length of time it takes to build a new refinery). For a fast-food chain, six months (the time it takes to obtain zoning approvals and construct new restaurants) may be the dividing line between short and long run.

MARGINAL PRODUCT   Let's consider the production decisions of the auto parts firm. Currently it is operating with a 10,000-square-foot plant. In the short run, this capital input is fixed. However, labor is a **variable input**; that is, the firm can freely vary its number of workers. Table 6.2 shows the amount of output obtainable using different numbers of workers. (This information is reproduced from the earlier production function and expanded slightly.) Notice that output steadily increases as the workforce increases, up to 120 workers. Beyond that point, output actually declines. It appears that too many workers within a plant of limited size is counterproductive to the task of producing parts.

TABLE 6.2

Production of Specialty Parts (10,000-Square-Foot Plant)

The second column shows the amount of total output generated by different amounts of labor. The third column shows the marginal product of labor—the extra output produced by an additional worker.

Number of Workers	Total Product	Marginal Product
10	93	
		4.2
20	135	
		4.5
30	180	
		5.0
40	230	
		3.3
50	263	
		3.0
60	293	
		2.8
70	321	
		2.5
80	346	
		2.2
90	368	
		2.0
100	388	
		1.2
110	400	
		0.3
120	403	
		−1.2
130	391	
		−1.1
140	380	

The last column of Table 6.2 lists the marginal product of labor (abbreviated MP_L). This **marginal product** is the additional output produced by an additional unit of labor, all other inputs held constant. For instance, increasing labor from 20 to 30 workers increases output by $180 - 135 = 45$ units, or $45/10 = 4.5$ units per worker. A further increase from 30 to 40 workers implies an MP_L of 5.0 units per worker. In algebraic terms, we can define labor's marginal product as $MP_L = dQ/dL$. In other words, labor's marginal product is the change in output per unit change in labor input.

Note that MP_L first rises (for increases up to 40 workers), then declines.[3] Rising marginal productivity (for a small labor force) can be explained on several grounds. When the workforce is small, the typical worker must be a jack-of-all-trades (and master of none). Increasing the number of workers provides opportunities for *specialization* of labor—workers devoting themselves to particular tasks—and this results in increased output. Furthermore, working with the firm's underutilized machinery and capital equipment, these additional workers will be very effective in increasing the rate of output.

Figure 6.1a graphs labor's total product (i.e., output) for workforces of various sizes. Consider the total product curve corresponding to a 10,000-square-foot plant. For small numbers of workers, the total product curve increases rapidly. As the number of workers increases, the curve's slope becomes less steep, then reaches a peak and declines. Of course, this "shape" reflects labor's marginal productivity. When MP_L is large, the total product curve is steep. As MP_L declines, the curve becomes less steep.

The product curve peaks when MP_L approaches zero and begins to decline when MP_L becomes negative. Figure 6.1a also displays labor's total product curve for a 20,000-square-foot plant (with output rates taken from Table 6.1). As indicated, the larger plant generates an increased rate of output for the same workforce. Finally, Figure 6.1b graphs labor's marginal product for a 10,000-square-foot plant. As the workforce varies, MP_L initially rises, peaks, and then steadily declines.

Graph the marginal product of labor if the firm produces output using a 30,000-square-foot plant. Compare this with the MP_L using a 10,000-square-foot plant. Explain the difference.

CHECK STATION 1

THE LAW OF DIMINISHING MARGINAL RETURNS   The declining marginal product of an input (like labor) represents one of the best known and most important empirical "laws" of production:

> The law of diminishing marginal returns states that, as units of one input are added (with all other inputs held constant), a point will be reached where the resulting additions to output will begin to decrease; that is, marginal product will decline.

---

[3] Indeed, labor's marginal product becomes negative for additional workers beyond 120; that is, total product actually declines when "too many" workers are employed. Of course, a profit-maximizing firm would never operate under such a labor plan. (By cutting its workforce, it would save on wage payments *and* increase output.)

FIGURE 6.1

Total Product and
Marginal Product

Part a graphs labor's
total product; part b
depicts labor's marginal
product.

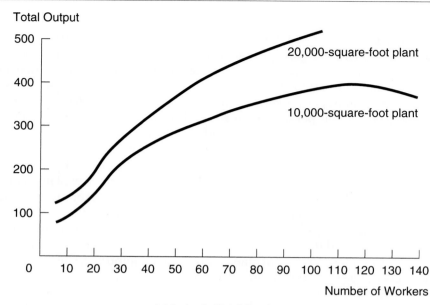

(a) Labor's Total Product

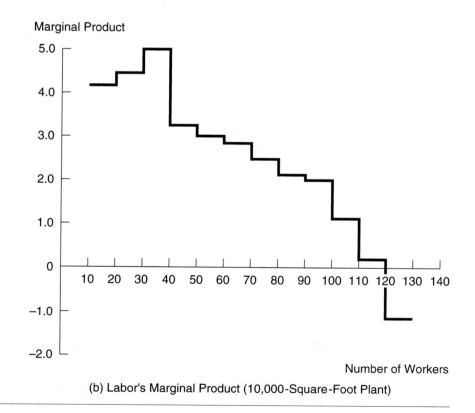

(b) Labor's Marginal Product (10,000-Square-Foot Plant)

In the preceding example, diminishing returns to labor occur for increases in the labor force beyond 40 workers. At this point the most productive jobs already are filled, so extra workers are assigned to less productive tasks. Furthermore, the firm already has exploited most or all of the gains from specialization and is efficiently utilizing its plant and capital equipment. Extra workers would indeed generate additional output but at a diminishing rate.

Optimal Use of an Input

The law of diminishing returns means that the firm faces a basic trade-off in determining its level of production. By using more of a variable input, the firm obtains a direct benefit—increased output—in return for incurring an additional input cost. What usage of the variable input is optimal? As always, the answer is found by measuring the firm's marginal profit (i.e., marginal revenue minus marginal cost) but this time from a unit increase in the *input*. For concreteness, suppose the auto parts firm seeks to increase output by expanding the number of labor-hours. Then the marginal profit of adding an hour of labor can be expressed as the difference between the marginal revenue per hour and the marginal cost per hour.

In analyzing this input decision, a definition is helpful. Marginal revenue product is the formal name for the marginal revenue associated with increased use of an input. To be precise, an input's **marginal revenue product** is the extra revenue that results from a unit increase in the input. The link between additional use of input and revenue can be thought of in two steps. To illustrate, suppose the auto parts supplier is considering increasing labor from 20 to 30 workers. According to Table 6.2, the resulting marginal product is 4.5 parts per worker. Suppose further that the supplier's marginal revenue per part is constant. It can sell as many parts as it wants at a going market price of $40 per part. Therefore, labor's marginal revenue product (MRP_L) is $(\$40)(4.5) = \$180$ per worker. Similarly, the MRP_L for a move from 30 to 40 workers is $(\$40)(5.0) = \$200$ per worker. More generally, labor's marginal revenue product can be expressed as

$$MRP_L = (MR)(MP_L),\qquad\qquad [6.2]$$

where MR denotes marginal revenue per unit of output.[4]

Now consider the marginal cost of using additional labor. In general, the **marginal cost of an input** is simply the amount an additional unit of the input adds to the firm's total cost. If the firm can hire as many additional workers as it wishes at a constant wage (say, $160 per day), this is the marginal cost of labor.[5] Thus, in this case, the marginal cost of labor is $MC_L = \$160$. (In some

---

[4] In calculus terms, $MRP_L = dR/dL = (dR/dQ)(dQ/dL) = (MR)(MP_L)$.

[5] It is important to distinguish between the marginal cost of an input and the marginal cost of an additional unit of output. Taking labor as an example, MC_L is defined as $\Delta C/\Delta L$, the cost of hiring an extra worker. In contrast, the added cost of producing an extra unit of *output* is $MC = \Delta C/\Delta Q$.

cases, however, the firm may have to bid up the price of labor to obtain additional workers; then MC_L will be increasing, not constant.)

How can the firm's managers use this information to determine its profit-maximizing workforce? The firm's marginal profit per worker is

$$M\pi_L = MRP_L - MC_L.$$

The additional profit from adding one more worker is the revenue generated by adding the worker net of the worker's marginal cost. The firm should continue to increase its labor force so long as the amount of additional profit from doing so is positive, that is, so long as the additional revenue (MRP_L) is greater than the additional cost (MC_L). Due to diminishing marginal returns, labor's marginal revenue product eventually will fall. When MRP_L exactly matches MC_L (i.e., when $M\pi_L = 0$), increasing the labor force any further will be unprofitable. Thus, labor should be increased until the marginal revenue product equals the marginal cost of labor, that is, until

$$MRP_L = MC_L. \tag{6.3}$$

After this point, the marginal cost of labor will exceed the marginal revenue product of labor and profits will decline. The following profit-maximization condition applies not only to labor but also to any other variable input:

> To maximize profit, the firm should increase usage of a variable input up to the point at which the input's marginal revenue product equals its marginal cost.

EXAMPLE 1   The human resources manager of the auto parts firm estimates that the marginal cost of hiring an extra worker is $P_L = \$160$ per day. With this information in hand, the firm can easily determine the optimal workforce for its 10,000-square-foot plant. Earlier we noted that a move from 20 to 30 workers implies an MRP_L of \$180 per worker (per day). Since this exceeds the daily cost per worker, \$160, this move is profitable. So, too, is a move from 30 to 40 workers ($MRP_L = \$200$). But an increase from 40 to 50 workers is unprofitable. The resulting MRP_L is ($40)(3.3) = \$132, which falls well short of the marginal labor cost. For further workforce increases, MRP_L continues to decline due to diminishing returns. Thus, the optimal size of the firm's labor force is 40 workers.

What would be the firm's optimal labor force if it had in place a 30,000-square-foot plant? From Table 6.1, we see that, for this plant size, labor's marginal product (and, therefore, its MRP_L) falls as more and more workers are hired. For instance, a move from 50 to 60 workers results in an MRP_L of \$212, a move from 60 to 70 workers an MRP_L of \$168, and a move from 70 to 80 workers an MRP_L of \$128. Given a labor price of \$160 per day, the firm profits by increasing its labor force up to a total of 70 workers (since $MRP_L > MC_L$ in this range). But an increase beyond this level reduces profitability ($MRP_L < MC_L$). The firm would best utilize the 30,000-square-foot plant by using 70 workers and producing 520 parts per day.

CHECK STATION 2

Let MR = \$40 and MC_L = \$160 per day. Using the relevant information from Table 6.1, determine the firm's optimal number of workers for a 20,000-square-foot plant. Repeat the calculation for a 40,000-square-foot plant.

EXAMPLE 2   A firm's production function is described by

$$Q = 60L - L^2,$$

where Q measures units of output and L is the number of labor-hours. Output sells for \$2 per unit, and the cost of labor is MC_L = \$16 per hour. How many workers should the firm hire, and how much output should it produce?

To answer these questions, we apply the fundamental rule

$$MRP_L = MC_L.$$

First, observe that labor's marginal product is $MP_L = \partial Q/\partial L = 60 - 2L$, which steadily declines as the labor force increases. In turn, labor's marginal revenue product is $MRP_L = (\$2)(60 - 2L) = 120 - 4L$. Setting this equal to \$16, we obtain $120 - 4L = 16$. The optimal amount of labor is L = 26 hours. From the production function, the resulting output is 884 units. Finally, the firm's operating profit (net of its labor cost) is $(\$2)(884) - (\$16)(26) = \$1,352$.

PRODUCTION IN THE LONG RUN

In the long run, a firm has the freedom to vary all of its inputs—its use of labor (of all kinds), land, capital (factories, machines, and inventories), and materials. Two aspects of this flexibility are important. First, firms face a number of important trade-offs in the way they produce output. A key trade-off involves the proportions of inputs used in production. For instance, a law firm may find it advantageous to economize on the size of its clerical staff by investing in computers and software specifically designed for the legal profession. In effect, it is substituting capital for labor. Steeply rising fuel prices have caused many of the major airlines to modify their fleets, increasing the number of smaller, fuel-efficient aircraft. Major department store chains sell their merchandise in stores of varying design and size, using smaller stores in downtown locations where rents are high, and larger, sprawling stores in suburbs, where land is much less expensive.

Second, firms face key decisions with respect to the *scale* of their operations. What is the most cost-effective way to expand the firm's operations in the long run? Would building and operating a new facility twice the size of the firm's existing plants achieve a doubling (or more than doubling) of output? Are there limits to the size of the firm beyond which efficiency drastically declines? These are all important questions that can be addressed using the concept of returns to scale.

Returns to Scale

The *scale* of a firm's operations denotes the levels of all the firm's inputs. A *change in scale* refers to a given percentage change in all inputs. (At a 15 percent scale increase, the firm would use 15 percent more of each of its inputs.) A key question for the manager is how the firm's output changes when the firm's inputs are proportionally increased. The concept of returns to scale can be used to address this question. **Returns to scale** measure the percentage change in output resulting from a given percentage change in inputs. There are three cases to consider: constant, increasing, and decreasing returns to scale.

Constant returns to scale is a benchmark case. **Constant returns to scale** occur if a given percentage change in all inputs results in an equal percentage change in output. For instance, if all inputs are doubled, output also doubles; a 10 percent increase in inputs would imply a 10 percent increase in output; and so on. Under constant returns, the firm's inputs are equally productive whether smaller or larger levels of output are produced. A common example of constant returns to scale occurs when a firm can easily replicate its production process. For instance, a manufacturer of electrical components finds that it can double its output by replicating its current plant and labor force, that is, by building an identical plant beside the old one. Similarly, a chain of dry cleaners can increase its volume of service by increasing its number of outlets (with a designated number of workers per outlet). So long as all necessary inputs are readily available, the firm can increase output in proportion to inputs via replication, and constant returns to scale will hold.

Increasing returns to scale occur if a given percentage increase in all inputs results in a greater percentage change in output. (This case often goes by the abbreviated term *returns to scale*.) For example, a 10 percent increase in all inputs causes a 20 percent increase in output. How can the firm do better than constant returns to scale? By increasing its scale, the firm may be able to use new production methods that were infeasible at the smaller scale. For instance, the firm may utilize sophisticated, highly efficient, large-scale factories. It also may find it advantageous to exploit specialization of labor at the larger scale. As an example, there is considerable evidence of increasing returns to scale in automobile manufacturing: An assembly plant with a capacity of 200,000 cars per year uses significantly less than twice the input quantities of a plant having a 100,000-car capacity. Frequently, returns to scale result from fundamental engineering relationships. Consider the economics of an oil pipeline from well sites in Alaska to refineries in the contiguous United States. Doubling the circumference of the pipe (call this s) increases the pipe's cross-sectional *area* by a factor of s^2, or *fourfold*—allowing a like increase in the flow capacity of the pipeline. Thus, a simple fact of elementary geometry provides a dramatic example of increasing returns.[6] To sum up, as long as there are increasing returns (whatever the source), it is better to use larger production facilities to supply output (at lower unit cost) instead of many smaller facilities.

Decreasing returns to scale occur if a given percentage increase in all inputs results in a smaller percentage increase in output. The most common explanations for decreasing returns involve organizational factors in very large firms. As the scale of the firm increases, so do the difficulties in coordinating and monitoring the many management functions. Coordinating the production and distribution of 12 products manufactured in four separate plants typically means incurring additional costs for management and information systems that would be unnecessary in a firm one-quarter the size. As a result, proportional increases in output require more than proportional increases in inputs.

Output elasticity provides a convenient measure of returns to scale. The **output elasticity** is the percentage change in output resulting from a 1 percent increase in all inputs. For constant returns to scale, the output elasticity is 1; for increasing returns, it is greater than 1; and for decreasing returns, it is less than 1. For instance, an output elasticity of 1.5 means that a 1 percent scale increase generates a 1.5 percent output increase, a 10 percent scale increase generates a 15 percent output increase, and so on.

Reexamine the production function in Table 6.1. Check that production exhibits increasing returns for low levels of input usage and decreasing returns for high levels of usage. Can you find instances of constant returns in the medium-input range?

CHECK STATION 3

A recent study of surface (i.e., strip) coal mining estimated production functions for deposits of different sizes.[7] The study was based on a survey of Illinois mines that included information (for each mine) on the production of coal (in tons), the amount of labor employed (in hours), the quantity of earthmoving capital (in dollars), and the quantity of other capital (also in dollars). Using these data in combination with sophisticated regression techniques, the study estimated production functions for mines that had a variety of geological characteristics. Significant economies of scale were found for most types of mines. The average elasticity of output with respect to inputs was 1.24. (A 20 percent increase in all inputs raised output by about 25 percent.) Typically, economies of scale were not exhausted until an annual output level of 4.8 million tons of coal was reached—a level higher than

Returns to Scale in Coal Mining

[6] As we shall see in Chapter 7, one can examine returns to scale not only at the plant level but also at the firm level. At the firm level, increasing returns to scale may occur in research and development, marketing, advertising, or distribution.

[7] G. A. Boyd, "Factor Intensity and Site Geology as Determinants of Returns to Scale in Coal Mining," *Review of Economics and Statistics* (1987): 18–23.

the actual operating scale of most mines. (Thus, further increases in the scale of mineral extraction would seem to be warranted.) In addition, there was evidence that increased use of large-scale, primary earthmoving equipment greatly enhanced the degree of returns to scale. In short, higher capital intensity implies greater returns to scale in mining.

Least-Cost Production

In the long run, the firm can vary all of its inputs. Because inputs are costly, this flexibility raises the question: How can the firm determine the mix of inputs that will minimize the cost of producing a given level of output? (With one variable input, this question was not at issue. With its factory already in place, the firm had no choice but to hire extra workers—paying them the requisite wages—to increase output.)

Let's return to the case of two inputs, labor and capital. Here the firm's production function is of the form

$$Q = F(L, K),$$

where L is the number of labor-hours per month and K is the amount of capital used per month. In producing a given level of output (call this Q_0), the firm can substitute freely between labor and capital. For instance, by using additional capital it could produce the same output, Q_0, using less labor and vice versa. In short, there is a trade-off between labor and capital in production.

What is the firm's optimal mix of labor and capital in producing output Q_0? We now show that the answer depends on the costs and marginal products of the inputs. We denote the firm's labor cost per hour (i.e., workers' wages plus other benefits) by P_L and its cost per unit of capital by P_K. Then the firm's total cost of using L and K units of inputs is

$$TC = P_L L + P_K K.$$

The firm seeks to minimize this cost, subject to the requirement that it use enough L and K to produce Q_0. We now state the following important result concerning optimal long-run production:

In the long run, the firm produces at least cost when the ratios of marginal products to input costs are equal across all inputs.

For the case of two inputs, we have

$$MP_L/P_L = MP_K/P_K. \tag{6.4}$$

More generally, for multiple inputs (three or more), a corresponding number of equalities holds among the ratios of marginal products to input prices.

Equation 6.4 shows that when total cost is minimized, the extra output per dollar of input must be the same for all inputs. To see why this must be true, assume to the contrary that the ratios in Equation 6.4 differ. As an example, let MP_L be 30 units per hour and P_L be \$15 per hour; in turn, let MP_K be 60 and P_K be \$40. Then $MP_L/P_L = 30/15 = 2$ units per dollar of labor, while $MP_K/P_K = 60/40 = 1.5$ units per dollar of capital. Because labor's productivity per dollar exceeds capital's, it is advantageous for the firm to increase its use of labor and reduce its use of capital. To be specific, the firm could maintain its present output level *by using two extra units of labor in place of one fewer unit of capital.* (The 60 units of output given up by reducing capital is exactly matched by (2)(30) = 60 units of output provided by the additional labor.) The net savings in total cost is \$40 (the saved capital cost) minus \$30 (the cost of two labor hours), or \$10. In short, if one input's productivity per dollar exceeds another's, the firm can produce the same output at lower cost by switching toward greater use of the more productive input. It should continue to make such switches until the ratios in Equation 6.4 come into equality. At that point, the firm will have found its least-cost input mix.

Suppose that initially $MP_L/P_L > MP_K/P_K$. Explain why the ratios will move toward equality as the firm switches to more labor and less capital.

CHECK STATION 4

EXAMPLE 3 A manufacturer of home appliances faces the production function $Q = 40L - L^2 + 54K - 1.5K^2$ and input costs of $P_L = \$10$ and $P_K = \$15$. Thus, the inputs' respective marginal products are

$$MP_L = \partial Q/\partial L = 40 - 2L$$

and

$$MP_K = \partial Q/\partial K = 54 - 3K.$$

From the previous discussion, we know that the firm's least-cost combination of inputs must satisfy $MP_L/P_L = MP_K/P_K$. This implies that

$$[40 - 2L]/10 = [54 - 3K]/15.$$

Solving for L, we find $L = K + 2$. This relation prescribes the optimal combination of capital and labor. For instance, the input mix K = 8 and L = 10 satisfies this relationship. The resulting output is $Q = (40)(10) - (10)^2 + (54)(8) - 1.5(8)^2 = 636$. The firm's total input cost is TC = (\$10)(10) + (\$15)(8) = \$220. In other words, the minimum cost of producing 636 units is \$220 using 10 units of labor and 8 units of capital. An alternative optimal mix of inputs is K = 18 and L = 20. We can check that this input mix produces 886 units at a minimum cost of \$470.

The National Football League (NFL) lives by the golden rule of team parity. Large-market teams in New York, Miami, or Dallas command greater revenues from ticket sales, concessions, TV and cable contracts, team products, and promotional deals. But small-market teams in Green Bay, Kansas City, and Cincinnati can nonetheless field winning teams. To achieve parity, the NFL has instituted a cap on team salaries, a system of revenue sharing, and more favorable player draft positions and schedules for weaker teams.[8]

How can a sports franchise construct a winning team with a strictly limited player budget ($74.6 million per team in 2003)? Coach Bill Belichick of the New England Patriots assembled teams that won the Super Bowl in 2002, 2004, and 2005 by carefully trading off player performance and price. The Patriots deliberately avoided superstars (considered to be overpriced) and relied instead on a mix of moderate-priced veterans and rookies obtained via free agency and the draft. The team traded marquee quarterback Drew Bledsoe and installed young Tom Brady in his place. Lawyer Milloy, an outstanding defensive player, was replaced with free-agent veteran Rodney Harrison, trading a $5.8 million salary for $3.2 million. Once an economics major at Wesleyan University, Belichick knew that each potential player must be evaluated based on his likely contribution to winning versus the annual salary for which he could be signed. Though Milloy's marginal product (i.e., ability and winning impact) was likely higher than Harrison's, this gain was not worth the salary price. Harrison was retained because $MP_H/P_H > MP_M/P_M$. As illustrated earlier by Equation 6.4, the key to optimally using multiple inputs is to compare MP-to-price ratios.[9]

By contrast, major league baseball, lacking a salary cap and having limited revenue sharing, suffers from severe competitive inequalities. (The league did institute a modest "luxury tax" in 2003. Teams with a payroll over a specified threshold have to pay a tax to the league.) The richest, large-market teams are able to sign the established top players at gargantuan salaries and, thus, assemble the best teams. Championship teams bring extra revenues to strong franchises and so help perpetuate their dominance. In 2003, the New York Yankees, the most winning team in baseball, earned an estimated $270 million in revenue and paid $184.5 million in player salaries, both figures being league highs. (The second highest salary bill by the Boston Red Sox was a "distant" $125 million. Tampa Bay paid just under $53.5 million in salaries.) During the spring of 2004, the Yankees signed free-agent superstar Alex Rodriguez. Freed from

[8] This account is based in part on L. Zinser, "Path to Super Bowl No Longer Paved with Stars," *The New York Times* (February 4, 2004), A1.

[9] The Patriots' objective is to maximize its team performance given limited total expenditures on salaries. This is closely related to the earlier least-cost problem: minimizing total salary expenditures subject to achieving a targeted level of team performance. The solution to the maximum-performance problem satisfies Equation 6.4, the same condition that pertains to the least-cost problem. For this reason, the two decisions often are referred to as "dual" problems. For instance, in Example 3, 636 units is the maximum output that can be obtained with an expenditure of $220, or equivalently, $220 is the minimum cost of producing 636 units. The answer to either problem is achieved using 10 units of labor and 8 units of capital.

any salary cap, the signing makes economic sense as long as the player's marginal revenue product is greater than his salary: $MRP_L > P_L$. Remembering that $MRP_L = (MR)(MP_L)$, we can see why a large-market team such as the Yankees gains the most from superstar signings. It enjoys much higher revenues and marginal revenues (MR) from strengthening its lineup. (It's also possible that a player's MP_L could differ across teams, for instance, if the player is a much better "fit" with his new team.)

In sum, under their respective ground rules, baseball's rich tend to get richer, while football's middle-class teams operate on the same level playing field.

A GRAPHICAL APPROACH   An alternative way to portray the firm's least-cost problem is via a graphical solution. Consider once again the production function of Example 3: $Q = 40L - L^2 + 54K - 1.5K^2$. We saw that the firm could produce $Q = 636$ units of output using $L = 10$ and $K = 8$ units of inputs. The same output, $Q = 636$, can be produced using different combinations of labor and capital: 6 units of labor and 12 units of capital, for instance. (Check this.)

An **isoquant** is a curve that shows all possible combinations of inputs that can produce a given level of output. The isoquant corresponding to $Q = 636$ is drawn in Figure 6.2a. The amounts of the inputs are listed on the axes. Three input combinations along the $Q = 636$ isoquant, ($L = 6$, $K = 12$), ($L = 10$, $K = 8$), and ($L = 14.2$, $K = 6$), are indicated by points A, B, and C, respectively. The isoquant's negative slope embodies the basic trade-off between inputs. If a firm uses less of one input, it must use more of the other to maintain a given level of output. A separate isoquant has been drawn for the output $Q = 800$ units. This isoquant lies above and to the right of the isoquant for $Q = 636$ because producing a greater output requires larger amounts of the inputs. Of course, we can describe the production function in increasing detail by drawing separate isoquants for more and more output levels (much the way one draws a contour map).

The slope of the isoquant measures the trade-off between the two inputs. For example, consider a movement from point B to point A in Figure 6.2a—a shift in mix from ($L = 10$, $K = 8$) to ($L = 6$, $K = 12$). Here an additional $12 - 8 = 4$ units of capital substitute for $10 - 6 = 4$ units of labor. But moving from point B to point C implies quite a different trade-off between inputs. Here 4.2 units of labor are needed to compensate for a reduction of only 2 units of capital. The changing ratio of input requirements directly reflects diminishing marginal productivity in each input. As the firm continually decreases the use of one input, the resulting decline in output becomes greater and greater. As a result, greater and greater amounts of the other input are needed to maintain a constant level of output. The isoquant's slope is steep on its upper left portion and flattens with movements downward along its length.

Using the production function, we can obtain a precise measure of the isoquant's slope. Consider again point B, where 10 units of labor and 8 units of capital are used. Recall from Example 3 that $MP_L = 40 - 2L$ and

FIGURE 6.2

Isoquants and Isocost
Lines

The two isoquants in
part a show the different
combinations of labor
and capital needed to
produce 636 and 880
units of output. The
isocost lines in part b
show combinations of
inputs a firm can acquire
at various total costs.

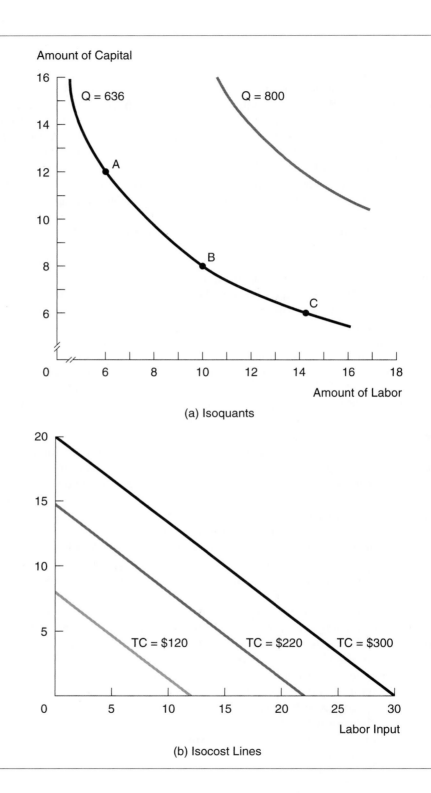

(a) Isoquants

(b) Isocost Lines

$MP_K = 54 - 3K$. Thus, at these input amounts, $MP_L = 40 - 2(10) = 20$ and $MP_K = 54 - 3(8) = 30$. The marginal product of an additional unit of labor is two-thirds that of a unit of capital. Since additional labor is only two-thirds as productive as capital, three additional units of labor are needed for every two-unit reduction in capital if a constant level of output is to be maintained. The slope of the isoquant (i.e., the slope of the tangent line at B) is

$$\Delta K/\Delta L = [-2 \text{ capital units}]/[+3 \text{ labor units}] = -2/3.$$

At A ($L = 6$, $K = 12$), the marginal products are $MP_L = 28$ and $MP_K = 18$. At this input combination, the isoquant's slope is $-28/18 = -1.55$. From the figure, we confirm that here the isoquant is quite steep.

The general rule is that the slope of the isoquant at any point is measured by the ratio of the inputs' marginal products:

$$\Delta K/\Delta L \text{ (for Q constant)} = -MP_L/MP_K.$$

Notice that the ratio is $-MP_L/MP_K$ and not the other way around. The greater is labor's marginal product (and the smaller capital's), the greater the amount of capital needed to substitute for a unit of labor, that is, the greater the ratio $\Delta K/\Delta L$. This ratio is important enough to warrant its own terminology. The **marginal rate of technical substitution (MRTS)** denotes the rate at which one input substitutes for the other and is defined as

$$MRTS = -\Delta K/\Delta L \text{ (for Q constant)} = MP_L/MP_K.$$

For example, at point B, the MRTS is $20/30 = .667$ units of capital per unit of labor; at point C, the MRTS is $28/18 = 1.55$.

Suppose the manager sets out to produce an output of 636 units at least cost. Which combination of inputs along the isoquant will accomplish this objective? The answer is provided by portraying the firm's least-cost goal in graphic terms. Recall that the firm's total cost of using L and K units of input is

$$TC = P_L L + P_K K.$$

Using this equation, let's determine the various combinations of inputs the firm can obtain at a given level of total cost (i.e., expenditure). To do this, we rearrange the cost equation to read

$$K = TC/P_K - (P_L/P_K)L.$$

To illustrate, suppose the firm faces the input prices of Example 3, $P_L = \$10$ and $P_K = \$15$. If it limits its total expenditures to $TC = \$120$, the firm can use any mix of inputs satisfying $K = 120/15 - (10/15)L$ or equivalently

$K = 8 - (2/3)L$. This equation is plotted in Figure 6.2b. This line is called an **isocost line** because it shows the combination of inputs the firm can acquire at a given total cost. We can draw a host of isocost lines corresponding to different levels of expenditures on inputs. In the figure, the isocost lines corresponding to TC = \$220 and TC = \$300 are shown also. The slope of any of these lines is given by the ratio of input prices, $\Delta K/\Delta L = -P_L/P_K$. The higher the price of capital (relative to labor), the *lower* the amount of capital that can be substituted for labor while keeping the firm's total cost constant.

By superimposing isocost lines on the same graph with the appropriate isoquant, we can determine the firm's least-cost mix of inputs. This is shown in Figure 6.3. For instance, to produce 636 units of output at minimum cost, we

FIGURE 6.3

Producing Output at Minimum Cost

The firm produces 636 units at minimum cost at point B, where the isoquant is tangent to the lowest possible isocost line. Point B corresponds to 10 units of labor and 8 units of capital.

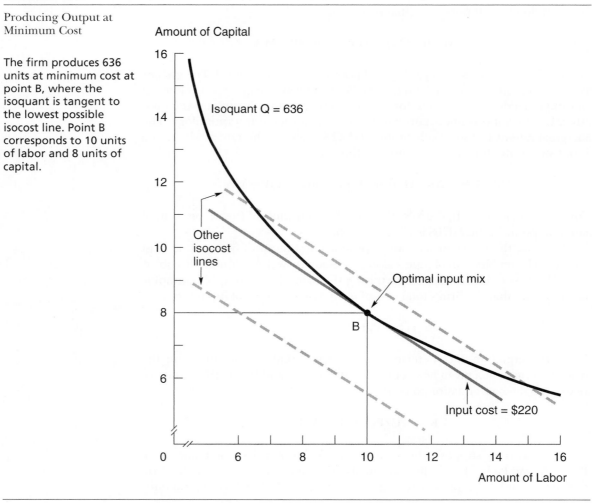

must identify the point along the isoquant that lies on the *lowest* isocost line. The figure shows that this is point B, the point at which the isocost line is tangent to the isoquant. Of course, point B confirms Example 3's original solution: The optimal combination of inputs is 10 units of labor and 8 units of capital. Since point B lies on the $220 isocost line, we observe that this is the minimum possible cost of producing the 636 units.

The important point is to recognize the general features of this solution. At the point of tangency, the slope of the isoquant and the slope of the isocost line are the same. The isoquant's slope is $-MP_L/MP_K$. In turn, the isocost line's slope is $-P_L/P_K$. Thus, the least-cost combination of inputs is characterized by the condition

$$MRTS = MP_L/MP_K = P_L/P_K.$$

The ratio of marginal products exactly matches the ratio of input prices.[10] (If one input is twice as expensive as another, optimal usage requires that it have twice the marginal product.) This relationship can be rearranged to read

$$MP_L/P_L = MP_K/P_K.$$

This is exactly the condition established in Equation 6.4. The marginal product per dollar of input should be the same across all inputs.

When Boeing's first twin-engine long-haul aircraft rolled out of the assembly hanger, it was in record time and represented the single most ambitious experiment in computer-aided design (CAD). Computer-aided design permits "virtual" manufacturing: realistic simulation of the most important aspects of products and processes.[11] Instead of constructing countless mock-ups of the new aircraft to ensure that its millions of complex parts fit together and function as intended, Boeing uses CAD to create its mock-ups elsewhere: in the billions of bits of information faithfully stored in its computers. These computerized designs can be tested and modified at will—before materials, labor, and equipment are committed to actual production. For Boeing, CAD greatly enhances precision, allows designs to be transmitted instantly among company personnel and subcontractors, and dramatically cuts the time it takes to translate design into production. Indeed, for high-tech, complex systems

Designing the Boeing 777

---

[10] The same condition is derived readily using the method of Lagrange multipliers introduced in the appendix to Chapter 2. The problem is to minimize $TC = P_L L + P_K K$ subject to $F(L, K) = Q_0$, where Q_0 denotes a given level of output. The Lagrangian is $£ = P_L L + P_K K + z(Q_0 - F(L, K))$. The optimality conditions are $\partial£/\partial L = P_L - z(\partial F/\partial L) = 0$, $\partial£/\partial K = P_K - z(\partial F/\partial K) = 0$, and $\partial£/\partial z = Q_0 - f(L, K) = 0$. Dividing the first condition by the second yields $P_L/P_K - (\partial F/\partial L)/(\partial F/\partial K) = 0$. It follows that $P_L/P_K = MP_L/MP_K$, after recognizing that $MP_L = \partial F/\partial L$ and $MP_K = \partial F/\partial K$.

[11] For an account of Boeing's experience, see "A Survey of Manufacturing Technology," *The Economist* (March 5, 1994): 7–11.

such as aircraft, more than 50 percent of eventual life-cycle product costs depend on early design decisions.

Computer-aided design is changing the ways managers think about production. Beyond the customary, tangible production inputs (labor, capital, and materials), managers have come to recognize *information* as a fourth input. By using information more intensively, production managers can economize on the use of the other three inputs, as Boeing has done successfully. The exact trade-off managers choose between information and the other production resources depends on the relative costs of the inputs. As computing costs decline, managers will increasingly turn to CAD systems, particularly when they deliver significant savings on expensive labor and capital.

Moreover, information has two features not shared by other inputs. First, information is not used up. Setting up information systems involves certain fixed costs, but, once established, information can be used and reused at relatively low marginal costs. Second, information enhances manufacturing flexibility. In modern information-based manufacturing, there are innumerable ways to produce a given quantity of output and myriad trade-offs among them. As the example of the Boeing 777 demonstrates, accelerated manufacturing and just-in-time production methods save time as well as money.

MEASURING PRODUCTION FUNCTIONS

In this section, we briefly discuss ways in which managers can estimate and measure production functions based on engineering or economic data. The first step in the estimation process is to specify the quantitative form of the production function. Although many forms are possible, our discussion focuses on the four most common specifications and their properties.

Linear Production

As the term suggests, a **linear production function** takes the form

$$Q = aL + bK + c, \qquad [6.5]$$

where a, b, and c are coefficients that must be estimated from the data. Clearly, this is a very simple form of production function—indeed, probably too simple. An immediate implication of linearity is that each input's marginal product is constant: $MP_L = a$ and $MP_K = b$. Constant marginal productivity may approximate production over a limited range of input usage. But at sufficiently high levels of inputs, it is at odds with the law of diminishing marginal productivity. In this sense, the linear form should be viewed as a somewhat extreme case.

Furthermore, linearity implies that the inputs are *perfect substitutes* for one another. As a concrete example, suppose the production function is $Q = 20L + 40K$, where labor and capital are measured in labor-hours and machine-hours, respectively. Because capital has twice the marginal product of labor, it follows that one machine-hour is a perfect substitute for *two* labor-hours. This in turn implies that the firm's input choice is "all or nothing" in the long run. If the rental rate per machine-hour is less than the wage cost of two labor-hours, the firm's least-cost means of expanding output is to use only capital. In contrast, if labor is the less expensive option, production should use labor exclusively. In general, so long as $MP_K/P_K > MP_L/P_L$, the firm should use capital exclusively (and vice versa if the inequality is reversed). Since marginal products are constant under linear production, one or the other inequality will hold. Put another way, only if marginal products decline (or input costs increase) will it be optimal for the firm to use both inputs.

Production with Fixed Proportions

Production with fixed proportions is the opposite extreme from linear production. Instead of perfect input substitutability, fixed-proportions production allows no substitutability. Output is produced with a given proportion of inputs. Simple examples include a taxi and its driver or a construction crane and its operator. In both cases, the required mix of labor to capital is one to one. An excess of either input—a machine without an operator or vice versa—does no good. Expansion of production requires balanced increases in the necessary inputs. Like linear production, fixed-proportions production should be thought of as an extreme case. Rarely is there no opportunity for input substitution. (For example, it is true that a crane needs an operator but, at a more general level, extra construction workers can substitute for construction equipment.)

However, there is an important implication of fixed-proportions production. In the face of an increase in an input's price, the firm *cannot* economize on its use, that is, substitute away from it. Thus, a petrochemical firm that uses fixed proportions of different chemicals to produce its specialty products is at the mercy of market forces that drive up the prices of some of these inputs.

Polynomial Functions

In the *polynomial form,* variables in the production function are raised to positive integer powers. As a simple example, consider the quadratic form

$$Q = aLK - bL^2K^2,$$

where a and b are positive coefficients. It is easy to check that each input shows diminishing returns. (For example, $MP_L = \partial Q/\partial L = aK - 2bK^2L$, which declines as L increases.) The quadratic form also displays decreasing returns to scale. A more flexible representation is the cubic form,

$$Q = aLK + bL^2K + cLK^2 - dL^3K - eLK^3,$$

where all coefficients are positive. We can show that this function displays increasing returns for low output levels and then decreasing returns for high output levels. The marginal product of an input (say, labor) takes the form

$$MP_L = \partial Q / \partial L = (aK + cK^2 - eK^3) + 2bKL - 3dKL^2.$$

We see that marginal product is a quadratic function in the amount of labor; that is, it is a parabola that rises, peaks, and then falls. Thus, this functional form includes an initial region of increasing marginal productivity followed by diminishing returns.

The Cobb–Douglas Function

Perhaps the most common production function specification is the **Cobb–Douglas function**

$$Q = cL^{\alpha}K^{\beta}, \qquad\qquad [6.6]$$

where c, α, and β denote parameters to be estimated. (Furthermore, α and β are between 0 and 1.) The Cobb–Douglas function is quite flexible and has a number of appealing properties. First, it exhibits diminishing returns to each input. To see this, note that $MP_L = \partial Q / \partial L = c\alpha K^{\beta}L^{\alpha - 1}$ and $MP_k = \partial Q / \partial K = c\beta L^{\alpha}K^{\beta - 1}$. Labor's marginal product depends on both L and K. It declines as labor increases, since L is raised to a negative power $(\alpha - 1 < 0)$. However, labor's marginal product shifts upward with increases in the use of capital, a complementary input. (Analogous results pertain to the other input, capital.)

Second, the nature of returns to scale in production depends on the sum of the exponents, $\alpha + \beta$. Constant returns prevail if $\alpha + \beta = 1$; increasing returns exist if $\alpha + \beta > 1$; decreasing returns exist if $\alpha + \beta < 1$. We can check these effects as follows. Set the amounts of capital and labor at specific levels, say, L_0 and K_0. Total output is $Q_0 = cL_0^{\alpha}K_0^{\beta}$. Now suppose the inputs are increased to new levels, zL_0 and zK_0, for $z > 1$. According to Equation 6.6, the new output level is

$$
\begin{aligned}
Q_1 &= c(zL_0)^{\alpha}(zK_0)^{\beta} \\
&= cz^{\alpha + \beta}L_0^{\alpha}K_0^{\beta} \\
&= z^{\alpha + \beta}Q_0,
\end{aligned}
$$

after regrouping terms and using the definition of Q_0. If the scale increase in the firm's inputs is z, the increase in output is $z^{\alpha + \beta}$. Under constant returns $(\alpha + \beta = 1)$, the increase in output is z; that is, it is identical to the scale increase in the firm's inputs. For instance, if inputs double (so that $z = 2$), output doubles as well. Under increasing returns ($\alpha + \beta > 1$), output increases in a greater proportion than inputs (since $z^{\alpha + \beta} > z$). Under decreasing returns ($\alpha + \beta < 1$), output increases in a smaller proportion than inputs.[12]

Third, the Cobb–Douglas function can be conveniently estimated in its logarithmic form. By taking logs of both sides of Equation 6.6, we derive the equivalent linear equation:

$$\log(Q) = \log(c) + \alpha \log(L) + \beta \log(K).$$

With data on outputs and inputs, the manager can employ the linear regression techniques of Chapter 4 using log (L) and log (K) as independent variables and log (Q) as the dependent variable. The statistical output of this analysis includes estimates of log (c) (the constant term) and the coefficients α and β.

EXAMPLE 4   Suppose the firm faces the production function $Q = L^{.5}K^{.5}$ and input prices are $P_L = \$12$ and $P_K = \$24$. (The inputs are equally productive, but capital is twice as expensive as labor.) The optimal input mix satisfies Equation 6.4 so that

$$[.5L^{-.5}K^{.5}]/12 = [.5L^{.5}K^{-.5}]/24.$$

After collecting terms, we get $K^{.5}/K^{-.5} = (12/24)L^{.5}/L^{-.5}$, or

$$K = .5L.$$

As noted, capital is twice as expensive as labor. As a result, for the Cobb–Douglas function, the firm employs half the number of units of capital as it does of labor.

Estimating Production Functions

To be useful to the manager, production functions must be estimated and constructed based on actual data gathered by the firm. These data come in a number of forms. One possibility is to use engineering data. The engineering approach can provide direct answers to a number of production questions: On average, how much output can be produced by a certain type of machine under different operating conditions? How many bushels of a particular crop can be grown and harvested on land (of known quality) using specified amounts of labor, capital, and materials (such as fertilizer)? Such information usually is

---

[12] One disadvantage of the Cobb–Douglas function is that it cannot allow simultaneously for different returns to scale. For instance, actual production processes often display increasing returns to scale up to certain levels of output, constant returns for intermediate output levels, and decreasing returns for very large output levels. The Cobb–Douglas function cannot capture this variation (because its returns are "all or nothing").

based on experience with respect to similar (or not so similar) production processes. Consequently, the estimated production function is only as accurate as the past production experience on which it is based. Sometimes there is little in the way of a past production track record, as in the case of new-product development efforts involving high risks and advanced technologies. The development of new weapons systems is a case in point. Although production and cost estimates are based on the best available engineering estimates (and possibly on tests of prototypes), they nonetheless are highly uncertain.[13]

A second source of production information is economic data in statistical form. For instance, a particular firm can make use of *time-series* data on its production facilities. In a time-series analysis, the firm's managers compile a production history, month by month or year by year. Of obvious importance is the record of the amounts of inputs (capital, labor, land, materials, and so on) used in production and the resulting level of output. Alternatively, the economic data may come in the form of a *cross section*. In this case, information is gathered for different plants and firms in a given industry during a single period of time. For instance, by observing production in the auto industry, one can address a number of important questions: For plants of fixed size (possibly employing different degrees of automation), what is the effect on output of expanding the labor force (i.e., adding extra shifts)? Does the industry exhibit economies of scale and, if so, over what range of outputs? (That is, will a 40 percent increase in plant scale deliver more than a 40 percent increase in output?)

These sources—although subject to measurement errors—generate very useful information for managers. Based on these data, the manager (often with the help of an operations research specialist) can estimate the mathematical relationship between levels of inputs and quantity of output. The principal statistical method for carrying out this task is regression analysis (the most important elements of which were discussed in Chapter 4). The end product of this analysis is a tangible representation of the firm's production function.

OTHER PRODUCTION DECISIONS

Within the limits of its production technology, the firm's managers face a number of important decisions. We have already discussed two of these fundamental decisions:

1. **Optimal use of a single input.** A firm maximizes its profit by increasing the use of a variable input to the point at which its marginal revenue product equals its marginal cost.

---

[13] Another limitation of engineering data is that they apply only to parts of the firm's activities, typically physical production operations. Thus, such data shed little light on the firm's marketing, advertising, or financial activities.

2. **Optimal mix of inputs.** A firm produces a given quantity of output at minimum cost by equating the marginal product per dollar spent on each input.

In this section, we focus on two additional decision problems: (1) the allocation of a single input among multiple production facilities and (2) the use of an input across multiple products. As will become clear, both decisions are examples of constrained maximization problems. Each can be solved readily using marginal analysis.

Multiple Plants

As a motivating example, consider an oil company that buys crude oil and transforms it into gasoline at two of its refineries. Currently it has 10 thousand barrels of oil under long-term contract and must decide how to allocate it between its two refineries. Clearly, the firm's goal is to allocate the available supply of crude so as to maximize the refineries' total output. The firm determines crude oil allocations, M_A and M_B, that will maximize total output,

$$Q = Q_A + Q_B,$$

subject to

$$M_A + M_B = 10 \text{ thousand.}$$

Increasing the quantity of crude to a refinery increases its output according to the refinery's production function.

The key to maximizing total output is to compare marginal products at the two refineries. Barrels of crude first should be allocated to the refinery whose marginal product is greater; let's say this is refinery A. As additional barrels are allocated to this refinery, its marginal product diminishes, and it becomes worthwhile to allocate oil to refinery B as well. In general, additional oil is split between the two refineries based on a comparison of marginal products.

In the final allocation of all 10 thousand barrels, output is maximized if and only if *the marginal products of both refineries are equal.* Why must this be the case? If marginal products differed (say, $MP_A < MP_B$), barrels should be shifted from the low-MP plant (refinery A) to the high-MP plant (refinery B). This raises total output because the extra output at B exceeds the reduction in output at A. In short, total output is maximized only when

$$MP_A = MP_B.$$

Let's apply this rule in a specific example. Based on extensive studies, management has estimated the following production functions for the refineries:

$$\text{Refinery A:} \quad Q_A = 24M_A - .5M_A^2$$
$$\text{Refinery B:} \quad Q_B = 20M_B - M_B^2,$$

where gasoline outputs are measured in thousands of gallons and quantities of crude oils are measured in thousands of barrels. Marginal products are

$$\text{Refinery A:} \quad MP_A = 24 - M_A$$
$$\text{Refinery B:} \quad MP_B = 20 - 2M_B.$$

Figure 6.4 shows the declining marginal product curve for each refinery and two possible allocations. One is a "naive" allocation calling for an equal split between the two facilities: $M_A = M_B = 5$ thousand barrels. Using the production functions, we find total output to be 182.5 thousand gallons. However, the figure immediately points out the inefficiency of such a split. At this division, the marginal product of the last barrel of crude at refinery A greatly exceeds the marginal product of the last barrel at refinery B ($19 > 10$). Barrels should be reallocated toward refinery A.

We can readily identify the optimal solution from Figure 6.4: $M_A = 8$ thousand barrels and $M_B = 2$ thousand barrels.[14] At these allocations, each refinery's marginal product is 16. (To check this, refer to the marginal product expressions just given.) The total output of gasoline from this allocation is 196 thousand gallons—a considerable improvement on the naive allocation. Furthermore, no other allocation can deliver a greater total output.

Multiple Products

Firms often face the problem of allocating an input in fixed supply among different products. The input may be a raw material—for instance, DRAM computer chips allocated to the various models of personal computers manufactured by the firm—or it may be capital. Frequently, the input in shortest supply is managerial labor itself. Which products of the firm are in greatest need of managerial attention? Which top-level managers are best suited to improve performance in a given product line?

Although seemingly quite different, allocating inputs across multiple plants and allocating inputs across multiple products share the same mode of analysis. In each case, the input is in limited supply and the key is to recognize the trade-off among the uses to which it can be put. Consider a variation on the oil

---

[14] We can find these allocations directly using the facts that $MP_A = MP_B$ and $M_A + M_B = 10$. Equating marginal products implies $24 - M_A = 20 - 2M_B$. Solving this equation and the quantity constraint simultaneously gives the solution $M_A = 8$ thousand barrels and $M_B = 2$ thousand barrels.

FIGURE 6.4

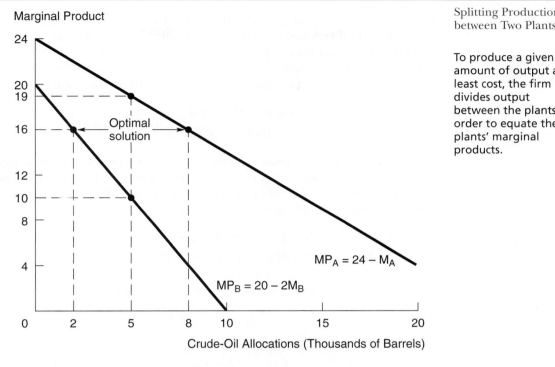

Marginal Product

To produce a given
amount of output at
least cost, the firm
divides output
between the plants in
order to equate the
plants' marginal
products.

Optimal
solution

$MP_A = 24 - M_A$

$MP_B = 20 - 2M_B$

Crude-Oil Allocations (Thousands of Barrels)

company's decision. Suppose two of the company's product managers are engaged in a heated debate. The first manager oversees the company's production and sale of gasoline; the second is responsible for production of synthetic fiber. Both products use crude oil as an essential input. The problem is that the current demands of the managers for this input exceed the firm's available crude oil supply, 20 thousand barrels. Each manager is arguing for a greater share of the input.

How can economic analysis be used to resolve this dispute? Given a limited resource and two products, gasoline and fiber, management's ultimate goal must be to allocate the crude oil where it is most profitable. To measure the impact on profit, we need specific information about the products' production functions and profits. However, let's first provide a general description of the decision problem. The firm's objective is to allocate crude oil to each product (in quantities M_G and M_F) to maximize total profit subject to the constraint of 20 thousand total barrels.

The form of this decision is very similar to that of the multiplant decision. Here total profit is maximized if and only if the input is allocated such that *the products generate identical marginal profits per unit of input.*[15]

[15] Here marginal profit is calculated *per unit input* because input is the appropriate decision variable.

$$M\pi_G = M\pi_F.$$

If fiber had a higher marginal profit per unit input than gasoline, gallons of crude should be switched from gasoline production to fiber production; the extra profit from additional production of fiber would exceed the lost profit from cutting back gasoline production, implying a net increase in total profit. Here is a concrete example. Suppose the production functions are

$$\text{Gasoline: } G = 72M_G - 1.5M_G^2$$
$$\text{Fiber: } F = 80M_F - 2M_F^2$$

Here gasoline output is measured in thousands of gallons, fiber output in thousands of square feet, and crude oil in thousands of barrels. The products' profits per unit output are $.50 per gallon for gasoline and $.75 per square foot for fiber. Then the respective marginal profits are

$$M\pi_G = (\$.50)MP_G = (\$.50)(72 - 3M_G) = 36 - 1.5M_G$$
$$M\pi_F = (\$.75)MP_F = (\$.75)(80 - 4M_F) = 60 - 3M_F.$$

Setting these equal to each other and rearranging gives

$$M_F = .5M_G + 8.$$

Solving this equation and the constraint $M_G + M_F = 20$ implies $M_G = 8$ thousand barrels and $M_F = 12$ thousand barrels. This allocation generates 480 thousand gallons of gasoline and 672 thousand square feet of fiber. The firm's total profit is $744 thousand (less the cost of the crude).

CHECK STATION 5   Find the optimal crude oil allocation in the preceding example if the profit associated with fiber were cut in half, that is, fell to $.375 per square foot.

FINAL REMARKS   With respect to both the plant and product decisions, two comments are in order. First, the appropriate marginal conditions are extended easily to the case of multiple (more than two) plants and decisions. (For instance, if there are three plants, the marginal product condition becomes $MP_A = MP_B = MP_C$.) Second, the decision framework changes significantly if management is able to vary the amount of the input. (When the input is in fixed supply, the sole issue is how to allocate it.) Over a longer period of time, the firm will be able to change the amount of the input by buying more or less crude oil. Here management's task is to determine the optimal amount of input to use at each plant or for each product. We already characterized the solution to this decision: For each plant or each product, use of the input should be expanded to the point where its marginal revenue product equals its marginal cost per unit input (i.e., the input's price).

Recall that the key issue for the office supply firm was how to divide its 18-person sales force between large accounts (firms already under contract with the company or a competitor) and new accounts (firms without a current rental contract). To address this problem, five senior sales managers have put to paper their best estimate of the profit functions for both types of accounts; these functions are shown in Figure 6.5. There is general agreement that the large accounts are more profitable than the new accounts. In Figure 6.5, the profit function for large accounts is uniformly greater than that for new accounts. (For instance, assigning five salespeople to the former generates $800,000, whereas assigning the same number to new accounts generates only $400,000.) In light of the profit curves, would senior sales managers be justified in allocating all 18 salespeople to large accounts?

Allocating a Sales Force Revisited

The answer is a resounding no! Management's objective is to assign its sales force to maximize total profit. Upon some reflection, we should recognize this as a fixed-input/multiple-product decision. (To be more precise, there are two different "service activities" that vie for the limited labor input.) Thus, the company should assign salespersons to the category of account that generates the greater marginal profit per unit input. Do not be misled by the fact that large accounts provide greater total profit

FIGURE 6.5

Profit Functions for an Office Supply Firm

The optimal division of salespeople is 8 individuals to "large" accounts and 10 to "new" accounts.

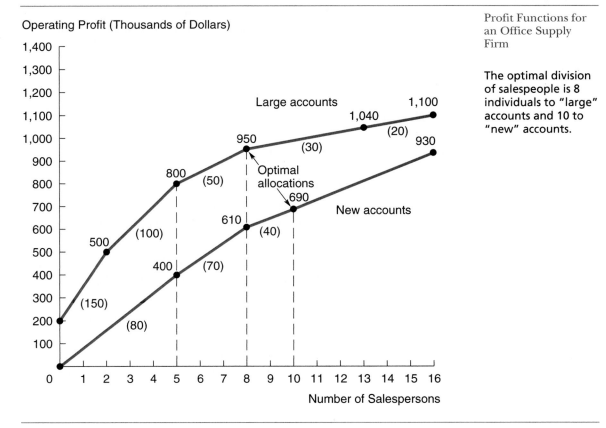

(for labor forces of equal size). What matters is a comparison of marginal profits. For convenience, Figure 6.5 lists marginal profits (in parentheses) for each type of account and for the different sizes of sales force. The profit function for large accounts indicates that a two-person sales force raises profit from $200,000 to $500,000, implying a marginal profit of $150,000 per person (presumably this minimal sales force is essential for retaining the firm's most loyal current clients); going from two to five salespeople increases profit by $100,000 per individual; and so on.

By now you should be able to determine the optimal allocation of the sales force: eight salespeople to large accounts and ten to new accounts. The sales force is assigned to accounts in order of marginal profits; that is, the highest marginal profit assignments are made first. The "first" five individuals serve large accounts. (Marginal profit is $150,000 and then $100,000 per person.) The "next" eight individuals serve new accounts. (Marginal profit is $80,000 and then $70,000 per person.) The "next" three individuals go to large accounts (marginal profit is $50,000). The "last" two salespeople serve new accounts (marginal profit is $40,000). By assigning eight and ten salespeople to large and new accounts, respectively, the firm earns a total operating profit of $950,000 + $690,000 = $1,640,000.

New accounts have a lower average profit per salesperson but claim a majority of the sales force. The intuitive explanation is that these accounts offer better profit opportunities at the margin. Once five salespeople have been assigned to maintain the large accounts, there is relatively little opportunity to increase profit in this area (presumably because of the difficulty in persuading competitors' clients to switch). In contrast, there is a relatively steady marginal profit to be earned in new accounts. Thus, this is where the majority of the salespeople should be placed.

SUMMARY

Decision-Making Principles

1. Production is the process of turning inputs into outputs.

2. To maximize profit, the firm should increase usage of a variable input up to the point where the input's marginal cost equals its marginal revenue product.

3. To minimize the cost of producing a particular amount of output, the firm should choose an input mix such that the ratio of the marginal product to the input's cost is the same across all inputs.

4. In allocating an input among multiple plants, the firm maximizes total output when marginal products are equal across facilities.

5. In allocating an input among multiple products, the firm maximizes total profit when marginal profits per unit input are equal across products.

Nuts and Bolts

1. The production function indicates the maximum amount of output the firm can produce for any combination of inputs.

2. The short run is a period of time in which the amount of one or more of the firm's inputs is fixed, that is, cannot be varied.
   a. Marginal product (MP) is the additional output produced by an additional unit of an input, all other inputs held constant.
   b. The law of diminishing returns states that, as units of one input are added (with all other inputs held constant), a point will be reached at which the resulting additions to output will begin to decrease; that is, marginal product will decline.
   c. An input's marginal revenue product (MRP) is the extra revenue generated by unit increase in the input. For input A,
   $$MRP_A = (MR)(MP_A).$$

3. The long run is an amount of time long enough to allow the firm to vary all of its inputs.
   a. Constant returns to scale occur if a given percentage change in all inputs results in an equal percentage change in output.
   b. Increasing (decreasing) returns to scale occur if a given increase in all inputs results in a greater (lesser) proportionate change in output.

4. Production functions are estimated by specifying a variety of mathematical forms and fitting them to production data derived from engineering studies, economic time series, or cross sections.

Questions and Problems

1. Explain the difference between diminishing returns and decreasing returns to scale.

2. "One-tenth of the participants produce over one-third of the output. Increasing the number of participants merely reduces the average output." If this statement were true, would it be consistent with the law of diminishing returns?

3. Does optimal use of an input (such as labor) mean maximizing average output (per unit of input)? Explain.

4. In November 1990, Chrysler Corporation announced plans to initiate three-shift or nearly continuous (21-hours-per-day) production at a number of its plants. Explain why Chrysler's decision might have been prompted by movements in its wage costs or capital costs, or both. Why would Chrysler have instituted this production change for its most popular (and profitable) vehicles, its minivans and Jeep Cherokee? What risks might such a plan pose?

5. Consider the production function $Q = 10L - .5L^2 + 24K - K^2$ for L and K in the range 0 to 10 units. Does this production function exhibit diminishing returns to each input? Does it exhibit decreasing returns to scale? Explain.

6. a. Suppose the inputs in Problem 5 can be purchased at the same price per unit. Will production be relatively labor intensive or capital intensive? Explain.

   b. Suppose input prices are $P_L = 40$ and $P_K = 80$ and the price of output is 10. Determine the optimal quantity of each input.

7. A 200-pound steer can be sustained on a diet calling for various proportions of grass and grain. These combinations are shown in the table.

Pounds of Grass	Pounds of Grain
50	80
56	70
60	65
68	60
80	54
88	52

   a. Plot the isoquant corresponding to the inputs necessary to sustain a 200-pound steer. Comment on its shape.

   b. The rancher's cost of grass is $.10 per pound; the cost of grain is $.07 per pound. He prefers a feed mix of 68 pounds of grass and 60 pounds of grain. Is this a least-cost mix? If not, what is? Explain.

   c. The rancher believes there are constant returns to scale in fattening cattle. At current feed prices, what input quantities should he choose if he wants to raise the steer's weight to 250 pounds?

8. A trendy French restaurant is one of the first businesses to open in a small corner of a commercial building still under construction. The restaurant has received rave reviews and has lines of diners waiting for tables most nights.

   a. In the short run (next few months), what measures should the restaurant take to maximize its profit? Explain.

   b. In the long run (next six months and beyond), how can it maximize its profit? (Assume that the impressive state of demand is permanent.)

9. Steel can be produced using three different methods: (1) a basic process using coke that produces steel ingots, (2) continuous casting, or (3) an electric furnace using steel scrap. The following table lists the average cost per ton of steel for each method.

Type of Cost	Basic Process	Continuous Casting	Electric Furnace
Materials	$150	$140	$120
Labor	$ 80	$ 75	$ 70
Capital	$100	$100	$ 60
Energy	$ 20	$ 15	$ 50
Other	$ 45	$ 40	$ 25

a. Production of steel by electric furnace is a relatively new development (beginning in the late 1970s) and accounts for a growing fraction of total steel sold. What is your prediction about the future production share of this method? Explain.

b. If there were a new energy crisis (causing energy prices to triple), how would this affect steelmakers' choices of production methods?

c. Suppose the price of steel scrap is expected to fall significantly over the next five years. What effect would this have on the choice of production method?

10. Making dresses is a labor-intensive process. Indeed, the production function of a dressmaking firm is well described by the equation $Q = L - L^2/800$, where Q denotes the number of dresses per week and L is the number of labor-hours per week. The firm's additional cost of hiring an extra hour of labor is about $20 per hour (wage plus fringe benefits). The firm faces the fixed selling price, $P = \$40$.

a. How much labor should the firm employ? What are its resulting output and profit?

b. Over the next two years, labor costs are expected to be unchanged, but dress prices are expected to increase to $50. What effect will this have on the firm's optimal output? Explain. Suppose instead that inflation is expected to increase the firm's labor cost and output price by identical (percentage) amounts. What effect would this have on the firm's output?

c. Finally, suppose once again that $MC_L = \$20$ and $P = \$50$ but that labor productivity (i.e., output per labor-hour) is expected to increase by 25 percent over the next five years. What effect would this have on the firm's optimal output? Explain.

11. In her last-minute preparations for final exams, a student has set aside five hours to split between studying for two subjects, finance and economics. Her goal is to maximize the average grade received in the two courses. (Note that maximizing the average grade and maximizing

the sum of the grades are equivalent goals.) According to her best guesses, grades vary with study as follows:

Study Hours	Finance Grade	Study Hours	Economics Grade
0	70	0	75
1	78	1	81
2	83	2	85
3	88	3	87
4	90	4	89
5	92	5	90

    a. List the marginal values of additional hours worked for each subject.
    b. How much time should the student spend studying each subject?
    c. Suppose the student also is taking an accounting exam and estimates that each hour of studying will raise her grade by three points. She has allotted two hours for studying accounting (in addition to the five hours already mentioned). Is this an optimal decision? Explain. (Assume her objective is to maximize her average grade across the three courses.)

12. Consider the production function $Q = 100L^{.5}K^{.4}$. Suppose $L = 1$ and $K = 1$ so that $Q = 100$.
    a. If L is increased by 1 percent, that is, to $L = 1.01$, with capital unchanged, what is the resulting percentage increase in output?
    b. Describe the nature of returns to scale for this production function.

13. A firm is producing a given amount of output at least cost using a mix of labor and capital (which exhibit some degree of substitutability). Using an isoquant graph, show that if one input price increases, least-cost production calls for the firm to lower the use of that input (and increase the use of the other).

* 14. Let $Q = L^{\alpha}K^{\beta}$. Suppose the firm seeks to produce a given output while minimizing its total input cost: $TC = P_L L + P_K K$. Show that the optimal quantities of labor and capital satisfy $L/K = (\alpha/\beta)(P_K/P_L)$. Provide an intuitive explanation for this result.

* 15. In a particular region, there are two lakes rich in fish. The quantity of fish caught in each lake depends on the number of persons who fish in each, according to $Q_1 = 10N_1 - .1N_1^2$ and $Q_2 = 16N_2 - .4N_2^2$, where N_1 and N_2 denote the number of fishers at each lake. In all, there are 40 fishers.
    a. Suppose $N_1 = 16$ and $N_2 = 24$. At which lake is the average catch per fisher greater? In light of this fact, how would you expect the fishers to redeploy themselves?
    b. How many fishers will settle at each lake? (*Hint:* Find N_1 and N_2 such that the average catch is equal between the lakes.)

    * Starred problems are more challenging.

c. The commissioner of fisheries seeks a division of fishers that will maximize the total catch at the two lakes. Explain how the commissioner should use information on the marginal catch at each lake to accomplish this goal. What division of the 40 fishers would you recommend?

Spreadsheet Problems

S1. A firm's production function is well described by the equation

$$Q = 2L - .01L^2 + 3K - .02K^2.$$

Input prices are $10 per labor-hour and $20 per machine-hour and the firm sells its output at a fixed price of $10 per unit.

a. In the short run, the firm has an installed capacity of K = 50 machine-hours per day, and this capacity cannot be varied. Create a spreadsheet (based on the example that follows) to model this production setting. Determine the firm's profit-maximizing employment of labor. Use the spreadsheet to probe the solution by hand before using your spreadsheet's optimizer. Confirm that $MRP_L = MC_L$.

b. In the long run, the firm seeks to produce the output found in part a by adjusting its use of both labor and capital. Use your spreadsheet's optimizer to find the least-cost input amounts. (*Hint:* Be sure to include the appropriate output constraint for cell I3.)

c. Suppose the firm were to downsize in the long run, cutting its use of both inputs by 50 percent (relative to part b). How much output would it now be able to produce? Comment on the nature of returns to scale in production. Has the firm's profitability improved? Is it currently achieving least-cost production?

	A	B	C	D	E	F	G	H	I
1									
2			OPTIMAL INPUTS						
3								Output	136.0
4								Price	10.0
5		Labor	20		Capital	50.0			
6		MP_L	1.600		MP_K	1.000		MR	10.00
7								Revenue	1360.0
8		MRP_L	16.0		MRP_K	10.0			
9		MC_L	10.0		MC_K	20.0		Cost	1200.0
10								Ave Cost	8.8
11									
12								Profit	160.0
13									

S2. A second firm's production function is given by the equation

$$Q = 12L^{.5}K^{.5}.$$

Input prices are \$36 per labor unit and \$16 per capital unit, and P = \$10.

a. In the short run, the firm has a fixed amount of capital, K = 9. Create a spreadsheet to model this production setting. Determine the firm's profit-maximizing employment of labor. Use the spreadsheet to probe the solution by hand before using your spreadsheet's optimizer.

b. Once again, the firm seeks to produce the level of output found in part a by adjusting both labor and capital in the long run. Find the least-cost input proportions. Confirm that $MP_L/P_L = MP_K/P_K$.

c. Suppose the input price of labor falls to 18. Determine the new least-cost input amounts in the long run. Provide an intuitive explanation for the change in inputs caused by the lower labor price.

Suggested References

The following reading surveys the use and estimation of production functions.

Gold, B. "Changing Perspectives on Size, Scale, and Returns: An Interpretative Survey." *Journal of Economic Literature* (March 1981): 5–33.

The following references offer case studies of production and economies of scale.

Basu, S., and J. G. Fernald. "Returns to Scale in U.S. Production: Estimates and Implications." *Journal of Political Economy* 105 (April 1997): 249–283.

Boyd, G. A. "Factor Intensity and Site Geology as Determinants of Returns to Scale in Coal Mining." *Review of Economics and Statistics* (1987): 18–23.

Cookenboo, L. "Production Functions and Cost Functions: A Case Study." in E. Mansfield (Ed.), *Managerial Economics and Operations Research.* New York: Norton, 1993.

Noulas, A. G., S. C. Ray, and S. M. Miller. "Returns to Scale and Input Substitution for Large U.S. Banks." *Journal of Money, Credit and Banking* 22 (February 1990): 94–108.

Managers' production strategies are discussed in:

Womack, J. P. "From Lean Production to Lean Enterprise." *Harvard Business Review* (March–April 1994): 93–103.

1. Labor's marginal product is uniformly greater (i.e., greater for any size of labor force) at a 30,000-square-foot plant than at a 10,000-square-foot plant.

2. At a 20,000-square-foot plant, the optimal labor force is 50 workers. (Here the MRP_L changes from \$180 to \$140.) At a 40,000-square-foot plant, the optimal labor force is 90 workers. (The MRP_L changes from \$180 to \$140.)

3. Doubling scale (starting from 10 workers and a 10,000-square-foot plant) more than doubles output. The same is true starting from 20 workers and a 20,000-square-foot plant. In contrast, doubling scale (starting from 50 workers and a 20,000-square-foot plant) produces less than double the output. Constant returns occur for a doubling of scale starting from 40 workers and a 10,000-square-foot plant or 30 workers and a 20,000-square-foot plant.

4. Given diminishing returns, using additional labor and less capital will lower the marginal product of labor and raise the marginal product of capital. Using extra labor also might bid up the price of labor. These effects move MP_L/P_L and MP_K/P_K into equality.

5. If fiber's profit is \$.375 per square foot, fiber's marginal profit becomes $M\pi_F = 30 - 1.5M_F$. Equating this to $M\pi_G$ implies $M_F = M_G - 4$. Together with $M_F + M_G = 20$, the solution is $M_F = 8$ thousand barrels and $M_G = 12$ thousand barrels. Given the reduced profit from fiber, the allocation of crude oil to this product is lowered (from 12 thousand to 8 thousand barrels).

Cost Analysis

Delete each element of capability until system capability is totally gone and 30 percent of the cost will still remain.

NORMAN AUGUSTINE, AUGUSTINE'S LAWS

Allocating Costs

A sporting goods firm recently experimented with producing a new line of shoes: cross-training shoes for boys 10 to 16 years old. The boys' shoe is very similar to the firm's main product, a best-selling women's athletic shoe. (The sizes are virtually the same; only the colors and logos differ.) Thus, the new line of shoes is easy and inexpensive to produce—indeed, there is excess production-line capacity to do so. Production of the women's shoe runs about 8,000 pairs per week, and the company recently began producing 2,400 pairs of boys' shoes per week. The firm's production managers estimate that the factory overhead cost shared between the two shoe lines comes to about $90,000 per week. (Overhead costs include shared factory space, machines, electricity, and some sales and support staff.) The company's policy is to allocate these shared fixed costs in proportion to the numbers of pairs of each line of shoes.

Currently the company charges an average price of $36 per pair for the boys' shoe. However, the total revenues generated at that price fail to cover the shoes' total costs: direct cost (primarily materials and labor) and the allocated overhead cost just mentioned. Faced with this apparent loss, top management is considering various options to achieve profitability.

- The firm's chief accountant suggests raising the price on the new line (say, to $40 per pair) to improve margins and better cover production costs.

- The marketing manager agrees this might be reasonable but cautions that sales are bound to drop.

- The head of production adds that unit costs will vary with volume as well.

He advocates producing at an output level at which direct costs per unit will be minimized.

In light of this conflicting advice, what type of cost analysis could guide the firm in determining its profit-maximizing course of action?

Cost analysis is the bedrock on which many managerial decisions are grounded. Reckoning costs accurately is essential to determining a firm's current level of profitability. Moreover, profit-maximizing decisions depend on projections of costs at other (untried) levels of output. Thus, production managers frequently pose such questions as: What would be the cost of increasing production by 25 percent? What is the impact on cost of rising input prices? What production changes can be made to reduce or at least contain costs? In short, managers must pay close attention to the ways output and costs are interrelated.

In this chapter, we build on Chapter 6's analysis of production to provide an overview of these crucial cost concepts. In the first section, we discuss the basic principles of *relevant costs*—considering the concepts of opportunity costs and fixed costs in turn. Next, we examine the relationship between cost and output in the short run and the long run. Then we turn to economies of scale, scope, and learning. Finally, we consider the importance of cost analysis for a number of key managerial decisions.

RELEVANT COSTS

A continuing theme of previous chapters is that optimal decision making depends crucially on a comparison of relevant alternatives. Roughly speaking, the manager must consider the relevant pros and cons of one alternative versus another. The precise decision-making principle is:

In deciding among different courses of action, the manager need only consider the differential revenues and costs of the alternatives.

Thus, the only relevant costs are those that differ across alternative courses of action. In many managerial decisions, the pertinent cost differences are readily apparent. In others, issues of relevant cost are more subtle. The notions of opportunity costs and fixed costs are crucial for managerial decisions. We will consider each topic in turn.

Opportunity Costs and Economic Profits

The concept of opportunity cost focuses explicitly on a comparison of relative pros and cons. The **opportunity cost** associated with choosing a particular decision is measured by the benefits forgone in the next-best alternative. Typical examples of decisions involving opportunity cost include the following:

- What is the opportunity cost of pursuing an M.B.A. degree?
- What is the opportunity cost of using excess factory capacity to supply specialty orders?
- What is the opportunity cost that should be imputed to city-owned land that is to be the site of a public parking garage downtown?

As the definition suggests, an estimate of the opportunity cost in each case depends on identifying the next-best alternative to the current decision. Consider the first example. Suppose the M.B.A. aspirant has been working in business for five years. By pursuing an M.B.A. degree full time, what is he giving up? Presumably, it is the income he could have earned from the present job. (This opportunity cost is larger or smaller depending on how remunerative the job is and on the chances for immediate advancement.) Therefore, the total cost of taking an M.B.A. degree is the explicit, out-of-pocket tuition cost plus the implicit (but equally real) opportunity cost.[1]

Next, consider the case of excess factory space. Assuming this space otherwise would go unused, its opportunity cost is zero! In other words, nothing is given up if the extra space is used to supply the specialty orders. More realistically, perhaps, one would assign a small opportunity cost to the capacity; committing the space to the specialty order might preclude using it for a more profitable "regular" order that might arrive unexpectedly.

Finally, consider the case of the city-owned land. Here the opportunity cost is whatever dollar value the land could bring in its next-best alternative. This might mean a different, more profitable city project. In general, an accurate estimate of the land's alternative value is simply its current market price. This price reflects what potential buyers are willing to pay for comparable downtown real estate. Unless the city has a better alternative for the land, its next-best option will be to sell the land on the open market.

As the first and third examples illustrate, opportunity costs for goods, services, or inputs often are determined by market prices (assuming such markets exist). For instance, the opportunity cost of the full-time M.B.A. student's time is his forgone wage (determined, of course, by labor-market conditions). The cost of the city-owned land is its market price. Note that if the city did not own the land, its cost would be explicit; it would have to pay the market price to obtain it. The fact of ownership doesn't change this cost; opportunity cost is still determined by the market price.[2]

---

[1] Here are some questions to consider: What is the opportunity cost of pursuing an M.B.A. degree part time at night while holding one's current job? For a 19-year-old, what is the opportunity cost of pursuing an undergraduate business degree?

[2] Of course, explicit costs and opportunity costs sometimes differ. For example, suppose an individual possesses financial wealth that earns an 8 percent rate of return. If that person were to borrow from a bank, the rate would be no lower than 11 percent. Then the opportunity cost of internally financing payment of M.B.A. tuition is lower than the market cost of obtaining a loan to do so.

The concept of opportunity cost is simply another way of comparing pros and cons. The basic rule for optimal decision making is this:

> Undertake a given course of action if and only if its incremental benefits exceed its incremental costs (including opportunity costs).

Thus, pursuing the M.B.A. degree makes sense only if the associated benefits—acquisition of knowledge, career advancement, higher earnings—exceed the total costs. Likewise, the factory space should be used only if the direct increase in cash flows exceeds the opportunity cost. Finally, the garage should be built only if its total benefits exceed its costs.

How would one estimate the full cost to an airline if one of its planes is held over for 24 hours in a western airport for repair?   **CHECK STATION 1**

ECONOMIC PROFIT   At a general level, the notion of profit would appear unambiguous: Profit is the difference between revenues and costs. On closer examination, however, one must be careful to distinguish between two definitions of profit. **Accounting profit** is the difference between revenues obtained and expenses incurred. The profit figures reported by firms almost always are based on accounting profits; it is the job of accountants to keep a careful watch on revenues and explicit expenses. This information is useful for both internal and external purposes: for managers, shareholders, and the government (particularly for tax purposes). With respect to managerial decision making, however, the accounting measure does not present the complete story concerning profitability. In this case, the notion of economic profit is essential. **Economic profit** is the difference between revenues and all economic costs (explicit and implicit), including opportunity costs. In particular, economic profit involves costs associated with capital and with managerial labor. Here is a simple illustration.

STARTING A BUSINESS   After working five years at her current firm, a money manager decides to start her own investment management service. She has developed the following estimates of annual revenues and costs (on average) over the first three years of business:

Management fees	$140,000
Miscellaneous revenues	12,000
Office rent	−36,000
Other office expenses	−18,000
Staff wages (excluding self)	−24,000

From this list, the new venture's accounting profit, the difference between revenues and explicit expenses, would be reckoned at $74,000.

Is going into business on one's own truly profitable? The correct answer depends on recognizing all relevant opportunity costs. Suppose the money manager expects to tie up $80,000 of her personal wealth in working capital as part of starting the new business. Although she expects to have this money back after the initial three years, a real opportunity cost exists: the interest the funds would earn if they were not tied up. If the interest rate is 8 percent, this capital cost amounts to $6,400 per year. This cost should be included in the manager's estimate. Furthermore, suppose the manager's compensation (annual salary plus benefits) in her current position is valued at $56,000. Presumably this current position is her best alternative. Thus, $56,000 is the appropriate cost to assign to her human capital.

After subtracting these two costs, economic profit is reduced to $11,600. This profit measures the projected monetary gain of starting one's own business. Since the profit is positive, the manager's best decision is to strike out on her own. Of course, the projected profit is hardly a sure thing. The attendant risks (of lower revenues or greater costs) may persuade the manager to retain her old job. (However, the intangible but real benefits of being one's own boss would weigh in favor of the new venture.) Note that the manager's decision would be very different if her current compensation were greater—say, $80,000. The accounting profit looks attractive in isolation. But $74,000 obviously fails to measure up to the manager's current compensation ($80,000) even before accounting for the cost of capital.

In general, we say that economic profit is zero if total revenues are exactly matched by total costs, where total costs include a normal return to any capital invested in the decision and other income forgone. Here *normal return* means the return required to compensate the suppliers of capital for bearing the risk (if any) of the investment; that is, capital market participants demand higher normal rates of return for riskier investments. As a simple example, consider a project that requires a $150,000 capital investment and returns an accounting profit of $9,000. Is this initiative profitable? If the normal return on such an investment (one of comparable risk) is 10 percent, the answer is no. If the firm must pay investors a 10 percent return, its capital cost is $15,000. Therefore, its economic profit is $9,000 − $15,000 = −$6,000. The investment is a losing proposition. Equivalently, the project's rate of return is 9,000/150,000, or 6 percent. Although this return is positive, the investment remains unprofitable because its return is well below the normal 10 percent requirement.

Now suppose the investment's return is 12 percent; that is, its accounting profit is $18,000. In this case, the project delivers a 2 percent "excess" return (i.e., above the normal rate) and would be economically profitable. Finally, suppose the project's accounting profit is exactly $15,000. Then its economic profit would be exactly zero: $15,000 − (.1)($150,000) = 0. Equivalently, we would say that the project just earned a normal (10 percent) rate of return.

Fixed and Sunk Costs

Costs that are **fixed**—that is, do not vary—with respect to different courses of action under consideration are irrelevant and need not be considered by the manager. The reason is simple enough: If the manager computes each alternative's profit (or benefit), the same fixed cost is subtracted in each case. Therefore, the fixed cost itself plays no role in determining the relative merits of the actions. Consider once again the recent graduate who is deciding whether to begin work immediately or to take an M.B.A. degree. In his deliberations, he is concerned about the cost of purchasing his first car. Is this relevant? The answer is no, assuming he will need (and will purchase) a car whether he takes a job or pursues the degree.

Consider a typical business example. A production manager must decide whether to retain his current production method or switch to a new method. The new method requires an equipment modification (at some expense) but saves on the use of labor. Which production method is more profitable? The hard (and tedious) way to answer this question is to compute the bottom-line profit for each method. The easier and far more insightful approach is to ignore all fixed costs. The original equipment cost, costs of raw materials, selling expenses, and so on are all fixed (i.e., do not vary) with respect to the choice of production method. The only differential costs concern the equipment modification and the reduction in labor. Clearly, the new method should be chosen if and only if its labor savings exceed the extra equipment cost. Notice that the issue of relevant costs would be very different if management were tackling the larger decision of whether to continue production (by either method) *or shut down*. With respect to a shut-down decision, many (if not all) of the previous fixed costs become variable. Here the firm's optimal decision depends on the magnitudes of costs saved versus revenues sacrificed from discontinuing production.

Ignoring fixed costs is important not only because it saves considerable computation but also because it forces managers to focus on the differential costs that are relevant. Be warned that ignoring fixed costs is easier in principle than in practice. The case of sunk costs is particularly important. A **sunk cost** is an expense that already has been incurred and cannot be recovered. For instance, in the earlier factory example, plant space originally may have been built at a high price. But this historic cost is sunk and is irrelevant to the firm's current decision. As we observed earlier, in the case of excess, unused factory capacity, the relevant opportunity cost is near zero.

More generally, sunk costs cast their shadows in sequential investment decisions. Consider a firm that has spent $20 million in research and development on a new product. The R&D effort to date has been a success, but an additional $10 million is needed to complete a prototype product that (because of delays) may not be first to market. Should the firm make the additional investment in the product? The correct answer depends on whether the product's expected future revenue exceeds the total *additional* costs of developing and producing the product. (Of course, the firm's task is to forecast accurately these future revenues and costs.) The $20 million sum spent to date is sunk and, therefore, irrelevant for the firm's decision. If the product's future prospects are unfavorable, the firm should cease research and development to avoid throwing good money after bad.[3]

CHECK STATION 2   A firm spent $10 million to develop a product for market. In the product's first two years, its profit was $6 million. Recently there has been an influx of comparable products offered by competitors (imitators in the firm's view). Now the firm is reassessing the product. If it drops the product, it can recover $2 million of its original investment by selling its production facility. If it continues to produce the product, its estimated revenues for successive two-year periods will be $5 million and $3 million and its costs will be $4 million and $2.5 million. (After four years, the profit potential of the product will be exhausted and the plant will have zero resale value.) What is the firm's best course of action?

The Sunk Costs of Nuclear Power Plants

Although 20 percent of U.S. energy consumption is supplied by nuclear power, no new nuclear plants have been initiated since 1978. The reason is a combination of simple economics and safety concerns. Plant construction has been plagued by cost overruns and safety problems. (Indeed, strict safety regulations have contributed to the overrun problem.) At the same time, costs have increased and revenue projections have declined. Why? Principally because of the low prices of alternative energy sources, oil and natural gas. As the prices of these fuels fell during the 1980s and 1990s, the economics of nuclear power became less and less attractive.

Inevitably, the managers of utilities with nuclear plants in the midst of construction were caught in a double bind. With hundreds of millions of dollars already spent, should they complete the facility or abandon it? Which was the lesser evil? Different utilities made different choices, based on admittedly imperfect forecasts of future revenues and costs. (As the unrepentant actress Mae West once said, "In a choice between two evils, my general rule is to pick the one I haven't tried yet.") In some cases, utilities abandoned plants that were 85 percent complete after having spent more than $1 billion. Yet these were perfectly rational decisions. In view of escalating costs, the last "15 percent" (along with obtaining requisite regulatory approvals) could have cost an additional $1 billion. In light of changing energy forecasts, completion was not warranted.[4]

---

[3] In fact, the original $20 million may well have been a "good money" investment; that is, the product's original prospects may have been sufficiently favorable to warrant investment. However, two years later, in view of declining prospects, the prudent action may be to drop the R&D effort.

[4] Unfortunately, the utilities did not always have the incentives to make the right decision. In many jurisdictions, regulators allow utilities to pass on the high capital costs of nuclear investments to customers (via higher electricity rates) only if facilities have been completed and are producing energy. In this case, the utility may choose to complete the facility despite adverse economies to recover (partially) its previously sunk cost.

It should be noted that private utilities were not alone in facing sunk-cost decisions during the 1980s and 1990s. The U.S. government halted public spending on scores of energy projects, including almost all synthetic-fuel programs ($25 billion spent), four nuclear plants under the Tennessee Valley Authority ($1.85 billion), a uranium-producing facility ($2.6 billion), and the politically sensitive Clinch Breeder Reactor ($1.5 billion). In light of changing economics, the Pentagon canceled development of the Sergeant York air defense gun ($1.8 billion), and Congress canceled the B-1A bomber ($4.7 billion), which since has been revived.

In 1989, Congress authorized the largest pure science project ever undertaken, the Supercollider program. The project called for 54 miles of underground tunnels—a racetrack for subatomic particles—and was designed to test the theories underlying the fundamental forces and particles of the universe. Unhappily, the project's cost estimates obeyed their own law of acceleration, rising over the years from $4.4 billion to $6 billion to $8.2 billion to $11 billion to $13 billion. In 1993, with $2 billion already spent and 15 miles of underground tunnels dug, Congress voted to abandon the program. Despite critics' contentions that government programs, once begun, seem to have lives of their own, the budget axe has been used effectively in scrapping uneconomical programs.

Perhaps the last word on sunk cost is provided by the story of the great sailing ship *Vassa*. When newly launched in Stockholm before a huge crowd that included Swedish royalty, the ship floated momentarily, overturned, and ignominiously (and literally) became a sunk cost.

Profit Maximization with Limited Capacity: Ordering a Best-Seller

The notion of opportunity cost is essential for optimal decisions when a firm's multiple activities compete for its limited capacity. Consider the manager of a bookstore who must decide how many copies of a new best-seller to order. Based on past experience, the manager believes she can accurately predict potential sales. Suppose the best-seller's estimated price equation is $P = 24 - Q$, where P is the price in dollars and Q is quantity in hundreds of copies sold per month. The bookstore buys directly from the publisher, which charges $12 per copy. Let's consider the following three questions:

1. How many copies should the manager order, and what price should she charge? (There is plenty of unused shelf space to stock the best-seller.)
2. Now suppose shelf space is severely limited and stocking the best-seller will take shelf space away from other books. The manager estimates that there is a $4 profit on the sale of a book stocked. (The best-seller will take up the same shelf space as the typical book.) Now what are the optimal price and order quantity?

3. After receiving the order in Question 2, the manager is disappointed to find that sales of the best-seller are considerably lower than predicted. Actual demand is $P = 18 - 2Q$. The manager is now considering returning some or all of the copies to the publisher, who is obligated to refund $6 for each copy returned. How many copies should be returned (if any), and how many should be sold and at what price?

As always, we can apply marginal analysis to determine the manager's optimal course of action, provided we use the "right" measure of costs. In Question 1, the only marginal cost associated with the best-seller is the explicit $12 cost paid to the publisher. The manager maximizes profit by setting MR equal to MC. Since $MR = 24 - 2Q$, we have $24 - 2Q = 12$. The result is $Q = 6$ hundred books and $P = \$18$. This outcome is listed in part a of Table 7.1a.

By comparison, what are the optimal order quantity and price when shelf space is limited, as in Question 2? The key point is that ordering an extra best-seller will involve not only an out-of-pocket cost ($12) but also an opportunity cost ($4). The opportunity cost is the $4 profit the shelf space would earn on an already stocked book—profit that would be forgone. In short, the total cost of ordering the book is $12 + 4 = \$16$. Setting MR equal to $16, we find that $Q = 4$ hundred and $P = \$20$. Given limited shelf space, the manager orders fewer best sellers than in Question 1. Table 7.1b compares the profitability of ordering 400 versus 600 books. The cost column lists the store's payment to the publisher ($12 per best-seller). Forgone profit is measured at $4 per book. We confirm that ordering 400 books is the more profitable option, taking into

TABLE 7.1

An Optimal Book Order

The optimal number of books to order and sell depends on demand, sales costs, and opportunity costs.

	Price	Sales Revenue	Cost	Forgone Profit	Final Net Profit
(a) $Q_s = 600$	$18	$10,800	$7,200	$ 0	$3,600
(b) $Q_s = 400$	20	8,000	4,800	1,600	1,600
[$Q_s = 600$]	18	10,800	7,200	2,400	1,200
(c) $Q_s = 200$	14	2,800	4,800	800	−1,600
$Q_r = 200$	6	1,200		0	
[$Q_s = 400$]	10	4,000	4,800	1,600	−2,400
[$Q_r = 0$]	6	0		0	
[$Q_s = 0$]	—	0	4,800	0	−2,400
[$Q_r = 400$]	6	2,400		0	

account the forgone profit on sales of other books. Indeed, the logic of marginal analysis confirms that this order quantity is optimal, that is, better than any other order size.

Finally, Question 3 asks how the manager should plan sales and pricing of the 400 best-sellers already received if demand falls to $P = 18 - 2Q$. The key here is to recognize that the original \$12 purchase price is irrelevant; it is a sunk cost. However, opportunity costs are relevant. The opportunity cost of keeping the best-seller for sale has two elements: the \$4 profit that another book would earn (as in Question 2) plus the \$6 refund that would come if the copy were returned. Therefore, the total opportunity cost is $6 + 4 = \$10$. Setting MR equal to MC implies $18 - 4Q = 10$, or $Q = 2$ hundred. The store manager should keep 200 books to be sold at a price of $18 - (2)(2) = \$14$ each. She should return the remaining 200 books to obtain a \$1,200 refund. As Table 7.1 indicates, this course of action will minimize her overall loss in the wake of the fall in demand. The table also shows that selling all 400 copies or returning all copies would generate greater losses.

THE COST OF PRODUCTION

As we noted in Chapter 6, production and cost are very closely related. In a sense, cost information is a distillation of production information: It combines the information in the production function with information about input prices. The end result can be summarized in the following important concept: The **cost function** indicates the firm's total cost of producing any given level of output. The concept of a cost function was first introduced in Chapter 2. In this section, we take a much closer look at the factors that determine costs. A key point to remember is that the concept of the cost function presupposes that the firm's managers have determined the least-cost method of producing any given level of output. (Clearly, inefficient or incompetent managers could contrive to produce a given level of output at some—possibly inflated—cost, but this would hardly be profit maximizing. Nor would the resulting cost schedule foster optimal managerial decision making.) In short, the cost function should always be thought of as a *least-cost function*. It usually is denoted as $C = C(Q)$ and can be described by means of a table, a graph, or an equation.

As in our study of production, our analysis of cost distinguishes between the short run and the long run. Recall that the short run is a period of time so limited that the firm is unable to vary the use of some of its inputs. In the long run, all inputs—labor, equipment, factories—can be varied freely. Our investigation of cost begins with the short run.

Short-Run Costs

In the basic model of Chapter 6, we focused on two inputs, capital and labor. In the short run, capital is a fixed input (i.e., cannot be varied) and labor is the sole variable input. Production of additional output is achieved by using additional hours of labor in combination with a fixed stock of capital equipment in the firm's current plant. Of course, the firm's cost is found by totaling its expenditures on labor, capital, materials, and any other inputs and including any relevant opportunity costs, as discussed in the previous section. For concreteness, consider a firm that provides a service—say, electronics repair. Figure 7.1 provides a summary of the repair firm's costs as they vary for different quantities of output (number of repair jobs completed).

The total cost of achieving any given level of output can be decomposed into two parts: fixed and variable costs. As the term suggests, **fixed costs** result from the firm's expenditures on fixed inputs. These costs are incurred regardless of the firm's level of output. Most overhead expenses fall into this category. Such costs might include the firm's lease payments for its factory, the cost of equipment, some portion of energy costs, and various kinds of administrative costs (payment for support staff, taxes, and so on). According to the table in Figure 7.1, the repair firm's total fixed costs come to $270,000 per year. These costs are incurred irrespective of the actual level of output (i.e., even if no output were produced).

Variable costs represent the firm's expenditures on variable inputs. With respect to the short-run operations of the repair firm, labor is the sole variable input. Thus, in this example, variable costs represent the additional wages paid by the firm for extra hours of labor. To achieve additional output (i.e., to increase the volume of repair jobs completed), the firm must incur additional variable costs. Naturally, we observe that total variable costs rise with increases in the quantity of output. In fact, a careful look at Figure 7.1 shows that variable costs rise increasingly rapidly as the quantity of output is pushed higher and higher. Note that the firm's total cost exhibits exactly the same behavior. (With fixed costs "locked in" at $270,000, total cost increases are due solely to changes in variable cost.) The graph in Figure 7.1 shows that the total cost curve becomes increasingly steep at higher output levels.

Average total cost (or simply **average cost**) is total cost divided by the total quantity of output. Figure 7.2 shows average costs for the repair company over different levels of output. (Check that the average cost values are computed as the ratio of total cost in column 2 of the table and total output in column 1.) The graph displays the behavior of average cost. Both the table and graph show that short-run average cost is U-shaped. Increases in output first cause average cost (per unit) to decline. At 30,000 units of output, average cost achieves a minimum (at the bottom of the U). As output continues to increase, average unit costs steadily rise. (We will discuss the factors underlying this average cost behavior shortly.) Finally, **average variable cost** is variable cost divided by total

FIGURE 7.1

A Firm's Total Costs

Total cost is the sum of fixed cost and variable cost.

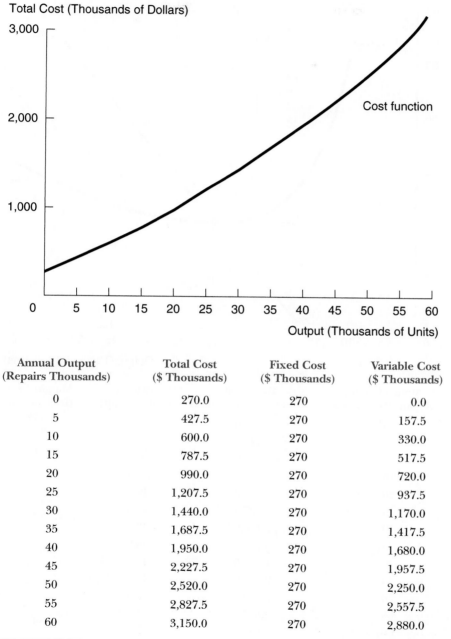

Annual Output (Repairs Thousands)	Total Cost ($ Thousands)	Fixed Cost ($ Thousands)	Variable Cost ($ Thousands)
0	270.0	270	0.0
5	427.5	270	157.5
10	600.0	270	330.0
15	787.5	270	517.5
20	990.0	270	720.0
25	1,207.5	270	937.5
30	1,440.0	270	1,170.0
35	1,687.5	270	1,417.5
40	1,950.0	270	1,680.0
45	2,227.5	270	1,957.5
50	2,520.0	270	2,250.0
55	2,827.5	270	2,557.5
60	3,150.0	270	2,880.0

FIGURE 7.2

A Firm's Average and
Marginal Costs

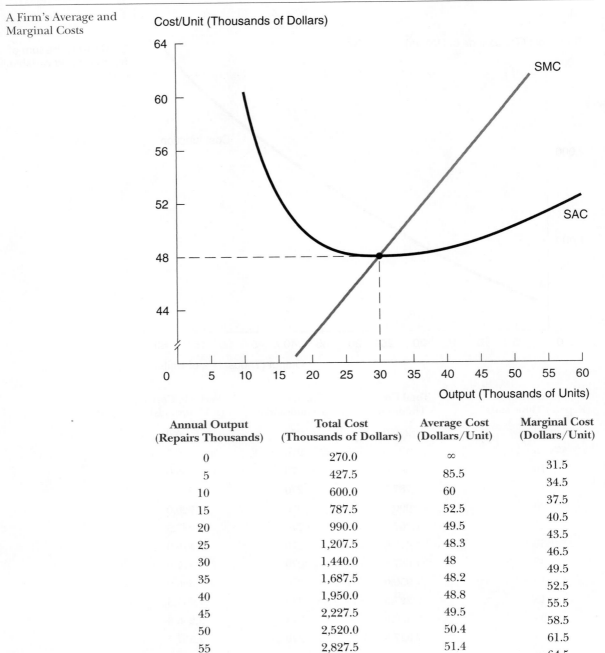

Cost/Unit (Thousands of Dollars)

Annual Output (Repairs Thousands)	Total Cost (Thousands of Dollars)	Average Cost (Dollars/Unit)	Marginal Cost (Dollars/Unit)
0	270.0	∞	
			31.5
5	427.5	85.5	
			34.5
10	600.0	60	
			37.5
15	787.5	52.5	
			40.5
20	990.0	49.5	
			43.5
25	1,207.5	48.3	
			46.5
30	1,440.0	48	
			49.5
35	1,687.5	48.2	
			52.5
40	1,950.0	48.8	
			55.5
45	2,227.5	49.5	
			58.5
50	2,520.0	50.4	
			61.5
55	2,827.5	51.4	
			64.5
60	3,150.0	52.5	

output. Because it excludes fixed costs, average variable cost is always smaller than average total cost.

Marginal cost is the addition to total cost that results from increasing output by one unit. We already are acquainted with the concept of marginal cost from the analyses of the firm's output and pricing decisions in Chapters 2 and 3. Now we take a closer look at the determinants of marginal cost. The last column of the table in Figure 7.2 lists the repair company's marginal costs for output increments of 5,000 units. For instance, consider an output increase from 25,000 to 30,000 units. According to Figure 7.2, the result is a total cost increase of 1,440,000 − 1,207,500 = \$232,500. Consequently, the marginal cost (*on a per-unit basis*) is 232,500/5,000 = \$46.50/unit. The other entries in the last column are computed in an analogous fashion. From either the graph or the table, we observe that the firm's marginal cost rises steadily with increases in output. Expanding output starting from a level of 40,000 units per month is much more expensive than starting from 20,000 units.

What factors underlie the firm's increasing short-run marginal cost (SMC)? The explanation is simple. With labor the only variable input, SMC can be expressed as

$$SMC = P_L/MP_L, \qquad\qquad [7.1]$$

where P_L denotes the price of hiring additional labor (i.e., wage per hour) and MP_L denotes the marginal product of labor.[5] To illustrate, suppose the prevailing wage is \$20 per hour and labor's marginal product is .5 units per hour (one-half of a typical repair job is completed in one hour). Then the firm's marginal (labor) cost is 20/.5 = \$40 per additional completed job. According to Equation 7.1, the firm's marginal cost will increase if there is an increase in the price of labor or a decrease in labor's marginal product. Moreover, as the firm uses additional labor to produce additional output, the *law of diminishing returns* applies. With other inputs fixed, adding increased amounts of a variable input (in this case, labor) generates smaller amounts of additional output; that is, after a point, *labor's marginal product declines*. As a result, marginal cost rises with the level of output. (Clearly, material costs are also variable and, therefore, are included in SMC. However, because these costs typically vary in proportion to output, they do not affect the shape of SMC.)

Now we can explain the behavior of short-run average cost (SAC). When output is very low (say 5,000 units), total cost consists mainly of fixed cost (since variable costs are low). Short-run average cost is high because total cost is divided by a small number of units. As output increases, total costs (which are mostly fixed) are "spread over" a larger number of units, so SAC declines. In the graph

[5] The mathematical justification is as follows. Marginal cost can be expressed as $MC = \Delta C/\Delta Q = (\Delta C/\Delta L)/(\Delta Q/\Delta L) = P_L/MP_L$. As the notation indicates, here we are looking at discrete changes in output and input. The same relationship holds with respect to infinitesimal changes (dC/dQ).

in Figure 7.2, notice that SAC lies well above SMC for low levels of output. So long as extra units can be added at a marginal cost that is lower than the average cost of the current output level, increasing output must reduce overall average cost. But what happens to average cost as marginal cost continues to rise? Eventually there comes a point at which SMC becomes greater than SAC. As soon as extra units become more expensive than current units (on average), the overall average begins to increase. This explains the upward arc of the U-shaped SAC curve. This argument also confirms an interesting result: *The firm's marginal cost curve intersects its average cost curve at the minimum point of SAC.*

We have described the firm's short-run cost function in tabular and graphic forms. The cost function also can be represented in equation form. The repair company's short-run cost function is

$$C = C(Q) = 270 + (30Q + .3Q^2), \qquad [7.2]$$

where output is measured in thousands of units and costs are in thousands of dollars. (You should check this equation against Figure 7.1 for various outputs.) The first term is the firm's fixed costs; the term in parentheses encompasses its variable costs. In turn, average cost is SAC = C/Q, or

$$SAC = 270/Q + (30 + .3Q). \qquad [7.3]$$

The first term usually is referred to as **average fixed cost** (fixed cost divided by total output); the term in the parentheses is **average variable cost**. According to Equation 7.3, as output increases, average fixed cost steadily declines while average variable cost rises. The first effect dominates for low levels of output; the second prevails at sufficiently high levels. The combination of these two effects explains the U-shaped average cost curve. Finally, treating cost as a continuous function, we find marginal cost to be

$$SMC = dC/dQ = 30 + .6Q. \qquad [7.4]$$

We observe that marginal cost rises with the level of output.

Long-Run Costs

In the long run, the firm can freely vary all of its inputs. In other words, there are no fixed inputs or fixed costs; *all costs are variable.* Thus, there is no point in distinguishing total costs and variable costs. We begin our discussion by stressing two basic points. First, the ability to vary all inputs allows the firm to produce at lower cost in the long run than in the short run (when some inputs are fixed). In short, flexibility is valuable. As we saw in Chapter 6, the firm still faces the task of finding the least-cost combination of inputs.

Second, the shape of the long-run cost curve depends on returns to scale. To see this, suppose the firm's production function exhibits *constant returns to scale* at all levels of output. This means that increasing all inputs by a given percentage (say, 20 percent) increases output by the same percentage. Assuming input prices are unchanged, the firm's total expenditure on inputs also will increase by 20 percent. Thus, the output increase is accompanied by an equal percentage increase in costs, with the result that average cost is unchanged. *So long as constant returns prevail, average cost is constant.*

Now suppose production exhibits increasing returns: A 20 percent increase in inputs generates a greater than 20 percent increase in output. The result is a fall in average cost per unit. *When increasing returns prevail, average cost falls as output increases.* Finally, we can apply analogous reasoning to show that *the presence of decreasing returns implies rising average costs.*

SHORT-RUN VERSUS LONG-RUN COST   Consider a firm that produces output using two inputs, labor and capital. Management's immediate task is to plan for future production. It has not leased plant and equipment yet, nor has it hired labor. Thus, it is free to choose any amounts of these inputs it wishes. Management knows that production exhibits constant returns to scale. Consequently, the firm's long-run average cost (LAC) is constant as shown by the horizontal line in Figure 7.3. Furthermore, we can show that the firm should plan

FIGURE 7.3

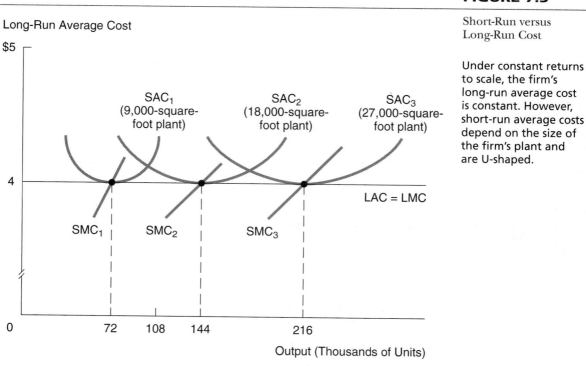

Short-Run versus
Long-Run Cost

Under constant returns to scale, the firm's long-run average cost is constant. However, short-run average costs depend on the size of the firm's plant and are U-shaped.

to use the same optimal *ratio* of labor to capital in production, regardless of the level of output. If the firm plans to double its level of output, it should also double the use of each input, leaving the proportions unchanged. These input proportions (in combination with prevailing input prices) determine the firm's average cost per unit. In Figure 7.3, $LAC = C/Q = \$4$. The long-run total cost function is $C = 4Q$. Thus, marginal cost (LMC) is also $4 per unit. As the figure shows, long-run marginal and average costs are constant and identical.

Figure 7.3 also shows the short-run average cost curves for three possible plants of varying sizes. The firm's plant (and equipment therein) represents the total capital input. The left curve is for a 9,000-square-foot plant, the middle curve for an 18,000-square-foot plant, and the right curve for a 27,000-square-foot plant. Notice that the smallest plant is optimal for producing 72,000 units of output. With such a plant in place (and using the right amount of labor), the firm can produce this output level at a minimum average cost of $4. If the firm planned to produce twice the level of output (144,000 units), it would use a plant twice the size (an 18,000-square-foot facility) and twice the labor. Finally, the largest plant is optimal for producing 216,000 units.

Once its plant is in place, however, the firm has considerably less flexibility. In the short run, its plant cannot be varied. Thus, if a 9,000-square-foot plant is in place, production of an output, such as 108,000 units (see Figure 7.3), means an increase in the average cost of production above $4. Why? To produce this output requires expanding the use of labor (since the plant is fixed). Because of diminishing returns, the extra output comes at an increasing marginal cost, and this drives up average cost as well.

Obviously, the firm may have many choices of plant size, not just three. Before its plant is in place, the firm has complete flexibility to produce *any* level of output at a $4 unit cost. (It simply builds a plant of the proper scale and applies the right proportion of labor.) But, once the plant is in place, any change in planned output must be achieved by a change in labor (the sole variable input). The result is a movement either right or left up the U of the relevant SAC curve. In either case, there is an increase in average cost.

Comparative Advantage and International Trade

In a host of industries, such as electronics, automobiles, computers, aircraft, and agricultural products of all kinds, competition is worldwide. The major industrial countries of the world compete with one another for shares of global markets. For numerous goods, a U.S. consumer has a choice of purchasing a domestically produced item or a comparable imported good made in a far-flung corner of the world—for instance, Europe, East Asia, or South America. Thus, a knowledge of international trade is essential for successful managers in increasingly global industries.

International trade is based on mutually beneficial specialization among countries. Why does one country concentrate on production and exports in certain goods and services and another country specialize in others? Important reasons for varying patterns of specialization include different resource endowments, differences in the amount and productivity of labor, and differences in capital. For instance, a nation with abundant agricultural resources, predominantly unskilled labor, and little capital is likely to specialize in production of basic foods. By contrast, a nation such as Japan, with a highly educated population and abundant capital but with relatively few natural resources, has an advantage in manufactured goods. Many observers believe that the United States' competitive advantage lies in high-tech goods and services. Relying on their research expertise and innovative ability, American firms excel in the development of technologically advanced goods and services. As these markets grow and mature, however, high-tech goods will likely evolve into commodity items, assembled and produced in large-scale facilities. It is not surprising that production of these goods tends to shift to other parts of the world over time.

To understand the basis for mutually beneficial trade, it is important to grasp the notion of comparative advantage. The easiest way to explain this concept is with a simple example. Table 7.2 offers a stylized depiction of trade involving two goods, digital electronic watches and pharmaceutical products, and two countries, the United States and Japan. Part a of the table shows the productivity of labor (i.e., output per hour) in each country for each good. For instance, on average U.S. workers produce 4 bottles of pills and 1 digital watch per labor-hour; their Japanese counterparts produce 2 bottles and .8 watches per labor-hour. According to the table, the United States is a more efficient manufacturer of both items; that is, U.S. workers are more productive in both sectors.

TABLE 7.2

Relative Costs in the United States and Japan

(a) Productivity	Pharmaceuticals (Bottles per Hour)	Digital Watches (Watches per Hour)
United States	4	1
Japan	2	.8

(b) Costs	Pharmaceuticals (per Bottle)	Digital Watches (per Watch)
United States	$3.75	$15
Japan	$5.00	$12.50
	(¥500)	(¥1,250)

However, labor productivity is only one factor influencing the cost of production. The other determinant is the price of the input, in this case, the price of labor. To compute the labor cost per unit of output, we need to know the prevailing hourly wage in each country. To keep things simple, suppose the U.S. wage in both sectors is $15 per hour, whereas the Japanese wage in both sectors is 1,000 yen (¥) per hour. Naturally, the Japanese wage is denominated in that country's currency, the yen. Now consider the labor cost per unit of each good in each country. For the U.S. pharmaceutical sector, this labor cost is simply ($15 per hour)/(4 bottles per hour) = $3.75 per bottle, using Equation 7.1. Part b of the table lists these costs for each country. For Japan, the cost in yen is shown in parentheses. For example, the labor cost per digital watch is 1,000/.8 = ¥1,250.

Finally, to make cross-country cost comparisons, we need one additional piece of information: the prevailing exchange rate between the two currencies. As its name suggests, the exchange rate denotes the amount of one country's currency that exchanges for a unit of another country's. Again, keeping things simple, suppose the current exchange rate in round numbers is 100 yen per dollar. (Furthermore, we suppose that this rate is expected to remain unchanged.) Using this exchange rate, it is a simple matter to convert the countries' costs per unit into a common currency, in this case the dollar. Japan's labor cost per bottle is ¥500, or $5.00 after dividing by the exchange rate of ¥100 per dollar. Similarly, its cost per digital watch is ¥1,250, or $12.50. Table 7.2b lists these conversions.

Table 7.2 conveys a specific message about the countries' relative costs for the goods. The United States has a unit labor cost advantage in producing pharmaceuticals ($3.75 compared to $5), whereas Japan has an advantage in producing watches ($12.50 compared to $15). Thus, one would envision the United States specializing in pharmaceuticals and Japan in digital watches. The predicted pattern of trade would have the United States exporting the former product and importing the latter from Japan. Indeed, actual trade flows in the 1990s between the two countries displayed exactly this pattern.

Table 7.2 also carries a general message: Productivity matters, but it is not the only thing that matters. After all, according to the table, the United States has an absolute productivity advantage in both goods. Yet Japan turns out to have a cost advantage in watches. The cost edge materializes because Japan has a **comparative advantage** in watches. That is, Japan's productivity disadvantage is much smaller in watches (where it is 80 percent as productive as the United States) than in pharmaceuticals (where it is only 50 percent as productive). After taking into account its lower wage rate, Japan indeed is the lower-cost watch producer.

Let us emphasize the point: Besides productivity, the countries' relative wages and the prevailing exchange rate also matter. For instance, if U.S. wages increased more rapidly than Japanese wages over the coming year, the U.S. cost advantage in pharmaceuticals would narrow, and Japan's cost advantage in watches would widen. Alternatively, suppose productivities and wages were unchanged in the two countries, but the exchange rate changed over the year. For instance, suppose the value of the dollar rose to ¥125 per dollar. (We say that the dollar has appreciated or, equivalently, that the yen has depreciated.) At this new exchange rate, Japan's labor costs per unit of output (converted into dollars) become 500/125 = $4 and 1,250/125 = $10 for the respective goods. With the appreciation of the dollar, Japanese goods become less costly (after converting into dollars). The U.S. cost advantage in pharmaceuticals has narrowed significantly ($3.75 versus $4), whereas the Japanese cost advantage in watches has widened. Accordingly, U.S. pharmaceutical exports should decline; these exports simply are not as attractive to Japanese consumers as before. In turn, a more expensive dollar (a cheaper yen) makes Japanese watch exports more attractive to U.S. consumers.

To sum up, relative productivities, relative wages, and the prevailing exchange rate combine to determine the pattern of cost advantage and trade. With respect to the exchange rate, depreciation of a country's currency increases its exports and decreases its imports. A currency appreciation has exactly the opposite effect.

RETURNS TO SCALE, SCOPE, AND LEARNING

Returns to Scale

Returns to scale are important because they directly determine the shape of long-run average cost. They also are crucial for answering such questions as: Are large firms more efficient producers than small firms? Would a 50 percent increase in size reduce average cost per unit? Although the exact nature of returns to scale varies widely across industries, a representative description is useful. Figure 7.4 depicts a long-run average cost curve that is U-shaped. This reflects increasing returns to scale (and falling LAC) for low output levels and decreasing returns (increasing LAC) for high levels. In the figure, the minimum level of long-run average cost is achieved at output level Q_{min}. As in Figure 7.3, short-run average cost curves for three plants are shown. Thus, output Q_{min} is produced using the medium-sized plant. If the costs of *all* possible plants were depicted, the lower "envelope" of the many SAC curves would trace out the figure's long-run average cost curve. To sum up, if the firm is free to use *any* size plant, its average production cost is exactly LAC.

As noted in Chapter 6, a number of factors influence returns to scale and, therefore, the shape of long-run average cost. First, *constant average cost* (due to constant returns to scale) occurs when a firm's production process can be replicated easily. For instance, the electronics repair firm may find it can double its rate of finished repair jobs simply by replicating its current plant and labor

FIGURE 7.4

U-shaped, Long-Run
Average Cost

The U shape is due to
increasing returns at
small outputs and
decreasing returns at
large outputs.

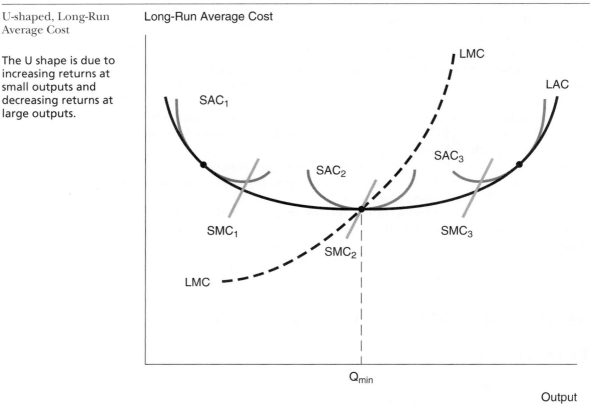

Long-Run Average Cost

force, that is, by building an identical repair facility beside the existing one and proportionally increasing its labor force. By duplication, the firm could supply twice the level of service at an unchanged average cost per job.

Second, *declining average cost* stems from a number of factors, including capital-intensive mass-production techniques, automation, labor specialization, advertising, and distribution. By increasing scale, the firm may be able to use new production methods that were infeasible at smaller outputs. It also may find it advantageous to exploit specialization of labor at the larger scale. The result of either kind of production innovation is a reduction in long-run average cost.

Fundamental engineering relationships may have the same effect. In the expanding market of the 1990s, operators of Caribbean cruise liners launched ever larger ships (the largest having over 2,000 berths, almost three times the industry average) to take advantage of scale economies. At twice the tonnage, a super-cruise liner can carry significantly more than twice the number of passengers while requiring only a small increase in crew. Accordingly, the cost per passenger declines markedly.

Declining average cost also may be due to the presence of a variety of fixed expenses. Frequently, significant portions of a firm's advertising, promotional, and distributional expenses are fixed or (at least) vary little with the firm's level of output. (For instance, a 30-second television advertisement represents the same fixed cost to a large fast-food chain and a small chain alike. But this expense comprises a much lower average cost per "burger" for the large chain.) Similarly, the costs to firms of many government regulations are (in the main) fixed. Accordingly, they represent a smaller average cost for the large firm. The U.S. automobile industry, perhaps the most highly regulated sector in the world, is a case in point.[6]

Finally, *increasing average cost* is explained by the problems of organization, information, and control in very large firms. As the firm's scale increases, so do the difficulties of coordinating and monitoring its many management functions. The result is inefficiency, increased costs, and organizational overload.[7]

A great many studies have investigated the shape of average cost curves for different industries in both the short and long runs. Almost all of these studies use regression techniques to generate equations that explain total cost as a function of output and other relevant explanatory variables (such as wages and other input prices). The data for this analysis can come from either a time series (the same firm over a number of months or years) or a cross section (a cost comparison of different firms within a single time period). Despite difficulties in estimating costs from accounting data and controlling for changing inputs (especially capital), technology, and product characteristics, these studies have produced valuable information about costs.

One general finding is that, for most goods and services, there are significant economies of scale at low output levels, followed by a wide region of constant returns at higher levels. In short, for a great many industries, long-run average cost tends to be L-shaped, as depicted in Figure 7.5b. This is in contrast to the usual textbook depiction of U-shaped long-run average cost shown in Figure 7.5a. A small number of products display continuously declining average costs. This case usually is described under the term *natural monopoly* and includes many (but not all) local utilities, local telephone service, and cable television. Figure 7.5c shows this case.[8]

---

[6] In the automobile industry, frequent product changes (a competitive necessity) have the same effect. Such changes require significant retooling every few years. A company's average cost of production depends in part on the number of units over which these retooling costs are spread.

[7] For many goods and services, transportation costs are an important factor in explaining increasing LAC. At a small scale, the firm can efficiently serve a local market. But delivering its good or service to a geographically far-flung market becomes increasingly expensive.

[8] A study of the long-run average cost of electricity generation found a shift from a continuously declining LAC in the 1950s to an L-shaped LAC in the 1970s. Even in this so-called natural monopoly, there appears to be room for multiple, efficient producers. See R. Christensen and G. Greene, "Economies of Scale in U.S. Power Generation," *Journal of Political Economy* (1976): 655–676.

FIGURE 7.5

Three Examples of Long-
Run Average Cost

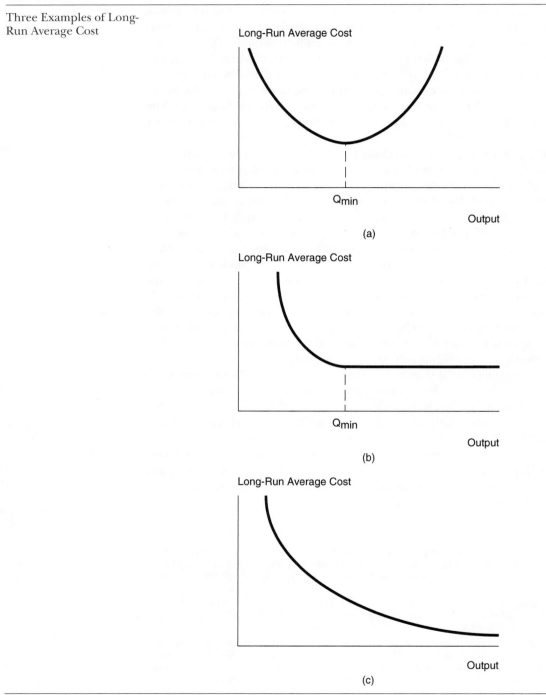

A useful way to summarize the degree of scale economies across industries is provided by the notion of efficient scale. **Minimum efficient scale (MES)** is the lowest output at which minimum average cost can be achieved. In parts a and b of Figure 7.5, minimum efficient scale is designated by Q_{min}. (In part b, this occurs where the average cost curve first achieves a minimum.) In part c, there is no minimum efficient scale because LAC continuously declines.

Minimum efficient scale is important in determining how many firms a particular market can support. For example, suppose market demand is 10 million units per year. If minimum efficient scale for the typical firm occurs at 100,000 units per year, the market can support 100 firms, each producing at minimum efficient scale. In contrast, if minimum efficient scale is 5 million units, the market can support only two firms producing efficiently. Finally, if average cost declines for all outputs (up to 10 million units), the market may be able to support only one firm efficiently.

As one might expect, estimates of MES vary widely across industries.[9] For instance, in the production of sulfuric acid (a standard chemical), the MES for a plant is about 4 percent of total U.S. consumption. The average cost disadvantage of producing at one-half of MES is only 1 percent. The clear implication is that there is ample room in the market for as many as 25 (1/.04) firms. By comparison, the MES for electric motors is about 15 percent of U.S. consumption and the cost disadvantage at one-half of MES is 15 percent. For production of commercial aircraft, MES is 10 percent of the U.S. market, and the cost disadvantage at one-half of MES is 20 percent. This suggests that the industry could support as many as 10 manufacturers. Economies of scale would not seem to explain why Boeing and Airbus dominate the worldwide market. Rather, the rise of these two aviation giants and the demise of Lockheed and McDonnell-Douglas more aptly are attributed to differences in the companies' management strategies and technological capabilities.

Economies of Scale in Public Schools

Over the last 20 years, there have been growing concerns about the quality and cost of public education. Parents, teachers, school administrators, and general taxpayers have an interest in maintaining quality schools while holding down costs. One crucial question is the extent to which economies of scale exist in public schools. Can schools with greater enrollments provide quality instruction at a lower cost per pupil?

Empirical studies of per-pupil costs across schools indicate the answer is yes. In a study of Maryland public elementary and middle-level schools, John Riew compared costs (in 1979) across a sample of schools of different sizes, using multiple regression analysis to measure the degree of scale economies.[10]

[9] Estimates of plant-level economies of scale for different industries are collected in W. Shepherd, *The Economics of Industrial Organization* (Upper Saddle River, NJ: Prentice Hall, 1997).

[10] See J. Riew, "Scale Economies, Capacity Utilization, and School Costs: A Comparative Analysis of Secondary and Elementary Schools," *Journal of Education Finance* (Spring 1986): 433–446.

The basic regression equations were designed to measure the relationship between a school's average operating costs per pupil (the dependent variable) and its enrollment (the main independent variable). The regression also included independent variables measuring teacher training, teacher experience, professional support staff, and teachers' aides to account for the separate effect of "school quality" indices on cost. Finally, the regressions included the school's utilization rate (the ratio of actual enrollment to the school's capacity). If, as expected, short-run average costs decline, increasing a school's utilization rate should mean a reduction in its average cost per pupil.

The regression results confirm that economies of scale are present in both types of schools. For elementary schools, average cost per pupil declines significantly over the range from 200 to 400 students before leveling off as enrollments approach 500 students. For a typical school, an increase in enrollment from 200 to 300 students, with all other variables held constant, affords a savings of $115 in average operating expenditures per pupil. In addition, if this increase also represents a rise in utilization (say, from 50 to 75 percent given a school capacity of 400 students), then there is an additional average cost reduction of $97. Thus, the combined average cost savings for this enrollment increase come to $212 per student.

For middle schools, economies of scale occur at higher enrollments, in a range between 500 and 900 students, and are exhausted as enrollments approach 1,000 students. An increase in enrollment from 600 to 800 students reduces the average cost per student by $142. The accompanying increase in utilization (say, from 60 to 80 percent given a school capacity of 1,000 students) produces an additional savings of $55. Thus, the combined average cost savings come to $197 per student.

The average cost savings are comparable with elementary and middle schools but occur at different enrollment levels and stem from a different mix of scale economies and utilization. For elementary schools, increasing utilization is the key to average cost savings. In this respect, massive enrollment declines during the 1970s and early 1980s contributed to cost escalation, whereas enrollment increases in the last decade should contribute to cost declines. For middle schools, scale economies are the most important factor. The efficient operation of these schools with their more varied programs, specialized teaching, and administrative functions requires a larger population of students.

Economies of Scope

Most firms produce a variety of goods. Computer firms, such as IBM and Toshiba, produce a wide range of computers from mainframes to personal computers. Consumer products firms, such as Procter & Gamble and General Foods, offer myriad personal, grocery, and household items. Entertainment firms, such as Walt Disney Corporation, produce movies, television programs, toys, theme park entertainment, and vacation services. In many cases, the justification for multiple products is the potential cost advantages of producing many closely related goods.

A production process exhibits **economies of scope** when the cost of producing multiple goods is less than the aggregate cost of producing each item separately. A convenient measure of such economies is

$$SC = \frac{C(Q_1) + C(Q_2) - C(Q_1, Q_2)}{C(Q_1) + C(Q_2)}.$$

Here $C(Q_1, Q_2)$ denotes the firm's cost of jointly producing the goods in the respective quantities; $C(Q_1)$ denotes the cost of producing good 1 alone and similarly for $C(Q_2)$. For instance, suppose producing the goods separately means incurring costs of \$12 million and \$8 million, respectively. The total cost of jointly producing the goods in the same quantities is \$17 million. It follows that $SC = (12 + 8 - 17)/(12 + 8) = .15$. Joint production implies a 15 percent cost savings vis-à-vis separate production.

There are many sources for economies of scope. In some cases, a single production process yields multiple outputs. Cattle producers sell both beef and hides; indeed, producing cattle for beef or hides alone probably is not profitable. In other cases, production of a principal good is accompanied by the generation of unavoidable by-products. Often these by-products can be fashioned into marketable products. Sawdust is a valuable by-product of lumber production. Tiny plastic pellets (the by-product of stamping out buttons) are used in sandblasting instead of sand. After the harvest, leftover cornstalks are used to produce alcohol for power generation. Still another source of economies is underutilization of inputs. An airline that carries passengers may find itself with unused cargo space; thus, it contracts to carry cargo as well as passengers. In recent years, many public school systems have made their classrooms available after hours for day-care, after-school, and community programs.

An important source of economies of scope is transferable know-how. Soft-drink companies produce many types of carbonated drinks, fruit juices, sparkling waters, and the like. Presumably, experience producing carbonated beverages confers cost advantages for the production of related drinks. Brokerage houses provide not only trading services but also investment advising and many banklike services, such as mutual funds with check-writing privileges. Insurance companies provide both insurance and investment vehicles. In fact, whole-life insurance is a clever combination of these two services in an attractive package.

Scope economies also may be demand related. The consumption of many clusters of goods and services is complementary. For instance, the same company that sells or leases a piece of office equipment also offers service contracts. A select number of firms compete for the sales of cameras and photographic film. Sometimes the delivery of multiple services is so common and ubiquitous that it tends to be overlooked. Full-service banks provide a wide range of services to customers. The leading law firms in major cities provide extensive services in dozens of areas of the law. (Of course, smaller specialty law firms coexist with these larger entities.) Many large hospitals provide care in all major medical specialties as well as in the related areas of emergency medicine, mental health care, geriatrics, and rehabilitative therapy.

CHECK STATION 3   Toshiba America Information Systems (a subsidiary of the parent Japanese company) sells laptop computers, printers, disk drives, copiers, facsimile machines, and telephone equipment in North America. Would you expect there to be economies of scope in these product lines? If so, what are the sources of these economies?

E-Commerce and Cost Economies

As noted in Chapter 3, the Internet and the emergence of e-commerce have significant impacts on the structure of firm costs.[11] A wide-ranging research study by Washington's Brookings Institution estimates that across the whole of the U.S. economy the adoption of information technology and e-commerce methods will produce total annual cost savings as high as $100 billion (about 1 percent of annual gross domestic product). Increased efficiency stems from reengineering the firm's supply chain and from reducing transactions costs of all kinds. The greatest potential savings emerge in information-intensive industries such as health care, financial services, education, and public-sector operations.

Recall that the hallmark of information economics is the presence of high fixed costs accompanied by low or negligible marginal costs. As a result, average costs decline sharply with output. The fixed costs of business capital investments are increasingly found in computers, software, and telecommunications (together comprising over 10 percent of capital expenditure), rather than in the traditional "bricks and mortar" of factories, assembly lines, and equipment. To date, a number of firms—Microsoft, Cisco Systems, Yahoo!, Oracle, eBay, Sun Microsystems, Google, and Dell Computers, to name a few—have taken advantage of information economics to claim increasing shares of their respective markets, thus benefiting from sharply declining average unit costs.

Information economics also provides new sources for economies of scope. Computer-aided design and manufacturing (CAD/CAM) systems can quickly switch from one product to another, allowing the production of many products and designs, all using similar inputs. Items ranging from microchips to aircraft are now engineered and manufactured with CAD/CAM. Micromarketing is the process of differentiating products and targeting more markets. For instance, most Americans are familiar with Nabisco's Oreo cookies. If you liked the original,

---

[11] For discussions of e-commerce and cost economies, see R. E. Litan and A. M. Rivlin, "Projecting the Economic Impact of the Internet," *American Economic Review*, Papers and Proceedings (May 2001): 313–317; J. Madrick, "The New Economy's Network Society Plays by Old-Economy Rules," *The New York Times*, July 6, 2000, C2; and H. R. Varian, "The Technology Sector's Rise and Fall Is a Tale as American as the Model T," *The New York Times*, December 14, 2000, C2.

there are now Fudge Covered Oreos, Oreo Double Stufs, and Oreo Big Stufs. Each of these products is targeted to a separate junk-food market. Before 1984, Procter & Gamble sold one type of Tide laundry detergent; now it sells four. Boeing uses computer-aided design to develop simultaneously several types of sophisticated aircraft for different buyers (domestic and international airlines).

Some experts suggest that relying on economies of scale—producing dedicated systems that are economical but inflexible—is no longer enough. The most successful firms in the future will also exploit the flexibility provided by economies of scope. For instance, the heady growth of Dell Computers (in the face of withering PC price wars) rests on its ability to produce, sell, and deliver made-to-order PC systems more efficiently than its competitors.

The Learning Curve

Profit-maximizing firms continually seek ways (including technological improvements) to reduce costs of production. An important source of cost reductions rests on the simple idea that the more you do something, the better you become at it. Thus, based on its cumulative production experience, management can be expected to learn about better methods of production that will achieve lower average cost. The **learning curve** embodies the inverse relationship between average cost and cumulative production; that is, as the firm's cumulative output increases, its average cost per unit tends to fall.

Learning can come from many sources. Workers often perform tasks more slowly at first until the production process becomes familiar. There may be several ways to complete a task, and it may take some experimentation to find the best way and to become comfortable with it. Typically, management must learn how to shape the production process and how to organize and schedule various tasks in production. Quality control for both inputs and output needs time to identify potential trouble areas. Engineering managers also learn from the production process. By redesigning parts of the product or changing specifications and tolerances on inputs, engineering managers can achieve more efficient and less costly production methods. Input suppliers, especially if there are specifically designed inputs, go through their own learning process.

There are many examples of firms that exploit the learning curve.[12] Here are just a few:

- On October 1, 1908, the price of the Ford Model T was set at $950. In the next 12 months, approximately 15,000 cars were sold. By August 1, 1916, costs had fallen markedly and prices had been reduced to $345. Sales in that year were approximately 577,000 units. Price eventually reached a low of $260 in 1924.

[12] See, for example, P. Ghemawat, "Building Strategy on the Experience Curve," *Harvard Business Review* (March–April 1985): 143–149.

- In the 1970s, Texas Instruments exploited the learning curve in C-MOS technology for handheld calculators. During the decade, the company witnessed a dramatic decline in the production cost of increasingly sophisticated calculators—from the neighborhood of $1,000 to under $10. Sales volumes went through the roof.

- Between 1959 and 1974, the Japanese motorcycle industry experienced average cost reductions of 12 to 24 percent for each doubling of cumulative output.

- For the past 30 years, the performance of integrated circuits has followed "Moore's Law" (coined in 1965 by Gordon Moore, a cofounder of Intel), which states that the computing power of the most advanced chips tends to double every 18 months.

The key to the learning curve is the dependence of average cost on *cumulative* output. If the firm produces a new product at a rate of 500 units per month, its cumulative output after one year is 6,000 units; after two years, it is 12,000 units; and after five years, it is 30,000 units. Learning is a function of cumulative output for the reasons just cited. Consequently, one would look for a fall in average cost as cumulative output increases over time. Figure 7.6a displays a representative learning curve. The curve shows average cost declining as cumulative output increases. The curvature in the graph is typical. The greatest opportunities for cost reductions come early in the new product's life. Thus, the curve falls steeply when cumulative output is low. Studies of learning curves across different industries find an average cost reduction of 20 percent for each doubling of cumulative output. By the time the product is relatively mature (cumulative output is large), further reductions in average cost are modest (thus, the curve becomes relatively flat).

Figure 7.6b underscores the difference between the learning curve and returns to scale. The shape of each long-run average cost curve reflects returns to scale. For instance, an increase from an output rate of 1,000 units per month to 1,500 units implies a $.10 drop in average cost per unit (along the upper curve of part b). This reflects increasing returns to scale. But the impact of cumulative learning is separate from returns to scale. The downward shift in LAC shown in the figure is due to the addition of a year's cumulative production experience. Holding the rate of output constant (at 1,000 units), learning-curve effects are responsible for a cost reduction of $.15. Of course, the firm may enjoy cost reductions from both sources. A move to an output rate of 1,500 in the second year means a cost reduction of $.25 per unit—$.10 due to returns to scale and $.15 due to learning. Although both effects play a role, they are logically distinct from each other. To illustrate, a study of the chemical processing industry found that average costs tend to fall 11 percent for each doubling of plant size (economies of scale) and 20 to 30 percent for each doubling of cumulative output (learning).[13]

[13] M. B. Lieberman, "The Learning Curve and Pricing in the Chemical Processing Industries," *Rand Journal of Economics* (Summer 1984): 213–228.

FIGURE 7.6

Returns to Scale and Learning-Curve Effects

Part a shows the learning-curve effect: Average cost declines as cumulative output increases. Part b distinguishes economies of scale (a reduction in average cost via a movement along the curve) from learning (a shift in the curve).

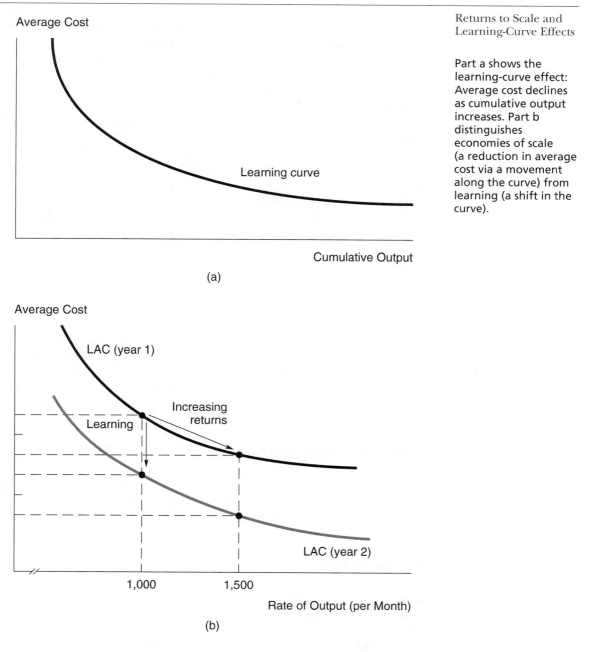

STRATEGIC IMPLICATIONS OF THE LEARNING CURVE   There are immediate strategy lessons for managers in industries where learning-curve effects are important. First, profit projections should be predicated on estimates of unit costs over time. An operation that is not profitable initially may become so after a few years of learning. In this sense, entry into the industry should be viewed as an investment. (Of course, an initial loser may grow into a perpetual loser. Sometimes the darkest hour comes just before the total blackout.) Moreover, occupying a position as a high-volume producer may confer a significant cost advantage over rivals. By accelerating sales (via price cuts or aggressive marketing), the firm adds to its cumulative production, thereby lowering its unit costs. Not only is this profitable in itself; lower costs enable the firm to further cut price and stimulate sales. In principle, this process can continue over time until learning-curve effects are exhausted.

Thus, when learning effects are important, the firm can profit by increasing its immediate level of output precisely because higher production today enhances future profits. (It is not hard to model formally this result.) The main idea is that the learning curve effect increases (shifts up) the marginal profit associated with extra output. Therefore, the new point of optimality (where $M\pi = 0$) necessarily occurs at a greater output level. However, the argument should not be taken to a false extreme. Learning-curve effects should not be used to justify the pursuit of *greater market share* as the firm's ultimate long-term goal. The firm's objective remains the pursuit of maximum total profit over the life of the product. Increasing market share (to a degree) is the right *means* to that end. But pursuing the false goal of market share *per se* could lead a firm to cut price and increase output by too much, thereby sacrificing total long-term profit.

COST ANALYSIS AND OPTIMAL DECISIONS

Knowledge of the firm's relevant costs is essential for determining sound managerial decisions. First, we consider decisions concerning a single product; then we examine decisions for multiproduct firms.

A Single Product

The profit-maximizing rule for a single-product firm is straightforward: So long as it is profitable to produce, the firm sets its optimal output where marginal revenue equals marginal cost. Figure 7.7 shows a single-product firm that faces a downward-sloping demand curve and U-shaped average cost curves. The firm's profit-maximizing output is Q* (where the MR and MC curves cross), and its optimal price is P* (read off the demand curve). The firm's economic

FIGURE 7.7

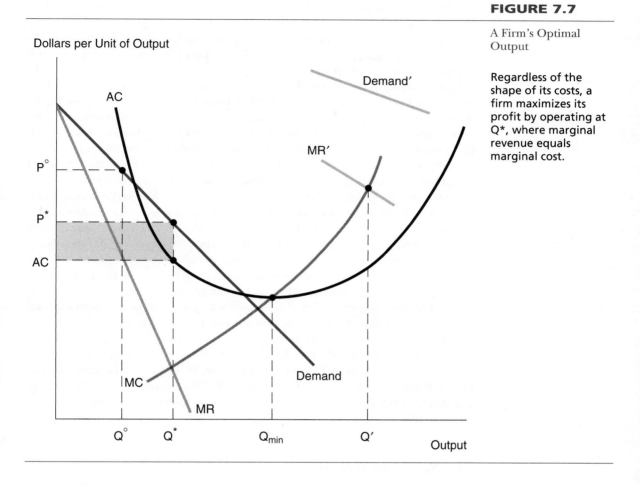

A Firm's Optimal
Output

Regardless of the
shape of its costs, a
firm maximizes its
profit by operating at
Q*, where marginal
revenue equals
marginal cost.

profit is measured by the area of the shaded rectangle in the figure. The rectangle's height represents the firm's profit per unit (P* − AC) and its base is total output Q*. (Remember that the firm's average cost includes a normal return on its invested capital. Therefore, a positive economic profit means that the firm is earning a greater-than-normal rate of return.) No alternative output and price could generate a greater economic profit.

By now, the application of marginal revenue and marginal cost should be very familiar. Nonetheless, it is worth pointing out two fallacies that occasionally find their way into managerial discussions. The first fallacy states that the firm always can increase its profit by exploiting economies of scale. But fully exploiting these economies means producing at minimum efficient scale—the point of minimum average cost. Figure 7.7 shows the problem with this contention: The profit-maximizing output Q* falls well short of Q_min. In fact, if the firm were to produce at Q_{min}, it would suffer an economic loss. (The demand line falls below the average-cost curve at Q_{min}.)

The general point is that the firm's optimal output depends on *demand* as well as cost. In Figure 7.7, the level of demand for the firm's product is insufficient to justify exploiting all economies of scale. However, we easily could depict a much higher level of demand—one that pushes the firm to an output well above Q_{min}, that is, into the range of increasing average cost. The figure shows part of a (hypothetical) demand curve and the associated marginal revenue curve that intersects marginal cost at output Q'. For this level of demand, Q' (a quantity much greater than Q_{min}) is the profit-maximizing output.

The second fallacy works in the opposite direction of the first. It states that if the current output and price are unsatisfactory, the firm should raise its price to increase profits. The intuitive appeal of this "rule" is obvious. If price is too low relative to average cost, the remedy is to increase price. However, this contention is not necessarily so. In Figure 7.7, raising price is appropriate only if the current price is lower than P^* (with output greater than Q^*). If price is already greater than P^*, further price increases only reduce profits. In fact, the figure can readily demonstrate the classic fallacy of managing the product out of business. Suppose management makes the mistake of setting its output at $Q°$. Here the firm's price $P°$ is slightly below average cost, so the firm is incurring a loss. As a remedy, the firm raises price. Does this improve profits? No. The increase in price causes a decrease in quantity (which is expected) but also an increase in average cost (perhaps unexpected). At a higher price and lower output, the firm still is generating a loss. If it raises price again, its volume will shrink further and its price still will fail to catch up with its increasing average cost. By using this strategy, the firm quickly would price itself out of the market.

The Shut-Down Rule

Under adverse economic conditions, managers face the decision of whether to cease production of a product altogether, that is, whether to shut down. Although the choice may appear obvious (shut down if the product is generating monetary losses), a correct decision requires a careful weighing of relevant options. These alternatives differ depending on the firm's time horizon.

In the short run, many of the firm's inputs are fixed. Suppose the firm is producing a single item that is incurring economic losses—total cost exceeds revenues or, equivalently, average total cost exceeds price. Figure 7.8 displays the situation. At the firm's current output, average cost exceeds price: $AC > P^*$; the firm is earning negative economic profit. Should the firm cease production and shut down? The answer is no. To see this, write the firm's profit as

$$\pi = (R - VC) - FC = (P - AVC)Q - FC. \qquad [7.5]$$

FIGURE 7.8

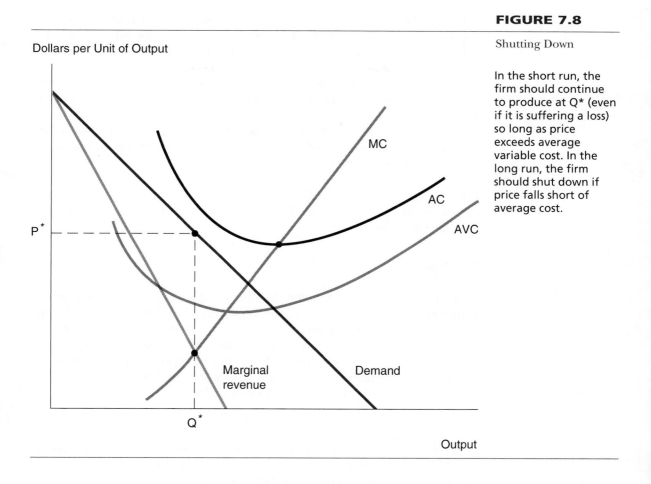

Dollars per Unit of Output

In the short run, the firm should continue to produce at Q* (even if it is suffering a loss) so long as price exceeds average variable cost. In the long run, the firm should shut down if price falls short of average cost.

The first term, $R - VC$, is referred to as the product's *contribution*. So long as revenue exceeds variable costs (or, equivalently, $P > AVC$), the product is making a positive contribution toward the firm's fixed costs. Observe that price exceeds average variable cost in Figure 7.8. (The average variable cost curve is U-shaped, and it lies below the AC curve because it excludes all fixed costs.) Therefore, continuing to produce the good makes a contribution to fixed costs. (In fact, output Q* delivers maximum contribution because $MR = MC$.) If instead the firm were to discontinue production ($Q = 0$), this contribution would be lost. In the short run, the firm is "stuck" with its fixed costs. It will incur these costs whether or not it produces output. If the firm shuts down, its profit will be $\pi = -FC$. (The firm will earn no revenues but will pay its fixed costs.) In sum, the firm should continue production because the product generates a positive contribution, thereby minimizing the firm's loss. The firm suffers an economic loss in the short run; nevertheless, this is better than shutting down. Thus, we have the following general rule:

> In the short run, the firm should continue to produce so long as price exceeds average variable cost. Assuming it does produce, the firm maximizes contribution (and minimizes any losses) by setting marginal revenue equal to marginal cost.

In the long run, all inputs and all costs are variable. (For instance, a firm that leases its plant and equipment can shed these costs if it chooses not to renew its two-year lease. The firm can also downsize its workforce over time.) In the long run, the firm should continue operating only if it expects to earn a nonnegative economic profit. A firm that suffers persistent economic losses will be forced to exit the industry.

CHECK STATION 4   Earlier we noted that the repair firm's cost function is $C = 270 + 30Q + .3Q^2$. Suppose demand is given by $P = 50 - .2Q$. What is the firm's optimal course of action in the short run? In the long run?

Multiple Products

In the previous section, we noted that the prevalence of multiproduct firms is explained by economies of scope. The implication of such economies is that the firm can produce multiple products at a total cost that is lower than the sum of the items' costs if they were produced separately. As we shall see, managers must be careful to pay attention to relevant costs in a multiproduct environment.

To illustrate, consider a firm that produces two products in a common facility. The firm's total cost of production is described as

$$C = FC + VC_1 + VC_2,$$

where FC denotes the total fixed costs shared by the products. The separate variable costs for the products also are included and depend directly on the output levels of each product. The firm's total profit is

$$\pi = (R_1 - VC_1) + (R_2 - VC_2) - FC, \qquad [7.6]$$

where R_1 and R_2 denote the products' revenues. As noted earlier, each term in parentheses is the product's contribution. The firm's total profit is the sum of its products' contributions minus its total fixed costs.

As we saw in the single-product case, the firm should continue producing an item only if $R > VC$ or, equivalently, $P > AVC$. Exactly the same principle applies to the multiproduct case. Furthermore, in the long run the firm should continue in business only if the total profit in Equation 7.6 is nonnegative; otherwise, it should shut down. The firm's output rule for multiple goods can be stated in two parts:

1. Each good should be produced if, and only if, it makes a positive contribution to the firm's fixed costs: $R_i > VC_i$ or, equivalently, $P_i > AVC_i$.

2. In the long run, the firm should continue operations if, and only if, it makes positive economic profits.

MULTIPLE PRODUCTS: A NUMERICAL EXAMPLE   Suppose a firm's total fixed cost is $2.4 million per year. For the first good, $P_1 = \$10$, $AVC_1 = \$9$, and $Q_1 = 1.2$ million; in turn, $P_2 = \$6.50$, $AVC_2 = \$4$, and $Q_2 = .6$ million. Total profit is $1.2 + 1.5 - 2.4 = \$.3$ million per year. Each product makes a positive contribution, and total contribution exceeds total fixed cost. Thus, the firm should stay in business. What if the second good's price is $5.50? In the short run, both goods continue to contribute toward fixed costs and, therefore, should be produced. In the long run, total contribution ($2.1 million) falls short of total fixed cost, so the firm should shut down. Finally, if the second good's price is $3.50, then $P_2 < AVC_2$. The firm should halt production of the second good immediately and cease operations altogether in the long run.

Robert Kaplan of the Harvard Business School has spent many years studying the ways large and small corporations use accounting systems to measure costs.[14] He points out that managerial accounting systems designed decades ago are no longer relevant for today's advanced technological environments. A multiproduct firm faces innumerable costs. At one extreme, some costs (so-called unit costs) vary directly with a good's output—materials, production-line labor and equipment, and so on. At the other extreme are fixed costs incurred whether or not the good is produced—costs associated with general adminis-tration, the firm's sales force, research and development, and salaries of high-level management, for instance. In between are quasi-variable costs—costs that are partially affected by a particular good's volume of output. At the production level, such costs include parts purchasing, product testing, and changes in product design or production techniques. At the sales level, these costs include marketing, distribution, processing, and customer service.

Almost all accounting systems allocate the last two categories—fixed and quasi-variable costs—across the firm's multiple products in proportion to the products' volumes. If a product accounts for 20 percent of a firm's output (whether by units, labor costs, or machine-hours), it is assigned 20 percent of these costs. These allocated costs are added to the product's direct unit costs to determine its total cost of production. According to this cost accounting system, the product is profitable if, and only if, its total revenues exceed its total costs.

Although cost accounting systems are useful in many respects, they can be misleading when it comes to economic decisions. There is a twofold prob-lem with any accounting method of allocating costs. First, for decision-mak-ing purposes, costs that are truly fixed (i.e., don't vary) with respect to

Accounting for Costs

---

[14]R. Kaplan, "Management Accounting for Advanced Technological Environments," *Science*, August 25, 1989, 819–823.

products' volumes should not be allocated at all. This is in keeping with the earlier proposition that fixed costs do not matter. According to Equation 7.6, contribution is the only relevant measure of a good's performance. Production should continue if contribution is positive and should cease if it is negative. Note that the good's accounting profit (by including a fixed-cost allocation) understates its contribution. Consequently, when it comes to product decisions, accounting profit can be very misleading.

In the preceding example, a typical accounting allocation would assign the $2.4 million in fixed costs to the products in proportion to output: $1.6 million to the first product and $.8 million to the second. (The first product comprises two-thirds of total output.) Thus, the first product's accounting profit would be $\pi_1 = (10 - 9)(1.2) - 1.6 = -\$.4$ million. Based on this measure, the product appears to be unprofitable. What if the firm discontinues its production? The firm will no longer earn any contribution from the first good. But there will be no decline in the $2.4 million fixed cost; now the entire fixed cost will be assigned to the second item. Left producing a single good, the firm will be unable to earn a profit (its *loss* will amount to $2.4 - 1.5 = \$.9$ million) and will be forced to shut down. Here allocating fixed costs leads to a disastrous series of decisions. As we noted earlier, the firm's optimal course of action is to produce both products. To repeat, assigning fixed costs to products is unnecessary (and potentially misleading). Instead, the only relevant long-run issue is whether the firm's total contribution covers these fixed costs in the aggregate.

A second problem with allocating costs is related to the first. To make sound decisions, managers need accurate and timely measures of their products' true variable costs. Allocating costs on the basis of arbitrary proportions is sure to lead to errors. Robert Kaplan discusses the case of Siemens, a German electrical manufacturer.[15] Among its many products, the company produces motors—standard motors in high volumes and a variety of custom motors in much lower volumes. Manufacturing custom motors requires many more tasks than does producing standard ones. More workers are needed to perform setups, make design changes, inspect output, schedule, move, and count inventories, and negotiate with vendors. Although generally aware of this differential cost burden, the company continued to allocate these collective costs according to accounting standards. Consequently, the high-volume standard motors received a cost allocation that far exceeded what might be estimated as their "true" costs. In effect, standard motors bore a large share of the custom motors' costs. Recognizing this, the company has adopted an activity-based cost (ABC) system that more accurately reflects the dependence of costs on product-related activities (rather than solely on output volumes). When effectively implemented, ABC systems allow managers to predict the cost implications of future product decisions and plan pricing policy accordingly.

[15] Ibid., 819–823.

In the example that opens this chapter, the managers of a sports shoe company were engaged in a debate over what strategy would lead to the greatest profit. Should production of the boys' shoes be increased? Cut back? Discontinued? The correct answers to these questions depend on a careful analysis of relevant costs. To clarify the situation, management has gathered the following information about different sales quantities:

Allocating Costs Revisited

Pairs of Shoes	Price	Revenue	Direct Cost	Allocated Cost	Total Average Cost
1,600	$40	$64,000	$66,400	$15,000	$50.88
2,400	36	86,400	74,400	20,769	39.65
3,200	32	102,400	85,600	25,714	34.79
3,600	30	108,000	92,400	27,931	33.43
4,000	28	112,000	100,000	30,000	32.50

The firm's production managers have supplied the data on direct (i.e., variable) costs. Recall that production of women's and boys' running shoes share $90,000 in fixed costs. The firm's accountants allocate this cost to the two lines in proportion to numbers of pairs. The output of women's shoes is 8,000 pairs. (Thus, if the volume of boys' shoes is 4,000 pairs, the product's output is one-third of the total; hence, its allocation is $(1/3)(\$90,000) = \$30,000$. Allocations for other outputs are computed in the same way.) Total average cost is the sum of direct and allocated costs divided by total output.

The firm currently is charging a price of $36 per pair and selling 2,400 pairs per week. How would management evaluate the current profitability of this strategy, and how might it improve its profits? First, consider the *wrong* method of approaching these questions. Management observes that when it sells 2,400 pairs, total average cost is $39.65 per pair. This exceeds the $36 selling price. Therefore, management believes its current strategy is unprofitable. What are its other options? An obvious possibility is to increase price to a level above $39.65, say, to $40. The table shows the results of this strategy. Volume drops to 1,600 pairs, but total average cost rises to $50.88. (Because the decline in volume is much greater than the reduction in total cost, average cost rises dramatically.) Price still falls well short of average cost. A price cut will do no better. The other prices in the table tell the same story: Average total cost exceeds price in all cases. Therefore, management concludes that the boys' running shoe cannot earn a profit and should be discontinued.

Let's now adopt the role of economic consultant and explain why management's current reasoning is in error. The problem lies with the allocation of the $90,000 in "shared" costs. Recall the economic "commandment": Do not allocate fixed costs. In a multiproduct firm, contribution is the correct measure of a product's profitability. A comparison of columns

3 and 4 in the table shows that the boys' shoe makes a positive contribution for four of the price and output combinations. Thus, the shoe should be retained. The firm's optimal strategy is to lower the price to P = $32. The resulting sales volume is Q = 3,200. Maximum contribution is $102,400 − $85,600 = $16,800. Beyond P = $32, however, any further price reduction is counterproductive. (The additional cost of supplying these additional sales units exceeds the extra sales revenue.) Thus, the production manager would be wrong to advocate a policy of minimizing direct costs per unit of output. We can check that of the five output levels, average variable cost is minimized at Q = 4,000. (Here AVC is $100,000/4,000 = $25 per pair.) Nonetheless, this volume of output delivers less contribution than Q = 3,200 because the accompanying drop in price is much greater than the decline in average variable cost. To sum up, the firm's correct strategy is to maximize the product's contribution.

SUMMARY

Decision-Making Principles

1. Cost is an important consideration in decision making. In deciding among different courses of action, the manager need only consider the differential revenues and costs of the various alternatives.

2. The opportunity cost associated with choosing a particular decision is measured by the forgone benefits of the next-best alternative.

3. Economic profit is the difference between total revenues and total costs (i.e., explicit costs and opportunity costs). Managerial decisions should be based on economic profit, not accounting profit.

4. Costs that are fixed (or sunk) with respect to alternative courses of action are irrelevant.

5. In the short run, the firm should continue to produce so long as price exceeds average variable cost. Assuming it does produce, the firm maximizes its profit (or minimizes its loss) by setting marginal revenue equal to marginal cost.

6. In the long run, all revenues and costs are variable. The firm should continue production if, and only if, it earns a positive economic profit. A multiproduct firm should continue operating in the long run only if total revenue exceeds total costs. There is no need to allocate shared costs to specific products.

Nuts and Bolts

1. The firm's cost function indicates the (minimum) total cost of producing any level of output given existing production technology, input prices, and any relevant constraints.

2. In the short run, one or more of the firm's inputs are fixed. Short-run total cost is the sum of fixed cost and variable cost. Marginal cost is the additional cost of producing an extra unit of output. In the short run, there is an inverse relationship between marginal cost and the marginal product of the variable input: $MC = P_L/MP_L$. Marginal cost increases due to diminishing returns. The short-run average cost curve is U-shaped.

3. In the long run, all inputs are variable. The firm chooses input proportions to minimize the total cost of producing any given level of output. The shape of the long-run average cost curve is determined by returns to scale. If there are constant returns to scale, long-run average cost is constant; under increasing returns, average cost decreases with output; and, under decreasing returns, average cost rises. Empirical studies indicate L-shaped (or U-shaped) long-run average cost curves for many sectors and products.

4. Many firms supply multiple products. Economies of scope exist when the cost of producing multiple goods is less than the aggregate cost of producing each good separately. Moreover, a firm's average cost of production falls over time as it "learns" to produce more efficiently. The learning curve describes the inverse relationship between a firm's average cost and its cumulative output.

5. Comparative advantage (not absolute advantage) is the source of mutually beneficial global trade. The pattern of comparative advantage between two countries depends on relative productivity, relative wages, and the exchange rate.

Questions and Problems

1. The development of a new product was much lengthier and more expensive than the company's management anticipated. Consequently, the firm's top accountants and financial managers argue that the firm should raise the price of the product 10 percent above its original target to help recoup some of these costs. Does such a strategy make sense? Explain carefully.

2. Comment on the following statement: "Average cost includes both fixed and variable costs, whereas marginal cost only includes variable costs. Therefore, marginal cost is never greater than average cost."

3. A company produces two main products: electronic control devices and specialty microchips. The average total cost of producing a microchip is $300; the firm then sells the chips to other high-tech manufacturers for $550. Currently, there are enough orders for microchips to keep its factory capacity fully utilized. The company also uses its own chips in the production of control devices. The average total cost (AC) of producing

such a device is $500 plus the cost of two microchips. (Assume all of the $500 cost is variable and AC is constant at different output volumes.) Each control device sells for an average price of $1,500.

a. Should the company produce control devices? Is this product profitable?

b. Answer part a assuming outside orders for microchips are insufficient to keep the firm's production capacity fully utilized.

c. Now suppose $200 of the average cost of control devices is fixed. (Assume, as in part a, that microchip capacity is fully utilized.) Should control devices be produced in the short run? Explain.

4. The year 1998 saw an unprecedented number of megamergers in the banking industry: NationsBank with BankAmerica, Bank One with First Chicago NBD, and Citicorp with Travelers Group to name the three largest mergers. These merged entities are hoping to offer one-stop shopping for financial services: everything from savings to home mortgages, investments, and insurance.

a. In the short run, what are the potential cost advantages of these mergers? Explain.

b. Is a $300 billion national bank likely to be more efficient than a $30 billion regional bank or a $3 billion state-based bank? What economic evidence is needed to determine whether there are long-run increasing returns to scale in banking?

c. Do you think the mergers are predicated on economies of scope?

5. An entrepreneur plans to convert a building she owns into a video-game arcade. Her main decision is how many games to purchase for the arcade. From survey information, she projects total revenue per year as $R = 10,000Q - 200Q^2$, where Q is the number of games. The cost for each game (leasing, electricity, maintenance, and so on) is $4,000 per year. The entrepreneur will run the arcade, but instead of paying herself a salary, she will collect profits. She has received offers of $100,000 to sell her building and a $20,000 offer to manage a rival's arcade. She recognizes that a normal return on a risky investment such as the arcade is 20 percent.

a. As a profit maximizer, how many games should she order?

b. What is her economic profit?

6. In 1971, Congress conducted hearings on emergency loan guarantee legislation for Lockheed Corporation, which was in the middle of a severe liquidity crisis due to losses on a number of military contracts. The loan guarantee was intended to allow the company to complete development of the L-1011 Tri-Star program (production of a new commercial aircraft).

a. One estimate of the average cost (in millions of dollars) per aircraft during the program was AC = $100(TQ)^{-.5} = 100/\sqrt{TQ}$, where TQ denotes the total number of aircraft produced to date. What is the average cost of the first aircraft? The 2nd? The 49th? The 100th? For every doubling of cumulative output, by what percentage does average cost decline?

b. Based on extensive economic testimony, Congress agreed with Lockheed management's contention that the aircraft eventually would be profitable and granted a $250 million loan guarantee. Economic experts estimated the break-even number of aircraft in a range between 200 (the company's view) and 400 (the skeptics' view). How would one go about making such an estimate?

c. Years later, having sold fewer than 200 aircraft, Lockheed publicly announced that it was abandoning the program. The day after the announcement, Lockheed's stock price rose 18 percent. What conclusions can one draw from this?

7. A firm's long-run total cost function is:

$$C = 360 + 40Q + 10Q^2.$$

a. What is the shape of the long-run average cost curve?

b. Find the output that minimizes average cost.

c. The firm faces the fixed market price of $140 per unit. At this price, can the firm survive in the long run? Explain.

8. Suppose the manufacturer of running shoes has collected the following quantitative information. Demand for the boys' shoe is estimated to be Q = 9,600 − 200P, or, equivalently, P = 48 − Q/200. The shoe's direct cost is C = $60,000 + $.0025Q^2$.

a. Check that these demand and cost equations are consistent with the data presented in the Allocating Costs Revisited section.

b. Find the firm's profit-maximizing price and output.

9. Suppose you are a theater owner fortunate enough to book a summer box-office hit into your single theater. You are now planning the length of its run. Your share of the film's projected box-office receipts is R = $10w − .25w^2$, where R is in thousands of dollars and w is the number of weeks that the movie runs. The average operating cost of your theater is AC = MC = $4 thousand per week.

a. To maximize your profit, how many *weeks* should the movie run? What is your profit?

b. You realize that your typical movie makes an average operating profit of $1.5 thousand per week. How does this fact affect your decision in part a (if at all)? Explain briefly.

c. In the last 25 years, stand-alone movie theaters have given way to cineplexes with 4 to 10 screens and megaplexes with 10 to 30 screens (yes, 30 screens!) under one roof. During the same period, total annual movie admissions have barely changed. What cost factors can explain this trend? In addition, what demand factors might also be relevant?

d. The film's producer anticipated an extended theater run (through Labor Day) and accordingly decided to move back the videocassette release of the film from Thanksgiving to January. Does the decision to delay make sense? Explain carefully.

10. A firm uses a single plant with costs $C = 160 + 16Q + .1Q^2$ and faces the price equation $P = 96 - .4Q$.

a. Find the firm's profit-maximizing price and quantity. What is its profit?

b. The firm's production manager claims that the firm's average cost of production is minimized at an output of 40 units. Furthermore, she claims that 40 units is the firm's profit-maximizing level of output. Explain whether these claims are correct.

c. Could the firm increase its profit by using a second plant (with costs identical to the first) to produce the output in part a? Explain.

11. Firm A makes and sells motorcycles. The total cost of each cycle is the sum of the costs of frames, assembly, and engine. The firm produces its own engines according to the cost equation:

$$C_E = 250,000 + 1000Q + 5Q^2.$$

The cost of frames and assembly is $2,000 per cycle. Monthly demand for cycles is given by the inverse demand equation $P = 10,000 - 30Q$.

a. What is the MC of producing an additional *engine?* What is the MC of producing an additional *cycle?* Find the firm's profit-maximizing quantity and price.

b. Now suppose the firm has the chance to buy an unlimited number of engines from another company at a price of $1,400 per engine. Will this option affect the number of *cycles* it plans to produce? Its price? Will the firm continue to produce engines itself? If so, how many?

12. Firm Z provides Internet access and a bundle of related information services to subscribers. The best estimate of subscriber demand is given by $P = 20 - 5Q$, where Q is the number of subscribers per month in millions and P is the monthly subscription price. In turn, firm Z purchases server capacity from firm N, paying a fixed charge of $2 million per month plus $10 per month for each subscriber. All other operating expenses for firm Z (for its employees, equipment, office space, and so on) come to a total of $2 million per month.

a. (i) To maximize its profit, how many subscribers should firm Z serve and at what monthly subscription price? (ii) Firm Z has contracted with firm N for the next six months (and is legally obligated to pay N under the contract). Unfortunately, Z discovers that its other operating expenses are closer to $4 million (rather than $2 million). Should firm Z continue to operate over the next six months? Beyond six months?

b. Firm Z has identified a segment of "hard-core, sophisticated users" who tend to "shop around" in choosing their preferred internet provider. These users also spend more time online, about 25 percent more time than the average regular subscriber. (In terms of capacity used, each hard-core user counts as 1.25 regular subscribers.) Should the firm offer a different subscription price to these users? Provide a brief qualitative explanation.

c. Firm N offers to provide firm Z monthly server capacity for up to 4 million subscribers at a flat fee of $15 million. Under this option, answer the questions in part a, section i (i.e., assume the firm's other operating expenses come to $2 million). From firm Z's perspective, are these new contract terms more or less attractive than the original terms in part a?

d. Assume that firm Z elects the new contract offered in part c. Now the firm recognizes that it can gain an additional source of revenue by allowing banner advertising on its site. It has recently signed advertising agreements with various Internet vendors. The effect of these agreements is to bring the firm $10 of advertising revenue for each subscriber to the site. What effect (if any) would this have on firm Z's profit-maximizing subscription price and number of subscribers?

13. As noted in Problem 5 of Chapter 3, General Motors (GM) produces light trucks in its Michigan factories. Currently, its Michigan production is 50,000 trucks per month, and its marginal cost is $20,000 per truck. With regional demand given by $P = 30,000 - 0.1Q$, GM sets a price of $25,000 per truck.

a. Confirm that setting $Q = 50,000$ and $P = \$25,000$ is profit maximizing.

b. General Motors produces the engines that power its light trucks and finds that it has some unused production capacity, enough capacity to build an additional 10,000 engines per year. A manufacturer of sports utility vehicles (SUVs) has offered to purchase as many as 25,000 engines from GM at a price of $10,000 per engine. GM's contribution is estimated to be about $2,000 per engine sold (based on a marginal cost of $8,000 per engine). Should GM devote some of its engine capacity to produce engines to sell to the SUV manufacturer? Does this outside opportunity change GM's optimal output of light vehicles in part a?

c. GM also assembles light trucks in a west coast facility, which is currently manufacturing 40,000 units per month. Because it produces multiple vehicle types at this megaplant, the firm's standard practice is to allocate

$160 million of factory-wide fixed costs to light trucks. Based on this allocation, the California production manager reports that the average total cost per light truck is $22,000 per unit. Given this report, what conclusion (if any) can you draw concerning the marginal cost per truck? If West Coast demand is similar to demand in Michigan, could the West Coast factory profit by changing its output from 40,000 units?

*14. A firm produces digital watches on a single production line serviced during one daily shift. The total output of watches depends directly on the number of labor-hours employed on the line. Maximum capacity of the line is 120,000 watches per month; this output requires 60,000 hours of labor per month. Total fixed costs come to $600,000 per month, the wage rate averages $8 per hour, and other variable costs (e.g., materials) average $6 per watch. The marketing department's estimate of demand is $P = 28 - Q/20,000$, where P denotes price in dollars and Q is monthly demand.

a. How many additional watches can be produced by an extra hour of labor? What is the marginal cost of an additional watch? As a profit maximizer, what price and output should the firm set? Is production capacity fully utilized? What contribution does this product line provide?

b. The firm can increase capacity up to 100 percent by scheduling a night shift. The wage rate at night averages $12 per hour. Answer the questions in part a in light of this additional option.

c. Suppose demand for the firm's watches falls permanently to $P = 20 - Q/20,000$. In view of this fall in demand, what output should the firm produce in the short run? In the long run? Explain.

*15. A manufacturing firm produces output using a single plant. The relevant cost function is $C = 500 + 5Q^2$. The firm's demand curve is $P = 600 - 5Q$.

a. Find the level of output at which average cost is minimized. (*Hint:* Set AC equal to MC.) What is the minimum level of average cost?

b. Find the firm's profit-maximizing output and price. Find its profit.

c. Suppose the firm has in place a second plant identical to the first. Argue that the firm should divide production equally between the plants. Check that the firm maximizes profit at total output Q* such that

$$MR(Q^*) = MC_1(Q^*/2) = MC_2(Q^*/2).$$

Find Q*. Explain why total output is greater than in part b.

d. In the long run, the firm can produce using as many or as few plants as it wishes (each with the preceding cost function). In this case, what kind of returns to scale hold? What are the firm's optimal output and price in the long run? How many plants will the firm use to produce the good? (*Hint:* Refer to the value of minimum AC you found in part a.)

Discussion Question Explain why the cost structure associated with many kinds of information goods and services might imply a market supplied by a small number of large firms. (At the same time, some Internet businesses such as grocery home deliveries have continually suffered steep losses regardless of scale. Explain why.) Could lower transaction costs in e-commerce ever make it easier for small suppliers to compete? As noted in Chapter 3, network externalities are often an important aspect of demand for information goods and services. (The benefits to customers of using software, participating in electronic markets, or using instant messaging increase with the number of other users.) How might network externalities affect firm operating strategies (pricing, output, and advertising) and firm size?

Spreadsheet Problems

S1. A firm's production function is given by the equation

$$Q = 12L^{.5}K^{.5},$$

where L, K, and Q are measured in thousands of units. Input prices are 36 per labor unit and 16 per capital unit.

a. Create a spreadsheet (based on the example shown) to model this production setting. (You may have already completed this step if you answered problem S2 of Chapter 6. An algebraic analysis of this setting appears in this chapter's Special Appendix.)

b. To explore the shape of short-run average cost, hold the amount of capital fixed at K = 9 thousand and vary the amount of labor from 1 thousand to 2.5 thousand to 4 thousand to 5.5 thousand to 7.5 thousand to 9 thousand units. What is the resulting behavior of SAC? Use the spreadsheet optimizer to find the amount of labor corresponding to minimum SAC. What is the value of SAC_{min}?

c. In your spreadsheet, set L = 9 thousand (keeping K = 9 thousand) and note the resulting output and total cost. Now suppose that the firm is free to produce this same level of output by adjusting both labor and capital in the long run. Use the optimizer to determine the firm's optimal inputs and LAC_{min}. (Remember to include an output constraint for cell I3.)

	A	B	C	D	E	F	G	H	I	J
1										
2			COST ANALYSIS							
3								Output	36	
4								Price	8.50	
5		Labor	1.00		Capital	9.00				
6		MP_L	18.00		MP_K	2.00		MR	8.00	
7								Revenue	306	
8		MRP_L	144.00		MRP_K	16.00				
9		MC_L	36.00		MC_K	16.00		Cost	180	
10								Ave. Cost	5.00	
11										
12								Profit	126	
13										

d. Confirm that the production function exhibits constant returns to scale and constant long-run average costs. (For instance, recalculate the answer for part c after doubling both inputs.)

e. Finally, suppose the firm's inverse demand curve is given by

$$P = 9 - Q/72.$$

With capital fixed at $K = 9$ thousand in the short run, use the optimizer to determine the firm's optimal labor usage and maximum profit. Then find the optimal amounts of both inputs in the long run. Explain the large differences in inputs, output, and profit between the short run and the long run.

S2. A multinational firm produces microchips at a home facility and at a foreign subsidiary according to the respective cost functions:

$$C_H = 120Q_H \quad \text{and} \quad C_F = 50Q_F + .5Q_F^2.$$

The firm sells chips in the home market and the foreign market where the inverse demand curves are

$$P_H = 300 - D_H \quad \text{and} \quad P_F = 250 - .5D_F,$$

respectively. Here D denotes the quantity *sold* in each market, and Q denotes the quantity *produced* in each facility. Chips can be costlessly shipped between markets so that D_H need not equal Q_H (nor D_F equal Q_F). However, total production must match total sales:

$$Q_H + Q_F = D_H + D_F.$$

a. Create a spreadsheet (based on the example that follows) to model the firm's worldwide operations. Find the firm's profit-maximizing outputs, sales quantities, and prices. Are chips shipped overseas? (*Hint*: The key to maximizing profit is to find sales and output quantities such that $MR_H = MR_F = MC_H = MC_F$. Also note that MC_H is constant. When using your spreadsheet's optimizer, be sure to include the constraint that cell F9—extra output—must equal zero. That is, total sales must exactly equal total output.)

b. Answer the questions in part a under an "antidumping" constraint; that is, the company must charge the *same* price in both markets. (*Hint*: Include the additional constraint that cell F12, the price gap, must equal zero.)

	A	B	C	D	E	F	G	H
1								
2		**WORLDWIDE CHIP DECISIONS**						
3								
4		Set Sales & Output Quantities (000's)						
5								
6			Home	Abroad	Total			
7								
8		Sales	10	10	20		Extra	
9						0	< Output	
10		Output	10	10	20			
11								
12		Price	290	245		45	< Price Gap	
13								
14		Revenues	2,900	2,450	5,350			
15		MR	280	240	—			
16								
17		Costs	1,200	550	1,750			
18		MC	120	60	—			
19								
20		Profit	1,700	1,900	3,600			
21								

Suggested References

The following articles provide good treatments of the strategic issues surrounding economies of scope and learning.
Ghemawat, P. "Building Strategy on the Experience Curve." *Harvard Business Review* (March–April 1985): 143–149.

Goldhar, J. D., and M. Jelinek. "Plan for Economies of Scope." *Harvard Business Review* (November–December 1983): 141–148.

The following articles examine the existence of scale and scope economies in a variety of settings.

Clark, J. "The Economies of Scale and Scope at Depository Financial Institutions: A Review of the Literature." *Economic Review* (Federal Reserve Bank of Kansas City, 1988): 16–33.

Koshal, R. K. and M. Koshal. "Do Liberal Arts Colleges Exhibit Economies of Scale and Scope?" *Education Economics* 8 (December 2000): 209–220.

Silk, A. J., and E. R. Berndt. "Scale and Scope Effects on Advertising Agency Costs." National Bureau of Economic Research, Working Paper No. w9965, September 2003.

Sung, N., and M. Gort. "Economies of Scale and Natural Monopoly in the U.S. Local Telephone Industry." *Review of Economics and Statistics* 82 (November 2000): 694–697.

Wholey, D., et al. "Scale and Scope Economies among Health Maintenance Organizations." *Journal of Health Economics* 15 (December 1996): 657–684.

The following article examines the economics of Lockheed's Tri-Star aircraft using estimates of the experience curve as a key ingredient.

Reinhardt, U. E. "Breakeven Analysis for Lockheed's Tri-Star: An Application of Financial Theory." *Journal of Finance* (September 1973): 821–838.

The following article reviews research estimating cost functions.

J. Panzar, "Determinants of Firm and Industry Structure," in R. Schmalensee and R. Willig (eds.), *Handbook of Industrial Organization* (Amsterdam: North Holland, 1989): 3–59.

The following article describes cost analysis at Bethlehem Steel Corporation.

Baker, G. L., et al. "Production Planning and Cost Analysis on a Microcomputer." *Interfaces* (July–August 1987): 53–60.

**CHECK STATION
ANSWERS**

1. The full cost to the airline of a grounded plane includes explicit costs—repair costs, overnight hangar costs, and the like. It also includes an opportunity cost—the lost profit on any canceled flights.

2. The past profits and development costs are irrelevant. If the firm drops the product, it recovers $2 million. If the firm continues the product, its additional profit is $5 + 3 - 4 - 2.5 = \$1.5$ million. Thus, the firm should drop the product.

3. The related electronics products would exhibit economies of scope for several reasons. First, they have many technological elements in common (e.g., expertise in copier technology carries over to facsimile machines). They also have some common components (microchips). Second, customers see the products as complementary. Thus, brand-name allegiance gained in computers could carry over to telephone equipment. Third, there are also likely economies in joint advertising, promotion, and distribution. (Toshiba's sales force can pursue sales on any or all of its products.)

4. The repair firm's marginal revenue is $MR = 50 - .4Q$ and its marginal cost is $MC = 30 + .6Q$. Setting MR equal to MC, we find $Q^* = 20$. From the price equation, $P^* = 50 - (.2)(20) = 46$. In turn, profit is $\pi = 920 - 990 = -70$. The firm incurs a loss in the short run, but this is preferable to shutting down ($\pi = -270$). It is earning a maximum contribution toward overhead. In the long run, the firm should shut down unless conditions improve.

Transfer Pricing

In the body of this chapter, we have focused on the production and sale of a firm's products to outside buyers. While this is the most common case, products are also sold among divisions within large firms. For example, major automobile companies consist of many divisions. The division that produces parts will transfer its output to separate assembly divisions responsible for automobiles, trucks, and vans. In turn, assembled vehicles are transferred to different sales divisions and finally to dealers. In the same way, within a major chemical manufacturer, one division may produce a basic chemical that is used as an input in the production of specialty chemicals and plastics, each housed in separate divisions.

The price the selling division charges to the buying division within the company is called the **transfer price**. The firm's objective is to set the transfer price such that the buying and selling divisions take actions that maximize the firm's total profit. Accomplishing this task requires an accurate cost assessment. To illustrate the issues at stake, consider a large firm that sells a variety of office electronics products, such as telephones, printers, desktop computers, and copiers. One division specializes in the production of microchips that serve as the "electronic brains" for many of the firm's final products, including copiers, laser printers, and facsimile machines. For the time being, we assume there is no outside market for the firm's specialty chips; they are produced only for use in the firm's final products. (We relax this assumption in the following section.)

What transfer price per unit should the chip division charge the copier (or any other) division?

The answer to this question is that *the firm should set the internal transfer price for the microchip exactly equal to its marginal cost of production.* Figure 7A.1 summarizes the demand and cost conditions associated with the production of copiers. The key point about the figure is understanding the "full" marginal cost of producing copiers. Managers of the copier division are well aware of the direct costs they incur in assembly. This marginal cost is shown as the upward-sloping MC_A curve in the figure. In addition, we must consider the marginal cost of producing the chips that are used in the copier. In Figure 7A.1, this marginal cost (labeled MC_M) is superimposed on the MC_A curve. The total marginal cost of producing copiers is the sum of the chip cost and the assembly

FIGURE 7A.1

Transfer Pricing

In the absence of an external market, the optimal transfer price for an intermediate product equals the item's marginal cost of production. Optimal output of the firm's final product occurs at Q*, where MR equals MC_T. Here MC_T includes the intermediate good's transfer price.

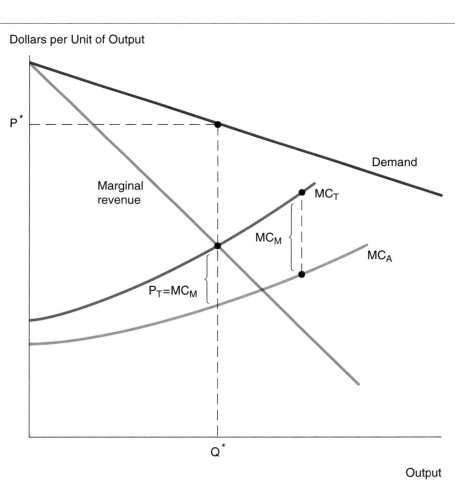

cost. In the figure, this total marginal cost curve is denoted by $MC_T = MC_A + MC_M$ and is drawn as the vertical sum of the two curves. (Note that MC_M is depicted as slightly upward sloping; that is, the gap between MC_A and MC_T steadily increases as output rises.)

The firm maximizes the total profit it earns on copiers by setting the quantity such that marginal revenue equals total marginal cost, $MR = MC_T$. In Figure 7A.1, the optimal quantity occurs at Q^* and the associated optimal selling price for the copier is P^*. What transfer price for chips will lead to this outcome? The appropriate transfer price should be set at $P_T = MC_M$. By paying this transfer price, the copier division incurs an additional cost of $MC_A + P_T = MC_A + MC_M$ for each extra copier it produces. By taking into account the true "full" cost of producing additional output, the copier division automatically maximizes the firm's total profit.

A MARKET FOR CHIPS If there is an external market in which microchips can be bought and sold, the profit-maximizing analysis must be modified. In this case, *the firm should set the internal transfer price for the microchip equal to the prevailing market price.* The reasoning is straightforward. Let $P°$ denote the prevailing market price. Obviously, the chip division cannot charge the copier division a transfer price that exceeds $P°$; the copier division would simply opt to buy chips from the outside market. Nor would the chip division be satisfied with a transfer price below $P°$; it would prefer to produce and sell chips exclusively for the outside market. Consequently, $P_T = P°$ is the only price at which internal transfers will occur.

Here is another way to arrive at this conclusion. The correct price to impute to internally produced chips should reflect the firm's true opportunity cost. Each chip that goes into the "guts" of the firm's copiers is a chip that could have been sold on the outside market at price $P°$. Since it is this market price that the firm gives up, the internal transfer price should be set accordingly.

TRANSFER PRICING: A NUMERICAL EXAMPLE Let the demand for copiers be given by $P = 4,000 - 3Q$, where Q is the number of copiers demanded per week and P is the price in dollars. The total cost of assembling copiers (excluding the cost of microchips) is given by $C_A = 360,000 + 1,000Q$. The cost of producing microchips is $C_M = 40,000 + 200Q_M + .5Q_M^2$, where Q_M is the quantity of chips. Suppose each copier uses *one* microchip. The total cost of producing copiers is $C_T = C_A + C_M = 400,000 + 1,200Q + .5Q^2$. In turn, the marginal cost of copiers is $MC_T = dC_T/dQ = 1,200 + Q$. Equivalently, $MC_T = MC_A + MC_M = 1,000 + (200 + Q) = 1,200 + Q$. Setting $MR = MC_T$ implies $4,000 - 6Q = 1,200 + Q$. Thus, $Q^* = 400$ and $P^* = 4,000 - (3)(400) = \$2,800$. At a production rate of 400 microchips per week, marginal cost is $MC_M = 200 + 400 = \$600$. Thus, in the absence of an external market for microchips, the appropriate transfer price is

$P_T = MC_M = \$600$. At an output of 400 chips, the average cost per chip is $AC_M = C_M/Q = \$500$. Thus, by selling its output to the copier division at $P_T = 600$, the chip division earns an internal profit of $(\$600 - \$500)(400) = \$40,000$ per week. The copier division's average total cost is $AC_A = C_A/Q + \$600 = \$2,500$ per copier. At $P^* = 2,800$, the division makes a profit of \$300 per copier, implying a total profit of \$120,000 per week. The combined profit of the divisions is $40,000 + 120,000 = \$160,000$.

Now, suppose an external market for chips exists and a chip's current market price is $P_M = \$900$. For each additional chip produced and sold, the chip division's marginal revenue equals \$900, the current market price. Setting $MR = MC$ implies $900 = 200 + Q_M$, where Q_M denotes the quantity of microchips. The solution is $Q_M = 700$. Next consider the copier division. The price it pays for chips is now $P_T = P_M = \$900$. Thus, its marginal cost (inclusive of the price of chips) is $MC_T = 1,000 + 900 = \$1,900$. Setting $MR = MC$ implies $4,000 - 6Q = \$1,900$. Thus, $Q^* = 350$ and $P^* = \$2,950$. To sum up, the chip division's total weekly output is 700 chips. Half of this output (350 chips) is transferred to the copier division; the other half is sold on the open market.

Questions and Problems

1. a. A senior manager argues that the chip division's main purpose is to serve the firm's final-product divisions. Accordingly, these services should be offered free of charge; that is, the transfer price for chips should be $P_T = 0$. Explain carefully what is wrong with this argument.

   b. Suppose the chip division treats the copier division as it would an outside buyer and marks up the transfer price above marginal cost. Explain what is wrong with this strategy.

2. In the numerical example, suppose the firm can purchase chips on the open market at a price of \$300. What production decisions should the divisions make in this case?

Short-Run
and Long-Run Costs

This appendix takes a closer quantitative look at the cost setting in Spreadsheet Problem S1 and illustrated in Figure 7.3. We start with the following economic facts. Let the firm's production function be given by

$$Q = 12L^{.5}K^{.5} = 12\sqrt{L} \cdot \sqrt{K} \qquad [7A.1]$$

where L and K are in thousands of units. The prices of labor and capital are $P_L = 36$ per unit and $P_K = 16$ per unit, respectively.

SHORT-RUN COSTS   We begin by deriving expressions for the firm's SAC and SMC. To do this, we fix the amount of capital at some level; call this $K°$. With capital fixed, we solve Equation 7A.1 for L:

$$L = Q^2/(144K°). \qquad [7A.2]$$

Total cost is

$$C = 16K° + 36L$$
$$= 16K° + Q^2/(4K°)$$

after substituting for L. In turn, short-run average cost is

$$SAC = C/Q = 16K°/Q + Q/(4K°) \qquad [7A.3]$$

and SMC = dC/dQ = Q/(2K°). It is easy to check that SAC is U-shaped. For instance, by setting K° equal to 9 thousand square feet, we obtain the SAC function:

$$SAC = 144/Q + Q/36.$$

This is the equation of the first SAC curve graphed in Figure 7.3. By setting K° = 18 thousand and K° = 27 thousand, we trace out the other SAC curves in the figure.

LONG-RUN COSTS   We can now confirm that the firm's LAC and LMC curves are constant, as shown in Figure 7.3. One way of doing so is to note that the level of LAC is given by the minimum point of each SAC curve. Returning to the SAC expression in Equation 7A.3, we can show that the point of minimum average cost occurs at output

$$Q = 8K°. \tag{7A.4}$$

To see this, remember that the SMC curve intersects the SAC curve at its minimum point. Equating the preceding expressions for SAC and SMC, we find 16K°/Q + Q/4K° = Q/2K°. The solution is $Q^2 = 64(K°)^2$, or Q = 8K°. After substituting Q = 8K° into Equation 7A.3, we find the firm's minimum average cost to be min SAC = 16K°/8K° + 8K°/4K° = 4/unit. In turn, substituting Q = 8K° into Equation 7A.2 implies

$$L = (4/9)K°. \tag{7A.5}$$

This equation specifies the necessary amount of labor to be used in conjunction with a plant of size K°.

In summary, Equation 7A.3 describes the short-run average cost of producing Q units of output using K° units of fixed capital, whereas Equation 7A.2 specifies the requisite amount of labor. For instance, the short-run average cost of producing 54 thousand units of output in a 9 thousand-square-foot plant is SAC = 144/54 + 54/36 = $4.17. The necessary amount of labor is $L = (54)^2/[(144)(9)] = 2.25$ thousand labor-hours. In turn, the LAC of producing Q units is $4 and is achieved using the amounts of capital and labor given by Equations 7A.4 and 7A.5. Thus, to produce 54 thousand units in the long run, the firm should use a 54,000/8 = 6.75 thousand-square-foot plant and (4/9)(6.75) = 3 thousand labor-hours.

Questions and Problems

1. a. Using Equation 7A.3, find the short-run average cost of producing 108 thousand units in a 9 thousand-square-foot plant. Determine the necessary quantity of labor.
   b. Would the same output be less expensive to produce using an 18 thousand-square-foot plant?

CHAPTER 8

Decision Making under Uncertainty

If Hell is paved with good intentions, it is largely because of the impossibility of foreseeing consequences.

ALDOUS HUXLEY

Gearing Down for a Recession

Selling yachts is a very cyclical industry. In a booming economy, large increases in personal disposable income greatly expand the demand for this high-priced luxury item. In the midst of a recession, sales of yachts sink and a sizable percentage of yacht dealers go under. You have owned a yacht dealership for the last two years and have made handsome profits during the good times. Currently you are in the process of deciding on the number of yachts to order from the manufacturer for the coming season. If the economy continues to grow as in the past, your order will be roughly the same as in the previous year. However, a number of economic forecasters are predicting a significant chance—40 percent—of a recession in the next six months. If a recession occurs, you can expect to sell no more than half the number of yachts sold in the past. Should you order for a rising economy or scale back for a recession? A wrong decision means large losses (in an unexpected recession) or forgone profits (in an unexpected boom).

In this chapter, we focus on decisions involving risks—situations in which the consequences of any action the decision maker might take are uncertain because unforeseeable events may occur that will affect his or her final situation. To analyze this type of problem, the decision maker should begin by

1. Listing the available alternatives, not only for direct action but also for gathering information on which to base later action;

2. Listing the outcomes that can possibly occur (these will depend on chance events as well as on the decision maker's own actions);

3. Evaluating the chances that any uncertain outcome will occur; and

4. Deciding how well the decision maker likes each possible outcome.

As this list indicates, decision making under certainty and uncertainty share a number of common features. Whatever the setting, the manager should be aware of all available actions, determine the consequences of each action, and formulate a criterion for assessing each outcome. The introduction of uncertainty, however, requires additional analysis and judgment. First, the manager must be aware of these uncertain events and how they will affect the outcome of any action he or she chooses. Moreover, after accounting for these uncertainties, the manager must assess or estimate the likelihood of alternative outcomes. Second, in decisions under risk, the manager has a course of action that is missing in decisions under certainty: the option to acquire additional information about the risks before making the main decision. Third, the manager must carefully assess the firm's attitude toward risk, that is, formulate a criterion that determines which risks are acceptable. This criterion then can serve as a guide for choosing among risky alternatives.

In this chapter, we begin our study of decision making under uncertainty. First, we review the fundamentals of uncertainty, probability, and expected value. Then we examine the use of decision trees as a guide for managerial choices, especially in sequential decisions. Finally, we explore the effect of risk aversion on managerial decisions: how a manager can assess attitudes toward risk and apply the expected-utility criterion as a decision guide.

UNCERTAINTY, PROBABILITY, AND EXPECTED VALUE

Uncertainty lies at the heart of many important decisions. Managers are often uncertain about outcomes that have a direct bearing on the firm's profit. For example, introducing a new product entails a multitude of risks, including the cost and timetable of development, the volume of sales in the product's first and subsequent years, and competitors' possible reactions. The example that opens this chapter suggests that uncertainty concerning the future course of the macroeconomy—consumer and business spending, price inflation, and interest rate movements—is an important factor for many industries and firms.

Uncertainty (or *risk*) is present when there is more than one possible outcome for a decision.[1] Roughly speaking, the greater the dispersion of possible outcomes, the higher the degree of uncertainty. The key to sound decision making under uncertainty is to recognize the range of possible outcomes and

---

[1] Throughout the discussion, we use the terms *risk* and *uncertainty* interchangeably.

assess the likelihood of their occurrence. Uncertainty is acknowledged in expressions such as "it is likely," "the odds are," and "there is an outside chance." The difficulty with such qualitative expressions is that they are ambiguous and open to different interpretations. One is prompted to ask, "How likely is likely?" The essential means for quantifying statements of likelihood is to use *probabilities*. It is far more useful for a meteorologist to state that there is a 60 percent chance of rain tomorrow than to claim that rain is likely. Probability has been described as the mathematical language of uncertainty. The key is to have a sound understanding of what probabilities mean.

The **probability** of an outcome is the odds or chance that the outcome will occur. In the usual parlance, we speak of probabilities as ranging between 0 and 1. (An event having a probability of 1 is a certainty; an event having a probability of 0 is deemed impossible.) Whatever the probability, the relevant question is: What is the basis for this assessment? Frequently there is an *objective* foundation for the probability assessment. The chance of heads on a single toss of a fair coin is 50 percent, or one-half. In a random draw, the chance of picking the lone black ball from a hat containing five balls is one in five, and so on.

When viewed closely, the main basis for assessments such as these is the notion of a probability *as a long-run frequency*. If an uncertain event (like a coin toss or a random draw) is repeated a very large number of times, the frequency of the event is a measure of its true probability. For instance, if a fair coin is tossed 1,000 times, the frequency of heads (i.e., the number of heads divided by the total number of tosses) will be very close to .5. If the actual long-run frequency turned out to be .6, we would be justified in asserting that the coin was unfair. The frequency interpretation applies to most statistical data. For example, if annual employment in a state's mining industry totals 40,000 workers and 80 workers die in mining accidents each year, the annual probability of a representative mine worker dying on the job is 80/40,000 or .2 percent.

It should be evident that in many (and perhaps most) situations, there is no chance that a situation will be repeated and, therefore, no way to assess probabilities on frequency grounds. In development of a new product (one that is unique to the marketplace), a firm knows that the product launch is a one-shot situation. The firm may believe there is a 40 percent chance of success, but there is no way to validate this by launching the product 100 times and watching for 40 successes. Similarly, a company about to enter into patent litigation faces the problem of predicting the likely outcome of a one-time legal suit. Still another example is a business economist attempting to put odds on the likelihood of a new oil price "shock" (say, a 50 percent rise in oil prices) over the next 18 months.

In dealing with such situations, decision makers rely on a *subjective* notion of probability. According to the *subjective* view, the probability of an outcome represents the decision maker's degree of belief that the outcome will occur. This is exactly the meaning of a statement such as "The chance of a successful product launch is 60 percent." Of course, in making a probability assessment, the manager should attempt to analyze and interpret all pertinent evidence and information that might bear on the outcome in question.[2] For the new product, this would include consumer surveys, test market results, the product's unique qualities, its price relative to prices of competing products, and so on. The point is that a subjective probability is not arbitrary or ad hoc; it simply represents the decision maker's best assessment, based on current information, of the likelihood of an uncertain event. In this sense, all probabilities—even those based on frequencies or statistical data—represent the decision maker's degree of belief.

Expected Value

The manager typically begins the process of analyzing a decision under uncertainty by using a probability distribution. A **probability distribution** is a listing of the possible outcomes concerning an unknown event and their respective probabilities. As we saw earlier, assessing relevant probability distributions is the first step in the manager's analysis. For example, the manager might envision the probability distribution shown in the table for the first year's outcome of a new-product launch.

Outcome	Sales Revenue	Probability
Complete success	$10,000,000	.1
Promising	7,000,000	.3
Mixed response	3,000,000	.2
Failure	1,000,000	.4

This probability distribution provides the best available description of the uncertainty surrounding the market's reception of the product. Note the considerable range of outcomes and the high likelihood of failure. (Revenue of $1 million is not enough to justify continuing the product.) Failure is the norm for even the most promising new products.

---

[2] Any probability forecast is based on the decision maker's currently available information. Consequently, if this information changes, so will the probability assessment. Thus, a disappointing market test would lead management to lower its probability assessment of product success. The point is that probability assessments are not engraved in stone; rather, they are constantly being revised in light of new information. In addition, various "experts" often hold different subjective probability assessments about an event based on different information or different interpretations of common information. (In contrast, the objective probability of "heads" in a single coin toss is immutable; that is, it is always one-half. Assuming there is no doubt about the fairness of the coin, this probability will not change with new information, nor will it be subject to dispute.) We take up the subjects of information acquisition and probability revision in Chapter 9.

From the probability distribution, we can compute the expected value of the uncertain variable in question. In the preceding example, expected revenue is $(.1)(\$10) + (.3)(\$7) + (.2)(\$3) + (.4)(\$1) = \$4.1$ million.

More generally, suppose the decision maker faces a risky prospect that has n possible monetary outcomes, $v_1, v_2, \ldots, v_n$, predicted to occur with probabilities $p_1, p_2, \ldots, p_n$. Then the expected monetary value of the risky prospect is

$$E(v) = p_1v_1 + p_2v_2 + \ldots + p_nv_n.$$

In the preceding numerical example, we have applied exactly this formula with respect to the four possible outcomes.

DECISION TREES

The **decision tree** is a convenient way to represent decisions, chance events, and possible outcomes in choices under risk and uncertainty. In fact, this simple diagram can incorporate all the information needed to "solve" the decision problem once the specific objectives of the decision maker have been established. The method is extremely versatile. When first encountered, choices under risk appear messy, ill defined, and puzzling. The actual choices, the potential risks, and the appropriate objective to pursue may all be far from clear. The individual should not be blamed for regarding his or her choice as "a riddle wrapped in a mystery inside an enigma," to borrow a phrase from Winston Churchill. However, sketching a crude decision tree almost always will clarify the options. The very structure of the tree emphasizes the ingredients (choices, outcomes, and probabilities) necessary for making an informed decision. The more precise the tree becomes (after drawing and redrawing), the more precise one's thinking becomes about the problem. The "finished" tree can then be evaluated to "solve" the decision problem. Probably more important, the decision tree provides a visual explanation for the recommended choice. One easily can pinpoint the "why" of the decision: which circumstances or risks weighed in favor of which course of action. And one can undertake any number of sensitivity analyses, altering the facts of the decision to determine the impact on the recommended course of action.

Decision trees can be simple or complex, spare or "bushy," small enough to evaluate by hand or large enough to require a computer. To illustrate the method, we start with a concise example.

An Oil Drilling Problem

An oil wildcatter must decide whether to drill at a given site before his option period expires. The cost of drilling is $200,000. This sum will be completely lost if the site is "dry," that is, contains no oil. The wildcatter estimates that, if he strikes oil, the total profit (before drilling costs) over the well's life will be $800,000. Thus, if there is a strike, the wildcatter will earn a $600,000 profit.

Figure 8.1 shows the decision tree for the wildcatter's problem. The tree depicts the sequence of events in the decision, reading from left to right. The problem starts with a point of decision, by convention represented by a square, from which emanate two branches: the decisions to drill or not to drill. If the choice is not to drill, the story ends there. The final profit outcome is $0, as indicated at the tip of the branch. If the choice is to drill, a chance event represented by a circle occurs. The chance event summarizes the risk associated with drilling. The two possible outcomes, a strike or a dry well, are shown on the branches emanating from the circular chance node. The respective monetary outcomes, $600,000 and −$200,000, are listed next to the branch tips.

We need one final piece of information to complete the description of the decision problem. This is the probability, in the wildcatter's best judgment, that the site will have oil. Suppose this probability is .4 (or a 40 percent chance). This is listed on the chance branch corresponding to "wet." Obviously, the probability of dry must be .6, because wet and dry sites are the only two outcomes. For the moment, let us suppose the wildcatter's probability assessment is based on a completed geological survey of the site, his judgment of how this site compares with other sites (with and without oil) that he has drilled in the past, and any other pertinent information. (In Chapter 9, we will say much more about interpreting, estimating, and revising probability projections of uncertain outcomes.)

All that remains is to specify a criterion by which the decision maker can choose a course of action under uncertainty. The criterion we employ at the outset of this chapter is expected value.

> The **expected-value criterion** instructs the manager to choose the course of action that generates the greatest expected profit.

FIGURE 8.1

The Wildcatter's Drilling Problem

By drilling, the wildcatter earns an expected profit of $120,000.

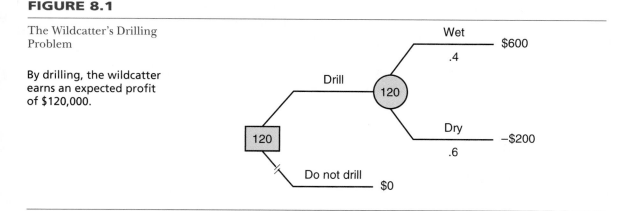

Let's apply the expected-value criterion to determine the wildcatter's best course of action. The "do not drill" option results in a certain outcome of $0. The expected profit from the "drill" option is

$$(.4)(600,000) + (.6)(-200,000) = 120,000.$$

Note that this expected profit is a weighted average of the possible outcomes, the weight for each outcome being its probability. The greater an outcome's probability, the more weight it has in determining the overall expected profit (i.e., the expected profit moves closer to it). For instance, if the strike chances were .5, the expected value would be a straight average of the possible profit and loss, or $200,000. Better strike odds produce a higher expected profit.

In Figure 8.1, the expected profit of $120,000 has been recorded at the chance node of the tree. This indicates that, before the chance event has been resolved (i.e., before the true outcome, oil or no oil, has been revealed), the expected value of the risky drilling prospect is $120,000. According to the expected-value criterion, the wildcatter's optimal decision is to drill. The double slashes through the decision tree's "do not drill" branch show that this choice has been ruled out.

A firm supplies aircraft engines to the government and to private firms. It must decide between two mutually exclusive contracts. If it contracts with a private firm, its profit will be $2 million, $.7 million, or −$.5 million with probabilities .25, .41, and .34, respectively. If it contracts with the government, its profit will be $4 million or −$2.5 million with respective probabilities .45 and .55. Which contract offers the greater expected profit?

CHECK STATION 1

GOOD AND BAD DECISIONS AND OUTCOMES   Suppose the wildcatter follows the expected-value criterion and drills the site. Unfortunately, the site turns out to be dry. The resulting $200,000 loss is a *bad outcome*. But this does not mean that the choice to drill the site was a *bad decision*. Given what the wildcatter knew then, the risk was worth taking. Roughly speaking, the chance of a very large profit outweighed the chance of a smaller (although sizable) loss. Drilling was a good decision that happened (unluckily) to end in a bad outcome. Alternatively, suppose the wildcatter chooses to drill a second site instead of the first. At the second site, the outcomes are $550,000 and −$220,000, with probabilities .3 and .7, respectively. The expected profit of the second site, $11,000, is barely positive. Upon drilling the second site, the wildcatter strikes oil. Certainly this is a good outcome. But even a lucky outcome cannot turn this into a good decision. In fact, the second site offers uniformly worse outcomes and worse odds than the first. Accordingly, it never should be chosen over the first site. (If the wildcatter has sufficient resources, both sites might be drilled profitably.)

The point is that a good decision must be judged on the basis of the information available before the fact, that is, at the time the choice must be made. Of course, hindsight is 20-20, but this is of no value to the manager. Moreover, 20-20 hindsight is misleading when it comes to evaluating past decisions. A bad outcome does not brand the decision as bad, nor does a good outcome mark a decision as good. What matters are the chances of the foreseeable good and bad outcomes at the point of decision. No matter how basic this point, it is surprising how often it is forgotten by decision makers in business and government. Perhaps the greatest virtue of using decision trees in evaluating and comparing risks is that it reminds us of the difference between good decisions and good outcomes.

Features of the Expected-Value Criterion

The depiction of the risk in Figure 8.1 hardly could be simpler. Thus, it comes as no surprise that the expected-value calculation is automatic, indeed, almost trivial. Nonetheless, it is important to recognize the general properties of this criterion that apply equally well to simple and complex risks.

The first (and most basic) feature of the expected-value standard is that it values a risky prospect by accounting not only for the set of possible outcomes but also for the probabilities of those outcomes. For instance, suppose the wildcatter must decide whether to drill on one site or another. (There are insufficient resources to drill on both.) The first site's possible profit outcomes are $800,000, $600,000, $160,000, −$60,000, and −$200,000; these outcomes occur with probabilities .05, .15, .2, .25, and .35, respectively. Consequently, the expected profit from drilling this site is (.05)(800) + (.15)(600) + (.2)(160) + (.25)(260) + (.35)(−200), or $77,000. The second site has the same five possible outcomes as the first but with probabilities .05, .2, .25, .2, and .3. Notice that the second site offers higher probabilities of "good" outcomes than the first site. Clearly, then, the second site should have a higher value than the first. The expected-value standard satisfies this commonsense requirement. Performing the appropriate computation will show that the second site's expected profit is $128,000, a significantly higher figure than the expected profit of the first site.

Second, the expected value of a risky prospect represents the average monetary outcome if it were repeated indefinitely (with each repeated outcome generated independently of the others). In this statistical sense, the expected-value standard is appropriate for playing the long-run averages. Indeed, many managers employ the expected-value criterion when it comes to often-repeated, routine decisions involving (individually) small risks. For instance, suppose you have the chance to bet on each of 100 tosses of a coin. You win a dime on each head and lose a nickel on each tail. This, you'll no doubt agree, is the epitome of a routine, often-repeated, low-risk decision. Here the expected-value criterion instructs you to bet on each toss. If you choose this profitable (albeit somewhat boring) course of action, your expected gain in the 100 tosses is $2.50. Your actual profit will vary in the neighborhood of $2.50, perhaps coming out a little above, perhaps a little below. The statistical "law of large numbers" applied to the independent tosses ensures that there is no real risk associated with the bet.

Third, in decisions involving multiple and related risks, the expected-value criterion allows the decision maker to compute expected values *in stages.* Figure 8.2 makes this point by presenting a "bushier" (and more realistic) tree for the wildcatter's drilling decision. The tree incorporates three risks affecting drilling profits: the cost of drilling and recovery, the amount of oil discovered, and the price of oil per barrel. As the tree depicts, the cost of drilling and recovery is the first uncertainty to be resolved and depends on the depth at which oil is found (or not found). In the wildcatter's judgment, oil may be struck at one of two depths or not at all. Thus, the tree depicts three branches emanating from the initial chance node. As an example, let's consider the second branch: oil found at 5,000 feet. This branch ends in a chance node from which three new branches emerge. These branches show the possible amounts of oil (barrels per year) that might be recovered; the third branch, for instance, has a total recovery of 16,000 barrels. Finally, each recovery branch ends in a chance node from which three new branches sprout. These indicate the possible different values of average oil prices over the life of the well. For example, the third branch lists a $15-per-barrel price. At the end of this branch, the last uncertainty is resolved and the wildcatter's profit, in this case $180,000, is finally determined. (Simply take the profit figures at face value. We have not supplied the revenues and costs on which they are based.)

The path from the leftmost chance node to the $180,000 profit outcome indicates one particular scenario that might occur: finding a 16,000-barrel oil field at 5,000 feet and selling it at a two-year average price of $15 per barrel. However, this outcome is but one of many possible outcomes contingent on the resolution of the multiple risks. In all there are $(2)(3)(3) + 1 = 19$ possible profit outcomes, one for each branch tip. The combination of multiple risks, each with multiple outcomes, means that the corresponding decision tree will be bushy indeed.

The bushy tree also requires a lengthier process of probability assessment because the wildcatter must evaluate probabilities for three distinct risks. The first three branches of the tree show his chances of striking (or not striking) oil at different depths. If he finds some oil at a given depth, the next question is how much. The secondary branches of the tree list the chances of finding different oil quantities. Note that the likelihood of different recovery amounts depends on the depth at which oil is first found, and the likelihood of very large deposits is better at 3,000 feet than at 5,000 feet. (Remember that these recovery probabilities are conditional on some oil being found at all. Shallow fields are likely to be large fields, but the chance of finding oil at 3,000 feet is only .13 in the first place.) Finally, once the recovery quantity is ascertained, the sole remaining uncertainty concerns the market price of oil. The chances listed on the third-level branches have been obtained from an expert's prediction of future prices. Note that the chances of different market prices per barrel are

FIGURE 8.2

A More Complicated
Drilling Decision

This decision tree contains
multiple risks that generate
19 possible outcomes.

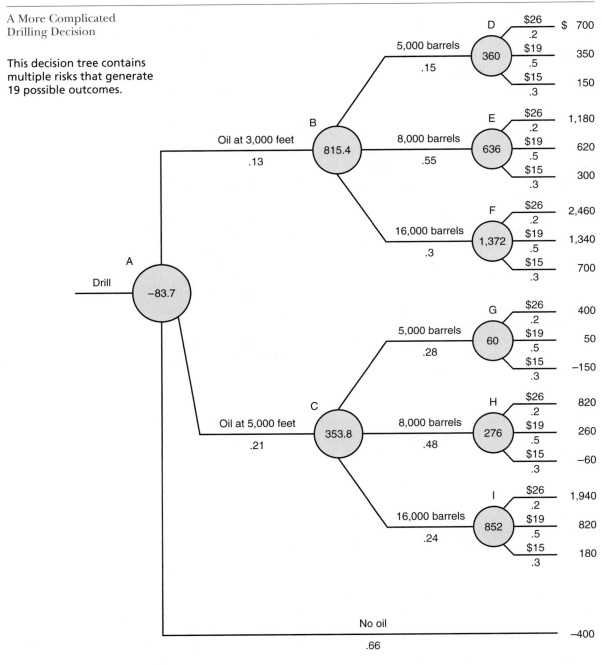

independent of the quantity of oil recovered (i.e., the chances are the same regardless of the recovery amount).

What is the wildcatter's expected value from drilling in the face of these multiple risks? To answer this question, we calculate the expected value in stages by "averaging back" the tree, starting at the branch tips and working to the left. To illustrate, consider the chance node D on the tree: a 5,000-barrel-per-year oil reserve at a depth of 3,000 feet. The three branches list the profit outcomes for this field depending on the (uncertain) oil price. The expected profit from such a field is simply the average of the possible profit outcomes weighted by the respective probabilities. Thus, the expected profit is (.2)(700) + (.5)(350) + (.3)(150) = $360 thousand, listed in chance node D. But what if the field had yielded 8,000 barrels per year? By an analogous calculation, we find the expected profit to be $636 thousand in this case, as shown in chance node E. The expected profits for the chance nodes F through I (corresponding to different-sized fields at different depths) have also been computed and listed on the tree. At this point, we have "averaged out" the price uncertainty.

In the next step, we average over the possible quantities of oil found. Chance node B shows the expected profit if oil is found at 3,000 feet, computed by averaging the expected profits at nodes D through F:

$$(.15)(360) + (.55)(636) + (.3)(1,372) = 815.4 \text{ thousand.}$$

Node C lists the expected profit ($353.8 thousand) for a field found at 5,000 feet.

The last step is to compute the overall expected profit of drilling. This is shown in the initial chance node A and is the average of the expected profits at B and C and the $400 thousand loss if no oil is found. As always, this expected value is computed using the branch probabilities as weights. Therefore, the expected profit from drilling is

$$(.13)(815.4) + (.21)(353.8) + (.66)(-400) = -\$83.7 \text{ thousand.}$$

The wildcatter has solved his decision problem by calculating the expected profit of drilling in stages. Since this is negative, the wildcatter should choose not to exercise his option on the site.

CHECK STATION 2

Suppose the chief executive of an oil company must decide whether to drill a site and, if so, how deep. It costs $160,000 to drill the first 3,000 feet, and there is a .4 chance of striking oil. If oil is struck, the profit (net of drilling expenses) is $600,000. If oil is not struck, the executive can drill 2,000 feet deeper at an additional cost of $90,000. The chance of finding oil between 3,000 and 5,000 feet is .2, and the net profit (after all drilling costs) from a strike at this depth is $400,000. What action should the executive take to maximize expected profit?

The Perils of International Business

For the last 30 years, globalization of business has been an enduring trend. Consumers in all parts of the world buy an increasing proportion of foreign goods, and a growing number of firms operate across national boundaries.

The prospects of rapid growth and high profits from untapped foreign markets are attractive to large firms. Telecommunication companies vie for shares of the Chinese market, expecting to quintuple the number of phone lines from 5 per hundred people to 25 (still only about one-third of the U.S. average). Ford has invested $6 billion in developing a "world" car to be marketed and sold all over the globe. Procter & Gamble and Kimberly-Clark compete for the disposable diaper market in Brazil. A parade of U.S. mutual-fund companies is rushing to Europe, Japan, and Australia in pursuit of those nations' retirement savings.

However, if opportunity is one side of the international business coin, the other side is risk. Leveraging successes enjoyed in local markets to far-flung foreign operations is far from certain. These risks come in many categories.

ECONOMIC CONDITIONS   The 1990s' recession in Europe and the late 1990s' financial crisis in Southeast Asia caused dramatic falls in business and consumer spending. Global firms with sales concentrated in these regions saw profits evaporate and losses mount.

UNCERTAIN COSTS   Because of low-skilled workforces, lack of capital, and primitive distribution systems, the cost of doing business in developing countries (especially China, India, Africa, and South America) is frequently high and uncertain. Foreign firms assembling electronics goods in Russia have been plagued by low worker productivity, vandalism, and crime.

DIFFERENT CULTURES   Brazilians spend a higher percentage of income on their children than do citizens of neighboring countries. They are eager for disposable diapers. Argentines are largely indifferent. Consumers in Southeast Asia are accustomed to buying light meals from street vendors, not from fast-food restaurants. To cite an extreme case of cultural miscalculation, General Motors introduced its popular Nova car model into South America. Only after disastrous sales did the company realize that *no va* means "does not go" in Spanish.

POLITICAL RISK   Tax and regulatory burdens, government bureaucracy and even corruption, and changing political parties and governments all contribute to the risk of doing business abroad. Over the past 40 years, international businesses have been decimated by unrest and civil war in places such as Cuba, Lebanon, El Salvador, Vietnam, and the Balkans. Today, outright expropriation is much less frequent but remains a risk.

EXCHANGE-RATE RISK   A firm that earns a significant part of its revenues abroad is subject to exchange-rate risk when converting these to its home currency. For instance, a depreciating Japanese yen means lower dollar profits from revenues earned in Japan. Similarly, the costs incurred by a foreign subsidiary are subject to exchange-rate risk. Thus, the depreciating currencies of Southeast Asia (by lowering the dollar-equivalent costs) make production in that part of the world more attractive to global firms.

Even the most experienced international firms face unforeseen risks and suffer missteps in foreign markets. Despite its marketing muscle and well-tested formula for operating stores, McDonald's has gained little market share in South Africa and the Philippines. Instead, it has been humbled by well-established local competitors catering to local tastes. In 1977, Coca-Cola was the leading soft drink in India before the company pulled up stakes refusing to divulge its secret formula to the Indian government. Returning in 1993, the company found itself a distant second to Thums Up, an imitation cola in a similar glass bottle, that won the allegiance of Indian consumers in Coke's absence. Admitting that its tried and true business formula was the wrong one for India, Coca-Cola's management purchased Thums Up and now aggressively markets that drink alongside "The Real Thing."

The lesson to take from these companies' experience is that international businesses, if they are to be successful, must be especially vigilant in identifying myriad risks and capturing them in carefully conceived, bushy decision trees.

SEQUENTIAL DECISIONS

Some of the most interesting and important business and economic problems call for a sequence of decisions to be made over time. For example, suppose a chemical firm is considering a large capital investment in a new petrochemical facility. The profitability of such an investment depends on numerous uncertain factors: future market demand, reactions of close competitors, and so on. Profits also depend on the future product and pricing decisions of the firm itself. It is not simply that the firm faces many decisions over time; the more important point is that the sequence of decisions is interdependent. A correct investment decision today presupposes that the company will make optimal (i.e., profit-maximizing) pricing decisions tomorrow if the plant is built. The following example illustrates this general point about sequential decisions.

In Chapter 1, we sketched a decision problem facing a pharmaceutical firm that must choose between two research and development approaches. Suppose the profits and probabilities of the competing methods are summarized in the table:

An R&D Decision Revisited

R&D Choice	Investment	Outcomes	Profit (Excluding R&D)	Probability
Biochemical	$10 million	Large success	$90 million	.7
		Small success	50 million	.3
Biogenetic	$20 million	Success	$200 million	.2
		Failure	0 million	.8

All profit figures are expressed in terms of present discounted values and, thus, are directly comparable to investment figures.

We observe that the biogenetic (G) approach requires a greater initial investment and is significantly riskier than the biochemical (C) alternative. In the worst case, the firm will write off the R&D effort, earning no commercial profit and, therefore, losing its $20 million investment. The biochemical approach is also uncertain but far less risky. A commercially viable drug is guaranteed. Even in its worst case, the firm makes a $40 million net profit. Straightforward calculations show that

$$E(\pi_C) = (.7)(90) + (.3)(50) - 10 = \$68 \text{ million,}$$

whereas

$$E(\pi_G) = (.2)(200) - 20 = \$20 \text{ million,}$$

where $E(\pi)$ denotes expected profit. Of the two methods, the company should pursue the biochemical approach.

However, the firm's decision analysis should not end here. It has a considerably wider range of options than first appears. Resources permitting, the firm might do well to hedge its bet by pursuing *both* R&D programs simultaneously. Depending on the results, the firm can decide which method to commercialize.

The decision tree in Figure 8.3 depicts the simultaneous R&D option. The tree lists four distinct possible R&D outcomes: one, both, or neither effort may

FIGURE 8.3

Simultaneous R&D
Investments

By investing in both
R&D methods,
the company earns
an expected profit
of $72.4 million.

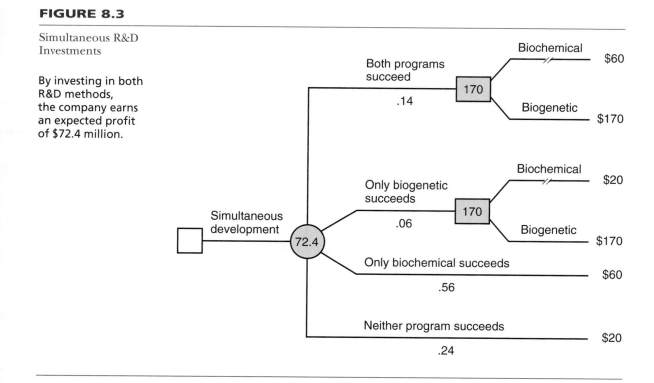

be successful. The probability of each joint outcome is the product of the probabilities of the individual outcomes because these risks are assumed to be independent. Thus, the chance that both methods will succeed is $(.7)(.2) = .14$, and so on. Note that the probabilities of the four possible outcomes sum to 1, as they must.

When the results of both R&D programs are in, the firm must decide which method to commercialize. If the biogenetic research effort fails (the lower two branches), the firm has no choice; it must go the biochemical route. If the biogenetic research is successful, the firm should commercialize this method because it offers the greater profit. (Note that the firm will produce the drug with only a *single* method—whichever is more profitable.) Thus, in the upper two branches, the drug is produced biogenetically. The profit is $200 million minus $30 million (the total investment in both methods), or $170 million. The other profit outcomes are computed in analogous fashion.

What is the firm's expected profit at the start of the simultaneous R&D effort? Multiplying the possible monetary outcomes by their respective probabilities, we compute this to be

$$(.14)(70) + (.06)(70) + (.56)(60) + (.24)(20) = \$72.4 \text{ million.}$$

Simultaneous development offers a larger expected profit than the next-best alternative, pursuing the biochemical approach exclusively. By undertaking both, the firm enjoys the security of biochemical's "sure thing" profits while still testing the biogenetic waters—a long shot that could provide a huge profit. Even in the likely event that the biogenetic option fails, the firm makes a profit. The decision tree instructs us that pursuing both approaches simultaneously increases the firm's expected profit by $72.4 - 68 = \$4.4$ million vis-à-vis pursuing the biochemical method alone.

However, the firm has not yet exhausted its options. Now it considers pursuing the R&D methods *sequentially*: one first, then (if necessary) the other. (We presume that stretching out the time devoted to sequential development is feasible and carries no significant cost to the firm. In other words, the firm is not racing to beat a rival to market.) The sequential development option raises an obvious question: Which method should it try first?

The decision tree in Figure 8.4 depicts the sequential strategy: biochemical R&D first, then biogenetic R&D. After the outcome of the first R&D effort is known, the firm can choose to commercialize it or invest in the second program. (If the biogenetic program is subsequently pursued and fails, the firm goes back and completes development of the biochemical approach.) The top square shows the firm's decision in the event the biochemical program is successful. Contrary to one's intuition, the firm should *not* proceed to immediate development; rather, its best course of action is to invest in the second R&D program, see the result, and, if it fails, fall back on the biochemical approach. The resulting expected profit from making this

FIGURE 8.4

Sequential R&D:
Biochemical First

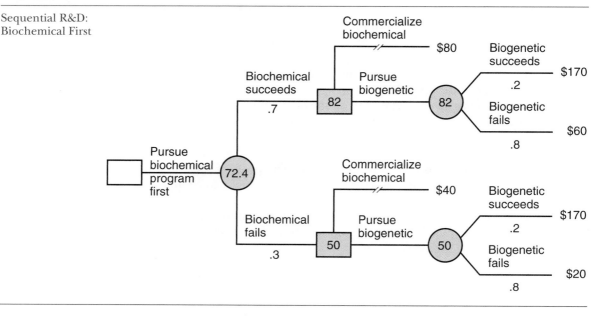

second R&D investment is $82 million—$2 million better than from immediately commercializing a biochemically based drug. What if the biochemical program is less successful? The lower decision square provides the answer. As we might expect, the firm's best action is to invest in the second R&D program; the expected profit of $50 million is $10 million greater than the alternative. Thus, regardless of the outcome of the biochemical program, the biogenetic program also should be pursued.

The drug company's overall expected profit at the outset, that is, at the tree's initial chance node is $(.7)(82) + (.3)(50) = \$72.4$ million. The expected profit from this sequential strategy is exactly the same as under simultaneous development. This result may seem surprising until we note that the two strategies call for the company to take exactly the same actions. Even under sequential development, the company's best strategy is to pursue both R&D methods, just as under simultaneous development. Despite the apparent differences in the decision trees, the strategies must have the same expected profit because they call for the same actions in all cases. Thus, this sequential strategy offers no advantage over committing to simultaneous development in the first place.

In contrast, the reverse sequential strategy—pursue the biogenetic program first, then the biochemical program if necessary—is advantageous.

FIGURE 8.5

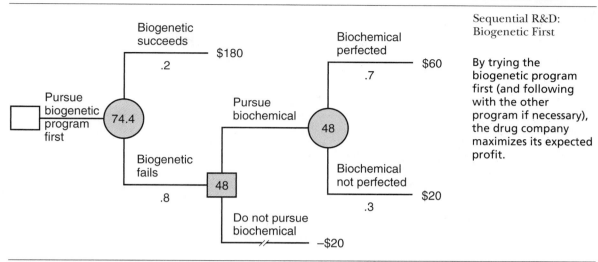

Sequential R&D:
Biogenetic First

By trying the
biogenetic program
first (and following
with the other
program if necessary),
the drug company
maximizes its expected
profit.

Figure 8.5 depicts this strategy. The tree shows that if the biogenetic program is successful, it should be commercialized (for an expected profit of $180 million). Otherwise, the biochemical program should be pursued and brought to market (for an expected profit of $48 million). To calculate the firm's expected profit when it first embarks on this sequential program, we average these two results. Thus, the overall expected profit is $(.2)(180) + (.8)(48) = \$74.4$ million. This sequential strategy provides $2 million more profit on average than the next-best alternative.

How do we account for the superiority of first pursuing the biogenetic method? To answer this question, let's compare the actions under the sequential and simultaneous programs. The actions are the same in each case, except when the biogenetic program achieves immediate success. Here the company need not pursue the biochemical program and so saves the $10 million investment—a sum it would have spent under simultaneous development. This saving occurs 20 percent of the time (when the biogenetic program is successful). Therefore, the company's expected savings from sequential development (relative to simultaneous development) is $(.2)(10) = \$2$ million. This accounts for the expected profit difference, $74.4 - 72.4$, between the two strategies. By postponing pursuit of the biochemical method, the firm is able to profit from the information concerning the success or failure of the risky biogenetic approach. The condensed decision tree in Figure 8.6 summarizes the expected profits for all of the company's possible actions.

FIGURE 8.6

Summary of
Pharmaceutical
Company's R&D
Options

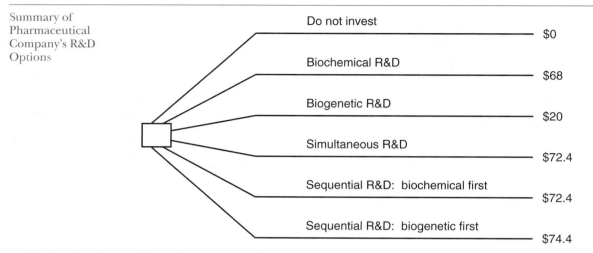

Do not invest	$0
Biochemical R&D	$68
Biogenetic R&D	$20
Simultaneous R&D	$72.4
Sequential R&D: biochemical first	$72.4
Sequential R&D: biogenetic first	$74.4

CHECK STATION 3   Firm A is deliberating whether to launch a new product. If firm B (its main competitor) does not bring out its own product (a 40 percent probability), firm A expects to earn $20 million over the product's life. If firm B introduces its own product, there is a 50 percent chance that the market will view it as superior to A's, in which case firm A will lose $30 million on the launch. If A's product is superior, its profit will be $10 million. Presuming its goal is to maximize expected profit, should firm A launch the product?

Risking a New York Blackout

On a July evening in 1977, separate lightning strikes hit two electrical transmission towers carrying power to New York City. It was clear that the city's electricity demand that evening, even with emergency generating capacity, would require the remaining transmission lines to carry power in excess of their short-term emergency rating. This presented a terrible dilemma to the systems operator in the control center of the Consolidated Edison Company of New York. If the demand–supply imbalance was not corrected quickly, the overload would cause the circuit breakers on the remaining lines to open, causing a citywide blackout. (After the 1965 blackout of much of the Northeast, circuit breakers were redesigned to open automatically so as to isolate transmission trouble spots.)

The operator's available information about the severity of the disaster was incomplete at best. He could communicate by phone with a limited number of controllers and operators in the system. Most important, the operator had only 15 to 25 minutes to take action! Careful consideration, extensive analysis, and exhaustive deliberation were out of the question. He could not follow "normal operating procedure" or turn to a page of instructions in an emergency operating manual. What should he have done?

One option was to do nothing, relying on the system to weather the imbalance. (Perhaps the city's demand for power would decline over the course of the evening.) Another option was to try to get more power generated within New York City. Should he have ordered circuit breakers on the damaged lines to be manually closed to restore limited transmission capacity? Unfortunately, there was a common difficulty with all of these alternatives. Even if the operator ordered the given measure immediately, he would not know whether it would be successful until after the fact.

The operator had another (albeit more drastic) alternative. In all likelihood, he could solve the demand–supply imbalance by "shedding load," that is, deliberately blacking out a portion of the city. Was this his best option? If so, how much load should he shed: enough (70 percent) to ensure against a complete disaster or a minimum amount (25 percent)? If you were in the operator's place, what kind of decision analysis would you undertake in 20 minutes? In his place, what would you have done?[3]

RISK AVERSION

Thus far, we have used the concept of expected monetary value as a guide to making decisions under uncertainty. A decision maker who follows the expected-profit criterion is said to be **risk neutral**. This standard is appropriate for a manager who is willing to play the averages. The evidence suggests, however, that individuals and firms are not neutral toward risks that are large relative to their financial resources. When it comes to significant risks, individuals and institutions adopt an attitude that is conservative toward losses. Thus, the use of the expected-profit criterion must be qualified.

A COIN GAMBLE   You are offered the following choice: You can receive $60 for certain (the money is yours to keep), or you can accept the following gamble. A fair coin is tossed. If heads come up, you win $400; if tails come up, you lose $200. Would you choose the sure $60 or accept the gamble on the coin toss? (In answering, imagine that real money—your own money—is at stake.)

When given this choice, the majority of individuals prefer the sure $60 to the gamble. This is not surprising given the magnitude of the risk associated with the coin toss. Notice, however, that choosing $60 is at odds with maximizing expected profit. The expected profit of the coin toss is $(.5)(400) + (.5)(-200) = \$100$. Thus, a risk-neutral decision maker would prefer the gamble to the sure $60. Refusing the bet shows that you are not risk neutral when it comes to profits and losses of this magnitude.

A precise way to express one's evaluation of the coin toss (or any risky prospect) is to name a certainty equivalent. The **certainty equivalent (CE)** is the

---

[3]This account is based on Robert Behn, "The Shed Load Decision," *Management Case* (Duke University, 1983) and "Con Ed Control Had Fifteen Minutes to Pull Switch," *The New York Times,* July 18, 1977. A summary of Con Ed's actions and their results follows the Check Station Answers at the end of the chapter.

amount of money for certain that makes the individual exactly indifferent to the risky prospect. Suppose that, after some thought, you determine you would be indifferent to the options of receiving $25 for certain or facing the risk of the coin toss. You are saying that your CE for the coin toss is $25. This CE is significantly smaller than the expected value of the bet, $100. This being the case, we would say that you are risk averse. An individual is **risk averse** if his or her certainty equivalent for a given risky prospect is less than its expected value.

Loosely speaking, the magnitude of one's aversion to risk is indicated by the shortfall of the CE below the expected value of the risky prospect; this difference (sometimes referred to as a *discount for risk*) measures the reduction in value (below expected value) due to a prospect's riskiness. Here the risk discount is 100 − 25 = $75. The discount depends on individual preferences as well as on the size of the risk. For instance, a second individual might prefer to avoid the coin toss altogether; that is, in a choice between the coin toss and receiving $0 for certain, this individual prefers $0. This preference makes good sense for someone who does not wish to bear the downside risk of the coin toss. Suppose this individual is indifferent to the options of *paying* $20 for certain or taking the coin toss. (He or she is willing to pay $20 to avoid the risk of the gamble.) Here the CE is −$20, and the risk discount is $100 − (−20) = $120. Clearly, the second decision maker is more risk averse than the first.

THE DEMAND FOR INSURANCE   Risk aversion provides a ready explanation concerning the demand for insurance. Insurance companies stand ready to compensate their policyholders in the event of losses (specified in the insurance contract) at a price in the form of the premium paid by the customer to the company. Risk-averse individuals are willing to give up monetary income to avoid risks. In effect, this is what they do when they purchase insurance.

To make the argument concrete, consider a couple who is about to purchase fire insurance to protect their home (which is valued at $150,000). The risk of a fire destroying their house is very small—about 1 in 300 in any given year. Nevertheless, the loss of their house would mean financial ruin. Thus, the couple finds it prudent to purchase insurance. In return for payment of a $500 annual premium, a 100 percent fire policy promises to pay whatever amount is necessary to rebuild and replace the house in the event of fire. In purely financial terms, the couple faces the following options. If they do not buy the policy, their wealth at the end of the year will be $150,000 if there is no fire or $0 if a fire occurs (a 1-in-300 chance). Their expected wealth is $149,500. (Check this.) By purchasing the policy, their net wealth is $150,000 − $500 = $149,500 at the end of the year. Their wealth is certain. Regardless of whether a fire occurs, they will have their house (or the money to rebuild it). Notice that whether or not they purchase insurance, the couple's expected wealth is the same, $149,500. Because they are risk averse, the couple prefers the certain $149,500 provided by insurance to the alternative of bearing the risk of fire. Thus, they purchase full insurance.

In this example, the company has offered the couple "actuarially fair" insurance; that is, the couple's premium ($500) just covers the company's expected payout under the policy: $(1/300)(\$150,000) = \$500$. Because of their large size and ability to pool different risks, insurance companies generally behave as though they are risk neutral. To illustrate, suppose the company insures 300,000 houses in a state against fire. Although it is impossible to predict which houses will be struck by fire, the law of large numbers indicates that very close to 1,000 homes in total will have fire losses. Thus, the total premiums ($150 million) will closely match the company's actual payout. Because of administrative costs in writing the policies, insurance companies typically charge premiums that exceed their expected losses. (Of course, competition among insurance companies limits the premiums any one company can charge.) But higher premiums do not eliminate (although they may reduce) the demand for insurance. Even if the fire insurance premium were $1,000 per year, the risk-averse couple might leap at the chance to buy coverage rather than go unprotected.[4]

| | Risk Management at Microsoft |

"Microsoft sees risk everywhere, in a dozen broad categories: financial, reputational, technological, competitive, customer, people (employees and contractors), operations, distributions, business partners, regulatory and legislative, political and strategic."[5] This might seem an unusual statement. After all, what could be more secure than the company's near-monopoly position in PC operating systems?

Yet, Microsoft's risk managers see things quite differently. Their job is to identify, quantify, and manage literally hundreds of risks, of which 20 to 30 may be most important at a given time. Of particular importance are regulatory risks (government antitrust actions) and uncertainties surrounding intellectual property rights. In the longer term, the emergence of new software markets and Microsoft's ability to influence or control the accompanying standards and platforms are crucial. Once managers have identified key risks, they can address the best way to manage them: by insurance, by a shared-risk joint venture, by diversification, or (in the extreme case) by ceasing the risky activity all together.

Risk management is becoming a pervasive part of big business. When faced with enormous uncertainties, management's stance is decidedly not risk neutral. Invariably, it is risk averse. Beyond the expected monetary returns associated with the separate risks on its radar screen, management must be

---

[4] The general rule is that a risk-averse individual always will insure fully against a risk if offered actuarially fair insurance. At higher premiums, a range of outcomes is possible: full insurance, partial insurance, or no insurance. A popular type of partial insurance involves provision for deductibles. With a deductible, the company pays only for the portion of losses above a specified monetary threshold. Thus, the policyholder buys insurance (at a reduced premium) for large losses but self-insures for small ones.

[5] This quotation and the synopsis in the text is drawn from E. Teach, "Microsoft's Universe of Risk," *CFO Magazine* (March 1997): 69–72.

concerned about its combined risk exposures. As noted earlier, it is wise to diversify by pursuing multiple risky R&D initiatives, instead of putting all the eggs in one basket. Firms operating in "dirty" industries must continuously assess the risks posed by changing environmental regulations. In the wake of the monumental losses associated with Hurricane Katrina, disaster insurers have been taking a microscope to their risk portfolios. Using computer models, they sift through decades of data on storm patterns and earthquakes to estimate risk probabilities. While looking out for excessive geographic concentration of insurance coverage, the insurers are also reassessing shoreline properties, scrutinizing building codes, raising premiums, dropping policies, reinsuring portions of their risks, and even selling "catastrophic" (CAT) bonds to investors. (With CAT bonds, an investor obtains a high interest return in "normal" circumstances but loses a portion, or all, of the principal if yearly hurricane damage claims exceed specified thresholds.)

An important insight offered by risk management is that many risks are interdependent. Decisions made in one area create (or mitigate) risks in another. Alerted to the risks of mass tort litigation for repetitive stress injury, Microsoft incorporated this cost ($2.82 per unit) when setting the licensing fee for its new innovative keyboards, thereby providing a prudent monetary reserve for this risk.

Expected Utility

How can a manager formulate a criterion, reflecting the firm's attitude toward risk, to guide his or her decisions? The formal answer to this question developed some 60 years ago by mathematical economists John Von Neumann and Oscar Morgenstern is called the expected-utility rule. (At the same time, Von Neumann and Morgenstern developed the field of game theory, which we will encounter in Chapter 13.)

The use of expected utility proceeds in two steps. First, the decision maker must think carefully about the firm's preferences concerning risks: what risks it is willing to accept and how to value those risks. In the process, the manager constructs a utility scale that describes this risk tolerance. Second, the manager analyzes the decision problem in much the same way as before, that is, constructs a decision tree showing relevant probabilities and possible monetary outcomes and then evaluates the tree. However, there is one crucial difference: In contrast to the risk-neutral manager, who averages *monetary values* at each step, the risk-averse decision maker averages the *utilities* associated with monetary values. At each point of decision, the manager selects the alternative that supplies the maximum expected utility. With this summary in hand, let's see exactly how the method works.

A RISK-AVERSE WILDCATTER   Once again, let's consider the wildcatter's basic decision problem, reproduced in Figure 8.7. Now suppose the wildcatter is risk averse; he is unwilling to rely on expected profits as his choice criterion.

FIGURE 8.7

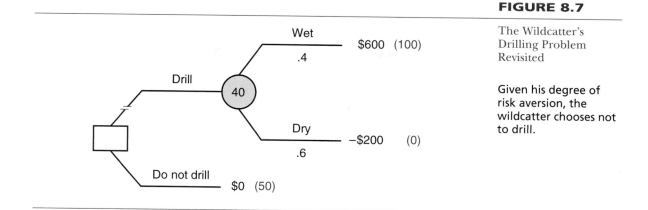

The Wildcatter's
Drilling Problem
Revisited

Given his degree of
risk aversion, the
wildcatter chooses not
to drill.

Instead, he seeks to determine a criterion for choosing among risky prospects
that reflects his own attitude toward risk. We now show how he can construct
a utility function that measures his own degree of risk aversion and how he can
use this function to guide his choices.

The wildcatter begins by attaching a utility value to each possible monetary outcome. Let's start with the decision to drill. Here the outcomes of
$600 thousand and −$200 thousand are the best and worst possible outcomes, respectively. The wildcatter is free to set these utility values arbitrarily so long as the best outcome receives the higher value. The usual
choice is to assign the worst outcome a utility value of zero. Thus, we would
write $U(-200) = 0$; that is, the utility associated with a loss of $200 thou-
sand is zero. In turn, let's arbitrarily set $U(600) = 100$. This establishes a
range of utility values from 0 to 100 for monetary outcomes between the
worst and best possible outcomes.

Using these utility values, wildcatter evaluates the option to drill by computing its expected utility. The **expected utility** is the probability of each outcome times its utility, summed over all outcomes. Thus, the expected utility of
drilling is

$$E(U_{drill}) = (.4)U(600) + (.6)U(-200)$$
$$= (.4)(100) + (.6)(0) = 40.$$

Now consider the "do not drill" option. In this case, the wildcatter's monetary result is $0 for certain. What utility value should the wildcatter assign this
outcome? To determine $U(0)$, the wildcatter compares $0 for certain with a
gamble offering $600 thousand (with probability p) and −$200 thousand (with
probability $1 - p$). The wildcatter measures his relative preference for $0 by
finding the probability p that leaves him indifferent to the options of $0 and

the gamble. Suppose that, after some mental trial and error, he judges his indifference probability to be p = .5; that is, he is indifferent to a certain $0 and to a 50-50 risk between $600 thousand and −$200 thousand. The fact that he is indifferent (at p = .5) allows us to find U(0). The expected utility of the 50-50 gamble is

$$(.5)U(600) + (.5)U(-200) = (.5)(100) + (.5)(0) = 50.$$

Since the wildcatter is indifferent to $0 for certain and this gamble, the two alternatives must have the same utility; that is, U(0) = 50.

Finally, the wildcatter uses expected utility as a guide for his decision. The simple rule is this:

> The decision maker should choose the course of action that maximizes his or her expected utility.

The expected utility of drilling is 40, whereas the utility of not drilling is 50. Thus, the wildcatter should elect not to drill the site. The decision tree in Figure 8.7 shows how the expected-utility rule is applied. Beside each monetary value in the tree is its associated utility. The expected utility of drilling is computed and listed by the chance circle. Finally, the "drill" decision branch has been crossed out because it has the lesser expected utility. The wildcatter's preferred option is not to drill.

In the more complicated examples to come, there will be many opportunities to practice the mechanics of expected utility. For the moment, the key point to remember is this: The decision maker's job is to assess utilities that express his or her attitude toward risk. There is no "formula" for determining the "right" utilities; they are purely personal and subjective.

In the preceding example, the wildcatter's key assessment is that $0 for certain is equivalent (in terms of his preferences) to a 50-50 risk between $600 thousand and −$200 thousand. Notice that this assessment reflects risk aversion on his part. The 50-50 risk has an expected value of $200,000. Yet the wildcatter's stated CE for this risk is $0; this is a considerable risk discount. With this assessment in hand, it becomes a simple matter to compare expected utilities: 40 for drilling versus 50 for not drilling. We also should note an equivalent way to explain the decision not to drill. Given his degree of risk aversion, the wildcatter prefers to drill only if the chances of striking oil are greater than .5. Because the actual probability of an oil strike on this site is only .4, he naturally chooses not to drill.

A MORE COMPLICATED OIL DRILLING PROBLEM   Part a of Figure 8.8 depicts a more complicated drilling prospect involving four possible monetary outcomes and associated probabilities. In addition, the wildcatter's utility value is listed beside

FIGURE 8.8

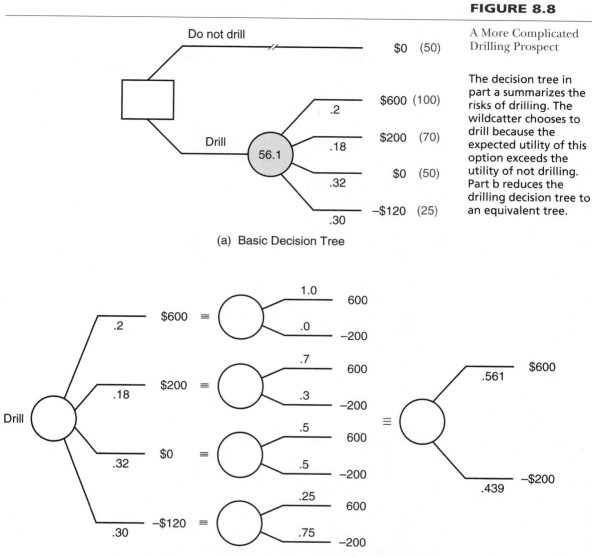

(a) Basic Decision Tree

(b) Reducing the Drill Option to an Equivalent Risk

A More Complicated Drilling Prospect

The decision tree in part a summarizes the risks of drilling. The wildcatter chooses to drill because the expected utility of this option exceeds the utility of not drilling. Part b reduces the drilling decision tree to an equivalent tree.

each monetary outcome. He continues to set $U(600) = 100$ and $U(-200) = 0$. Accordingly, $U(0)$ remains 50. The wildcatter also has assessed $U(200) = 70$ and $U(-120) = 25$. In other words, he is indifferent to the options of $200 thousand for certain and a 70-30 risk between the outcomes, $600 thousand and −$200 thousand. Similarly, he is indifferent to *losing* $120 thousand for certain or a 25-75 risk between the same two outcomes.[6] Therefore, these utilities are U(200) = (.7)(100) + (.3)(0) = 70 and U(−120) = (.25)(100) + (.75)(0) = 25.

Now the wildcatter is ready to compare his two options. The expected utility of drilling is (.2)(100) + (.18)(70) + (.32)(50) + (.3)(25) = 56.1. The utility of not drilling is U($0) = 50. Thus, drilling offers the higher expected utility and should be elected.[7]

* WHY THE EXPECTED-UTILITY METHOD WORKS　The preceding discussion shows *how* the expected-utility rule works. It is also worth checking *why* it works. Part b of Figure 8.8 demonstrates the reasoning behind the expected-utility rule. Beside each monetary outcome is listed an equivalent (in terms of preference) risk over the best and worst outcomes. By his own admission, the wildcatter is indifferent to a given monetary outcome versus the equivalent risk. Therefore, we can substitute the equivalent risk for each monetary outcome in the decision tree. Substituting equivalent risks will not change how the wildcatter feels about the drill option. (This assumption usually is called the *substitution principle.*) We make the substitution by (mentally) deleting the monetary outcome and, in its place, connecting the equivalent risk to the branch tip. Although the decision tree looks very bushy, the substitution has an important implication: Now the only outcomes in the tree are $600 thousand and −$200 thousand, the best and worst outcomes. If we add up the *total* probability of obtaining $600,000, we obtain the reduced tree on the right. The probability is computed as

$$(.2)(1.0) + (.18)(.7) + (.32)(.5) + (.30)(.25) = .561.$$

(Note that four branch paths on the tree end in $600 thousand. Each path involves a pair of chance branches, so we use the product rule for probabilities.) Thus, the actual drilling risk is equivalent (has been reduced) to a simpler risk offering a .561 chance at $600,000 and a .439 chance at −$200 thousand.

Now the wildcatter's decision is straightforward: Drilling is preferred to not drilling because, by his own admission, the wildcatter rates $0 for certain as equivalent to a .5 chance of the best outcome, and this is less than the .561 equivalent chance offered by drilling. We have gone to some

---

[6] Notice that −$200,000 is not an actual drilling outcome. (The worst actual outcome is −$120,000.) However, this fact makes no substantive difference in assigning utilities. The wildcatter is free to assign any outcome as the lowest or "zero-utility" value so long as this monetary outcome is lower than all actual outcomes.

[7] We note in passing that the original drilling site and the second drilling site have identical expected profits: $120,000. (Check the expected value of the second site.) Loosely speaking, the original site is more risky than the second. (It has a greater upside potential as well as greater downside risk.) Here the risk-averse wildcatter rejects the first site while choosing to drill the second.

* The analysis in this section is advanced and can be omitted without loss of continuity.

trouble to see through the logic of the wildcatter's choice. But notice that applying the expected-utility rule determines the decision in *exactly* the same way (albeit more compactly). We found the expected utility of drilling to be 56.1. Since this is greater than the utility of not drilling (50), drilling is the better option. Henceforth, we can apply the expected-utility rule with confidence that it properly evaluates the relative risks of different courses of action.

Expected Utility and Risk Aversion

Figure 8.9 shows the wildcatter's utility curve over a range of monetary outcomes. This curve is constructed by plotting utilities for particular monetary values and then drawing a smooth curve through those points. As pictured, the utility curve is concave, that is, becomes less and less steep. The concavity of the

FIGURE 8.9

The Wildcatter's Utility Curve

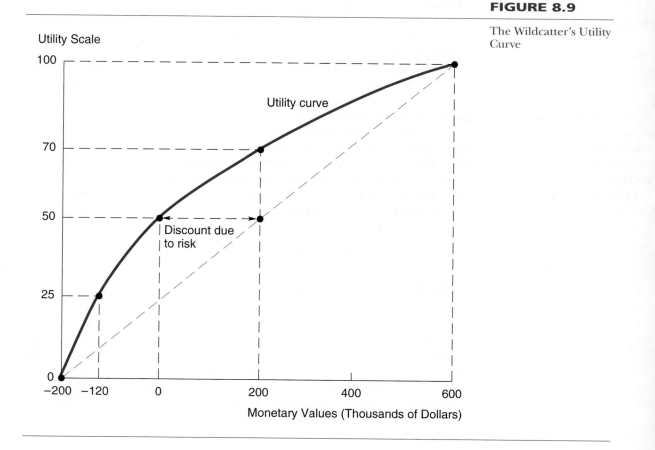

curve reflects the wildcatter's risk aversion. To see this, consider a simple two-outcome risk—say, a 50-50 chance of $600 thousand or −$200 thousand. By definition, the expected utility of this risk is $(.5)(100) + (.5)(0) = 50$. Pinpoint 50 on the vertical utility scale, read over to the curve, and then read down to the certainty equivalent value. As we saw earlier, this is $0. Now, instead of reading off the curve at $U = 50$, read over to the dashed line connecting the endpoints of the curve. Reading down, we arrive at the monetary value $200 thousand. This is exactly the expected value of the risky prospect: $(.5)(600) + (.5)(−200) = 200 thousand. The point is that the expected value of any risky prospect always lies along a straight-line utility curve. *A risk-neutral manager has a linear utility graph.* In fact, the horizontal gap between the CE (read off the curve) and the expected value (read off the line) exactly measures the discount due to risk aversion. For any concave curve, it is always true that the CE falls to the left of (i.e., is lower than) the corresponding expected value.

Figure 8.10 shows three typical utility curves. The concave curve reflects risk aversion, and the linear graph reflects risk neutrality. The third curve is convex, that is, becomes steeper and steeper. It is easy to check that an individual displaying such a curve is risk loving and prefers to bear risk. More precisely, the individual's CE for any risk is greater than (lies to the right of) its expected value.

With the utility graph in hand, the decision maker can supply requisite utility values and routinely evaluate decision trees. Besides assigning utility values to outcomes, the decision maker can use the graph in reverse. For instance, the expected utility of the second oil site (56.1) merits drilling. A direct expression of how much the site is worth to the wildcatter is given by its certainty equivalent. To find the CE, start at a utility of 56.1 in Figure 8.9, read over to the utility curve, and then read down to the corresponding monetary value—in this case, about $50 thousand. This is the value the wildcatter places on the site. Thus, he would not sell out if offered $30 thousand–but would do so readily if offered a certain $60 thousand (or any sum greater than $50 thousand).

CHECK STATION 4　Consider a 50-50 risk between $600 thousand and $0. Check that the expected utility of this risk is 75. Using the utility graph, find the CE of this risk. Compare the risk's CE and its expected value. Why is the gap between the two relatively small?

Once a utility curve has been assessed, the manager can use the expected-utility rule repeatedly and routinely to guide his or her decisions. Each particular decision carries accompanying profits and losses. But what ultimately matters is the impact of the firm's many decisions on its monetary wealth position. As a general rule, it is best to assess a utility function over final monetary wealth. For example, suppose the wildcatter begins the year with $1.8 million. He thinks about the potential range of his realized *wealth* two years from now. (This range depends on the number and riskiness of sites he might explore.) In a worst-case scenario he

FIGURE 8.10

Three Utility Functions

A risk-averse individual (part a) has a concave utility function. A risk-neutral individual (part b) has a linear utility function. A risk-loving individual (part c) has a convex utility function.

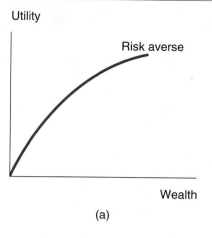

Utility

Risk averse

Wealth

(a)

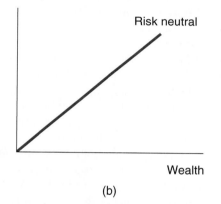

Utility

Risk neutral

Wealth

(b)

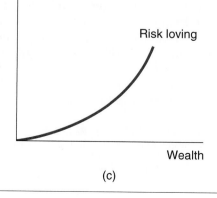

Utility

Risk loving

Wealth

(c)

might end with debts of $1.5 million. In the best case, his wealth might reach $5 million. Thus, he should assess his utility curve over this wide range.

To sum up, the manager must think hard about tolerance for risks over different final wealth positions. In doing so, the manager assesses a utility graph that best represents his or her attitude toward risk.[8] Once the utility curve is in hand, the manager can analyze the problem by means of the usual decision tree after supplying utility values for possible final monetary wealth positions. Finally, the manager averages back the tree and selects the course of action that has the highest expected utility.

Nonmonetary Examples

Application of the expected-utility rule is not limited to decisions involving monetary outcomes. The following examples make the point.

AN R&D RACE   Once again, consider a firm that is in the process of developing a product. It must decide which of two R&D methods—call these A and B—to pursue. (It will choose only one; it lacks the resources to try both.) The methods have comparable costs, and both ultimately will lead to successful product introductions at comparable profits. The sole uncertainty concerns each method's time until completion. Figure 8.11 shows the range of completion times and probabilities for each method. One more fact is important: The firm is in a neck-and-neck race with a competitor developing a similar product. The first company to get a product to market will have a huge competitive advantage. By all estimates, the competitor's date of product completion is 18 months from now. Which method should the firm choose?

A natural first step is to compare the expected times of completion (ETCs) for the two methods. From Figure 8.11, we see that the ETC of method A is 18.4 months and that of method B is 19.4 months. By this criterion, method A would be chosen because it promises an earlier date of completion on average.

Although method A is faster on average, it is not necessarily the firm's better choice. Remember that it is paramount that the firm beat the competitor to market. If the principal concern is completing the project before the competition—that is, before 18 months from now—method B is the better choice. Why? Because it offers a .52 chance of completion in 18 months or sooner. The chance for method A is only .41. By this criterion, only two outcomes matter: completion "in time" (before 18 months) or "too late" (later than 18 months). Here a miss is as good as a mile. Completion in 21 months is not significantly better than completion in 26 months. Because the ETC criterion does not cap-

---

[8] There is a variety of methods decision makers can use to assess utility curves. One such method is presented in Problem 14 at the end of this chapter. In the process of utility assessment, the manager can gain considerable insight about his or her risk preferences. A common finding is that decision makers become considerably less risk averse when starting from a high (rather than a low) financial wealth base.

FIGURE 8.11

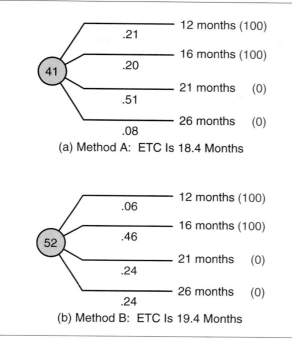

(a) Method A: ETC Is 18.4 Months

(b) Method B: ETC Is 19.4 Months

An R&D Race

Even though method A is faster on average, the firm should choose method B because B offers the greater chance of beating the rival to market.

ture the all-or-nothing deadline present in the problem, following ETC (the wrong criterion) can lead to an incorrect decision.

We can easily capture this reasoning by assigning appropriate utility values to the possible outcomes. If making the deadline is all or nothing, any outcome before 18 months is a "best" outcome and is assigned utility U = 100. Any outcome after the deadline (no matter how close) is a "worst" outcome and has utility U = 0. From the decision tree in Figure 8.11, the expected utility for method A is

$$(.21)(100) + (.20)(100) + (.51)(0) + (.08)(0) = 41.$$

In turn, the expected utility for method B is

$$(.06)(100) + (.46)(100) + (.24)(0) + (.24)(0) = 52.$$

In effect, method B is preferred because it offers the greater chance, .52, of beating the 18-month deadline.[9]

[9] Of course, the situation may not be completely all or nothing. Completion in 12 months may be somewhat better than completion in 16 months, and both are *significantly* better than a 21- or 26-month completion. Thus, we might assign U(16) = 90 (instead of 100). Even with this change, however, method B is preferred (i.e., offers the greater expected utility).

A SURGICAL DECISION   A 60-year-old woman suffers from cardiovascular disease and currently is on a program of medication, strict diet, and limited physical activity. A heart bypass operation, if successful, can restore her to near-perfect health. The operation, however, carries the risk of death—an estimated 4 percent risk for individuals with her medical history. Should the patient elect to undergo the operation?

Here the key issue is whether the potential benefit of the operation is worth the risk. (We assume the operation's cost is not an issue for the patient; health insurance will cover the monetary cost.) Figure 8.12 offers a convenient way to think about this issue. On the one hand, the patient can forgo the operation and continue in her present impaired health status. On the other hand, she can elect the operation, with the chance of returning to normal health and the risk of death. Figure 8.12b asks the patient to express how safe the operation must be to induce her to take it. Thus, the patient names the probability of success (labeled p) that will leave her *indifferent* to the choices of the two courses of action. As shown, her response is p = .88; that is, the chance of a successful operation would have to be 88 percent to leave her indifferent. To put this

FIGURE 8.12

A Medical Decision

According to part b, the patient is indifferent to the options of her current health status or a 12 percent risk of death from surgery. Since the actual surgical risk is 4 percent, the decision tree in part a shows that her best decision is to elect surgery.

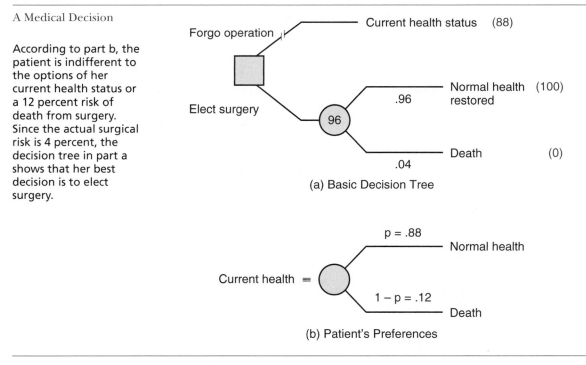

(a) Basic Decision Tree

(b) Patient's Preferences

another way, given her current health status, she would be willing to risk a $1 - p = .12$ chance of death (but no higher) from the operation.[10]

Note that the patient's answer expresses only her relative *preferences* among the risky outcomes; it has nothing to do with the actual risk of the operation. Presumably the surgeon's opinion (and possibly second opinions) provides the best information about the actual risk. However, the patient herself is the "expert" when it comes to assessing the degree of risk she is willing to accept (expressed by $p = .88$).

With her risk preference suitably expressed, the patient's decision is straightforward. Recall that the operation's actual mortality risk is estimated to be .04. Since the probability of success (.96) exceeds the patient's required degree of safety (.88), the patient should elect surgery. Exactly the same conclusion is reached using the utility values listed next to the medical outcomes in Figure 8.12a. The best outcome, a return to perfect health, has $U = 100$. The worst outcome, death, has $U = 0$. According to her own assessment, the patient's current health status has $U = 88$. The operation is the best decision because it offers the greater expected utility: $E(U) = (.96)(100) + (.04)(0) = 96$.

To solve the yacht dealer's problem posed at the beginning of the chapter, we supply the following information. The dealer incurs fixed costs amounting to $150,000 per year and obtains yachts from the manufacturer at an average cost of $10,000 each. In a growing economy, the demand for yachts is described by $P = 20 - .05Q$; in a slumping economy, demand is $P = 20 - .1Q$, where P is measured in thousands of dollars.

Gearing Down for a Recession Revisited

Let's start by finding the dealer's profit-maximizing yacht order for each type of economy. Setting MR = MC, we find the dealer's optimal quantity and price to be $Q_G = 100$ and $P_G = \$15,000$ for a growing economy; the resulting profit is $\pi_G = \$350,000$. For the recession economy, we find $Q_R = 50$, $P_R = \$15,000$, and $\pi_R = \$100,000$. Of course, the dealer must place the order now, before knowing the true direction of the economy. Let's suppose the dealer must choose to order a round lot of either 50 or 100 yachts. (Other possibilities are considered in Problem 15 at the end of the chapter.) In light of a 60 percent chance of growth, which order, 50 or 100, has the higher expected profit?

The decision tree in Figure 8.13 answers this question. If 100 yachts are ordered, the dealer's profit is either $350,000 or −$150,000. Under slumping demand, the best the dealer can do is sell all 100 yachts at a price of $10,000 each. (At this quantity, revenue is maximized; that is, MR = 0.) If 50 yachts are ordered, the possible outcomes are $225,000 and $100,000. The first outcome occurs when the dealer plans for a recession but is pleasantly surprised by growing demand and sells the 50 yachts at a price of $17,500 each. (Note that this price is obtained from the demand curve for a growing economy.)

<hr>

[10] This response depends on how bad her current health status is relative to "perfect" health. For instance, if her current health status were only slightly impaired, her point of indifference might be $p = .97$. If her current health were something like "living death," however, the point of indifference might be $p = .5$. In other words, the patient believes "My current state is so bad that I'd trade it for a 50-50 chance at a normal life or else death."

FIGURE 8.13

Ordering Yachts under
Uncertainty

The dealer's better course
of action is to order 50
yachts.

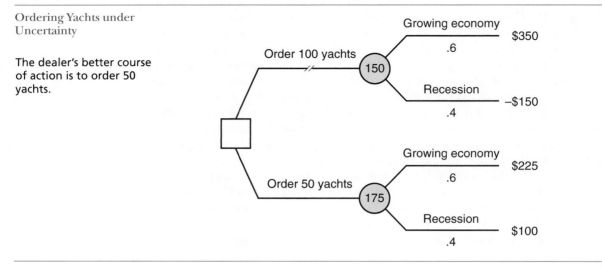

Direct calculation shows that ordering 50 yachts generates an expected profit of $175,000, whereas ordering 100 yachts produces only $150,000. Thus, a risk-neutral dealer prefers the smaller (50-yacht) order. (A risk-averse dealer shares this preference, because ordering 50 yachts is less risky than ordering 100.) This result might conflict with one's intuition. After all, a growing economy is more likely than not, and ordering 100 yachts is optimal in this case; therefore, one would judge 100 yachts to be the better choice. What's wrong with this reasoning? The key point is that the cost of making a wrong decision differs across the two actions. Taking a large yacht order is very costly (generates a large loss) if a slumping economy causes inventory to be sold at bargain prices. The "cost" of placing a limited order and having too little inventory to accommodate a growing economy is relatively small. (At least the dealer can raise prices.) As a result, the expected profit associated with the small order is significantly greater than that of the large order.

SUMMARY

Decision-Making Principles

1. In choosing among risky prospects, sound decision making means assessing the foreseeable good and bad outcomes and their respective chances. Thus, decisions must be judged according to the information available at the time the choice is made, not with the benefit of 20-20 hindsight.

2. When a series of related decisions is to be made, an "optimal" initial choice depends on foreseeing and making "optimal" choices for the decisions that follow.

3. To make sound decisions, the manager must also assess his or her own (or the company's) attitude toward risk. A risk-averse decision maker assesses a (certainty equivalent) value for a risky prospect that is smaller than the prospect's expected value.

Nuts and Bolts

1. The decision tree is the basic tool for making decisions under uncertainty. The tree must include branches for (a) all possible actions of the decision maker and (b) all chance events that can affect outcomes. Each chance branch should be assigned a probability. In decisions involving profits and losses, each branch tip should be assigned a monetary value.

2. The decision tree should accurately depict the chronology of the decision setting, that is, the sequence of decision nodes and chance nodes.

3. The expected-value criterion values a risky prospect by taking a weighted average of the possible monetary outcomes, the weight for each outcome being its probability:

$$E(v) = p_1v_1 + p_2v_2 + \ldots + p_nv_n.$$

The expected-value criterion is appropriate for a risk-neutral decision maker who is willing to play the averages.

4. More generally, the principle of expected-utility maximization provides a consistent guide to decisions. In applying this principle, the manager constructs a utility graph that portrays his or her attitude toward risk. If the manager is risk neutral, this graph will be linear; if risk averse, it will be concave.

5. Whatever his or her attitude toward risk, the manager "solves" the decision tree by a process of "averaging and eliminating"—starting from the right and moving left. The expected utility (profit) at any chance node is found by averaging—multiplying branch utilities (or profits) by probabilities. At any decision node, the decision maker selects the alternative having the greatest expected utility (profit). All inferior decision branches are eliminated. The movement from right to left means that the last uncertainties are averaged first and the last decisions are evaluated first.

Questions and Problems

1. a. Average back the decision tree in the accompanying figure, supplying expected monetary values for points A through E.
    b. One of your fellow managers is worried that there are no probabilities given for the branches leading from point D. In order to solve the tree, he decides to assign a .5 probability to each branch. Do you agree with this procedure or not? Explain.

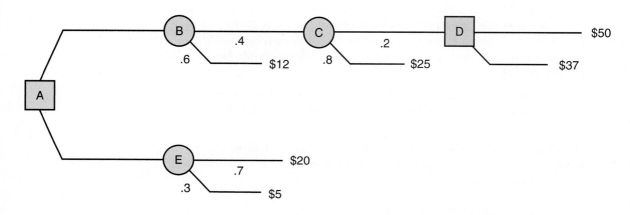

2. In 1976, the parents of a 7-year-old boy sued a New York hospital for $3.5 million. The boy was blinded shortly after he was born two weeks prematurely. His parents claimed that hospital doctors administered excessive oxygen to the baby and that this caused the blindness. The case went to trial, and just as the jury announced it had reached a verdict, the lawyers for the two sides arrived at an out-of-court settlement of $500,000.
    a. If you were the parents, how would you decide whether to accept the settlement or wait for the jury's decision? What probability assessments would you need to make? Would you have accepted the settlement?
    b. Answer the questions in part a, taking the hospital's point of view.

3. For five years, a firm has successfully marketed a package of multitask software. Recently, sales have begun to slip because the software is incompatible with a number of popular application programs. Thus, future profits are uncertain. In the software's present form, the firm's managers envision three possible five-year forecasts: maintaining current profits in the neighborhood of $2 million, a slip in profits to $.5 million, or the onset of losses to the tune of −$1 million. The respective probabilities for these outcomes are .2, .5, and .3.

    An alternative strategy is to develop an "open," or compatible, version of the software. This will allow the firm to maintain its market position, but the effort will be costly. Depending on how costly, the firm envisions four possible profit outcomes: $1.5 million, $1.1 million, $.8 million, and $.6 million, with each outcome considered equally likely.

a. Which course of action produces greater expected profit?

b. Roughly speaking, which course of action appears to be less risky? If management were risk averse, would this fact change its preferred course of action?

4. A European consortium has spent a considerable amount of time and money developing a new supersonic aircraft. The aircraft gets high marks on all performance measures except noise. In fact, because of the noise, the consortium's management is concerned that the U.S. government may impose restrictions at some of the American airports where the aircraft can land. Management judges a 50-50 chance that there will be some restrictions. Without restrictions, management estimates its (present discounted) profit at $125 million; with restrictions, its profit would be only $25 million. Management must decide now, before knowing the government's decision, whether to redesign parts of the aircraft to solve the noise problem. The cost of the redesign program is $25 million. There is a .6 chance that the redesign program will solve the noise problem (in which case, full landing rights are a certainty) and a .4 chance it will fail.

Using a decision tree, determine the consortium's best course of action, assuming management is risk neutral.

5. A firm faces uncertain revenues and uncertain costs. Its revenues may be $120,000, $160,000, or $175,000, with probabilities .2, .3, and .5, respectively. Its costs are $150,000 or $170,000 with chances .6 and .4, respectively. (Revenues and costs are independent.)

a. How many possible profit outcomes exist? Draw a decision tree listing these profit outcomes at the branch tips. Compute the firm's expected profit by folding back the tree. (It does not matter which uncertainty, demand or cost, is resolved first in the tree.)

b. Without a decision tree, calculate *separately* the firm's expected revenue and expected cost. What is the firm's expected profit? (This result underscores a great computational convenience of the expected-value criterion. Expected profit is equal to expected revenue minus expected cost; that is, expectations can be taken separately.)

6. Global Studios is thinking of producing a megafilm, *Aqua World*, which could be a megahit or a megaflop. Profit is uncertain for two reasons: (1) The cost of producing the film may be low or high, and (2) the market reception for the film may be strong or weak. There is a .5 chance of low costs (C), and a .5 chance of high costs. The probability of strong demand (D) is .4; the probability of weak demand is .6. The studio's

profits (in millions of dollars) for the four possible outcomes are shown in the table.

Low C/Strong D	Low C/Weak D	High C/Strong D	High C/Weak D
80	40	0	−80

a. Should the studio produce the film? Use a decision tree to justify your answer.

b. The studio is concerned that Kevin Costmore, the film's director and star, might let production costs get out of control. Thus, the studio insists on a clause in the production contract giving it the right to terminate the project after the first $30 million is spent. By this time, the studio *will know for certain* whether total production costs are going to be low (i.e., under control) or high (out of control). How much is this termination clause worth to the studio (vis-à-vis the situation in part a)?

7. In 1996, McDonald's (MD) launched Campaign 55, reducing the prices of its "flagship" sandwiches with the objective of regaining market share. Before the launch, suppose MD's management envisioned two possible outcomes: a strong customer response or a weak response. Industry experts were not very optimistic about the campaign. They assessed the probability of a strong response to be .25. MD forecasted an expected profit of $50 million if the response proved to be strong. If the immediate customer response was weak, management believed that all was not lost. If MD could persuade the majority of its franchisees to back and help fund the campaign, the resulting profit would be $20 million. However, if the majority rose up against the campaign, the red ink would fly, and McDonald's profit would be −$100 million. MD considered these two outcomes to be *equally likely*.

a. Given these assessments, construct a decision tree to determine MD's expected-profit-maximizing course of action.

b. Suppose that MD has the flexibility to try the campaign but to terminate it if the initial response is weak, thereby limiting its total loss to $20 million. (It must "pull the plug" before knowing whether the franchisees are for or against the campaign.) Again, construct a decision tree to determine MD's expected-profit-maximizing strategy.

8. Firm A is facing a possible lawsuit by legal firm B. Firm B represents the family of Mr. Smith, who was killed in a motel fire (allegedly caused by faulty wiring). Firm A was the builder of the motel. Firm A has asked its legal team to estimate the likely jury award it will be ordered to pay in court. Expert legal counsel anticipates three possible court outcomes:

awards of $1,000,000, $600,000, or $0, with probabilities .2, .5, and .3, respectively. In addition to any awards, firm A's legal expenses associated with fighting the court case are estimated to be $100,000.

Firm A also has considered the alternative of entering out-of-court settlement negotiations with firm B. Based on the assessments of its lawyers, firm A envisions the other side holding out for one of two settlement amounts: $900,000 (a high amount) or $400,000 (a more reasonable amount). Each demand is considered equally likely. If presented with one of these settlement demands, firm A is free to accept it (in which case firm B agrees to waive any future right to sue) *or* reject it and take its chances in court. The legal cost of pursuing a settlement (whether or not one is reached) is $50,000.

Determine the settlement or litigation strategy that minimizes firm A's expected total cost (any payment plus legal fees).

* 9. Filene's Basement, a Boston-based department store, has a policy of marking down the price of sale items each week that they go unsold. You covet an expensive brand of winter coat that is on sale for $100. In fact, you would be willing to pay as much as $120 for it. Thus, you can buy it now (for a profit of $120 − $100 = $20) or wait until next week, when the price will be reduced to $75 if the coat is still available. The chances of its being available next week are 2/3. If it is available in week 2, you can buy or wait until week 3. There is a 1/2 chance it will be sold between weeks 2 and 3 and a 1/2 chance it will be available at a reduced price of $60. Finally, if it is available in week 3, you can buy or wait until week 4. There is a 1/4 chance it still will be available, at a price of $50 (and a 3/4 chance it will be sold in the meantime). Week 4 is your last chance to buy before the coat is withdrawn.
   a. How long should you wait before buying? Illustrate via a decision tree.
   b. Filene's has 120 of these winter coats for sale. What is its expected total revenue from the pricing scheme in part a? (One-third of the coats sell in the first week, one-half of the remaining coats in the second week, and so on. All coats in week 4 are sold for $50.)
   c. Alternatively, Filene's can set a single price for all coats. Its demand curve is P = 180 − Q. Would it prefer a common-price method or the price-reduction method in part b? Explain.

10. As CEO of firm M, you and your management team face the decision of whether to undertake a $200 million R&D effort to create a new megamedicine. Your research scientists estimate that there is a 40 percent chance of successfully creating the drug. Success means securing a worldwide patent worth $550 million (implying a net profit of $350 million). However, firm W (your main rival) has just announced that it is

---

* Starred problems are more challenging.

spending $150 million to pursue development of the same medicine (by a scientific method completely independent of yours). You judge that firm W's chance of success is 30 percent. Furthermore, if both firms are successful, they will split equally the available worldwide profits ($275 million each) based on separate patents.

a. Given its vast financial resources, firm M is risk neutral. Should it undertake the $200 million R&D effort? (Use a decision tree to justify your answer.)

b. Now suppose that it is feasible for firm M to delay its R&D decision until after the result of firm W's R&D effort (success or failure) is known. Is it advantageous for firm M to have this "second move"? (Use a decision tree to justify your answer.)

c. Instead, suppose that firm A and firm B can form a joint venture to pursue either or both of their R&D programs. What is the expected profit of simultaneously pursuing *both* programs? *Hint:* Be sure to compute the probability that *both efforts fail* (in which case the firms' combined loss is 200 + 150 = $350 million.). Alternatively, could the joint venture profitably pursue a *single* program?

11. Consider once again the R&D strategies of the pharmaceutical company described earlier in this chapter. Suppose the company's management is risk averse and has assessed the following utility values for the set of possible outcomes (in millions of dollars).

Outcome	Utility	Outcome	Utility
$200	100	$70	59
180	95	60	55
170	92	50	50
100	71	40	44
80	64	20	32
		0	0

Compute the expected utility of pursuing the biochemical approach alone. Next, find the expected utility of pursuing the biogenetic approach first, then continuing with the biochemical approach if necessary. In light of these calculations, what action do you recommend for the company? How has the company's risk aversion influenced its decision?

12. Consider once again the dilemma facing Consolidated Edison's system operator. To keep things simple, we focus on one of the decisions he faced: to maintain load or to shed load. Suppose his choices are to shed 50 percent of the load (which will "solve" the problem at the cost of

blacking out 50 percent of New York City) or maintain full load (risking the chance of a total blackout).

a. The operator envisions three possible scenarios by which the system might weather the demand–supply imbalance at full load. The first scenario he considers "improbable," the second is a "long shot," and the third is "somewhat likely." How might he translate these verbal assessments into a "round-number" estimate of the probability that 100 percent load can be maintained? What probability estimate would you use?

b. Consider the three outcomes: 100 percent power, 50 percent power, and 0 percent power (i.e., a total blackout). It is generally agreed that 0 percent power is "more than twice as bad" as 50 percent power. (With 50 percent power, some semblance of essential services, police, fire, hospitals, and subways, can be maintained; moreover, with a deliberate 50 percent blackout, it is much easier to restore power later.) What does this imply about the utility associated with 50 percent power? (For convenience, assign 100 percent power a utility of 100 and 0 percent power a utility of 0.)

c. Construct a decision tree incorporating your probability estimate from part a and your utility values from part b. What is the operator's best course of action? Explain.

*13. Firm A is about to embark on a risky development project that offers a .2 chance of a $4 million profit and a .8 chance of a $0 profit. Unexpectedly, firm B proposes a joint venture. In return for its expertise, firm B will receive 25 percent of any profit. With firm B aboard, the chance of success is expected to rise to .25. After much deliberation, firm A decides to turn down the joint venture and continue on its own.

Two years pass, and firm A has overcome most of the development hurdles. The estimated chances of success are now .8. Now firm C offers to pay firm A $3 million for all rights (and profits) concerning the development project. Deciding to take the sure $3 million, firm A now sells out.

Show that whatever firm A's attitude toward risk, the pair of decisions just outlined is contradictory. (*Hint*: There are only three outcomes across the two decisions: $4 million, $0, and $3 million, with the associated utilities 100, 0, and u, respectively.) Show that no value of u is consistent with firm A's pair of choices.

14. In attempting to quantify its attitude toward risk, top management of the pharmaceutical company has reported certainty equivalent values for a variety of 50-50 risks. These are summarized in the following table.

Outcome of 50-50 Risk	Certainty Equivalent
$200 and $0	$ 50
$200 and $50	112
$50 and $0	13
$200 and $112	153
$112 and $50	70
$50 and $13	28
$112 and $13	50

For instance, the company's CE for a 50-50 risk between $200 million and $0 is $50 million, and so on.

a. Use these responses to determine utility values for each of the monetary values in the second column. (*Hint*: Set U($200) = 100 and U($0) = 0. Show that U($50) = 50, U($112) = 75, and so on.) Construct a utility graph by plotting points and drawing a smooth curve. (You may wish to check the utility values in Problem 11 against your curve.)

* b. Consider the mathematical utility function U = $7.1\sqrt{y}$, where U is the utility value corresponding to monetary outcome y. Check that this function is an accurate description of the pharmaceutical company's attitude toward risk. Is the company very risk averse?

* 15. Put yourself in the yacht dealer's shoes. You currently are considering other order quantities in addition to 50 and 100. Find the optimal order quantity, that is, the exact quantity that maximizes your expected profit. (*Hint*: From the two demand curves, find the expected-price equation, that is, the expected sale price for any given quantity of yachts. Given this expected-price equation, apply the MR = MC rule to maximize expected profit.)

16. a. You are given $1,000 to keep. You then are offered a choice between receiving an additional $500 for certain or taking a 50-50 gamble with outcomes of $1,000 and $0. Which would you choose?

b. You are given $2,000 to keep. You then are offered a choice between paying $500 for certain or taking a 50-50 gamble with outcomes of $0 and −$1,000. Which would you choose?

c. The majority of individuals choose the sure $500 in part a but select the gamble in part b. Show that this combination of choices is inconsistent. What does this suggest about the way in which decision makers should think about risks?

Discussion Question In 1997, after spending more than $.5 billion in development and after extensive test marketing, Procter & Gamble in partnership with Frito-Lay and Nabisco launched a series of snack food products made with Olestra, a "no fat" substitute. The campaign launch promised that consumers would enjoy the same flavor of potato chips or crackers but with zero fat. Although touted as a miracle product, Olestra faced a number of uncertainties: ultimate consumer demand, willingness to pay, and pricing; product cost, quality, and shelf life; regulatory approval; and, most important, medical side effects (stomach cramps and the ugly specter of diarrhea in some consumers).

Use this example and other management cases discussed weekly in the business press to make a list of the many categories of risks faced by managers. In particular lines of business, what categories of risks are the most crucial for the firm's profit? Provide examples of firm strategies to eliminate, mitigate, or insure against these risks.

Suggested References

The following texts are among the best and most complete treatments of decisions under uncertainty.

Kleindorfer, P. R., H. S. Kunreuther, and P. J. H. Schoemaker. *Decision Sciences*, Chapters 4 and 5. Cambridge: Cambridge University Press, 1993.

Raiffa, H. *Decision Analysis*. New York: McGraw-Hill, 1997. (Paperback)

Savage, S., *Decision Making with Insight*. Belmont, CA: Thomson Learning, 2003.

The next two references survey the experimental evidence on decision making under uncertainty.

Camerer, C. "Individual Decision Making" in J. H. Kagel and A. E. Roth (Eds.). *The Handbook of Experimental Economics*. Princeton, NJ: Princeton University Press, 1995.

Davis, D. D., and C. A. Holt. *Experimental Economics*, Chapter 8. Princeton: Princeton University Press, 1993.

The following reference is a fascinating account of the many risks and decisions involved in Ford's redesign of its popular Taurus model.

Walton, M. *Car Wars*. New York: Norton, 1999. (Paperback)

The following two references offer comprehensive guides to decision-tree applications and software:

Keefer, D. L., C. W. Kirkwood, and J. L. Corner, "Perspective on Decision Analysis Applications, 1990–2001," *Decision Analysis* (March 2004): 4–22.

Maxwell, D. T. "Decision Analysis: Adding Insight VI, *OR/MS Today* (June 2002): 44–51.

Internet sites dealing with decision making under uncertainty include:

www.analycorp.com

Sam Savage's wonderful guide to risk at www.analycorp.com/uncertainty
Decision-tree software published by Decision Support Services, www.treeplan.com
and Palisade's commercial software, www.palisade.com/html/Articles/case.html

1. The firm's expected profit under the private contract is
   $(.25)(\$2) + (.41)(\$.7) + (.34)(-\$.5) = \$.617$ million. Under the
   government contract, the firm's expected profit is
   $(.45)(\$4) + (.55)(-\$2.5) = \$.425$ million. In terms of expected value,
   the private contract is the better alternative.

2. The executive's expected profit of drilling to *only* 3,000 feet is
   $(.4)(600) + (.6)(-160) = \$144$ thousand. By quitting after 3,000 feet,
   the executive takes a loss of $160,000. What is her expected profit if
   she drills deeper? It is $(.2)(400) + (.8)(-250) = -\$120$ thousand.
   The expected loss from drilling deeper is smaller than that from
   quitting. Finally, the expected profit from drilling 5,000 feet (if
   necessary) is $(.4)(600) + (.6)(-120) = \$168$ thousand. This is the
   executive's best course of action.

3. We calculate firm A's expected profit from launching the product in
   two steps. If firm B brings out its own product (probability 60
   percent), A's expected profit is $(.5)(\$10) + (.5)(-\$30) = -\$10$
   million. If B does not bring out a product (probability 40 percent), A's
   profit is $20 million. Thus, firm A's overall expected profit is
   $(.4)(\$20) + (.6)(-\$10) = \$2$ million. To maximize expected profit,
   the firm should launch the product.

4. The expected utility of a 50-50 risk between $600,000 (U = 100) and
   $0 (U = 50) is $(.5)(100) + (.5)(50) = 75$. From Figure 8.9, we see
   that the CE of this risky prospect is about $220,000. In contrast, the
   expected value of this risk is $300,000. To confirm this expected value
   using the figure, draw a line between the $600,000 and $0 points on
   the graph. Then find .75 on the utility scale, read over to the line, and
   read down to the monetary value of $300,000. Note that the risk
   discount (the horizontal gap between the utility curve and the dashed
   line) is smaller here than for the $600,000 versus -$200,000 risk. This
   illustrates a general principle: The smaller the range of risk, the closer
   the CE is to the expected value.

What decision did the Con Ed operator take, and what was the result? The operator initially
attempted to reroute power, thinking that only one transmission line was down. He also reduced
voltage and called for added emergency power from city generators. About 30 minutes into the
emergency, he shed about 25 percent of the system's load. Unfortunately, this proved to be too little, too late. Eleven minutes after load was shed, New York City blacked out completely. It took 25
hours to restore power to all parts of the city.

CHAPTER 9

The Value
of Information

The race isn't always to the fastest nor the battle to the strongest, but that is the way you should bet.

DAMON RUNYAN

Forecasting the economy is big business. Scores of forecasters, many using econometric models that contain hundreds of equations, are paid handsomely by private businesses for predictions of the future course of the economy. Like the yacht dealer in the previous chapter, businesses strive for early warnings of swings in the economy. The fluctuation in stock market prices is one such early signal. Steady and sustained increases in stock prices (as summarized by the Dow Jones Industrial Average or the S&P 500 index) point to a growing economy over the next six to nine months. Prolonged stock market drops signal a coming recession. In fact, stock market movements have been a key leading indicator of recessions. Each of the eight postwar U.S. recessions has been preceded by a sustained fall in stock prices. (These price drops have come between 6 to 12 months in advance of the onset of the recession.) How should a decision maker (the yacht dealer, for instance) judge the chances of a recession after observing a rising stock market or after a falling market?

The Stock Market and the Economy

Future historians will remember the last half of the twentieth century as the dawning of the Age of Information. Information is the business of a significant and growing portion of the private sector. A key question is how information can be used to make better plans and decisions in business, government, the sciences, and even in personal matters. The pervasive role of information in decision making is illustrated by the following questions: Should a consumer products firm undertake an expensive test-market program before launching a new and highly promising product? What scientific research approaches should the government support in the long-term war on cancer? How should a firm use macroeconomic forecasts of the economy to make inventory and capacity decisions? What do polls and statistical analyses indicate about the likely outcome of the upcoming presidential election? What tests are appropriate during pregnancies of older women to screen for severe fetal genetic defects? What database is pertinent for predicting stock market returns for a particular company or companies in an industry segment? How can information on public risks—such as those posed by nuclear power, steel fatigue in aging bridges or aircraft, coastal hurricanes, environmental pollution, the spread of infectious diseases—be used to prevent disasters?

These are all broad and important questions. The aim of this chapter is to provide a way of thinking about information, in particular, about how it can be used to make better decisions. We consider a trio of questions: When should a manager acquire additional information before making his or her main decision? How should the manager modify probability assessments of uncertain events in light of this information? How should the manager make decisions with this information in hand? Together, the answers to these questions provide the foundation for determining the value of information in decisions under uncertainty.

THE VALUE OF INFORMATION

The Oil Wildcatter Revisited

Let's return to the oil drilling decision of the previous chapter but with one additional option: Suppose the wildcatter forms a partnership with a well-known geologist to explore for oil. At a cost, the partnership can take a seismic test to obtain better information about the site before drilling. To begin, we consider a *perfect* seismic test. Suppose the geologist conducts the test and that she categorizes its outcome as either "good" or "bad." By "good" she means that oil is present (the site is wet) for certain; by "bad" she means the site is definitely dry. (Another way to say this is that wet sites always test good and dry sites always test bad.) It should be clear that, for decision-making purposes, this perfect test is very valuable. If the outcome is good, the partnership drills, strikes oil with certainty, and gains a $600,000 profit. If it is bad, it knows there is no oil and so avoids a loss by choosing not to drill.

The decision tree in Figure 9.1 displays this strategy. Notice that the tree begins not with a decision square but with a chance circle. The outcome of the test is resolved first: good or bad. Then two decision squares appear because a choice must be made in two separate cases: after a good seismic test or after a

FIGURE 9.1

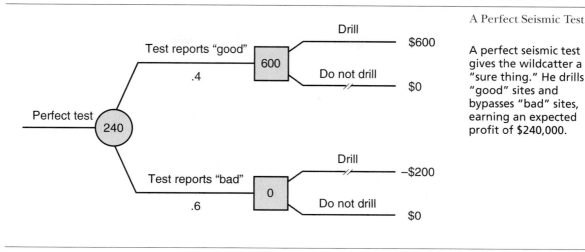

A Perfect Seismic Test

A perfect seismic test gives the wildcatter a "sure thing." He drills "good" sites and bypasses "bad" sites, earning an expected profit of $240,000.

bad one. The course of action—drill if and only if the test is good—is also shown on the tree.

How well-off is the partnership with the perfect seismic test? In Figure 9.1, we have computed the expected profit at the outset, before the test result is in. Recall that the partners judge the probability of oil to be $\Pr(W) = .4$. Since good tests occur precisely when the site is wet, the frequency of a good test is also .4. Similarly, $\Pr(B) = .6$. Therefore, the initial expected value is $(.4)(600,000) + (.6)(0) = \$240,000$. Forty percent of the time, the seismic result is good, and there is a $600,000 drilling profit. The rest of the time, the result is bad, no drilling occurs, and the profit is zero.

How much is the test information worth to the partnership? The answer is provided by the concept of the expected value of information. The **expected value of information (EVI)** is simply the difference between the decision maker's expected value with the test information and without it. Thus, we can write the expected value of information as

$$\text{EVI} = \text{Expected value with information}$$
$$- \text{Expected value without information.}$$

Recall from the discussion in Chapter 8 that, without the test, the best decision was to drill; the resulting expected profit was $120,000. In the present decision, the EVI is $240,000 - 120,000 = \$120,000$.

The EVI measures the benefit of the test. So far we have not specified the test's cost. Suppose the test costs $50,000. Since the benefit exceeds the cost, the partners should elect the test. Their expected net gain is

EVI − (Test cost) = 120,000 − 50,000 = $70,000. If the cost were $150,000, however, the test would not be worth its expense. The general rule is

> A decision maker should acquire costly information if and only if the expected value of the information exceeds its cost.

Before leaving this simple example, let's check exactly where the increase in expected profit came from. Refer once again to Figure 9.1. As the tree indicates, only good sites are drilled. But now consider the effect if all sites, good and bad, were drilled, as would be the case if the test information were not available. From the tree, we see that the partners would lose $200,000 from drilling bad/dry sites. Thus, the advantage of the test is that it saves this amount by screening out these sites. This savings occurs 60 percent of the time, because this is the frequency of dry sites. The partner's expected gain from the seismic test (compared to always drilling) is (.6)(200,000) = $120,000. This is exactly the EVI calculated earlier. The test allows the partners to resolve the uncertainty—wet or dry—before committing to a decision to drill or not to drill. In this way, they save the cost of drilling dry sites.

Imperfect Information

Although illustrative, the preceding example is unrealistic because it is unlikely that the partners ever could obtain perfect information before drilling. We now consider the decision to drill in light of an *imperfect* seismic test. Again, we assume the test results are categorized as "good" or "bad," but now the test is imperfect. The partners are aware of the recent record of test outcomes as listed in Table 9.1. We address the same questions as before: Should the partners invest in the test, and, if so, what drilling decision should they make based on its result?

Table 9.1 provides a record of 100 past sites (judged to be roughly similar to the current site) where seismic tests have been conducted. It provides a two-way classification of each site's outcome: the result of the test (good or bad) versus the true state of the site (wet or dry). The top left-hand entry shows that 30 of the 100 sites tested good and proved to contain oil. The other entries have similar interpretations. Loosely speaking, there is a correlation

TABLE 9.1

Past Seismic
Test Record (100 Sites)

		Actual State of the Site		
		Wet (W)	Dry (D)	Total
Seismic	**Good (G)**	30	20	50
Result	**Bad (B)**	10	40	50
	Total	40	60	100

between the test and the actual outcomes, demonstrated by the preponderance of cases lying on the main diagonal of the table: Good tests are likely to be associated with wet sites and bad tests with dry sites. However, there are a significant number of false reports (G&D and B&W). The test results, therefore, are far from perfect.

Let's use the historical frequencies in the table as an easy way to develop a number of probabilities essential for evaluating the seismic test option. First, note that the overall frequency of wet sites is 40 out of 100, or 40 percent. (See the total at the bottom of the column labeled "Wet.") Thus, this past record is consistent with the initial probability assessment of the site under consideration. Second, it is natural to inquire as to the chances of striking oil if the site has tested good or, alternatively, if it has tested bad. Looking at the first row of the table, we find that among 50 sites that tested good, 30 also turned out to be wet. The notation $Pr(W|G)$ is used to denote the probability that the site is wet given (or conditional on) a good test. From the table, we find that $Pr(W|G) = 30/50 = .6$. Alternatively, if the test is bad, what are the chances of finding oil? Of the 50 sites that tested bad, 10 were wet. Therefore, we have $Pr(W|B) = 10/50 = .2$.

Let's review what the table is telling us. Before taking the test, the best estimate of the chance of striking oil is $Pr(W) = .4$. This usually is termed the **prior probability** (i.e., before new information is obtained). After taking the test, the partners will revise their probability assessment based on the test outcome. One of two **conditional probabilities** will be relevant. The initial assessment is revised upward after a good test, $Pr(W|G) = .6$, and downward after a bad result, $Pr(W|B) = .2$. Another important piece of data in the table is that 50 out of 100 sites tested good and 50 tested bad. That is, the probability that a site will test good is .5.

One other point should be made. As presented, Table 9.1 lists the number of cases in each cell. By placing a decimal point before each entry, we give the cells a slightly different interpretation. Now each is understood to be a frequency or probability. For instance, the upper left entry becomes .3; that is, 30 percent of all sites tested good and proved to be wet. We use the notation $Pr(W\&G) = .3$ to denote the probability of this joint outcome. Similar interpretations and notation hold for the other entries. This new interpretation has no effect on the conditional probabilities found earlier. For example, the chance that the site is wet after a bad test is $Pr(W|B) = .1/.5 = .2$, exactly the same as the preceding result. Because of its flexibility and wide application, we employ a probabilistic interpretation in the remainder of this chapter.

It is important to see how the seismic information can improve the partners' decision. Figure 9.2 makes this point by depicting the new decision tree, which incorporates the seismic results. We start by emphasizing the sequence of events in the tree. As in Figure 9.1, the first event is the test result: good or bad. This is represented by the chance node (the circle) from which the possible test results emanate. After seeing the result, the partners must decide

FIGURE 9.2

An Imperfect Seismic Test

A "good" seismic test boosts the chance of striking oil to .6. A "bad" seismic test lowers it.

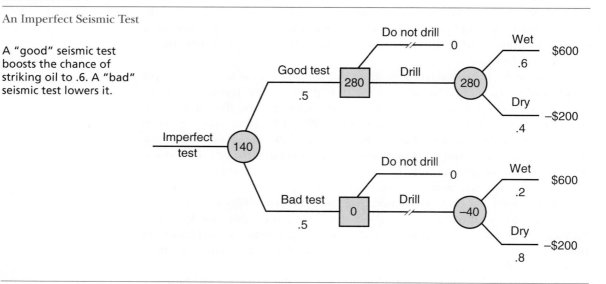

whether or not to drill. These decisions are denoted by the two squares appearing on the good and bad test branches. Finally, for the "drill" option, the tree shows the chance event, wet or dry, along with the revised probabilities. After a good test, striking oil carries a 60 percent chance; after a bad test, the chance is only 20 percent. (In contrast to the case of a perfect seismic test, a good result does not guarantee oil, and a bad result does not rule it out.)

With the decision tree in hand, the optimal decision strategy is easy to determine. Consider the upper decision square. If the test is good, drilling offers an expected profit of $280,000 and should be undertaken. After a bad test, drilling has an expected profit of −$40,000 (since the chance of finding oil is only 20 percent). Thus, the partners should employ a contingent strategy: Drill the site if the seismic test is favorable and forgo it if the test is unfavorable. How much profit do they stand to gain using this strategy? To answer this question, we simply calculate the expected profit at the initial chance node, before the test outcome is known. As we noted previously, a good test is expected to occur 50 percent of the time, in which case drilling earns an expected profit of $280,000. The other 50 percent of the time, a bad test occurs, no drilling takes place, and the profit is $0. Thus, the expected profit at the initial chance node is simply (.5)(280,000) + (.5)(0) = $140,000. Remembering that the expected profit without the test is $120,000, we find the test has an EVI of 140,000 − 120,000 = $20,000. This test is much less valuable than the perfect seismic test examined earlier. Nonetheless, if the test is inexpensive enough (i.e., costs less than $20,000), the partners should elect it.

REVISING PROBABILITIES

In many situations, the decision maker possesses potentially valuable information but in a form that is not readily usable. Typically, the decision maker must ask: How does this piece of information alter my assessment of an uncertain event? Does it make the event more or less likely? By how much should I revise the event's probability? A considerable body of research has studied the ways in which individuals make probabilistic predictions. The overwhelming evidence from these studies is that one's intuition often is a poor guide when it comes to probability assessment and revision. (See the discussion of intuitive prediction later in the chapter.) Fortunately, some basic results in probability provide a formal method for handling this task.

To illustrate the method, suppose the partners lack the seismic record listed in Table 9.1. Instead, they have the following summary information about the accuracy of the seismic test. The vendor of the test certifies that, in the past, sites that were actually wet tested "good" three-quarters of the time and dry sites tested "bad" two-thirds of the time. In algebraic terms, we have $\Pr(G|W) = 3/4$ and $\Pr(B|D) = 2/3$. As before, the partners assess a 40 percent chance that the site is wet based on their information prior to the seismic test, $\Pr(W) = .4$.

How can the partners derive $\Pr(W|G)$ and $\Pr(W|B)$, the two key probabilities they need to solve their decision tree? The most direct way is to compute the table of joint probabilities in Table 9.1. Consider the calculation of one such joint probability, $\Pr(W\&G)$, appearing in the upper left corner of the table. The partners reason as follows: According to their prior judgment, the site is wet 40 percent of the time. A wet site can be expected to test good three-quarters of the time. Therefore, the site is both wet and good three-quarters of 40 percent of the time, or 30 percent of the time. In algebraic terms, we have $\Pr(W\&G) = (3/4)(.4) = .3$. What is the probability that the site is dry and (falsely) tests good? Since $\Pr(D) = .6$ and only one-third of dry sites test good, the joint probability is $\Pr(D\&G) = (1/3)(.6) = .2$. The other joint probabilities are computed in similar fashion. The basic result is that any joint probability can be expressed as the product of a prior probability and a conditional probability. In the first calculation, we made use of the result

$$\Pr(W\&G) = \Pr(G|W)\Pr(W). \qquad [9.1]$$

Once we have the table of joint probabilities, it is a simple matter to compute the probabilities needed for the decision tree. The probability of a given test result—say, $\Pr(G)$—is found by adding across the appropriate row. In algebraic terms,

$$\Pr(G) = \Pr(W\&G) + \Pr(D\&G), \qquad [9.2]$$

so that $\Pr(G) = .3 + .2 = .5$. Note that a good test can occur when the site is really wet *and* when the site is really dry.

Next, we calculate revised probabilities. The chance that the site is wet given a good seismic test is computed as

$$\Pr(W|G) = \frac{\Pr(W\&G)}{\Pr(G)}, \qquad [9.3]$$

so that $\Pr(W|G) = .3/.5 = .6$. Similarly, we have $\Pr(W|B) = \Pr(W\&B)/\Pr(B)$ $= .1/.5 = .2$. Of course, these are precisely the answers we found earlier from the joint probability table. But, in this case, the partners did not begin with the table in front of them; rather, they started with a prior probability, $\Pr(W)$, and with information on the accuracy of the test, $\Pr(G|W)$ and $\Pr(B|D)$. From these facts, they were able to calculate the necessary probabilities: $\Pr(G)$, $\Pr(W|G)$, and $\Pr(W|B)$.

CHECK STATION 1   Suppose the partners face the same seismic test just discussed but are less optimistic about the site; the prior probability now is $\Pr(W) = .28$. Construct the joint probability table, and compute $\Pr(W|G)$ and $\Pr(W|B)$.

Bayes' Theorem

With a little practice, the step-by-step mechanics of calculating revised probabilities become routine. In fact, the sequence of steps can be condensed easily. For example, if we replace $\Pr(W\&G)$ in Equation 9.3 with the right-hand side of Equation 9.1, we obtain

$$\Pr(W|G) = \left[\frac{\Pr(G|W)}{\Pr(G)}\right][\Pr(W)]. \qquad [9.4]$$

This equation is the most common form of **Bayes' theorem** (named after Reverend Thomas Bayes, who wrote an essay on the subject in 1763). Bayes' theorem expresses the conditional probability needed for the decision in terms of the reverse conditional probability and the prior probability.[1]

---

[1] An expanded version of Bayes' theorem is obtained by taking the right-hand side of Equation 9.2 and substituting it for the denominator in Equation 9.4:

$$\Pr(W|G) = \frac{\Pr(G|W)\Pr(W)}{\Pr(G|W)\Pr(W) + \Pr(G|D)\Pr(D)}.$$

The partners have available numerical values for all the right-hand-side variables and, thus, can calculate $\Pr(W|G)$ directly. Note that the numerator is $\Pr(G\&W)$, and this term is repeated in the denominator along with $\Pr(G\&D)$. From this version of Bayes' theorem, we see that the magnitude of $\Pr(W|G)$ depends directly on the frequency of the event "good and wet" relative to the frequency of "good and dry."

Bayes' theorem is more than a numerical formula. More generally, it expresses the way new information affects a decision maker's probability assessments. The decision maker begins with a prior probability assessment; this is the second bracketed term in Equation 9.4. He or she revises this prior assessment in light of new information. Note that the revised probability, $Pr(W|G)$, depends directly on the prior probability, $Pr(W)$. Other things being equal, the larger one's prior probability, the larger will be one's revised probability. (The only exception is in the case of *perfect* information, where $Pr(W|G)$ is unity regardless of the prior assessment.)

Of course, the other factor affecting the revised probability is the new information itself (the first bracketed term in Equation 9.4). If the factor $[Pr(G|W)/Pr(G)]$ is greater than 1—that is, if $Pr(G|W)$ is greater than $Pr(G)$—the information will cause the partners to revise upward their probability of striking oil. But this is exactly what we would expect. If the frequency of a good test is greater for wet sites than the overall frequency of good results (for all sites, wet and dry), this means that a good test is a positive indicator of oil. The bigger the ratio $Pr(G|W)/Pr(G)$, the larger the upward revision. Let's look at a quick example illustrating Bayes' theorem.

HEALTH RISKS FROM SMOKING   About one in twelve American adults is a heavy smoker. One way to assess the health risk of heavy smoking is to study the population of individuals who have lung cancer. Among individuals suffering from lung cancer, the proportion of heavy smokers is one in three. Based on these facts, by what factor does the risk of lung cancer increase due to heavy smoking?

Using Bayes' theorem is the key to answering this question. Analogous to Equation 9.4, we write

$$Pr(LC|S) = \left[\frac{Pr(S|LC)}{Pr(S)} \right] Pr(LC)$$

where LC denotes lung cancer and S a heavy smoker. We know that $[Pr(S|LC)/Pr(S)] = (1/3)/(1/12) = 4$. Then, from the preceding equation, we conclude that $Pr(LC|S) = 4Pr(LC)$. In words, the risk of lung cancer for a smoker is *four* times the overall risk of lung cancer (for smokers and non-smokers together).

The partners face the same seismic test as earlier and (as in Check Station 1) hold the prior probability $Pr(W) = .28$. Determine the optimal actions in light of the test, and calculate the resulting expected profit. What is the value of the test?

CHECK STATION 2

VALUELESS INFORMATION   Not all new information is of value to the decision maker. The key question in evaluating new information is: What impact does it have in revising the decision maker's initial probability assessment? Consider again Bayes' theorem (Equation 9.4) in the context of the oil drilling problem:

$$Pr(W|G) = \left[\frac{Pr(G|W)}{Pr(G)}\right]Pr(W).$$

Suppose the test's past track record is such that $Pr(G|W) = Pr(G)$. In words, this says the chance of getting a good test for sites containing oil is no greater than the overall frequency of good tests at all sites, wet and dry. Clearly, the test would appear to have little predictive value; its result is completely uncorrelated with the true condition of the site, wet or dry. Bayes' theorem confirms that the test is *valueless*. Since the first factor in Equation 9.4 is 1, it follows that $Pr(W|G) = Pr(W)$. The new probability is identical to the prior probability; there is no probability revision. This being the case, the partners' decisions will not be affected by the outcome of the test. Obviously, then, their expected profit also will be unchanged; that is, the expected value of this new information will be zero. Such information is worthless.

CHECK STATION 3   The partners wish to evaluate the quality of a new seismic test before deciding to pay for it. They assess the following joint probabilities: $Pr(W\&G) = .32$, $Pr(B\&D) = .12$, $Pr(B\&W) = .08$, and $Pr(G\&D) = .48$. What is the value of the test?

There is one other important case in which new information or a test result would have no value. This occurs when the decision maker's optimal decision is unaffected by the test result even though the outcome may cause him or her to revise the probabilities. The decision maker takes the same actions with or without the test and so earns the same expected profit in each instance. Again the EVI is zero. Here's an illustrative example.

A NEW SEISMIC TEST   Suppose the quality of a new seismic test is summarized in the table. What is the EVI of this test?

	Wet (W)	Dry (D)	Total
Good (G)	.1	.1	.2
Bad (B)	.3	.5	.8
Total	.4	.6	1.0

From the table, we easily calculate that $Pr(W|G) = .1/.2 = .5$ and $Pr(W|B) = .3/.8 = .375$. After seeing a good test, the partners drill and attain an expected profit of $200,000. After a bad test, what expected profit would drilling bring? The requisite calculation is

$$E(\pi) = (.375)(600,000) + (.625)(-200,000) = 100,000.$$

Since drilling is profitable, the partners should drill even in light of a bad test result.

What is the overall expected profit with the test? After good tests (20 percent of the time), the partners drill and earn $200,000. After bad tests (the other 80 percent of the time), they also drill and earn $100,000. Thus, their expected profit is $(.2)(200,000) + (.8)(100,000) = \$120,000$. But this is exactly the same profit they earn without the test. After a little thought, this should not be a surprise. Without the test, the optimal action is to drill. With the test, the optimal action is to drill. Since they take the same actions with or without the test, they earn the same expected profit in each instance.

What is the general lesson to be learned from this example? Acquiring new information is beneficial if and only if it has the potential to affect the manager's actual decisions. If it does not, the information is of no value.[2]

OTHER APPLICATIONS

For pedagogical purposes, we have made intensive use of the oil drilling example. However, it is important to stress the *general* application of information issues in all types of business and public policy decisions. In a host of settings, the decision maker is confronted with the task of quantifying his or her uncertainty, that is, estimating a probability. Here are some examples:

- The largest consumer-products firms launch between 15 and 25 new products each year from a potential pool of 50 to 100 candidates. How can the firms' product managers judge the likely success rates of different products? Which kinds of products (and marketing campaigns) have been most successful in the past? Based on surveys and market tests, how should the companies reassess their products' chances of success?

- In the relentless pursuit of quality, a parts supplier for the automobile industry seeks to reduce its rate of product defects. How does it estimate its defect rate? How can it identify the key factors that affect this rate? Would modifying its production-line process reduce the rate?

- Do a chemical company's emissions into the air (at levels within legal standards) pose a health risk for its workers or the surrounding residents? Are the emissions responsible for an increased rate of certain types of cancer in the community? Is the cancer rate actually elevated, and, if so, what other factors (age or other characteristics of the population, or even chance) would account for this?

---

[2] This point holds regardless of the decision maker's attitude toward risk. Given the opportunity to acquire information, a risk-averse manager solves the same decision tree as his or her risk-neutral counterpart but uses expected utility as a guide. Information is valuable if the expected utility with the information (after accounting for its cost) exceeds the expected utility without it.

In the preceding examples and in most other similar problems, there is no shortage of historical data that may have a bearing on the probability being estimated. The tough questions are: What is the best way to interpret the data? How can the manager identify factors that distinguish when a risk will be high or low? These are not easy questions to answer. Nonetheless, the road to the answers almost always begins with constructing two-dimensional tables of probabilities. Such tables look much like those in the wildcatter example. The column headings list the actual risk or uncertain event of concern to the decision maker. The row headings summarize the way in which the decision maker has categorized the data—identifying factors that influence the relevant risk. Here are two examples.

The Science of Baseball

The national pastime of baseball has been called a "game of inches." The umpire calls a pitch a ball instead of a third strike, and the next pitch is hit for a home run. A ball hit just beyond the shortstop's reach becomes a game winner. Baseball is also a game of decisions and statistics. Managers make dozens of moves and decisions during a ball game. General managers put together team rosters (drafting players, making trades) by continually gauging talent, again based on player statistics.

For the last five years, the Oakland Athletics under General Manager Billy Beane have been the leading proponents of "money ball"—using statistical analysis to build the strongest winning team with a limited total payroll.[3] "Old-school thinking judged a prospective ballplayer by whether he had the traditional "tools": the abilities to hit, field, throw, and run. Scouts believed they could judge these talents simply by watching a prospect play. This subjective assessment could be backed up by traditional hitting statistics (batting average, home run, and runs batted in) and pitching statistics (win–loss record and earned run average).

Beane was one of the first to realize that these old-school methods were often biased and inefficient. How good a ballplayer looked on the field was far less important than how many runs he produced (or for a pitcher how many opposing runs he prevented). A new breed of baseball analysts was uncovering much better hitting and pitching statistics to predict winning performance. Oakland's record between 1999 and 2004 proved the point. Oakland was the second most winning team during this span (and in the top 10 each year) despite having one of the lowest payrolls (between 25th and 28th among 30 major league teams). Almost a dozen teams have since followed Oakland's statistical lead. In building a winning team today, the right statistics (and, of course, money) talk.

[3] On building a winning ball team using the "new" statistics, see M. Lewis, *Money Ball* (New York, NY: W. W. Norton & Company, 2003). Bill James was the first to apply a modern statistical approach to baseball. An excellent discussion of statistical averages and managerial decisions appears in J. Thorn and P. Palmer, *The Hidden Game of Baseball* (Garden City, NY: Doubleday, 1985).

Statistics and playing the averages also matter on the field, 162 games a year. Put yourself in the shoes of the manager of the local team. It is the seventh inning of a 3-to-3 ball game. The opposing team has runners on first and third bases due to an infield single and an error. There is one out, and the opposing team's left-handed "cleanup" hitter is coming to bat. Should you allow your starting right-handed pitcher to face the batter, or should you use your ace left-handed relief pitcher?

In pondering this decision, you have no shortage of probabilistic information. Begin with the opposing hitter's batting average. Let's say he is a .300 hitter (i.e., has averaged three base hits in every 10 times at bat). This is a fine performance. However, in his last 10 games, the player has hit poorly, averaging only .240. But today he already has hit a double against the starting pitcher. However, he is slow of foot and frequently hits into double plays (which your starting pitcher is adept at inducing). Yet, the relief pitcher may be the better bet. The cleanup hitter averages only .255 against left-handers, and the relief pitcher has allowed opposing hitters only a .235 batting average. A telling factor, however, is that the hitter has 11 hits in 24 lifetime attempts against your left-hander.

Our purpose in this example is not to establish the manager's optimal decision (although second-guessing is fun); rather, it is to make the point that any decision requires categorizing the past data on the basis of the most relevant predictive factors. This example is complicated because for every factor working in one direction, there seems to be another factor working in the other. Nonetheless, the only way to make the best-informed decision is to take all relevant factors into account.

To sum up, from a manager's or general manager's point of view, baseball is a game of tendencies and percentages. The difference between a fine .300 hitter and a poor .200 hitter is one extra hit in every 10 times at bat. Small as it seems, this difference looms large over a 162-game season. Earl Weaver, the former manager of the Baltimore Orioles, was a vigorous proponent of baseball by the numbers. In making pitching decisions, he kept tabs on the batting record of each opposing hitter against each of his team's pitchers. Not everyone (especially his pitchers) agreed with this approach. As Jim Palmer, Baltimore's Hall of Fame pitcher put it, "The only thing Earl Weaver knows about pitching is that as a player he couldn't hit it."

Predicting Credit Risks

Let's revisit the fourth introductory example of Chapter 1. How can a bank assess and accurately predict the creditworthiness of a new business customer? In recent years, banks have increasingly turned to statistical measures, compiling computerized composite credit "scores" for customers. The bank's aim is to distinguish high-risk and low-risk accounts, closing or reducing credit limits on the former and increasing limits on the latter.

Consider how the method works in screening traditional business loans. The loan division of a bank has spent considerable time and energy developing a scoring system for predicting the default rates on different loan accounts.[4] The scoring formula incorporates key characteristics of the customer, the type and purpose of the loan, and forecasts of future economic conditions, all of which influence or indicate the risk of default. Bank officers put each loan into one of four categories on the basis of these scores. After a year's experience with the system, the bank is ready to assess its performance. In doing so, it has constructed the data in Table 9.2a. The table shows the breakdown of "performing" (paying) loans in the four categories and defaulted loans (also by category) over the past year.

Last year, the overall rate of default by the bank's business customers was one in 10 loan accounts. The overall quality of business customers seeking loans this year is expected to be unchanged from last (as is the general business climate). How should the bank use this information in making loan decisions? Table 9.2b provides the answer. This table computes the joint probabilities of all possible events by multiplying prior and conditional probabilities. For example, the proportion of all loans that are designated in class A and that default is

$$\text{Pr(default\&A)} = \text{Pr(A|default)Pr(default)}$$
$$= (.1)(.1) = .01$$

The other entries in the joint probability table are calculated in similar fashion.

The bank's final step (Table 9.2c) is to compute revised probabilities: the default risk for each designated loan category. These risks are approximately 5, 5, 13, and 25 percent for the respective categories. We can draw several observations from these results. First, as we might expect, loans identified as "high-risk" (class D) have by far the greatest probability of default. Presumably these loans were extended under much stricter conditions—higher interest rates, stiffer collateral conditions, lower loan amounts—because of their risk. Still, it is natural to ask whether the bank's loan officers (at the time of granting) recognized exactly how risky class D loans actually were. (Perhaps at the time they saw them as 15 to 20 percent risks.) In light of the actual 25 percent default rate, the bank may be well advised to stop making class D loans altogether (or make them under even more stringent conditions).

A second observation is that the actual default risks for class A and class B loans are indistinguishable. The scoring system seemingly does not work very well in gauging small risks; that is, it makes a distinction when none exists. This suggests taking a closer look at the class A (zero-risk) loans that actually failed.

---

[4] For an account of banks' scoring methods, see M. Quint, "Banks Raise Scrutiny of Credit Cards," *The New York Times* (March 27, 1991), D1 and R. Simon, "Looking to Improve Your Credit Score? Fair Isaac Can Help," *The Wall Street Journal*, (March 19, 2002), A1.

TABLE 9.2

Assessing Loan Risks

Part a lists the frequency of loan categories by actual default experience.

Part b lists the joint probabilities of all outcomes.

Part c shows the conditional probabilities.

(a) Frequencies of Loan Categories by Actual Default Record

Category	Performing Loan	Defaulted Loan
A (zero risk)	.2	.1
B (solid)	.4	.2
C (uncertain)	.3	.4
D (high risk)	.1	.3
Total	1.0	1.0

For example, 10 percent of all defaulted loans were (incorrectly) judged to be "zero" risk at the time the money was lent.

(b) Joint Probabilities

Category	Performing Loan	Defaulted Loan	Total
A (zero risk)	.18	.01	.19
B (solid)	.36	.02	.38
C (uncertain)	.27	.04	.31
D (high risk)	.09	.03	.12
Total	.90	.10	1.00

(c) Conditional Probabilities

$Pr(default|A) = .01/.19 = .05$

$Pr(default|B) = .02/.38 = .05$

$Pr(default|C) = .04/.31 = .13$

$Pr(default|D) = .03/.12 = .25$

Do these loans share common attributes? Could the scoring system be modified to identify these loans as low-risk class B loans? To sum up, the scoring system provides valuable information bearing on actual loan performance. However, the bank probably has further work to do in refining the system.

INTUITIVE PREDICTION

By now you should be familiar with and practiced in the simple mechanics of computing probabilities based on new information. Of course, the typical manager (and, to be sure, the average person) does not have Bayes' theorem on the tip of his or her tongue; rather the manager probably uses informal prediction methods based on personal judgment, experience, and intuition. However, there are two main problems with informal approaches.

The first difficulty is that the logic underlying the prediction often is "uncheckable" or at least hard to pin down. What factors led the individual to make that prediction? How would this forecast change under different circumstances or assumptions? Some sort of logical analysis is necessary to answer these questions. Even forecasters with track records of accurate predictions must be able to explain the reasons for their forecasts to others. Again, formal analysis is essential. To take an extreme case, how confident would you be in a forecaster, no matter how accurate the track record, if he or she confessed to using astrological tables or a Ouija board?

The second difficulty is that forecasts based informally on intuition, judgment, and experience frequently are inaccurate or biased. For instance, a common layperson's belief is that a large head, forehead, or brain is a sign of intelligence. But scientific evidence shows this hypothesis to be false. Perhaps the best way to understand the difficulties in making probabilistic predictions is to test yourself on some short (but subtle) examples.

Illustrative Prediction Problems

For each of the following examples, use your informal judgment to come up with your own best probability estimate of the event in question. After recording your intuitive responses, you may wish to use a formal method (a joint probability table or Bayes' theorem) to find solutions. Keep yourself honest by writing down your responses before turning to the answers that follow.

EXAMPLE 1   An individual, picked at random from the U.S. labor force, is described in the following short psychological sketch:

> Steve is shy and withdrawn, with little interest in people or the world of reality. He has a need for order and structure and a passion for detail.

Which of the following is Steve's most likely occupation: (1) farmer, (2) salesperson, (3) librarian, (4) airline pilot, or (5) doctor?

EXAMPLE 2   You are presented with three boxes. Each box has two compartments. In one box there is a gold coin in each compartment. In the second, there is a silver coin in each compartment. In the third, there is a gold coin in one compartment and a silver coin in the other. The compartments are closed, and the boxes (identical from the outside) are randomly mixed. You choose one box and are allowed to open one compartment. Suppose you see a silver coin. What are the chances that the coin in the other compartment is silver?

EXAMPLE 3   During his annual medical examination, a 59-year-old man had a chemical test on a sample of his stool. Blood in the stool is a possible indication of cancer of the bowel. This cancer is relatively rare; for a man this age, the incidence of bowel cancer is about 1 in 1,000. It is also quite curable provided it is identified early, while still small. In answer to his questions, the man is told that a test is available and is 95 percent accurate; that is, if cancer is present, the test will be positive with 95 percent probability. Likewise, if there is no cancer, the test will be negative 95 percent of the time. Suppose the test result is positive. What is the chance that the man has cancer of the bowel?

Answers to the Prediction Problems

EXAMPLE 1   For this question, the most common response by far is librarian, followed by farmer and airline pilot. Apparently the psychological sketch fits the commonly perceived stereotype of a librarian. Overlooked in this answer is one crucial fact: The individual has been picked at random from the labor force. This being the case, one's prior probability (before reading the sketch) should be heavily weighted toward salesperson. Salespeople comprise roughly 15 percent of the labor force; farmers are next, at under 3 percent; and librarians comprise only a fraction of 1 percent. How much should the sketch alter these prior probabilities? Surely very little, since we have but two sentences about Steve, and they are not very informative or discriminating. Perhaps half of all persons might be described as orderly and passionate about detail. Up to a quarter of the population might regard themselves as "shy." Moreover, not all librarians are shy, nor are all salespersons gregarious. In short, the observation that the worker has been picked at random is the overriding determinant of his likely occupation. Nonetheless, most people overlook this fact and invest too much confidence in the relatively uninformative sketch.

EXAMPLE 2   The nearly unanimous answer to this question is 50 percent. One reasons that the draw rules out the gold-gold box, leaving either the silver-silver or gold-silver boxes as equally likely. Despite its overwhelming intuitive appeal, this answer is wrong. The chances are two in three that the other coin will be silver. An easy way to see this is to note that there is a total of three silver coins in the boxes, and the coin you see is equally likely to be any of the three. But two of these coins reside in the all-silver box, meaning its neighbor is silver. Only one of the silver coins has a gold neighbor. Thus, upon seeing a silver coin, the odds are two to one against the other coin being gold. Bayes' theorem provides a neat confirmation of this correct answer:

$$\Pr(SS \text{ box}|S) = \left[\frac{\Pr(S|SS \text{ box})}{\Pr(S)}\right]\Pr(SS \text{ box}).$$

On the right-hand side, the first term is 1.0 (a silver coin is a certainty from the SS box), the second term is .5 (the overall chance of picking a silver coin is $1/2$), and the last term (the prior chance of picking the SS box at random) is $1/3$. Thus, we find $\Pr(SS \text{ box}|S) = 2/3$.

EXAMPLE 3   On the basis of the near-perfect test, most respondents see cancer as very likely, in the range of 50 to 95 percent. However, the correct chance is only about 2 percent. This surprising answer can be confirmed by using Bayes' theorem or by applying the following simple reasoning. Suppose a thousand 59-year-old men were to be tested. According to the prior probability, one man actually would have cancer; with near certainty, he would test positive. Of the remaining 999 healthy men, 95 percent would test negative. But 5 percent, or 50 men, would record false positives. In all, one would expect 51 positives, 1 true and 50 false. Thus, $\Pr(\text{cancer} \mid +) = 1/51$, or about 2 percent. Why is this probability so low? It is because the disease is very rare in the first place. Because the test is not quite perfect, the false positives tend to "swamp" the true positives. Thus, the revised probability is much lower than intuition would suggest. We should note that the test caused a large probability revision: a 20-fold increase from 1 in 1,000 to 2 in 100. In this sense, the test is quite informative. Thus, it may be very valuable in guiding subsequent medical treatment.

These examples are representative of a host of examples (used by economists and psychologists in their research) showing the systematic errors individuals make in predicting probabilities. A number of important conclusions emerge from this research. First, individuals are *overconfident* in their abilities to make such predictions. Consequently, their prediction mistakes (large and recurrent as they may be) always come as a surprise. (Even for professional forecasters, the common saying is "often wrong, never in doubt.") Second, individuals make mistakes in combining new and old information. In many cases, individuals put too much weight on seemingly compelling information (the psychological sketch or the positive medical test) and too little weight on the underlying prior probability of the event in question. In other cases, they fail to appreciate the weight that should be given statistical information (particularly when based on large, random samples).

To sum up, the evidence on individual intuitive prediction delivers a cautionary message. The use of formal analysis guided by Bayes' theorem offers a much better guide to probabilistic prediction.

**The *Challenger*
Disaster and
NASA's Risk
Analysis**

On January 28, 1986, the space shuttle *Challenger* exploded 74 seconds after takeoff, killing schoolteacher Christa McAuliffe and the six astronauts on board. The presidential commission that investigated the disaster faulted a series of decisions by NASA surrounding the flight.[5] Beset by escalating costs and three previous launch delays, NASA went ahead with the January launch despite the knowledge of potential risks.

[5] This account is drawn from a number of sources: W. Biddle, "What Destroyed the Challenger?" *Discover Magazine* (April 1986): 40–47; D. L. Chandler, "NASA's System for Assessing Risks Is Faulted," *Boston Globe* (March 5, 1988), 26; and J. E. Russo and P. J. Schoemarker, *Decision Traps* (New York: Simon and Schuster, 1990), 196–198.

The commission's principal criticism focused on NASA failures to recognize and accurately assess key launch risks. The explosion was caused by a blowout of the O-ring seal between two sections of the booster rocket. Moreover, on the basis of their experience with earlier shuttle flights, NASA and Morton Thiokol, the maker of the booster rocker, were aware of possible O-ring problems. O-ring wear had been observed on 7 of the 30 previous shuttle launches. Of course, the rockets had always done the job on the previous launches. So who could argue with a run of 30 successes?

If some O-ring damage was occurring, what was the proximate cause? NASA scientists had a vague concern about the link between low launch temperatures and O-ring failures. (Excessive cold might cause the rubber rings to become brittle.) These concerns became more salient when a cold front and 30-degree temperatures were forecast for January 28. Because of the cold, a prominent Morton Thiokol engineer recommended against the launch. But this advice was overruled, and the warning was not communicated to top NASA officials. The temperature was 36 degrees Fahrenheit at launch time.

The following temperature line shows the data that NASA scientists gathered on the eve of the launch. The diagram shows the launch temperatures

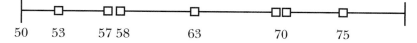

for the previous seven shuttle flights that had experienced O-ring wear. These "problem" launches occurred at both high and low temperatures, so the diagram reveals no discernible association between low launch temperatures and O-ring wear. Five of the seven flights had shown wear on a single O-ring. But the launch at 53 degrees Fahrenheit had experienced wear on three rings. An indication of low-temperature problems, perhaps? However, the launch at 75 degrees also exhibited abnormal wear, this time on two O-rings. It is not surprising that NASA scientists saw no real O-ring risks from low-temperature launches.

Was there evidence available that NASA overlooked? The answer is yes. NASA's crucial error was its failure to appreciate the evidence of the 23 "uneventful" flights. In fact, every one of the launches that were free of O-ring damage occurred at temperatures of 65 degrees and above. Against this background, the incidence of O-ring wear at relatively low temperatures looks quite damning. For instance, it is instructive to list the outcomes of all 30 launches in a simple 2-by-2 table.

	O-Ring Wear	No O-Ring Wear	Total
Temperature > 65°	3	23	26
Temperature < 65°	4	0	4
Total	7	23	30

The message of the table should be clear. Once we have separated out the most frequent outcome, high-temperature launches showing no wear, we are left with four launches made at lower temperatures (below 65°), *all of which experienced O-ring damage.* Thus, the table offers strong evidence that low-temperature launches entail O-ring risks.

By failing to incorporate the results of the "uneventful" flights in addition to the "problem" flights, NASA came up short in its risk assessment. To put this as simply as possible, data in all four cells of a 2-by-2 table are needed to establish an association between any two factors. Why did NASA miss such an apparently simple association? The investigative panel pointed to one important reason. NASA diligently compiled a checklist of over 4,500 "critical" risk factors. However, all these factors seemed to be treated equally, with no effort to distinguish the "most critical" factors. NASA should have set priorities according to the likelihood of each factor leading to system failure. Indeed, tests conducted for the presidential panel after the shuttle disaster showed that O-ring failure was much more sensitive to changes in temperature than had been previously imagined. If NASA had recognized the need to acquire this test information in advance, it would have certainly abandoned the cold-weather launch.

OPTIMAL SEARCH

Many management situations involve searching and uncovering (at a cost) a number of uncertain opportunities. Each option has its own cost and probability distribution concerning possible payoffs, independent of the other options. Options are explored (or searched) in sequence in whatever order is preferred. When management stops exploring new options, it selects the most profitable one from among its current options. Management's task is to find the best sequential search strategy, that is, the order in which to pursue options and when to stop.

Optimal Stopping

The sequential R&D decision in Chapter 8 illustrates one kind of optimal search. There the drug company could pursue (at a cost) either of two highly uncertain scientific methods in either order. After learning the results, it commercialized only one process: the one that proved more profitable. A related R&D problem offers another example of optimal search.

ESCALATING INVESTMENTS IN R&D   An electronics firm can initiate an important R&D program by making a $3 million investment. There is a 1/5 chance that the program will meet with immediate success (i.e., within the year), earning the firm a return of $10 million for a net profit of $7 million. If success does not come, the firm can invest another $3 million with the chance of success now 1/4. If this second stage fails, the firm can invest again, and so on, up to a total of five investments. The investment cost for each stage is $3 million, the ultimate return from a successful completion of the program (sooner or later) is $10 million, and the chances of success are 1/5, 1/4, 1/3, 1/2, and 1 for the investments. Should a risk-neutral firm pursue this program, and if so, at what stage (if any) should it stop?

This kind of decision is called an **optimal-stopping** problem. When (if ever) should the firm stop reinvesting? In a moment, we will use a decision tree to solve the problem. First, use your unaided judgment to select the best strategy. What did you choose? A cross section of student responses typically reveals a wide variety of opinion. To the nearest 10 percent, roughly 20 percent of students choose not to invest, 30 percent elect to invest all the way if necessary, and the remainder choose to stop after a certain number of failures. In fact, the most popular choice (about one-third of the responses) is to stop after three failures. Typical reasoning is that the "prize" is worth $10 million, so the firm should spend no more than $9 million (three failures) in pursuing it.

However, a little reflection shows that this reasoning is faulty. Stopping after a $9 million loss clearly is inferior to investing all the way. With the latter strategy, a $10 million "success" is ensured at a cost of no more than $15 million; the firm's loss is $5 million at worst.

The key to a correct analysis lies in recognizing the repetitive nature of the firm's decision problem. Having invested and failed, the firm faces the same decision as before under nearly the same conditions. Money already invested is a sunk cost and so is irrelevant as far as future actions are concerned. The relevant variables are the incremental investment cost, the profit from future success, and the probability of success. The first two variables are unchanged throughout, whereas the last increases stage by stage. This observation leads to an important conclusion: *If it is ever worth investing initially, it is worth continuing to invest because the odds of success get better and better (and no other facts change).* Thus, the firm can narrow its courses of action down to two: Either it should invest all the way or it should not invest at all.

The decision tree in Figure 9.3 shows the firm's best course of action. Note the repetitive nature of the tree. Decisions alternate with chance nodes. The firm continues to travel down the tree for as long as it invests and fails to achieve success. At each branch tip, the firm's resulting profit (net of all costs accumulated to date) is shown. As always, the optimal decision is found by averaging back the tree from right to left. Thus, the last decision encountered is the first one analyzed. If it comes to that decision, the firm obviously should invest a fifth time. (A $5 million loss from continuing is better than a $12 million loss from quitting.) Similarly, a comparison of expected values at each point of decision shows that the firm should invest a fourth time, a third time, and so on. Averaging back the tree, we find the initial investment to be profitable. Its expected value is $1 million. Thus, investing all the way is the optimal course of action.

FIGURE 9.3

A Sequential R&D Decision

Because the odds of success increase with each investment, the firm's best strategy is to continue to invest in the project. Its overall expected profit is $1 million.

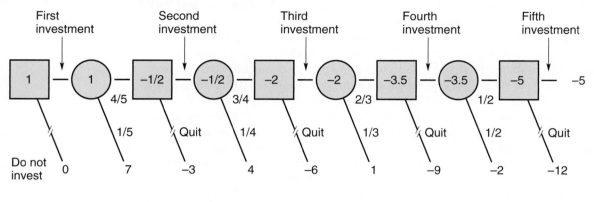

Because of the ever-increasing probabilities in the preceding example, the optimal-stopping strategy is to start and *never* stop. The more the company spends on the program, the closer it gets to ultimate success. Here the basic uncertainty is not whether success will come but whether it will come sooner or later. Of course, not all R&D programs share this feature. The riskiest research programs—those that depend on breakthroughs beyond the "current state of the art"—may never succeed, regardless of the size of the investment. (If it were simply a matter of spending money, the war on cancer would have been won during Gerald Ford's presidency or sooner.) As money is spent and failures continue to mount, the decision maker must realistically revise downward the probability of success. Thus, one would expect the success probabilities to *decrease* stage by stage.

With declining probabilities, the firm should give up the investment (irrespective of how much money has been sunk) when the revised probability of success falls sufficiently low. This stopping rule can be summarized by a cutoff probability (call this p*) below which the firm should not invest. In fact, the cutoff value for the multistage decision is exactly the same as for the single-stage problem; it must satisfy the zero-profit condition

$$p^*\pi - c = 0,$$

or, equivalently,

$$p^* = c/\pi,$$

where π denotes the profit upon success and c is the investment cost. At p*, the investment is a break-even proposition (i.e., the expected profit is zero). For any lower probability of success, the investment earns an expected loss and should not be pursued. For example, let π = \$20 million, c = \$3 million, and the success probabilities be .25, .21, .17, .13, .07, and .01. Since the cutoff value is p^* = 3/20 = .15, the firm should invest up to \$9 million (three investments), if necessary, before abandoning the program.

Optimal Sequential Decisions

In addition to optimal-stopping problems, managers face a variety of sequential decisions involving the order of actions. Chapter 8's R&D decision is one such example. Although such decisions usually are more complicated than stopping problems, many have simple enough structures that they can be solved without decision trees. Here is an example.

SEQUENCING R&D INVESTMENTS   Suppose a firm can choose one of several programs to develop a new product. Regardless of which method it uses, the firm earns a predictable profit (call this π) upon successful development. However, the methods have differing investment costs (c) and probabilities of success (p). In what order should the firm pursue the methods?

The surprising, simple answer is that the methods should be pursued in order of their probability-to-cost ratios, p/c. The program with the greatest p/c ratio should be tried first. If it succeeds, the firm's search is over; if it fails, the program with the next highest ratio should be tried next; and so on. To check this result, consider the case of two programs, A and B. If the firm pursues A first, its expected net benefit is

$$p_A\pi - c_A + (1 - p_A)(p_B\pi - c_B)$$
$$= p_A\pi + p_B\pi - p_Ap_B\pi - c_A - c_B + p_Ac_B. \qquad [9.5]$$

Here the firm's expected gross profit is $p_A\pi + p_B\pi - p_Ap_B\pi$. The cost of the two programs is $c_A + c_B$. However, if A is successful, the firm saves c_B. This happens with a probability of p_A and accounts for the last term in the second line of Equation 9.5. If program B is pursued first instead, the firm's expected net benefit is identical to the second line of Equation 9.5 except that the last term is p_Bc_A. Therefore, pursuing A first is more profitable than pursuing B first if and only if $p_Ac_B > p_Bc_A$, or, equivalently, $p_A/c_A > p_B/c_B$. Thus, the programs should be pursued in order of their probability-to-cost ratios. When there are more than two programs, the demonstration is analogous.

It is interesting to note that this solution also applies to the classic problem of searching in one of a number of locations for a lost object. Suppose the goal is to find the object in the fewest number of searches on average. It is assumed that all locations have the *same cost* of search. With equal search

374 Chapter 9 The Value of Information

costs, the preceding solution instructs us to begin the search in the location with the highest likelihood of success and, if the object isn't there, to try the next most likely spot, and so on. Of course, this is exactly what we would expect. If search costs differ, the way to minimize expected search costs is to search in order of p/c. This is the best we can do, but it cannot change the fact that one always finds the item in the last place one looks! We can sum up this discussion as follows:

> A risk-neutral firm should (1) continue to invest in an R&D program as long as $p > c/\pi$ and (2) determine the sequence of investments in descending order of p/c.

CHECK
STATION 4 An industrial buyer is negotiating with firm A to procure spare parts. In the buyer's judgment, firm A's best final price offer will be $120, $140, or $165 per part with respective probabilities of .15, .25, and .6. Knowing A's best offer, the buyer can accept it or go on to negotiate with a second supplier, firm B, whose possible prices are $130 and $180, each equally likely. (If the buyer rejects firm A's price, it cannot go back to the firm later.) What plan of action minimizes the buyer's expected price? Could the buyer do better by first approaching firm B and using firm A as a backup?

THE VALUE OF ADDITIONAL ALTERNATIVES

We all are aware of the advantage of increasing the number of available options. Choosing among a larger number of alternatives is always preferable to selecting from a smaller number. Clearly, the decision maker benefits if his or her most preferred option is in the larger set of alternatives and not in the smaller. For someone with a real sweet tooth, the dessert selection is the first part of the menu that person studies in a gourmet restaurant. We all know the sinking feeling that comes on learning from the server that the dessert we crave is no longer available.

Of course, in most managerial decisions the available alternatives do not come so neatly packaged; rather, the manager's task is to uncover and seek out additional options. The difficulty is that the manager typically pursues a strategy of search in an uncertain environment. He or she can make only probabilistic predictions about the additional alternatives that might be uncovered and whether one of these would be worth choosing.

Simultaneous Search

Frequently, a decision maker can augment the number of alternatives from which he or she will choose later—usually at some cost. It is natural to ask: What is the expected benefit from expanding the domain of choice? Is doing so worth the cost? Consider the following example.

SEARCHING FOR THE BEST PRICE   With the aid of its investment banker, a firm is seeking to sell one of its divisions at the highest attainable price. The investment banker is hopeful that it can find as many as eight to ten potential buyers for the division. Its best assessment is that the offer of a typical potential buyer will be centered around $52 million, with a range of plus or minus $12 million. In fact, it assesses a *uniform distribution* for the offer; that is, it regards all values between $40 million and $64 million as *equally* likely. The investment banker also believes that buyer offers will, by and large, be independent of one another. (Each buyer's offer comes from the equally likely range just given, regardless of others' offers.) In looking for the best sale price, what strategy should the firm pursue? What is the best price it can get, on average, from contacting outside buyers?

Let's consider the second question first. Suppose the firm contacts a *single* buyer. Then the *average* price it can obtain is $52 million. In turn, what if the investment banker can find two potential buyers, allowing the firm to choose the *higher* price of the two? How high will this "better" price be on average? The answer is $56 million. For the moment, the exact number is less important than understanding that the firm fares better on average from choosing the higher of the two price offers than by being locked into a single price. Of course, it does even better if it has the opportunity to pick the highest price from among three potential buyers, better still with four buyers, and so on.

Table 9.3 lists the expected maximum price attainable as the number of buyers varies up to nine. As we would expect, the "best" price rises steadily with the number of buyers. In fact, there is a simple formula for computing the expected maximum value among a number of variables (call this number n) drawn independently from a uniform distribution. The expected maximum value is

$$E(V_{max}) = \left(\frac{1}{n+1}\right)L + \left(\frac{n}{n+1}\right)U \qquad [9.6]$$

where L is the lowest possible value and U is the greatest possible value. In our example, we have $L = 40$ and $U = 64$. For instance, if $n = 3$, then $E(V_{max}) = (1/4)(40) + (3/4)(64) = 58$. Observe that the expected maximum value is a *weighted* average of the extreme values, L and U, the weights being $1/(n+1)$ and $n/(n+1)$. For a single buyer ($n = 1$), the weights are .5 and the expected price is a straight average of the minimum and maximum values (i.e., halfway between them). As the number of buyers increases, the expected maximum price approaches the upper end of the possible value range because the weight on U approaches 1.[6]

---

[6] We can rearrange Equation 9.6 in the form
$$E(V_{max}) = L + [n/(n+1)][U - L].$$
In short, the expected value of V_{max} is $n/(n+1)$ of the way between the lower and upper bounds.

TABLE 9.3

Expected Maximum Prices When Choosing from Different Numbers of Buyers	Expected Maximum Price (Millions of Dollars)		
	Number of Buyers	Uniform Distribution	Normal Distribution[a]
The greater the number of buyers from which to choose, the higher the seller's expected price.	1	52.0	52.0 (0)
	2	56.0	56.5 (.56)
	3	58.0	58.8 (.85)
	4	59.2	60.2 (1.03)
	5	60.0	61.3 (1.16)
	6	60.6	62.2 (1.27)
	7	61.0	62.8 (1.35)
	8	61.3	63.4 (1.42)
	9	61.6	63.9 (1.49)

[a] Numbers in parentheses indicate the difference between the expected price and the mean of the normal distribution—measured in number of standard deviations. For instance, on average, the highest of three prices drawn independently from a normal distribution lies .85 standard deviations above the distribution mean. In our example, the distribution mean is 52 and the standard deviation is 8. Therefore, the expected price is found to be $52 + (.85)(8) = 58.8$, as shown.

The preceding result generalizes as follows: For any distribution of values (not only the uniform), the expected maximum value increases with the number of independently drawn alternatives. The last column of Table 9.3 shows the expected maximum value when values come from a normal (bell-shaped) distribution. (The mean is 52 and the standard deviation is 8.)[7] Although the uniform and normal distributions are very different in shape, they display a qualitatively similar pattern of maximum values. Note that expected maximum values are higher for the normal than for the uniform distribution. Roughly speaking, this is because the uniform distribution has a fixed upper limit of possible values, whereas the normal distribution does not.

Table 9.3 shows the expected benefit from pursuing additional buyers. Clearly, if this pursuit is costless, the firm should seek out as many buyers as it can possibly find. More realistically, suppose finding additional buyers is costly— in fact, the total fee the firm can expect to pay its investment banker depends on how wide and costly a search the banker makes on the firm's behalf. For concreteness, suppose the banker sets its fee according to the number of buyers it enlists, charging an average cost of $1 million per found buyer. From the firm's point of view, how many potential buyers should it instruct the banker to enlist?

[7] The mean and standard deviation have been set so that the normal distribution roughly "matches" the uniform one above. Remember that two-thirds of the time a normally distributed variable falls within one standard deviation of the mean. For the uniform distribution here, the probability of a value within plus or minus 8 around the mean is also two-thirds.

As always, marginal analysis offers a direct answer. Additional buyers should be sought so long as the expected marginal benefit (MB) exceeds the extra cost (MC). From Table 9.3, we find the optimal number to be four in the uniform case. (From three to four buyers, MB is $1.2 million and exceeds MC, but from four to five, MB is less than MC.) The firm's expected price (net of investment banking fees) is $59.2 - 4 = \$55.2$ million. For the normal distribution, in turn, the optimal number of buyers is five. By experimenting with different search costs, we easily can confirm that the lower the cost of the search, the greater the number of buyers the firm should seek.

In the preceding example, what would be the effect on the optimal number of buyers if a typical buyer's value were uniformly distributed between $46 and $70? (Note that the expected value of the typical buyer has increased by $6, but the dispersion, that is, standard deviation, is unchanged.) What would be the effect if a typical buyer's value were distributed uniformly between $46 and $58? (Here the typical buyer's expected value is unchanged but the standard deviation has been cut in half.)

CHECK STATION 5

The Stock Market and the Economy Revisited

As noted at the beginning of the chapter, the stock market has dropped precipitously prior to all eight postwar recessions. In light of a sustained stock market drop, some analysts have concluded that there will be a forthcoming recession. Do you agree?

The answer is not a simple "yes." As a famous economist once said, "The stock market has predicted 14 of the last 8 recessions." Thus, in at least six instances, stock prices have fallen without a subsequent economic recession. In these cases, stock price movements were a false indicator of the future course of the economy. Thus, a rough estimate for the chances of a recession given a stock market drop is 8/14 or 57 percent.

Table 9.4a illustrates the point by recording the historical record of growth and recession combined with stock market movements. While the U.S. economy has suffered eight periods of recession in the postwar period, the norm has been a growing economy. (The table shows that the economy grew in 32 out of 40 periods, or roughly 80 percent of the time.) The stock market fell prior to all eight recessions, but it also fell prior to periods of economic growth. From the second row of Table 9.4, we see that after a prolonged drop in the stock market (S−), the probability of a coming recession (R) is $\Pr(R|S-) = 8/14$, or 57 percent.

Now let's return to the yacht dealer's decision introduced in Chapter 8. Recall that the dealer assessed a .6 chance for a growing economy (G). This is more pessimistic than historical experience would suggest. Based on this forecast, the dealer's optimal course of action was to order 50 yachts, thereby earning an expected profit of $175,000. We now can ask: How should the dealer revise this forecast of economic conditions in light of stock market movements? How many yachts should the dealer order?

The historic record provides measures of the stock market's accuracy in forecasting the course of the economy. From Table 9.4a, we see that $\Pr(S-|R) = 8/8 = 1.0$,

TABLE 9.4

The Stock Market as a
Leading Indicator
of the Economy

(a) The Historical Record	Economy Grows (G)	Recession (R)	Total
Stocks Rise (S+)	26	0	26
Stocks Drop (S−)	6	8	14
Total	32	8	40

(b) The Yacht Dealer's Assessed Probabilities	Economy Grows (G)	Recession (R)	Total
Stocks Rise (S+)	.4875	0	.4875
Stocks Drop (S−)	.1125	.4	.5125
Total	.6000	.4	1.000

$Pr(S+|G) = 26/32 = .8125$, and $Pr(S-|G) = 6/32 = .1875$. Using this information, the yacht dealer can construct part b of the table. Note that the intent is to assess *current* prospects for the economy. Thus, the dealer starts with his current assessment, his *prior probability*, $Pr(G) = .6$. The upper-left entry lists the joint probability that stocks rise (S+) and the economy grows (G). This is computed as:

$$Pr(S+\&G) = Pr(S+|G)Pr(G) = (.8125)(.6) = .4875.$$

Similarly,

$$Pr(S-\&G) = Pr(S-|G)Pr(G) = (.1875)(.6) = .1125.$$

The second column is self-explanatory. We can readily compute revised probabilities from part b of the table:

$$Pr(G|S+) = .4875/.4875 = 1.0$$

and

$$Pr(G|S-) = .1125/.5125 = .22.$$

The decision tree in Figure 9.4 completes the solution. In light of a rising stock market, there is no chance of a recession. Accordingly, the dealer should order 100 yachts, anticipating an expected profit of $350,000. If the stock market falls, there is a 78 percent chance of a recession. The best the dealer can do is to order 50 yachts, earning an expected profit of $127,500. Averaging the cases of rising and falling stock prices, the dealer has an overall expected profit of $(.4875)(350,000) + (.5125)(127,500) = \$236,000$. The dealer does well to gear the size of the order to future prospects of the economy as signaled by stock movements. The dealer's expected value of information is $EVI = 236,000 - 175,000 = \$61,000$.

FIGURE 9.4

Yacht Orders and the
Stock Market

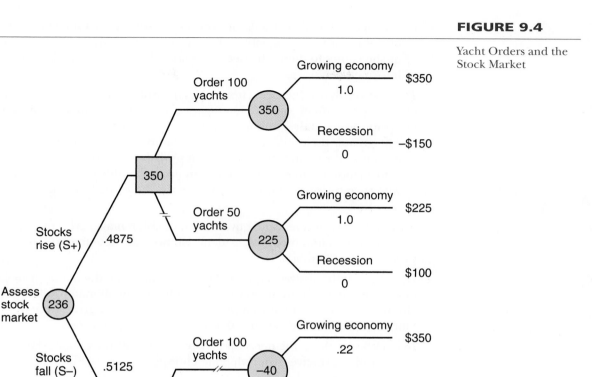

SUMMARY

Decision-Making Principles

1. Any new information source is potentially valuable in influencing
   forecasts of uncertain events and, thus, guiding better decisions.
   a. The decision maker should acquire additional information if and only
      if its expected value (in making better decisions) exceeds its cost.

b. The decision maker should not commit needlessly to a single course of action for the foreseeable future. By crossing bridges only when he or she comes to them, the decision maker can expect to make better-informed decisions.

2. The logic of Bayes' theorem shows that any probability forecast is based on a combination of the decision maker's previous information (his or her prior probabilities) and newly acquired information.
a. The greater the initial degree of uncertainty or the stronger the new evidence, the greater the subsequent probability revision.
b. Information is valueless if it results in no probability revisions or, even with such revisions, it does not change the individual's optimal decisions.

3. Although most business and government decision makers rely on informal prediction methods, evidence shows that these methods are prone to error and bias.

4. Optimal search involves sequential decisions in which the manager seeks out and evaluates alternatives from which he or she ultimately will choose. The manager's search propensity increases the greater the marginal benefit of search and the smaller the marginal cost.

5. In search situations, the decision maker is better off the greater the number of alternatives from which to choose.

Nuts and Bolts

1. Calculation of revised probabilities is accomplished using a joint probability table (with rows listing the test results and columns listing the uncertain outcomes) or employing Bayes' theorem.

2. New information (such as a test result) appears at the beginning, prior to the main decision, in the decision tree. A decision square follows each possible test outcome.

3. As always, the decision tree is solved by averaging out and folding back. The expected profit computed at the beginning of the tree measures the expected benefit from making decisions contingent on the acquired information.

4. The expected value of information is the difference between the decision maker's expected profit with the information and without it.

5. In a simultaneous search setting, the manager determines the optimal number of alternatives so that the marginal benefit of an additional alternative matches its marginal cost.

Questions and Problems

1. It is time to buy a new car, and you have done a considerable amount of research on the matter over the past weeks. From several articles in consumer magazines and scrutiny of numerous auto-buying Web sites, you have reviewed an impressive body of information on different models' repair records, road handling, specifications and features, comfort, customer satisfaction, and so on. You have test-driven a half-dozen candidates and discussed prices with several dealers for each model. All things considered, you have decided to buy Model M and will finalize your purchase in the next few days. However, after attending a party last night, you are less certain. An acquaintance spent the better part of the evening recounting the disastrous experience he had with his new Model M. He got rid of the car after six months of electrical, steering, and handling problems. He is considering suing the dealer and claims you are crazy even to consider buying Model M. What do you do now?

2. Just prior to baseball's spring training season, you are asked to assess the probability that a particular baseball team will win the coming World Series.
   a. How would you go about making this assessment? In what sense is this assessment subjective?
   b. If you knew absolutely nothing about baseball, what would be the appropriate probability assessment? As an avid sports fan, how would you modify this "naive" assessment? How would your assessment change day by day as the season progressed?

3. A health club has sent promotional material to a mailing list consisting of local college students, area doctors, and lawyers. The accompanying table shows the record of individuals taking up the club's introductory offer in the first two weeks of the promotion.

	Frequency of Respondents		
	Responded	**Did Not Respond**	**Total**
Students	.08	.16	.24
Doctors	.05	.13	.18
Lawyers	.09	.49	.58
Total	.22	.78	1.00

   a. What is the chance that a typical college student will respond to the promotion? A typical doctor? A typical lawyer? With respect to which group is the promotion most effective?
   b. How might the information in the table be useful to marketing and advertising managers?

4. The table that follows (compiled from police reports) shows the driving safety records for three age groups over the last year in a large metropolitan area.

	Number of Drivers Having:		
	No Accidents	1 Accident	2 or > Accidents
Age 17–30	90,243	12,050	1,822
Age 31–55	243,125	21,443	2,822
Over 55	149,674	16,621	2,293

a. An analyst points out that of 57,051 drivers involved in accidents last year, drivers aged 31 to 55 accounted for 24,265 cases, or some 43 percent of the total—a far greater proportion than any other age group. Should one conclude that this age group has the highest-risk drivers?

b. Which age group has the worst accident record? The best? Explain.

c. A separate analysis shows that for drivers aged 35 to 45, the rate of accidents (one or more per year) is 9.3 per 1,000 drivers. For drivers aged 65 to 75, the rate is 8.4 per 1,000 drivers. However, most studies show that members in the younger group are much safer drivers than those in the older group. Why might a simple comparison of accident rates per driver be misleading? What other important factor(s) should be taken into account?

5. Consider once again the decision to redesign an aircraft (Problem 4 in Chapter 8).

a. Find the expected value of perfect information about the redesign program. Calculate separately the expected value of perfect information about the U.S. government's decision.

b. Suppose the management of the consortium questions its engineers about the success or failure of the redesign program prior to committing to it. Management recognizes that its engineers are likely to be biased in favor of the program. It judges that if the program truly will succeed, the engineers will endorse it 90 percent of the time, but even if the program will fail, they will endorse it 50 percent of the time. What is the likelihood of success in light of an endorsement? What if the engineers do not endorse the program?

6. Consider the following simplified version of the television game show *Let's Make a Deal*. There is a grand prize behind one of three curtains; the other two curtains are empty. As a contestant, you get to choose a curtain at random. Let's say you choose curtain 3. Before revealing what's behind the curtain, the game show host always offers to show you what one of the other curtains contains. She shows you that curtain 2 is empty; in fact, she

always shows you an empty curtain. (You know that's how the game works; so does the audience and everybody else.) Now you must decide: Do you stick with your original choice, curtain 3, or switch to curtain 1? Which action gives you the better chance of finding the grand prize?

7. On behalf of your company, you are preparing a price bid to supply a fixed quantity of a good to a potential buyer. You are aware that a number of competitors also are eager to obtain the contract. The buyer will select the lowest bid. Your cost is $100,000. If yours is the winning bid, your profit is the difference between your bid and your cost. If not, your profit is zero. You are considering three possible bids:
   - Bid $110,000; the probability of winning is .9.
   - Bid $130,000; the probability of winning is .5.
   - Bid $160,000; the probability of winning is .2.
   a. Assuming your company's aim is to maximize its expected profit, which bid should you submit?
   b. In part a, your cost is $100,000 for certain. Now suppose it is uncertain: either $80,000 or $120,000, with each cost equally likely. Will this fact change your bidding behavior in part a? Explain briefly.
   c. Suppose it is possible to gain information about the cost so that you will know exactly what the cost will be ($80,000 or $120,000) before submitting a bid. Use a decision tree to find the value of this information.

8. Recall the earlier example of assessing the risk of loan defaults. Suppose the bank's top managers are divided on whether to adopt the scoring system permanently. A number of top officers believe their intuitive judgment about risks is superior to an "artificial" score. Accordingly, the bank decides to test its judgment against the scoring system. The managers will make their own designations of loans to the four categories and see how well they can identify problem loans. Their track record over the past year is shown in the table:

Category	Performing Loan	Defaulted Loan
A (zero risk)	.25	.20
B (solid)	.30	.25
C (uncertain)	.40	.45
D (high risk)	.05	.10
Total	1.00	1.00

   a. Predict the probability of default for each loan category. (Assume the overall default rate is 10 percent: Pr(default) = .1.)
   b. How do these risk assessments, based on judgment and intuition, compare with the earlier predictions based on credit scores? Which seems to provide more valuable information? Explain.

9. Firm B is considering whether to pursue an R&D effort to develop a powerful new microchip. One concern with the chip's design is that the chip might generate too much heat operating at high speeds. Indeed, there is the risk that the heat problem will doom the R&D effort. Firm B's scientists believe that there is a .5 chance that the R&D effort will succeed (S) and a .5 chance it will fail (F). If the effort succeeds, there is a second risk. Firm B has filed several patents concerning the design of the chip. If these patents are upheld in court, it will have the exclusive right to produce the chip. However, a competitor, firm Z, has been pursuing a similar chip design and has filed its own patents. If the courts decide in favor of firm Z, both firms will be free to produce similar chips and will share the market. Firm B's legal department estimates a .6 chance that its patents will be upheld giving it exclusive production rights.

The following table lists firm B's possible profit outcomes.

Failed R&D Investment:	−$40 million
Successful R&D/Exclusive Production Rights:	$50 million
Successful R&D/Shared Production Rights:	$ 5 million

a. Firm B must decide now whether to undertake the R&D investment. What course of action maximizes its expected profit? (Use a decision tree to justify your answer.)

b. Suppose instead that firm B can postpone its R&D decision for six months, by which time it will have learned the court's ruling on its patent. What is its expected profit if it waits? Depending on the court outcome, what actions should it take?

c. Suppose instead that firm B can build a 75 percent speed, prototype chip before committing to the full-scale R&D investment. The prototype chip will either run cool (C) or hot (H). The firm's scientists believe that the prototype will certainly run cool if the R&D effort is to succeed: $\Pr(C|S) = 1.0$. If the R&D effort is doomed to fail, the scientists believe that the prototype chip will run hot with probability 2/5: $\Pr(H|F) = .4$. Find $\Pr(S|C)$ and $\Pr(S|H)$.

d. Should the firm build the prototype chip at a cost of $2 million? Use a decision tree to justify your answer. (Assume that the firm *cannot* wait for the patent outcome.)

* 10. A government agency suspects that one of the firms it has hired under a cost-plus contract is padding its bills to the government. If padding is going on and if the agency can prove its case in court, it estimates it could save $2 million in disallowed costs. However, the cost of bringing a large-scale legal action against the firm is considerable, about $500,000. The agency's auditors believe that there is a 20 percent chance that padding is

* Starred problems are more challenging.

going on. Its lawyers reckon that there is a 75 percent chance of proving and winning the legal case (if padding is indeed taking place).

a. Assuming the agency is risk neutral, use a decision tree to determine its best course of action.

b. Suppose the agency can conduct a preliminary investigation (conduct audits and interview dozens of employees) before deciding whether to bring a case. From the investigation, the agency can expect one of two results: a "clean" outcome (C) or a "questionable bill of health" (Q). If cost padding really is going on, there is a 75 percent chance that the investigation will signal Q. If there really is no cost padding, then the chance of C is 80 percent. (There is a 20 percent chance that would-be whistle-blowers, such as disgruntled employees, will allege questionable practices even when no padding is going on.) If an investigation results in outcome Q, what is the chance that cost padding is going on?

c. Use a decision tree to determine the expected value to the agency of conducting an investigation.

*11. An oil wildcatter is considering drilling a site that she judges to be wet with probability .2 and dry with probability .8. Her profit from an oil strike is $1 million, and her loss from a dry hole is $-$.8 million.

a. Before drilling, the wildcatter can pay for a seismic test that will return an outcome of good or bad. In the past, wet sites have tested good 75 percent of the time, and dry sites have tested good 25 percent of the time. What is the test's EVI?

b. For a comparable fee, the wildcatter can find out whether a recently drilled well nearby struck oil (O) or not (N). If the wildcatter's site were wet, the nearby well also would be wet with certainty. If the site were dry, the nearby well also would be dry with probability .75. What is the EVI in this case?

c. Suppose the wildcatter purchases *both* sources of information. Now what is the EVI?

12. A firm anticipates an R&D program requiring as many as three stages. A successful program (sooner or later) will earn the firm a commercial profit of $20 million. The investment costs for the respective stages are $5 million, $3 million, and $4 million, and the conditional probabilities of success are .2, .3, and .1. What is the firm's optimal investment policy? What is its expected profit?

13. A firm is looking for the best (i.e., lowest) price from one of two sellers. It can approach each seller only once (and at no cost). Seller X's price is distributed uniformly between $30 and $40. Seller Y's price is distributed uniformly between $32 and $38. Which seller should the firm approach first, and what is the maximum price it should accept?

14. Suppose you will be shown three "prizes" in order. You know absolutely nothing about how valuable the prizes might be; only after viewing all

three can you determine which one you like best. However, after you see a prize and decline it, there is no "going back." You must select a prize immediately after seeing it, before seeing any subsequent prize.

a. Your sole objective is to obtain the best of the three prizes. (Second best does not count.) A random selection provides a one-third chance of getting the best prize. Find a strategy that provides a greater chance and compute the actual chance.

b. What if there is a large number of prizes (say, 10, 50, or 100)? Describe in general terms the kind of strategy that would maximize your chances of obtaining the *best* prize. (Do not try to compute an exact answer.)

Discussion Question In August 1999, Bridgestone/Firestone Inc. recalled 6.5 million tires in the wake of a number of tire-related rollover accidents involving the Explorer SUV produced by Ford Motor Company. Although Firestone tires have an admirable overall quality record and the Explorer ranks second in its safety record among eight leading brands of SUV, 88 fatalities in the United States and as many as 50 fatalities overseas have been linked to the combination of Firestone tires (three particular brands) mounted on the Explorer. A review of the Firestone/Ford disaster shows that both companies (as well as the National Highway Safety Administration) lacked the data to allow early recognition of this accident risk. (To this day, there is no way to "prove" the exact causes of the tire failures. Evidence and analysis of the safety risk are purely statistical.)

a. Ironically, the low overall rate of tire-related accidents made it more difficult to detect the particular Firestone/Ford risk. Why would this be the case? Until 1999, Firestone relied exclusively on the low rate of tire claims under warranty to conclude that its tires were safe. Why might reliance on warranty data alone be a mistake?

b. The rate of tire failure is associated with multiple factors. The Explorer accidents with Firestone tires tended to occur at high speeds and at high temperatures. In addition, low tire pressures, recommended by Ford to increase ride comfort, tended to create more road friction and heat. (Carrying heavy loads has the same effect.) Precisely because the risk was associated with multiple, simultaneous factors, it was much more difficult to detect. Why would this be the case? (*Hint*: Screening factors *individually* produced no obvious warning signals.)

c. Ford believed that the major fault was with Firestone's tires. Firestone contended that its tires were absolutely safe under its recommended operating conditions—that the Explorer's design and operation were the major culprits. What kind of information would one gather to assess these rival arguments? Explain.

Spreadsheet Problems

S1. Individual investors face a daunting choice of thousands of mutual (stock and bond) funds and fund managers. The following (stylized) spreadsheet example tries to distinguish superior fund managers from the throng of average managers based on their past track records of performance. Suppose there are three types of mutual fund managers: **S**uperior (20 percent of the population), **A**verage (60 percent), and **I**nferior (20 percent). In any six-month period, superior managers earn positive returns 70 percent of the time, average managers 60 percent of the time, and inferior managers just 50 percent of the time. At the risk of oversimplifying, we assume an average six-month gain of 25 percent (at an annual rate) versus a possible loss of 15 percent. Thus, the superior manager's expected return is computed as: $(.7)(25) + (.3)(-15)$ = 13 percent. Similarly, an average fund manager's expected return is 9 percent and an inferior manager's expected return is only 5 percent. These rates of return mimic real-life fund performance and are listed in the top of the spreadsheet.

    Consider the strong 10-year track record of Manager G. This fund has had positive returns in 15 (six-month) periods and negative returns in only 5 periods. This long and strong track record suggests that G is a superior manager. Using the spreadsheet, our task is to compute the revised probability: $Pr(S|15 \text{ of } 20)$. To do this, we first compute the converse probability: $Pr(15 \text{ of } 20|S)$, the likelihood of such a track record if Manager G is truly superior (i.e., has a .7 chance of earning a positive return in any particular six-month period). This likelihood follows a binomial probability and is shown to be about 18 percent in cell D15. This probability is computed using the Excel formula:

$$= \text{BINOMDIST(C15, B15, D9, 0)}.$$

Here the first argument (cell C15) is the number of binomial successes, the second argument is the total number of trials, the third argument is the probability of success on each trial, and the last argument is always zero. By similar formulas, we compute $Pr(15 \text{ of } 20|A)$ and $Pr(15 \text{ of } 20|I)$ in cells E16 and F16. (Notice that it is much less likely that such a strong track record would be recorded by an average fund or especially by an inferior fund.)

    a. Complete the joint probability table by computing the missing entries in cells E20 and F20. (Cell D20 has been calculated for you.) In turn, compute the revised probabilities (i.e., $Pr(S|15 \text{ of } 20)$ and so on) in row 24.

	A	B	C	D	E	F	G	H	I	J	K
1											
2			**EVALUATING FUND MANAGERS**								
3											
4				**Possible Annual Returns**							
5				25	or	−15					
6											
7				**Fund Manager Types**							
8				Superior	Average	Inferior					
9			Prob(Up)	0.7	0.6	0.5					
10			Exp Return	13	9	5					
11											
12					Likelihood						
13			Track Record	Superior	Average	Inferior					
14		Years	Ups								
15		20	15	0.179	0.075	0.015					
16											
17					Joint Probability						
18			Track Record	Superior	Average	Inferior					
19		Years	Ups					Total			
20		20	15	0.036	?	?		?			
21										Expected	
22			Prior Prob	0.2	0.6	0.2				Return	
23											
24			Revised Prob	?	?	?		1.000		?	

b. Even with an impressive past performance record, how confident are you that Manager G is of the superior type? If you invest your money with Manager G, what return would you predict on average? (Compute the expected return in cell J24 using the revised probabilities found in part a.)

c. Experiment with different performance records (cells B15 and C15) and greater differences between types of fund managers (cells D9 and F9). What effect does each factor have on one's ability to identify superior managers?

Suggested References

Clemin, R. T., and T. Reilly. *Making Hard Decisions with Decision Tools Suite Update.* Belmont, CA: Thomson Learning, 2003.

Lawrence, D. B. *The Economic Value of Information.* New York: Springer-Verlag, 1999.

Savage, S. L. *Decision Making with Insight.* Belmont, CA: Thomson Learning, 2003.

Both Thomson Learning texts are fine treatments and come packaged with decision tree software.

Camerer, C. "Individual Decision Making." In J. H. Kagel and A. E. Roth (Eds.). *The Handbook of Experimental Economics.* Princeton, NJ: Princeton University Press, 1995.

Howard, R. A., J. E. Matheson, and D. W. North. "The Decision to Seed Hurricanes." *Science* (June 16, 1972): 1191–1202. *This article is a classic application concerning the value of information.*

Kahneman, D., P. Slovic, and A. Tversky. *Judgment under Uncertainty: Heuristics and Biases.* Cambridge: Cambridge University Press, 1982. *This volume contains many classic articles on the pitfalls of intuitive probability assessments.*

Salop, S. C. "Evaluating Uncertain Evidence with Sir Thomas Bayes: A Note for Teachers," *Journal of Economic Perspectives* (Summer 1987): 155–160. *Salop argues strongly for the application of probabilities and statistical techniques in the evaluation of legal evidence.*

The following references present theory and experimental evidence concerning optimal search.

Abrams, E., et al. "An Experimental Comparison of Two Search Models." *Economic Theory* 16 (November 2000): 735–49.

DeGroot, M. *Optimal Statistical Decisions.* New York: McGraw-Hill, 1970, Chapter 13.

Diamond, P. "Search Theory." In *The New Palgrave: A Dictionary of Economics*, edited by J. Eatwell, M. Milgate, and P. Newman. New York: Macmillan, 1987, 271–286.

Genesove, D. "Search at Wholesale Auto Auctions." *Quarterly Journal of Economics* 110 (February 1995): 23–49.

A comprehensive Web site for free access to downloadable and Web-based statistical software is:

www.statistics.com/content/javastat.html. *This site has an easy-to-use Bayes' theorem calculator (click on Bayesian methods or go directly to* http://members.aol.com/johnp71/bayes.html*).*

1. The joint probability table can be written as follows:

	W	D	
G	.21	.24	.45
B	.07	.48	.55
Total	.28	.72	

For example, $\Pr(G\&W) = \Pr(G|W)\Pr(W) = (3/4)(.28) = .21$. Thus, $\Pr(W|G) = .21/.45 = .47$ and $\Pr(W|B) = .07/.55 = .13$.

2. With a good test, the partners drill. Their expected profit is then $E(\pi) = (.47)(600) + (.53)(-200) = \$176$ thousand. If the test is bad, they do not drill and earn $0. Thus, their overall $E(\pi)$ is $(.45)(176) = \$79.2$ thousand. Without the test, the $E(\pi)$ from drilling is $(.28)(600) + (.72)(-200) = \$24$ thousand. The value of the test is $55.2 thousand.

3. This test is valueless: $\Pr(W|G) = .32/.8 = .4$, and $\Pr(W|B) = .08/.2 = .4$. The test never causes a probability revision. It reports "good" 80 percent of the time, whether or not the site is wet: $\Pr(G|W) = \Pr(G|D) = .8$.

4. If firm A offers $120 or $140, the buyer will accept (because the expected price from firm B is $155). Thus, the buyer's expected profit of approaching A first is $(.15)(120) + (.25)(140) + (.6)(155) = \$146$. If the buyer approaches B first, it accepts $130 but rejects $180 (in which case, it faces A's expected price of $152). The buyer's expected profit is $(.5)(130) + (.5)(152) = \$141$. Approaching B first is the best course of action.

5. A distribution between $46 and $70 has *no* effect on the optimal number of buyers. The marginal benefit (MB) of contacting an extra buyer depends on the dispersion of prices, and this is unchanged. For a distribution between $46 and $58, the standard deviation is half as great as originally and so is marginal benefit. The optimal number of buyers is either two or three (a tie). The MB of adding a third buyer is $1 million, identical to MC.

Sequential Search

Earlier in the text, we examined the problem of simultaneous search for the best alternative. This appendix considers the more challenging problem in which the firm engages in sequential search, thus uncovering one alternative at a time. Consider once again the firm seeking to sell one of its divisions for the best possible price. Now, the company instructs its banker to seek out buyers one at a time. At a cost, it can identify an initial potential buyer and hear its price. The firm then has the option to accept the offer if the price is sufficiently attractive; if it refuses, it can approach another buyer; and so on. If the firm has refused a buyer's price once, can it accept the offer later? The answer depends on whether the offer still will be outstanding (or whether the would-be buyer will have changed its mind or already used its limited resources to make an alternative acquisition).

In modeling the search environment, it is useful to distinguish two different cases. We speak of **search with recall** in the event that the decision maker always can select from among *all* alternatives uncovered to date. For **search without recall**, the decision maker's sole opportunity to choose a new alternative occurs immediately upon discovering it (i.e., before he or she observes any subsequent alternatives). Clearly, the decision maker is always better off with the recall option than without it (since the recall option expands the possible choice strategies). The interesting question is: How can the decision maker best exploit the search opportunities under either recall option?

SEARCH WITH AND WITHOUT RECALL   First, consider the problem of finding the best (i.e., highest) price when the decision maker can approach a number of buyers with recall. The classic problem posits that each of the buyer's prices is drawn independently from a common distribution and that approaching each buyer involves a constant search cost (call this c). Let $F(P)$ denote the cumulative distribution function for the typical price P. This function measures the probability that the buyer's actual price is *below* the value P. In the company's problem, for instance, each buyer's price is uniformly distributed between \$40 million and \$64 million. Here, the associated probability function is $F(P) = (P - 40)/24$. From the formula, we see that the chance of the price being below 40 is zero; the chance that the price is below 52 is .5 (this is the distribution median); and so on.

For search with recall, it is easy to see that the decision maker's strategy comes down to setting a minimally acceptable price, a so-called cutoff price. If the current price is good enough—that is, exceeds this cutoff (call it P*)—the decision maker accepts it and terminates the search. If the current price falls below P*, the search continues. In fact, there is a simple way to characterize this optimal cutoff price. We can show that P* satisfies

$$P^* = [1 - F(P^*)]E(P|P \geq P^*) + F(P^*)P^* - c. \qquad [9A.1]$$

The left side of this equation is the payoff from accepting price P*. The right side is the expected payoff (net of cost c) from searching and possibly getting a better price. Here the second term on the right side accounts for the case in which the search yields a new price that is worse than P*. This occurs with probability $F(P^*)$, in which case the decision maker falls back on the price in hand, P*. The first term accounts for the case of a price better than P*. The term $E(P|P \geq P^*)$ stands for "the expected value of P, conditional on P being greater or equal to P*." Taken as a whole, Equation 9A.1 states simply that the decision maker should set the optimal cutoff price so as to be indifferent to the options of accepting it immediately or rejecting it and searching again.

In fact, Equation 9A.1 can be rearranged to read

$$[1 - F(P^*)]E(P - P^*|P \geq P^*) - c = 0. \qquad [9A.2]$$

Here the first term measures the decision maker's expected *gain* from the search. This gain is the product of the probability of finding a better price and the expected increase in price. The equation says that P* is set such that this expected gain just matches the cost of the search.[1] Note that the firm's decision

---

[1] If the expected net gain of the search were positive at p*, this cutoff price could not be optimal. The firm could do better by searching more frequently (i.e., by setting a higher cutoff at a point where there was no longer any net gain from the search). Conversely, if the net gain were negative, the firm could do better by lowering its cutoff price.

to stop or search depends only on the firm's current price, the distribution of possible prices, and the cost of the search.[2] It does not depend on how many buyers the firm already has approached or how many potential buyers remain.

Now consider the opposite case of a search without recall: Selection of past prices is impossible. Again the firm's strategy can be described by a cutoff price. Facing a fixed number of possible buyers, the firm cannot afford to be as choosy without recall as it can with recall; that is, its cutoff price will be lower. To illustrate this point, let's return to the example of selling a division. Table 9A.1 lists the firm's optimal cutoff prices with and without recall for three different values of search costs.

Let's interpret the table's first entry, 57.1. Here the firm has some current price in hand and must decide whether to accept it or pay $1 million for a single additional price quote, allowing it to select the better of the two prices. The firm's best strategy is to accept the current price if and only if it is greater than the cutoff price, $P^* = 57.1$. The fact that it always can fall back on its current price encourages a search.[3] (If the next buyer's price is less favorable than the first buyer's, all the firm has lost is its search cost.) But what if it does not have this fall-back option? If the firm chooses to search without the opportunity of recall, it must give up its current price. If it searches for one more buyer, its

TABLE 9A.1

Optimal Search with and without Recall

	Number of Additional Buyers		
	One	**Two**	**Unlimited**
Cost is 1.0:			
p* with recall	57.1	57.1	57.1
p** without recall	51.0	53.5	57.1
Cost is 2.0:			
p* with recall	54.2	54.2	54.2
p** without recall	50.0	52.4	54.2
Cost is 3.0:			
p* with recall	52.0	52.0	52.0
p** without recall	49.0	50.7	52.0

Each potential buyer's price is distributed uniformly between $40 million and $64 million. Cost is the (constant) marginal cost of approaching an additional buyer. All figures are in millions of dollars.

[2] We can show that p* increases if c falls and/or the dispersion of possible buyer values increases. Intuitively, the decision maker will reject a larger region of prices (preferring to search) when the search becomes less costly or when the potential gain from the search increases (due to greater price dispersion).

[3] This cutoff price was computed using Equation 9A.2. Starting from 57.1, what does the buyer stand to gain, on average, from seeking an additional price? The chance of bettering 57.1 is $(64 - 57.1)/24$, or .29. The conditional expected value of this better price is $(57.1 + 64)/2 = 60.55$, so the overall expected gain is $(.29)(60.55 - 57.1) = 1.0$. Thus, we see that the expected gain from the search (starting from a 57.1 price) exactly matches the cost of the search.

expected net price is $52 - 1 = \$51$ million. Obviously this becomes its cutoff. This accounts for the values of P** in the first column of Table 9A.1. The computation of P** in the case of two or more buyers is much more complicated and will not be taken up here. The main point of the table is to confirm the general point stated earlier:

> The firm's cutoff prices with recall are always greater than its cutoff prices without recall.

When the search is without recall, the firm benefits from increasing the number of additional buyers it can approach. Adding an extra buyer (moving from one additional buyer to two) increases the firm's expected value from the search. As a result, it searches more often: P** increases. In fact, if the firm has an unlimited number of buyers from which to choose, we see, from the last column of Table 9A.1, that P** = P*. The firm sets the *same* cutoff price with or without recall. Here the absence of recall is no disadvantage because the firm need never worry about running out of buyers and being stuck with an unfavorable price. Any time the firm will choose to search with recall, it also will choose to search without recall. With unlimited buyers, it pursues the same strategy and earns the same profit in either case.

A further point follows from this discussion:

> Other things being equal, the expected profit from sequential search always exceeds the expected profit from simultaneous search.

Under a simultaneous search, the decision maker is required to choose the number of alternatives at the outset, before any outcomes are realized. Under a sequential search, the decision maker acquires information along the way before deciding whether to pay to sample additional alternatives.

The earlier example of finding the best price makes the point. Recall that the firm's best simultaneous search strategy is to solicit offers from four firms, netting an expected price of $55.2 million. By comparison, suppose the firm can approach any number of buyers sequentially at the same $1 million cost per buyer. In this case, the firm's expected net price (with or without recall) is $57.1 million. This expected profit is given precisely by the firm's optimal cutoff price. (The quoted price is found from Table 9A.1.) To see why this is so, note that the firm's expected profit from the search is given by the right side of Equation 9A.1, and this profit, in turn, is exactly equal to the firm's cutoff price (the left side of the equation). In this example, sequential search has an almost $2 million profit edge over simultaneous search.[4]

---

[4] The principles of optimal search also are directly applicable for a risk-averse decision maker. The practical effect of risk aversion is to tend to reduce the marginal benefit of search for the simple reason that the certain bird in the hand is more valuable than the uncertain and costly search for the better bird in the bush. Moreover, because of its greater flexibility, a sequential search tends to increase its edge over a simultaneous search as the decision maker becomes increasingly risk averse.

SECTION II

Competing within Markets

In the previous chapters, we have examined managerial decisions of typical firms facing demand and cost conditions. Although we have noted specific products and industries, we have carried out the analyses without explicit reference to types of economic environments. In this section's five chapters, we take a closer look at the market environments in which firms compete.

Economists and management scientists traditionally divide markets into four main types: perfect competition, monopolistic competition, oligopoly, and pure monopoly. These market types differ with respect to several key attributes: the number of firms, the extent of barriers to entry for new firms, and the degree to which individual firms control price. In perfect competition and monopolistic competition, many sellers supply the market, and new sellers can enter the industry easily. In a pure monopoly, in contrast, a single firm is the industry. There are no direct competitors, and barriers to new entry are prohibitive. Oligopoly represents an intermediate case: The industry is dominated by a small number of firms and is marked by significant but not prohibitive entry barriers.

The extent to which firms influence price also varies across the market structures. A typical firm in a perfectly competitive market is so small that it has no influence over price; rather, the market—via the forces of supply and demand—determines the current price. In contrast, the pure monopolist—a pharmaceutical company selling a wonder drug under patent, for instance—has maximum power to raise prices. Oligopoly represents a middle ground between perfect competition and pure monopoly. When a small number of large firms dominate a market, price competition tends to be blunted with higher prices being one result.

Market structure also has a direct bearing on the role of government regulation. In markets where competition is vigorous, government regulation is unnecessary and inappropriate. Regulation is necessary, however, to prevent the potential monopolization of markets and prohibit anticompetitive practices by firms, and to oversee the pricing, production, and investment decisions of natural monopolies.

The following chapter examines perfect competition, and Chapter 11 analyzes the instances of pure monopoly and monopolistic competition. Chapter 12 considers competition within oligopolies. Chapter 13 focuses on game theory, a basic tool for analyzing competitive strategies within markets. Chapter 14 concludes this section by examining the role of government in regulating private markets and in providing public goods and services in the absence of private markets.

CHAPTER 10

Perfect Competition

Everything is worth what its purchaser will pay for it.

Anonymous

There has been an ongoing debate between economists and ecologists for the past 30 years about whether or not the world is running out of resources. (This is a renewal of a centuries-old debate that began with Malthus.) Many ecologists have argued that resources are limited and that economic growth and unchecked population increases are draining these resources (a barrel of oil consumed today means one less barrel available tomorrow) and polluting the environment. Leading economists have pointed out that the cry about limited resources is a false alarm. Technological innovation, human progress, and conservation have meant that the supply of resources has more than kept pace with population growth and can do so indefinitely. Food, water, and other resources are more abundant today than at any time in the past, and living standards around the globe are higher.

One example of this debate was a bet made in 1981 between Paul Ehrlich, a well-known scientist, and Julian Simon, an eminent economist.[1] Simon challenged ecologists to pick any resources they wished and any future date. He then made a simple bet: The prices of the chosen resources would be lower at the future date than they were at the present time. With the help of economists and other scientists, Ehrlich selected five resources (copper, chrome, nickel, tin, and tungsten) for which he predicted increasing scarcity over the next decade. He hypothetically purchased $200

---

[1] This account is based on John Tierney, "Betting the Planet," *The New York Times Magazine* (December 2, 1990), 52.

worth of each metal at 1981 prices. Then the two sides waited and watched price movements over the next 10 years.

What can the economics of supply and demand tell us about this debate (and this bet)?

This chapter and the three that follow focus on the spectrum of industry structures. Markets are typically divided into four main categories: perfect competition, monopolistic competition, oligopoly, and pure monopoly. Table 10.1 provides a preview of these different settings by considering two dimensions of competition: the number of competing firms and the extent of entry barriers. At one extreme (the lower right cell of the table) is the case of perfect competition. Such a market is supplied by a large number of competitors. Because each firm claims only a very small market share, none has the power to control price. Rather, price is determined by supply and demand. As important, there are no barriers preventing new firms from entering the market.

At the other extreme (the upper left cell of the table) lies the case of pure monopoly. Here a single firm supplies the market and has no direct competitors. Thus, as we shall see, the monopolist (if not constrained) has the ultimate power to raise prices and maximize its profit. Clearly, prohibitive entry barriers are a precondition for pure monopoly. Such barriers prevent rival firms from entering the market and competing even-handedly with the incumbent monopolist.

Oligopoly (shown in the second row of Table 10.1) occupies a middle ground between the perfectly competitive and monopolistic extremes. In an oligopoly, a small number of large firms dominate the market. Each firm must anticipate the effect of its rivals' actions on its own profits and attempt to fashion profit-maximizing decisions in response. Again, moderate or high entry barriers are necessary to insulate the oligopolists from would-be entrants.

Finally, monopolistic competition (not shown in the table) shares several of the characteristics of perfect competition: many small firms competing in the market and an absence of entry barriers. In this sense, it would occupy the same cell as perfect competition. However, whereas perfect competition

TABLE 10.1

Comparing Market Structures

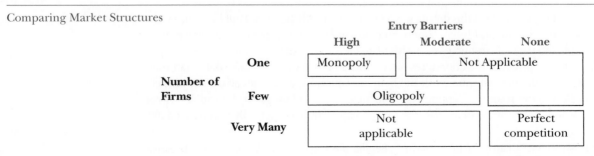

		Entry Barriers		
		High	Moderate	None
Number of Firms	One	Monopoly	Not Applicable	
	Few	Oligopoly		
	Very Many	Not applicable		Perfect competition

is characterized by firms producing identical standardized products, monopolistic competition is marked by product differentiation. In short, the two dimensions of competition shown in Table 10.1, though useful, do not do the full job in distinguishing different market structures.

THE BASICS OF SUPPLY AND DEMAND

A thorough knowledge of the workings of supply and demand and how they affect price and output in competitive markets is essential for sound managerial decision making. For example, if a manager's own product or service is sold in a perfectly competitive industry, he or she is naturally concerned with a prediction of future prices in the market. Should the firm gear up production with the expectation of price increases? Alternatively, the manager's firm may buy its inputs and intermediate goods in competitive markets. For instance, consider a firm that produces beer and soft-drink cans. Currently, 60 percent of its cans are aluminum and 40 percent are steel. The firm recognizes that the price of aluminum is quite volatile. If aluminum prices were predicted to rise by 15 percent, the firm would be ready to change its can output from aluminum to steel. In short, whether the focus is on input markets or output markets, a solid understanding of future price movements is essential.

In a perfectly competitive market, price is determined by the market demand and supply curves. We will consider each of these entities in turn.

The **demand curve** for a good or service shows the total quantities that consumers are willing and able to purchase at various prices, other factors held constant.[2] Figure 10.1 depicts a hypothetical demand curve D for shoes in a local market. As expected, the curve slopes downward to the right. Any change in price causes a movement along the demand curve.

The **supply curve** for a good or service shows the total quantities that producers are willing and able to supply at various prices, other factors held constant. In Figure 10.1, the supply curve for shoes (denoted by S) is upward sloping. As the price of shoes increases, firms are willing to produce greater quantities because of the greater profit available at the higher price. Any change in price represents a movement along the supply curve.

The **equilibrium price** in the market is determined at point E where market supply equals market demand. Figure 10.1 shows the equilibrium price to be $25 per pair of shoes, the price at which the demand and supply curves intersect. At the $25 price, the quantity of output demanded by consumers exactly matches the amount of output willingly offered by producers. The corresponding equilibrium quantity is 8,000 pairs. To see what lies behind the notion of

---

[2] In Chapters 2 and 3, we already have presented an extensive analysis of the demand curve facing an individual firm. In the present discussion, we focus on total demand in the market as a whole. Except for this difference, all of the earlier analyses apply.

FIGURE 10.1

Supply and Demand

The intersection of supply and demand determines the equilibrium price ($25) and quantity (8,000 pairs).

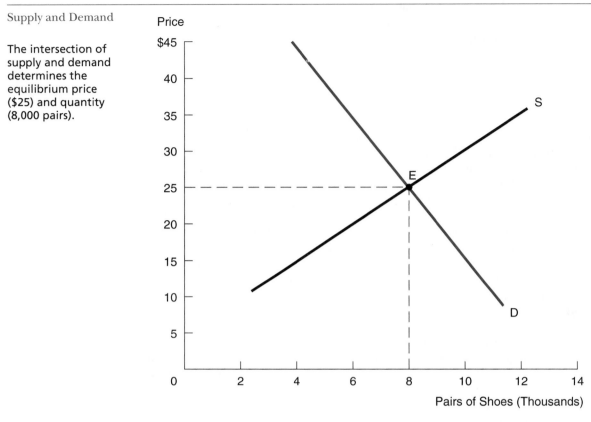

demand–supply equilibrium, consider the situation at different prices. Suppose the market price were temporarily greater than $25 (say, $35). At this higher price, the amount of shoes firms supply would greatly exceed the amount consumers would purchase willingly. Given the surplus of supply relative to demand, producers would be forced to reduce their prices to sell their output. Price reductions would occur until equilibrium was restored at the $25 price.

Similarly, if the price were temporarily lower than $25, consumer demand would outstrip the quantity supplied. The result would be upward pressure on price until the equilibrium price was restored.

If we augment the demand and supply graph with quantitative estimates of the curves, we can pinpoint equilibrium price and quantity more precisely. Suppose the market demand curve in Figure 10.1 is described by the equation

$$Q_D = 13 - .2P,$$

where Q_D denotes the quantity of shoes demanded (in thousands of pairs) and P is the dollar price per pair. Let the market supply curve in the figure be given by

$$Q_S = .4P - 2.$$

Then, if we set supply equal to demand $(Q_S = Q_D)$, we have $13 - .2P = .4P - 2$, or $.6P = 15$; therefore, $P = 15/.6 = \$25$. Inserting $P = \$25$ into either the demand equation or the supply equation, we confirm that $Q_D = Q_S = 8$ thousand units.[3]

SHIFTS IN DEMAND AND SUPPLY   Changes in important economic factors can shift the positions of the demand and/or supply curves, causing, in turn, predictable changes in equilibrium price and quantity. For example, suppose the local economy is coming out of a recession and that consumer incomes are rising. As a result, a greater quantity of shoes would be demanded even at an unchanged price. An increase in demand due to any nonprice factor is depicted as a rightward shift in the demand curve. Shifting the entire curve means that we would expect an increase in the quantity demanded at *any* prevailing price.[4] Such a shift is shown in Figure 10.2a.

What is the result of the shift in demand? We see from the figure that the new equilibrium occurs at a higher price and greater quantity of output. This is hardly surprising. The increase in demand causes price to be bid up. In the process, the amount supplied by firms also increases. The change from the old to the new market equilibrium represents a movement along the stationary supply curve (caused by a shift in demand).

Now consider economic conditions that might shift the position of the supply curve. Two principal factors are changes in input prices and technology improvements. For instance, increases in input prices will cause the supply curve to shift upward and to the left. (Any effect that increases the marginal cost of production means that the firm must receive a higher price to be induced to supply a given level of output.) Technological improvements, however, allow firms to reduce their unit costs of production. As a consequence, the supply curve shifts down and to the right. Such a shift is shown in Figure 10.2b. The result is a greater market output and a lower price. The favorable shift in supply has moved the equilibrium toward lower prices and greater quantities along the unchanged demand curve.

---

[3] The same answer would be found if we began with the curves expressed in the equivalent forms $P = 65 - 5Q_D$ and $P = 5 + 2.5Q_S$. Setting these equations equal to one another, we find $65 - 5Q = 5 + 2.5Q$. It follows that $Q = 60/7.5 = 8$ thousand. Inserting this answer into either equation, we find $P = \$25$.

[4] It is important to distinguish between shifts in the demand curve and movements along the curve. The effect of a change in price is charted by a movement along the demand curve. (An increase in price means fewer units demanded, but the demand curve has not shifted.) By contrast, the demand curve shifts with a change in any *nonprice* factor that affects demand.

FIGURE 10.2

Shifts in Supply
and Demand

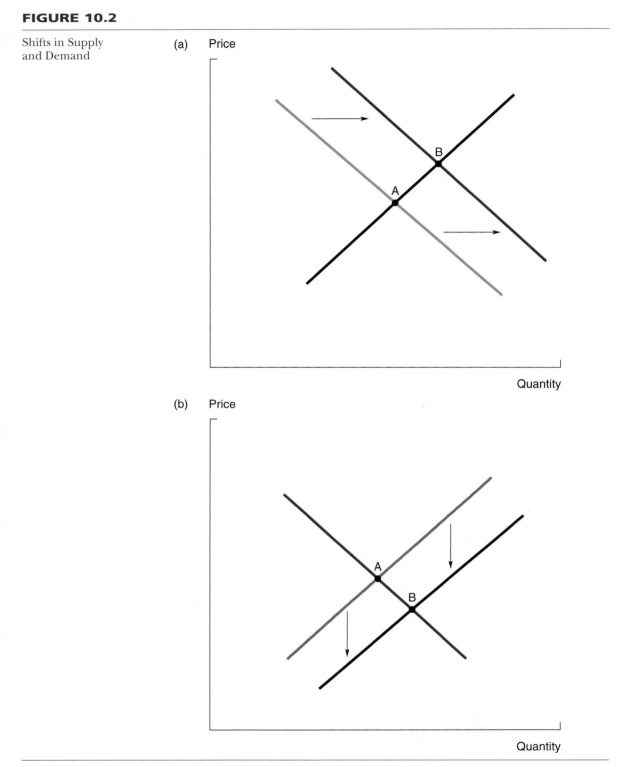

(a)   Price

Quantity

(b)   Price

Quantity

In 1999, the respective worldwide demand and supply curves for copper were $Q_D = 15 - 10P$ and $Q_S = -3 + 14P$, where Q is measured in millions of metric tons per year. Find the competitive price and quantity. Suppose that in 2000 demand is expected to fall by 20 percent, so $Q_D = (.8)(15 - 10P) = 12 - 8P$. How much are world copper prices expected to fall?

CHECK STATION 1

Volatile Oil Prices

The five-year period between 1999 and mid-2004 witnessed renewed volatility in the price of crude oil. Crude oil prices varied from $15 per barrel at the beginning of the period to over $60 by mid-2005. How do the basic economic forces of supply and demand explain these dramatic price fluctuations?

Consider the year 2002 (in the middle of this period) and a time of relatively stable prices. Strong economic growth in the United States and Europe and economic recovery in Asia boosted oil demand. At the same time, the Organization of Petroleum Exporting Countries (OPEC), comprising about 37 percent of total world supply, held fast to its production quotas in order to stabilize the average price of crude in the range of $25 to $28 per barrel. To get a quantitative understanding of the resulting price effects, consider the following bare-bones demand and supply model. Let normal worldwide oil demand in 2002 be described by the equation $Q_D = 90 - .6P$, and let normal oil supply be $Q_S = 75$ million barrels per day. Equating demand and supply, $Q_D = Q_S$, implies $90 - .6P = 75$, or $P = \$25$ per barrel, a good prediction of the actual price. (In graphical terms, the downward-sloping demand curve intersects the vertical supply curve at a price of $25.)

Now backtrack to early 1999. The rock-bottom average crude prices at the beginning of that year stemmed from a combination of ample supplies and depressed demand. The aftermath of the 1998 economic slowdown in East Asia (the financial crisis and Japan's continued recession) contributed to reduced overall demand. At the same time, OPEC was providing ample oil supplies (members were overproducing their supply quotas) and Western producers were also awash in oil. As an illustration, 1999 supply was about 76 million barrels per day, and 1999 demand was 5 million barrels per day less than in 2002, implying the demand equation $Q_D = 85 - .6P$. Now setting demand equal to supply implies a $15 per barrel equilibrium price (again firmly in the range of actual prevailing prices). In 1999, both depressed demand (a leftward shift in the demand curve) and extra supply (a slight rightward shift in the supply curve) combined to cause a large drop in price relative to the normal level of $25 per barrel. (Check this qualitatively by constructing the appropriate graph with shifting demand and supply curves.)

Finally consider events in 2004. Between 2002 and 2004 demand grew significantly, implying a new demand curve: $Q_D = 104 - .6P$. But in the first half of 2004, crude supply was about 80 million barrels per day, up only slightly from the 2002 level. The continuing war in Iraq and oil worker strikes in Venezuela each cut about 2 million barrels per day of supply. These cuts were balanced by increased production by Saudi Arabia and other OPEC and non-OPEC producers. Increased demand and limited supply meant an oil price surge—namely, $Q_D = 104 - .6P = 80$, which implied an actual price of $P = \$40$ per barrel. Oil prices continued to rise during 2005, fueled by surging demand (particularly from fast-growing China) and fears of new supply disruptions from natural disasters (Hurricane Katrina) and terroristic threats.

Because the crude oil demand and supply curves are inelastic, relatively small quantity changes can lead to large price fluctuations. It is easy to check that the 2004 crude oil demand curve is relatively steep. (Plot the curve for yourself.) Demand is quite price inelastic: $E_P = (dQ/dP)(P/Q) = (-.6)(40/80) = -.3$, at $P = \$40$ and $Q = 80$. Furthermore, we have been dealing with a vertical, perfectly inelastic supply curve. Although supply might vary little in the short run (three months), higher prices will certainly induce some supply increase in the longer run (six months and longer). Suppose that the long-run supply response in 2004 is estimated according to the equation $Q_S = 70 + .4P$. (This equation is consistent with supply behavior under the more stable price experience of 2003: 80 million barrels supplied at a price of \$25 per barrel.) Now, higher prices induce greater oil supplies; the longer-run supply curve is not vertical. Setting 2004 demand, $Q_D = 104 - .6P$, equal to supply implies $104 - .6P = 70 + .4P$, so that the longer-run equilibrium price is \$34 per barrel with a global output of 83.6 million barrels per day. According to this equilibrium analysis, the longer-run increase in supply is expected to bring prices down from above \$40 per barrel to the mid-\$30 range.

COMPETITIVE EQUILIBRIUM

Perfect competition is commonly characterized by four conditions.

1. **A large number of firms supply a good or service** for a market consisting of a large number of consumers.
2. **There are no barriers with respect to new firms entering the market.** As a result, the typical competitive firm will earn a zero economic profit.
3. **All firms produce and sell identical standardized products.** Therefore, firms compete only with respect to price. In addition, all consumers have perfect information about competing prices. Thus, all goods must sell at a single market price.
4. **Firms and consumers are price takers.** Each firm sells a small share of total industry output, and, therefore, its actions have no impact on price. Each firm takes the price as given—indeed, determined by supply and demand. Similarly, each consumer is a price taker, having no influence on the market price.

It is important to remember that these conditions characterize an ideal model of perfect competition. Some competitive markets in the real world meet the letter of all four conditions. Many other real-world markets are effectively perfectly competitive because they approximate these conditions. At present, we will use the ideal model to make precise price and output predictions for perfectly competitive markets. Later in this and the following chapters, we will compare the model to real-world markets.

In exploring the model of perfect competition, we first focus on the individual decision problem the typical firm faces. Then we show how firm-level decisions influence total industry output and price.

Decisions of the Competitive Firm

The key feature of the perfectly competitive firm is that it is a **price taker**; that is, it has no influence on market price. Two key conditions are necessary for price taking. First, the competitive market is composed of a large number of sellers (and buyers), each of which is small relative to the total market. Second, the firms' outputs are perfect substitutes for one another; that is, each firm's output is perceived to be indistinguishable from any other's. Perfect substitutability usually requires that all firms produce a standard, homogeneous, undifferentiated product and that buyers have perfect information about cost, price, and quality of competing goods.

Together, these two conditions ensure that the firm's demand curve is perfectly (or infinitely) elastic. In other words, it is horizontal like the solid price line in Figure 10.3a. Recall the meaning of *perfectly elastic demand*. The firm can sell as much or as little output as it likes along the horizontal price line ($8 in the figure). If it raises its price above $8 (even by a nickel), its sales go to zero. Consumers instead will purchase the good (a perfect substitute) from a competitor at the market price. When all firms' outputs are perfect substitutes, the "law of one price" holds: All market transactions take place at a single price. Thus, each firm faces the same horizontal demand curve given by the prevailing market price.

THE FIRM'S SUPPLY CURVE   Part a of Figure 10.3 also is useful in describing the supply of output by the perfectly competitive firm. The cost characteristics of the typical firm in the competitive market are as shown in the figure. The firm faces a U-shaped, short-run average cost curve and an increasing short-run marginal cost curve. (Recall that increasing marginal cost reflects diminishing marginal returns.)

Suppose the firm faces a market price of $8. (For the moment, we are not saying how this market price might have been established.) What is its optimal level of output? As always, the firm maximizes profit by applying the MR = MC rule. In the case of perfectly elastic demand, the firm's marginal revenue from selling an extra unit is simply the price it receives for the unit: MR = P. Here the marginal revenue line and price line coincide. Thus, we have the following rule.

A firm in a perfectly competitive market maximizes profit by producing up to an output such that its marginal cost equals the market price.

FIGURE 10.3

Price and Output under
Perfect Competition

In part a, the firm
produces 6,000 units
(where P = MC) and
makes a positive
economic profit. In
part b, the entry of new
firms has reduced the
price to $6, and the firm
earns zero economic
profit.

Cost and Revenue per Unit

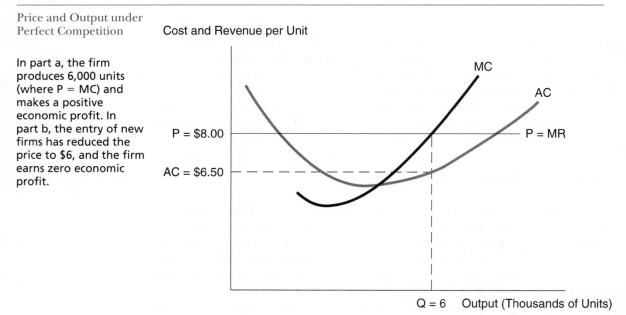

(a) A Competitive Firm's Optimal Output

Cost and Revenue per Unit

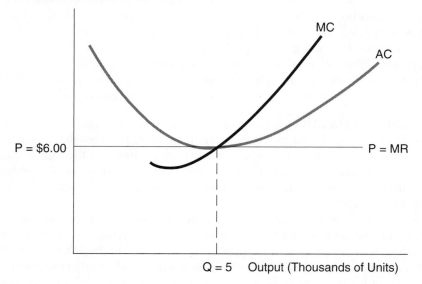

(b) Long-Run Equilibrium in a Competitive Market

In Figure 10.3, the intersection of the horizontal price line and the rising marginal cost curve (where P = MC) identifies the firm's optimal output. At an $8 market price, the firm's optimal output is 6,000 units. (Check for yourself that the firm would sacrifice potential profit if it deviated from this output, by producing either slightly more or slightly less.) Notice that if the price rises above $8, the firm profitably can increase its output; the new optimal output lies at a higher point along the short-run marginal cost curve. A lower price implies a fall in the firm's optimal output. (Recall, however, that if price falls below average variable cost, the firm will produce nothing.) By varying price, we read the firm's optimal output off the marginal cost curve. The firm's **short-run supply curve** is simply the portion of the short-run marginal cost curve lying above average variable cost.

The typical firm in a perfectly competitive market has a cost structure described by the equation:

$$C = 25 - 4Q + Q^2,$$

CHECK STATION 2

where Q is measured in thousands of units. Using the profit-maximizing condition, P = MC, write an equation for the firm's supply curve. If 40 such firms serve the market, write down the equation of the market supply curve.

LONG-RUN EQUILIBRIUM   Perfectly competitive markets exhibit a third important condition: In the long run, firms can freely enter or exit the market. In light of this fact, it is important to recognize that the profit opportunity shown in Figure 10.3a is *temporary*. Here the typical firm is earning a positive economic profit that comes to $\pi = (\$8.00 - \$6.50)(6,000) = \$9,000$. But the existence of positive economic profit will attract new suppliers into the industry, and as new firms enter and produce output, the current market price will be bid down. The competitive price will fall to the point where all economic profits are eliminated.

Figure 10.3b depicts the long-run equilibrium from the firm's point of view. Here the firm faces a market price of $6 per unit, and it maximizes profit by producing 5,000 units over the time period. At this quantity, the firm's marginal cost is equal to the market price. In fact, long-run equilibrium is characterized by a "sublime" set of equalities:

$$P = MR = LMC = min\ LAC.$$

In equilibrium, we observe the paradox of profit-maximizing competition:

The simultaneous pursuit of maximum profit by competitive firms results in zero economic profits and minimum-cost production for all.[5]

[5] Remember that a zero economic profit affords the firm a normal rate of return on its capital investment. This normal return already is included in its estimated cost.

In short, the typical firm produces at the point of minimum long-run average cost but earns only a normal rate of return because P = LAC.

Market Equilibrium

Let's shift from the typical firm's point of view to that of the market as a whole. Figure 10.4 provides this marketwide perspective. The current equilibrium occurs at E, where the market price is $6 per unit (as in Figure 10.3b) and the industry's total quantity of output is 200,000 units. This output is supplied by exactly 40 competitive firms, each producing 5,000 units (each firm's point of minimum LAC). The market is in equilibrium. Industry demand exactly matches industry supply. All firms make zero economic profits; no firm has an incentive to alter its output. Furthermore, no firm has an incentive to enter or exit the industry.

FIGURE 10.4

Competitive Price and
Output in the Long Run

An increase in demand
from D to D' has two
effects. In the short run,
the outcome is E'; in the
long run (after entry by
new firms), the outcome
is E*.

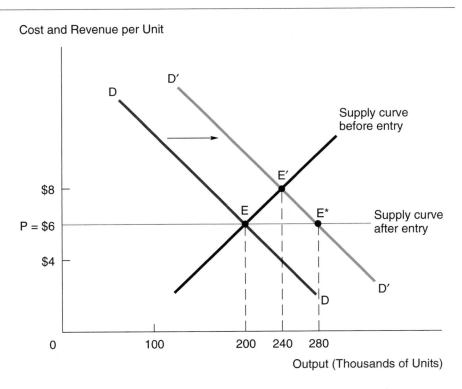

In the perfectly competitive market described in Check Station 2, what is the equilibrium price in the long run? (*Hint:* Find the typical firm's point of minimum average cost by setting AC = MC.) Find the output level of the typical firm. Let industry demand be given by the equation $Q_D = 320 - 20P$. Find total output in the long run. How many firms can the market support?

Now consider the effect of a permanent increase in market demand. This is shown as a rightward shift of the demand curve (from DD to D'D') in Figure 10.4. The first effect of the demand shift is to move the market equilibrium from E to E'. At the new equilibrium, the market price has risen from $6 to $8 and industry output has increased to 240,000 units. The higher level of output is supplied by the 40 incumbent firms, each having increased its production to 6,000 units. (According to Figure 10.3a, this is precisely the firm's profit-maximizing response to the $8 price.) The equilibrium at E' is determined by the intersection of the new demand curve and the total supply curve of the 40 firms currently in the industry. This supply curve also is shown in Figure 10.4 and is constructed by summing horizontally the individual firms' supply curves (i.e., marginal cost curves) in Figure 10.3. (Check Station 4 will ask you to derive the market equilibrium by equating demand and short-run supply.)

The shift in demand calls forth an immediate supply response (and a move from E to E'). But this is not the end of the story. Because the firms currently in the market are enjoying excess profits, new firms will be attracted into the industry. Price will be bid down below $8 and will continue to be bid down so long as excess profits exist. In Figure 10.4, the new long-run equilibrium result is at E*. Price is bid down to $6 per unit, its original level. At this price, total market demand is 280,000 units, a 40 percent increase above the 200,000 units sold at equilibrium E. In turn, industry supply increases to match this higher level of demand. How is this output supplied? With the price at $6 once again, each firm produces 5,000 units. Therefore, the total output of 280,000 units is supplied by 280,000/5,000 = 56 firms; that is, 16 new firms enter the industry (in addition to the original 40 firms). In the long run, the 40 percent increase in demand has called forth a 40 percent increase in the number of firms. There is no change in the industry's unit cost or price; both remain at $6 per unit.

Starting from the long-run equilibrium in Check Station 3, suppose market demand increases to $Q_D = 400 - 20P$. Find the equilibrium price in the short run (before new firms enter). (*Hint:* Set the new demand curve equal to the supply curve derived in Check Station 2.) Check that the typical firm makes a positive economic profit. In the long run—after entry—what is the equilibrium price? How many firms will serve the market?

LONG-RUN MARKET SUPPLY   The horizontal line in Figure 10.4 represents the case of a *constant-cost* industry. For such an industry, the long-run market supply curve is a horizontal line at a level equal to the minimum long-run average cost of production. Recall that any long-run additions to supply are furnished by the entry of new firms. Furthermore, in a constant-cost industry, the inputs needed to produce the increased industry output can be obtained without bidding up their prices. This is the case if the industry in question draws its resources from large, well-developed input markets. (If the industry is a "small player" in these input markets, an increase in its demand will have a negligible effect on the inputs' market prices.) For instance, the market for new housing exhibits a nearly horizontal long-run supply curve. In the long run, the industry's two main inputs—building materials and construction labor—are relatively abundant and provided by nationwide markets.[6]

For an *increasing-cost* industry, output expansion causes increases in the price of key inputs, thus raising minimum average costs. Here the industry relies on inputs in limited supply: land, skilled labor, and sophisticated capital equipment. For instance, if U.S. drilling activity increased by 30 percent (perhaps due to increases in world oil prices), the typical oil company's average cost per barrel of oil could be expected to rise for a number of reasons. First, the increase in drilling would bid up the price of drilling rigs and sophisticated seismic equipment. Second, skilled labor (such as chemical engineering graduates), being in greater demand, would receive higher wages. Third, because the most promising sites are limited, oil companies would resort to drilling marginal sites, yielding less oil on average. For an increasing-cost industry, the result of such increases in average costs is an upward-sloping long-run supply curve.

MARKET EFFICIENCY

You probably are familiar with one of the most famous statements in economics—Adam Smith's notion of an "invisible hand":

> Every individual endeavors to employ his capital so that its produce may be of greatest value. He generally neither intends to promote the public interest, nor knows how much he is promoting it. He intends only his own security, only his gain. And he is in this led by an invisible hand to promote an end which was no part of his intention. By pursuing his own interest he frequently promotes that of society more effectively than when he really intends to promote it.[7]

One of the main accomplishments of modern economics has been to examine carefully the circumstances in which the profit incentive, as mediated by

---

[6] Here it is important to distinguish between long-run and short-run supply. In the short run, an increased local demand for new housing can bid up the wages of construction labor (and, to some extent, materials) until additional workers are attracted into the market. In addition, if available land is limited in rapidly growing metropolitan areas, its price may increase significantly

[7] Adam Smith, *The Wealth of Nations* (1776).

competitive markets, promotes social welfare.[8] Although economists are fond of proving theorems on this subject, the present approach is more pragmatic. Our aim is to examine the following proposition: *Competitive markets provide efficient amounts of goods and services at minimum cost to the consumers who are most willing (and able) to pay for them.* This statement is one expression of the notion of *market efficiency.* Of course, getting to the heart of market efficiency requires a careful explanation of what the "efficient" amount of a good or service means.

Private Markets: Benefits and Costs

The main step in our examination of market efficiency is the valuation (in dollar terms) of benefits and costs. We begin the analysis with a single transaction and move on to the thousands of transactions that take place within markets. Consider the following example.

THE DEMAND AND SUPPLY OF DAY CARE   A couple is seeking to obtain up to 10 hours of day care per week for their 2-year-old. Through informal inquiries in their neighborhood, they have found a grandmother who has done baby-sitting and some day care in the past and comes highly recommended. The grandmother is not sure whether she is willing to commit to 10 hours. Before any discussion of price takes place, the couple has thought hard about their value for day care. They have decided that the maximum amount they are willing to pay is $8 per hour (that is, they would be indifferent to the options of getting day care at this price and not getting it at all). For her part, the grandmother has decided that her minimum acceptable price is $4. (Thus, $4 is the best estimate of her "cost" based on the value of her time and the strain of taking care of a 2-year-old. All things considered, she just breaks even at this price.) Can the couple and the grandmother conclude a mutually beneficial agreement? How can we measure the parties' gains from an agreement?

The answer to the first question clearly is yes. Any negotiated price between $4 and $8 would be mutually beneficial. What about the second question? If the parties are equally matched bargainers, we might expect the final price to be $6. The grandmother makes a profit of $2 per hour, or $20 per week. Similarly, the couple makes a $2-per-hour "profit"; that is, they pay only $6 for a day-care hour that is worth $8 to them. Their "profit" per week is $20. The couple's gain (or any consumer's gain in general) is customarily labeled **consumer surplus**. Although it goes under a different name, the couple's gain is identical in kind (and here in amount) to the grandmother's profit.

---

[8] The study of the relationship between private markets and public welfare usually is referred to as *welfare economics.*

Figure 10.5 makes the same point in graphical terms. The couple's $8 value is drawn as a horizontal demand curve (up to a maximum of 10 hours per week). The grandmother's $4 cost line and a $6 price line are shown also. The grandmother's profit is depicted as the area of the rectangle between the price and cost lines. In turn, the couple's consumer surplus is shown as the area of the rectangle between the value and price lines. The areas of the profit and consumer surplus rectangles are both $20. The total gain from trade—the sum of consumer surplus and profit—is given by the area of the rectangle between the value and cost lines and comes to $40.

An agreement calling for 10 hours of day care per week delivers the maximum total gain to the parties together. For this reason, we call such a transaction *efficient*. In contrast, an agreement that called for only 5 hours of day care per week would furnish only $20 of total gain ($10 to each side). Although this agreement is better than nothing, it would rightly be labeled *inefficient* because it generates less than the maximum total gain. (More than 10 hours is infeasible because the grandmother is willing to supply 10 hours at most.)

FIGURE 10.5

A Day-Care Transaction

This transaction provides the couple with a consumer surplus of $20 per week and the grandmother with a profit of $20 per week.

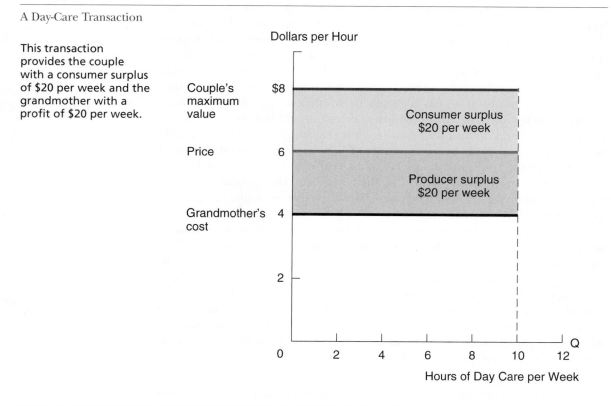

We note two simple, but important, points about the efficiency concept. First, the actual price negotiated is *not* a matter of efficiency. An agreement calling for 10 hours of day care at a price of $7 (or at any other price between $4 and $8) would generate the same total profit, $40 per week. Of course, at $7 the total gain is redistributed. The grandmother's profit is $30 per week, and the couple's is $10. But the total gain has not changed. In algebraic terms, the total gain is

$$CS + \pi = (8 - P)Q + (P - 4)Q = 4Q.$$

In computing this total gain, the price paid by the buyer to the supplier just cancels out; that is, the terms involving the price P disappear. Note that for 10 hours of care ($Q = 10$), the total gain is $40.

Second, starting from any inefficient agreement, there is a different efficient agreement that is better for both parties. In short, the best split of the "pie" for both parties is attained when the "pie" is made as big as possible in the first place. For instance, suppose the parties agreed on 7 hours of day care per week at a price of $7. This inefficient agreement generates gains to the grandmother and couple of $21 and $7, respectively. Clearly, both parties would benefit from a 10-hour deal at an appropriate price. For instance, a price concession by the grandmother to $6.50 with a 10-hour deal would bring her $25 in profit and the couple $15 in consumer surplus. Both parties are better off than with the 7-hour agreement.

THE DAY-CARE MARKET   Let's now extend the previous analysis to the large day-care market that emerged in the 1980s and 1990s. Figure 10.6 shows the weekly demand curve for day care in a given geographical region. There is nothing remarkable about this bare-bones demand curve. Depending on the going hourly price for day care, more or less millions of day-care hours will be demanded. The lower the price, the greater the number of hours purchased. However, one aspect of this demand curve (or any demand curve) is important: Besides showing the quantity consumed at any price, *the demand curve shows the monetary value that consumers are willing to pay for each unit.* For instance, the "first" few units consumed are valued at roughly $12, the demand curve's price intercept. Even at a rate this high, some parents (with high incomes, rotten kids, or both) are willing to pay the high price for day care. But what about the 8 millionth hour of day care consumed? For this hour to be purchased, the hourly price must drop to $4. Put simply, the value of any unit of day care is given by the price the consumer is willing to pay for it.[9] (Thus, it is hard to

---

[9] This valuation method is based on the notion of *consumer sovereignty*. Each individual is the best judge of the value he or she derives from a purchase. When all the individual purchases are added together, we obtain a market demand curve—the best measure of aggregate value from day-care services. Thus, under the doctrine of consumer sovereignty, it would be improper for a government authority to place either an arbitrarily high value (say, $30 per hour) or low value (e.g., $.50 per hour) on day-care services.

FIGURE 10.6

Regional Demand for
Day Care

At a price of $4, the
total demand for day
care is 8 million hours
per week. Parents
receive a total consumer
surplus of $32 million.

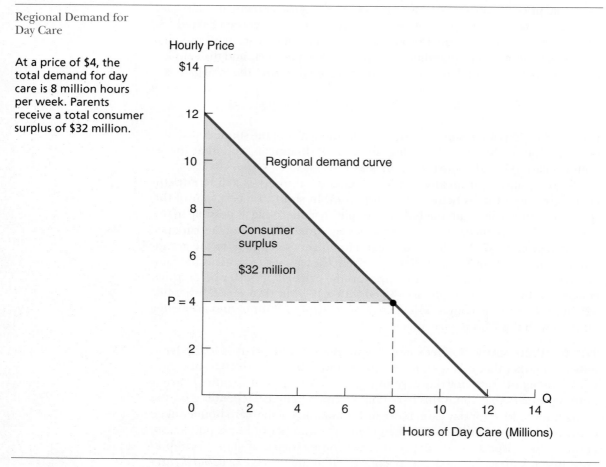

claim that the 8 millionth hour is worth $4.50 because the would-be consumer
of this hour is unwilling to pay that high a price.) In short, the value of a particular unit is given by the height of the demand curve at that quantity.[10] For
this reason, the demand curve can be thought of as a **marginal benefit curve**.

Now suppose the going price for day care is in fact $4 per hour, with the result
that 8 million hours are purchased per week. What is the *total* consumer surplus
enjoyed by purchasers? The answer is straightforward: Consumer surplus is measured by the triangle inscribed under the demand curve and above the price line.
After all, the demand curve indicates what consumers are *willing* to pay and the

[10] Caution: We are *not* saying that *each* of the 8 million day-care hours consumed at a price of $4 is *worth*
$4. We mean only that the last, 8 millionth, unit is worth $4. The other hours are worth much more, as
shown by the rising height of the demand curve as we move to smaller and smaller quantities.

price line indicates what they *actually* pay, so the difference (added up over all units consumed) is their total surplus. Recall that the area of a triangle is given by one-half of its height times its base. Thus, the consumer surplus from 8 million hours demanded at a $4 price comes to $(.5)(12 - 4)(8) = \$32$ million.[11]

To complete the description of the market, let's consider the supply of day care. A day-care supply curve is shown in Figure 10.7. Notice that the main part of the supply curve is provided by low-cost suppliers at $2.50 per hour. Let's say these suppliers enjoy significant economies of scale while maintaining quality day care. In fact, as we shall see, "grandmotherly" day care at $4 per hour will become a thing of the past. Less efficient, high-cost grandmothers will be priced out of the day-care market.

Now we are ready to take a closer look at market efficiency. To begin, we know that, in a competitive day-care market, the intersection of supply and demand determines price and quantity. In Figure 10.7, the competitive price is $2.50 and quantity is 9.5 million hours per week. Now we can make our key point: *This competitive outcome is efficient; that is, it delivers the maximum total dollar benefit to consumers and producers together.* This is particularly easy to see in Figure 10.7, because day-care suppliers earn zero profits: Price equals average cost. All gain takes the form of consumer surplus. It is easy to check that the total surplus measures out to $(.5)(12 - 2.5)(9.5) = \$45.125$ million.

An equivalent way to confirm that the competitive level of output is efficient is to appeal to the logic of marginal benefits and costs. We have argued that the height of the demand curve at a given output level Q measures the marginal benefit (in dollar terms) of consuming the last (Qth) unit. Similarly, the height of the supply curve indicates the marginal cost of producing the Qth unit. At a competitive equilibrium, demand equals supply. A direct consequence is that marginal benefit equals marginal cost. Equating marginal benefits and marginal costs ensures that the industry supplies the "right" quantity of the good—the precise output that maximizes the total net benefits (consumer benefits minus supplier costs) from production.

In contrast, at a noncompetitive price—say, $4—only 8 million day-care hours would be demanded. At this reduced output, the marginal benefit (what consumers are willing to pay for additional day-care hours) is $4, and this is greater than the marginal cost of supplying extra hours, $2.50. Thus, there is a net welfare gain of $4.00 - 2.50 = \$1.50$ for each additional day-care hour supplied. More generally, so long as the demand curve lies above the supply curve (MB > MC), there is a net gain (MB − MC > 0) from increasing the output of day care. Conversely, at any output level beyond the competitive quantity (say, 11 million hours), the marginal benefit of extra hours falls short of the marginal

---

[11] An equivalent way to find consumer surplus is to reason as follows. The first unit consumed earns a surplus of $12 - 4 = 8$. The last (i.e., 8 millionth) unit consumed earns a surplus of $4 - 4 = 0$. Since demand is linear, the average surplus per unit is $(8 + 0)/2 = \$4$. We multiply this by 8 million units to arrive at a total surplus of $32 million.

FIGURE 10.7

A Competitive Day-Care Market

The competitive price ($2.50) and output (9.5 million hours) are determined by the intersection of the supply and demand curves.

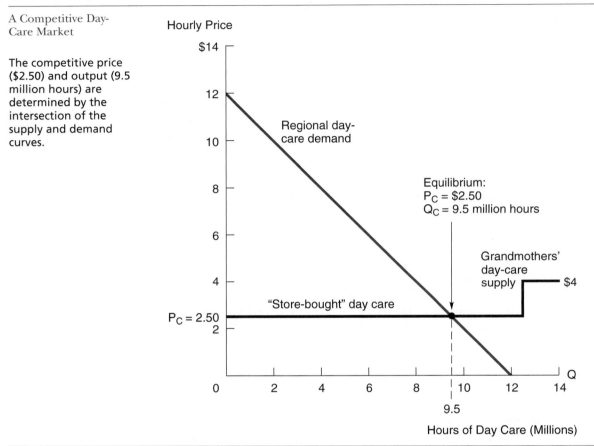

Hourly Price

Regional day-care demand

Equilibrium:
$P_C = \$2.50$
$Q_C = 9.5$ million hours

Grandmothers' day-care supply — $4

"Store-bought" day care

$P_C = 2.50$

9.5

Hours of Day Care (Millions)

cost of supply (MB < MC). Producing these units is a "losing" proposition. Thus, there is a net gain from cutting output back to the competitive level.[12]

[12] In mathematical terms, consider the objective of maximizing the sum of consumer surplus and producer profit:

$$\text{Surplus} + \text{Profit} = (B - R) + (R - C) = B - C,$$

where B denotes the total consumer benefits associated with a given level of output, R is total revenue paid by consumers to producers, and C is the total cost of production. The revenue term is simply a transfer between consumers and producers and does not affect the objective. Thus, maximizing this sum is equivalent to maximizing net benefits, B − C. At the optimal level of output, it must be the case that MB = MC.

Furthermore, the competitive equilibrium achieves this optimal level of output. To see this, consider the demand and supply curves, denoted by the functions $D(Q)$ and $S(Q)$, respectively. The competitive price and output are determined by the intersection of supply and demand, $D(Q_C) = S(Q_C) = P_C$. By our earlier argument, $D(Q) \equiv MB(Q)$ and $S(Q) \equiv MC(Q)$ for all Q, where MB and MC denote the marginal benefit and cost functions, respectively. It follows that $MB(Q_C) = MC(Q_C) = P_c$. Thus, the competitive level of output is efficient.

Figure 10.7 provides a visual depiction of our original proposition:

> Competitive markets provide efficient levels of goods and services at minimum cost to the consumers who are most willing (and able) to pay for them.

Think of this statement in three parts, focusing on production, consumption, and total output in turn. First, in a competitive market, the active firms are necessarily least-cost suppliers; all other higher-cost would-be suppliers are priced out of the market. (In our example, grandmothers cannot compete; "store-bought" day care is more efficiently supplied than "home-made.") The supply curve in Figure 10.7 is not drawn arbitrarily; rather, it describes the *lowest* possible costs of production. In this sense, *production is efficient.*

Second, competitive markets obey the "law of one price"; that is, all buyers and suppliers face the same price. In particular, this means that only consumers who are most willing (and able) to pay this price (i.e., those who reside on the highest portion of the demand curve) will actually end up with the goods. In this sense, *consumption is efficient.*

Third, given the market selection of minimum-cost producers and maximum-value consumers, the optimal output is achieved at the competitive intersection of supply and demand. Since $P_C = MB = MC$, it is impossible to alter output—above or below the competitive level—and increase net benefits. In this sense, *the level of output is efficient.*

What are the efficiency implications of a government program to provide universal, *free* day care?

CHECK STATION 5

EFFICIENCY AND EQUITY   It is important to emphasize that efficient markets are not necessarily equitable or fair. The outcomes of competitive markets directly reflect the distribution of incomes of those who buy and sell in these markets. An inability to pay excludes many people from the economic equation. In trying to solve the problems of poverty, malnutrition, inadequate health care, and the like, the government has the responsibility of addressing equity issues (as well as efficiency issues).

DYNAMIC, MARKETWIDE EFFICIENCY   In our examination of competitive efficiency, we have focused on a *single* market and found that the efficient level of output occurs at the intersection of demand and supply, where $P_C = MB = MC$. Can this "invisible hand" result be extended to encompass at once all the innumerable markets in a modern economy? The generalization to multiple markets is more complicated than it might seem at first. When dealing with many markets, it is not quite correct to focus on them separately, one at a time. After all, demands for different goods and services in the economy are interdependent. Changing the price of one good affects not only its consumption but also the consumption of substitute and complementary goods. Similarly, any change in price and output in one market generates marginal benefits and costs not only for that good but also for other affected markets. Given these interdependencies, can we draw any conclusions about the workings of private markets and economic efficiency?

Modern economic theory provides an elegant and important answer to this question: *If all markets in the economy are perfectly competitive, the economy as a whole is efficient, that is, delivers an efficient quantity of each good and service to consumers at least cost.* In short, a system of competitive markets in which all goods and services and all inputs (including labor) can be freely bought and sold provides a solution to the economic problem of resource allocation.[13] Indeed, no matter how well intentioned, government measures that interfere with competitive markets can cause welfare losses.

A final virtue of competitive markets is that they are dynamically efficient; that is, they respond optimally to changes in economic conditions. If a new product or service can be supplied at a cost below the price consumers are willing to pay, profit-seeking firms will create and supply a market where none formerly existed. If demand for an existing product rises, so will price, thus attracting new entrants and further supply. At the new equilibrium, the efficiency condition, $P = MB = MC$, will be restored. Alternatively, if costs decline, the efficient response is achieved via a fall in price, causing consumption to increase to a new optimal level. Finally, markets encourage the pursuit of technological innovations. Firms have a continuous incentive to search for and adopt more profitable methods of production.

With respect to dynamic efficiency, the choice of the day-care market for illustration was not completely frivolous. In the 1980s and 1990s, the emergence of dual-career families (combined with a second baby boom) created an unprecedented demand for day care. Organized child-care facilities have claimed an increasing share of this care (now some 25 percent) at the expense of care in the child's own home or by relatives. Three-year-old toddlers are now "clients" for child-care chains such as Kinder-Care, Petite Academy, and Children's Discovery Centers, to name a few of the larger operations. These chains are competing vigorously to become the "McDonald's" of day care: a market leader delivering a standardized service at a reasonable cost. Day-care chains face numerous problems, including poorly paid care providers, high turnover, uninspired programs, and debate among experts about the child development risks of impersonal care. Can "store-bought" day care deliver the type of service parents really want? This remains an open question.

---

[13] The proof of the foregoing "efficiency theorem" is beyond the scope of this book. It can be shown that a perfectly competitive economy is *Pareto efficient*; that is, it is impossible to reorganize the economy to make some economic agent (an individual or a firm) better off without making some other agent worse off.

The "invisible hand" theorem—that perfectly competitive markets ensure maximum social benefits—is best thought of as a benchmark. Although many markets in the United States meet the requirements of perfect competition, notable cases of market failures also exist. Market failures usually can be traced to one of three causes: (1) the presence of monopoly power, (2) the existence of externalities, or (3) the absence of perfect information. In Chapter 14, we analyze each of these sources of market failure.

Market Competition and the Internet

Is competition on the Internet one further step toward the textbook case of perfect competition?[14] The affirmative view holds that Internet competition, where consumers can easily find and identify the cheapest prices, should squeeze prices and profit margins to the bone. The early evidence suggests that the Internet can promote competition and efficiency in several respects. First, transacting online provides buyers and sellers much better information about available prices for competing goods. Clearly, the ability of customers to find better prices for standardized goods increases competition and induces more favorable prices. For instance, Internet prices for books and CDs tend to be 9 percent to 16 percent lower than traditional retail prices. Internet prices also display considerably less dispersion than do retail prices.

Second, the Internet increases the geographic range of markets and the variety of items sold in those markets. Hundreds of fragmented transactions are readily enlisted in unified markets. For example, a consumer could expend the time and effort to find a used copy of a John Grisham legal mystery by going to several bookstores and paying about $4 (half the new-book price). Or the consumer could use the Internet's unified used-book market, where scores of the same title sell for $2.50 including shipping. The important point is that unified markets directly increase overall economic efficiency. (See Problem 13 for a good example of this point.) However, unified markets need not always imply lower prices. For instance, with numerous buyers seeking scarce copies of original Nancy Drew mysteries (dust jackets intact), the Internet price averages $20 to $30 per copy. By comparison, the rare buyer who is lucky enough to find the same book on a bookstore shelf might pay only $5 to $15. As always the price effect of moving to a unified market depends on the relative increases in supply versus demand. An additional key benefit of online markets is greater product variety. One research study discovered that some 45 percent of all books sold online at Amazon were "rare" titles (ranked below the top 100,000).

---

[14] For interesting discussions of market competition and the Internet, see "A Perfect Market: Survey of E-commerce," *The Economist* (May 15, 2004) special supplement; E. Brynjolfsson, Y. Hu, and M. D. Smith, "Consumer Surplus in the Digital Economy: Estimating the Value of Increased Product Variety at Online Booksellers," *Management Science* (November 2003): 1580-1596; M. E. Porter, "Strategy and the Internet," *Harvard Business Review* (March 2001): 63–78; R. E. Litan and A. M. Rivlin, "Projecting the Economic Impact of the Internet," *American Economic Review*, Papers and *Proceedings* (May 2001): 313–317; and H. R. Varian., "The Usual Decorous Waltz between Prices and Sales Becomes a Lively Tango in the World of Online Sales," *The New York Times* (December 19, 2002), C2.

Using fitted demand curves, the study estimated the associated consumer surplus for these purchases with dramatic results. Consumer surplus averaged about 70 percent of the purchase price of each rare title. In total, the ability to find a wide variety of rare books was worth about $1 billion in 2000. By comparison, Amazon's low prices saved consumers about $100 million. Item variety proved to be worth 10 times more than price reductions.

Third, in many important instances, a firm's use of the Internet lowers costs: from finding and serving customers to ordering and procuring inputs, to lowering inventories. Selling online also may reduce the need for "bricks-and-mortar" investments, and online promotion and marketing may take the place of a direct sales force. Specific examples of cost savings abound: The cost of selling an airline ticket online is $20 cheaper than the cost of selling through a travel agent. Online automobile sales reduce the need for dealerships and vehicle inventories. Online stock trades are much less costly than brokered trades. Just as important, the Internet lowers the internal costs of the firm by serving as a platform for sharing and disseminating information throughout the firm and for better managing all aspects of the supply chain. Of course, each firm is constantly in pursuit of lower costs—via online initiatives or in any other areas—as a way to gain a competitive advantage over its rivals. However, if all (or most) firms in a given market successfully exploit e-business methods to lower unit costs, the upshot is that the entire industry supply curve shifts downward. In a perfectly competitive market, these cost reductions are passed on, dollar for dollar, in lower prices to consumers. In the long run, only the most efficient firms will serve the market and economic profits again converge to zero. Fourth, by lowering barriers to entry, online commerce moves markets closer to the perfectly competitive ideal. The e-business environment frequently means a reduced need for capital expenditures on plant, equipment, and inventories as well as for spending on highly trained direct sales forces. Elimination or reduction of these fixed costs makes it easier for numerous (perhaps small) firms to enter the market and compete even-handedly with current competitors.

What aspects of the online business environment are at odds with perfect competition? First, numerous e-business goods and services are highly differentiated. (They do not fit the "standardized" designation of perfect competition.) Differentiation allows the firm to raise price without immediately losing all sales. (Its demand curve is downward sloping, not horizontal.) For example, the firm can potentially command higher prices for ease of use, better customer service and support, faster shipping, and customized offers and services. Even in cyberspace, a firm's ability to earn positive economic profits depends on how well it differentiates its product and how effectively it establishes a strong brand name. Thus, a loyal customer of Amazon.com will continue to shop there for the ease, convenience, and product selection, even if prices are somewhat higher than at other sites. (Moreover, information goods usually exhibit high switching costs: Consumers are reluctant to learn to use a new software system or to navigate through an unfamiliar Web site.) Second, network externalities and economies of scale confer market power. The firm with the largest user network (e.g., Microsoft in PC operating systems, eBay in online auctions, America Online in instant messaging, Oracle in database software) will claim increasing market share and be able to command premium prices. In addition, the presence of economies of scale (due to high fixed costs and low marginal costs) means that market leaders (such as Google and Apple's itunes) will command a significant average-cost advantage relative to smaller rivals. All of these factors create barriers to entry, preventing new rivals from penetrating the market. Thus, shielded from price competition, the market leaders are able to earn positive economic profits.

Although e-business offers obvious avenues for increased competition, it does not eliminate the potential for claiming and exploiting market power in a number of traditional ways. As management expert Michael Porter puts it, "Because the Internet tends to weaken industry profitability, it is more important than ever for companies to distinguish themselves through strategy."

INTERNATIONAL TRADE

As noted in Chapter 7, international trade is based on mutually beneficial specialization among countries, that is, on comparative advantage. The final section of this chapter underscores two additional points. First, when free trade is the norm, patterns of trade follow the rules of worldwide supply and demand. If a country's demand outstrips its available supply, it will make up the difference via imports from the rest of the world. Second, the proposition that competitive markets are efficient applies not only to individual markets within a nation but also to all global markets. Free trade is the basis for worldwide efficient production. When nations erect trade barriers, economic welfare is diminished.

GLOBAL TRADE IN WATCHES   In Chapter 7's trade example, the United States imported digital watches from Japan because of the latter's comparative advantage in production. Let us extend that illustration by providing a full specification of supply and demand for the two countries. (To keep things simple, we focus only on trade in watches between the United States and Japan; we need not worry about other countries.) In the United States, the demand curve for watches is given by:

$$Q_U^D = 50 - 2P_U,$$

where Q_U^D denotes the quantity of watches per year (in millions) and P_U denotes the price per watch in dollars. In turn, the U.S. supply curve for watches is

$$Q_U^S = -10 + 2P_U.$$

As expected, if the price per watch increases, the quantity demanded falls while the quantity supplied increases. The corresponding demand and supply curves for Japan are

$$Q_J^D = 22.5 - .01P_J,$$

and

$$Q_J^S = -105 + .1P_J.$$

Note that Japanese demand and supply depend on P_J, the price per watch quoted in yen. How does one handle the two sets of prices denominated in different currencies? As long as the cost of transporting watches is negligible, free trade ensures that watches must sell at the same price (after converting to a common currency) throughout the world. Why? If the U.S. and Japanese prices were not equivalent, then a firm could act as a "middleman," buying watches at the lower price and shipping them to be sold at the higher price. This kind of profitable trading or "arbitrage" would quickly eliminate any price differences.

To continue the numerical solution, suppose the exchange rate is ¥100 per dollar. Then equivalent prices mean that

$$P_J = 100P_U.$$

For instance, a U.S. price of $10 per watch is equivalent to a Japanese price of ¥1,000 per watch.

If the worldwide market for watches is perfectly competitive, then the equilibrium price of watches will be at a level where *total world demand for watches exactly matches total world supply*:

$$Q_U^D + Q_J^D = Q_U^S + Q_J^S. \qquad [10.1]$$

We can use this equation and the preceding demand and supply expressions to solve for the equilibrium price P_U. We have

$$[50 - 2P_U] + [22.5 - P_U] = [-10 + 2P_U] + [-105 + 10P_U],$$

after replacing P_J with $100P_U$ in the Japanese demand and supply expressions. After combining terms and simplifying, we have

$$187.5 = 15P_U.$$

Therefore, $P_U = 187.5/15 = \$12.50$. The equivalent price in Japanese yen is ¥1,250 per watch.

At the \$12.50 price, U.S. firms supply $-10 + 2(12.50) = 15$ million watches while U.S. consumers demand $50 - 2(12.50) = 25$ million watches. The United States imports exactly 10 million watches from Japan to make up the difference. At this same price, Japanese firms produce 20 million watches, but Japanese consumers demand only 10 million. (Check these figures for yourself.) Thus, Japan exports the surplus, namely 10 million watches, to the United States.

What if one country's demand were expected to change in the coming year? For instance, suppose the U.S. demand curve is expected to shift toward greater demand at any given price. To be specific, let the new U.S. demand equation be $Q_U^D = 65 - 2P_U$. Then it is easy to solve the worldwide demand–supply equation to find $P_U = \$13.50$. At this price, U.S. demand is $65 - 2(13.50) = 38$ million watches while U.S. supply is $-10 + 2(13.50) = 17$ million watches. Thus, the United States will now import 21 million watches. As one would expect, the increase in demand causes a significant increase in U.S. imports from Japan.

Finally, what is the effect of an exchange rate change in the coming year? To be specific, what if the dollar were to increase in value (i.e., appreciate) by 34 percent to a rate of ¥134 per dollar? Recall from the discussion in Chapter 2 that a dollar appreciation tends to lower the price (in dollars) of the goods that the United States imports; thus, these imports should increase. Similarly, countries that export goods to the United States are eager to ramp up production and earn revenues in (more valuable) dollars. Let's check these effects using the current numerical example. Again we equate total world demand to total world supply, now making the substitution $P_J = 134P_U$ throughout to reflect the new exchange rate. Thus, Equation 10.1 becomes

$$[50 - 2P_U] + [22.5 - 1.34P_U] = [-10 + 2P_U] + [-105 + 13.4P_U].$$

This simplifies to $187.5 = 18.74P_U$ or $P_U = \$10$. The dollar price of U.S. imports has, indeed, fallen. At this lower price, U.S. demand is 30 million units, while U.S. supply is only 10 million units. Thus, U.S. imports will increase to 20 million units. Japan is willing to supply these imports because the yen price of watches has risen to $P_J = ¥1,340$ (from the former ¥1,250 price). This higher price spurs Japanese firms to increase their output and induces Japanese consumers to cut back their purchases. Japan exports its excess output, exactly 20 million units, to the United States.

The Efficiency of Free Trade

The chapter's earlier analysis demonstrated that perfectly competitive markets are efficient. More generally, worldwide competition promotes global efficiency. Firms from all over the world compete for sales to consumers of different nations. Free competition means that the good in question will sell at a single world price (net of transport costs). Only the most efficient lowest-cost firms will supply the good. Only consumers willing and able to pay the world price will purchase the good. Finally, exactly the right amount of the good will be supplied and consumed worldwide. In competitive equilibrium, global output occurs at a quantity such that P = MB = MC. The quantity of output is efficient. In a nutshell, this is the efficiency argument for free trade.

TARIFFS AND QUOTAS   In reality, worldwide trade is far from free. Traditionally, nations have erected trade barriers to limit the quantities of imports from other countries. Most commonly, these import restrictions have taken the form of tariffs, that is, taxes on foreign goods, or direct quotas. The usual rationale for this is to protect particular industries and their workers from foreign competition. Since World War II, the industrialized nations of the world have pushed for reductions in all kinds of trade barriers. Under the General Agreement on Tariffs and Trade (GATT), member nations meet periodically to negotiate reciprocal cuts in tariffs. Since the mid-1980s, there has been a resurgence of protectionist sentiment in the United States, aimed in part at insulating domestic industries from competition and, in part, as retaliation against alleged protectionist policies by Japan and Europe.

Although there is a number of strategic reasons why a country might hope to profit from trade barriers, the larger problem is the efficiency harm imposed by these restrictions. To illustrate this point, we return to the watch example.

RESTRICTED TRADE IN WATCHES   With free trade, the United States imported 10 million watches at an equilibrium world price of $12.50 per watch. Figure 10.8a depicts the U.S. demand and supply curves from the original example. The horizontal line at P = $12.50 represents the world price. The length of the line segment CD measures the volume of imports, 10 million watches (the difference between U.S. consumption and U.S. production). Now suppose the United States enacts trade restrictions prohibiting the import of Japanese watches altogether. Then the no-trade equilibrium price would occur at the intersection of domestic supply and demand. In the figure, this price is $15, and total output is 20 million watches.

What is the net effect of prohibiting watch imports? Domestic watch producers benefit, while domestic consumers are harmed. We now show that the cost to consumers exceeds the benefit to producers, thus causing a net loss in the aggregate. To see this, note that the extra profits earned by domestic producers due to the price increase (from $12.50 to $15) are given by the area of trapezoid ABCE. (The extra profit lies between the old and new price lines and above the industry supply curve.) However, the increase in price has sliced into the total surplus of consumers. The reduction in consumer surplus is measured by trapezoid ABDE. (This is simply the area between the two price lines and under the demand curve.) When we compare trapezoids ABDE and ABCE,

FIGURE 10.8

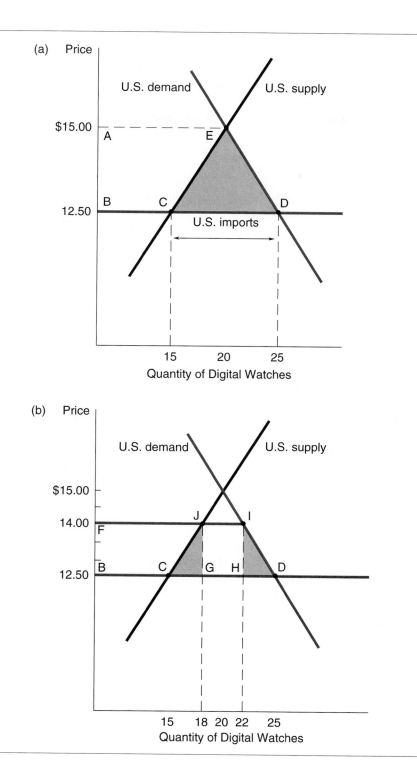

Figure a shows a complete restriction on trade. Figure b shows a tariff.

we see that consumer losses exceed producer gains by the shaded triangle ECD. This triangle measures the harm done to society, or the so-called "deadweight" loss attributable to the trade prohibition.[15]

Figure 10.8b depicts the effect of a less dramatic trade restriction. In this instance, U.S. trade authorities have imposed a 12 percent tariff on Japanese imports, raising the price of watches to $(1.12)(\$12.50) = \$14$. As shown in the figure, the tariff reduces total U.S. consumption to 22 million watches, while increasing domestic production to 18 million watches. (Check these figures using the original U.S. supply and demand equations.) Thus, U.S. imports are $22 - 18 = 4$ million watches. Though less extreme, the impact of the tariff is qualitatively similar to that of a complete trade prohibition. Compared to free trade, consumer surplus is reduced by trapezoid FBDI (the area between the two price lines). Producer profits are increased by trapezoid FBCJ. The trade authority also collects tariff revenue, given by rectangle JGHI, on the 4 million watches imported. Comparing the loss in consumer surplus to these twin gains, we see that the nation as a whole suffers a net loss measured by the areas of the two shaded deadweight loss triangles.

We make two final observations. First, a tariff is superior to the alternative of a quota that achieves an equivalent reduction in imports. A quota of 4 million units would have exactly the same result as the 12 percent tariff, except that it would raise no revenue. After eliminating the revenue rectangle JGHI, we find the total deadweight loss of the quota to be trapezoid CDIJ. Second, moves to higher and higher tariffs steadily diminish imports, increase deadweight losses, and ultimately raise little revenue. In the present example, as the tariff is raised toward 20 percent, the price of watches approaches $15, and imports fall closer and closer to zero. Obviously, tariff rates that eliminate nearly all imports generate very little revenue.

Betting the Planet Revisited

Simon's bet rested on the simple economics of supply and demand. If ecologists were correct in their assertion that the world was running out of essential resources, then the prices of these scarce resources should rise. Basing his opinion on his own research, Simon was confident that the ecologists were wrong and that resources would be more abundant tomorrow than today so that their prices would fall.

Who was right? When the bet was settled in 1991, the prices of all five metals had declined over the decade. The same quantities of the metals that were worth $1,000 in 1981 had a total market value of only $618 in 1991. The explanations? Increases in supply kept up with increases in demand; mining companies found new deposits and used more efficient methods to recover and refine ores; the metals often were replaced by cheaper substitutes; and the tin cartel collapsed and tin prices collapsed with it.

[15] For more on deadweight loss, see the discussion of market failure in Chapter 14.

Ehrlich wrote Simon a check for the difference between the prices then and now—$382 plus accumulated interest over the decade. Using price as the market test, the "boomster" had won his bet with the "doomster."

Does this result settle the larger debate concerning the depletion of resources? The answer is no. Although supplies of many resources are more abundant now than in the past, this does not mean that resource supplies will outstrip demand indefinitely. The depletion of many resources—from old-growth forests to fishing banks—and the extinction of many species of plants and animals remain continuing concerns.

SUMMARY

Decision-Making Principles

1. Whatever the market environment, the firm maximizes profit by establishing a level of output such that marginal revenue equals marginal cost.

2. In perfect competition, the firm faces infinitely elastic demand: Marginal revenue equals the market price. Thus, the firm follows the optimal output rule $P = MC$. In long-run equilibrium, the firm's output is marked by the equalities $P = MR = MC = AC_{min}$, and the firm earns zero profit.

3. Economic transactions are voluntary. Buyers and sellers participate in them if and only if the transactions are mutually beneficial.

4. Competitive markets provide the efficient amounts of goods and services at minimum cost to the consumers who are most willing (and able) to pay for them. Worldwide competition and free trade promote global efficiency.

Nuts and Bolts

1. In a perfectly competitive market, a large number of firms sell identical products, and there are no barriers to entry by new suppliers. Price tends toward a level where the market demand curve intersects the market supply curve. In the long run, price coincides with minimum average cost, and all firms earn zero economic profits.

2. The total value associated with an economic transaction is the sum of consumer and producer surplus. Consumer surplus is the difference between what the individual is willing to pay and what she or he actually pays.

3. For any market, the height of the demand curve shows the monetary value that consumers are willing to pay for each unit. Consumer surplus in the market is given by the area under the demand curve and above the market price line.

4. In equilibrium, a competitive market generates maximum net benefits. The optimal level of output is determined by the intersection of demand and supply, that is, where marginal benefit exactly equals marginal cost.

Questions and Problems

1. The renowned Spaniard Pablo Picasso was a prolific artist. He created hundreds of paintings and sculptures as well as drawings and sketches numbering in the thousands. (He is said to have settled restaurant bills by producing sketches on the spot.)
   a. What effect does the existence of this large body of work have on the monetary value of individual pieces of his art?
   b. Might his heirs suffer from being bequeathed too many of his works? As the heirs' financial adviser, what strategy would you advise them to pursue in selling pieces of his work?

2. Consider the regional supply curve of farmers who produce a particular crop.
   a. What does the supply curve look like at the time the crop is harvested? (Show a plausible graph.)
   b. Depict the crop's supply curve at the beginning of the growing season (when farmers must decide how many acres to cultivate).
   c. Depict the crop's supply curve in the long run (when farmers can enter or exit the market).

3. Potato farming (like farming of most agricultural products) is highly competitive. Price is determined by demand and supply. Based on Department of Agriculture statistics, U.S. demand for potatoes is estimated to be $Q_D = 184 - 20P$, where P is the farmer's wholesale price (per 100 pounds) and Q_D is consumption of potatoes per capita (in pounds). In turn, industry supply is $Q_S = 124 + 4P$.
   a. Find the competitive market price and output.
   b. Potato farmers in Montana raise about 7 percent of total output. If these farmers enjoy bumper crops (10 percent greater harvests than normal), is this likely to have much effect on price? On Montana farmers' incomes?
   c. Suppose that, due to favorable weather conditions, U.S. potato farmers as a whole have bumper crops. The total amount delivered to market is 10 percent higher than that calculated in part a. Find the new market price. What has happened to total farm revenue? Is industry demand elastic or inelastic? In what sense do natural year-to-year changes in growing conditions make farming a boom-or-bust industry?

4. In a competitive market, the industry demand and supply curves are $P = 200 - .2Q_d$ and $P = 100 + .3Q_s$, respectively.

a. Find the market's equilibrium price and output.

b. Suppose the government imposes a tax of $20 per unit of output on all firms in the industry. What effect does this have on the industry supply curve? Find the new competitive price and output. What portion of the tax has been passed on to consumers via a higher price?

c. Suppose a $20-per-unit sales tax is imposed on consumers. What effect does this have on the industry demand curve? Find the new competitive price and output. Compare this answer to your findings in part b.

5. The Green Company produces chemicals in a perfectly competitive market. The current market price is $40; the firm's total cost is $C = 100 + 4Q + Q^2$.

a. Determine the firm's profit-maximizing output. More generally, write down the equation for the firm's supply curve in terms of price P.

b. Complying with more stringent environmental regulations increases the firm's fixed cost from 100 to 144. Would this affect the firm's output? Its supply curve?

c. How would the increase in fixed costs affect the market's long-run equilibrium price? The number of firms? (Assume that Green's costs are typical in the market.)

6. Firm Z, operating in a perfectly competitive market, can sell as much or as little as it wants of a good at a price of $16 per unit. Its cost function is $C = 50 + 4Q + 2Q^2$. The associated marginal cost is $MC = 4 + 4Q$ and the point of minimum average cost is $Q_{min} = 5$.

a. Determine the firm's profit-maximizing level of output. Compute its profit.

b. The industry demand curve is $Q = 200 - 5P$. What is the total market demand at the current $16 price? If all firms in the industry have cost structures identical to that of firm Z, how many firms will supply the market?

c. The outcomes in part a and b cannot persist in the long run. Explain why. Find the market's price, total output, number of firms, and output per firm in the long run.

d. Comparing the short-run and long-run results, explain the changes in the price and in the number of firms.

7. In a perfectly competitive market, industry demand is given by $Q = 1,000 - 20P$. The typical firm's average cost is $AC = 300/Q + Q/3$.

a. Confirm that $Q_{min} = 30$. (*Hint*: Set AC equal to MC.) What is AC_{min}?

b. Suppose 10 firms serve the market. Find the individual firm's supply curve. Find the market supply curve. Set market supply equal to market demand to determine the competitive price and output. What is the typical firm's profit?

c. Determine the long-run, zero-profit equilibrium. How many firms will serve the market?

8. In a competitive market, the industry demand and supply curves are $P = 70 - Q_D$ and $P = 40 + 2Q_S$.
   a. Find the market's equilibrium price and output.
   b. Suppose that the government provides a subsidy to producers of $15 per unit of the good. Since the subsidy reduces each supplier's marginal cost by 15, the new supply curve is $P = 25 + 2Q_S$. Find the market's new equilibrium price and output. Provide an explanation for the change in price and quantity.
   c. A public interest group supports the subsidy, arguing that it helps consumers and producers alike. Economists oppose the subsidy, declaring that it leads to an inefficient level of output. In your opinion, which side is correct? Explain carefully.

9. Demand for microprocessors is given by $P = 35 - 5Q$, where Q is the quantity of microchips (in millions). The typical firm's total cost of producing a chip is $C_i = 5q_i$, where q_i is the output of firm i.
   a. Under perfect competition, what are the equilibrium price and quantity?
   b. Does the microchip industry (as described earlier) display increasing, constant, or decreasing returns to scale? What would you expect about the real microchip industry? In general, what must be true about the underlying technology of production for competition to be viable?
   c. Under perfect competition, find total industry profit and consumer surplus.

10. Consider once again the digital watch numerical example.
    a. Suppose U.S. demand for watches increases to $Q_U^d = 65 - 2P_U$ at the same time that the dollar depreciates from ¥100 per dollar to ¥90 per dollar. Find the dollar price of watches and the amount of U.S. watch imports.
    b. Does the dollar depreciation offset the impact of the increased U.S. demand for watches? Explain.

11. The market for rice in an East Asian country has demand and supply given by $Q_D = 28 - 4P$ and $Q_S = -12 + 6P$, where quantities denote millions of bushels per day.
    a. If the domestic market is perfectly competitive, find the equilibrium price and quantity of rice. Compute the triangular areas of consumer surplus and producer surplus.
    b. Now suppose that there are no trade barriers, and the world price of rice is $3. Confirm that the country will import rice. Find Q_D, Q_S, and the level of imports $Q_D - Q_S$. Show that the country is better off than in part a (by again computing consumer surplus and producer surplus).
    c. The government authority believes strongly in free trade but feels political pressure to help domestic rice growers. Accordingly, it decides

to provide a $1 per bushel subsidy to domestic growers. Show that this subsidy induces the same domestic output as in part a. Including the cost of the subsidy, is the country better off now than in part b? Explain.

12. a. When a best-selling book was first released in paperback, the Hercules Bookstore chain seized a profit opportunity by setting a selling price of $9 per book (well above Hercules' $5 average cost per book). With paperback demand given by $P = 15 - .5Q$, the chain enjoyed sales of $Q = 12$ thousand books per week. (Note Q is measured in thousands of books.) Draw the demand curve and compute the bookstore's profit and the total consumer surplus.

   b. For the first time, Hercules has begun selling books online—in response to competition from other online sellers and in the quest for new profits. The average cost per book sold online is only $4. As part of its online selling strategy, it sends weekly emails to preferred customers announcing which books are new in paperback. For this segment, it sets an average price (including shipping) of $12. According to the demand curve in part a, only the highest-value consumers (whose willingness to pay is $12 or more) purchase at this price. Check that these are the first 6 thousand book buyers on the demand curve. In turn, because of increased competition, Hercules reduced its store price to $7 per book.

   At $P = $7, how many book are bought in Hercules' stores? (Make sure to exclude online buyers from your demand curve calculation.) Compute Hercules' total profit, then compute the sum of consumer surplus from online and in-store sales. Relative to part a, has the emergence of online commerce improved the welfare of book buyers as a whole? Explain.

* 13. The following table summarizes the demand for water by potential buyers and water holders in two water districts of a southwestern state:

		District 1				District 2	
Agent	Value	Quantity Demanded	Quantity Held	Agent	Value	Quantity Demanded	Quantity Held
H1	$35	3	3	H4	$28	4	5
H2	42	4	2	H5	32	3	3
H3	25	4	5	H6	24	6	6
B1	50	4	0	B4	48	3	0
B2	37	2	0	B5	30	4	0
B3	26	3	0				

* Starred problems are more challenging.

Here the label H denotes current water holders and B stands for potential buyers. For instance, agent H1 holds 3 acre-feet of water and values this water at $35 per acre-foot. In contrast, agent B1 currently possesses no water but has a demand for 4 acre-feet, each valued at $50.

a. Suppose pairs of water holders and would-be water buyers attempt to negotiate mutually beneficial transactions. If H1 negotiates with B1, H2 with B2, and so on, what transactions will take place in each district? What is the total dollar benefit from these transactions in each district?

b. Suppose instead that water can be bought freely and sold within each district but not between districts. What will be the price in each district? What is the total dollar benefit from the resulting transactions?

c. Answer part b assuming water is freely traded between districts.

Discussion Question Over the last 30 years in the United States, the *real* price of a college education (i.e., after adjusting for inflation) has increased by almost 70 percent. Over the same period, an increasing number of high school graduates have sought a college education. (Nationwide college enrollments almost doubled over this period.) While faculty salaries have barely kept pace with inflation, administrative staffing (and expenditures) and capital costs have increased significantly. In addition, government support to universities (particularly research funding) has been cut.

a. College enrollments increased at the same time that average tuition rose dramatically. Does this contradict the law of downward-sloping demand? Explain briefly.

b. Use supply and demand curves (or shifts therein) to explain the dramatic rise in the price of a college education.

Spreadsheet Problems

S1. In a perfectly competitive market, the cost structure of the typical firm is given by $C = 25 + Q^2 - 4Q$, and industry demand is given by $Q = 400 - 20P$. Currently, 24 firms serve the market.

a. Create a spreadsheet (similar to the given example) to model the short-run and long-run dynamics of this market. (*Hint*: Enter numerical values for the Price, # Firms, and Q_F cells; all other cells should be linked by formulas to these three cells.)

b. What equilibrium price will prevail in the short run? (*Hint*: Use the spreadsheet's optimizer and specify cell F8, the difference between demand and supply, as the target cell. However, instead of maximizing this cell, instruct the optimizer to set it equal to zero. In addition, include the constraint that P − MC in cell F14 must equal zero.)

  c. What equilibrium price will prevail in the long run? (*Hint*: Include cell C8, the number of firms, as an adjustable cell in addition to cells B8 and B14, and add the constraint that total profit in cell G8 must equal zero.)

	A	B	C	D	E	F	G	H
1								
2				EQUILIBRIUM IN A PERFECTLY				
3				COMPETITIVE MARKET				
4								
5				The Industry				
6		Price	# Firms	Supply	Demand	D − S	Tot. Profit	
7								
8		10	24	192	200	8	552	
9								
10								
11				The Typical Firm				
12		Q_F	MC	Cost	AC	P − MC	Firm Profit	
13								
14		8	12	57	7.13	−2	23	
15								
16								
17		SR: (1) D − S = 0 and (2) P = MC; Adjust: P & Q_F						
18		LR: (1) and (2) and (3) P = AC; Adjust: P & Q_F & # Firms						
19								

S2. The industry demand curve in a perfectly competitive market is given by the equation $P = 160 − 2Q$, and the supply curve is given by the equation $P = 40 + Q$. The upward-sloping supply curve represents the increasing marginal cost of expanding *industry* output. The total *industry* cost of producing Q units of output is $C = 800 + 40Q + .5Q^2$. (Note that taking the derivative of this equation produces the preceding industry MC equation.) In turn, the total benefit associated with consuming Q units of output is given by the equation $B = 160Q − Q^2$. (Total benefit represents the trapezoidal area under the demand curve. It is also the sum of consumer surplus and revenue. Note that taking the derivative of the benefit equation produces the original industry demand curve $MB = 160 − 2Q$.)

a. Create a spreadsheet similar to the given example. Only the quantity cell (C5) contains a numerical value. All other cells are linked by formulas to the quantity cell.
b. Find the intersection of competitive supply and demand by equating the demand and supply equations or by varying quantity in the spreadsheet until MB equals MC.
c. Alternatively, find the optimal level of industry output by maximizing net benefits (cell F9) or, equivalently, the sum of consumer and producer gains (cell F10). Confirm that the perfectly competitive equilibrium of part b is efficient.

	A	B	C	D	E	F	G
1							
2				EFFICIENCY OF			
3				PERFECT COMPETITION			
4							
5		Quantity	32		Price	96	
6							
7		Benefit	4,096		Con Surplus	1,024	
8		P = MB	96				
9					B − C	1,504	
10		Revenue	3,072		CS + Profit	1,504	
11		MR	32				
12					Profit	480	
13		Cost	2,592				
14		MC	72				
15							

Suggested References

Adams, W., and J. R. Brock (Eds.). *The Structure of American Industry.* New York: Prentice-Hall, 2000, especially Chapter 1.

This volume devotes separate chapters to describing the market structures of the major sectors in the American economy—from agriculture to banking, from cigarettes to beer, from automobiles to computers.

Salathe, L., and S. Langley, "An Empirical Analysis of Alternative Export Subsidy Programs for U.S. Wheat." *Agricultural Economics Research* (Winter 1986): 111–132.

The article surveys studies on the demand and supply of wheat.

The following readings discuss Internet and e-commerce competition:

Borenstein, S., and G. Saloner. "Economics and Electronic Commerce." *Journal of Economic Perspectives* (Winter 2001): 3–12.

Brynjolfsson, E., Y. Hu, and M. D. Smith. "Consumer Surplus in the Digital Economy: Estimating the Value of Increased Product Variety at Online Booksellers." *Management Science* (November 2003): 1580–1596.

The following volume assesses the effects of airline deregulation in promoting competition and lowering prices. It also estimates the increase in consumer surplus resulting from airline deregulation.

Morrison, S. A., and C. Winston. *The Evolution of the Airline Industry.* Washington, DC: Brookings Press, 1995.

The following book and articles provide readable treatments of competitiveness, free trade, and protectionism.

Bagwhati, J. *In Defense of Globalization.* Oxford, UK: Oxford University Press, 2004.

Baldwin, R. E. "Are Economists' Traditional Trade Policy Views Still Valid?" *Journal of Economic Literature* (June 1992): 804–829.

Bhagwati, J. "Free Trade: Old and New Challenges." *The Economic Journal* 104 (March 1994): 231–246.

"Research on Free Trade." *The American Economic Review* 83, Papers and Proceedings (May 1993): 362–376.

"A Survey of Globalization." *The Economist* (September 29, 2001).

The best Internet sources for analyzing free trade are the writings of Professor Jagdish Bhagwati of Columbia University: www.columbia.edu/~jb38.

CHECK STATION ANSWERS

1. Equating $Q_D = 15 - 10P$ and $Q_S = -3 + 14P$ implies $18 = 24P$, or $P = 18/24 = \$.75$ per pound. Given the drop in demand, we equate $12 - 8P = -3 + 14P$, implying the new price $P = \$.68$. Though demand has fallen 20 percent, price has declined by just some 10 percent.

2. Setting $P = MC$ implies $P = 2Q_F - 4$, or $Q_F = (P + 4)/2$. With 40 firms, the supply curve is $Q_S = 40(P + 4)/2 = 20P + 80$.

3. To find the point of minimum average cost, we set $AC = MC$. This implies $25/Q + Q - 4 = 2Q - 4$, or $25/Q = Q$. After multiplying both sides by Q, we have $Q^2 = 25$ or $Q_{min} = 5$. Thus, each firm will produce 5 thousand units. In turn, $AC_{min} = 6$. Thus, the long-run price is also $P = \$6$. At this price, $Q_D = 320 - (20)(6) = 200$ thousand units. The requisite number of firms to supply this demand is $200/5 = 40$. (This exactly matches the number of current firms.)

4. From Check Station 1, the short-run supply curve is $Q_S = 20P + 80$. Setting Q_D equal to Q_S implies $400 - 20P = 20P + 80$. Therefore, we have $P = \$8$. In turn, $Q_F = (8 + 4)/2 = 6$ thousand units and $Q_S = (40)(6) = 240$ thousand units. With price greater than average cost, each firm is making a positive economic profit. In the long run, $P = AC_{min} = \$6$, implying $Q_D = 400 - (20)(6) = 280$ thousand units, supplied by $280/5 = 56$ firms.

5. If day care is free ($P = \$0$), the outcome will be inefficient: Too much day care will be demanded and consumed. The marginal benefit of the last hours consumed will be nearly zero, that is, much less than the hours' marginal cost $MB < MC$. (However, there may be beneficial distributional consequences.)

CHAPTER 11

Monopoly

Monopoly: the earnings of many in the hands of one.

EUGENE DEBS

Everyone has stories to tell, good and bad, about New York cabbies. However, the largely untold story is that New York's taxis (like those of most other major cities) are highly regulated. Minimum standards of service and fares are set by a city commission. Even more important, this commission directly limits the number of taxis via its licensing authority. By law, each authorized "yellow" cab must carry a medallion. The number of medallions has been nearly unchanged for 65 years. In 1937, the number for New York City was 11,787. After "token" increases in 1996 and 2004, today, there are 12,487 licensed taxis!

The commission is caught in a continuous crossfire from consumer advocates, government officials, and representatives of taxi companies and drivers. Are fares too high or not high enough? Should additional medallions be issued, or would this be bad for the industry? Does the industry need tighter regulation, or is the regulatory burden already too great? As you read this chapter, think about the ways in which an economic analysis could be applied to address these questions.

PURE MONOPOLY

A **pure monopoly** is a market that has only one seller: a single firm. It is worth noting at the outset that pure monopolies are very rare. It is estimated that less than 3 percent of the U.S. gross domestic product (the dollar value of all goods and services) is produced in monopolistic markets. (Here a monopoly is defined as a market in which a single firm has 90 percent or more of the market.) Nonetheless, the case of pure monopoly is important not only in its own right but also because of its relevance for cases of near monopolies in which a few firms dominate a market. The monopoly model also explains the behavior of cartels—groups of producers that set prices and outputs in concert.

There are two main issues to address in analyzing monopoly. First, one must understand monopoly behavior—how a profit-maximizing monopolist determines price and output. Second, one must appreciate that a precondition for monopoly is the presence of **barriers to entry,** factors that prevent other firms from entering the market and competing on an equal footing with the monopolist.

Let's start by considering a monopolist's price and output decision. Being the lone producer, the monopolist is free to raise price without worrying about losing sales to a competitor that might charge a lower price. Although the monopolist has complete control over industry output, this does not mean it can raise price indefinitely. Its optimal price and output policy depends on market demand. Because the monopolist *is* the industry, its demand curve is given simply by the industry demand curve. Figure 11.1 depicts the industry demand curve and long-run costs for the monopolist. Given information on demand and cost, it is straightforward to predict monopoly price and output. As a profit maximizer, the monopolist should set its output such that marginal revenue (derived from the industry demand curve) equals the marginal cost of production. In the figure, this output, Q_M, is shown where the monopolist's marginal revenue and marginal cost curves intersect. According to the industry demand curve, the corresponding monopoly price is P_M. The area of the shaded rectangle measures the monopolist's total excess profit. This profit is the product of the monopolist's profit per unit, $P_M - AC$ (the rectangle's height), and total output, Q_M (the rectangle's base).

We should make two related remarks about the potential for excess profits under pure monopoly. First, monopoly confers a greater profit to the firm than it would if the firm shared the market with competitors. We have seen that economic profits in perfect competition are zero in the long run—not so for the monopolist. Second, even when the firm occupies a pure-monopoly position, its excess profits depend directly on the position of industry demand versus its cost. Figure 11.2 makes the point by depicting three different industry demand

FIGURE 11.1

A Monopolist's Optimal
Price and Output

The monopolist
maximizes its profit by
producing an output
such that MR equals
MC.

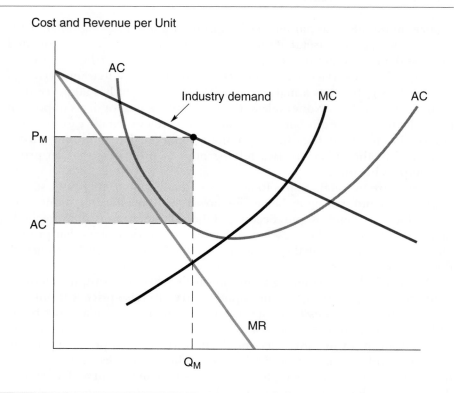

Cost and Revenue per Unit

curves. It should be evident that only curve D_1 offers significant excess profits. Demand curves D_2 and D_3 offer very little in the way of profit possibilities. Although they differ with respect to elasticities, both curves barely exceed the monopolist's average cost. The lesson here is that pure monopoly enables the firm to earn excess profit, but the actual size of this profit depends on a comparison of demand and cost. For instance, if other goods or services are close substitutes for the monopolist's product, industry demand may be relatively elastic and afford relatively little excess profit (curve D_2). If it is to increase its profit substantially, the monopoly firm must find a way to lower its average cost of production or to raise market demand. (However, there may be no demand at all for the monopolist's unique product. The U.S. patent office overflows with inventions that have never earned a dime.)

Monopolies, Past and Present

For many managers, acquiring a monopoly position in a market is akin to an all-consuming search for the Holy Grail. However, it is worth remembering how few and far between monopolies are in the American marketplace. The adage

FIGURE 11.2

Dollars per Unit of Output

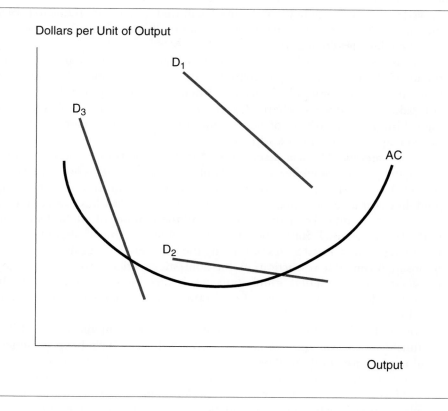

Output

The industry demand curve facing a monopolist might be D1, D2, or D3. Only curve D1 affords the opportunity for significant economic profits.

"Many are called, but few are chosen" certainly applies to the monopoly quest. Here are three examples of "once, but not necessarily future" monopolies.

The **Xerox Corporation** accounted for over 95 percent of photocopier sales in the United States—a classic monopoly—until the late 1960s. In the 1970s, Xerox's U.S. market share fell sharply. New firms, such as Canon, Sharp, Royal, and Savin, successfully entered the copier market, particularly in the low- and medium-price segments. Currently, these four firms and Xerox make up this market with roughly comparable market shares. In the high-price, high-volume, copier-duplicator segment, Xerox, IBM, and Eastman Kodak divide the market (again roughly equally).

How did Xerox lose its monopoly position? During the 1970s, many of the company's original patents expired, making it much easier for firms to market similar copiers. In 1975, Xerox was forced to sign a consent decree with the Federal Trade Commission agreeing to license its copier patents to other manufacturers. Perhaps more important, competitors were able to innovate around Xerox's patents and develop comparable or superior copiers. In the early

1970s, Xerox stumbled by introducing a line of medium-volume copiers that proved unreliable. Finally, when the market moved from copier rental to copier purchase, new entry was facilitated because far less financial muscle was needed to sell copiers than to maintain a rental base.

Today, Xerox offers the widest product line and competes in more parts of the world than any other copier manufacturer. However, copiers have become much more of a "commodity" business, where numerous companies produce comparable copiers and where efficient assembly is as important as techno-logical innovation. Instead of being a monopolist, Xerox is merely one of a dozen major players in the world copier industry.[1]

The **American Medical Association (AMA)** has the responsibility for over-seeing the practice of medicine in the United States. Among its other activities, the AMA establishes procedures for licensing physicians and implementing guidelines for medical schools. In this latter role, the AMA has exercised con-trol over the number of medical schools and the number of medical students in the United States. Prior to 1965, the AMA influenced the number of doctors practicing in the United States by limiting the number of medical students and imposing formidable restrictions on the domestic practice of foreign-educated physicians. One result of this limitation was elevated incomes for physicians. In the 1960s, doctors' earnings put them in the upper 20 percent of the income distribution.

Since the 1980s, the AMA's control of the number of medical students has diminished and immigration laws for foreign doctors have been loosened, resulting in a greater than 40 percent increase in the supply of doctors. By one estimate, this supply increase has "cost" the average doctor 20 to 25 percent in annual income.[2] In short, the erosion of the AMA's monopoly restrictions on the supply of physicians has meant a reduction in the excess returns earned by the medical profession.

The **National Collegiate Athletic Association (NCAA)** establishes and enforces the myriad rules governing intercollegiate athletics. Though inter-collegiate athletics are certainly a part of the college experience and educa-tion, they are also "big business," returning hundreds of thousands of dollars to universities with the most successful programs. Some top college coaches make seven-figure salaries. Athletic shoe companies pay top teams to wear their products. By its authority, the NCAA has monopoly control over this business. The organization determines the size and number of scholarships in different sports and the number of games played. It negotiates most of the lucrative radio and television agreements for major collegiate sports, such as football and bas-ketball. Most important, the NCAA limits the "salaries" paid to athletes to the

---

[1] For a more extensive analysis, see T. Bresnahan, "Post-Entry Competition in the Plain Paper Copier Market," *American Economic Review* (May 1985): 15–19.

[2] See Monica Noether, "The Effect of Government Policy Changes on the Supply of Doctors: Expansion of a Competitive Fringe," *Journal of Law and Economics* (1986): 231–262.

cost of tuition plus room and board. Of course, the NCAA and university presidents argue strenuously that student athletes should not be paid. Whether one agrees with this view or not, a basic fact remains. The enormous profitability of intercollegiate sports is a direct result of the NCAA's "monopoly-like" behavior—in particular, output restrictions that keep revenues high and scholarship rules that keep costs low.[3]

A common measure of monopoly power is given by the Lerner index, defined as $L = (P_M - MC)/P_M$, where P_M denotes the monopolist's price and MC is marginal cost. For a profit-maximizing monopolist, how does the Lerner index depend on the elasticity of industry demand? (*Hint:* Recall the price-markup rule of Chapter 3.) What do you see as the advantages and disadvantages of using the Lerner index as a measure of monopoly power?

CHECK STATION 1

Barriers to Entry

A **barrier** is any factor that blocks or impedes entry of new firms into a particular market. There is a wide variety of barriers to entry that are more or less important, depending on the market under consideration. In some cases, one or more of these barriers are sufficient to support a single dominant firm in the market. In others, entry barriers are not absolute but limit the market to a small number of firms. It is also useful to speak of *barriers to competition*—that is, factors that, while not precluding rivals from the market, insulate a given firm from direct competition. Sources of entry barriers include the following.

ECONOMIES OF SCALE   When average cost falls significantly with increases in scale, a new firm must enter the market with a large market share to be competitive. If this addition to industry output requires a significant drop in market price, entry will be unprofitable. In so-called natural monopolies, average cost continually decreases with output, implying that a single firm achieves the lowest possible unit cost by supplying the entire market. For instance, it is cheaper for one company to lay a single network of cables to provide cable TV to a particular town or region.

CAPITAL REQUIREMENTS   In some industries (automobiles, defense, oil refining, deep-sea drilling), the capital requirements of production are enormous. In others (chemicals, pharmaceuticals, electronics), large investments in research and development are necessary. When large sunk costs are required,

---

[3] For an extensive economic analysis of the NCAA, see J. R. Fizel and R. W. Bennett, "College Sports," in W. and J. Brock, *The Structure of American Industry* (Upper Saddle River, NJ: Prentice-Hall, 2001).

entry is particularly risky. (If, after entry, a firm finds itself suffering losses, it will be largely unable to recover its investment.)

PURE QUALITY AND COST ADVANTAGES   Sometimes a single firm has absolute quality or cost advantages over all potential competitors. Cost advantages may be due to superior technology, more efficient management, economies of scope, or learning. For these reasons, Intel dominates the market for microchips, Wal-Mart is the world's leading chain of discount department stores, and Boeing and Airbus share the global aircraft market. In many e-commerce markets, network externalities (making larger networks more valuable to customers) bestow an important quality advantage on the market leader (eBay in online auctions for instance). Although there are many close substitutes, Coca-Cola continues to guard the secret for its best-selling soft drink. In the 1970s and 1980s, the Department of Defense used sole-source procurements to purchase major weapon systems, claiming that only a single qualified supplier existed. A dramatic expression of the monetary return to "being one of the best" is the annual income of a "superstar" such as Tiger Woods, Shaquille O'Neal, Tom Cruise, or Julia Roberts.

PRODUCT DIFFERENTIATION   Once an incumbent has created a preference for a "unique" product or brand name via advertising and marketing campaigns, it has erected considerable barriers to new entrants that seek to compete for its customers. Producers of retail goods and services thrive on product differentiation, real or perceived. Producers of ready-to-eat breakfast cereals carry product differentiation to an extreme. The dominant producers have "packed" the product space with a proliferation of brands, making it almost impossible for a new firm to secure a market niche. *Switching costs* can be an important barrier to competition in markets for information-intensive goods and services. When customers have "invested" in learning to use a particular software program, navigate a Web site, or set up online accounts, they are less likely to switch to competitive (perhaps even superior) alternatives.

CONTROL OF RESOURCES   A barrier to entry exists when an incumbent firm (or firms) controls crucial resources—mineral deposits, oil supplies, even scientific talent. At the local level, a retailer's "choice" location may provide protection from entry by would-be competitors. Ownership of unique items (fine art, antiques) confers a degree of monopoly power (albeit limited by the availability of substitutes). For instance, the price of a unique item at auction is determined by what the market will bear, not by competitive supply. The best-known examples of monopoly power based on resource control include French champagne, De Beers (diamonds), and OPEC (crude oil).

PATENTS, COPYRIGHTS, AND OTHER LEGAL BARRIERS   A patent grants the holder exclusive rights to make, use, or sell an invention for 20 years. A patent can apply to an idea, process, or system as well as to an invention. A copyright prohibits the unauthorized copying of a particular work. Patents and copyrights constitute important barriers to entry in computers, machinery, electronics, publishing, pharmaceuticals, defense, and chemicals. In many instances (local utilities, cable television firms, vendors on state highways and in national parks), the government grants legal monopolies for extended periods of time.

STRATEGIC BARRIERS   Finally, the dominant firm (or firms) may take actions explicitly aimed at erecting entry barriers. Securing legal protection (via patent or copyright) is only one example. A monopolist may exercise limit pricing, that is, keep price below monopoly levels to discourage new entry. It may threaten retaliatory pricing. For the same reasons, it may engage in extensive advertising and brand proliferation, not because this is profitable in itself (it may not be) but to raise the cost of entry for new competitors. Finally, the monopolist may intentionally create excess productive capacity as a warning that it can quickly expand capacity should a new firm attempt to enter. We will reexamine strategic barriers in Chapter 13.

Intel's Monopoly

Intel Corporation is by far the most powerful and profitable producer of microchips in the world. In the early 1970s, Intel invented the microprocessor, the computer on a chip that serves as the "brain" of the personal computer. Since then, it has produced a series of chips, most recently the Pentium 4, each faster and cheaper than the last. In 2000, the company registered $34 billion in sales and over $9 billion in profits. It accounted for 82 percent of the world's PC chip market, and its market dominance in advanced microprocessors was well over 90 percent. Thus, Intel held a virtual monopoly in the microchip market.[4]

In recent years, however, new competitors have increasingly pushed into Intel's markets. In the 1990s, Advanced Micro Devices, Inc. (AMD) set out to sell compatible microchips while avoiding Intel's patents. Intel has repeatedly sued AMD for patent infringement, but despite some legal successes, Intel has been unable to bar AMD from selling cloned chips. Other recent court cases have gone against Intel, effectively granting companies the right to sell compatible chips. In the mid-1990s, other chips emerged as competitors in particular market segments: the Power PC chip shared by IBM, Motorola, and Apple, Hewlett-Packard's RISC chip, and Sun's SPARC chip, to name a few. Today, AMD competes head-to-head with Intel in developing technologically advanced chips, increasing its share of the chip market to almost 20 percent.

In response to these challenges, Intel has not been a "quiet" or complacent monopolist. It repeatedly has entered into litigation to protect its patent rights. It launched the "Intel Inside" marketing and advertising campaign aimed at convincing computer purchasers that its chip is superior to the clones. In segments where new competitors pose the greatest threat, the company has

---

[4] This account is drawn from industry reports and D. Clark, "With New Chips, Intel Hopes PCs Turn into Media Servers," *The Wall Street Journal* (June 17, 2004): B1, and D. Clark, "Big Bet Behind Intel Comeback in Chips, Speed Isn't Everything," *The Wall Street Journal* (November 18, 2003): A1.

sought to preserve its market share by aggressively cutting chip prices, even on its Pentium 4 chip. Intel also has increased its annual capital spending for new factory expansion to some $7.5 billion, and it has increased its annual R&D spending to over $5 billion.

By far its most important response has been to accelerate the pace at which it develops and introduces new chips. In 1994, Intel introduced the Pentium chip, followed shortly thereafter by the Pentium Pro and the Pentium II. The company launched the Pentium III chip in 1998, the Pentium 4 in 2000, and an enhanced Pentium 4 chip in 2003. In recent years, Intel has pursued a new strategy of advanced chip specialization—developing separate chips for laptops (the energy-efficient Pentium M), home entertainment systems, WIFI and mobile gadgets, and servers. Both Intel and AMD have raised the 32-bit standard by introducing efficient 64-bit chips. In effect, the company relies on continuous innovation to keep several "monopoly" steps ahead of the competition. The company knows that today's dominant chip will quickly be challenged by competitors' clones, causing prices and profits to erode. Indeed, Intel expects today's best-selling chip to be displaced by the company's next and newest chip. As a company spokesperson put it, "We eat our young." Despite tough challenges, Intel continues to maintain a monopoly position in the world market for microprocessors.

CHECK STATION 2   What kinds of entry barriers helped protect Intel's monopoly position? What actions did Intel take to impede market entry?

PERFECT COMPETITION VERSUS PURE MONOPOLY

Recall from Chapter 10 that a perfectly competitive market delivers output to consumers at the lowest sustainable price. (If prevailing prices were any lower, firms would incur losses and leave the market.) In a pure monopoly, in contrast, a single firm is the sole supplier of a good or service. The monopolist uses its market power to restrict output and raise price.

The simplest way to compare and contrast the basic price and output implications for purely monopolistic and purely competitive industries is by means of a graph. Figure 11.3 displays demand and cost curves for an unspecified good or service. The industry demand curve D has the usual downward slope. For any given industry price, it predicts total industry-wide sales. The horizontal cost line S depicts the long-run unit cost of supplying different industry levels of output. The cost line reflects the fact that output can be expanded in the long run at a constant cost (at least for the range of output shown in the graph). We can now use these demand and cost facts to predict long-run price and output for a perfectly competitive industry versus the *same* industry organized as a pure monopoly.

Under perfect competition, industry price and output are determined at the intersection of the demand and supply curves. The total industry output is split

FIGURE 11.3

Perfect Competition
versus Pure Monopoly

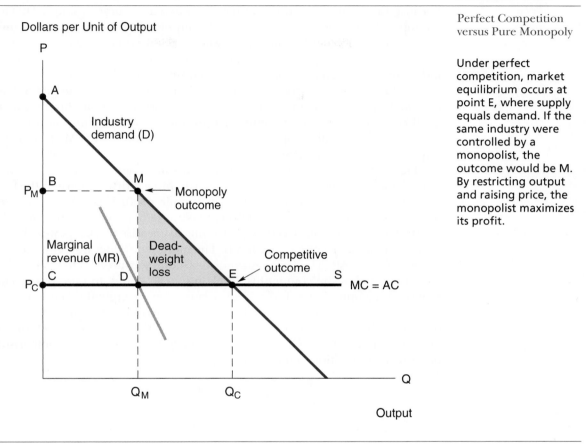

Dollars per Unit of Output

Under perfect
competition, market
equilibrium occurs at
point E, where supply
equals demand. If the
same industry were
controlled by a
monopolist, the
outcome would be M.
By restricting output
and raising price, the
monopolist maximizes
its profit.

among a large number of firms, each producing at a constant cost per unit.
Competitive price and output are P_C and Q_C, respectively. Note that P_C is identical to the typical supplier's cost per unit; that is, the typical competitive firm makes
zero economic profit. If the market price ever rises above unit cost, opportunities
for positive economic profits will induce suppliers, including new entrants, to
increase output. This supply influx will drive price back down to the unit cost level.[5]

[5] We have spoken of the "typical" firm as though all competitive firms were identical. Of course, this
need not be literally true. Some firms may be more efficient producers and, therefore, have lower
costs than the average firm. For instance, suppose one firm owns an input (say, a piece of land) that
is twice as productive as the comparable inputs of other firms. Although we could view this as a cost
advantage, the likelihood is that the productivity edge already is reflected in the price of the input.
(Land that is twice as productive carries double the market price.) Thus, many seeming cost advantages disappear. Any that remain can be incorporated easily into the supply curve. The supply
curve begins with the production of the lowest-cost producers and then slopes upward until a horizontal segment of "typical" cost producers is reached.

Now suppose the *same* industry is controlled by a single firm, a monopolist. Because the monopolist is the industry, its demand curve is simply D. The monopolist can supply as much or as little output as it wishes at a constant unit cost given by S. What price and output will a profit-maximizing monopolist set? As always, marginal analysis supplies the answer: The firm will set output where industry-wide marginal revenue equals marginal cost. Figure 11.3 shows MR (derived from the industry demand curve in the usual way). The line S does double duty: Besides being a supply curve, it measures the monopolist's marginal cost curve. (The monopolist can produce additional units at this unit cost.) The monopolist's optimal output is Q_M (where MR = MC), and the required market-clearing price is P_M.

Figure 11.3 provides a graphical comparison of perfect competition and pure monopoly. Under competition, long-run price is driven down to the lowest sustainable level (where industry economic profit is zero). As a consequence, a competitive market delivers maximum benefits to consumers. In contrast, the monopolist has the opportunity to exercise market power, that is, to raise price above competitive levels. The monopolist does not set price and output capriciously. The key to maximizing monopoly profit is to restrict output to well below the competitive level and, in so doing, to raise price. The monopolist's optimal level of output occurs where marginal revenue equals marginal cost. Note that monopoly output is always smaller than competitive output. In the figure, the intersection of MR and MC occurs to the left of the intersection of D and MC. Thus, we have the following summary comparison of perfect competition and pure monopoly:

$$P_M > P_C$$
$$Q_M < Q_C$$

and

$$(\text{maximum}) \quad \pi_M > \pi_C = 0.$$

Competition delivers output at a minimum price and implies zero industry profits. Monopoly delivers maximum industry profits by limiting output and raising price.

Finally, the presence of monopoly represents a major deviation from the efficiency of perfect competition. In Figure 11.3, the net benefit attained under perfect competition is measured by the area of the large consumer-surplus triangle ACE. (Producers make zero economic profits because $P_C = AC$ in the long run.) By contrast, under pure monopoly, the monopolist raises price, thereby earning a pure economic profit (rectangle BCDM) but leaving a smaller triangle of surplus for the consumer (triangle ABM). Thus, under monopoly, the sum of consumer surplus and producer profit is given by the trapezoidal area ACDM, which is smaller than the total gains under perfect competition by the triangle MDE.

The triangle MDE is referred to as the **deadweight loss** attributed to monopoly. The economic critique of monopoly is not simply that the firm gains at the expense of consumers when it elevates price. (In terms of total welfare, the firm's profit counts equally with the consumers' surplus. Indeed, consumers could well be shareholders of the monopolist and share in the profit directly.) Rather, the important point is that the monopolist's elevation of price and restriction of output causes a reduction in *total* welfare. The reduction in consumer surplus (relative to the competitive outcome) exceeds the excess profit earned by the monopolist. The deadweight-loss triangle (MDE) measures the size of the total welfare loss.

Put another way, this deadweight loss would be regained if market output were increased from Q_M to Q_C. For these additional units, *consumers' marginal benefits exceed suppliers' marginal costs.* Consequently, producing this output would increase social welfare. As we will see later in this chapter, the common government response to the so-called case of "natural" monopoly is to regulate lower prices and increased output. Similarly, as noted in Chapter 14, the government undertakes a broad spectrum of antitrust initiatives to restrain or prohibit specific actions and behavior that would lead to monopolization of markets.

Suppose the industry demand curve in Figure 11.3 shifted up and to the right. What would be the effect on price, output, and profit under competition and under monopoly? Answer these questions again, supposing unit costs increased.

CHECK STATION 3

Cartels

A **cartel** is a group of producers that enter into a collusive agreement aimed at controlling price and output in a market. The intent of the cartel is to secure monopoly profits for its members. Successful maintenance of the cartel not only has an immediate profit advantage; it also reduces the competitive uncertainties for the firms and can raise additional entry barriers to new competitors.

In the United States, collusive agreements among producers (whether open or tacit) represent violations of antitrust laws and are illegal.[6] Some cartels outside the United States have the sanction of their host governments; in others, countries participate directly. The best known and most powerful cartels are based on control of natural resources. In the 1990s and today, the Organization of Oil Exporting Countries (OPEC) controls about 40 percent of the world supply of oil. De Beers currently controls the sale of more than 90 percent of the world's gem-quality diamonds.

The monopoly model is the basis for understanding cartel behavior. The cartel's goal is to maximize its members' collective profit by acting as a single

[6] The law permits trade and professional associations; these organizations sometimes formulate and sanction industry practices that some observers deem anticompetitive. In the 1950s, widespread collusion among electrical manufacturers in contract bidding was uncovered and prosecuted.

monopolist would. Based on the demand it faces, the cartel maximizes profit by restricting output and raising price. Ideally, the cartel establishes total output where the cartel's marginal revenue equals its marginal cost. For instance, if cartel members share constant and identical (average and marginal) costs of production, Figure 11.3's depiction of the monopoly outcome would apply equally to the cartel. The cartel maximizes its members' total profits by restricting output and raising price according to Q_M and P_M, where marginal revenue equals marginal cost.[7]

Output restriction is essential for a cartel to be successful in maximizing its members' profits. No matter how firm its control over a market, a cartel is not exempt from the law of demand. To maintain a targeted price, the cartel must carefully limit the total output it sells. Efforts to sell additional output lead to erosion of the cartel price. The larger the additions to supply, the greater the fall in price and, therefore, the greater the decline in the cartel's total profit. This observation underscores the major problem cartels face: *Cartels are inherently unstable.* The reason lies in the basic conflict between behavior that maximizes the collective profits of the cartel and self-interested behavior by individual cartel members.

To see this, return to the cartel's optimal price and output, P_M and Q_M, in Figure 11.3. Suppose the cartel agrees to set total output at Q_M and assigns production quotas to members. The self-interest of each member is to *overproduce* its quota. The member can sell this additional output by cutting price very slightly. (Remember that one member's additional output is small enough to put little downward pressure on price.) What effect does this added output have on the member's profit? Figure 11.3 shows that the cartel price is well above marginal cost. Thus, even allowing for a slightly discounted selling price, selling the extra output is very profitable. Each member has an incentive to "cheat" on its agreed-upon output quota. But if all members overproduce, this behavior is self-defeating. If all members increase output (say, by 10 to 15 percent), flooding the market with extra output will have a significant downward effect on price. The total output of the cartel will be far greater than Q_M, price will fall below P_M, and the cartel's profit inevitably must drop. Thus, overproduction is a constant threat to the cartel's existence. In the presence of wholesale cheating, the cartel may fall apart.

OPEC's Cartel Behavior

The 11 member nations of OPEC meet twice a year to discuss the cartel's target price for crude oil and to allot members' production quotas. These deliberations are of great interest to other oil-producing countries, private oil companies, and, of course, oil consumers. Like a continuing drama with many

---

[7]When costs differ across cartel members, there is more to determining the relevant marginal cost curve. To maximize profit, the cartel first should draw its production from the member(s) with the lowest marginal costs. As output increases, the cartel enlists additional supplies from members in ascending order of marginal cost. The cartel's marginal cost curve will be upward sloping and is found by horizontally summing the members' curves. This ensures that cartel output is obtained at minimum total cost.

acts, the OPEC negotiations center on (1) an assessment of the world demand for oil, (2) the appropriate limit on total OPEC supply, and (3) the division of this supply among cartel members.

A key issue for OPEC is to determine the level of total output and the corresponding oil price that will sustain maximum long-run profits for the cartel. Here experts are divided. In the 1980s, many Western economists criticized OPEC for setting prices that were too high with respect not only to consumer welfare but also to the cartel's own interests. In this view, OPEC's pursuit of exceedingly high prices served to increase its short-term profits. However, in the longer run (five to ten years), high cartel prices induced oil consumers to conserve energy or to turn to other energy sources, thereby, permanently lowering oil demand. If Figure 11.3 is taken to represent long-run demand, OPEC was, in effect, setting output below Q_M and price above P_M, undermining the interests of both oil consumers and OPEC. Based on its own analyses, OPEC has publicly refuted these contentions, claiming that it provides adequate supplies and fair prices to the consuming nations of the world.

In the last decade, OPEC has had a mixed record in limiting its supply and maintaining high oil prices.[8] In the middle years of the 1990s, cartel members' quotas were almost fixed; total cartel output was strictly limited to 24.5 to 25 million barrels per day. However, as cartel members increasingly exceeded their individual quotas, OPEC's actual total output crept upward, exceeding 27 million barrels per day in 1998. A number of financially distressed countries—Indonesia, Nigeria, and Libya—consistently overproduced their quotas. In 1997 and 1998, Venezuela opened its arms to oil producers, exceeding its official quota by some 25 percent. Until 1997, oil prices were relatively stable, in the neighborhood of $20 per barrel. But events in 1998 were far different. Because of continued oversupply, the financial crisis in Southeast Asia, and a mild winter in the Northern Hemisphere, oil demand fell sharply and with it oil prices to a nine-year low of less than $13 per barrel. After emergency discussions in March 1998, OPEC and four noncartel producers, most notably Mexico and Norway, agreed on output cuts of about 1.5 million barrels per day, barely enough to prop oil prices above $15 per barrel.

From 1998 to spring 2001, OPEC was largely successful in negotiating lower total output levels for the cartel. Official cartel output quotas successively fell from 26 million to 25.2 million and finally to 24.2 million total barrels per day. Until 2001, the combination of strong worldwide oil demand and OPEC's limitations on supply supported oil prices in excess of $25 per barrel. However, economic conditions facing OPEC in 2001 were much more precarious. With the worldwide economic slowdown, increased supplies by Iraq and Russia, and inevitable quota cheating by its own members, OPEC faced the prospect of soft and falling oil prices. In the fall of 2001, OPEC ministers accused nonmember Russia of freeloading on

---

[8] This synopsis is based on industry reports and on N. Banerjee, "OPEC Raises Quota; Not Much More Oil May Flow," *The New York Times* (June 4, 2004): C1; "Still Holding Customers Over a Barrel," *The Economist* (October 25, 2003): 61; and B. Bahree and T. Herrick, "OPEC's Move to Maintain Output Alerts Russia to Possible Price War," *The Wall Street Journal* (October 1, 2001): A2.

TABLE 11.1

Production Quotas of
OPEC Members (as of
August 2004)

Quotas are expressed in
millions of barrels of oil
per day.

Country	Quota
Algeria	.83
Indonesia	1.35
Iran	3.82
Iraq	N.A.*
Kuwait	2.09
Libya	1.39
Nigeria	2.14
Qatar	.67
Saudi Arabia	8.45
United Arab Emirates	2.27
Venezuela	2.99
Total	26.00

*N.A. = not applicable

the cartel's efforts to limit output.[9] Unless Russia limited its production (which had surged by 500,000 to 700,000 barrels per day to rival the output of Saudi Arabia), OPEC threatened to engage in a market-share war even at the expense of price cuts. OPEC members were exceeding their quotas by an estimated 1 million total barrels per day, and oil prices again fell to below $20 per barrel.

From 2002 to the present, OPEC has prospered due to a combination of steadily increasing oil demand and limited supply. The surge in demand has been lead by the rapid economic growth in China and surprisingly strong consumption in the United States. Disruptions in Venezuela and Nigeria and the United States' invasion of Iraq have contributed to supply shortfalls. With OPEC's official quota in the neighborhood of 24 billion barrels per day, oil prices steadily rose to above $30 per barrel (spiking then falling back after the March 2003 invasion of Iraq). In the summer of 2004, surging demand and fears of terrorist attacks that could disrupt supplies, pushed spot prices to $50 per barrel and higher. In line with surging demand, OPEC behaved like a profit-maximizing monopolist by increasing its output, raising its official quota from 23.5 million to 26 billion barrels per day. Table 11.1 shows the OPEC members' quotas set in August 2004. (Though a member of OPEC, Iraq has no official quota.)

[9] A related problem is that an oil producer is typically better off being outside the cartel, where it can take advantage of a high, cartel-maintained price without limiting its own output. There have been no new OPEC members since 1973, and the 1990s have seen the defection of two members, Ecuador and Gabon, from the cartel. Many oil producers, including Mexico, Malaysia, Norway, Russia, and Egypt, support OPEC's initiatives while refusing membership.

Nonetheless, OPEC continued to overproduce this higher quota by more than 1 million barrels per day. While recent economic circumstances have continued to sustain high oil prices, OPEC remains a textbook example of the competing tensions within cartels—the need to limit output for the collective good of the cartel and the individual incentive to increase output for a member's (or nonmember's) own account.

Suppose that the demand curve facing OPEC is given by $P = 62 - Q$ and that each member's cost of producing oil is $AC = MC = \$10$. Find the cartel's profit-maximizing total output and price. If instead of keeping to this output, all members overproduced their quotas by 20 percent, what would be the effect on OPEC's total profit?

CHECK STATION 4

Natural Monopolies

A **natural monopoly** occurs when the average cost of production declines throughout the relevant range of product demand. Utilities—water, electric power, gas, and telephone—typically fall into this category. Figure 11.4 shows a natural monopoly (say, in the generation of electricity) that displays steeply declining average cost.

Natural monopoly poses obvious difficulties for the maintenance of workable competition. First, it is costly and inefficient for multiple competing firms to share the market. A single firm can always produce a specified quantity of output—call this Q—at lower average cost than it could if the same total quantity were supplied by n firms, each producing Q/n. (Use Figure 11.4 to confirm this.) For six local firms to make the large capital investment to supply electricity is unnecessarily duplicative and costly. With a facility of suitable capacity, a single firm is better suited to be the sole source of supply. Second, even if the market, in principle, could support more than one firm, the inevitable result would be the emergence of a single dominant monopolist. This is simply to say that any firm that increases output can achieve lower unit costs and so price the competition out of the market. Thus, we would expect that the first firm to enter the market and expand its output will grow to control the industry.

Government decision makers play an active and direct role in the regulation of natural monopoly. The principal regulatory aim is to target industry price and output at the efficient competitive level. Let's use Figure 11.4 to display the natural-monopoly outcome, with and without price regulation. In the absence of any regulation (i.e., under a policy of laissez-faire), the firm acts as a pure monopolist. The resulting outcome is the price–quantity pair Q_M and P_M, where the firm's marginal revenue equals its marginal cost. Here the marginal benefit of the last unit consumed is equal to the monopoly price, which, of course, is well above the marginal cost of production. An increase in output from the monopoly level would improve welfare (since MB > MC).

FIGURE 11.4

A Natural Monopoly

Regulators seek to implement average-cost pricing where the demand curve intersects the AC curve.

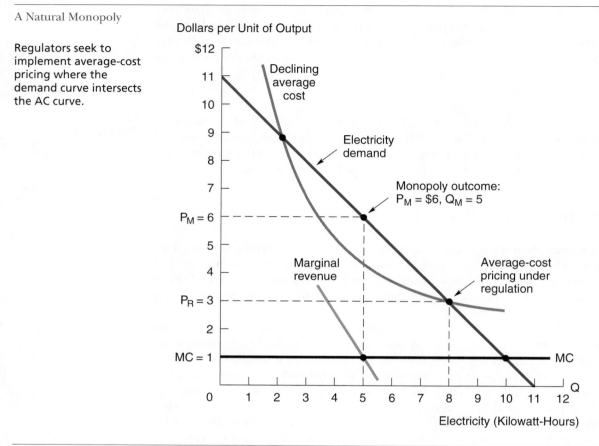

The regulator can induce an increase in output by limiting the natural monopolist to a price that delivers a "fair" rate of return on the firm's investment. This is accomplished by instituting **average-cost pricing**. The appropriate price and quantity are determined by the intersection of the demand and average cost curves in Figure 11.4. At price P_R, the firm earns zero "economic" profit; that is, price exactly equals average cost, where AC includes a provision for a normal return on invested capital. Relative to the unregulated outcome, the lower average-cost-based price spurs a significant increase in output and, therefore, in welfare.

However, average-cost pricing does not exhaust the opportunities for welfare gains. At output $Q_R = 8$, the demand curve still lies above marginal cost; that is, MB > MC. Output should be expanded and price lowered. In fact, optimal price and output can be determined by the intersection of the demand

and marginal cost curves. This outcome is referred to as **marginal-cost pricing** because it fulfills the efficiency condition P = MB = MC. Consumers are encouraged to purchase more output so long as their value exceeds the (low) marginal cost of production.

If marginal-cost pricing is efficient, why isn't it universally used? The practical difficulty with this pricing scheme should be evident. Price falls short of the firm's declining average cost—P = MC < AC—so the firm makes persistent losses. One way to maintain P = MC while making good this loss is to have the government subsidize the decreasing-cost producer. (Government-owned utilities often follow this route, financing deficits from general tax revenues.) An alternative method is for the utility to institute so-called "two-part" pricing. Here each customer pays a flat fee (per month) for access to output and then pays an additional fee, equal to marginal cost, according to actual usage. Thus, customers are encouraged to consume output at marginal cost. At the same time, the flat-fee charge allows the firm to cover average cost; that is, it covers the firm's large fixed costs. Although beneficial, two-part pricing is not a perfect remedy for the pricing problems associated with declining average cost. The problem is that the fixed fee may deter some potential customers from purchasing the service altogether even though their marginal benefit exceeds marginal cost.

Average-cost pricing is the most common regulatory response, and it goes a long way toward implementing the virtues of competitive pricing in the natural-monopoly setting. However, it is far from perfect. First, the regulator/rate setter faces the problem of estimating the monopolist's true costs over the relevant range of potential output. At regulatory rate hearings, the natural monopolist has a strong incentive to exaggerate its average cost to justify a higher price. Imperfect or biased cost estimates lead to incorrect regulated price and output. Second, the regulated monopolist has a reduced incentive to minimize its cost of production. Indeed, if the regulatory agency were able to maintain $P_R = AC$ at all times, any cost change would be immediately reflected in a price increase. The firm would have no economic incentive (although it might have a political one) to hold costs down. Interestingly, the presence of "regulatory lag"—the fact that prices are reset periodically, sometimes after long delay—bolsters the firm's cost-cutting incentives. In the typical case of escalating costs, the monopolist profits from cost-cutting measures during the period over which the regulated price is fixed.

Finally, critics of price regulation point out that over time government intervention has spread into many areas that are a far cry from natural monopolies—trucking, airlines, and banking, for example. Furthermore, they point out that, by intention or not, regulation frequently reduces true competition: Regulated rates can hold prices *up* as well as down. In this sense, regulators are "captured" by the firms over which they are supposed to exercise control, in effect maintaining a status quo protected from new competition. For instance, until the emergence of airline deregulation, the express purpose of the Civil

Aeronautics Board (the governing regulator) was to fix prices and limit entry into the airline market. In the late 1970s, the CAB, under economist Alfred Kahn, changed course dramatically, freeing fares and allowing the entry of no-frills airlines. The result was the present era of significantly lower airfares.

A "Natural" Telecommunications Monopoly?

Before 1996, most communities in the United States received local telephone service and cable television services by single, separate companies. Created by the breakup of AT&T in the 1980s, the "Baby Bells" provided local telephone services across the geographic regions of the country. Customarily, local authorities granted a legally protected monopoly to a single cable company. Regulators argued for a single provider on the grounds of natural monopoly. By building a single network to serve all households, the cable monopolist would enjoy significant economies of scale, allowing it to deliver low-cost services to subscribers. During this time, many cable companies were largely unregulated and were shielded from competition. Not surprisingly, they tended, over time, to raise monthly fees for basic services.

Economic analysis is useful in exploring the alternatives of regulation and competition in the ever-expanding domain of telecommunications. If one believes that telecommunications has the economic features of a natural monopoly, then granting one firm a regulated monopoly to provide services over a single network is the appropriate response. Alternatively, if one believes competition to be viable in telecommunications, regulatory effort should be aimed at removing all entry barriers. Telecommunication companies, cable firms, satellite operators, telecom-cable merged companies, and other firms should all be allowed to offer competing services. Competition might mean the creation of multiple networks in each service area. Or, if economies of scale are important, it might mean a single broadband network, with the controlling firm obligated to allow access to any multimedia company.

Over the last decade, the advent of deregulation and the development of advanced telecommunications services have reduced monopoly barriers and greatly increased competition.[10] Today, local telephone services are provided by the Baby Bells, long-distance companies, Internet companies, and cable companies. The same companies plus independent firms offer long-distance services. Network broadcasters, cable companies, and satellite operators provide television services. Cable, DSL, and dial-up services offer Internet connectivity. Telecommunication companies of all stripes provide cellular and wireless communications. (However, cellular firms must acquire the necessary spectrum licenses to provide these services.) In short, a host of firms (coming from different original markets) are competing to offer the most attractive bundled services to consumers—Internet services, hundreds of television channels, movies on demand, and so on.

---

[10] For a history and economic analysis of telecommunications markets, see N. Economides, "Telecommunications Regulation: An Introduction," New York University Working Paper #CLB 03-35 (September 2003).

There is much evidence supporting the viability of competition. For instance, in jurisdictions where multiple cable firms compete, economic studies have found that subscribers on average pay two to three dollars less per month than in jurisdictions with a monopoly provider of comparable services. (Indeed, some studies indicate that the degree of competition is more important than firm costs in explaining cable prices.) The availability of competing substitutes, such as satellite providers, also induces lower cable prices. (In the same way, rural areas unable to receive multiple network broadcasts face higher cable prices.) Evidence from the long-distance telephone market, where MCI, Sprint, the Baby Bells and independent companies compete successfully with AT&T, also underscores the price-lowering benefits of increased competition. Likewise, in the cellular market, intense competition by the same players and others has lowered prices dramatically. (Since 2003, allowing number portability when switching providers has had an additional price-lowering effect.) By comparison, local telephone competition has been somewhat disappointing. Prices to consumers have fallen, mainly due to regulations requiring the local network owner to provide access to competitor firms at low fees. Thus, lower retail prices have stemmed from lower regulated retail prices rather than from new network capacity. (In 2004, these access fees were deregulated with the ultimate economic effect still uncertain.)

In short, many economists advocate a "hands-off" regulatory approach to allow the process of free entry and competition to uncover the most efficient ways of providing telecommunications services.

MONOPOLISTIC COMPETITION

In perfect competition, all firms supply an identical standardized product. In monopoly, a single firm sells a unique product (albeit one that may have indirect substitutes). As the term suggests, **monopolistic competition** represents a mixture of these two cases. The main feature of monopolistic competition is *product differentiation*: Firms compete by selling products that differ slightly from one another. Product differentiation occurs to a greater or lesser degree in most consumer markets. Firms sell goods with different attributes (claimed to be superior to those of competitors). They also deliver varying levels of support and service to customers. Advertising and marketing, aimed at creating product or brand-name allegiance, reinforce (real or perceived) product differences.

Product differentiation means that competing firms have some control over price. Because competing products are close substitutes, demand is relatively elastic, but not perfectly elastic as in perfect competition. The firm has some discretion in raising price without losing its entire market to competitors. Conversely, lowering price will induce additional (but not unlimited) sales. In analyzing monopolistic competition, one often speaks of "product groups." These are collections of similar products produced by competing firms. For instance, "designer dresses" would be a typical product group, within which there are significant perceived differences among competitors.

The determination of appropriate product groups always should be made on the basis of substitutability and relative price effects. Many, if not most, retail stores operate under monopolistic competition. Consider competition among supermarkets. Besides differences in store size, types of products stocked, and service, these stores are distinguished by locational convenience—arguably the most important factor. Owing to locational convenience and other service differences, a spectrum of different prices can persist across supermarkets without inducing enormous sales swings toward lower-priced stores.

Monopolistic competition is characterized by three features. First, firms sell differentiated products. Although these products are close substitutes, each firm has some control over its own price; demand is not perfectly elastic. Second, the product group contains a large number of firms. This number (be it 20 or 100) must be large enough so that each individual firm's actions have negligible effects on the market's average price and total output. In addition, firms act independently; that is, there is no collusion. Third, there is free entry into the market. One observes that the last two conditions are elements drawn from perfect competition. Nonetheless, by virtue of product differentiation (condition 1), the typical firm retains some degree of monopoly power. Let's consider the output and price implications of these conditions.

Part a of Figure 11.5 shows a short-run equilibrium of a typical firm under monopolistic competition. Because of product differentiation, the firm faces a slightly downward-sloping demand curve. (If it raises price slightly, it loses some, but not all, customers to competitors.) Given this demand curve, the firm maximizes profit by setting its marginal revenue equal to its marginal cost in the usual way. In the figure, the resulting output and price are Q and P, respectively. Because price exceeds average cost, this typical firm is earning positive economic profits.

In a long-run equilibrium, the free entry (or exit) of firms ensures that all industry participants earn zero economic profits. Thus, in the long run, the outcome in part a of Figure 11.5 is not sustainable. Attracted by positive economic profits, new firms will enter the market. Because it must share the market with a greater number of competitors, the typical firm will find that demand for its product will be reduced; that is, its demand curve will shift to the left. Part b of Figure 11.5 shows the firm's new long-run demand curve. As in part a, the firm is profit maximizing. The firm's optimal output is Q_E, where marginal revenue equals marginal cost. However, even as a profit maximizer, the firm is earning *zero* economic profit. At this output, its price, P_E, exactly equals its average cost. In fact, the firm's demand curve is tangent to (and otherwise lies below) its average cost curve. Any output other than Q_E, greater or smaller, implies an economic loss for the firm.

FIGURE 11.5

Monopolistic
Competition

In part a, the firm
produces output Q
(where MR = MC) and
makes a positive
economic profit. In
part b the entry of
new firms has reduced
the firm's demand
curve to the point
where only a zero
economic profit is
available.

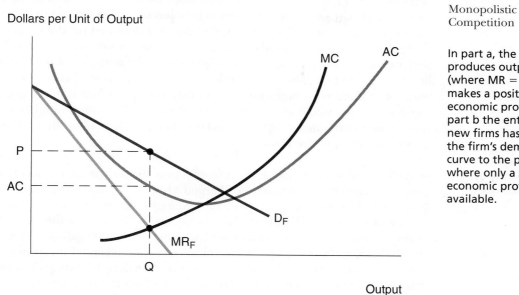

Dollars per Unit of Output

Output

(a) The Firm Earns Excess Profit

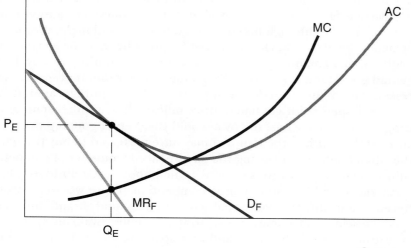

Dollars per Unit of Output

Output

(b) Long-Run Equilibrium—the Firm Earns Zero Economic Profit

A comparison of Figures 10.3 and 11.5 shows the close correspondence between the graphical depictions of monopolistic competition and perfect competition. The essential difference centers on the individual firm's demand curve—either downward sloping (reflecting differentiated products) or infinitely elastic (indicating standardized products that are perfect substitutes). In both cases, the long-run equilibrium is marked by the tangency of the demand line with the average cost curve. Under perfect competition, this occurs at the point of minimum average cost. In contrast, the typical firm in monopolistic competition (by virtue of its differentiated product) charges a higher price (one above minimum average cost) and supplies a smaller output than its counterpart in a competitive market.

Is This Any Way to Maximize Profits?

In 1981, a Boston-based gas station owner set the highest gasoline prices in the nation.[11] During that summer, he charged $1.69 per gallon for unleaded gas during the daytime and $2.59 per gallon at night, when other downtown gas stations were closed. (His all-time high price was $3.99.) Even at these extreme prices, however, the station owner sold an average of 3,000 gallons per week, half of this at night. Despite catcalls, pickets, and even vandalism from angry motorists during the gasoline crisis, the owner "stuck by his pumps"; he even charged $1 for air. As he put it, "People think of gas stations as public mammary glands, but they're wrong. This is a business and it's important to generate profits from every part of it. If I can use a resource, like air, to pay for the electric bill, so much the better. If you allow capitalism in its true form, it works beautifully."

The station owner was an avowed profit maximizer, albeit not a very attractive one. How did he profit by his dual-price policy? The answer is price discrimination.[12] Although his costs varied little day and night, the elasticity of demand varied greatly. He maximized his profit by charging a higher price at night, when demand is much more inelastic than during the day. In fact, we could go so far as to say that he operated under different market structures, day and night. At night, he appeared to have a pure local monopoly. Motorists desperate for gas had to drive miles to find another station open during those hours. Thus, the owner sold gas even at gouging prices. (Of course, at those prices the motorist may have preferred to buy five gallons rather than a full tank.) During the day, he faced a number of competitors within blocks and numerous stations in neighboring Cambridge. That is, the market resembled monopolistic competition. There was some product differentiation due to locational convenience and brand allegiance. Nonetheless, in normal times excess profits are limited by relatively free entry of new firms. (The gasoline crisis and accompanying supply shortage afforded sellers short-run, excess profits.)

[11] E. Keerdojan, "There's No Oil Glut for a Price Glutton," *Newsweek* (July 6, 1981), 14.

[12] See the extensive discussion of price discrimination in Chapter 3.

Over the last 65 years, New York City's taxi commission has kept the number of medallions (legally required to drive a taxi) nearly fixed. Currently, there are 12,487 cabs to serve a population of some 8 million. Cabs are never around when New Yorkers want them. Yet the market price of medallions (bought and sold weekly) is over $250,000. It would seem there is significant unfilled demand for taxi service and a substantial profit to be had from supplying it.

New York City's Taxicabs Revisited

The New York taxi market is a classic case of a monopoly restriction on output—sanctioned and maintained by government regulation. Although there are economic grounds for government regulation in many aspects of this service (fare rates, safety and maintenance of cabs, conduct of drivers), an absolute restriction on entry does not appear to be one of them. Consider the following hypothetical—but plausible—illustration. Weekly demand for trips is

$$Q = 7 - .5P,$$

where Q denotes the number of trips in millions and P is the average price of a trip in dollars. The taxi meter rates currently established by the commission (after a 25 percent hike in 2004) imply an average fare of $P = \$10$ per trip. The current number of licensed taxis is 12,487, and a taxi, if fully utilized, can make a maximum of 140 trips per week. The typical taxi's cost of carrying Q_t weekly trips is

$$C = 910 + 1.5Q_t.$$

This cost includes wages paid to the driver, a normal rate of return on the investment in the taxi, depreciation, and gasoline.

These facts allow us to prepare an economic analysis of the taxi market that addresses a number of policy questions. Is there an insufficient supply of cabs? The answer is yes. If fully utilized, the current number of taxis can supply $(12,487)(140) = 1,748,180$ trips per week. But demand is $Q = 7 - .5(10) = 2$ million trips. (The supply shortfall is 13 percent of total demand.) Are medallion holders (fleet owners and individual taxi owners) earning excess profits? The answer is yes. The cost per week is $910 + (1.5)(140) = \$1,120$ for a fully utilized cab. The average cost is $\$1,120/140 = \$8$ per trip. Cab owners enjoy an excess profit of $(\$10 - 8)(140) = \$280$ per week, or $\$14,560$ per year. A medallion entitles the owner to this excess profit each and every year. Thus, it is not surprising that the market value of a medallion is $250,000 or more. (At a price of $250,000, the medallion earns an annual real return of $14,560/250,000 = 5.8$ percent; this is in line with real returns for other assets of comparable riskiness.)

Are consumer interests being served? Surely not. At the very least, the commission should increase the number of medallions by 13 percent so that trip supply can match trip demand at the $10 fare. Current medallion holders would continue to earn $280 excess profit per week (along with new holders), so they would feel no adverse effects. A more dramatic policy change would be to do away with the medallion system and allow free entry into the taxi market by anyone who wishes to drive a cab. What would be the likely outcome of this deregulation? Attracted by excess profits, new taxis would enter the market. If fare regulations remained unchanged $(P = \$10)$, the influx of taxis would mean fewer trips per taxi and zero economic profits for all taxis in equilibrium. Alternatively, the commission could set lower fares (say, P = $9.50) in conjunction with free entry, allowing price to decline with the influx of supply. A third option is to allow free entry and, at the same time, deregulate fares. A number of cities (e.g., San Diego and Seattle) have tried to introduce free competition into taxi markets. Drivers are free to discount fares below the standard meter rates (with these discounts being posted on the cabs' doors). Supply (augmented by free entry) and demand would then determine prevailing taxi fares—presumably at levels well below those set by regulation.

Finally, our economic analysis provides a ready explanation for the reluctance of commissions in major cities like New York to increase the number of medallions. A large increase in medallions would reduce the profit associated with holding a medallion and, therefore, decrease the value of the medallion itself. (Allowing perfectly free entry would eliminate these profits altogether and reduce the value of a medallion to zero.) Fierce lobbying by taxi drivers and taxi companies has persuaded city governments to retain the current medallion system.

SUMMARY

Decision-Making Principles

1. Whatever the market environment, the firm maximizes profit by establishing a level of output such that marginal revenue equals marginal cost.

2. A monopolist sets MR = MC, where MR is determined by the industry demand curve. The magnitude of monopoly profit depends on demand (the size and elasticity of market demand) and on the monopolist's average cost.

3. In monopolistic competition, the firm's long-run equilibrium is described by the conditions MR = MC and P = AC.

Nuts and Bolts

1. Under pure monopoly, a single producer is shielded from market entrants by some form of barrier to entry. To maximize profit, the monopolist restricts output (relative to the competitive outcome) and raises price above the competitive level.

2. A cartel is a group of producers that enter into a collusive agreement aimed at controlling price and output in a market. The cartel restricts output and raises price to maximize the total profits of its members. The incentive for individual members to sell extra output (at discounted prices) is the main source of cartel instability.

3. A natural monopoly occurs when the average cost of production declines throughout the relevant range of product demand. Regulation via average-cost pricing is the most common response to natural monopoly.

4. In monopolistic competition, a large number of firms sell differentiated products and there are no barriers to entry by new suppliers. Because each firm faces a slightly downward-sloping demand curve, price exceeds minimum average cost.

Questions and Problems

1. In 1989, the *Detroit Free Press* and *Detroit Daily News* (the only daily newspapers in the city) obtained permission to merge under a special exemption from the antitrust laws. The merged firm continued to publish the two newspapers but was operated as a single entity.
   a. Before the merger, each of the separate newspapers was losing about $10 million per year. What forecast would you make for the merged firms' profits? Explain.
   b. Before the merger, each newspaper cut advertising rates substantially. What explanation might there be for such a strategy? After the merger, what prediction would you make about advertising rates?

2. A pharmaceutical company has a monopoly on a new medicine. Under pressure by regulators and consumers, the company is considering lowering the price of the medicine by 10 percent. The company has hired you to analyze the effect of such a cut on its profits. How would you carry out the analysis? What information would you need?

3. Firm S is the only producer of a particular type of foam fire retardant and insulation used in the construction of commercial buildings. The inverse demand equation for the product is

$$P = 1,500 - .1Q,$$

where Q is the annual sales quantity in tons and P is the price per ton. The firm's total cost function (in dollars) is

$$C = 1,400,000 + 300Q + .05Q^2.$$

   a. To maximize profit, how much foam insulation should firm S plan to produce and sell? What price should it charge?
   b. Compute the firm's total profit.

4. Until recently, the market for air travel within Europe was highly regulated. Entry of new airlines was severely restricted, and air fares were set by regulation. Partly as a result, European air fares were and continue to be higher than U.S. fares for routes of comparable distance. Suppose that, for a given European air route (say, London to Rome), annual air travel demand is estimated to be $Q = 1,500 - 3P$ (or, equivalently, $P = 500 - Q/3$), where Q is the number of trips in thousands and P is the one-way fare in dollars. (For example, 600 thousand annual trips are taken when the fare is $300.) In addition, the long-run average (one-way) cost per passenger along this route is estimated to be $200.

a. Some economists have suggested that during the 1980s and 1990s there was an implicit cartel among European air carriers whereby the airlines charged monopoly fares under the shield of regulation. Given the preceding facts, find the profit-maximizing fare and the annual number of passenger trips.

b. In the last five years, deregulation has been the norm in the European market, and this has spurred new entry and competition from discount air carriers such as Ryan Air and EasyJet. Find the price and quantity for the European air route if perfect competition became the norm.

5. Consider a natural monopoly with declining average costs summarized by the equation $AC = 16/Q + 1$, where AC is in dollars and Q is in millions of units. (The total cost function is $C = 16 + Q$.) Demand for the natural monopolist's service is given by the inverse demand equation $P = 11 - Q$.

a. Determine the price and output of the unregulated natural monopolist.

b. Suppose a regulator institutes average-cost pricing. What is the appropriate price and quantity?

c. Answer part b assuming the regulator institutes marginal-cost pricing. What is the enterprise's deficit per unit of output? How might this deficit be made up?

6. Consider once again the microchip market described in Problem 9 of Chapter 10. Demand for microprocessors is given by $P = 35 - 5Q$, where Q is the quantity of microchips (in millions). The typical firm's total cost of producing a chip is $C_i = 5q_i$, where q_i is the output of firm i.

a. Suppose that one company acquires all the suppliers in the industry and thereby creates a monopoly. What are the monopolist's profit-maximizing price and total output?

b. Compute the monopolist's profit and the total consumer surplus of purchasers.

7. Let's reconsider the case of gasoline price gouging.

a. Suppose that, during the day, the station owner's demand is given by $P_D = 2.06 - .00025Q_D$. The marginal cost of selling gasoline is $1.31 per gallon. At his current $1.69 price, he sells 1,500 gallons per week. Is this price–output combination optimal? Explain.

b. The station owner sells an equal number of gallons at night, setting $P_N = 2.59. Suppose elasticity of demand is $E_P = -3$. According to the optimal markup rule (in Chapter 3), is this price profit maximizing?

c. The station owner is able to sell gasoline day and night at high prices. Why aren't there more gas stations in downtown locations in major cities? Explain.

8. Suppose that, over the short run (say, the next five years), demand for OPEC oil is given by $Q = 52.5 - 1.25P$ or, equivalently, $P = 42 - .8Q$.

(Here Q is measured in millions of barrels per day.) OPEC's marginal cost per barrel is $10.

a. What is OPEC's optimal level of production? What is the prevailing price of oil at this level?

b. Many experts contend that maximizing short-run profit is counterproductive for OPEC in the long run because high prices induce buyers to conserve energy and seek supplies elsewhere. Suppose the demand curve just described will remain unchanged only if oil prices stabilize at $20 per barrel or below. If oil price exceeds this threshold, long-run demand (over a second five-year period) will be curtailed to $Q = 60 - 2P$ (or $P = 30 - .5Q$). OPEC seeks to maximize its total profit over the next decade. What is its optimal output and price policy? (Assume all values are present values.)

9. Firms A and B make up a cartel that monopolizes the market for a scarce natural resource. The firms' marginal costs are $MC_A = 6 + 2Q_A$ and $MC_B = 18 + Q_B$, respectively. The firms seek to maximize the cartel's total profit.

a. The firms have decided to limit their total output to $Q = 18$. What outputs should the firms produce to achieve this level of output at minimum total cost? What is each firm's marginal cost?

b. The market demand curve is $P = 86 - Q$, where Q is the total output of the cartel. Show that the cartel can increase its profit by expanding its total output. (*Hint*: Compare MR to MC at $Q = 18$.)

c. Find the cartel's optimal outputs and optimal price. (*Hint*: At the optimum, $MR = MC_A = MC_B$.)

10. Consider a regulated natural monopoly. Over a 10-year period, the net present value of all the investment projects it has undertaken has been nearly zero. Does this mean the natural monopoly is inefficient? Does it mean the regulatory process has been effective? Explain.

11. Consider again the New York taxi market, where demand is given by $Q = 7 - .5P$, each taxi's cost is $C = 910 + 1.5Q_t$, and $AC_{min} = \$8$ at 140 trips per week.

a. Suppose that, instead of limiting medallions, the commission charges a license fee to anyone wishing to drive a cab. With an average price of $P = \$10$, what is the maximum fee the commission could charge? How many taxis would serve the market?

b. Suppose the commission seeks to set the average price P to maximize total profit in the taxi industry. (It plans to set a license fee to tax all this profit away for itself.) Find the profit-maximizing price, number of trips, and number of taxis. How much profit does the industry earn? (*Hint*: Solve by applying $MR = MC$. In finding MC, think about the extra cost of adding fully occupied taxis and express this on a cost-per-trip basis.)

c. Now the city attempts to introduce competition into the taxi market. Instead of being regulated, fares will be determined by market conditions. The city will allow completely free entry into the taxi market. In a *perfectly competitive* taxi market, what price will prevail? How many trips will be delivered by how many taxis?

d. Why might monopolistic competition provide a more realistic description of the free market in part c? Explain why average price might fall to, say, only \$9.00. At P = \$9.00, how many trips would a typical taxi make per week? (Are taxis underutilized?) How many taxis would operate?

*12. Firm 1 is a member of a monopolistically competitive market. Its total cost function is $C = 900 + 60Q_1 + 9Q_1^2$. The demand curve for the firm's differentiated product is given by $P = 660 - 16Q_1$.

a. Determine the firm's profit-maximizing output, price, and profit.

b. Attracted by potential profits, new firms enter the market. A typical firm's demand curve (say, firm 1) is given by
$P = [1{,}224 - 16(Q_2 + Q_3 + \ldots + Q_n) - 16Q_1]$, where n is the total number of firms. (If competitors' outputs or numbers increase, firm 1's demand curve shifts inward.) The long-run equilibrium under monopolistic competition is claimed to consist of 10 firms, each producing 6 units at a price of \$264. Is this claim correct? (*Hint:* For the typical firm, check the conditions MR = MC and P = AC.)

c. Based on the cost function given, what would be the outcome if the market were perfectly competitive? (Presume market demand is $P = 1{,}224 - 16Q$, where Q is total output.) Compare this outcome to the outcome in part b.

*13. A single buyer who wields monopoly power in its purchase of an item is called a *monopsonist*. Suppose that a large firm is the sole buyer of parts from 10 small suppliers. The cost of a typical supplier is given by $C = 20 + 4Q + Q^2$.

a. Suppose that the large firm sets the market price at some level P. Each supplier acts competitively (i.e., sets output to maximize profit, given P). What is the supply curve of the typical supplier? Of the industry?

b. The monopsonist values the part at \$10. This is the firm's break-even price, but it intends to offer a price much less than this and purchase all parts offered. If it sets price P, its profit is simply:

$$\pi = (10 - P)Q_s,$$

where Q_s is the industry supply curve found in part a. (Of course, Q_s is a function of P.) Write down the profit expression and maximize profit with respect to P. Find the firm's optimal price. Give a brief explanation for this price.

* Starred problems are more challenging.

Discussion Question Pharmaceutical companies can expect to earn large profits from blockbuster drugs (for high blood pressure, depression, ulcers, allergies, sexual dysfunction) while under patent protection. What is the source of these profits? Upon patent expiration, numerous rival drug companies offer generic versions of the drug to consumers. (The original developer continues to market the drug under its trade name and usually offers a second generic version of the drug as well.) Discuss the effect of patent expiration on market structure, pricing, and profitability for the drug.

Spreadsheet Problems

S1. Imagine that the perfectly competitive market described in Chapter 10, Problem S1, were transformed into a pure monopoly. (What were formerly independent small firms are now production units owned by the monopolist.) The cost structure of the typical unit continues to be given by $C = 25 + Q^2 - 4Q$, and industry demand is $Q = 400 - 20P$ or, equivalently, $P = 20 - .05Q$. Currently, the monopolist has 30 production facilities in place.

   a. Create a spreadsheet similar to the example shown. Enter numerical values for cells B14 and C8; all other cells should be linked by formulas to these two cells.

	A	B	C	D	E	F	G
1							
2			Monopolist Controls				
3			the Market				
4							
5			Industry				
6		Output	Plants	Price	MR	Tot Profit	
7							
8		180	30	7	−2	150	
9							
10							
11			Typical Production Unit				
12		Q_F	MC	Cost	AC		
13							
14		6	8	37	6.17		
15							
16		Short Run: Maximize total profit. Adjust Q_F					
17		Long Run: Maximize total profit. Adjust Q_F & # firms					
18							

b. In the short run, the monopolist can change output level Q_F but cannot vary the number of production facilities. Use the spreadsheet optimizer to maximize the firm's short-run profit.

c. In the long run, the monopolist can change output level Q_F and the number of production facilities. Use the spreadsheet optimizer to maximize the firm's long-run profit.

S2. Suppose a monopolist controls the industry described in Problem S2 of Chapter 10. The industry demand curve remains $P = 160 - 2Q$. In addition, total production costs are unchanged: $C = 800 + 40Q + .5Q^2$. Create the requisite spreadsheet and use the spreadsheet's optimizer to determine the monopolist's profit-maximizing output.

S3. a. Create a spreadsheet (based on the example shown) to model the monopolistically competitive market of Problem 12. The individual firm's demand curve is $P = 1,224 - 16(Q_2 + Q_3 + \ldots + Q_n) - 16Q_1$, and its cost function is $C = 900 + 60Q_1 + 9Q_1^2$. Six firms currently serve the market. Enter numerical values for cells B14 and D8; all other cells should be linked by formulas to these two cells.

b. Holding the number of firms fixed, adjust the typical firm's output to find the short-run equilibrium. Specify cell G14 (MR − MC) as the target cell, and set it equal to zero (rather than maximizing it).

c. Determine the long-run equilibrium by adjusting the number of firms and each firm's output, while setting total profit equal to zero.

	A	B	C	D	E	F	G	H
1								
2				Equilibrium Under				
3				Monopolistic Competition				
4								
5				Industry				
6		Q	Price	# Firms	MR		Tot Profit	
7								
8		60	264	6	104		1,440	
9								
10								
11				Typical Firm				
12		Q_F	Cost	MC	AC		MR−MC	
13								
14		10	2,400	240	240.0		−136	
15								
16		SR: (1) MR = MC: Adjust Q_F						
17		LR: (1) MR = MC and (2) Profit = 0: Adjust Q_F & # firms						
18								
19								

Suggested References

Adams, W., and J. Brock (Eds.). *The Structure of American Industry.* Upper Saddle, River NJ: Prentice-Hall, 2001.

Chapter 12 describes the NCAA's cartel and the control of intercollegiate athletics.

Carlton, D. W., and J. M. Perloff. *Modern Industrial Organization,* Chapters 4, 5, and 7. Reading, MA: Addison-Wesley, 2004.

Darrat, A. F., O.W. Gilley, and D. J. Meyer. "Petroleum Demand, Income Feedback Effects, and OPEC's Pricing Behavior: Some Theoretical and Empirical Results." *International Review of Economics and Finance* (1992): 247–259.

Joskow, P. L. "Restructuring, Competition, and Regulatory Reform in the U.S. Electricity Sector." *Journal of Economic Perspectives* (Summer 1997): 119–138.

Joskow notes that natural monopoly elements are more important in electricity transmission than in generation and discusses opportunities for competition and deregulation.

Plott, C. R., A. B. Sugiyama, and G. Elbaz. "Economies of Scale, Natural Monopoly, and Imperfect Competition in an Experimental Market." *Southern Economic Journal* 61 (October 1994): 261–287.

Tirole, J. *The Theory of Industrial Organization,* Chapter 1. Cambridge, MA: MIT Press, 1989.

Tirole's opening chapters provide a theoretical overview of pure monopoly.

OPEC's official Web site is www.opec.org.

**CHECK STATION
ANSWERS**

1. Note that the Lerner index is just the monopolist's optimal markup. According to the markup rule in Chapter 3, $(P - MC)/P = -1/E_p$. In short, if the monopolist is profit maximizing, the Lerner index should be equal to the inverse of the industry's price elasticity of demand. This index indicates the degree to which the monopolist can elevate price above marginal cost. However, it does not measure the magnitude of monopoly profit (since no account is made for the firm's total quantity of output or its fixed costs).

2. Intel's entry barriers stemmed from (1) pure quality and cost advantages (Intel's chips were cheaper and faster than anyone else's), (2) patents (which the company vigorously defended), (3) product differentiation (the Intel Inside campaign), and possibly (4) economies of scale. Besides items (2) and (3), Intel impeded entry by cutting prices on its chips and expanding factory capacity for producing chips. In 1991, it announced the development of the Pentium chip (exaggerating its features), thereby deterring its major customers (computer manufacturers) from experimenting with rival chips.

3. In a competitive market, the increase in demand would generate an equal long-run increase in supply. There is no increase in price. Under monopoly, the demand shift causes a rightward shift in the MR curve. As a result, the monopolist increases output as well as price. What if there is a cost increase instead? In the competitive market, price increases dollar for dollar with cost. (Firms' economic profits remain zero.) The monopolist's optimal response is to cut output

(MR = MC occurs at lower Q) and pass on only part of the cost increase in the form of a higher price. (For linear demand and cost, the price increase is one-half the cost increase.)

4. OPEC maximizes its profit by setting MR = MC. Thus, we have $62 - 2Q = 10$, implying Q = 26 million barrels per day. In turn, $P = 62 - 26 = \$36$ per barrel and $\pi = (36 - 10)(26) = \$676$ million per day. If the cartel overproduces by 20 percent, the new quantity is 31.2, the new price is \$30.80, and OPEC's profit falls to $\pi = (30.8 - 10)(31.2) = \$649$ million, a 4 percent drop.

Oligopoly

It is in rare moments that I see my business clearly: my customers, my organization, my markets and my costs. Then why do I still lie awake at night? I'm trying to figure the damn strategies of my competitors!

A MANAGER'S LAMENT

In the early 1990s, the infant-formula industry accounted for annual sales of some $2 billion. Abbott Laboratories, Bristol-Myers Squibb, and American Home Products Corporation dominated the market with 50 percent, 37 percent, and 9 percent market shares, respectively. The growth of the overall market had been uneven. Until the early 1970s, breast-feeding of babies was on the decline, sinking to a low of 20 percent of mothers. Formula makers prospered by offering mothers the convenience of bottled milk. Twenty-five years of research, however, convinced pediatricians that mother's milk is the "optimum" baby food. In the 1990s, about 50 percent of American mothers breast-fed their babies.

The three dominant companies employed strikingly similar business practices. The formulas they sold were nearly identical (and must have the same nutrients by federal law). The companies charged virtually the same wholesale prices. They increased prices by an average of 8 percent annually over the decade (while milk prices increased by 2 percent annually). They produced a 13-ounce can at a marginal cost of about $.60 and sold it for an average wholesale price of $2.10. With average total cost estimated to be about $1.70 per can, the companies enjoyed nearly a 25 percent profit margin. The companies engaged in almost no advertising; instead, they promoted and marketed their formulas via giveaway programs to hospitals and

Collusion in the Infant-Formula Industry

doctors. Such programs were very effective. Research has shown that 90 percent of mothers stick to the formula brand the hospital gives them.

The cozy oligopoly enjoyed by the three companies attracted would-be entrants and government scrutiny. In the late 1980s, Carnation and Gerber entered the formula market by advertising directly to consumers. However, the American Academy of Pediatrics opposed this strategy, arguing that direct advertising would influence mothers not to breast-feed. Consequently, the two companies' sales comprised less than 5 percent of the market. In addition, the federal government took an interest in formula pricing. Under its Women, Infants, and Children Program (WIC), the government subsidized formula for disadvantaged families. Administered by the states, the WIC program accounted for about one-third of all formula sales. In most states, families received WIC vouchers that could be exchanged for any brand of formula, with the companies giving the government a discount (about $.50 per can) off the regular wholesale price. However, a number of states instituted competitive bidding—awarding all WIC sales in the state to the firm making the lowest price bid.

The history of the infant-formula industry raises a number of questions. Does viable competition exist in the industry? Are barriers to entry significant? Are prices excessive? What effect might competitive bidding have on market structure, pricing, and profitability in the infant-formula industry?

In the previous two chapters, we focused on perfect competition and pure monopoly, the polar cases of market structure. However, many markets occupy positions between these extremes; that is, they are dominated by neither a single firm nor a plethora of firms. Oligopoly is the general category describing markets or industries that consist of a small number of firms. Because of oligopoly's importance and because no single model captures the many implications of firm behavior within oligopoly, we devote the entire chapter to this topic.

A firm within an oligopoly faces the following basic question: How can it determine a profit-maximizing course of action when it competes against an identifiable number of competitors similar to itself? This chapter and the succeeding chapter on game theory answer this question by introducing and analyzing competitive strategies. Thus, we depart from the approach taken previously where the main focus was on a "single" firm facing rivals whose actions are predictable and unchanging. In crafting a competitive strategy, a firm's management must anticipate a range of competitor actions and be prepared to respond accordingly. Competitive strategy finds its most important applications within oligopoly settings. By contrast, in a pure monopoly, there are no immediate competitors to worry about. In pure competition, an individual firm's competitive options are strictly limited. Industry price and output are set by supply and demand, and the firm is destined to earn a zero profit in the long run.

The strategic approach extends the single-firm point of view by recognizing that a firm's profit depends not only on the firm's own actions but also on the actions of competitors. Thus, to determine its own optimal action, the firm must correctly anticipate the actions and reactions of its rivals. Roughly speaking, a manager must look at the competitive situation not only from his or her own point of view but also from rivals' perspectives. The manager should put himself or herself in the competitor's place to analyze what that person's optimal decision might be. This approach is central to game theory and is often called *interactive* or *strategic* thinking.

The outline of this chapter is as follows. In the first section, we describe how to analyze different types of oligopolies beginning with Michael Porter's five-forces model. Next, we introduce the concept of market concentration, as well as the link between concentration and industry prices. In the second section, we consider two kinds of quantity competition: when a market leader faces a number of smaller competitors and when competition is between equally positioned rivals. In the third section, we examine price competition, ranging from a model of stable prices based on kinked demand to a description of price wars. Finally, in the fourth section, we explore two other important dimensions of competition within oligopolies: the effects of advertising and of strategic precommitments.

OLIGOPOLY

An **oligopoly** is a market dominated by a small number of firms, whose actions directly affect one another's profits. In this sense, the fates of oligopoly firms are *interdependent*. To begin, it is useful to size up an oligopolistic industry along a number of important economic dimensions.

For 25 years, Michael Porter's five-forces model has provided a powerful synthesis for describing the structures of different industries and guiding competitive strategy.[1] Figure 12.1 provides a summary of the five-forces framework.

FIGURE 12.1

The Five-Forces Framework

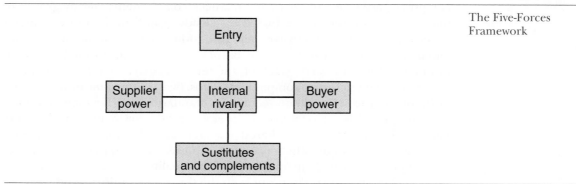

[1] The five-forces model is examined at length in M. E. Porter, *Competitive Strategy: Techniques for Analyzing Industries and Competitors* (New York: Simon and Schuster, 1998).

The core of Porter's analysis centers on internal industry rivalry: the set of major firms competing in the market and how they compete. Naturally, the number of close rivals and their relative size, position, and power are crucial. (The following section looks closely at the notion of industry *concentration* to measure the number and sizes of firms.) Entry into the market is the second most important factor in sizing up the industry. We have already seen that free entry predisposes a perfectly competitive market to zero economic profits in the long run. Conversely, significant barriers to entry (as listed and described in Chapter 11) are a precondition for monopoly. Ease of entry is also crucial for analyzing oligopoly. Boeing and Airbus compete vigorously to sell new aircraft, but barriers to entry due to economies of scale protect them from new competitors. By contrast, numerous new discount airlines in the United States and Europe have dramatically changed the competitive landscape in the air travel market. Similarly, a small independent studio (putting together a good script, directing talent, and up-and-coming actors) can produce a well-reviewed and profitable hit movie despite the formidable clout of the major studios.

The impacts of substitutes and complements directly affect industry demand, profitability, and competitive strategy. In a host of industries, this impact is ongoing, even relentless. For instance, trucking and railways are *substitutes*, competing modes of transport in the long-haul market. Soft-drink consumption suffers at the hands of bottled water, sports drinks, and new age beverages. In other cases, the emerging threat of new substitutes is crucial. Cable companies have long challenged network television (with satellite TV a third option) and now vigorously compete for local telephone customers. Since the millennium, online commerce has steadily increased its sales, often at the expense of "bricks-and-mortar" stores. The fast growth of new hybrid automobiles poses a long-term threat to traditional gasoline-powered vehicles.

More recently, new attention and analysis have been paid to the industry impact of *complementary* goods and activities. As noted already in Chapter 3, computer hardware and software are crucial complements. Steady growth in one market requires (and is fueled by) steady growth in the other. Though Barnes & Noble superstores compete with online seller Amazon, its sales are enhanced by its own online arm, barnesandnoble.com. Coined by Adam Brandenberger and Barry Nalebuff, the term *coopetition* denotes cooperative behavior among industry "competitors." Thus, firms in the same industry often work together to set common technology standards (e.g., for high-definition television or DVDs) so as to promote overall market growth. Firms in the same market also might join in shared research and development programs. Coopetition also occurs when a company and its input supplier cooperate to streamline the supply chain, improve product quality, or lower product cost. In short, oligopoly analysis embraces both the threat of substitutes and the positive impacts of complementary activities.

Finally, the potential *bargaining power* of buyers and suppliers should not be overlooked. For instance, the pricing behavior of a final goods manufacturer depends on the nature of the customers to whom it sells. At one extreme, its customers—say, a mass market of household consumers—may have little or no bargaining power. The manufacturer has full discretion to set its price as it wants (always taking into account, of course, overall product demand and the degree of competition from rival firms). At the other extreme, a large multinational corporate buyer will have considerable bargaining clout. Typically, such a buyer will have the power to negotiate the final terms of any contract (including price), and indeed it might hold the balance of power in the negotiation. (The producer might need the large buyer much more than the buyer needs the producer.) In the extreme, the buyer might organize a procurement and ask for competitive bids from would-be goods producers. In this way, the buyer uses its power to maximize competition among the producers so as to secure the best contract terms and price. (Negotiation and competitive bidding are the subjects of Chapters 16 and 17, respectively.) Of course, the same analysis applies to the firm's relationships with its suppliers. We know from Chapter 10 that the firm will receive the best possible input prices if its suppliers compete in a perfectly competitive market. On the other hand, if the number of suppliers is limited or if actual inputs are in short supply, bargaining power shifts to the suppliers who are able to command higher prices.

Industry Concentration

As noted earlier, an oligopoly is dominated by a small number of firms. This "small number" is not precisely defined, but it may be as small as two (a duopoly) or as many as eight to ten. One way to grasp the "numbers" issue is to appeal to the most widely used measure of market structure: the **concentration ratio**. The four-firm concentration ratio is the percentage of sales accounted for by the *top* four firms in a market or industry. (Eight-firm and twenty-firm ratios are defined analogously.) Concentration ratios can be computed from publicly available market-share information. Ratios also are compiled by the U.S. Census Bureau and released by the government at five-year intervals. Table 12.1 lists concentration ratios for selected goods and services compiled from both sources. Notice the progression from highly concentrated to less concentrated industries.

Market concentration has a ready interpretation. The higher the concentration ratio, the greater is the degree of market dominance by a small number of firms. Indeed, a common practice is to distinguish among different market structures by degree of concentration. For example, an **effective monopoly** is said to exist when the single-firm concentration ratio is above 90 percent—$CR_1 > 90$. A market may be viewed as **effectively competitive** when CR_4 is below 40 percent. If $CR_4 < 40$ percent, the top firms have individual market shares averaging less than 10 percent, and they are joined by many firms with still smaller market shares. Finally, one often speaks of a **loose oligopoly** when 40 percent $< CR_4 < 60$ percent and a **tight oligopoly** when

TABLE 12.1

Concentration Ratios
for Selected Goods

	Concentration Ratio		
Product or Service	**4 Firms**	**8 Firms**	**20 Firms**
Long-distance telephone	92	97	
Glass containers	91	97	
Warehouse clubs	90	99	
Laundry machines	90	NA	
Beer	90	93	
Ammunition	89	94	
Aircraft	85	96	
Breakfast foods	83	94	
Tobacco	83	93	
Refrigerators	82	97	
Photocopying machines	81	85	
Motor vehicles	80	96	
Running shoes	79	97	
Office supply stores	78	80	
Rental cars	77	95	
Flat glass	77	99	
Aircraft engines	77	82	
Carbon black	76	100	
Burial caskets	74	80	
Contact lens	72	98	
Photographic film	70	83	
Vacuum cleaners	69	92	
Tires	68	86	
Men's underwear	68	84	
Bookstores	65	71	
Cable television	63	77	
Cellular phone service	61	81	
Metal cans	58	87	
Pet food	58	80	
Snack foods	57	64	
Internet service	56	66	
Farm machinery	53	60	
Coffee	53	66	
Elevators	53	66	
Semiconductors	53	64	
Motion pictures	51	67	
Stockings	51	66	
Television broadcasting	51	61	

TABLE 12.1

(Continued)

Product or Service	Concentration Ratio		
	4 Firms	8 Firms	20 Firms
Men's shoes	50	68	
Leather	49	67	
Personal computers	45	69	
Office furniture	45	59	
Fast food	44	57	
Book publishing	42	57	
Toys	41	58	
Boatbuilding	41	49	
Lawn equipment	40	57	
Software	39	46	
Rubber	37	46	
Paper mills	34	55	
Domestic air flights	34	51	
Soap	34	46	
Paint	32	47	
Newspapers	32	45	
Electric power	31	46	
Grocery stores	31	43	
Oil refining	29	49	
Pumps	28	36	
Ice	24	31	43
Hotels	22	28	36
Milk	21	31	50
Bolts, nuts, etc.	19	28	41
Funeral homes	19	21	23
Basic chemicals	16	29	49
Women's dresses	14	24	39
Jewelry	12	20	34
Furniture	11	18	28
Lumber and wood	11	17	26
Hospitals	10	13	20
Gasoline stations	9	15	26
Concrete	7	11	20
Musical groups and artists	7	12	21
Used car dealers	7	9	10
Auto repair	2	3	5
Florists	1.7	2.3	4

Source: U.S. Bureau of the Census, 2002, and industry reports.

$CR_4 > 60$ percent. Monopolistic competition, discussed in the previous chapter, typically falls in the loose-oligopoly range.

About three-quarters of the total dollar value of goods and services (gross domestic product, GDP) produced by the U.S. economy originate in competitive markets, that is, markets for which $CR_4 < 40$. Competitive markets include the lion's share (85 percent or more) of agriculture, forestry, fisheries, mining, and wholesale and retail trade. Competition is less prevalent in manufacturing, general services, and construction (making up between 60 percent and 80 percent of these sectors). In contrast, pure monopoly accounts for a small portion of GDP (between 2 and 3 percent). Tight oligopolies account for about 10 percent of GDP, whereas loose oligopolies comprise about 12 percent.[2] In short, as Table 12.1 shows, although concentrated markets are relatively rare in the U.S. economy, specific industries and manufactured products are highly concentrated.

Because the notion of concentration ratio is used so widely, it is important to understand its limitations. The most serious limitation lies in the identification of the *relevant market*. A market is a collection of buyers and sellers exchanging goods or services that are very close substitutes for one another. (Recall that the cross-elasticity of demand is a direct measure of substitution. The larger the impact on a good's sales from changes in a competitor's price, the stronger the market competition.) Concentration ratios purport to summarize the size distribution of firms for relevant markets. However, it should be evident that market definitions vary, depending on how broadly or narrowly one draws product and geographic boundaries.

First, in many cases the market definitions used in government statistics are too broad. An industry grouping such as "pharmaceutical products" embraces many distinct, individual product markets. Numerous firms make up the overall consumer-drug market (concentration is low), but individual markets (drugs for ulcers and blood pressure) are highly concentrated. Similarly, government statistics encompass national markets and, therefore, cannot capture local monopolies. Newspapers are a dramatic case in point. Based on CR_4, the newspaper industry would seem to be effectively competitive for the United States as a whole. But for most major cities, one or two firms account for nearly 100 percent of circulation.[3]

Second, the census data exclude imports—a serious omission considering that the importance of imports in the U.S. economy has risen steadily (to some 13 percent of GDP today). In many industries (automobiles, televisions, electronics), the degree of concentration for U.S. *sales* (including imports) is much

---

[2] As one might expect, categorization of market structures by concentration is not hard and fast. The preceding data are based on W. G. Shepherd, *The Economics of Industrial Organization* (Prospect Heights, IL: Waveland Press, 1997), Chapter 3.

[3] The Bureau of the Census presents concentration ratios starting for broad industry categories and progressing to narrower and narrower groups (so-called "six-digit" categories). The categories in Table 12.1 are at the five- and six-digit levels. As we would expect, concentration tends to increase as markets are defined more narrowly. Many researchers believe that five-digit categories best approximate actual market boundaries.

less than the concentration for U.S. *production*. Thus, many industries are far more competitive than domestic concentration ratios would indicate.

Finally, using a concentration ratio is not the only way to measure market dominance by a small number of firms. An alternative and widely used measure is the Herfindahl–Hirschman Index (HHI), defined as the sum of the squared market shares of all firms:

$$HHI = s_1^2 + s_2^2 + \cdots s_n^2$$

where s_i denotes the market share of firm i and n denotes the number of firms. For instance, if a market is supplied by five firms with market shares of 40, 30, 16, 10, and 4 percent, respectively, $HHI = 40^2 + 30^2 + 16^2 + 10^2 + 4^2 = 2,872$. The HHI index ranges between 10,000 for a pure monopolist (with 100 percent of the market) to zero for an infinite number of small firms. If a market is shared *equally* by n firms, HHI is the n-fold sum of $(100/n)^2$, or $(n)(100/n)^2 = 10,000/n$. If the market has five identical firms, $HHI = 2,000$; if it has 10 identical firms, $HHI = 1,000$. The Herfindahl–Hirschman Index has a number of noteworthy properties:

1. The index counts the market shares of all firms, not merely the top four or eight.
2. The more unequal the market shares of a collection of firms, the greater is the index because shares are squared.
3. Other things being equal, the more numerous the firms, the lower is the index.

Because of these properties, the HHI has advantages over concentration ratios; indeed, the HHI is used as one factor in the Department of Justice's Merger Guidelines. (Under antitrust laws, the government can block a proposed merger if it will substantially reduce competition or tend to create a monopoly.) Concentration ratios and the HHI are highly correlated. Because they are available more readily (and easier to compute), concentration ratios are quoted more widely.

CONCENTRATION AND PRICES

Concentration is an important factor affecting pricing and profitability within markets.

Other things being equal, increases in concentration can be expected to be associated with increased prices and profits.

One way to make this point is to appeal to the extreme cases of pure competition and pure monopoly. Under pure competition, market price equals average cost, leaving all firms zero economic profits (i.e., normal rates of return). Low concentration leads to minimum prices and zero profits. Under a pure monopoly, in contrast, a single dominant firm earns maximum excess profit by optimally raising the market price. Given these polar results, it is natural to hypothesize a positive relationship between an industry's degree of monopoly (as measured by concentration) and industry prices. For instance, the smaller the number of firms that dominate a market (the tighter the oligopoly), the greater is the likelihood that firms will avoid cutthroat competition and succeed in maintaining high prices. High prices may be a result of tacit collusion among a small number of equally matched firms. But even without any form of collusion, fewer competitors can lead to higher prices. The models of price leadership and quantity competition (analyzed in the next section) make exactly this point.

There is considerable evidence that increases in concentration promote higher prices. The customary approach in this research is to focus on particular markets and collect data on price (the dependent variable) and costs, demand conditions, and concentration (the explanatory variables). Price is viewed in the functional form

$$P = f(C, D, SC),$$

where C denotes a measure of cost, D a measure of demand, and SC seller concentration. Based on these data, regression techniques are used to estimate this price relationship in the form of an equation. Of particular interest is the separate influence of concentration on price, other things (costs and demand) being equal. The positive association between concentration and price has been confirmed for a wide variety of products, services, and markets—from retail grocery chains to air travel on intercity routes; from cement production to television advertising; from auctions of oil leases and timber rights to interest rates offered by commercial banks. More generally, a large-scale study of manufacturing (using five-digit product categories) for the 1960s and 1970s shows that concentration has an important effect on prices for consumer goods and materials (and a smaller positive effect for capital and producer goods).[4]

Is an increase in monopoly power necessarily harmful to the interests of consumers? The foregoing discussion citing the evidence of higher prices would say yes. However, an alternative point of view claims that monopoly (i.e., large firms) offers significant efficiency advantages vis-à-vis small firms.[5]

[4] See C. Kelton and L. Weiss, "Change in Concentration, Change in Cost, Change in Demand, and Change in Price," in Leonard Weiss, (Ed.), *Concentration and Price*. (Cambridge: MIT Press, 1989). This book provides a comprehensive collection and critical analysis of the price-concentration research.

[5] This view often is referred to as the *University of Chicago–UCLA approach*, because much of the research originated at these schools. For discussion and critique, see M. Salinger, "The Concentration–Margins Relationship Reconsidered," *Brookings Papers: Microeconomics 1990*, 287–335.

According to this hypothesis, monopoly reflects superior efficiency in product development, production, distribution, and marketing. A few firms grow large and become dominant *because* they are efficient. If these cost advantages are large enough, consumers can obtain lower prices from a market dominated by a small number of large firms than from a competitive market of small firms. Thus, a price comparison between a tight oligopoly and a competitive market depends on which is the greater effect: the oligopoly's cost reductions or its price increases. For example, suppose that, in the competitive market, $P_c = AC_c$ and, in the tight oligopoly, $P_o = 1.15AC_o$. Absent a cost advantage, the oligopoly exhibits higher prices. But if the oligopoly's average cost advantage exceeds 15 percent, it will have the lower overall price.

The evidence concerning monopoly efficiency is mixed at best. It is hard to detect significant efficiency gains using either statistical approaches or case studies. Large firms and market leaders do not appear to be more efficient or to enjoy larger economies of scale than smaller rivals. (They do profit from higher sales and prices afforded by brand-name allegiance.) Nonetheless, the efficiency issue offers an important reminder that greater concentration per se need not be detrimental. Indeed, the government's antitrust guidelines mentioned earlier cover many factors—concentration, ease of entry, extent of ongoing price competition, and possible efficiency gains—in evaluating a particular industry.

Global Airfares

Fares on air routes around the world offer a textbook case of the link between concentration and prices. Numerous research studies have shown that average fares on point-to-point air routes around the globe vary inversely with the number of carriers. Indeed, the degree of competition on a particular route is a much stronger predictor of airfares than the distance actually traveled.

The effect of competition can be seen in several ways. Airline deregulation in the United States began in 1978. Fares were deregulated and air routes were opened to all would-be carriers. In the first decade of deregulation, the average number of carriers per route increased from 1.5 to almost 2. During the same period, deregulated fares proved to be about 20 percent below what they would have been absent deregulation.[6] Since 1988, average airfares have continued to decline (after adjusting for general inflation and higher fuel costs).

However, in recent years, the advent of the "hub system" and the industry consolidation via mergers have meant reduced competition on many routes. American Airlines accounts for about 70 percent of all flights to and from Dallas–Fort Worth, while United Airlines accounts for a like traffic proportion in Denver. Together, the two airlines account for about 87 percent of all flights at Chicago's O'Hare Airport. Delta Airlines controls over 75 percent of the traffic in Atlanta, Cincinnati, and Salt Lake City. Northwest dominates its hubs in Detroit and Minneapolis. Fares at hub airports dominated by a single airline

---

[6] See S. Morrison and C. Winston, "Airline Deregulation and Public Policy," *Science* (August 18, 1989): 707–711.

tend to be more than 20 percent higher than those in comparable routes. Conversely, on routes where discount airlines have entered and competed successfully with incumbent carriers, fares have dropped by 30 to 50 percent. Nonetheless, discount carriers complain of barriers to entry (few or no takeoff and landing slots) and the predatory practices (incumbents' sudden price cuts and flight increases) that keep them from competing on key routes.

Air route competition in Europe and the rest of the world is far behind developments in the United States. European governments have a long history of protecting national carriers from competition by foreign airlines. The result is far fewer competing carriers on the major European air routes and, therefore, elevated fares. Because of protectionist policies, an intranational fare (Paris to Marseilles) may be much higher than an intra-European fare (Paris to Athens), which, in turn, is higher than an international fare (Paris to New York). Indeed, protection from competition has led to inefficiency and high operating costs (especially among the state-owned airlines). Because of high wages and low labor productivity, operating costs at European airlines are more than 40 percent above those of U.S. airlines. In short, high concentration within Europe coincides with high costs (not economies of scale). Despite elevated prices, most European airlines have struggled to break even. Only recently have discount carriers like Ryanair and EasyJet begun to penetrate important European markets, spurring incumbent carriers to cut unnecessary costs and to reduce fares.

Finally, in other parts of the world, from Southeast Asia to South America, true route competition remains dormant. Enjoying monopoly status on many routes, South American airlines charge some of the highest fares in the world. The dawn of deregulation and competition in Brazil is expected to set off a free fall in fares. Since the early postwar years, a Japanese–U.S. treaty has reserved flights between the countries to three carriers: Northwest Airlines, United Airlines, and Japan Airlines. In 1998, after four years of negotiations, a new agreement allowed a limited number of transpacific flights by U.S. airlines and increased cargo flights to Japan by Federal Express in return for broad access to North America by Japan Airlines and Nippon Airways. With the fall in concentration, transpacific passengers have benefited from lower fares and more frequent flights.

QUANTITY COMPETITION

There is no single "ideal" model of competition within oligopoly. This is hardly surprising in view of the different numbers of competitors (from two upward) and dimensions of competition (price, product attributes, capacity, technological innovation, marketing, and advertising) encompassed by oligopoly. In this section, we examine quantity competition in a pair of settings. In the following section, we take up different kinds of price competition.

A Dominant Firm

In many oligopolistic industries, one firm possesses a dominant market share and acts as a leader by setting price for the industry. (Price leadership also is possible among equals.) Historically, one can point to dominant firms, such as General Motors in the automobile industry, Du Pont in chemicals, and U.S. Steel. Firms that currently hold dominant market shares include IBM in mainframe computers, eBay in online auctions, Federal Express in overnight delivery, Intel in microchips, and Microsoft in PC software, to name just a few.

What are the implications of price leadership for the oligopoly market? To supply a precise answer to this question, we must construct a tractable and realistic model of price behavior. The accepted model assumes the dominant firm establishes the price for the industry and the remaining small suppliers sell all they want at this price. The small firms have no influence on price and behave competitively; that is, each produces a quantity at which its marginal cost equals the market price. Figure 12.2 depicts the resulting combined supply curve for these small firms. The demand curve for the price leader, labeled d in the figure, is found by subtracting the supply curve of the small firms from the total industry demand curve. In other words, for any given price (see P* and P′ in the figure), the leader's sales quantity is equal to total market demand minus the supply of the small firms, that is, the horizontal distance between curves D and S.

Once the dominant firm anticipates its net demand curve, it sets out to maximize its profits in the usual way: It establishes its quantity where marginal revenue (derived from curve d) equals marginal cost (curve MC). In Figure 12.2, the leader's optimal price is P*, its output is Q*, and the small firms' combined output is Q_S. A numerical example illustrates the result. Suppose that total market demand is given by $Q_D = 248 - 2P$ and that the total supply curve of the 10 small firms in the market is given by $Q_S = 48 + 3P$. The dominant firm's marginal cost is MC = .1Q. Then the dominant firm determines its optimal quantity and price as follows. The firm identifies its net demand curve as $Q = Q_D - Q_S = [248 - 2P] - [48 + 3P] = 200 - 5P$, or equivalently, $P = 40 - .2Q$. Setting MR = MC implies $40 - .4Q = .1Q$, or Q* = 80 units. In turn, $P^* = 40 - (.2)(80) = \$24$. Therefore, $Q_S = 48 + (3)(24) = 120$; thus, each of the 10 small firms supplies 12 units.

In effect, the dominant firm makes the first (and, of course, the most important) strategic move in the market, with the remaining smaller firms responding to its actions. The important strategic consideration for the dominant firm is to anticipate the supply response of the competitive fringe of firms. For instance, suppose the dominant firm anticipates that any increase in price will induce a significant increase in supply by the other firms and, therefore, a sharp reduction in the dominant firm's own net demand. In other words, the more price elastic is the supply response of rivals, then the more elastic is the dominant firm's net demand. Under such circumstances, the dominant firm does best to refrain from raising the market price.

FIGURE 12.2

Optimal Output for a
Dominant Firm

The dominant firm's net
demand curve is the
difference between
industry demand and
the competitive supply
of small firms.

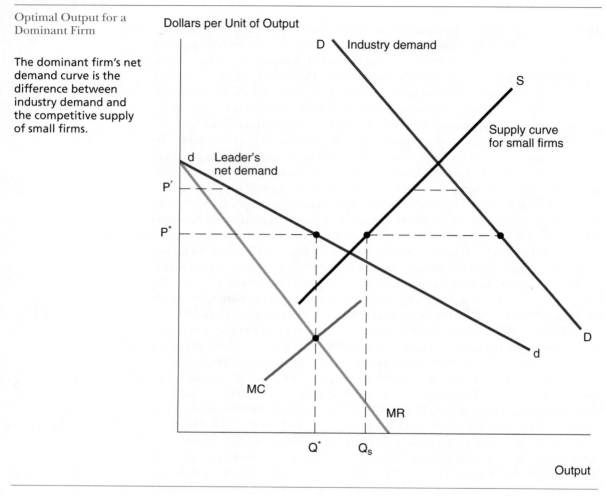

Competition among Symmetric Firms

Now let's modify the previous setting by considering an oligopoly consisting of a
small number of *equally positioned* competitors. As before, a small number of firms
produce a standardized, undifferentiated product. Thus, all firms are locked into the
same price. The *total* quantity of output supplied by the firms determines the prevailing market price according to an industry demand curve. Via its quantity choice,
an individual firm can affect total output and, therefore, influence market price.

A simple but important model of quantity competition between duopolists
(i.e., two firms) was first developed by Augustin Cournot, a nineteenth-century
French economist. To this day, the principal models of quantity competition

bear his name. Knowing the industry demand curve, each firm must determine the quantity of output to produce—with these decisions made independently. As a profit maximizer, what quantity should each firm choose? To answer this question, let's consider the following example.

DUELING SUPPLIERS   A pair of firms compete by selling quantities of identical goods in a market. Each firm's average cost is constant at $6 per unit. Market demand is given by $P = 30 - (Q_1 + Q_2)$, where Q_1 and Q_2 denote the firms' respective outputs (in thousands of units). In short, the going market price is determined by the *total* amount of output produced and sold by the firms. Notice that each firm's profit depends on both firms' quantities. For instance, if $Q_1 = 5$ thousand and $Q_2 = 8$ thousand, the market price is $17. The firms' profits are $\pi_1 = (17 - 6)(5) = \$55$ thousand and $\pi_2 = (17 - 6)(8) = \$88$ thousand, respectively.

To determine each firm's profit-maximizing output, we begin by observing the effect on demand of the competitor's output. For instance, firm 1 faces the demand curve

$$P = (30 - Q_2) - Q_1. \qquad [12.1]$$

The demand curve (as a function of the firm's own quantity) is downward sloping in the usual way. In addition, the demand curve's price intercept, the term in parentheses in Equation 12.1, depends on the competitor's output quantity. Increases in Q_2 cause a parallel downward shift in demand; a decrease in Q_2 has the opposite effect. Given a prediction about Q_2, firm 1 can apply marginal analysis to maximize profit in the usual way. The firm's revenue is $R_1 = (30 - Q_2 - Q_1)Q_1 = (30 - Q_2)Q_1 - Q_1^2$. Marginal revenue, in turn, is

$$MR = \partial R_1 / \partial Q_1 = (30 - Q_2) - 2Q_1.$$

Setting marginal revenue equal to the $6 marginal cost, we find that $30 - Q_2 - 2Q_1 = 6$, or

$$Q_1 = 12 - .5Q_2. \qquad [12.2]$$

Firm 1's profit-maximizing output depends on its competitor's quantity. An increase in Q_2 reduces firm 1's (net) demand, its marginal revenue, and its optimal output. For example, if firm 1 anticipates $Q_2 = 6$, its optimal output is 9; if it expects $Q_2 = 10$, its optimal output falls to 7. In other words, Equation 12.2 sets a schedule of optimal quantities in response to different competitive outputs. For this reason, it is often referred to as the *optimal reaction function*. A similar profit maximization for firm 2 produces the analogous reaction function:

$$Q_2 = 12 - .5Q_1. \qquad [12.3]$$

Now we are ready to derive the quantity and price outcomes for the duopoly. The derivation rests on the notion of *equilibrium*.[7] Here is the definition: In **equilibrium**, each firm makes a profit-maximizing decision, anticipating profit-maximizing decisions by all competitors.

Before we discuss this definition further, let's determine the equilibrium quantities in the current example. To qualify as an equilibrium, the firms' quantities must be profit maximizing against each other; that is, they must satisfy both Equations 12.2 and 12.3. Solving these equations simultaneously, we find $Q_1 = Q_2 = 8$ thousand. (Check this.) These are the unique equilibrium quantities. Since the firms face the same demand and have the same costs, they produce the same optimal outputs. These outputs imply the market price, $P = 30 - 16 = \$14$. Each firm's profit is $64,000, and total profit is $128,000.

CHECK STATION 1   Suppose the duopoly example is as described in the preceding example except that the second firm's average cost is $9 per unit. Find the firms' equilibrium quantities.

The duopoly equilibrium "lies between" the pure-monopoly and purely competitive outcomes. The latter outcome occurs at a quantity sufficiently large that price is driven down to average cost, $P_c = AC = \$6$, so that industry profit is zero. According to the demand curve, the requisite total quantity is $Q_c = 24$. In contrast, a monopolist—either a single firm or the two firms acting as a cartel—would limit total output (Q) to maximize industry profit:

$$\pi = (30 - Q)Q - 6Q.$$

Setting marginal revenue (with respect to *total* output) equal to marginal cost implies $30 - 2Q = 6$. The result is $Q_M = 12$ thousand and $P_M = \$18$ thousand. Total industry profit is $144,000. In sum, the duopoly equilibrium has a lower price, a larger total output, and a lower total profit than the pure-monopoly outcome.

The analysis behind the quantity equilibrium can be applied to any number of firms; it is not limited to the duopoly case. Suppose n firms serve the market and the market-clearing price is given by

$$P = 30 - (Q_1 + Q_2 + \ldots + Q_n).$$

Then firm 1's marginal revenue is $MR = [30 - (Q_2 + \ldots + Q_n)] - 2Q_1$. Setting MR equal to the firm's $6 MC yields

$$Q_1 = 12 - .5(Q_2 + \ldots + Q_n). \qquad [12.4]$$

Analogous expressions hold for each of the other firms. The equilibrium is found by simultaneously solving n equations in n unknowns. In fact, the easiest

---

[7] This concept frequently is called a Cournot equilibrium or a Nash equilibrium, after John Nash, who demonstrated its general properties.

method of solution is to recognize that the equilibrium must be symmetric. Because all firms have identical costs and face the same demand, all will produce the same output. Denoting each firm's output by Q^*, we can rewrite Equation 12.4 as

$$Q^* = 12 - .5(n - 1)Q^*,$$

implying the solution

$$Q^* = 24/[n + 1]. \qquad [12.5]$$

Notice that in the duopoly case ($n = 2$), each firm's equilibrium output is 8 thousand, the same result we found earlier. As the number of firms increases, each firm's profit-maximizing output falls (becomes a smaller part of the market). What is the impact on *total* output? Total output is

$$Q = nQ^* = 24n/(n + 1)$$

and approaches 24 thousand as the number of firms becomes large (say, 19 or more). In turn, the equilibrium market price approaches $30 - 24 = 6$; that is, *price steadily declines and approaches average cost*. It can be shown that this result is very general. (It holds for any symmetric equilibrium, not only in the case of linear demand.) The general result is as follows:

> As the number of firms increases, the quantity equilibrium played by identical oligopolists approaches the purely competitive (zero-profit) outcome.

In short, quantity equilibrium has the attractive feature of being able to account for prices ranging from pure monopoly ($n = 1$) to pure competition (n very large), with intermediate oligopoly cases in between.

PRICE COMPETITION

In this section, we consider two basic models of price competition. The first is a model of stable prices based on kinked demand. The second is a model of price wars based on the paradigm of the prisoner's dilemma.

Price Rigidity and Kinked Demand

Competition within an oligopoly is complicated by the fact that each firm's actions (with respect to output, pricing, advertising, and so on) affect the profitability of its rivals. Thus, actions by one or more firms typically will trigger competitive reactions by others; indeed, these actions may trigger "second-round" actions by the original firms. Where does this jockeying for competitive position settle down? (Or does it settle down?) We begin our discussion of pricing behavior by focusing on a model of *stable* prices and output. Many oligopolies—steel, automobiles, and cigarettes, to name a few—have enjoyed relatively stable prices over extended periods of time. (Of course, prices adjust over time to reflect general inflation.) Even when a firm's cost or demand fluctuates, it may be reluctant to change prices.

Price rigidity can be explained by the existence of **kinked demand curves** for competing firms. Consider a typical oligopolist that currently is charging price P*. Why might there be a kink in its estimated demand curve, as in Figure 12.3? Suppose the firm lowers its price. If price competition among firms is fierce, such a price cut is likely to be matched by rival firms staunchly defending their market shares. The upshot is that the firm's price reduction will generate only a small increase in its sales. (The firm will not succeed in gaining market share from its rivals, although it could garner a portion of the increase in industry sales owing to lower marketwide prices.) In other words, when it comes to price reductions, demand is relatively inelastic. Conversely, suppose the firm raises its price above P*. By holding to their present prices, rival firms can acquire market share from the price raiser. If the other firms do not follow, the firm will find its sales falling precipitously for even small price increases. In short, demand is elastic for price increases. This explains the demand curve's kink at the firm's current price.

In view of kinked demand, the firm's profit-maximizing price and quantity are simply P* and Q*. This is confirmed by noting that the firm's marginal revenue curve in Figure 12.3 is discontinuous. The left part of the MR curve corresponds to the demand curve to the left of the kink. But MR drops discontinuously if price falls slightly below P*. The presence of the vertical discontinuity in MR means that P* and Q* are optimal so long as the firm's marginal cost curve crosses MR within the gap. The dotted MC curve in the figure shows that marginal cost could decrease without changing the firm's optimal price. (Small shifts in demand that retain the kink at P* would also leave the firm's optimal price unchanged.) In short, each firm's price remains constant over a range of changing market conditions. The result is stable industry-wide prices.

The kinked demand curve model presumes that the firm determines its price behavior based on a prediction about its rivals' reactions to potential price changes. This is one way to inject strategic considerations into the firm's decisions. Paradoxically, the willingness of firms to respond aggressively to price cuts is the very thing that sustains stable prices. Price cuts will not be attempted if they are expected to beget other cuts. Unfortunately, the kinked demand curve model is incomplete. It does not explain why the kink occurs at the price P*. Nor does it justify the price-cutting behavior of rivals. (Price cutting may not be in the best interests of these firms. For instance, a rival may prefer to hold to its price and sacrifice market share rather than cut price and slash profit margins.) A complete model needs to incorporate a richer treatment of strategic behavior.

FIGURE 12.3

Optimal Output with
Kinked Demand

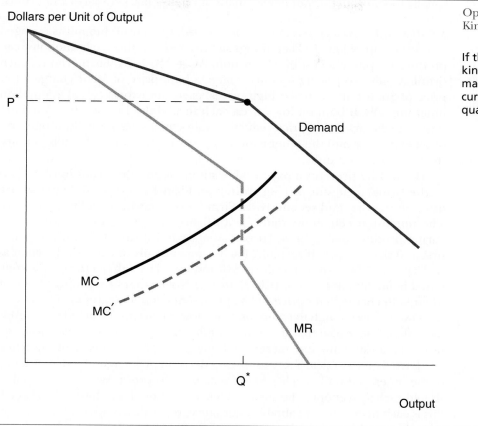

Dollars per Unit of Output

P*

Demand

MC

MC'

MR

Q*

Output

If the demand curve is
kinked, the firm's
marginal revenue
curve has a gap at
quantity Q*.

An oligopolist's demand curve is P = 30 − Q for Q smaller than 10 and P = 36 − 1.6Q for Q greater than or equal to 10. Its marginal cost is 7. Graph this kinked demand curve and the associated MR curve. What is the firm's optimal output? What if MC falls to 5? **CHECK STATION 2**

Price Wars and the Prisoner's Dilemma

Stable prices constitute one oligopoly outcome but not the only one. In many markets, oligopolists engage in vigorous price competition. To this topic we now turn.

A surprising number of product lines are dominated by two firms, so-called duopolists. Examples are Pepsi versus Coke, Nike versus Reebok (running shoes), Procter & Gamble versus Kimberley-Clark (disposable diapers), and Disney-MGM versus Universal (movie theme parks). When the competing goods or services are close substitutes, price is a key competitive weapon and usually the most important determinant of relative market shares and profits.

A PRICE WAR   As a concrete example, consider a pair of duopolists engaged in price competition. To keep things simple, suppose that each duopolist can produce output at a cost of $4 per unit: AC = MC = $4. Furthermore, each firm has only two pricing options: charge a high price of $8 or charge a low price of $6. If both firms set high prices, each can expect to sell 2.5 million units annually. If both set low prices, each firm's sales increase to 3.5 million units. (The marketwide price reduction spurs total sales.) Finally, if one firm sets a high price and the other a low price, the former sells 1.25 million units, the latter 6 million units.

Table 12.2 presents a payoff table summarizing the profit implications of the firms' different pricing strategies. Firm 1's two possible prices are listed in the first and second rows. Firm 2's options head the two columns. The upper-left cell shows that if both firms charge high prices, each will earn a profit of $10 million. (It is customary to list firm 1's payoff or profit first and firm 2's payoff second.) Each company's profit can be calculated as $\pi = (P - AC)Q = (8 - 4)(2.5) = \$10$ million. The other entries are computed in analogous fashion. (Check these.) Notice that firm profits are lower when both charge lower prices. (The price reduction increases the firms' total sales but not by enough to compensate for lower margins. Demand is relatively inelastic.) Notice also that if one firm undercuts the other's price, it wins significant market share and, most important, profit at the expense of the other.

Each firm must determine its pricing decision privately and independently of the other. Naturally, each seeks to maximize its profit. What pricing policy should each firm adopt? The answer is that each should set a low price. Indeed, this is each firm's more profitable alternative, regardless of what action its rival takes. To see this, let's look at the payoffs in Table 12.2 from firm 1's point of view. To find its best strategy, firm 1 asks a pair of "what if" questions about its rival. What if firm 2 were to charge a high price? Then, clearly, firm 1 does best by setting a low price, that is, undercutting. (A profit of 12 is superior to a profit of 10.) Alternatively, if firm 2 sets a low price, firm 1's profit-maximizing response is to set a low price, that is, to match. (Here, 7 is better than 5.)

TABLE 12.2

A Price War

Each firm's optimal strategy is to set a low price.

			Firm 2	
			High Price	Low Price
Firm 1	High Price		10, 10	5, 12
	Low Price		12, 5	7, 7

Because the firms face symmetric payoffs, exactly the same logic applies to firm 2. In short, self-interest dictates that each firm set a low price; this is the better strategy for each, regardless of the action the other takes.

The upshot of both sides charging low prices is profits of 7 for each—lower than the profits (10 each) if they both charged high prices. Both would prefer the larger profits enjoyed under a high-price regime. Yet the play of self-interested strategies is driving them to low prices and low profits. One might ask: Why can't the firms achieve the beneficial, high-price outcome? The answer is straightforward. To set a high price, anticipating that one's rival will do likewise, is simply wishful thinking. Although high prices are collectively beneficial, this outcome is *not* an equilibrium. Either firm could (and presumably would) profitably undercut the other's price. An initial high-price regime quickly gives way to low prices. As long as the firms act independently, the profit incentive drives down prices.

Before leaving this example, we make an additional point. The strategic behavior of rational firms can be expected to depend not only on the profit stakes as captured in the payoff table but also on the "rules" of the competition.[8] In the present example, the rules have the firms making their price decisions independently. There is no opportunity for communication or collusion. (In fact, any kind of price collusion is illegal under U.S. antitrust laws.) We say that the firms behave *noncooperatively*. However, the "rules" would be quite different if the firms were the two largest members of an international cartel. Opportunities for communication and collusion would be freely available. Clearly, the firms would strive for a *cooperative* agreement that maintains high prices. However, it is worth remembering a lesson from Chapter 11's analysis of cartels: A collusive agreement can facilitate a mutually beneficial, cooperative outcome, but it hardly guarantees it. Cartels are unstable precisely because of the individual incentives to cut price and "cheat." Thus, even a collusive agreement is not ironclad.

In the price war, suppose that some consumers display a strong "brand" allegiance for one firm or the other. Consequently, any price difference between the duopolists is expected to produce a much smaller swing in the firms' market shares. Specifically, suppose that if one firm charges a price of $6 and the other $8, the former sells 4 million units and the latter 2 million (instead of the original 6 million and 1.25 million sales). All other facts are as before. How does this change the payoffs in Table 12.2? What price should each firm set? Explain.

CHECK STATION 3

THE PRISONER'S DILEMMA   So frequent are situations (like the preceding example) in which individual and collective interests are in conflict that they commonly are referred to as the **prisoner's dilemma**. The origin of the term

---

[8] The example of price competition also serves as an introduction to game theory. Payoff tables, the rules of the game, and the analysis of optimal strategies are all topics taken up in greater depth in Chapter 13.

comes from a well-known story of two accomplices arrested for a crime. The police isolate each suspect in a room and ask each to confess and turn state's evidence on the other in return for a shortened sentence. Table 12.3 shows the possible jail terms the suspects face. If the police can garner dual confessions, the suspects will be charged and convicted of a serious crime that carries a five-year sentence. Without confessions, convictions will be for much shorter jail terms.

Obviously, each suspect seeks to *minimize* time spent in jail. A careful look at Table 12.3 shows that each prisoner's best strategy is to confess. (If his or her accomplice stays mum, confessing brings the shortest sentence, one year. If the partner confesses, so too must the suspect to avoid a maximum term.) Without the benefit of communication, there is no way for the partners to agree to stay mum. The individual incentive is for each to turn state's evidence. By cleverly constructing the configuration of possible jail terms, the authorities can induce the suspects to make voluntary confessions, resulting in five-year prison terms.

The prisoner's dilemma should be viewed as a general model rather than as a special (perverse) case. Once one has the model in mind, it is easy to identify countless situations in which it applies:

- In the superpowers' arms race, it is advantageous for one country to have a larger nuclear arsenal than its rival. But arms escalation by both sides improves neither side's security (and probably worsens it).

- A cartel has a collective interest in restricting output to earn a monopoly profit. At the same time, cartel members can increase their individual profits by cheating on the cartel, that is, exceeding their quotas. (Recall the discussion in Chapter 11.)

- Abnormally cold winter temperatures bring the threat of a shortage of natural gas for heating buildings and homes. State and city officials urge residents to turn down their thermostats to conserve natural gas. Unfortunately, the result is a negligible reduction in use. (Why should I suffer low temperatures when my personal energy saving will have no discernible impact on the shortage?)

- The utilization of public resources, most commonly natural resources, presents similar dilemmas. For instance, many countries fish the Georges Bank in the North Atlantic. Each country's fleet seeks to

TABLE 12.3

The Prisoner's Dilemma

			Suspect 2	
Each suspect's optimal strategy is to confess and turn state's evidence on the other.			**Stay Mum**	**Confess**
	Suspect 1	**Stay Mum**	2 years, 2 years	8 years, 1 year
		Confess	1 year, 8 years	5 years, 5 years

secure the greatest possible catch. But the simultaneous pursuit of maximum catches by all countries threatens depletion of the world's richest fishing grounds. Similarly, firms in many industries generate air and water pollution as manufacturing by-products, and it is hardly in their self-interest to adopt costly pollution controls. Nonetheless, the collective, social benefit of reducing pollution may be well worth the cost.

- The more widely antibiotics are prescribed, the more rapidly drug-resistant microorganisms develop.

In each of these cases, there is a significant collective benefit from cooperation. However, the self-interest of individual decision makers leads to quite different—*noncooperative*—behavior. The key to overcoming the prisoner's dilemma is to form an agreement that binds the parties to take the appropriate cooperative actions. To halt the arms race, the interested parties must bind themselves to a verifiable arms control treaty. Cartel members can agree to restrict output in order to maximize the collective profit of the cartel. A negotiated treaty on fishing quotas is one way to preserve Georges Bank. The American Medical Association has proposed guidelines calling for conservative practices in prescribing antibiotics. In the natural-gas example, a binding agreement among consumers is impossible; rather, the way to encourage cuts in consumption is via higher natural gas prices.

In the prisoner's dilemma example, suppose that a minimum sentencing law requires that a defendant entering into a plea bargain must serve a minimum of three years. What entries will this affect in Table 12.3? Explain why this law is likely to backfire in the present instance.

CHECK STATION 4

Attack on a Skater

On January 6, 1994, an unknown assailant attacked figure skater Nancy Kerrigan, injuring her right knee and preventing her from competing in the U.S. Olympic trials. Within days, the police and FBI followed a trail of clues left by the inept perpetrators. They subsequently arrested three men, one of whom was the former bodyguard of rival skater Tonya Harding. At first, Miss Harding and Jeff Gillooly (her former husband, with whom she was living) repeatedly denied any knowledge of the attack. However, after more than 10 hours of interviews with federal investigators, Miss Harding admitted that she learned of Gillooly's involvement several days after the attack. When Gillooly later found out about Harding's statement (she had repeatedly assured him she had not implicated him), he named her as a key figure in planning the attack.

In their own inimitable way, Harding and Gillooly entangled themselves in a classic prisoner's dilemma: whether to hold out or implicate the other. Once again, the cliché that fact imitates theory seems to have been vindicated. Indeed, the case ended in dueling plea bargains. Gillooly pleaded guilty to one charge of racketeering, subject to a maximum jail term of two years, and was fined

$100,000. Harding pleaded guilty to minor charges for which she received probation, paid a $100,000 fine, and was forced to withdraw from competitive skating. However, an earlier court injunction enabled her to compete in the Winter Olympics, where she finished eighth. Nancy Kerrigan, who was placed on the U.S. team, finished second and won the Olympic silver medal.

Would the pair have escaped prosecution if they had refused to implicate one another? To this question we probably will never know the answer.

BERTRAND PRICE COMPETITION   An extreme case of price competition originally was suggested by Joseph Bertrand, a nineteenth-century French economist. Suppose duopolists produce an undifferentiated good at an identical (and constant) marginal cost, say $6 per unit. Each can charge whatever price it wishes, but consumers are very astute and always purchase solely from the firm giving the lower price. In other words, the lower-price firm gains the entire market, and the higher-price firm sells nothing.

To analyze this situation, suppose that each firm seeks to determine a price that maximizes its own profit while anticipating the price set by its rival. In other words, as in the previous example of quantity competition, we focus on equilibrium strategies for the firms. (The difference is that here the firms compete via prices, whereas previously they competed via quantities.) What are the firms' equilibrium prices? A little reflection shows that the unique equilibrium is for each firm to set a price equal to marginal cost: $P_1 = P_2 = \$6$. This may appear to be a surprising outcome. In equilibrium, $P = AC = MC$ so that both firms earn zero economic profit. With the whole market on the line, as few as two firms compete the price down to the perfectly competitive, zero-profit level.

Why isn't there an equilibrium in which firms charge higher prices and earn positive profits? If firms charged different prices, the higher-price firm (currently with zero sales) could profit by slightly undercutting the other firm's price (thereby gaining the entire market). Thus, different prices cannot be in equilibrium. What if the firms were currently charging the same price and splitting the market equally? Now either firm could increase its profit by barely undercutting the price of the other—settling for a slightly smaller profit margin while doubling its market share. In summary, the possibilities for profitable price-cutting are exhausted only when the firms already are charging $P = AC = MC$ and earning zero profits.

The Bertrand model generates the extreme result that price competition, by as few as two firms, can yield a perfectly competitive outcome. It should be emphasized that this result depends on two extreme assumptions—that (1) all competition is on the basis of price and (2) the lower-price firm always claims the entire market. We already have seen that quantity competition leads to quite a different outcome. Furthermore, even if price is the most important competitive dimension, market shares are unlikely to be all or nothing.[9] In

---

[9] A good example of the Bertrand model is the case of competitive bidding. Here the firm that submits the lowest bid price gains the exclusive award of a supply contract. Competitive bidding is taken up in Chapter 17.

models with some degree of product differentiation, competition leads to price reductions, but equilibrium prices remain above the perfectly competitive level.

OTHER DIMENSIONS OF COMPETITION

Thus far, our focus has been on quantity and price competition within oligopolies. In this final section, we briefly consider two other forms of competition: advertising and strategic precommitment.

Advertising

For firms competing in an oligopoly, advertising can be a powerful means of promoting sales. Indeed, firms that sell differentiated goods spend enormous sums on advertising. We begin this section by analyzing a single firm's optimal advertising decision. Later, we consider advertising as a competitive weapon within oligopoly.

OPTIMAL ADVERTISING   Consider a consumer-products firm that must determine not only the price at which to sell one of its goods but also the associated level of advertising expenditure. At a given price, an increase in advertising will raise sales to a greater or lesser extent.

One way to picture the firm's decision problem is to write its demand function as $Q(P, A)$. Here the demand function Q shows that the quantity of sales depends on price P and advertising expenditure A. The firm's total profit in terms of P and A can be written as

$$\pi = P \cdot Q(P, A) - C[Q(P, A)] - A. \qquad [12.6]$$

Profit is simply revenue minus production cost minus total advertising cost. We see that determining the level of advertising involves a basic trade-off: Raising A increases sales and profits (the net value of the first two terms) but is itself costly (the third term). As always, the optimal level of advertising is found where marginal profit with respect to A is zero. Taking the derivative of Equation 12.6 and setting this equal to zero, we find

$$M\pi_A = \partial\pi/\partial A = P(\partial Q/\partial A) - (dC/dQ)(\partial Q/\partial A) - 1 = 0$$

or

$$(P - MC)(\partial Q/\partial A) = 1. \qquad [12.7]$$

The left-hand side of this equation is the marginal profit of an extra dollar of advertising, computed as the increase in quantity $(\partial Q/\partial A)$ times the profit contribution per unit. The right-hand side is the MC of advertising ($1). Optimal advertising spending occurs when its marginal benefit (in terms of profit) equals its marginal cost.

EXAMPLE   Let the demand for a good be given by $Q = 10,000P^{-5}A^{.5}$ and let MC = \$.80. Let's use marginal analysis to find the firm's optimal price, output, and level of advertising. Noting that $E_P = -5$, we can solve for price using the markup rule $P = [E_P/(1 + E_P)]MC = (-5/-4)(.8) = \$1.00$. For the constant elasticity demand function, optimal price does not depend on the level of advertising expenditure. (This markup is relatively low because demand is quite price elastic.) With $P = 1.00$ and $MC = .8$, the firm's contribution is \$.20 per unit. Thus, net profit is

$$\pi = .2Q(P, A) - A$$
$$= (.2)(10,000A^{.5}) - A.$$

In turn, we find $M\pi_A = 1,000A^{-.5} - 1 = 0$. A rearrangement gives $A^{.5} = 1,000$. Therefore, $A = (1,000)^2 = \$1,000,000$. Finally, substituting $A = \$1,000,000$ into the demand equation yields $Q = 10,000,000$.

ADVERTISING WITHIN OLIGOPOLY   To consider the impact of advertising in an oligopoly, we must move from a single firm's point of view and ask: What is the effect when a small number of oligopolists simultaneously pursue optimal strategies? To illustrate the possibilities, we briefly consider two polar cases.

1. **Product Differentiation.** One role of advertising is to underscore real or perceived differences between competing products, that is, to promote product differentiation and brand-name allegiance. Thus, the aim of a firm's advertising is to convince consumers that its product is different and better than competing goods, for example, "Coke is the real thing," "Only Rolaids spells relief," and "Tropicana Orange Juice tastes like fresh squeezed, not concentrate." From the firm's point of view, the ideal result of such advertising is to create a large segment of loyal consumers—customers who will not defect to a rival product, even if the competitor offers a lower price or enhanced features.

   In economic terms, increased product differentiation lessens the substitutability of other goods while reducing the cross-price elasticity of demand. In other words, it tends to blunt competition between oligopolists on such dimensions as price and performance. (For instance, because of heavy advertising, Dole pineapples and Chiquita bananas enjoy much higher price markups than generic fruit.) The individual oligopolistic firm finds it advantageous to differentiate its product. Moreover, the firms' simultaneous advertising expenditures may well result in increased profits for the oligopoly as a whole.[10]

---

[10] To construct the most extreme case, suppose that a small amount of advertising has the power to create a mini-monopoly for each differentiated product. Then the profits from higher monopoly prices would far outweigh the cost of the advertising.

2. **Informational Advertising.** A second major role of advertising is to provide consumers better information about competing goods. Claims that "We offer the lowest price" (or "best financing" or "50 percent longer battery life" or "better service" or "more convenient locations") clearly fall into this category. Advertising copy frequently provides direct descriptions of products including photographs.

The effect of purely informational advertising is to make consumers more aware of and sensitive to salient differences among competing products. When *imperfect information* is the norm, some firms might charge higher-than-average prices or deliver lower-than-average quality and still maintain modest market shares. Informational advertising tends to eliminate those possibilities and forces firms to compete more vigorously for *informed* consumers. The result is lower prices (and/or improved product quality) and lower industry profits.[11]

Across the spectrum of oligopoly, both reasons for advertising—to differentiate products and to provide information—are important. Both effects provide firms an economic incentive to advertise. (Indeed, only under perfect competition—where products are standardized and consumers already have perfect information—would we expect advertising to be absent.) However, the implications for firms and consumers (whether advertising enhances or blunts competition) tend to work in opposite directions. Not surprisingly, a number of commentators and policy makers have attacked pervasive advertising as anti-competitive. (In novelist F. Scott Fitzgerald's words, "Advertising is a racket. Its contribution to humanity is exactly minus zero.") However, it is mainly an empirical question as to which aspect of advertising—its procompetitive or anti-competitive effect—tends to be stronger and more important.

There have been numerous research studies concerning the effect of advertising in different industries over different time periods.[12] Overall, findings are mixed. Advertising about price has been found to lower average prices for consumer products, such as toys, gasoline, pharmaceuticals, and eyeglasses. (For instance, consumers in states that ban eyeglass advertising pay higher prices than consumers in states that allow it.) There is evidence that advertising (once vigorously fought by state and national bar associations) can lower the price of legal services. In short, in certain markets, advertising plays an

---

[11] To cite another extreme case, suppose that informational advertising's sole effect is to shuffle sales from one oligopolist to another; no amount of advertising can increase total industry sales. Furthermore, each oligopolist has some product feature for which it pays to advertise. The result is a classic prisoner's dilemma. Advertising is in each oligopolist's self-interest. But, collectively, advertising is self-defeating. Total sales do not increase and market shares remain unchanged. Thus, from the industry's point of view, the total sum spent on advertising is wasted.

[12] A fine survey and discussion of these studies can be found in D. W. Carlton and J. M. Perloff, *Modern Industrial Organization*, Chapter 14 (Reading MA: Addison-Wesley, 2004).

important role in providing price information. However, there is also countervailing evidence that advertising and product differentiation can create entry barriers and increase industry concentration and profits. (Here the evidence is somewhat mixed. Whether high levels of advertising cause increased concentration or are *caused by it* is an open question.)

Strategic Commitments

A comparison of quantity competition and price competition yields a number of general propositions about the strategic actions and reactions of competing firms. Consider once again the case of symmetric firms competing with respect to quantities. A key part of that example was the way in which one firm's quantity action affected the other's—that is, how the competitor would be expected to react. If one firm (for whatever reason) were to increase its quantity of output, then the profit-maximizing response of the other would be to decrease its output. (Roughly speaking, the greater is one firm's presence in the market, the less demand there is for the other.) Equation 12.3's reaction function shows this explicitly. We say that the firms' actions are **strategic substitutes** when increasing one firm's action causes the other firm's optimal reaction to decrease. Thus, the duopolists' quantity decisions are strategic substitutes.

By contrast, price competition works quite differently. If one firm changes its price (up or down), the optimal response for the competing firm is to change its price in the same direction. (One firm's price cut prompts a price cut by its rival. Conversely, if one firm raises its price, the other can afford to raise its price as well.) The earlier example of Bertrand (winner take all) price competition exhibits exactly this behavior. Similar (but less dramatic) price reactions occur when competition is between differentiated products. (Here a price cut by one firm will attract only a portion of the other firm's customers and so prompts only a modest price reaction.) We say that the firms' actions are **strategic complements** when a change in one firm's action causes the other firm's optimal response to move in the *same* direction.

A comparison of competition between strategic substitutes and strategic complements leads to the following proposition.

> In a host of oligopoly models, competition involving prices (strategic complements) results in lower equilibrium profits than competition involving quantities (strategic substitutes).

This result underscores the key difference between firm strategies under price competition and quantity competition. When firms compete along the price dimension, a rival's lower price leads to the firm lowering its own price. In short, competition *begets* more competition. By contrast, under quantity competition, a rival's increase in output induces a lower quantity of output by the firm itself. In this sense an increase in output *deters* a competitive response. In general, price competition is more intense than quantity competition (which is self-limiting). The upshot is that equilibrium price setting tends to lead to lower profits for the firms than equilibrium quantity setting.

Of course, it is important to keep this result in perspective. Price competition is not always "destructive"; the particular equilibrium outcome depends, as always, on underlying demand and cost conditions. (For instance, Check Station 3 displays favorable demand conditions in which equilibrium behavior leads to *high* prices.) In other words, the comparison of equilibrium outcomes requires holding other factors constant. (End-of-chapter Problems 9 and 10 provide a good example of this.) The result does suggest an interesting strategic message. Frequently, firms find themselves surveying any number of strategic dimensions—price, quantity, advertising, and so on—and have the opportunity to "pick their battles." Most oligopoly models suggest that it is wise to avoid price competition (because this involves strategic complements) and to compete on quantity and advertising (where both involve strategic substitutes).

COMMITMENTS   Suppose a firm is about to engage in quantity competition but also faces an earlier decision. For instance, the firm has the opportunity to invest in a new production process that has the advantage of lowering its marginal cost of production. Should the firm commit to this process investment? A complete answer to this question depends on anticipating the investment's effect on the subsequent quantity competition. Looking just at the firm's own behavior, we know that the lower MC induces a higher optimal output. But the strategic effect also matters. Because the firms' quantities are strategic substitutes, an increased output by the first firm will induce a lower output by the rival. This reduction in competing output further spurs the firm to greater output and increases its profitability. (Check Station 1 provides a good example of these equilibrium output effects.) In short, the original commitment to invest in capacity might well be profitable exactly *because* of its strategic effect on competitor behavior.

Economists Drew Fudenberg and Jean Tirole have explored the general principals underlying this example.[13] When the subsequent competition involves strategic substitutes, a "tough" commitment by one of the firms will advantageously affect the ensuing equilibrium. Here "tough" denotes any move that induces an increase in the firm's own output and (in turn) a decrease in the rival's output. Making product quality improvements, increasing advertising spending, and lowering unit costs would all qualify as tough commitments. Indeed, Fudenberg and Tirole characterize any of these moves as part of a "Top-Dog" strategy, an aggressive strategy that induces the rival to back off.

---

[13] See D. Fudenberg and J. Tirole, "The Fat-Cat Effect, the Puppy-Dog Ploy, and the Lean and Hungry Look," *American Economic Review* (1984): 361–366. An additional source is J. Bulow, J. Geanakopolos, and P. Klemperer, "Multimarket Oligopoly: Strategic Substitutes and Complements," *Journal of Political Economy* (1985): 488–511.

(Chapter 13 uses game theory to consider further instances that confer this kind of first-mover advantage.) The extreme case of this strategy occurs if the firm's first move has such a dramatic effect on the economics of its rival that the latter's best response is to exit the market altogether. In effect, the top dog has driven its rival from the market.

Interestingly, the logic of strategic commitment is exactly reversed when the subsequent competition involves strategic complements. Consider once again price competition. Here a "tough" commitment that implies lower prices by the initiating firm also induces lower prices by the competitor. But a lower rival price is exactly what the first firm *does not want* to happen. (The tough first move would only make sense if it succeeded in driving the competitor out of the market altogether.) Instead, the firm in question should adopt a "Fat-Cat strategy" to use Fudenberg and Tirole's label. This means making a "soft" first move, such as engaging in product differentiation—real (via product innovation) or perceived (via increased advertising spending). The effect of any soft move is to allow for a higher price for the firm itself and to induce a higher price by the competitor. The point of the initial commitment is to soften or blunt the subsequent price competition.

In summary, a tough strategic commitment is advantageous when the subsequent competition involves strategic substitutes; a soft commitment is appropriate when strategic complements are involved.

Collusion in the Infant-Formula Industry Revisited

We can use concepts developed in this chapter to shed light on the structure and conduct of the infant-formula industry. First, the industry was dominated by three large firms that made up 96 percent of total sales, a clear triopoly. Thus, there existed preconditions for the exercise of market power. Second, there is abundant evidence that leading firms enjoyed excess profits over the past decade, profit margins of as much as 25 percent above average costs. Third, pricing behavior of the firms is striking: All had nearly identical patterns of price increases well in excess of the cost of milk (the main ingredient in formula). The companies succeeded in these price increases despite some decline in formula use (and a resurgence in breast-feeding). Certainly, this pricing behavior raises the suspicion of tacit collusion among the companies to maintain orderly (and increasing) prices. Indeed, an investigation of these pricing practices for possible collusion was undertaken by the Federal Trade Commission.

The formula industry meets a fourth acid test of entrenched oligopoly: The market was insulated from competition by new entrants. Despite their size and prowess in other markets, Carnation and Gerber accomplished few inroads in the U.S. infant-formula market. The crucial entry barrier stemmed from the major companies' direct giveaway programs to hospitals and doctors. With 90 percent of mothers continuing to use the formula brought home from the hospital, the companies enjoyed the ideal captive market. Furthermore, the American Academy of Pediatrics allied itself with the dominant firms to press for a prohibition on all advertising of infant formula. Doctors leading the academy argued that formula advertising discourages breast-feeding. But Carnation and Gerber advertised aggressively and insisted it was the only chance they had to bring their products before the public. Carnation filed a lawsuit against the academy and the formula producers, accusing them of conspiring to prevent it from marketing formula. A Bristol-Myers memo revealed in a Florida lawsuit stated, "It is probably in our best interests to forestall any form of consumer advertising." The chief of Florida's antitrust division added, "I have walked into my pediatrician's office and have had him try to convince me not to buy Carnation even though it is cheaper." Clearly, the direct giveaway program combined with impediments to advertising represented a formidable barrier to entry.

What is the likely economic impact of competitive bidding for formula sales under the Women, Infants, and Children (WIC) program? As noted, most states allow vouchers to be exchanged for any brand of formula. These states have seen company discounts averaging $.50 per can. Formula companies lobbied strongly against "winner-take-all" bidding, arguing that awarding the WIC contract to one bidder would restrict a family's choice of formula. (The companies went so far as to warn Texas officials that they might no longer supply free formula to hospitals.) The experience in "winner-take-all" bidding indicates why the companies resisted it. Competition was intense. With one-third of the total market up for bid, winning discounts averaged $1.00 per can. Indeed, the winning discount reached a high of $1.50 per can in Michigan. (Here the net price of $.60 roughly matched estimated marginal cost. Thus, this bidding instance appears to have achieved the Bertrand equilibrium.) However, with recent reductions in winning discounts, a number of state regulators have begun investigations of company collusion and bid rigging. Nonetheless, competitive bidding offers the advantage of lower prices and the real possibility of competition by new entrants.[14]

In the late 1990s, the three major formula producers reached a settlement with the Federal Trade Commission in its price-fixing investigation. Although admitting no wrongdoing, the firms agreed to make reimbursements to formula customers in eight states. Since 2000, a number of generic formula makers have made small market-share gains by advertising their offerings and giving samples to doctors and mothers. Surprisingly, the Academy of Pediatricians dropped its opposition to advertising, and today aggressive advertising (for better or worse) is the norm for all industry players.

---

[14] Accounts of the history of the formula market, the advertising controversy, and experiments with competitive bidding include B. P. Noble, "Price-Fixing and Other Charges Roil Once-Placid Market," *The New York Times* (July 28, 1991): C9, B. Meier, "Battle for Baby Formula Market," *The New York Times* (June 15, 1993): C1, M. Brick, "Makers of Generic Baby Formula Win Round in Court," *The New York Times* (May 2, 2001): C5, and G. Retsinas, "The Marketing of a Superbaby Formula," *The New York Times* (June 1, 2003): BU1.

SUMMARY

Decision-Making Principles

1. The key to making optimal decisions in an oligopoly is anticipating the actions of one's rivals.

2. In the dominant-firm model, smaller firms behave competitively, that is, take price as given when making their quantity decisions. Anticipating this behavior, the dominant firm maximizes its profit by setting quantity and price (and applying MR = MC) along its *net* demand curve.

3. When competition is between symmetrically positioned oligopolists (the Cournot case), each firm maximizes its profit by anticipating the (profit-maximizing) quantities set by its rivals.

4. Intense price competition has the features of the prisoner's dilemma; optimal behavior implies mutual price cuts and reduced profits.

5. Advertising should be undertaken up to the point at which increased profit from greater sales just covers the last advertising dollar spent.

Nuts and Bolts

1. An oligopoly is a market dominated by a small number of firms. Each firm's profit is affected not only by its own actions but also by actions of its rivals.

2. An industry's concentration ratio measures the percentage of total sales accounted for by the top 4 (or 8 or 20) firms in the market. Another measure of industry structure is the Herfindahl–Hirschman Index (HHI), defined as the sum of the squared market shares of all firms. The greater the concentration index or the HHI, the more significant is the market dominance of a small number of firms. Other things being equal, increases in concentration can be expected to be associated with increases in prices and profits.

3. There are two main models of quantity rivalry: competition with a dominant firm or competition among equals. In each model, equilibrium quantities are determined such that no firm can profit by altering its planned output. In the quantity-setting model, the equilibrium approaches the perfectly competitive outcome as the number of (identical) firms increases without bound.

4. If a firm expects price cuts (but not price increases) to be matched by its rivals, the result is a kink in the firm's demand curve. Prices will be relatively stable (because price changes will tend to be unprofitable).

5. The prisoner's dilemma embraces such diverse cases as price wars, cartel cheating, arms races, and resource depletion. In each instance, self-interested behavior by interacting parties leads to an inferior outcome for the group as a whole.

Questions and Problems

1. Venture capitalists provide funds to finance new companies (start-ups), usually in return for a share of the firm's initial profits (if any). Of course, venture capitalists look to back experienced entrepreneurs with strong products (or at least product blueprints). But potential competitors and the structure of the market into which the new firm enters also are important. According to conventional wisdom, the best start-up prospects involve entry into loose oligopolies. What economic factors might be behind this conventional wisdom?

2. In granting (or prohibiting) proposed acquisitions or mergers in an industry, government regulators consider a number of factors, including the acquisition's effect on concentration, ease of entry into the market, extent of ongoing price competition, and potential efficiency gains. In 1985, the Department of Transportation allowed United Airlines to acquire Pan American World Airways Pacific Division, including its U.S.–Japan routes. Before the acquisition, market shares on routes between the United States and Japan were Japan Airlines (30 percent), Northwest (30 percent), Pan Am (19 percent), and United (7 percent), with four other carriers accounting for the remaining 14 percent. Entry by new airlines along these routes was difficult and expensive. Nonetheless, price competition (due in large part to United's efforts to gain market share) was substantial.
    a. What would be the (approximate) effect of the acquisition on the market's concentration ratio? On the HHI?
    b. At the time, a Justice Department guideline called for prohibition of an acquisition that would raise HHI by more than 100 points in industries that already are highly concentrated (defined as a starting HHI exceeding 1,800). How would this guideline apply to United Airlines' proposed acquisition?
    c. The Department of Transportation recognized that United's acquisition would integrate its domestic route network with the newly acquired Pacific routes. Would this make United a stronger competitor? Would route integration be beneficial to airline travelers?

3. The OPEC cartel is trying to determine the total amount of oil to sell on the world market. It estimates world demand for oil to be $Q_W = 60 - .5P$,

where Q_W denotes the quantity of oil (in millions of barrels per day) and P is price per barrel. The cartel's marginal cost is approximately $20 per barrel.

a. Determine OPEC's profit-maximizing output and price.
b. OPEC's economists recognize the importance of non-OPEC oil supplies. These can be described by the estimated supply curve $Q_S = 1.5P - 20$. Write OPEC's net demand curve. Find its optimal output and price. What portion of the world's total oil supply comes from OPEC?

4. Firm A is the dominant firm in a market where industry demand is given by $Q_D = 48 - 4P$. There are four "follower" firms, each with long-run marginal cost given by $MC = 6 + Q_F$. Firm A's long-run marginal cost is 6.

a. Write the expression for the total supply curve of the followers (Q_S) as this depends on price. (Remember that each follower acts as a price taker.)
b. Find the net demand curve facing firm A. Determine A's optimal price and output. How much output do the other firms supply in total?

5. Two firms serve a market in which demand is described by $P = 40 - 5(Q_1 + Q_2)$. Each firm's marginal cost is 20.

a. Suppose each firm maximizes its own profit, treating the other's quantity as constant. Find an expression for firm 1's optimal output as it depends on firm 2's. In equilibrium, what common level of output will each firm supply?
b. Suppose, instead, that the firms collude in setting their outputs. What outputs should they set and why?

6. Firms M and N compete for a market and must independently decide how much to advertise. Each can spend either $10 million or $20 million on advertising. If the firms spend equal amounts, they split the $120 million market equally. (For instance, if both choose to spend $20 million, each firm's net profit is $60 - 20 = \$40$ million.) If one firm spends $20 million and the other $10 million, the former claims two-thirds of the market and the latter one-third.

		Firm N's Advertising	
		$10 million	$20 million
Firm M's Advertising	$10 million	?, ?	?, ?
	$20 million	?, ?	40, 40

a. Fill in the profit entries in the payoff table.

b. If the firms act independently, what advertising level should each choose? Explain. Is a prisoner's dilemma present?

c. Could the firms profit by entering into an industry-wide agreement concerning the extent of advertising? Explain.

7. In each of the following cases, provide a brief explanation of whether a prisoner's dilemma is present. If so, suggest ways the dilemma can be overcome.

a. When there is a bumper crop (a large supply and, therefore, low prices), farmers incur losses.

b. Individual work effort has been observed to suffer when managers are grouped in teams with all team members receiving comparable compensation based on the overall performance of the group.

8. Suppose four firms engage in price competition in a Bertrand setting in which the lowest-price firm will capture the entire market. The firms differ with respect to their costs. Firm A's marginal cost per unit is $8, firm B's is $7, firm C's is $9, and firm D's is $7.50.

a. Which firm will serve the market? What price (approximately) will it charge?

b. Would your answer change if firms A and B had somewhat greater fixed costs of production than firms C and D?

9. Two firms produce differentiated products. Firm 1 faces the demand curve $Q_1 = 75 - P_1 + .5P_2$. (Note that a lower competing price robs the firm of some, but not all, sales. Thus, price competition is not as extreme as in the Bertrand model.) Firm 2 faces the analogous demand curve $Q_2 = 75 - P_2 + .5P_1$. For each firm, AC = MC = 30.

a. Confirm that firm 1's optimal price depends on P_2 according to $P_1 = 52.5 + .25P_2$. *Hint:* Set up the profit expression:
$\pi_1 = (P_1 - 30)Q_1 = (P_1 - 30)(75 - P_1 + .5P_2)$ and set
$M\pi = \partial \pi_1/\partial P_1 = 0$ to solve for P_1 in terms of P_2. Alternatively, set
$MR_1 = MC$ and solve for Q_1 and then P_1 in terms of P_2.

b. Explain why a lower price by its competitor should cause the firm to lower its own price.

c. In equilibrium, the firms set identical prices: $P_1 = P_2$. Find the firms' equilibrium prices, quantities, and profits.

10. Suppose instead that the firms in Problem 9 compete by setting quantities rather than prices. All other facts are the same. It is possible to rewrite the original demand equations as $P_1 = [150 - (2/3)Q_2] - (4/3)Q_1$ and $P_2 = [150 - (2/3)Q_1] - (4/3)Q_2$. In words, increases in the competitor's output lowers the intercept of the firm's demand curve.

    a. Set $MR_1 = MC$ to confirm that firm 1's optimal quantity depends on Q_2 according to $Q_1 = 45 - .25Q_2$. Explain why an increase in one firm's output tends to "deter" production by the other.

    b. In equilibrium, the firms set identical quantities: $Q_1 = Q_2$. Find the firms' equilibrium quantities, prices, and profits.

    c. Compare the firms' profits under quantity competition and price competition (Problem 9). Provide an intuitive explanation for why price competition is more intense (i.e., leads to lower equilibrium profits).

11. Firm Z faces the price equation $P = 50 + A^{.5} - Q$, and the cost function $C = 20Q + A$, where A denotes advertising spending.

    a. Other things (price) held constant, does an increase in advertising spending lead to greater sales? Does advertising spending represent a fixed cost or a variable cost?

    b. Find the firm's profit-maximizing quantity as a function of A. (*Hint*: Treating A as fixed, we have $MR = 50 + A^{.5} - 2Q$.) Do the same for the firm's price. Explain these results.

    c. Using the results in part b, write the firm's profit expression in terms of A alone. Find the firm's optimal level of advertising. Find its optimal quantity and price.

*12. a. Using the marginal condition in Equation 12.7, show that an equivalent condition for the optimal level of advertising is $(P - MC)Q/A = 1/E_A$, where $E_A = (\partial Q/Q)/(\partial A/A)$ is the elasticity of demand with respect to advertising. In words, the ratio of advertising spending to operating profit should equal E_A. Other things being equal, the greater this elasticity, the greater the spending on advertising.

    b. Use the markup rule, $(P - MC)/P = -1/E_P$, and the equation in part a to show that $A/(PQ) = -E_A/E_P$. (*Hint*: Divide the former by the latter.) According to this result, the ratio of advertising spending to dollar sales is simply the ratio of the respective elasticities.

    c. In 1986, General Motors Corporation was ranked 5th of all U.S. firms in advertising expenditure, and Kellogg Co. was ranked 30th. But advertising spending constituted 17 percent of total sales for Kellogg and only 1 percent for GM. Given the result in part b, what must be true about the firms' respective price and advertising elasticities to explain this difference?

Discussion Question Choose a good or service that is supplied by a small number of oligopoly firms. (Examples range from athletic shoes to aircraft to toothpaste, or choose a product from the industry list in Table 12.1.) Gather

*Starred problems are more challenging.

information on the good from public sources (business periodicals, trade magazines, or government reports) to answer the following questions.

a. Who are the leading firms and what are their market shares? Compute the concentration ratio for the relevant market.

b. What are the most important dimensions (price, technological innovation, advertising and promotion, and so on) on which firms compete?

c. What has been the history of entry into the market? What kinds of barriers to entry exist?

Spreadsheet Problems

S1. A dominant firm in an industry has costs given by $C = 70 + 5q_L$. The dominant firm sets the market price, and the eight "small" firms coexisting in the market take this price as given. Each small firm has costs given by $C = 25 + q^2 - 4q$. Total industry demand is given by $Q_d = 400 - 20P$.

a. Create a spreadsheet similar to the example to model price-setting by the dominant firm. (If you completed Problem S1 of Chapter 10, you need only make slight modifications in that spreadsheet.)

	A	B	C	D	E	F	G	H	I	J
1										
2				Dominant Firm						
3				Price Leadership						
4										
5				Market Supply & Demand			Dominant Firm			
6		Price	# S. Firms	Q_s	Q_d		Q_d-Q_s	Cost	Profit	
7										
8		8	8	48	240		192	1030	506	
9										
10										
11					Small Firms					
12		q	MC	Cost	AC		P − MC	Profit		
13										
14		6	8	37	6.167		0	11.0		
15										
16										
17			Small firms' supply is determined by P = MC.							
18			Large firm maximizes profit given net demand.							
19										

b. Experiment with prices between P = 7 and P = 16. For each price, determine the small firms' supply by setting q such that P = MC. Taking into account the supply response of the eight other firms, what price seems to be most profitable for the dominant firm?

c. Use your spreadsheet's optimizer to find the dominant firm's optimal price. (*Hint*: Adjust cells B8 and B14 to maximize cell I8 subject to the constraint G14 equal to zero.)

S2. A firm faces a price equation $P = 12.5 + .5A^{.5} - .25Q$ and a cost equation $C = 5Q + A$, where Q denotes its output and A denotes its level of advertising expenditure.

a. Create a spreadsheet to describe the firm's profit as it varies with output and advertising. Set advertising spending at 50 and find the firm's optimal level of output.

b. Use your spreadsheet's optimizer to find the firm's optimal output and level of advertising spending.

Suggested References

The following texts provide comprehensive treatments of market structure and oligopoly.

Adams, W., and J. Brock (Eds). *The Structure of American Industry.* Upper Saddle River, NJ: Prentice Hall, 2001.

Besanko, D., D. Dranove, M. Shanley, and S. Schaefer. *Economics of Strategy.* New York: John Wiley & Sons, 2003. (Chapters 7, 11, and 12 examine industry structure and the five-forces model. Chapter 8 discusses strategic commitment.)

Carlton, D. W., and J. M. Perloff. *Modern Industrial Organization.* Reading, MA: Addison-Wesley, 2004.

Dixit, A., and S. Skeath. *Games of Strategy.* New York: W. W. Norton, 2004.

Shepherd, W. G. *The Economics of Industrial Organization.* Prospect Heights, IL: Waveland Press, 1999.

Tirole, J. *The Theory of Industrial Organization,* Chapters 3, 5 and 7. Cambridge: MIT Press, 1989.

McGahan, A. M., and M. E. Porter, "How Much Does Industry Matter Really?" *Strategic Management Journal* 18 (Summer 1997): 167–185.

The preceding article provides a statistical analysis of firm profitability. It finds that variations in profitability depend on firm characteristics and strategies (accounting for 32% of profit variations), market structure (19%), other factors (7%), and random fluctuations (42%).

Powerful and intriguing analyses of the prisoner's dilemma include:

Axelrod, R. M. *The Evolution of Cooperation.* New York: Basic Books, 1985.

Axelrod, R. M. *The Complexity of Cooperation.* Princeton: Princeton University Press, 1997.

Fine articles on advertising and product bundling include:

Adams, W. J., and J. L. Yellin. "Commodity Bundling and the Burden of Monopoly." *Quarterly Journal of Economics* (1976): 475–498.

Greuner, M. R., D. R. Kamerschen, and P. G. Klein. "The Competitive Effects of Advertising in the US Automobile Industry, 1970–94." *International Journal of the Economics of Business* 7 (2000): 245–261.

Silk, A. J., L. R. Klein, and E. R. Berndt. "The Emerging Position of the Internet as an Advertising Medium." *Netnomics* 3 (2001): 129–148.

Concentration ratios gathered by the U.S. Bureau of the Census are available online at:

www.census.gov/epcd/www/concentration.html.

1. Firm 1's optimal reaction function remains $Q_1 = 12 - .5Q_2$. To determine its optimal output, firm 2 sets marginal revenue equal to 9: $30 - Q_1 - 2Q_2 = 9$; therefore, $Q_2 = 10.5 - .5Q_1$. Solving these equations simultaneously, we find $Q_1 = 9$ and $Q_2 = 6$. In equilibrium, the lower-cost firm claims a majority market share.

2. The kink occurs at $Q = 10$. At outputs less than 10, $MR = 30 - 2Q$. For outputs greater than 10, $MR = 36 - 3.2Q$. Evaluating each expression at $Q = 10$, we see that MR jumps from 10 to 4. So long as MC is between 10 and 4, the firm's optimal output is 10 and its optimal price is 20.

3. In the off-diagonal entries in Table 12.2, both the low-price firm and the high-price firm earn $8 million in profit. This change completely reverses the firms' incentives. Regardless of what action the other takes, each firm's profit-maximizing strategy is to set a *high* price. (Comparing possible profits, 10 is greater than 8, and 8 is greater than 7.) Strong brand allegiance removes the incentive to cut price.

4. The minimum sentencing law changes the off-diagonal payoffs in Table 12.3. Now a unilateral confession brings a three-year term (not a one-year term). Now it is in each prisoner's best interest to stay mum, provided he expects his partner to do likewise (two years is better than three years). By limiting the scope of plea bargaining, the law has impeded the prosecutor's ability to secure longer prison terms.

Bundling and Tying

Besides pricing its separate products, oligopolistic firms frequently choose to **bundle** their products, that is, to sell two or more products as a package. Under the right circumstances, bundling can be considerably more profitable than separate sales. Consider the following example.

BUNDLING FILMS   A movie studio has two films ready for sale to two theater chains. Each chain consists of 500 multiscreen theaters. Table 12A.1 shows the values each chain places on each film. For instance, chain 1 is willing to pay up to $13,000 per screen per week for film X; chain 2 will pay only $7,000, and so on. (The differences in value reflect the respective geographic patterns of the chains' theaters and the fact that some films tend to "play better" in some regions and cities than others.)

  The movie studio has a number of options in pricing films. If it sells film X separately and charges $7,000 per screen per week, it will sell to both chains, earning total revenue of $7,000,000 per week.[1] If it charges $13,000 instead, it would sell only to chain 1, earning $6,500,000 in revenue. Clearly, the $7,000

---

[1] Here and throughout, we are presuming that a chain will purchase the film at a price equal to its value; in fact, purchasing or not would be a matter of indifference. If you are worried about this knife-edge case, think of the studio as charging a slightly lower price, say, $6,995, in order to provide the chain a strictly positive incentive to buy. (Note that this makes no essential difference in the revenue calculations.)

price is the better option. Similarly, one can check that the studio's optimal price for film Y is $6,000 per screen per week. At these prices, the films will be sold to both chains and will produce $13,000,000 in total revenue.

What if the studio were to sell the films as a package at a bundled price? The last column of Table 12A.1 shows the combined value each chain puts on the film package. Clearly, the studio's optimal bundled price is $P_B = $18,000$. At this price, both chains purchase the bundle, and the studio earns $18,000,000 per week. Bundling has increased the studio's revenue by $5,000,000, or some 38 percent. What is the source of this additional profit? The answer lies in the fact that each chain's values for the films are *negatively* correlated. That is, the chain with the higher value for one film has the lower value for the other. Since higher and lower values are offsetting, the chains have very similar *total* values for the bundled package. By bundling films, the studio can set a price ($18,000) that extracts nearly all of each chain's total value (or consumer surplus) for the films, without pricing either chain out of the market.

Notice that bundling holds no advantage over separate pricing if the chains' values for film Y are reversed. In this scenario, chain 1 puts higher values ($13,000 and $11,000) on both films. Each chain's values are *positively* correlated; that is, high values go with high values, low values with low values. You should check that the studio's optimal bundled price is $P_B = 7,000 + 6,000 = $13,000$. In other words, the bundled price is simply the sum of the separate film prices. Sold separately or as a bundle, the films deliver exactly the same revenue.

Bundling can be profitable even when the goods' values are *uncorrelated*. Consider once again the studio's pricing problem, but now let each chain have uncorrelated values. In particular, suppose that each of the 1,000 theaters that

TABLE 12A.1

Selling Films: Separate Sales versus Bundling

(a)

Theater Chains		Film X	Film Y	Bundle
		Values ($000)		
Theater Chains	Chain 1	13	6	19
	Chain 2	7	11	18

Depending on the circumstances, a firm can increase its revenue via bundling.

(b)

		Film X	Film Y	Bundle
		Values ($000)		
Theater Chains	Chain 1	13	6	19
	Chain 2	7	11	18
	Chain 3	15	2	17
	Marginal Cost	5	5	10

make up the two chains values film X at $13,000 or $7,000, with each value equally likely. In turn, each theater values film Y at $11,000 or $6,000, again with each value equally likely. (Like coin tosses, a theater's value for one film is independent of its value for the other.) Thus, the same numbers in Table 12A.1a apply but with new interpretations. As before, the studio's optimal separate film prices are $P_X = \$7,000$ and $P_Y = \$6,000$, inducing all theaters to purchase both films. Now consider the demand for the films as a bundle. From the values in Table 12A.1, the possible bundled values are $13,000 (25 percent of theaters), $18,000, (25 percent), $19,000 (25 percent), and $24,000 (25 percent). If the studio sets $P_B = \$13,000$, all theaters purchase the film. However, the studio can do better by raising its price to $P_B = \$18,000$, inducing 75 percent of the theaters to purchase the bundle. To check this, note that only the "$13,000" theaters refuse to buy. The studio's revenue is $(18,000)(750) = \$13,500,000$. In short, even with independent demands, bundling has a revenue advantage over separate sales. (Check for yourself that raising the bundled price above $18,000 is counterproductive.)

MIXED BUNDLING   Thus far, our discussion has centered on the potential advantages of so-called pure bundling vis-à-vis separate sales. Of course, firms frequently offer customers both options: to purchase the bundle or to buy only one of the goods at a separate price. This policy is termed **mixed bundling**.

Table 12A.1b demonstrates the advantage of mixed bundling. Following our original interpretation, chains 1 and 2 have negatively correlated values for the films (the same values as before). We have modified the example in two ways. First, we have added a third buyer, chain 3, which places a very low value on film Y. (Think of chain 3's theaters spread throughout retirement communities. Film X is *Everyone Loves Gramma* and film Y is *Horror on Prom Night*.) Second, we have introduced a cost associated with producing and selling the film. (The $5,000 cost in the example reflects the studio's cost of creating extra prints of the film for distribution to theaters.)[2]

Now consider the studio's possible pricing strategies. Its most profitable pure-bundling strategy is to set $P_B = \$17,000$ and to sell to all three chains (1,500 theaters), giving it total profit: $\pi = (17,000 - 10,000)(1,500) = \$10,500,000$. (Check that setting $P_B = \$18,000$ and selling only to chains X and Y is less profitable.) Alternatively, the studio can pursue mixed bundling: pricing the bundle at $P_B = \$18,000$ and pricing the separate films at $P_X = \$15,000$ and $P_Y = \$12,000$. Given these prices, chains 1 and 2 purchase the bundle, while chain 3 purchases only film X. Therefore, the studio's total profit is: $(18,000 - 10,000)(1,000) + (15,000 - 5,000)(500) = \$13,000,000$. Relative to pure bundling, mixed bundling has increased the studio's profit by $2,500,000.

---

[2] In Table 12A.1a, we ignored marginal costs for the purpose of keeping things simple. It is easy to check (after computing profits rather than revenues) that pure bundling becomes even more advantageous if marginal costs are present.

What is the source of this $2,500,000 advantage? First, the studio gains by raising the bundled price paid by chains 1 and 2 from $17,000 (under pure bundling) to $18,000, thereby increasing its profit by $1,000,000. Second, under pure bundling, chain 3 was induced to buy film Y—a film that costs $5,000 per print but only returns $2,000 to chain 3 in value. Mixed bundling precludes this purchase and transfers the savings, $(5,000 - 2,000)(500) = \$1,500,000$, to the studio in added profit. In short, these two gains, $1,000,000 + $1,500,000, account for the total $2,500,000 increase in profit.

In this example, mixed bundling is more profitable than pure bundling, but this need not be the case in general. As the example shows, the potential advantage of mixed bundling occurs when there are significant marginal costs associated with separate goods and some consumers place very low values on some goods. Under these circumstances, allowing separate purchases via mixed bundling benefits both buyer and seller. Absent these conditions, pure bundling or even separate sales may be more profitable.

Finally, the case of mixed bundling clearly underscores a basic point: At bottom, bundling (of either sort) is a form of price discrimination.[3] In effect, bundling represents a quantity discount; the price of the package is far less than the sum of the separate goods' prices. As the foregoing example showed, a particular customer may put a much lower value on one item in the bundle than another. By offering the "second" item in the bundle at minimal extra cost, the firm lures additional purchasers and increases its revenue in the process.

TYING   Closely related to bundling, **tying** occurs when a firm selling one product requires (or attempts to require) the purchase of another of its related products. For instance, 30 years ago customers who leased Xerox copiers were required to buy Xerox paper. Although strict requirements are rare today, companies continue to try to induce customers to purchase related items. Kodak promotes its quality film and developing paper as ideal for its cameras. Microsoft Corporation claims that its applications programs work best with its Windows operating systems. General Motors insists that genuine GM replacement parts are essential for its cars and trucks.

A firm has several reasons for tying. First, it is one way to ensure peak performance for the good or service. By ensuring quality, the firm protects its brand name and reputation. For instance, McDonald's insists that all its franchise restaurants buy materials and food from itself. Second, the firm can use tie-in sales as a subtle form of price discrimination. By charging a price above marginal cost for the complementary product (e.g., copier paper), the firm can effectively require intensive users of its main product (the copier) to pay a higher (total) price than average users. Thus, the firm can effectively segment

---

[3] Price discrimination and related practices are discussed in the latter half of Chapter 3.

the market according to differing demands. Third, even if there are no differences in buyers, tying presents the opportunity to gain a "captive audience" of buyers for the complementary product. The result is relatively inelastic demand and substantial price markups and profits for the firm. (For instance, the average list price of an American-made automobile is about $18,000. But the cost of buying all its parts separately, at replacement-part prices, would be over $50,000, even before assembly.) In some cases, a firm might well find it advantageous to discount its main product (even price it below average cost) in order to generate a customer base for highly profitable tie-in sales.

THE BUNDLED SOFTWARE WARS   The year 1993 marked the beginning of the "suite" wars among software suppliers. Suites are bundles of application programs, such as word processing, spreadsheets, and graphics, sold as a package at steeply discounted prices. The "street" price of a suite is only 35 to 50 percent of the total cost of the programs purchased separately.

The software suite is a classic (and an extraordinarily successful) example of mixed bundling. Suite sales have been growing much faster than the sales of individual computer programs. For Microsoft Corporation, which pioneered this selling strategy, suites have been the key to winning the battles in the word-processing and spreadsheet arenas. One reason for this success is the extra value suites deliver to customers. Suites integrate the look and feel of the bundled programs (not to mention the documentation), thus making them much easier and more powerful to use. A second reason for the suite appeal is the chance to extract increased revenue from purchasers. As in our earlier examples, a customer who purchases the complete bundle of programs at a discount price might have bought only one or two at separate prices. A third reason is that suites tend to blunt the cutthroat competition for software consumers. When a customer chooses one company's suite over another, he or she tends to be linked to that company for years to come, through upgrades and new products.

A fourth reason stems from the competitive strategy of Microsoft itself. In the early 1990s, the company sold over 85 percent of the operating systems used in personal computers but was an "also ran" in the separate markets for word-processing programs and spreadsheet programs. In 1992, Corel's WordPerfect and IBM's Lotus 1-2-3 programs were the runaway market leaders in word processing and spreadsheets. By creating a new market for bundled and integrated applications, Microsoft elevated its Word and Excel programs to market leaders. In 1995, more than half of all business offices used WordPerfect and Lotus 1-2-3. Today, Microsoft's Office suite commands 95 percent of the suite market (with 3 percent for Lotus's Smartsuite and 2 percent for Corel's WordPerfect suite). Microsoft has won the suite wars.

Problems

1. Peter's Restaurant lists separate prices for all the items on its dinner menu. Chez Pierre offers only a fixed-price complete dinner (with patrons choosing from a list of appetizers, entrées, and desserts). Casa Pedro offers complete dinners at a fixed price and an à la carte menu. Under what different circumstances might these respective pricing schemes make economic sense? Explain briefly.

*2. A firm sells two goods in a market consisting of three types of consumers. The table shows the values consumers place on the goods. The unit cost of producing each good is $10.

		Good	
		Good X	Good Y
	A	$8	$20
Consumers	B	14	14
	C	20	8

Find the optimal prices for (1) selling the goods separately, (2) pure bundling, and (3) mixed bundling. Which pricing strategy is most profitable?

---

*Starred problems are more challenging.

CHAPTER 13

Game Theory and Competitive Strategy

It is a remarkable fact that business strategies are played largely in the mind. Only a small part of the play appears in overt action. Its full scope and depth lie in the players' looking backward and forward and running through their minds their alternative moves and countermoves.

JOHN McDONALD, THE GAME OF BUSINESS

A Battle for Air Passengers

Three airlines (A, B, and C) are competing for passengers on a lucrative long-haul air route. At present, the carriers are charging identical fares ($225 for a one-way ticket), the result of a truce in recent price wars. The airlines currently compete for market share via the number of scheduled daily departures they offer. Each airline must make a decision on its desired number of departures for the coming month—without knowing its rivals' plans ahead of time. Each airline is aware of the following facts:

1. The size of the total daily passenger market is stable irrespective of the number of departures offered. At current prices, an estimated 2,000 passengers fly the route each day.

2. Each airline's share of these total passengers equals its share of the total flights offered by the three airlines. (For example, if airline A offers twice as many flights as each of its rivals, it claims half of all passengers and B and C obtain 25 percent shares.)

3. The airlines fly identical planes and have identical operating costs. Each plane holds a maximum of 200 passengers. Regardless of the plane's loading (full, half full, and so on), each one-way trip on the route costs the airline $20,000.

As the manager of one of these airlines, how many departures should you schedule for the coming month? After seeing the first month's results (your rivals' choices and the resulting airline profits), what decisions would you make for the second month and subsequent months?

In pursuing his or her objectives, how should a decision maker choose a course of action in competition with rivals who are acting in their own interests? This is the essential question addressed by the discipline of **game theory**. We will apply this approach to the specific problem of firms competing within a market. In this context, we could just as well call our approach "strategic profit analysis." Nonetheless, the more general term, *game theory*, remains apt. This name emphasizes the kind of logical analysis evident in games of pure strategy—chess, poker, even war games. As we shall see, strategic considerations are equally important when firms vie for market share, engage in patent races, wage price wars, and enter new markets. Indeed, it is fair to say that over the last 25 years, the game-theoretic approach has been at the heart of the most important advances in understanding competitive strategies.

The key presumption of game theory is that each decision maker (or "player") acts rationally in pursuing his or her own interest and recognizes that competitors also act rationally.[1] Although rational behavior may be directed toward a variety of goals, the usual operational meaning is that all players pursue profit-maximizing strategies and expect competitors to do likewise. (In this sense, the models of quantity and price competition discussed in the preceding chapter are game-theoretic models.)

SIZING UP COMPETITIVE SITUATIONS

A convenient way to begin our discussion is with an overview of the basic game-theoretic elements of competitive situations. We begin with elements *common to all* competitive situations.

1. **Players and Their Actions.** If it is to have a strategic interest, the competitive situation must involve two or more players whose choices of actions affect each other. (It is customary to use *player* as a catch-all term. Depending on the context, a player may be a private individual, a manager, a firm, a government decision maker, a military leader, a representative of a group or coalition, you name it.) In the example

[1] The publication in 1944 of *The Theory of Games and Economic Behavior*, by Oskar Morgenstern and John Von Neumann, launched the discipline of game theory. The first 35 years were marked by theoretical advancements and applications to economics, international relations, and conflict studies. The last 25 years have seen an explosion of interest in extending and applying game theory in such diverse areas as management science, economics, political science, evolutionary biology, and especially competitive strategy.

opening this chapter, the players are the managers of three competing airlines. Each must decide what action to take—what number of daily departures to fly along the air route in question. By deliberate intent, this example considers only one kind of action. Generally, an airline's operations on a single air route involve decisions about prices, schedules, plane configurations, in-flight services, advertising, and so on. In the broader context of industry competition, an airline strategy would encompass marketing decisions (advertising, the use of computerized reservation systems, and frequent-flier programs), investment decisions (ordering planes, expanding terminals, and choosing hubs), manpower and labor decisions, and merger and acquisition strategies.

2. **Outcomes and Payoffs.** The firm's action, together with actions taken by its rivals, determines the outcome of the competition. (If risks of the type discussed in Chapters 8 and 9 are important, there will be a range of outcomes with probabilities attached.) In the battle for air passengers, the three airlines' numbers of departures completely determine their market shares (and the number of tickets they sell). Associated with any outcome is a payoff that embodies each competitor's ultimate objective or goal. For a private firm, such as an airline, this payoff usually is measured in terms of monetary profit. (In some instances, the payoffs take the form of costs that are to be minimized.) In other situations, payoffs take nonmonetary forms. In a war, payoffs might be expressed in terms of territory taken, number of enemy killed, and so on. In the race for the U.S. presidency, payoffs might be counted in electoral college votes. In trade negotiations, payoffs might be measured by the size and extent of tariff reductions. In short, a payoff summarizes and measures the preferences of a given player.

3. **Underlying "Rules."** Just as important as the players, actions, outcomes, and payoffs are the formal and informal rules that govern the behavior of the competitors. One category of rules includes generally agreed-upon competitive practices, laws, and specific industry regulations. For instance, before 1978, the airline industry operated under strict government regulations. Airlines could not change fares or service on new routes without prior regulatory approval. In the current era of deregulation, price and entry constraints have been dropped. Nonetheless, myriad antitrust rules and regulations prohibit price collusion, unfair practices, and mergers that would increase monopoly power. A second category of "rules" provides a framework to model the competition. They specify whether competitors take actions simultaneously or sequentially. If sequentially, who moves first, second, or last? These rules also describe

what each competitor knows about the others' preferences and previous moves at the time it takes action. In the battle for air passengers, airlines set their number of departures independently and without knowing their competitors' decisions. Quite different strategic issues would arise if one airline always was first to set its departure schedule with the other two free to set their schedules afterward.[2]

Equally important, competitive situations *differ* across a number of dimensions.

1. **Number of Competitors.** The number of competitors is one fundamental way to categorize competitive situations. We distinguish between settings with two competitors (so-called two-person games) and those with more than two (n-person or many-person games). In a two-person game, you and your adversary have conflicting interests to a greater or lesser degree. In the preceding chapter, we considered quantity and price competition between duopolists. In Chapter 16, we will examine two-party negotiations between buyer and seller, management and labor, and plaintiff and defendant. Frequently, one can analyze multicompetitor settings as if they involved only two parties: the firm in question and all other competitors. This is true in the battle for air passengers. One airline's market share depends on its own number of departures and on the *total* departures by its competitors (not the particular breakdown). Thus, an airline need only anticipate the average decisions of its competitors to determine its own best response.

When there are more than two interested parties, new analytical considerations enter. First, one has to distinguish the differing interests of the multiple parties. For instance, when a mediator or arbitrator intervenes in two-party disputes, this third party's actions and preferences influence the final outcome. Second, with multiple parties, there is the possibility (even the likelihood) that some of the competitors will form coalitions to deal more effectively with the others. Cartels form to attempt to exercise market power as a group; companies form trade associations to lobby for common interests; workers join unions; and nations sign mutual aid treaties. When coalitions are present, an important issue is their stability. How likely is it that members of one coalition will break with their original

---

[2]Again, there is a ready analogy with parlor games: card games, chess, checkers, Go, and other board games. Any conventional game specifies the players, their available actions, their payoffs (including what constitutes winning), and the rules (the order of play, the limits of communication, and so on).

partners to join others, form new coalitions, or strike out on their own? Which group would it be most advantageous to join?

2. **Degree of Mutual Interest.** There are some situations in which the interests of the competitors are strictly opposed; one side's gain is the other side's loss. At the end of a poker game, for example, there is simply an exchange of dollars. Since winnings are balanced by losses, the total net gain of the players together is equal to zero. In the terminology of game theory, this type of competitive situation is called a **zero-sum game**. The zero-sum game may be thought of as one extreme—that of pure conflict. At the other extreme are situations of pure common interest—situations in which "competitors" win or lose together, and both prefer the same outcome. Real-world examples of either pure cooperation or pure conflict, however, are the exception. The vast majority of competitive situations lies between these extremes. Here the players exhibit varying degrees of common interest and competition. Because different outcomes can lead to very different (and nonoffsetting) gains and losses for the competitors, these situations are designated **non-zero-sum games**.

As we shall see, the battle for air passengers is a non-zero-sum competition. Certainly, airlines are competing for passengers and are out to gain them, possibly at their rivals' expense. But they also recognize that flooding the market with flights can be suicidal for all. (After all, total demand is limited and extra flights are costly.) In Chapter 16, labor and management find themselves in a similar position during contract negotiations. Each side seeks to secure better contract terms for itself. But both have an interest in avoiding a costly strike. In short, a realistic description of managerial strategies in competitive settings must take into account elements of common interest as well as conflict.

3. **Communication and Agreement among Competitors.** In the battle for passengers, the competing airlines make independent decisions. If the battle turns bitter and all airlines set numerous flights, the eventual outcome may well be losses for all carriers. By contrast, if rival airlines were allowed to communicate their intentions and coordinate their operations, one would expect them to agree to mutual flight reductions. (One also would expect cooperation on other competitive dimensions, such as higher prices, less generous frequent-flier programs, and so on.)

A competitive situation is called **noncooperative** if players are unable (or are not allowed) to communicate and coordinate their behavior. For instance, the airlines, like almost all competing firms in the United States, are required by law to play noncooperatively; any form of collusion is prohibited. The situation is **cooperative** if players can communicate before taking action and form binding agreements about what joint actions to take. A cartel, such as OPEC, in which a group of firms agrees on price and output policy, is an example of a cooperative setting.

In general, the more the players' interests coincide, the more significant is their ability (or inability) to communicate. In a two-person zero-sum game, communication cannot benefit either competitor. My gain is your loss, so there is nothing to agree about. On the other hand, when there is pure common interest, the problem is entirely one of communication. In settings involving both common and conflicting interests, communication, if permitted, plays a complex role in determining the outcome. Sometimes competitors can communicate to a limited degree (as with public pronouncements) but must stop short of actual agreement on a mutual course of action. Frequently, these communications—threats, promises, or even bluffs—are intended to influence a competitor's behavior. Other times, firms take actions to "signal" their intent to one another, without explicitly communicating. In addition, tacit communication can play a role, as when "understandings" among competitors develop. Finally, in negotiation settings, parties are free to communicate as they please in attempting to reach an agreement. Of course, the give-and-take of communication, including offers and counteroffers, is crucial for negotiations.

4. **Repeated or One-Shot Competition.** Another important distinction is whether the competition is one shot or ongoing—that is, whether the same parties will be involved in similar situations in the future. For instance, competition among airlines is ongoing. Similarly, when management and union representatives negotiate a contract, they recognize that the bargaining will repeat itself three or so years down the road when the new contract expires. By contrast, a buyer and seller negotiating a house sale are unlikely to meet again. In one-shot situations, competitors usually are out for all they can get. In an ongoing competition, they often behave much differently. All they can get now is tempered by the impact on what they might get in the future. If management negotiates too stringent a contract this time, the union may be more militant the next time. As we shall see, if a noncooperative situation is repeated or ongoing, a clear opportunity is provided for tacit communication and understanding to take place over time.

5. **Amount of Information.** The degree of information one competitor has about another is one of the most important factors in a competitive situation. In many industries, secrecy is crucial. Detroit's automakers carefully guard their new designs. At the same

time, some firms invest large sums attempting to obtain information about their competitors. Indeed, some feel that much can be gained by analyzing a competitive situation, particularly a bargaining one, in terms of the information firms possess about one another. Management usually knows who its main rivals are, but it may have only sketchy knowledge of their intentions, views, and ultimate objectives. Normally, the firm has limited information about the innermost workings of its competitors' organizations, such as their resource-allocation decisions and costs. This raises the questions: What would management like to know about its competitors? What would management like them to believe about its own intentions?

In the rest of this chapter, we focus primarily on two-party settings under perfect information, that is, where the firms have all immediately relevant information about each other. (Examples of competitive settings with imperfect information and two or more players are presented in Chapters 16 and 17.) Our discussion spans the differences raised in items 2, 3, and 4. We take up zero-sum and non-zero-sum games and explore the implications of repetition and tacit communication.

ANALYZING PAYOFF TABLES

The starting point for a game-theoretic analysis of any competitive situation is a description of the players, their strategies, and their payoffs. Here is a motivating example.

JOCKEYING IN THE TV RATINGS GAME   The profits of the three major television networks—CBS, NBC, and ABC—depend significantly on the ratings achieved by their prime-time programs. The higher the ratings, the higher the price the network can charge for advertising and the greater the number of advertising spots it can sell. To keep things simple, we restrict our attention to NBC and CBS (the two ratings leaders during the last decade) and focus on their programming decisions for the 8-to-9 P.M. and 9-to-10 P.M. slots on a particular weeknight. The networks must decide which hour-long programs from last season to pencil into the slots. Each network's main concern is when to schedule its "hit" show—at 8 P.M. or 9 P.M. The other time slot will be filled by a "run-of-the-mill" program.

Here the focus of competition is between two players, NBC and CBS. Each network has two possible actions, or strategies: to run its hit show at 8 P.M. or 9 P.M. The essential elements of any two-player competitive decision can be described by a two-dimensional **payoff table**. According to the standard format, the first player's alternative actions are listed along the rows of

TABLE 13.1

	CBS			
	Schedule Hit at 8 P.M.		Schedule Hit at 9 P.M.	
NBC Schedule Hit at 8 P.M.	36 (21 + 15)	33 (19 + 14)	39 (25 + 14)	28 (11 + 17)
Schedule Hit at 9 P.M.	30 (13 + 17)	36 (20 + 16)	32 (16 + 16)	30 (16 + 14)

A TV Ratings Battle

Each network's dominant strategy is to schedule its "hit" at 8 P.M. The left-hand entry in each cell lists NBC's total number of viewers (in millions). The right-hand entry lists CBS's total viewers. Figures in parentheses divide total viewers between 8 P.M. and 9 P.M.

the table; the second player's possible actions are listed along the columns. The payoff table in Table 13.1 is an example. NBC's possible actions are listed along the rows and CBS's actions along the columns. For any combination of actions, the resulting payoffs to the networks are shown under the corresponding row and column. By convention, the first (i.e., row) player's payoff is listed first. In the table, each network's payoff is measured by the projected *total* number of viewers (in millions) over the two-hour period. For instance, if each network leads with its hit show at 8 P.M., NBC's audience will be 36 million viewers and CBS's will be 33 million. The table also shows the number of viewers during each hour. Although the disaggregated figures are of some interest in their own right, what ultimately matters to each network is its total audience.[3]

In the ratings battle, each network's sole interest is in maximizing its total audience.[4] With this goal in mind, what is each network's optimal action? Table 13.1 provides a relatively simple answer: Each network should schedule

[3] The hourly viewer numbers reflect a number of facts. First, the total number of viewers is larger during the 8-to-9 P.M. slot than during the 9-to-10 P.M. slot. Second, during a given hour, the more highly rated a network's show (and the less highly rated its competitor), the larger the network's audience. Third, a portion of viewers watching a network's show from 8 to 9 P.M. continues to stay tuned to that network during the 9-to-10 P.M. slot.

[4] In different contexts, a player's payoff may take many forms: a monetary value (such as revenue, cost, or profit), a litigation victory, the number of electoral votes won, market share, and so on. The general point is that the payoff is meant to capture *everything* the decision maker cares about—his or her ultimate objective or utility to be maximized (or, if a cost, to be minimized). One implication of this point is that comparisons of player payoffs are *not* meaningful. For instance, if player 1 faces the payoff entries (5, −3), he derives no welfare from the fact that the other player makes a loss. The player's welfare is completely captured by his own five units of profit. The player fares better with the payoff (6, 10). In short, his or her motives are neither competitive nor altruistic; they are simply self-interested.

its hit show in the 8-to-9 P.M. slot. To confirm this, first take NBC's point of view. To find its own best course of action, NBC must anticipate the behavior of its rival. Obviously, there are two cases to consider:

1. If CBS schedules its hit at 8 P.M., NBC should follow suit. By doing so, its total audience is 36. NBC's alternative—placing its hit at 9 P.M.— would deliver a smaller audience of 30. Leading with its hit is NBC's best response if CBS leads with its hit.

2. If CBS schedules its hit at 9 P.M., NBC's best response would continue to be leading with its hit. (An audience of 39 million is better than an audience of 32 million.)

In short, regardless of CBS's action, NBC's audience-maximizing response is to schedule its hit at 8 P.M.

A **dominant strategy** is a best response to *any* strategy that the other player might pick. Thus, we have shown that scheduling its hit at 8 P.M. is NBC's dominant strategy. By similar reasoning, CBS's dominant strategy is to lead with its hit. (If NBC schedules its hit at 8 P.M., CBS prefers a 33 million audience to a 28 million audience; if NBC puts its hit at 9 P.M., CBS prefers a 36 million audience to a 30 million audience.) The predicted outcome of the ratings battle is for each network to use its dominant strategy, that is, schedule its hit at 8 P.M. This results in audience shares of 36 million and 33 million, respectively.

As a simple variation on this example, suppose CBS is aware that scheduling its hit against NBC's hit would be suicidal. (Imagine NBC's hit to be the top-rated show.) To illustrate, change CBS's top-left entry in Table 13.1 from 33 to 25. How does this change CBS's behavior? Now CBS's best response is to put its hit at 9 P.M. if NBC schedules its hit at 8 P.M. (Of course, CBS's best response is to put its hit at 8 P.M. if NBC schedules its hit at 9 P.M.) In other words, CBS should set its schedule to avoid a showdown of hit shows. CBS no longer has a dominant strategy; rather, its best response depends on what NBC does. Nonetheless, its optimal action is easy to determine. NBC surely will choose to schedule its hit at 8 P.M., because this is its dominant strategy. Anticipating this, CBS should place its hit at 9 P.M. as a best response.[5] The network outcomes are audiences of 39 million and 28 million viewers, respectively.

In this variation on the basic example, CBS's optimal action requires a simple kind of *reflexive* thinking: putting itself in NBC's shoes. Notice that the predicted outcome has the property that each player's strategy is a best response against the chosen strategy of the other. Thus, neither network could improve its profit by second-guessing the other and moving to a different strategy.

---

[5] This mode of reasoning often is referred to as *iterated dominance.* In general, the elimination of a *dominated* strategy of a competitor may allow a player to eliminate one or more of his or her own strategies from consideration.

Consider the following competition between two department stores, each of which must decide what kind of clothing to promote. Does either store have a dominant strategy? What is the predicted outcome?

		Store 2	
		Promote Girls' Clothes	Promote Women's Clothes
Store 1	Promote Girls' Clothes	0, 0	4, 2
	Promote Children's Clothes	2, 2	2, 4

Equilibrium Strategies

What action should a decision maker take to achieve his objectives when competing with or against another individual acting in her own interests? The principal answer supplied by game theory is this:

> In settings where competitors choose actions independently of one another (and so cannot collude), each player should use an equilibrium strategy, one that maximizes each player's expected payoff against the strategy chosen by the other. This is known as a *Nash equilibrium.*

In both versions of the ratings battle example, the predicted outcome satisfies this definition, that is, is an equilibrium. The following example illustrates a competitive setting in which *neither* side has a dominant strategy. Nonetheless, each side has an equilibrium strategy, and that is how each should play.

MARKET-SHARE COMPETITION   Consider two duopolists who compete fiercely for shares of a market that is of *constant* size. (The market is mature with few growth opportunities.) Each firm can adopt one of three marketing strategies in an attempt to win customers from the other. The payoff table in Table 13.2 depicts the percentage increase in market share of firm 1 (the row player). For instance, if both firms adopt their first strategies, firm 1 loses (and firm 2 gains) two share points. As described, the market-share competition is a **zero-sum game**. The competitors' interests are strictly opposed; one side's gain is the other side's loss. This being the case, it is customary to list only the row player's payoffs. The row player seeks to maximize its payoff, while the column player seeks to keep this payoff to a minimum. By doing so, firm 2 maximizes its own increase in market share.

TABLE 13.2

			Firm 2		
Competitive Advertising in a Mature Market			C1	C2	C3
		R1	$\boxed{-2}$	-1	④
In this zero-sum game, the firms' equilibrium strategies are R2 and C2.	Firm 1	R2	5	$\boxed{②}$	3
		R3	⑦	-3	$\boxed{-5}$

In the advertising competition, there is a single equilibrium pair of strategies: R2 versus C2. The resulting payoff (two here) is called the *equilibrium outcome*. To check that this is an equilibrium, consider in turn each firm's options. Against C2, the best firm 1 can do is use R2. Switching to R1 or R3 means suffering a loss of market share. Similarly, the best firm 2 can do against R2 is use C2. If it switches to C1 or C3, it grants firm 1 a greater share increase, implying a greater loss in market share for itself. Thus, the strategies R2 and C2 are profit maximizing against each other and constitute a Nash equilibrium.

To check that this is the only equilibrium, let's identify each firm's best response (i.e., its most profitable action) to any action taken by its competitor. Firm 1's best response to C1 is R3, to C2 is R2, and to C3 is R1. Certainly, if firm 1 could anticipate firm 2's action, it would use its best response against it. In Table 13.2, the payoffs from firm 1's best responses to firm 2's possible actions are circled. The circles offer visual proof of the fact that firm 1 has no dominant strategy. (Why? If a strategy were dominant, all the circles would line up along the same row.) The table also identifies firm 2's best responses: Its best response to R1 is C1, to R2 is C2, and to R3 is C3. The resulting payoffs are enclosed in squares. (Firm 2 has no dominant strategy.) The circles and squares make it easy to identify the equilibrium outcome and strategies. A payoff is an equilibrium outcome if and only if it is enclosed by *both* a circle and a square; that is, it must be a best-response strategy for both players. Thus, we confirm that 2 is the unique equilibrium outcome; R2 versus C2 are the equilibrium strategies that generate this outcome.

The best a "smart" player can expect to get in a zero-sum game against an equally smart player is his or her equilibrium outcome. If either side deviates from its equilibrium play, it reduces its own payoff and increases the competitor's payoff. Indeed, there should be no real uncertainty about how the game will be played. Each side should anticipate equilibrium behavior from the other. The resulting equilibrium outcome is called the *value* of the game.[6]

---

[6] A zero-sum game always possesses an equilibrium. The value of the game is unique; there cannot be two equilibria having different values. However, equilibrium behavior may require the use of randomized actions (so-called "mixed" strategies) by the players. We discuss the use of mixed strategies in the appendix to this chapter.

The following payoff table lists the respective market shares of the two firms and provides an alternative way of viewing the advertising competition. Indeed, it is derived directly from Table 13.2 under the assumption that the firms' initial shares are 45 percent and 55 percent, respectively. For instance, according to Table 13.2, the play of R1 versus C1 results in a two-percentage-point loss for firm 1; this translates into 43 percent and 57 percent market shares in the table. Given the form of the payoff table, explain why this competition can be referred to as a constant-sum game. Determine the equilibrium. Is there any strategic difference between a zero-sum game and a constant-sum game?

| | | Firm 2 | | |
		C1	C2	C3
	R1	43, 57	44, 56	49, 51
Firm 1	R2	50, 50	47, 53	48, 52
	R3	52, 48	42, 58	40, 60

A REMINDER   It is important to distinguish clearly between a Nash equilibrium that involves dominant strategies and one that does not. Here is the difference:

> In a dominant-strategy equilibrium, each player chooses an action that is a best response against any action the other might take.
>
> In a Nash equilibrium, each player takes an action that is a best response to the action the other takes.

Both kinds of equilibria share the essential feature of stability. In equilibrium, there is no "second-guessing"; it is impossible for either side to increase its payoff by unilaterally deviating from its chosen strategy.

The concepts differ in one important respect. When a player has a dominant strategy, there is no circumstance in which doing anything else ever makes sense. The player always should use this strategy. Of course, in many, if not most, competitive situations, players will not have available a single strategy that is dominant. However, as in the market-share competition, there still will be a Nash equilibrium. Here each side's action is a best response against the other's. As long as each competitor is smart enough to recognize the Nash equilibrium and expect the other to do likewise, this is how each should play.

But what if one player is not so smart? Consider the market-share battle once again. Suppose the manager of firm 2 is convinced that firm 1 plans to use strategy R3. This might not seem to be a very smart move by firm 1. (Perhaps it is lured to R3 by the mistaken hope of a +7 payoff.) But let's say that there is ample evidence that this is how firm 1 will play. (It already has begun launching the R3 advertising campaign.) Then, surely, firm 2 should choose C3, gaining a 5 percent share increase at firm 1's expense. By changing from C2 to C3, firm 2 can profit from firm 1's mistake. The point is this: In a Nash equilibrium (unlike a dominant-strategy equilibrium), there exist some circumstances where it might pay to use a nonequilibrium strategy. If one player deviates from equilibrium (by mistake or for any other reason), the other player may be able to improve its payoff by deviating also.

Are we recommending nonequilibrium play in Table 13.2 for either firm? Certainly not. Equilibrium play is quite transparent and should be grasped readily by both sides.[7] But, in a different setting where there is reason to anticipate one player deviating from equilibrium play, the other player may be able to profit from that action by deviating (optimally) as well.

CHECK STATION 3   In Chapter 12's example of dueling suppliers, each firm had constant unit costs $AC = MC = \$6$, and market demand was described by $P = 30 - (Q_1 + Q_2)$, where output is measured in thousands of units. The following payoff table lists the firm's profits for three levels of output. Choose one entry and check that the payoffs are correct. Does either firm have a dominant strategy? From the table, the firms appear to prefer outputs of 6,000 units each. Explain why this is not an equilibrium outcome. Find the firms' equilibrium quantities. (Confirm that this matches the answer derived algebraically in Chapter 12.)

		Firm 2's Quantity (000s)		
		6	8	10
	6	72, 72	60, 80	48, 80
Firm 1's Quantity (000s)	8	80, 60	64, 64	48, 60
	10	80, 48	60, 48	40, 40

THE PRISONER'S DILEMMA ONCE AGAIN   Before concluding this section, we take a brief second look at the paradigm of the prisoner's dilemma (PD) introduced in Chapter 12. The top portion of Table 13.3 reproduces the price-war payoffs of Table 12.2. The middle portion of the table portrays a different sort of PD: an arms race between a pair of superpowers. Finally, the bottom portion uses symbolic payoffs to represent the generic features of the prisoner's dilemma.

---

[7] There is an additional argument for the equilibrium play of R2 and C2. Each strategy is very *robust*; that is, it does well against a range of behavior by the other side. For instance, what if firm 1 assessed the following probabilities for firm 2's actions: C1 (.2 probability), C2 (.6), and C3 (.2)? In firm 1's view, there is considerable room for firm 2 to make a mistake one way or the other. Using these probabilities and the payoffs in Table 13.2, we compute firm 1's *expected* payoff from R2 to be: $(.2)(5) + (.6)(2) + (.2)(3) = 2.8$. As one easily can check, firm 1 earns a much greater expected payoff from R2 than it does from R1 or R3. A little bit of sensitivity analysis shows that it pays to use R2, unless firm 2 is very likely to use C1 or C3. A similar analysis shows that firm 2's choice of C2 is also robust; that is, C2 remains a best response over a wide range of probabilities for firm 1's actions.

TABLE 13.3

(a) A Price War

Firm 2

		High Price	Low Price
Firm 1	High Price	10, 10	5, 12
	Low Price	12, 5	7, 7

In each case, the play of dominant strategies leads to inferior group outcomes.

(b) An Arms Race

Superpower 2

		Disarm	Build Arms
Superpower 1	Disarm	10, 10	$-50, 12$
	Build Arms	20, -50	$-20, -20$

(c) A Generic
     Prisoner's Dilemma

Player 2

		Cooperate	Defect
Player 1	Cooperate	R, R	S, T
	Defect	T, S	P, P

T = Temptation
R = Reward
P = Penalty
S = Sucker

$$T > R > P > S$$

Although particular payoffs vary, the strategic implications of the three payoff tables are the same. Assuming noncooperative play (i.e., no possibility of communication or collusion), self-interest dictates the play of dominant strategies. In the price war, a low price is most profitable, regardless of the competitor's price. Similarly, an arms buildup is the dominant strategy in the arms race. Finally, in the generic prisoner's dilemma, defection from the cooperative solution is the dominant strategy. Note that the temptation payoff from defecting is greater than the reward payoff from cooperation. In turn, the penalty payoff if both players defect is greater than the sucker payoff if only one player cooperates. In short, the logic of dominant strategies inevitably leads to the inferior penalty payoffs under noncooperative play.

What if the "rules" of the competition allow communication between players and binding agreements are possible (i.e., compliance with any agreement can be monitored and enforced)? Under these cooperative ground rules, players should agree to take actions to achieve the mutually beneficial "upper-left" payoffs. Thus, firms would want to agree to charge high prices, and superpowers would strive to negotiate a binding and verifiable arms-control treaty. We will say more about the possibilities of reaching such agreements in our later discussion of repeated competition.

COMPETITIVE STRATEGY

Strategic decisions by managers embrace an interesting mixture of competition and cooperation. Firms compete via price wars, patent races, capacity expansion, and entry deterrence. But they also cooperate via joint ventures, the adoption of common standards, and implicit agreements to maintain high prices. The following competitive situations illustrate this blend of competition and cooperation.

A COMMON STANDARD FOR HIGH-DEFINITION DVDs   By holding several times the amount of information, the next generation of digital video disks (DVDs) will provide strikingly clear picture quality for movies, video games, and computer graphics. Although the technological hurdles have been overcome, a key strategic question remains: Which technology standard and format for DVDs will be adopted worldwide? In one camp, Sony Corporation leads a number of companies including Samsung, Philips, Dell Computer, and Hewlett-Packard promoting the so-called Blu-ray format. The opposing side, led by Toshiba Corporation and backed by NEC Corporation and Microsoft, have developed the HD format.[8] Each format has its advantages, but each is incompatible with the other. For more than two years, the corporate players have been forming alliances and pushing their preferred formats. Negotiations concerning the standards dispute have been overseen by the DVD forum, an industry group having some 200 corporate members. However, there has been no resolution of the conflict to date. To complicate matters, China has recently proposed a third DVD format that it alone would control.

Table 13.4 shows the (hypothetical) payoffs to the two opposing camps associated with the competing standards. Not surprisingly, the Sony group's greatest payoff occurs if all sides adopt the Blu-ray format, whereas the Toshiba group's greatest payoff comes with the HD format. However, *coordination* is crucial. Both sides receive much lower payoffs if different, incompatible technologies are chosen (the off-diagonal entries).

[8] This account is based on P. Dvorak, N. Wingfield, and S. McBride, "Technology Titans Battle over Format of DVD Successor," *The Wall Street Journal*, March 15, 2004, A1, and K. Chen, "China Will Keep Pursuing Digital Standards," *The Wall Street Journal*, April 23, 2004, B1.

TABLE 13.4

The Battle for a
Common Technology
Standard

		Toshiba Group	
		Adopt Blu-ray Format	**Adopt HD Format**
Sony Group	**Adopt Blu-ray Format**	100, 50	30, 20
	Adopt HD Format	0, 0	60, 90

The two equilibria
have both sides adopt-
ing the Blu-ray format
or both sides adopting
the HD format.

The payoff table in Table 13.4 has two equilibria: Both adopt the Blu-ray format (upper-left cell), or both adopt the HD format (lower-right cell). Each is an equilibrium because if one side adopts a given format, the best the other can do is follow suit. (Check this.) Coordination on a common standard is in each side's own best interest. The catch is that the sides have strongly opposed views on which standard it should be. We would expect the outcome to be one of the equilibria—but which one? That is a matter of bargaining. In general, rational bargainers should agree on a common standard, but such an agreement is not guaranteed. In fact, the opposing camps have reached no agreement to date. Each plans to go ahead with its own format.

Fortunately, mutual advantage is a strong force behind the emergence of common standards. Twenty years ago, there existed a plethora of operating systems in the emerging personal computer market. Today Microsoft Windows is the dominant standard (85 percent market share).[9] More generally, the world has moved toward a number of common standards: metric measurement, left-hand-steering automobiles, and common principles of international law. (Obviously, countries retain different languages, currencies, customs, and law, even though English, the U.S. dollar, and most recently the euro serve as de facto, partial standards.)

Competitive situations such as that embodied in Table 13.4 are ubiquitous. (Standards setting is but one example.) In fact, they commonly are referred to under the label "battle of the sexes." In that domestic version, husband and wife must decide whether to attend a ball game or the ballet on a given night. Each strongly prefers the other's company to attending an event alone. The two equilibria have husband and wife making the same choice. But which choice? The wife prefers that they both attend the ball game; the husband

[9] The computer industry is a hotbed for battles over standards. Once allies in the development of MS-DOS, IBM and Microsoft Corporation long ago went in separate directions, backing different advanced operating systems, OS/2 and Windows, respectively. The battle over competing versions of UNIX, another powerful operating system, appears to have ended with AT&T's version the winner. The battle for control of the JAVA software standard—between Sun's "pure" JAVA version and Microsoft's "custom" JAVA—continues.

prefers the ballet. Based on past experience, we will not hazard a guess as to the outcome of the domestic discussion and negotiations. The general point is that the battle of the sexes is a model applicable to any bargaining situation.

Market Entry

Consider once again Chapter 1's example of market competition between the two giants of the book business—Barnes & Noble and Borders Group. Each chain is aggressively expanding its number of superstores across the country, often in direct competition with the other. Often the chains are jockeying for the same real estate sites in the same cities.

To model the ongoing competition between the chains, suppose that both are considering a new superstore in a midsize city. Though the city is currently underserved by the area's bookstores, each chain recognizes that book-buying demand is sufficient to support only one superstore profitably. There is not enough market room for two stores. If both chains erect new superstores and split the market, both will suffer losses. (Each firm's net cash flow will be insufficient to cover the high fixed costs of opening a new store.) Table 13.5 shows the firms' payoffs. If one firm stays out, it earns zero profit (regardless of the other firm's action). If it enters, its profit is \$4 million or −\$4 million depending on whether the other firm enters. Clearly, neither firm has a dominant strategy. However, it is easy to identify the two off-diagonal outcomes as equilibria. If firm 1 enters, firm 2's best response is to stay out. Thus, entry by firm 1 alone is an equilibrium. By the same reasoning, entry by firm 2 alone is an equilibrium. ("Both firms entering" is not an equilibrium, nor is "both firms staying out." Check this.)

Rational competitors should reach one of the equilibria, but it is difficult to say which one. Each firm wishes to be the one that enters the market and gains the profit. One way for a player (say, Borders) to claim its desired equilibrium is to be the first to enter. Here there is a **first-mover advantage**. Given the opportunity to make the first move, Borders should enter and preempt the market. Barnes & Noble's best second move is to stay out. By stealing a march on the opposition—that is, being first to market—a firm obtains its preferred equilibrium. Even if the firms require the same amount of time to launch a

TABLE 13.5

Market Entry

There are two equilibria. If one firm enters the market, the other should stay out.

		Borders	
		Stay Out	Enter
Barnes & Noble	Stay Out	0, 0	0, 4
	Enter	4, 0	−4, −4

superstore, Borders can claim a first-mover advantage if it can make a *credible* commitment to enter the market. To be credible, Borders' behavior must convince its rival of its entry commitment;[10] a mere threat to that effect is not enough. A campaign announcing and promoting the new store would be one way to signal the firm's commitment; another would be entering into a binding real estate lease. Of course, sometimes both firms commit to entry with disastrous results.

Boeing and Airbus (a European consortium) compete to sell similar aircraft worldwide. The following table depicts the players' actions and hypothetical payoffs. What are the equilibrium outcomes? How does the outcome change if European governments pay a $40 million production subsidy to Airbus?

CHECK STATION 4

		Airbus	
		Produce	**Do Not Produce**
Boeing	**Produce**	$-20, -20$	$80, 0$
	Do Not Produce	$0, \ \ 80$	$0, 0$

Next versus Sun

A dramatic example of a market-entry battle was the competition in the early 1990s between Next, Inc. and Sun Microsystems, Inc. Next, the brainchild of Steven Jobs, a cofounder of Apple Computer, challenged Sun on two related fronts: in producing powerful corporate workstation computers and in developing "object-oriented" software for workstations and other computers. (This type of software allows programmers to create customized programs by quickly plugging together modular pieces of software rather than starting from scratch.) Because it was already a dominant producer of workstations, Sun enjoyed a powerful first-mover advantage. In vying for dominance in object-oriented software, both companies entered on equal footing. The competition on both fronts was brutal. In Mr. Jobs's words, "They would rather see us dead than alive." The question was whether the market could support two rival systems or even one.

In 1993, Next withdrew as a producer of workstations, having made little headway against Sun and the makers of increasingly powerful PCs, which had become low-cost substitutes for workstations. Next was, indeed, "dead" in the workstation market. However, the outcome in the software rivalry came as a shock to industry observers. In November 1993, the two companies announced an alliance to develop and promote Nextstep, Next's object-oriented software.

---

[10] Competitive situations such as these often are referred to as games of "chicken." Two trucks loaded with dynamite (or two cars loaded with teenagers) are racing toward each other along a one-lane road. The first to swerve out of the way is chicken. The only equilibrium has one side holding true to course and the other swerving. Here the issue of commitment is made in dramatic terms.

Under the agreement, Sun would invest $10 million in Next in return for a 1.5 percent ownership of the company and access to NextStep.

According to the companies, the software alliance could not have come about while they were bitter rivals on the hardware front. Indeed, the alliance was a major strategy reversal for Mr. Jobs. Next, like Apple Computer before it, had been based on "closed" systems, that is, hardware and software that were incompatible with other industry products. Under the alliance, Next would develop NextStep as an open system, compatible with all major computer types.

Bargaining

One of the most fertile domains for applying game theory is in the realm of bargaining and negotiation. The following example is intended to suggest some of the strategic issues that arise in bargaining settings.

BARGAINING OVER THE TERMS OF A TRANSACTION   Two firms, a buyer and a seller, are in negotiations concerning the sale price of a good. Both sides know that the seller's cost to produce the good is $80,000 and that the buyer's value for the good (the maximum amount the firm can pay) is $120,000. Suppose that, before negotiations begin, each side has formulated its final and best offer, a price beyond which it will not concede in the negotiations. In particular, each is considering one of three possible final offers: $90,000, $100,000, or $110,000.

The firms' offers determine the final price as follows. First, if the firms' price offers are incompatible—that is, the seller insists on a price greater than the buyer is willing to pay—there is no agreement, and each side earns a zero profit. Second, if the players' final offers match, then this is the final price. Third, if the buyer's offer exceeds the seller's demand, the final price is midway between the two offers—as if the players conceded at equal rates toward this final price.

Table 13.6 lists the payoffs that result from different combinations of final offers in this stylized bargaining game. For instance, the three zero-profit outcomes in the upper-left portion of the table are the result of incompatible offers. Alternatively, if the buyer's offer is $100,000 and the seller's offer is $90,000, the final price is $95,000. Therefore, the buyer's profit is 120,000 − 95,000 = $25,000 and the seller's profit is 95,000 − 80,000 = $15,000. These profits are shown in the middle-right entry. The other profit entries are computed in analogous fashion.

Table 13.6 displays three distinct equilibria. In the "middle" equilibrium, each side makes a price offer of $100,000 and this is the final agreement. Facing this offer, the best the player can do is match it. Asking for less diminishes one's profit, and asking for more results in a disagreement and a zero profit. Thus, this is an equilibrium. In the lower-left equilibrium, the final price favors the

TABLE 13.6

A Stylized Bargaining
Game

Even the simplest bar-
gaining situations
involve multiple
equilibria.

		Seller Final Offers ($000s)		
		110	100	90
Buyer Final	90	0, 0	0, 0	㉚, ⑩
Offers	100	0, 0	⑳, ⑳	25, 15
($000s)	110	⑩, ㉚	15, 25	20, 20

seller, whereas in the upper-right equilibrium, the final price favors the buyer. Each of these is a legitimate, though not necessarily fair, equilibrium. For instance, against a seller who "plays hardball" and sets $110,000 as her final price, the best the buyer can do is concede by offering $110,000 as well. Twenty-five percent of something is better than 50 percent of nothing.

To keep things simple, we have limited the buyer and seller to three offers. Of course, in actual bargaining, each side's final offer could lie anywhere in the range from $80,000 to $120,000. In general, all matching offers in this range constitute equilibria. The problem is that there are *too many* equilibria. The equilibrium concept does rule out certain outcomes. For instance, the bargaining game should never end in a disagreement. Nevertheless, there are matching equilibrium offers that have the bargainers splitting the total gains from an agreement in any proportion (10-90, 40-60, 70-30, and so on). In Chapter 16, we will say much more about how bargaining tactics can influence which equilibrium is reached.

Sequential Competition

In the competitive settings analyzed thus far, players have taken one-shot actions. Of course, many realistic competitive settings involve a series of actions over time. One firm may make a move, its rival a countermove, and so on. In a **sequential game**, players take turns moving. To portray the sequence of moves, we use a **game tree**. A game tree is a near cousin to the decision trees we encountered in Chapters 8 and 9. However, a game tree goes beyond an ordinary decision tree by including all players' actions in the diagram. As we shall see, when one party makes its current decision, it must look ahead and try to anticipate the actions and reactions of its competitors at their turns in the game tree. To illustrate the method, we start with a compact example.

A multinational firm (MNF) is pondering whether to accept a developing country's (DC) invitation to invest in the development of a copper mine on its soil. Management of MNF is contemplating an agreement in which MNF and DC split the profits from the mine equally. By its estimates, each side's profit is

**An International
Mineral Lease**

worth about $50 million (in net present value). Both sides are aware that any agreement, being unenforceable, is not really binding. For instance, after MNF has sunk a large investment in the project, DC's leaders could decide to break the agreement and expropriate the mine. Given DC's desperate economic condition, this is a real possibility. In such a case, MNF would suffer a loss of $20 million. The value of the nationalized mine—run less efficiently by DC—would be $80 million. Finally, each side must look to the other to launch the mineral project. MNF sees no other countries in which to invest, and DC has found no other companies capable of launching the mine.

Given this description, we can use the game tree in Figure 13.1 to portray the sequence of actions by MNF and DC. (Such a depiction is commonly called the *extensive form* of the game.) The first move is MNF's: whether to invest or not. If MNF does invest, the next move (at the time the mine becomes operational) is DC's: whether to honor the 50-50 agreement or to expropriate the mine. In the game tree, squares represent points of decision, and monetary payoffs are shown at the branch tips of the tree. Here both players' payoffs are shown: MNF's first, then DC's. (Political considerations aside, we presume that the monetary payoffs accurately portray the objectives of the parties.) Furthermore, although it is easy to envision other actions and reactions by the parties, we have kept things simple: one move for each player.

At the initial move, should MNF invest in the mine? To answer this question, MNF's management need only look ahead to DC's subsequent move and the ensuing payoffs. Once the mine is operational, DC can be expected to expropriate it; DC certainly prefers an $80 million payoff to a mere $50 million from cooperation. Foreseeing this (and the resulting $20 million loss), MNF

FIGURE 13.1

Moving toward an
International Agreement

Game trees are solved
from right to left.
Anticipating that DC will
expropriate, MNF chooses
not to invest in the
first place.

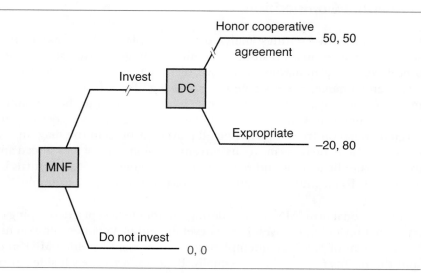

wisely decides not to invest. The parties find themselves on the horns of a dilemma. Both would gain handsomely from a cooperative agreement. But under the current circumstances, such an agreement is unenforceable. DC's position is particularly vexing. It can promise MNF that it will not expropriate the mine. But talk is cheap. Given the economic stakes, the promise is not credible. Even if DC intended to honor the agreement out of the goodness of its heart, how could it credibly convince MNF of its good intentions?

If the desirable cooperative outcome is to be achieved, the parties must structure an agreement that alters DC's incentives to expropriate. DC will honor an agreement only if it is more profitable to do so than to expropriate. This basic point suggests a number of remedies. One solution is for MNF to give DC an 81-19 split of the $100 million total gain from the mine. Although this might not seem particularly "fair," it does induce DC's compliance. Thus, MNF can invest confidently, counting on a $19 million return. Alternatively, the 50-50 split can be maintained with a monetary penalty exacted if DC breaches the agreement. For instance, as part of an agreement, DC would place $31 million (let's say) in an account with an international agency, such as the World Bank. This money would be forfeited to MNF if DC were to expropriate the mine. Clearly, DC prefers the $50 million from the agreement to the $80 - 31 = \$49$ million net profit from expropriation.

ENTRY DETERRENCE   In the earlier example of market entry, two firms made simultaneous decisions whether or not to enter a market. Let's modify the situation and presume that one firm, the incumbent, already occupies the market and currently holds a monopoly position. A second firm is deciding whether to enter. If entry occurs, the incumbent must decide whether to maintain or cut its current price. The game tree in Figure 13.2a depicts the situation. The new firm has the first move: deciding whether or not to enter. (Because of high fixed costs, entry is a long-term commitment. The new firm cannot test the waters and then exit.) The incumbent has the next move: maintaining or cutting its price. As the game tree shows, entry is profitable if a high price is maintained but leads to losses if price is cut.

A natural strategy for the incumbent is to threaten to cut price if the new firm enters. If this threat is believed, the new firm will find it in its best interest to stay out of the market. Without a competitor, the incumbent can maintain its price and earn a profit of 12. If the threat works, it will not actually have to be carried out. The beauty of the threat is that the incumbent will have accomplished its goal at no cost. However, the game-tree analysis reveals a significant problem with this strategy. Such a threat lacks credibility. If the new firm were to take the first move and enter the market, the incumbent would not rationally cut price. Once the market has become a duopoly, the incumbent firm's profit-maximizing choice is to maintain price. (A profit of 6 is better than a profit of 4.) In fact, maintaining price is a dominant strategy for the incumbent; high prices are preferred whether or not entry occurs. Thus, the equilibrium is for one firm to enter and the other to maintain price.

FIGURE 13.2

Deterring Entry

In part (a), E is not deterred by I's empty threat to cut price. In part (b), I deters entry by committing to a limit price before entry occurs.

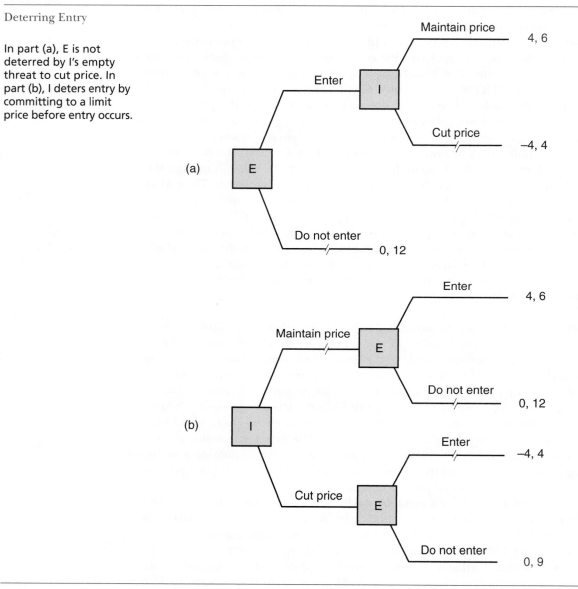

This example of entry deterrence underscores once again the importance of strategic commitment. If the incumbent could convince the entrant of its commitment to a low price, this would forestall entry. Perhaps one way to accomplish this goal is for the incumbent to cut price *before* the other firm enters to show its commitment to this low price. If the incumbent can move first and cut its price once and for all, the other firm's best response will be to stay clear of the market. The incumbent certainly would prefer this outcome; its profit is 9, higher than its profit (6) from moving second and accommodating entry. This possibility is depicted in Figure 13.2b's game tree. Be sure to note the reversal in the order of the moves.

Maintaining a lower-than-monopoly price to forestall entry is called **limit pricing**. Cutting price before entry is intended as a signal of the incumbent's price intentions post entry. But is it a credible signal? Again, the real issue is commitment. If the incumbent can bind itself to a low-price policy (now and in the future), the new firm will be convinced that entry is a losing proposition. This might be accomplished with long-term price agreements with customers or by staking the firm's reputation on its low prices. In most cases, however, pricing practices can be undone relatively rapidly and costlessly. The operative question is: If the entrant were to enter, would the incumbent continue to limit price or would it revert to a high price that best serves its self-interest? If the incumbent is expected to revert, limit pricing loses its credibility and its deterrence effect. Reversion can be depicted by adding a final pricing decision in Figure 13.2b's game tree. Clearly, cutting price in advance does no good if the incumbent is expected to undo the price cut after entry.

How might the incumbent convince a new firm that it will cut prices post entry? One way is to invest in additional capacity that makes it inexpensive—indeed, profitable—to increase output should a new firm enter.[11] Putting this capacity in place means incurring immediate fixed costs but allows the incumbent to expand output at a low marginal cost. For example, suppose capacity expansion costs $4 million directly so that all incumbent payoffs are reduced by 4. At the same time, the added capacity reduces the cost of expanding output (following a price cut) by $3 million. The incumbent's payoff is $6 - 4 = \$2$ million if it sets a high price after entry; its payoff is $4 - 4 + 3 = \$3$ million if it cuts price after entry. Now the firm's profit incentive is to cut price. Knowing this, the new firm will rationally forgo entry. The incumbent's net payoff is $12 - 4 = \$8$ million, some $2 million better than the original equilibrium.

Strategies to block entry make up one category of entry barriers noted in Chapter 11. A **strategic entry barrier** is defined as any move by a current firm designed to exclude new firms by lowering the profitability of entry. Credible limit pricing and maintenance of excess capacity are two such strategies. High levels of advertising, saturating the product space by proliferating the number of brands, or making product improvements that require high levels of R&D are others. Many of these strategies are *not profitable in themselves*. For example, spending on advertising may increase the firm's own costs faster than it increases revenues. However, if such a move raises the cost of entry, it may be

---

[11] Analysis and discussion of capacity strategies appear in A. Dixit, "Recent Developments in Oligopoly Theory," *American Economic Review* (1982): 12–17, and in M. B. Lieberman, "Strategies for Capacity Expansion," *Sloan Management Review* (1987): 19–27.

profitable overall by excluding new firms (and, thus, reducing competition). In some circumstances, incumbent firms actually may welcome costly government regulations if these policies have the effect of limiting entry.

BACKWARD AND FORWARD IN GAME TREES   Moving beyond these compact examples, one can construct game trees to model more complicated competitive settings, for instance, ones that involve multiple sequential moves by more than two players. As long as the number of moves is finite (so the game cannot go on forever) and all players have perfect information about previous moves, the optimal moves of the players can be found by backward induction, that is, by solving the game tree from right to left. In other words, to determine a player's optimal action at any point of decision, one must first pin down the optimal plays for all future moves. The resulting sequences of optimal moves constitute the players' equilibrium strategies. Thinking ahead is the watchword for sequential games. Or, in the words of the philosopher Soren Kierkegaard, "Life can only be understood backwards, but it must be lived forwards."

We note in passing that many parlor games, ranging from the simple to the complex, are sequential games of perfect information. The game of tic-tac-toe fits this description and is easy to solve by working backward. Properly played, the game should end in a stalemate.[12] Chess is a vastly more complicated game than tic-tac-toe but is also a sequential game of perfect information. In principal, one could solve chess backward from all possible endings to arrive at the optimal sequence of opening moves. At present, of course, this is a practical impossibility. (Chess experts have worked out optimal end-game strategies when only a few pieces remain on the board.) Instead, chess champions "make do" with looking ahead six or seven moves (and countermoves) in evaluating a given strategy.[13]

These examples highlight an important result in game theory:

> Any sequential game with perfect information can be solved backward to obtain a complete solution.

Some day, chess will be completely solved. We will know whether optimal play always will produce a draw, a win for "white" (the opener), or a win for "black." Of course, when that day comes, chess will cease to be an interesting game.

---

[12] Of course, the game tree for tic-tac-toe is a bushy mess. The first player can make one of nine moves, the second player one of eight moves, and so on. Since the game cannot end before five moves, there must be at least $9 \times 8 \times 7 \times 6 \times 5 = 15,120$ branches in the game tree. The practical way to solve such games is to reduce the problem by considering a limited number of actions. Because of symmetry, many of the actions in tic-tac-toe are strategically identical. For instance, there are really only three different opening moves: corner, side, or middle.

[13] The most advanced, "artificially intelligent" computer programs for chess are able to evaluate millions of moves per second up to 10 moves ahead. The best of these programs have attained grandmaster standings; they play superlative, but somewhat unimaginative, chess.

Backward induction is the most important ingredient for thinking clearly about competitive strategy, but it is not the only ingredient. Sometimes an action taken by one player today, without altering the game tree itself, can change the beliefs and, therefore, the subsequent behavior of other players. This process involves **forward induction**: Current actions influence future ones (instead of the other way around).

As a simple (hypothetical) example, consider two professional baseball teams residing in the same city. Years ago, both teams were profitable, but today attendance is off and both are making losses. The team owners recognize that the city now can profitably support only one team. By all estimates, the team that stays will be worth $100 million (based on future admissions revenues), while the team that moves to a less desirable city will be worth only $50 million. But which team will be the one that stays? For the time being, it is impossible to say. There are two equilibria—one with the first team staying and the second leaving and one with exactly the reverse roles—and either is a possible outcome. (This "exit" game is the near cousin of the simultaneous "entry" game we already have encountered.)

Now let's add an interesting twist. Suppose the first team's owners receive a well-publicized offer to sell the team for $65 million. (This offer comes from an investor group in another city that covets the team.) The first team's management answers with a well-publicized *refusal*. The import of this refusal should be evident. Management is sending a clear and credible signal that it is here to stay; that is, it is insisting on the first, favorable equilibrium. To put this another way, it would be completely irrational to refuse the $65 million and to settle later for the unfavorable equilibrium worth only $50 million. Granting the rationality of the first team's leaders, the second team's management has no choice but to acquiesce to the second equilibrium and make plans for leaving town.[14] In short, an action that one player *didn't take* (but could have) has a profound influence on the beliefs and actions of the other player. Forward induction has pinpointed the second outcome as the only rational equilibrium.

Another way one player can influence another's beliefs and actions is via signalling.[15] In many competitive settings, players have imperfect information about key characteristics of their rivals. As one example, suppose that Dowpont, a chemical company, is seeking to acquire Petrico, an oil company, by means of a tender offer. Petrico's management is willing to sell, provided it can get the highest price for the company. Petrico's stock price has stayed near $50 per share over the last year. In the wings is Nexoff, a second oil company, which is also a potential suitor. Commentators are anticipating a bidding war. Some believe that Petrico might be worth as much as $60 to $80 a share under either Dowpont's or Nexoff's management. Today, Dowpont takes the initiative by

---

[14] Remember, the ultrarational owners we're proposing are hypothetical! On the available evidence, it seems that otherwise savvy businesspeople "lose most of their marbles" as soon as they acquire a professional sports team.

[15] Another signalling example will be discussed in Chapter 15.

offering to buy shares at a price of $70 from any of Petrico's stockholders. After careful deliberation, Nexoff decides not to make a competing offer. A short time later, Dowpont quietly completes the acquisition of Petrico.

What has happened here? Why were business analysts wrong in predicting a bidding war? A plausible explanation is that Dowpont's $70 bid carried a preemptive message to Nexoff:

> "We might have made a low initial offer of $55 per share, which you would likely raise and we would raise again. In this kind of 'auction' the high bidder would eventually acquire the company. However, both firms, winner and loser alike, would incur the substantial costs of engaging in multiple rounds of bidding. By bidding at $70 per share instead, we are signalling that our acquisition value for the firm is very high—$80 per share, say. Don't incur the costs of entering an auction you are likely to lose—unless, of course, you think your value is even higher than ours."

Nexoff "heard" something close to this message. Suppose that it judged its own value to be $75. Even though this is greater than Dowpont's bid ($70), it is still less than Dowpont's implied value ($80). Thus, Nexoff was wise to avoid a bidding war it could not win.

For Dowpont's preemptive strategy to work, it must be credible. That is, higher bids must signal higher values. Obviously, if Dowpont's value for the oil company was only $65 per share, it would never bid $70. More generally, Dowpont's optimal bidding strategy specifies the bid it makes depending on the value it places on the oil company. Holding a low value, Dowpont places a low bid with little preemptive value. But, with a higher value, Dowpont is willing to pay a higher price to increase the chances of preempting the competition. Knowing this, Nexoff can infer the neighborhood of Dowpont's value from its bid. It enters the bidding competition only if its own value is greater than Dowpont's inferred value.

As a final note, signalling can provide an alternative explanation for limit pricing. In making its entry decision, an entrant certainly will be concerned about the cost structure of the incumbent firm. After all, entry could lead to disastrous losses (because of low prices and limited market share) against an incumbent with low unit costs. It is reasonable to suppose that a potential entrant has only limited information about these costs. How can the incumbent send a credible message that its costs are, indeed, low? By charging a low price prior to entry. To work as a credible signal, the price must be low enough to distinguish a low-cost incumbent from a high-cost one. That is, the high-cost incumbent must have no incentive to imitate this low price.[16]

---

[16] The intuition behind this result is appealing. Unfortunately, the construction of the limit-pricing equilibrium is complicated. For a thorough discussion, see P. Milgrom and J. Roberts, "Sequential Equilibria," *Econometrica* (1982): 443–459.

Repeated Competition

Frequently, firms encounter one another in repeated competition. For instance, duopolists may compete with respect to prices and/or quantities, not just in a single period of time but repeatedly. Similarly, an incumbent monopolist may encounter a number of would-be entrants over time. How does repetition of this sort affect strategy and behavior?

Repeated competition introduces two important elements into the players' strategic calculations. First, players can think in terms of *contingent* strategies. For instance, one firm's pricing decision this month could depend on the pricing behavior of its rival during prior months. (The firm might want to "punish" a rival's price cuts with cuts of its own.) Second, in repeated play, the present isn't the only thing that counts; the future does as well. Accordingly, a player may choose to take certain actions today in order to establish a *reputation* with its rivals in the future. As we shall see, the use of contingent strategies and the formation of reputations serve to broaden the range of equilibrium behavior.

REPEATED PRICE COMPETITION   As one example of a repeated game, suppose the price competition shown in Table 13.3a is played not once, but repeatedly over time. Thus, when the firms independently set prices in January, they know they will face new price decisions in February and in March and in each succeeding month into the indefinite future. Recall that in one-time play, charging a low price is each firm's dominant strategy. As a result, firms find themselves in a low-profit prisoner's dilemma. But what if the game is played indefinitely? One possibility is for the players to charge low prices every period (i.e., simply to repeat the single-stage equilibrium). Charging low prices indefinitely is one equilibrium of repeated competition, albeit a very unattractive one. After all, who wants to be trapped in a prisoner's dilemma forever?

Are there other more favorable possibilities? Common sense would suggest that players would strive to coordinate on a cooperative, high-price strategy. The question is how firms can keep this kind of implicit agreement from breaking down. One way is to exploit the power of contingent strategies. Consider the following **punitive** (or grim) strategy:

> The firm (1) sets a high price in the first period, (2) sets a high price in every succeeding period, provided the other firm does likewise, and (3) sets low prices forever after, if the other firm ever charges a low price.

In short, any defection from the cooperative high-price outcome is penalized by immediate and perpetual defections to low prices.

Let's check that the firms' mutual play of this punitive strategy constitutes an equilibrium in the repeated competition. If each firm adheres to this strategy, each charges a high price in the first and all other periods. Each earns a profit of 10 each period forever. Alternatively, could a firm benefit by unilaterally deviating from the punitive strategy? What if the firm deviated by charging a low price, say, in the first period (as good a time as any)? In this period, it increases its profits from 10 to 12. However, this triggers low prices from the other firm forever. Thus, the best it can do is to continue with low prices as well, earning a profit of 7 each period henceforth. Clearly, a one-time 2-unit profit increase is not worth a 3-unit profit reduction into perpetuity.[17] Accordingly, the firm's interest is to maintain its reputation for cooperative play throughout the repeated competition. To sum up, the play of punitive strategies, by holding out the threat of retribution, supports a cooperative, high-price equilibrium.

The general lesson is that, in infinitely repeated competition, the threat of punishment can be sufficient to enforce a cooperative equilibrium. Indeed, swift but limited penalties may be sufficient to support cooperation. For instance, the "tit-for-tat" strategy is much less drastic than the punitive strategy just described. Under tit-for-tat,

> The firm (1) sets a high price in the first period, and (2) in each succeeding period, echoes (i.e., imitates) the competitor's previous price.

The point of **tit-for-tat** is to deliver a *limited* punishment for defections from cooperation. If the competitor cuts price one period, the firm cuts its price next period. But if and when the competitor returns to a high price, the firm returns to high prices too. As with the punitive strategies, the mutual play of tit-for-tat supports a cooperative high-price equilibrium. With both using tit-for-tat, the firms cooperate indefinitely. Neither can gain by a unilateral defection; a one-period gain is not worth triggering an ongoing cycle of defections.

The mutual play of tit-for-tat, or of the punitive strategy, succeeds in supporting a cooperative equilibrium. But these are only two of an endless number of possible contingent strategies. Not surprisingly, there has been considerable research interest in strategies for playing the repeated prisoner's dilemma. An intriguing result of this research is how well tit-for-tat performs in achieving cooperation. Tit-for-tat has four virtues. First, it is *nice*; it is never the first to defect. Second, it is *retaliatory*; it immediately punishes an unwarranted defection. Third, it is *clear*; a competitor can immediately see that it doesn't pay to mess with tit-for-tat. Fourth, it is *forgiving*; by mimicking the competitor's

---

[17] The astute reader will recognize that this conclusion depends on how the firm weighs future versus present profits. Firms discount future profits. For discount rates of any reasonable magnitude, neither firm has an incentive to cut price. (However, in the extreme case of an extraordinarily high discount rate, future profits would carry almost no weight and the firm would opt for the immediate price cut.) For more on discounting, see Chapter 19.

previous move, it always is ready to return to cooperation. This last feature is the big difference between the punitive strategy (which satisfies the first three features) and tit-for-tat.[18]

OTHER ASPECTS OF REPUTATION   We have seen that a repeated game allows a player to create and maintain a reputation for cooperation. Reputation can play an analogous role in related contexts.

As a simple example, suppose a seller can produce medium-quality goods or high-quality goods. A typical buyer is willing to pay a premium price for a high-quality item, and the seller could make a greater profit from delivering high quality. The trouble is that the two types of good are indistinguishable at the time of purchase. Only after the buyer has purchased and used the good is the difference in quality apparent. If only a *single*, one-time transaction is at stake, we can argue (without needing a payoff table) that the only equilibrium has the seller offering medium-quality goods at a low price. Why? Because a seller's claim for high quality would not be credible. Any buyer who believed the claim and paid a premium price would be exploited by a self-interested seller who delivered medium quality instead.

Of course, you might plausibly protest that honesty should be the best policy for the seller. This is true—*provided* the seller has an incentive to establish a reputation for delivering high-quality goods now and in the indefinite future. Here is a simple way to establish a high-quality equilibrium. If a seller ever delivers a medium-quality item at a premium price, the buyer in question refuses to pay a premium price to that seller ever again and instructs all other buyers to treat the seller the same way. Given this purchasing behavior by buyers, any seller has the incentive to deliver high-quality items and maintain its reputation.

Finally, although reputation provides a basis for repeated cooperation in the pricing and quality contexts, this need not always be the case. In other contexts, a firm's advantage may lie in establishing a reputation for toughness. For instance, in the market-entry game in Table 13.5, we saw that the key to success was to preempt the market by being the first to enter. Now suppose there is a multitude of markets across the country to enter and conquer. How can a firm successfully expand and claim its fair share (or more than its fair share) of these markets? The experience of Wal-Mart Stores Inc. provides a classic example. While other national discount store chains were declaring bankruptcy, Wal-Mart aggressively expanded into small southwestern cities—localities that would support one discount store but not two.

---

[18] The political scientist Robert Axelrod has been a pioneer in investigating the repeated prisoner's dilemma. In a famous series of experiments, he asked economists, management scientists, and game theorists to devise strategies to be used in repeated prisoner's dilemmas, such as price competition. What strategy performed best on average when paired in turn against all other strategies? Tit-for-tat! For more on repeated competition and the features of successful strategies, see R. Axelrod, *The Evolution of Cooperation* (New York: Basic Books, 1984).

What has been the chain's experience in cities where it has met competition from other retailers? It has relied mainly on its reputation for "staying the course." Thus, Wal-Mart has been willing to suffer losses while waiting for its competitor to exit the market. By maintaining a tough reputation, this "preempt and persist" strategy is credible in each new market Wal-Mart enters. Finally, what has been Wal-Mart's response to new entrants in markets where it already holds a monopoly position? In many cities, the economics are essentially as described in Figure 13.2a's game tree. It is more profitable to maintain price after entry than to cut price. In isolation, Wal-Mart's threat to cut price is not credible and would not deter new entry. But the very fact that Wal-Mart is a chain of stores—some 2,000 stores facing an endless number of would-be entrants—profoundly alters its incentives. Wal-Mart credibly can pledge that it will fight entry by *always* cutting prices afterward. According to this pledge, if it once acquiesces to entry, it forever sacrifices its reputation for toughness and will acquiesce to future entrants that challenge its other stores. By staking its reputation in this way, Wal-Mart succeeds in deterring entry in equilibrium; the short-term profit gain from accommodating entry (even once) is not worth the permanent cost (in reduced future profits) from destroying its reputation for toughness.

A FINAL NOTE ON FINITE COMPETITION   We have seen that unlimited repetition can support cooperation in equilibrium. Of course, competition need not go on indefinitely. For instance, one might imagine that there is some probability the competition will end after any stage. As long as this probability is small enough, the previous analysis, in support of the cooperative equilibrium, continues to hold. However, what happens when the number of periods of competition are limited rather than infinite, that is, when the final period (even one very far in the future) is known? Here the logic of cooperation breaks down. To see this, consider once again the example of price competition played over a fixed number of periods. To find each firm's optimal actions, we work backward. In the last period, each firm's dominant strategy is to cut price, so this is what each does. (No threat of future price cuts can change this because there is no tomorrow.) What about the next-to-last period? With prices sure to be low in the last period, each firm's best strategy is to cut price then as well. In general, if low prices are expected in subsequent periods, each firm's best strategy is to cut prices one period earlier. Whatever the fixed number of periods—3 or 300—this logic carries all the way back to period 1: The only equilibrium is the repeated play of low prices.

Thus, we have something of a paradox. When the duration of price competition is limited, superrational players always will look ahead and see that a price war is coming. Self-interest dictates that it is better to cut price earlier than later. Both sides would prefer high prices, but rational players know that high prices are not stable. Is there a way back to the cooperative, high-price outcome? The answer is yes, if one admits the possibility of "near-rational" play.

Suppose there is a small chance that one or both sides will play cooperatively because they fail to look ahead to the end of the game. (Perhaps they believe the competition will go on indefinitely.) Injecting this "little bit" of irrationality is a good thing. Now, even a perfectly rational player finds it in his or her self-interest to charge a high price and maintain a cooperative equilibrium (at least until near the end of the competition).[19]

Multiple Players and Evolutionary Strategies

Many strategic situations involve multiple competitors choosing independent actions, with the combination of choices influencing individual payoffs. These environments move beyond the two-player category and cannot be immediately summarized in simple row-and-column payoff tables. Nonetheless, they can be addressed and analyzed using algebraic and graphic methods. We begin with three examples.

CARTEL BEHAVIOR   As noted in Chapter 11, cartels frequently struggle to limit output and maintain high prices. Suppose that a 10-member cartel has suffered a major setback in internal negotiations. Now each member must make an independent decision between one of two actions: to maintain its current output (stick to its quota) or to increase its output by 20 percent. The graph in Figure 13.3a depicts this situation. The two upward-sloping lines show the typical member's profit if it pursues either choice. Notice that the "Exceed Quota" line lies strictly above the "Honor Quota" line. That is, each member earns a greater profit by overproducing its quota. However, a member's exact profit also depends on the others' actions—specifically on the number of members who stick to their quotas (measured along the horizontal axis). For instance, at point A all 10 members choose to abide by their quotas and each obtains a payoff of 20. By contrast, at point B all 10 members are exceeding their quotas (on the horizontal axis, 0 are honoring their quotas), and each earns a profit of only 10 due to depressed prices. Finally, at points C and D, five members are abiding by their quotas and five are overproducing; the former members' payoffs are 14, and the latter's are 17.

Absent the possibility of collusion, each cartel member's course of action is clear—each should choose its dominant strategy, overproducing its quota. Regardless of the others' actions, producing more always delivers a higher profit than producing less. The prisoner's dilemma should be evident. The interest of each member is to supply extra output (since its extra output has only a small downward effect on price). But when all members increase output,

[19] For an analysis of the repeated prisoner's dilemma along these lines, see D. Kreps, P. Milgrom, J. Roberts, and R. Wilson, "Rational Cooperation in the Finitely Repeated Prisoners' Dilemma," *Journal of Economic Theory* (1982): 245–252. For an insightful discussion of reputation, see R. Wilson, "Reputations in Games and Markets," in A. Roth (Ed.), *Game-Theoretic Models of Bargaining* (New York: Cambridge University Press, 1985).

FIGURE 13.3

Three Examples of
Multiperson Dilemmas

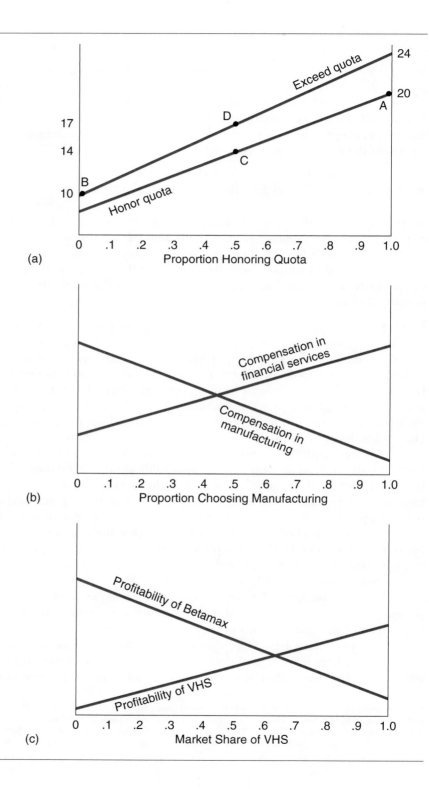

the total increase in supply has a significant impact on price, causing all to earn lower profits.

CHOOSING A CAREER   Armed with a business degree, a graduate is mulling over a career in one of two fields: manufacturing or financial services. (These account for the lion's share of business employment in the region.) The graph in Figure 13.3b shows the payoffs associated with the job choices. The horizontal axis lists the percentage of job seekers over a two-year period pursuing manufacturing (with the remaining percentage opting for financial services). Clearly, the payoffs (average salaries) in each sector depend on the relative numbers of job seekers. At the extreme, if nearly all job seekers choose manufacturing, the abundance of applicants bids down the average wage dramatically. With a shortage of candidates in financial services, the average compensation is bid up accordingly.

Suppose the graduate cares only about expected monetary compensation. Armed with the payoff graph, which career should she choose? Here, there is no easy answer, no dominant strategy. Clearly, the more remunerative choice depends on the relative number of job seekers pursuing the two career paths. From the figure, we see that the "road less traveled" is the more profitable. But which road will that be? With job seekers continually making career decisions (new candidates and managers switching careers), one would expect the markets to converge to an equilibrium. The aforementioned illustration in which almost all candidates pursue manufacturing is clearly not an equilibrium. Manufacturing candidates would do better (earn higher wages) by pursuing financial services instead. Astute job seekers would quickly migrate in this direction. The equilibrium should be clear. When both careers offer the *same* payoff, there is no incentive to change from one to the other. In the figure, this occurs when about 45 percent of the candidates pursue manufacturing (and 55 percent pursue financial services).

COMPETING STANDARDS   Figure 13.3c shows the economics of the competing standards for videocassette recorders—Matsushita's VHS and Sony's Betamax. Although Betamax was first to market in 1975 and offered superior playing quality, Sony chose not to license its technology to competitors and offered recorders that played only one-hour tapes. Thus, early in the competition, consumers and producers gave a slight edge to VHS. Quickly, this edge widened as the many producers of VHS recorders came up with new innovations, and the number of film titles in VHS format multiplied. Within 10 years, the Beta format had all but disappeared.

According to Figure 13.3c, the standards battle has two possible equilibria: the market adopts one standard and renders the other obsolete. Which standard ultimately gains the ascendancy is a matter of "critical mass." Once the market tips toward one standard, it continues to gain more and more followers until it claims the entire market. In Figure 13.3c, Beta's value curve is on average slightly higher (more favorable) than VHS's. Nonetheless, once VHS claimed more than 60 percent of the market (at which point the VHS value line exceeded the Beta value line), Beta was doomed to extinction. In short, the ultimate winner is not preordained by economic forces; rather, it is "path dependent," that is, dependent on the pattern of early adoptions.

The examples of career choices and competing standards suggest that competition over time often determines the ultimate market outcome. This is often referred to as economic evolution or "natural" selection. The idea, familiar from biology, is that the most profitable ("fittest") behaviors will tend to grow and predominate in the population. Inferior strategies will be eliminated—either because they do poorly and go bankrupt or because firms discontinue them and adapt their behavior toward more profitable strategies. In multiplayer competition, it is probably too much to expect that all agents play optimally all of the time. However, over time, competitors can be expected to learn and adapt toward superior strategies. Thus, the system evolves over time toward optimal play. The following example illustrates the point.

EVOLUTION AND EQUITABLE BARGAINING   Table 13.7 revisits the stylized bargaining game introduced in Table 13.6. However, instead of one-shot bargaining, let's now suppose that bargaining occurs repeatedly. Imagine a large population of managers who go through their lives bargaining. That is, they bargain repeatedly with different randomly encountered partners. In each encounter, a bargainer can choose one of three basic strategies: tough (demanding 75 percent of the total trading profit), fair (asking for 50 percent), or soft (asking for only 25 percent). As we saw earlier, a player's best strategy depends on the behavior of the bargaining rival. According to Table 13.7, tough is best against soft; fair is best against fair; and soft is best against tough.

An individual bargaining repeatedly against a large population of partners is concerned with the expected profit associated with each bargaining strategy. To take a simple example, suppose one-third of the bargaining population is currently using each of the strategies. Then the expected profit of using the soft strategy is $(1/3)(10) + (1/3)(15) + (1/3)(20) = \$15$ thousand. In turn, the expected profits of using the fair and tough strategies are \$15 thousand and \$10 thousand, respectively.

If the forces of economic evolution are at work, we would expect that strategies with superior profits would tend to grow in the population (via

TABLE 13.7

Repeated Bargaining

A strategy's expected profit depends on the strategy proportions across the bargaining population.

		Population Strategies		
		Tough	Fair	Soft
An Individual's Strategy	Tough	0	0	30
	Fair	0	20	25
	Soft	10	15	20

learning and imitation), whereas inferior strategies would tend to diminish. Thus, the first-order effect is for the soft and fair strategies to grow in the population and the tough strategy to shrink. There is also a second-order effect. As the proportion of tough bargainers shrinks, it becomes less advantageous to be soft. In addition, with an increasing proportion of fair bargainers, it becomes more and more profitable on average to also be fair. Thus, as the bargaining setting evolves, the profit advantage goes more and more to the fair bargainers. Over time, the number of fair bargainers approaches 100 percent of the population.

In addition to tracing the preceding dynamics, there is a direct way to identify this evolutionary outcome. It is simply the symmetric equilibrium of Table 13.7. If one's bargaining rival always insists on its fair share, then the best one can do is also play fair by agreeing to this split. However, it is important to note that the fair split is not the only symmetric equilibrium. A second equilibrium has 50 percent of the population playing soft and 50 percent playing tough. For these proportions, playing soft has an expected profit of $(.5)(20) + (.5)(10) = \$15$ thousand, and playing tough has an identical expected profit of $(.5)(30) + (.5)(0) = \$15$ thousand, according to Table 13.7. With these strategies earning the same expected profit, both are equally viable in evolutionary terms. It may come as a surprise that none of the population uses the fair strategy in this equilibrium! To see why, we observe that the fair strategy's expected profit is $(.5)(25) + (.5)(0) = \$12.5$ thousand. Against a population of exclusively tough and soft players, the fair strategy has an inferior expected profit. Thus, it is not viable in this equilibrium.

The evolution of repeated bargaining among the player population will ultimately converge to one of the two equilibria. But the question is, which one? As in the earlier example of VHS versus Betamax, the ultimate market outcome is path dependent; it depends in part on the initial "market shares" of the competing strategies. Nonetheless, the present example permits the following conclusion. Starting from most initial proportions, the evolution of bargaining is overwhelmingly likely to end in the fair-share equilibrium. Thus, apart from its equity appeal, the fair-share strategy also has a strong evolutionary advantage.[20]

To sum up, though more than two players are involved, the analysis of multiperson competitive situations proceeds in the same way as before. In one-shot competitions, rational players should adopt equilibrium strategies. Furthermore, in repeated-play settings, evolutionary forces—the economic selection of superior strategies and the demise of inferior ones—can promote convergence to equilibrium behavior over time.

---

[20] As Spreadsheet Problem 3 in this chapter shows, bargaining evolves to the soft–tough equilibrium only if the fair strategy begins with a very small proportion (less than 15 percent) of the population. For a complete account of the notion of economic evolution and this bargaining example, see R. Hansen and W. Samuelson, "Evolution in Economic Games," *Journal of Economic Behavior and Organization* (1988): 315–338.

A Battle for Air Passengers Revisited

The first step for each airline is to prepare estimates of its profits for alternative numbers of departures it might schedule. We know that daily demand is 2,000 trips at a price of $225 per trip. In other words, the airlines are competing for shares of a market having $450,000 in total revenue. The cost for each additional daily departure is $20,000. Let's derive an expression for airline A's profit. We denote the airlines' numbers of departures by a, b, and c, respectively. Then airline A's profit (in thousands of dollars) can be expressed as

$$\pi_a = 450\frac{a}{(a + b + c)} - 20a.$$

Here A's share of total revenue is $a/(a + b + c)$. For instance, if all airlines fly identical numbers of flights, they obtain one-third market shares, or $150,000 in revenue each. If airline A provides half the total flights, it claims half the total revenue, and so on. The second term in the profit expression is the total cost of providing this number of departures. (Analogous expressions apply for the other airlines.) Inspection of this equation reveals the airline's basic trade-off: By flying more flights, it claims a greater share of revenue, at the same time incurring additional costs. Moreover, the larger the number of competitors' flights, the smaller the airline's revenue share. If all airlines fly "too many" flights, they all incur large costs, but the result remains a revenue standoff.

Table 13.8 lists the typical airline's payoff table. Note two things about the table. First, it has condensed the decisions of the other two airlines into one variable: the total number of competitor flights. (The columns list numbers of these flights ranging from 5 to 17.) From the profit equation, we observe that an airline's profit depends only on the number of its own flights (a) and the total number of competitor flights (b + c). For example, if airline A mounts five flights and B and C have a total of five flights, A's profit is $(5/10)(450) - (5)(20) = \$125$ thousand, as shown in Table 13.8. Second, only the airline's own profit is listed (to save space). As we would expect, each firm's profit is highly

TABLE 13.8

An Airline's Payoff Table

The airline's best responses are highlighted. In equilibrium, each of the three airlines flies five daily departures.

		Total Number of Competitors' Flights												
		5	6	7	8	9	10	11	12	13	14	15	16	17
	2	50.0	50.0	50.0	50.0	41.8	35.0	29.2	24.3	20.0	16.3	12.9	10.0	7.4
Own	3	75.0	75.0	75.0	62.7	52.5	43.8	36.4	30.0	24.4	19.4	15.0	11.1	7.5
Number	4	100.0	100.0	83.6	70.0	58.5	48.6	40.0	32.5	25.9	20.0	14.7	10.0	5.7
of Flights	5	125.0	104.5	87.5	73.1	60.7	50.0	40.6	32.4	25.0	18.4	12.5	7.1	2.3
	6	125.5	105.0	87.7	72.9	60.0	48.8	38.8	30.0	22.1	15.0	8.6	2.7	−2.6
	7	122.5	102.3	85.0	70.0	56.9	45.3	35.0	25.8	17.5	10.0	3.2	−3.0	−8.8
	8	116.9	97.1	80.0	65.0	51.8	40.0	29.5	20.0	11.4	3.6	−3.5	−10.0	−16.0

sensitive to the number of flights flown by its competitors. By reading across the payoffs in any row, we see that an airline's profit falls drastically as the number of competing flights increases.

If the three airlines are going to compete month after month, how might they set their number of departures each period? In answering this question, we consider two possible benchmarks: equilibrium behavior and collusive behavior.

To help identify equilibrium behavior, best-response payoffs are highlighted in Table 13.8. For example, if its competitors schedule only five total flights, the airline's best response is six flights, earning it \$125,500 (the highest payoff in column 1); against 13 flights, the airline's best response is four flights; and so on. The table shows that no airline has a dominant strategy. (The more numerous the competitors' flights, the fewer flights the airline should fly.) However, it is striking that the best responses congregate closely around five flights (ranging from three to six). In fact, the unique equilibrium has each of the airlines mounting exactly five flights. To confirm this, note that if the competitors fly five each (or 10 total), the airline's best response also is to fly five. (You might want to check by trial and error that no other combination of flights is an equilibrium.) In equilibrium, each airline's profit is \$50,000; total flights number 15, and industry profit is \$150,000.

What if the airlines could tacitly collude in determining the total number of daily departures? Because market revenue is fixed at \$450,000, the best the industry can do is carry the 2,000 passengers at least cost, that is, by using the fewest flights. This requires 10 daily departures (fully loaded), since capacity per plane is 200 passengers. Total industry profit is $450,000 - (10)(20,000) = \$250,000$. If the airlines fly three, three, and four flights, their respective profits are \$75,000, \$75,000, and \$100,000. One possibility is a tacit agreement among the airlines limiting the number of departures—ostensibly to achieve efficient loadings—perhaps alternating delivery of the tenth flight.

Remember, however, that such a tacit understanding is very fragile. If the other airlines limit themselves to six total flights, the last airline's best response is six flights, not four. Although it maximizes industry profit, collusive behavior does not constitute an equilibrium. Any airline can profit by unilaterally increasing its number of departures. Historically, airlines competed vigorously for passengers by offering the convenience of frequent departures—but on flights that were far from filled. With the emergence of the airline hub systems in recent years, the number of departures has stabilized.

SUMMARY

Decision-Making Principles

1. The formal study of competitive behavior by self-interested players is the subject of game theory. In competitive settings, determining one's own optimal action depends on correctly anticipating the actions and reactions of one's rivals.

2. A dominant strategy is a best response (i.e., maximizes the player's profit) with respect to *any* strategy that a competitor takes. If a dominant strategy exists, a rational individual should play it.

3. In a (Nash) equilibrium, each player employs a strategy that maximizes his or her expected payoff, given the strategies chosen by the others. Game theory predicts that the outcome of any competitive situation will be an equilibrium: a set of strategies from which no player can profitably deviate.

4. In sequential competition, the manager must think ahead. His or her best course of action depends on anticipating the subsequent actions of competitors.

Nuts and Bolts

1. Payoff tables are essential for analyzing competitive situations. A payoff table lists the profit outcomes of all firms as these outcomes depend on the firms' own actions and those of competitors.

2. In a zero-sum game, the interests of the players are strictly opposed; one player's gain is the other's loss. By contrast, a non-zero-sum game combines elements of competition and cooperation.

3. When players take independent actions (play noncooperatively), the solution of the game involves the play of equilibrium strategies.

4. When there are multiple equilibria, it is often advantageous to claim the first move.

5. If players can freely communicate and reach a binding agreement, they typically will try to maximize their total payoff.

6. A game tree lists the sequence of player actions and their resulting payoffs. It is possible to solve any game with perfect information by backward induction.

7. In repeated games, the use of contingent strategies and the formation of reputations serve to broaden the range of equilibrium behavior.

Questions and Problems

1. Give a careful explanation of a Nash equilibrium. How is it different from a dominant-strategy equilibrium?

2. Is it ever an advantage to move first in a zero-sum game? When is it an advantage to have the first move in a non-zero-sum game? Provide an example in which it is advantageous to have the second move.

3. Consider the accompanying zero-sum payoff table.
   a. Does either player have a dominant strategy? Does either have a dominated strategy? Explain.
   b. Once you have eliminated one dominated strategy, see if some other strategy is dominated. Solve the payoff table by iteratively eliminating dominated strategies. What strategies will the players use?

Firm Z

		C1	C2	C3
	R1	−1	−2	4
Firm Y	R2	0	2	2
	R3	−2	4	0

4. a. Identify the equilibrium outcome(s) in each of the three payoff tables.

I.

	C1	C2
R1	12, 10	10, 4
R2	4, 8	9, 6

II.

	C1	C2
R1	12, 10	4, 4
R2	4, 4	9, 6

III.

	C1	C2
R1	12, 10	4, 4
R2	4, −100	9, 6

   b. In each table, predict the exact outcome that will occur and explain your reasoning.
   c. In table III, suppose the column player is worried that the row player might choose R2 (perhaps a one-in-ten chance). Given this risk, how should the column player act? Anticipating the column player's thinking, how should the row player act?

5. Firms J and K produce compact-disc players and compete against one another. Each firm can develop either an economy player (E) or a deluxe player (D). According to the best available market research, the firms' resulting profits are given by the accompanying payoff table.
   a. The firms make their decision independently and each is seeking its own maximum profit. Is it possible to make a confident prediction concerning their actions and the outcome? Explain.

Firm K

		E	D
	E	30, 55	50, 60
Firm J	D	40, 75	25, 50

   b. Suppose that firm J has a lead in development and so can move first. What action should J take, and what will be K's response?
   c. What will be the outcome if firm K can move first?

6. Two firms dominate the market for surgical sutures and compete aggressively with respect to research and development. The following payoff table depicts the profit implications of their different R&D strategies.
   a. Suppose that no communication is possible between the firms; each must choose its R&D strategy independently of the other. What actions will the firms take, and what is the outcome?
   b. If the firms can communicate before setting their R&D strategies, what outcome will occur? Explain.

		Firm B's R&D Spending		
		Low	Medium	High
	Low	8, 11	6, 12	5, 14
Firm A's R&D Spending	Medium	12, 9	8, 10	6, 8
	High	11, 6	10, 8	4, 6

7. In 2003, Saudi Arabia and Venezuela (both members of OPEC) produced an average of 8 million and 3 million barrels of oil a day, respectively. Production costs were about $10 per barrel and the price of oil averaged $28 per barrel. Each country had the capacity to produce an additional 1 million barrels per day. At that time, it was estimated that each 1-million-barrel increase in supply would depress the average price of oil by $3.
   a. Fill in the missing profit entries in the payoff table.
   b. What actions should each country take and why?
   c. Does the asymmetry in the countries' sizes cause them to take different attitudes toward expanding output? Explain why or why not. Comment on whether or not a prisoner's dilemma is present.

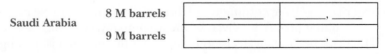

		Venezuela	
		3 M barrels	4 M barrels
Saudi Arabia	8 M barrels	_____, _____	_____, _____
	9 M barrels	_____, _____	_____, _____

8. Consider the following zero-sum game.
   a. Does either player have a dominant strategy? Does either have a dominated strategy? Explain.
   b. Find the players' equilibrium strategies.

		Player C		
		C1	C2	C3
	R1	13	12	10
Player R	R2	14	6	8
	R3	3	16	7

9. The following payoff table depicts service competition between two hospitals in a southeastern city. (Each payoff represents profit in millions of dollars.)

		Hospital B's Service		
		Basic	All Purpose	Speciality
Hospital A's Services	Basic	5, 7	5, 4	12, 6
	All Purpose	4, 5	8, 7	7, 4
	Speciality	6, 10	3, 12	3, 3

a. Does either hospital have a dominant strategy (or any dominated strategy)? Assuming they determine their strategies independently of one another, what are the hospitals' respective (Nash) equilibrium strategies? Explain briefly.

b. Suppose instead that the hospitals merge and, therefore, coordinate their service decisions. Which actions should they take? Explain briefly.

c. What general economic reasons might there be for a hospital merger to generate an increase in total profit? Would the hospitals' customers be likely to benefit from the merger? Under what circumstances? Explain carefully.

10. Firm A and firm B are battling for market share in two separate markets. Market I is worth $30 million in revenue; market II is worth $18 million. Firm A must decide how to allocate its three salespersons between the markets; firm B has only two salespersons to allocate. Each firm's revenue share in each market is *proportional* to the number of salespeople the firm assigns there. For example, if firm A puts two salespersons and firm B puts one salesperson in market I, A's revenue from this market is $[2/(2 + 1)]$30 = $20 million and B's revenue is the remaining $10 million. (The firms split a market equally if neither assigns a salesperson to it.) Each firm is solely interested in maximizing the *total* revenue it obtains from the two markets.

a. Compute the complete payoff table. (Firm A has four possible allocations: 3–0, 2–1, 1–2, and 0–3. Firm B has three allocations: 2–0, 1–1, and 0–2.) Is this a constant-sum game?

b. Does either firm have a dominant strategy (or dominated strategies)? What is the predicted outcome?

11. One way to lower the rate of auto accidents is strict enforcement of motor vehicle laws (speeding, drunk driving, and so on). However, maximum enforcement is very costly. The following payoff table lists the payoffs of a typical motorist and a town government. The motorist can obey or disobey motor vehicle laws, which the town can enforce or not.

		Town	
		Enforce	Don't Enforce
Motorist	Obey	0, −15	0, 0
	Don't Obey	−20, −20	5, −10

    a. What is the town's optimal strategy? What is the typical motorist's behavior in response?

    b. What if the town could commit to a strict enforcement policy and motorists believed that this policy would be used? Would the town wish to do so?

    c. Now suppose the town could commit to enforcing the law part of the time. (The typical motorist cannot predict exactly when the town's traffic police will be monitoring the roadways.) What is the town's optimal degree (i.e., percentage) of enforcement? Explain.

12. In the following game tree, players A and B alternate moves. At each turn, a player can terminate the game or pass the move to the next player. By passing, the player increases the rival's potential payoff by five units and reduces her own by one unit. Thus, as long as both players pass the move on to one another, their payoffs increase.

    a. Suppose you are paired with another student with whom you will play the game. Just based on your judgment (no analysis), how would you play?

    b. Now analyze the game tree by working backward. What actions should the players take? What is the outcome? Briefly explain this result.

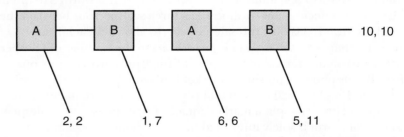

13. The following payoff table lists the profits of a buyer and a seller. The *seller acts first* by choosing a sale price ($9, $8, or $6). The buyer then decides the quantity of the good to purchase (two units, four units, six units, or eight units).

    a. Suppose the buyer and seller transact only once. Does the buyer have a dominant strategy? Depending on the price quoted, what is his best response? What price should the seller set? Explain carefully.

    b. Suppose the seller and buyer are in a multiyear relationship. Each month, the buyer quotes a price and the seller selects her quantity. How might this change each player's behavior?

c. Now suppose the buyer and seller are in a position to negotiate an agreement specifying price and quantity. Can they improve on the result in part a? Which quantity should they set? What price would be equitable? Explain.

Buyer Quantities

		2 Units	4 Units	6 Units	8 Units
	P = $9	10, 6	20, 5	30, 0	40, −8
Seller Prices	P = $8	8, 8	16, 9	24, 6	32, 0
	P = $6	4, 12	8, 17	12, 18	16, 16

14. Consider the following payoff tables. In the first period, each firm determines its price (high or low). In the second period, each firm chooses a design standard (design 1 or design 2). They both gain if they choose the same compatible standard. They receive no gain if they choose different incompatible standards.

I.

Firm 2

		H	L
Firm 1	H	4, 4	1, 6
	L	6, 1	3, 3

II.

Firm 2

		D_1	D_2
Firm 1	D_1	5, 5	0, 0
	D_2	0, 0	2, 2

a. What are the equilibria of each payoff table considered separately?
b. In the two-stage competition, check whether the following strategies are in equilibrium.
   i. Both players use H followed by D_1.
   ii. Both players use H followed by D_1 if the opponent used H originally and D_2 otherwise.
   What do your answers suggest about a way out of the prisoner's dilemma?

Discussion Question Over the last decade, the Delta Shuttle and the U.S. Air Shuttle have battled for market share on the Boston–New York and Washington, DC–New York routes. In addition to service quality and dependability (claimed or real), the airlines compete on price via periodic fare changes. The hypothetical payoff table lists each airline's estimated profit (expressed on a per-seat basis) for various combinations of one-way fares.

U.S. Air Shuttle Fares

		$139	$119	$99
Delta Shuttle Fares	$139	$34, $38	15, 42	6, 32
	$119	42, 20	22, 22	10, 25
	$ 99	35, 7	27, 9	18, 16

a. Suppose that the two airlines select their fares independently and "once and for all." (The airlines' fares cannot be changed.) What fares should the airlines set?

b. Suppose, instead, that the airlines will set fares over the next 18 months. In any month, each airline is free to change its fare if it wishes. What pattern of fares would you predict for the airlines over the 18 months?

c. Pair yourself with another student from the class. The two of you will play the roles of Delta and U.S. Air and set prices for the next 18 months. You will exchange written prices for each month. You then can determine your profit (and your partner's profit) from the payoff table. The competition continues in this way for 18 months, after which time you should compute your total profit (the sum of your monthly payoffs). Summarize the results of your competition. What lessons can you draw from it?

Spreadsheet Problems

S1. Four large used-car dealers compete for customers in a city where demand for used automobiles is constant at about 800 cars per month. By an implicit agreement, the dealers set comparable prices on their cars, with the result that price wars and competitive discounting are extremely rare. All dealers claim to have the lowest prices, but the facts say otherwise. The average (variable) cost of a used car to the dealer (procuring and readying it for sale) is $2,400. The average sale price per car is $4,000.

The dealers do compete with respect to the number and types of cars in their showrooms. The typical prospective buyer visits a number of dealers looking for the "right" car. The greater the number of cars a dealer has available, the better is its chance of making a sale. In fact, a particular dealer's share of the total market is proportional to the number of cars it holds in its showroom. Thus, dealer 1's profit can be expressed as $\pi_1 = 3,200,000[x_1/(x_1 + x_2 + x_3 + x_4)] - 2,400x_1$. The profit expressions for the other dealers are analogous.

The partial spreadsheet that follows lists the profit of a typical dealer (for various inventories) when it faces competitors with different average inventories. For instance, if dealer 1 stocks an inventory of 250 cars when the other dealers do likewise, then dealer 1's inventory is 25 percent of the total. Thus, it sells exactly $(.25)(800) = 200$ cars at a price of $4,000 each, while paying for 250 cars at $2,400 each. Its net profit is $200 thousand.

a. Create a spreadsheet to complete the entries in the following payoff table. (*Hint*: To compute cell G10, enter the formula:

$$= 3200*\$B10/(\$B10 + 3*G\$5) - 2.4*\$B10.$$

Then simply copy this formula into the other cells of the table. Adding dollar signs creates the appropriate absolute references to the dealers' inventory levels. For the row player's action, the sign always goes before the alphabetical coordinate, $B10. For the column player's action, it goes before the numerical reference, G$5. Also, in cells D7–D10 and E7, dealer 1 sells its entire inventory; thus, its payoffs are computed accordingly.)

	A	B	C	D	E	F	G	H	I	J	K
1											
2				USED-CAR DEALERS							
3											
4	Dealer 1's			Average Auto Inventory of the Other Three Dealers							
5	Inventory			175	200	225	250	275	300	325	
6											
7		175		280.0	280.0	238.8	185.4				
8		200		320.0	320.0	251.4	193.7				
9		225		360.0	332.7	260.0	198.5				
10		250		400.0	341.2	264.9	200.0				
11		275									
12		300									
13		325									
14		350									
15											

b. Find dealer 1's best inventory response to the various inventory actions of the other dealers. (Circle the greatest profit entry in each column of the table.)

c. What is the equilibrium inventory level for each of the four dealers?

d. If the dealers colluded to limit inventories, what would be the maximum monopoly profit they could earn collectively? Would individual dealers have an incentive to cheat on their inventories? Explain.

e. What would be the effect of free entry into the used-car business?

S2. In Problem 10, suppose that each firm has a $10 million direct sales budget to allocate between the two markets. Again, revenues in the markets are split in proportion to direct sales dollars spent.

a. Create a three-entry spreadsheet to find firm A's total revenue if it spends $7 million in market I (and the remainder in market II) while firm B spends $6 million there. Which firm earns the greater total revenue?

b. Use the spreadsheet optimizer to find firm A's optimal spending split if firm B's split is $7 million–$3 million.

c. Find firm A's optimal spending splits, if firm B spends, $5 million, $6 million, $6.25 million, $9 million, or $9.5 million in market I. What is the symmetric equilibrium of this spending game? Provide an intuitive explanation for the equilibrium.

S3. In the stylized bargaining game of Table 13.7, we considered the long-run viability of the three bargaining strategies labeled tough, fair, and soft. The following partial spreadsheet shows the evolution of these strategies. In the spreadsheet, the story begins with 40 percent of all bargainers playing tough, 20 percent playing fair, and 40 percent playing soft. The resulting expected payoffs are 12, 14, and 15, respectively, and the average payoff for the three strategies is $(.4)(12) + (.2)(14) + (.4)(15) = 13.6$.

Because the fair and soft payoffs exceed the overall average, the proportions using these strategies will increase at the expense of the tough strategy. In general, strategy i's proportion in period $t + 1$ is computed according to

$$x_i(t + 1) = x_i(t)[1 + .01(r_i(t) - r(t))],$$

where r_i denotes strategy i's expected payoff and r the overall average payoff. According to this equation, the population proportion of the soft strategy will increase from .40 in period 1 to $(.4)(1 + .01(15 - 13.6)) = .406$ in period 2. Similarly, the tough and fair proportions (cells D14 and E14) become .394 and .201. The preceding evolutionary equation implies that the new proportions add up exactly to 1. (In the spreadsheet, the proportions are rounded to three decimal places.) The coefficient .01 ensures a gradual, smooth evolution, but a larger or smaller coefficient could have been used.

	A	B	C	D	E	F	G	H	I	J	K	L	M
1													
2		EVOLUTION IN A BARGAINING GAME											
3													
4		Payoff Table											
5				Tough	Fair	Soft							
6		Tough		0	0	30							
7		Fair		0	20	25							
8		Soft		10	15	20							
9													
10					Proportions					Expected Payoffs			
11		Period		Tough	Fair	Soft	Total		Tough	Fair	Soft	Average	
12													
13		1		0.4	0.2	0.4	1.00		12.00	14.00	15.00	13.60	
14		2		0.394	0.201	0.406	1.00		12.17	14.16	15.06	13.74	
15		3		0.387	0.202	0.411	1.00		12.33	14.31	15.12	13.87	
16		4		0.381	0.203	0.416	1.00		12.48	14.45	15.17	14.00	
17		5		0.376	0.203	0.421	1.00		12.63	14.59	15.23	14.12	
18		6		0.370	0.204	0.426	1.00		12.77	14.73	15.28	14.24	
19		7		0.365	0.205	0.430	1.00		12.90	14.86	15.33	14.35	
20		8		0.359	0.206	0.434	1.00		13.03	14.98	15.37	14.45	
21		9		0.354	0.208	0.438	1.00		13.15	15.11	15.42	14.55	
22		10		0.349	0.209	0.442	1.00		13.26	15.23	15.46	14.65	

a. Reproduce the sample spreadsheet extending it to 150 periods. Simply complete rows 13 and 14 and then copy row 14 (and its formulas) into the next 148 rows. Be sure to use the reference $L13 for the average payoff.
b. What strategy or strategies dominate after 150 periods? Explain.
c. Experiment with different initial proportions in row 13. What happens if fair behavior is very rare, say, below 10 percent in the population? Explain the new evolutionary outcome.
d. What happens if the initial proportions are exactly .3333, .1333, and .5333? By varying the proportions slightly, show that this result is unstable.

Suggested References

The following references are classic treatments of game theory.

Schelling, T. C. *The Strategy of Conflict.* Cambridge: Harvard University Press, 1990.

Von Neumann, J., and O. Morgenstern. *Theory of Games and Economic Behavior.* Princeton, NJ: Princeton University Press, 1944.

Recent appraisals of game theory include:

Camerer, C. "Progress in Behavioral Game Theory." *Journal of Economic Perspectives* (Fall 1997): 167–188.

Gul, F. "A Nobel Prize for Game Theorists: The Contributions of Harsanyi, Nash, and Selton." *Journal of Economic Perspectives* (Summer 1997): 159–174.

A number of texts provide comprehensive and up-to-date treatments of game theory.

Camerer, C. *Behavioral Game Theory.* Princeton: Princeton University Press, 2003.

Dixit, A., and S. Skeath, *Games of Strategy.* New York: Norton, 1999.

Fudenberg, D., and J. Tirole. *Game Theory.* Cambridge: MIT Press, 1994.

Kreps, D. M. *Game Theory and Economic Modelling.* New York: Oxford University Press, 1991.

Myerson, R. *Game Theory.* Cambridge: Harvard University Press, 1997 (Paperback).

Osborne, M. J. *An Introduction to Game Theory.* New York: Oxford University Press, 2004.

Rasmusen, E. *Games and Information.* Cambridge: Blackwell, 2001 (3rd Edition).

For applications of game theory to competitive strategy and business problems, we highly recommend:

Dixit, A. K., and B. J. Nalebuff. *Thinking Strategically: The Competitive Edge in Business, Politics, and Everyday Life.* New York: W. W. Norton, 1993 (Paperback).

McMillan, J. *Games, Strategies, and Managers.* New York: Oxford University Press, 1996.

The following readings apply game theory to the study of market competition.

Gilbert, R. "The Role of Potential Competition in Industrial Organization." *Journal of Economic Perspectives* (Summer 1989): 107–127.

McAfee, R. P., and John McMillan. "Competition and Game Theory." *Journal of Marketing Research* (August 1996): 263–267.

Roberts, J. "Battle for Market Share: Incomplete Information, Aggressive Strategic Pricing, and Competitive Dynamics," in T. Bewley (Ed.) *Advances in Economic Theory.* Cambridge: Cambridge University Press, 1987.

Game theory resources on the Web include:

www.economics.harvard.edu/~aroth/alroth.html. *Professor Alvin Roth's home page has an extensive number of links to game theory sites.*

http://levine.sscnet.ucla.edu/general.htm. *Professor David Levine of UCLA provides some absorbing readings and games.*

www.comlabgames.com. *This site has software for playing and designing games.*

CHECK STATION ANSWERS

1. Store 1 does not have a dominant strategy, but store 2 does. Regardless of store 1's action, store 2's optimal choice is to promote women's clothing. Anticipating this behavior, store 1's best response is to promote girls' clothing. Despite the seeming symmetry of the example, store 1 fares much better than store 2.

2. This competition is a constant-sum game because the players' payoffs in each cell add up to the same sum. (Here the market shares always add up to 100.) The method of circles and squares pinpoints the

equilibrium at R2 and C2. This is exactly the same outcome as in the zero-sum version in Table 13.2. There is no strategic difference between a zero-sum game and its constant-sum counterpart.

3. If its rival produces six units, the firm's best response is either eight or ten units. (Actually, an amount not shown, nine units, would be absolutely best.) If its rival produces eight units, the firm's best response is eight units. If its rival produces 10 units, the firm's best response is either six or eight units (actually, seven is best). This shows that neither firm has a dominant strategy. The firms might hope to produce six units each, but this is not an equilibrium. Either could gain at the other's expense by increasing output (ideally, to nine units). The sole equilibrium has each firm producing eight units—the same answer as found in Chapter 12.

4. Originally, there are two equilibria: Boeing alone produces or Airbus alone produces. With the government subsidy, Airbus's dominant strategy is to produce. Knowing this, Boeing gives up the market.

Mixed Strategies

Whenever a player selects a particular course of action with certainty, we refer to this as a *pure* strategy. All of the applications in the main body of this chapter have involved pure-strategy equilibria, for instance, R2 versus C2 in the market-share competition. However, in other settings, optimal play frequently requires the use of *mixed (or randomized)* strategies. Here a player randomizes between two or more pure strategies, selecting each with fixed probabilities. Consider a second version of the market-share competition.

MARKET COMPETITION REVISITED Suppose that the firms have only their first and third strategies available. The payoff table in Table 13A.1a is identical to that of Table 13.2 except that the second strategy of each player is omitted. Now, there is no pure-strategy equilibrium. Instead, the players' best responses "cycle" and never settle down to any pair of strategies. For example, beginning at R1, C1, firm 1 would gain by switching to R3. But R3, C1 is not stable since now firm 2 would gain by switching to C3. But R3, C3 will give way to R1, C3 (after firm 1 switches) and, in turn, this gives way to R1, C1 (after firm 2 switches). We are back to where we began.

Although there is no equilibrium in pure strategies, the payoff table does have a unique equilibrium when players use particular mixed strategies. To qualify as a mixed-strategy equilibrium:

> The player's chosen probabilities must ensure that the other player earns the same expected payoff from any of the pure strategies making up his or her mixture.

TABLE 13A.1

Mixed Strategies in a
Zero-Sum Game

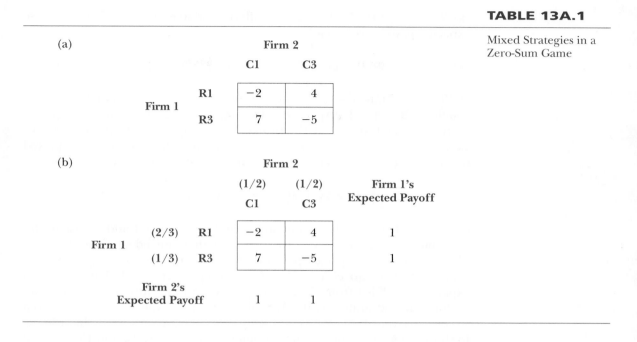

(a)

		Firm 2	
		C1	C3
Firm 1	R1	−2	4
	R3	7	−5

(b)

			Firm 2		Firm 1's
			(1/2)	(1/2)	Expected Payoff
			C1	C3	
Firm 1	(2/3)	R1	−2	4	1
	(1/3)	R3	7	−5	1
Firm 2's Expected Payoff			1	1	

This statement is quite a mouthful and requires some explaining. Why must the opponent's pure strategies earn the *same* expected payoff? To see this, let's turn back to the market-share competition. Suppose firm 1 decided to randomize between R1 and R3, each with probability .5. This is a plausible mixed strategy but, as we shall see, is not in equilibrium. Suppose firm 2 anticipates firm 1 using this 50-50 mixture. What is firm 2's best response? Suppose firm 2 considers C1. Because firm 1's actual action is uncertain, firm 2 must compute its expected payoff. From Table 13A.1a, the expected payoff is $(.5)(-2) + (.5)(7) = 2.5$. Alternatively, using C3, firm 2's expected payoff is $(.5)(4) + (.5)(-5) = -.5$. Clearly, firm 2 always prefers to play C3. (Remember, firm 2 is trying to *minimize* the expected market-share increase of firm 1.) But, if firm 2 always is expected to play C3, then it would be foolish for firm 1 to persist in playing the 50-50 mixture. Firm 1 should respond to C3 by playing R1 all the time. But then firm 2 would not want to play C3, and we are back in a cycle of second guessing. In short, mixed strategies when one player's pure strategies have different expected payoffs cannot be in equilibrium.

Now we are ready to compute the "correct" equilibrium probabilities for each firm's mixed strategy. Start with firm 1. Let x denote the probability it plays R1 and $1 - x$ the probability it plays R3. If firm 2 uses C1, its expected payoff is $(x)(-2) + (1 - x)(7)$. If, instead, it uses C3, its expected payoff is

$(x)(4) + (1 - x)(-5)$. Firm 2 is indifferent between C1 and C3 when these expected payoffs are equal:

$$-2x + 7(1 - x) = 4x - 5(1 - x), \qquad [13A.1]$$

or $12 = 18x$. Thus, $x = 2/3$. In equilibrium, firm 1 uses R1 and R3 with probabilities $2/3$ and $1/3$, respectively. Turning to firm 2, let y denote the probability it plays C1 and $1 - y$ the probability it plays C3. If firm 1 uses R1, its expected payoff is $(y)(-2) + (1 - y)(4)$. If, instead, it uses R3, its expected payoff is: $(y)(7) + (1 - y)(-5)$. Equating these expected payoffs implies:

$$-2y + 4(1 - y) = 7y - 5(1 - y), \qquad [13A.2]$$

or $9 = 18y$. Thus, $y = 1/2$. In equilibrium, firm 2 uses C1 and C3, each with probability $1/2$. In Table 13A.1b, we display these mixed strategies.[1] Finally, what is each firm's expected payoff when it uses its mixed strategy? If we substitute $x = 2/3$ into either side of Equation 13A.1, we find that firm 2's expected payoff is 1 from either of its pure strategies. Thus, the expected payoff for its mixed strategy is also 1. Similarly, firm 1's expected payoff is 1 from either of its strategies. These expected payoffs also are shown in Table 13A.1b. In short, when both sides use their optimal mixed strategies, firm 1's expected gain in market share (and firm 2's expected loss) is 1 percent.

REMARK   In this equilibrium, neither side can improve its expected payoff by switching from its mixed strategy. In fact, a player actually does not lose by switching to some other strategy proportion. For instance, as long as firm 2 uses its 50-50 mixed strategy, firm 1 earns the same expected payoff from *any* mixture of R1 and R3 (one-third/two-thirds, 50-50, etc.). The penalty for switching from equilibrium proportions comes in a different form: A smart opponent can take advantage of such a switch. Using its equilibrium strategy, firm 1 *guarantees* itself an expected payoff of 1 against the equilibrium play of

---

[1] There is a simple rule for finding the mixed strategies in a 2-by-2 payoff table like this one. Firm 1's mixed strategy proportions are $x = (d - c)/[(d - c) + (a - b)]$ and $1 - x = (a - b)/[(d - c) + (a - b)]$. Firm 2's proportions are $y = (d - b)/[(d - b) + (a - c)]$ and $1 - y = (a - c)/[(d - b) + (a - c)]$. To find the R1 chance, take the difference between the entries in the *opposite row* $(d - c)$ and then divide by the sum of the row differences, $(d - c) + (a - b)$. The same opposite-row rule works for the R2 chance, and an *opposite-column* rule works for computing firm 2's mixed strategy proportions.

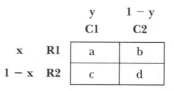

TABLE 13A.2

Mixed Strategies in a
Non-Zero-Sum Game

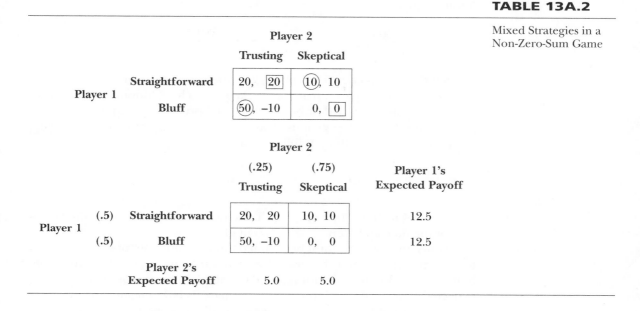

firm 2 or against any other play. If firm 1 were to switch to nonequilibrium strategy proportions (let's say, 60-40 proportions), it gives firm 2 the chance to gain at its expense by switching to C3. (Against a 60-40 mix by firm 1, the expected payoff of C3 is .4.) Firm 1's original advantage (an expected payoff of +1 in equilibrium) now would be eroded. In short, wandering from the original equilibrium play is ill-advised.

A GAME OF TRUST   Table 13A.2 depicts a *non-zero-sum* game that might be called a game of trust. Each player has two actions. The players' highest payoffs occur if player 1 is "straightforward" and player 2 is "trusting." The catch is that player 1 might try to take advantage of a trusting partner by playing the "bluff" strategy. In turn, player 2, recognizing this possibility, could take a "skeptical" position, and so on. The greater the incidence of bluffing and/or skepticism, the lower is the sum of the players' payoffs. Thus, this behavior is detrimental. One finds the basic features of this game in many economic settings. For instance, a contractor might be tempted to pass on unexpected cost overruns to a more or less trusting government agency. Alternatively, in an out-of-court settlement, party A might try to extract excessive monetary compensation from party B.

The circles and squares in Table 13A.2 show the best responses for the respective players. We see that there is no pure-strategy equilibrium. To find the mixed-strategy equilibrium, we follow the approach used earlier. Player 1's proportions must leave player 2 indifferent between being trusting or skeptical.

It follows that

$$20x - 10(1 - x) = 10x + 0(1 - x).$$

The left side of this equation is player 2's expected payoff from being trusting; the right side is her payoff from being skeptical. The solution is $x = .5$. Thus, player 1 is straightforward or bluffs with equal probability. In turn, player 2's proportions (y and $1 - y$) must leave player 1 indifferent between being straightforward or bluffing. It follows that

$$20y + 10(1 - y) = 50y + 0(1 - y).$$

This reduces to $10 = 40y$ or $y = .25$. Thus, player 2 should be trusting 25 percent of the time and skeptical 75 percent of the time.

Notice that player 2 must be inclined toward skepticism precisely in order to keep player 1 honest. If player 2 were too trusting, player 1 always would bluff. Table 13A.2b shows these mixed strategies and the players' resulting expected payoffs. Both players' expected payoffs fall well short of the 20 in profit each would enjoy in the upper-left cell. However, the straightforward and trusting strategies do not constitute a viable equilibrium.

A fundamental result in game theory holds that every game (having a finite number of players and actions) has at least one Nash equilibrium. Thus, if a payoff table lacks a pure-strategy equilibrium, there will always be a mixed-strategy equilibrium. Deliberately taking randomized actions might seem strange at first. But, as the examples indicate, mixed strategies are needed to sustain equilibrium. Indeed, in a zero-sum game lacking a pure-strategy equilibrium, mixed strategies are required to protect oneself against an opponent's opportunistic play.

Finally, many games may have both pure-strategy and mixed-strategy equilibria. One example is the market-entry game in Table 13.5. We already have identified a pair of pure-strategy equilibria in which one firm enters and the other stays out. There is also a mixed-strategy equilibrium in which each firm enters with probability .5. When the competitor enters with this frequency, the firm's expected profit from entering is 0, the same as if it stayed out. Obviously, this equilibrium is not very desirable for the firms. If they compete for new markets repeatedly, the firms mutually would prefer to divide up the available markets by alternating between the two pure-strategy equilibria.

Problems

1. A stranger in a bar challenges you to play the following zero-sum game. The table lists your payoffs in dollars.

		Him	
		C1	C2
You	R1	−16	24
	R2	8	−16

    What is your optimal mixed strategy? What is your opponent's? How much should you expect to win or lose on average?

2. The following payoff table offers a simple depiction of the strategy choices of the Allies and Germany with respect to the 1944 D-Day invasion during World War II. The Allies can land at either Calais or Normandy, and Germany can mount a defense at one, but not both, locations. Payoffs can be interpreted as the Allies' probability of ultimately winning the war. Find the mixed-strategy equilibrium. Explain briefly these optimal strategies. What is the value of the game, that is, the Allies' winning chances?

		Germany	
		Calais	Normandy
Allies	Calais	.6	.9
	Normandy	.8	.6

CHAPTER 14

Regulation, Public Goods, and Benefit–Cost Analysis

How many people does it take to screw in a light bulb?
Economist: None, the market will do it.
Consumer Advocate: None, the regulators will do it.

DENNIS CARLTON AND JEFFREY PERLOFF

The FDA, AZT, and AIDS

Azidothymidine, or AZT, retards multiplication of the AIDS virus in cells and was the first drug approved for treatment of the disease. The drug was discovered in 1964 and was acquired by Burroughs Wellcome Co. a decade later. When the AIDS epidemic struck, Wellcome sent the drug to the National Institutes of Health where government scientists conducted the first test-tube tests and human trials. If the Food and Drug Administration (FDA) approved the drug, Wellcome's patent would give it the exclusive right to market and sell AZT.

FDA approval came in March 1987 and was hailed as a success story by the medical community and AIDS activists. Drug development and approval is a lengthy process. On average, total lead time for the approval of a new drug (preclinical and clinical trials, and FDA approval) is seven to nine years. For AZT, the FDA approval phase was expedited to a "record" four months (as opposed to an average time of 28 months). However, soon after AZT's introduction, the company was attacked for the "excessive" price it set for the drug. At a price to distributors of $1.50 per capsule, the cost of treatment for patients with advanced cases of AIDS ranged between $5,000 and $8,000 per year. This made AZT one of the highest-priced drugs ever sold.

In its defense, Wellcome justified the high price as a way of recovering the enormous costs of developing AZT. Though the company refused to divulge AZT's R&D costs, the cost of developing a major new drug (R&D, testing, and FDA approval) averages $200 million. Critics contended that the government's sponsorship of the drug's testing significantly reduced the company's costs. In 1989, federal lawmakers and a host of interest groups sought an investigation of Wellcome's pricing policies and called for the government to require the company to lower prices. Subsequently, the company voluntarily reduced AZT's price by 20 percent.

The story of AZT's development and introduction raises a number of questions. What roles should private firms and government regulators play in bringing therapeutic drugs to market? How should safety be ensured? How should prices be set?

Ours is a mixed economy. Private markets provide an astonishing variety of goods and services. But there are many things they cannot guarantee, including safe streets, clean air, national security, an educated citizenry, and protection from potential carcinogens. Indeed, government sets the most basic ground rules, without which private markets could not function. Government policies and laws define and enforce the basic property rights of business firms and individuals. The government also plays an important role in overseeing and regulating many markets with the aim of ensuring open and free competition. Finally, the government has a direct hand in determining the levels of many public goods, from defense expenditures to highways. Private goods are produced and priced by profit-maximizing firms and purchased by consumers and other firms. In contrast, spending on public goods is undertaken by government and financed via general tax revenues or by public borrowing.

In this chapter, we consider the role of government in economic decision making. Clearly, government sets the ground rules for society in general and economic activity in particular. If we look more closely at government's role, we can identify three broad categories of economic function: microeconomic, macroeconomic, and distributive. Government's microeconomic role is to provide certain public goods and services, undertake public investments, and regulate operations of private markets. Government's macroeconomic task is to help steer the course of the aggregate economy: reducing the frequency and severity of recessions, promoting economic growth, and maintaining low rates of inflation and unemployment. In its distributive role, government attempts to reduce income inequality; ensure minimum health, education, and living standards; and improve the welfare of the poor. (The instruments for carrying out these activities include the tax system, assistance and welfare programs, and direct government provision of certain services.) Although we treat these three roles as separate functions, many government programs may serve two or more of them simultaneously. For instance, a packaged program of increased taxes may be used to help rein in a booming macroeconomy, redistribute income, and finance spending on particular government budget categories.

Macroeconomic and redistributive policies are vast subjects in themselves. This chapter focuses on the microeconomic function of government. In this sphere, the government has two main roles: (1) to regulate private markets when there are failures (imperfections) that would otherwise result in inefficient production or consumption, and (2) to provide the "right" amounts of certain public goods and services—goods that are not, or cannot, be provided via private markets. Part I of this chapter focuses on regulation; Part II applies benefit–cost analysis to evaluate public programs.

I. MARKET FAILURES AND REGULATION

To begin, it is important to remember that private markets depend on well-defined property rights. In modern economies, the person on the street sometimes takes property rights for granted. (This is not so in some developing countries, where government politics, judicial failures, and even corruption have hindered the development of private markets.) It is government that defines property rights and enforces and protects them. Thus, private transactions between sellers and buyers start with the seller owning the good and conclude with the buyer obtaining legal possession of the item (in exchange for payment). Besides individuals, firms and other organizations have legal rights to undertake transactions, enter into contracts, and create new corporate entities.

Thus, private markets depend on the rule of law created and maintained by government and enforced by the police and the courts. Even today, the legal definition of property rights can change. For instance, new rules allow for the trading of pollution permits, strive to strengthen protection of intellectual property, and have even created property rights to genomic material. Numerous recent court rulings have held that downloading music over the Internet via networked users violates the property rights of the music's creators (unless they grant their permission) and is, therefore, illegal. In summary, well-functioning private markets would not exist without the underpinning of government.

In the concluding section of Chapter 10, we demonstrated that perfectly competitive markets are efficient. In plain language, *competitive markets provide the right amounts of goods and services at minimum cost to the consumers who value them most highly.* In graphical terms, the efficient level of output occurs at the intersection of demand and supply. Recall that the demand curve reflects the marginal benefits to consumers, whereas the supply curve reflects the marginal costs of suppliers. Thus, equating demand and supply in a perfectly competitive market ensures that $P_c = MB = MC$.

The "invisible hand" theorem—that perfectly competitive markets ensure maximum social benefits—is best thought of as a benchmark. Although many markets in the United States closely approximate the requirements of perfect competition, notable cases of market failure also exist. Market failures usually can be traced to three causes: (1) the presence of monopoly power, (2) the existence of externalities, or (3) the absence of perfect information. In the next three sections, we examine each of these cases in turn.

MARKET FAILURE DUE TO MONOPOLY

Monopolistic markets (pure monopoly, monopolistic competition, or oligopoly) represent a major deviation from the efficiency standard. Relative to pure competition, the exercise of monopoly power elevates prices, thereby increasing the monopolist's profit at the expense of consumer welfare. Even more important is the fact that monopoly is harmful in the aggregate. Consumers lose more than monopolistic producers gain. Thus, total welfare falls.

Recall from Chapter 11 that monopoly's welfare shortfall represents a deadweight loss. Turning back to Figure 11.3, we see that the deadweight loss is measured by the triangle MDE. The perfectly competitive outcome (point E) delivers maximum social benefit in the form of the large consumer-surplus triangle ACE. By contrast, under monopoly (point M), total social benefit is measured as the sum of consumer surplus (triangle ABM) and the monopolist's excess profit (rectangle MBCD). Thus, we confirm that the welfare difference between perfect competition and pure monopoly is measured by the deadweight loss triangle MDE.

Let industry demand be given by $P = 20 - 2Q$ and industry unit cost by $AC = MC = 8$. Find output and price under pure monopoly and under perfect competition. Calculate the deadweight loss due to monopoly.

CHECK STATION 1

The welfare implications under pure monopoly can be extended to the intermediate cases of monopolistic competition and oligopoly. When there is competition among a small number of firms, prices are raised above the competitive level but fall short of the pure monopoly level. Accordingly, smaller deadweight losses occur under these market conditions. For a given market, the magnitude of these losses depends on the kind of oligopolistic behavior exhibited by firms, the concentration ratio in the market, and the elasticity of market demand, among other factors. A number of researchers have attempted to measure the deadweight loss due to monopolistic elements across the U.S. economy. Depending on the assumptions employed (and "heroic" assumptions are required), estimates of monopoly costs vary from .5 to 6 percent of GDP. Recent estimates have been predominantly in the lower part of this range, below 2 percent of GDP.[1]

Rent Seeking

Because monopoly allows a firm to earn excess profits, companies will invest resources in order to secure a monopoly position. This includes activities directed at the political system (lobbying), the court system (litigation), and the regulatory system (for example, at the patent office). Economists call the excess profits that monopolists earn "rents" and call the quest for these rents "rent

---

[1] For a survey and critique of these results, see A. J. Daskin, "Deadweight Loss in Oligopoly: A New Approach," *Southern Economic Journal* (July 1991): 171–185.

seeking." Economic theory suggests that firms will compete for rents up to the point at which it no longer profits them to do so. That is, they will compete until most of the excess profits from monopoly have been dissipated through the costs of rent-seeking activity. Rent-seeking activity represents a social loss. (If everyone stopped doing it, social welfare would increase even if monopoly remained.)

If the monopolist dissipates its excess profits through rent-seeking activity, the total welfare loss of monopoly includes not just the deadweight loss MDE in Figure 11.3 but also the area MBCD. The lure of monopoly profits prompts firms to undertake wasteful spending that effectively dissipates any actual profits. Interestingly, estimates of rent-seeking losses (including resources spent by society to prevent rent seeking) typically are higher (sometimes much higher) than the estimated deadweight losses due to actual monopolization of markets.[2]

Government Responses

Antitrust action often is taken to prevent the emergence of monopoly power and restore competition to a monopolistic industry. The United States Congress has passed a number of important pieces of antitrust legislation. The Sherman Act of 1890 prohibits conspiracies and combinations in restraint of trade, monopolization of any kind, or attempts to monopolize. The Clayton Act of 1914 identifies and prohibits specific types of anticompetitive behavior. The act forbids types of price discrimination aimed at reducing competition in an industry. (Recall that price discrimination occurs when a producer sells the same type of goods to different buyers at different prices.) It also prohibits tying agreements that are used for the purpose of reducing competition. In a tying agreement, the producer states it will sell a customer a product only if the customer agrees not to buy that product (or another product) from a competitor. The act also prohibits corporations from buying up competitors' shares of stock or having board members in common with competitors if this practice will lessen competition. The Federal Trade Commission Act of 1914 outlaws "unfair methods of competition" and created the Federal Trade Commission to define and enforce this law. In addition, there are a number of other pieces of legislation designed to foster competition.

The government can bring suit to enforce the provisions of the various antitrust laws. In addition, both the Sherman Act and the Clayton Act allow private parties who are injured by anticompetitive behavior to bring suit for damages. If successful, the suing party receives three times the value of the actual injury. Suits by either the government or private parties have several aims and results:

[2] For a good discussion see, J. R. Hines, Jr., "Three Sides of Harberger Triangles," *Journal of Economic Perspectives* (Spring 1999): 167–188.

1. **Breaking Up Monopolies.** Relying on the Sherman Act, the government may sue to break up a corporation that has attained a monopoly or near monopoly in an industry. In 1911, the government broke up Standard Oil of New Jersey (which controlled over 90 percent of the refining and sales of petroleum products) into 30 independent corporations. In 1982, AT&T, after being sued by the government, agreed to be broken into 23 independent local telephone companies. These operating companies became seven regional phone companies offering local telephone service. The long-distance service, Western Electric, and Bell Laboratories were retained in the corporation that kept the name AT&T. Other suits by the government have been less successful. The courts refused to break up U.S. Steel in 1920 and IBM in 1982. In 2001, the newly elected administration of President George W. Bush abandoned attempts to break up Microsoft.

2. **Preventing Monopolies from Arising.** The government seeks to keep corporations with economic power from engaging in practices that are designed to minimize or eliminate competition. Such practices include bundling and tying arrangements, price discrimination, and price-fixing. In the 1990s, a number of legal suits against such practices were brought; however, winning such cases in court is difficult. Nintendo of America, the dominant video-game maker, successfully defended an antitrust action brought by Atari Corporation. In a 1995 settlement with federal regulators, Microsoft agreed to share information about its Windows operating system with software developers and to stop requiring PC manufacturers to pay license fees for Windows on all units shipped (whether or not Windows was installed). A second landmark case brought by the Justice Department against Microsoft between 1998 and 2001 ended in a carefully constructed settlement.

   Illegal **predatory pricing** occurs when a large company sets price below cost in order to drive smaller companies out of business. The dominant firm then raises prices once the competitors are driven out. (Companies do not reenter since they know that entry will lead to another round of price-cutting.) The problem for courts is to distinguish predatory pricing from virtuous price competition. In 1993, the United States Supreme Court cleared Brown and Williamson Tobacco Corporation of predatory pricing charges brought by the Brook Group, a rival seller of generic cigarettes. The court raised the standard for proving predatory pricing, requiring proof that the accused company deliberately priced at a loss, that this behavior had a reasonable chance of driving rivals out of business, and that the accused would profit as a result. Although

American Airlines was cleared of predatory pricing charges in the early 1990s, antitrust authorities were conducting investigations in 2001, alleging that large airlines routinely slashed prices and added extra flights on routes where discount airlines began offering service.

3. **Preventing Mergers That Reduce Competition.** The government also has acted to prevent mergers in which the result would be a monopoly or near-monopoly position or in which the merger would significantly reduce competition. In 1962, the government successfully sued to prevent the merger of Brown Shoe and Kinney Shoe, respectively the fourth and eighth largest manufacturers of shoes at the time. The effect of the merger was likely to foreclose other manufacturers from using Kinney as a retailer. In 1964, the government successfully sued to prevent the merger of the second largest producer of metal containers with the third largest producer of glass containers. With mergers and acquisitions booming in the late 1980s, the merger policies the Reagan and Bush administrations were predominantly "hands off." In the 1990s, the Clinton administration closely scrutinized a number of mergers. Subject to minor conditions, regulators approved the mega-mergers of Kimberly-Clark and Scott Paper; Chase Manhattan and Chemical Bank; Citicorp and Travelers Group; and Boeing and McDonnell-Douglas. However, regulators blocked proposed mergers of Staples and Office Depot (office supply superstores), Rite-Aid and Revco (prescription drug suppliers), and Microsoft's acquisition of Intuit (maker of Quicken financial software), on the basis of economic evidence that reduced competition would result. In 1998, the Justice Department blocked the proposed merger of the defense giants Lockheed Martin and Northrup Grumman. In 2001, the European Union's Antitrust Commission blocked a proposed merger between General Electric and Honeywell International, though it had the blessing of U.S. authorities. Likewise, European regulators blocked a music joint venture between Time Warner and EMI Group. However, U.S. regulators approved a number of mergers—Exxon's merger with Mobil, Pepsi's buyout of Quaker Oats, and Chevron's purchase of Texaco—in which anticompetitive effects were deemed minimal. In other cases—such as Oracle's hostile takeover of PeopleSoft—the courts have upheld the acquisition despite regulatory opposition.

4. **Preventing Collusion.** As we know, firms need not be monopolies to exercise monopoly power. Firms can form cartels and collaborate to reduce output and increase price. Such cartels have the same effect on social welfare as do monopolies, and such behavior is illegal. Price-

fixing (in which corporations jointly decide what price to set) also is illegal. In 1927, the court found that the makers of toilets had acted illegally when they met to fix prices and limit quantities. More difficult is the problem of price-fixing when there is no explicit agreement to do so. Even absent an agreement, the court may find "conscious parallelism," that is, a situation in which all producers act in the same way at the same time while being aware that other producers are doing likewise.

In the 1990s, the government successfully challenged the practice of Ivy League universities meeting and exchanging information on planned tuition increases, faculty salaries, and financial aid policies. It also won a collusion suit against the producers of baby formula. In 1996, the giant agribusiness firm Archer Daniels Midland pleaded guilty to fixing the price of citric acid (a food additive) and lysine (a feed additive) and paid a $100 million fine. In 1997, thirty brokerage firms paid $900 million to settle claims that they fixed prices. In 2000, government antitrust authorities brought a successful price-fixing case against six global vitamin makers, followed by price-fixing charges against the world's leading auction houses, Sotheby's and Christie's. Ultimately, Sotheby's was fined $45 million (private lawsuits have run to over $100 million), and its chairman was sentenced to a year in prison and fined $7.5 million. In September 2004, Infineon Corporation agreed to pay one of the largest fines ever, $160 million, for its role in fixing the prices of memory chips. Currently, the government is pursuing charges of price-fixing against chemical industry leaders Du Pont, Dow Chemical, and Bayer, among others.

Antitrust Policy in the 1990s

In the 1990s the Justice Department and the Federal Trade Commission took pragmatic approaches to antitrust regulation. American antitrust policy was born in opposition to the great wave of mergers and consolidations at the close of the nineteenth century. The original philosophy of the trustbusters was that market dominance and monopoly were bad in and of themselves. Until the 1960s, this remained the prevailing view. (To cite an extreme instance, in 1966, the government prevented the merger of two Los Angeles grocery chains that shared just 8 percent of the local market.) However, by the 1970s and 1980s, the Chicago School approach had assumed dominance in the antitrust arena. According to this school, the forces of free market competition are far more effective at limiting monopolies than government regulators. Absent prohibitive barriers to entry, a firm's market power would only be temporary. High profits would attract new entrants attenuating the monopolist's power. Following this approach, the Reagan and Bush administrations used their antitrust powers sparingly.

Antitrust thinking in the 1990s built on the Chicago approach but also accepted new reasons for government action.[3] The first concern of antitrust authorities was not size per se. Rather, it was whether the firm in question had the power to unduly raise prices. For instance, the combination of Staples and Office Depot would have claimed only about 4 percent of the national office supply market. However, competition between the superstores virtually defined a new market: steeply discounted, one-stop shopping for high-volume office supplies. The government's economic analysis predicted that (even with merger efficiencies), prices would rise by 15 percent or more in markets where the stores formerly competed head to head. Thus, on average, the merger's cost to consumers was found to outweigh the benefits.

However, under different circumstances—for instance, if the sixth and seventh largest firms were to combine to compete even-handedly with the top three firms—mergers could be pro-competitive. This benefit–cost approach (see more on this later in the chapter) means that antitrust intervention must proceed on a case-by-case basis. In 1997, the government initiated an investigation of possible predatory pricing by the major airlines aimed at crushing the challenge of discount airlines. Similarly, the government succeeded in extracting a settlement from NASDAQ brokers because its economic analysis confirmed unusually wide price spreads that were consistent with a pattern of tacit collusion by brokers.

The United States versus Microsoft

The most important test of antitrust regulation in the digital age was the Justice Department's landmark antitrust suit against Microsoft. In the *Microsoft* case, antitrust regulation had to grapple with the forces of network externalities and the control of standards. Recall from Chapter 3 that network externalities exist when software users obtain greater value with a larger network of other connected customers. A key characteristic of network economies is the strong tendency for one dominant standard to emerge to the exclusion of others. (Recall Chapter 13's game-theoretic analysis of competing standards.) Clearly, the global network of Microsoft's Windows-based operating system (and Office applications) benefited from enormous network effects. With over 90 percent of the PC market, Windows established itself as the dominant standard. Furthermore, because switching costs are so high, we would expect the dominant standard to persist over time. (When customers have "invested" in learning to use an operating system or set of software applications, they are less likely to switch to competitive, perhaps even superior, alternatives.) In short, the economic preconditions were in place to support Microsoft's dominant market position.

But, despite its market dominance, Microsoft was not immune from the forces of competition. In the mid-1990s, the most important threats to

[3] See L. Uchitelle, "Broken System? Tweak It They Say: Economists Tiptoe on New Regulation," *The New York Times* (July 28, 2002), p. BU 1, and J. R. Wilke and B. Davis, "Lines That Divide Markets Likely to Blur under Bush," *The Wall Street Journal* (December 15, 2000), A18.

Microsoft were posed by Sun Microsystems' Java language and by Netscape's Internet browser. Java offered a universal, open-source platform for running software applications. Moreover, Java would run on any number of operating systems: Windows, but also Unix, Linux, Mac OS, or whatever new technology came along. Widespread use of Java could effectively sap the power Microsoft derived from control of the Windows standard. Any other operating system (working with Java) could compete with Windows on equal terms. Similarly, Netscape's browser, because it could operate as an intermediary between the operating system and applications (particularly Internet applications), posed its own challenge. If the browser succeeded in becoming a standard, Microsoft would find its market power diluted by the countervailing strength of Netscape.

Against this competitive background, Microsoft's market position and behavior could be viewed from two opposing perspectives. The first position, forwarded by one economic camp and adopted by Microsoft in its defense, held that antitrust intervention was unwarranted. A policy of laissez-faire saw Microsoft's dominance as the natural result of network externalities and control of the dominant PC software standards. Microsoft argued strongly that its strategy of integrating more and more functions into its operating system and of developing powerful applications delivered maximum value to consumers. Yes, the company currently enjoyed a dominant market position, but in the longer run, the abundant technological competition in software (the emergence of the Internet, networked systems, and rival operating systems) would constitute the surest measures of healthy market competition.

The second position held that Microsoft, starting from the position of market dominance outlined previously, undertook innumerable actions to limit new competition and prohibit future entry. Moreover, absent such actions, the forces of competition would have eroded the company's market dominance. According to this view, Microsoft sought to erect strategic entry barriers in order to maintain its monopoly position to the detriment of rivals and consumers. For example, Microsoft deliberately chose to bundle its own browser, Internet Explorer, with Windows, giving Explorer prominence on the desktop and hoping to discourage the separate use of Netscape's Navigator browser. In its dealings with PC makers, chip makers, and software developers the company took calculated actions to prevent the distribution and adoption of new rival technologies. For example, Microsoft warned PC manufacturers that if they did not favor Internet Explorer, they would lose their Windows licenses. Similarly, it required PC makers to install and prominently display Internet Explorer (notwithstanding the makers' and consumers' preference for Netscape Navigator). By threatening to turn to rival chip maker Advanced Micro Devices, Microsoft prevented Intel from joining with Sun to improve the performance of Java on Intel's chips. Finally, Microsoft's leverage extended to software applications developers. Any developer doing business with the company (and receiving advance information about new versions of Windows) was contractually required to use Internet Explorer and Microsoft's proprietary version of Java.

In April 2000, trial judge Thomas Jackson ruled that Microsoft had used anticompetitive means to maintain a monopoly for its PC operating system and had attempted to monopolize the Web-browser market. In a subsequent ruling, he ordered the remedy urged by Clinton's Justice Department: that Microsoft should be divided into two entities, an operating systems (OS) company and a software applications company. The split would prevent Microsoft from using its monopoly in the former area to extend its market power in the latter. Each company would be left to compete (free of antitrust restrictions) in its separate markets. Thus, the OS company (in seeking to maximize its own profits) would freely transact with any and all applications developers and Internet providers. Similarly, the software applications company would naturally seek out any and all platforms (including rival operating systems and Internet access providers) to purvey its software. Finally, the two companies might to a degree compete with one another (e.g., the OS company might include more and more applications in its offerings).

However, the story was far from over. In June 2001, the Appeals Court upheld the trial court's findings of monopolization but overruled the proposed breakup. Ultimately, the court required representatives from Microsoft and President Bush's Justice Department to attempt a negotiated settlement of the case. The result was a carefully crafted five-year agreement with the following main features. Microsoft agreed to (1) sell Windows under the same terms to all PC makers, (2) allow PC makers to install non-Microsoft software as they pleased, and (3) disclose technical information to software rivals so that their products could run smoothly on Windows. A three-person technical committee residing at the company's headquarters would have broad powers to monitor Microsoft's compliance. Finally, Microsoft was not restricted from entering new markets or from adding any features it wanted to its operating system.

To sum up, the settlement represented a middle ground, seeking to limit specific anticompetitive practices by Microsoft. How effectively the settlement will work and whether it will succeed in promoting increased competition and innovation remain to be seen.[4]

MARKET FAILURE DUE TO EXTERNALITIES

An **externality** is an impact or side effect that is caused by one economic agent and incurred by another agent or other agents. The classic case is pollution of any kind—air, water, or noise. Pollution is a by-product of the provision of certain goods and services, and harmful side effects are experienced by a diverse population—the users of a waterway, local residents who suffer deteriorated

---

[4]For a variety of economic views, see D. S. Evans et al., *Did Microsoft Harm Consumers? Two Opposing Views* (Washington, DC: AEI Press, 2000). The views and testimony of leading economists are available online: T. Bresnahan (www.stanford.edu/%7Etbres/research.htm), F. Fisher (www.usdoj.gov/atr/cases/f2000/2057.htm), and C. Shapiro (www.usdoj.gov/atr/cases/f4600/4642.htm).

air quality, or immediate neighbors who must endure aircraft noise. Externalities can be negative, as in the cases of pollution, traffic congestion, and cigarette smoke. But externalities also can be positive, that is, produce beneficial side effects. For instance, the pursuit of basic science and research (often government sponsored) generates a host of spin-off benefits (i.e., the development of profitable products) to private firms. (But, contrary to popular belief, the development of nonstick coating was not a by-product of the space program.) Likewise, an individual property owner reaps external benefits from living near open conservation land or on a street with beautifully maintained homes.

The difficulty posed by externalities lies in the fact that the party generating the externality has no incentive to consider the external effects on the other affected parties. The general rule is this:

> Left to its own devices, the party in question will act so as to produce too much of a negative externality and too little of a positive externality.

In short, externalities—either positive or negative—are a potential source of economic inefficiency.

To illustrate the externality problem, consider the production of a chemical whose by-product is the generation of significant air pollution. Figure 14.1 shows the demand and supply conditions prevailing in the competitive market for the chemical. As always, the market equilibrium occurs at the intersection of demand and supply, here at price P_c = \$4 per liter and industry output Q_c = 10 million liters. In the absence of any externality, this competitive outcome would be efficient.

However, an externality, namely, pollution, is present. To keep things simple, we assume that a known, fixed amount of pollutant—say, 1 cubic foot of noxious gas—is generated per liter of chemical produced. As Figure 14.1 shows, the *external* or *social* cost comes to \$1 per cubic foot of pollution and per liter of chemical produced. The exact way this external cost might be estimated and quantified comes under the heading of benefit–cost analysis. Briefly put, the basic approach is to identify the negative impacts of pollution, principally the health effects (increased illness, a statistical increase in mortality) as well as the more mundane economic effects (increased cleaning bills and so on) and aesthetic effects. Once identified, the next step is to estimate dollar costs for these impacts. Thus, the \$1 pollution cost is meant to encompass all these effects and their associated economic costs.

In Figure 14.1, the \$1 external cost associated with pollution is shown added on top of the chemical industry supply curve, MIC, to form the new curve, MTC. The original supply curve embodies the *internal* cost of producing the chemical—specifically, the marginal internal cost. This marginal cost is simply \$4 per liter. However, the true, full cost of producing the chemical is the sum of all costs per unit, internal and external. Thus, the full cost of expanding

FIGURE 14.1

Production Accompanied
by an Externality

An unregulated
competitive market
produces too much of
the externality. In
contrast, the optimal
outcome occurs where
demand equals MTC.

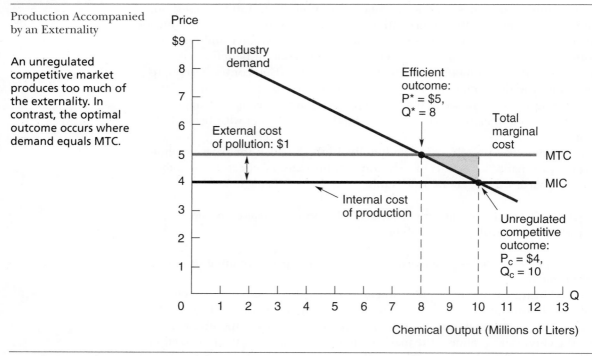

output comes to MIC + MEC = \$4 + \$1 = \$5. In the figure, this is shown by
the curve MTC.

Once the externality is recognized, it is easy to pinpoint the industry's efficient level of output using the logic of marginal benefits and costs. Optimal
industry output occurs at the intersection of the demand curve and the "full"
supply curve, at output level Q* = 8 million liters. Here the marginal benefit
from the last unit consumed exactly matches the full (internal plus external)
marginal cost of producing this unit.[5] The efficient level of output is lower than
the competitive outcome Q_c = 10 million liters. By failing to recognize the externality, the competitive market produces too much output and associated pollution, relative to the efficient outcome. Figure 14.1 also shows the deadweight loss
from the excess production, Q_c − Q*—the triangular shaded area where marginal benefits to consumers fall below the full marginal costs of supply.

At bottom, the inefficiency problems associated with externalities are
caused by incorrect pricing. The competitive price of \$4 reflects only the

---

[5] For the interested students, the figure's demand curve is given by MB = 9 − .5Q. The competitive equilibrium, P_c = \$4 and Q_c = 10 million, is found by setting MB = MIC. The efficient level
of output, P* = \$5 and Q* = 8 million, satisfies MB = MIC + MEC.

marginal internal costs of the chemical. But the full marginal cost is higher by the amount of the marginal external cost (here, $1). In the figure, the correct market price is actually $5, where $P^* = MB = MTC$. This simple observation suggests a direct way for a government regulator to implement the efficient outcome:

> An efficient means of regulation is to tax the producer of a negative externality an amount exactly equal to the associated marginal external cost.

In the chemical example, the external cost of pollution is $1 (per extra cubic foot of pollutant), so this is the appropriate tax. In other words, each chemical firm pays a tax, $T = \$1$, for each cubic foot of pollution it discharges. What is the effect of this tax on the typical chemical producer? By continuing to produce the chemical with pollution as a by-product, the firm incurs an "out-of-pocket" cost (per additional unit of output) equal to $MIC + T = MIC + MEC$. Since the tax is set exactly equal to the marginal external cost (MEC), the producer of the externality is made to pay its true social cost. In this way, setting the right tax ($T = MEC$) serves to "internalize the externality." With the tax in place, the relevant industry supply curve is MTC (up from MIC, the pretax curve), and the competitive market equilibrium becomes $P^* = \$5$ and $Q^* = 8$ million liters, precisely the efficient outcome.[6]

Suppose the $1 pollution tax is instituted. Among the affected groups—chemical consumers and suppliers, the government, and the general citizenry—who gains and who loses from the program, and by how much? What is the net gain to society as a whole?

CHECK STATION 2

Now consider the typical firm's incentives with respect to pollution cleanup. Specifically, suppose the firm has available the technology to chemically treat and eliminate harmful pollutants. For concreteness, take the cleanup cost to be $.50 per unit of pollution. Let's start with an obvious point. Absent any pollution fee or tax, there is absolutely no incentive for the firm to engage in cleanup, even though this action would be relatively inexpensive; cleanup simply means incurring additional costs. However, suppose the $1 fee per unit of pollution is in place. Now the firm's cleanup incentive is obvious. By cleaning up, it saves itself the fee ($1 per unit) it otherwise would pay. It is cheaper to eliminate the pollution (a $.50 per unit cost) than to pollute and pay the government tax. Thus, the firm's cost-minimizing strategy is 100 percent cleanup. How does this affect price and output in the chemical market? In Figure 14.1, the (external) cost of pollution is replaced by the (internal) cost of cleanup.

---

[6] Note that the full cost increase due to the externality is passed on in the form of a higher price to purchasers of the chemical. This should not be viewed as somehow "unfair." Rather, before the pollution tax, consumers were enjoying an unduly low price, one that did not reflect the full social cost of producing the chemical. Internalizing the externality means that the competitive price will now (fairly) reflect all relevant production costs.

The market price becomes $4.50 (reflecting the full cost of production and treatment), and total production increases from 8 million to 9 million liters.

With a $1 tax and a treatment cost of $.50, complete cleanup is both privately and socially efficient. From a societal viewpoint, it is less costly for the firm to expend resources for cleanup than for "society" (i.e., the region as a whole) to suffer the external costs of pollution (impaired health and other harmful side effects). Instead, what if the cost of cleanup is $1.50 per unit? Facing a $1-per-unit pollution fee, the typical firm finds it cheaper to pay the tax than to clean up, so no pollution treatment occurs. It is important to recognize that this result is also efficient! Since the cost of cleanup exceeds the resulting benefit, it simply is not worth eliminating the pollution. To put this another way, it is economically inappropriate to dictate 100 percent cleanup in pursuit of the single-minded goal of environmental "cleanliness" regardless of cost; rather, the efficient economic decision is based on a comparison of benefits and costs. If the cost of cleanup exceeds the benefits, cleanup is not warranted. By levying a fee that exactly matches pollution's external cost, the government regulator ensures that the typical firm's cost-minimizing response will be economically efficient.

Remedying Externalities

The adverse effects of externalities can be ameliorated by a number of means, including (1) government taxes, standards, or permits, or (2) monetary payments between the affected parties established via bargaining or by the courts. We will take up each of these approaches in turn.

We already introduced the argument for imposing taxes and fees on the economic agent causing the externality. Let's take a closer look at the benefits and costs of eliminating the externality. Figure 14.2 reconsiders pollution cleanup in its own right, separately from its implications for the output of the chemical industry. The rising marginal cost curve shows that it becomes increasingly costly for firms to clean up pollution more and more completely (i.e., to the point of 100 percent cleanup). The falling marginal benefit curve shows that health gains from cleanup (although positive) exhibit diminishing returns. Air and water that are almost completely clean pose negligible health risks. The optimal amount of cleanup occurs at Q*, where MB = MC. This point is well short of complete elimination. Beyond this level, the extra benefits are not worth the costs.[7]

The government can implement program Q* through either pollution fees or quantity standards. The appropriate fee is set at the value of marginal

---

[7] This economic point may seem patently obvious. Nonetheless, it is at odds with the Environmental Protection Agency's legislative mandate to promote and improve the quality of the environment without regard for cost.

FIGURE 14.2

Optimal Regulation of
an Externality

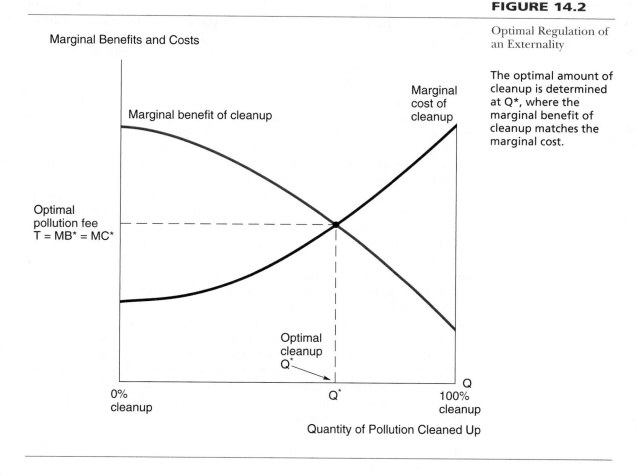

Marginal Benefits and Costs

Marginal benefit of cleanup

Marginal
cost of
cleanup

Optimal
pollution fee
T = MB* = MC*

Optimal
cleanup
Q*

0%
cleanup

Q*

100%
cleanup

Q

Quantity of Pollution Cleaned Up

The optimal amount of
cleanup is determined
at Q*, where the
marginal benefit of
cleanup matches the
marginal cost.

benefit, MB*. Alternatively, the regulator could attain the same result by requiring Q* as the minimum abatement standard. In short, when the regulator has perfect knowledge of the marginal benefit and cost schedules, either regulatory regime can be used to attain the desired result.

In the realistic case of imperfect information, however, externality fees have certain advantages over standards. For example, suppose the regulator is in a good position to estimate the benefits from cleanup but is in the dark about the industry's cost of cleanup. Clearly, the choice of standard involves guesswork and potential error. If the regulator overestimates cleanup costs, the standard will be too lax; if it underestimates these costs, the standard will be too stringent.

Pollution fees, although also subject to error, allow more flexibility. Suppose the regulator mistakenly sets too low a tax; let's say that T < MB* in

Figure 14.1. Since firms clean up only to the point where the marginal cost of doing so equals the tax ($MC = T$), the result will be relatively little cleanup. The regulator will see that additional cleanup affords a marginal benefit above marginal cost—$MB > T = MC$. Thus, it can adjust the tax upward until, by trial and error, the resulting level of cleanup satisfies $MB^* = T = MC^*$, thereby achieving the social optimum.

The advantage of fees over standards is even more pronounced when we recognize the enormity of regulating the myriad sources of pollution. Could a regulatory body, no matter how well informed, be expected to know the marginal benefits and costs associated with each pollution source and set optimal standards? Clearly, such individual standards would be subject to considerable error. In contrast, the value of the tax approach is that all generators of a given externality would be charged the same fee. This uniform fee is set to reflect the estimated externality cost. Whatever their differing costs of abatement, each firm cleans up pollution to the point where its marginal cost equals the tax: $T = MC_1 = MC_2 = \ldots = MC_n$. (Firms for which cleanup is cheap undertake greater pollution abatement.) Marginal costs are equated across all firms, ensuring that the total amount of pollution is eliminated at least cost. The fee system achieves full efficiency when the tax matches MB^*.

Regulators have used externality fees in a variety of areas. London, for example, has imposed a congestion fee for driving in the central city. Analysts credit this fee (about \$8 per day for driving downtown) with reducing traffic, shortening wait times, and more than doubling average speed in the city.[8]

Another regulatory response to an externality, such as pollution, is the introduction of **transferable emissions permits**. The regulator sets the number of permits to allow the discharge of a fixed total quantity of pollution. However, these permits can be bought and sold freely among firms. One would expect a ready market for these permits to emerge. Which firms would end up obtaining and using the permits? Those paying the highest price and for which the permits are most valuable—namely, profitable businesses producing pollution that is costly to clean up. This is exactly the efficient solution the regulator is seeking. A certain amount of pollution is permitted; the rest is cleaned up at least cost. (The going market price of permits indicates the marginal cost of cleanup.)

To sum up, the trading of pollution permits implies that the required amount of pollution will be cleaned up at least total cost. Nonetheless, the regulator still faces the problem of determining the allowable total amount of pollution (presumably via benefit–cost analysis), and this task is far from easy. Despite these difficulties, emissions trading programs have been highly successful. Trading permits for sulfur dioxide (the pollutant responsible for acid rain) has been responsible for a 30 percent drop in these emissions. More recently, 12 northeastern states have developed a permit system to reduce ozone, and the Environmental Protection Agency joined with 22 states to

[8] See "Ken's Coup," *The Economist* (March 22, 2003), 51.

launch a trading system in nitrogen-oxide emissions. In 2004 the European Union began a system of trading in carbon dioxide emissions, a primary greenhouse gas. This approach has worked in other areas as well. To prevent overfishing in the Northeast Atlantic, the New England Fishery Management Council has restricted the number of fishing days but has allowed fishermen to lease their days to other rivals.

PRIVATE PAYMENTS   When the affected parties are few in number and property rights are clearly defined, externalities can be resolved efficiently without government intervention. By appropriately structuring payments, the parties themselves can remedy the problem.

A classic example is the case of an upstream mill that releases pollutants into a waterway to the detriment of a downstream fishery. Table 14.1 depicts three abatement actions the mill might take and the resulting costs to each party. Of the three options, 50 percent abatement is the efficient solution because this minimizes the total cost incurred by the parties. How might this result actually come to pass? The Coase theorem (developed by Ronald Coase) provides a simple answer: *Bargaining between the affected parties will result in an efficient outcome, regardless of the property-rights assignment.*[9] To illustrate, suppose the fishery has the right to clean water. Absent any other agreement, it could demand 100 percent cleanup. However, a quick check of Table 14.1 demonstrates the mutual advantage of an agreement at 50 percent cleanup. The mill saves $70,000 in cleanup costs, while the loss to the fishery is only $30,000. Thus, a payment of, say, $50,000 from mill to fishery in exchange for the right to 50 percent discharge would be mutually beneficial.

TABLE 14.1

Private Remedies for an Externality

Mill's Action	Mill's Cost	Fishery's Cost
0% cleanup	$0	$100,000
50% cleanup	50,000	30,000
100% cleanup	120,000	0

Fifty percent cleanup is the course of action that minimizes the parties' total cost. This efficient outcome can be reached via self-interested bargaining between the parties, regardless of who holds the property right concerning water use.

[9] Coase, R., "The Problem of Social Cost," *Journal of Law and Economics* (1960): 1–31.

Suppose, instead, that the mill has the right to pollute (i.e., to elect 0 percent cleanup). Now the fishery must pay the mill to reduce its pollution. Nonetheless, the efficient agreement remains at 50 percent cleanup. A payment by the fishery of $60,000 (or, more generally, any payment between $50,000 and $70,000) would be mutually beneficial. No matter where they start, the parties always have an economic incentive to negotiate their way to an efficient outcome because this outcome affords the greatest joint gain.

Another solution to the problem is to give the party harmed by the externality the right to sue for damages. If an externality is produced, the injured party brings the case to court and will be awarded monetary damages (from the defendant) equal to the economic cost it suffers. This system of private damages is exactly analogous to an externality tax. The initiator of the externality is made to pay the full external cost of his or her actions. The difference is that the payment is private; it goes to the injured party, not the government. As an illustration, suppose the fishery holds the right to clean water and can sue for full damages. The mill has three options: 100 percent cleanup at a cost of $120,000 and no damages paid; 50 percent cleanup at a cost of $50,000 and damages of $30,000 (the harm done to the fishery); or 0 percent cleanup and damages of $100,000. Clearly the mill's cost-minimizing action is 50 percent cleanup. This is precisely the efficient outcome.

Global Warming

The world is faced with an environmental problem of unprecedented complexity. Across the globe, countries contribute to global warming through the emission of greenhouse gases (GHG)—primarily carbon dioxide (CO_2) but also methane and nitrous oxides. Sources of these gases include fossil-fuel energy use, industrial and agricultural processes, and forest burning. Even if atmospheric concentrations of these gases were stabilized now, experts predict that the average global temperature will rise by 1 to 2 degrees Fahrenheit over the next 25 years.

Although some climate change is indisputable, the degree and significance of these effects are far from certain. There remains scientific uncertainty concerning the expected net increase in GHG gases under different scenarios (including natural absorption of these gases by the oceans), and the ultimate global temperature impact of emissions. (A common estimate is that a doubling in the CO_2 level will cause an increase of 3 degrees centigrade, or about 5.4 degrees Fahrenheit in the mean global temperature level.) In addition, the economic consequences of an increase in global temperature are uncertain. One result of warming is a rise in sea levels, implying significant coastline regression across the globe. A second result is regional climatic changes (caused chiefly by alterations in global wind patterns and ocean currents)—less rainfall in the American Midwest and central Canada, more frequent typhoons in the Indian peninsula, possible alteration of the gulf stream, and reduced water levels in the world's major rivers. A third consequence (largely unknown) is the effect of a CO_2-rich atmosphere on agricultural yields (crop growth, plant diseases, and so on).

A simple fact explains why international cooperation is necessary to address the problem of global warming. Greenhouse gases entering the atmosphere from any particular point source are distributed equally around the globe within 12 months. The degree of global warming depends on the total amount of GHGs regardless of their source. The atmosphere, like many other environmental resources (the open seas, fishing stocks, endangered species), belongs to no countries and all countries. Thus, global warming represents the ultimate externality.

Countries can reduce emissions by a variety of means: reining in heavy industry (at the cost of reducing the rate of economic growth), using cleaner energy sources (including nuclear power), adopting more fuel-efficient technologies, turning toward greater conservation measures, and replanting forests. However, all of these measures are costly. It is in no single country's interest to institute unilateral reductions in GHGs. Yet, all countries potentially could benefit if multilateral reductions were undertaken. Thus, the nations of the world face a kind of Hobson's choice: reducing GHG emissions entails enormous economic costs. In the long run, however, *not* reducing these emissions may be even more costly.

In principle, the solution to the global warming problem is the same as for any externality. The externality (in this case, total GHG emissions) should be reduced up to the point where the marginal benefit (in terms of a cooler Earth) from any additional reduction just matches the marginal cost (the cost of reducing emissions, including possibly reduced economic growth). Indeed, starting with the 1992 Environmental Summit in Rio de Janeiro, the nations of the world have explored targets and timetables for global emissions reductions. An alternative means of achieving efficient reductions is the implementation of a global "carbon" tax, whereby fossil fuels, automobile emissions, and the like are taxed according to the amount of CO_2 they contribute to the atmosphere.

However, two aspects make the global warming problem particularly difficult. The first is the uncertainty about the magnitudes of benefits and costs. Some policy makers call for significant GHG cuts (25 to 40 percent), emphasizing the large benefits of reducing global warming and manageable costs. Other experts, particularly economists, call for modest reductions, pointing out that the economic harm stemming from global warming is likely to be minimal and that the cost of reducing emissions beyond 15 to 25 percent increases exponentially. As yet, there is no consensus on the optimal amount of GHG reductions.

The second problem is distributional. The wealthy industrial countries tend to place the highest value on environmental preservation. (After all, environmental protection is a normal good; as income increases, more of it is desired.) However, many of the opportunities for low-cost emission reductions reside in the developing world. Thus, there is a mismatch: The developed world lacks the opportunities for low-cost reductions, while the developing world lacks the financial resources to pay for reductions. Thus, payments (or other forms of aid) from industrial nations to developing ones would seem to be a prerequisite for a worldwide reduction plan.

The Kyoto Treaty, supported by more than 160 nations in 1997 and reaffirmed in 2001, marks an important step in addressing global warming. By this agreement, the major industrialized nations promised to reduce emissions by an average 5.2 percent below 1990 levels by 2008 to 2012. Developing nations pledged reductions but were not bound by specific amounts or a timetable. At the urging of U.S. negotiators, part of the plan calls for a worldwide trading program in carbon dioxide emissions. By this mechanism, developing nations could collect significant monetary sums from industrialized countries for reducing GHG emissions below specified targets. The terms of the treaty specified that it would become legally binding once ratified by industrial nations accounting for 55 percent of the world's carbon emissions. The treaty became binding in February 2005. To date, the Bush administration has withheld ratification by the United States. Although concerned about climate change, the current administration contends that the cost to the U.S. economy will be too great and that developing countries must also be required to reduce emissions.[10]

Promoting Positive Externalities

A positive externality occurs when a particular activity has beneficial side effects on other parties. For instance, efforts to improve literacy and education levels in a particular segment of the population benefit not only the individuals themselves but also society as a whole. (Better education raises labor productivity, reduces crime, and promotes government stability.) By limiting the onset and spread of disease, vaccination programs protect the general population including those who are not vaccinated. The growth of cities as centers of commerce stems from positive externalities. In order to grow, businesses need other businesses nearby (as input suppliers or customers), a ready labor force, and financial institutions from which to borrow. With the help of markets, each segment generates benefits for the others. These are just a few examples of positive externalities.

Left to their own devices, economic agents in unregulated markets tend to undertake too little of activities that generate positive externalities. (This is simply the converse of the previous proposition that agents generate too much negative externalities.) The appropriate government intervention is either to mandate or subsidize greater levels of these beneficial activities. In the United States, education is publicly provided and is mandatory through certain grade levels. Similarly, vaccinations against common diseases can be obtained for free and are mandatory. The following example illustrates the use of subsidies to promote beneficial activities.

[10] For more on the economics of global warming, see W. J. McKibbin and P. J. Wilcoxen, "The Role of Economics in Climate Change Policy," *Journal of Economic Perspectives* (Spring 2002): 107–129, and "Symposium on Global Climate Change," *Journal of Economic Perspectives* (Fall 1993): 3–86.

PROMOTING RESEARCH   In the United States, private universities and firms undertake the vast majority of basic research leading to new scientific and technological knowledge. As a concrete example, consider a firm engaged in basic research that is contemplating embarking on an R&D program to produce a superior flame-retardant fabric. The firm estimates the expected gross profit of the program (in present-value terms) to be $12 million. It also recognizes that the program will generate external benefits to society as a whole (to consumers and other firms who develop copycat fabrics). These external benefits come to an estimated $6 million. Finally, the firm's total cost of undertaking the R&D program is $15 million.

As far as the firm is concerned, the program's net profit is $12 - 15 = -\$3$ million. Thus, the firm will choose not to undertake the program. Taking account of total benefits, however, the program *should* be undertaken. (In total, net benefits come to $12 + 6 - 15 = \$3$ million.) Clearly, the profit motive alone is not enough to induce the firm to go ahead. What incentive is needed? Simply stated, the government should offer the firm a "carrot," that is, an R&D subsidy. What kind and magnitude of subsidy? The answer is straightforward. The crux of the externality problem is that the firm faces paying the entire cost of the R&D program but reaps only two-thirds of the total benefit ($12 million of the $18 million total). Accordingly, the remedy is a "one-third" subsidy. For every $1.00 of the firm's R&D expenditures, the government reimburses or pays for $.33. With the subsidy, the firm's net R&D cost becomes $(2/3)(15) = \$10$ million. Therefore, its net profit becomes $12 - 10 = \$2$ million, and the firm elects to undertake the program.

The general rule (of which this example is a specific case) is this: *To induce efficient behavior, the subsidy should be set equal to the ratio of external benefit to total benefit.*

THE PATENT SYSTEM   In the United States, patent law grants the holder exclusive rights to an invention for 20 years. An invention must take the form of a product or process. Intangible knowledge (say, a mathematical theorem) is not patentable. Moreover, the invention must contain a minimum degree of novelty. A mere improvement does not constitute a patentable invention. At the time the patent is granted, the invention becomes public knowledge.

What is the economic rationale for patent laws? Their most important role is to provide incentives for firms (and individuals) to pursue inventions and innovations. Absent patent protection, why should an inventor work to develop an invention or why should a firm incur the costs to bring it to market? If one did, another firm could duplicate any successful invention and so profit at the expense of the inventor. If the invention were publicly available to all, potential customers would be unwilling to pay a high price to the inventing firm when they could use the knowledge themselves for free. In short, without patent protection, a firm that creates an invention would be able to claim only a small portion of the profit generated by the invention. Thus, it would be in the same position as the research firm in the preceding example. Creation of knowledge generates a large positive externality. (After all, new knowledge cannot be used up and one person's use of it does not diminish another's.) Patent protection encourages the process of invention by allowing the inventor to capture a greater portion of the external benefits.

Patent laws represent a trade-off. On one hand, they provide strong incentives for research and invention in the first place. On the other hand, the patent grants the successful inventor a monopoly over the sale of knowledge embodied in the invention. Like any monopolist, the inventor will set a high price to maximize his or her profit. Because some would-be customers will be unwilling to pay this monopoly price, the knowledge will not be as widely used as it might be.[11] As in any monopoly, there is a deadweight loss due to underprovision. To sum up, patent protection represents a trade-off between encouraging invention before the fact and disseminating knowledge after the fact.

As a practical matter, patent laws do not provide complete protection against imitation. Copycat firms frequently succeed in making just enough changes in the process or product to avoid patent infringement. Nonetheless, patents make imitation more difficult and more costly. Thus, by bequeathing the firm a partial monopoly, patent laws provide a positive profit incentive for invention.[12]

COPYRIGHT   Copyright law provides protection for expressive works, such as music, drama, literature, film, and even software. The Copyright Act of 1790 protected material for 14 years, renewable for another 14 years while the author was still alive. By 1998, this protection had been raised to the life of the author plus 70 years.

Media attention continues to focus on the contours of copyright law, especially in the area of music where technological advances (video recorders, DVD recorders, and the like) have made copying and downloading easy and inexpensive. In the late 1970s, Universal Pictures and Disney sued Sony and other makers of video recorders to prohibit the sale of the recorders, alleging that such recording violated copyright law. The federal district court ruling in Sony's favor remains the underpinning of current controversies involving the downloading of music. In 2001, the Court of Appeals (Ninth Circuit) upheld an injunction that effectively shut down Napster, a popular music and file exchange service. In that case, the court objected to Napster making copyrighted songs available from its main server. However, courts have refused to prevent the distribution of software that allows direct file sharing among users without the benefit of a central server. Though the music industry has recently

---

[11] Indeed, if the actual marginal cost of additional people using this knowledge is essentially zero, then maximizing social benefits requires making the invention available to all for free.

[12] For a study of patent effectiveness, see E. Mansfield, "Patents and Innovation: An Empirical Study," *Management Science* (1986): 173–181.

begun suing individual violators, illegal downloads continue to dominate the market. To further fight the downloading problem, the industry has aggressively promoted paid download services such as iTunes, MusicMatch, Rhapsody, and even a new paid Napster.

Regulatory Reform and Deregulation

Efficient regulation depends on a careful consideration of benefits and costs. Regulatory reforms in the 1980s and 1990s have made slow but steady progress in this direction.[13] As we have seen, the government has adopted a pragmatic approach to antitrust interventions, assessing the net benefits of mergers, pricing tactics, and other business behavior on a case-by-case basis. In regulations pertaining to the workplace, the environment, new products, and safety, the secular trend is similar. In many cases, these regulations were born in legislative language that ignored considerations of cost. The 1970 Clean Air Act specifically excludes a consideration of costs in setting air quality standards. The Food and Drug Administration is not obligated to use benefit–cost tests in ascertaining product safety, and the Occupational, Safety and Health Act (OSHA) seeks to ensure "safe and healthful working conditions." However, over time regulatory agencies have increasingly turned to a comparison of benefits and costs. The means of regulation are also changing. Performance of OSHA regulators is less a matter of counting enforcement actions and more of solving workplace problems cooperatively.

One important area of reform is deregulation.[14] For instance, consider the regulation of natural monopolies discussed in Chapter 11. In principle, the regulator sets the firm's price at average cost, allowing it only a normal rate of return. In practice, identifying and implementing this ideal price is difficult. Critics point out that, by intention or not, regulation frequently reduces true competition: Regulated rates can hold prices *up* as well as down. In this sense, regulators are "captured" by the firms over which they are supposed to exercise control—in effect, maintaining a status quo protected from new competition. Regulatory critics go on to point out that, over time, government intervention has spread into many areas that are a far cry from natural monopolies: trucking, airlines, and banking, for example. Regulations that limit market entry and fix prices frequently do more harm than good in markets where competition otherwise would be viable.

Beginning in the late 1970s, policy makers have increasingly adopted regulatory reforms calling for deregulation. Deregulation focused on a wide variety of industries, including airlines, banking, brokerage firms, cable television, natural gas, railroads, trucking, and telecommunications. In most instances, deregulation (partial or complete) took the form of opening entry

---

[13] See W. K. Viscusi, "Economic Foundations of the Current Regulatory Reform Efforts," *Journal of Economic Perspectives* (Summer 1996): 119–134.

[14] For an economic assessment of deregulation, see C. Winston, "Economic Deregulation: Days of Reckoning for Microeconomists," *Journal of Economic Literature* (September 1993): 1263–1289.

into markets and removing operating and price restrictions. Did the predicted benefits of deregulation come to pass? On balance, the answer is yes. For instance, in the railroad and trucking industries, firms have engaged in vigorous price competition and have become more efficient once free of restrictive regulations. Competition also has been vigorous in the areas of banking and brokerage services.

Perhaps most successful has been the case of airline deregulation. Deregulation has produced entry by no-frills airlines, greater competition along high-traffic routes, lower average fares, greater variety and frequency of service, and increased airline efficiency (stemming from hub-and-spoke operations and reduced labor costs) with some reduction in service quality. Although a number of carriers have failed, overall airline profitability largely is unchanged (vis-à-vis what it would be absent deregulation). With the mergers of several surviving airlines, industry concentration has increased. Overall, consumers have benefited significantly from the 25 years of airline deregulation.

MARKET FAILURE DUE TO IMPERFECT INFORMATION

In our previous discussion of market efficiency, we took for granted that the consumer is the best judge of the value he or she will enjoy from the purchase of a good or service; that is, the buyer fully understands the benefits and costs associated with any transaction undertaken. This is a good working presumption for many, if not most, transactions. However, some economic transactions involve significant uncertainties, such as with respect to product quality, reliability, or safety. In these cases, consumers may well systematically misjudge values, with the result that perfectly free markets will fail to deliver maximum benefits.

There are numerous cases of market inefficiencies due to imperfect information, ranging from the routine to the dramatic. As a simple example, consider two lines of household batteries marketed by competing firms. The first firm's battery is a best-seller; it is cheaper to produce and, thus, carries a lower price (10 percent lower) than the competition. But, according to objective tests, the second firm's battery lasts 18 percent longer on average. If consumers possessed *perfect* information about the batteries, the second battery brand could well be the better seller because it delivers more power per penny. However, only a minority of consumers (perhaps diligent readers of *Consumer Reports*) are knowledgeable about the lives of different brands of batteries. Most consumers decide mainly on initial purchase price. Thus, in the presence of imperfect information, a free competitive market will have no way to rid itself of the less-efficient product.

Much more serious examples of market failures occur in the realm of product safety. For instance, consider a hypothetical (or perhaps not so hypothetical) children's toy, a miniature missile launcher. Let's say the toy already is popular in Europe, where it was first marketed. Now it is ready to assault the United States. Without a doubt, demand is there. The real question is whether society wants missile launchers in the hands of its 10-year-olds. The European experience suggests that one test of an expert rocketeer is to hit a challenging target at 20 paces—say, the wide-open mouth of one's little brother or sister. Lesser experts may succeed only in hitting eyes, ears, and so on. Moreover, the typical parent may know very little about these potential risks. In light of the European record of injuries and even near fatalities, the prudent regulatory response would be to ban the product in the United States altogether.

When consumers possess imperfect information or misinformation, market outcomes typically will fail the efficiency test. Consequently, there is a potential role for government to intervene in markets to improve their performance. Such intervention is justified on grounds of "paternalism"—that government regulators (with superior information) will mandate better production and consumption decisions than would take place in the free market. In many well-known instances, the argument for government paternalism and, therefore, for regulation is very strong. The government bans some drugs, taxes alcohol and cigarettes (placing warning labels on the latter), mandates compulsory education up to a certain grade (while limiting child labor), and prohibits the sale of unsafe products.

At the same time, we should recognize that government regulation is not an ideal remedy. Frequently, the choice is between imperfect markets and imperfect regulation or, sometimes, between market failure and regulatory failure. For instance, the automobile is probably the single most regulated product today. Regulations govern general performance, reliability, safety, fuel economy, and emissions. The majority of these regulations represent improvements over what would be offered in an unregulated market. But almost all these regulations are costly, and not all constitute unambiguous improvements. Later in this chapter, we will pay special attention to how the discipline of benefit–cost analysis can be used to evaluate when and how to regulate for maximum advantage.

Assessing Risks

The modern world is full of more and more things to worry about: global warming, earthquakes, asbestos in buildings, hazardous chemicals, toxins in fish, just to name a few. In making informed decisions—whether to choose air bags on a new car, use lawn pesticides, or go skiing—consumers must grapple with risk assessments all the time. Psychologists have questioned ordinary people to see how accurately they can gauge risks. In a classic study, the psychologist Paul Slovik asked 15 national experts and 40 members of the League of Women's

TABLE 14.2

Risky Choices

How would you rank the following items in order of risk?

Activity or Technology	Your Risk Ranking	Activity or Technology	Your Risk Ranking
Alcoholic beverages	_____	Motor vehicles	_____
Antibiotics	_____	Mountain climbing	_____
Bicycles	_____	Nuclear power	_____
Commercial aviation	_____	Pesticides	_____
Contraceptives	_____	Police work	_____
Electric power	_____	Power mowers	_____
Fire fighting	_____	Private aviation	_____
Food coloring	_____	Railroads	_____
Food preservatives	_____	Skiing	_____
Handguns	_____	Smoking	_____
High school and college football	_____	Spray cans	_____
Home appliances	_____	Surgery	_____
Hunting	_____	Swimming	_____
Large construction	_____	Vaccinations	_____
Motorcycles	_____	X-rays	_____

Voters to rank the everyday risks listed in Table 14.2. You can use the alphabetically ordered list of activities in the table to test your own "risk aptitude." Before turning to Table 14.3, rank the items in Table 14.2 from 1 to 30 in descending order of risk. (In constructing your ranking, consider the total risk to society of the activity or technology.)[15]

Table 14.3 lists the activities and compares the rankings of experts and ordinary people (members of the league). Scanning the list, one observes some general level of agreement between the two rankings. Certain items (handguns, motorcycles, smoking) are ranked as high risk, others as low risk (antibiotics, home appliances, power mowers) by both groups.

More interesting, however, are the gaps between people's risk perceptions and experts' judgments.[16] Psychologists have found that several factors affect the average person's risk perception. Risks that loom largest in people's perceptions are those that are most visible, imposed (rather than voluntary or

---

[15] These research results appear in Paul Slovik, "Perception of Risk," *Science* (1987): 280–285.

[16] We are not claiming that the experts' assessments are perfectly accurate. Indeed, the appropriate regulatory policy with respect to a given item depends on a careful evaluation of the benefits versus the costs of reducing risk. The point remains, however, that perception is often a far cry from reality.

TABLE 14.3

Ranking Risks:
Perception versus
Reality

Activity	Voters	Experts	Activity	Voters	Experts
Alcoholic beverages	6	3	Motor vehicles	2	1
Antibiotics	28	24	Mountain climbing	15	29
Bicycles	16	15	Nuclear power	1	20
Commercial aviation	17	16	Pesticides	9	8
Contraceptives	20	11	Police work	8	17
Electric power	18	9	Power mowers	27	28
Fire fighting	11	18	Private aviation	7	12
Food coloring	26	21	Railroads	24	19
Food preservatives	25	14	Skiing	21	30
Handguns	3	4	Smoking	4	2
High school and college football	23	27	Spray cans	14	26
			Surgery	10	5
Home appliances	29	22	Swimming	19	10
Hunting	13	23	Vaccinations	30	25
Large construction	12	13	X-rays	22	7
Motorcycles	5	6			

under one's own control), man-made (rather than natural), and potentially catastrophic (rather than mundane). For these reasons, the average person tends to overstate the risks from nuclear power, hunting, mountain climbing, skiing, private aviation, and police work. The same person tends to understate the risks from swimming, X-rays, contraceptives, and food preservatives.

Compare your own rankings to those in Table 14.3. Were your assessments closer to those of the average person or those of the experts?

II. BENEFIT–COST ANALYSIS AND PUBLIC GOODS PROVISION

Benefit–cost analysis is a method of evaluating public projects and programs.[17] Most important, it aids public managers in making current and future decisions—in choosing among alternative courses of action. Accordingly, benefit–cost analysis is used in planning budgets, building dams and airports, controlling disease, planning for safety, and spending for education and research. It also finds a place in evaluating the costs and benefits of regulation:

[17] By some historical accident, there is no clear agreement on the proper term for this method of analysis; *benefit–cost analysis* and *cost–benefit analysis* are used interchangeably.

when and how government should intervene in private markets to influence consumption and production decisions. In exploring problems posed by market failures and their remedies, we already have been utilizing benefit–cost analysis. In short, almost any government program is fair game for the application of the benefit–cost approach. We begin by discussing the economic rationale for the government's provision of certain kinds of public goods. We then go on to outline the basics of benefit–cost analysis.

PUBLIC GOODS

Although there is no single, definitive dividing line between the private and public sectors, it is useful to focus on the economic reasons why some goods and services are provided by government rather than by private markets. We already considered the case of market-supplied private goods. We now turn to the opposite case of pure public goods.

A **pure public good** is one that is nonrival and nonexclusive. Roughly speaking, it can be said that "if anyone enjoys the public good, everyone enjoys it." We can think of a pure public good as the extreme case of an externality: All benefits are external. The prototypical example of a pure public good is national defense. Defense is nonrival; that is, all citizens within the protected area enjoy the benefits of defense. (One state's enjoyment of national defense does not subtract from another state's enjoyment.) Furthermore, national defense is nonexclusive: It is impossible (or certainly impractical) to single out and exclude a particular town or region from the national-defense network. A considerable range of other goods, from local police protection to municipal mosquito abatement, shares these two properties of pure public goods.

Whether or not it is exclusive, a nonrival public good has the feature that increased benefits can be provided to additional people at zero (or negligible) marginal cost. An uncongested highway or bridge has this property. The marginal cost of additional users is zero or nearly so. Even though exclusion is feasible, it should not be employed. As we shall see, the greatest collective benefit occurs when the highway is toll free. At a price of zero, no one is excluded and usage is maximized at no additional cost. More generally, so long as they are not congested, publicly provided nonrival goods (lending libraries, parks and playgrounds, and the like) should be provided without restriction so as to be intensively used.

Public Goods and Efficiency

Under the basic benefit–cost rule, the government should undertake a project or program if and only if its total benefits exceed its total costs. Thus, a stretch of highway should be built if the collective benefits to users (discounted over the course of its life) exceed its total costs—the cost of land taken, highway construction, and annual maintenance. Because the highway allows thousands of trips per day simultaneously, we naturally sum the benefits over all these trips to compute collective benefits.

The question of whether or not to build a highway can be put more generally: What is the optimal size highway to build? Here, highway "size" is taken to mean length in miles. A longer span of multilane, high-speed roadway delivers faster and more numerous trips to more destinations at an additional construction cost per mile. Consider the planning problem of a government highway commission that has gathered the information depicted in Figure 14.3. The horizontal axis lists highways of different lengths (in miles) that might be built. The MC curve shows the marginal cost (in millions of dollars) of constructing additional miles of highway. The figure also presents demand curves for highway trips for two distinct groups: commercial users (business trucks, vans, and the like) and noncommercial users ("ordinary" drivers). Each demand curve measures the marginal benefit for the group from the greater number of trips (and greater convenience) afforded by extra miles of highway.

Identifying a highway of optimal size turns on a comparison of marginal benefit and marginal cost. The key point to recognize is that *the total marginal benefit to the groups together is found by taking the vertical sum of the separate marginal benefit (demand) curves.* For instance, according to Figure 14.3, a 10-mile-long highway delivers a marginal benefit of $1.75 million per mile to commercial vehicles and $1 million per mile to ordinary drivers. Since these trips are nonrival (i.e., the highway has more than enough capacity for both groups), the total marginal benefit is $2.75 million. More generally, the uppermost "demand" curve shows the sum of the groups' marginal benefits by size of highway. Once total marginal benefit is established, we can determine the optimal size of the public project in the usual way. In the figure, a 17.5-mile highway generates the maximum social net benefit. At this size, total marginal benefit equals marginal cost.

Two observations concerning the provision of a public good such as the highway are in order. First, there is the problem of financing the project. As pointed out earlier, to maximize usage (and, therefore, benefits), the highway should be toll free.[18] Consequently, highway costs are paid for out of government tax revenues or via new government borrowing. Unlike a private good, which is paid for only by individual users, the highway is truly a collective good. Although specific groups benefit from the good more than others, all taxpayers contribute to its cost.

Second, there is the practical difficulty of accurately estimating marginal benefits. Highway usage is by no means easy to project or to value (in dollar terms).

---

[18] Governments do set highway tolls to pay back the cost of construction or to raise revenue even after all borrowing has been retired. To the extent that these tolls reduce usage, they are economically inefficient.

FIGURE 14.3

Optimal Output of a Pure Public Good

A highway of optimal length (17.5 miles) equates the total marginal benefit of users to the marginal cost of construction.

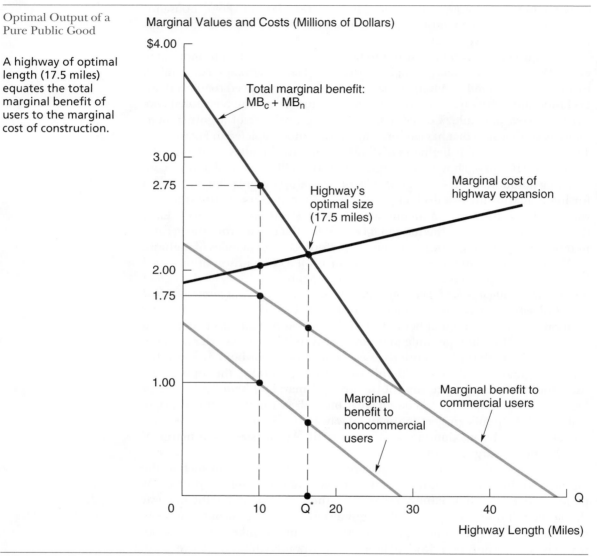

A sample of commercial and noncommercial users can be canvassed concerning their potential usage and value. Obviously, however, these results are subject to a margin of error. One problem is that the sample may be unrepresentative. Another is that potential users may deliberately misrepresent their values. Intensive users, eager for the highway to be built (and knowing it will be collectively financed), have an incentive to overstate their values. Infrequent users have the incentive to understate their values—to report zero or even negative values—to block spending on the highway. To the extent that marginal benefits (and marginal costs) are in error, so, too, will be the provision of the public good.

Not surprisingly, spending decisions on public goods frequently are determined as much by politics as by benefit–cost analyses. For instance, the highway decision could be taken out of the commission's hands and voted on directly by state representatives. The virtue of voting is that it is broadly "representative" of constituents' (or at least legislature members') preferences. However, many well-known, unavoidable difficulties are encountered with systems of voting. Voting often leads to inconsistent results and, in some circumstances, is subject to undue influence, or even manipulation, by interested parties—all within its ground rules. Perhaps the greatest difficulty is that a voter's ballot, yea or nay, cannot reflect the magnitude of the individual's true benefit or cost from the project. Thus, a project may receive majority approval even though the dollar gains of the majority fall well short of the total cost incurred by the minority. Conversely, an economically worthwhile project with benefits diffused over a vast, nonvoting constituency may well be blocked by a "special" interest group that gets out its vote.

We can sum up the present discussion by reemphasizing the sharp contrast between purely public and purely private goods. The typical private good is both rival and exclusive. (The purchase of a good—say, toothpaste—by one consumer makes it unavailable to any other consumer. Moreover, any consumer is excluded from purchasing the item if he or she is unable or unwilling to pay the good's price.) As a consequence, private goods avoid the valuation problems encountered by public goods. The marginal value of a private good is simply the current price consumers are willing to pay for it.[19]

THE BASICS OF BENEFIT–COST ANALYSIS

It is best to think of benefit–cost analysis in three steps. For a given course of action, the method (1) identifies all impacts (pro and con) on all affected members of society; (2) values these various benefits and costs in *dollar terms*; and (3) recommends undertaking the program if and only if doing so produces a positive total *net* benefit to society—that is, if and only if total benefits exceed total costs. The aim of the method is economic efficiency: ensuring that public resources are put to their best possible uses.

---

[19] We also can contrast the way marginal benefits are summed for the two classes of goods. Since pure public goods are nonrival, individual demand curves are summed *vertically* to find total marginal benefit. For private, rival goods, market demand (i.e., aggregate marginal benefit) is determined as the *horizontal* sum of individual demand curves.

Applying the Net Benefit Rule

According to the third step in benefit–cost analysis, the decision of whether or not to undertake a given program hinges on the project's net benefit. The program should be undertaken if and only if

$$\text{Net benefit} = \text{Total benefit} - \text{Total cost} > 0,$$

that is, only if total benefit exceeds total cost. (As we shall see, if benefits and costs occur over time, we must calculate the present discounted value of each using an appropriate rate of interest.) The rule is simple: The choice is between the status quo (which, by definition, has a net benefit of zero) and the project. A project with positive net benefit is an improvement on the status quo.

We can extend this basic rule to the case of several mutually exclusive public programs. For instance, suppose the Department of the Interior is considering building a dam along a major river in the Pacific Northwest. The dam can be built in one of two locations, according to one of three designs. Thus, there are six possible dam plans: seven alternatives, including the option of not building. Among these mutually exclusive alternatives, *the one with the maximum net benefit should be selected.* (If all dam plans imply negative net benefits, not building the dam delivers the highest net benefit, namely, zero.)

A second variation on the basic rule is applicable to public investment decisions involving resource constraints. Suppose that, if the dam is built, it will generate 1.5 million acre-feet of water per year. This water can be employed in a number of competing uses, including allocation to city residents, local industry, or farmers, among other segments. From a benefit–cost point of view, the water should be allocated in a way that maximizes total net benefit. A simple rule for allocating the limited supply of water is to compute the *net benefit per acre-foot* of water in each use. For instance, suppose the city's net benefit comes to $100/acre-foot, industry's to $120/acre-foot, and farmers' to $60/acre-foot. Then industry's demand should be satisfied first, followed by the city's demand, and finally the farmers' demand.

The objective of these benefit–cost rules is to promote economic efficiency. While all would agree on the need to use resources wisely, the way benefit–cost analysis carries out this goal has come under criticism. Two points in the debate center on the use of dollar values in step 2 of benefit–cost analysis and the *value judgment* concerning efficiency versus equity implicit in step 3.

Dollar Values

Critics of benefit–cost analysis point out the difficulty (and perhaps impossibility) of estimating dollar values for many impacts. How does one value clean air, greater national security, unspoiled wilderness, or additional lives saved?

How does one value a benefit that will occur in 50 years' time? As we shall see, the most difficult valuation problems arise when benefits and costs are highly uncertain, nonmarketed, intangible, or slated to occur in the distant future.

Proponents of benefit–cost analysis do not deny these difficulties; rather, they point out that any decision depends, explicitly or implicitly, on some kind of valuation. For instance, suppose a government agency refuses to authorize $80 million for spending on highway safety programs that are projected to result in 50 fewer highway deaths annually. The implication is that the lives saved are not worth the dollar cost. Given the realities of limited resources, it is hard to argue that lives are priceless or impossible to value. The agency's decision indicates that, in its reckoning, the value of such a life saved is less than $1.6 million. Virtually all economic decisions involve trade-offs, issues of dollar values and costs. The fact that these problems are difficult is no justification for ignoring or avoiding them. The strength of the benefit–cost approach is that it highlights these trade-offs, at the same time acknowledging that many values are imprecise or uncertain.

Efficiency versus Equity

The third step underscores a fundamental tenet of benefit–cost analysis: that only total benefits and costs matter, not their distribution. Thus, a program should be undertaken if it is beneficial in the aggregate, that is, if its total dollar benefits exceed total costs. But what if these benefits and costs are unequally distributed across the affected population? After all, for almost any public program there are gainers and losers. (Indeed, any citizen who obtains no benefit from the program is implicitly harmed. He or she pays part of the program's cost either directly via higher taxes or indirectly via reduced spending on programs the person would value.) Shouldn't decisions concerning public programs reflect distributional or equity considerations?

Benefit–cost analysis justifies its focus on efficiency rather than equity on a number of grounds. The first and strongest ground is that the goals of efficiency and equity need not be in conflict, provided appropriate compensation is paid among the affected parties. Consider a public program that generates different benefits and costs to two distinct groups, A and B. Group A receives a benefit of $5 million; group B suffers a loss of $3 million. The immediate impact of the project is clearly unequal. Nonetheless, if the gainers pay the losers, both groups can profit from the program. The requisite payment must exceed $3 million but not exceed $5 million.

The potential for mutually beneficial compensation exists so long as the program's total net benefit is positive. There are myriad instances in which compensation is paid. For instance, the extension of a desperately needed highway (which would generate significant regional benefits) inevitably means taking land and private homes by eminent domain. Compensation for these localized losses is accomplished by paying the owners fair market value for the properties. Though compensation is paid in specific cases, over all public programs, compensation is the exception rather than the rule. In the vast majority of cases, winners do not compensate losers at all.

The second argument for ignoring equity relies on a form of division of labor. Distribution is best addressed via a progressive tax system and through transfer programs that direct resources to low-income and other targeted groups. According to this argument, it is much more efficient to use the tax and transfer system directly than to pursue distributional goals via specific public investments. Blocking the aforementioned project on equity grounds has a net cost: forgoing a $5 million gain while saving only $3 million in cost. Redistribution via taxes and transfers conserves dollars; there is no net loss. But, of course, how well the tax system addresses distribution problems is open to debate.

A third argument in the efficiency–equity debate focuses on the aggregate impact of applying the benefit–cost rule over many projects. The contention is that by following this rule—that is, undertaking only net beneficial projects—long-run total benefits are maximized *and* project-specific inequities will tend to even out. Clearly, this last contention is an empirical issue. It will find support if the incidence of benefits and costs is independent across projects and if the law of large numbers is applicable.[20]

We make one final observation about the efficiency–equity debate. Although it is not common practice, benefit–cost analysis nonetheless is amenable to the introduction of distributional issues. As step 1 indicates, the benefit–cost method identifies, untangles, and disaggregates the various benefits and costs of all affected groups. This, in itself, is an essential part of making distributional judgments. The method's key value judgment about equity emerges when these benefits and costs are reaggregated: *All groups' benefits or costs carry equal dollar weight.* To many observers, the equal-weight standard is appealing and seems eminently fair. As an alternative approach, one can deliberately employ *unequal* weights to reflect equity concerns. For instance, if group B in the preceding example consists of low-income residents, their dollars might be accorded twice the weight of group A's dollars. With these weights, the benefit–cost analysis now becomes $5 - (2)($3) = -1 million. Thus, the program would not be implemented on equity grounds. A similar distributional analysis would support investing in a program (even it its net benefit is negative) if its benefits accrue to the neediest in society and its costs fall on the most affluent.

---

[20] Obviously, this argument would be of little consolation to a person whose home is taken by a highway (without full compensation). He or she relocates and finds out that a prison is planned for next door and a waste dump for a location upwind.

EVALUATING A PUBLIC PROJECT

In this section, we apply benefit–cost analysis to a public investment decision: building a bridge. The decision is not simply whether to invest in the bridge or save one's money. Instead, there are other questions: Is the public investment better than the alternative of regulating the private transport market? Would private investment and control of the bridge be a still better alternative?

Public Investment in a Bridge

A task force of state and city planners is considering the construction of a harbor bridge to connect downtown and a northern peninsula. Currently residents of the peninsula commute to the city via ferry (and a smaller number commute by car, taking a slow, "great circle" route). Preliminary studies have shown there is considerable demand for the bridge. The question is whether the benefit to these commuters is worth the cost.

The planners have the following information. The ferry currently provides an estimated 5 million commuting trips annually at a price of $2 per trip; since the ferry's average cost per trip is $1, its profit per trip is $1. The immediate construction cost of the bridge is $85 million. With proper maintenance, the bridge will last indefinitely. Annual operating and maintenance costs are estimated at $5 million. Plans are for the bridge to be toll free. Since the bridge will be a no-cost perfect substitute for the ferry, it will price the ferry out of business. The planners estimate the bridge will furnish 10 million commuting trips per year. The discount rate (in real terms) appropriate for the project is 4 percent. Based on this information, how can the planners construct a benefit–cost analysis to guide its investment decision?

The simplest way to proceed is to tabulate a benefit–cost analysis for the status quo (the ferry) and one for the bridge and determine which delivers the greater net benefit. Figure 14.4 shows the demand curve for commuter trips from the peninsula and the resulting benefit–cost calculations for the ferry and bridge. The demand curve in part a shows that, at the ferry's current $2-per-trip price, 5 million trips are taken (point F). If a toll-free bridge is built, 10 million trips will be made (point B). The planning board believes demand is linear; consequently, the demand curve is a straight line. (Check that its equation is $P = 4 - .4Q$, where Q is measured in *millions* of trips.)

Now we can use the demand curve to compute net benefits for the ferry and bridge alternatives. Let's start with the ferry. Currently, the ferry delivers benefits to two groups: the ferry itself (its shareholders) and commuters.

FIGURE 14.4

A Benefit–Cost Analysis
of Building a Bridge

The bridge should be
built because its
projected net benefit
is positive.

Affected Groups	Annual Flow	Net Present Value
Ferry Operator	−5.0 (profit)	−125
Ferry Commuters	−5.0 (consumer surplus)	−125
Bridge Commuters	20.0 (consumer surplus)	500
Taxpayers	−5.0 (maintenance cost)	−125
	(capital cost:)	−85
TOTAL NET BENEFIT		40

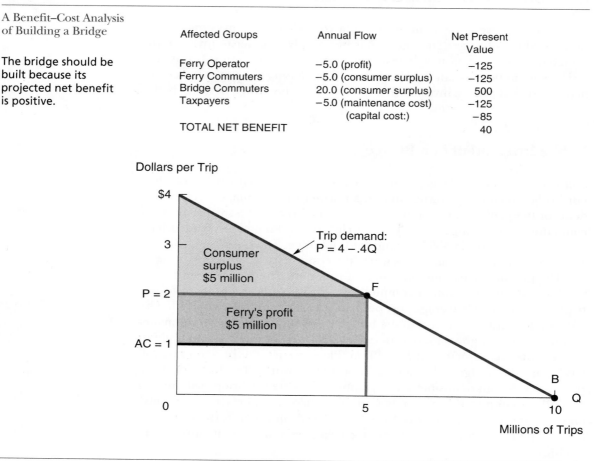

As indicated in Figure 14.4, the ferry's annual profit is $(2.00 - 1.00)(5) = \$5$
million. How do we measure the commuters' collective benefit? As for any
good or service, this benefit takes the form of *consumer surplus*—the difference between what consumers are willing to pay and the actual price
charged. The triangular area between the demand curve and the $2 price
line (up to their point of intersection at 5 million trips) measures the total
consumer surplus enjoyed by ferry commuters. The area of this triangle is
given by $(.5)(4.00 - 2.00)(5) = \$5$ million. Thus, the sum of profit plus con-
sumer surplus is $10 million per year. Supposing this benefit flow is expected

to continue at this level indefinitely, the resulting net present value is $10/.04 = \$250$ million.[21]

Now let's consider the benefit–cost calculation for the bridge in Figure 14.4. The first line under the bridge's accounting shows the adverse effect on the ferry: It is put out of business, so its profit is zero. The last two lines show the burden on taxpayers; they must foot the bill for the construction and maintenance costs of the bridge. Because the bridge charges no toll, it generates no revenue. The second line makes the key point: *The entire benefit of the bridge takes the form of consumer surplus,* the dollar benefits commuters enjoy above the (zero) price they pay. Consumer surplus is given by the triangle inscribed under the demand curve and above the zero price line. The dollar value is $(.5)(4.00)(10) = \$20$ million per year. In present-value terms, this benefit comes to $500 million against a total cost (also in present-value terms) of $210 million. Thus, the net benefit of the bridge is $290 million. Since this is greater than that of the status quo (the ferry), the bridge should be built. The advantage of the bridge relative to ferry is $290 - 250 = \$40$ million.

PUBLIC PRICING   Here's a point that should not be overlooked: The decision to build the bridge crucially depends on charging the "right" toll. In the present example, no toll is charged. The right price is zero because there is a negligible cost (no wear and tear or congestion) associated with additional cars crossing the bridge. Thus, a zero price ensures maximum use of the bridge and maximum benefit (with no associated cost). Setting any positive price would exclude some commuters and reduce net benefit. But what if there were significant costs associated with additional use of a public good? The general principle behind optimal pricing is simple: *The optimal price should just equal the marginal cost associated with extra usage.* For instance, because large tractor-trailer trucks cause significant road damage to highways, they should pay a commensurate toll. In general, user fees should be set at a level that just covers the marginal cost of the service being delivered.

Suppose the planning authority sets a $2 toll per trip on the bridge (the same price as the ferry). Compute the net (discounted) benefit of the bridge and compare it to that of the ferry. In what sense is this pricing policy self-defeating?

CHECK STATION 3

REGULATING THE FERRY   Before concluding that building the bridge is warranted, government decision makers should consider another option: regulation of the private market. In our example, regulation means limiting the price the ferry operator can charge. From a benefit–cost point of view, the optimal

---

[21] Recall that the present value of a perpetual annuity is $PV = CF/r$, where CF is the annual cash flow and r is the yearly interest rate. In the present example, it probably would be more realistic to predict annual traffic (on the ferry or the bridge) to grow at some rate per year (g). In this case, present value is given by $PV = CF/(r - g)$.

regulated price is simply the price that would prevail in a perfectly competitive market. With free entry of competitors into the market, the ferry's price would be driven down to the zero-profit point, P = $1. Thus, this is the price the government should set for the (natural monopolist) ferry operator.

At a $1 price, the ferry delivers 7.5 million trips and makes a zero profit. Commuters realize total consumer surplus that comes to (.5)(4.00 − 1.00)(7.5) = $11.25 million per year. The present value of the net benefit associated with ferry regulation is 11.25/.04 = $281.25 million. Building the bridge, with a discounted net benefit of $290 million, has a slight edge over the regulatory alternative and continues to be the best course of action.

CHECK STATION 4   Could a private firm profitably build and operate the bridge? Assume it faces the same costs and interest rate as the government. In addition, the private bridge is expected to share the market with the ferry, unless it prices the latter out of business. What toll should the private bridge operator charge? Can it realize a profit?

VALUING BENEFITS AND COSTS

The main issues with respect to valuing benefits and costs concern the role of market prices and ways of valuing nonmarketed items.

Market Values

In most cases, market prices provide the correct values for benefits and costs. This result is exactly what one would expect in light of the discussion in Chapter 10. There we saw that competitive markets are efficient. In such markets, the price of the good or service is an exact measure of its marginal benefit to consumers and its marginal cost to producers: P = MB = MC. For instance, if construction of the bridge requires 50,000 cubic yards of concrete and the price of concrete is $100 per cubic yard, the total cost of this input is $5 million. Whether the concrete actually is obtained via an increase in total production (at a $5 million additional cost to producers), or whether it means displacing some other consumption (causing $5 million in lost benefit to previous consumers), is immaterial. Of course, the same principle applies to the cost of any input to production—capital, labor, land, and so on. It also applies to valuing the benefits of program outputs. For instance, suppose the chief benefit of constructing a water project is the irrigation of new tracts of land. The market value of the resulting crops (net of associated costs) would represent the dollar benefits of the project.

Correct valuation of benefits and costs, based on market prices, may require modifications in some circumstances. We know that the current market price reflects the valuation of marginal units (i.e., the last units consumed).

But if the output impact is large, a significant amount of consumer surplus will be created above and beyond revenue generated at the going market price. This surplus should be counted in the benefit–cost analysis. Thus, the zero toll is hardly an accurate measure of the benefit per trip generated by the bridge. All of its benefit takes the form of consumer surplus.

A second problem concerns price distortions. Taxes are one source of distortions. For instance, suppose the government sets a tariff on the import of an agricultural good with the intent of protecting domestic farmers from foreign competition. The result is that the domestic price for this crop is $1 above the world price. How should one value the new crops grown using water from a federal dam? The difficulty is that instead of a single price reflecting marginal benefit and marginal cost, there are two prices. If all the crop is sold on the world market, that is the appropriate price, and similarly for the home market. If the crop is sold on both markets, the appropriate value is a weighted average of the separate prices.[22]

A third instance involves unemployment. If resources are fully employed, utilizing them for one purpose instead of another is costly. The opportunity cost is the lost product they would have earned in their alternative use. This general point applies specifically to the labor market. The cost of hiring a worker to build the bridge is given by the going market *wage* for labor of comparable skill. This wage reflects that worker's productivity in an alternative, private construction job. But what if the new worker was formerly unemployed? Now the market wage is not an accurate measure of the opportunity cost. Presumably this cost reflects only the worker's lost leisure time, not his or her lost productivity elsewhere. To put this another way, if the benefit–cost analysis takes the market wage as a cost, it also should count as a benefit the income (net of forgone leisure) enjoyed by the new worker. Thus, the benefit–cost sum would include

$$-\text{Wage} + (\text{Wage} - \text{Lost leisure}).$$

The first term is the out-of-pocket cost of hiring the worker; the second term is the value of the new job created. Note that the wage term cancels out in the sum. This confirms that the ultimate opportunity cost of hiring the *unemployed* worker is simply the value of lost leisure time.

Nonmarketed Benefits and Costs

One gains a renewed appreciation for the role of market prices when one considers the difficulties in valuing nonmarketed items. For instance, heroic efforts are required to evaluate the performance of public elementary and secondary schools

[22] Another source of price distortions stems from the presence of monopoly. Under monopoly pricing, $P = MB > MC$. Suppose cement for the bridge is supplied by a monopolist. In that instance, it matters whether the cement is obtained via an increase in supply or from a reduction in another customer's consumption. In the first case, the appropriate cost to society is MC; in the second, it is MB. Yet another source of price distortions is externalities.

(let alone the dollar value of this education). How can one identify superior schools? Should performance be judged in terms of teacher–student ratios, average test scores, or dropout rates? All of these measures provide highly imperfect indices of performance. Indeed, educators agree there is no perfect measure.

One turns to such measures for a very simple reason: Because public education is provided collectively (i.e., financed out of local tax revenues), there is no "market" value for this essential service. Parents do not pay market prices for their children's education, nor are they free (with some special exceptions) to choose among public schools. Contrast these difficulties with the problem of valuing education provided by private schools. Here the value is clear; it is at least as much as the price parents actually pay in tuition. For purposes of measuring economic value, there is no need for a doctoral dissertation on the determinants of school performance; the market price is enough. If, for whatever reason, a private school fails to deliver a quality education, parents will stop paying the high market price.

The same point about valuation applies to all nonmarketed goods: national security, pollution, health risks, traffic congestion, even the value of a life. Being nonmarketed, all of these goods are difficult to value. In the absence of market prices, other valuation methods are necessary. Roughly speaking, there are three approaches to valuing nonmarketed goods and so-called "intangibles": (1) direct elicitation of values, (2) values based on indirect market prices, and (3) socially determined values.

DIRECT ELICITATION   A straightforward way to find out what people really want is to ask them. Researchers often use direct surveys and opinion polls to acquire information about benefits and costs. For instance, consider a program of subsidized "free" day care for low-income, single parents. Cost estimates for such a program are available, but the dollar value of benefits is more elusive. A direct approach is to identify and survey the recipient population: "How much would 20 hours of day care per week, located within 20 minutes of your residence, be worth to you? What about 40 hours per week?" The survey would inquire about a range of day-care options as a way to gauge what form of day care is most valuable. Perhaps between 500 and 1,000 completed surveys would become the basis for estimates of potential participation rates and average dollar values for alternative kinds of day-care offerings.

Policy makers use surveys as a means of valuation in a host of public projects and programs. Surveys have been used to help ascertain the benefits of air quality improvement (including improved visibility in Los Angeles from smog reduction), the benefits of public transport, the cost of increased travel time due to traffic, the value of local public goods (expanding an elementary school or building a new town library), the risks of occupational hazards, the costs of nearby "undesirable facilities," such as prisons and waste facilities, and so on.

Direct elicitation carries a number of advantages. The method is current and direct. It is relatively uncomplicated and controllable: The survey can be designed to ask the "right" questions of the "right" sample population. Because it asks what people want, the method is politically appealing. However, the survey approach is costly and subject to many commonly acknowledged sources of errors. To the extent that those surveyed are not perfectly representative of the entire targeted group, the survey will suffer from sampling bias. The broader difficulty is in the expressed monetary valuations themselves. Since survey questions are invariably hypothetical, answers that express the individual's true preferences are difficult to obtain. Accurate benefit valuation requires precisely worded questions: "As a chemical worker, how much would it be worth to you (in monetary terms) if your risk of injury on the job were reduced by 25 percent?" But precise questions often meet with very imprecise answers.[23] A more general question is easier to answer: "Would you give up $2,000 in annual salary if your job as a chemical worker could be made 'safe'?"; "Are you in favor of continued construction of nuclear power plants?" However, such questions are less applicable to the valuation task at hand.

INDIRECT MARKET MEASURES   A second approach to estimating values holds that actions speak louder than words and seeks to infer values for nonmarketed items from individual behavior in "related" markets. A number of examples illustrate the method.

1. As mentioned earlier, the benefit of a public secondary school education is difficult to estimate because it does not carry a market price. An obvious approach is to turn to labor markets for help. What is the expected difference in labor earnings (in present-value terms) between a high school graduate and a ninth-grade dropout?[24] The answer to this question offers a ready measure of the economic value of these years of schooling (although not necessarily the full personal value).

2. How much is an individual's time worth? The answer to this question is pertinent to transportation issues: the cost of traffic congestion, the benefit of centrally locating an airport. Again, labor markets suggest a

---

[23] Surveys of low-income groups face an additional problem. For these groups, value responses reflect both willingness to pay and ability to pay. Consider two alternative survey questions: (1) If a new day-care facility were built in your neighborhood, how much would you be willing to pay for 20 hours of day care per week? (2) You are currently using 20 hours of day care per week. If the facility were to close down, how much money per week would be needed to compensate you for the loss of day-care services? The answer to the first question (constrained by the respondent's ability to pay) might be much lower than the answer to the second ($3 per hour, say, compared to $6 per hour). Since the goal of the day-care program is to efficiently address the needs of the local, low-income population, many would argue that the second response (free of the income constraint) represents the superior benefit estimate.

[24] To measure properly the value of schooling *alone*, this comparison must allow for other factors. Thus, differential earnings should be computed for individuals of comparable intelligence and socioeconomic status.

maximum value: the hourly wage one can earn on the job. If one chooses an additional hour of work over leisure, then the worker must value leisure higher than the going wage rate.

3. Environmental costs and benefits also are intangible; they find no ready expression in the market. The cost of air pollution takes many forms: aesthetic costs (poor air and visibility) and health costs (added sick days, increased morbidity and mortality). A large body of medical and statistical research has attempted to estimate the effect of pollution on health (controlling for myriad other factors) and the dollar cost of these health-related impacts. An alternative approach compares property values in high-pollution areas versus those in otherwise comparable low-pollution areas. The difference in property values reflects the cost the "market" assesses for pollution.

SOCIALLY DETERMINED VALUES   Society, via its norms and laws, places monetary values on many nonmarketed items. Workers' compensation laws determine monetary payments in the event of industrial injuries. Judges and juries determine the extent of damages and appropriate compensation in contract and tort proceedings. In divorce cases, the court frequently is asked to determine the monetary value of a homemaker's contribution to the family. Government regulations implicitly determine societal values. For instance, federal law requires special access for the handicapped in public buildings and public transit. Presumably, the cost of meeting this requirement represents a lower bound for the value society places on easy access.

CHECK STATION 5   How might each of the preceding approaches provide dollar values in the following situations: (a) the costs (across all dimensions to all affected parties) of accidents in the chemical industry and (b) the cost of noise pollution for residents near busy airports?

VALUING LIVES   Perhaps the most controversial application of benefit–cost analysis occurs in the valuation of lives. On the one hand, many of us would like to believe human life is "priceless" or, in some sense, beyond monetary measure. On the other hand, a host of government programs involves significant safety benefits, not only in the form of injuries prevented but also in terms of lives saved. The issue in all such decisions is whether the benefits (including lives saved) are worth the cost. As mentioned earlier, the decision *not* to spend $80 million on a program expected to save 50 lives means the cost per life saved, $1.6 million, is too high. In short, spending or not spending on public safety programs implicitly or explicitly involves valuing lives.

A number of approaches to estimating the dollar value of a life have been taken. All of the approaches have drawbacks and none can claim to justify a precise dollar value. Instead, the goal is to determine a possible range of dollar values encompassing the value of a life. A first approach, the *earnings* method, appeals to the labor market for an answer. Boldly stated, the value of a representative life is measured by the present value of an individual's lifetime wage earnings. To illustrate the method, we use a deliberately oversimplified example. Consider a 22-year-old individual whose annual current earnings are $40,000. Over the course of his working life (say, 50 years), his real earnings (adjusted for inflation) are expected to be constant. Using a real interest rate of 3 percent, the present value of his earnings comes to $1,028,000. (From a financial table, we find the present value of a $1 annuity spanning 50 years to be $25.7. Thus, a $40,000 annuity has a present value of (40,000)(25.7) = $1,028,000.) Depending on the precise assumptions, studies that have used the earnings approach have produced estimates in the general neighborhood of $1 million per life. Of course, many would argue that the presumption "you're worth what you earn" constitutes a gross understatement of a life's value. (One would never want to apply this method to unemployed or retired people.)

A second approach examines the amounts of compensation individuals demand for bearing the risk of death. Wages in high-risk jobs provide market evidence concerning this issue. Other things being equal, high-risk jobs—law enforcement, firefighting, skyscraper construction, mining, lumberjacking, oil drilling, to name a few—pay higher wages. A number of studies have used statistical methods to estimate the relationship between wage premiums and mortality risks. Again we employ an oversimplified example. Construction work on skyscrapers is a high-risk occupation. By some estimates, the *additional* mortality risk (relative to a comparable low-risk job) is in the neighborhood of 2 per 1,000 *per year.* Suppose the wage premium paid to such workers (again relative to a comparable low-risk job) is $5,000 per year. What conclusions can we draw from these facts? If a construction firm hires, say, 1,000 workers, it pays a total wage premium (due to risk) of $5 million and 2 deaths will occur on average. The implied value of a life is 5,000,000/2 = $2,500,000.

Proponents argue that the risk–cost trade-off embodied in private markets is the best guide to valuing lives when it comes to government decisions. Like the earnings approach, the risk compensation method provides a ballpark estimate of the value of a life. The approach has the advantage that it attempts to measure the cost (in terms of compensation) of additional risks. However, the method also is likely to underestimate a life's dollar value. An individual who chooses a high-risk occupation can be expected to be more risk loving than the average person and, therefore, demand a lower wage premium. (If compensation for the average person were closer to $7,000, the value of a life would be $3,500,000.) Additionally, workers in dangerous occupations may be inadequately informed about the true risks. Values for lives inferred from such decisions may reflect (at least partially) poor judgment, as well as calculated risks. Also, many high-risk jobs may go to people who, due to their socioeconomic status, have few other options. Value estimates using this approach tend to be considerably higher than those based on lifetime earnings—in the range of $3 million to $6 million.[25]

More recently, this approach has been applied beyond the labor market. It has been used to estimate values for lives based on observed consumer behavior in product purchase decisions, for instance, consumers' willingness to pay for added safety features in automobiles. In addition, several questionnaire surveys have been aimed at the same issue. In this method, a large sample of citizens (1,000 or more) are asked to make choices (hypothetical) involving different dollar/risk trade-offs from which average values for lives can be inferred.[26]

The FDA, AZT, and AIDS Revisited

The regulation of therapeutic drugs, such as AZT, poses particularly difficult problems because three kinds of market failure are present at once. First, external benefits associated with the discovery and marketing of new drugs are enormous. Thus, strong patent protection for developers of new drugs is essential to provide incentives for investment in high-cost and risky R&D in the first place. But patent laws remedy one kind of market failure at the expense of a second. Under patent protection, the developer has a 20-year monopoly on the sale of the drug and, naturally, attempts to establish monopoly prices in order to maximize available profit. The presence of monopoly means that prices will be inefficiently high and output will be restricted below the efficient level. (After the fact, social benefits would be maximized if new drugs were priced at marginal cost.)

A third type of market failure stems from imperfect information. On their own, consumers have no means to assess the benefits and risks of new drugs; nor does the average physician who might prescribe the drug. Thus, before any new drug is commercialized, laboratory and clinical studies are required to confirm its benefits and to identify potential side effects and risks. The medical research community, in conjunction with drug companies, carries out these tests. The Food and Drug Administration evaluates the test results and decides whether or not to approve the drug. In fact, the FDA approval process relies on two basic benefit–cost rules: (1) approve the drug if and only if its expected benefits exceed its costs, and (2) design the type, length, and extent of the prior tests, so that the expected benefit of additional information about the drug just matches the extra dollar costs of the tests. In short, in accord with Chapter 9's discussion concerning the value of information, the costs of the FDA evaluation process should be weighed against the benefits. Thus, tough information requirements of drug licensing account for the lengthy testing and approval process (seven or more years).

Given these multiple market failures, how should the government set its trade-offs in regulating new drugs? The answers are simpler in principle than in practice. Ideally, the

---

[25] The Department of Transportation has used a value for a life of approximately $3 million, whereas the Environmental Protection Agency currently uses a value of $3.7 million.

[26] A final approach is based on socially determined values (as discussed earlier). In a case of wrongful death suit brought to court, a jury's task is to set the size of any monetary award to be paid to surviving family members.

government should grant the developer the right to sell a new drug at a price that offers the firm a normal rate of return given the risks of the development process. Thus, this prescription parallels the rule of average-cost pricing, discussed earlier in the context of natural monopoly (Chapter 11). A significant difference, however, involves the caveat concerning the risks of research and development. Drug research is not only costly, but, in addition, only a small fraction of the drugs on which R&D efforts are devoted are brought to market. Properly measured, the total cost of a particular successful drug includes the variable cost associated with production, the huge fixed costs devoted to the drug's own R&D, and the development costs of the expected number of "dry holes" that never make it to market. The regulator must track down and measure all of these costs if it is to institute "correct" average-cost pricing.

Because of the difficulty in measuring average costs, the majority of health analysts are reluctant to move toward formal price regulations for new drugs.[27] Research studies provide some evidence of above-normal returns earned by pharmaceutical companies. But price regulations designed to eliminate excess profits could go too far, leaving drug companies with below-normal returns and severely retarding new drug development. More modest government strategies aimed at increasing the availability of new drugs include (1) increasing government subsidies to needy individuals to pay for the costs of drugs, (2) disseminating information about generic drug substitutes, and (3) using managed-care purchasing arrangements to negotiate lower drug prices.

The government does have a significant role to play on other fronts. Given the enormous external benefits of new drug development, the government should continue to sponsor and subsidize scientific studies by universities, private firms, and its own research groups. Finally, for many new drugs, such as AZT, the FDA should accelerate its approval process (notwithstanding the high costs of doing so). For the most promising drugs, the considerable benefits of early introduction and dissemination justify these additional costs.

SUMMARY

Decision-Making Principles

1. There are three main causes of market failure: monopoly power, externalities, and imperfect information. Each case offers a potential role for government regulation.

2. Benefit–cost analysis identifies all impacts (pro and con) on all affected members of society, values these benefits and costs in dollar terms, and sums all benefits and subtracts all costs to determine net benefit. A project should be adopted or a regulation enacted if, and only if, it has a

---

[27] For economic assessments of drug development and policy recommendations, see E. Porter, "Do New Drugs Always Have to Cost so Much?" *The New York Times* (November 14, 2004), BU5, and F. M. Scherer, "Pricing, Profits, and Technological Progress in the Pharmaceutical Industry," *Journal of Economic Perspectives* (Summer 1993): 97–116.

positive net benefit. This last rule does not formally account for distributional effects. Nonetheless, the cataloguing of costs and benefits should alert the policy maker to the equity and distributional consequences of the program.

Nuts and Bolts

1. Deadweight loss measures the reduction in net benefits when the level of output differs from the efficient (i.e., competitive) outcome. Under monopoly, the deadweight loss triangle stems from the production of too little output. Rent seeking measures the costs that occur when firms expend resources to obtain monopoly power. Measures to promote and/or restore competitive behavior are the most effective remedies for monopoly.

2. An externality is an impact or side effect that is caused by one economic agent and incurred by another agent or agents. An efficient means of regulation is to tax the producer of a negative externality an amount exactly equal to the associated marginal external cost. Under conditions conducive to bargaining, externalities also may be resolved via monetary payments between the affected parties.

3. Pure public goods are nonrival and nonexclusive. The optimal quantity of a pure public good is determined where the sum of the marginal benefits to all affected groups equals the good's marginal cost.

4. The basic benefit–cost decision rules are as follows:
   a. Distributional consequences aside, undertake a single public investment if and only if the present value of net benefits is positive.
   b. In a choice among mutually exclusive alternatives, select the one with the highest present value of net benefits.
   c. In public decisions involving resource constraints, select combinations of programs that maximize total net benefits subject to the constraints.

5. When efficiently functioning markets exist for a program's inputs and outputs, we can value the associated benefits and costs at market prices. The valuation of nonmarketed impacts and "intangibles" follows one of three approaches: (a) direct elicitation of values, (b) values based on indirect market values, and (c) values based on public policy.

Questions and Problems

1. Suppose Coca-Cola and Pepsi announced plans to merge into a single global soft-drink company. What would be the possible effects on soft-drink consumers of such a union? What kind of regulatory scrutiny should the U.S. government cast on the proposed merger?

2. In each of the following situations, explain whether an externality is present.
   a. Mine safety has improved in recent years. Nonetheless, mining accidents result in 50 to 100 deaths per year and thousands of lost workdays due to injury.
   b. Large brokerage and financial service companies conduct intensive introductory training programs for new hires, many of whom, once trained, leave the company within the first year to work for competitors.
   c. The volume of email spam has grown exponentially in the last five years. (One proposed remedy is to require a sender's computer to solve a 5-second problem every time it sends an email.)
   d. A husband and wife who have put off buying a house suddenly find themselves priced out of the market by rocketing real-estate prices.

3. Consider the market for studded tires used to fight hazardous road conditions during the winter months. Industry demand is given by $P = 170 - 5Q$, where Q is the number of tires in thousands, and P is the price per tire in dollars. Studded tires are supplied in a competitive market at an average cost of \$60 per tire.
   a. Determine the competitive price and quantity of studded tires.
   b. Over their lifetimes, studded tires cause considerable road damage. The best estimate of total road damage is $C = .25Q^2$. Consequently, the marginal cost of an extra studded tire on the road is given by $MC = .5Q$. The MC per tire increases the greater the number of tires grinding down the road. Accounting for this road damage, a regulator seeks to determine the quantity of tires that will maximize net social benefit. Find this quantity. (*Hint*: Find the quantity at which the competitive price equals the full cost of an extra tire.) At this quantity, what is the resulting market price? Compute the net social benefit.
   c. By what regulatory means could this outcome be obtained? Explain.
   d. Suppose firms can manufacture low-impact studded tires that do negligible road damage at an extra cost of \$12 per tire. Assuming optimal regulation (as in part b or part c), which type of tire will be produced? Explain.

4. Explain whether you agree or disagree with each of the following statements concerning the role of government. In each case, indicate whether your position is based (implicitly or explicitly) on benefit–cost analysis or on some other criterion.
   a. The Consumer Product Safety Commission should uphold strict safety standards for all children's toys.
   b. OSHA should relax many of its workplace safety regulations, for instance, by relying on workers to take precautions rather than requiring expensive safety devices on machines and tools.

    c. Mass transit, all public buildings, and all institutions receiving federal funds must be modified where necessary to ensure access for disabled individuals.

    d. The Department of Agriculture should curtail the use of pesticides by farmers.

    e. Given its large projected deficit, the federal government should postpone capital spending to repair 100-year-old bridges.

5. Two large manufacturing firms are major sources of airborne pollutants in a metropolitan area. Currently, each firm generates about 15 million units of pollution per year. The firms' costs of reducing pollution are $C_1 = 2Q_1 + .1Q_1^2$ and $C_2 = .15Q_2^2$, where Q_1 and Q_2 denote the amounts of pollution cleaned up by the respective firms. The social benefit of reducing pollution is estimated to be $B = 9Q - .2Q^2$, where Q denotes the total amount of pollution cleaned up; that is, $Q = Q_1 + Q_2$.

    a. Write the expressions for the marginal benefit and marginal costs of cleanup, that is, MB, MC_1, and MC_2.

    b. Suppose the EPA seeks to implement pollution standards that maximize net benefits to society $(B - C_1 - C_2)$. Find the optimal values of Q_1 and Q_2 by setting $MB = MC_1 = MC_2$. Explain why the firms face different quantity standards.

    c. Suppose, instead, that the regulator sets a uniform pollution tax of $4 per unit. How much pollution will each firm clean up?

    d. What tax should the regulator set to implement the optimal cleanup amounts in part b? Explain.

6. Three blocs of nations are beginning negotiations aimed at reducing the emissions of greenhouse gases (GHGs). The blocs are the United States, the European Community, and a coalition of developing countries (DNs). Table A shows each bloc's current GHG emissions and the annual cost of reducing emissions to lower levels. The extent of global warming depends on the *total* GHG emissions of the three blocs. Each bloc would benefit from global emission reductions; a slowdown in warming would mean avoiding significant economic and environmental costs. Table B lists these benefits (measured vis-à-vis the status quo). In both tables, emissions are measured in billions of tons per year.

    a. Is global warming a kind of prisoner's dilemma? Is it in the self-interest of any of the blocs to reduce emissions unilaterally? Explain briefly.

    b. In preliminary talks, Europe has sought an agreement calling for "shared sacrifices"—that is, multilateral emission reductions. However, because of large budget deficits, neither the United States nor Europe is prepared to extend monetary aid to the developing world in compensation for its reductions. Does there exist a multilateral reduction plan that benefits all blocs?

TABLE A

Costs of Reducing Emissions ($ Billions per Year)

	United States		Europe		Developing Nations	
Population	250 million		400 million		2 billion	
National Income	$10 trillion		$12 trillion		$4 trillion	
	Emissions	Cost	Emissions	Cost	Emissions	Cost
Status Quo	1.2	$ 0	1.0	0	1.4	0
	1.0	22	.8	18	1.2	12
	.8	60	.6	42	1.0	30
	.6	100	.4	80	.8	48

TABLE B

Benefits from Emission Reductions ($ Billions per Year)

Total Emissions	United States	Europe	DNs	Total Emissions	United States	Europe	DNs
3.6	0	0	0	2.6	28	40	46
3.4	6	8	10	2.4	32	45	54
3.2	12	16	20	2.2	36	50	60
3.0	18	24	30	2.0	40	55	66
2.8	24	32	38	1.8	44	60	72

c. Suppose, instead, that financial payments between blocs are feasible. Identify the efficient global reduction plan. How much reduction should each bloc undertake, and what sort of compensation is necessary? (*Hint*: Any incremental emission reduction should be undertaken as long as the *additional* global benefit exceeds the *extra* cost.)

7. A city must decide whether to build a downtown parking garage (for up to 750 cars) and what rate to charge. It is considering two rates: a flat $1.50-per-hour rate or an all-day rate averaging $1 per hour (based on a $10 daily rate and an average 10-hour stay). Parking demand is $Q = 900 - 300P$, where Q is the number of cars in the garage each hour and P is the hourly rate. The capital cost of the garage is estimated to be $20 million and its annual operating cost to be $.62 million (regardless of the number of cars utilizing it) over its estimated 40-year life. The city's discount rate is 8 percent. At 8 percent, $1 per year for 40 years has a present value of $11.90. (Use the factor of 11.9 to multiply yearly net benefits to obtain a present value.)

a. Sketch the demand curve (per hour) and calculate total benefits—the sum of consumer surplus and revenue—from the garage under either rate. (Multiply by 10 hours per day and 260 working days per year to find annual values.) Should the city build the facility? If so, which of the two rates should it charge?

b. Could a private developer profitably build and operate the garage? Which of the two rates would it set? (Assume it faces the same demand, costs, and discount rate as the city.)

8. a. A commonly used benefit–cost rule is to undertake a program if and only if its ratio of benefits to cost (both in present-value terms) is greater than 1 (B/C > 1). Does this rule make sense?

b. A city is deliberating what to do with a downtown vacant lot that it owns. Should it build a parking garage or a public library? According to its studies, the benefit–cost ratio for the garage is 2 and the ratio for the library is 1.5. Accordingly, the city decides to build the garage. Is this conclusion justified, or is additional information needed? Explain carefully.

c. A state must decide which of its deteriorating bridges to repair within its limited budget. The total number of such bridges (some currently closed for safety reasons) is between 450 and 500. The state has gathered estimates of repair costs and projected traffic benefits for each bridge. It has decided to repair those bridges with the greatest benefit–cost ratios until its budget is exhausted. Does this strategy make sense? Explain carefully.

9. A state in the northwestern United States faces a number of problems concerning the production of its paper products. The wood pulp industry (from which paper is made) is monopolized and generates a significant amount of pollution. As the state's secretary of commerce, you have hired three analysts to help you think through several government policy alternatives. The demand for wood pulp is given by $P = 500 - 10Q$, where Q is measured in thousands of units. The long-run cost of production exhibits constant returns to scale: $LAC = LMC = 150$. Producing a unit of wood pulp generates one unit of pollution. The marginal external cost is estimated to be 100 per extra unit of pollution.

a. Analyst A advises no government intervention at all. In this case, what quantity and price will prevail in the (monopolized) industry?

b. Analyst B is mainly worried about the monopolization of the industry and, therefore, recommends that you promote competition through regulation and antitrust policy. What quantity of pulp would a perfectly competitive industry produce?

c. Analyst C is worried about the pollution externality and, therefore, recommends a tax of 100 per unit of pulp output (on the currently monopolized industry). What quantity of pulp will the monopolized industry produce under the tax?

d. Which of the analysts' recommendations would you support? Do you have a better policy? Explain. (*Hint*: Identify the socially efficient level of pulp production to help clarify your answer.)

10. In the early 1970s, the governor of Maine assembled a task force to evaluate several oil company proposals to develop a deep-water harbor for tankers and to build a refinery at Machias, a seaport at the northeastern end of the state's rocky and unspoiled coast. Following are miscellaneous facts that may (or may not) be relevant to a benefit–cost analysis of the proposal.

(1) The harbor and refinery would process 30,000 barrels of crude oil per day into home-heating oil, gasoline, and other fuels.

(2) The complex would provide cheaper oil to the state and to the Northeast in general. (Neighboring New Hampshire imports much of its oil from Canada.)

(3) Recently, a tanker broke up off the Maine coast, causing a major oil spill. Coastal property owners believe the harbor and refinery would jeopardize the value of their land.

(4) Industries in the region, including utilities, construction companies, and the state's railroads, vigorously support the project.

(5) Unemployment in the region is 3 percent above the national average.

(6) The growth of Maine's tourist industry (the state's biggest industry) has leveled off in recent years.

(7) Several oil companies are competing for the project.

a. Outline a benefit–cost analysis of the proposed project.

b. Select three or four benefits or costs and explain how they might be valued. Describe some of the major uncertainties inherent in the benefit–cost analysis. What additional information about these risks would be useful?

11. A state highway safety agency must allocate its budget for the next fiscal year. A total funding of $32 million has been granted for reducing fatalities and property damage due to automobile accidents. However, detailed funding decisions concerning specific programs remain to be made. The table lists pertinent data on four major programs.

To solve its budget problem, the council still must formulate a trade-off between lives saved and property damage prevented. The council is aware that a certain government agency employed $1.6 million as the value of a life saved. To make a start on its decision, members of the council have agreed to use this figure, enabling it to put a dollar value on the total benefits (from lives and property saved) of a given expenditure on each program.

Project	Upper Limit on Expenditures	Expected Fatalities Prevented per Millions of Dollars Expended	Expected Reduction in Property Damage per Millions of Dollars Expended
Seat-belt advertising	$14,000,000	2.9	$0
Research in improved highway safety	12,000,000	.6	3,200,000
Research in improved auto design	9,000,000	1.6	1,500,000
Dollars spent lobbying for tougher drunk-driving penalties	16,000,000	2.3	200,000

a. Find the budget allocation that generates the greatest total benefits. (*Hint*: Where should the first dollars be spent, the next dollars, and so on?)

b. Suppose the council increases the value of a life to $2.4 million. How does the value placed on a life influence the council's budget allocation? Explain briefly.

12. An industrial state has been generating increasing amounts of hazardous waste and is considering construction of a waste treatment facility. The key question is where to locate it. The attitude of most cities and towns toward the facility is "Not in my backyard!" Under state law, towns have the absolute right to refuse such a facility. The state is encouraging private waste disposal companies to negotiate with towns that might be willing to accept the facility. The table summarizes annual benefits and costs (in millions of dollars) associated with the five leading sites. Only *one* site will be chosen for the facility. Note that the state's industries as a whole will benefit from having an in-state facility. In addition, the sites offer the developer potential profits but will generate substantial costs for the host towns.

Affected Groups	Site				
	A	B	C	D	E
State industry	4	4	3	2	3
Developer's:					
revenue	12	12	12	12	12
cost	−6	−9	−7	−7	−8
Host town's cost	−7	−5	−4	−8	−2

a. What is the developer's most profitable site? Suppose the developer negotiates with a number of towns. At which site would you predict the final agreement to be reached? Does this site generate maximum net benefits?

b. Suppose only sites A, B, and D are feasible. Is a negotiated agreement between the developer and the town possible? According to the benefit–cost standard, where should the facility be located? How could this outcome be implemented? Explain.

Discussion Question In the aftermath of the September 11, 2001, terrorist attacks in New York City and Washington, DC, there has been renewed concern about airport security. To date, security services at major airports have been provided by a small number of private firms under contract with the airlines.

a. Many commentators and policy makers have argued that airport security should not be left as the responsibility of private firms. Identify the possible sources of market failure (if any) that might lead to security standards that are too weak. What kinds of economic information could one gather as evidence for or against market failure?

b. Supposing that a strong case for market failure were made, what are the possible remedies? How could one apply benefit–cost analysis to craft the most effective remedy? (In answering questions a and b, a first step is to gather relevant information concerning the economics of airport security from the business press and online.)

Spreadsheet Problem

S1. Consider once again the combination of market failures outlined in Problem 9. Recall that the demand for wood pulp is described by $P = 500 - 10Q$, where Q is measured in thousands of units. The long-run cost of production exhibits constant returns to scale: $LAC = LMC = 150$. Producing a unit of wood pulp generates one unit of pollution, and the marginal external cost is estimated to be 100 per extra unit of pollution.

a. Create a spreadsheet similar to the one shown to model this setting. In the spreadsheet, cells B10, C10, and D10 contain numerical values. The entries in rows 15 and 19 and cell E10 are computed by formulas linked to the numerical cells. *Hints*: Remember that consumer surplus is found by using the formula for the area of a triangle, in this case: $.5*(500 - E10)*B10$. Total benefit is the sum of consumer surplus, net profit, and government tax revenue minus the external costs associated with pollution.

	A	B	C	D	E	F	G	H
1								
2		COPING WITH AN EXTERNALITY						
3								
4			Market Demand		LMC = LAC		MC$_{EXT}$	
5			P = 500 − 10Q		150		100	
6								
7								
8		Quantity	Tax	Clean Up (u)	Price			
9								
10		10	0	0	400			
11								
12								
13		Con Surp	Net Profit	Govt Rev	External Cost		Total Benefit	
14								
15		500	2,500	0	1,000		2,000	
16								
17			Gross Profit	tax+clnup cost	tax − MCu			
18								
19			2,500	0	0			
20								

b. Using the spreadsheet, confirm the output and price results for each of the analyst's recommendations in Problem 9. Then find the optimal regulatory policy using the spreadsheet's optimizer. That is, maximize total benefit by adjusting the output and tax cells.

c. Now suppose that the wood pulp producers can clean up part or all of their pollution at a cost. The total cost of "cleaning up" u units of pollution is $5u^2$ (i.e., it increases quadratically). By cleaning up pollution, producers avoid any tax. Thus, the government's tax revenue is given by $R = t(Q - u)$, and the firms' total pollution related costs are $t(Q - u) + 5u^2$ (cell D19). Find the optimal output, tax, and cleanup. [*Hint*: Maximize total benefits subject to cell E19 equaling zero. Remember that the firms will reduce pollution up to the point that the tax/unit equals the MC of cleaning up an extra unit (and note that MC = 10u).] Explain your results.

Suggested References

The following references provide advanced discussions of the theory and practice of regulation.

"Symposium on Antitrust Policy." *Journal of Economic Perspectives* (Fall 2003): 3–50.

"Symposium on the Microsoft Case." *Journal of Economic Perspectives* (Spring 2001): 25–80.

Viscusi, W. K., J. M. Vernon, and J. E. Harrington. *The Economics of Regulation and Antitrust.* Lexington MA: D. C. Heath and Company, 2000.

The following articles are classic treatments concerning the difficulties of regulation and the remedies provided by private negotiation.

Coase, R. R. "The Problem of Social Cost." *Journal of Law and Economics* (October 1960): 1–44.

Stigler, G. J. "The Theory of Economic Regulation." *Bell Journal of Economics* (Spring 1971): 3–21.

The following references survey the state of environmental regulation.

Freeman, A. M., "Environmental Policy Since Earth Day I: What Have We Gained?" *Journal of Economic Perspectives* (Winter 2002): 125–146.

Nordhaus, W. D., and J. Boyer. *Warming the World: Economic Models of Global Warming.* Cambridge, MA: MIT Press, 2000.

"Symposium on Global Climate Change." *Journal of Economic Perspectives* (Fall 1993): 3–86.

The following references provide fine treatments and several case studies of benefit–cost analysis.

Dorfman, R. "Why Benefit–Cost Analysis Is Widely Disregarded and What to Do about It." *Interfaces* (September–October 1996): 1–6.

Gramlich, E. M. *A Guide to Benefit–Cost Analysis.* New York: Waveland Press, 2000.

The following article discusses how to value lives.

Viscusi, W. K., and J. E. Aldy. "The Value of a Statistical Life: A Critical Review of Market Estimates Throughout the World," Discussion Paper No. 392, Harvard Law School, November 2002.

Comprehensive online guides to antitrust policy include www.mywiseowl.com/articles/Antitrust, www.ftc.gov/bc/compguide/index.htm, and www.antitrustinstitute.org/links.cfm.

For the economic merits of energy and carbon taxes, see:

www.globalpolicy.org/socecon/glotax/carbon/.

CHECK STATION ANSWERS

1. Under competition, $P_c = AC = 8$ and $Q_c = 6$. Under monopoly, $MR = MC$. Therefore, $MR = 20 - 4Q = 8$, so $Q_m = 3$ and $P_m = 14$. The deadweight loss is $(1/2)(P_m - P_c)(Q_m - Q_c) = 9$.

2. Who gains and who loses from instituting the pollution tax? Chemical suppliers continue to earn zero profits. The government collects $(\$1)(8) = \$8$ million. Pollution is reduced from 10 million to 8 million units for a social benefit of $2 million. Consumers suffer from the increase from $P = \$4$ to $P = \$5$. Their loss in consumer surplus is given by the trapezoidal area between these price lines and under the demand curve. This area is computed as $(\$1)(8 + 10)/2 = \$9$ million. Thus, the total net benefit is $8 + 2 - 9 = \$1$ million.

3. At a $2 toll with 5 million trips, the bridge generates $10 million in revenue and creates $5 million in consumer surplus. After subtracting the maintenance cost, the bridge's annual total net benefit is $10 million, so its net present value is $10/.04 - 85 = \$165$ million. By limiting traffic, the toll sacrifices consumer surplus. As a result, the

bridge is not worth building with this pricing policy; its net benefits are lower than the status quo, the ferry.

4. The best the firm can do is price the ferry out of the market by charging P = $1 (or a penny below). At this price, demand is 7.5 million trips, so the firm's annual profit (net of maintenance) is $2.5 million. The net present value of profit is $2.5/.04 - 85 = -\$22.5$ million. Building the bridge is a losing proposition for a private firm.

5. a. (1) A survey would provide direct information on workers' risk perceptions.

   (2) An indirect market approach would examine the wage premium in risky jobs. For example, wages might be $5,000 per year higher for a chemical worker than for a comparable factory worker as compensation for job risk.

   (3) Workers' compensation might represent societal values. (If the government, via medical insurance, pays part of the costs of accidents, this cost also should be included.)

   b. (1) A survey would attempt to evaluate the severity of noise problems based on the testimony of residents.

   (2) The cost of noise pollution would be reflected in lower property values near airports.

   (3) Unfortunately, society does not compensate affected homeowners for noise-related costs. However, the government sets restrictions on airline routes to reduce the worst incidences of noise pollution.

SECTION III

Decision-Making Applications

The five final chapters examine a number of important applications that are amenable to the types of analysis developed in the first sections of this book. The settings considered include asymmetric information, competitive strategy in the contexts of negotiation and competitive bidding, decisions involving constraints, and investment choices over time.

Chapter 15 considers the implications of asymmetric information—the case in which an agent on one side of a transaction has superior information to his or her counterpart on the other side. Asymmetric information presents a barrier to efficient transactions whether in markets or within firms. In turn, a firm's organizational design aims to minimize the costs posed by asymmetric information.

Negotiation, bargaining, and dispute resolution play important roles in many managerial situations. Chapter 16 explores the economic factors that create opportunities for mutually beneficial agreements. It also takes a game-theoretic approach to analyzing negotiation strategies under imperfect information. Chapter 17 considers an important application of decision making under uncertainty: competitive bidding. In an auction setting, a single seller seeks to obtain the highest price from competing buyers. Alternatively, in the procurement context, a single buyer solicits bids from potential suppliers. The focus is on two main questions: How should firms determine their bidding strategies? In turn, how can the auctioning party design the competitive bidding system for maximum advantage?

The final two chapters consider decisions involving economic constraints and investment choices, respectively. Chapter 18 takes up linear programming, a method for determining optimal decisions in the presence of specific resource constraints. The linear programming approach can be applied in a host of settings: production problems, marketing plans, and transportation schemes, to name a few. Chapter 19 considers a firm's investment decision—plans that may involve cash outlays and inflows extending over many years. For instance, the decision to build a new plant involves current capital expenditures in return for additional profits in the future. Whether to invest in research and development or to launch a new product involves the same kind of trade-offs. The chapter's analysis provides the means for evaluating risky and complex investment projects.

CHAPTER 15

Asymmetric Information and Organizational Design

I was to learn later in life that we tend to meet any new situation by reorganizing, and what a wonderful method it can be for creating the illusion of progress while producing confusion, inefficiency, and demoralization.

PETRONIUS ARBITER, 210 B.C.

Incentive Pay at Du Pont's Fiber Division

Beginning in January 1989, Du Pont's fiber division began an experiment in incentive pay of unprecedented scope for a company of its size. *The Wall Street Journal* characterized the plan as the "most extensive and innovative ever tried at a major U.S. corporation." Under the plan, managers and employees of every rank would forgo raises in exchange for a piece of the action.[1] Employees would receive bonuses based on the division's overall performance relative to an annual profit goal.

To see how the plan would work, consider two workers, a fiber division worker and a Du Pont worker in another division, each currently earning $50,000 per year. The other worker might expect an average wage increase of 4 percent per year for the next three years, raising this worker's salary to about $56,200. If the fiber division attained 100 percent of its annual profit goal in the three years, the fiber-division worker would receive a comparable increase. However, if the fiber division achieved only 80 percent of its profit goal, the fiber-division worker would fall 3 percent behind his or her counterpart, receiving only about $54,500 in third-year salary. If the division came in below 80 percent, the penalty would increase to 6 percent, putting the third-year salary at only $52,900. In turn, the fiber-division worker could earn up to 12 percent more than his or her counterpart (for a third-year wage of about $63,000) if the division achieved 150 percent or more of its profit goal.

[1] L. Hayes, "All Eyes on Du Pont's Incentive-Pay Plan," *The Wall Street Journal* (December 5, 1988), A1.

629

> At its introduction, nearly all of the division's 20,000 employees (and four of the five affected labor unions) adopted the plan. The enthusiasm was in part due to the fact that the first-year profit goal was set at a modest level, and partial-year sales results almost guaranteed beating it. The salary incentives also seemed to affect workers' behavior, prompting many to suggest ways to cut costs and enhance revenues. Nonessential programs became candidates for termination. Some workers said the plan would change their viewpoints: from fixation on their particular jobs to the big picture of company performance.
>
> The rise in pay-for-performance plans in the 1990s and into the 2000s has raised a number of questions. What are the benefits and costs of plans such as Du Pont's? What risks do they entail? Over time, how can management evaluate how well its plan is working?

In Chapters 8 and 9, we considered decision making under uncertainty and the value of information solely from the individual manager's point of view. Dealing with risk and acquiring better information are equally relevant in decisions involving multiple decision makers, whether they operate within markets, across organizations, or within the same organization. Particularly important examples involve asymmetric information—situations in which one party knows more than another about key economic facts. As we shall see, the presence of asymmetric information has a number of implications. First, managers must be careful to draw correct inferences from the behavior of others. Second, asymmetric information can lead to market failures, that is, can impede profitable transactions between buyers and sellers. Third, it can create incentive problems. One party may undertake behavior that is not in the best interest of another party with which it interacts.

The first section of this chapter considers the effect of asymmetric information on economic transactions among multiple parties. The second section explores how firms can best organize themselves to deal with the constraints posed by asymmetric information.

ASYMMETRIC INFORMATION

In situations characterized by asymmetric information, one party knows more than another about key economic facts. The presence of asymmetric information can lead to two important effects, *adverse selection* and *moral hazard*, each of which we take up in turn.

Adverse Selection

As noted in Chapter 8, managers must make accurate probability assessments to make well-informed decisions. But as the next example shows, these assessments must take into account the likely behavior of other decision makers.

A BENEFITS PROGRAM   After considerable planning, a company's human resources department has introduced a medical program for its employees and their spouses that will pay for maternity-related health expenses (checkups, hospital stay, medicines, and so on). Employees who elect this coverage pay an additional premium. The firm estimates that 1 in 20 of its employees will have a new baby in a given year. (This estimate comes from records for the last 10 years.) Accordingly, the company has set the premium to cover its expected payouts at this 1-in-20 rate. Postscript: In the first two years of the program, the company has lost an enormous amount of money on the program. Employees covered by the plan are having babies at the rate of 1 in 10 per year. Is this bad luck or bad planning?

The company's losses are not due to bad luck. Today's workforce does not differ in its composition or behavior from that of the last 10 years. Instead, the firm's losses are due to *adverse selection*. The following table lists the hypothetical, but plausible, numbers for the first year of the program. Notice that the overall rate of new babies is 200/4,000 or 1 in 20, exactly the average rate of the previous 10 years. The rate of having babies has not changed. However, *among policyholders*, the rate of having babies is 1 in 10 (100/1,000); among nonpolicyholders, it is 1 in 30. This result should not surprise us. Couples who are planning to add to their families will tend to elect the policy; those who are not will forgo the coverage. This behavior usually is termed *self-selection*. From the company's point of view, the result is called **adverse selection**. Couples who are most likely to have babies (and know this) will most likely elect the coverage.

	Baby	No Baby	Total
Policy	100	900	1,000
No policy	100	2,900	3,000
Total	200	3,800	4,000

In general, adverse selection occurs because of asymmetric information. Individuals have better information about their true risks than the insurance provider does. As a result, individuals at the greatest risk elect insurance coverage. To avoid losses on their policies, insurance companies must anticipate this behavior and set their premiums accordingly. In the preceding example, the company would have to double its premium to break even.

A "LEMONS" MARKET   Asymmetric information plays an important role in many other markets. The used-car market is a famous example.[2] First, there is considerable uncertainty about the quality of used cars; not all used cars (even

---

[2] The classic article on this topic is G. A. Akerlof, "The Market for 'Lemons': Quality Uncertainty and the Market Mechanism," *Quarterly Journal of Economics* (1970): 488–500.

the same model year) are alike. Second, one cannot easily observe the quality of the car by inspection. Third, the seller knows a lot more about the quality of the car than the buyer. After all, the seller has had experience with the car and may be selling it for a reason.

To take an extreme case, consider a car of the current model year that is six months old and has been driven only 4,000 miles. As a used car, it now may sell for as little as 75 percent of its original sale price. How can one account for the large discount in price? Adverse selection is the answer. For any given car model and year with equivalent mileage, some cars run like "dreams," others are "lemons," with a wide quality range in between. Before purchasing a used car, a buyer should consider, "What kinds of used cars would sellers most likely offer for sale?" The answer is low-quality cars, including the lemons. After all, why would a person sell a reliable car? The fact that the car is for sale should make the buyer suspicious.

To see this more concretely, consider a new-model car that sells for a certain price. Because of quality variations, the actual value of the car may range as much as $3,000 above or below this price. After buying the car, the purchaser becomes familiar with its true quality. One year later, a number of car owners are contemplating selling their cars. For concreteness, suppose that, depending on quality, potential sellers assess their cars' values across a range of $8,000 to $14,000. (The lemon's value is $8,000; a prize car is worth $14,000.) All values in this range are considered equally likely (i.e., one-third of all cars have values between $8,000 and $10,000, one-third have values between $10,000 and $12,000, and one-third have values between $12,000 and $14,000). Finally, suppose potential used-car purchasers are eager to buy. On average, they are willing to pay $1,000 more for the typical used car than the seller's value.

If both sides could assess a given car's true value, buyer and seller could readily conclude a mutually beneficial sale. (The range of car values would present no problem.) A car valued by the seller at, say, $9,000 would be worth $10,000 to the typical buyer, and both parties would know this. Thus, the sides could be expected to bargain to a price between these two values—say, $9,500— and both would benefit from the sale. The same logic applies to a car of any quality, lower or higher. So long as *both* sides know the car's value, a mutually beneficial transaction is possible.[3]

How does asymmetric information make a difference? Because a typical buyer cannot distinguish quality, he or she must be concerned that the quality of the car purchased merits the price paid (at least on average). The potential seller, however, knows exactly the car's value. What can we say about the equilibrium price in this used-car market? To answer this question, consider an $11,000 price. This is the average seller value (the midpoint of the $8,000 to $14,000 range). If *all* cars were sold at this price, sellers as a whole would just break even and buyers would obtain an average profit of $1,000 (since their

---

[3] If neither side knew the car's true value, a similar logic would apply. Again, all cars would sell, regardless of quality. In this case, the average seller's value is $(8,000 + 14,000)/2 = $11,000$. In turn, the average buyer's value is $12,000. Thus, all used cars would sell for prices between these two values.

average value is $12,000). But adverse selection dictates that only "lower-quality" cars—that is, only cars that sellers value at less than $11,000—will be sold. A seller will not sell a car for $11,000 if he or she knows it to be worth more. In short, only cars with seller values between $8,000 and $11,000 will be offered for sale. With all values in this range equally likely, the average seller value is $9,500 (the midpoint of this range). In turn, the buyer's average value for these cars is 9,500 + 1,000 = $10,500. Rational buyers will *not* accept $11,000 as the equilibrium price, because this price exceeds the average value of the cars offered on the market.

If $11,000 is not the equilibrium price, what is? It is easy to check that $10,000 is the necessary equilibrium. At this price, only cars with seller values between $8,000 and $10,000 are offered for sale. Thus, buyers can expect to obtain cars worth (to them) between $9,000 and $11,000, or $10,000 on average. Equilibrium occurs when the expected value for buyers just matches their purchase price. (At a lower price, buyer demand would exceed seller supply; at any higher price, the expected profit for buyers would be negative.) In equilibrium, low-value cars (lemons and their slightly higher-quality brethren) dominate the market. Only one-third of the potential supply of cars is sold, and prices are driven down until they reflect actual average quality.

Adverse selection (with asymmetric information as its source) is a general phenomenon. The market for used cars is but one example. Insurance markets represent another. For many of the elderly, medical insurance is unavailable or very expensive. Why? Elderly people in poor health are much more likely to purchase insurance; thus, the proportion of this group in the insured pool increases, forcing up premiums. (The increased premiums may induce the most healthy, elderly people to drop their coverage, further worsening the proportions.)

The market for credit is another example. Banks, credit card companies, and other lenders face the problem of distinguishing between low-risk borrowers (those who will repay their debts) and high-risk borrowers (those who may not). If a bank charges the same interest rates to both types of borrowers, it will tend to attract the worst credit risks. This will force interest rates up and further worsen the pool of credit risks.

Used-car dealers serve as middlemen, procuring large numbers of vehicles from many sources and reselling them to the public. Is adverse selection present when the dealer buys vehicles? When the dealer sells vehicles? In each case, what measures might the dealer take to mitigate adverse consequences?

CHECK STATION 1

Signaling

In the presence of asymmetric information, the manager must anticipate the effects of self-selection and price accordingly. Additionally, a manager may seek better information to distinguish the different risk classes. For instance, auto insurers place drivers into different risk classes according to past driving record (as well as age and gender) and set premiums accordingly. A used-car buyer might have a licensed mechanic thoroughly check out a prospective purchase. Banks and other lenders devote significant time and resources to assessing borrowers' computerized credit histories. By obtaining better information (albeit at a cost), the manager can go a long way toward reducing or even eliminating the problem of adverse selection.

Asymmetric information poses a problem for the informed party as well. For instance, a seller may know he or she has a high-quality used car but may be unable to sell it for its true value due to adverse selection. Similarly, an individual who cannot prove he or she is a good credit risk may have to pay the same (high) interest rates as high-risk candidates. In general, "high-quality" individuals wish to distinguish themselves from their "low-quality" counterparts. They can do this in several ways. One way is by developing a reputation. For example, a seller may seek to build and maintain a reputation for delivering high-quality goods and services. A business that depends on repeat purchases and word of mouth will find its long-term interest served by accurately representing the quality of its goods. A second method is to offer guarantees or warranties. A warranty serves two related purposes. First, it protects customers against quality problems or defects in the products. Second, the warranty offer itself signals product quality. A producer of a high-quality product can afford to offer an extensive warranty because guaranteeing a reliable product will cost the producer very little. A producer of a low-quality product will choose not to offer such a warranty because it is much more expensive for it to do so. In short, the offer of a warranty provides a (low-cost) way for high-quality producers to distinguish themselves from low-quality producers. Signaling quality in this way allows high-quality producers to charge higher prices for their goods and services. Of course, warranties may not always produce the desired result. In 2002 Amtrak withdrew a warranty whereby dissatisfied customers were entitled to free future train travel. Amtrak found itself issuing more and more warranties for situations which it could not control, including weather delays and delays due to having to cede priority to freight trains.[4]

Signaling is a common response to the presence of asymmetric information. A particularly important example occurs in job markets. At the time of hiring, a firm may find it difficult to predict how productive different job candidates will be. Certainly, management will have much better information after the worker has been on the job for six months or a year, but by that time, management may have invested considerable resources in on-the-job training for the worker and may have little flexibility in modifying its decisions. (Terminating unproductive workers is difficult and costly.)

---

[4] See B. Mohl, "Amtrak Satisfaction Guarantee Was Doomed from the Outset," *The Boston Sunday Globe* (November 3, 2002), M8.

If the firm cannot distinguish between high- and low-quality workers at the time of hiring, the best it can do is offer the same wage (based on average productivity) to all new workers. (Low-quality workers are paid more than their worth and high-quality workers less than their worth.) But the workers themselves are well aware of their abilities, skills, and energy. High-productivity workers would like to signal their true abilities to potential employers and thereby obtain higher-paying jobs. One way to signal their true value is via education.[5]

Thus, education not only provides general knowledge—ways of thinking as well as specific skills—that can increase an individual's productivity, it also serves as a signal. Even if it did not contribute to productivity, education would continue to signal productivity. Individuals of high innate ability generally progress further and more quickly through the educational ranks. More productive persons tend to have greater benefits and lower costs from additional years of education and will invest more heavily in education than will their less productive counterparts. Other things being equal, the higher an individual's educational achievement (measured by years of schooling, advanced degrees, and so on), the greater his or her potential productivity. In short, educational attainment serves as an important signal, distinguishing persons of different productivities.

We sum up this discussion with two comments. First, for signaling to work, high-quality firms or individuals must have an incentive to use the signal; their lower-quality counterparts do not. This typically requires lower cost of signaling for the former group than for the latter. Second, signaling is not costless. Students sometimes pursue college or higher degrees simply to earn a "job credential" rather than for the education itself. So long as signaling is part of the equation, individuals will have an incentive to overinvest in education.[6]

Principals, Agents, and Moral Hazard

The preceding examples share the feature that the actions of one party (the one with better information) affect the welfare of a second party. Knowing their plans for starting a family, a couple decides whether to enroll in the health benefits program. Individuals who know their own talents well make education and job plans that affect employers. These relationships often are referred to as **principal–agent** problems. The party who takes the action is the agent; the affected party—who has only limited information about and control over the agent—is the principal.

[5] The classic treatment of this topic is A. M. Spence, *Market Signaling* (Cambridge: Harvard University Press, 1974). Professors Spence and Ackerlof (see footnote 1) shared the 2001 Nobel prize in economics (with J. Stiglitz) for the cited research in asymmetric information.

[6] In contrast, if all firms had perfect knowledge of all persons' productivities, there would be no signaling role. An individual would increase his or her level of education if and only if the long-term benefit (in terms of increased productivity and wages) exceeded the additional cost of schooling.

As we have seen, examples of principal–agent relationships abound. A physician (agent), who has superior knowledge, takes actions that affect the welfare of his or her patient (principal). A supplier (agent) may or may not live up to his or her contractual obligations to serve a buyer (principal). Within the firm, employees (agents) may not have the incentives to act according to their employer's (principal's) wishes. And although the law requires that management act in the best interests of stockholders, the stockholders typically lack the information to know whether management is indeed making decisions in the stockholders' interest.

The problem of **moral hazard** occurs when an agent has incentives to act in its own interests, contrary to the interests of the principal. The following principal–agent setting combines the dual problems of moral hazard and adverse selection.

A BUILDING CONTRACT   Because of its spectacular growth, a business firm (the principal) has decided to proceed with a new regional headquarters building. It has entered into a building contract with a construction firm (the agent) with which it has worked in the past. Based on preliminary architectural plans, the estimate of the final completion cost is $6.5 million. Both sides acknowledge that this estimate is highly uncertain; final cost could well be as low as $6 million or as high as $7.5 million. Recognizing this uncertainty, the parties have drawn up a cost-plus contract. That is, the firm will reimburse the builder for all allowable costs, plus a provision for a normal rate of profit. The contract also sets the completion date for two years from commencement of the project, but this target is also uncertain.

Beyond the element of risk and uncertainty, the more subtle aspect of the building contract is that the business firm is less well-informed about the contractor's likely capabilities and completion cost than the contractor itself. As in the example of the insurance benefits program, this information asymmetry exposes the business firm to the risk of adverse selection. Is the contractor's $6.5 million estimate legitimate? The contractor might know that its costs are likely to be higher than it is willing to say. Perhaps it knows that ongoing trouble with some of its subcontractors is likely to delay completion. To put it another way, the business firm may be largely unaware about whether a rival contractor could undertake the project at a lower cost or on a more favorable timetable.

Here, because of its informational disadvantage, the firm may well find itself doing business with a high-cost contractor. Even if another lower-cost contractor were anxious to compete for the job, it might have no way to prove to the firm that it was superior. Indeed, less-efficient contractors have been known to pursue "buy-in" strategies—quoting lower profit rates and claiming lower cost estimates to win cost-plus contracts. The result is adverse selection.

The business firm faces a second risk. Under the cost-plus contract, the contractor is not responsible for any cost overruns and does not benefit from any cost underruns. Thus, it has no incentive to complete the project efficiently and at minimum cost. In fact, without cost incentives, it might indulge in various kinds of managerial "slacking" or in the extreme case might pass questionable costs (or allocate undue fixed costs) to the client. Here the presence of moral hazard means that the contractor has an incentive to act in its own interests, not the client's. Unable to monitor perfectly the contractor's actions (cost management, accounting practices, and the like), the business firm is at risk to pay inflated costs.

In this example, the business firm faces the twin, but logically distinct, risks of adverse selection and moral hazard. Here is the distinction:

> Adverse selection occurs when the agent (whose interests are at odds with the principal's) holds unobservable or hidden information.
>
> Moral hazard occurs when an agent (whose interests are at odds with the principal's) takes unobservable or hidden actions.

For example, a life insurance policy may attract those with serious health problems (adverse selection) and may cause those covered to begin to engage in more risky behavior (moral hazard). Likewise, an employment contract may attract lower-productivity employees (adverse selection) and give those workers incentives to engage in self-serving actions at the expense of the employer (moral hazard). As the next two examples show, the problem of moral hazard is pervasive.

HEALTH INSURANCE AND MEDICAL EXPENDITURES   The United States offers some of the most sophisticated health and hospital care in the world. However, a significant minority—some 40 million Americans—cannot afford adequate health care because they lack private or government-funded health insurance. Moreover, health-care costs and expenditures continue to increase at rapid rates. In 2003, health-care expenditures constituted about 15 percent of U.S. gross domestic product.

Health insurance protects individuals and families against the financial risk of illness. Like any other type of insurance, medical coverage responds to the fact of uncertainty. In return for premiums rendered, the insurer agrees to pay for prespecified categories of medical expenses.

Paradoxically, the very benefit that insurance bestows is also responsible in part for the escalation of health expenditures. To see why this is so, simply note that medical decisions (like all other choices) involve a comparison of benefits and costs. Physicians and patients face myriad choices concerning hospitalization, diagnostic tests, possible surgery, mode of long-term care, medicinal regimes, and so on. A well-functioning health-care system should weigh the health benefits of these choices against the corresponding costs. Consider the effect of health insurance. On average, such insurance pays for between 80 and 90 percent of an individual's major medical expenses. Thus, in making medical decisions, patient and physician alike are largely "freed" from the discipline of cost. (If insurance coverage were 100 percent, there would be no incentive to weigh costs against benefits.)

The upshot is that insurance increases the demand for health-care services. Insured patients will undertake spending on hospital stays, procedures, and tests so long as the expected marginal health benefits exceed the patient's share of additional costs. With the patient's share as low as 10 percent of true costs, patient and physician have an obvious incentive to spend too much (from a cost–benefit viewpoint) on health-care services. Of course, this spending is not really free. It must be paid for by higher insurance premiums and increased burdens on government-sponsored insurance programs. Interestingly, there is no clear line here between principals and agents. Society as a whole (the principal) demands a well-functioning and affordable system of health-care provision and insurance. However, the existence of insurance induces patients and physicians (the agents) to overspend on health care. This is the moral hazard.

What is the way out of this dilemma? There are two responses, but each is only a partial remedy. One approach is to monitor and regulate the choices of patient and physician. These efforts range from promulgating voluntary standards of medical practice to controlling which medical procedures in which circumstances the insurance will reimburse. These prescriptions can reduce medical expenditures but at the risk of compromising the discretion of the attending physician. Since the mid-1990s, health insurers and health maintenance organizations (HMOs) have aggressively pursued cost-containment strategies, often sparking conflicts with physicians.

A second response is to improve the *incentives* for cost control. For example, insurers could reduce the rate of insurance coverage and make the patient pay a greater percentage of the cost. Advocates of this approach argue that raising patient payment rates to 20 to 30 percent would retain the main benefits of insurance while providing much stronger incentives for reduced expenditures, in particular eliminating expenditures having low or uncertain marginal benefits. In 2004 the employees of Whole Foods Market, Inc. adopted such a program. In this scheme, employee premiums are low (zero for most workers) but the deductible (the amount an employee must pay before the insurance kicks in) is $1,500. In addition, each year Whole Foods puts a fixed amount of money into a medical account for each employee. If the employee does not use this money, it is carried forward to future years. Thus, in their medical and health-care decisions, workers should begin acting as if they are spending their own money, at least up to the amount of the deductible.[7] Whether such incentive plans will always lead consumers to wiser health decisions is still an open question. A 2004 Rand Corporation study found that worker copayments reduced the use of prescription drugs but increased visits to emergency rooms,

[7] See R. Lieber, "New Way to Curb Medical Costs: Make Employees Feel the Sting," *The Wall Street Journal Online* (June 23, 2004), A1.

raising the concern that patients, made to pay for a significant share of their health costs, were not buying the medicine they needed. This in turn could lead to more expensive treatment in the future.[8]

An alternative approach targets physician incentives. The traditional fee-for-service approach simply reimburses doctors for the cost of treatment. In its place, *fixed* payments for treatments, separated into diagnosis-related groups, provide strong cost incentives. For instance, a hospital that receives a fixed payment for a surgical appendectomy has a strong incentive to keep down costs. If its cost exceeds the fixed payment, it bears the loss; if its cost is below the fixed payment, it garners the profit. An increasingly popular payment scheme, the *capitation* approach, takes incentives to the limit. Under capitation, an HMO pays a group of doctors one fixed annual payment per patient. The fee per patient is set at the estimated cost of caring for each enrollee. At the end of the year, if total costs come in below total fees, the doctors pocket the profit. Conversely, if costs outpace fees, the doctors absorb the loss.

CHECK STATION 2

The capitation approach gives full decision-making control to physicians. One result might be a greater focus on preventive care. Explain why. Might adverse selection (exercised by the physician group) and moral hazard (also exercised by the physician group) be a problem? What risks do doctors face under capitation? On the patients' side, might there be a risk of compromised health-care quality? Explain.

Federal Deposit Insurance and Bank Failures

Since the 1930s, the prevention of widespread bank failures has been a key goal of bank regulation.[9] Regulations govern the conduct of banks and monitor bank behavior. Rules govern bank charter, provide for periodic bank examinations, and set up capital and investment requirements. The government also provides deposit insurance. The Federal Deposit Insurance Corporation (FDIC) and the Federal Savings and Loan Insurance Corporation (FSLIC) insure bank deposits against defaults in return for annual premiums paid by participating banks.

Deposit insurance serves an important purpose: to guarantee public confidence in banks in troubled financial times. Recall that during the Great Depression (before we had deposit insurance) banks experienced frequent "runs"—frenzied withdrawals by depositors. Widespread financial failures affect not only depositors but also adversely affect consumer spending, business profits, investment, and employment.

Obviously, 100 percent deposit insurance would eliminate the risk of bank runs. Under current rules, however, the government insures individual accounts only up to $100,000; there is no coverage for losses above this amount.

[8] See V. Fuhrmans, "Higher Co-Pays May Take Toll on Health," *The Wall Street Journal* (May 19, 2004), D1.

[9] See P. A. Meyer, *Money, Financial Institutions, and the Economy* (Homewood, IL: Irwin, 1985), Chapter 15, for a complete treatment of the issues discussed in this section.

One rationale for this limit is to insure small depositors, who probably are less able than large investors to gauge a bank's solvency. More importantly, 100 percent insurance creates a significant moral hazard: It induces excessive risk taking by some banks. In particular, an aggressive bank would have the incentive to create a high-risk, high-return portfolio of loans. Accordingly, it could offer high rates of return to attract large deposits. These depositors would know that they are 100 percent insured, even if the bank became financially distressed because its risky loans performed poorly. In short, the $100,000 limit acts as an important constraint against this type of moral hazard on the part of banks.

Or does it? When the giant bank Continental Illinois ran into severe difficulties in 1984, the FDIC broke its rule of limited insurance by announcing that it would cover all deposits (with no limit). With few exceptions (Penn Square Bank being one), the way in which the FDIC has handled bank insolvencies has resulted in nearly 100 percent deposit coverage. In particular, a philosophy of a bank being "too big to be allowed to fail"—that is, the practice of government bailouts for the largest banks—is not only costly in itself, but it also encourages excessive risk taking. This effect was one large factor in the savings and loan crises of the late 1980s and early 1990s.

In a sense, the dilemma of deposit insurance involves two types of moral hazard. Full insurance induces some banks to take excessive risks, increasing the chance of bank insolvencies—the very event the program sought to prevent. This is one type of moral hazard. The regulatory body itself is prone to a second type of moral hazard. Before the fact, it professes to offer limited insurance. But after the fact (in the event of a failure), it has a strong incentive to bend the rules and offer full insurance to minimize the wider financial repercussions of large bank failures. In the wake of the financial crises in Southeast Asia, Japanese regulatory authorities struggled to decide whether to let a significant segment of the financial system fail or whether to bail out the largest banks.

How can we escape this double dilemma? One way is for regulators to maintain the current system but commit firmly to limited insurance. Alternatively, regulators could adopt "risk-based" insurance. This plan would obligate high-risk banks to pay higher premium rates for their insurance. Conservative, well-managed banks would pay lower rates. (This raises the question of whether regulators can distinguish accurately between these two groups.)

The message of this section is that the principal–agent relationship comes with an associated cost. While possessing the necessary information to make an appropriate decision, the agent also has interests that conflict to a lesser or greater degree with those of the principal. Certainly, the parties will attempt to mitigate these problems. As the examples have shown, this might mean monitoring or limiting the agent's decision-making discretion or improving the agent's incentives. Nonetheless, the loss in group welfare because of suboptimal decisions or costly controls represents a real **agency cost**. As we shall see in the next section, an important task of managers is to organize large-scale firms in ways that minimize these agency costs.

ORGANIZATIONAL DESIGN

Large-scale firms are ubiquitous in industrialized economies and take many different forms. At the same time, millions of transactions take place in markets of all kinds. Having examined the economics of different market structures in previous chapters, we now take a closer look at the organization of firms. What economic factors determine the size and breadth of firms? Why do some economic transactions take place within firms, whereas others are transacted via markets? What can economic analysis say about the likely ways in which firms are organized? This section considers each of these questions.

The Nature of the Firm

As recently as 100 years ago the typical firm in the industrial world was a very small concern, managed by its owner and employing a small number of workers. Only the railroads, steel producers, and a handful of other manufacturers constituted the realm of large firms. Today in the United States alone, there are about 30 corporations of more than 100,000 employees each. Although firms range in size from the single proprietor to the largest *Fortune* 500 companies, the vast majority of managers work for firms with 50 or more employees. Thus, in the present discussion we focus primarily on this category.

We begin our study of the firm with the following proposition first articulated by Ronald Coase.[10]

> Firms will be organized to minimize the total cost of production including transaction costs.

This efficiency proposition for private organizations is the counterpart of the efficiency standard pertaining to perfectly competitive markets. (Recall Chapter 10's discussion.) In brief, competition among firms will ensure that only the most efficient organizational forms will survive and prosper. To put this another way, if the firm's present organization were unnecessarily costly, then improved management would be able to increase profit to the benefit of the firm's shareholders.

In applying Coase's proposition, let's start with the owner-managed firm, the norm in the nineteenth century and still represented today. The proprietor of a small business (a clothing producer at the turn of the century, let's say) was both owner and manager. The proprietor procured the necessary equipment, hired workers, and made all important decisions (what items to produce and in what quantities). As sole manager and decision maker, the owner also claimed all profits (and paid all losses) from the business. The owner held the

---

[10] R. Coase, "The Nature of the Firm," *Econometrica* (1939): 386–405.

relevant information about how to run the business and had a strong incentive to take optimal actions because his or her ultimate profit depended on it. In short, the business of transforming inputs into outputs operated on a small scale and with the simplest of organizational structures. With management and ownership vested in one individual, the informational and moral hazard problems (posed earlier in this chapter) were minimized.

Contrast the small firm of the nineteenth century with the large-scale firm of today. As noted in Chapters 6 and 7, because of economies of scale and scope, average costs decline at higher levels of output. This fact offers a first explanation for large firm size. Of course, the increase in scale makes the business of transforming inputs into outputs much more complicated. No longer can a single owner-manager take on all management and decision-making responsibilities.

> The modern firm distributes information and management responsibilities among a wide group of inside managers. Today's firm is an organization based on a set of agreements and contracts, both explicit and implicit.

The first statement asserts that the modern firm is not a monolith. The second statement acknowledges the importance of contractual obligations. The firm's very functions depend on contractual relationships of all kinds: employment contracts, supplier agreements, and financial contracts. Quite simply, combining capital, labor, and other inputs using mass-production techniques requires an organization based on long-standing agreements.

The large-scale firm presents an interesting and important trade-off. On the one hand, increases in scale and scope offer the advantage of declining average costs. On the other hand, the division of management responsibilities raises myriad principal–agent problems of the kind discussed earlier in this chapter. Thus, top management must design an organizational structure that preserves the advantages of large-scale production while mitigating the attendant agency problems, thereby minimizing agency costs.

The design of organizational structure involves:

1. Determining the boundaries of the firm,

2. Dividing decision-making responsibilities within the firm, and

3. Crafting mechanisms for monitoring and rewarding managers and other firm employees (including hiring, promotion, and remuneration).

The first item raises a number of issues, in particular the question of which activities should the firm undertake itself and which activities should it leave to outside contractors and suppliers. The crux of the second item is the degree to which the firm should centralize or decentralize decision making. The third item directly addresses the problem of melding agents' behavior and interests to those of the firm as a whole.

Before going on, we make two observations. First, the three listed aspects of organizational design depend on each other. For example, outsourcing means relinquishing some decision-making control. Decentralizing, where lower-level managers have significant discretion, requires sound incentive and reward systems. The way decision making is decentralized is also important. Certain divisions within the firm may work better with monitoring and incentive structures than others. Second, organizational structures can be either formal or informal. Formal structures carefully define decision-making authority and set up specific mechanisms to monitor and reward. Informal structures, often known by the term *corporate culture*, create goals and expectations and foster a social environment that informally rewards good performance.

The Breadth of the Firm

Any firm must decide whether to undertake an economic activity in-house or to outsource the activity. In analyzing this choice, let's start simply. Most firms rely on outside markets to procure their most basic inputs, everything from telephone service and office equipment to automobiles and fuel. Furthermore, we know from Chapter 10 that competitive markets ensure efficient provision of standardized goods and services at the lowest sustainable prices. Thus, the firm will likely obtain these standardized goods from outside suppliers more cheaply than producing them itself. (Often the firm would not be able to produce these items in large enough quantity to take advantage of economies of scale, leaving it with higher average costs.)

In turn, consider the economic circumstances that might favor undertaking an activity in-house. Roughly speaking, the firm will undertake those activities that require extensive coordination in production or make use of specific inputs. For example, consider the activities of a large law firm. Providing legal services is labor intensive and requires lawyers trained in a number of specialties. A law firm also requires office space, equipment, a law library, and considerable administrative resources. Surely, the law firm will procure its office space via the commercial real estate market and purchase routine supplies and equipment. However, the firm's "bread and butter" legal services will be coordinated and provided in-house. Complex cases require lawyers of many specialties (from first-year associates to senior partners) to work together to meet clients' needs. Established relationships within the firm make this easier to do. It is hard to imagine a law firm contracting out its basic legal services, for instance, hiring a freelance lawyer by the hour to conduct a complex litigation case. Similarly, paying for its lawyers to use an outside law library would be expensive and inefficient. (However, law firms do pay for the outside provision of electronic legal databases.)

TABLE 15.1

The Choice between In-House Production and Outsourcing	**Factors Favoring In-House Production**	**Factors Favoring Outsourcing**
	1. Firm-specific good or service	1. Standardized good or service
	2. Outside risks: input quality, supply disruptions	2. Competitive market available
	3. High degree of coordination required	3. Low degree of coordination required

Table 15.1 lists the most important factors favoring in-house production over outsourcing. Besides the factors already discussed, the presence of outsourcing uncertainty confers an advantage on taking activities in-house. Thus, for a state-of-the-art high-tech component, the firm may not be able to ensure the same quality through outsourcing that it can achieve through in-house production. Additionally, the firm may find it easier to handle redesigns in-house than through outsourcing. Negotiating redesign provisions with an outside supplier (such as which side should bear the additional cost) could be costly and acrimonious. In short, when risks loom large, the firm might want to fall back on the maxim: If you want something done right, do it yourself.

OUTSOURCING AT GM   General Motors is ambitiously imitating Japanese production practices, not in the United States but in Brazil.[11] GM's Brazilian factories are more efficient, flexible, and profitable than those in the United States, owing to a simple change in how they produce vehicles. Instead of making cars from the ground up, GM's Brazilian operations use parts preassembled by outside suppliers: dashboards, side panels, parts of the drive train. Indeed, the Brazilian factories are L-shaped or T-shaped to maximize the number of exterior loading docks by which suppliers hourly deliver preassembled parts. Using outside suppliers allows the carmaker to conserve on valuable factory space and reduce its labor force, significantly cutting costs in the process. General Motors plans to bring these production methods to the United States despite the protests of its predominantly unionized labor force.

Assigning Decision-Making Responsibilities

A general principle guides the division of management responsibilities within the firm.

> An optimal organizational structure for the firm should assign decision responsibilities to those managers with the best information on which to act.

[11] This account is based on K. Bradsher, "G.M.'s Plant in Brazil Raises Fears Closer to Home," *The New York Times* (June 16, 1998), A1.

This maxim reminds us of Chapter 9's principal message. Superior information is valuable precisely because it supports better decisions. Thus, good organizational design places decisions as close as possible to the relevant information.

A corollary to this proposition follows. Organizations should distribute tasks to best generate and utilize specialized information. This is not a new insight. After all, division of labor and specialization characterize the modern firm. However, specialization not only enhances productivity in the traditional sense but also greatly improves the quality of decisions. Imagine the following nightmare. You are a top executive whose daily calendar calls for you to make six crucial decisions: from solving a production problem in your West Coast plant to deciding on a new marketing plan, to dealing with federal regulators. You are woefully unprepared to decide any of these issues. (This is sort of like the exam no one told you about and for which you never studied.) By comparison, suppose you are an executive waking up to face six big decisions in your bread-and-butter area of responsibility. Well prepared by years of experience and accumulated knowledge, you eagerly tackle these challenges.

Modern firms typically divide responsibilities along functional lines—production, marketing, finance, and so on. This type of structure has obvious advantages and less obvious disadvantages. One risk is that functional managers may lose sight of the bigger picture. Even with divided responsibilities, business is a system, and functional areas must work together. Obviously, a materials manager must communicate with a production manager. The latter cannot plan to increase jeans production without the necessary denim and thread on order. Similarly, a manufacturing manager greatly benefits by learning of customers' needs and complaints from the marketing manager.

An alternative organizational design divides responsibility by line of product or service. Product lines represent natural profit centers. Consequently, a product manager would oversee product decisions in the pursuit of maximizing profit. Midlevel managers would still occupy functional jobs within this product division. Management can also divide by the type of customer (business versus residential, for instance) or even by geographical regions. Indeed, some corporations choose to combine the advantages of product and functional divisions. For example, the marketing managers from the firm's several divisions might meet periodically as a team for coordination and consultation. The firm can also organize cross-divisional manufacturing and finance teams.

Airbus's Dysfunctional Organization

In 2000, the Airbus Industrie consortium finally transformed itself into a corporation.[12] Backed financially by its four European parents, the commercial aircraft manufacturer lived the first 30 years of its existence as a consortium of French, British, German, and Spanish aerospace companies, plus a marketing

[12] This account is based on D. Michaels, "Airbus Revamp Brings Sense to Consortium, Fuels Boeing Rivalry," *The Wall Street Journal* (April 3, 2001), A1; D. Michaels, "Europe's Airbus Ready to Spread Wings as a Company," *The Wall Street Journal* (June 23, 2000), A15; and J. Tagliabue, "Airbus to Become an Independent Corporation," *The New York Times* (January 14, 1997), D1.

unit charged with negotiating the sale of aircraft. During the 1990s, the Airbus consortium succeeded in increasing its market share to about 40 percent of the global commercial aircraft market (to Boeing's 60 percent). However, critics claimed that Airbus bought market share by selling aircraft at a loss, all the while receiving financial transfusions from its national governments.

Under its former organizational structure, Airbus was its own worst enemy. According to a long-standing political compromise, the construction of each new aircraft was carved up in fixed shares among the partners. Germany and France (each with 37.9 percent stakes) built parts of the fuselage and assembled finished planes. Britain (20 percent stake) built the main wings, and Spain (4.2 percent stake) built parts of the tail. (General Electric produced the engines in a joint venture with a French company.) Of the four consortium members, only the privatized British Aerospace managed to break even during the 1990s. This slice-and-dice organizational approach produced inefficiency, duplication, and waste. For years, work on new jetliners was divided in fixed shares computed by complicated formulas.

Although many firms have functional organizations, Airbus's structure might best be described as dysfunctional—decentralization by default. The partners regarded each other as unreliable outside suppliers. Management meetings among the members resembled games of "liar's poker." Each member tried to charge the highest possible prices to other members for parts it supplied and to pay the lowest prices to other members for parts it bought. Each fanatically guarded and kept secret its financial information. Not surprisingly, coordination and logistical problems were common.

In 2000, after much infighting, Airbus transformed itself into one company with one set of financial books and one chief executive. Airbus continues to produce its aircraft components in different European locations, but it now tightly integrates production, assembly, scheduling, and delivery. The organization has aggressively cut costs, centralized procurement, and expanded sales. Management can now evaluate the profitability of its major decisions, whether the issue be pricing, aircraft features, or information technology. In 2003, Airbus delivered more planes than Boeing for the first time in its history. The company then began assembly of a 550-seat super-jumbo aircraft that was due to begin service in 2006. (Boeing has taken a different tack, betting its fortunes on a new lighter, more efficient midsize model, the 7E7.) Although Airbus still faces numerous challenges, changing its organizational structure appears to have been a key factor in moving the company forward.

DECENTRALIZATION   The trend toward dividing organizations along functional and product lines creates pockets of specialized information dispersed throughout the business organization. This phenomenon virtually precludes the possibility of completely centralized decisions by top executives and the board of directors. As a practical matter, even the most engaged CEO can make only a small fraction of the decisions involved in managing a modern business. To an increasing degree, the norm in the modern corporation is decentralization.

Decentralized decision making follows the efficiency norm that organizations should assign decision responsibilities as closely as possible to the loci of relevant information. Presumably, an experienced regional sales manager with his or her ear close to the ground can best make periodic marketing, promotion, and pricing decisions. In general, as the number of contingencies grows, so does the importance of decentralized decision making. For instance, in the absence of market segmentation, a single decision maker might do a credible job identifying a profit-maximizing price in a peaceful, unchanging market. However, with scores of ever-changing market segments, setting a spectrum of prices centrally becomes daunting, even hopeless. When plans depend on case-by-case contingencies, decision making should be decentralized and close to the relevant information source.

Let's now consider the contrary point of view and ask: Under what circumstances does efficiency favor centralized decisions? The answer: When decisions are highly interdependent, that is, when managers must coordinate choices. For instance, management's optimal output decision depends simultaneously on demand and cost. Thus, we should not delegate the output decision to a production manager (or a marketing manager) alone. Each would have only part of the relevant information to determine Q^*. Accordingly, the output decision should be in the hands of more centralized managers who use demand and cost information from both the production and marketing segments of the firm. (Overall advertising expenditures also depend on and affect output and, therefore, also qualify for centralized decision making.) However, once centralized management has determined output, it can delegate many of the other decisions, such as the exact details of the advertising campaign, promotions, and input decisions to the appropriate functional areas.

A second argument for centralization arises in the face of significant principal–agent problems. Imagine that a regional manager has the best information to make a particular decision, but that the manager's interests conflict with the firm's objectives. Absent controls or incentives to bend the manager's interests to the firm's, it would be foolish to delegate this decision. Instead, upper-level management should make the decision, following the right incentives, even if it has imperfect information. Table 15.2 summarizes factors bearing on the choice between centralization and decentralization.

TRANSFER PRICES   Large, multidivisional firms must coordinate activities among its divisions. To do this, divisions often provide goods or services to each other. For instance, a firm's automotive division might receive finished engines from its parts unit, while at the same time rely on the firm's in-house marketers and advertisers to spur sales. **Transfer prices**—the prices that selling divisions charge to buying divisions within the firm—help coordinate internal actions. (See the Appendix to Chapter 7 for a full discussion and analysis.) The key to

TABLE 15.2

The Choice between
Centralization or
Decentralization

Factors Favoring Centralization	Factors Favoring Decentralization
1. High degree of coordination required	1. Low degree of coordination required
2. Concentration of decision-relevant information	2. Dispersion of decision-relevant information
3. Significant principal–agent problems	3. Compatible interests and objectives

maximizing the firm's total profit is to *set each transfer price equal to the marginal cost* of the good or service in question. This ensures that the firm uses its internal resources efficiently. For instance, the automotive division should pay a transfer price for engines that reflects marginal cost; therefore, these costs are recorded dollar for dollar in computing the auto division's profitability. (Of course, accounting for all marginal costs is also crucial for setting optimal prices and quantities for finished vehicles.) As we saw in the case of Airbus, setting appropriate transfer prices is not always easy. The supplying division often pushes for a higher transfer price simply to enhance its own measure of profit. Of course, this price gouging comes at the expense of the buying division. Understating the transfer price can also lead to incorrect decisions, resulting in overproduction of both the transfer good and the final product. (In the extreme, treating the internal service—because it does not produce a final sale—as if it were free encourages overutilization of the resource while ignoring its true cost altogether.) In short, setting transfer prices according to marginal cost is essential for efficient coordination within the multidivisional firm.[13]

TEAMS   Management's choice between centralization and decentralization is not all or nothing. In a hybrid system of decision responsibilities, centrally located management periodically reviews (and perhaps modifies) decisions made by decentralized managers. The growing use of teams also represents a hybrid sharing of information and decision responsibility. Teams work best when no single manager has the information to take an optimal action. Teams pool information and perspectives. Five heads are less likely than one to make a mistaken or biased decision. Indeed, this is part of the reasoning behind 12-person juries. Multiple perspectives can aid in general problem solving and in uncovering new, alternative courses of action. Of course, team decision making is costly in terms of human resources and risks difficulties in reaching a decision consensus. Though management teams are a growing trend, the indiscriminant use of teams can produce unproductive results.

[13] As noted in Chapter 7's appendix, if the firm's supplying division also sells its output to the external market, the appropriate transfer price is simply the market price. We should also note that transfer pricing is not the only means of ensuring coordination. Setting coordinated budgets for the divisions can accomplish the same end.

In principle, how would an organization determine the optimal size of a team?

**DHL Worldwide
Express**

In the mid-1990s, DHL Worldwide Express led the market in international document and parcel delivery, claiming over 40 percent of the worldwide market.[14] The company achieved annual revenues of over $2 billion and before-tax profits of more than $110 million. Recognized for its premium services (speedy delivery, package customs clearance, and tracking), the company also charged premium prices. However, corporate headquarters was concerned that its pricing structure was inconsistent. Although the company compiled a worldwide book of list prices for delivery of documents and parcels to and from different parts of the world, regional managers exercised wide discretion in offering discounts (small or steep) to particular customers for different types of deliveries. Indeed, some multinational customers complained of widely different rates for deliveries of comparable distance.

A fundamental question faced DHL headquarters. Should the company encourage decentralized decision making allowing considerable price discretion to its regional managers? Or should it pursue a centralized approach, reining in managers and instituting a highly uniform pricing policy? We can begin to answer these questions based on the economics of the global delivery market and in light of the organizational concepts already discussed. First, demand conditions (and cost conditions) varied significantly in different parts of the world. Particular routes experienced much higher volumes of shipments than others. Competition was absent in some parts of the world, cutthroat in others. For instance, DHL held a virtual monopoly in many parts of Africa but faced a price war with two strong competitors (TNT and FedEx) on selected Southeast Asian routes. In addition, the worldwide delivery market consisted of various different services. Because of customers' urgent need for documents, the document segment was typically less price sensitive than the package segment and, therefore, commanded higher markups. Demand also varied by customers. For example, banks and financial institutions sending documents typically displayed much less elastic demand than a wholesaler making regular high-volume shipments of spare parts.

In light of these facts, DHL headquarters acknowledged that optimal pricing required careful case-by-case decisions and that regional managers had the best information to make these decisions. (As noted in Chapter 3, the company should pursue a policy of price discrimination using the optimal markup rule.) As one regional manager stated, "The name of the pricing game is customization." Thus, headquarters endorsed a decentralized decision approach with two limitations. Large discounts from the list price "book" proposed by local managers would first require higher-level approval. Second, to ensure consistency and customer goodwill, local managers would have only limited pricing discretion on important multinational accounts.

[14] This account is based on "DHL Worldwide Express," Harvard Business School Case, 1997.

The company implemented a centralized scheme with respect to one aspect of regional pricing. Headquarters had recently implemented a sophisticated information system to estimate delivery costs anywhere in the world. Tracking the marginal cost of delivery from point A to point B was complex because the company used a hub system. Units picked up at A went to a regional staging location, then along a least-cost route to one of 12 hubs, then to a second regional staging location, and finally to destination B. Before the adoption of this information system, regional managers could not accurately estimate marginal costs along the company's far-flung routes. Using the new centralized information system, regional managers can now access data on marginal cost by route and mark up price accordingly.

Monitoring and Rewarding Performance

The modern firm is built on formal and informal systems of carrots and sticks to motivate managers and other workers to take actions in the interest of the organization. These include merit evaluations, raises, bonuses, promotions, lateral transfers, perquisites, admonishments, pats on the back, and even firings. While acknowledging this wide range, we choose to focus on formal monetary reward structures and pose the following question: To what degree can pay-for-performance mechanisms mitigate moral hazard problems in organizations? In our answer, we examine two specific problems: motivating workers and maximizing executive performance.

MOTIVATING WORKERS   Probably the most pervasive form of principal–agent relationship is that of employer and worker. For the relationship to work successfully, the firm (the principal) must motivate the worker (the agent) to act in the employer's interests. Workers have knowledge and abilities advantageous to their companies, but they also have their own needs and desires that may differ from the firm's objectives. Workers may simply wish to labor less hard and to enjoy life more, thereby sacrificing potential profits of the company.

Consider the following simplified model of the employer–worker relationship. The worker chooses and controls the amount of effort he or she puts into the job. An increased level of effort raises the workers' output, thereby increasing the company's profit. However, increased effort is also costly to the worker; that is, it generates disutility. Tying compensation to effort is one way to induce higher effort levels. Thus, the employer seeks to put in place an optimal employment contract—one that maximizes its profit by compensating the worker for his or her effort.

If both the employer and employee have full information, they can easily design the optimal contract. Employer and worker should agree to an effort level that maximizes the net profit from the employment relationship: $\pi - D$, where π denotes the firm's profit and D denotes the worker's disutility. As a hypothetical example, suppose that a second-year associate at a small law firm works an average of 55 hours per week in return for a $55,000 annual salary. At this level of effort, the associate generates $80,000 in additional profit for the firm and experiences a personal disutility valued at $40,000. Here the net profit from the employment relationship is $80,000 - 40,000 = \$40,000$. The firm's share of this is $80,000 - 55,000 = \$25,000$, and the associate's share is $15,000 (the difference between the actual pay and the least amount he would accept in compensation for the disutility of the job). Both sides know these facts and know that working shorter or longer hours would diminish net profits. For instance, working 70 hours a week might generate increased billings and raise profit to $90,000, but it would also imply a disutility of $60,000, reducing the net profit to $30,000. Thus, employer and worker settle on the efficient (55 hour per week) work arrangement.

Asymmetric information introduces potential complications. Frequently, the firm cannot observe and measure the worker's effort or output (or both). Let's start with two pieces of good news.

> If effort is observable, then the parties can always implement an optimal contract even if output can only be measured approximately.

To see why, suppose that output depends not only on the worker's effort but also on uncertain elements beyond the worker's control. (In the legal setting, a complicated litigation case might take many legal hours to prepare and try in court and still have an uncertain financial outcome.) In this case, the optimal contract will specify the level of effort that maximizes the *expected* net profit from the relationship. As long as the worker complies with this level of effort, he or she receives the stipulated monetary compensation. This is sometimes referred to as a "forcing" contract. The contract terms are designed to force the worker to take the optimal level of effort; otherwise the worker is penalized. (Of course, both sides benefit from the efficient work agreement.) A second result follows:

> If output is observable and depends deterministically on effort, then the parties can always implement an optimal contract even if effort is unobservable.

In this case, there is no way to observe the worker's effort directly. (Perhaps, hours worked do not accurately reflect effort. An associate might spend many hours in the law library daydreaming or, even worse, may exaggerate the number of hours worked.) However, by observing the worker's output, the employer can infer the worker's effort indirectly. Thus, the employment contract would compensate the associate, provided that his or her legal output was acceptable; that is, the output produced net profits in the neighborhood of $80,000. (This is also called a "forcing" contract, but here output and profit are the variables that are monitored.)

Here is the bad news associated with asymmetric information:

> If effort and output are both imperfectly observable, then the parties will be unable to implement a "first-best" optimal employment contract because of moral hazard.

The stylized example in Table 15.3 demonstrates this result. The worker can choose one of four effort levels—low, medium, high, or super—in order of increasing disutilities. The additional gross profit attributed to the worker depends *probabilistically*, not deterministically, on the level of effort. According to the table, gross profits are uncertain (either $100,000 or $50,000), and raising the level of effort increases the probability of achieving the high-profit outcome. Thus, higher effort increases expected gross profit on average, but the employer cannot infer the worker's effort level from the profit outcome. (Even a super effort might result in a low-profit result.)

If both employer and employee could observe effort, the parties would implement an optimal agreement calling for *high* effort. From Table 15.3a, we see that high effort generates the greatest net profit, $40,000. (Notice that it is *not* efficient to insist on a super effort because the net profit is only $30,000.) Item 1 in Table 15.3b lists the results of the high-effort contract. As shown, the firm pays $60,000 in salary to the worker, thereby claiming slightly more than half of the available net profit for itself. (In general, the exact wage bargain struck, perhaps higher or lower, would depend on labor market conditions.)

Now suppose that the employer cannot observe effort. The employer's natural concern is that the worker will choose a low level of effort (thereby minimizing disutility) while continuing to pocket the $60,000 salary. The employer's concern is justified. Absent any other incentives, low effort is exactly what the worker will choose. The potential divergence between the employer's and worker's interests is the essence of the moral hazard problem in the employment relationship. This outcome is shown in item 2 of Table 15.3b. The upshot is that the employer's expected profit is reduced to $0, and the parties' total expected profit falls to $25,000.

What can an employer do? One option is simply to anticipate low effort and adjust the salary down to $45,000, securing a $15,000 net profit from the employment relationship. This outcome (item 3 of Table 15.3b) is better than $0 but still far short of the $25,000 that is possible under a perfectly enforceable fixed-wage contract. A second option is to offer an *incentive* contract. What if the employer offers to pay the worker a base salary of $10,000 plus one-half of all gross profits the employee generates on the job? Does this profit-sharing arrangement raise the incentive to supply extra effort? The answer is yes. As shown in item 4 of Table 15.3b, the worker maximizes his or her profit (salary less disutility) by choosing a *medium* level of effort. The incentive contract has induced additional effort and has increased the total profit pie. Nevertheless, the worker still does not have sufficient incentive to adopt optimal behavior, that is, exert high effort. (Under high effort, the worker's expected compensation is

TABLE 15.3

Employment Contracts

a. Effort and Profits

Effort Level	Gross Profits $100K or $50K	Expected Gross Profit	Disutility	Expected Net Profit
Super	.8 and .2	$90,000	$60,000	$30,000
High	.7 and .3	$85,000	$45,000	$40,000
Medium	.5 and .5	$75,000	$39,000	$36,000
Low	.2 and .8	$60,000	$35,000	$25,000

b. Different Contracts

	Effort Level	Compensation	Employer Profit	Worker Profit	Total Profit
Observable Effort					
1. Forcing Contract	High	$60,000	$25,000	$15,000	$40,000
Unobservable Effort					
2. Fixed Wage	Low	$60,000	$ 0	$25,000	$25,000
3. Fixed Wage	Low	$45,000	$15,000	$10,000	$25,000
Incentive Pay					
4. (1/2 Profit + $10,000)	Medium	$60,000/$35,000	$27,500	$ 8,500	$36,000
5. (Profit − $25,000)	High	$75,000/$25,000	$25,000	$15,000	$40,000

$(.5)(85,000) + 10,000 = \$52,500$. Thus, the worker's net profit is $52,500 - 45,000 = \$7,500$, or $1,000 less than the medium-effort outcome.)

As this example shows, raising the worker's profit share is the key to inducing extra effort. In fact, allowing the worker to keep 100 percent of his or her contribution to profit ensures an optimal choice of effort. Now the worker's interest is identical to the overall objective of profit maximization. Taking full account of the extra benefits and costs (disutility) of additional effort, the worker adopts optimal behavior. Unfortunately, even this solution has problems. First, 100 percent profit participation represents a very risky contract for the worker. After all, the gross profit outcome in Table 15.3 will be either $100,000 or $50,000. That's a significant risk. Furthermore, under the terms of item 5's contract, the worker guarantees the employer a profit of $25,000 and bears all the residual risk. Any risk-averse worker will demand a premium for bearing this risk. To put this another way, besides the disutility of effort, the personal "cost" to the worker associated with risk bearing could well be on the order of $5,000 or more. Thus, imposing this risk on the worker shrinks the total pie by this amount. Second, because the employer has a guaranteed profit, the employer's incentives are negligible. Typically, the employer's actions and efforts will contribute to the worker's ultimate output. Now the moral hazard "shoe" is on the other foot. Will the employer adopt optimal behavior? Absent incentives, the answer is problematic.

In the interest of realism, we can generalize this stylized example and extend it in a number of directions. (The appendix to this chapter presents just such an extended model.) Whatever the specific model, the degree of contractual incentives remains the key issue. Suppose that (1) the worker's output depends mainly on effort (and only partly on factors beyond his or her control); and (2) the worker's choice of effort has a large impact on profit. Both of these factors argue for high-powered incentives (i.e., high profit-sharing rates). As in the preceding example, profit sharing induces greater worker effort, mitigating (though not eliminating) the moral hazard problem.

Integration or Franchising?

Should a firm sell its product by using its own integrated workforce or instead by contracting with a franchisee? Researchers have used the employer–worker contracting model with great success to explain the in-house versus franchising choice. As we noted in Chapter 2, the franchise arrangement embodies high-powered incentives for the franchisee; the franchise manager's effort and choices directly influence the franchise's profits. By contrast, under an integrated employment relationship, the employee faces low-powered incentives; typically the employee has limited managerial discretion and little (or zero) profit sharing.

A recent survey that reviewed scores of research studies on franchising shows that the "real world" accords well with the theoretical models.[15] (The studies covered all business sectors having a significant incidence of franchising: traditional and fast-food restaurants, gasoline service stations, hotels and motels, retail chains, and so on.) The empirical regularities of these studies are striking. Across all these sectors, the incidence of franchising consistently increased when the agent's effort (rather than other uncontrollable factors) was the main determinant of output and profit. Conversely, researchers found a greater incidence of workforce integration when the firm could monitor employee effort levels and decisions at low cost. (In other words, franchising's high-powered incentives were unnecessary when effort could be monitored and controlled directly.) Finally, researchers found that franchising was more prevalent in sectors where management decisions depended on information about local market conditions. As noted earlier in Table 15.2, the dispersion of decision-relevant information favors decentralized decisions, that is, external franchising.

CHECK STATION 4   Using the facts in Table 15.3, confirm that the worker's profit share must be just greater than 60 percent to ensure that the worker adopts an efficient level of effort.

EVALUATING INDIVIDUAL PERFORMANCE   An understanding of incentives in the principal–agent problem leads to an additional result.

---

[15] See F. Lafontaine and M. E. Slade, "Incentive Contracting and the Franchise Decision," Chapter 5 in K. Chatterjee and W. Samuelson (Eds.) *Game Theory and Business Applications* (Boston: Kluwer Academic Publishers, 2001).

> All information bearing on an individual's effort and contribution to profit should be included in the measure of performance. Any variables not bearing on effort or profit contribution should be excluded.

This proposition is sometimes called the *informativeness* principle. In other words, the more precise the measure of performance (combined with the appropriate incentive structure), the more efficient will be the agent's behavior (and the smaller will be the resulting agency cost). The proposition makes intuitive sense. Pertinent performance information should not be ignored, nor should irrelevant information be included.

The difficulty, of course, is in accurately monitoring and measuring performance. Frequently, it is difficult to disentangle and identify the contribution of a particular worker. Rather, the worker's effort and performance influence the firm's profit in conjunction with the contributions of many other workers and in combination with market forces. In short, measured output may simultaneously depend on myriad factors beyond the worker's control. This presents two problems. First, imperfect performance measurement reduces the incentives for efficient behavior. Second, using aggregate measures exposes the worker to significant risks in the compensation scheme.

Once again, the corporate reward system faces a trade-off. Rather than tie compensation solely to aggregate performance measures, many companies turn to subjective measures to evaluate individual employee performance. For example, supervisors evaluate the performance of employees on an annual or semiannual basis. The supervisor may give numerical ratings (say, on a 10-point scale) for a number of aspects of job performance. Alternatively, the employer may give the employee a number of annual goals and then evaluate the employee on whether and how well he or she accomplishes these goals.

There is an additional evaluation problem. Sometimes it is difficult to know "how much performance is good performance." This is sometimes known as the benchmark problem. How does the evaluation system set realistic goals on which to calibrate performance? Companies have a number of sources of information in establishing the correct benchmark. Industrial engineers and efficiency experts could perform studies that examine efficient ways of completing tasks. Their findings could provide the appropriate benchmark. Alternatively, firms may use actual past performance as a benchmark. This gives realistic data as to performance possibilities but it also can lead to strategic behavior on the part of workers who are torn between the benefit of exceeding the current benchmark and the cost of establishing higher benchmarks for the future. Frequently, firms base benchmarks on the historic average performance of a large group of comparable workers.

Individual evaluations attempt to separate worker performance from all the other factors that affect output. Thus, they lower the agency costs stemming from extraneous risks. However, because such evaluations are in part subjective, they may suffer from error and influence.

EVALUATING GROUP PERFORMANCE   Frequently, group performance is easier to measure than individual performance for many of the reasons noted previously. Rewarding group performance may encourage cooperation among employees who can all share in the fruits of their collective achievement. However, rewarding group performance does introduce new uncertainties into the compensation of the employee. That is, an employee's compensation and promotion are now tied to the efforts of others. More important, rewarding group performance may discourage optimal effort (indeed, encourage shirking), especially when the firm cannot easily observe individual effort.

For example, suppose that a team consists of five workers whose annual bonuses will depend on the measured success of the group. Suppose that the group cannot observe individual effort but that if all team members exert 15 percent extra effort, group performance will rise by a like amount and each member will reap an additional $25,000 in bonus. Because each member reckons the disutility of extra effort at $10,000, agreeing to become a high-performing team benefits all (the net advantage is $15,000 each). But there is a catch. (Have you spotted the prisoner's dilemma yet?) Each member's personal incentive is to "free ride" on the efforts of the others. By exerting extra effort, the member raises the average performance of the group by only one-fifth of 15 percent, or 3 percent. (Remember, there are *five* team members.) In turn, the marginal individual benefit to exerting extra effort is only one-fifth of $25,000, or $5,000. The benefit of the extra effort is not worth the worker's disutility. The upshot of all attempting a free ride is that no one exerts extra effort. (Indeed, the larger the group, the greater is the incentive to free ride.) In short, the group incentive system is dysfunctional.

Information Technology and Organizational Structure

The emergence of low-cost information storage, retrieval, and transmission systems is changing the organization of firms in numerous ways. Information technology (IT) reduces the firm's costs for traditional activities such as reaching customers, promoting and pricing its goods and services, and managing its supply chain. However, recent research shows that IT investments add the most value when accompanied by complementary changes in the firm's organization.[16]

BOUNDARIES OF THE FIRM   Traditionally, economic activities have been undertaken within the firm because they are cheaper to do internally than through an external market. However, as IT has reduced the cost of external transactions, firms have transferred a portion of these in-house activities to external suppliers and markets. For instance, since the late 1990s, General Motors—the paragon of the traditional vertically integrated firm—has discontinued or spun off many of its component-manufacturing operations. (The spin-off of its Delphi Automotive Systems created a separate firm with $28

---

[16] This account is based on research results in E. Brynjolfsson and L. M. Hitt, "Beyond Computation: Information Technology, Organizational Transformation, and Business Performance," *Journal of Economic Perspectives* (2000): 23–48.

billion in sales.) Today, e-procurement systems allow companies to transact cheaply and efficiently with hundreds of external suppliers.

INTERNAL INFORMATION SHARING   Research has found that the greatest benefit of IT systems lies in facilitating information sharing across dispersed business units and functions. The chief of a conglomerate might rightly lament, "If our firm only knew what our firm knows." In other words, even when a firm is rich in its "knowledge capital," it may suffer from information overkill, loss, or waste. By contrast, an effective IT system allows efficient information sharing. For example, a production manager can share innovation in one assembly line with the firm's other six geographically dispersed lines. The marketing department can electronically make available customer information to the production and distribution departments. Early research evidence suggests that the advent of low-cost information sharing transforms organizational structure by cutting across traditional functional divisions. For instance, besides her traditional departmental responsibilities, a marketing manager might work online as a member of an interdisciplinary team charged with managing a new-product launch. In a firm's traditional hierarchy, one of the boss's functions was to gather and process information from lower-level workers. Wed to an effective IT system for sharing information, a longitudinal organizational structure (with fewer levels in the management hierarchy) can achieve the same result.

DECENTRALIZATION   In some respects, IT systems foster decentralized decision making within firms. As noted earlier, delegation allows the local manager (with superior information and experience) to make appropriate decisions. At the same time, effective IT systems make it easier for higher company executives to monitor the local manager's actions and performance and to coordinate those actions with others (if coordination is necessary). Because IT systems make it easier to monitor and measure worker performance, they go hand in hand with greater reliance on incentive pay for managers. (Recall that incentive pay is most effective in motivating effort when a worker's output can be accurately measured.) In addition, IT systems tend to displace human managers in handling routine, rule-based job functions. For instance, today it takes only a handful of managers to operate and monitor a large-scale, automated cement-making plant. In short, the ranks of IT-intensive firms will increasingly be filled by highly skilled information managers and decision makers.

Yet even in the IT-intensive firm, there is room for coordinated, centralized decision making at the "top." Consider, for instance, carrying out a company-wide mandate to "eliminate any and all problems associated with serving the firm's largest customer." Identifying the cause (or possibly the multiple interrelated causes) of a late or incorrect order might require communication and coordination among myriad departments: materials, quality control, production, distribution, and customer service. A task force, led by top management and enlisting all elements of the supply chain, could best troubleshoot the problem.

Separation of Ownership and Control in the Modern Corporation

An important example of the principal–agent problem occurs in large publicly held corporations. Such corporations are owned by vast numbers of shareholders (principals) and managed by directors (agents). Although they hold no management rights, shareholders elect the board of directors that oversees corporate management.

This organizational form confers significant benefits in the financing of the firm. In issuing equity shares, the corporation becomes the recipient of a vast supply of financial capital, funds that would be difficult or impossible to secure from a single owner or even from a limited number of partners. Indeed, even if the necessary funds could be raised from a small number of inside owners, such financing would be suboptimal from the perspective of risk bearing. An owner with, say, $10 million of eggs in a single corporate basket does not have a well-diversified portfolio. Broad-based equity markets allow investors to diversify across many firms and business sectors with the added protection of limited liability. (Limited liability means that the shareholders risk losing their investment but no more than that. Creditors of the corporation cannot pursue the personal assets of shareholders.)

However, shared ownership in the modern corporation does not imply shared control. Setting day-to-day management decisions according to shareholder votes, besides being extraordinarily costly and impractical, would surely generate poor decisions. Thus, efficiency considerations dictate that the organization vests decision-making responsibilities and control in a cadre of professional managers acting on behalf of shareholders.

The problematic aspect of this form of organization is that shareholders have little practical control over the selection of top management or how top management performs once in place. Two roadblocks prevent shareholders from wielding voting power over the board and top management. The first is the practical fact that management controls the voting and proxy process. (A shareholder uses a proxy to direct management in how to vote the shareholder's shares.) Top executives of U.S. corporations can use corporate funds to solicit proxies. By contrast, insurgent shareholders (those seeking to change management) receive compensation for their proxy solicitation only if they are successful in the proxy battle.

The second obstacle stems from the difficulties of collective shareholder actions. With the exception of large institutional investors, typical shareholders own a very small fraction of the outstanding voting shares of a large corporation. Small shareholders recognize that their individual votes will have a negligible effect on the outcome of any voting contest. Consequently, few shareholders will take the considerable time, effort, and cost of understanding the competing solicitations in a proxy battle. (This phenomenon is sometimes called rational apathy.) With most uninformed shareholders casting their votes for current management, the chance is small that a challenge, no matter how meritorious, will succeed. Thus, although the cost is considerable, the expected gain from waging a proxy battle is likely to be small. The upshot is that the vast majority of director elections involve incumbents without challengers.

Suppose a small group of shareholders is convinced (and rightly so) that a change in top management would increase the value of the firm by $10 million. However, the group of challengers collectively holds only 1 percent of the voting shares. Thus, their gain from the change would be $100,000. Suppose that a reasonable estimate of the challengers' cost of waging a proxy fight is $150,000. Weighing the potential gain against the cost, the group would mount the proxy fight only if the chances of winning are high. (Again, if they win they receive reimbursement for their costs.) Given the difficulties in educating and subsequently enlisting hundreds of poorly informed small shareholders, the chances of winning the fight might be 30 percent at best. In this case, the group's expected gain from waging the battle is $(.3)(100,000) + (.7)(-150,000) = -\$75,000$. Thus, the challenger group has absolutely no financial incentive to launch this proxy fight. Despite the $10 million collective benefit from a management change, the fragmentation of share holdings precludes a meaningful voting contest.

Frequently, an inventor-entrepreneur who launches a new firm occupies the role of chief officer and owns between 50 percent and 100 percent of the firm. Ten years later, the same inventor-entrepreneur might have reduced his or her ownership share to well below 50 percent and have transferred decision-making responsibilities to a cadre of other top managers. Explain why.

CHECK STATION 5

LIMITING THE POWER OF TOP MANAGEMENT   Because shareholders possess limited control over the selection and performance of top management, one would expect significant principal–agent problems. Top-level managers have the necessary information and presumably the expertise to make optimal decisions. However, managers often pursue their own agendas and undertake plans that conflict with the interests of shareholders. For instance, executives might engage in "empire building," thereby incurring unnecessary costs (inflated management salaries, executive jets, and the like). Alternatively, in pursuit of the prestige of being market-share leaders, executives might be prone to expand the firm's operations far past the point of profit maximization. As the classical economist Adam Smith so eloquently put it:

> The directors of such companies . . . , being the managers rather of other people's money than of their own, it cannot well be expected that they should watch over it with the same anxious vigilance with which the partners in a private copartnery frequently watch over their own. . . . Negligence and profusion, therefore, must always prevail, more or less, in the management of the affairs of such a company.[17]

[17] Adam Smith, *The Wealth of Nations*, Book 5, Chapter 1, Part 3, Article 1.

Because of these concerns, a number of mechanisms exist to mitigate the principal–agent problems inherent in large corporations.

1. **External Enforcement of Managerial Duties** In the United States, there are two types of enforcement. The first is enforcement through private rights of action. State statutes and common law impose on directors the "duty of care" and the "duty of loyalty," among others. Shareholders may sue directors who act negligently or who line their own pockets to the detriment of the corporation. In our legal system, private attorneys have ample incentives by the fees they might earn in derivative or class-action suits to prosecute such cases. In effect, such a system provides private attorneys general who operate to enforce managerial duties. For example, shareholders have sued the management of Disney for its neglect in monitoring the compensation package of a former executive. This compensation package resulted in the payout of tens of millions of dollars to the executive even though he spent just months at the company before leaving. The second mechanism involves direct government enforcement authorized by state and federal securities acts. For example, the government may sue or prosecute executives for insider trading or fraud.

   There remain a number of open questions concerning managerial duties. Should the law impose broad duties or narrow ones? Should the law mandate duties or should the corporation be able to specify duties in its corporate charter? Who should enforce the duties, private investors (through derivative and class-action suits) or the government? For instance, consider the debate concerning mandatory or optional duties. Under an optional (opt-out) regime, the law would provide a standard set of duties that is potentially appropriate for a large number of corporations. However, the law would allow individual corporations to opt out of these duties through provisions in the corporate charter. Proponents of the opt-out regime assert that the same set of provisions is unlikely to be optimal for every corporation. Advocates of mandatory duties doubt the intent of top management to impose duties on itself, especially given the aforementioned principal–agent problems.

2. **The Market for Corporate Control** Another limitation on executive power comes from the market for corporate control. Tender offers (friendly or hostile) by corporate acquirers provide incentives for efficient management. If the firm's top executives manage poorly and, therefore, depress the market value of the public corporation, other firms will quickly identify a profitable acquisition opportunity. For instance, suppose that actions taken by an inferior management team

cause the firm's stock price to fall to $40 per share. By removing current management and refocusing the firm's business strategy, a would-be acquirer could increase firm value to $65 per share. Then a tender offer (in which an acquirer offers to buy shares from the public) at a premium relative to market (say $50 per share) would be profitable for the firm's shareholders and the acquirer alike. If shareholders tender a majority of their shares to the acquiring firm, then the acquiring firm has the ability (through the voting power of these shares) to remove current management and install its own. Indeed, some argue that the ever-present threat of a takeover provides strong incentives for management to pursue maximum firm value in the first place. Even though shareholders lack direct control, the market for corporate control forces managers to act to maximize firm value or risk a takeover and the resultant loss of their jobs.

In addition to these current mechanisms, several proposals strive to reduce the principal–agent problems inherent in the modern corporate form:

1. **Shareholder Empowerment** These proposals seek to give public shareholders a stronger voice in management by endowing them with greater management rights and by reducing the costs of involvement. Some reforms aim at altering voting rules to provide for binding shareholder resolutions. Other measures seek to reduce the cost of shareholder challenges (e.g., by allowing shareholders to use limited corporate resources in their challenges). Still other proposals seek to encourage cooperation among large institutional shareholders. Collectively, these institutions (pension funds, insurance funds, and investment funds) frequently hold sufficient numbers of shares to wield significant voting power. Because empowerment reforms seek to reduce the separation of ownership and control, they reduce agency costs but at the risk of unduly restricting top management's decision-making discretion.

2. **Corporate Governance Reforms** In the United States, corporate boards are typically composed of inside and outside directors. Inside directors are drawn from the ranks of top management and run the day-to-day operations of the corporation. Outside directors (other businesspeople or top managers of other firms) provide general oversight of the corporation. Given the limited compensation paid, outside directors are far less entrenched in their roles than inside directors. Accordingly, monitoring by outside directors can mitigate principal–agent problems.

    As an example, consider a hostile takeover in which both inside and outside directors stand to lose their jobs. For the inside directors, this loss can be enormous, including surrender of an executive position and the large income, important responsibilities, and prestige that go with it. For the outside director, all that is lost is a very part-time job and a very part-time salary. Thus, the inside director might strongly oppose the tender offer, whereas the outside director, largely free from a conflict of interest, would act more objectively.

As critics point out, strong outside directors often cannot rein in top management. Outside directors are typically chosen by inside directors, and their continued employment depends on getting along with the insiders. In addition, inside directors typically control the flow of information to outsiders. Corporate governance reform proposals aim at increasing the independence and influence of outside directors. Reform plans often include one or more of the following proposals: increasing the number of outside directors (most proposals specify a majority of outside directors); removing inside directors from nominating new directors and from setting directorial compensation; setting mandatory retirement ages or term limits for directors; and prohibiting interlocking directorships (where inside directors of one company are outside directors of another and vice versa).

FINANCIAL INCENTIVES   As noted in the previous section, incentive contracts can mitigate principal–agent problems. The same reasoning applies to a corporation's top management. By crafting pay-for-performance compensation plans, the organization can give managers greater incentives to maximize share value. This mechanism serves to reduce the costs associated with the separation of ownership and control.

Consider a corporation whose stock is currently trading at a price of $100 per share. Now compare three possible executive compensation schemes. At year-end, Executive 1 receives a flat bonus of $200,000 cash. Executive 2 receives $100,000 cash plus $100,000 worth of restricted shares (i.e., 1,000 shares). The restricted shares cannot be traded for three years. Finally, Executive 3 receives $100,000 cash plus $100,000 worth of warrants. Each warrant gives the holder the right to purchase the corporation's stock at a strike price of $100 per share. Suppose the trading price of this derivative instrument is $10 per warrant, so Executive 3 receives 10,000 warrants.

The three schemes have the same cash value. But which one provides the greatest incentive to maximize the corporation's share value three years hence? Executive 1 received no equity interest in the firm. Her compensation is independent of the share price, so she has no direct financial incentive in that regard. Executive 2 holds 1,000 shares. Therefore, for every dollar that his management skills can raise the share price, he profits by $1,000. Finally, Executive 3 holds 10,000 warrants. If the share price three years hence is no greater than $100 (the strike price), these warrants will be worthless. But suppose her management skills are instrumental in raising the share price above $100. For each

$1 increase in share price above $100, Executive 3's 10,000 warrants increase in value by $10,000. (For instance, if the three-year price is $120, each warrant is worth $20, the difference between the strike price and the current price.) Thus, the third pay-for-performance scheme gives by far the greatest executive incentive to maximize share value.

Linking executive compensation to the firm's performance serves to align management's interests with those of shareholders. Managers who take actions that succeed in raising shareholder values receive awards via greater monetary compensation; those who preside over poorly performing companies are penalized in their compensation. The key is to design top executive compensation to be responsive to performance. It is fair to ask: How well do the compensation schemes for top executives actually work?

Executive Compensation and Incentives

The research of Michael Jensen and Kevin Murphy, who studied compensation for chief executive officers of 250 of the largest U.S. corporations, provides one answer.[18] Their study carefully accounted for all monetary sources of CEO incentives: base salary, annual bonus, stock ownership, and stock options. The last three items allow direct rewards for superior performance. The authors employed least-squares regression techniques to estimate the relationship between changes in each CEO's combined compensation (the dependent variable) and two-year changes in the corporate value of his or her company (the independent variable). Their results were conclusive: Annual changes in executive compensation were *largely independent* of changes in corporate performance. Accounting for all sources of compensation, a $1,000 increase in corporate value corresponded to a mere $2.59 increase in compensation for the median CEO of the 250 companies. This appears to be a very small incentive indeed.

Jensen and Murphy suggest straightforward measures to strengthen CEO incentives. First, CEOs should own substantial amounts of company stock. For instance, the financial "wizard" Warren Buffet owns almost 45 percent of Berkshire Hathaway, the conglomerate he controls. Obviously, Buffet has a keen incentive to increase his company's value (which over the last 25 years has grown at an average annual rate of some 28 percent). Second, CEO compensation should be more responsive to performance. The compensation of Michael Eisner, the CEO of Walt Disney, is 10 times more sensitive to corporate performance than that of the median CEO in the Jensen Murphy study. Strengthening incentives in this direction should improve performance. Third, companies should fire poorly performing CEOs (a rare event over the last 20 years).

As U.S., European, and Japanese companies continue to experiment with pay-for-performance (PFP) systems, the debate about their effectiveness will continue. Critics contend PFP systems are deficient for a number of reasons: Companies cannot easily measure executive performance; PFP schemes reward

[18] See Michael Jensen and Kevin Murphy, "CEO Incentives—It's Not How Much You Pay, But How," *Harvard Business Review* (May–June 1990): 138–153; Jensen and Murphy, "Performance Pay and Top-Management Incentives," *Journal of Political Economy* (April 1990): 225–264.

the wrong types of behavior; and monetary compensation does not always sufficiently motivate behavior. (Does a promised promotion or a pat on the back do better?) Even proponents of PFP systems frequently disagree on the appropriate degree of incentives. In principle, the optimal degree of incentive depends on two factors: the degree to which the affected agent can influence the performance measure, and the agent's degree of risk aversion. For instance, basing a salesperson's compensation on something over which he or she has no control (e.g., the performance of the production department) precludes any incentive effect. Alternatively, if the actions of a hypothetical CEO account for only a small portion of variations in corporate performance (say, 10 percent), the compensation link can be geared down correspondingly.

Because of year-to-year fluctuations in corporate performance, PFP systems frequently produce large variations in an agent's compensation. (By contrast, a fixed salary scheme produces minimal variation.) In Chapter 8, we saw that risk-averse agents require extra compensation to bear these risks. In general, structuring an optimal PFP scheme depends on a trade-off between fostering the desired incentives and insuring the agent against undue monetary risks.[19] Because this task is easier in principle than in practice, we can expect a continued debate concerning the role of incentive pay in promoting corporate performance.

ENRON, TYCO, WORLDCOM   What do the spectacular recent failures of some of our largest corporations say about the organizational design of the modern firm? Of course, business failure in itself does not necessarily imply organizational failure. Even with the most able management and the most efficient organization, business carries numerous risks. Consumer tastes change; input availability and price can fluctuate dramatically; new ideas can create new markets and destroy others; natural disasters can alter fortunes. Nevertheless, faulty organizational design and poor decision making can have devastating effects.

Prior to its collapse in December 2001, Enron earned over $100 billion in revenues and had 20,000 employees. It had pioneered online energy trading and had moved into other areas such as broadband communications. However, some of its energy contracts allowed customers to pay for future energy supplies at a fixed price. Enron moved many of its risky activities to affiliated companies, often run by Enron personnel. This removed the activities from Enron's books but did not remove the risk from the corporation. Because its businesses required huge amounts of credit and, thus, a good credit rating, Enron pursued these off-the-books strategies in order to retain access to capital at reasonable borrowing rates. Other questionable accounting practices inflated the value of Enron's assets. In late 2001, some of these assets began to perform poorly. This, in turn, exposed the company's hidden fragile capital structure, and the firm's credit rating fell. Investors began selling its stock and Enron collapsed.

---

[19] For a lucid analysis of this trade-off, see John McMillan, *Games, Strategies, and Managers* (Oxford University Press, New York, 1996), Chapter 9.

By 1997, WorldCom, Inc., through internal growth and its acquisition of MCI, had become the second-largest long-distance provider in the country. After the collapse of Enron, investors at WorldCom became suspicious of accounting irregularities and filed a class-action suit that ultimately exposed one of the biggest fraudulent accounting schemes of all time. Accounting fraud also undid Tyco International, a conglomerate that produced a wide variety of products. Tyco's chief executive officer, chief financial officer, and general counsel stole hundreds of millions of dollars from the company through fraudulent accounting and illegal stock transactions. In still another instance of improper practices, Marsh & McLennan Company's insurance brokers have been sued by the state of New York for accepting kickbacks to steer clients (their principals) to particular insurance companies.

All of these cases represent the principal–agent problem run amuck—in particular, informational and monitoring failures. Through accounting fraud, the participants in these schemes were able to remove the transactions from the view of their principals, the investing public. Without proper monitoring, the participants could then act in their own interests to the detriment of their principals.

The government policy response to these scandals has focused on increased monitoring and penalties. In 2002, Congress passed the Sarbanes-Oxley Act, which raised firm reporting requirements and increased fines and jail time for violations. For example, the act mandates that the chief executive officer and the chief financial officer personally certify the firm's financial statements. It also requires real-time disclosure of changes in a firm's financial condition. Fines for violations can now reach $5 million (plus disgorgement) and violators can go to prison for up to 20 years.

As a second response to the scandals, Congress strengthened the role of the United States Sentencing Commission.[20] The commission's job is to establish effective penalties for organizations that violate federal laws. Its guidelines call for increased penalties for organizations with a history of violations or of tolerance for illegal activities. The guidelines also permit reduced penalties for firms that report illegal activities, take responsibility for them, and cooperate with the prosecuting authorities. Penalties are also reduced for organizations deemed to have effective compliance and ethics programs. In 2004, the commission strengthened the requirements for such compliance programs. To qualify for mitigation, the program must include (1) standards and procedures to prevent and detect criminal conduct, (2) responsibility at all levels and adequate resources, and authority for the program, (3) training at all levels, (4) auditing, monitoring, and evaluating program effectiveness, (5) nonretaliatory internal reporting systems, (6) incentives and discipline to promote compliance, and (7) reasonable steps, upon detection of a violation, to prevent further similar offenses. In short, recent government policies are meant to provide strong incentives for firms to prevent illegal behavior (and to expose it should it happen).

---

[20] Information from "An Overview of the United States Sentencing Commission and the Federal Sentencing Guidelines," publication of the United States Sentencing Commission, 2004.

<table>
<tr>
<td>

Incentive Pay at Du Pont's Fiber Division Revisited

</td>
<td>

In October 1990, only two years into its three-year plan, Du Pont announced that it was ending its experiment to link workers' compensation in its fibers division to division profits.[21] Although it promised to give workers and managers a greater sense of responsibility for (and stake in) the success of the fiber business, the plan had a number of unintended, though predictable, consequences. Instead of becoming more deeply involved and paying greater attention to profitability, many workers grew more alienated, believing they had little or no control over profits. The plan also raised tensions among employees whose bonuses now depended on the efforts of others. Many workers blamed management for wasting money and being a drag on profits. They resented the fact that managers were protected by other bonus plans geared to firmwide profits.

The failure to achieve the 1990 profit goal (set 4 percent above the 1989 goal), however, sealed the fate of the plan. With its principal customers—the automobile and housing industries—crippled by the 1990 economic recession, the fiber division's profit prospects were dismal. After earning a modest bonus in the first year, employees stood to lose 2 to 4 percent of their pay in the second. This fact sealed the death of the plan.

The aforementioned problems are exactly in line with this chapter's analysis. In effect, the bonus system enrolled all fiber-division employees in a 20,000-person team! Although one could spew bromides on how everyone should work together, the incentive effects drove people apart. Any individual employee had virtually no impact on the division's profits and, thus, had little personal incentive to pay attention to profitability. Instead, part of the worker's compensation was placed at risk, determined by factors beyond his or her control. It is evident that the performance plan utterly failed the informativeness test. Indeed, many workers rebelled at pay cuts triggered by the economic downturn, a factor they deemed irrelevant so far as their performance was concerned. For all these reasons, the plan failed.

</td>
</tr>
</table>

SUMMARY

Decision-Making Principles

1. Under asymmetric information, the decision maker must take into account the dual problems of adverse selection and moral hazard.

2. Many contractual relationships involve an agent in possession of superior information taking actions for another party. The principal must provide incentives or controls to induce the agent to act in the principal's behalf.

3. Modern firms divide information and management responsibilities among a wide group of managers. The firm is an organization based on a set of agreements and contracts, both explicit and implicit.

---

[21] See R. Koenig, "Du Pont Plan Linking Pay to Fibers Profit Unravels," *The Wall Street Journal* (October 25, 1990), B1.

4. According to the efficiency principle, business firms will organize to minimize the total cost of production, including transaction costs. Designing an efficient organization involves determining the boundaries of the firm, assigning decision responsibilities to managers with the best information on which to act, and providing control and incentive systems to minimize agency costs.

Nuts and Bolts

1. Adverse selection occurs when an agent (whose interests are at odds with the principal's) holds unobservable or hidden information. Warranties, contingent agreements, establishing a reputation, and signaling can help mitigate adverse selection problems.

2. Moral hazard occurs when an agent (whose interests are at odds with the principal's) takes unobservable or hidden actions. Principals can design controls and incentives to mitigate (though not eliminate) moral hazard problems. The resulting reduction in welfare from moral hazard is frequently labeled an agency cost.

3. A firm will choose to undertake an activity in-house rather than rely on outsourcing when the activity requires a high degree of coordination.

4. A firm will benefit from decentralized decision making when specialized information is dispersed among different management segments and when delegated decisions exhibit a low degree of interdependence.

5. Firms require control and incentive systems when an agent's objective differs from the firm's. Compensating the agent the exact amount he or she contributes to profit solves the incentive problem but exposes the agent to additional risk.

6. The modern corporation is characterized by separation of ownership and control. The owner-shareholders have little direct control over management. However, performance incentives, the external enforcement of executive duties, corporate governance reforms, and the market for corporate control can help mitigate principal–agent problems.

Questions and Problems

1. Carmakers acknowledge that a small percentage of new automobiles are "lemons." In the early 1980s, Chrysler Corporation succeeded in winning back lost market share by offering buyers the chance to return their new cars for up to 30 days if they were not satisfied. In this way, the "new" Chrysler sought to demonstrate its confidence in product quality.

Suppose Chrysler made the following estimates for the program: (1) 4 percent of its new cars were lemons; (2) one-half of all lemons would be discovered and returned; and (3) 1 out of every 16 "normal-quality" cars would be returned because of minor problems, buyer change of heart, and so on.

   a. Of all the cars returned, what portion are lemons? For a buyer satisfied after month 1, what is the chance that that person will later find that he or she owns a lemon?

   b. How might Chrysler decide whether the program's benefits in screening for quality are worth its costs?

2. In the early 1990s, lawsuits charged Sears with massive fraud in its auto repair centers, alleging that mechanics were convincing customers that they needed expensive repairs when, in fact, they were unnecessary. Sears entered into a multimillion-dollar agreement to settle the case out of court. In addition, in a bid to win back business it had lost during the highly publicized case, Sears announced that its sales staff would no longer be paid on commission.

   a. In your view, were the abuses by the mechanics a result of adverse selection, moral hazard, or both?

   b. The management of Sears stated that it was unaware of the abuses. What are the incentives for management to monitor its employees to prevent such wrongdoing?

   c. What is the disadvantage of ending the commission system?

3. Suppose prospective clerical workers fall into one of two categories in equal numbers: high productivity (HP) and low productivity (LP). An HP worker's value to the firm is $30,000 per year; an LP worker's value is $20,000 per year. A firm hires workers who stay an average of five years.

   a. At the time of hiring, the firm cannot distinguish HP and LP workers. In this case, what wage will it offer its new hires?

   b. One option is for workers to attend college before taking a job. Suppose college has no effect on clerical productivity (its other virtues notwithstanding). For an HP worker, the expected total cost of attending a four-year college (accounting for possible scholarships) is $40,000. The expected cost for an LP worker is $60,000. Can HP workers effectively signal their productivity by attending college? What if the average job stay is only three years?

4. As a benefit to employees, many universities offer their clerical and administrative employees free tuition for themselves and their families. Why might universities prefer this to simply offering the employees more money?

5. Five couples are having dinner at a fancy French restaurant. They expect that the total dinner bill will be split evenly five ways. How might this prior knowledge affect the diners' menu selections? (What if one couple mistakenly believes there are to be separate checks?)

6. When a corporation offers shares of stock or other securities to the public, it hires an underwriter to conduct the sale. (The underwriter is an investment bank such as Morgan Stanley or Merrill Lynch.) Most commonly, firms and investment bankers use a procedure known as "firm commitment" underwriting. In this arrangement, the underwriter buys the shares from the company and then sells them to the public. If the offering is undersubscribed or if the price must be subsequently lowered to unload the shares, the underwriter, not the firm, suffers the loss. Why do firms and underwriters use this procedure? What is in it for each? How does this means of sale affect the buying public?

7. Since the mid-1980s, baseball teams have bid vigorously for free agents—players with six or more years of service who are free to sign with a new team. After signing a five-year contract with a new team for an exorbitant amount, a free-agent pitcher has had three consecutive lackluster seasons.
   a. How might adverse selection explain this outcome?
   b. How might moral hazard cause this outcome? Explain.
   c. What advice would you give owners in bidding for free agents?

8. Many companies give out perquisites (the corner office, company cars, etc.) strictly on the basis of seniority. Likewise, companies frequently allocate tasks based on seniority. For example, many airlines assign routes to pilots and flight attendants based on seniority. What are the advantages and disadvantages of the seniority system?

9. Team decision making frequently mitigates information and coordination problems. What are some of the costs of teams?

10. For planning purposes, company headquarters seeks to obtain accurate information about the productive capacity of one of its plants. The plant manager knows that the facility's capacity is $Q = 10,000$ units but knows that headquarters is in the dark. Using a bonus system, headquarters also wants to encourage the manager to strive for maximum plant output.

   a. Headquarters decides to use the bonus system:

   $$B = .5(Q - Q_T),$$

   where the plant manager forecasts the likely output Q_T. If actual output Q exceeds Q_T at the end of the year, the bonus increases. If Q falls short of Q_T, the bonus is reduced. Under this system will the manager report the plant's true capacity, 10,000 units? Explain.

   b. Suppose instead that headquarters uses the bonus system:

   $$B = .4Q_T + .3(Q - Q_T), \text{ if } Q > Q_T, \quad \text{and}$$
   $$B = .4Q_T + .5(Q - Q_T), \text{ if } Q < Q_T.$$

   Will the manager report the plant's true capacity? Will the manager strive for maximum output? Explain.

Discussion Question

a. In 1999, Procter & Gamble and Ford Motor Co., two of the world's largest spenders on advertising, changed the way they paid their advertising agencies. Formerly, these agencies' fees were set as a percentage of each firm's total advertising spending (primarily through television, magazines, and newspapers). The agencies focused their efforts on large campaigns built around impact ads. The new system pays the agency a modest base fee (based on spending) plus an incentive fee that varies directly with the total sales of the products promoted by the ads. How do you think agencies will react to the new system? Is the new pay structure better for one or both sides than the old one? Explain.

b. Exide Corp., a worldwide battery maker, built its organizational structure on 10 separate country units. Country managers, particularly in Europe, aggressively sought to expand their sales and profits—by price cuts, exports, and advertising—frequently in competition with the company's other geographic units. In 2000, the company made a dramatic organizational change, abolishing its geographic units and dividing its structure into six global product lines (automotive batteries, industrial batteries, consumer batteries, and so on). What are the potential advantages and disadvantages of this organizational change?

c. In a proposed 2004 takeover of King Pharmaceuticals by Mylan Laboratories, Perry Corporation, an investment firm and holder of a large amount of King shares, stood to gain $28 million, but only if shareholders of Mylan approved the deal. In order to facilitate this transaction, Perry Corporation purchased 26.6 million shares of Mylan while selling short the same number of shares. The short sale gives Perry Corporation a $1 profit for every dollar that a Mylan share falls and a $1 loss for every dollar that a Mylan share increases, thus completely offsetting for Perry the effect of any share price change. Carl Icahn, the second largest shareholder and an opponent of the takeover, described Perry Corporation's move as a "travesty." Though this financial maneuver is not illegal, some corporate governance activists contend that it should be. What do you think? Explain why.

Spreadsheet Problem

S1. Suppose that the gross profit generated by a particular worker is given by $\pi = 1,000e + u$, where e denotes the worker's effort (measured as an index between 0 and 50) and u is a random variable with a mean of zero and a positive standard deviation. Thus, profit depends not only on the worker's effort but also on random factors beyond his or her control. The worker's disutility associated with effort is given by $D = 10e^2$. The employer compensates the worker with an incentive contract of the form $P = W + b\pi$, where W is a fixed wage component and b is the worker's profit share. For concreteness, let e = 30, and suppose that the contract calls for W = $10,000 and b = .3. Then the expected gross profit attributable to the worker is $30,000. The employer's expected wage payment is $10,000 + (.3)(30,000) = $19,000, and the employer's expected profit is $30,000 - 19,000 = $11,000. In turn, the worker's expected profit (net of any disutility) is $19,000 - 10(30)^2 = $10,000.

Under an incentive contract, the variability in the worker's wage (i.e., the risk) increases with the profit share b. A risk-averse worker will *discount* the expected profit listed earlier by a risk premium to account for the burden of risk. To be precise, we suppose that the risk premium takes the form $R = 10,000b^2$. The maximum premium, $10,000, occurs under 100 percent profit sharing (b = 1). Of course, for b = 0, the wage is fixed, so there is no risk and no risk premium. For b = .3, the premium is $900, so the worker's risk-adjusted profit is $10,000 - 900 = $9,100. In general, the worker's risk adjusted profit is given by:

$$\pi_W = W + b(1000e) - 10e^2 - 10,000b^2.$$

a. Create a spreadsheet similar to the example given on page 672. For the contract with W = $10,000 and b = .3, find the worker's optimal level of effort. (*Hint*: Use the spreadsheet's optimizer to maximize the worker's risk-adjusted profit in cell E12. Alternatively, adjust the worker's effort until $M\pi_W = 1000b - 20e$ in cell E17 is exactly equal to zero.)

b. Find the worker's optimal effort levels for sharing rates of .4, .6, .8, and 1.0. What pattern do you detect?

c. Using the optimizer, find the sharing rate and level of effort that together maximize the employer and worker's total profit. (*Hint*: Adjust cells C7 and D7 to maximize cell C17 subject to the constraint that $M\pi_W$ in cell E17 is equal to zero.) Does this optimal contract carry a strong or weak profit incentive?

d. If e were observable, then the parties could write a forcing contract with a fixed wage (b = 0) payable as long as the worker delivers an optimal level of effort. What level of effort maximizes total profit? Compare the total profits attained in parts c and d.

	A	B	C	D	E	F
1						
2		**AN OPTIMAL INCENTIVE CONTRACT**				
3						
4		Fixed	Profit	Worker's	Expected	
5		Wage (W)	Share (b)	Effort	Gross Profit	
6						
7		10,000	0.30	30	30,000	
8						
9		Expected	Worker's	Worker's	Risk-Adjusted	
10		Compensation	Risk Premium	Disutility	Profit	
11						
12		19,000	900	9,000	9,100	
13						
14		Employer's	Total		Worker's	
15		Profit	Profit		Marginal Profit	
16						
17		11,000	20,100		−300	
18						

Suggested References

The following articles are some of the classic treatments of asymmetric information, principal–agent problems, and organizational design.

Akerlof, G. "The Market for 'Lemons': Quality Uncertainty and the Market Mechanism." *Quarterly Journal of Economics* (1970): 488–500.

Alchian, A. A., and H. Demsetz. "Production, Information Costs, and Economic Organization." *American Economic Review* (1972): 777–795.

Brynjolfsson, E., and L. M. Hitt. "Beyond Computation: Information Technology, Organizational Transformation, and Business Performance." *Journal of Economic Perspectives* (2000): 23–48.

Coase, R. "The Nature of the Firm." *Economica* (1937): 386–405.

Jensen, M. C., and W. Meckling. "Theory of the Firm: Managerial Behavior, Agency Costs and Ownership Structure." *Journal of Financial Economics* (1976): 305–360.

Radner, R. "Hierarchy: The Economics of Managing." *Journal of Economic Literature* (1992): 1382–1415.

Riley, J. G. "Silver Signals: Twenty-Five Years of Screening and Signalling." *Journal of Economic Literature* (2001): 432–478.

Shleifer, A., and R. W. Vishny. "A Survey of Corporate Governance." *Journal of Finance* (1997): 737–783.

Spence, A. M. *Market Signaling.* Cambridge: Harvard University Press, 1974.

The following texts offer superb treatments of organizational design.

Brickley, J. A., C. W. Smith, and J. L. Zimmerman. *Managerial Economics and Organizational Architecture.* Chicago: McGraw-Hill, 2003.

Milgrom, P., and J. Roberts. *Economics, Organization and Management.* Englewood Cliffs, NJ: Prentice Hall, 1992.

Pratt, J. W., and R. J. Zeckhauser. *Principals and Agents: The Structure of Business.* Boston: Harvard Business School Press, 1985.

An interesting place to begin an Internet search is Erik Brynjolfsson's home page (with links to research on organizational structure and information technology): http://ebusiness.mit.edu/erik.

1. A used-car dealer faces two types of adverse selection problems. First, the dealer is in the business of buying cars and must take care to avoid low-quality vehicles. Thus, it is wise to have staff mechanics to inspect vehicles before purchase. The dealer must also sell used cars to the suspecting public. By developing a good reputation and by offering warranties, the dealer can mitigate these adverse selection problems as well.

2. Under capitation, after being paid its up-front fees, the physicians' group pays for all costs. Therefore, it has the strongest possible incentive to practice preventive care (provided, of course, that it is cost-effective). A possible problem with this approach is the presence of adverse selection. A doctors' group has an incentive to enlist the healthiest segments of the population and to turn its back on those in poor health. Under capitation, doctors face substantial financial risks. (At the end of the year, the costs paid out may exceed the capitation revenues received.) This raises a new moral hazard problem. Heightened cost incentives might induce doctors to compromise the quality of care (to maintain their incomes).

3. Optimizing the size of a team involves trading off the marginal benefits of adding another member (another perspective and source of information) against the additional cost. Besides the cost in human resources, added costs would include the difficulty in communicating and reaching consensus and the heightening of free-rider problems. As always, the optimal trade-off occurs where MB = MC.

4. Suppose the worker's profit share is exactly 60 percent. Now if the worker changes from medium effort to high effort, his expected compensation increases by $(.6)(85,000 - 75,000) = \$6,000$, according to Table 15.3. The resulting change in disutility is $45,000 - 39,000 = \$6,000$. Thus, the worker is exactly indifferent to exerting the extra effort. Raising the profit share slightly above 60 percent tips the decision to high effort (the optimal choice).

5. This is a classic manifestation of the growing separation of management and control in successful, growing firms. Formerly, the inventor was best equipped to shepherd the firm's new product. At this later stage in the product life cycle, efficiency may dictate the institution of professional managers. The drop in the entrepreneur's ownership stake is probably also a reflection of efficient financial diversification on his or her part.

**CHECK STATION
ANSWERS**

A Principal–Agent Model

Throughout this chapter, the principal–agent relationship has appeared in numerous places: medical and federal deposit insurance, workers' contracts, franchising policies, and executive compensation. Thus, it pays to build a formal description of this relationship. We now describe and analyze a bare-bones model.

Suppose a risk-neutral principal hires a risk-averse agent to work (undertake effort) to produce output π. (We value output in dollar terms, so π can be thought of as the net profit generated by the agent.) The exact output realized depends on the agent's level of effort (e) and on other, uncertain factors beyond the agent's control. For instance, a salesperson might devote the same effort in contacting clients in March as in February, but his or her actual sales results might vary significantly between the months. We model output by the equation

$$\pi = ke + u, \qquad [15A.1]$$

where the coefficient k represents the agent's marginal product (output per unit of effort) and u is the component of output (plus or minus) due to uncertain factors. The random factor u is taken to have a mean of zero and a variance of σ^2.

The agent measures his welfare according to the wage (W) received from the principal and the cost of the effort expended. We model the cost (or disutility) of the worker's effort as $C_E = .5ce^2$, where c denotes a numerical coefficient and e is taken to vary between 0 (no effort) and 1 (100 percent effort). Note that the marginal cost of effort increases with e; expending more and more extra effort becomes more and more costly. Thus, the agent faces a trade-off. The agent benefits by increasing e and raising output π (by which he might increase his wage reward), but the extra effort comes at a personal cost. The agent's overall welfare or utility (call this U_A) depends on the wage received, net of the cost of effort: $W - C_E = W - .5ce^2$.

Now consider the wage contract between principal and agent. The agent's wage is given by

$$W = a + b\pi. \tag{15A.2}$$

Here the principal is able to observe and measure the agent's output π but not his effort e. Accordingly, the agent's wage in Equation 15A.2 depends on output but not effort. Specifically, the agent receives a fixed wage portion (a) plus a profit-sharing portion ($b\pi$) that depends directly on his output. We note two extreme cases: $b = 0$ corresponds to a fixed-wage contract, whereas $b = 1$ means that the agent's compensation varies dollar for dollar with output. For b between 0 and 1, the agent's wage involves partial profit sharing. Accordingly, we speak of b as the agent's profit-sharing rate.

Because the agent is risk averse, we need to focus on the agent's *certainty equivalent wage*. As noted in Chapter 8, the individual values a risky payment at an amount below the payment's expected value. This reduction in value is termed the agent's *risk premium* (*RP*). Thus, we write the agent's certainty equivalent wage as

$$\begin{aligned} W_{CE} &= E[W] - RP \\ &= E[a + b\pi] - RP \\ &= E[a + b(ke + u)] - RP \\ &= a + bke - RP, \end{aligned}$$

where E denotes expectation. (Here we have substituted from Equations 15A.1 and 15A.2 and used the fact that the expected value of u is 0.) The agent's risk premium depends on the degree of risk inherent in the wage and on his personal degree of risk aversion. The variance of his wage is exactly $b^2\sigma^2$, and this we take as the appropriate summary measure of wage risk. Thus, we can write the agent's risk premium as $RP = .5rb^2\sigma^2$, where the coefficient r denotes the agent's degree of risk aversion. The more risk averse is the agent, then the greater is r. (If the agent were risk neutral, then r would be 0.)

We are now ready to write an expression for the agent's overall level of welfare

$$\begin{aligned} U_A &= W_{CE} - C_E \\ &= [a + bke - RP] - .5ce^2 \\ &= a + bke - .5rb^2\sigma^2 - .5ce^2. \end{aligned} \tag{15A.3}$$

In turn, the principal's level of welfare is

$$U_P = E[\pi - W]$$
$$= E[\pi - (a + b\pi)]$$
$$= (1 - b)ke - a.$$

Finally, the total welfare of principal and agent together is

$$U_T = U_P + U_A = ke - .5rb^2\sigma^2 - .5ce^2. \qquad [15A.4]$$

The parties' total welfare is the expected profit, $\pi = ke$ (after adding together each side's respective profit share), net of the agent's cost of effort and risk premium (the cost of bearing risk).

Given that the agent seeks to maximize his overall level of welfare, what level of effort will he expend? To maximize U_A with respect to e, we use the marginal condition

$$dU_A/de = bk - ce = 0.$$

Therefore, $e^* = bk/c$, where the asterisk denotes the optimal level of effort. Note that $b = 0$ implies $e^* = 0$. If the agent receives a fixed wage, $W = a$, that does not depend on performance, there is no point in expending costly effort. The agent's optimal level of effort increases with b and k. A greater profit-sharing rate or greater productivity means a closer connection between the worker's remuneration and his effort; with more to gain in either case, he works harder. Not surprisingly, effort varies inversely with its cost (c).

Let's now characterize an efficient wage contract. The goal of efficiency (recall the discussion in Chapter 10) is to maximize the *total welfare* of the parties. First, substitute the formula for the agent's effort ($e^* = bk/c$) into Equation 15A.4.

$$U_T = U_P + U_A = k(bk/c) - .5rb^2\sigma^2 - .5c(bk/c)^2$$

$$= bk^2/c - .5rb^2\sigma^2 - .5b^2k^2/c \qquad [15A.5]$$

An efficient contract sets the sharing rate b to maximize total welfare in Equation 15A.5. Note that total profit does not depend on the fixed wage (a). Varying the fixed wage simply redistributes the split of the total profit. The optimality condition with respect to b is

$$dU_T/db = k^2/c - rb\sigma^2 - bk^2/c = 0.$$

Therefore,

$$b^* = \frac{k^2/c}{r\sigma^2 + k^2/c}$$

or

$$b^* = \frac{1}{rc\sigma^2/k^2 + 1}. \qquad\qquad [15A.6]$$

(In the last step, we have simplified the expression by dividing numerator and denominator by the common factor k^2/c.)

Equation 15A.6 summarizes the factors that determine the optimal rate of profit sharing. First, note that if the agent were risk neutral ($r = 0$), the optimal contract would set $b^* = 1$; the agent would be paid each extra dollar of profit earned. As noted earlier in the chapter, this induces the agent to supply the profit-maximizing level of effort (taking into account the cost of effort). Similarly, if effort is very productive (k is very large), efficiency implies a high sharing rate, again, to induce a high effort level. Conversely, if output is very risky or the agent is very risk averse (high σ^2 or high r), an efficient contract sets a low profit-sharing rate, minimizing the agent's exposure to profit risk. Finally, if effort is very costly (high c), the efficient contract sets a low profit-sharing rate and elicits a modest level of effort from the agent.

The bare-bones principal–agent model can be generalized in many useful directions. We conclude by extending the setup to allow the principal to monitor *imperfectly* the agent's effort. Suppose the principal observes:

$$H = e + v,$$

where v is a random factor with mean 0 and standard deviation σ_v. The principal cannot measure and observe the agent's true effort e. Rather, it observes a proxy (H for "hustle") that may overestimate or underestimate e. The principal then offers a wage contract of the form

$$W = a + b\pi + dH.$$

In this new contract, greater effort by the agent is (imperfectly) rewarded by means of the positive coefficient d. For this contract, we can derive the agent's optimal level of effort: $e^* = (bk + d)/c$. Although we will not write down their formulas, the optimal coefficients b^* and d^*—in particular their relative magnitudes—are of some interest. First, both coefficients are positive. This follows from the *informativeness* principle (noted earlier in the chapter) that all performance information should be used in setting compensation. Second, an efficient wage contract places the greater weight on the performance measure (π or H) having the greater precision, that is, smaller variance. For instance, if effort can be measured with relative precision (σ_v is small relative to σ), then d^* will be large and b^* will be small. Conversely, if effort is very imprecisely observed, profit sharing (b^*) will carry the greater relative weight.

CHAPTER 16

Bargaining and Negotiation

To get to the Promised Land, you have to negotiate your way through the wilderness.

H. COHEN

Wooing David Letterman

In January 1993, David Letterman made it official—he would be leaving *Late Night* on NBC for a new 11:30 P.M. show on CBS beginning in the fall. A tangled web of negotiations preceded the move. In the 1990s, NBC's unbeatable late-night lineup, *The Tonight Show* and *Late Night*, accounted for huge net revenues of some $100 million per year. In 1992, NBC chose the comedian Jay Leno, instead of Letterman, to succeed Johnny Carson as the host of *The Tonight Show* in an effort to keep its lock on late-night programming. Accordingly, CBS, a nonentity in late-night television, saw its chance to woo David Letterman.

After extensive negotiations, CBS offered Letterman a $14 million salary to do the new show (a $10 million raise over his salary at NBC). In addition, Letterman's own production company would be paid $25 million annually to produce the show. (By comparison, NBC produces *The Tonight Show* in house at an annual cost of $15 million.) However, NBC was unwilling to surrender Letterman to CBS without a fight. The network entered into secret negotiations with Letterman's representative, Michael Ovitz, exploring the possibility of dumping Leno and giving *The Tonight Show* to Letterman.

One group of NBC executives stood firmly behind Leno. Another group preferred replacing Leno to losing Letterman to CBS. Giving Letterman *The Tonight Show* would mean paying him much more, as well as buying out Leno's contract.

Moreover, the network still would face certain risks: Would Letterman's brand of irreverent comedy appeal to the more mainstream television audience in the earlier time slot? What show would replace *Late Night*? Even if it retained Letterman as host of *The Tonight Show*, NBC had to face the fact that its new lineup (with an undetermined late-night entry) would produce only about $75 million in annual net revenue. In the end, NBC offered *The Tonight Show* to Letterman—but with the condition that he wait a year until Leno's current contract was up.[1]

David Letterman faced the most difficult decision of his life. He had been hurt and angry when NBC had bypassed him for *The Tonight Show*, and he yearned for a chance to showcase his talents in the earlier time slot. Should he make up and stay with NBC or take a new path with CBS? In the end, he chose to leave. CBS executives were elated. Over a five-year horizon, they expected the new Letterman show to generate $35 million in net revenue per year. Over a longer period (assuming the establishment of a second show following Letterman's), net revenues surely would increase, perhaps substantially.

The Letterman negotiations raise a number of questions. How well did Michael Ovitz do in squeezing the most out of CBS on behalf of Letterman? In its negotiations, what (if anything) could NBC have done differently to keep its star?

Negotiation and bargaining are important features of many economic settings. Examples include negotiating the terms of a sales transaction, management–labor bargaining, and settling a dispute out of court, to name just a few. Generally speaking, these are situations in which both parties stand to benefit from a cooperative agreement. Nonetheless, a significant degree of conflict remains because each side seeks to secure an agreement at terms most favorable to itself.

Many economic transactions are completed by means of bargaining under bilateral monopoly, that is, in settings in which a single seller faces a single buyer. In contrast to organized markets, in which competition among large numbers of buyers and sellers determines price and quantity, in bargaining settings the competition is one on one. Although the analysis of market competition obviously deserves attention (see Chapters 10, 11, and 12), it is worth remembering that there are other important means of resource allocation.

Our objectives in this chapter are twofold. In the first two sections, we analyze the economic forces underlying the bargaining setting: What economic factors create the opportunity for mutually beneficial agreements? What form do economically efficient bargains take? Next, we examine bargaining strategy from the perspective of decision making under uncertainty: What bargaining strategy maximizes management's expected profit from the transaction? What

---

[1] This account is based on B. Carter, *The Late Shift: Letterman, Leno, and the Network Battle for the Night*, (New York: Hyperion, 1994); K. Auletta, "Late-Night Gamble," *The New Yorker* (February 1, 1993): 38–46, and B. Carter, "A Letterman Deal with ABC Was Just a Signature Away," *The New York Times* (March 18, 2002): C1.

are the risks of such a strategy? Finally, we apply the principles of negotiation to the takeover dispute between Texaco and Pennzoil introduced in Chapter 1.

THE ECONOMIC SOURCES OF BENEFICIAL AGREEMENTS

It takes two to tango and three to form a menage à trois. In other words, economic agents enter into transactions because the transactions are mutually beneficial. A well-crafted agreement is better for both parties than no agreement at all. Moreover, some agreements are better (for both parties) than others. Given this observation, it is natural to explore the economic factors that create the opportunities for mutually beneficial agreements. We begin our discussion by considering a typical negotiated transaction involving a buyer and a seller.

SELLING A WAREHOUSE   Two firms are locked in negotiations concerning the sale of a warehouse, the equipment therein, and a considerable inventory of industrial machinery. The main issue is price. The present owner is closing down its current operation in a move to redirect its resources into other businesses. The warehouse is in a valuable location for the would-be buyer, who also could make direct use of the equipment and machinery inventory. The buyer has examined the warehouse and contents and, after considerable figuring, has estimated its value for the transaction at $600,000; that is, the potential buyer is indifferent to the options of paying $600,000 to complete the purchase or forgoing the transaction altogether. The seller sets its value for the transaction at $520,000; this is the net amount the firm estimates it would obtain, on average, from selling the warehouse and contents via a broker or at auction. The buyer and seller values are referred to as **reservation prices** or **walk-away prices**.

Given the values held by buyer and seller, it is evident that a mutually beneficial agreement is possible. In particular, both parties would prefer an agreement at a price between $520,000 and $600,000 to the alternative of no agreement at all. For convenience, we denote the sale price by P. The seller's profit from such a transaction is P − $520,000, whereas the buyer's gain is $600,000 − P. If there is no agreement on a price (and, therefore, no sale), each party earns zero profit. Clearly, any price such that $520,000 ≤ P ≤ $600,000 affords positive profits for both parties. This price range between the buyer and seller walk-away prices is referred to as the **zone of agreement**. Observe that the total gain (the sum of buyer and seller profit) from such a transaction is

$$(600,000 - P) + (P - 520,000) = 600,000 - 520,000 = \$80,000.$$

The total gain (or trading gain) is measured by the difference between the buyer and seller values, that is, the size of the zone of agreement.

FIGURE 16.1

The Zone of
Agreement and the
Payoff Frontier

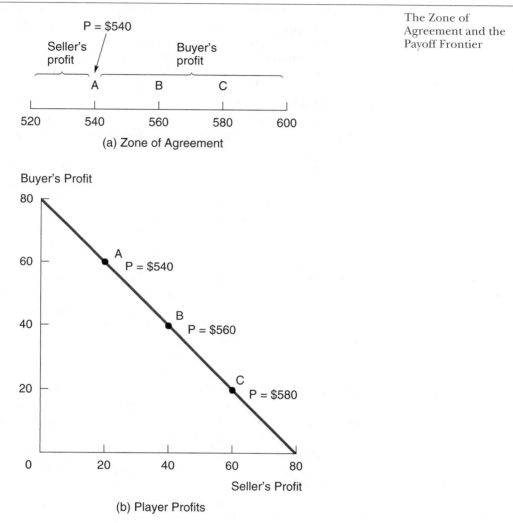

(a) Zone of Agreement

(b) Player Profits

Figure 16.1 presents two views of the buyer–seller transaction. Part a shows the zone of agreement and possible negotiated prices within it. A price of $540,000 is shown at point A. At this price, the buyer claims $60,000 in profit and the seller claims $20,000. Obviously, at higher negotiated prices, the seller's profit increases and the buyer's profit falls dollar for dollar. Part b displays this profit trade-off explicitly. The parties' profits from transactions at various prices are graphed on the axes. The profits from a $540,000 price appear at point A.

Prices of $560,000 and $580,000 (and the corresponding profits) are listed at points B and C, respectively. The downward-sloping line shows the profit implications for all possible prices within the zone of agreement. This is commonly called the **payoff frontier**. If the parties fail to reach an agreement, they obtain zero profits, as marked by point 0 at the origin of the graph.

Figure 16.1 reemphasizes a simple but important point about the gains from a negotiated agreement. An agreement at any price between $520,000 and $600,000 is better for both parties than no agreement. The "no agreement" outcome is said to be *inefficient* because there exist one or more alternative outcomes that are better for both parties. We say that *an outcome is efficient if no other outcome exists that is better for both parties.*[2] By this definition, all of the outcomes along the payoff frontier are efficient. For instance, consider an agreement at a $520,000 price. Any change in price that makes one party better off necessarily makes the other worse off; that is, there is no other agreement that is better for both parties. Thus, this agreement is efficient.

This example, simple as it is, illustrates the mixture of cooperative and competitive elements in bargaining. The parties must cooperate to reach some mutually beneficial agreement. But, of course, the price at which an agreement occurs is a matter of competition: The buyer prefers a low price, the seller a high price. In the negotiation literature this situation is called a *distributive* bargain because the parties can be thought of as bargaining (via price) over the distribution of the total profit (in this case, $80,000) available from the transaction. The actual price they negotiate depends in part on the bargaining abilities of the parties and on notions of equity and fairness. For instance, a final price in the vicinity of $560,000 (implying $40,000 in profit for each side) might be negotiated by equally matched bargainers who are in agreement that the total bargaining profit should be divided equitably. For the moment, however, our analysis has identified the zone of agreement without offering a prediction of which price within this zone will be the agreement terms.

Two additional points can be drawn from the example. First, the source of the trading gains is the difference in the parties' values. Because the seller's value for the warehouse and items is less than the buyer's value, completion of the transaction creates a trading gain that both sides share. In contrast, if the agent values were reversed (i.e., the seller's value was $600,000 and the buyer's value $520,000), no mutually beneficial transaction would be possible. Second, the values or reservation prices of the parties are influenced by the alternative transactions available to them. In the present circumstances, for instance, the buyer estimates the monetary value for the warehouse at $600,000. Clearly, if the buyer learned of the availability of another warehouse at a comparable location at an unexpectedly low price, its walk-away price for the current transaction would fall markedly. Similarly, if the buyer revised downward its estimate

---

[2] More accurately, an agreement is efficient if there is no other agreement that makes one party better off without making the other worse off.

of the potential profit from the warehouse operation (because of adverse economic conditions in general), its walk-away value also would fall. Of course, the importance of outside opportunities pertains equally to the seller. In short, the alternative transactions available to the parties directly or indirectly set the respective walk-away prices between which negotiated agreements can occur.

In 1983, Harper & Row Company made a phenomenal profit as the hardcover publisher of *In Search of Excellence*, the long-time best-selling business book. Warner Books held the rights to release the book in paperback—rights that were to begin in November 1983. Prior to that date, Harper & Row and Warner entered into negotiations to postpone the paperback release until April 1984. After lengthy discussions, they concluded the deal at an undisclosed price. What was the basis for this mutually beneficial agreement?

**CHECK
STATION 1**

Resolving Disputes

As we have seen, negotiation is a frequent means of securing new transactions. It also plays an essential role in dispute resolution. Examples include management–labor negotiations, international negotiations, conflicts between government regulators and business, and legal disputes. As we will see, the resolution of an ongoing dispute offers exactly the same kind of mutual benefits as the forging of a new agreement. The following typical example makes the point.

A PATENT CONFLICT   A small manufacturer of a specialty pump used in oil refineries and nuclear reactors has filed a $4 million lawsuit against a leading pump company for patent infringement. Three years after the small firm successfully introduced its pump, the large firm began to sell a similar pump at lower prices. The small firm claims its rival "reverse engineered" its pump and then copied it, making only small modifications. At the time of development, the small firm filed numerous patents on the pump's "unique" valves and circuitry—patents that it claims have been infringed on. The large company has filed its own patents and claims the pump it developed is unique (and, indeed, is more similar in design to its own 10-year-old model than to the small firm's model).

The firms' legal representatives are conducting negotiations aimed at reaching an out-of-court settlement. Both sides recognize that a full-scale trial will be very costly—in all likelihood more costly for the small firm because, unlike its larger rival, it does not maintain an in-house legal department. How should each side approach the negotiations? Can the parties reach a mutually beneficial out-of-court agreement?

For either side, an optimal negotiating strategy depends critically on its best estimate of the expected monetary outcome if the case goes to court. After all, the court outcome is the relevant alternative to a negotiated agreement.

The problem is that the court outcome is highly uncertain. The court's award of monetary damages (if any) can vary over a wide range. Under a "no infringement" ruling, the large firm would owe zero damages. Alternatively, if a broad infringement is found, the large firm could be ordered to cease sale of the pump altogether and pay maximum damages. Outcomes in between include narrowly defined infringements (of a particular valve, for instance) with damages based on larger or smaller estimates of the resulting economic loss suffered by the small company.

Given these multiple uncertainties, each side would be well advised to take a cue from Chapters 8 and 9 and construct a decision tree incorporating the sequence and probabilities of the different possible outcomes and monetary consequences. Suppose each side has done this and has averaged back its tree to compute the expected litigation value of the case (i.e., the amount on average that the court will order the large firm to pay the small firm). Let v_S and v_L denote the small and large firms' respective expected values. Because the two sides are likely to see the risks and possible outcomes differently, these estimates will also differ from each other. In addition, the firms have in hand estimates of the total costs (legal and other) of fighting the case in court. We denote these costs by c_S and c_L, respectively.

With this information in hand, it is easy to evaluate the monetary implications for each side of going to court. The small firm's expected profit, net of court costs, is $v_S - c_S$. The large firm's expected expense, including court costs, is $v_L + c_L$. Thus, a proposed out-of-court settlement (call this P) is beneficial for both sides if and only if

$$v_S - c_S \le P \le v_L + c_L. \qquad [16.1]$$

This range of out-of-court settlements constitutes the zone of agreement. To illustrate, suppose the firms' assessments of the case are identical. Let's say that the expected litigation value is $v_S = v_L = \$1$ million, and court costs are $c_S = \$200,000$ and $c_L = \$160,000$, respectively. Then any out-of-court settlement (i.e., a payment from the large firm to the small firm) between $800,000 and $1.16 million is mutually beneficial. As always, the size of the zone of agreement measures the total benefit at stake in reaching an agreement.

The collective benefit from an agreement is exactly equal to the sum of the court costs the disputants save by avoiding litigation. (Let's check this: The size of the zone of agreement is $1,160,000 - 800,000 = \$360,000$, which is exactly the sum of the court costs.) The exact terms of the agreement dictate how this benefit is split. For instance, under an agreement at P = $1 million, the parties settle for what each agrees is the expected litigation outcome. In the process, each side saves its court costs. (Under an agreement at P = $980,000, each side saves $180,000 relative to its expected litigation outcome.)

Differences in Values

The preceding discussion and examples illustrate a basic principle:

| Differences in values create opportunities for parties to craft mutually beneficial agreements.

The following applications involve decisions under uncertainty and explore two sources of value differences: differences in probability assessments and differences in attitudes toward risk.

PROBABILITY ASSESSMENTS   Even if two parties have identical preferences, they may assess different values for a transaction due to different probability assessments and forecasts. For instance, an agreement may be supported by each side's *optimistic* belief that the transaction is substantially better than no agreement at all. As Mark Twain said, "It is differences of opinion that make horse races." Many transactions involve an element of a "bet": Each side believes it has a better assessment of the transaction's value than the other and will gain (possibly) at the other's expense. Of course, differences in probability assessments also can work against negotiated agreements. The following application makes the point.

SETTLEMENT NEGOTIATIONS REVISITED   Let's return to the patent dispute, but now suppose the firms hold different, conflicting assessments about the litigation value of the case. The small firm believes there is a .6 chance that its side will win the case (i.e., there will be a finding of patent infringement). The large firm assesses a .6 chance that *it* will win the case (i.e., no infringement will be found). Both sides estimate an expected damage award of $2 million for an infringement finding and no damages otherwise. Therefore, the parties' expected values are $v_S = (.6)(\$2.0) = \$1.2$ million and $v_L = (.4)(2.0) = \$.8$ million. Accounting for the parties' legal costs (as in constraint 16.1), the least the small firm will accept out of court is $1 million, whereas the most the large firm will offer is $960,000. Thus, there is no zone of agreement. In general, a negotiated settlement is possible if and only if there is some price, P, such that constraint 16.1 is satisfied. An equivalent constraint is

$$v_S - v_L \leq c_S + c_L, \qquad\qquad [16.2]$$

which is derived by rearranging constraint 16.1. A mutually beneficial settlement is possible if and only if the difference between the parties' litigation expectations is smaller than the combined court costs.

Company A seeks to purchase a can manufacturing facility from its current owner, company B. Both parties agree that the potential value of the facility depends on the outcome of a "bottle bill" recently proposed in the state legislature. The proposed bill requires a deposit on all soft-drink cans. If the bill passes, use of cans will fall significantly. (Cans will be replaced by larger glass and plastic containers.) If the bill is defeated, the value of the facility is estimated to be $4 million; if it is passed, the value will fall to $3 million. The transaction costs (lawyers' fees and so on) of completing the deal are estimated to be $50,000 for each side. Under what circumstances is a mutually beneficial transaction possible?

RISK AVERSION   Recall from the discussion in Chapter 8 that a risk-averse agent assesses the value for an uncertain outcome to be significantly lower than its expected value (EV). This value is termed the outcome's certainty equivalent (CE). In algebraic terms, CE < EV. The greater the agent's risk aversion and/or the riskiness of the outcome, the greater the gap between the certainty equivalent and expected value.

The presence of risk aversion motivates transactions that minimize and/or distribute risks among the parties. For instance, consider the patent dispute once again. We saw that, when each side assessed its winning chances at 60 percent, the parties' expected payoffs (court costs included) were $1 million and −$960,000; thus, no settlement was possible. However, because the litigation outcome is highly uncertain, we can expect each risk-averse disputant to value going to court at a CE value considerably below its EV. For example, suppose the small firm judges its CE value for going to court at $800,000 (including court costs), and the large firm sets its CE at −$1,100,000. Now there is a $300,000-wide zone of agreement in the settlement negotiations. The presence of risk aversion makes a *certain* out-of-court settlement more attractive than a risky outcome in court (even though each side is optimistic about the outcome at trial).

As a general principle, transactions should be designed so that risks are assumed by the party best able to bear them. Consider the wildcatter in Chapter 8 who holds an option to drill for oil on a geological site. Suppose the wildcatter estimates the expected profit of the site to be $140,000 but, being risk averse, assesses the CE value of the site to be considerably less than this—say, $100,000. Should the wildcatter explore the site or sell the option to a giant exploration company that drills scores of wells in all parts of the world? Suppose the large drilling company is risk neutral. If its geologists agree with the wildcatter's probabilistic assessments, the company's value for the site is $140,000. Consequently, the option can be sold at a mutually beneficial price between $100,000 and $140,000. The option should be transferred to the risk-neutral party because that party values the site more highly.

A classic case of a transaction designed for optimal risk bearing is the cost-plus contract used in high-risk procurements. The risks concerning performance, cost, and timetable of delivery in defense procurement—for instance, in the development of a new weapons system or aircraft—are enormous. As a result, the usual fixed-price contract, in which the defense contractor is paid a fixed price and bears all production risk, is impractical (that is, the firm would set an extremely high fixed price—add a substantial risk premium—to compensate for possible cost overruns). Given its vast financial wealth, the federal government arguably can be characterized as risk neutral. The government, rather than the firm, should bear the contract risk. Under a cost-plus contract, the government reimburses the firm for all allowable costs and pays it a fixed profit amount in addition. The large variability in cost is borne by the government buyer, whereas the contractor's profit is guaranteed. The government benefits by paying the firm a much lower profit fee than would be required if the firm were the risk bearer.[3]

When both parties are risk averse, the optimal response to uncertainty is **risk sharing**. Returning to the oil example, suppose a second drilling firm is identical to the first; that is, it is equally risk averse and holds the same probability assessments. Then the site has a CE value of $100,000 to either party. Because there is no difference in value, there is no possibility of mutual benefit from an outright sale. But consider what happens if the two companies form a partnership to share equally (i.e., 50-50) all profits and losses from drilling. The expected value of each side's 50 percent profit share is, of course, $70,000. What is each side's CE for its share? Because each outfit now is exposed to considerably smaller risks, this CE will be *higher* than $50,000 (one-half the CE of 100 percent ownership), although still lower than $70,000. In effect, each firm is more nearly risk neutral when its risk is reduced proportionally. Let's say each outfit's CE is $60,000. Then the total value of drilling as a partnership is $60,000 + 60,000 = $120,000$. By selling a 50 percent profit share (for, say, $50,000), the original option holder is better off (its total value increases from $100,000 to $110,000) as is the purchaser (with an expected profit of $60,000 - 50,000 = $10,000$). Thus, risk sharing has promoted a mutually beneficial transaction.[4]

Suppose five identical, risk-averse wildcatters form a partnership to share equally the profit or loss from the site discussed earlier. What is the effect on each outfit's expected profit and CE? What about the total value of the partnership (i.e., the sum of the individual CEs)? As a thought experiment, extend the example to a 20-member syndicate. What happens to the total value of the syndicate as the risk is split among more and more firms?

CHECK STATION 3

---

[3] One disadvantage of the cost-plus contract is that it offers the firm very little incentive to keep costs down.

[4] Since the two firms are identical, 50-50 risk sharing constitutes an optimal (i.e., value-maximizing) contract.

Contingent Contracts

Agreements containing contingency clauses are a widespread response to the presence of risk and uncertainty in economic transactions. Under a contingent contract, the terms of the sale depend, in clearly defined ways, on the outcomes of future events. Cost-plus contracts designed for high-risk procurements comprise one broad class of contingent contracts. The widespread use of variable-rate mortgages is another important example. Such contracts facilitate risk sharing; the use of contingent pricing typically means that both sides' returns depend on the outcomes of uncertain economic variables. Contingent contracts also can facilitate transactions when parties hold conflicting probability assessments. The following example makes the point.

CONTINGENT PRICING IN AN ACQUISITION   Firm A is negotiating to buy a division of firm T. The difficulty is that the value of the division depends on whether it wins the bidding for a major contract from the government. If it wins, the division will be worth $20 million under current management and $22 million if acquired by firm A. If it loses, it will be worth $10 million under current management and $12 million if acquired by firm A. In either case, the division is worth more to firm A than to firm T, due to synergies with firm A's other operations. Firm T judges a .7 probability that the division will win the contract, but firm A judges this probability to be only .4. Is a mutually beneficial agreement possible?

To answer this question, first consider a straight cash buyout. Firm T values the division at $(.7)(20) + (.3)(10) = \$17$ million. The price must be at least this high to be acceptable. In turn, firm A computes the expected value at $(.4)(22) + (.6)(12) = \$16$ million, so it will pay no more than this. Consequently, a cash buyout is impossible. Both sides agree that the division will be worth more under firm A than under firm T (regardless of the contract outcome). But the parties' different, conflicting probability assessments make a straight cash purchase impossible.

However, the acquisition can be consummated if a contingent pricing clause is included. Suppose the parties agree that the purchase price will be $21 million if the government contract is won and $11 million if it is not. Clearly, these price terms provide each side a $1 million profit regardless of the government contract outcome. Contingent pricing neatly overcomes the obstacle posed by conflicting probability beliefs.

The use of contingent contracts is a common response to risk and uncertainty in purchase and sale arrangements. Warranties and guarantees are obvious examples. Here the terms of the agreement are adjusted in light of future events. Another response to uncertainty is the use of incentive contracts, which call for both buyer and seller to share the burden of cost overruns. Acquisition of an enterprise at a purchase price that depends on the firm's future earnings is still another example. Corporate acquisitions paid for with securities of the acquiring firm embody an element of contingent pricing. If the acquisition is truly valuable, the securities of the merged company will appreciate.

MULTIPLE-ISSUE NEGOTIATIONS

Thus far, we have considered single-issue agreements, in which price is the only object of negotiations. Here an agreement within a range of prices is mutually preferred to no agreement at all. The negotiation setting becomes more complicated when the terms of an agreement involve multiple issues, such as performance specifications, service requirements, or product attributes, as well as price. When multiple issues are at stake, the parties cannot be satisfied in simply finding an agreement; rather, the goal is to uncover an optimal agreement—one that, roughly speaking, is best for both parties.

Even if the parties have conflicting interests on each of many separate issues, diligent negotiations can arrive at a well-crafted agreement that is better for both sides than alternative agreements. The simplest of examples suffices to make the point. Consider two members of a legislative committee whose interests are directly opposed on each of two issues. Ms. A strongly favors issue 1 and weakly opposes issue 2. Mr. B strongly favors issue 2 and weakly opposes issue 1. Can these members fashion a mutually beneficial voting agreement? The answer is yes. They should agree to "swap votes" so that both vote affirmatively on each issue. By gaining a vote on the issue that is more important to him or her, each member is better off after the swap (even though the member votes against his or her strict self-interest on the unimportant issue). This example illustrates a principle that is applicable to bargaining in general:

> In multiple-issue negotiations, so long as there are differences in the value (importance) parties place on issues, there will be opportunities for mutually beneficial agreements of a *quid pro quo* nature.

In multiple-issue bargaining involving monetary transfers, the key to the attainment of efficiency is to structure agreements to maximize the *total* value the parties derive from the transaction. The logic of this result is quite simple. The transacting parties should form an agreement that maximizes the size of the profit "pie" to be split. Then negotiation of an overall price for the transaction has the effect of dividing the pie between the parties. Any such division of the maximal total value is efficient; one side cannot gain without the other side losing. In turn, any division of a less-than-maximal total value is necessarily inefficient. An appropriately priced maximal-value agreement delivers higher profits for both sides. We offer a concrete example to illustrate this result.

A COMPLEX PROCUREMENT   The Department of Defense (DOD) is in the process of negotiating a procurement contract for aircraft engines with an aeronautics firm. The contract will specify the number of engines to be delivered, the time of delivery, and the total price to be paid by DOD to the contractor. The firm has assessed its total cost of supplying various quantities of engines by different deadlines. For its part, DOD has assessed monetary values (its maximum willingness to pay) for different contracted deliveries. Table 16.1 lists the parties' costs and values.

Suppose DOD and the firm tentatively are considering a contract for 40 engines in four years at a price of $39 million. Is this contract mutually beneficial? Could both parties do better under a different contract at the "right" price? Of the nine possible combinations of order sizes and delivery dates, which should the parties adopt?

From Table 16.1, we find the parties' profits under the 40-engine, four-year contract ($39 million price) as follows: The firm's profit is $39 - 36 = \$3$ million; DOD's profit is $42 - 39 = \$3$ million. Clearly, this is a mutually beneficial agreement. However, it is evident from the table that the parties can improve on these contract terms. The value-maximizing contract calls for 80 engines to be delivered in three years. This contract offers a total profit of $85 - 70 = \$15$ million. (This is just the difference between DOD's value and the firm's cost.) At a $77.5 million price, each side earns a $7.5 million profit—some two-and-one-half times the profit under the four-year, 40-engine agreement. The three-year, 80-engine contract is efficient. All other contracts offer lower total profits and, therefore, are inefficient.

TABLE 16.1

A Multiple-Issue Procurement Contract

A contract calling for 80 engines to be delivered in three years provides the greatest total profit ($15 million) to the parties.

(a) The Firm's Costs (Millions of Dollars)

Number of Engines	Time of Delivery		
	2 Years	3 Years	4 Years
40	40	38	36
60	60	55	51
80	80	70	65

(b) Department of Defense Values (Millions of Dollars)

Number of Engines	Time of Delivery		
	2 Years	3 Years	4 Years
40	50	46	42
60	72	69	63
80	90	85	78

Continuous Variables

In the preceding procurement example, identifying an efficient agreement was made easier by the limited number of distinct contract alternatives. In the next example, the two issues at stake can be varied continuously. Nonetheless, the same principles apply in finding an efficient agreement.

A QUANTITY–PRICE CONTRACT   A buyer and seller are negotiating the terms of a delivery contract specifying price and output quantity (Q). The buyer's total value from purchasing Q units is $B = 3Q - Q^2/20$. The seller's cost of producing Q units is $C = Q^2/40$. The parties seek an agreement as to the quantity, Q, and the total payment from buyer to seller (call this R). What order quantity is part of an efficient agreement?

A direct way to characterize an efficient agreement is to find the value-maximizing order quantity. The sum of buyer and seller profits is

$$(B - R) + (R - C) = B - C.$$

Total net benefit $(B - C)$ is maximized by setting marginal benefit equal to marginal cost: $MB = dB/dQ = 3 - Q/10$ and $MC = dC/dQ = Q/20$. Setting these equal to each other gives $Q = 20$. At this quantity, the buyer's benefit is $B = 3(20) - 20^2/20 = 40$, and the seller's cost is $C = 20^2/40 = 10$. The relevant negotiation region for the payment, R, is the range between 10 and 40, and the maximum total profit is $40 - 10 = 30$. (This assumes each party faces a zero profit from a disagreement; i.e., each has no other profitable alternative.)

A graphical analysis provides additional insight into the meaning of efficiency when continuous variables are the object of negotiation. In Figure 16.2, the axes list the variables, Q and R. Thus, any point on the graph represents possible terms of an agreement. The next step is to show the profit implications of any agreement. This is done by means of profit contours, the series of curves in the figure.[5] The black curves show the seller's profit contours; the colored curves are the buyer's. For instance, the lowest seller contour (marked $\pi_S = 0$) shows all combinations of Q and R that provide exactly a zero profit. This is identical to the firm's cost curve: $R = C = Q^2/40$. The curve is upward sloping; to maintain a zero profit, the firm must receive a higher R for producing a larger Q. The next highest contour ($\pi_S = 7$, only part of which is shown) shows Q and R combinations yielding a profit of 7. In general, higher

---

[5] In a great many economic settings, a slightly different terminology is used. Figure 16.2 often is called an *Edgeworth box*, and the contours are called *indifference curves*. For instance, we examined an individual's indifference curves in the appendix to Chapter 3. When the individual gains from an increase in either variable, the indifference curves will be downward sloping. (To leave the individual indifferent, a reduction in one variable must be compensated by an appropriate increase in the other.)

FIGURE 16.2

A Quantity–Price
Contract

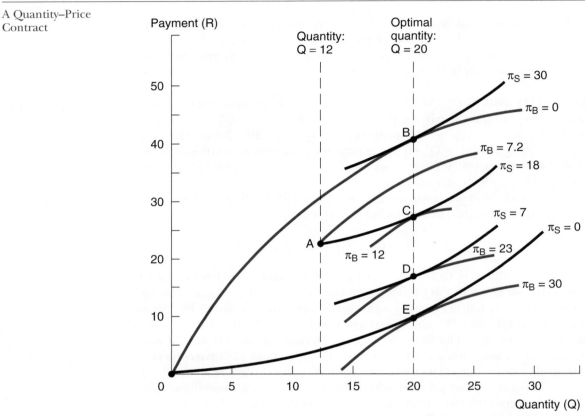

profit contours are simply vertical displacements of lower ones. The seller's profit increases as one moves north or west in the diagram, that is, as R increases (for fixed Q) or Q falls (for fixed R).

The interpretation of the buyer's contours (the colored curves) is analogous, but the orientation is reversed: The buyer profits from lower R and/or higher Q, that is, from south and east movements in Figure 16.2. In particular, note that the zero-profit contour is uppermost in the figure and that the buyer's profit increases with moves to lower contours.[6] How can we use these profit contours to identify efficient agreements? The answer is provided by the following important result:

---

[6] Both players' contours are upward sloping but have opposite curvatures. The seller's contours are convex because cost increases more and more steeply with increases in Q. The buyer's contours are concave because the marginal benefit from extra Q declines.

| An agreement is efficient if, and only if, it lies on buyer and seller profit contours that are tangent to each other.

To confirm this result, let's start with an extreme example of an *inefficient* outcome: the no-agreement outcome (corresponding to $Q = R = 0$) shown as point 0. Note that the parties' contours through point 0 form a kind of "cat's eye." Any agreement within the cat's eye is better for each side (i.e., lies on a higher profit contour) than the disagreement outcome. Point A (corresponding to $Q = 12$ and $R = 21.6$) is an example. Although point A is an improvement over point 0, it still is not efficient. Note that the buyer and seller contours cross each other at point A, leading to a new (smaller) cat's eye. Both sides can earn higher profits by moving within this cat's eye. As a general rule, so long as the parties' profit contours cross, the current agreement is inefficient; that is, both sides can profit by moving to a new agreement within the cat's eye.

When are all mutually beneficial improvements exhausted? This occurs at any point in Figure 16.2 where the profit contours are tangent (i.e., no longer cross). At points of tangency, such as B, C, D, and E, any movement to the northeast or southwest is counterproductive, that is, lowers both sides' profits. Any other movement raises one side's profit at the expense of the other's. Consequently, points of tangencies represent efficient agreements. In the figure, we observe that the set of tangencies lies along the vertical line at an output of 20 units. This confirms what we already showed algebraically: 20 units is the optimal (i.e., value-maximizing) output. By varying R (the vertical position in the figure), we redistribute this maximum total profit between the parties.

We can sum up our discussion in this section with the following proposition:

| When there are available monetary transfers that redistribute bargainers' payoffs dollar for dollar, an efficient agreement is one that maximizes the parties' total value from the transaction.

NEGOTIATION STRATEGY

Negotiations inevitably produce tension between the forces of competition and cooperation. To reach a mutually beneficial agreement, both sides must cooperate. More than that, they must strive to uncover better agreements. Yet each side's ultimate objective is to secure the most favorable agreement for itself. Of course, along the payoff frontier securing better terms for oneself implies less favorable terms for the other side. Thus far, our discussion has focused on identifying efficient agreements, that is, outlining the best the parties can do together. However, for a variety of reasons, bargaining as actually practiced often falls far short of optimal outcomes. In his seminal work on bargaining, *The Strategy of Conflict*, Thomas Schelling puts the problem this way:

Most bargaining situations ultimately involve some range of possible outcomes within which each party would rather make a concession than fail to reach agreement at all. In such a situation any potential outcome is one from which at least one of the parties, and probably both, would have been willing to retreat for the sake of agreement, and very often the other side knows it. Any potential outcome is therefore one that either party could have improved by insisting; yet he may have no basis for insisting, since the other knows or suspects that he would rather concede than do without an agreement. Each party's strategy is guided mainly by what he expects the other side to insist on; yet each knows that the other is guided by reciprocal thoughts. The final outcome must be a point from which neither expects the other to retreat.[7]

To put this another way, any set of terms falling inside the zone of agreement can be supported as an *equilibrium* outcome. As an example, consider two parties bargaining over the division of the total profit from a mutually beneficial transaction. Bargaining takes place in the simplest possible way: Each side makes a *single* offer, naming his or her share of the total profit. If the offers are compatible (i.e., add up to less than 100 percent of the total profit), there is an agreement (each party getting his or her offer); otherwise, there is no agreement. Here any pair of offers summing to exactly 100 percent constitutes an equilibrium. For instance, offers of 50 percent each are in equilibrium. Neither side can profit by (1) demanding more, because this leads to a disagreement and zero profit, or (2) demanding less, because this directly lowers his or her profit. In turn, the offers 80 percent and 20 percent (or any other pair of compatible offers, no matter how inequitable) are also in equilibrium. The cold truth is that, against an opponent whose nonnegotiable demand is for 80 percent of the profit, the best one can do is settle for the remaining 20 percent. To sum up, any division of the profit (equitable or inequitable) is an equilibrium outcome.

Via the dynamic process called bargaining, parties will arrive at some final outcome. But the multitude of equilibrium outcomes makes it difficult to predict which one. Clearly the final outcome depends significantly on the bargainers' expectations—expectations that are modified via the exchange of offers and counteroffers during the negotiations. In some sense, bargaining ceases when expectations converge, at a point where neither side can expect the other to concede further. Then either an agreement is signed or, if the sides stubbornly hold to conflicting expectations, a disagreement results.

Perfect Information

If both sides have perfect information—that is, there is no uncertainty about the economic facts of the negotiation—profit-maximizing bargainers always should reach an efficient agreement. The reason is simple. To settle for an

---

[7] T. C. Schelling, *The Strategy of Conflict* (Cambridge: Harvard University Press, 1990).

inefficient agreement is to leave money on the table. This cannot be profit maximizing; there exist alternative terms providing greater profit for both parties. We should emphasize, however, that what is true in theory does not always hold in practice. Even under perfect information, identifying and implementing efficient agreements is far from easy. Consider the following example.

A MANAGEMENT–LABOR CONFLICT   In recent years, researchers have given renewed attention to bargaining behavior in settings where delays in reaching agreements are very costly. Here a key issue is whether self-interested bargaining of the offer/counteroffer form will lead to early agreements, which avoid these costs. Consider the following highly stylized description of a labor negotiation. Management and labor are in dispute over a single issue: the size of the average wage increase under a new contract. Management would like no increase, whereas labor wants a $1.60-per-hour increase. Both sides recognize that each $1 wage rise increases the total amount paid to labor by $4 million over the course of the contract. Prior to a strike deadline, labor is awaiting management's best offer. If the offer is attractive, it will accept; otherwise, it will declare a strike. During the strike, formal offers will be made at two-week intervals, alternating between the parties. Either side can accept the other's offer at any time. If no agreement is reached in 12 weeks' time (after labor has the last chance to make an offer), an arbitrator will set the wage increase, which both sides expect to be $1 per hour. By the time an arbitration decision is reached, each side will have suffered significantly from 12 weeks of strike costs. For management, the cost is $200,000 per week (in lost profit); for labor, the cost is $100,000 per week (in lost wages). How should the sides bargain to their best advantage?

Table 16.2 depicts the answer to this question. Since the timing of offers is crucial, note carefully that each side has the chance to make three offers, beginning with management and ending with labor. Beside each such opportunity, the table lists the party's optimal offer and the resulting payoffs if the offer is accepted. In the same way we analyze a decision tree, we determine optimal offers by working backward, starting with labor's last offer. The key is to recognize that *each side's optimal offer is designed to be barely acceptable to the other.* For instance, labor's last offer is $1.10. If management accepts this, management's total expense (wage plus strike costs) is $(4)(1.10) + (10)(.2) = \$6.4$ million. (Here the first term is the total wage cost; the second term is the cost of 10 strike weeks.) If it rejects the offer, the case goes to arbitration and its total cost is also $6.4 million—$4 million in wages plus 12 weeks in strike costs. Clearly, $1.10 is the maximum demand management will accept.[8] Labor's net profit

---

[8] Don't be troubled by the fact that management is indifferent to the options of accepting or rejecting the offer. A marginal adjustment in the offer (say, to $1.098 per hour) ensures management acceptance (in line with its strict preference) at negligible cost to labor. For convenience, we report the offers in round numbers.

TABLE 16.2

	Week	Wage Offer	By	Labor's Payoff[a]	Management's Payoff[a]
Equilibrium Offer Sequence for a Strike Negotiation	0	1.15	Management	4.6	−4.6
In equilibrium, management makes an initial offer of $1.15, which labor accepts.	2	1.20	Labor	4.6	−5.2
	4	1.10	Management	4.0	−5.2
	6	1.15	Labor	4.0	−5.8
	8	1.05	Management	3.4	−5.8
	10	1.10	Labor	3.4	−6.4

[a] Assuming the current offer is accepted.

from the agreement is $(4)(1.10) − (10)(.1) = \$3.4$ million. Note that this is $.6 million better than its payoff if the case goes to arbitration. The $.6 million is exactly equal to the total strike costs collectively saved by the parties from a week-10 agreement rather than the arbitration decision *two* weeks later. Labor's optimal take-it-or-leave-it offer claims all the savings for itself.

The argument for management's week-8 offer is analogous; an offer of $1.05 is designed to be barely acceptable to labor. (Labor could hold out for its $1.10 offer, but strike costs would eat up the difference.) This time, management claims all of the $.6 million collective gain. Working backward from week 8 to week 6 to week 4 and so on, we trace out the equilibrium sequence of offers.

The striking (pardon the pun) conclusion is that *rational disputants are predicted to reach an immediate agreement without suffering any strike costs.* Specifically, management's initial offer of $1.15 is set to be just acceptable to labor—that is, as good as what labor could get from its next offer, set to be acceptable to management, and so on. Two further points deserve attention. First, although strikes never occur and arbitration is never invoked, the terms of the initial agreement are influenced by the parties' payoffs in the event of "ultimate" disagreement. For instance, if the predicted arbitrated settlement were $1.50 (instead of $1.00), the initial settlement would move in labor's favor. This is simply another example of the general rule that the location of the zone of agreement depends on the parties' disagreement alternatives. In fact, since the parties make the same number of offers, the disputants' "gains" from the initial agreement, relative to their disagreement payoffs ($2.8 million and −$6.4 million), are *equal*. Second, the relative positions of the parties' disagreement payoffs depend on the relative cost of delay and the length of time until arbitration. When delay is more costly for one side than for the other, the disagreement payoffs reflect this fact. The longer the strike period, the greater the profit disadvantage for the party with the greater cost of delay.

In principle, negotiators who possess perfect information about the bargaining environment and who exercise perfect foresight should always reach an efficient agreement (one that imposes no delay costs) at the start. In practice, strikes frequently occur, bargainers misjudge opponents' intentions, and the parties have far-from-perfect foresight. Different notions of equity often are the driving forces behind bargaining behavior. For example, one could make an argument for each of the following agreements as being equitable: (1) $1.15, because this offers the parties equal gains relative to ultimate disagreement; (2) $1.00, because this duplicates the arbitrator's predicted decision; and (3) $.80, because this splits the difference between the disputants' opening positions, $1.60 and $0. When conflicting notions of equity are present, agreement is unlikely to be immediate. As a result, real-life bargainers often suffer the costs of impasse, lockout, and strike.[9]

Find the terms of the initial agreement when (1) the arbitrated settlement (A) is $.50 or (2) labor's strike cost is $50,000 per week (with A = $1.00).

CHECK STATION 4

Imperfect Information

Thus far, our discussion has implicitly assumed each bargainer has perfect information about the benefits and costs (both to itself and its bargaining partner) of potential agreements. A more realistic description of the bargaining setting posits imperfect information on the part of the bargainers. Typically each side has only limited information about its own values for potential agreements and, at best, will have only probabilistic information about the other side's values. Under imperfect information, issues of bargaining strategy become increasingly important. In a simple price negotiation, for instance, neither side knows for certain how far it can push the other before an agreement becomes impossible. Indeed, neither can be certain whether there is a zone of agreement. The negotiation process itself conveys information about possible acceptable agreements, but this information cannot be taken at face value. In everyday bargaining, the parties typically start with exaggerated and incompatible demands. It would be foolish for one side to concede immediately to the other's opening offer. Similarly, it would be unwise for one side to "lay its cards on the table" and reveal its true value for the transaction at the outset. In short, bargaining strategy calls for a significant element of bluff.

[9] Economists have tested this negotiation model in controlled laboratory experiments using student subjects. The evidence indicates that bargainers fail to reach immediate agreements. Although agreements occur relatively early, bargainers suffer some strike costs. In addition, the dollar settlements predicted by the model find only weak support from the experimental evidence. For a review of the experimental evidence, see A. E. Roth, "Bargaining Experiments," in J. H. Kagel and A. E. Roth (Eds.), *The Handbook of Experimental Economics* (Princeton, NJ: Princeton University Press, 1995).

The theory of negotiation under uncertainty yields an important result:

| In bargaining settings under imperfect information, optimal bargaining behavior
| is incompatible with the attainment of efficient agreements all of the time.

Imperfect information presents a barrier to the attainment of efficient agreements both during and after the actual negotiations. As we shall see, it generally is in the self-interest of each side to keep its values private—indeed, to misrepresent its values during the negotiations for the purpose of assuming a "tough" bargaining stance. The result is a predictable number of missed and/or inefficient agreements. The presence of uncertainty *after* an agreement is signed also poses problems. For instance, if agreements are difficult to monitor or enforce, there may be insufficient incentives for one or both parties to fulfill the terms of the agreement. The following example shows clearly how optimal bargaining behavior can result in a failure to attain certain beneficial agreements.

A TENDER OFFER   Firm A (the acquirer) is about to make a first-and-final price offer for the outright purchase of family-owned firm T (the target). Firm A is confident the target will be worth $1.6 million under A's own management. It has only a vague idea of firm T's reservation price, that is, the minimum price current management will accept. Its best guess is that this value (denoted by v) is *uniformly distributed* between $1 million and $2 million; that is, all possible values in this range are equally likely. What is the firm's best offer? How often will a sale be concluded?

Clearly, the acquirer can confine its attention to offers in the $1 million to $1.6 million range. Firm A faces an obvious trade-off between the probability and profitability of agreements. The higher its offer, the greater the chance of acceptance, but the lower the transaction profit. The firm's expected profit from offer P is

$$E(\pi) = [1.6 - P]\Pr(P \text{ is accepted})$$

$$= (1.6 - P)(P - 1) = -1.6 + 2.6P - P^2. \qquad [16.3]$$

Here, we have used the fact that $\Pr(P \text{ is accepted}) = P - 1$. For instance, as predicted by this expression, the offer, P = $1.5 million, is accepted half the time (by a target with a value anywhere between $1 million and $1.5 million). The higher offer, P = $1.8 million, is accepted with probability .8, and so on. To maximize expected profit, we set

$$M\pi = dE(\pi)/dP = 2.6 - 2P = 0.$$

Thus, the optimal offer is P* = $1.3 million. The probability that this price will be accepted is .3, implying that the acquirer's maximum expected profit is

$90,000. The point to underscore is this: The acquirer maximizes its expected profit by taking a calculated risk; it shades its offer well below its true value even though this tactic poses the risk of missing possible agreements (whenever the target's value is between $1.3 million and $1.6 million).

The lesson of this example carries over to the case of multiple offers and counteroffers. In equilibrium, a self-interested bargainer always should hold out for terms that are strictly better than its true reservation price, thereby incurring the risk that some possible agreements are missed. Put another way, suppose one side always is willing to concede up to its true value, if necessary, to reach an agreement. Clearly, the other side could take advantage of this purely cooperative behavior by "waiting the player out"—agreeing to terms only after the player has made full concessions. To protect itself against this "waiting" strategy, a player must be willing to risk disagreement. As movie producer Sam Goldwyn once said, "The most important thing in acting is honesty. Once you've learned to fake that, you've got it made." To a degree, the same can be said of bargaining: Under imperfect information, a certain amount of dissembling, playing one's cards close to the vest, is essential. Otherwise, one is prone to the danger of being read like an open book by an opponent.

Haggling in Cyberspace

We all know how retail goods are bought and sold in developed economies. Sellers post their prices, and buyers (personal or commercial) decide whether and how much to purchase. By contrast, the growth of electronic commerce promises to turn upside down the tradition of sellers' posting fixed prices.[10] Hundreds of Web sites bring buyers and sellers together to name their prices and to complete transactions at a click of a mouse. To date, haggling in cyberspace works in a variety of different ways.

SEARCHING FOR THE BEST PRICE If you want to buy a new sports utility vehicle, do you visit the nearest dealer showrooms? Or do you find and purchase your vehicle electronically without leaving your computer? A variety of auto Web sites on the Internet match buyers with dealers. For a fee, dealers are listed on the network. Potential buyers specify the type of vehicle they seek and are connected to dealers with available cars, typically at discounted prices. Diverse items from sporting goods to airline seats to electronic equipment to vacation time-share rentals can be purchased this way. Indeed, there are Web search engines (so-called "bots," short for *robots*) that comb Web sites for the best prices each time a buyer request is made. Thus, buyers can engage in a simultaneous search (see Chapter 9) at minimal cost.

ONLINE AUCTIONS As the name suggests, these Web sites list items to be sold by auction: used cars, jewelry, rare books, airline tickets, wine, computers, even Omaha steaks, to name some typical items. Auctions are typically open

---

[10] This account is based on K. Belson, "Digital Dealmakers Meet in the Middle," *The New York Times* (September 11, 2003): D1; A. Davis, "For Dueling Lawyers, the Internet is Unlikely Referee," *The Wall Street Journal* (May 12, 1999): B1; H. Green, "Good-Bye to Fixed Pricing," *Business Week* (May 4, 1998); 71; and S. Hansell, "Hackers' Bazaar," *The New York Times* (April 2, 1998): D1.

for anywhere from 24 hours to five days and usually close at the stroke of noon. Buyers submit bids electronically, highest bids are continuously listed and updated, and the highest bid at the auction's close wins the item. If multiple, identical units are for sale, buyers also specify quantities.

ELECTRONIC EXCHANGES   Here standardized items are sold via so-called double auctions at which buyers name "bid" prices and sellers name "ask" prices. Bid and ask prices are matched electronically according to well-defined rules, thereby completing transactions. Natural gas supplies, electricity, computer parts, and other commodities are sold on these exchanges.

What are the economic implications of these electronic trading systems? Clearly, they are mutually beneficial. Consumers get the opportunity to find or name the best price. Suppliers benefit by selling excess inventories, gaining revenues while incurring minimal transaction costs. (Firms have been more cautious in selling new goods electronically, wary of cannibalizing retail sales.) In addition, electronic sales typically promote competition. By bringing large numbers of buyers and sellers together, electronic exchanges approximate perfectly competitive markets. Similarly, Web sites that permit consumers to comparison shop can be expected to promote competition among sellers. In both cases, we would expect competition to narrow the range of sale prices for identical items (approximating the theoretical "law of one price," with that price determined by supply and demand). Conversely, as we show in Chapter 17, electronic auctions marshal competition among buyers to secure the best price for the seller.

Some types of electronic trading mechanisms put a premium on bargaining and negotiation. Under some trading rules, a buyer who searches out a best posted sale price has the discretion to make a counteroffer at a lower price to the seller. In turn, the seller can make his own counteroffer, leading to full-fledged bargaining. The Web site www.priceline.com allows buyers to name their price for airline tickets. A buyer logged in to the site lists the date, cities to travel between, and the price he or she wishes to pay for the ticket. Priceline matches each request with the unfilled seats of eight domestic airlines (including the top six) and says yes or no by e-mail within an hour. Thus, the service allows customers to bargain for discounted fares. At the same time, significant restrictions—buyers earn no frequent flier miles and must accept the flight (with up to one intermediate stop) and departure time offered—preclude high-fare business travelers from taking advantage of the system.

Finally, there are a number of Internet sites meant to facilitate dispute resolution and legal settlements. Rather than go to court, the disputing parties can exchange settlement offers online, and the site's computer software not only controls the communication of offers but also might act as a mediator by suggesting alternative settlements. The Web site cybersettle.com facilitates the settlement of hundreds of moderate-dollar (but nagging) insurance claims. Frequently, the disputants can come to an early agreement when the computer feedback tells them their offers aren't very far apart. Thus, the advantage of online dispute resolution is its speed and low cost.

REPETITION AND REPUTATION   Thus far, we have focused on a one-time negotiation between a pair of interested parties. As a natural consequence, the parties' bargaining behavior has been motivated solely by the immediate profit available from an agreement. Now let's consider the effect if one or both parties are expected to face different bargaining situations repeatedly. For instance, labor contracts typically are no longer than three years. Thus, even when the current contract is signed and sealed, labor and management are well aware they will be negotiating a new contract in two or three years' time. Alternatively, one side may find itself repeatedly negotiating with scores of different parties over time. As an example, representatives of insurance companies negotiate hundreds of tort and liability claims each year.

Repeated negotiation (with the same or different parties) introduces the key strategic element of *reputation*; that is, the firm recognizes that its behavior in the current set of negotiations can influence the expectations of its future bargaining partners. In a one-time bargaining setting, in contrast, the firm's actions are motivated solely by immediate profit; issues of reputation do not enter.

One important effect of reputation formation in repeated negotiations is to limit the scope of purely opportunistic behavior. To illustrate, consider current contract negotiations between two firms, A and B. Due to many bargaining factors in its favor, A is confident it can negotiate a contract giving it 90 percent of the total profit from an agreement. If it expects never to bargain with B again, A surely will push for these favorable terms. But what if B and A are likely to bargain with each other over many subsequent contracts? Negotiating too good a contract poses the risk of souring the entire bargaining relationship. (Perhaps B would spurn A and seek out a new bargaining partner in the future.) Accordingly, A may rationally choose not to take full advantage of its short-term bargaining power.

Reputation effects also suggest that B, the weaker bargaining party, may be unwilling to concede the lion's share of the short-term gain to A. In a one-shot bargain, accepting 10 percent of something is better than nothing. But in repeated bargaining, B must be concerned about its reputation. Large concessions now may spur the other party to take a tougher bargaining stance in the future. Thus, B has an interest in establishing a reputation as a tough but fair bargainer. Sometimes this reputation effect means sacrificing or delaying short-term agreements. For instance, strikes frequently occur because one or both sides seek to establish their long-term reputations. Insurance companies typically take a tough stance toward settling claims of uncertain merit. Viewing the claim by itself, the company might find it cheaper to settle than to go to court. Nonetheless, on reputation grounds, it pays to fight to deter questionable claims in the future.

Finally, the repeated bargaining relationship has a *disciplining* role—a role we already noted in Chapter 13 in our discussion of the repeated prisoner's dilemma. Recall that, in the one-shot prisoner's dilemma, the dominant-strategy equilibrium calls for noncooperation. In contrast, in the infinitely repeated prisoner's dilemma, continual cooperation is an equilibrium. The key to this equilibrium is one side's credible threat to punish the other's noncooperation with a retaliatory response. In short, bargaining partners that are "married" to each other have obvious incentives to maintain a cooperative relationship.

Texaco versus Pennzoil Revisited

In light of our discussion, how can we account for the prolonged conflict between Pennzoil and Texaco recounted in Chapter 1? Recall the main events. The dispute began with Pennzoil's 1984 legal suit claiming that Texaco acquired Getty Oil by interfering with Pennzoil's prior acquisition agreement and contract with the company. In 1985, a Texas jury awarded Pennzoil $10.5 billion in damages from Texaco, an amount that withstood (albeit slightly reduced) subsequent court rulings and Texaco's filing for bankruptcy. More than four years after the initial suit, the dispute ended with a settlement, approved by the bankruptcy court, in which Texaco paid Pennzoil $3 billion in cash.

The overriding feature of the conflict was the enormous collective costs borne by the parties throughout the dispute. The most direct and best evidence of these costs is provided by the changes in stock market valuations of the two companies during the conflict. Financial economists have shown that the dispute reduced the companies' combined equity values by $3.4 billion.[11] (Of course, Pennzoil's stock market value rose upon the initial Texas verdict. The point is that the fall in value of Texaco shares far exceeded this.) Only a small part of the collective fall in value can be attributed to legal costs—some $600 million as an upper-bound estimate. More important were the costs posed for Texaco of insolvency and bankruptcy: the potential disruption of current operations of the company as a whole and the harm done to buyer and supplier relationships. Following the settlement in late 1987, the combined stock market values of the companies rose some $2.6 billion. Thus, the best estimate of the ultimate cost of the Texaco–Pennzoil conflict is $.8 billion.

In view of these costs, why did the parties take so long to settle? Was their behavior consistent with rational bargaining behavior? Our earlier discussion of out-of-court settlements provides one possible reason: differing expectations of the parties as to the ultimate court outcome. This reason would appear to have been important early in the dispute, before the Texas jury's decision and in the initial appeals process. Because Texaco believed Pennzoil's suit to be totally without merit, no serious settlement negotiations

[11] D. M. Cutler, and L. H. Summers. "The Costs of Conflict Resolution and Financial Distress," *Rand Journal of Economics* (1988): 157–172.

took place before the jury decision. Most legal and economic experts attacked the jury's decision as being of dubious merit and expected it to be overturned or the damages substantially reduced. Thus, even at this stage, there was substantial uncertainty about the ultimate legal disposition of the dispute. The disputants might still have held radically different expectations about various court outcomes, leaving no ground for a settlement. However, one would expect that, as the appeals process progressed, the disputants—guided by similar expert legal advice—would have had little reason to differ in their assessments. Indeed, some commentators have argued that changes in the firms' stock market values were the most accurate barometers of court expectations. For six litigation events during the dispute that went against Texaco, there were significant concurrent falls in Texaco's stock price. Three events that were favorable to Texaco were marked by positive stock price movements.[12] In any case, the enormous drop in the total value of the companies would appear to have been much larger than any difference in expectations. According to Equation 16.2, the parties should have ended the dispute, thus saving these enormous costs.

A second explanation for the delay in settlement has to do with the liability of Texaco's directors.[13] Whether the ultimate payment by Texaco was $3 billion (in a settlement) or $11 billion (if the jury verdict was ultimately upheld), the directors faced the risk of losing all of their assets if they were found personally liable for the loss. Under these circumstances, a director rationally would prefer to fight the decision in the courts (pursuing a small chance of vindication) rather than settle and be sued. It is significant that the directors were relieved of personal liability in the bankruptcy court's final settlement.

Finally, issues of bargaining strategy probably help explain the settlement delay and final acceptance. First, Pennzoil aggressively sought its bond and lien rights, enforcement of which would have been very costly for Texaco (and may have provoked bankruptcy). In doing so, Pennzoil was attempting to exercise "leverage"; that is, it sought to obtain better terms in a settlement by imposing high costs on the other party. Texaco responded in kind, first by fighting against the bond enforcement and then, when that failed, abruptly declaring bankruptcy. After eight months of costly and unresolved bankruptcy proceedings, the parties agreed to a $3 billion settlement. Ironically, this amount almost exactly split the difference between the disputants' last offers before bankruptcy: $4.1 billion and $2 billion. Given the real risk that protracted bankruptcy could destroy much of Texaco's value, Pennzoil rationally accepted the $3 billion settlement, even though the odds that its $11 billion award would be sustained probably were better than 50-50.

---

[12] Ibid.

[13] See R. H. Mnookin and R. Wilson, "Rational Bargaining and Market Efficiency: Understanding Texaco vs. Pennzoil," *University of Virginia Law Review* (1989): 295–334.

Wooing David Letterman Revisited

When Willie Sutton was asked why he robbed banks, he replied, "Because that's where the money is." In some sense, this advice applies to the Letterman bargaining. Good negotiators should find their way to where the money is; that is, they should conclude value-maximizing deals. Let's step back and evaluate Letterman's possible deals with NBC or CBS.

Table 16.3 lists the main possibilities and the monetary consequences to each of the parties in the negotiations. (Values are annual estimates over the three years of Letterman's contract.) For comparison purposes, the first agreement shows the original status quo. NBC obtains $100 million in revenue and clears $63 million in profit after paying "star" salaries and $15 million to produce each show. Letterman earns $5 million, and CBS is out of the late-night business.

Now consider the new agreement. According to analysts' projections, NBC's net revenue is expected to drop to about $50 million per year. With its revenue cut in half (and only a modest savings in star salaries), NBC's profit is decimated. CBS's projected revenues are not quite sufficient to cover its costs. Did Michael Ovitz squeeze out the best deal for Letterman from CBS? The answer certainly seems to be yes. Clearly, CBS views snagging Letterman as an investment: Future revenue growth from Letterman is judged to be worth the initial loss.

The third column shows Letterman's good fortune. Besides his own salary, Letterman's production company stands to earn $10 million in profit ($25 million in revenue, minus $15 million in "normal" production costs). The "top" entry of $9 million requires some explanation. This estimate represents the personal value Letterman puts on getting the 11:30 slot. Again and again during the negotiations, Letterman stated how much being able to perform for the broader mainstream audience meant to him. The $9 million is a guesstimate of how much the 11:30 slot is worth to him. In short, the total value of the deal to Letterman includes not only his monetary compensation but also the value he puts on moving to 11:30.

What if NBC had dumped Leno and offered Letterman the earlier time slot at terms matching CBS's offer? The third agreement shows the consequences. NBC preserves most of its original revenue but must pay Letterman's price and also must buy out Leno (his salary plus about a $3 million annual penalty). NBC's profit from this option is even less than its profit if Letterman defects to CBS. Thus, in addition to its loyalty to Leno, NBC seems to have had a financial reason for not matching CBS's deal.

What is harder to explain is why NBC did not pay what was necessary to keep Letterman in his 12:30 slot. The fourth agreement has NBC giving Letterman $35 million per year, thereby beating CBS's deal. By doing so, NBC retains its $100 million late-night gold mine and earns $33 million in net profit. This is nearly twice the profit NBC can hope for if it loses Letterman. Given the monetary estimates in Table 16.3, this is the value-maximizing agreement. In this agreement, the parties' combined value is $68 million. By comparison, the combined value is somewhat less than $50 million in either the second or third agreements. Keeping NBC's late-night lineup intact

TABLE 16.3

	NBC	CBS	Letterman	Total	The Letterman Negotiations
1. Letterman at NBC, 12:30					
Revenue	100	0			
Letterman's salary	−5		5		
Leno's salary	−2				
Cost of two shows	−30	___	___		
	63	0	5	68	
2. Letterman to CBS, 11:30					
Revenue	50	35	9*		
Letterman's salary		−14	14		
Leno, 1 new host	−3				
Shows: costs, profits	−30	−25	10 (25 − 15)		
	17	−4	33	46	
3. Letterman at NBC, 11:30					
Revenue	75	0	9*		
Letterman's salary	−14		14		
Buy out Leno	−5				
Shows: costs, profits	−41	___	10		
	15	0	33	48	
4. Letterman gets big raise					
Revenue	100	0			
Letterman's salary	−25		25		
Leno's salary	−2				
Shows: costs, profits	−40	___	10		
	33	0	35	68	
5. Letterman to CBS, 12:30					
Revenue	60?	40?			
Letterman's salary		−14	14		
Leno, 1 new host	−3				
Shows: costs, profits	−30	−25	10		
	27	1	24	52	

*Letterman's personal value for the 11:30 P.M. slot.

appears to be where the money is.[14] CBS's entry into the late-night sweepstakes (via the second or third deals) has two value-reducing effects. First, it slices up the market, thus lowering total revenue. (Indeed, ABC's competing news show, *Nightline*, was probably the main beneficiary of the talk-show wars.) Second, adding a third show raises the networks' total costs. For completeness, the table shows a fifth possible deal in which

[14] Note that the fourth agreement produces exactly the same total value ($68 million) as the original status quo. Of course, the main difference is how this profit is divided. By virtue of CBS's competitive offer, NBC is forced to concede a substantial payoff to Letterman.

Letterman agrees to a 12:30 show with CBS. Although such a move avoids an 11:30 head-to-head battle, the parties' total value is still significantly less than a "don't-rock-the-boat" agreement.

If money were the only thing that mattered, Letterman and NBC appear to have missed a mutually beneficial agreement. Of course, one can argue over the exact revenue and cost implications of the deals. (However, a quick sensitivity analysis shows that NBC's retaining Letterman at 12:30 remains the efficient agreement, short of drastic alterations in the revenue and cost figures.) Nonmonetary factors, particularly Letterman's disappointment when he was spurned as Johnny Carson's successor, may offer the best explanations for the ultimate negotiated outcome.

Does history ever repeat itself? In 2002, ABC made an aggressive effort to lure Letterman from CBS after negotiations to renew his contract had become acrimonious. The ABC offer was the financial equal both for Letterman and his production company of what CBS had on the table, and Letterman pondered the decision for nine days while on vacation in St. Barts. Among other considerations, Letterman was concerned about the fallout of displacing the venerable ABC news show, *Nightline*, if he made the move. At the same time, CBS set in motion a contingency plan to attract late-night host Conan O'Brien from NBC should it lose Letterman. In the end, Letterman decided to stay with CBS.

SUMMARY

Decision-Making Principles

1. The impetus for all negotiations is mutual gain—to forge an agreement that is better for both sides than a disagreement. This is true whether the sides are attempting to form a new agreement or to resolve a long-standing dispute.

2. The zone of agreement lies between the parties' values for the transaction (assessed relative to what each would get in a disagreement). In terms of negotiation strategy, the amount of profit one side can claim from an agreement depends on an assessment not only of its own walk-away value but also that of the other side (because this sets a limit on the other side's ability to compromise).

3. Negotiations involve a mixture of competition and cooperation. They are as much about value "creating" as value "claiming." An efficient agreement maximizes the parties' total value from the transaction. Value is created by trading on differences. Parties should adopt an issue as part of an agreement, provided the benefits to one side exceed the costs to the other.

Nuts and Bolts

1. Mutually beneficial transactions are based on differences in bargainer values. In single-issue transactions, the difference between the bargainers' reservation prices determines the total profit available from an agreement. Differences in values can result from differences in preferences, probability assessments, or attitudes toward risk.

2. An outcome is efficient if there exists no other alternative that is better for both parties. The payoff frontier shows the set of efficient agreements. For any movement along the frontier, any gain for one bargainer necessitates a loss for the other.

3. When monetary transfers are freely available, an agreement is efficient if and only if it is value maximizing, that is, generates the greatest total profit to the bargainers together. The size of the transfer determines the distribution of the total profit between the bargainers.

4. Under perfect information, rational bargainers always should achieve an efficient agreement. Moreover, any agreement on the payoff frontier (provided it is preferred by both parties to a disagreement) can be supported as an equilibrium bargaining outcome.

5. In bargaining settings under imperfect information, optimal bargaining behavior may preclude the attainment of efficient agreements. For instance, disputants will prefer to incur the cost of going to court if the difference in their litigation expectations exceeds their collective court costs. In simple price bargaining, a buyer strategically understates its true value, while the seller overstates its value (or cost), with the result that mutually beneficial agreements may be lost. Similarly, strategic considerations in multiple-issue negotiations can prevent the attainment of value-maximizing agreements.

Questions and Problems

1. A plaintiff is suing a defendant for $100,000. The cost of going to court is $15,000 for each side.
   a. The parties agree there is a 50 percent chance of the plaintiff's winning the case. What is the range of mutually beneficial agreements that the parties might negotiate in an out-of-court settlement? What if each side believes *its* winning chance is 60 percent?
   b. Suppose the damages are $200,000, and each side sees its winning chance at 60 percent. What are the prospects for an out-of-court settlement?

c. Suppose the plaintiff is bringing a nuisance suit. The plaintiff has no chance of winning in court, and both sides know it. Would it be rational for the defendant to settle the case out of court nonetheless? Explain. What legal rules can you suggest that might serve to deter nuisance suits?

2. In labor negotiations, failure to reach a contract agreement frequently results in a labor strike or work slowdown. In each of the following situations, identify which side—labor or management—is better positioned to obtain favorable contract terms from the other.
   a. Demand for the firm's products is booming, and the firm is earning record profits.
   b. The labor union has over $20,000 per worker in its strike fund.
   c. A recession in the region has led to increased unemployment.

3. The developer of a new shopping mall is negotiating the terms of a store lease with a sporting goods firm. The developer is pressing the store for an increase in monthly rent. The store offers to pay the developer 1 percent of its first year's revenues in return for a lower monthly rent, and the developer agrees. Why might this more complicated contract be mutually beneficial? Explain briefly.

4. Firm S supplies inputs to firm B. Because producing the input is quite complicated, some defects are inevitable. Firm S can reduce the rate of defects at a cost. In turn, defective parts lower firm B's profits (because of lost sales and unhappy customers). The firms' profits and costs (in thousands of dollars) are shown in the table.
   a. Should firm B insist on 0 percent defects? Why or why not?
   b. What level of product quality is part of an efficient agreement? Explain.

	B's Profit	S's Cost		B's Profit	S's Cost
0% Defects	100	80	6% Defects	50	25
2% Defects	86	58	8% Defects	26	20
4% Defects	72	37	10% Defects	24	16

5. An upstream paper mill releases moderate amounts of pollutants into a waterway. A downstream fishery suffers an economic cost from this pollution of $100,000 annually. This cost burden would fall to $30,000 if the pollution were reduced by 50 percent. Complete (100 percent) cleanup would cost the mill $120,000, whereas a 50 percent cleanup would cost $50,000.
   a. Currently, the mill has the legal right to pollute. Can the parties come to a mutually beneficial agreement to reduce pollution? If so, how much pollution should be reduced?
   b. Answer part a assuming the fishery has the legal right to clean water.

6. The United Mine Workers (UMW) and the Association of Coal Producers are attempting to negotiate a new contract in which the issues at stake are a wage increase, the introduction of a right-to-strike clause, and a proposal that nonmining jobs at sites be opened up to nonunion workers. Each $1.00 increase in the hourly wage would raise the association's total wage bill by $40 million. Besides the wage issue, the UMW feels very strongly about the right-to-strike clause; in fact, it would be willing to give up $.75 in wage increases to secure it. It feels less strongly about reserving nonmining work for the union and is willing to give up only $.50 in wages to retain this provision. For its part, the association has attempted to calculate the impact of each of these provisions. It judges that accepting the right-to-strike clause might increase its costs by $50 million in the long run and that opening site work to nonunion labor would save it $60 million.

   a. Under an efficient agreement, how should the parties decide the right-to-strike and reserved-work issues?

   b. As a variation on this example, suppose the current administration in Washington has invoked emergency legislation to freeze mining wages (as well as other prices and wages in the economy). The result is that the right-to-strike and reserved-work clauses are the only issues under negotiation; any wage change is prohibited. Now how should the parties decide these issues to mutual advantage?

7. Firm B and firm S are in the process of negotiating a contract whereby S will synthesize a hormone for B. Besides the payment from B to S, three issues are involved: (1) whether the hormone will be 95 percent or only 80 percent pure, (2) whether the target date for completion will be three or five years, and (3) whether B will lend two of its expert biochemists to S to aid in the development. Firm B has estimated its values for various combinations of issues, and firm S has estimated its costs. These amounts are shown in the table:

	Firm B Values			Firm S Costs	
	3 Years	5 Years		3 Years	5 Years
95%	180	100	95%	140	80
80%	160	60	80%	90	50
No biochemists	0	0		0	0
Biochemists	−30	−30		−40	−20

Lending the biochemists is purely an additive factor; doing so reduces B's value but also reduces S's cost. For example, a three-year contract for a 95 percent pure hormone with the loan of the biochemists has a value to B of $180 - 30 = 150$ and a cost to S of $140 - 40 = 100$.

    a. With three issues (two outcomes each), there are eight possible contracts. Which contracts are inefficient (i.e., produce worse outcomes for both sides than some other contract)?

    b. Given that dollar-for-dollar compensation can be paid between the parties, which of the eight contracts is optimal? Explain.

8. Firm A seeks to acquire (privately owned) firm T whose ultimate dollar value is uncertain because of its possible liability for the past production of hazardous waste. The table shows A's and T's respective values (in \$ millions) for the firm conditional on whether the firm is found to be liable. Note that A and T have different contingent values and different probability assessments (shown in parentheses) as to T's liability. Both firms are risk neutral.

	Value of Firm T	
	T not Liable	T Liable
A's Value	50 (.5)	20 (.5)
T's Value	40 (.8)	30 (.2)

    a. Firm A is hoping to acquire T in a 100 percent cash transaction. Is a mutually beneficial 100 percent cash transaction possible? Explain.

    b. Instead, suppose that firm A considers acquiring T, paying all or in part with its own stock. (The owners of T are prohibited from selling the stock they receive for two years.) If A acquires T and subsequently T is found liable, both sides expect that A's stock price will fall by 50 percent. Is a mutually beneficial *100 percent stock* transaction possible? (Provide an example to show whether the answer is yes or no.)

    c. The firms are considering a provision in the acquisition allowing T's senior managers (who will continue to work for the combined firm) to buy back (at a predetermined price) ownership of T in the event that the firm is found liable. Does such a provision make sense? Provide a qualitative explanation.

9. In the quantity–price contract example in Figure 16.3, we noted that the order quantity, $Q = 20$, is efficient. We can demonstrate that seemingly reasonable contracting methods can lead to inefficient results: too little output being produced and sold. As before, let benefits and costs be $B = 3Q - Q^2/20$ and $C = Q^2/40$, respectively. Each side knows the other's benefit or cost function. The contracting method is as follows: The seller names a price for its output, and the buyer chooses the quantity to purchase at this price.

a. Find the buyer's profit-maximizing purchase quantity as it depends on the seller's quoted price P. (*Hint*: The buyer sets Q to maximize $\pi_B = B - PQ = 3Q - Q^2/20 - PQ$. Treating P as a parameter, set $d\pi_B/dQ$ equal to zero. You should find that $P = 3 - Q/10$ or, equivalently, $Q = 30 - 10P$.)

b. Find the seller's optimal price. (*Hint*: The easiest approach is to use the price equation, $P = 3 - Q/10$, treat Q as the decision variable, and set MR = MC to find optimal quantity and price.)

c. Explain why an inefficient outcome results when the seller quotes a take-it-or-leave-it price per unit.

10. Firms A and B are negotiating to conclude a business deal worth $200,000 in total value to the parties. At issue is how this total value will be split. Firm A knows B will agree to a 50-50 split, but it also has thought about claiming a greater share by making a take-it-or-leave-it offer. The firm judges that B would accept a 45 percent share with probability .9, a 40 percent share with probability .85, and a 35 percent share with probability .8. What offer should A make to maximize its expected profit?

* 11. Suppose two firms, X and Y, are bargaining over how to split a total stake of $120,000. As in the earlier management–labor example, the firms alternate offers. Delay is very costly to both parties. During the time between offers, the value of the stake shrinks by 50 percent. When X makes the first offer, $120,000 is to be split; failing an immediate agreement, by the time Y makes the next offer, the stake is $60,000; at X's next turn, the stake is $30,000; and so on.

a. Suppose three offer rounds (X, then Y, then X) are allowed. What equilibrium offers will the parties make? Which offer will be accepted?

b. What if there are four offer rounds? Is making the first offer advantageous?

c. Suppose offers can be made indefinitely, with the stake continually shrinking. Show that X demands $80,000 for itself in the first round and Y agrees, that is, accepts $40,000. In other words, X claims two-thirds of the total stake. *Hint*: As in the earlier examples, X demands a fraction of the stake (call this z) such that Y is indifferent to the options of agreeing, that is, accepting $120,000(1 - z)$, or waiting one turn and making its own offer. Note that, at its turn, Y will demand $60,000(z)$ for itself, leaving the remainder for X. Use these facts to solve for z.

* 12. A buyer has value v_b for a potential acquisition and believes the seller's reservation price has the cumulative probability distribution F(v). The buyer chooses P to maximize its expected profit:

$$\pi_b = (v_b - P)\Pr(P \text{ accepted}) = (v_b - P)F(P).$$

* Starred problems are more challenging.

Find the buyer's marginal profit and set it equal to zero. Show that the buyer's optimal price satisfies $P = v_b - F(P)/f(p)$, where $f(v) = dF(v)/dv$ is the associated density function. Note that the buyer shades down its value in making its optimal bid.

* 13. Firm A is attempting to acquire firm T but is uncertain about T's value. It judges that the firm's value under current management (call this v_T) is in the range of $60 to $80 per share, with all values in between equally likely. A estimates that, under its own management, T will be worth $v_A = 1.5v_T - 30$. (Note that v_A is strictly greater than v_T except when v_T equals 60.) Firm A will make a price offer to purchase firm T, which T's current management (knowing v_T) will accept or reject. Show that all possible offers result in an *expected loss* for firm A, even though T is always worth more under A's control than under T's. (In this example, asymmetric information implies an adverse selection problem similar to those discussed in Chapter 15.)

14. Firm X can produce a necessary component in-house at a cost of 10 or purchase it from one of three suppliers (A, B, or C) whose costs are 8, 7, and 5, respectively. X can approach the firms in any order, attempt to negotiate an agreement with the first, and, if this fails, go on to the second, and so on. There is no cost to approaching a new firm, but X can negotiate with each firm only once. In any negotiation, the firms will split equally the available total profit (if any). Here total profit is measured relative to each side's next-best alternative; for X, this alternative is a deal with any supplier not yet tried.

Show that X's optimal strategy is to approach C first, then B, then A, if necessary. Do X and C reach an agreement? At what price? What do your answers suggest about the benefits of competition?

Discussion Question Traditionally, negotiation and litigation have been the two prevailing methods of dispute resolution. These alternative methods lie at opposite extremes of a spectrum. The negotiation process is private, voluntary, informal, and unstructured, aimed at reaching a mutually beneficial agreement involving only the parties themselves. The litigation (or adjudication) process is public and follows formal rules whereby both sides of the dispute are heard and a binding outcome is determined by a third party (judge or jury).

The last 20 years have seen increased use of alternative methods for resolving disputes—mediation and arbitration in particular. In mediation, a third party is engaged to help the parties reach a mutually beneficial agreement. In arbitration, a third party hears the dispute and renders a binding decision.

a. Using available reference sources (in print or on the Internet), provide summaries of the mediation and arbitration processes.
b. Provide a critical assessment of the advantages and disadvantages of each method in reaching efficient agreements (and in terms of time and cost). How do the methods compare to the alternatives of negotiation and litigation?

Spreadsheet Problem

S1. A French firm (company F) is negotiating with a German firm (company G) to buy aircraft engines. Under discussion is the price to be paid (in German deutsche marks), quality (high or low), warranty (full or partial), and the delivery schedule (two, three, or five years). The spreadsheet that follows shows company G's values in marks (DM) and company F's costs in French francs (Fr) for possible agreements. For instance, delivery of high-quality engines under full warranty in two years implies a cost (in German marks) to company G of $68 + 10 = 78$ million DM. Company G receives 65 million DM (cell H13) implying a profit of $65 - 78 = -13$ million DM (cell K13). In turn, company F's value (in francs) for the deal is $238 + 18 = 256$ million Fr. The exchange rate is 3 francs for each deutsche mark. Thus, company F's final profit is $256 - (3)(65) = 61$ million Fr (cell L13).

   a. Create a spreadsheet similar to the sample spreadsheet given. Put the numerical value of 1 in cell C7, C9, I7, or I9, and put zeros in the remaining three cells. The placement of the 1 (a so-called dummy variable) specifies the exact agreement. For instance, putting the 1 in cell C7 indicates high-quality engines under full warranty. Similarly, put a 1 in cell C12, C13, or C14 to indicate the delivery schedule. Then compute company F's profit (cell L13) according to the formula

$$= (C7*D7 + C9*D9 + I7*G7 + I9*G9$$

$$+ \ C12*D12 + C13*D13 + C14*D14) - 3*H13.$$

	A	B	C	D	E	F	G	H	I	J	K	L	M
1													
2		A FRENCH–GERMAN CONTRACT											
3													
4					Warranty								
5		Quality		Full			Partial						
6				F	G		F	G					
7		High	1	238	68		180	42	0		Sum		
8											1		
9		Low	0	144	24		92	18	0				
10													
11		Delivery		F	G		F's Payment to G				G's Profit	F's Profit	
12		2 Years	1	18	10			(DMs)			(DMs)	(Frs)	
13		3 Years	0	0	0			65			−13	61	
14		5 Years	0	−24	−12								
15													
16		Sum	1										
17													

This formula works because all zero-valued dummies disappear, leaving only the values (238 plus 18) for the actual agreement. Company G's profit is computed as its revenue payment minus its cost by an analogous formula.

b. Find the zone of agreement by maximizing company F's profit subject to company G's profit being equal to 0, and vice versa. Use your spreadsheet's optimizer, listing F's payment and the seven dummy variables as the adjustable cells. Include the constraints that all dummies must be greater than or equal to 0. In addition, the sum of the first four dummies (computed in cell K8) must equal 1, and the sum of the last three dummies (computed in cell C16) must also equal 1. Finally, do not forget the constraint that one firm's profit is equal to 0.

c. Find one or more points on the efficient frontier, setting one company's profit equal to a positive value and maximizing the other's profit. What agreement terms are efficient? Explain.

Suggested References

The following book is the best-selling practical guide to reaching mutually beneficial agreements.

Fisher, R., W. Ury, and B. Patton. *Getting to Yes*. New York: Houghton Mifflin, 1992.

The following are rigorous and readable texts on bargaining.

Brams, S. J. *Negotiation Games: Applying Game Theory to Bargaining and Arbitration*. New York: Routledge, 2003.

Osborne, M., and A. Rubinstein. *Bargaining and Markets*. Boston: Academic Press, 1990.

Raiffa, H. *The Art and Science of Negotiation*. Cambridge: Harvard University Press, 1982.

Roth, A. (Ed.). *Game-Theoretic Models of Bargaining*. Cambridge: Cambridge University Press, 1985. *(See especially the chapters by Chatterjee, Myerson, Samuelson, and Wilson.)*

Schelling, T. C. *The Strategy of Conflict*. Chapters 2 and 3. Cambridge: Harvard University Press, 1990.

A rigorous treatment of bargaining theory is contained in

Kennan, J., and R. Wilson. "Bargaining with Private Information." *Journal of Economic Literature* (March 1993): 45–104.

Experimental and empirical evidence on bargaining is provided in:

Babcock, L., and G. Loewenstein. "Explaining Bargaining Impasse: The Role of Self-Serving Biases," *The Journal of Economic Perspectives* 11 (Winter 1997): 109–126.

Camerer, C. F. *Behavioral Game Theory*. Chapters 2 and 4, Princeton, NJ: Princeton University Press, 2003.

Cramton, P., and J. S. Tracy. "Strikes and Holdouts in Wage Bargaining: Theory and Data." *The American Economic Review* 82 (1992): 100–121.

Roth, A. E., "Bargaining Experiments," in J. H. Kagel and A. E. Roth (Eds.), *The Handbook of Experimental Economics*. Princeton, NJ: Princeton University Press, 1995.

There are numerous Web sites offering negotiation resources and support. Among the best are:

Harvard Law School's Project on Negotiation, www.pon.harvard.edu.

InterNeg, http://interneg.org/interneg/index.html (negotiation games and simulations, training and external links).

Stanford University's Center on Conflict and Negotiation, www.stanford.edu/group/sccn.

1. Clearly, Warner must be paid by Harper to postpone the paperback release, because the postponement will cost Warner five months' worth of paperback profits. The price, P, paid must at least cover this lost profit (denoted by π_W); that is, $P \geq \pi_W$. Harper, in turn, gains five months' worth of hardcover profit from the agreement (call this profit π_H). It will pay no more than the profit it gains: $P \leq \pi_H$. Therefore, a mutually beneficial agreement is possible if and only if $\pi_W \leq P \leq \pi_H$, that is, so long as the extra hardcover profit exceeds the lost paperback profit. The zone of agreement stretches from π_W to π_H. Notice that changing the date of the paperback release is a profitable response to an event that was unforeseen: that this particular title would be such a hot seller. Once this is known, extending the exclusive hardcover run becomes the profit-maximizing course of action.

2. A transaction is possible if and only if firm A (the buyer) is more optimistic that the bill will be defeated (and, therefore, sees a higher expected value for the facility) than is firm B. Firm A's value, net of the transaction cost, is $(p_A)(4) + (1 - p_A)(3) - .05$, where p_A is the firm's assessed probability that the bill will be defeated. In turn, firm B's minimum walk-away price is $(p_B)(4) + (1 - p_B)(3) + .05$. Note that the seller's walk-away price is augmented by the transaction cost. After some rearrangements, we find that firm A's value is greater than firm B's if and only if $p_A > p_B + .1$.

3. The smaller the portion of risk he or she holds, the more risk neutral the decision maker becomes. Thus, with risks split five ways, the gap between the prospect's expected value and its CE value (the sum of the CE values of syndicate members) will shrink. If risk were shared by a large number of members (say, 100), the individual risk would be trivial, and the total CE value would approach the prospect's expected value.

4. If the arbitrated settlement (A) is $.50, an argument analogous to the one in the text predicts an initial wage settlement of $.65. If labor's strike cost is $50,000 per week (with A = $1), management's minimally acceptable offer to labor is always $.025 lower than labor's next offer. The offer progression (working from last to first) is 1.10, 1.075, 1.175, 1.15, 1.25, and 1.225. Thus, management must offer $1.225 to ensure labor's immediate acceptance.

CHAPTER 17

Auctions and Competitive Bidding

Two rules for succeeding in business: (1) Never underestimate the importance of money, and (2) everything is up for bid.

ANONYMOUS

Bidding to Televise the Olympics

Three years before each Olympic Games, a competition takes place that is just as intense as the Olympiad itself—namely, the high-stakes bidding competition by the U.S. networks to televise the games. The following table shows the spectacular growth in the price paid for these television rights. Part of the revenue growth is attributable to price inflation over the past 30 years. Part, too, is due to the growth in U.S. television audiences. (Larger audiences allow networks to charge higher rates to advertisers.)

Winning Bids for Televising the Olympics (Millions of Dollars)

Summer Games		Winter Games	
1976 Montreal	(ABC) $25	1976 Innsbruck	(ABC) $10
1980 Moscow	(NBC) $87	1980 Lake Placid	(ABC) $15.5
1984 Los Angeles	(ABC) $300	1984 Sarajevo	(ABC) $91.5
1988 Seoul	(NBC) $300–400	1988 Calgary	(ABC) $309
1992 Barcelona	(NBC) $401	1992 Albertville	(CBS) $243
1996 Atlanta	(NBC) $456	1994 Lillehammer	(CBS) $295
2000 Sydney	(NBC) $705	1998 Nagano	(CBS) $375
2004 Athens	(NBC) $793	2002 Salt Lake City	(NBC) $545
2008 Beijing	(NBC) $894	2006 Turin	(NBC) $613
2012 London	(NBC) $1,181	2010 Vancouver	(NBC) $820

However, the greatest part of the revenue increase is owing to the skill with which Olympic organizers have arranged the bidding competition. Since 1976, when ABC was awarded the games without any real competition (before the other networks had a chance to bid), the organizers have implemented a number of bidding innovations.[1] For instance, in 1980, the Soviets organized a ruthless bidding competition involving multiple rounds. At each stage, the current leader was announced, and losers were required to up the bidding by at least 5 percent. For the 1988 Seoul summer Olympics, the organizers limited the competition to two rounds of sealed bids. NBC's winning bid included a novel revenue-sharing agreement: a $300 million guaranteed payment plus two-thirds of any gross advertising revenues in excess of $600 million (up to a maximum $500 million total payment).

For the 1992 winter games, the Olympic Committee specified single sealed bids, before returning to multiple bidding rounds (adding a minimum required bid of $360 million) for the 1992 summer games. In 1995, a surprising turn occurred in the competition for the rights to the games from 2000 to 2008. NBC made early (high) preemptive offers that the organizers mulled and accepted, thereby short circuiting the bidding competition altogether. However, in 2003, the committee returned to rounds of competitive bidding for the 2010 and 2012 games.

The history of the Olympics bidding raises a number of questions. As a network representative, how should you determine the size of your bid? What difference do the bidding rules make? How should the organizing committee marshal the bidding competition to maximize its revenue?

This chapter studies an important application of decision making under uncertainty: the use of auctions and competitive bidding. Indeed, auctions are among the oldest forms of economic exchange. One of the earliest references was given by Herodotus, who noted a peculiar auction used by the ancient Babylonians—as a way of distributing wives. In modern economies, a common means of selecting a best alternative is by soliciting competitive bids. In the simplest (and also most common) bidding settings, the objective is to get the best price. This is the case in the networks' bidding for the Olympic Games television rights. Here, a single seller faces a number of competing buyers, and "best" price means highest price.

The two most frequently used methods are the English and sealed-bid auctions. In the familiar English ascending auction, the auctioneer calls for higher and higher bids, and the last and highest bid claims the item. The English auction enjoys a secure place in a bewildering variety of settings—the sale of art and antiques, rare gems, tobacco and fish, real estate and automobiles, and liquidation sales of all kinds. By contrast, in a sealed-bid auction, buyers submit private bids, bids are opened, and the highest bidder claims the item and pays its bid. The sale of public and private companies has been accomplished by

---

[1] John McMillan provides an incisive analysis of this competition. See Chapter 12 of J. McMillan, *Games, Strategies, and Managers* (New York: Oxford University Press, 1992).

sealed-bid auction as have the sales of real estate, best-seller paperback rights, theater bookings of films, U.S. Treasury securities, and offshore oil leases, to name a few. A third kind of auction method is the Dutch auction, used in the sale of a variety of goods but especially in the sale of flowers in Holland. The auctioneer's initial price is set very high, and then the price is lowered at intervals. The first buyer who announces a bid obtains the item at the current price.

Auctions are also a common means for conducting competitive procurements. Here, a single buyer solicits bids from a number of competing suppliers with the objective of obtaining the lowest possible price. In complex procurements, the ultimate objective is best thought of as source selection. The buyer seeks to select the "best" supplier, measured not only in terms of price but also by product quality, management capability, service performance, and the like. The most common institution for complex procurements is the submission of sealed bids (possibly in multiple rounds) before the buyer makes a final selection.

Whatever the particular institution or setting, auctions share the common feature that competition exists on only one side of the market. The auctioning party occupies a monopoly position and faces competing buyers or sellers. The auction determines at once with whom a transaction will take place and at what terms. Thus, the study of auctions raises two main questions: As a competitor, how should a firm bid to maximize its profit? In turn, how can the auctioning party design competitive bidding institutions for maximum advantage? This chapter considers each of these issues in turn.

THE ADVANTAGES OF AUCTIONS

Competitive bidding institutions are widespread because of the advantages they bring in obtaining the best price. As a means of effecting transactions, auctions take a place alongside competitive markets, posted prices, and negotiated transactions. Auctions are viable when a well-functioning, competitive market fails to exist. In other words, a producer of a standardized good that is bought and sold in a competitive market at predictable prices hardly can expect to have much success holding its own auction; any would-be buyers already can obtain the good from the market at the best available price. Thus, a prerequisite for an auction sale is that the good be differentiated from others. Indeed, auctions are a ready means of sale for unique items: artwork, antiques and other rare objects, paperback rights, oil and mineral leases, and the like.

Roughly speaking, auctions occupy a middle ground between posted pricing and negotiated prices. A common means of sale (and the universal means for U.S. retail sales) is for sellers to post prices, leaving buyers the choice to purchase at that price or not at all. Ideally, posted prices should be set in line with supply and demand. But, given the difficulty in judging these forces (or changes in them), this is not always the case. At the other extreme are negotiated prices, which are freely flexible. Although it has obvious advantages, pricing flexibility also has its costs. Negotiations can be time-consuming and expensive. Moreover, in the bargaining process, both buyer and seller have a significant influence on the final price. If everything is negotiable, a seller surrenders much of its monopoly power over price.

Auctions can be viewed as combining the best of the posted and negotiated pricing worlds. An auction ensures that competition among buyers sets the final price—the highest price the market will bear. In effect, the auction allows the seller to compare all buyer offers simultaneously and choose the best one. The auction is less time-consuming than rounds of one-on-one negotiations, and it preserves the seller's monopoly position. Auctions are more flexible than posted pricing. The current state of market demand determines the good's price, not the seller's best guess as to demand. The following examples illustrate these points.

A STOCK REPURCHASE   A company is considering buying back a portion of its common stock. Top management believes the value of its company's stock to be about $80 per share. (The current market price of $67 is indicative of the market's "undervaluing" the firm's shares.) Management is considering offers to buy back shares at one of three possible prices: $70, $72, and $74. However, there is a great deal of uncertainty about how many shares might be tendered at these prices. The following table lists the number of shares tendered (in millions) at the different prices for three kinds of shareholder response: strong, medium, and weak. Of course, management does not know which of the cases will hold; its best prediction is that all three are equally likely.

Shareholder Response

Price	Strong	Medium	Weak
$70	13	9	6
72	14	12	8
74	18	15	12

The company reckons its profit from any repurchase at $(\$80 - P)Q$, where P is the price it pays and Q is the quantity of shares it succeeds in buying. What price offer should the firm make to maximize its expected profit?

A simple expected-value analysis identifies the optimal offer as $70. With this offer, the firm earns a profit of $130 million, $90 million, or $60 million, depending on the market response. For instance, under strong demand, the firm's profit is $(80 - 70)(13) = \$130$ million. Since each market response is equally likely, the firm's expected profit is $93.3 million. It is easy to check that both the $72 and $74 offers deliver lower expected profits.

Now suppose that instead of setting a buyback price, the firm uses a particular kind of auction to repurchase shares. In this system, each shareholder tenders any number of shares at a price he or she names. After all tenders are collected, the firm buys shares (as many or as few as it wishes) at a *single common price* consistent with the tenders submitted.[2] For example, if the response proves to be strong, the firm has a number of options. By choosing a common price of $70, it could buy back 13 million shares (from all shareholders who named prices of $70 or below). It could name $72 as the common price and repurchase 14 million shares, or it could name $74 and repurchase 18 million shares.

By waiting for the shareholders' response, as revealed by the "auction," the firm can select the best repurchase price, given current market conditions. It is easy to check that the firm's most profitable offer is contingent on demand. If demand proves strong, the firm's best price is $70 (yielding $130 million in profit). If demand is medium, its best price increases to $72. Here, the firm's resulting profit is $(80 - 72)(12) = \$96$ million. If demand is weak, its best offer is $74 (with $72 million in profit). Using the auction method, what is the firm's expected profit? Since each response is equally likely, the firm's expected profit is simply $(1/3)(130) + (1/3)(96) + (1/3)(72) = \$99.3$ million. The firm's expected profit has increased by $6 million relative to the profit under its best posted price, $70, which is fixed regardless of the market response. Using the auction method, the firm effectively has acquired perfect information about demand. As noted in Chapter 9, the difference in expected profit—in this case $6 million—measures the expected value of perfect information. To sum up, in an uncertain environment, this auction method has a clear advantage over posted pricing.

BIDDING VERSUS BARGAINING   In Chapter 16, we considered the classic example of bilateral monopoly, where a single seller faced a single buyer with the aim of negotiating a mutually beneficial price. The following example illustrates the potential benefit of competitive bidding versus bargaining in securing a better price.[3] With the aid of its investment banker, a firm is seeking to sell its division at the highest possible price. The division is worth $40 million under the company's own management. The investment banker is hopeful that it can find as many as four to six potential buyers for the division. The banker believes the range of buyer values to be between $40 million and $64 million with all values in the range equally likely. In addition, the banker believes that buyers' values are independent of one another. Thus, if one buyer is willing to pay $44 million, the next buyer's independent value might be $55 million (or any other equally likely value in the $40–$64 million range).

---

[2] The financial community commonly refers to this procedure as a Dutch auction. However, this label is misleading because the method is very different from the usual Dutch auction described later in this chapter.

[3] You encountered an earlier version of this example in Chapter 9's discussion of optimal search.

What price could the firm expect to obtain in negotiations with a *single* buyer? There is certainly room for a mutually beneficial agreement. For instance, if the buyer's actual value were $52 million, a negotiated price of $46 million (halfway between the parties' values) would generate a profit of $6 million for each side. If the bargainers were equally matched, one would expect the final price to be close to this split-the-difference prediction. Moreover, since $52 million is the single buyer's expected value for the transaction, one-on-one bargaining by equally matched parties should result in a price of $46 million on average.

The firm can obtain a much higher sale price on average by putting the division up for competitive bid and enlisting as many potential buyers as possible. Suppose the firm solicits sealed price bids from the buyers. In placing its bid, each buyer will assess the (independent) monetary value it places on the division and will submit a sealed bid below this value, aiming to win the division at a profit. As we show later in the chapter, with six buyers, the price paid by the highest bidder will be *$60 million on average.*

The firm obtains a much better price for its division by soliciting bids from multiple competitors than from a single one-on-one negotiation. The sources of the advantage are twofold. First, as the number of potential buyers increases, it is more likely that one will hold a high value (in the upper part of the $40–$64 million range) and make a high bid. Second, the increase in the number of competitors forces each bidder (including the high-value buyer) to place a bid near to its true value. This implies lower profit for the bidder and a better price for the seller. In an auction, the bidder must compete against other would-be buyers, instead of against the seller alone, as in a one-on-one negotiation. In sum, competitive bidding serves to marshal the competition among a number of buyers to deliver the best price to the seller.

CHECK STATION 1

In attempting to sell an item, firm S has approached buyer A, whose last best price offer is $24. It now plans to approach firm B but is uncertain of the price it might get. Its best assessment is that B's final price offer lies in the range $20 to $28, with all (continuous) values in between equally likely. Show that firm S can improve its payoff (to $25 on average) by selling to the firm offering the better price.

Why Didn't Paramount Put *Titanic* TV Rights Up for Bid?

Days after the movie *Titanic* opened in American theaters, NBC negotiated one of the biggest bargains in television history, securing the TV rights to the film for a mere $30 million.[4] *Titanic* was projected to be the highest grossing film of all time, yet the price of the NBC deal was less than half the prices paid for *Men in Black* and *The Lost World: Jurassic Park*, films that attained less than half the level of theater revenues.

[4] For a full account, see B. Carter, "Why NBC Was Alone at the Helm in Bidding for Rights to *Titanic*," *The New York Times* (April 27, 1998): D1.

Paramount Pictures negotiated exclusively with NBC, choosing not to put the film up for bid among the other networks. The film's opening weekend showed a solid but not spectacular box office ($28 million), and critics' reviews ranged from favorable to mixed. Before opening, the film's publicity was all bad, centering on its enormous production costs and concerns about its 195-minute length. Fearing that box-office revenues would decline as weeks passed (the pattern for most films), Paramount was impatient to close a television deal while the film was faring well.

NBC was just as eager to deal. With ABC and CBS executives on Christmas break, NBC had the negotiation table to itself. More important, NBC's entertainment chief had attended the film on opening night and marveled at the response of teenage girls and parents alike. After hard bargaining, discussion centered on prices in the $22 million to $25 million range with Paramount insisting on an escalator clause that would raise NBC's payment depending on the strength of the film's theater revenues. NBC closed the bargaining by making a take-it-or-leave-it offer: a flat $30 million offer with no escalation clause and a "short fuse." Paramount sealed the deal.

Within days, the howls of protest sounded. The ABC and CBS television networks asked why they were denied the chance to bid. Paramount's production partner, 20th Century Fox, threatened to bring suit for Paramount's failure to auction the film and to include an escalator clause (popularly known as idiot insurance because it protects studios from selling eventual hits too cheaply). Ironically, Fox had passed on its right of first refusal to acquire the TV rights at a price below $30 million. According to industry estimates, *Titanic* could have sold for $60 million to $70 million (not including escalator provisions) had the film been auctioned two weeks after opening. By failing to enlist the best price via competitive bidding, Paramount may have left over $40 million in forgone profit on the cutting room floor.

BIDDER STRATEGIES

A firm's optimal bid in a given situation depends on many factors: its value for the good at auction, its assessment of the extent of bidding competition, and most important, the type of auction in which it competes.

To model bidding behavior, we begin by considering the so-called **independent private value** setting. Here, each bidder assesses an *individual value* (or *reservation price*) for the item up for bid. We denote buyer i's value by v_i, for i = 1, ... n, where n denotes the number of bidders. (In the converse case of a competitive procurement, each firm would hold a private cost estimate c_i.) Each bidder's value is independent of the others' and private, that is, known only to itself. Although values are private, all bidders are aware of the common probability distribution from which buyer values are independently drawn. (After the fact, buyers hold different values. But before the fact, one buyer is no more likely to have a high value than any other.) If winning bidder i obtains the item at price P, its profit is simply $v_i - P$. We now consider three common types of auction.

English and Dutch Auctions

In the oral, ascending **English auction**, bids continually increase until the last and highest bidder wins the item at his or her bid price. Optimal bidder strategies in the English auction are remarkably simple:

> When buyers hold independent private values, each buyer's dominant strategy in an English auction is to bid for the good up to the buyer's reservation price if necessary.

In the English auction, a buyer never should place a bid above his or her true value; this would imply a loss if the bid were to win. Nor should the buyer stop short of his or her value; this needlessly precludes earning a profit should a slightly higher bid win. Bidding up to full value (if necessary) is optimal regardless of the competitors' values or the bid strategies they might use; that is, this strategy is dominant. Notice that the bidding stops when the price barely rises above the next-to-last bidder's value. Thus, the auction delivers the good to the buyer holding the highest value among the bidders. The price stops at a level approximately equal to the second-highest reservation price, v_{2nd}.

The seller can achieve exactly the same price result using a closely related auction method: the so-called **Vickrey auction** or **second-price auction**. In the Vickrey auction, bidders submit sealed bids and the highest bidder claims the item but pays a price equal to *the second-highest bid* (instead of paying his own bid). Although they appear to be quite different, the English and Vickrey auctions are strategically equivalent when bidders hold private values. To see this, imagine that each buyer in an English auction were to authorize a personal representative to bid on the buyer's behalf. Each buyer privately submits its reservation price to this representative, instructing him to bid up to this value if necessary. Once all bidder submissions are reported, the auction house could hold a "virtual" English auction. It simply identifies the two highest submissions, "bids" them against one another, until the price just matches the second-highest submission (whereupon this bidder is dropped from the auction), and thereby awards the item to the high bidder at the second-highest bid price. It is easy to check (see Problem 1) that each buyer's dominant strategy is to report its true reservation price. Thus, the final prices in the Vickrey and English auctions are identical: $P_{2nd} = P_E = v_{2nd}$. Later, we will return to variations on the Vickrey auction when multiple items are up for bid.

Dutch auctions are used to sell many commodities worldwide, including produce, fish, and, most notably, flowers in Holland. In a Dutch auction, the auctioneer starts the sale by calling out a high price and then lowers the price by small increments until a bid is made. The first bidder obtains the item at the current price.

Optimal bidding strategies are significantly different in the Dutch and English auctions. The Dutch bidder faces a decision under uncertainty. Once the price descends below the bidder's reservation price, the bidder must decide how long to wait—that is, until how low a price—before placing a bid. A buyer with value 10 might choose not to bid when the price has fallen to 9, hoping to win the bid when the price drops to 8.5. The risk, of course, is that another buyer will be first to bid and win the item at a price of 8.7. Thus, the decision when to bid depends on one's value and the assessed strength of the competition (as embodied in the number of rival buyers and their likely values for the item). By contrast, the English bidder faces no such risk because there is always the opportunity to better the current price.

It is also interesting to compare the Dutch and sealed-bid auctions. In the latter, buyers submit sealed price bids, and the highest bidder wins the item at his or her bid price. The two auctions appear to be very different in form, but as some simple reasoning can readily show, the two methods are strategically identical for bidders. In each auction, a buyer must choose how high to bid (or how low to let the price drop), trading off the probability and profitability of winning. Holding a given reservation value and facing the same set of rivals, any buyer should make the same bid in either auction. After all, a Dutch bidder could just as well write down its bid-in price beforehand. If all bidders did this, the Dutch auction could be run as a sealed-bid auction: Prices are "opened" and the highest-price buyer obtains the item at its bid-in price. In short, the Dutch and sealed-bid auctions are expected to induce identical bidding behavior and to generate, therefore, identical expected sale prices.

Flower sales in Amsterdam occupy the pinnacle of the Dutch auction. Auctions take place in a building roughly the size of 10 football fields. Each day thousands of lots of flowers are brought for sale before hundreds of bidders occupying steeply tiered seats in separate auction halls. To expedite sales, prices are displayed on the hand of a computerized "clock." The price descends with the downward counterclockwise sweep of the clock hand, and buyers bid by pushing a button that stops the hand and automatically records the sale price. Sales are completed at the rate of 600 transactions an hour (one every six seconds). Flowers for sale come not only from Holland but also by air from Europe, Israel, Africa, and parts of Asia. Upon sale, the flowers are shipped to Canada, the United States, and scores of other developed countries.

Sealed-Bid Auctions

Sealed competitive bidding is frequently used to sell unique items: certain antiques, real estate, oil leases, or timber and mineral rights by the U.S. government. Submitting a bid in a sealed-bid auction is a classic example of decision making under uncertainty. Each bidder faces a fundamental trade-off between the probability and profitability of winning. In raising its bid to purchase an item, the company increases its chances of winning but lowers its profit from winning. (Similarly, in a competitive procurement, a lower price increases a supplier's chance of being selected but reduces its potential profit.) Given this trade-off, it is natural to ask: What bid will maximize the bidder's expected profit?

STRATEGY AGAINST A BID DISTRIBUTION   The key to formulating a profit-maximizing bidding strategy is to anticipate the distribution of competing bids. Obviously, to win the auction, the firm must beat the best competing bid. If the firm could predict this bid perfectly, its most profitable bid would be the one that wins by the smallest margin. But a perfect prediction clearly is impossible; at best, the firm possesses a probability assessment of competing bids. Based on this assessment, the firm determines its optimal (i.e., profit-maximizing) bid.

As an example, consider a typical sealed-bid auction—say, for a small suburban office building expected to receive bids from three firms. Each bidding firm plans to occupy the building (if it wins the auction) and places a greater or lower value on the building, depending on its main features: location, office space, amenities, and so on. Needless to say, an additional desired feature is a low purchase price at auction. Let's consider the bidding problem faced by a typical firm, say firm 1. Its bidding strategy begins with an assessment of its reservation price, that is, its monetary value for the building. For concreteness, suppose its reservation price is $v_1 = \$342$ thousand. This value can be thought of as a break-even price. The firm is just indifferent to the alternatives of acquiring the building at this price or not acquiring it at all. It never would pay more and would be happy to pay less.[5]

Firm 1's profit from winning the auction at bid b is $342 thousand − b, the difference between its value and its bid. If it does not win the auction, its profit is, of course, zero. It follows that the firm's expected profit is

$$E(\pi) = [342 - b][Pr(b \text{ wins})],$$

where the second term denotes the probability that bid b wins (i.e., is the highest bid). The key to determining a profit-maximizing bid is to assess accurately the way the firm's winning chances depend on its bid. Recognizing that it faces two other bidders for the building, the firm has thought carefully about its winning chances and has made the probability assessments listed in the third column of Table 17.1. As we would expect, the firm's winning chances increase steadily with its bid. Looking at the last

---

[5] In fact, the $342,000 estimate probably represents an expected value; that is, the company recognizes that the value of the building is more or less uncertain. Given this uncertainty, a risk-neutral buyer values the building at its expected value.

column of the table, we see that the firm's expected profit is minimal (1) for very low bids, which have little chance of winning, and (2) for bids near its reservation price, since these generate little profit. Expected profit is maximized at a bid of $328 thousand, which the firm predicts has a 49 percent winning chance. This is firm 1's optimal bid.

The firm's probability assessment of its winning chances usually is based on its past bidding experience: how often its bids have won auctions against varying numbers of competitors in the past. A useful way to think about the firm's winning chances is in terms of the distribution of the best (i.e., highest) competing bid. The probability of the firm's winning is simply the probability that the best competing bid (BCB) is smaller than the firm's own bid. Figure 17.1 shows the graph of the cumulative distribution of BCB (labeled H). The curve's height indicates the probability that the best competing bid is smaller than the value shown on the horizontal axis. For instance, at $320 thousand the height of the curve is .25, meaning that there is a .25 chance that the highest competing bid will be lower than $320 thousand (and, of course, a .75 chance that it will be higher than this value). The median of the BCB distribution is about $328 thousand (actually, very slightly higher). There is a 50 percent probability of BCB being lower than the median value.

The BCB distribution curve is important because it precisely measures the firm's winning chances for its various bids. Thus, a bid at the distribution median has a .5 chance of winning the auction because half the time the best competing bid will be below this value. According to the BCB curve, a $320 thousand bid has a .25 chance of winning, and so on. Using the BCB curve, there is a simple geometric means of describing the firm's optimal bid. In Figure 17.1, a vertical line has been drawn at the firm's reservation price, $342 thousand. Suppose the firm chooses bid b. Then the firm's profit, if the bid wins, is $342 thousand − b. This profit is measured by the horizontal distance

TABLE 17.1

Finding a Profit-Maximizing Bid (Thousands of Dollars)	Bid	Winning Profit	Probability of Winning	Expected Profit
	$300	$42	.00	$0.00
Raising a sealed bid increases the probability, but lowers the profitability, of winning. A bid of $328,000 maximizes the buyer's expected profit.	310	32	.06	1.92
	320	22	.25	5.50
	326	16	.42	6.76
	328	14	.49	6.86
	332	10	.64	6.40
	336	6	.81	4.86
	340	2	1.00	2.00

FIGURE 17.1

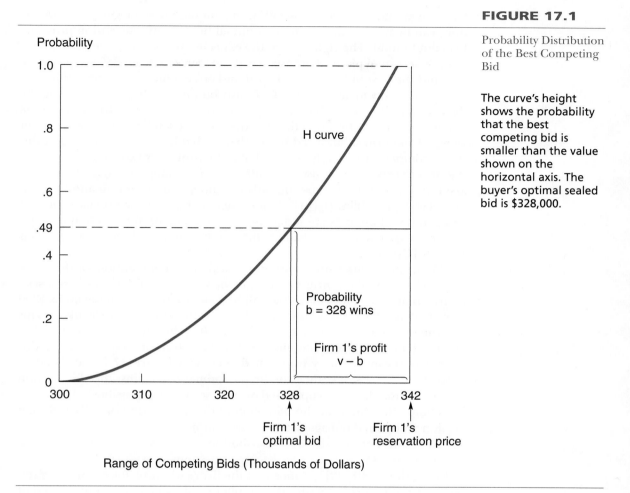

Probability Distribution
of the Best Competing
Bid

The curve's height
shows the probability
that the best
competing bid is
smaller than the value
shown on the
horizontal axis. The
buyer's optimal sealed
bid is $328,000.

between $342 thousand and b. The probability that the bid wins the auction is given by the height of the curve H(b). It follows that the firm's expected profit, $(342 - b)H(b)$, is measured by the area of the rectangle inscribed under the BCB curve.

Maximizing the firm's expected profit is equivalent to choosing a bid that maximizes this rectangle's area.[6] The figure shows the firm's optimal bid, $328 thousand, and the associated inscribed rectangle. This rectangle has a

---

[6] The interested reader may wish to apply calculus to find the optimal bid. A bidder with value v that submits bid b earns an expected profit of $E(\pi) = (v - b)H(b)$. Marginal profit is $M\pi = dE(\pi)/db = (v - b)h(b) - H(b)$, where $h(b) = dH/db$ is the density function of the BCB distribution. Setting $M\pi$ equal to zero, we find $b = v - H(b)/h(b)$. The optimal bid is below the firm's value, v, and the size of this discount is given by $H(b)/h(b)$.

larger area than any other possibility. In general, the same geometric procedure can be used to determine an optimal bid for any reservation price the firm might hold. The right side of the expected-profit rectangle simply is set at the reservation price. (For instance, if the firm's value is $330 thousand, we can find the best bid to be $320 thousand after some experimentation.)

A useful way to arrive at the BCB distribution is to begin by assessing the distribution for a *typical* competing bid. For instance, let $G(b)$ denote the cumulative distribution function for the bid of a *single* competitor. In other words, if the firm submits bid b, the chance that it will better the bid of this single competitor is simply $G(b)$. What if the firm faces two competitors? For the firm to win, its bid must be greater than *both* competing bids. Under the assumption that the competing bids are independent of one another, this occurs with probability $[G(b)]^2$. More generally, suppose the firm faces $(n - 1)$ competitors whose bids are independent and come from the common distribution $G(b)$. Then the probability that bid b is greater than all the others is $H(b) = [G(b)]^{n-1}$.

To illustrate this result, consider the sealed-bid competition for the office building, again taking firm 1's point of view. Suppose the firm's best assessment is that each competitor's bid will be somewhere between the limits $300 thousand and $340 thousand, with all values in between equally likely. This assessment implies[7] $G(b) = (b - 300)/40$. Therefore, it follows that $H(b) = [(b - 300)/40]^2$, because the firm faces two competitors. In fact, this is exactly the probability function depicted in Figure 17.1 and listed in Table 17.1. As we saw earlier, the firm's optimal bid against this distribution is $328 thousand. To sum up, based on an assessment of possible bids by a typical competitor, the firm should compute the distribution of BCB and then fashion an optimal bid against this distribution.

Now consider how the BCB distribution is affected if the number of bidders increases, say, to five firms. Facing four competitors, firm 1 would assess $H(b) = [(b - 300)/40]^4$. Notice that the firm's win probability for any given bid goes down drastically with the number of bidders. For example, a bid of $330 thousand has a .75 chance of beating any single bidder, a .56 chance of beating two other bids, but only a .32 chance of beating four others. Not surprisingly, the increase in the number of competitors causes firm 1 to increase its optimal bid. In fact, there is a second effect reinforcing firm 1's raise in bid: With the increase in competition, firm 1 would expect other firms to raise their bids as well. Thus, the bid distribution of the typical firm, $G(b)$, will be shifted toward higher bids. In short, firm 1 faces an increase not only in the number of competing bids but also in their levels. For both reasons, its optimal bid increases.

---

[7] To check this formula, note that G is .5 at the distribution median, $320,000. At a bid of $330,000, G is .75 as expected. For a uniformly distributed value (as here), $G = (b - L)/(U - L)$, where L and U denote the lower and upper limits of the distribution, respectively.

Your firm is competing in a sealed-bid auction for a piece of computer equipment valued (by the firm) at $30,000. You are contemplating one of four bids: $18,000, $20,000, $24,000, and $27,000. Given the bid distribution of a typical buyer, these bids would win against a single competitor with respective probabilities .4, .6, .8, and .9. What is the firm's optimal bid against one competitor? Against two competitors? Against three competitors?

EQUILIBRIUM BIDDING STRATEGIES[8]   Thus far, we have taken the point of view of a single firm whose task is to formulate an optimal bid, given a prediction about the distribution of competing bids. Although this approach has certain advantages, it also suffers from two problems. First, firms often are severely limited in their information about their competitors' bidding behavior; that is, there may be little empirical basis (i.e., a history of past bidding tendencies) for assessing H(b) or G(b). An "optimal" bid that assumes the "wrong" competing bid distribution will show a poor profit performance. Second, a purely empirical approach involves only one-sided optimization. It ignores the important fact that competitors are profit maximizers—that they themselves are attempting to set optimal bids. (Rather, it simply takes the bid distribution as given.)

A key point is the significant element of *interdependence* among bidding strategies. As we saw earlier, one firm's optimal bid depends on the number of competitors and how those competitors are expected to bid. For instance, higher bids from competitors may call for higher bids from the firm itself. Recall that in Chapter 13 we introduced the concept of equilibrium strategies in the context of oligopoly competitive interdependence. Equilibrium analysis is equally applicable to sealed competitive bidding. Firms' strategies constitute an equilibrium if each firm is profit maximizing against the behavior of the others, that is, if there is no opportunity for any firm to make a profitable unilateral deviation from its current bidding strategy.

The simplest example of equilibrium bidding occurs when buyers compete for a good with a known **common value**. For example, suppose all bidders have the same reservation price for the office building, say, $348 thousand (and all recognize this as the common value). *The unique equilibrium has each bidder submitting a sealed bid exactly equal to this common value*, so this value becomes the final price. The seller obtains full value for the item. Any set of bids with the high bid below $348 thousand is not in equilibrium, because any one of the losing bidders can increase its profit by slightly topping the current high bid.[9] Profit-increasing deviations are exhausted when bids match the item's full value.

With this simple observation in hand, let's examine equilibrium bidding in the case of differing private values. Again, there are n bidders, with bidder i

---

[8] The material in this section is difficult and can be skipped without loss of continuity.
[9] In the real world, prices below full value would be temporary at best. In repeated auctions, losing bidders would certainly raise their bids, seeking to claim any positive profit. These upward bid adjustments cease when there is no longer any bid profit available, that is, when all buyers are bidding full value.

holding value v_i and placing sealed bid b_i. Buyer values are drawn independently from a *common* distribution; that is, each buyer's value comes from the common, cumulative probability distribution $F(v)$. To illustrate, consider the office building example and assume for the moment that there are only *two* bidders. Suppose each buyer's value is *uniformly distributed* between $300 thousand to $360 thousand. (This means that all values in this range are possible and equally likely.) Furthermore, bidder values are *independent* of one another. Knowing its own value, but not knowing its opponent's, how should each buyer determine its optimal bid? The answer is provided by the equilibrium bidding strategy

$$b_i = (.5)(300) + .5v_i,$$

where values and bids are measured in thousands of dollars. Using this strategy, a buyer with value $300 thousand bids $300 thousand; with value $340 thousand it bids $320 thousand; and with value $360 thousand (the maximum value) it submits a maximum bid of $330 thousand. In short, the buyer bids a price midway between its true value and the lowest possible value (here, $300 thousand).

Let's check that this strategy constitutes an equilibrium. Consider a typical firm (say, firm 1) whose expected profit is

$$E(\pi) = [v_1 - b_1][Pr(b_1 \text{ wins})]. \qquad [17.1]$$

The competing *bids* of its rival, firm 2, are distributed uniformly between $300 thousand and $330 thousand (since firm 2 is presumed to employ the equilibrium bidding strategy just shown). Thus, bid b_1 wins with probability $(b_1 - 300)/30$. For instance, a bid of $300 thousand never wins, a bid of $315 thousand wins with probability .5, and a bid of $330 thousand wins with certainty. Substituting the probability expression into Equation 17.1 yields

$$E(\pi) = (v_1 - b_1)\left(\frac{b_1 - 300}{30}\right). \qquad [17.2]$$

The bidder's marginal profit is $M\pi = dE(\pi)/db_1 = [v_1 - 2b_1 + 300]/30$. Setting this equal to zero implies

$$b_1 = (.5)(300) + .5v_1. \qquad [17.3]$$

Note that the firm's expected profit is zero for the extreme bids, $300 thousand (which never wins), and v_1 (for which the firm makes no profit). The firm's optimal bid is halfway between these extremes. Thus, we have confirmed that the suggested equilibrium strategy is indeed optimal for the typical firm and for any value the firm might hold.

Two firms compete in a sealed-bid auction with each firm's private value uniformly distributed between \$0 and \$50. (i) Suppose firm 2 is expected to use the (nonequilibrium) bidding strategy, $b_2 = .6v_2$. Confirm that firm 1's optimal response is $b_1 = .5v_1$. (In other words, firm 1 still does best by bidding "one-half its value" as in Equation 17.3.) (ii) Against $b_2 = .4v_2$, show that firm 1's optimal sealed-bid strategy remains $b_1 = .5v_1$.

CHECK STATION 3

How are equilibrium bidding strategies affected by changing the number of competing firms? Let buyer values be uniformly and independently distributed between lower and upper bounds, denoted by L and U, respectively. (In the preceding example, L is \$300 thousand and U is \$360 thousand.) Then the common equilibrium strategy when n firms compete is simply

$$b_i = \left(\frac{1}{n}\right)L + \left(\frac{n-1}{n}\right)v_i. \qquad [17.4]$$

The firm's equilibrium bid is a weighted average of the firm's actual value and the lowest possible bidder value. Note that, as the number of bidders increases, the equilibrium bid rises and comes closer and closer to the firm's value. Holding $v_i = \$348$ thousand, the firm bids \$324 thousand when it is one of two bidders, but \$342 thousand when it is one of eight bidders.[10]

In fact, there is a very simple rule describing equilibrium bidding strategies with any number of bidders and any common probability distribution:

> In a sealed-bid auction, the equilibrium bidding strategy of the typical risk-neutral buyer is to submit a bid, b_i, equal to the expected value of the highest of the $n-1$ other buyer values, conditional on these values being lower than v_i. Formally stated, $b_i = E(v'|v' \le v_i)$, where v' denotes the largest of the other bidders' personal values.

Since this bidding rule is something of a mouthful, a concrete example is useful. Consider, once again, the office building auction—this time with two buyers. Suppose firm 1's value is v_1. Since firm 1 knows its opponent's value is uniformly distributed between \$300 thousand and \$360 thousand, the distribution of this value, v', *conditional on* v' being smaller than v_1, is uniform between \$300 thousand and v_1. Therefore, the conditional expected value of v' is simply $(.5)(300) + .5v_1$—the average of \$300 thousand and v_1. This is the firm's best bid. But this is exactly the equilibrium bidding strategy depicted in Equation 17.3. More generally, if there are $n-1$ other bidders whose personal

[10] Here is how to check Equation 17.4's equilibrium strategy. With this strategy, each buyer's bids are in the range L to $(L/n) + [(n-1)/n]U$. Therefore, bid b_i wins with probability $[(b_i - L)/((n-1)(U-L)/n))]^{n-1}$. Thus, the firm's expected profit can be written in the form of $k(v_i - b_i)(b_i - L)^{n-1}$, after collecting miscellaneous constant terms into the coefficient k. Therefore, marginal profit is $k[(n-1)(v_i - b_i)(b_i - L)^{n-2} - (b_i - L)^{n-1}]$. Setting this equal to zero and canceling out the common factor $(b_i - L)^{n-2}$ yields Equation 17.4. Thus, we have confirmed that using the proposed strategy is an equilibrium.

values are distributed uniformly between 300 and v_1, the expectation of the greatest of these values is $300/n + [(n − 1)/n]v_1$. This confirms Equation 17.4's equilibrium strategy.[11]

Although there is no easy intuitive argument to explain the preceding bidding rule, one comment is in order. The key to crafting an optimal bid is to assume for a moment that yours is the highest value. (If this is not the case, the buyer will be outbid by a rival anyway.) Accordingly, the buyer bases its bid on the expected value of v', *conditional on* v' being smaller than v_1.

To sum up, we have examined two approaches to finding the firm's optimal bidding strategy. The first approach takes the *distribution of opposing bids* as given and asks what is the firm's profit-maximizing bid strategy in response. The equilibrium approach starts from a prediction concerning the underlying *values of the firms* and identifies bid strategies such that each buyer is profit maximizing against the bidding behavior of its competitors. By the way, the BCB distribution in Figure 17.1 is derived from equilibrium bidding behavior among three bidders, each with a value distributed uniformly between $300 thousand and $360 thousand. Here, the common equilibrium bidding strategy is $b_i = (1/3)(300) + (2/3)v_i$. In turn, competing bids range from $300 thousand to $340 thousand. Therefore, the BCB distribution is given by $H(b) = [(b − 300)/40]^2$ and this is graphed as the H curve in Figure 17.1.

Common Values and the Winner's Curse

Frequently, bidders are uncertain about the "true" value of an item put up for competitive bid. For instance, the United States periodically sells offshore oil leases via sealed-bid auctions. The value of any lease is highly uncertain, depending on whether oil is found, at what depth and at what cost, and future oil prices. Except for differences in costs, the profit from the lease is likely to be similar across firms. Thus, to a greater or lesser degree, the tract has a **common value** for all bidders. The difficulty is that this value is unknown.

In making its bid, the individual firm typically first will form an estimate of the tract's potential value. Obviously, this estimate will be subject to error and firms may hold very different estimates of value. How should a profit-maximizing firm bid in this situation?

Figure 17.2 depicts bidding behavior when the item for bid has a common unknown value. The true (but unknown) value is labeled V. Centered at V is the distribution of possible bidder estimates (curve E). The figure depicts a normal distribution of estimates. On average, estimates reflect the true value, V, but there is considerable dispersion. Some buyers underestimate and others overestimate the true value. The figure also depicts a typical distribution of bids

---

[11] For uniformly distributed values, the equilibrium bidding strategy can be expressed in a neat formula. This is not the case for many other distributions, such as the normal distribution. However, tables of conditional expected values for many distributions are readily available.

FIGURE 17.2

The Winner's Curse

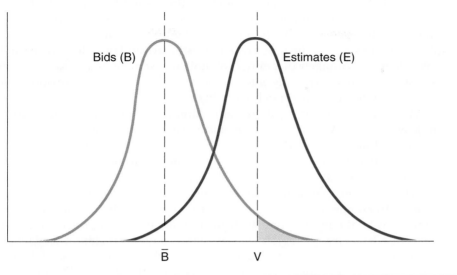

When the value of the item is highly uncertain, a winning bid drawn from the right tail of the bid distribution may exceed the true value of the item.

(curve B). Obviously, each bidder, seeking a profit, submits a bid well below its estimate of value. This explains why the bid distribution is centered well to the left of (i.e., below) the estimate distribution.

Here is an important observation to draw from Figure 17.2. A winning bid drawn from the right tail of the bid distribution may exceed the true value of the item. The shaded tail shows the portion of the distribution of bids that exceeds the true value. For a bid in this region, the buyer is said to fall prey to the **winner's curse**. After the fact, the auction winner finds that the good obtained is worth less than the price paid for it. The source of the winner's curse lies in the fact that the winning bidder has been too optimistic and has grossly overestimated the good's value. When the firm's (upward) estimation error exceeds its bid discount, it buys the good at a price greater than its value.

From the bidder's point of view, the key to avoiding the winner's curse is to recognize that the act of winning conveys information about the bidder's estimate relative to others. In all likelihood, winning means that the bidder probably overestimated the true value. Put another way, *conditional on winning the auction, the buyer should figure the item's true value to be significantly less than its original estimate.* The upshot is that each buyer should estimate the tract's value by first discounting its original estimate before making a bid.

The potential size of the winner's curse depends on two factors: the degree of uncertainty surrounding the item's value and the number of bidders. Obviously, the winner's curse is impossible if there is no uncertainty. No firm knowingly will bid above the item's true value. The larger the dispersion of estimates and, therefore, the dispersion of bids, the greater the chance that a winning bidder will pay too much. A more subtle point is that an increase in the number of bidders raises the frequency of the winner's curse. As the number of bidders rises, so will the range of actual estimates and bids. If there are only two bidders, it is unlikely that either will hold an estimate in the extreme right tail. But when there are many bidders, the presence of one or more optimistic, right-tail bidders becomes much more likely.

A buyer's optimal estimate of value (and bid) should take into account these two factors. A proper estimate of the item's "acquisition" value (its value conditional on winning) declines with an increase in uncertainty about the item or with an increase in the number of bidders. To bid profitably, a buyer must lower its bid accordingly.[12]

There is evidence of the winner's curse in real-life competitive bidding settings. In competitive procurements, it is commonly held that the winner simply may be the most optimistic firm (the one that most grossly underestimated the true cost of the job) rather than the most efficient one. The evidence of frequent cost overruns is due partly to the winner's curse and partly to poor contract incentives to minimize costs. Estimates in the 1970s and 1980s suggest that the U.S. government has received close to full value for its off-shore oil leases. In aggregate, tract winners may not have been cursed, but they did not reap excessive profits. Recently the winner's curse has been advanced as a reason for the unprecedented prices paid in corporate takeovers involving multiple bidders. A significant portion of these acquisitions have proven to be failures at any price.

FINAL NOTE   When the item up for bid has a common but uncertain value, bidding at an English auction becomes more subtle and complex than in a private, independent value setting. Because of winner's curse considerations, the bidder cannot simply plan to bid up to its value estimate. Observing the number of active bidders and when they drop out conveys information about competitors' estimates and, therefore, the item's unknown value. Thus, the buyer's upper bid limit should incorporate these observations.

CHECK STATION 4   You are uncertain about the value of an item up for bid in a sealed-bid auction. You believe that the value is between $3,000 and $4,000. You expect to bid against a single rival whom you realize is much more knowledgeable about the item's value. In fact, your rival can perfectly predict the item's market value (i.e., knows the precise value between $3,000 and $4,000). You are thinking of bidding $3,300 for the item. Assess the potential profitability as well as the potential risks of this bid.

[12] The computation of conditional values and equilibrium sealed-bidding strategies is quite complicated and, thus, is not pursued here.

OPTIMAL AUCTIONS

Earlier in this chapter, we noted the advantages of competitive bidding relative to posted prices and negotiated prices. We again take the perspective of the auctioning party—a seller who is interested in maximizing the revenue from an auction sale or a buyer who seeks the best terms (including minimum cost) from a competitive procurement.

Expected Auction Revenue

What are the expected-revenue consequences of different types of auctions? Which type of auction generates maximum expected revenue? In answering these questions, it is convenient to restrict attention to the two most common auctions: the English and sealed-bid auctions. Consider once again the symmetric, private-value model, in which buyer values are drawn independently from the same distribution. For this setting, we can state the following remarkable result:

> Suppose the private-value model holds and that risk-neutral buyers adopt equilibrium bidding strategies. Then the English, sealed-bid, Dutch, and Vickrey auctions all generate identical expected revenues.

This important proposition is called the **revenue equivalence theorem**. We already know that (1) the English and Vickrey auctions are equivalent and (2) the Dutch and sealed-bid auctions are equivalent. Thus, it remains to show that the English and sealed-bid auctions generate the same expected revenues—a result that follows from our earlier characterization of equilibrium bidding strategies. In the English auction, each buyer bids up to its true value (if necessary). The bidding stops when the next-to-last bidder drops out, at a price approximately equal to the second highest value among the bidders. Thus, the seller's expected revenue is simply

$$E(P_E) = E(v_{2nd}),$$

where v_{2nd} denotes the second highest buyer value. In the sealed-bid auction, each buyer uses the equilibrium bidding strategy

$$b_i = E(v'|v' \leq v_i),$$

where v' is the largest of the other bidders' personal values. Note that the *winner's* bid is set at a price that is equal, on average, to the next-best—that is, *second*-highest—valuation. Thus, under either the English or sealed-bid auction, the average purchase price is the same—equal to the expectation of the second-highest buyer value. Obviously, as the number of bidders increases, the expected price rises under either auction.

A UNIFORM EXAMPLE   Suppose there are n buyers with reservation prices independently and uniformly distributed between lower and upper bounds L and U, respectively. In other words, any value between L and U is considered equally likely. It is a statistical fact that the expected value of the largest of the n independent values (call this v_{max}) is given by

$$E(v_{max}) = \left(\frac{1}{n+1}\right)L + \left(\frac{n}{n+1}\right)U. \qquad [17.5]$$

In words, the expected value of the greatest of n independent, uniformly distributed values lies $n/(n+1)$ of the way toward the upper bound. For instance, if there are three bidders and values range from 100 to 200, the expectation of the greatest value lies three-quarters of the way between 100 and 200, that is, at 175. As the number of bidders increases (and the factor $n/(n+1)$ approaches 1), $E(v_{max})$ increases toward U.

In turn, the expectation of the second-highest value (v_{2nd}) is given by

$$E(v_{2nd}) = \left(\frac{2}{n+1}\right)L + \left(\frac{n-1}{n+1}\right)U. \qquad [17.6]$$

In words, $E(v_{2nd})$ lies $(n-1)/(n+1)$ of the way toward the upper bound. This is illustrated by the position of $E(v_{2nd})$ in Figure 17.3. Of course, this point indicates the average price (corresponding to the second-highest buyer value) achieved by an English auction.

Now let's compare this to the result in a sealed-bid auction. Here the winning buyer bases his bid on v_{max}, the highest outstanding value. The $E(v_{max})$ is also shown in the figure. But the winning bidder shades his optimal bid below his private value. In equilibrium, his bid corresponds to the expectation of the next-highest value, $E(v_{2nd})$, so the degree of shading exactly balances the advantage of basing the bid on the highest value. In the uniform case, his value

FIGURE 17.3

Expected Prices When
Buyer Values Are
Uniformly Distributed

The English and sealed-
bid auctions have
identical revenues.

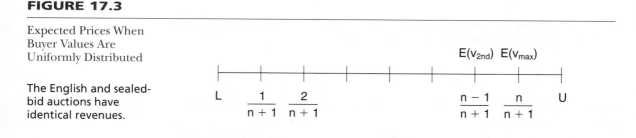

is $n/(n + 1)$ toward U, but he applies the factor $(n - 1)/n$ in shading his bid below his value (see Equation 17.4). Multiplying $n/(n + 1)$ by $(n - 1)/n$ results in an expected winning sealed bid exactly $(n - 1)/(n + 1)$ of the way toward U. This is exactly the same price as in the English auction.

Suppose there are four bidders with values independently and uniformly distributed between 0 and 100. Compute the expected price at an English auction. Write down the typical buyer's equilibrium strategy in a sealed-bid auction and then compute $E(v_{max})$ and $E(b_{max})$. Confirm that the auctions deliver the same expected price.

CHECK STATION 5

Revenue equivalence should be viewed as a benchmark, a result that holds in a prescribed set of circumstances. As we shall see, modifying the basic auction setting can confer a revenue advantage on one type of auction or the other. For instance, suppose the private-value model is replaced by a **common-value setting**. One can show that *in the common-value setting, the English auction produces greater revenue, on average, than the sealed-bid auction.* Although the proof of this result requires advanced mathematical methods, the intuition is grasped easily.[13] Recall that, in the common-value setting, buyers must discount their bids below their private estimates to avoid the winner's curse. Roughly speaking, the greater the uncertainty about the item's value, the greater is this bid discount. (The discount also increases with the number of bidders.) The next point to recognize is that a buyer faces less uncertainty in the English auction than in the sealed-bid auction. The English auction conveys more information because each buyer can observe roughly the price levels at which rivals drop out of the bidding, and this provides indirect information about their estimates. All in all, the English auction's informational advantage translates into a revenue advantage for the seller.[14]

Next, consider the effect of **bidder risk aversion** on bidding strategies and auction performance. (Thus far, the presumption has been that bidders are risk neutral, always seeking to maximize expected profit.) Interestingly, risk aversion has no effect on bidding behavior in an English auction. Bidding up

---

[13] The first formulation and proof of this result can be found in P. Milgrom and R. Weber, "A Theory of Auctions and Competitive Bidding," *Econometrica* (1982): 1089–1122.

[14] However, one should modify these revenue comparisons in light of actual bidding behavior observed in scores of auction experiments. Numerous experiments with independent private values show that bidding behavior in the English auction closely tracks the dominant strategy of bidding according to one's true value. By contrast, sealed-bidding behavior tends to be above the equilibrium benchmark. As a result, the sealed-bid auction tends to raise higher revenues than the English auction. A similar pattern holds in auction experiments with a common unknown value. Sealed bids are significantly elevated relative to the equilibrium benchmark (whereas English bids are only slightly elevated). In these experiments, sealed bidders fall prey to the winner's curse (overpay for items) when the item's value is highly uncertain and when competition is high (five or more bidders). In these conditions, bidders fail to recognize the drastic bid discounts needed to avoid the winner's curse. Thus, in actual practice, it appears that the sealed-bid auction holds a slight revenue advantage over the English auction. For an overview of the experimental evidence, see W. Samuelson, "Auctions in Theory and Practice," Chapter 10 in K. Chatterjee and W. Samuelson (Eds.), *Game Theory and Business Applications* (Boston: Kluwer Academic Publishers, 2001).

to full value (if necessary) is a dominant strategy regardless of the bidder's attitude toward risk. Things are different, however, in a sealed-bid auction. Here risk aversion implies higher bids by buyers—the more risk averse the buyer, the higher is the bid. As always, the optimal bid depends on the trade-off between the probability and profitability of winning. The upshot is that a risk-averse buyer raises its bid, settling for a smaller but *more certain* profit.[15] Thus, risk aversion on the part of bidders tends to confer a revenue advantage on the sealed-bid auction relative to the English auction. (One other effect can be mentioned. If a bidder's value for an item is uncertain, an increase in risk aversion implies a reduction in the bidder's certainty equivalent value, which in turn lowers bids. However, this value reduction is the same regardless of the auction method being used.)

Finally, the revenue equivalence result presumes that buyers' private values are drawn independently from a common probability distribution. Allowing for **value asymmetry** (buyer values drawn from different distributions) upsets revenue equivalence. Roughly speaking, the English auction tends to have a revenue advantage when two or more bidders have similar distributions of values (and, therefore, tend to bid up the price close to their reservation values). Conversely, the sealed-bid auction does better when the value ranges are quite different. As an extreme example, suppose there are two bidders with v_1 uniformly distributed between 100 and 150 and v_2 uniformly distributed between 0 and 50. In the English auction, buyer 2 always drops out before buyer 1 and the expected price is only $E[P_E] = E[v_{2nd}] = 25$. In the sealed-bid auction, buyer 1's optimal bid is $b_1 = 50$, just enough to guarantee winning the auction. Thus, the sealed-bid auction yields twice the expected revenue of the English auction.[16]

RESERVE PRICES   A common feature of auctions is the setting of a reserve price. If the high bid in the auction does not exceed the seller's minimum or **reserve price**, the good is withdrawn from sale.[17] A reserve price serves two related purposes: It protects the seller from auctioning the good for too low a price, and it potentially can elevate the final bid price. To see how a reserve price works, let v_s denote the seller's value (or reservation price) for the item being sold. This reservation price could represent the personal value the seller

---

[15] Suppose the firm that bids for the office building has utility function $U = 10\sqrt{y}$, where y is the firm's bidding profit. Using Table 17.1, we can confirm that the firm's utility-maximizing bid is $332 (whereas its profit-maximizing bid was $328).

[16] For less dramatic asymmetric distributions, the sealed-bid auction continues to hold a revenue advantage, though a narrower one. Let one buyer's values be uniformly distributed between 0 and 60 and the other's between 30 and 90. Here expected English revenue is calculated to be 28.75. In the sealed-bid auction, expected revenue is 34.4 (about 20 percent) higher.

[17] The reserve price may be public or silent. A public reserve is announced prior to the bidding and establishes where the bidding starts. A silent reserve price is established by having a representative of the auction house bid on the seller's behalf up to the agreed-upon minimum. In either case, if no buyer bids above the minimum, the item goes unsold and is returned to the seller.

places on the item (e.g., the personal value for a painting). Alternatively, it might represent a fallback price at which the seller knows she can sell the item outside the auction. (For instance, the seller already may have been offered $320,000 for the office building.) Clearly, the seller never should accept an auction price below v_s. In fact, one can show that the seller should set the reverse price P_{min} to be strictly greater than her value; that is, $P_{min} > v_s$. (This is analogous to a seller demanding a price in excess of her reservation value in the negotiation settings discussed in Chapter 16.) By setting such a reserve price, the seller risks the possibility that the highest bid, b_{max}, will not attain P_{min}, even when a mutually beneficial transaction exists, that is, when $v_s < b_{max}, < P_{min}$. The advantage of the reserve price is that it forces buyers to bid higher than they otherwise might to meet the reserve.[18]

Competitive Procurement

Thus far, we have presented an analysis of bidding strategy in the case of auctions for the sale of goods or services. Exactly analogous results apply in the case of competitive procurements, that is, when a number of firms submit bids to supply a good or service and the lowest bid is selected to fulfill the contract. Here each supplier seeks to maximize its expected bidding profit given by

$$E(\pi) = (b - c)\Pr(b \text{ wins}),$$

where c denotes the firm's cost. Other things being equal, a higher bid implies a greater profit from the contract but a lower probability of being the winning (i.e., lowest) bid. Taking this trade-off into account, the firm's optimal bid involves *marking up* its bid price above cost. Increasing the number of competitors causes the firm to set a lower markup in its optimal bid.[19] In addition, winner's curse considerations will lead bidders to increase their bids when there is a common, unknown element to the firms' costs.

However, there is an important difference in the contractual terms used in sale auctions and in a large number of procurements. Auctions almost always involve a sale at a *fixed* price. By contrast, many competitive procurements rely on contingent contracts as an efficient response to the presence of risk and uncertainty. At the time of contract signing, the ultimate quality, cost, and time

---

[18] When revenue equivalence holds, one can show that the English and sealed-bid auctions using the right reserve price are optimal auctions; that is, each produces the maximum revenue of all possible auction procedures.

[19] In equilibrium, a risk-neutral firm sets its bid at the expected value of the next lowest competing cost, conditional on this cost being greater than the firm's own cost. For instance, if each firm's cost is distributed uniformly between L and U, firm 1's equilibrium bid is $b_i = [(n - 1)/n]c_i + U/n$. Note that b_i is a weighted average of c_i and U and that b_i approaches c_i as the total number of bidders increases.

of delivery of the good or service all may be subject to considerable risk. Thus, it is common for the procurement contract to permit risk sharing between the buyer and winning contractor.

Incentive contracts are used widely in high-risk procurement environments (defense programs, research and development, and so on). Under such a contract, the supplier's profit is given by

$$\pi = \pi_T + b(c_T - c),$$

where c is the ultimate cost of the procurement (unknown at the time the contract is signed). The remaining three variables are specified in the contract: π_T is the firm's target profit, c_T is its target cost, and b is its sharing rate. If the actual cost matches the target cost ($c = c_T$), then the firm earns its target profit: $\pi = \pi_T$. For positive sharing rates, the supplier and the buyer share in cost overruns and underruns. For instance, if b = .4, then each extra dollar of cost is paid 40 percent by the firm and 60 percent by the buyer. For b = 1, the buyer writes a **fixed-price contract**; the supplier is responsible dollar for dollar for cost overruns. At b = 0, the buyer writes a **cost-plus contract**; here the buyer pays for all overruns and the firm is guaranteed a fixed profit of π_T. For sharing rates between 0 and 1, the buyer writes an **incentive contract**.

The trade-off between risk sharing and efficient firm selection is at the heart of determining the "degree of incentive" (i.e., the value of b) in the contract terms. Under a fixed-price contract, the winning supplier bears all costs and, therefore, has an obvious efficiency incentive (i.e., will strive to keep costs to a minimum). Since it bears full-cost responsibility, a firm's price bid will necessarily reflect its likely production cost (plus a provision for profit). Consequently, by choosing the lowest competitive bid, the buyer also will be selecting the lowest-cost firm. However, the disadvantage of the fixed-price contract is that it allows no risk sharing. Being risk averse, the winning supplier will require a much higher profit margin for bearing procurement risk and will pass this premium on to the buyer via a higher price bid.

At the opposite extreme, a cost-plus contract insures the supplier completely against uncertainty about program cost. Accordingly, a risk-averse supplier requires a much lower guaranteed profit fee (than with a fixed-price contract). However, under a cost-plus contract, the firm has no incentive to minimize cost (since the buyer picks up the tab). Furthermore, if cost-plus contracts are set, the bidding competition is much less likely to select the most efficient supplier.

In general, the buyer minimizes its expected procurement cost by fashioning an incentive contract. (That is, neither the fixed-price nor cost-plus extremes are optimal.) Determining an optimal incentive contract (the "right" value of b) depends on a basic trade-off among the goals of risk sharing, efficient firm selection, and incentives for cost reductions.

MULTI-OBJECT AUCTIONS

Auction institutions and buyer strategies become more complicated when multiple objects are up for sale and values are nonadditive. By nonadditive, we mean that buyer values for collections of objects need not equal the sum of values for individual objects. Subsets of items may be substitutes or complements. For instance, a buyer might exhibit downward-sloping demand, that is, declining values for additional units acquired. (Here units are partial substitutes.) Alternatively, items might be worth considerably more in combination than they are separately. For instance, a piece of real estate may be worth much more undivided than when sold separately in pieces. Likewise, regional and national combinations of spectrum rights can be expected to be worth considerably more than the separate parts.

The Spectrum Auctions

In the late 1990s, the Federal Communications Commission (FCC) held a series of auctions to sell portions of the electromagnetic airwave spectrum to be used for wireless communication and data services. The auctions drew dozens of bidders, large and small, and have raised some \$23 billion in winning bids to date. Numerous economists and game theorists advised the FCC on the design of the auctions. The spectrum auctions were designed to (1) ensure multiple providers in regional markets (i.e., multiple licenses were sold in each market), (2) allow bidders to assemble multiple geographical licenses (to build efficient nationwide networks), and (3) raise revenue for the government. A key aspect of the FCC auctions was the recognized complementarities among licenses. For instance, a particular bidder might hold a very high reservation price for a combination of 16 licenses that allowed it to form a nationwide cellular network. However, its reservation price would decline significantly for only 12 of the desired licenses, and its value for only 6 licenses might be severely limited. In selling the spectrum, the FCC instituted an unprecedented auction method: *simultaneous multiple rounds of bidding on all licenses.* In each round, bidders could submit bids for any and all licenses. At the end of the round, the new high bids were announced, and bidding would proceed to the next round. In fact, the first two broadband auctions took 112 rounds (and 3 months) and 184 rounds (and 5 months), respectively. The results were auspicious. Not only did the auctions raise unprecedented revenue sums, but also winning bidders were able to assemble valuable combinations of licenses.

Notice the importance of keeping the bidding open on licenses simultaneously. If licenses were auctioned sequentially, assembling combinations of licenses would be fraught with difficulties. (Imagine that licenses A to Z were auctioned sequentially, and a particular bidder needed to assemble A, G, M, and Z. The bidder would face an obvious "exposure" problem. Should the buyer bid aggressively on the first license A, not knowing if it can attain the other licenses?) The simultaneous open auction allowed buyers to watch the movements in license prices round by round and adjust their bidding strategies accordingly (giving up on high-priced licenses or entering the bidding for cheaper licenses).

A number of experts proposed that the simultaneous multiround auction should also allow package (or combinatorial) bidding. Thus, a firm could bid on the package such as A, G, M, Z as well as on individual licenses. At each round of bidding, the FCC would identify and announce the current winning bids (those that maximized its total revenue). Allowing package bidding would have provided much more bidder flexibility (and possibly increased total revenue). However, the FCC prohibited package bidding on the grounds that it tended to favor large bidders making package bids and that it was inordinately complex to implement. To see why package bids might be unduly advantaged, suppose that the highest *stand-alone* values for licenses A, G, M, and Z are $10 million each and the second-highest values are $8 million. Then the individual prices would tend to be bid up to slightly above $8 million each, for a total of $32 million. Now suppose another bidder values the *package* at $35 million and places a bid (say, $34 million) that beats the sum of the individual bids. The bidding is still open, but now the individual bidders face a "free-rider" problem. If they were allowed to communicate and collude, they could beat the package bid (their total value of $40 million exceeds the other bidder's package value). But with collusion prohibited, none of the bidders will be eager to raise its own bid price unilaterally. Thus, the package bid is likely to prevail, even though the efficient allocation would have the licenses sold separately.

The FCC continues to consider allowing package bids in future spectrum auctions. A number of auction experts have proposed using a modified Vickrey auction in which buyers submit *sealed bids* for all items and combinations of items. Based on the bids, the seller implements the value-maximizing allocation of the items. The important feature of the Vickrey auction is that a winning bidder pays a price set according to the "cost" (in terms of reduced value) that his award imposes on the *other* buyers. (Problem 12 provides a concrete example.) Because a buyer's price is always independent of its bid, each buyer's dominant strategy is to bid its actual values for all items and combinations of items. Thus, in addition to the revenue it generates, the Vickrey auction is guaranteed to produce an efficient allocation of the items.

Bidding to Televise the Olympics Revisited

In light of our analysis of competitive bidding, what conclusions can we draw about the networks' fight for the Olympics television rights? First, consider the positions of the bidders themselves. Bidding for the Olympics four or more years before the fact is fraught with uncertainty. Much of this uncertainty is common to all bidders. A network's advertising revenues from televising the Olympics depend on the number of viewers advertisers expect. Of course, viewer interest (in particular, American viewer interest) depends on a number of factors: intrinsic interest in the various events and athletes and whether the telecast is live. Other sources of revenue, such as reselling the rights for cable television transmission, are also uncertain. Similarly, the cost of broadcasting the Olympics (depending on inflation, exchange-rate changes, or predictions of future wages) has a significant (unknown) common-value component. At the same time, revenues and costs also can differ substantially across networks. Previous Olympics broadcasting experience may enhance revenues (ABC was once regarded as *the* Olympics network) and reduce costs. Broadcasting the Olympics gives a boost to a network's ratings, thereby enhancing profitability of other programs. Analysts believe that this boost is more important to the third-place network in the ratings, spurring an aggressive bid. In short, Olympics bidding displays a mix of common-value and private-value elements.

The history of the bidding suggests that the three networks have engaged in vigorous competition for the games. The norm has been for Olympics organizers to insist on multiple rounds of bidding in an attempt to extract maximum revenue from the winner. To the extent that multiple bidding rounds approximate an English auction, each buyer should be willing to bid up to its estimate of what the games are worth, conditional on its being the winner. How successfully did the networks carry out this strategy? The evidence suggests that the winning networks have earned losses, sometimes large ones, as frequently as they have turned profits. ABC suffered a $65 million loss on the 1988 Calgary games and a smaller loss on the 1984 Los Angeles games. CBS broke even on the 1992 Albertville games, whereas NBC made a $25 to $30 million profit on the 1988 Seoul games (a much smaller profit than it had expected). In the last decade, the profit record has been equally mixed. NBC incurred a $100 million loss on the 1992 Barcelona games but made a $70 million profit on the 1996 Atlanta games and a modest profit ($40 million or less) on the 2000 Sydney Olympics. The Salt Lake City winter games of 2002 marked NBC's finest Olympics hour. Major events shown live in prime time, the strong showing by American athletes, the figure skating judging scandal, and post 9/11 patriotism all contributed to unusually high revenues, generating a $75 million profit for the network.

On average, it appears that the networks have paid full value or even more than full value for the Olympics telecasts. The networks' mixed records might owe to a run of bad luck (realized revenues unpredictably falling below estimates), but there is no hard evidence to support this view. Did the networks tend to overestimate revenues (and/or underestimate costs)? The record suggests a qualified yes. Winning bids have been consistently higher than organizers' preauction predictions of what the broadcasting rights are worth. (The organizers' lower predictions have proved more accurate than the networks'.)

Indeed, NBC's enormous Barcelona loss stemmed in part from the pay-per-view fiasco (based on inflated revenue predictions as to the price cable viewers would pay for simulcast coverage) and in part on cost overruns. In addition, the winner's curse played a major role in NBC's Barcelona loss. In the first bidding round, all three networks placed comparable bids between $350 and $360 million. In the second and final round, NBC raised its bid to $401 million; its rivals had increased theirs by a token few million.

Conditional on its winning the bidding (and given its competitors' much more pessimistic assessments), NBC should have realized that its estimate and bid were grossly overoptimistic.[20]

Finally, how have the organizers done in marshalling the bidding competition to their advantage? Very well, it would appear. They have used multiple bidding rounds to encourage higher bids. (Recall that the English auction is superior to the sealed-bid auctions if common-value elements are important.) The organizers also repeatedly have set minimum reserve prices to elevate bids. This was particularly effective in bidding for the 1994 Lillehammer games. CBS paid the $300 million reserve that the other networks refused to meet; thus, CBS was forced to pay a higher price than would have been forthcoming in an open ascending auction without a reserve. For the Seoul games, organizers experimented with a revenue-sharing arrangement: NBC paid $300 million plus two-thirds of any advertising revenue earned in excess of $600 million. As noted earlier, when bidders are risk averse, revenue sharing serves to elevate values and bids by spreading risk across the contracting parties. (Inexplicably, organizers rejected the networks' revenue-sharing bids for the Barcelona games, insisting on fixed prices.) In sum, Olympics organizers have adeptly crafted the bidding institutions to increase their revenue.

In 1995, NBC added a new wrinkle to the network competition. A month before the bidding was to begin, it delivered a secret preemptive offer for the 2000 summer games in Sydney and the 2002 winter games in Salt Lake City. The prices were 54 percent and 48 percent greater than the previous summer and winter record bids but came with the proviso that the offers would be immediately withdrawn if the Olympics committee approached other bidders. Believing that the price was more than it could expect at auction (something we will now never know), the Olympics committee accepted NBC's terms. Industry observers at the time judged that NBC was paying close to full value. (As noted earlier, NBC profited in both Olympics, mainly due to unexpectedly strong revenues.) Later in 1995, NBC took an even greater risk. It made a second preemptive bid for the 2004, 2006, and 2008 games at still higher prices even before the sites had been determined. In addition, the network agreed to revenue sharing once advertising revenues reached a sufficient threshold. Only time will tell whether NBC has pulled off a shrewd gamble (preempting a bidding competition that might have forced it to higher prices) or whether its love affair with the Olympics had led it to grossly overpay.

In June 2003, the Olympics committee returned to competitive bidding offering broadcast rights (plus Internet, video-on-demand, and pay-per-view rights) for the 2010 and 2012 games with the sites still to be determined. This time the winner would be determined by sealed bids. Before the final bidding, CBS and AOL Time Warner dropped out of the competition. Again NBC was the winner, beating ABC and Fox and paying some $2 billion in total for the two games.

---

[20] After making the winning bid for the 1996 games, Dick Ebersol, the president of NBC Sports, guaranteed a profit on the deal, saying his past predictions were 100 percent correct. He neglected to say that he had "passed" on making a prediction for the Barcelona games.

SUMMARY

Decision-Making Principles

1. By maximizing the number of competitors and letting price be determined by "what the market will bear," competitive bidding institutions compare favorably with the alternatives of one-on-one negotiation and posted pricing.

2. In a sealed-bid auction, each buyer faces a basic trade-off: The lower its bid, the greater its profit if it is accepted but also the lower the chance the bid will win.

3. If bidders are risk neutral and have symmetrically distributed independent private values, the expected price (in equilibrium) is identical in the English and sealed-bid auctions.

Nuts and Bolts

1. In an English auction in which bidders have private values, each buyer's dominant strategy is to bid up to its value if necessary.

2. a. In a sealed-bid auction, the manager should assess the probability distribution of the best competing bid, $H(b)$, and determine the optimal bid by maximizing $E(\pi) = (v - b)H(b)$. If $G(b)$ is the bid distribution of a single competitor, then $H(b) = [G(b)]^{n-1}$.

    b. An alternative approach is to determine an equilibrium bidding strategy—one that is profit maximizing against competitors that also are using profit-maximizing strategies. If bidders are risk neutral and values are drawn independently from a common distribution, the common equilibrium bidding strategy is $b_i = E(v'|v' \leq v_i)$, where v' denotes the largest of the other bidders' personal values.

3. The winner's curse occurs when the highest bidder—having won because of excessive optimism about the item's value—finds it has paid more than the item is worth. When there is common-value uncertainty, bidders must discount their original estimates of value, that is, determine the item's value conditional on winning the auction, in order to avoid the winner's curse.

Questions and Problems

1. In a second-bid auction, buyers submit sealed bids, and the highest bidder obtains the item for sale but pays the seller an amount equal to the *second-highest bid*.

    a. Suppose buyers hold different private values for the item. Show that each player's dominant strategy is to bid his true value in this sealed-bid auction. (*Hint*: Check that the bidder cannot gain by either understating or overstating his reservation price in making his bid.)

    b. In the setting of independent, private values, the English and second-bid auctions lead to identical bids and outcomes. Explain why.

    c. The major auction houses allow buyers who will not be in attendance to submit bids prior to the public auction. A representative of the house bids on the buyer's behalf up to but not in excess of the submitted bid. A submitted bid of $1,200 could well win the item for a price of $900 when the bidding stops in the actual English auction. What is the optimal submitted bid for a buyer with private value v_i? Explain.

2. Private companies frequently approach your consulting firm to undertake special projects and provide advice to management. As a senior consultant, one of your jobs is to quote a price for these projects based on an estimate of cost and firm resources (i.e., consultants available to work on them). Your firm recognizes that it is competing with other consulting firms for its potential clients' business.

    Over the last six months, you have bid on ten separate projects and have won nine of them. You are establishing a reputation as someone who really can bring in business. Some managers in the firm are worried, however, about a shortage of resources (i.e., available consultants) to complete these jobs. Is yours a "good" bidding record? Describe carefully how you would make this assessment.

3. The Internal Revenue Service has organized a sealed-bid auction to sell an office building whose owners have failed to pay back taxes.

    a. As a real-estate developer, you estimate the value of the building to be $2.9 million. You believe that a typical competitor's bid will be in the range of $2 million to $3 million (with all values in between equally likely) and that bids are independent of one another. You are considering bids of $2.4 million, $2.6 million, and $2.7 million. Which bid provides the greatest expected profit against one other bidder? Against two other bidders?

    b. Now suppose that you face two other bidders and believe that a typical competitor's *value* for the building lies between $2 million and $3.5 million with all values in between equally likely. (Again, your value is $2.9 million.) Assuming your two rivals employ equilibrium bid strategies, what is your equilibrium bid?

4. In many situations, a seller of an item entertains bids from a number of buyers but allows one buyer to obtain the good by *matching* the highest

competing offer. Consider the owner of a house who must sell the property immediately. These are only two potential buyers, one of whom currently rents the house. The owner agrees to solicit a final price from the outside buyer and allow the renter to match it if he wishes. All the parties believe that the buyers' values for the house are independent of each other and that, for each buyer, values between $200,000 and $260,000 are equally likely.

a. How should the renter decide whether or not to match the outside offer?

b. What offer should the outside buyer make if her value is $240,000? More generally, what offer should she make as a function of her value, v?

c. What is the seller's expected revenue? Confirm that it is lower than under either the English or sealed-bid auctions.

5. Reliant Press produces business forms for large customers: major banks, insurance companies, and the government. More than half of its sales are by competitive bid. Its largest facility receives an average of 10 bid requests per week and responds to 90 percent of them. The firm typically is one of three or four bidders on any job. In making its bids, Reliant has applied highly variable markups above cost (anywhere from 30 to 90 percent). As part of a review of its bid performance, the firm's chief of sales recently ordered the collection of bid data for the past four months; these data are shown in Table 1. Table 2 shows the information the firm collected on the *lowest* competing bid for each auction during this period.

a. Based on the information in Table 1, what is the firm's optimal markup?

TABLE 1

Bid Success by Markup

Markup	Number of Bids	Number of Winning Bids
30%	7	6
40	9	7
50	12	7
60	17	9
70	23	9
80	31	8
90	20	4
100	9	1
Total	128	51

TABLE 2

Distribution of Lowest
Competing Bids

Markup (Range)	Number of Lowest Competing Bids
19% and below	6
20–29	10
30–39	11
40–49	17
50–59	20
60–69	17
70–79	15
80–89	14
90–99	11
100% and above	7
Total	128

b. Answer part a using the information in Table 2. Do the tables support similar policy actions? Which table embodies better information?

6. A half-dozen firms are competing to secure a highway contract from a local government via sealed bid. When bids are opened, the winning firm's bid is 40 percent below the next-lowest bid.
   a. How might you explain such a low bid? Given such a bid, what risks does the winning bidder face? Explain.
   b. Is such a low bid unambiguously "good" for the local government? What potential risk does the government face? (In terms of the auctioning party's risk, how does a procurement differ from an auction sale?) How might the government protect itself from this risk?

7. Movie distributors sell films to local exhibitors via sealed competitive bids. Exhibitors complain about the system of "blind" bidding—that is, they are often forced to bid on a film sight unseen (before the film is even completed). At the risk of oversimplifying, suppose a typical film might be worth $10,000 per week (a hit), $6,000 (OK), or $2,000 (a dog). Each of these outcomes is considered equally likely for the typical unseen film.
   a. Suppose three risk-neutral exhibitors are bidding for a film. What is the expected value of the typical film under blind bidding? In a sealed-bid auction where equilibrium bids are placed, what is the distributor's expected revenue from the competition? Could the distributor increase its expected revenue by delaying the bidding until after the film can be viewed (so its value will be known)? Explain. How do your answers change if exhibitors are risk averse?

b. Could a distributor increase its expected revenue by selectively screening only its best films but making the bidding on the rest of the films blind?

c. Suppose three exhibitors bid for a film after viewing it. Exhibitor A is extremely astute and so can make a precise prediction of the film's value. Exhibitors B and C have only imprecise information about this value. Could the distributor increase its expected revenue by excluding one of the bidders? If so, which one?

8. In many sealed-bid auctions, one expects that an increase in the number of bidders will cause each potential buyer to raise his or her equilibrium bid. In some cases, the impact is just the reverse; a buyer is wise to lower his or her bid against a greater number of competitors.

a. Explain why this might be the case.

b. Explain carefully the general result that the seller gains from an increase in the number of bidders. If more numerous bidders cause buyers to lower their bids, how can the seller still gain?

9. Identical items are sold at English auction by one of two methods. One is to auction single items, one at a time. The other is to hold an initial English auction in which the high bidder has the right to buy the lot or a portion of it (at the price he or she bids per unit). If the bidder purchases only some of the items, the remainder are immediately reauctioned under the same ground rules.

a. Suppose seven identical items are auctioned one by one. What complication does this present for bidders? Which items, the first or the last, would you expect to sell for the lowest prices on average?

b. Suppose the winning bidder can buy all or some of the seven items and any leftovers are reauctioned. In what sense does this procedure resemble a Dutch auction? How might this affect buyers' bidding strategies?

10. Firms J and K are competing to supply high-tech equipment to a government buyer. Firm J's expected production cost is $105 million and its profit requirement (on top of this) is $5 million. (The firm demands this profit because it can earn this amount on a comparable contract.) Firm K has an expected cost of $95 million and a profit requirement of $7 million. The government buyer has limited information about the firms, so it does not know which has the lower total cost (direct cost plus profit).

a. Suppose the government stipulates a cost-plus contract and plans to choose the firm that submits the lower-profit bid. Which firm will it select? Is the selection process efficient?

b. Suppose, instead, that the government sets a fixed-price contract and the firms submit total cost bids. Which firm will be selected? Why might firms insist on a higher required profit under a fixed-price contract than under a cost-plus contract?

    c. Finally, suppose the government uses an incentive contract and sets the firm's sharing rate at $b = .25$ and the cost target at $c_T = 100$. Which firm can be expected to submit the lower required-profit bid? Will the efficient firm be selected?

11. Firm S plans to sell an office building via an English auction. The firm expects two buyers to bid, each with a value uniformly distributed between \$300,000 and \$360,000. In addition, firm S knows it can sell the building to a third outside buyer for \$300,000 if the auction does not produce a better price.

    a. Suppose firm S sets the auction reserve price at $P_{min} = \$300,000$. Show that the expected price in the English auction is \$320,000.

    b. Suppose instead that firm S sets $P_{min} = \$330,000$. What is the chance that neither buyer will meet this price? What is the chance that exactly one buyer will meet this price? What is the chance that both buyer values exceed this price? Conditional on both values being above \$330,000, what will be the expected price in the English auction?

    c. Averaging over the three possibilities in part b (by the appropriate probabilities), compute the seller's expected revenue. Confirm that it is to the seller's advantage to set the higher reserve price.

12. Three buyers, firms X, Y, and Z, are bidding for two items F and G. The bidders' (nonadditive) values for the items are as follows.

	Items		
	F	G	FG
Firm X	3	3	12
Firm Y	6	1	8
Firm Z	1	4	7

Each firm knows its own values but has only a probabilistic assessment of its rivals' possible values.

    a. Suppose there is an English auction for F and then an English auction for G. Why might firm X be willing to bid above its value for F (say, to a level of 5)? Explain the dilemma firm X faces in bidding for F. Given the values in the table, is the final bidding outcome likely to be efficient?

    b. Now suppose there is a third English auction for the combination FG. (The items are sold as a bundle if the high bid for FG exceeds the sum of the separate bids for F and G.) Will this lead to a new, improved bidding outcome? Now suppose firm Z's value for G is 8 (instead of 4) and its value for FG is 9. How might a "free-rider" problem lead to an inefficient bundled sale?

c. In a modified Vickrey auction, bidders report values for all items and combinations of items; items are allocated to maximize total value; and each winning bidder pays a price equal to *the forgone value its bid imposes on the other buyers*. Here firm X wins bundle FG (the value-maximizing allocation) and pays $6 + 4 = 10$ (the sum of the forgone values of the other buyers). (i) Explain why each buyer's dominant strategy is to report truthful values. (ii) Again suppose firm Z's value for G is 8 (instead of 4). What allocation and what payments occur in the Vickrey procedure?

Discussion Question New issues of U.S. Treasury bills are sold at auction. The government decides on the total quantity of bills to be sold and seeks to pay the lowest possible interest rates on these bills. Private parties submit sealed bids specifying the quantity of bills sought and the interest rate they require. A purchaser is allowed to submit multiple bids for different quantities at different interest rates. (A purchaser also can place a "noncompetitive" or "market" bid that is filled at the *average* interest rate as determined by the auction.)

a. Explain why the ability to submit multiple bids is valuable to buyers. How should purchasers determine their interest-rate bids?
b. How should the government select winning bids in the bill auction?
c. Suppose rules of the auction called for the government to pay all winning bidders the same interest rate—a rate equal to the highest accepted bid. How would this rule change affect bidding behavior? How might it affect the average interest rate the government pays?

Spreadsheet Problem

S1. The histogram of best (i.e., lowest) competing bids in Table 2 of Problem 5 mirrors closely a normal distribution with a mean of 60 and a standard deviation of 30. Create a spreadsheet modeled on the sample given to find the firm's optimal bid markup. In the sample spreadsheet, note that a bid at a 60 percent markup has a .5 chance of winning and implies an expected profit of $(.5)(60) = 30$.

a. First, experiment with other markups in your search for maximum expected profit.
b. Use your spreadsheet's optimizer to find the optimal markup.
c. Find the firm's optimal markups if the BCB distribution has a (less favorable) mean of 40 or if it has a (more favorable) mean of 80. (*Hint*: Cells F7 to F10 should be computed utilizing the normal distribution function included with your spreadsheet. This function typically takes the form:

Normal(value, mean, standard deviation).

Thus, you can simply change the value of the mean in cell C5 to 40 or 80 and reoptimize the problem.)

	A	B	C	D	E	F	G	H
1								
2					**OPTIMAL STRATEGY WHEN BCB**			
3					**IS NORMALLY DISTRIBUTED**			
4								
5		Mean =	60		Markup	Pr(win)	E(Profit)	
6		St Dev =	30					
7					20	0.9088	18.176	
8					40	0.7475	29.900	
9					60	0.5000	30.000	
10					80	0.2525	20.199	
11								
12								

Suggested References

The following selections survey and compare different auction institutions.

Klemperer, P. *Auctions: Theory and Practice.* Princeton, NJ: Princeton University Press, 2004.

Milgrom, P. *Putting Auction Theory to Work.* Oxford: Oxford University Press, 2004.

Samuelson, W. "Auctions in Theory and Practice." Chapter 10 in K. Chatterjee and W. Samuelson (Eds.), *Game Theory and Business Applications.* Boston: Kluwer Academic Publishers, 2001.

"Symposium on Auctions." *Journal of Economic Perspectives* (Summer 1989): 3–50.

The following articles review the rich body of experimental evidence on bidder behavior and auction performance.

Kagel, J. H. "Auctions: A Survey of Experimental Research." in J. H. Kagel and A. E. Roth (Eds.), *The Handbook of Experimental Economics*, Princeton, NJ: Princeton University Press, 1995.

Lucking-Reiley, D. "Using Field Experiments to Test Equivalence Between Auction Formats: Magic on the Internet." *American Economic Review* (1999): 1063–1080.

Thaler, R. H. "The Winner's Curse." *Journal of Economic Perspectives* (Winter 1988): 191–202.

The next group of readings uses game theory and other advanced methods to characterize the equilibrium outcomes of auctions. (These articles presume a high degree of mathematical sophistication.)

Klemperer, P. *The Economic Theory of Auctions.* Cheltenham, UK: Edward Elgar, 1999.

McAfee, R. P., and J. McMillan. "Auctions and Bidding." *Journal of Economic Literature* (1987): 699–738.

Milgrom, P., and R. Weber. "The Theory of Auctions." *Econometrica* (1982): 1089–1122.

Riley, J. G., and W. Samuelson. "Optimal Auctions." *American Economic Review* (1981): 381–392.

Vickrey, W. "Counterspeculation, Auctions, and Competitive Sealed Tenders." *Journal of Finance* (1961): 8–37.

The following articles discuss real-world auction applications.

Bajari, P., and A. Hortacsu. "Economic Insights from Internet Auctions." *Journal of Economic Literature* 42 (2004): 457–486.

Symposium on the Spectrum Auctions. *Journal of Economics and Management Strategy* 6 (1997): 431–675.

McAfee, R. P., and J. McMillan. "Analyzing the Airwaves Auctions." *Journal of Economic Perspectives* (Spring 1996): 159–176.

Bikhchandani, S., and C. Huang. "The Economics of Treasury Security Markets." *Journal of Economic Perspectives* (Summer 1993): 117–134.

Hansen, R. G. "Sealed Bid versus Open Auctions: The Empirical Evidence." *Economic Inquiry* (1986): 125–142.

Auction sites on the Internet include:
www.ebay.com,
www.paulklemperer.org/index.htm (auction resources gathered by Professor Paul Klemperer)
www.webcom.com/agorics/auctions/auction1.html *(a valuable discussion of all kinds of auctions).*

CHECK STATION ANSWERS

1. Selecting the better of two offers is always advantageous relative to precommitting to one offer or the other. There is a .5 chance that firm B will beat firm A's $24 price. Firm B's expected price, conditional on it being greater than $24, is $(24 + 28)/2 = \$26$. Thus, firm S's overall average price is $(.5)(24) + (.5)(26) = \$25$.

2. Against one bidder, $20,000 is optimal; the expected profit is $(.6)(10,000) = \$6,000$. Against two bidders, $24,000 is optimal; the expected profit is $(.8)^2(6,000) = \$3,840$. Against three bidders, $24,000 is still optimal; the expected profit is $(.8)^3(6,000) = \$3,072$.

3. i) Given $b_2 = .6v_2$, firm 2's bids are uniformly distributed between 0 and 30. Thus, buyer 1's expected profit is $E(\pi) = (v_1 - b)(b/30)$. Setting $dE(\pi)/db = 0$ implies $(v_1 - 2b)/30 = 0$, or $b_1 = .5v_1$. ii) For $b_2 = .4v_2$, we have $E(\pi) = (v_1 - b)(b/20)$ and $dE(\pi)/db = (v_1 - 2b)/20$. Again, firm 2 should bid $b_1 = .5v_1$ for $v_1 \leq 40$. For all $v_1 > 40$, the firm should bid 20, just outbidding the highest possible bid of firm 2. In sum, firm 1's equilibrium bidding does very well (is nearly optimal), even if the competitor pursues nonequilibrium bidding strategies.

4. The less well-informed buyer must be wary of the winner's curse. Any time that the buyer wins the bidding, it must be because the better-informed rival has made a lower bid knowing that the item's value is low. The disadvantaged buyer only wins low-value items and tends to overpay for them. It is best to stay out of the auction altogether.

5. The expected price at the English auction is $(.4)(0) + (.6)(100) = \$60$. In the sealed-bid auction, bids are $b_i = [(n - 1)/n]v_i = .75v_i$. Thus, $E(b_{max}) = .75E(v_{max})$, since the buyer with the highest value makes the highest bid. From Equation 17.5, $E(v_{max}) = [n/(n + 1)]100 = 80$. Therefore, $E(b_{max}) = (.75)(80) = \$60$. The auctions deliver the same expected revenue.

CHAPTER 18

Linear Programming

Management is the art of doing the best one can within constraints and occasionally getting around them.

ANONYMOUS

An Investment Problem

A portfolio manager has $20 million to invest in a fund consisting of the following bonds:

Bond Category	Quality Rating	Maturity (Years)	Yield (Percent)
Treasury bills	5	.4	4.0
Treasury bonds	5	4.0	6.0
Corporate bonds	3.5	3.2	4.4
Municipal bonds	3	2.0	5.6
Junk bonds	1	2.5	8.0

He has listed the bonds in descending order of quality rating (treasury securities carry the lowest risk, junk bonds are most risky). The second column lists average maturity (in years) for each category. The final column shows the expected return or yield (in percent per year, after tax) for each bond. Junk bonds have the greatest expected return, followed by treasury bonds.

> The manager intends to create a bond fund by investing proportions of the $20 million in the different securities and has announced an investment goal of a high-quality, medium-maturity portfolio. In particular, the fund's average quality rating should be at least 3.5 and its average maturity should be no shorter than 1.5 years and no longer than 2.5 years.
>
> The portfolio manager seeks to create a bond fund that offers the highest expected return subject to the quality and maturity requirements given. To accomplish this goal, what proportion of the $20 million should he invest in each bond?

In the investment problem, the analyst seeks to maximize the portfolio return subject to various constraints. Constrained optimization problems of this sort form the core of a distinct managerial field known as operations research (O.R.). Indeed, we all enjoy the benefits of operations research applications in our everyday lives although we may not know it. Suppose you decide to take your family to Disney World:[1]

> Operations research will be your invisible companion, scheduling the crews and aircraft, pricing the plane tickets and hotel rooms, even helping to design capacities on the theme park rides. If you use Orbitz to book your flights, an O.R. engine sifts among millions of options to find the cheapest fares. If you get directions from MapQuest, another O.R. engine spits out the most direct route. If you ship souvenirs home, O.R. tells UPS which truck to put the packages on, exactly where on the truck the packages should go to make them fastest to load and unload, and what route the driver should follow to make his deliveries efficiently.

All of these operations involve maximizing or minimizing subject to constraints. The most basic and important tool of operations research is linear programming. **Linear programming (LP)** is a method of formulating and solving decision problems that involve explicit resource constraints. Analysts use the LP method to solve problems such as the investment problem and a host of other decision questions: How should a firm allocate its advertising expenditure among various media? What quantities of two jointly manufactured goods should a firm produce with a fixed amount of labor and inputs? How should a federal agency allocate its limited budget between two competing safety programs? What quantities of output should a consumer-products firm transport from each of its factories to each of its retail outlets to minimize transportation cost?

What do these problems have in common? First, all seek to find the best values of certain variables: the right advertising mix, the most profitable product quantities, the appropriate budget allocation. These values, which the decision

---

[1] This account comes from V. Postrel, "Operation Everything," *The Boston Globe* (June 27, 2004): D1.

maker controls, are **decision variables**. Second, each decision has an explicit objective, be it maximum profit, minimum cost, or maximum number of lives saved. Third, constraints limit the possible values of the decision variables. For example, limited labor supply may constrain the quantity of output. Similarly, the federal agency cannot spend more than its available budget, and the consumer-products firm must supply the quantities to its retail outlets subject to its factories' production capacities. Thus, in each case, the heart of the problem is finding (calculating) values for the decision variables that best meet the given objective while satisfying various constraints.

With respect to the first two features, decision variables and objectives, the LP method resembles the optimization methods we have encountered already. Like the pricing and output decisions of Chapters 2 and 3, LP decisions rely on marginal analysis (of a special kind) for their solution. Unlike those decisions, however, LP problems incorporate explicit resource constraints. The interplay of these constraints creates new and interesting economic trade-offs.

In this chapter, we take a systematic approach to managerial decisions involving economic constraints. First, we describe a number of constrained decision problems and show how they can be formulated and solved mathematically as linear programs. Next, we examine the important concept of shadow prices for resources. Then we introduce more complex linear programming decisions and illustrate the kinds of solutions furnished by computer programs. In the appendix to this chapter, we explore the simplex algorithm, which many computer programs use to solve linear programs.

LINEAR PROGRAMS

We can analyze a host of managerial decisions using linear programming. Here is a representative example:

FINDING AN OPTIMAL COMPUTER MIX   Consider a personal computer (PC) manufacturer that produces two versions of its popular desktop computer. The standard version has a high-capacity (80-gigabyte) hard disk, a conventional disk drive, and a rewritable DVD drive. The economy version, which sells at a lower price, has a 40-gigabyte hard drive and a conventional rewritable CD drive. The prices, variable costs, and contributions of the models are shown in the table.

	Standard PC	Economy PC
Price	$1,600	$1,000
Variable cost	1,100	700
Contribution	500	300

The firm has ample components (such as monitors and keyboards) from which to assemble PCs but a limited capacity (given available factory space and necessary equipment) for producing DVD drives and hard-disk drives. The firm's maximum weekly outputs are 200 DVD drives and 20,000 gigabytes of hard-drive capacity. The firm can split its hard-drive capacity in any way between the two models. For instance, it could devote all of its hard-drive capacity to 250 standard models or, alternatively, to 500 economy models. Or it could produce other combinations—for instance, 200 standard models and 100 economy models.

In addition, the firm assembles computers using a 50-person labor force that supplies 2,000 hours of labor per week. The two models require roughly equal assembly time—an average of five labor-hours each. How many computers of each type should the firm produce to maximize its profit? Answering this question requires two steps: (1) formulating the firm's decision as a linear program—a set of mathematical equations that precisely describes the firm's available options, and (2) solving these mathematical equations.

The formulation stage begins with the identification of the relevant decision variables. The firm must determine two key quantities: the number of standard models (S) and the number of economy models (E). The firm seeks to maximize the total contribution (π) it obtains from these products. We can express this contribution algebraically as

$$\pi = 500S + 300E. \qquad \text{[OF]}$$

The goal to be maximized—in this instance, total contribution—is the **objective function (OF)**.

Next we identify the production constraints. The company cannot produce an unlimited number of computers. It faces three principal constraints. First, the firm can produce only 200 DVD drives a week. This means that, at most, it can produce 200 standard models. Also, it can produce a maximum of 20,000 gigabytes of hard drives. Finally, the firm has only 2,000 hours of labor to devote to production of PCs. The algebraic representations of these constraints are:

$$S \leq 200 \qquad \text{[D]}$$
$$80S + 40E \leq 20,000 \qquad \text{[H]}$$
$$5S + 5E \leq 2,000. \qquad \text{[L]}$$

As the labels in brackets indicate, the inequalities correspond to the DVD drive, hard-disk drive, and labor constraints, respectively. The right-hand side of each inequality lists the total capacity (or supply) of the particular input. The left-hand side shows the total amount used of each resource if the firm produces quantities S and E of the models. For instance, producing S standard models requires S number of DVD drives—one drive per machine. Thus, according to the first constraint, DVD capacity limits the weekly output of standard models to 200.

Next consider the hard-disk constraint. Production of the models in the quantities S and E together requires 80S + 40E gigabytes of hard-disk capacity. For instance, producing 100 of each model per week would require a total of (80)(100) + (40)(100) = 12,000 gigabytes of capacity, which is safely within the 20,000 gigabytes available. Finally, consider the labor constraint. Here the firm uses a total of 5S + 5E hours of labor. The total amount of labor cannot exceed 2,000.

The complete mathematical description of the problem consists of the objective function (to be maximized), the three resource constraints, and two nonnegativity constraints, S ≥ 0 and E ≥ 0. These last two constraints simply reflect the impossibility of producing negative quantities. Although obvious (even trivial) to the decision maker, we must include them to get the right answer. (Computer programs don't have the same intuition as managers.)

We now have a fully formed linear program. What makes it linear? All of the expressions, for both the objective function and the constraints, are linear. In a linear expression, we can multiply the variable by a constant, we can add or subtract these multiplied variables, and we can add a constant to the expression. But this is all; we cannot multiply two variables together, we cannot raise variables to powers, we cannot take square roots of variables, or anything else. Roughly speaking, the linearity assumption requires that the key quantities in the actual managerial problem—revenues, costs, and profits—vary proportionally with changes in the firm's decision variables. For instance, if the firm can sell its product at fixed prices, its revenue is proportional to output, thus satisfying linearity. However, if the firm faces a downward-sloping demand curve (the usual circumstance in Chapters 2 and 3), revenue is a nonlinear function of output; that is, the revenue graph is curved. The linear programming method cannot handle this case. (Instead, we can use a related method, nonlinear programming.)

Graphing the LP Problem

We can solve small-scale linear programs, like the PC example, using graphical methods. This approach provides the numerical solution and also offers insight as to the factors that determine the optimal decision. The method consists of the following steps.

1. Construct a graph, placing a decision variable on each axis.
2. Graph each constraint as though it were binding, that is, as if it held with strict equality.
3. Find the feasible region, the area of the graph that simultaneously satisfies all constraints.
4. Superimpose contours of the objective function on the feasible region to determine the optimal corner of the region.

5. Solve the appropriate equations of the LP problem to determine the optimal values of the decision variables at the corner solution.

Let's apply this procedure to solve the computer company's production problem. Figure 18.1 plots the firm's decision variables, S and E, on the horizontal and vertical axes, respectively, and plots the three resource constraints as straight lines. The area OABCD represents the "feasible region" of all *possible* combinations of the two computer models. For each resource, the constraint line in the graph depicts model combinations that use up exactly the available resource. Any point lying to the right of any of the resource constraint lines represents quantities that the firm cannot produce. For example, if the point lies to the right of the DVD constraint, it represents an output combination that requires more than 200 DVD drives. Any point to the left of this line requires fewer than 200 drives. In turn, the equation $80S + 40E = 20,000$ describes the

FIGURE 18.1

Production Constraints for a PC Manufacturer

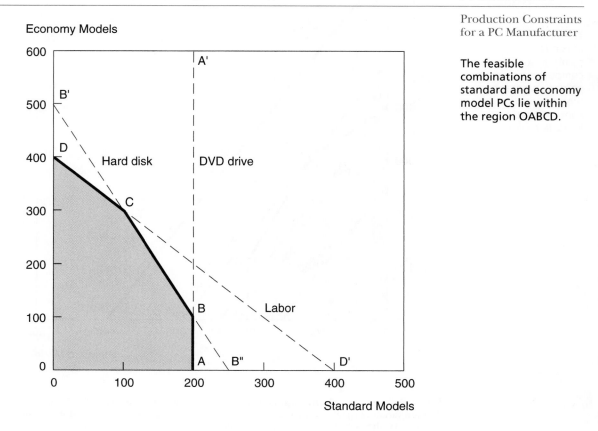

The feasible combinations of standard and economy model PCs lie within the region OABCD.

binding hard-disk constraint and appears on the graph as the line B′B″.[2] Finally, the binding labor constraint is given by the equation $5S + 5E = 2,000$ and is graphed as DD′. The firm's feasible region of production consists of S and E combinations that simultaneously satisfy all three constraints: the shaded area bounded by OABCD.

The company still has to determine the output combination (the point in the feasible region) that maximizes total contribution. To find this point, we draw in contribution contours—lines indicating combinations of S and E that yield a fixed value of contribution. For instance, we can graph the contour corresponding to a contribution of $75,000 by using the equation $500S + 300E = 75,000$. This contour is shown in Figure 18.2. (Check this by

FIGURE 18.2

Production Constraints with Contribution Contours

The firm's profit-maximizing combination of computers occurs at point C, where the highest contribution contour touches the feasible region.

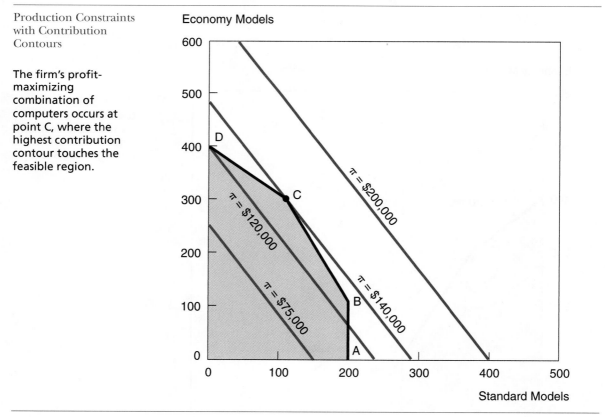

[2] The easiest way to graph any constraint line is to pinpoint its two intercepts; that is, set one of the decision variables equal to zero and solve for the other. Doing this for the hard-disk equation, we find E = 0 with S = 250 and, in turn, S = 0 with E = 500. Thus, the horizontal intercept is 250 (at B″) and the vertical intercept is 500 (at B′).

noting that the horizontal intercept is S = 150, since the firm can earn $75,000 by producing only standard models. In turn, the vertical intercept is E = 250.) Figure 18.2 also depicts contours corresponding to contributions of $120,000, $140,000, and $200,000. Note that increasing the contribution causes a parallel (northeast) shift in the contour. Obviously, larger production quantities are necessary to generate the greater contribution. Note, however, that the contour slopes do not change because the ratio of contributions is always $500 to $300.

The optimal solution is found at the corner of the feasible region that touches the highest contribution contour. In Figure 18.2, this occurs at point C. Here the contour corresponding to $140,000 contribution just touches the feasible region. As the figure shows, this is the best the firm can do. The firm can consider other feasible production plans, but any such plan lies on a lower contribution contour. For instance, point B's plan (200 standard models and 100 economy models) produces only $130,000 in contribution (i.e., lies on a lower contour). At point D the firm earns even less. However, "pie in the sky" production plans are irrelevant. The firm cannot attain a higher contribution—say, $200,000— because such a contour lies wholly outside the feasible region.

We can reinforce the visual solution to the LP problem by using marginal analysis. Suppose the firm takes point D as a candidate for its optimal production plan. Using marginal analysis, the firm asks whether it could increase its contribution by moving to some other point on the edge of the feasible region. Suppose it considers moving in the direction of C, producing more standard models and fewer economy models. (Note that segment DC portrays the binding labor constraint.) To produce an extra standard model requires five additional hours of labor; with all labor utilized, this means producing one fewer economy model (which frees up five labor-hours). Would such a move improve the firm's profit? It certainly would! The net increase in contribution is $200. (The gain is $500 in contribution for the extra standard unit minus $300 in lost contribution from the economy unit that is no longer produced.)[3] Thus, the firm should make the one-unit switch. But, having switched one unit, it can increase its profit by switching a second unit (by exactly the same logic). It can continue to increase its profit by moving along segment DC until it attains the production plan corresponding to point C. Here it can no longer improve its profit because it runs up against the hard-disk capacity constraint. Having exploited all its options for increasing its profit, the firm has arrived at its optimal product mix.[4]

---

[3] In algebraic terms, the change in profit is $\Delta\pi = 500\Delta S + 300\Delta E$. But, along the binding labor constraint, $5S + 5E = 2,000$. Thus, it follows that the trade-off between changes in S and E is given by $5\Delta S + 5\Delta E = 0$, or, equivalently, $\Delta E = -\Delta S$; that is, producing one more S ($\Delta S = 1$) means producing one less E ($\Delta E = -1$). Thus, we can write the change in profit as $\Delta\pi = 500\Delta S + 300(-\Delta S) = 200\Delta S$, after substituting for ΔE. The firm increases its profit by increasing S and reducing E.

[4] Check for yourself that, starting from point B, the firm also profits by moving toward point C. How much does contribution increase if it produces an extra economy unit?

What are the precise model quantities at point C? Since point C lies on the constraint lines corresponding to hard disks and labor, we know that these constraints are binding; that is, the optimal mix uses up all available hard-disk capacity and labor. Thus, S and E satisfy the constraints, $80S + 40E = 20,000$ and $5S + 5E = 2,000$. Solving these two equations in two unknowns, we find that $S = 100$ and $E = 300$. Total contribution is $\pi = (500)(100) + (300)(300) = \$140,000$ after inserting the optimal quantities into the objective function.

CHECK STATION 1   A farmer raises two crops, wheat and barley. Wheat sells at $1.60 per bushel and barley at $1.00 per bushel. The production of each crop requires land and labor in differing amounts. Each 1,000 bushels of wheat requires one acre of farmland and four labor-hours per week. An equal quantity of barley also requires one acre but requires only two hours of labor per week. The farmer has ten acres of land and an average of 32 hours of labor per week to devote to wheat and barley production. How much of each crop should the farmer produce? In your answer, formulate and graph the appropriate LP problem.

A Minimization Problem

The production problem the PC company faces is typical of a large class of profit-maximization problems. A second important class of decisions involves cost minimization. The next example illustrates the point.

REGULATION AT LEAST COST   An environmental regulatory agency is launching a program to reduce water pollution in one of the region's major rivers. As a first step, it has set standards for two key measures of water quality. It seeks (1) to increase the level of dissolved oxygen (essential to fish and other life in the estuary) by 6 milligrams (mg) per liter and (2) to reduce the concentrations of chlorides by 70 mg per liter. Its aim is to meet both these standards at minimum cost by allocating funds between two programs.

- Program 1: Direct treatment of effluents. Each $1 million spent in this program will increase dissolved oxygen by 3 mg/liter and reduce chlorides by 10 mg/liter.

- Program 2: Flow regulation. Each $1 million spent in this program will increase dissolved oxygen by 1 mg/liter and reduce chlorides by 20 mg/liter.

How much should the agency spend on one or both programs to meet its goals?

Let's formulate and solve the agency's problem. As always, we begin by identifying the decision variables. Here the agency must choose how much to spend on direct treatment and how much to spend on flow regulation. We label the spending (in millions of dollars) on the respective programs by D and F. The agency seeks to minimize the total cost (C) of the programs, subject to meeting its goals.

$$\text{Minimize: C = D + F.} \qquad\qquad \text{[OF]}$$

The goals it must meet can be expressed by the following inequalities.

$$\text{Subject to: } 3D + F \geq 6 \qquad\qquad \text{[O]}$$
$$10D + 20F \geq 70. \qquad\qquad \text{[C]}$$

The first inequality reflects the fact that the programs together must increase oxygen by 6 mg/liter. The right-hand side lists this minimum requirement. The left-hand side shows the total amount of oxygen generated by the programs. For instance, spending $2 million on each program (D = F = 2) would increase oxygen by $(3)(2) + 2 = 8$ mg/liter, which would more than meet the goal. In turn, the left-hand side of the second constraint shows the reduction in chlorine: 10 mg per million spent on the first program plus 20 mg per million on the second. The nonnegativity constraints, $D \geq 0$ and $F \geq 0$, complete the formulation.

Figure 18.3 shows the graph of the feasible region. The main point to observe is the impact of the "greater than or equal to" constraints. The feasible region lies above the two-sided boundary AZB. (Make sure you understand that the constraint lines are properly graphed. Check the intercepts!) Obviously, large values of F and D (i.e., greater spending on the programs) will make it easier to meet the dual improvement goals, but the point is to do it at *minimum* cost. When it comes to cost contours, the object is to get to the lowest one (i.e., the one farthest to the southwest) while meeting both goals. Figure 18.3 shows the relevant part of the "least-cost" contour. Note that it touches the feasible region at point Z, the corner formed by the binding oxygen and chlorine constraints. The precise amounts to spend on each program are found by solving the equations $3D + F = 6$ and $10D + 20F = 70$. The solution $D = 1$ and $F = 3$ is the result.[5] In short, $1 million and $3 million should be spent on the respective programs. The least-cost total outlay is $4 million.

ALGEBRAIC SOLUTIONS   The mathematics for solving small-scale linear programs involves two main steps: (1) identifying the correct set of simultaneous equations and (2) solving these equations for the optimal values of the decision variables. In the preceding example we used simple graphics to solve the first step. (Caution: We cannot simply assume certain constraints will be binding

---

[5] Recall that there are two equivalent ways to solve simultaneous equations. The first method is by *substitution*. For instance, in the regulator's problem, we transform the equation $3D + F = 6$ to the form $F = 6 - 3D$. Then we insert this expression for F into the second equation, $10D + 20F = 70$. We are left with one equation in one unknown: $10D + 20(6 - 3D) = 70$. The solution is $D = 1$. Putting this value back into the first equation, we find $F = 6 - (3)(1) = 3$. The second method is by *elimination*. It is easiest to eliminate F by multiplying both sides of the first equation by 20 to obtain $60D + 20F = 120$. Then we subtract the second equation from this expression. Note that 20F in each equation cancels out, leaving $60D - 10D = 120 - 70$; this implies $D = 1$ and $F = 3$. Either method works equally well.

FIGURE 18.3

Clean-Water Funding

At point Z, $1 million is spent on program D and $3 million on program F. This plan meets the oxygen and chloride constraints at minimum total cost.

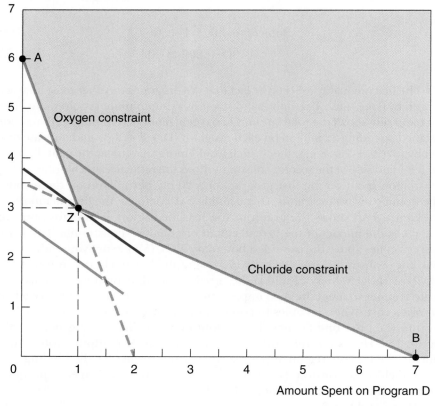

Amount Spent on Program F

Oxygen constraint

Chloride constraint

Amount Spent on Program D

and go ahead and solve them. In the computer example, there are five inequalities, including the nonnegativity constraints, only two of which are binding equalities in the optimal solution. Without a graph or other analysis, which two constraints will be binding is a pure guess.)

Once you understand the general points of the graphical method, you may be interested in a quick way of finding the optimal corner. The method relies on a comparison of slopes:

> The optimal corner is formed by the constraints whose slopes most closely bracket the slope of the objective function.

To apply this rule, we simply note the slope of each constraint from the graph. In the computer problem, the slopes of the labor constraint, hard-disk constraint, and DVD constraint are -1, -2, and $-\infty$, respectively. The slope of the contribution contour is $-5/3$, and this falls between the first two slopes. Accordingly, the optimal output in Figure 18.2 occurs at point C, where the hard-disk and labor constraints are binding. Similarly, in the regulator's problem (Figure 18.3), point Z is optimal because the slope of the cost contour (-1) falls between the slope of the oxygen constraint (-3) and the chlorine constraint ($-1/2$).

FORMULATION ISSUES   In some cases, LP problems have no solution or the solution is unbounded. Consider the following formulation:

$$\text{Maximize: } 3x + y$$
$$\text{Subject to: } x + 2y \leq 12$$
$$x + y \geq 15.$$

The difficulty here lies in the constraints. It is impossible to find values of the decision variables that simultaneously satisfy both inequalities. (Graph the constraints to confirm this.) In short, the problem itself is infeasible. It lacks a feasible region and, therefore, has no possibility of an optimal solution.[6]

A different formulation difficulty arises if we make a slight modification in the preceding example. Suppose that the variable y is omitted in the first constraint so that the inequality reads $x \leq 12$. The new problem has a feasible region—in fact, too large a region. The feasible region consists of all points to the left of the vertical line $x = 12$ and above the downward-sloping line $x + y = 15$. Now the feasible region is unbounded; it extends vertically indefinitely. Clearly, we can make the value of the objective function as large as we like by making y as large as possible—all the while keeping x below 12. This linear program has an unbounded solution, which tells us that we have poorly formulated the problem. After all, in the real world, no firm has the opportunity to make an infinite profit. Somehow we have omitted the real constraints that limit the firm's profitability.

SENSITIVITY ANALYSIS AND SHADOW PRICES

The solution of the basic linear program provides management with its optimal decision. The solution is also the starting point for considering a range of related decisions and what-if questions. For instance, managers of

---

[6] This kind of infeasibility can arise quite naturally. In this problem, for instance, let the decision variables denote the quantity of two products. Total production is limited due to fixed capacity (the first constraint). At the same time, the firm has contracted to deliver a minimum of 15 total units to a buyer (the second constraint). Here there is no solution because the firm has contracted to deliver more than it possibly can supply.

the computer firm recognize that changing market prices are a fact of life in the PC industry. How might the firm change its production mix in response to changes in product prices? As a second example, the firm might consider increasing (at a cost) one or more of its production capacities (e.g., labor or hard-drive capacity). How much would such an increase in capacity be worth, and would it be worth the cost?

Sensitivity analysis is important in almost all decision contexts but especially so in linear programming problems. As we shall see, analysts use computers to solve almost all medium- and large-scale LP problems. Standard computer output provides not only the numerical solution to the problem in question but also a wide variety of sensitivity analyses. Thus, a solid understanding of sensitivity analysis is essential in order to take full advantage of the power of linear programming.

Changes in the Objective Function

It is natural to ask how changes in the coefficients of the objective function affect the optimal decision. In the computer firm's production problem, for instance, the current contributions are $500 and $300 per unit of each model type. Obviously, if market prices or variable unit costs change, so will the contributions. How would such changes affect the firm's optimal production mix?

As a concrete example, suppose the firm anticipates that the current industry price of $1,000 for an economy model will fall to $900 in the coming months. Thus, the firm expects that contribution per unit of the economy model will fall to $900 - 700 = \$200$ as a result. Assuming an unchanged contribution for model S, the firm's new objective function is

$$\pi = 500S + 200E.$$

With the sizable drop in E's contribution per unit, intuition suggests that the firm should reduce the output of E and increase the output of S. Figure 18.4 indicates that this is indeed the case. It shows the same feasible region as Figure 18.2, but the slopes of the contribution contours change. In Figure 18.4, the highest contribution contour touches the feasible region at point B, where the hard disk and DVD constraints are binding. (The slope of the new contribution contour is $-500/200 = -2.5$, and this falls between the slopes of these two constraint lines, -2 and $-\infty$.) We find the values of the decision variables at optimal corner B by solving the equations $S = 200$ and $2S + E = 500$. The optimal values are $S = 200$ and $E = 100$, and maximum contribution is $120,000. In contrast, if the firm were to maintain its old production mix, $S = 100$ and $E = 300$ (at point C), it would earn a contribution of only $110,000. To sum up, the firm should respond to the fall in economy model contribution by shifting to a greater quantity of standard models.

FIGURE 18.4

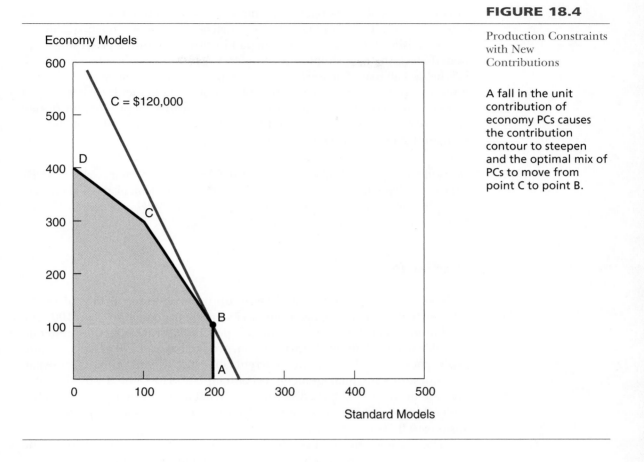

Economy Models

Production Constraints
with New
Contributions

A fall in the unit
contribution of
economy PCs causes
the contribution
contour to steepen
and the optimal mix of
PCs to move from
point C to point B.

Standard Models

A general conclusion emerges from this example: The optimal production plan depends on the *relative* contributions of the two models. To see this, write the objective function in the form $\pi_S S + \pi_E E$, where π_S and π_E denote the contribution per unit for the respective models. The slope of the contribution contour is $\Delta E/\Delta S = -\pi_S/\pi_E$. Depending on the ratio of model contributions, one of the following three plans is optimal:

Point B (S = 200, E = 100) provided $-\infty < -\pi_S/\pi_E \le -2$

Point C (S = 100, E = 300) provided $-2 \le -\pi_S/\pi_E \le -1$

Point D (S = 0, E = 400)   provided $-1 \le -\pi_S/\pi_E \le 0$

Note that a small change in the contribution ratio has no effect on the optimal plan so long as the requisite inequality continues to hold. For instance, if the price cut is to $960 (only 4 percent), the new contribution ratio will be 500/260. Production plan C will continue to be optimal because the second inequality still will be satisfied. (Of course, with the fall in price, the firm's profit will drop; nonetheless, the firm should stick to plan C.) If the contribution of model E falls below half that of model S, production plan B will become optimal.[7] Finally, if the contribution of E exceeds that of S, producing model E exclusively will produce the most total contribution. In other words, as production of one model becomes relatively less and less profitable, the optimal plan shifts to increasing amounts of the other model.

CHECK STATION 2   How will the farmer's mix of crops be affected if the price of wheat increases to $2.25? If it falls to $.90? What if both crop prices fall by 15 percent? How high would the ratio P_W/P_B have to be to induce the farmer to produce only wheat? How low would the ratio have to be for him to produce only barley?

Shadow Prices

Let's return to the original version of the computer firm's problem. Management is operating according to its optimal production plan: 100 standard models and 300 economy models per week, which together generate $140,000 in contribution. At this solution, production uses 100 percent of hard-disk capacity and all of the firm's current labor supply. This prompts some natural questions for management to contemplate: How much would profits increase by increasing hard-disk capacity? What about by increasing the labor force? As we shall see, the notion of shadow prices for resources provides the answers to these questions.

The **shadow price** of a resource measures the change in the value of the objective function associated with a unit change in the resource. To illustrate, let's compute the shadow price associated with hard-disk capacity. Suppose the firm increases this capacity from 20,000 to 22,000. Figure 18.5 shows the capacity increase as a rightward shift in the hard-disk constraint line. With the increase in capacity, point C moves to the southeast. Nonetheless, the newly positioned point C remains the optimal corner; that is, the firm should continue to utilize all of its disk capacity and labor. The hard-disk and labor constraints are $80S + 40E \leq 22,000$ and $5S + 5E \leq 2,000$, respectively. Solving these as binding constraints, we find the optimal production plan to be $S = 150$ and $E = 250$. The firm's new contribution is $(500)(150) + (300)(250) = \$150,000$. The 2,000-unit increase in disk capacity has resulted in a $10,000 profit increase. Thus, the shadow price of an extra unit of capacity is $10,000/2,000 = \$5$.

---

[7] If the slope of the objective function contour happens to be identical to the slope of a given constraint, any production point along the constraint is optimal. For instance, if $-\pi_S/\pi_E = -2$, maximum total contribution is attained at points B and C and any other point along segment BC.

FIGURE 18.5

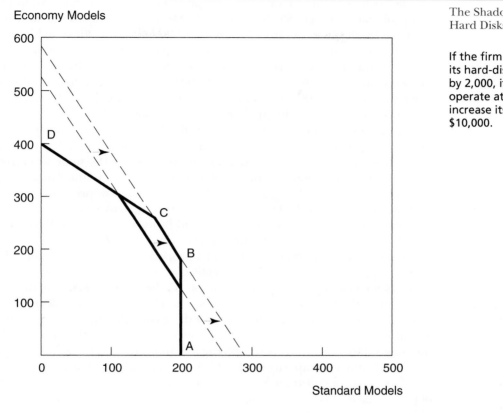

Economy Models

If the firm can increase
its hard-disk capacity
by 2,000, it will
operate at point C and
increase its profit by
$10,000.

Standard Models

To find the shadow price associated with additional hours of labor, we set
up an analogous calculation. Suppose the firm expands its labor force to 2,100
hours per week. The binding constraint equations are now $5S + 5E = 2,100$
and $80S + 40E = 20,000$. Thus, the optimal production plan is $S = 80$ and
$E = 340$. The new contribution is $(500)(80) + (300)(340) = \$142,000$. The
addition of 100 labor-hours per week increases contribution by $2,000.
(Remember, the old contribution was $140,000.) Therefore, the shadow price
of labor (per hour) is $2,000/100 = \$20$.

Each individual resource constraint has a shadow price. Each shadow price
measures the change in the objective function from a change in that resource *alone*,
that is, with the amounts of all other resources held constant. As is usual in sensitivity analyses, we trace the impact of one effect at a time. Also, *each shadow price is constant so long as the same constraints are binding in the optimal solution.* This price
measures both the benefit of added capacity and the cost of reduced capacity. For
instance, we saw that a 2,000-unit increase in hard-disk capacity raised profit by

$10,000 (implying a shadow price of $5). By the same token, we can confirm that having 3,000 extra units of capacity raises profit by $15,000, whereas having 1,000 extra units raises profit by $5,000. In fact, a 2,000-unit drop in capacity (a move from 20,000 to 18,000) causes a $10,000 fall in contribution (from $140,000 to $130,000). In each case, the shadow price per unit change in capacity is $5—a constant.

Now consider what happens if we expand hard-disk capacity beyond a total of 24,000 units—say, from 24,000 to 24,400 units. If we were to draw the new constraint in Figure 18.5, we would find that it lies entirely outside (i.e., to the right of) the downward-sloping labor supply constraint. Clearly, the hard-disk constraint is no longer binding. Instead, the DVD and labor constraints are binding, implying $S = 200$ and $5E + 5S = 2,000$. Thus, the optimal product mix is $S = 200$ and $E = 200$. The optimal mix remains the same when hard-disk capacity is increased beyond 24,000 or any higher amount. Any additions to capacity beyond 24,000 go unused. What is the shadow price of each extra unit of capacity beyond 24,000? Zero! The extra capacity has no effect on the feasible region, the firm's optimal plan, and its maximum profit. Because the change in profit from the extra units is zero, the shadow price is zero as well.

Thus, we have demonstrated a third property concerning shadow prices: *Any resource that is not used fully in the optimal solution (i.e., has a nonbinding constraint) has a shadow price of zero.* For example, in the original version of the problem (Figure 18.2), C is the optimal corner, where $S = 100$ and $E = 300$. Because this production plan uses only 100 DVD drives and 200 units of capacity are available, the shadow price of DVD capacity is zero. Clearly, the firm would be no worse off with less capacity (unless capacity were reduced below 100, in which case the shortage of capacity would affect the optimal production plan).

To sum up, a constraint's shadow price measures the improvement in the objective that results from relaxing the constraint or, conversely, the decline in the objective from tightening the constraint.

CHECK STATION 3   For the farmer's problem, compute the shadow prices of land and labor. How many additional hours would the farmer have to expend before the shadow price of labor fell to zero?

OPTIMAL DECISIONS AND SHADOW PRICES   Shadow prices that emerge from a linear program's optimal solution measure implicit values for the firm's limited resources. In the short run, these resources may be fixed. But in the longer run, the firm frequently can expand or contract its resources, usually at some cost. Shadow prices are essential for making these decisions. For instance, suppose the computer producer can hire extra labor at a cost of $15 per hour (wages plus fringe benefits). Should it do so? The answer is yes. The additional contribution per labor-hour is $20 (simply the shadow price for labor found earlier). Because the cost is only $15, the firm makes a net profit of $20 - 15 = \$5$ per labor-hour hired. It profitably can hire extra labor up to the point where labor's shadow price falls below $15. This occurs at a total labor supply of 2,500 labor-hours. At this point, the labor constraint becomes nonbinding (lies just outside the DVD and hard-disk constraint lines); thus, its shadow price falls to zero. Therefore, starting from 2,000 labor-hours, the firm could profit from hiring as many as 500 extra hours.

Now, suppose the firm could engage a subcontractor to provide an extra 2,000 units of hard-disk capacity *and* 100 hours of labor for a fixed fee of $18,000. Should the firm accept this deal? Again, the answer is derived directly from knowledge of the resource shadow prices. The total value to the firm of the extra capacities is simply $(2,000)(5) + (100)(20) = \$12,000$. Here the values of the separate capacity increases (using the respective shadow prices) are summed to arrive at the firm's total benefit. Because this benefit is less than the $18,000 cost, the firm should refuse the deal.

Finally, shadow prices play a crucial role in evaluating new activities. To illustrate, suppose the firm is contemplating the production and sale of a new super-turbo computer (T). Each unit of this model has an expected contribution of $700, contains a 120-gigabyte hard disk and one DVD drive, and requires 10 hours of labor. Should the firm produce this model? One way to answer this question is to formulate the new, larger LP problem as follows:

$$\text{Maximize:} \quad 500S + 300E + 700T$$

$$\text{Subject to:} \quad S + T \le 200$$
$$80S + 40E + 120T \le 20,000$$
$$5S + 5E + 10T \le 2,000.$$

Using an LP computer program to solve this problem, we find that $S = 100$, $E = 300$, and $T = 0$. Despite the higher unit contribution, no units of the turbo model should be produced because its assembly would require a large quantity of "expensive" labor.

We can reach the same conclusion much more quickly using the shadow prices from our original problem. Suppose the firm considers producing one turbo unit, $T = 1$. The direct benefit is simply the unit's contribution, $700. What is the implicit cost of this unit? Because producing the unit uses the firm's limited resources, the firm will be able to produce fewer units of the other models, and total contribution from those models must fall. This loss in contribution is an opportunity cost. Measuring this cost is straightforward. Producing a single turbo unit uses 120 gigabytes of hard-disk capacity valued at $5 per unit (its shadow price), one unit of DVD capacity valued at $0 (remember, its shadow price is zero), and 10 hours of labor valued at $20 each. The total cost is

$$(120)(5) + (1)(0) + (10)(20) = \$800.$$

Thus, if the firm produced this turbo unit, the change in its total contribution would be $700 - 800 = -\$100$. Producing a single turbo unit (or indeed any number of units) is a losing proposition. (If the firm produced 10 units, it would generate 10 times the loss, or $-\$1,000$.) Of course, if the unit contribution were predicted to be $900, a comparison of benefit and opportunity cost would show that the firm should introduce the turbo PC. This benefit–cost comparison would not indicate how many turbo units the firm should produce. The precise, optimal value of T can be determined only by solving the new linear program just illustrated.

Thus, we have the following general rule:

> A firm can profitably introduce a new activity if and only if the activity's direct benefit exceeds its opportunity cost, where opportunity cost is the sum of the resources used, valued at their respective shadow prices.

CHECK STATION 4   The farmer considers planting a third crop, soybeans. The price of soybeans is $1.75 per bushel. Growing 1,000 bushels of soybeans requires two acres of land and four hours of labor per week. Is soybean production profitable? Explain.

In closing this section, it is worth making one further point about the relationship between marginal analysis and the optimal solutions of linear programs. Earlier we saw that a new activity is excluded (its quantity is set equal to zero) if its unit benefit is less than its unit cost. What about activities that are *included* in the optimal solution? Recall that both standard and economy computers are part of the PC firm's optimal production mix. The marginal benefit of producing an extra standard model is $500 (its contribution). Using the resource shadow prices, its marginal cost is computed as

$$(80)(5) + (1)(0) + (5)(20) = \$500.$$

In the optimal solution, marginal benefit and marginal cost are identical. Similarly, for the economy model, marginal benefit is $300 and marginal cost is

$$(40)(5) + (0)(0) + (5)(20) = \$300.$$

Again marginal benefit and marginal cost are identical. The following general result holds for any linear program:

> For any decision variable that is positive in the optimal solution, its marginal benefit equals its marginal cost, where the latter is computed according to the resource shadow prices.

Thus, once again we find that the relationship $M\pi = MB - MC = 0$ holds at the optimum solution.

Allocating HIV Resources

In the fall of 1999, the Centers for Disease Control and Prevention called for a panel of health scientists, economists, and policy experts to formulate a framework and strategy for HIV prevention in the United States. A member of that panel, Edward Kaplan of Yale University, has described the work of the panel in analyzing the problem of HIV prevention.[8] The panel concluded that a key goal was "to prevent as many new HIV infections as possible within the resources available for HIV prevention." Though this broad goal might seem obvious, current health-care measures often pursue other ends. As Kaplan notes, formulating the problem as a constrained maximization problem was, at least at first, foreign to many on the panel who were not economists.

The panel modeled the strategy for HIV prevention as a linear programming problem. The key question was: How should the budget for prevention ($412 million in 1999) allocate funds across dozens of alternative prevention programs, with myriad constraints, to maximize the number of HIV cases prevented? Prevention programs range from counseling at-risk populations to screening blood donations to preventing mother-to-child transmissions to funding needle exchanges for intravenous drug users. The panel marshaled the available economic and medical data to solve a variety of LP problems under different scenarios (from pessimistic to optimistic). They found that an optimal resource policy could prevent about 3,900 new HIV infections per year at the $412 million funding level. Investigation of the relevant shadow prices showed that increasing funding would lead to greater HIV prevention but at a diminishing rate.

In contrast to the optimal plan, current U.S. prevention policy roughly allocates funds to different programs, regions, and targeted populations in proportion to reported AIDS cases and prevents only an estimated 3,000 infections. (Though spending more dollars where there are more AIDS cases probably makes sense for *treatment*, it is not the best plan for maximum *prevention*. Proportional allocation also contains a perverse incentive: The allocation should reward health authorities for preventing AIDS cases, not for reporting more numerous cases.) Overall, the most cost-effective prevention programs (derived with the LP approach) can increase prevention by some 30 percent compared to current programs. Kaplan also notes that if the allocation included funds for needle-exchange programs (currently, federal law prohibits funding for such programs), annual preventions would increase to some 5,300. To sum up, Kaplan credits the resource allocation model with organizing the tough thinking needed to combat AIDS.

FORMULATION AND COMPUTER SOLUTION FOR LARGER LP PROBLEMS

Skill in recognizing, formulating, and solving linear programming problems comes with practice. This section presents four decision problems that represent a cross section of important management applications of linear programming. Once you are comfortable with these applications, the other decision problems you encounter will begin to look familiar, and their formulation and

[8] E. Kaplan, "Allocating HIV Resources," *OR/MS Today* (February 2001): 26–29.

solution will be almost automatic. In addition, you will be able to formulate larger-scale problems and then solve them using standard computer programs. The final two problems display the kinds of LP solutions such programs provide with emphasis on interpretating the computer output.

PRODUCTION FOR MAXIMUM OUTPUT   A manufacturing firm can produce a good using three different production methods, each requiring different amounts of labor and capital—two inputs in fixed supply. The firm has 60 machine-hours and 90 labor-hours per day to devote to the product. The processes require the following inputs to produce one unit of output.

	Process 1	Process 2	Process 3
Machine-Hours	.5	1	2
Labor-Hours	2	1	.5

The firm seeks to maximize output by using the processes singly or in combination. How much output should it produce and by which processes?

The LP formulation is as follows:

$$\text{Maximize:}\quad x_1 + x_2 + x_3$$

$$\text{Subject to:}\quad .5x_1 + x_2 + 2x_3 \le 60$$

$$2x_1 + x_2 + .5x_3 \le 90.$$

All decision variables are nonnegative.

The decision variables (x_1, x_2, and x_3) denote the quantities of output produced via each process. The firm wishes to maximize total output, the sum of the outputs produced by each process subject to the constraints that the total amounts of labor and capital used to produce total output cannot exceed available supplies of inputs.

This problem involves two constraints (plus three nonnegativity constraints) and three decision variables. Here the previous graphical method will not work because there are more decision variables than axes of the graph. However, we can find the solution graphing the two *constraints* on the axes instead. The method is shown in Figure 18.6, where available input supplies—rather than decision variables—are placed on the axes. The rectangle OLMK represents the feasible region, whose sides indicate the available amounts of capital and labor (60 and 90 units, respectively).

The next step is to graph a contour of the objective function. Figure 18.6 shows two such contours. The inner contour shows combinations of inputs necessary to produce 40 units of output; the outer contour corresponds to producing 70 units. For instance, if the firm seeks to produce 40 units, it can do so

FIGURE 18.6

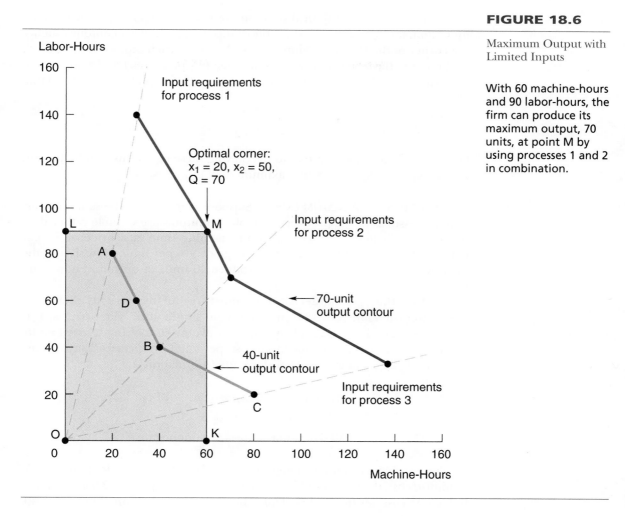

Labor-Hours

Maximum Output with
Limited Inputs

With 60 machine-hours
and 90 labor-hours, the
firm can produce its
maximum output, 70
units, at point M by
using processes 1 and 2
in combination.

Machine-Hours

via process 1, using 20 machine-hours and 80 labor-hours; this input combination is shown as point A in the figure. Alternatively, it could use process 2, using 40 units of each input (point B), or process 3, using 80 and 20 units (point C).

To complete the production contour we draw the segments connecting these points. For instance, the firm could produce the 40 units using a combination of processes 1 and 2. Consider the outputs $x_1 = 20$, $x_2 = 20$, and $x_3 = 0$. Total production is 40 units, using a total of $10 + 20 = 30$ machine-hours and $40 + 20 = 60$ labor-hours. This pair of inputs occurs at point D in Figure 18.6, halfway along the segment joining A and B. In general, by using processes 1 and 2 in various proportions to produce 40 units in total, we trace out the line segment AB. Similarly, combinations of processes 2 and 3 use inputs described by the line segment BC.

To complete the graphical solution, we find the highest production contour attainable given the fixed supply of inputs. The highest contour touches the corner of the feasible region at point M, where each input is fully utilized. At this point, the firm produces output using only processes 1 and 2. Returning to the mathematical formulation, we know from the graph that $x_3 = 0$ and that

$$.5x_1 + x_2 = 60$$
$$2x_1 + x_2 = 90$$

because both constraints are binding. Solving these equations simultaneously, we find $x_1 = 20$, $x_2 = 50$, and maximum total output is 70.

PRODUCTION AT MINIMUM COST   Suppose that we have the same production processes as in the previous example, but inputs are variable rather than fixed. In particular, the firm can rent machine time at a price of $8 per machine-hour and can hire labor at a wage of $10 per hour. How should the firm use the available processes to produce 40 units of output at minimum cost?

To find the optimal decision, we must formulate correctly the objective function. The cost of producing a single unit via process 1 is $(.5)(\$8) + (2)(\$10) = \$24$. (The cost is simply the sum of inputs used multiplied by their prices.) The total input costs per unit for processes 2 and 3 come to $18 and $21, respectively. Therefore, the formulation is

Minimize: $24x_1 + 18x_2 + 21x_3$
Subject to: $x_1 + x_2 + x_3 = 40.$
All decision variables are nonnegative.

This problem is simple enough that it can be solved by just looking at it. To minimize cost, the firm should produce exclusively via process 2 because it has the lowest cost per unit ($18). Thus, the optimal production plan is $x_2 = 40$, $x_1 = x_3 = 0$.

Remark   The solution to the minimum-cost problem features a single binding constraint. Furthermore, the optimal production plan uses only a single process. In the solution to the maximum-output problem, two of the three constraints are binding. The optimal production plan involves two processes (whose values are found by solving the two binding constraints simultaneously). The findings for these examples illustrate a general result:

> In any linear programming problem, the number of decision variables that take nonzero values in the optimal solution always is equal to the number of binding constraints.

Therefore, in decision problems in which the number of decision variables (call this number N) greatly exceeds the number of constraints (call this M), at least N − M decision variables will be zero in the optimal solution.

Computer Solutions

Solving linear programming problems graphically is impractical for problems in which the decision variables and constraints number three or more. Fortunately, many computer programs are available to solve large-scale linear programming problems. Indeed, a major airline routing its aircraft can find itself facing a linear programming problem involving thousands of decision variables and hundreds of constraints. Computers can efficiently solve even problems this large. In its broad description, the computer solution is much the same however large the problem. Typically, the user inputs a mathematical formulation of the problem, that is, the objective function and all constraints. The computer program then produces optimal values of all decision variables, the optimal value of the objective function, and the shadow prices associated with the constraints.

The last 15 years have seen the development of dozens of *spreadsheet-based* linear programming packages.[9] The user enters basic data, including constraints, directly into a spreadsheet. The program then carries out all arithmetic calculations and displays the optimal solution and shadow prices in the original spreadsheet. A key advantage is that this output can be used as inputs into larger related spreadsheets. The following examples illustrate a typical spreadsheet-based LP program.

A STAFFING PROBLEM   A major city has minimum requirements for the number of police officers on duty during each four-hour period (see the following table). Because split shifts are prohibited, each officer must work eight consecutive hours.

Officers receive standard pay rates for shifts 1 and 2, time and a quarter for shifts 3 and 4, and time and a half for shifts 5 and 6. How can the police department find a daily work schedule that will minimize its total wage cost?

Shift	Time	Required Number of Police Officers
1	8 A.M.–12 P.M.	150
2	12–4 P.M.	100
3	4–8 P.M.	250
4	8 P.M.–12 A.M.	400
5	12–4 A.M.	500
6	4–8 A.M.	175

[9] For a review of these software packages, see R. Fourer, "Linear Programming Survey," *OR/MS Today*, (December 2003): 34–43. An updated version of this comprehensive survey of LP software packages is available online at http://lionhrtpub.com/orms.

The formulation of this decision problem is as follows.

Minimize: $x_1 + 1.125x_2 + 1.25x_3 + 1.375x_4 + 1.5x_5 + 1.25x_6$

Subject to: $x_1 + x_6 \geq 150$

$$x_2 + x_1 \geq 100$$

$$x_3 + x_2 \geq 250$$

$$x_4 + x_3 \geq 400$$

$$x_5 + x_4 \geq 500$$

$$x_6 + x_5 \geq 175$$

All decision variables are nonnegative.

Here $x_1, x_2, \ldots, x_6$ denote the number of officers who *begin* duty with shifts $1, 2, \ldots, 6$. The objective function lists the total number of "regular-time" salaries of the force. (The city pays an officer beginning duty in shift 1 regular time for eight hours. One beginning in shift 2 receives four hours of regular time pay and four hours at time and a quarter; overall, he or she counts as a 1.125 officer. We similarly calculate the pay for officers beginning shifts 3 through 6.) The left-hand side of the first constraint lists the number of police on duty during the 8 A.M. to 12 P.M. period. (This is the sum of x_1 and x_6, the numbers of officers beginning shifts at 8 A.M. and ending shifts at noon.) This number must be no fewer than the 150-person requirement. We express the other five constraints in the same way.

The manager enters the objective function and the relevant constraints into the spreadsheet. Table 18.1 shows the completed spreadsheet (including the problem's optimal solution and shadow prices). In the table, the decision variables appear in row 6 and are in colored type for easy identification. We can vary these as we wish and observe the effect on the objective. The values shown here are the optimal values generated by executing Excel's optimization program, Solver. In actual practice, the user is free to enter any initial values. For instance, the user could begin by setting all six variables at 300 officers—values that far exceed required staffing levels. The manager can also experiment with other values. Cell I5 lists the objective, the total number of regular-time police officers (the value of which the manager wants to minimize). The value in this cell has been computed by using the objective function equation in the LP formulation.

Rows 8 and 10 represent the constraints. The fixed values in row 10 denote the required number of officers on the six shifts (the right side of the preceding inequalities). The computed values in row 8 list the numbers of officers actually present during the time periods. For instance, the value in cell C8 is the sum of cells B6 and C6, and so on. Finally, each value in row 12, the so-called extra officers, is the difference between the actual (row 8) and required (row 10) number of personnel.

To direct the computer to solve the LP problem, one must complete the Solver menu (shown below the spreadsheet in Table 18.1). In the menu, we

TABLE 18.1

Linear
Programming
Solution for Police
Staffing Problem

The department
meets its
hourly staffing
requirements at
minimum total
cost.

	A	B	C	D	E	F	G	H	I	J
1										
2		8 A.M.–12	12–4 P.M.	4–8 P.M.	8 P.M.–12	12–4 A.M.	4–8 A.M.			
3										
4	Shift Costs	1	1.125	1.25	1.375	1.5	1.25		Total Cost	
5									1,150	
6	# of Officers	150	175	75	325	175	0			
7										
8	# per 8-Hour Shift	150	325	250	400	500	175			
9										
10	Officers Required	150	100	250	400	500	175			
11										
12	Extra Officers	0	225	0	0	0	0			
13										
14	Shadow Price	1.0	0	1.125	0.125	1.25	0.25			

Solver Parameters   [?] [X]

Set Target Cell: $I$5

Equal to: ◯ Max   ◉ Min

By Changing Cells:

$B$6 : $G$6

Subject to Constraints:

$B$12 : $G$12 ≥ 0
$B$6 : $G$6 ≥ 0

[Solve]

[Close]

[Options]

[Add]

[Change]

[Delete]

have entered target cell I5 (total cost) to be minimized by varying cells B6 to G6 (the numbers hired beginning in each time period). The constraints specify that cells B12 through G12 must be greater than or equal to zero. That is, there cannot be a shortage of officers (i.e., a negative number of extra officers) on any shift. The final constraint states that all decision variables must be nonnegative.

Upon execution, the spreadsheet-based optimization program instantly computes all optimal values consistent with satisfying all constraints. From the spreadsheet solution in Table 18.1, we see that the minimum total number of regular-time officers is 1,150, as shown in cell I5. Note that the bare minimum number of officers is present on five of the six shifts; only the second shift has excess numbers. Moreover, officers begin work on five of the six shifts; no officers begin work on shift 6 at 4 A.M. (This illustrates the earlier general result: Since there are five binding constraints, there are exactly five nonzero decision variables.)[10]

The spreadsheet also lists the shadow price associated with each constraint. For instance, the shadow price of requiring an extra officer on the fourth shift (moving from 400 to 401 officers) is .125. How can this extra officer be obtained for only a *fractional* increase in the workforce? The answer is by hiring one fewer officer beginning in shift 2 (where we already have surplus personnel) and hiring one more officer beginning in shift 3. This trade satisfies the new constraints. The net increase in cost comes from the difference between the hourly costs on shifts 2 and 3: 1.25 − 1.125 = .125. This confirms the shadow price.

A SCHOOL BUSING PROBLEM   Each year, a municipality contracts with a private bus company for the transportation of students in the primary grades to and from school. As a management consultant to the city, you must structure a busing plan. The city's annual payment to the bus company will depend on the number of "kid-miles" the company carries. (For instance, carrying 20 children 2 miles each amounts to 40 kid-miles, as does carrying 8 children 5 miles each.)

The city's three elementary schools draw students from four distinct geographic neighborhoods. The city's planning department has furnished figures on the number of students in each neighborhood, the capacity of each school, and the distance from each school to each neighborhood. Figure 18.7 shows a map of the school district and provides the pertinent data. You must formulate a busing plan that will minimize total transportation cost. Before turning to the LP formulation and the computer solution in Table 18.2, try coming up with an optimal bus plan on your own, using the information in Figure 18.7.

From the data in Figure 18.7, we can develop the following LP formulation:

Minimize: $2.0N1 + 3.0E1 + \ldots + 3.0W3 + 2.2S3$

Subject to: $N1 + E1 + W1 + S1 \leq 360$

$N2 + E2 + W2 + S2 \leq 400$ School capacities

$N3 + E3 + W3 + S3 \leq 260$

$N1 + N2 + N3 = 240$

$E1 + E2 + E3 = 120$ Neighborhood
$W1 + W2 + W3 = 400$ Enrollments

$S1 + S2 + S3 = 200$

All decision variables are nonnegative.

[10] This is not the only optimal plan. A second solution of the LP problem is $x_1 = 75$, $x_2 = 250$, $x_3 = 0$, $x_4 = 400$, $x_5 = 100$, and $x_6 = 75$. This plan also requires the minimum number of regular-time officers (1,150).

FIGURE 18.7

Data for a School
Busing Problem

The number of
elementary school
children in the
neighborhoods and
the student capacities
of the schools are
listed in parentheses.

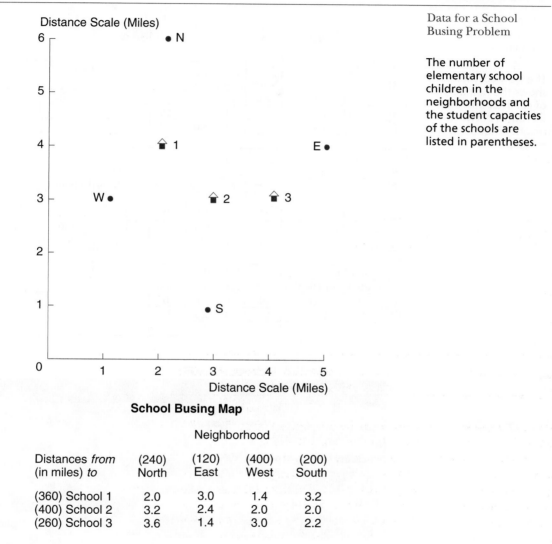

School Busing Map

Neighborhood

Distances *from* (in miles) *to*	(240) North	(120) East	(400) West	(200) South
(360) School 1	2.0	3.0	1.4	3.2
(400) School 2	3.2	2.4	2.0	2.0
(260) School 3	3.6	1.4	3.0	2.2

The formulation begins with recognizing that a busing plan has 12 decision variables: the number of children from each of four neighborhoods bused to each of three schools; for instance, the variable N1 denotes the number of students from the north neighborhood bused to school 1, and so on. Remember that the city wants to minimize the total number of kid-miles traveled. As the formulation shows, the objective function is found by multiplying the number of students along a given route by the distance along the route (e.g., 2.0N1)

TABLE 18.2

Linear Programming
Solution for Busing
Problem

The least-cost solution
shows the numbers
of children bused on
six routes between
neighborhoods and
schools.

	A	B	C	D	E	F	G	H	I
1									
2	Distances						Total Kid-Miles		
3		North	East	West	South				
4	School 1	2.0	3.0	1.4	3.2		1792		
5	School 2	3.2	2.4	2.0	2.0				
6	School 3	3.6	1.4	3.0	2.2				
7									
8									
9	Students					Total	Capacity	Extra	Shadow
10		North	East	West	South	in School	in School	Spaces	Prices
11									
12	School 1	240	0	120	0	360	360	0	0.8
13	School 2	0	0	280	120	400	400	0	0.2
14	School 3	0	120	0	80	200	260	60	0
15									
16	Total Kids Bused	240	120	400	200				
17	Students in District	240	120	400	200				
18	Difference	0	0	0	0				
19	Shadow Prices	2.8	1.4	2.2	2.2				
20									

Solver Parameters   ? ☒

Set Target Cell: $G$4

Equal to: ○ Max   ● Min

By Changing Cells:

$B$12 : $E$14

Subject to Constraints:

$H$12 : $H$14 ≥ 0
$B$18 : $E$18 = 0
$B$12 : $E$14 ≥ 0

Solve

Close

Options

Add

Change

Delete

and summing. The first three constraints pertain to school capacities: The total number of students going to each school cannot exceed the school's capacity. The last four constraints pertain to neighborhood enrollments: For each neighborhood, all school-age children ride the bus to some school. (If the left-hand side of the equality fell short of the right-hand side, many happy children would be left on street corners without being picked up for school.)

Table 18.2 shows the computer solution. Note that the north and east children go to the schools closest to them, and the west and south students go to either their nearest second-nearest schools. School 3 has extra spaces. The city pays for the minimum number of kid-miles: 1,792. The table also lists shadow prices associated with each school and each neighborhood. For instance, the shadow price associated with busing an extra child from the north neighborhood is 2.8; this results from busing the student to school 1 (2 miles). But, because school 1 already is at capacity, the extra north child displaces a west child who goes to school 2 instead of school 1 (an extra distance of .6 miles). In turn, the extra west child going to school 2 displaces a south child who now travels an extra distance of .2 miles to school 3. Thus, the listed shadow price represents a total increase in miles of 2.0 + .6 + .2 = 2.8.

Confirm that the shadow prices associated with school 1 and the west neighborhood are correct.

CHECK STATION 5

An Investment Problem Revisited

Recall that the manager wants to construct a portfolio of securities that offers the highest expected after-tax return, subject to the following requirements: (1) The portfolio's average quality rating is at least 3.5, and (2) the portfolio's average maturity is at least 1.5 years but no greater than 2.5 years.

Bond Category	Quality Rating	Maturity (Years)	Yield (Percent)
Treasury bills	5	.4	4.0
Treasury bonds	5	4.0	6.0
Corporate bonds	3.5	3.2	4.4
Municipal bonds	3	2.0	5.6
Junk bonds	1	2.5	8.0

The LP formulation is:

Maximize: $4.0B + 6.0T + 4.4C + 5.6M + 8.0J$

Subject to: $5B + 5T + 3.5C + 3M + 1J \geq 3.5$
$.4B + 4.0T + 3.2C + 2.0M + 2.5J \geq 1.5$
$.4B + 4.0T + 3.2C + 2.0M + 2.5J \leq 2.5$
$B + T + C + M + J = 1.0.$

All decision variables are nonnegative.

TABLE 18.3

Linear Programming Solutions for an Optimal Portfolio

By dividing funds among treasury bills, treasury bonds, and junk bonds, the investor earns a maximum expected return (6.23 percent) while meeting three investment requirements.

	A	B	C	D	E	F	G	H	I	J	K	L	M
1													
2		T-Bills	T-Bonds	Corp Bonds	Munis	Junk		Portfolio		Requirement	Gap	Shadow	
3												Price	
4	Proportions	0.260	0.365	0	0	0.375		1					
5													
6	Returns	4	6	4.4	5.6	8		6.23					
7													
8	Ratings	5	5	3.5	3	1		3.5		3.5	0	0.708	
9													
10										1.5	1	0	
11	Maturities	0.4	4	3.2	2	2.5		2.5					
12										2.5	0	0.555	
13													

Solver Parameters ? X

Set Target Cell: $H$6

Equal to: ● Max   ○ Min

By Changing Cells:

$B$4 : $F$4

Subject to Constraints:

$K$8 : $K$12 ≥ 0
$H$4   = 1
$B$4 : $F$4   ≥ 0

Solve

Close

Options

Add

Change

Delete

The portfolio manager must determine the proportions of the individual's total dollar investment to invest in the securities. These proportions are denoted by B, T, C, M, and J for the respective securities. (For instance, if the manager divided the portfolio equally among the five assets, the values would be B = T = C = M = J = .2.) The actual size of the manager's investment fund does not enter into the formulation. The optimal proportions will be the same whether the manager is investing $20,000 or $20 million.

The objective function lists the average (or expected) return of the portfolio. The first constraint indicates that the portfolio's average risk rating must be at least 3.5. The second and third constraints list the bounds on the portfolio's average maturity. The final constraint ensures that the portfolio proportions sum exactly to 1.

What portfolio will maximize the investor's expected return, subject to the risk and maturity constraints? From Table 18.3, we see that the optimal portfolio puts 26 percent of the individual's total dollar investment in treasury bills, 36.5 percent in treasury bonds, and the remainder in junk bonds. This portfolio has a risk rating of exactly 3.5 (which just meets this constraint), has a maturity of exactly 2.5 years (which just meets the upper maturity constraint), and delivers a maximum portfolio return of 6.23 percent.

The spreadsheet also lists the relevant shadow prices as calculated by the LP program. The shadow prices associated with the risk and maturity constraints are of some interest. The former shadow price shows that allowing a unit reduction in the portfolio's risk index (reflecting a tolerance for greater risk) would raise the portfolio's expected return by .708 percent. According to the latter shadow price, increasing the average maturity of the portfolio by a year would increase the expected return by .555 percent. (In either case, the portfolio would shift toward a greater share of junk bonds and a smaller share of treasury bills.)

SUMMARY

Decision-Making Principles

1. Linear programming is a method of formulating and solving decision problems that involve explicit resource constraints. The range of LP problems includes product mix, cost minimization, transportation, scheduling, inventory, and financial and budgeting decisions.

2. To qualify as a linear program, all decision variables must enter linearly into the objective function and into all constraints. So long as the LP problem is feasible, an optimal solution always exists at one of the corners of the feasible region. The optimal corner can be found by graphical means or by computer algorithms.

3. The shadow price of a resource shows the change in the value of the objective function associated with a unit change in the resource. Thus, the shadow price measures the improvement in the objective from relaxing a constraint or, conversely, the decline in the objective from tightening a constraint. A nonbinding constraint has a shadow price of zero.

4. Decision makers should adopt a new activity if and only if the activity's direct benefit exceeds its opportunity cost. We measure this opportunity cost by the sum of the resources used in the activity valued at their respective shadow prices.

Nuts and Bolts

1. Formulating linear programs requires identifying the relevant decision variables, specifying the objective function, and writing down the relevant constraints as mathematical inequalities.

2. Solving linear programs requires identifying the binding constraints and solving them simultaneously for the optimal values of the decision variables.

3. For two-variable problems, the optimal solution can be found by graphing the feasible region (framed by the binding constraint lines) and superimposing contours of the objective function. The optimal corner is found where the highest contour (or, for minimization problems, the lowest contour) touches the feasible region. The optimal corner determines which constraints are binding.

4. The shadow price of a constraint is found by changing the right-hand side of the inequality by a unit, solving the binding constraints for the decision variables, and recomputing the objective function. The shadow price is simply the change between the new and old values of the objective.

Questions and Problems

1. Explain whether linear programming techniques can be used in each of the following economic settings.
   a. There are increasing returns to scale in production.
   b. The objective function and all constraints are linear, but the number of decision variables exceeds the number of constraints.
   c. The firm faces a downward-sloping linear demand curve. (To sell more output, it must lower its price.)
   d. The firm can vary the amounts of two basic chemicals in producing a specialty chemical, but, for quality control reasons, the relative proportions of chemicals must be between 40/60 and 60/40.

2. Which of the following formulations can be solved via the LP method?
   a. Maximize: $x + 2y$, subject to: $x + y \geq 2$ and $3x - y \geq 4$.
   b. Maximize: xy, subject to: $x + y \leq 2$ and $3x - y \geq 4$.
   c. Maximize: $x + 2y$, subject to: $x + y \leq 2$ and $3x - y \geq 4$.

d. Maximize: x + 2y, subject to: x + y ≤ 2 and 3x + y ≥ 8.

e. Maximize: x + 2y, subject to: x + y ≤ 2 and x/(x + y) ≤ .7.

3. A manager has formulated the following LP problems. Use graphical methods to find the optimal solutions. (In each, all variables are nonnegative.)

a. Maximize: 10x + 15y, subject to: 2x + 5y ≤ 40 and 6x + 3y ≤ 48.

b. Minimize: .75x + y, subject to: x + .5y ≥ 10 and x + y ≥ 16.

4. Consider an LP problem in which a firm produces multiple goods (A and B) using two inputs (X and Y) in limited supply. Suppose a technological advance increases the amount of good A that can be produced per unit of input X. How will this change the feasible region? How will this affect the quantities of the goods produced in the profit-maximizing solution to the LP problem? (To answer these questions, be sure to graph the two resource constraints.)

5. An athlete carefully watches her intake of calcium, protein, and calories. Her breakfast diet consists mainly of milk and cereal, whose prices and nutrient contents appear in the following table:

	Milk (1 oz)	Cereal (1 oz)
Calcium	2	2
Protein	2	6
Calories	6	2
Price	$.10	$.15

She seeks a diet that supplies at least 50 units of calcium, 90 units of protein, and 66 calories at minimum cost.

a. Formulate, graph, and solve this decision problem. What is the minimum cost of meeting the nutrient requirements?

b. Calculate and provide an economic interpretation of the shadow price associated with calcium.

6. A firm produces tires by two separate processes that require different quantities of capital (K), labor (L), and raw materials (M). Process 1 requires one unit of K, four units of L, and two units of M to produce a tire yielding a $4 profit. Process 2 requires one unit of K, two units of L, and four units of M to produce a tire yielding a $6 profit. The available supply of capital is 10; of labor, 32; and of raw materials, 32.

a. Formulate and solve (by graphing) the firm's profit-maximization problem.

b. Find the shadow prices of raw materials and labor.

7. Consider again the investment problem that opened the chapter.
   a. Suppose the portfolio manager limits the portfolio to treasury bills and treasury bonds. Using a graph, find the proportions of each type of bond that maximize expected return subject to the risk and maturity constraints.
   b. Now suppose the manager can invest in any of the five securities but cares only about the risk constraint. Determine the optimal portfolio.
   c. Answer part b, assuming the manager cares only about the maturity constraints.

8. A soft-drink producer must decide how to divide its spending between two forms of media: television advertising and magazine advertising. Each 30-second commercial on prime-time network television costs $120,000 and, by the company's estimate, will reach 10,000 viewers, 5,000 of whom are in the prime consumer age group 15 to 25. A single-page ad in a leading human-interest weekly magazine costs $40,000 and reaches 5,000 individuals, of whom 1,000 are in the 15 to 25 age group. In addition, the company plans to hold a sweepstakes contest to promote its new soft drink. (A requirement for entry is to enclose the coded label from the new drink.) The company believes the print ad will be more effective in generating trial purchases and entries. Each magazine spot is expected to produce 500 entries and each television spot 250 entries. Finally, the company's goal in its promotion campaign is to reach at least 600,000 total viewers and 150,000 young viewers and to produce 30,000 or more contest entrants.

   How many spots of each kind should the soft-drink producer purchase to meet these three goals and do so at minimum cost?

9. A lumber company uses labor (L) and capital (K) to produce joint products, hardwood (H) and plywood (P). These items can be produced by one of two processes:
   • Process 1: 1 unit of L and 2 units of K to yield 2 units of H and 1 unit of P
   • Process 2: 2 units of L and 2 units of K to yield 2 units of H and 4 units of P

   Profit contribution is $2 per unit of H and $1 per unit of P. The firm has 110 units of L and 160 units of K available.
   a. Formulate and solve the firm's profit-maximization problem. (*Hint*: Don't be distracted by the fact that the processes produce joint products. The correct decision variables are the levels of each process.)
   b. Find the shadow price of labor.
   c. Answer part a, assuming the contribution of P rises to $3 per unit.

Discussion Question Following the example in the text, consider two HIV prevention programs: (1) intensive counseling of high-risk individuals and (2) instituting a needle-exchange program for intravenous drug users. Counseling has an estimated cost of $1,500 per individual per year and is expected to prevent .2 new HIV cases per individual helped. The needle-exchange program costs $500 per individual and prevents .1 new HIV cases per individual.

a. Which program is more effective at HIV prevention *per individual treated*? Which program is more cost-effective, that is, more effective *per dollar spent*? Do your answers raise a dilemma as to which program to fund?

b. Suppose that a regional health organization has a total budget of $450,000 to spend on the two programs and has identified 1,000 high-risk individuals. In coordinating the two prevention programs, it sets two variables, C and N, for the respective numbers to be counseled or furnished clean needles. (Given their very different orientations, the programs are mutually exclusive; each individual is enrolled in a single program.) If the organization's goal is to prevent as many new HIV cases as possible, how many individuals should it enroll in each program?

c. What is the organization's optimal allocation if the at-risk population numbers only 250? Show that it will have unused funds.

d. Finally, what is the organization's optimal allocation if the at-risk population numbers 500? Be sure to show the appropriate LP formulation.

Spreadsheet Problems

S1. An electronics firm has production plants in Oregon and Tennessee. It ships its products overseas from three ports: Los Angeles, New Orleans, and New York. Transportation costs between plants and seaports are shown in the table.

	Los Angeles	New Orleans	New York
Oregon	$14	$26	$30
Tennessee	24	10	12

The maximum capacity of the Oregon plant is 9,000 tons; the capacity of the Tennessee plant is 10,000 tons. The minimum daily quantities shipped overseas from Los Angeles, New Orleans, and New York are 5,000, 7,000, and 6,000 tons, respectively.

a. The company's objective is to minimize the cost of transporting its product from plants to ports while fulfilling its daily overseas shipping requirements. Formulate the appropriate LP problem.

b. Attempt to solve the LP problem by inspection. Find the company's minimum-cost transport plan using a standard LP computer program.

c. Find and interpret the shadow price associated with the 6,000 minimum daily shipment to New York.

S2. A manufacturer produces six products from six inputs. Each product requires different combinations and amounts of inputs. The following table shows the profit and raw materials requirements for each product. The last column shows the total amounts of raw materials available.

Products	1	2	3	4	5	6	Total Amounts of Inputs
Profits	60	70	48	52	48	60	
Inputs Required:							
Aluminum	.5	2	—	2	1	—	400
Steel	2	2.5	1.5	—	.5	—	580
Plastic	—	1.5	4	—	.5	—	890
Rubber	1.5	—	.5	1	.5	2.5	525
Glass	1.5	2	1.5	1	1	2	650
Chrome	.5	2	.5	2	1.5	2	620

a. Formulate the appropriate linear program.

b. Find the company's most profitable production plan using a standard LP computer program.

S3. A refinery processes two types of crude oil, heavy (H) and light (L), into its final product, fuel oil (F). Two different production processes (which can be used singly or simultaneously) are available.

- Process 1: 1 unit of H and 2 units of L to yield 2 units of F at a cost of $1.00.

- Process 2: 1 unit of H and 1 unit of L to yield 1.5 units of F at a cost of $.70.

The refinery must determine its production plan for the summer cycle (May–October) and the winter cycle (November–April). It has contracts to purchase 100 units of H and 150 units of L in each cycle and to deliver 125 units of F in the summer and 170 units of F in the winter. (The company is free to sell more than these contract amounts.) The summer unit fuel price is $1.00, and the winter price is expected to be $1.20. Finally, the refinery's goal is to maximize profit.

a. Formulate the refinery's problem as *two separate* linear programs—one for the summer cycle and one for the winter cycle. Explain (in a sentence or two) why this is possible. Solve using a spreadsheet. (*Hint*: The appropriate decision variables for the problems are the levels of the two processes used in production during the two cycles. Denote these variables by s_1, s_2, w_1, and w_2.)

b. Now suppose the refinery has facilities to store *crude oil* over the course of the year, but it *cannot* store the final product, fuel oil. Any excess crude that is not processed incurs a $.05 per unit charge for storage between cycles. The refinery only considers storing "summer" crude for winter production (and not vice versa). Formulate a single linear program by which the firm can maximize annual profit. Solve using a spreadsheet. (*Hint*: Introduce the additional decision variables I_H and I_L denoting the amounts of crude held in inventory between summer and winter. With these two new variables, modify and integrate the twin LP's in part a into a single LP. How do the inventory variables affect the constraints pertaining to crude supplies in summer and winter?)

c. How does the refinery benefit from inventory holding, and why does it benefit? (A general qualitative answer will suffice.)

Suggested References

The following reference is one of many fine, applied programming texts.

Vanderbei, R. J., *Linear Programming: Foundations and Extensions.* Boston: Kluwer Academic Publishers, 1996.

The following articles describe typical managerial applications and are very readable.

Kaplan E., "Allocating HIV Resources," *OR/MS Today* (February 2001): 26–29. The panel's full report is available online at www.nationalacademies.org (search for "No Time to Lose" full text). The direct link is www.nap.edu/books/0309071372/html

Kimes, S. E., and J. A. Fitzsimmons. "Selecting Profitable Sites at La Quinta Motor Inns." *Interfaces* (March–April 1990): 12–20.

Klingman, D. et al., "The Successful Deployment of Management Science throughout Citgo Petroleum Corporation." *Interfaces* (January–February 1987): 4–25.

1. The formulation of the farmer's problem is

Maximize: $R = 1.6W + 1.0B$

Subject to: $W + B \leq 10$ (land)

$4W + 2B \leq 32$ (labor),

where W and B denote the amounts (in thousands of bushels) of wheat and barley, respectively. Graphing the problem reveals that both constraints are binding. Solving simultaneously the equations $W + B = 10$ and $4W + 2B = 32$, we find $W = 6$ thousand bushels and $B = 4$ thousand bushels. The resulting revenue is $13,600.

2. So long as P_W/P_B is between 1 and 2, the crop mix $W = 6$ and $B = 4$ is optimal. (For instance, a 15 percent fall in both prices has no effect on the ratio.) A rise in the price of wheat to $2.25 puts the ratio

outside this range, causing the farmer to produce only wheat. The new solution is W = 8 and B = 0, with only the labor constraint binding. A fall in the price of wheat to $.90 causes the farmer to produce only barley. Now the solution is B = 10 and W = 0.

3. To find the shadow price of land, solve the equations W + B = 11 and 4W + 2B = 32 to arrive at W = 5 thousand bushels and B = 6 thousand bushels. The farmer's new revenue is $14,000. Land's shadow price is the difference between the old and new revenues, $14,000 − $13,600 = $400. To find the shadow price of labor, solve the equations W + B = 10 and 4W + 2B = 33 to arrive at W = 6.5 and B = 3.5. Labor's shadow price is $13,900 − $13,600 = $300. Labor's shadow price becomes zero when the supply of labor increases to 40 hours per week. At this level, the labor constraint line lies (just) outside the land constraint line.

4. Producing 1,000 bushels of soybeans has an opportunity cost of

$$(2)(\$400) + (4)(\$300) = \$2,000.$$

The direct revenue from selling the 1,000 bushels is $1,750. Since this revenue falls short of the cost, soybeans (in this or any other amount) should not be grown.

5. a. *School 1's shadow price:* The extra spot in school 1 will be filled by a west student who was attending school 2. This saves .6 kid-miles, because school 1 is this much closer to the west neighborhood than is school 2. In turn, the freed space in school 2 is filled by a south student (who was attending school 3) for a .2 kid-mile savings. The total gain in kid-miles is .6 + .2 = .8.

   b. *West neighborhood's shadow price:* The extra west student attends school 2 (an extra 2.0 kid-miles), displacing a south student who now moves to school 3 (an extra .2 kid-miles). Thus, the total increase in kid-miles is 2.2.

The Simplex Method

Linear programming problems of any complexity are solved with high-speed computers using one of a number of mathematical algorithms. One of the most widely used and powerful algorithms is the **simplex method**, originally developed following World War II by the mathematician George Dantzig. Recall that the optimal solution of any LP problem lies at a corner of the feasible region. Roughly speaking, the simplex method examines corners in a systematic way to find the optimum. Although we can rely on computer programs to implement the method, it is important to understand how it works.

The farmer's crop decision introduced in Check Station 1 offers a convenient example for demonstrating the simplex method. The LP formulation of this decision is

$$\text{Maximize:} \qquad R = 1.6W + 1.0B$$

$$\text{Subject to:} \qquad W + B \le 10$$

$$4W + 2B \le 32.$$

Here the farmer's decision variables are the amounts of wheat (W) and barley (B) to raise. Together, the crops cannot use up more than the available supplies of land (constraint 1) and labor (constraint 2).

The first step in the simplex method is to convert the inequality constraints to equalities. To do this, we introduce two slack variables, denoted by L and M, one for each inequality. These **slack variables** represent the unused amounts of the respective resources. The constraints now are rewritten as

$$W + B + L = 10$$
$$4W + 2B + M = 32.$$

Here L denotes the amount of "free" land not used for the crops, and M denotes the number of free hours of labor. Note that the slack variables are subject to the same nonnegativity constraints as the decision variables: $L \geq 0$ and $M \geq 0$. A negative slack variable would mean that the farmer's crop plan demanded more than the available amount of the resource in question. (For example, the plan $W = 3$, $B = 8$ would imply $L = -1$, from the first equation. This crop plan requires 11 acres, but only 10 are available. The farmer is "short" one acre: $L = -1$.)

The rewritten constraints represent two equations in four unknowns. By themselves, they cannot be solved. However, if we specify values for any two of the four variables, we can solve the equations for the remaining variables. This is exactly what the simplex method does. Furthermore, particular solutions correspond to corners of the feasible region. Figure 18A.1 makes the point. The feasible region is graphed as the four-cornered region ABCO. Each corner can be obtained from the preceding equations by setting two variables to zero and solving for the other two.

Point A: $B = 0$, $M = 0$ Point B: $M = 0$, $L = 0$
Point C: $W = 0$, $L = 0$ Point O: $W = 0$, $B = 0$.

For instance, at point B, each of the slack variables is zero; that is, all of each input is used up. The solution for the crop amounts is $W = 6$, $B = 4$. At point O, in contrast, no crops are produced. The solution for the slack variables, obviously, is $L = 10$, $M = 32$. A pair of definitions will be useful in what follows: A **basic variable** is one that takes a positive value in a given solution; a **nonbasic variable** is one that takes a zero value in the solution. For instance, at point B, the basic variables are W and B and the nonbasic variables are L and M.

The simplex method starts from an initial (arbitrary) corner and proceeds to other corners step by step. The elegance of the method is that it converges to the optimal corner in a small number of steps. For instance, a large-scale business problem may involve scores of decision variables, a large number of constraints, and hundreds of corners. The simplex method need search only a small fraction of corners before arriving at the optimum.[1]

---

[1] Obviously, the present problem (having only three profitable corners) is simple enough to be solved by enumeration. The simple setting makes it easy to understand the simplex method but does not do it real justice.

The Farmer's Problem

The most profitable crop mix occurs at point B, where 6,000 bushels of wheat and 4,000 bushels of barley are planted.

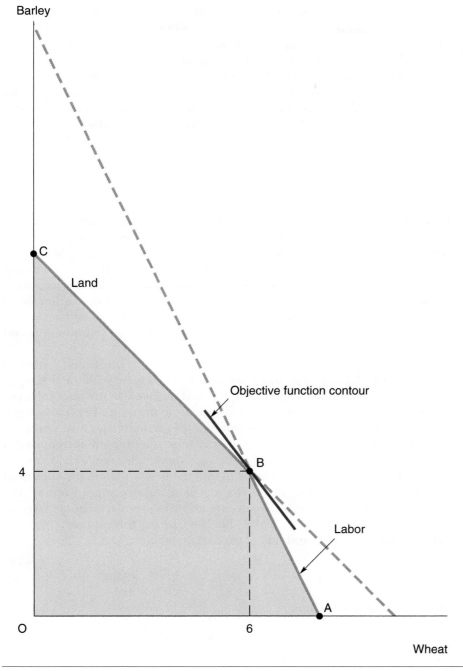

The algorithm works as follows. The simplex method moves from one corner to the next such that each new solution (1) remains feasible and (2) achieves at least as great a value of the objective function as its predecessor. In the final step, the method achieves an optimum; that is, no move to a superior neighboring corner is possible. Movement from one corner to the next is achieved by manipulating the constraint equations.

To solve the farmer's problem, it is convenient to start with the simple, albeit not very profitable, corner at point 0. Here L and M are basic variables and W and B are nonbasic (i.e., take zero values). The simplex method begins by rearranging the constraint equations so that each basic variable appears on the left-hand side. Thus, we rearrange the earlier equations to read

$$L = 10 - W - B \qquad\qquad [18A.1]$$
$$M = 32 - 4W - 2B.$$

In this form, we can check that L = 10 and M = 32 when W and B are zero.

The simplex method moves to a neighboring corner by exchanging one basic variable for one nonbasic variable. First, we consider bringing W into the solution, that is, changing it from a nonbasic to a basic variable. We do this by increasing its value from zero while maintaining B at zero. We observe, from Equation 18A.1, that W can take a value as high as 8 before causing M to become negative (i.e., infeasible). Note that the second equation is the real constraint on feasibility. Thus, if W were brought into the solution, it would replace M (i.e., M would become zero).

Alternatively, what if we brought B into the basic solution? Holding W equal to zero, we can increase B up to 10 before L becomes zero. With the first equation acting as the feasibility constraint, B would replace L in the basic solution. Between W and B, the simplex method chooses to introduce the "most promising" variable—the one that contributes the greatest revenue per unit. Introducing W increases revenue by 1.6 per unit. Alternatively, introducing B increases revenue by 1.0 per unit. Accordingly, the simplex method chooses W.

Each time a new variable is brought into the basic solution, the constraint equations must be modified so that the new basic variable appears only on the left-hand side of the equation. To accomplish this, we rearrange the second (binding) equality: W = 8 − .25M − .5B. Next, we use this expression to eliminate W from the right-hand side of the first equation in 18A.1:

$$L = 10 - (8 - .25M - .5B) - B = 2 + .25M - .5B.$$

The new equations become

$$L = 2 + .25M - .5B \qquad\qquad [18A.2]$$
$$W = 8 - .25M - .5B.$$

Setting the nonbasic variables to zero, we find L = 2 and W = 8. The simplex method has moved from point O (where no crops are produced) to point A (where only wheat is produced).

The next step repeats the procedure. Starting from the current position at point A, simplex considers a move to the neighboring corner B. (A move back to corner O need not be considered; this simply would undo the algebraic manipulations to date and reduce revenue back to zero.) Moving to point B means introducing B into the basic solution. Such a move is warranted if it increases revenue. Let's compute the revenue consequence of introducing B. Producing and selling a unit of B raises revenue directly by 1.0 (the sale price of the unit). By Equation 18A.2, it also implies producing .5 fewer units of W. Thus, the net revenue impact of adding a unit of B is

$$\Delta R / \Delta B = 1.0 - (.5)(1.6) = .2.$$

Because the change is positive, simplex adopts this move.[2]

Maintaining M equal to zero, B can be increased to 4 before L becomes zero (i.e., all land is exhausted). Rearranging the first equation in 18A.2, we find that B = 4 − 2L + .5M. Using this expression to eliminate B from the right-hand side of the second equation in 18A.2, we find that W = 8 − .25M − .5(4 − 2L + .5M) = 6 + L − .5M. Thus, the new pair of equations is

$$W = 6 + L - .5M \qquad\qquad [18A.3]$$
$$B = 4 - 2L + .5M.$$

Setting the nonbasic variables to zero, we find W = 6 and B = 4.

Is it possible to move to a more profitable corner? Ruling out a return to A, the simplex method considers a move to C by bringing M into the solution. Increasing M by a unit offers no direct increase in revenue. (After all, M does not appear in the objective function.) It does, however, allow a .5-unit increase in B while requiring a .5-unit fall in W (from Equations 18A.3). The total revenue impact of such a move would be

$$\Delta R / \Delta M = (.5)(1.0) + (-.5)(1.6) = -.3.$$

Increasing M reduces revenue. Thus, a move to point C is unwarranted. Because no movement to any neighboring corner is profitable, the simplex method establishes point B as the optimal solution. The complete solution is W = 6, B = 4, R = 13.6, and L = M = 0.

---

[2] Adding a unit of B also reduces L by .5 via the first equation of 18A.2. However, the reduction in this slack variable (the amount of unused land) has no revenue impact and, thus, is of no consequence.

Here is a summary of the steps in the simplex method:

1. Start with a feasible corner solution (usually a slack solution).
   a. Rewrite inequalities as equalities by inserting a slack variable on the left-hand side of each equation.
   b. Set the nonbasic variables to zero and solve for the basic variables.
2. Consider a movement to one of the neighboring corners.
   a. For a unit increase in each nonbasic variable, compute the resulting increase in the objective.
   b. Find the "most promising" variable and the corresponding binding constraint.
3. Move to the most promising neighboring corner.
   a. Isolate the variable to be introduced on the left-hand side of the binding-constraint equation.
   b. Use this equation to eliminate the new basic variable from the right-hand sides of all the other equations.
   c. Set the nonbasic variables to zero and solve the new equations for the basic variables.
4. Repeat steps 2 and 3 until the optimal corner is reached.
   a. Terminate the algorithm when introducing any nonbasic variable has a negative effect on the objective.

CHAPTER 19

Capital Budgeting

How to have your cake and eat it too? Lend it out at interest.

ANONYMOUS

Boeing's New Jet

Since 2003, Boeing Corporation has been working toward the production of a new superefficient, passenger-friendly, 200–300 seat aircraft, dubbed the Dreamliner 7E7. The plane will use new composites, consume 20 percent less fuel than comparable models, and feature large windows, roomy overhead compartments, and improved air quality. With a range of 6,400 nautical miles and a speed of 85 percent the speed of sound, the aircraft will serve direct routes (bypassing hub airports) and should appeal to time-sensitive travelers who prefer nonstop service. The design responded to Boeing's archrival, Airbus Industrie, which had begun development of a new 550-seat superjumbo jet. Thus, Boeing has abandoned its longtime hold on the jumbo-jet segment and the legacy of its 747 aircraft. Boeing expected to spend around $8 billion and to develop the aircraft with first deliveries occurring in 2008. Management planned to sell the plane to major airlines at a price of $120–$150 million per plane (depending on the model, on demand, etc.), gaining an estimated profit of $12.5 million per plane. Aggressively pursuing customer orders for future deliveries, Boeing's sales force planned for deliveries of over 100 aircraft in 2008 and 2009 combined, with annual sales rising to a peak of over 200 aircraft per year in 2018, before falling off near the end of its product life. In all, Boeing hoped to sell 2,500 aircraft over the Dreamliner's 20-year lifetime.

A number of commercial airlines, including Continental Airlines and Japan Airlines, have already placed preliminary orders for the new plane. Airline experts estimated that the value added to passengers due to greater comfort, speed, and range would justify fare increases of some 15 to 20 percent. Many airline executives believe that these higher fares, coupled with lower fuel costs, will more than compensate for the premium purchase price—some $20 million more than a conventional jet.

If Boeing is correct in its projections of future deliveries, how should it assess the long-term profitability of the new aircraft? In light of unexpected outcomes (such as higher development costs or lower orders), how would it reassess (and possibly cancel) the program? For its part, how should a commercial carrier such as Continental Airlines determine whether to purchase the Dreamliner or a conventional jet?

Capital budgeting is the process of making long-term investment decisions. Such investment decisions involve outlays and inflows that may extend over many years. Examples range far and wide. The decision to build a new plant may involve the investment of money over several years in exchange for returns that (if all goes well) will extend far into the future. Investment in research and development may require cash outlays for many years before the arrival of a commercial product that generates profits for the firm. With a new product in hand, the firm often must make significant up-front expenditures in advertising, promotion, and distribution to launch the product. The respective decisions to produce and purchase the Dreamliner are two other investment examples.

In this chapter, we focus on techniques for evaluating such investment projects. First, we examine the concepts of present value and discounting. Then we discuss how managers can use the present-value criterion to guide investment decisions. Finally, we examine the notion of an investment's internal rate of return and consider ways to estimate an appropriate discount rate that reflects a project's risk.

PRESENT VALUE AND DISCOUNTING

How can a firm go about comparing (and aggregating) revenues and costs that occur over varying points in time? The answer to this question requires an understanding of the concept of present value. As the term suggests, the **present value (PV)** of any monetary sum accruing in the future is the monetary amount today that is equivalent in value to the future sum. The issue of equivalence arises because any monetary sum held today earns interest over time. It is much more valuable to hold $1,000 today than to receive $1,000 five years from now—the $1,000 today will earn interest during the next five years. The examples of this section illustrate the concept and computation of present value.

Interest Rate Calculations

Suppose a firm holds $100,000 in short-term liquid funds in a bank account paying 10 percent interest annually. If left in the account for a year, the original funds will grow to $(1.1)(\$100,000) = \$110,000$. In algebraic terms,

$$FV_1 = (1 + r)B, \qquad\qquad [19.1]$$

where B denotes the original sum (the principal), r the annual rate of interest (expressed as a decimal rather than a percentage), and FV_1 the accumulated balance after one year. Thus, FV_1 stands for the **future value (FV)** (one year hence) associated with today's current holding of $100,000. Equation 19.1 demonstrates that one always can compute FV_1 given knowledge of the current sum, B, and the interest rate, r.

An alternative interpretation emerges when we rearrange Equation 19.1:

$$B = \frac{FV_1}{1 + r}. \qquad\qquad [19.2]$$

In this form, we think of B as the present value associated with the amount FV_1 accruing one year from now. To illustrate, let's change the circumstances of the example slightly. Suppose the firm expects to receive $110,000 in a year's time. What sum of money (if held today) would be equivalent to the future $110,000? The commonsense answer is $100,000. (This amount today will grow to exactly $110,000 in a year.) Equation 19.2 gives the same answer: $B = (110,000)/(1.1) = \$100,000$.

Extending the example, let's compute the future value of today's $100,000 if held in the bank account for *two* years. After one year, the balance has grown to $110,000. After the second year, the $110,000 balance will grow by an additional 10 percent. In other words, we must multiply $110,000 by the factor 1.1 to arrive at the new balance: $(1.1)(110,000) = \$121,000$. Notice that starting from the original $100,000 amount, we can find the final balance, $121,000, by applying the factor 1.1 twice; that is,

$$FV_2 = 1.1[(1.1)100,000] = \$121,000.$$

Within the brackets, we multiply the $100,000 sum by 1.1 to arrive at $110,000 after the first year. By applying the 1.1 factor outside the brackets, we determine the final amount after the second year.[1] In algebraic terms,

---

[1] We should recognize that, in this example, interest is compounded annually. This means that each year the firm earns interest on its whole balance to date, including its accumulated interest to date. In other words, the firm earns interest on its interest.

$$FV_2 = (1 + r)[(1 + r)B],$$

or

$$FV_2 = (1 + r)^2 B. \hspace{3cm} [19.3]$$

In general, if r is the annual interest rate, the future value after n years of B dollars today is

$$FV_n = (1 + r)^n B. \hspace{3cm} [19.4]$$

The following example makes the point.

EXAMPLE 1   Suppose we invest $100,000. At 10 percent annual interest, the future value after four years is $146,410. After seven years, the future value is $194,872. How did we find these future values? The easiest method is to compute the so-called future-value factors, $(1.1)^4$ and $(1.1)^7$. For instance, the former is 1.4641. Multiplying this factor by the original balance yields $146,410. Observe that, due to compounding, future values grow relatively quickly over time. Earning 10 percent annual interest, the original $100,000 almost doubles in seven years. Tables of future-value factors (by varying interest rates and number of years) are readily available and save the tedium of calculation by hand. The same results can be quickly obtained using a financial calculator or a standard spreadsheet program.

CHECK STATION 1   At an annual interest rate of 12 percent, what is the future value one year from now of $560 today? At the same interest rate, what is the future value of $560 five years from now?

Valuing Future Cash Flows

A **cash flow (CF)** denotes a pattern of monetary amounts received (or paid) by the firm over time. For instance, by making a significant monetary investment now, a firm may expect to obtain increasing annual profits over the life of the investment program—say, 15 years. We can extend the reasoning from the previous section to value *any* future cash flow, no matter how complicated. Let's begin with the simplest cash flow, a one-time monetary payment received by the firm n years from now. Assume that the annual interest rate will remain steady over this time period. Then the present value of this future receipt is

$$PV = \frac{CF_n}{(1 + r)^n}. \hspace{3cm} [19.5]$$

Here CF_n denotes the cash flow the firm receives in year n and PV is its present value today. Equation 19.5 is simply a rearrangement of Equation 19.4 (along with a change in notation: PV in place of B and CF_n in place of FV_n).

EXAMPLE 2 Suppose the firm expects to receive a cash inflow of $146,410 four years from now. At 10 percent, the present value of this receipt is $(146,410)/(1.1)^4 = \$100,000$. If, instead, the firm were to receive a $200,000 payment six years from now, the present value would be $(200,000)/(1.1)^6 = \$112,895$.

Notice that pushing a cash flow further into the future lowers its present value. In Equation 19.5, the term in the denominator, $(1 + r)^n$, becomes larger and larger as n increases. Equation 19.5 expresses the fact that any future cash flow must be discounted to determine its true present value. The higher the interest rate and/or the more delayed the cash flow, the greater the degree of discounting.

CHECK STATION 2 (a) Find the present value of $500 received four years from now if the effective annual interest rate is 6 percent. Of $500 received 16 years from now. (b) Answer the questions in part a assuming a 12 percent interest rate.

What if the firm expects to obtain a number of monetary receipts at different years in the future? Then the present value of the entire stream of future monetary receipts is simply the sum of the receipts' individual present values.

EXAMPLE 3 A firm expects to receive $146,410 four years from now *and* $200,000 six years from now. Using our earlier results from Example 2, we find the (total) present value of this cash flow to be $100,000 + $112,895 = $212,895.

In general, the present value of any cash flow can be expressed as

$$PV = \sum_{n=0}^{T} \frac{CF_n}{(1 + r)^n}. \qquad [19.6]$$

Here the symbol Σ denotes summation over the discounted cash flows in the years 0, 1, 2,..., T. An equivalent way to write the equation is $PV = CF_0 + CF_1/(1 + r) + CF_2/(1 + r)^2 + \ldots + CF_T/(1 + r)^T$. In the formula, CF_0, the cash flow received today, is not discounted because $(1 + r)^0$ is simply 1. Obviously, the present value of any cash flow depends on the underlying interest rate, the number and size of future receipts, and when they occur. The following example illustrates the computation of present values for varying cash flows.

EXAMPLE 4 A textile firm is considering building a new facility that will allow it to increase production. Building the plant will require an immediate capital outlay of $500,000 and will take one year. The firm expects that the plant, when in operation, will generate an addition to the firm's operating profit of $200,000 per year (based on annual revenues of $1,100,000 and annual operating costs of $900,000) for the next five years beginning one year from now.[2] The annual interest rate applicable over this time period is 12 percent. What is the present value associated with building the plant?

Because we will be working with increasingly complex cash flows, it is useful to represent them on a time line. Figure 19.1a displays the time line for the present example. All monetary amounts are in thousands of dollars. Note that monetary inflows (cash received) appear above the time line; the initial capital expenditure (an outflow) appears as a negative value below the line. The present value associated with this cash flow is

$$PV = -500 + \frac{200}{1.12} + \frac{200}{(1.12)^2} + \frac{200}{(1.12)^3} + \frac{200}{(1.12)^4} + \frac{200}{(1.12)^5}$$

$$= -500 + (178.6 + 159.4 + 142.3 + 127.1 + 113.5)$$

$$= -500 + 720.9$$

$$= \$220.9 \text{ thousand.}$$

Notice that the $500,000 immediate capital expense is not discounted; it is already a present value since it is incurred today. The combined present value of the firm's future profits (the terms in parentheses) comes to $720,900. Thus, the *net* present value of the cash flows associated with building the plant is 720,900 − 500,000 = $220,900. *Net* refers to the fact that it takes into account all cash flows, including the initial investment.

We can make the present example more realistic by introducing taxes. Suppose the firm pays a flat 34 percent tax rate on its taxable income. The $200,000 annual profit flows are taxable with one exception: The firm is allowed a deduction for the depreciation of its production facility over its lifetime. Under the tax law, the firm can depreciate the building on a straight-line basis over five years. This simply means the firm can take a deduction of $100,000 (one-fifth of the total $500,000 capital cost) against its annual income for each of the next five years. Thus, its yearly taxable income is 200,000 − 100,000 = $100,000. At the 34 percent rate, its tax is $34,000, with the result that the firm's after-tax cash flow is $166,000. Thus, we can take the effect of taxes into account by inserting $166,000 into the cash-flow time line (see part b of Figure 19.1) and into the present-value calculation. Accounting for taxes, the present value of building the plant becomes

$$PV = -500 + \frac{166}{1.12} + \frac{166}{(1.12)^2} + \frac{166}{(1.12)^3} + \frac{166}{(1.12)^4} + \frac{166}{(1.12)^5}$$

$$= -500 + 148.2 + 132.3 + 118.1 + 105.5 + 94.2$$

$$= -500 + 598.4$$

$$= \$98.4 \text{ thousand.}$$

[2] Five years is the firm's estimate of the remaining life of the product. After this time, profits will cease. Furthermore, it expects that the plant will be closed and bring little or nothing in the way of resale value.

FIGURE 19.1

Building a Plant: A
Cash-Flow Time Line

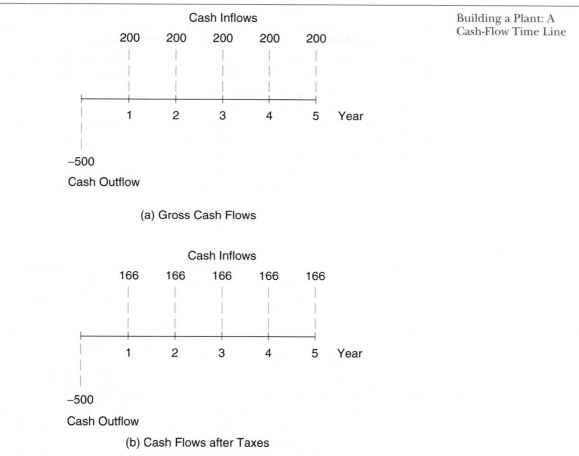

(a) Gross Cash Flows

(b) Cash Flows after Taxes

ANNUITIES   Many investment problems involve periodic cash flows of fixed amounts. Such cash flows commonly are referred to as **annuities**. For instance, the decision to build the plant generates a five-year level annuity (in the amount of $166,000 after taxes). In that example, we calculated the present value of the annuity by hand. Fortunately, the present values of annuities of different durations and at different interest rates have been tabulated and are readily available. (See, for example, Table 19A.2 in the chapter appendix.) A typical annuity table lists the present value of *$1* per year for each of the next T years at a given interest rate r; that is, the table lists present values for different combinations of T and r. For example, one such entry would correspond to a five-year annuity at a 12 percent discount rate: $T = 5$ and $r = .12$. The present value of such an annuity paying $1 per year is

$$\frac{1}{1.12} + \frac{1}{(1.12)^2} + \frac{1}{(1.12)^3} + \frac{1}{(1.12)^4} + \frac{1}{(1.12)^5} = 3.605.$$

In other words, at a 12 percent discount rate, a five-year annuity paying $1 at each installment has a present value of $3.605. The entry 3.605 is listed in the annuity table. If the annual payment were $100 instead of $1, the corresponding present value would be $(3.605)(100) = \$360.50$. In the decision to build the plant, the annual cash flow is $166,000; therefore, the associated present value is $(3.605)(166,000) = \$598,400$. This is exactly the present value found earlier by direct calculation. Accounting for the $500,000 initial outlay, the net present value of building the plant is $98,400.

A **perpetual annuity**—or, simply, a **perpetuity**—is an annuity that goes on forever. For example, suppose the annual $166,000 cash flow is expected to occur indefinitely, year after year. At a 12 percent interest rate, what is the present value of such a perpetual annuity? There exists an important, and very simple, rule for finding the net present value of any perpetuity. The present value is simply

$$PV = \frac{CF}{r}, \qquad [19.7]$$

where CF denotes the constant annual cash flow and r is the discount rate. In words, the present value of a perpetuity is found by dividing the periodic payment by the annual interest rate. For instance, in the plant example, $PV = \$166,000/.12 = \$1,383,333$.

Here is an easy way to confirm the logic of this rule.[3] Imagine putting an amount of principal, say, $150,000, in a bank account and leaving it there forever. You never will touch the principal but will withdraw the interest each year. What amount of cash flow (in the form of interest) will the $150,000 generate? If the interest rate is, say, 6 percent, the interest earned after the first year is $9,000. You withdraw this cash flow (perhaps to spend), leaving the original $150,000 in the account. After another year, an additional $9,000 cash flow is generated and withdrawn, and this process goes on year after year. The initial $150,000 in principal, thus, generates $9,000 per year forever. Whatever the interest rate and amount of original principal (B), the annual cash flow is simply $CF = rB$. Rearranging this expression (and recognizing the invested principal as a present value), we arrive at Equation 19.7.

Finally, we sometimes need to value a *growing perpetuity*. Suppose an annuity pays CF after the first year and the payment rises by g percent each year thereafter. A growing perpetuity has a present value of

$$PV = \frac{CF}{(1+r)} + \frac{CF(1+g)}{(1+r)^2} + \frac{CF(1+g)^2}{(1+r)^3} + \frac{CF(1+g)^3}{(1+r)^4} + \ldots$$

---

[3] Consider an infinite sum of the form $a(1 + x + x^2 + \ldots)$, where a can take on any value and x is any value less than 1. The value of this sum is $a/(1 - x)$. A perpetual annuity corresponds to the case $a = CF/(1 + r)$ and $x = 1/(1 + r)$. Substituting these values yields $PV = a/(1 - x) = CF/r$.

Here the term 1 + g is applied repeatedly to future cash flows to account for growth. (For instance, 5 percent annual growth corresponds to g = .05.) The sum of this infinite series reduces to a very simple form:

$$PV = \frac{CF}{r - g}.$$ [19.8]

The appropriate denominator is simply the difference between the rate at which cash flows are discounted (r) and the rate at which cash flows grow (g). For instance, if next year's cash flow is $1,000 and 8 percent growth is expected in cash flows thereafter, the resulting present value (discounting at r = .12) becomes PV = $1,000/(.12 − .08) = $25,000.

EXAMPLE 5   In forecasting long-run cash flows, inflation often causes cash flows to grow. Returning to the firm's plant investment decision, suppose the firm expects future dollar profits to grow by 4 percent per year due solely to price inflation. Cash flows will continue into perpetuity, and the firm's discount rate remains at 12 percent. The resulting present value is PV = $166,000/(.12 − .04) = $2,075,000. Here we do not have to go to the trouble of computing the ever-increasing cash flows; we simply use $166,000. Roughly, this can be thought of as a real, that is, inflation-adjusted, cash flow. In real terms, the firm earns a constant operating profit each year of $166,000. In turn, r − g = .12 − .04 = .08, or 8 percent. We can think of this rate, as a "real" interest rate; that is, it equals the nominal interest rate minus the expected rate of inflation. Thus, we have two equivalent ways to compute present values while properly accounting for inflation: (1) listing cash flows in nominal dollars and discounting by a nominal interest rate, or (2) listing cash flows in real (i.e., inflation-adjusted) dollars and discounting by a real interest rate. As the preceding example shows, often it is simpler to think of (and compute) cash flows in real terms.

Discounting and Valuation

The interest rate used in present-value calculations is known as the **discount rate** (or sometimes the **hurdle rate**). Before calculating the present value of a cash flow, we must specify the discount rate. In the preceding discussion, we assumed that placing money in a bank account generates cash flows at a known (and certain) rate of interest. Consider a simple bank account investment that is risk free and offers 5 percent interest. It follows that *any* other risk-free investment should be held to a comparable discount rate. Such an investment will be considered profitable if and only if it has a positive net present value when its cash flows are discounted at 5 percent. For example, suppose that, under the terms of a "special" banking account, an investment of $1,000 today produces a payback of $1,250 after five years. Is this a profitable investment? The answer is no. At a 5 percent discount rate, the net present value of this investment is

$$PV = -\$1,000 + \frac{(\$1,250)}{(1.05)^5}$$

$$= -1,000 + 979 = -\$21.$$

An individual would do better putting his or her money in an ordinary account that pays 5 percent annual interest and leaving it there. There is nothing special about the "special" account.

Now, let's change the setting slightly and suppose the future cash flows are uncertain. Assume the decision maker can estimate the *expected values* of future cash flows but recognizes that the actual, realized cash flows will vary. How should one assess the expected value of this risky investment? In general, we should use a higher discount rate to value a risky investment than to value a sure investment. This higher discount rate reflects risk aversion on the part of the firm's investors. More generally, it stems from the basic trade-off between risk and return embodied in all financial markets. Investors in financial markets (in stocks, bonds, money market funds, and other securities) require a higher rate of return for bearing additional risk. Thus, the 12 percent discount rate applied to the firm's investment in the new plant indicates that there is some degree of risk associated with the project.

The moral is that the discount rate used in present-value calculations depends on the riskiness of the expected cash flow. In valuing a risky project, one approach is to look to the financial markets to judge the kinds of required rates of return associated with other investment projects of comparable risk. Later in the chapter, we will explore the implications of the capital asset pricing model for estimating appropriate discount rates.

To sum up, net present value measures the monetary value to the firm (in today's dollars) of any investment project. We can compute the present value from the project's associated cash flows using Equation 19.6. Examination of that equation, or of any of the earlier examples, shows that

> The net present value associated with positive future cash flows is greater (1) the greater the cash flows themselves, (2) the sooner they occur, and (3) the lower the interest rate used for discounting.

CHECK STATION 3   Calculate the net present value of building the plant using after-tax cash flows and assuming the appropriate discount rate is 24 percent (due to the high risk of the project).

Suppose that you have won $1 million in the state lottery. According to the rules of the game, the lottery will pay this to you in 20 equal annual payments of $50,000 with the first payment coming immediately. As you are by now well aware, this prize is worth considerably less than the advertised $1 million. Using the valuation techniques described in this chapter, you could determine the present value of this prize. It perhaps should not surprise you that there are companies willing to buy this cash flow from you. Two companies, Singer Asset Finance Co. of West Palm Beach, Florida, and Sterling Capital of New York, currently dominate this market.[4] Employees of these "prize brokers" track down lottery winners and offer to buy all or part of their winnings for lump sums of cash. They then turn around and resell these cash flows to investors that include large institutions such as John Hancock Mutual Life Insurance Co. of Boston and SunAmerica Inc. of Los Angeles. More recently, brokers have begun to securitize lottery winnings. That is, after buying winnings from a large number of lottery winners, the brokers bundle them into one fund and then sell shares in the fund.

How much could you expect to receive up front from a finance company in return for surrendering all rights to future payments? A 20-year jackpot totaling $1 million might fetch an immediate lump-sum payment of $450,000 to $500,000. This is considerably less than the present value of these future payments. The reduced payment allows for myriad legal fees and provides a substantial profit for the finance company. Yet, many lottery winners are anxious to sell for good and bad reasons. Many take the lump-sum option to relieve themselves of burdensome debts. However, others choose to transact simply because they are impatient for the money or because they are poorly informed about the value of what they are giving up. Indeed, some brokers and finance firms have been accused of preying on lottery winners, using aggressive (some would say fraudulent) negotiation tactics to take a large part of their money. In response, a number of state lotteries have begun to let winners opt for an immediate lump-sum award option.

A similar industry has sprung up around structured settlements for injured plaintiffs. For example, an injured plaintiff may settle with an insurance company for monthly payments over an extended period of time. A broker will offer a lump-sum payment for all or part of these cash flows. These brokers then resell these cash flows to investors and institutions.

Collecting Now:
Lotteries and
Liability
Settlements

MAKING INVESTMENT DECISIONS

Capital budgeting helps guide the manager's investment decisions. Suppose the manager has undertaken a careful cash-flow analysis of a particular investment. He or she has computed the investment's present value using an

---

[4] This account is based on V. O'Connell, "How Major Players Turn Lottery Jackpots into a Guaranteed Bet," *The Wall Street Journal* (September 23, 1997): A1, and V. O'Connell, "Thriving Industry Buys Insurance Settlements from Injured Plaintiffs," *The Wall Street Journal* (February 25, 1998): A1.

appropriate discount rate. What should the manager do now? We address this question in three related contexts:

1. Only a single investment is under consideration.
2. The choice is among multiple, mutually exclusive investment options.
3. Multiple investments can be undertaken but are subject to a resource constraint.

A Single-Investment Decision

In the single-investment scenario, the firm must decide between investing in the project or rejecting it (sticking with the status quo). The manager's optimal rule is straightforward:

> The firm should undertake the project if and only if the project's net present value is positive.

In Example 3 above, we saw that building the plant has a net present value of $98,400. The PV measures precisely the monetary value of this opportunity. By building the facility, the manager is increasing the total value of the firm by $98,400. Indeed, it is best to think of the value of the firm itself as the present value of its future cash flows from all of its operations, that is, its investments and production of goods and services. With the acceptance of each positive-NPV investment project, the total value of the firm increases. (Of course, by the same reasoning, the firm should reject any negative-NPV investment.) In short, the present-value rule provides a simple screen concerning investment decisions.

THE INTERNAL RATE OF RETURN   An alternative, equivalent way to evaluate a single-investment decision uses the investment's internal rate of return. An investment's **internal rate of return (IRR)** is the discount rate at which the project's cash flows have a present value of zero. In algebraic terms, this rate of return is found by setting the fundamental present-value expression in Equation 19.6 equal to zero, after assigning cash-flow estimates for CF_0, CF_1, ..., CF_T, and then solving for r. As a practical matter, we use calculators or computers to find the internal rate of return. (For instance, most financial calculators compute an IRR at the touch of a key.) The tabular portion of Figure 19.2 lists the present value of building the plant at alternative discount rates. With these data in hand, we can determine the project's IRR by trial and error.

Notice that the project's PV steadily falls as the discount rate increases. (The higher the discount rate, the less valuable the project's future cash flows.) At what discount rate does the project's present value become zero? The answer (to the nearest decimal) is 19.7 percent. This is the project's internal rate of

FIGURE 19.2

Building a Plant:
PVs at Different
Discount Rates

Discount Rate	Present Value
0.0%	$330,000
6.0	195,250
12.0	99,400
18.0	19,100
19.0	7,600
19.7	−263
20.0	−3,500
24.0	−44,300
30.0	−95,700

Investment's Present-Value Curve

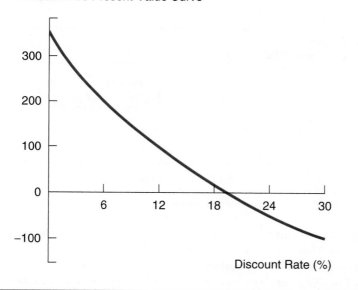

return. The graph in Figure 19.2 depicts a present-value curve for the project over a range of discount rates.

From either part of Figure 19.2, the following proposition emerges:

The firm should undertake an investment project if and only if the project's internal rate of return is greater than the discount rate.

By definition, the project has a present value of zero when the prevailing discount rate exactly matches the project's IRR. At any lower discount rate (r < IRR), the project's PV is positive, so the project is worth undertaking.

FIGURE 19.3

The Difference between
Discount Rate and
Internal Rate of Return

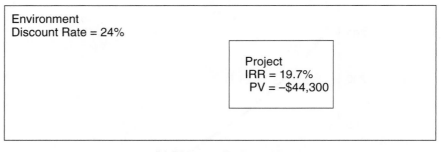

At a higher discount rate ($r > IRR$), its PV is negative and the project should be rejected. This confirms the proposition.[5]

It is important not to confuse the discount rate with the internal rate of return. The discount rate represents the rate of return of *alternative* investments in the same risk class. In this sense, it reflects the environment in which the firm operates. The internal rate of return is the rate of return on the project itself. Figure 19.3 underscores this difference. Observe that the investment project in question, building the plant, has an IRR of 19.7 percent. In part a of the figure, the surrounding environment is characterized by a discount rate of 12 percent for comparable risks. In such an environment, the net present value of the project is $98,400, and the project is worth undertaking. Part b places the same investment in a different environment, one characterized by a 24 percent discount rate. The internal rate of return on the project remains the same.

[5] The proposition holds provided the investment's present value slopes downward and crosses the x axis only once, as in Figure 19.2. This will occur whenever an investment (a negative cash flow) is followed by returns (positive cash flows). If the present-value curve has a different form (including multiple crossings), using the IRR criterion is more complicated. We then must modify the proposition.

(This is, in fact, why we call it the *internal* rate of return; it is not affected by the environment.) But now the investment is a poor bargain relative to the environment and, indeed, has a negative present value. In this setting, it should be rejected.

In sum, in a single-project decision, the investment should be undertaken if and only if (1) its present value (discounted at rate r) is positive or, equivalently, (2) its IRR is greater than r.

Mutually Exclusive Choices

In decisions involving multiple investment choices, the following proposition holds.

| In a choice among a number of mutually exclusive investment alternatives, the manager should choose the one that offers the greatest present value.

This proposition makes immediate sense. A project's PV measures the incremental value its cash flows add to the firm. If management wants to maximize the firm's total value, it should choose the project with the highest present value.

EXAMPLE 6   Before electing to build a new plant, the firm's management considers a second option: to contract with an outside supplier to increase its output. According to the firm's estimates, this option would require an upfront payment to the supplier of $100,000 and would generate incremental profits of $40,000 per year for each of the next five years (the life of the project). The associated risks of the options are comparable. Should the firm increase production by investing in-house or out of house?

The answer is that building the plant is the better option. Recall that, at a discount rate of 12 percent, its PV is $98,400. By comparison, the PV of using the outside supplier is

$$PV = -\$100 + \frac{40}{1.12} + \frac{40}{(1.12)^2} + \frac{40}{(1.12)^3} + \frac{40}{(1.12)^4} + \frac{40}{(1.12)^5} = \$44,190$$

This is somewhat less than half the PV of building the plant.

Here is an important point. When choosing among mutually exclusive alternatives, the IRR criterion is *not* a reliable guide. The current example makes the basic point. As we can check readily, the IRR associated with the outside-supply option is 28.7 percent! At face value, it would appear that going with the outside supplier is the more attractive option. Figure 19.4 demonstrates why this face-value reasoning is faulty. The figure depicts the present-value curves for each investment option. As claimed, the IRR of contracting with the outside supplier is 28.7 percent, well in excess of the 19.7 percent IRR

FIGURE 19.4

Comparing the Present
Values of Mutually
Exclusive Projects

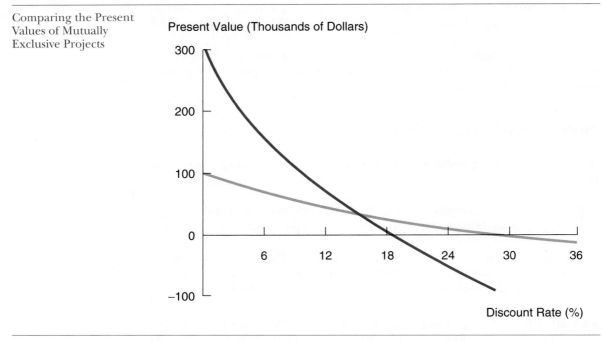

of building the plant. Nonetheless, the relevant issue is each option's net present value in the current environment, that is, at a discount rate of 12 percent. The slope of the outside-supply PV curve is much flatter than that of the inside-supply curve. Consequently, at a 12 percent discount rate, the latter's PV is much greater than the former's.

Notice that the slopes of the PV curves depend on the relative *scales* of the cash flows. Contracting outside is a small-scale investment, with modest future cash flows. Not surprisingly, its PV is limited. As an experiment, consider what would happen if the outside-supply option's cash flows were multiplied tenfold. (The initial investment is now $1,000,000, and the annual inflows are $400,000.) The present value would increase to $441,900. This option now would be clearly superior to producing in-house. The present-value curve would slope upward to the left much more steeply (10 times so) than before. But the new IRR would be 28.7 percent, exactly the same as in the base case. (Make sure you understand why.) In short, the IRR often gives the wrong message about the worth of an investment project. To sum up, because it is invariant with respect to scale, the IRR criterion should not be applied when selecting among mutually exclusive investments. The correct investment criterion relies on a comparison of present values.

Assume the discount rates associated with the inside- and outside-supply options are 18 percent and 12 percent, respectively, due to their differing degrees of risk. Compare the PVs of the two investment options to determine which should be undertaken.

CHECK STATION 4

Choices with Constrained Resources

Frequently, the manager faces an "embarrassment of riches": many investment projects with positive PVs but only limited funds with which to undertake them. In such cases, the manager seeks to undertake the set of investments that has a maximum total net present value subject to not exceeding the available funds. How should the manager prioritize the investment alternatives? Which should he or she choose to undertake? Consider the following application.

EXAMPLE 7   A firm has $1 million to invest and faces the following potential investment projects.

Project	Initial Investment	Net Present Value	NPV per $ Invested
A	$1,000,000	$2,000,000	2.0
B	400,000	1,400,000	3.5
C	300,000	1,200,000	4.0
D	100,000	600,000	6.0
E	200,000	500,000	2.5
F	200,000	300,000	1.5
G	100,000	50,000	.5

If the firm were not constrained, it would undertake all the programs because all have positive net present values (NPVs). Unfortunately, the firm has limited funds. To determine which projects to accept, the first step is to divide each project's NPV by the amount of the initial required investment. The NPVs per dollar invested are listed in the last column of the preceding table. The firm should choose the programs with the highest NPV's per dollar invested first. In descending order, these programs are D, C, B, and E. The manager stops listing additional programs because, together, these programs exhaust the $1 million in funds available. The total NPV from funding these programs is $3.7 million. If the manager simply had adopted the project with the highest NPV (project A), the total NPV would have come to only $2 million. Funding programs B through E, therefore, is optimal.[6]

---

[6] Because of investment indivisibilities, we must use common sense when ranking projects according to the PV per dollar of investment. If the budget had been $900,000 instead of $1,000,000, the top four programs would not have fit within it. The best the firm could do is substitute G for E to meet its budget. (Or perhaps it really could come up with the necessary additional $100,000.)

To summarize, under resource constraints, the manager should prioritize investment projects in order of the NPV generated per unit of the limited resource. In popular parlance, the goal is to identify investments that give the biggest bang for the buck (or in whatever currency the constrained resource is measured).

DETERMINING THE DISCOUNT RATE

To use NPV analysis, we need to estimate the rate of return for projects in a comparable risk class. Different investment projects carry different risks and, therefore, should be subject to different discount rates. Often, however, the precise determination of the appropriate discount rate is problematic. Therefore, techniques have been developed to get an approximate estimate of the appropriate discount rate.

The Weighted Average Cost of Capital

The weighted average cost of capital method makes the simplifying assumption that the project in question has the same risk characteristics as does the firm in general. If the firm has predominantly safe investments, the current project probably is safe as well; if the firm has more risky investments, the project likely is also more risky. That is, of course, only an approximation, but it is useful because it is easier to determine the appropriate rate for the firm than for an individual project. After all, in most cases, the stock and bond markets price the firm's shares and debt.

The firm's **weighted average cost of capital (WACC)** is the average of the rate of return on the firm's debt and the rate of return on its equity. To see how the approach works, let's suppose the firm has 40 percent debt and 60 percent equity. Suppose further that the firm pays 9.9 percent on its debt and returns 19.5 percent on its stock. Then the weighted average cost of capital is

$$\text{WACC} = (9.9)(.4) + (19.5)(.6) = 15.7\%.$$

How do we determine the firm's returns on its debt and equity? In general, a company is always borrowing money, often through bond offerings. To borrow money, the firm must pay interest; thus, it is easy to obtain the interest on debt. However, we should keep in mind that, because we are evaluating after-tax cash flows, we must calculate the after-tax interest rate. Since firms get a tax deduction for interest expenses, every dollar of interest paid shields a dollar of profits from taxation. Assuming the marginal tax rate is 34 percent, this saves the firm $.34 on the dollar. Thus, each dollar of before-tax interest really costs the firm $.66. In short, to find the after-tax rate of return on debt, we multiply the before-tax rate by .66. In this case, the before-tax rate on the firm's debt is 15 percent. Therefore, the after-tax rate is 9.9 percent.

Finding the rate of return on equity is more difficult. We could directly observe how well the stock has performed in, say, the last five years and use that rate of return. (For example, we could calculate the internal rate of return of an investment in shares five years ago if cashed in today.) Unfortunately, this method lacks precision because returns depend not only on firm-specific risks but also on general market conditions.

To obtain a more precise measure of the rate of return on equity, analysts divide the return on a stock into two components, a risk-free component and a component determined by risk:

$$r_s = r_f + r_p, \qquad\qquad [19.9]$$

where r_s is the return on the stock, r_f is the risk-free rate of return, and r_p is the risk premium. To find the risk-free rate, we typically look at the current rate of return on short-term bonds issued by the federal government.

How do we go about estimating the risk premium of a firm's stock? Modern finance theory posits that, for any security, there is a predictable relationship between risk and the expected return. We can estimate this risk–return trade-off using the **capital asset pricing model**. This model posits that a firm's risk (and, therefore, its expected rate of return) depends on its correlation with movements in the stock market as a whole. *Beta* measures the relationship between the individual stock's return and the return of the stock market; that is, it measures the systematic risk of the stock.[7] We interpret the beta of a firm's stock as follows. If the company has a beta of 1, the systematic risk of the stock is the same as the market (as measured by the S&P 500 or some other broad-based index). This means the stock should have the same risk premium as the market. If the beta is 2, the stock should have twice the risk premium of the market. A number of financial studies have documented the historic differences between the long-run rate of return on stocks and the risk-free rate of return. Over the last 50 years, the annual rate of return on stocks has averaged 12 percent and the return on risk-free, short-term treasury securities has averaged 3.5 percent. Thus, the risk premium on the stock market is about 8.5 percent.

We can rewrite Equation 19.9 as

$$r_s = r_f + \beta(r_m - r_f), \qquad\qquad [19.10]$$

where β denotes beta and $r_m - r_f$ is the market risk premium. Continuing our example, suppose the beta on the firm's stock is 1.4 and short-term government

[7] A stock's beta typically is estimated using regression techniques. Specifically, the realized risk premiums of the stock are regressed on the realized risk premiums of the market. Typically, this is done using monthly returns over a period of 60 months, that is, five years. Fortunately, managers do not have to carry out their own beta analyses because a number of financial reporting firms perform this service and report the results.

bonds currently have a return of 7.6 percent. Then the firm's cost of equity is $r_s = 7.6 + (1.4)(8.5) = 19.5$ percent. Using this value in combination with the firm's cost of debt, the manager determines the firm's weighted average cost of capital. The WACC found earlier was 15.7 percent.

Managers should use the WACC formulation with care. Some justify the use of the weighted average cost of capital because this is what it costs the firm to raise money to finance the project. If this were the case, however, we would notice two things. One is that all projects would use the same discount rate irrespective of their risk; that is, the manager would be indifferent between two projects with the same expected cash flows even if one were highly risky and the other very safe. This cannot be true. It also would mean that the net present value of projects would depend on their financing. The same project would have a lower or higher net present value depending on whether it was financed by equity or debt. This also is not true. The sole justification for using the weighted average cost of capital is that this project has approximately the same risk as the company as a whole. If the project's risk is far greater than that of the firm as a whole, a higher discount rate should be used. If the project has lower risk, then a lower rate is appropriate.[8]

A FINAL REMINDER   As with all methods of decision making, the manager should engage in a thorough sensitivity analysis. This applies especially to capital budgeting. In estimating cash flows, we should include both optimistic and pessimistic scenarios and compute NPV using a range of discount rates. Computing the project's IRR is a step in this direction. Plotting a complete present-value curve for the project is especially beneficial. If the decision to invest comes out the same under varying assumptions, the manager can have some degree of confidence that he or she is making a sound decision. If the decision is highly sensitive to these assumptions, the manager probably should take a closer look before leaping.

Boeing's New Jet Revisited

To evaluate Boeing's development of the Dreamliner, consider the projections given in Figure 19.5's spreadsheet.[9] Note the following:

1. During the five years of development, the firm has budgeted its investment costs at $8.0 billion spread somewhat unevenly over years 2004 to 2008.

2. Projected sales begin in 2009 with 30 projected deliveries and peak in 2020 with 219 deliveries, before declining thereafter. (The projected deliveries come from a thor-

---

[8] Other methods may lead to better estimates in specific cases. For example, if a company is entering a new business, it might be better to use the WACCs of other companies already in the business.

[9] This account and the data herein are based on Tompkins and Bruner, "The Boeing 7E7," *Case Study*, Darden Business Publishing, University of Virginia (2004), M. Brelis, "Faster vs. Bigger," *The Boston Globe* (May 6, 2001): C1, and other published sources.

FIGURE 19.5

Hypothetical Cash
Flows for the
Dreamliner

	A	B	C	D	E	F	G	H	I	J	K	L	M	N	O	P	Q
1																	
2																	
3				NPV		IRR		WACC									
4				$3.52		13.7%		0.092									
5																	
6								Cash-Flow Time Line									
7																	
8		Year		2004	2005	2006	2007	2008	2009	2010	2011	2012	2013	2014	2015	2016	
9																	
10		Devel. Cost		−0.8	−1.2	−3.3	−2.3	−0.4									
11		Planes Sold		x	x	x	x	x	30	64	108	82	84	104	119	136	
12		Cash Flow		−0.8	−1.2	−3.3	−2.3	−0.4	0.375	0.816	1.405	1.088	1.137	1.435	1.675	1.953	
13																	
14																	
15		Year		2017	2018	2019	2020	2021	2022	2023	2024	2025	2026	2027	2028		
16																	
17		Planes Sold		150	185	192	219	185	160	149	108	105	95	100	125		
18		Cash Flow		2.197	2.764	2.926	3.404	2.933	2.587	2.458	1.817	1.802	1.663	1.785	2.276		
19																	

oughgoing analysis of airline fleets.) The company projects that it will deliver 2,500 aircraft during twenty years of production.

3. Because of inflation, the firm's nominal profit per plane, initially $12.5 million, is
expected to grow by 2 percent per year.

4. These projections represent expected cash flows and are far from certain.

Based on these facts, we can confirm the cash flow estimates in Figure 19.5. For instance,
the expected cash flow in 2011 is $(12.5)(1.02)^2(108) = \$1,405$ million (after incorporat-
ing two years of price inflation).

It remains to specify the discount rate. Since the future risks of the Dreamliner program probably resemble the risks of the firm as a whole, we consider Boeing's weighted
average cost of capital. In 2001, when Boeing evaluated this project, Boeing's capital structure consisted of 43 percent debt and 57 percent equity. The company's beta was about
.6. (On average, its stock return was less volatile than the market.) With a forecasted nominal risk-free rate of 5 percent, its cost of equity is

$$r_s = 5.0 + (.6)(8.5) = 10.1\%.$$

Here, as earlier, we have taken 8.5 percent as the market risk premium. Finally, the firm's weighted average cost of capital is

$$WACC = (.43)(8.0) + (.57)(10.1) = 9.2\%.$$

Discounting these expected cash flows at 9.2 percent (using the financial formula for net present value provided by the spreadsheet program), we find the present value of the Dreamliner program (as of 2004) to be PV = $3.52 billion. If all goes according to plan, the program will add an appreciable amount to the value of the company. However, one can check that the IRR of the program is 13.7 percent (again using the formula function provided by the spreadsheet program). If Boeing finds its cost of capital rising above this rate (due to changed financial conditions), the investment in the new plane would no longer be profitable.

Continental Airlines faces its own investment problem and takes a somewhat different analytical approach. Are the greater fares and profits associated with the aircraft worth the higher price (an added $20 million above the price of a conventional jet)? Airline executives estimate that higher fares and lower fuel costs will translate into $1.5 million in added profit earned each year for each plane over its 20-year life. Deciding to look at the problem *in real terms*, management believes that fares and costs (such as pilots' wages and fuel prices) will just keep pace with inflation for the foreseeable future. Therefore, management reckons that the $1.5 million profit advantage will remain constant in real terms over the plane's life.

The crux of Continental's problem is to determine the appropriate real interest rate to use in discounting these real cash flows. In this respect, the WACC of the firm as a whole offers little guidance. Airline stocks tend to be more volatile than the stock market as a whole and, therefore, to have high betas. But management sees the real cash flows of the Dreamliner purchase decision as being relatively safe. As a first approximation, it sees the beta of the investment as zero (i.e., the project's risks are uncorrelated with stock market movements). Accordingly, it believes the investment should be discounted at the long-term *real* risk-free rate. Most studies estimate this rate to be in the neighborhood of 2.5 to 3 percent.

What is the present value of the purchase decision? Using Table 19A.2 in the appendix to this chapter, we note that, at 3 percent, a $1 annuity over 20 years has a PV of $14.88. Therefore, the PV of purchasing the Dreamliner is

$$PV = -20 + (14.88)(1.5) = \$2.3 \text{ million per plane.}$$

Ordering a number of these planes for its fleet appears to be an attractive proposition for Continental.

SUMMARY

Decision-Making Principles

1. Many (if not most) investment projects have a time element. A typical investment project involves initial outlays followed by cash inflows.

2. Managers should evaluate projects on the basis of cash flows. This requires taking taxes and depreciation into consideration.

3. Present value incorporates the notion that a future dollar is worth less than a dollar today. Three present-value decision rules help guide investment decisions:
   a. A single investment project should be undertaken if and only if (1) its net present value is positive or, equivalently, (2) its IRR exceeds r.
   b. Among multiple, mutually exclusive investment projects, the one with the highest present value (assuming this is positive) should be chosen.
   c. In the presence of funding constraints, investment projects should be undertaken in the order of present value per dollar invested.

4. To discount cash flows, firms should use the prevailing interest rate for projects in the same risk class.

5. As with all decision-making techniques, managers should perform sensitivity analysis before making a final decision. This involves considering both optimistic and pessimistic forecasts of the expected cash flows as well as using a range of estimates for the discount rate.

Nuts and Bolts

1. The value of the firm is the total present value of its cash flows from all its activities (its investments, goods and services production, and so on).

2. An investment's present value is found by discounting its future cash flows:

$$PV = \sum_{n=0}^{T} \frac{CF_n}{(1 + r)^n}.$$

3. The internal rate of return on an investment is the interest rate at which its present value is exactly zero.

4. If a project has approximately the same risk as the firm as a whole, managers can use the weighted average cost of capital as the discount rate. The WACC is a weighted average of the rates of return on the firm's debt and equity.

Questions and Problems

1. A private company is considering building and operating a downtown parking garage. The company would site the garage on company-owned land, and construction would require demolition of a small, company-owned apartment building. Which of the following items constitute an incremental benefit or cost of the investment?
   a. The market value of the apartment building
   b. Site preparation costs

  c. The cost of site work and grading done last year

  d. The portion of the company's administrative costs allocated to the new garage

  e. Future parking revenues from the garage

  f. Future depreciation

  g. Reduction in the company's overall taxes due to a statewide investment tax credit

2. Describe how you would compute the net present value of a personal investment decision, such as whether to pursue an M.B.A. degree, purchase a car, or pay a higher price for an energy-saving refrigerator.

3. A tax-exempt, private university is considering whether to build a new dormitory. The university's financial vice president has the following facts. The university plans to start construction in 2009 and will complete it in two years at a total cost of $10 million. The university estimates that the building, once completed, will generate cash flows (from room charges) of $2 million per year for 20 years. The university's cost of borrowing is 10 percent. Would you recommend going ahead with the dormitory?

4. A state commission runs a lottery in which it sells 1 million $1 tickets, one of which will be selected as the grand-prize winner. The winner will receive $1 million payable in 20 annual installments of $50,000 each, with the first payment today. At an interest rate of 8 percent, what is the present value of the winner's monetary receipts? What is the lottery commission's profit?

5. In evaluating an investment, a manager forecasts cash flows to increase 2 percent in real terms over the life of the project. There is little or no uncertainty associated with these cash flows. Thus, the manager believes they should be discounted at a risk-free rate of return. The current treasury bill rate is 6 percent; therefore, the manager uses this rate for discounting. Is the manager's approach correct? Provide a short critique.

6. Your firm is considering two mutually exclusive projects with the following cash flows.

	Year 0 (Today)	Years 1–11	Year 12
Project A	−$400,000	$41,000	$400,000
Project B	−120,000	17,000	165,000

  a. Which project (if either) should your firm adopt if the discount rate is 4 percent? What if the discount rate is 12 percent? 20 percent?

  b. Estimate the IRR for each project.

7. A firm is attempting to decide which of two machines to purchase. The machines serve exactly the same purpose, so the only issue is their cost.

Machine A costs $30,000; it will last three years and cost $8,000 to run each year. Machine B costs $20,000; it is expected to last only two years and to cost $12,000 to run each year.

At an interest rate of 10 percent, which machine costs less? (Be careful to account for the different working lives of the machines. You may wish to compare them over a six-year horizon.)

8. A company is trying to decide which of two computer systems to install. System A costs $1 million and will increase operating profits by $500,000 per year. Its useful life is five years. Because of rapid technological change, it will have no salvage value at the end of this time. System B costs $1.5 million and will increase operating profits by $800,000 per year. Its useful life also is five years, and it too will have no salvage value. For tax purposes, the company can depreciate either computer system on a straight-line basis.
   a. Suppose the company's tax rate is 40 percent and its cost of capital for either computer system is 10 percent. Which system should it buy?
   b. If no depreciation is allowed, which computer system is the better choice?

9. Consider a firm that is funded entirely by equity. It is considering a risky investment project. The treasury bill rate is 6 percent, and the expected return on the stock market is 12 percent.
   a. If the investment's beta is 1.5, what is its required return?
   b. Suppose the investment's beta is .8 and its IRR is 9 percent. Does this investment have a positive present value? Explain.

10. A software firm has 130 programmers to be assigned to different projects. Due to a scarcity of experienced programmers, the firm cannot hire new ones in the near future. Each project requires a specific number of programmers to meet its goals. The following table summarizes the dollar values and labor requirements of the various projects.

Project	NPV	Number of Programmers
A	$1,000,000	40
B	800,000	20
C	1,200,000	50
D	600,000	30
E	500,000	25
F	440,000	20
G	525,000	35

What assignment of personnel maximizes the firm's total value? Explain.

11. a. As part of a joint venture, another firm extends your firm money up front in return for a share of future profits. The cash flow pattern for your firm is +$5,000, −$3,000, −$4,000. Compute the associated IRR. For what range of discount rates would the partnership be beneficial to your firm? (Be careful with your answer.)

   b. Consider the cash-flow pattern −$1,000, +$3,000, −$2,500. Compute the associated PV at the following interest rates: 0, 5, 15, and 50 percent. Does an IRR exist? What do you conclude about the value of this investment?

   c. Consider the cash-flow pattern −$5,000, +$11,500, −$6,600. Compute the associated PV at the following interest rates: 0, 5, 10, 15, 20, and 50 percent. Does the project have a single IRR? At what discount rates is the project justified?

12. When the armed forces downsized in the 1990s, the Department of Defense offered thousands of military personnel a choice of severance packages. The individual could accept an immediate lump-sum payment of $50,000 or instead $8,000 per year for 30 years. (In the event of death, the annuity would continue to pay to the individual's named recipient.)

   a. Which package would you choose? Explain exactly how you would determine your choice.

   b. In counseling its personnel, the military provided pamphlets comparing the financial implications of the two plans. In making the comparisons, it used the prevailing interest rate on money market funds (a risk-free 7 percent rate at the time). Despite the military's recommendation of the annuity, about 70 percent of enlisted personnel and 50 percent of officers chose the lump sum. In your view, does this behavior make financial sense? Can you suggest reasons (rational or irrational), why individuals tended to choose the immediate financial reward?

Discussion Question At age 25, you have just received your M.B.A. degree and have been offered an attractive job at a salary of $50,000. You expect to work until age 65 and then retire and live off your savings for another 20 years. Over the years, you expect your average wage increases to just keep pace with the rate of inflation. Thus, your *real* wage will remain $50,000. After paying all variety of income taxes (federal, state, and social security), your after-tax income (again in real terms) is $40,000 per year.

You will invest any money you save each year in a portfolio of bonds and stocks. Your portfolio is modestly risky and is projected to earn an expected *real* return (i.e., above inflation) of 4 percent per year.

a. Compute the present value of your lifetime earnings profile (both before tax and after tax). You have received a second job offer, at a first-year salary of $40,000, which is expected to increase in real terms at a rate of 2 percent per year. In purely financial terms, which job (and wage profile) do you prefer? In answering this question, first use your unaided judgment, then compare present discounted values.

b. You have accepted the $50,000 salary and have determined to save a fixed fraction of your income in your working years to maintain a level standard of living throughout your life, including retirement. (Please ignore uneven expenses such as medical expenses in later life or other sources of income such as social security benefits. Or assume that the latter will exactly pay for the former.) What portion of your salary should you save? What if your goal is to raise your real standard of living by 1 percent each year (over your 60-year life span)? In each case, first provide a judgmental estimate and then provide a financial calculation.

c. What is wrong with modeling your life-cycle consumption and savings decisions as if your earnings and portfolio returns are deterministic? How might earnings and investment risks influence your savings decision?

Spreadsheet Problems

S1. A New York company is considering an investment in a new technology for its main activity, sign making. The new technology is a sign printer that prints four-color images onto a wide range of backings. The new printer will cost the company about $100,000 but will generate before-tax cash flows of $25,000 beginning one year from now and continuing for eight years. The firm's effective marginal tax rate is 40 percent. However, the firm will be able to depreciate the printer over five years using straight-line depreciation. This allows the company a $20,000 tax deduction for each of the next five years. The company believes it will be able to sell the printer for about $10,000 after eight years. Finally, the appropriate discount rate for the investment is 10 percent.

a. Create a spreadsheet based on the example given to model this investment decision. Complete the missing entries in columns F and G.

b. Use your spreadsheet's financial functions to compute the investment's present value and internal rate of return. Do you endorse the investment?

c. Suppose that $20,000 is a more realistic estimate of annual before-tax cash flows. Again, compute the investment's present value and internal rate of return.

	A	B	C	D	E	F	G	H
1								
2		**BUYING A PRINTER**						
3								
4		Initial Cost	100,000		NPV	IRR		
5		Cash Flow	25,000		?	?		
6		Salvage Value	10,000					
7		Tax Rate	0.40					
8		Discount Rate	0.10					
9								
10				Before-Tax			After-Tax	
11			Year	Cash Flow	Depreciation	Tax	Cash Flow	
12								
13			0	−100,000	0	0	−100,000	
14			1	25,000	20,000	2,000	23,000	
15			2	25,000	20,000	?	?	
16			3	25,000	20,000	?	?	
17			4	25,000	20,000	?	?	
18			5	25,000	20,000	?	?	
19			6	25,000	0	?	?	
20			7	25,000	0	?	?	
21			8	35,000	0	?	?	
22								

    d. Find the investment's present value and internal rate of return if all the original facts are unchanged but the appropriate discount rate is 15 percent.

S2. A company has entered into an unusual five-year contract calling for a sizable up-front payment and an even greater final payment. At the same time, the contract allows the firm to earn steady cash flows over the five years. As a result, the firm's after-tax, net cash flows are as follows: −$10,000, $7,000, $7,000, $7,000, $7,000, and −$20,000 in years 0 to 5.

    a. Create a spreadsheet to compute the net present value of this contract using discount rates between 0 percent and 50 percent at 5 percent intervals. Graph your results.

    b. Find the internal rate of return. Under what circumstances would you support entering into this contract?

Suggested References

The following references are leading finance textbooks that provide extended treatments of capital budgeting.

Bodie, Z., and R. Merton. *Finance*, Chapter 6. Upper Saddle River, NJ: Prentice Hall, 2000.

Brealey, R., and S. Myers. *Principles of Corporate Finance*, Chapters 2, 3, 5, and 6. New York: McGraw-Hill, 2004.

Frederick, S., G. Loewenstein, and T. O'Donoghue, "Time Discounting and Time Preference: A Critical Review." *Journal of Economic Literature* (2002): 351–401.

This article discusses individual discount rates based on consumption-savings experiments.

Reinhardt, U. E., "Break-Even Analysis for Lockheed's TriStar: An Application of Financial Theory," *Journal of Finance* (1973): 821–838.

This article presents a careful net-present-value analysis of Lockheed's investment in a new aircraft.

The Bodie and Merton text has an excellent Web site: www.prenhall.com/bodie. Select Chapter 6 and browse current events, Internet exercises, and the research area.

The CNN financial network hosts a valuable financial Web site at www.cnnfn.com. One way to find company betas is to go to the Yahoo home page (www.yahoo.com) and choose "stock quotes."

1. $FV_1 = (560)(1.12) = \$627.20$; $FV_5 = (560)(1.12)^5 = \$986.91$.
2. a. $PV = (500)/(1.06)^4 = \$396.05$; $PV = (500)/(1.06)^{16} = \$197.73$.
   b. $PV = (500)/(1.12)^4 = \$317.76$; $PV = (500)/(1.12)^{16} = \$81.56$.
3. At a discount rate of 24 percent, the PV of building the plant is $-\$44,300$.
4. At 18 percent, the PV of building the plant is $19,110$. At 12 percent, the PV of going outside is $44,190$. Going outside is the more profitable option.

CHECK STATION ANSWERS

Present Value Tables

TABLE 19A.1

Discount Factors: Present Value of $1 to Be Received after t Years $= 1/(1 + r)^t$

Number of Years	Interest Rate per Year														
	1%	2%	3%	4%	5%	6%	7%	8%	9%	10%	11%	12%	13%	14%	15%
1	.990	.980	.971	.962	.952	.943	.935	.926	.917	.909	.901	.893	.885	.877	.870
2	.980	.961	.943	.925	.907	.890	.873	.857	.842	.826	.812	.797	.783	.769	.756
3	.971	.942	.915	.889	.864	.840	.861	.794	.772	.751	.731	.712	.693	.675	.658
4	.961	.924	.888	.855	.823	.792	.763	.735	.708	.683	.659	.636	.613	.592	.572
5	.951	.906	.863	.822	.784	.747	.713	.681	.650	.621	.593	.567	.543	.519	.497
6	.942	.888	.837	.790	.746	.705	.666	.630	.596	.564	.535	.507	.480	.456	.432
7	.933	.871	.813	.760	.711	.665	.623	.583	.547	.513	.482	.452	.425	.400	.376
8	.923	.853	.789	.731	.677	.627	.582	.540	.502	.467	.434	.404	.376	.351	.327
9	.914	.837	.766	.703	.645	.592	.544	.500	.460	.424	.391	.361	.333	.308	.284
10	.905	.820	.744	.676	.614	.558	.508	.463	.422	.386	.352	.322	.295	.270	.247
11	.896	.804	.722	.650	.585	.527	.475	.429	.388	.350	.317	.287	.261	.237	.215
12	.887	.788	.701	.625	.557	.497	.444	.397	.356	.319	.286	.257	.231	.208	.187
13	.879	.773	.681	.601	.530	.469	.415	.368	.326	.290	.258	.229	.204	.182	.163
14	.870	.758	.661	.577	.505	.442	.388	.340	.299	.263	.232	.205	.181	.160	.141
15	.861	.743	.642	.555	.481	.417	.362	.315	.275	.239	.209	.183	.160	.140	.123
16	.853	.728	.623	.534	.458	.394	.339	.292	252	.218	.188	.163	.141	.123	.107
17	.844	.714	.605	.513	.436	.371	.317	.270	.231	.198	.170	.146	.125	.108	.093
18	.836	.700	.587	.494	.416	.350	.296	.250	.212	.180	.153	.130	.111	.095	.081
19	.828	.686	.570	.475	.396	.331	.277	.232	.194	.164	.138	.116	.098	.083	.070
20	.820	.673	.554	.456	.377	.312	.258	.215	.178	.149	.124	.104	.087	.073	.061
25	.780	.610	.478	.375	.295	.233	.184	.146	.116	.092	.074	.059	.047	.038	.030
30	.742	.552	.412	.308	.231	.174	.131	.099	.075	.057	.044	.033	.026	.020	.015

For example, if the interest rate is 10 percent per year, the present value of $1 received at year 5 is $.621.

TABLE 19A.1 (*continued*)

								Interest Rate per Year							
Number of Years	16%	17%	18%	19%	20%	21%	22%	23%	24%	25%	26%	27%	28%	29%	30%
1	.862	.855	.847	.840	.833	.826	.820	.813	.806	.800	.794	.787	.781	.775	.769
2	.743	.731	.718	.706	.694	.683	.672	.661	.650	.640	.630	.620	.610	.601	.592
3	.641	.624	.609	.593	.579	.564	.551	.537	.524	.512	.500	.488	.477	.466	.455
4	.552	.534	.516	.499	.482	.467	.451	.437	.423	.410	.397	.384	.373	.361	.350
5	.476	.456	.437	.419	.402	.386	.370	.355	.341	.328	.315	.303	.291	.280	.269
6	.410	.390	.370	.352	.335	.319	.303	.289	.275	.262	.250	.238	.227	.217	.207
7	.354	.333	.314	.296	.279	.263	.249	.235	.222	.210	.198	.188	.178	.168	.159
8	.305	.285	.266	.249	.233	.218	.204	.191	.179	.168	.157	.148	.139	.130	.123
9	.263	.243	.225	.209	.194	.180	.167	.155	.144	.134	.125	.116	.108	.101	.094
10	.227	.208	.191	.176	.162	.149	.137	.126	.116	.107	.099	.092	.085	.078	.073
11	.195	.178	.162	.148	.135	.123	.112	.103	.094	.086	.079	.072	.066	.061	.056
12	.168	.152	.137	.124	.112	.102	.092	.083	.076	.069	.062	.057	.052	.047	.043
13	.145	.130	.116	.104	.093	.084	.075	.068	.061	.055	.050	.045	.040	.037	.033
14	.125	.111	.099	.088	.078	.069	.062	.055	.049	.044	.039	.035	.032	.028	.025
15	.108	.095	.084	.074	.065	.057	.051	.045	.040	.035	.031	.028	.025	.022	.020
16	.093	.081	.071	.062	.054	.047	.042	.036	.032	.028	.025	.022	.019	.017	.015
17	.080	.069	.060	.052	.045	.039	.034	.030	.026	.023	.020	.017	.015	.013	.012
18	.069	.059	.051	.044	.038	.032	.028	.024	.021	.018	.016	.014	.012	.010	.009
19	.060	.051	.043	.037	.031	.027	.023	.020	.017	.014	.012	.011	.009	.008	.007
20	.051	.043	.037	.031	.026	.022	.019	.016	.014	.012	.010	.008	.007	.006	.005
25	.024	.020	.016	.013	.010	.009	.007	.006	.005	.004	.003	.003	.002	.002	.001
30	.012	.009	.007	.005	.004	.003	.003	.002	.002	.001	.001	.001	.001	.000	.000

TABLE 19A.2

Annuity Table: Present Value of $1 per Year for Each of t Years $= 1/r - 1/[r(1 + r)^t]$

Interest Rate per Year

Number of Years	1%	2%	3%	4%	5%	6%	7%	8%	9%	10%	11%	12%	13%	14%	15%
1	.990	.980	.971	.962	.952	.943	.935	.926	.917	.909	.901	.893	.885	.877	.870
2	1.970	1.942	1.913	1.886	1.859	1.833	1.808	1.783	1.759	1.736	1.713	1.690	1.668	1.647	1.626
3	2.941	2.884	2.829	2.775	2.723	2.673	2.624	2.577	2.531	2.487	2.444	2.402	2.361	2.322	2.283
4	3.902	3.808	3.717	3.630	3.546	3.465	3.387	3.312	3.240	3.170	3.102	3.037	2.974	2.914	2.855
5	4.853	4.713	4.580	4.452	4.329	4.212	4.100	3.993	3.890	3.791	3.696	3.605	3.517	3.433	3.352
6	5.795	5.601	5.417	5.242	5.076	4.917	4.767	4.623	4.486	4.355	4.231	4.111	3.998	3.889	3.784
7	6.728	6.472	6.230	6.002	5.786	5.582	5.389	5.206	5.033	4.868	4.712	4.564	4.423	4.288	4.160
8	7.652	7.325	7.020	6.733	6.463	6.210	5.971	5.747	5.535	5.335	5.146	4.968	4.799	4.639	4.487
9	8.566	8.162	7.786	7.435	7.108	6.802	6.515	6.247	5.995	5.759	5.537	5.328	5.132	4.946	4.772
10	9.471	8.983	8.530	8.111	7.722	7.360	7.024	6.710	6.418	6.145	5.889	5.650	5.426	5.216	5.019
11	10.37	9.787	9.253	8.760	8.306	7.887	7.499	7.139	6.805	6.495	6.207	5.938	5.687	5.453	5.234
12	11.26	10.58	9.954	9.385	8.863	8.384	7.943	7.536	7.161	6.814	6.492	6.194	5.918	5.660	5.421
13	12.13	11.35	10.63	9.986	9.394	8.853	8.358	7.904	7.487	7.103	6.750	6.424	6.122	5.842	5.583
14	13.00	12.11	11.30	10.56	9.899	9.295	8.745	8.244	7.786	7.367	6.982	6.628	6.302	6.002	5.724
15	13.87	12.85	11.94	11.12	10.38	9.712	9.108	8.559	8.061	7.606	7.191	6.811	6.462	6.142	5.847
16	14.72	13.58	12.56	11.65	10.84	10.11	9.447	8.851	8.313	7.824	7.379	6.974	6.604	6.265	5.954
17	15.56	14.29	13.17	12.17	11.27	10.48	9.763	9.122	8.544	8.022	7.549	7.120	6.729	6.373	6.047
18	16.40	14.99	13.75	12.66	11.69	10.83	10.06	9.372	8.756	8.201	7.702	7.250	6.840	6.467	6.128
19	17.23	15.68	14.32	13.13	12.09	11.16	10.34	9.604	8.950	8.365	7.839	7.366	6.938	6.550	6.198
20	18.05	16.35	14.88	13.59	12.46	11.47	10.59	9.818	9.129	8.514	7.963	7.469	7.025	6.623	6.259
25	22.02	19.52	17.41	15.62	14.09	12.78	11.65	10.67	9.823	9.077	8.422	7.843	7.330	6.873	6.464
30	25.81	22.40	19.60	17.29	15.37	13.76	12.41	11.26	10.27	9.427	8.694	8.055	7.496	7.003	6.566

For example, if the interest rate is 10 percent per year, the present value of $1 received in each of the next 5 years is $3.791.

TABLE 19A.2 (*continued*)

							Interest Rate per Year								
Number of Years	16%	17%	18%	19%	20%	21%	22%	23%	24%	25%	26%	27%	28%	29%	30%
1	.862	.855	.847	.840	.833	.826	.820	.813	.806	.800	.794	.787	.781	.775	.769
2	1.605	1.585	1.566	1.547	1.528	1.509	1.492	1.474	1.457	1.440	1.424	1.407	1.392	1.376	1.361
3	2.246	2.210	2.174	2.140	2.106	2.074	2.042	2.011	1.981	1.952	1.923	1.896	1.868	1.842	1.816
4	2.798	2.743	2.690	2.639	2.589	2.540	2.494	2.448	2.404	2.362	2.320	2.280	2.241	2.203	2.166
5	3.274	3.199	3.127	3.058	2.991	2.926	2.864	2.803	2.745	2.689	2.635	2.583	2.532	2.483	2.436
6	3.685	3.589	3.498	3.410	3.326	3.245	3.167	3.092	3.020	2.951	2.885	2.821	2.759	2.700	2.643
7	4.039	3.922	3.812	3.706	3.605	3.508	3.416	3.327	3.242	3.161	3.083	3.009	2.937	2.868	2.802
8	4.344	4.207	4.078	3.954	3.837	3.726	3.619	3.518	3.421	3.329	3.241	3.156	3.076	2.999	2.925
9	4.607	4.451	4.303	4.163	4.031	3.905	3.786	3.673	3.566	3.463	3.366	3.273	3.184	3.100	3.019
10	4.833	4.659	4.494	4.339	4.192	4.054	3.923	3.799	3.682	3.571	3.465	3.364	3.269	3.178	3.092
11	5.029	4.836	4.656	4.486	4.327	4.177	4.035	3.902	3.776	3.656	3.543	3.437	3.335	3.239	3.147
12	5.197	4.988	4.793	4.611	4.439	4.278	4.127	3.985	3.851	3.725	3.606	3.493	3.387	3.286	3.190
13	5.342	5.118	4.910	4.715	4.533	4.362	4.203	4.053	3.912	3.780	3.656	3.538	3.427	3.322	3.223
14	5.468	5.229	5.008	4.802	4.611	4.432	4.265	4.108	3.962	3.824	3.695	3.573	3.459	3.351	3.249
15	5.575	5.324	5.092	4.876	4.675	4.489	4.315	4.153	4.001	3.859	3.726	3.601	3.483	3.373	3.268
16	5.668	5.405	5.162	4.938	4.730	4.536	4.357	4.189	4.033	3.887	3.751	3.623	3.503	3.390	3.283
17	5.749	5.475	5.222	4.990	4.775	4.576	4.391	4.219	4.059	3.910	3.771	3.640	3.518	3.403	3.295
18	5.818	5.534	5.273	5.033	4.812	4.608	4.419	4.243	4.080	3.928	3.786	3.654	3.529	3.413	3.304
19	5.877	5.584	5.316	5.070	4.843	4.635	4.442	4.263	4.097	3.942	3.799	3.664	3.539	3.421	3.311
20	5.929	5.628	5.353	5.101	4.870	4.657	4.460	4.279	4.110	3.954	3.808	3.673	3.546	3.427	3.316
25	6.097	5.766	5.467	5.195	4.948	4.721	4.514	4.323	4.147	3.985	3.834	3.694	3.564	3.442	3.329
30	6.177	5.829	5.517	5.235	4.979	4.746	4.534	4.339	4.160	3.995	3.842	3.701	3.569	3.447	3.332

Answers to Odd-Numbered Problems

Chapter 1

1. Managerial economics is the analysis of important management decisions using the tools of economics. Most business decisions are motivated by the goal of maximizing the firm's profit. The tools of managerial economics provide a guide to profit-maximizing decisions.

3. The six steps might lead the soft-drink firm to consider the following questions. Step 1: What is the context? Is this the firm's first such soft drink? Will it be first to the marketplace or is it imitating a competitor? Step 2: What is the profit potential for such a drink? Would the drink achieve other objectives? Is the fruit drink complementary to the firm's other products? Would it enhance the firm's image? Step 3: Which of six versions of the drink should the firm introduce? When (now or later) and where (regionally, nationally, or internationally) should it introduce the drink? What is an appropriate advertising and promotion policy? Step 4: What are the firm's profit forecasts for the drink in its first, second, and third years? What are the chances that the drink will be a failure after 15 months? Should the firm test market the drink before launching it? Step 5: Based on the answers to the questions in Steps 1 through 4, what is the firm's most profitable course of action? Step 6: In light of expected (or unexpected) developments in the first year of the launch, how should the firm modify its course of action?

5. What types of constraints confront the hazardous waste firm?

   a. Technological constraints dictate the currently available array of methods for treating, recycling, incinerating, or burying the waste.

   b. Economic constraints include the firm's monetary costs of different treatment methods as well as the price that the firm can command from customers for its services.

   c. Legal and regulatory constraints encompass environmental and safety laws, required tax payments, and so on.

   d. The most important political constraints include convincing the residents and leaders of the host town to accept the facility and satisfying the concerns of environmental activists.

   e. Time constraints include the need for timely approval ("time is money") and the problem of safe "permanent" disposal of hazardous wastes (say, for 200 years in underground sites).

Chapter 2

1. This statement confuses the use of average values and marginal values. The proper statement is that output should be expanded so long as marginal revenue exceeds marginal cost. Clearly, average revenue is not the same as marginal revenue, nor is average cost identical to marginal cost. Indeed, if management followed the average-revenue/average-cost rule, it would expand output to the point where AR = AC, in which case it is making zero profit per unit and, therefore, zero total profit!

3. In planning for a smaller enrollment, the college would look to answer many of the following questions: How large is the expected decline in enrollment? (Can marketing measures be taken to counteract the drop?) How does this decline translate into lower tuition revenue (and perhaps lower alumni donations)? How should the university plan its downsizing? Via cuts in faculty and administration? Reduced spending on buildings, labs, and books? Less scholarship aid? How great would be the resulting cost savings? Can the university become smaller (as it must) without compromising academic excellence?

5. a. The firm exactly breaks even at the quantity Q such that $\pi = 120Q - [420 + 60Q] = 0$. Solving for Q, we find $60Q = 420$ or $Q = 7$ units.

   b. In the general case, we set $\pi = PQ - [F + cQ] = 0$. Solving for Q, we have $(P - c)Q = F$ or $Q = F/(P - c)$. This formula makes intuitive sense. The firm earns a margin (or contribution) of $(P - c)$ on each unit sold. Dividing this margin into the fixed cost reveals the number of units needed to exactly cover the firm's total fixed costs.

   c. Here MR = 120 and MC = dC/dQ = 60. Because MR and MC are both constant and distinct, it is impossible to equate them. The modified rule is to expand output as far as possible (up to capacity) because MR > MC.

7. a. The marginal cost per book is MC = 40 + 10 = \$50. (The marketing costs are fixed, so the \$10 figure mentioned is an average fixed cost per book.) Setting MR = MC, we find MR = 150 − 2Q = 50, implying Q* = 50 thousand books. In turn, P* = 150 − 50 = \$100 per book.

   b. When the rival publisher raises its price dramatically, the firm's demand curve shifts upward and to the right. The new intersection of MR and MC now occurs at a greater output. Thus, it is incorrect to try to maintain sales via a full \$15 price hike. For instance, in the case of a parallel upward shift, P = 165 − Q. Setting MR = MC, we find MR = 165 − 2Q = 50, implying Q* = 57.5 thousand books, and in turn, P* = 165 − 57.5 = \$107.50 per book. Here OS should increase its price by only \$7.50 (not \$15).

   c. By using an outside printer, OS is saving on fixed costs but is incurring a higher marginal cost (i.e., printing cost) per book. With a higher marginal cost, the intersection of MR and MC occurs at a low optimal quantity. OS should reduce its targeted sales quantity of the text and raise the price it charges per book. Presumably, the fixed-cost savings outweigh the variable cost increase.

9. The fall in revenue of waiting each additional month is MR = dR/dt = −8. The reduction in cost of a month's delay is MC = dC/dt = −20 + .5t. The optimal introduction date is found by equating MR and MC: −8 = −20 + .5t, which implies .5t = 12 or t* = 24 months. The marketing manager's 12-month target is too early. Delaying 12 more months sacrifices revenue but more than compensates in reduced costs.

11. $\pi = -423 + 10.4P - .05P^2$ implies $M\pi = 10.4 - .1P$. Setting $M\pi = 0$, we obtain 10.4 − .1P = 0, or P = \$104 thousand. This is exactly the optimal price found earlier.

13. Setting MR = MC, one has: a − 2bQ = c, so that Q = (a − c)/2b. We substitute this expression into the price equation to obtain P = a − b[(a − c)/2b] = a − (a − c)/2 = a/2 + c/2 = (a + c)/2. The firm's optimal quantity increases after a favorable shift in demand— either an increase in the intercept (a) or a fall in the slope (b). But quantity decreases if it becomes more costly to produce extra units, that is, if the marginal cost (c) increases. Price is raised after a favorable demand shift (an increase in a) or after an increase in marginal cost (c). Note that only \$.50 of each dollar of cost increase is passed on to the consumer in the form of a higher price.

15. a. The profit function is $\pi = -10 - 48Q + 15Q^2 - Q^3$. At outputs of 0, 2, 8, and 14, the respective profits are -10, -54, 54, and -486.

b. Marginal profit is $M\pi = d\pi/dQ = -48 + 30Q - 3Q^2 = -3(Q-2)(Q-8)$, after factoring. Thus, marginal profit is zero at $Q = 2$ and $Q = 8$. From part a, we see that profit achieves a local minimum at $Q = 2$ and a maximum at $Q = 8$.

Chapter 3

1. The fact that increased sales coincided with higher prices does not disprove the law of downward-sloping demand. Clearly, other factors—an increase in population and/or income, improved play of the home team, or increased promotion—could have caused increased ticket sales, despite higher prices.

3. a. $Q = 400 - (1,200)(1.5) + (.8)(1,000) + (55)(40) + (800)(1) = 2,400$.

b. $E_P = (dQ/dP)(P/Q) = (-1,200)(1.50)/2,400 = -.75$.

$E_A = (dQ/dA)(A/Q) = (.8)(1,000)/2,400 = .333$.

c. Since demand is inelastic, McPablo's should raise prices, increasing revenues and reducing costs in the process.

5. a. With demand given by $P = 30,000 - .1Q$ and $MC = \$20,000$, we apply the $MR = MC$ rule to maximize profit. Therefore, $MR = 30,000 - .2Q = 20,000$ implies $Q = 50,000$ vehicles and $P = \$25,000$. GM's annual profit is: $(25,000 - 20,000)(50,000) - 180,000,000 = \$70,000,000$.

b. According to the markup rule (with $MC = \$20,800$ and $EP = -9$), $P = [-9/(-9 + 1)][20,800] = \$23,400$. Because of very elastic demand, GM should discount its price in the foreign market (not raise it by $800).

c. This is a pure selling problem (the trucks have already been produced) so the goal is to maximize revenue. Setting $MR = 0$ implies $30,000 - 2Q = 0$, or $Q = 15,000$ vehicles and $P = \$15,000$. GM should discount the price (rather than hold it at $20,000) but not so low as to sell the whole 18,000 inventory. It should sell only 15,000 (and perhaps donate the other 3,000 to charity).

7. The consultant should recommend an immediate price increase. As noted in the text, if demand is inelastic, the firm can always increase profit by raising price, thereby raising revenue and reducing cost.

9. Given the low price elasticity, the very high markup for Prilosec is not at all out of line. (The tremendous health and pain-relief benefits of the drug account for the low price elasticity.) We know that $MC = \$.60$ per dose,

P = $3.00 per dose, and E_P is in the range -1.4 to -1.2. To test whether or not the current price is optimal, apply the markup rule: $P = [E_P/(1 + E_P)]MC$. For $E_P = -1.4$, the optimal price is $P^* = \$2.10$. In turn, for $E_P = -1.2$, $P^* = \$3.60$. Finally, for $E_P = -1.3$, $P^* = \$2.60$. Though the optimal price is quite sensitive to the precise estimate of elasticity, the high $3.00 price is consistent with elasticity within the estimated range.

11. How should the manager set prices when taking different levels of costs into account? The answer is to apply the markup rule: $P = [E_P/(1 + E_P)]MC$. For instance, if changes in economic conditions cause the firm's marginal costs to rise, the correct action is to increase price (even though there may have been no change in price elasticity). For the same reason, an electric utility is justified in charging higher electric rates in the summer when supplying sufficient electricity to meet peak demand is very costly.

13. a. The garage owner should set prices to get the maximum revenue from the garage. The owner should offer higher hourly rates for short-term parking and all-day rates (at a lower average cost per hour). This prevents short-term parkers from taking advantage of the lower rate.

    b. Start by setting $MR = 0$ for each segment. (This maximizes revenue in each separate segment.) The resulting optimal quantities are $Q_S = 300$ and $Q_C = 200$. Notice that the garage is not completely filled. The optimal prices are $P_S = \$1.50$ per hour and $P_C = \$1$ per hour.

    c. With only 400 places in the garage, the strategy in part b is not feasible. The best the operator can do is to fill up the garage and maximize revenue by ensuring that the marginal revenue is the same for the segments. Equating $MR_S = MR_C$ and rearranging implies $Q_S = Q_C + 100$. Together with the fact that $Q_S + Q_C = 400$, one finds $Q_S = 250$ and $Q_C = 150$. The requisite prices are $P_S = \$1.75$ per hour and $P_C = \$1.25$ per hour.

Chapter 4

1. Survey methods are relatively inexpensive but are subject to potential problems: sample bias, response bias, and response accuracy. Test marketing avoids these problems by providing data on actual consumer purchases under partially controlled market conditions. Test marketing is much more costly than survey methods and suffers from two main problems. First, some important factors may be difficult to identify and control. Second, test market results are not a perfect guide to actual market experience down the road.

3. a. Both t-values (based on 60 months of data) are much greater than 2, implying that both coefficients are significantly different from zero.

   b. The equation says that the expected return on Pepsi's stock roughly follows the expected return on the S&P 500. (The coefficient .92 is the stock's "beta.") Nonetheless, there remains a large random element in any individual stock's return. Day-to-day stock prices follow random walks. Explaining even 28 percent (R-squared of .28) of the variation in the stock's monthly return is impressive.

   c. Setting $R_{S\&P} = -1$ implies $R_{PEP} = .06 - .92 = -.86$ percent expected return over the next month.

5. a. According to the t-statistics, all explanatory variables are significant *except* income.

   b. This coefficient measures the price elasticity of demand, $E_P = -.29$. A 20 percent price hike implies a 5.8 percent sales drop.

   c. With $E_Y = -.09$, sales hardly vary with income.

7. a. Although the time coefficient is negative ($b = -.4$), its t-value is well below 2, indicating that the coefficient is not statistically different from zero. The water table has been stable over the decade.

   b. Think of yearly rainfall as one thinks of tosses of a coin. Even though each coin toss is random and independent of the other tosses, it is still possible to have an unusually large number of heads or tails in 10 trials by pure luck. Thus, the second expert is foolish to claim that dry years and wet years necessarily will cancel each other out.

Chapter 5

1. a. Since the scrap used by the company comes from beer and soft-drink cans, the first step is to forecast the consumption of these drinks over the next decade. Beer consumption depends on the size of the population ages 18 to 45; soft-drink consumption depends on the size of the population ages 10 to 25. Demographers can supply these population numbers. The next step is to predict trends in the types of beer and soft-drink containers: (1) the share of plastic and glass bottles versus cans, and (2) the share of steel cans versus aluminum cans. The company could forecast trends in these shares by using information on past shares available in industry publications.

   b. The main demographic factors are the size of the consuming age groups. These population numbers change slowly and are relatively easy to forecast. Economic factors include shifts in soft-drink and beer demands—changes that are harder to predict. For instance, sports drinks, bottled water, ice teas, and new-age beverages have all chipped away at soft-drink consumption. Political factors might also play a role. For instance, bottle bills and recycling programs may have significant impacts on the availability of can scrap. Finally, technology might matter; new can-making processes might reduce the amount of leftover scrap generated.

3. a. Structural forecasts have the advantage of being based on explicit economic models. (For instance, demand depends on price, income, and so on.) Including a host of relevant variables ought to improve the estimated relationship. (However, as mentioned in the text, structural forecasts are subject to the usual sources of error.) Time-series estimates, however, use only the past pattern of a given variable to predict future values. Thus, this method economizes on the use of information. The time-series approach can produce accurate forecasts provided (i) there is a regular pattern to past changes in the variable, and (ii) other economic variables are not important factors.

b. The time-series approach probably would provide sound five-year forecasts of the city's total cable subscriptions. Subscriptions could be expected to follow an S-shaped growth curve: initially slow growth, then rapid growth (as residents become familiar with cable programming), then a leveling off of total subscribers (as the market becomes saturated). By tracking past growth, one identifies where subscriptions currently are on the S-curve and where they are headed.

c. The forecast for a single cable vendor depends in part on a forecast of total growth, as previously. However, its total sales also depend on obvious factors that affect its market share—quality of programming, its relative price, advertising, the number of rival cable operators, and so on. To forecast growth in its subscribers, the firm should use a structural model that includes these factors as explanatory variables.

5. a. The estimated trend equation is $S = 95 + 5.5t$, using OLS regression.

b. Although the equation's R-squared is .69, the t-value on the time trend is only 2.12. With 2 degrees of freedom, the critical value for significance is 4.30. With only four observations, there is not enough data to say whether there is a true upward trend.

c. The forecast for year 5 is $95 + (5.5)(5) = 122.5$. From the regression output, the standard error of this forecast is 5.81.

7. a. The reduced-form equation is $Q_t = .95Q_{t-1} + 1.25Q_{t-1} - 1.25Q_{t-2}$.

b. The forecast for year 3 is $Q_3 = (2.2)(120) - (1.25)(100) = 139$. The forecasts for the next six years are 155.8, 169, 177.1, 178.3, 170.9, and 162.4. The total number of subscribers falls between years 7 and 8 because the lost subscribers outnumber new subscribers. Because of the subscriber drop between years 7 and 8, there are no new subscribers in year 9.

Chapter 6

1. Diminishing returns states that an input's marginal product declines as one increases its use past some point (holding other inputs constant). Decreasing returns to scale states that increasing all inputs in proportion generates a less-than-proportional increase in output. A production function can exhibit diminishing returns without decreasing returns to scale, or vice versa.

3. Maximizing average output is typically nonoptimal. First, we should emphasize that maximizing total output and maximizing average output are two different things. For instance, in Table 6.2, the firm's maximum output is 403 units using 120 workers. In contrast, the firm would maximize its average product by using 10 workers producing only 93 units. Second, optimal use of an input requires comparing extra output (and revenue) against the input's extra cost. As we have seen, optimum input use typically means producing below the level of maximum output.

5. The production function $Q = 10L - .5L^2 + 24K - K^2$ has marginal products $MP_L = 10 - L$ and $MP_K = 24 - 2K$. Both marginal products decline; therefore, there are diminishing returns. Starting from any L and K, doubling the use of both inputs generates less than double the level of output. Thus, the production function exhibits decreasing returns to scale.

7. a. The isoquant for the 200-pound steer has the usual convex curvature.

   b. The cost of the 68-60 mix is ($.10)(68) + ($.07)(60) = $11.00 per day. The cheapest diet is a 56-70 mix; its cost is $10.50 per day.

   c. For a 200-pound steer, the cheapest mix is 56-70. Given constant returns to scale, feeding a 250-pound steer would require (250/200) = 125 percent of this amount. A 70-87.5 mix (at a cost of $13.125) is needed.

9. a. Production of steel by electric furnace has the lowest average cost per ton; therefore, its share of production would be expected to increase over time.

   b. A tripling of energy prices would leave continuous casting ($400) as the least-cost production method.

   c. A fall in the price of steel scrap would favor production by electric furnace (the only process that uses scrap).

11. a. The grade improvements offered by extra hours of studying finance are 8, 5, 5, 2, and 2 points. For economics, the improvements are 6, 4, 2, 2, and 1 points.

   b. The "first" hour should be devoted to finance (an 8-point increase), the next hour to economics (6 points), the next 2 hours to finance (5 points each hour), and the "last" hour to economics (4 points). The student's predicted grades are 88 and 85.

c. This allocation is optimal. Devoting 5 hours to finance and economics offers the greatest point opportunities. Devoting 2 additional hours to accounting will produce more extra points (3 points each hour) than devoting an additional hour to finance (2 points) or economics (2 points).

13. Here is a graphical explanation. The firm's initial (optimal) input mix occurs where the lowest isocost line is tangent to its isoquant. If the price of labor increases, this changes the slope of the isocost line (so that labor "trades" for fewer units of capital). The new tangency with the same isoquant must occur at a mix using less labor and more capital.

15. a. For $N_1 = 16$ and $N_2 = 24$, the average catch at the first lake is $Q_1/N_1 = [(10)(16) - .1(16)^2]/16 = 8.4$ fish, and the average catch at the second lake is $Q_2/N_2 = [(16)(24) - .4(24)^2]/24 = 6.4$ fish, respectively. Lured by the greater average catch, some number of fishers will leave the second lake for the first.

b. Movement between lakes will cease when all individuals obtain the same average catch. Equating the average catches at the lakes implies $10 - .1N_1 = 16 - .4N_2$. In addition, $N_1 + N_2 = 40$. Solving these two equations simultaneously implies $N_1 = 20$ and $N_2 = 20$. The total catch at the two lakes is 320 fish.

c. The commissioner seeks to maximize $Q_1 + Q_2$ subject to $N_1 + N_2 = 40$. The optimum solution to this constrained maximization problem implies that the marginal catch of the last fisher should be equal across the lakes. Here, $MQ_1 = dQ_1/dN_1 = 10 - .2N_1$ and $MQ_2 = dQ_2/dN_2 = 16 - .8N_2$. Setting $MQ_1 = MQ_2$ and using $N_1 + N_2 = 40$, we find that $N_1 = 26$ and $N_2 = 14$. The marginal catch at each lake is 4.8 fish; the maximum total catch is $[(10)(26) - (.1)(26)^2] + [(16)(14) - (.4)(14)^2] = 338$ fish.

Chapter 7

1. The fact that the product development was lengthier and more expensive than initially anticipated is no reason to charge a higher price. These development costs have been sunk and are irrelevant for the pricing decision. Price should be based on the product's relevant costs (the marginal cost of producing the item) in conjunction with product demand (as summarized by the product's price elasticity).

3. a. The profit associated with an electronic control device (ECD) is $\pi_E = 1,500 - [500 + (2)(300)] = \$400$. If the firm sells the two microchips separately (instead of putting them into an ECD), its total profit is $\pi_M = (550 - 300)(2) = \$500$. Thus, the firm should devote all of its capacity to the production of microchips for direct sale. Producing ECDs is not profitable.

b. If there is unused microchip capacity, the firm earns $400 in additional profit for each ECD sold. Producing ECDs now becomes profitable.

c. If $200 (of the $500 average cost) is fixed, each ECD's contribution becomes $\pi_E = 1,500 - [300 + (2)(300)] = \$600$. The firm should produce ECDs in the short run; this is more profitable than selling chips directly.

5. a. Setting MR = MC implies $10,000 - 400Q = \$4,000$. Thus, $Q^* = 15$ games.

b. The contribution is R − VC = ($150,000 − 45,000) − ($4,000)(15) = $45,000. The opportunity cost of the entrepreneur's labor is $20,000, and the required annual return on the $100,000 investment is 20 percent or $20,000. Thus, her economic profit is $45,000 − 20,000 − 20,000 = $5,000.

7. a. Given the cost function $C = 360 + 40Q + 10Q^2$, it follows that $AC = 360/Q + 40 + 10Q$. Clearly, average cost is U-shaped.

b. To find the point of minimum average cost, set AC = MC: $360/Q + 40 + 10Q = 40 + 20Q$. Thus, $360/Q = 10Q$ or $Q^2 = 36$. Therefore, $Q_{min} = 6$ units and $AC_{min} = 360/6 + 40 + (10)(6) = 160$.

c. Because AC_{min} exceeds the market price (P = 140), the firm incurs losses if it operates. In the long run, it will shut down.

9. a. To maximize profit set MR = MC. Therefore, $10 - .5w = 4$ or $w = 12$ weeks. Profit is $84 - 48 = \$36$ thousand.

b. The "total" marginal cost (including the opportunity cost of lost profit) of showing the hit an extra week is $4 + 1.5 = \$5.5$ thousand. Setting MR = MC = 5.5 implies w = 9 weeks.

c. On the cost side, there are economies of scale and scope. (With shared fixed costs, 10 screens under one roof is much cheaper than 10 separate theaters.) Demand economies due to variety probably also exist. Filmgoers will visit your screens knowing that there's likely to be a movie to their liking.

d. Obviously, video rentals and sales compete with (and potentially cannibalize) theater revenues. The delay makes sense as long as the extra theater profits from extending the run exceed the video profits given up.

11. a. We have $MC_E = 1,000 + 10Q$ and $MC = 3,000 + 10Q$. Setting MR = MC implies $10,000 - 60Q = 3,000 + 10Q$. Thus, $Q = 100$ cycles and $P = \$7,000$.

b. Purchasing engines implies a marginal cost of $2,000 + 1,400 = \$3,400$ (compared to the MC in part a of $4,000). Again setting MR = MC implies $Q = 110$ and $P = \$6,700$. However, the firm should continue to produce some engines itself (up to the point where $MC_E = 1,400$). Setting $1,000 + 10Q_E = 1,400$ implies $Q_E = 40$ engines. The firm should produce 40 engines and buy the remaining $110 - 40 = 70$.

13. a. We are given that $MC = \$20,000$, and from the price equation, we derive $MR = 30,000 - .2Q$. Setting $MR = MC$ implies $Q = 50,000$, confirming that GM's current output level is profit maximizing.

b. The outside sales option means that GM faces an opportunity cost. Every engine sold to the SUV manufacturer generates an additional contribution of \$2,000. GM should not only employ the unused capacity to produce engines for external sale, it should also cut back somewhat its production of light trucks. The effective MC per truck is now $\$20,000 + 2,000$ (where the latter is the opportunity cost per engine.) The shift upward in MC implies a lower optimal output level (40,000 trucks to be exact).

c. Fixed costs should not be mixed with variable costs in determining output and price decisions. Removing the allocated fixed cost means taking out $160,000,000/40,000 = \$4,000$ per unit. Thus, the true marginal cost per unit is $\$22,000 - \$4,000 = \$18,000$. Note that the actual MC in the West Coast factory is lower than the MC in the Michigan plants. Thus, GM should expand its West Coast output (to 60,00 units to be exact).

15. a. $C = 500 + 5Q^2$. Minimum average cost occurs at the quantity Q such that $MC = AC$. We know that $MC = 10Q$ and $AC = 500/Q + 5Q$. Setting these equal implies $10Q = 500/Q + 5Q$. Collecting terms, we find that $5Q^2 = 500$ or $Q = 10$. At this output, minimum average cost equals 100.

b. Setting $MR = MC$ implies $600 - 10Q = 10Q$. Therefore, $Q = 30$; in turn, $P = 600 - (5)(30) = 450$, and $\pi = 13,500 - 5,000 = 8,500$.

c. If either MC differed from MR, the firm could increase its profit by redirecting output. Setting $MR = MC_1 = MC_2$ implies $600 - 10Q^* = 10(Q^*/2)$. Therefore, $Q^* = 40$. Each plant produces 20 units at a cost of 2,500 (from the original cost function). Finally, we find $P^* = 400$, and $\pi = 16,000 - 5,000 = 11,000$.

d. If the firm can use as many plants as it likes, it enjoys constant returns to scale. It should set the number of plants so that each is producing 10 units (where $MC = \min AC = 100$). In short, 100 is the relevant long-run marginal cost. Setting $MR = MC$ implies $600 - 10Q = 100$. Therefore, $Q = 50$. In turn, $P = 350$ and $\pi = (350 - 100)(50) = 12,500$. The number of plants is $50/10 = 5$.

Chapter 8

1. a. The expected values at points E, D, C, B, and A in the decision tree are $15.5, $50, $30, $19.2, and $19.2.

   b. The manager is confused. Point D is a point of decision: The manager simply should select the top branch (50 is greater than 37). Thus, the value at point D is $50. Putting probabilities on the branches makes no sense.

3. a. The expected value of continuing with its current software strategy is $(.2)(2) + (.5)(.5) + (.3)(-1) = \$.35$ million. The expected value of an "open strategy" is $(.25)(1.5) + (.25)(1.1) + (.25)(.8) + (.25)(.6) = \$1.0$ million. Thus, the "open" strategy is preferred.

   b. The "open" strategy is less risky in the sense of having a narrower range of possible outcomes. Managerial risk aversion would be an added reason to pursue this strategy.

5. a. The tree lists the six possible outcomes (in thousands of dollars) and the expected value of each chance circle. Overall expected profit is $1,500.

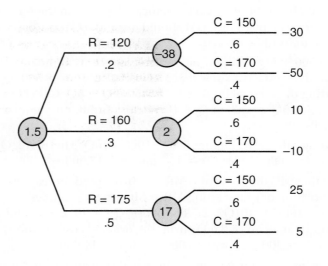

   b. E(revenue) $= (.2)(120,000) + (.3)(160,000) + (.5)(175,000) = \$159,500$. Expected cost is $(.6)(150,000) + (.4)(170,000) = \$158,000$. Thus, the expected profit is $\$159,500 - \$158,000 = \$1,500$, the same result as in part a.

7. a. If the customer response is weak, MD's expected profit is: $(.5)(20) + (.5)(-100) = -\$40$ million. MD's overall profit (averaging

over strong and weak customer responses) is $(.4)(50) + (.6)(-40)$ $= -\$4$ million. The company should not have launched the campaign.

b. If the customer response is weak, the company does better by "pulling the plug"—a \$20 million loss is better than an expected \$40 million loss from continuing. The overall expected profit from launching the campaign (and terminating it in the face of a weak customer response) is: $(.4)(50) + (.6)(-20) = \$8$ million. Given the flexibility to terminate, the company should launch the campaign.

9. a. The appropriate decision tree is shown in the figure. The optimal decision is to wait and buy the coat in the second week if it is still available. The buyer's expected profit is \$30.

   b. Under the price-reduction method, 40 coats are sold at \$100, 40 coats (half of the remaining 80) are sold at \$75, 30 coats (3/4 of the remaining 40) are sold at \$60, and 10 are sold at \$50. The store's total revenue comes to \$9,300.

   c. With demand given by $P = 180 - Q$, the firm maximizes revenue by selling 90 coats at a price of \$90. (Check this by setting $MR = 0$.) This resulting revenue, \$8,100, is less than the revenue of the price-reduction scheme.

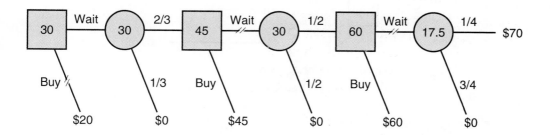

11. The expected utility of pursuing the biochemical approach alone is

$$E(U_{Chem}) = .7U(80) + .3U(40) = (.7)(64) + (.3)(44) = 58.$$

The accompanying decision tree depicts the strategy of trying the biogenetic approach first and then pursuing the biochemical approach if necessary. The expected utility of this strategy is 57.5. Thus, pursuing the biochemical approach alone has a slight edge over sequential development. Since sequential development has the greater risk (i.e., dispersion of possible outcomes), a risk-averse firm chooses the biochemical approach.

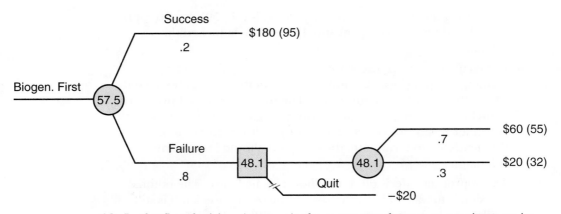

13. In the first decision (see tree), the company chooses to continue on its own, implying 20 > .25u. Thus, u < 80. In the subsequent decision, the company sells out, implying u > 80. These two inequalities (and, therefore, the two decisions) are contradictory.

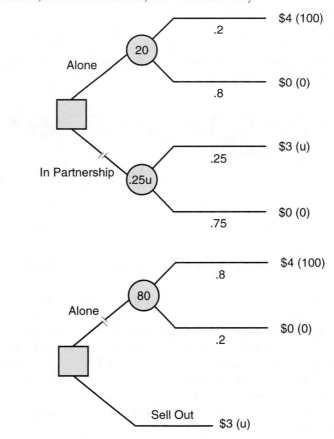

*15. The dealer must commit to ordering and selling some number of yachts (say, Q) before knowing the course of the economy. Recall that the two price equations are given by $P_G = 20 - .05Q$, and $P_R = 20 - .1Q$. Then the expected price required to sell Q yachts is $.6P_G + .4P_R = 20 - .07Q$. Expected profit is simply expected revenue minus cost. This is maximized by setting expected MR equal to MC ($10 thousand). Thus, $MR = 20 - .14Q = 10$. So the optimal (round) number of yachts is $Q = 71$. This number is closer to 50 than to 100. This should not be surprising since we found earlier that ordering 50 was better than ordering 100. Here we see that the optimal order size (one that is better than any other quantity) is 71 yachts.

Chapter 9

1. As tough as it may be to do, you should ignore your friend's story. His experience represents a single data point. You already have gathered the best available information on the relative merits of different models. You had a clear choice based on this information; your friend's singular experience should not be enough to change your probabilities or your mind.

3. a. The chance of a student responding is $Pr(R|S) = .08/.24 = 1/3$. The chance of a doctor responding is $Pr(R|D) = .05/.18 = .277$. The chance of a lawyer responding is $Pr(R|L) = .09/.58 = .155$. The promotion is most effective with students.

   b. The table identifies the market segments being reached by the promotion. More important, it measures the effectiveness of the promotion with respect to each segment.

5. a. The following decision trees show the consortium's expected profits from having perfect information in each instance.

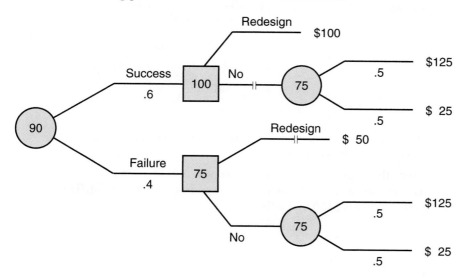

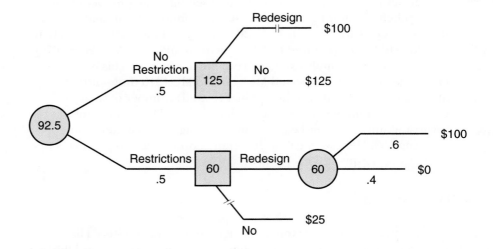

b. According to Bayes' theorem:

$$\Pr(\text{Success}|\text{Endorsement}) = \frac{\Pr(E|S)\Pr(S)}{\Pr(E|S)\Pr(S) + \Pr(E|F)\Pr(F)}$$

$$= \frac{(.9)(.6)}{[(.9)(.6) + (.5)(.4)]}$$

$$= \frac{.54}{.74} = .73.$$

$$\Pr(\text{Success}|\text{No Endorsement}) = \frac{\Pr(N|S)\Pr(S)}{\Pr(N|S)\Pr(S) + \Pr(N|F)\Pr(F)}$$

$$= \frac{(.1)(.6)}{[(.1)(.6) + (.5)(.4)]}$$

$$= \frac{.06}{.26} = .23.$$

7. a. A bid of $130,000 is the best choice. Its expected profit is
   $(.5)(30,000) = \$15,000$.

   b. Here the expected cost is $100,000, which is identical to the certain
   cost in part a. Thus, there is no change in expected profit. The
   optimal bid is $130,000 as before.

c. As the decision tree shows, your company's expected profit with perfect cost information is $17,500. Thus, the
EVI $= 17{,}500 - 15{,}000 = \$2{,}500$.

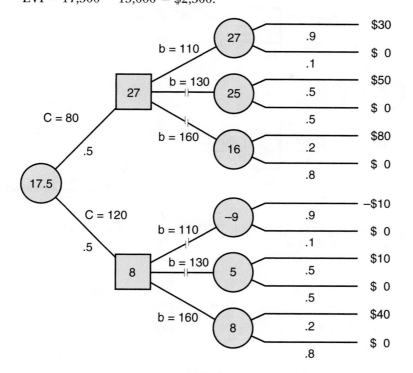

9. a. The firm should not take the R&D program (expected profit $= -\$4$ million).

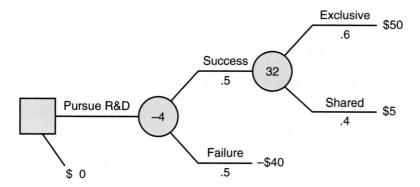

b. The firm should undertake the R&D if it learns it has exclusive rights (expected profit $= \$5$ million); otherwise it should not invest (expected profit $= -\$17.5$ million). Its overall expected profit is $(.6)(5) = \$3$ million.

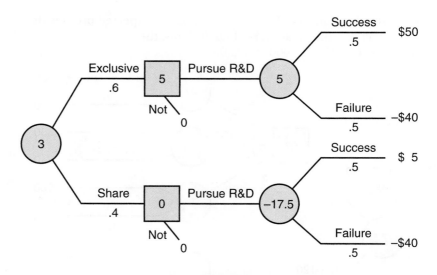

c. According to the joint table, $\Pr(S|C) = .5/.8 = .625$ and $\Pr(S|H) = 0/.2 = 0$.

Prototype	Risky Outcomes		
	Success	Failure	Total
Cool	.5	.3	.8
Hot	0	.2	.2
	.5	.5	

d. If the prototype chip runs cool, the expected profit from pursuing the R&D investment is $(.625)(32) + (.375)(-40) = \$5$ million, so it is worth investing. If the chip runs hot, the R&D program will fail with certainty, so the firm should walk away. Therefore, the firm's overall expected profit from testing the chip is $(.8)(5) + (.2)(0) = \$4$ million. Testing makes sense because its expected value ($4 million) is greater than its cost ($2 million).

11. a. For the seismic test, the revised probabilities are $\Pr(W|G) = .15/.35 = 3/7$, and $\Pr(W|B) = .05/.65 = 1/13$. Even if the test is good, the site isn't worth drilling; the expected profit is $(3/7)(1,000,000) + (4/7)(-800,000) = -\$28,571$. Thus, the seismic test has no value.

b. If the wildcatter learns the results of the nearby site, the revised probabilities are $Pr(W|O) = .2/.4 = .5$, and $Pr(W|N) = 0/.6 = 0$. If the result is O, the wildcatter drills and earns an expected profit of $100,000. If the result is N, he walks away. Because $Pr(O) = .4$, the overall expected value is $(.4)(100,000) = \$40,000$.

c. The accompanying table shows the joint probabilities if both sources of information are available. Note that there are four possible observations. The top-left entry is $Pr(G\&O\&W)$. It is computed as $Pr(G\&O\&W) = Pr(G|W)Pr(O|W)Pr(W) = (.75)(1.0)(.2) = .15$. The other entries are found in a similar fashion. From the table, we compute the revised probabilities to be $Pr(W|G\&O) = .75$, $Pr(W|B\&O) = .25$, $Pr(W|G\&N) = 0$, and $Pr(W|B\&N) = 0$. The wildcatter should drill only if both indications are favorable (G&O), in which case the expected profit is:

$$(.75)(1,000,000) + (.25)(-800,000) = \$550,000.$$

Since $Pr(G\&O) = .2$, the overall expected profit is:
$(.2)(550,000) = \$110,000$.

	Site Is		
	Wet	Dry	Total
G&O	.15	.05	.20
B&O	.05	.15	.20
G&N	0	.15	.15
B&N	0	.45	.45
Total	.20	.80	1.00

13. The firm should approach seller X first. If it rejects X's price, its expected price from Y is $(32 + 38)/2 = \$35$. Thus, it should buy from X only if X's price is below $35. With this cutoff price in mind, it will buy from X half of the time at an expected price of $(30 + 35)/2 = \$32.5$. The firm's overall expected price is $(.5)(32.5) + (.5)(35) = \$33.75$. (Half of the time it buys from X and half of the time it rejects X's price and buys from Y.)

If the firm approaches Y first, it buys immediately only if the offered price is less than $(30 + 40)/2 = \$35$. In turn, its expected purchase price, if it buys from Y, is $(32 + 35)/2 = \$33.5$. Thus, the firm's overall expected price is $(.5)(33.5) + (.5)(35) = \$34.25$. The message of this example is that the firm should start its search with the supplier whose best price is more uncertain (i.e., is more widely dispersed).

Chapter 10

1. a. According to the "law" of supply and demand, the existence of a large body of Picasso's artwork will tend to lower the value of any individual piece of work.

    b. If demand for Picasso's work is inelastic, increasing the number of pieces sold (by driving down prices) will reduce total revenue. The artist's heirs should try to limit supply by spreading sales of his artwork over long time periods.

3. a. Setting $Q_D = Q_S$ implies $184 - 20P = 124 + 4P$ or $24P = 60$. Therefore, $P = \$2.50$ and $Q = 134$ pounds per capita.

    b. This increase represents only .7 percent of total supply and will have little price effect. The new quantity supplied is $(1.007)(134) = 135$. Rearranging the demand curve, we have $P = 9.20 - .05Q$. Therefore, we find that $P = 9.20 - (.05)(135) = \$2.45$. Montana farmers' revenue should increase by about 8 percent (based on a 10 percent quantity increase and a 2 percent price drop).

    c. If the total harvest is 10 percent above normal, $Q_S = (1.10)(134) = 147.4$ pounds per capita and $P = 9.20 - (0.5)(147.4) = \$1.83$. Farm revenue drops from $(2.50)(134) = \$335$ to $(1.83)(147.4) = \$269.74$, a 19.5 percent drop. Demand is inelastic. A modest quantity increase caused a large price drop and this is detrimental to farmers' incomes. Since varying harvest conditions can cause significant price and revenue changes, today's farm profits quickly can become tomorrow's losses.

5. a. The Green Company's marginal cost is $MC = dC/dQ = 4 + 2Q$, and the price is $P = \$40$. Setting $MC = P$ implies $4 + 2Q = 40$ or $Q = 18$ units. More generally, setting $MC = P$ generates the supply curve $4 + 2Q = P$ or $Q = (P - 4)/2$.

    b. With the increase in fixed cost, the firm should continue to produce 18 units. Its profit is $\pi = R - C = (40)(18) - [144 + (4)(18) + (18)^2]$ $= 720 - 540 = 180$. Of course, the firm will supply no output if price falls below the level of minimum average cost. We set $MC = AC$ and find that average cost is a minimum at $Q = 12$. In turn, min $AC = 28$. Thus, the firm's supply is zero if price falls below 28.

    c. In part a (when fixed costs are 100), min $AC = 24$ at a quantity of 10 units for each firm. Thus, the original long-run equilibrium price is 24. With elevated fixed costs, one would expect the long-run price to rise to 28 (the new minimum level of AC). At this higher price, total demand is reduced. However, each firm's output would rise from 10 units to 12 units. With reduced total demand and greater output per firm, the number of firms must decline.

7. a. Average cost is AC $= 300/Q + Q/3$. Thus, total cost is
$C = 300 + Q^2/3$, which implies MC $= (2/3)Q$. Setting AC $=$ MC
implies $300/Q + Q/3 = (2/3)Q$, or $300/Q = Q/3$. Thus, $Q_{min} = 30$.
In turn, min AC $= (2/3)(30) = 20$.

   b. A firm's supply curve is found by setting P $=$ MC $= (2/3)Q_F$.
Therefore, $Q_F = 1.5P$. With 10 firms, total supply is $Q_S = 10Q_F = 15P$.
Setting $Q_D = Q_S$ implies $1,000 - 20P = 15P$. Thus, we find P $= 28.57$
and Q $= 428.57$. At $Q_F = 42.86$, each firm's AC is 21.3. Thus, its profit
is $(28.57 - 21.3)(42.86) = 311.6$.

   c. In long-run equilibrium, P $=$ min AC $= 20$. In turn,
Q $= 1,000 - (20)(20) = 600$. The number of firms is $600/30 = 20$.

9. a. Here MC $=$ AC $= 5$. Thus, $P_C = 5$. From the price equation,
$5 = 35 - 5Q$, implying $Q_C = 6$ million.

   b. The industry displays constant returns to scale (constant LAC). The
real microchip industry probably displays increasing returns to scale
(declining LAC). For competition to be viable, returns to scale must
be exhausted at volumes well below total market demand.

   c. Total profit is zero. Consumer surplus is $(.5)(35 - 5)(6) = 90$.

11. a. Setting $Q_D = Q_S$ implies $28 - 4P = -12 + 6P$, so P $= \$4$ and Q $= 12$
million bushels of rice. To find consumer surplus and producer surplus,
we graph the demand and supply curves, noting the vertical intercepts
($\$7$ and $\$2$, respectively). Thus, consumer surplus is $\frac{1}{2}(7 - 4)(12) = \$18$
million, and producer profit is $\frac{1}{2}(4 - 2)(12) = \$12$ million.

   b. With free trade, the world price establishes the new prevailing price,
P $= \$3$. From the demand and supply equations, we find $Q_D = 16$ and
$Q_S = 6$, so imports $= 16 - 6 = 10$ million bushels. In turn, consumer
surplus is $\frac{1}{2}(7 - 3)(16) = \$32$ million, and producer profit is
$\frac{1}{2}(3 - 2)(6) = \$3$ million. Free trade has increased total welfare.

   c. Offering rice growers a $\$1$ per bushel subsidy means a (subsidized)
price of $\$4$ and restores domestic supply to $Q_S = 12$ million bushels
(as in part a). Producer profit is once again $\$12$ million, but the cost
to taxpayers of the subsidy is $(\$1)(12) = \$12$ million. Thus, total
welfare is $32 + 12 - 12 = \$32$ million (less than under the free trade
"level playing field" of part b).

*13. a. District 1's total gain is $(50 - 35)(3) + (26 - 25)(3) = 48$. (Pair 2
cannot trade since the buyer's value is below the seller's.) District 2's
total gain is $(48 - 28)(3) = 60$. (Only pair 4 trades.) The districts'
combined gain is 108.

   b. District 1's market price will be between 35 and 37 (say, at $\$36$), with
B1, B2, and H3 buying from H3 and H1. Its total gain is

$(50 - 36)(4) + (42 - 36)(2) + (37 - 36)(2) + (36 - 25)(5) +$
$(36 - 35)(3) = 128$. District 2's market price will be \$28 with B4 and
B5 buying from H6 and H4. Its total gain is
$(48 - 28)(3) + (30 - 28)(4) + (28 - 24)(6) + (28 - 28)(1) = 92$.
The districts' combined gain is 220.

c. Now the common price in the districts is P = \$28 with B1, B4, H2, B2,
and B5 buying from H6, H3, and H4. Thus, the total gain is
$(50 - 28)(4) + (48 - 28)(3) + (42 - 28)(2) + (37 - 28)(2) +$
$(30 - 28)(4) + (28 - 24)(6) + (28 - 25)(5) + (28 - 28)(4) = 241$.
A single "common" market provides the maximum total gain.

Chapter 11

1. a. The merger should mean the end of the prevailing cutthroat
competition. The merged firm should set out to achieve the available
monopoly profit.

   b. Formerly, cutting rates made sense in order to claim additional clients
from one's rival. After the merger, the newspapers will raise rates
(again seeking the monopoly level).

3. a. The monopolist sets MR = MC, implying $1{,}500 - .2Q = 300 + .1Q$,
or $Q_M = 4{,}000$. In turn, $P_M = 1{,}500 - (.1)(4{,}000) = \$1{,}100$.

   b. Total profit is $4{,}400{,}000 - [1{,}400{,}000 + 1{,}200{,}000 + 800{,}000]$
$= \$1{,}000{,}000$.

5. a. We know that $P = 11 - Q$ and $C = 16 + Q$. Setting MR = MC, we have
$11 - 2Q = 1$. Thus, the monopolist sets $Q_M = 5$ million and $P_M = \$6$.

   b. The regulator sets P = AC. Thus, $11 - Q = 16/Q + 1$. After
multiplying both sides by Q, this becomes a quadratic equation with
two roots: $Q = 2$ and $Q = 8$. Naturally, the regulator selects the larger
output level, so we have $Q_R = 8$ million and $P_R = \$3$.

   c. Under marginal-cost pricing, $P^* = MC = \$1$ and $Q = 11 - P = 10$
million. At this quantity, AC is $26/10 = \$2.60$. The shortfall of price
below average cost is $2.60 - 1 = \$1.60$ per unit.

7. a. The combination $Q_D = 1{,}500$ gallons and $P_D = \$1.69$ is profit maximizing.
This quantity satisfies MR = MC: $2.06 - (.0005)(1{,}500) = 1.31$.

   b. The \$2.59 price at night is not optimal. According to the markup rule,
the price should be $P = [-3/(1 - 3)]1.31 = \$1.96\frac{1}{2}$.

   c. Although his contribution margin is very high, this does not mean that
he is enjoying large profits. The high fixed cost of downtown real estate
is the main factor limiting his profit. This factor explains why one finds
skyscrapers, not gas stations, in the downtown sections of major cities.

9. a. To produce a fixed amount of output (in this case, 18 units) at minimum total cost, the firms should set outputs such that $MC_A = MC_B$. This implies $6 + 2Q_A = 18 + Q_B$, or $Q_B = 2Q_A - 12$. Using this equation together with $Q_A + Q_B = 18$, we find $Q_A = 10$ and $Q_B = 8$. The common value of marginal cost is 26.

   b. We know that $P = 86 - Q$, implying $MR = 86 - 2Q$. Marginal revenue at $Q = 18$ is $86 - (2)(18) = 50$. This exceeds either firm's marginal cost (26); therefore, the cartel can profit by expanding output.

   c. Setting $MR = MC_A = MC_B$ implies $86 - 2(Q_A + Q_B) = 6 + 2Q_A = 18 + Q_B$. The solution is $Q_A = 13$ and $Q_B = 14$. The cartel price is $P = 59$, and the common value of MR and the MCs is 32.

11. a. At $P = \$10$, 2 million trips are demanded. In the text, we saw that each fully utilized taxi had an average cost per trip of $8 and, therefore, earned an excess profit of $(10 - 8)(140) = \$280$ per week. The commission should set the license fee at $L = \$280$ to tax away all this excess profit. Assuming that 14,286 taxis operate (just enough to meet the 2 million trips demanded), the commission collects a total of $4 million in license fees.

   b. The rearranged demand curve is $P = 14 - 2Q$. We saw that the extra cost of adding a fully occupied taxi is $1,120 per week, or $8 per trip. The relevant MC per trip is $8. Setting $MR = MC$, we have $14 - 4Q = 8$. Thus, $Q_M = 1.5$ million trips and $P_M = \$11$. The maximum total profit for the industry is $\pi = (11 - 8)(1.5) = \$4.5$ million. The number of taxis $1,500,000/140 = 10,714$.

   c. If the market could be transformed into a perfectly competitive one, the result would be $P_C = \min AC = \$8$, $Q_C = 7 - (.5)(8) = 3$ million trips, and number of taxis = 21,428.

   d. Taxi trips are not perfect substitutes. If a taxi charges a fare slightly higher than the industry norm, it will not lose all its sales. (Customers in need of a taxi will take the one in hand rather than wait for a slightly cheaper fare.) Since there is room for product differentiation and price differences, the taxi market probably is best described as monopolistic competition. In this setting, all cabs make zero profit (due to free entry). If price settles at $P = \$9$, then $AC = \$9$ for each cab. This AC occurs at about 121 trips per week; each taxi is 86 percent utilized. Trip demand is 2.5 million supplied by $2,500,000/121 = 20,661$ taxis.

*13. a. Each supplier maximizes profit by setting $P = MC$. Since $MC = 4 + 2Q$, this implies $Q_F = (P - 4)/2$. With 10 firms, $Q_S = 5P - 20$.

   b. The buyer's profit is $\pi = (10 - P)Q_S = (10 - P)(5P - 20)$. To maximize profit, set $d\pi/dP = 0$. The result is $70 - 10P = 0$, implying $P = \$7$ and $Q_S = 15$. The firm offers a price that is less than its value ($10) but high enough to induce an optimal supply.

Chapter 12

1. The conventional wisdom points to entry in loose oligopolies for two reasons: (i) The market offers positive economic profits (unlike a perfectly competitive market), and (ii) since the market is not dominated by large firms, a new entrant has the potential to reap significant market-share gain over time (unlike a tight oligopoly).

3. a. As a monopolist, OPEC sets MR = MC. After a rearrangement, its demand curve is $P = 120 - 2Q_W$. Thus, $120 - 4Q_W = 20$, or $Q_W = 25$ million barrels per day. The optimal price is $70 per barrel.

   b. OPEC's net demand curve is $Q_N = Q_W - Q_S = 80 - 2P$. Rearranging this, we have $P = 40 - .5Q_N$. Setting MR = MC, we have $40 - Q_N = 20$, or $Q_N = 20$ million barrels per day. In turn, $P = \$30$ and $Q_S = 25$. OPEC accounts for about 44 percent (20/45) of world oil production.

5. a. For firm 1, $MR_1 = MC$ implies $40 - 5Q_2 - 10Q_1 = 20$, or $Q_1 = 2 - .5Q_2$. In equilibrium, $Q_1 = Q_2$ so we can solve the preceding equation to find $Q_1 = Q_2 = 1.333$.

   b. If the firms collude, they set $MR = 40 - 10Q = 20$, or $Q = 2$. With total output split equally, each firm supplies 1 unit.

7. a. Yes, there is a prisoner's dilemma in the sense that when all farmers have large crops, they all make losses. One solution is for farmers to agree to withhold excess supplies from the market in order to maintain higher prices.

   b. If each member's compensation is based on the team's overall performance, there is the incentive to take a "free ride" on the efforts of other members. (If it is a 10-member team, each member contributes only 10 percent to the overall performance.) Countering the prisoner's dilemma may mean monitoring work effort or increasing the rewards for individual performance.

9. a. For firm 1, $P_1 = 75 + .5P_2 - Q_1$. Setting $MR_1 = MC$, we have $75 + .5P_2 - 2Q_1 = 30$, implying $Q_1 = 22.5 + .25P_2$. Substituting this solution for Q_1 into the price equation, we find $P_1 = 52.5 + .25P_2$.

   b. A lower P_2 shifts firm 1's demand curve inward, causing it to set a lower price.

   c. Solving $P_1 = 52.5 + .25P_1$, we find $P_1 = P_2 = 70$. From the demand equations, $Q_1 = Q_2 = 40$. Each firm's profit is 1,600.

11. a. Rearranging the price equation shows that raising A increases sales. Advertising spending is a fixed cost (doesn't vary with output).

    b. Setting MR = MC, we have $50 + A^{.5} - 2Q = 20$ or $Q = 15 + .5A^{.5}$. Substituting this solution for Q into the price equation, we find

$P = 35 + .5A^{.5}$. If advertising is increased, the firm should plan for increased sales at a higher price.

c. $\pi = (P - 20)Q - A = (15 + .5A^{.5})(15 + .5A^{.5}) - A = 225 + 15A^{.5} - .75A$. Setting $d\pi/dA = 0$ implies $7.5/A^{.5} - .75 = 0$. Thus, $A = 100$. In turn, $Q = 20$ and $P = 40$.

Chapter 13

1. In a Nash equilibrium, each player's chosen strategy is optimal, given the strategy of the other. Thus, neither side can profit by unilaterally deviating. By comparison, a dominant strategy is optimal against *any* strategy the other player might choose.

3. a. Firm Y has no dominant strategy nor any dominated strategy. For firm Z, C3 is dominated by C1.

   b. Once C3 is eliminated from consideration, R1 is dominated by R2. With R1 eliminated, C2 is dominated by C1. Thus, C1 is firm Z's optimal choice, and R2 is firm Y's optimal response.

5. a. There are two equilibria: Firm J develops E and firm K develops D, and vice versa. Thus, one cannot make a confident prediction as to which outcome will occur.

   b. If firm J moves first, it should choose E, knowing firm K will then choose D.

   c. Similarly, firm K's first move should be to choose E.

7. a.

		Venezuela	
		3 M barrels	4 M barrels
Saudi Arabia	8 M barrels	144, 54	120, 60
	9 M barrels	135, 45	108, 48

   b. Saudi Arabia's dominant strategy is to produce 8 million barrels. Venezuela's dominant strategy is to produce 4 million barrels.

   c. The basic asymmetry is in the size of the countries' outputs. By cutting price, Venezuela can expand output by 33 percent. For the same price cut, Saudi Arabia enjoys only a 12.5 percent increase. Venezuela profits from the extra output; Saudi Arabia does not. One might call this a "one-sided" prisoner's dilemma.

9. a. Neither side has a dominant strategy. Hospital B's "Specialty" strategy is dominated by its "Basic" strategy. Using the method of circles and

squares, one finds that in equilibrium both hospitals offer "All Purpose" services generating payoffs of (8, 7).

b. A merged hospital would coordinate its actions to maximize total profit. Accordingly, B delivers "Specialty" services and A delivers "Basic" services (18 in total profit).

c. A merged hospital could increase profits by reducing costs and/or improving quality (due to economies of scale and scope or by closing redundant services). Without hospital competition, the merged entity could also profit from increased market power (i.e., the ability to raise fees). The former effect could benefit patients via lower prices or improved services; the latter effect (higher prices) would be detrimental to consumers.

11. a. The town's dominant strategy is nonenforcement. Anticipating this, the typical motorist chooses to disobey the law. The outcome is (5, −10).

b. If the town can make the "first move" by committing to 100 percent enforcement, the situation changes. The typical motorist's best response is to obey, leading to the outcome (0, −15). Note, however, that enforcement (because of its high cost) is still not in the best interest of the town (−15 is worse than −10).

c. Now the town enforces the law with probability p. The typical motorist will obey the law if and only if his expected payoff from doing so (0) exceeds the payoff if he doesn't, $-20p + 5(1 - p)$. Setting these payoffs equal to one another implies p = .2. As long as the enforcement probability is slightly greater than 20 percent, motorists will obey the law. The town's enforcement cost is $(.2)(-15) = -3$. Probabilistic enforcement, which successfully deters, is the town's least costly strategy.

13. a. The buyer has no dominant strategy. She buys two units at P = $9, four units at P = $8, and six units at P = $6. Anticipating this behavior, the seller should set P = $8.

b. With multiple rounds, the buyer could vary its purchases to encourage lower prices (by purchasing six units at P = $6, two units otherwise). If this succeeds, the resulting payoff is (12, 18).

c. Maximum total profits (32) are achieved at Q = 8 units. A negotiated price of P = $6 (an equal profit split) appears to be equitable.

Chapter 14

1. Although there could be some cost economies from such a merger, the main effect on consumers likely would be higher soft-drink prices. Aggressive price competition to claim market share would be a thing of

the past. Because the merged entity would account for over 80 percent of total soft-drink sales, the United States Justice Department would be likely to fight such a merger on the grounds it would create a monopoly.

3. a. The competitive price of studded tires is $P_C = AC = \$60$. The price equation $P = 170 - 5Q$ can be rearranged as $Q = 34 - .2P$. Thus, one finds the competitive quantity to be $Q_C = 34 - (.2)(60) = 22$ thousand tires.

   b. The full MC of an extra tire is $60 + .5Q$. Equating industry demand to marginal cost, we find $P = 170 - 5Q = 60 + .5Q$. Therefore, the optimal quantity is $Q^* = 20$ thousand tires. The optimal price is $170 - (5)(20) = \$70$. Net social benefit is the sum of consumer surplus and producer profit, net of external costs. Consumer surplus is $(.5)(170 - 70)(20,000) = \$1,000,000$. Producer profit is $(70 - 60)(20,000) = \$200,000$. External costs are:
   $$C = .25Q^2 = (.25)(20)^2 = \$100 \text{ thousand.}$$
   Thus, net social benefit is $\$1,100,000$.

   c. At $Q^* = 20$ thousand tires, the marginal external cost is $.5Q^* = \$10$ per studded tire. Set a tax of $\$10$ per studded tire to obtain the optimal result in part b. The competitive market price, including tax, becomes $60 + 10 = \$70$.

   d. At an added cost of $\$12$, low-impact studded tires are not cost-effective. At a market price of $\$70$ (as in part b or c), they cannot compete profitably and should not be produced.

5. a. The firms' costs are $C_1 = 2Q_1 + .1Q_1^2$ and $C_2 = .15Q_2^2$. It follows that $MC_1 = 2 + .2Q_1$; $MC_2 = .3Q_2$. In turn, $MB = 9 - .4Q = 9 - .4(Q_1 + Q_2)$.

   b. Setting $MB = MC_1 = MC_2$, we find $Q_1 = 5$ and $Q_2 = 10$, and the common marginal value is $\$3$. It is economically efficient for firm 2 to clean up more pollution than firm 1 since its marginal cost of cleanup is lower.

   c. Each firm cleans up to the point where $MC = \$4$. Using the MC expressions in part a, we find $Q_1 = 10$ and $Q_2 = 13.33$.

   d. The optimal tax is $\$3.00$ (equal to the common value of $MB = MC_1 = MC_2$). Facing this tax, the firms choose $Q_1 = 5$ and $Q_2 = 10$, as in part b.

7. a. Sketching the demand curve, we find the price intercept to be $\$3.00$ and the quantity intercept to be 900 cars. At a rate of $\$1.50$, 450 cars will park each hour, implying revenue of $\$675$ per hour. In turn, consumer surplus is $(.5)(\$3 - \$1.50)(450) = \$337.50$ per hour. At a rate of $\$1.00$, 600 cars will park each hour, generating revenue of $\$600$ per hour. Consumer surplus is $(.5)(\$3 - \$1)(600) = \$600$ per hour. The $\$1$ rate generates the greater total benefit, $\$1,200$ per hour. The

annual benefit is $(2,600)(\$1,200) = \$3,120,000$. Thus, the net benefit of the garage (in present-value terms) is
$(11.9)(3,120,000 - 620,000) - 20,000,000 = \$9,750,000$.

b. The private developer would use the $1.50/hour rate because it offers the greater revenue. The annual profit is
$(2,600)(\$675) - 620,000 = \$1,135,000$. The net present value of the garage is $(11.9)(1,135,000) - 20,000,000 = -\$6,493,000$. The garage is not profitable.

9. a. Setting MR = MC, we have $500 - 20Q = 150$, or $Q_M = 17.5$ thousand units and $P_M = \$325$.

b. Under perfect competition, $P_C = LAC = \$150$ and $Q_C = 35$ thousand.

c. With a $100 tax, the monopolist's MC is 250. Setting MR = MC, we find $Q_M = 12.5$ thousand and $P_M = \$375$.

d. The efficient solution calls for a double dose of regulation: Promote perfect competition while taxing the externality. The efficient price is $P_C = LMC + MEC = 150 + 100 = \$250$. The corresponding (efficient) level of output is 25 thousand units. This is the optimal solution. All of the analysts' recommended outcomes are inefficient. (Of the three, the part a outcome, $Q = 17.5$ thousand, is the best. It comes closest to the efficient outcome, implying the smallest deadweight loss).

11. a. The total benefits (B) for the programs (per $1 million spent) are:
   - Program 1. B = $(2.9)(\$1.6 \text{ million}) + \$0 = \$4.64$ million
   - Program 2. B = $(.6)(\$1.6 \text{ million}) + \$3.2 \text{ million} = \$4.16$ million
   - Program 3. B = $(1.6)(\$1.6 \text{ million}) + \$1.5 \text{ million} = \$4.06$ million
   - Program 4. B = $(2.3)(\$1.6 \text{ million}) + \$.2 \text{ million} = \$3.88$ million

   Thus, program 1 should be funded up to its limit ($14 million), then program 2 (up to $12 million), and then the remaining $6 million on program 3.

b. With $2.4 million as the value per life, the program benefits are now:
   - Program 1. B = $(2.9)(\$2.4 \text{ million}) + \$0 = \$6.96$ million
   - Program 2. B = $(.6)(\$2.4 \text{ million}) + \$3.2 \text{ million} = \$4.64$ million
   - Program 3. B = $(1.6)(\$2.4 \text{ million}) + \$1.5 \text{ million} = \$5.34$ million
   - Program 4. B = $(2.3)(\$2.4 \text{ million}) + \$.2 \text{ million} = \$5.72$ million

   Again, program 1 should be funded up to its limit ($14 million), then program 4 (up to $16 million), and the remaining $2 million on program 3. With a greater value for each life, the programs saving the most lives are fully funded.

Chapter 15

1. a. We know that $Pr(L) = .04$, $Pr(R|L) = .5$, and $Pr(R|N) = 1/16$, where L denotes lemon, R denotes return, and N denotes normal car. The joint table is

	Lemon (L)	Normal (N)	Total
Return (R)	.02	.06	.08
Keep (K)	.02	.90	.92
Total	.04	.96	1.00

For instance, one computes the first row: $Pr(L \& R) = (.5)(.04) = .02$, and $Pr(N \& R) = (1/16)(.96) = .06$. Thus, we find $Pr(L|R) = .02/(.08) = .25$. Of all cars returned, 25 percent are lemons. In turn, $Pr(L|K) = .02/.92 = .021$.

   b. We see that the return policy screens out half of the lemons (a substantial benefit to customers) but at the cost that about 6 percent of normal-quality cars will be returned as well.

3. a. With equal chances of both types of workers, the firm offers a wage of $25,000 (equal to the workers' average productivity).

   b. By attending college, HP workers can distinguish themselves from LP workers (i.e., signal their higher productivity). Consider an equilibrium in which workers with college educations are paid $30,000, and all others are paid $20,000. By going to college, HP workers increase their incomes by $10,000 per year or $50,000 over their expected five-year job tenure. Since these added earnings exceed the cost of a college education ($40,000), it pays HP workers to go to college. Not so for LP workers whose college costs are $60,000. Thus, the signaling outcome is, indeed, an equilibrium. However, if the average job stay is only three years, this signaling equilibrium breaks down.

5. If the bill is split five ways, each time a couple orders an extra menu item (say, an expensive shrimp cocktail or a baked Alaska dessert), its share of the extra cost is only 20 percent. The other couples pay for 80 percent of the cost. Moral hazard occurs because couples will tend to overindulge themselves in expensive items because they bear only a fraction of the costs. The couple who mistakenly expects separate checks is in double jeopardy. By economizing, the couple forgoes a lavish meal yet pays for the others' extravagance.

7. a. Having only imperfect information, the winning bidder may have been overly optimistic about the player's "true" long-run ability. (For instance, the winning team may not have known that the pitcher had a sore arm, a bad attitude, and so on.) The winning bidder might ask itself, "If this pitcher is so great, why didn't his original team retain him?"

   b. If a ball player is guaranteed exorbitant sums for the duration of his contract, he may have a reduced incentive to give a 100 percent effort on the field (and, therefore, perform poorly). Obviously, his incentive increases in the last year of his contract if he expects to become a free agent.

   c. An owner should estimate what a player is worth based on the best available information and place a bid somewhat below this estimate in order to acquire the ball player at a profit.

9. Although team decision making can generate valuable information and promote problem solving (five heads are better than one), it is also costly (enlisting additional human resources) and time-consuming. In addition, team decision making may suffer from free-rider problems; that is, team members may shirk and expect other members to pick up the slack. For these reasons, it is important to limit the size of workable teams.

Chapter 16

1. a. The plaintiff's expected court receipt (net of legal costs) is $50,000 - 15,000 = \$35,000$. The defendant's expected court payment (including legal costs) is $50,000 + 15,000 = \$65,000$. The zone of agreement lies between these two amounts. If each side believes its winning chances are 60 percent, then the plaintiff's expected court receipt is $45,000 and the defendant's expected court payment is $55,000. The parties' optimistic (and conflicting) opinions have reduced the zone of agreement.

   b. When the potential damages are $200,000, the expected court outcomes of the disputants become $105,000 and $95,000. Now there is no zone of agreement. The plaintiff's minimally acceptable settlement exceeds the defendant's maximum acceptable payment.

   c. Facing a nuisance suit, the defendant knows it will win its court case but still faces an expected cost equal to its legal fees. Thus, it rationally might settle out of court for any amount smaller than this. For example, it might well settle a nuisance suit for $5,000 if it knows that defending the suit will cost $10,000. The most immediate way to deter nuisance suits is to make the losing party pay the other side's legal (i.e., court) costs.

3. Paying the developer 1 percent of the store's first year's revenue might be beneficial for two reasons. First, if the parties are risk averse, this arrangement is one way to share the risk of uncertain revenues. Second, the arrangement might depend on different probability assessments of the parties. For instance, the store may be relatively pessimistic (and the developer may be optimistic) about the volume of shoppers coming to the new mall.

5. a. Since the mill has the right to pollute, the fishery must pay it to clean up. With 50 percent cleanup, the benefit to the fishery is $100,000 - 30,000 = \$70,000$. The mill's cost is \$50,000, so the total net benefit (relative to no cleanup) is \$20,000. A 100 percent cleanup, however, costs more than it is worth: $\$120,000 > \$100,000$. Thus, a 50 percent cleanup (at a price between \$50,000 and \$70,000) is mutually beneficial.

   b. The same 50 percent reduction would be negotiated if the fishery held the legal right to clean water. Moving from 100 percent cleanup to 50 percent cleanup costs the fishery \$30,000 in reduced profit, but saves the mill \$50,000 in abatement costs. Since the total net benefit from this change is positive (\$20,000), the parties can benefit mutually from the cleanup. Here the mill will pay the fishery an amount between \$30,000 and \$50,000. A further move to zero percent cleanup is not warranted. (The fishery's reduction in profit exceeds the mill's cost saving.)

7. a. The eight possible agreements (and associated payoffs) are

   1. 95%, 3yr, w/o Bio.: 180, −140   2. 95%, 5yr, w/o Bio.: 100, −80

   3. 80%, 3yr, w/o Bio.: 160, −90   4. 80%, 5yr, w/o Bio.: 60, −50

   5. 95%, 3yr, w/Bio.: 150, −100   6. 95%, 5yr, w/Bio.: 70, −60

   7. 80%, 3yr, w/Bio.: 130, −50   8. 80%, 5yr, w/Bio.: 30, −30

   Only agreements 1, 3, 7, and 8 are efficient. Agreements 2, 4, and 6 are dominated by agreement 7. Agreement 5 is dominated by agreement 3.

   b. Agreement 7 is optimal since the parties' total gains, $(130 - 50)$, are maximized.

9. a. The buyer maximizes $\pi_B = B - PQ = 3Q - Q^2/20 - PQ$. Therefore, set $M\pi_B = 3 - Q/10 - P = 0$ and rearrange as $P = 3 - Q/10$ or $Q = 30 - 10P$. This describes the buyer's optimal purchase behavior as a function of P.

   b. To maximize profit, the seller sets MR = MC. We derive MR from the preceding price equation, $P = 3 - Q/10$; therefore, $MR = 3 - Q/5$. From the cost function, $C = Q^2/40$, we know that $MC = dC/dQ = Q/20$. Setting $3 - Q/5 = Q/20$, we find $Q = 12$. In turn, $P = 1.80$ and so $R = 21.6$. The seller's profit is $R - C = 21.6 - 3.6 = 18$. The buyer's profit is $B - R = 28.8 - 21.6 = 7.2$.

  c. Acting as a monopolist, the seller quotes a price that leads to the purchase of too few units (12 units instead of 20). The monopoly price is the source of the inefficiency.

11. a. As in the text example, we work backward starting from the last offer. If an agreement is not reached earlier, X sets its last offer equal to the size of the remaining stake, $30,000. Thus, at the second offer, Y can demand only $30,000 for itself, leaving $30,000 for X. (If Y gave any less to X, then X would refuse.) At the first offer, X demands $90,000 for itself, giving $30,000 to Y (which Y accepts). Thus, the $90,000-$30,000 split is offered and immediately accepted.

  b. With four offer rounds, the offers from last to first give the following amounts to X: $0, $15,000, $15,000, and $75,000. Firm X makes the first offer and claims more than half of the total stake.

  c. Let z denote the fraction of the current stake that the offerer demands for itself. At the first offer, X demands $120,000z, leaving Y with the remaining $120,000(1 − z). If Y refuses, it offers ($60,000)z. Since z is designed to leave Y indifferent between accepting or rejecting X's offer, it follows that $120,000(1 − z) = (.5)(120,000)z$, or $1 − z = .5z$. The solution is $z = 1/(1 + .5) = 2/3$ and the initial offer is $80,000.

13. The value of the target under current management ranges between $60 and $80 per share, with an expected value of $70 (since all values are equally likely). What if firm A offered a price of $70? Current management accepts this price when v_T is between $60 and $70. (Obviously, if $v_T > 70$, firm T will not sell.) Thus, when its offer is accepted, the acquisition value to firm A ranges between $60 and $75. (Remember that $v_A = 1.5v_T − 30$.) This means that firm A's expected acquisition value is $67.5. On average, it obtains a company worth less than the price it pays! The trick is to realize that companies that accept its offer are likely to be low-value companies. One can check that firm A cannot earn a positive profit at *any* price between $60 and $80.

Chapter 17

1. a. Each buyer should bid $b_i = v_i$. If the buyer bids above her value, it makes a difference only when she outbids an opponent who bids $b_j > v_i$, in which case she obtains the good for a price b_j above her value. In short, bidding above one's value makes no sense. If she bids below her value, she cannot improve the price she pays. (This is fixed at the second-highest bid.) But she risks losing the item if her bid is below the second-highest bid (i.e., if $b_i < b_j < v_i$). Bidding below one's true value is disadvantageous. Thus, the bidder's dominant strategy is $b_i = v_i$.

b. In the English auction, the bidding stops at (or just above) the second-highest value. In the second-price auction, the final price is set at the second-highest bid (which corresponds to the second-highest value).

c. The absent buyer should report a bid equal to his true value, $b_i = v_i$. If he wins, he pays only the price required to win the auction, which may be well below his reported bid. In short, he should report his true value so that the auction house can bid on his behalf (exactly as he would himself if he were present at the auction).

3. a. Against a single rival, the optimal bid is \$2.4 million implying an expected profit of $(2.9 - 2.4)(.4) = \$.2$ million. Against two rivals, the optimal bid is \$2.6 million implying an expected profit of $(2.9 - 2.6)(.6)^2 = \$.108$ million.

   b. Each firm's equilibrium bidding strategy is

$$b_i = (1/3)(2) + (2/3)v_i.$$

   Thus, the optimal bid is $(1/3)(2) + (2/3)(2.9) = \$2.6$ million.

5. a. From Table 1 we can compute the expected profit for any bid by multiplying the bid markup by the fraction of bids won. For example, the expected profit from bidding at a 60 percent markup is $(9/17)(60) = 31.76$. This is the greatest expected profit for any bid. (By comparison, the expected profits from 50 percent and 70 percent markups are 29.17 and 27.39, respectively.)

   b. Table 2 lists a total of 128 lowest competing bids. If Reliant Press were to use a 20 percent markup, it would lose to only 6 of these 128 LCBs (i.e., bids with markups of 19 percent or below). Thus, the firm's expected profit is $(122/128)(20) = 19.06$. If it bids 50 percent, its expected profit is $(84/128)(50) = 32.8$. If it bids 60 percent, its expected profit is $(64/128)(60) = 30.0$. If it bids 70 percent, its expected profit is $(47/128)(70) = 25.7$. The 50 percent markup offers the greatest expected profit of all alternatives (with the 60 percent markup a close second). The distribution of LCBs represents more complete information than the number of wins in Table 1. The latter table has only a small number of observations for each bid. Because of random factors (bids just winning or just losing), the recorded fraction of winning bids might vary considerably from the "true" long-run win probability.

7. a. Under blind bidding, each firm's reservation price is simply the expected value of the film. The common expected value for each bidder is $(1/3)(10,000) + (1/3)(6,000) + (1/3)(2,000) = \$6,000$, and this will be the equilibrium bid for each in a sealed-bid auction. Thus, the distributor's revenue from the auction will exactly equal the expected value of the film. If the distributor delays the bidding until

the uncertainty is resolved, exhibitors will bid the full (certain) value of the film. Again the expected revenue is $6,000. However, if exhibitors are risk averse, their reservation values (and, therefore, bids) will be below the film's expected value under blind bidding. Bids for previewed films will be unaffected (since these films carry no risk). With risk-averse bidders the exhibitor increases its expected revenue by previewing the films.

b. Selective screening works only if bidders are naive. Sophisticated bidders will anticipate that unscreened films are likely to have lower expected box-office receipts than the rest of the films. They will bid accordingly.

c. Against an astute bidder, the less well-informed theaters must bid cautiously to avoid the winner's curse (i.e., winning films that the astute bidder knows are poor box-office bets). This kind of bid deterrence allows the astute bidder to obtain films at bids below their full value with the effect that the seller's revenue is reduced. What if the astute bidder were excluded from the bidding? The equilibrium bids of the uninformed bidders are $b = E(v)$. Each buyer's expected bidding profit is zero, and the seller obtains a price that reflects the full value of the movie. The seller gains by excluding the astute bidder, thereby removing the information asymmetry.

9. a. In sequential bidding for identical items, a potential buyer must decide whether or not to try to win the first item or try to get the second, third, . . . , or last item more cheaply. In equilibrium, one would expect all items to sell for the same expected price. (If expected prices differed, buyers would change their bidding behavior, evening out the prices.)

b. When items can be bought as a lot, the high initial bidder may take one item, some items, or all items at the bid price. Leftover items are reauctioned and typically sell for lower average prices. The risk of waiting for a lower price is that there may be no items left. In this sense, the procedure resembles a Dutch auction.

11. a. At an English auction, the expected price is
$[2/(n + 1)]300 + [(n - 1)/(n + 1)]360 = (2/3)(300) + (1/3)(360) = \$320$ thousand.

b. The chance is .5 that an individual buyer's value is less than $330 thousand. The chance that both values are less than the reserve is $(.5)(.5) = .25$. The chance that one bidder will meet the reserve is .5. The chance that both values exceed the reserve is .25. If both values are above $330 thousand, the expected auction price is
$(2/3)(330) + (1/3)(360) = \$340$ thousand.

c. With P_{min} = $330 thousand, the seller's expected revenue is (.25)(300) + (.5)(330) + (.25)(340) = $325 thousand. This is $5 thousand more than the expected revenue in part a (with P_{min} = $300 thousand).

Chapter 18

1. a. Increasing or decreasing returns to scale implies that either the objective function or some constraint is nonlinear. Thus, the LP formulation cannot be used.

   b. The LP method can handle any number of decision variables. The earlier problem of producing a maximum level of output contained more variables (3) than constraints (2).

   c. A downward-sloping demand curve implies a nonlinear revenue function. (The revenue function is linear only if the demand curve is horizontal, i.e., the price is constant.) Thus, the LP formulation cannot be used.

   d. Here the constraints are $Q_1/Q_2 \geq .4$ and $Q_1/Q_2 \leq .6$. These can be rewritten as $Q_1 - .4Q_2 \geq 0$, and $Q_1 - .6Q_2 \leq 0$, respectively. Since these are both linear, the LP formulation applies.

3. a. The slope of the objective function ($-10/15$) lies between the slopes of the two constraints ($-2/5$ and $-6/3$). Therefore, the optimal solution has both constraints binding: $2x + 5y = 40$ and $6x + 3y = 48$. The solution is $x = 5$ and $y = 6$. The value of the objective function is 140.

   b. The slope of the objective function ($-.75$) lies outside the slopes of the two constraints ($-1/.5$ and $-1/1$). Therefore, the optimal solution has $y = 0$ and only the second constraint is binding: $x + y = 16$. Thus, $x = 16$ and the minimum value of the objective function is 12.

5. a. The formulation is

   Minimize: $.1M + .15C$

   Subject to: $2M + 2C \geq 50$ (calcium)

                   $2M + 6C \geq 90$ (protein)

                   $6M + 2C \geq 66$ (calories),

   where M and C are the nonnegative quantities of milk and cereal. A graph shows that the lowest contour touches the feasible region at the corner formed by the protein and calcium constraints. (The slopes of these constraints are $-1/3$ and -1, respectively; the slope of the typical cost contour is $-.1/.15 = -2/3$.) Solving $2M + 2C = 50$ and $2M + 6C = 90$, we find $C = 10$ and $M = 15$. The minimum cost of a healthy diet is $3.

b. If we increase the calcium requirement by a small amount (say, by 4 units to 54), the new solution becomes $C = 9$ and $M = 18$. The cost of meeting this higher health requirement is $3.15. Therefore, the shadow price of an extra unit of calcium is $.15/4 = \$.0375$.

7. a. The formulation is

Maximize: $4B + 6T$

Subject to: $5B + 5T \geq 3.5$

$.4B + 4T \geq 1.5$

$.4B + 4T \leq 2.5$

$B + T = 1.0.$

Since bonds have better returns, the investor would like to make T as large as possible. Clearly, the first two constraints never are binding. However, the last two constraints do bind the proportion of bonds. Solving $.4B + 4T = 2.5$ and $B + T = 1$, we find $B = .417$ and $T = .583$. The expected return of this portfolio is 5.17 percent.

b. The formulation is

Maximize: $4B + 6T + 4.4C + 5.6M + 8J$

$5B + 5T + 3.5C + 3M + 1J \geq 3.5$

$B + T + C + M + J = 1.0.$

Notice that treasury bonds dominate (are more profitable and safer) than treasury bills, corporate bonds, and municipal bonds. Eliminating these three securities reduces the binding constraints to $5T + J = 3.5$ and $T + J = 1$. The solution is $T = .625$ and $J = .375$. The portfolio's expected return is 6.75 percent.

c. If risk is not an issue, the manager should invest 100 percent of the portfolio in junk bonds ($J = 1$) earning a maximum rate of return and just meeting the maturity constraint.

9. a. Let x_1 and x_2 denote the levels of the two processes. At a unit level, process 1 produces 2 units of H and 1 unit of P for a total contribution of $(\$2)(2) + (\$1)(1) = \$5$. The contribution of process 2 is $(\$2)(2) + (\$1)(4) = \$8$ at the unit level. Thus, the LP formulation is

$$\text{Maximize:} \qquad 5x_1 + 8x_2$$

$$\text{Subject to:} \qquad x_1 + 2x_2 \leq 110$$

$$2x_1 + 2x_2 \leq 160.$$

In the graphic solution, both constraints are binding. The optimal solution is $x_1 = 50$ and $x_2 = 30$. Total contribution is \$490.

b. Let the supply of labor increase to 120. The new solution is $x_1 = 40$ and $x_2 = 40$, and total contribution increases to \$520. Labor's shadow price is $30/10 = \$3$.

c. If the contribution of plywood rises to \$3, the new objective function becomes maximize $7x_1 + 16x_2$. The slope of the objective function $(-7/16)$ no longer lies between the slopes of the input constraints $(-1/2$ and $-1)$. Therefore, only the labor constraint is binding and the firm only uses the second process (i.e., $x_1 = 0$). Solving the binding labor constraint, we have $x_2 = 55$. The firm's maximum contribution is $(16)(55) = \$880$.

Chapter 19

1. a. The market value of the apartment building is clearly the main opportunity cost (already in present-value terms) of the garage and should be debited against the garage's benefits.

   b. Site-preparation expenditures constitute incremental costs.

   c. Last year's site work is a sunk cost that is irrelevant to the investment decision.

   d. Allocated administrative expenses appear to be fixed costs that should not be debited as incremental costs of the garage.

   e. Future parking revenues are the main incremental benefit of the garage.

   f. Depreciation itself is not a cash flow, but it is a source of tax savings.

   g. As in part f, the statewide tax credit will lead to incremental tax savings that are counted as a reduced incremental cost.

3. The NPV is $-5 + -5/1.1 + 2/(1.1)^2 + \ldots + 2/(1.1)^{21}$, assuming the \$10 million initial cost is divided evenly over the first two years and revenues begin in two years. From the table in the appendix, we find that, at 10 percent, a \$1 annuity for 20 years starting next year has a PV of \$8.514. The same annuity starting in two years has a PV of $8.514/1.1 = \$7.74$. Thus, the dormitory's NPV is $-5 - 4.55 + (2)(7.74) = \$5.93$ million. The dormitory should be built.

5. Because the manager has estimated cash flows in real terms, she also should use a real discount rate. The 8 percent treasury bill rate is in nominal terms and is much higher than the appropriate real rate.

7. The six-year cash-flow pattern (in thousands of dollars) for machine A is $-38, -8, -8, -38, -8, -8$, implying a total cost (in present-value terms) of $-\$90,866$. For machine B, the cash flow pattern is $-32, -12, -32, -12, -32, -12$, implying a total cost of $-\$107,678$. Machine A is the lower-cost option. (If machine B's life were three years, it would be the better alternative. Check this.)

9. a. The required rate is $r_f + \beta(r_m - r_f) = 6 + (1.5)(12 - 6) = 15$ percent.

   b. Here the required rate is $6 + (.8)(12 - 6) = 10.8$ percent. Because this discount rate is greater than the investment's IRR (9 percent), the investment has a negative net present value and should not be undertaken.

11. a. The IRR satisfies $5,000 - 3,000/(1 + r) - 4,000/(1 + r)^2 = 0$. Using a financial calculator, a spreadsheet, or an algebraic solution, we find that $r = .234$ or 23.4 percent. Here an initial positive cash flow precedes future negative cash flows—the reverse of the usual pattern. Accordingly, the joint venture should be undertaken only if the discount rate is *greater* than the IRR (23.4 percent).

   b. The NPVs are $-\$500, -\$410, -\$282$, and $-\$111$ at interest rates of 0, 10, 15, and 50 percent, respectively. The NPV is negative at *all* discount rates. Therefore, no IRR exists for this pattern of cash flows.

   c. The NPVs are $-\$100, -\$34, \$0, \$9.5, \$0$, and $-\$267$ at interest rates of 0, 5, 10, 15, 20, and 50 percent, respectively. This investment project has two IRRs, 10 percent and 20 percent. The project's NPV is positive only at discount rates between 10 and 20 percent.

Index